Alcohol-Induced Disorders
Alcohol Intoxication
Alcohol Withdrawal
Alcohol Intoxication Delirium
Alcohol Withdrawal Delirium
Alcohol-Induced Persisting Dementia
Alcohol-Induced Persisting Amnestic Disorder
Alcohol-Induced Psychotic Disorder
Alcohol-Induced Mood Disorder
Alcohol-Induced Anxiety Disorder
Alcohol-Induced Sexual Dysfunction
Alcohol-Induced Sleep Disorder
Alcohol-Related Disorder Not Otherwise Specified

Amphetamine Use Disorders
Amphetamine-Induced Disorders
Caffeine-Induced Disorders
Cannabis Use Disorders
Cannabis-Induced Disorders
Cocaine Use Disorders
Cocaine-Induced Disorders
Hallucinogen Use Disorders
Hallucinogen-Induced Disorders
Inhalant Use Disorders
Inhalant-Induced Disorders
Nicotine Use Disorder
Nicotine-Induced Disorder
Opioid Use Disorders
Opioid-Induced Disorders
Phencyclidine Use Disorders
Phencyclidine-Induced Disorders
Sedative, Hypnotic, or Anxiolytic Use Disorders
Sedative, Hypnotic, or Anxiolytic-Induced Disorders
Polysubstance-Related Disorder
Other (or Unknown) Substance Use Disorders
Other (or Unknown) Substance-Induced Disorders

SCHIZOPHRENIA AND OTHER PSYCHOTIC DISORDERS

Schizophrenia
Paranoid Type
Disorganized Type
Catatonic Type
Undifferentiated Type
Residual Type

Schizophreniform Disorder
Schizoaffective Disorder
Delusional Disorder
Brief Psychotic Disorder
Shared Psychotic Disorder (Folie a Deux)
Psychotic Disorder Due to a General Medical Condition
Substance-Induced Psychotic Disorder
Psychotic Disorder Not Otherwise Specified

MOOD DISORDERS

Mood Episodes
Major Depressive Episode
Manic Episode
Mixed Episode
Hypomanic Episode

Depressive Disorders
Major Depressive Disorder
Dysthymic Disorder
Depressive Disorder Not Otherwise Specified

Bipolar Disorders
Bipolar I Disorder
 single manic episode
 most recent episode hypomanic
 most recent episode manic
 most recent episode mixed
 most recent episode depressed
 most recent episode unspecified
Bipolar II Disorder: one or more major depressive
 episodes with hypomanic episodes
Cyclothymic Disorder
Bipolar Disorder Not Otherwise Specified

Other Mood Disorders
Mood Disorder Due to a General Medical Condition
Substance-Induced Mood Disorder
Mood Disorder Not Otherwise Specified

Continued on inside of back cover

Abnormal Psychology

in a Changing World

FOURTH EDITION

Jeffrey S. Nevid
St. John's University

Spencer A. Rathus
Montclair State University

Beverly Greene
St. John's University

Prentice Hall
Upper Saddle River, New Jersey 07458

Library of Congress Cataloging-in-Publication Data

Nevid, Jeffrey S.
　　Abnormal psychology in a changing world / Jeffrey S. Nevid,
　Spencer A. Rathus, Beverly Greene. — 4th ed.
　　　　p.　　　cm.
　　Includes bibliographical references and index.
　　ISBN 0–13–030005–5
　　　1. Psychology, Pathological.　　　2. Psychiatry.　　I. Rathus, Spencer
　A.　II. Greene, Beverly.　　III. Title.
　RC454.N468　2000
　616.89—dc21　　　　　　　　　　　　　　　　　99-28720
　　　　　　　　　　　　　　　　　　　　　　　　　　　CIP

Editorial Director: Charlyce Jones Owen
Editor-in-Chief: Nancy Roberts
Executive Editor: Bill Webber
Editorial Assistant: Tamsen Adams
Marketing Assistant: Judie Lamb
AVP/Director of Production and Manufacturing:
　Barbara Kittle
Senior Production Editors: Barbara DeVries/Alison Gnerre
Manufacturing Manager: Nick Sklitsis
Buyer: Lynn Pearlman
Line Art Coordinator: Guy Ruggiero

Artist: Maria Piper
Creative Design Director: Leslie Osher
Interior and Cover Design: Kenny Beck
Director, Image Resource Center: Melinda Reo
Manager, Rights & Permissions: Kay Dellosa
Image Specialist: Beth Boyd
Photo Research: Julie Tesser
Cover Art: Paul Klee (1879–1940) Swiss. "Color
　Shapes" 1914. Barnes Foundation, Pennsylvania/
　Superstock, Inc.

This book was set in 10.5/12 Berkeley Book by TSI Graphics
Group and was printed and bound by World Color.
The cover was printed by The Lehigh Press, Inc.

Acknowledgments begin on page 645, which
constitutes a continuation of the copyright page.

© 2000, 1997, 1994, 1991 by Prentice-Hall, Inc.
Upper Saddle River, NJ 07458

Printed in the United States of America
10 9 8 7 6 5 4 3 2 1

ISBN 0-13-030005-5

Prentice-Hall International (UK) Limited, London
Prentice-Hall of Australia Pty. Limited, Sydney
Prentice-Hall Canada Inc., Toronto
Prentice-Hall Hispanoamericana, S.A., Mexico
Prentice-Hall of India Private Limited, New Delhi
Prentice-Hall of Japan, Inc., Tokyo
Pearson Education Asia Pte. Ltd., Singapore
Editora Prentice-Hall do Brasil, Ltda., Rio de Janeiro

BRIEF CONTENTS

CONTENTS

CHAPTER 3

Methods of Therapy and Treatment   89

CHAPTER 4

Stress, Psychological Factors, and Health 129

CHAPTER 5

Anxiety Disorders 169

CHAPTER 9

Substance Abuse and Dependence 305

Classification of Substance-Related Disorders 307

CHAPTER 13

Abnormal Behavior in Childhood and Adolescence   447

CHAPTER 14

Cognitive Disorders and Disorders Related to Aging   485

CHAPTER 15

Violence and Abuse 515

CHAPTER 16

Abnormal Psychology and Society 553

PREFACE

Abnormal psychology is among the most popular areas of study in psychology and for good reason. The problems it addresses are of immense personal and social importance—problems that touch the lives of us all in one way or another. They include problems that are all too pervasive, such as depression, sexual dysfunction, obesity, and alcohol and substance abuse. They include problems that are less common but have a profound impact on all of us, such as schizophrenia.

The problems addressed in this book are thus not of the few. The majority of us will experience one or more of them at some time or another. Or a friend or loved one will experience them. Even those who do not personally experience these problems will be touched by society's response—or lack of response—to them.

We approached the writing of this text with the belief that a textbook should do more than offer a portrait of a field of knowledge. It should be a teaching device—a means of presenting information in ways that arouse interest and encourage understanding and critical thinking. Toward these ends, we speak to the reader in a clear expository style. We attempt to render complex material accessible. We put a human face on the subjects we address by including many case examples drawn from our own clinical files and those of other mental health professionals. We stimulate and involve students through carefully chosen pedagogical features, questionnaires, highlights, and applications. And yes, we keep abreast of our ever-changing subject by bringing to our readers a wealth of new scientific information drawn from the leading scientific journals and organizations.

We also approach our writing with the belief that a better understanding of abnormal psychology is gained by considering the roles of a broad range of biological, psychological, and sociocultural factors and their interactions in the development of abnormal behavior patterns. We emphasize the need for an interactionist approach as a running theme throughout the text.

NEW TO THE FOURTH EDITION

Previous users will notice some changes in organization and content that we hope will make the text an even better instructional package. We have kept the number of chapters to 16, knowing full well that many instructors like to follow a syllabus that allows for about a chapter a week during a regular semester. The first 14 chapters cover the essential bases of ab-

normal psychology and all of the major diagnostic groupings. Chapter 15 provides students with exposure to models for understanding various forms of interpersonal aggression. Chapter 16 focuses on legal and ethical issues that relate to the interface of society and abnormal behavior, such as the insanity defense and psychiatric commitment.

New Chapter on "Eating Disorders, Obesity, and Sleep Disorders" (Chapter 10)

We've taken a fresh look at our organizational plan and decided to bring together information on eating disorders, obesity, and sleep disorders in a separate chapter. The problems addressed in this chapter are faced by many young people of college age. Moreover, these disorders are not neatly classified within any of the other diagnostic groupings. Though obesity is classified as a medical disorder, we feel it is important for students to understand the important roles of psychological and behavioral factors in the development and treatment of this disorder.

Expanded Focus on Interactionist Approaches

We have expanded upon our interactionist theme in two ways. First, we introduce a new feature called *"Tying It Together."* Students often feel as though one theoretical perspective must ultimately be right and the others wrong. The *"Tying It Together"* feature helps students integrate the theoretical discussions presented in the text and examine possible causal pathways in psychological disorders involving interactions of psychological, sociocultural, and biological factors. We hope to impress upon students the importance of taking a broader view of these complex problems by considering the influences of multiple factors and their interactions. Second, we have expanded upon our coverage of the leading interactionist model, the diathesis-stress model, as a way of understanding the development of psychological disorders ranging from mood disorders to schizophrenia.

New Introductory Chapter (Chapter 1)

A revamped introductory chapter combines coverage of historical and theoretical perspectives as well as research methodologies in the field of abnormal behavior. We know many students and instructors want to get to the material on the specific types of psychological disorders as early as possible in the semester. Many texts in abnormal psychology don't begin reviewing types of disorders until nearly the middle of the text. By incorporating background material in the introductory chapter, we can begin our exploration of the specific disorders as early as Chapter 4.

New Pedagological Features—Study Review Questions

We offer a new pedagogical feature—study review questions that follow the summary section in each chapter. These questions are connected with the learning objectives that begin each chapter, thus providing an opportunity for students to assess whether they have acquired the key information presented in the chapter.

Expanded Coverage of Sociocultural Aspects of Abnormal Psychology

We are gratified by the many comments we have received over the years about our integration of material relating to sociocultural issues. The sociocultural aspects of abnormal psychology refer to ethnicity, gender, sexual orientation, socioeconomic status, and level of education. The Fourth Edition continues to highlight the importance of sociocultural factors in our understanding of abnormal behavior.

Moreover, we have updated our discussion of sociocultural issues by incorporating such recent developments as the following:

- Update on evidence of cultural biases in psychological assessment
- Update on sociocultural factors in interpersonal violence
- New evidence on diagnostic biases leading to an overdiagnosis of schizophrenia in people of color
- New evidence on relationships between mental health and acculturation status of Mexican Americans
- Update on ethnic differences in risk factors for coronary heart disease
- Update on gender differences in rates of major psychological disorders
- New research on sociocultural and interpersonal factors in eating disorders and obesity.

We continue to include attention to these important sociocultural issues:

- Culture-bound and culture-related syndromes
- Ethnic differences in the prevalence of various mental health problems
- Relationships between acculturation and mental health problems of immigrant groups, with special emphasis on Hispanic Americans

- Perspectives on gender differences and gender role stereotypes in the diagnosis of depression
- Culturally-sensitive approaches to psychotherapy, including a special feature on cultural and linguistic issues in treating African Americans, Asian Americans, Hispanic Americans and Native Americans
- Racial and ethnic differences in utilization of mental health services and response to psychotropic medication.

Thorough Updating of Developments in the Field

We have approached each new edition of the text with the realization that our readers expect us to remain current with the literature. They expect us to take a fresh look at each topic and to incorporate new research findings. Toward this end, the fourth edition integrates scientific developments drawn from studies representing more than **1,000** new sources.

Here is but a small sampling of recent research developments incorporated in the Fourth Edition:

- New evidence on accuracy of computer-based diagnostic programs
- New evidence on effectiveness of psychotherapy in ordinary clinical practice
- New evidence on effectiveness of intensive outreach efforts in helping homeless people with psychiatric problems
- Incorporation of the new Institute of Medicine (IOM) criteria for classifying prevention programs
- New evidence on relationships between stress and physical disorders
- New evidence on relationships between social support and risk of the common cold
- New evidence of relationships between optimism and immune system functioning
- Developments in psychosocial treatment of cancer patients and people with HIV and AIDS
- New evidence of emotional factors in coronary heart disease
- Updated information on genetic factors in various psychological disorders
- New research on behavioral treatment of OCD and cognitive behavioral treatment of panic disorder
- New information on childhood abuse in people with multiple personalities and BPD
- New research on stress and depression
- New information on cognitive factors in depression
- New evidence of effectiveness of CBT and interpersonal psychotherapy on depression
- New evidence of diagnostic overlap among personality disorders

- New research on use of cognitive behavior therapy and antidepressant drugs in treating bulimia and the role of serotonin in regulating appetite
- New information on importance of exercise in maintaining weight loss
- New evidence of prevalence of eating disorders in young men
- Update on use of cognitive behavior therapy in treating binge eating disorder (BED)
- New statistics on the treatment of sex offenders
- Updated information on the effectiveness of sex therapy
- New development in biological treatments of erectile dysfunction
- New evidence of the benefits of attentional training in treating schizophrenia patients
- Updating of genetic factors in schizophrenia
- Latest developments in the search for brain abnormalities in schizophrenia
- Update on prevalence, gender differences, and biological factors in dyslexia
- Update on causal factors and treatment of ADHD, conduct disorder, anxiety disorders and depression in childhood
- Update on depression in late adulthood
- Update on genetic factors in Alzheimer's disease and treatment alternatives
- New information on relationships between violent behavior and psychological disorders
- New evidence on relationships between serotonin and aggressive behavior
- Update on prevalence and effects of different forms of interpersonal violence.

FEATURES OF THE TEXTBOOK

Textbooks walk balance beams, as it were, and they can fall off in three directions, not just two. Textbooks, that is, must do justice to their subject matter while they also meet the needs of instructors and students.

In subject matter, this textbook is comprehensive, providing depth and breadth. It covers the history of societal responses to abnormal behaviors, historic and contemporary models of abnormal behaviors, methods of assessment, psychological and biological models of treatment, contemporary issues, the comprehensive range of problem behaviors set forth in the DSM, and a number of other behavioral problems that entail psychological factors—most notably in the interfaces between psychology and health.

This book also contains a number of features that are intended to keep it "on the beam" as a vehicle for instruction and learning:

"Focus on Diversity" Features

This feature highlights recent developments concerning multicultural issues, gender, and sexual orientation. Illustrative "Focus on Diversity" features include:

- Ethnicity and Mental Health
- Acculturation and Mental Health
- Culture-Bound Syndromes
- Ethnic Matching of Clients and Therapists
- Feminist Therapy
- Koro and Dhat Syndromes: Far-Eastern Somatoform Disorders?
- Risk of Suicide among Native American Youth
- Gender Differences in Depression

We build upon these "Focus on Diversity" features by including several new *controversial* discussions that we believe will stimulate both student interest and critical evaluation of social issues:

- Psychological Resilience In Marginalized Groups
- Gender Identity Disorder: A Disorder or Culture Specific Creation?
- Homophobia: Social Prejudice or Personal Psychopathology?

Truth-or-Fiction? Items

Each chapter begins with Truth-or-Fiction? items that whet students' appetites for the subject matter within the chapter. Instructors and students have repeatedly reported that these items stimulate and challenge students. Some of the items are intended to be generally motivating ("Innocent people were drowned in medieval times as a way of certifying that they were not possessed by the Devil"). Others highlight interesting research findings ("In some ways, many "mentally healthy" people see things *less* realistically than do people who are depressed"). Still others encourage students to take a scientific look at the subject matter by questioning folklore and preconceptions (e.g., beliefs that women are more likely to be raped by strangers than by men they know).

Learning Objectives

Following the Truth-or-Fiction? items is a double-duty list of learning objectives. Why "double-duty"? First, these objectives are organized according to the major headings within the chapter, so they provide students with an advance organizer. Second, they provide students with concrete educational goals for each chapter.

Truth-or-Fiction-Revisited Sections

The Truth-or-Fiction? items are revisited in these sections at the points in the text where the topics are discussed. Students are thus given feedback concerning the accuracy of their preconceptions in the light of the material being addressed. Truth-or-Fiction? items are now numbered to make it easier for students to connect the opening questions with the answers given later in the chapter.

"A Closer Look" Features

"A Closer Look" features highlight new developments and provide students with questionnaires (e.g., "Are You Type A?") and applications (e.g., "Suicide Prevention") that enable them to apply information in the text to their own lives. The Fourth Edition includes several new "Closer Look" features:

- Preventing Psychological Disorders
- Writing as Therapy
- "You Gotta Have Friends" (friendship patterns and risk of the common cold)
- Emotions and the Heart
- EMDR: A Fad or a Find?
- The Recovered Memory Controversy
- St. John's Wort–A Natural "Prozac?"
- Serotonin and Aggression: Does it Put the Brakes on Violent Impulses?

Self-Scoring Questionnaires

Self-scoring questionnaires (for example, "Are you Type A?," "Fear of Fat Scale," and the "Life Orientation Test") involve students in the discussion at hand and permit them to evaluate their own behavior. In some cases, students may become more aware of troubling concerns, such as states of depression or problems with drug or alcohol use, that they may wish to bring to the attention of a professional. We have screened the questionnaires to ensure that they will provide students with useful information to reflect upon as well as serve as a springboard for class discussion.

Chapter Summaries

Chapter summaries are organized according to the major headings within the chapters. Students who use the SQ3R method may be advised by their instructors to read them before the chapters as a way of surveying the material and helping form questions to guide their reading.

Glossary

Key terms are boldfaced in the text and defined in the glossary. The origins of key terms are often discussed. By learning to attend to commonly found Greek and Latin word origins, students can acquire skills that will help them decipher the meanings of new words. These decoding skills are a valuable objective for general education as well as a specific asset for the study of abnormal psychology.

ANCILLARIES

No matter how comprehensive a textbook is, today's instructors and students require a complete teaching package to advance teaching and comprehension. *Abnormal Psychology in a Changing World* is accompanied by the following ancillaries:

Supplements for Instructors

Instructor's Resource Manual   Written by *Gary W. Piggrem* of DeVry Institute of Technology, the Instructor's Resource Manual is a true "course organizer" as it integrates Prentice Hall resources for teaching Abnormal Psychology. Includes updated *Lecture Suggestions, Discussion Questions* for the ABC NEWS/PRENTICE HALL video library, and more suggested *Student Activities*. ISBN 0-13-030006-3

Test Item File   Written by *Gary W. Piggrem* of DeVry Institute of Technology, this popular and comprehensive test bank has been updated to include new questions on revised text material. It now contains over 4000 multiple choice, true/false, and short answer/essay questions. Particular care has been given to the revision of the essay questions, which are now more comprehensive. ISBN 0-13-030015-2

Prentice Hall Custom Testing   This new testing system, a computerized version of the Test Item File, offers a two-track design for constructing tests: *EasyTest* for novice users and *FullTest* for more advanced users. In addition, Prentice Hall Custom Testing offers a rich selection of features such as On-Line Testing and Electronic Gradebook.
Windows PH Custom Test ISBN 0-13-030014-4
Macintosh Custom Test ISBN 0-13-030012-8

Prentice Hall Color Transparencies for Abnormal and Clinical Psychology Series II   A new set of full color transparencies has been created to accompany this text. Culminating from illustrations within the text as well as from outside sources, Series II was designed with lecture hall visibility and convenience in mind.
ISBN 0-13-080451-7

ABCNEWS   ABC News/Prentice Hall Video Library, Abnormal Psychology Series III   Segments from award-winning ABC News programs, including *20/20, Primetime Live,* and *Nightline* cover issues such as drugs and alcoholism, psychotherapy, autism, crime motivation, and depression, plus many more. ISBN 0-13-080449-5

Patients as Educators: Video Cases in Abnormal Psychology by James H. Scully, Jr., M.D., and Alan M. Dahms, Ph.D., Colorado State University This exclusive video contains a series of 10 patient interviews illustrating a range of disorders. Each interview is preceded by a brief history of the patient and a synopsis of some major symptoms of the disorder, and ends with a summary and brief analysis. ISBN 0-13-093022-9

Supplements for Students

Practice Test and Review Manual Written by Patty Rosenberger and Cori Ann Ramirez, both of Colorado State University, this guide has been expanded upon from the previous edition. Each chapter features learning objectives, a detailed chapter outline, list of key terms and people in a matching exercise format, practice multiple choice questions and practice short answer/essay questions. ISBN 0-13-030007-1

New York Times Abnormal Psychology Supplement *The New York Times* and Prentice Hall are sponsoring Themes of The Times, a program designed to enhance access to current information of relevance in the classroom. Through this program, the core subject matter provided in the text is supplemented by a collection of time-sensitive articles from one of the world's most distinguished newspapers, *The New York Times*. These articles demonstrate the vital, ongoing connection between what is learned in the classroom and what is happening in the world around us.

To enjoy the wealth of information in *The New York Times* daily, a reduced subscription rate is available. For information, call toll-free: 1-800-631-1222.

Prentice Hall and *The New York Times* are proud to co-sponsor Themes of the Times. We hope it will make the reading of both textbooks and newspapers a more dynamic, involving experience.

Psychology on the Internet: A Student's Guide Tap into World Wide Web sites in the area of psychology with the help of this innovative new guide from Prentice Hall! Designed to add a new dimension to your learning experience, this valuable guide will also help navigate your journey through cyberspace. Revolutionary and resourceful, it makes surfing the net simple—so get connected now and ride the wave of information's future! ISBN 0-13-022074-4

Companion Website

An interactive website is available for instructors and students who use *Abnormal Psychology in a Changing World, Fourth Edition*. Visitors will find a range of interactive resources, including a free, interactive student study guide, a virtual discussion group/chat area, and related links and resources. The quizzes available in every chapter can be e-mailed to instructors or teaching assistants. Please visit this site at: http://prenhall.com/nevid.

WebCT

For instructors interested in distance learning, Prentice Hall and Web-CT Educational Technologies offer a fully customizable, on-line course with www links, on-line testing, and many other course management features using the popular WebCT on-line course architecture. See your local Prentice Hall representative or visit our special Demonstration Central website at *http://www.prenhall.com/demo* for more information.

ACKNOWLEDGMENTS

The field of abnormal psychology is a moving target, as the literature base that informs our understanding is continually expanding. We are deeply indebted to a number of talented individuals who helped us hold our camera steady in taking a portrait of the field, focus in on the salient features of our subject matter, and develop our snapshots through prose.

First, our professional colleagues, who reviewed our manuscript through the first several editions and continue to help us refine and strengthen the material:

Gary Greenberg, Ph.D.
Connecticut College

Sally Bing, Ph.D.
University of Maryland Eastern Shore

Robert Kapche, Ph.D.
California State University, Long Beach

Christiane Brems, Ph.D.
University of Alaska Anchorage

Bernard Gorman, Ph.D.
Nassau Community College

Stuart Keeley, Ph.D.
Bowling Green State University

Bob Hill, Ph.D.
Appalachian State University

Larry Stout, Ph.D.
Nicholls State University

Joseph J. Palladino, Ph.D.
University of Southern Indiana

Harold Siegel, Ph.D.
Nassau Community College

Max Zwanziger, Ph.D.
Central Washington University

Carol Pandey, Ph.D.
L.A. Pierce College

Esther D. Rosenblum, Ph.D.
University of Vermont

J. Langhinrichsen-Rohling, Ph.D.
University of Nebraska-Lincoln

Second, but by no means second-rate, are the publishing professionals at Prentice-Hall who helped guide the development of this edition, especially Bill Webber, Executive Editor; Barbara DeVries and Alison Gnerre, Senior Production Editors, and Julie Tesser, photo researcher.

Finally, we (J.S.N. and S.A.R.) especially wish to thank the two people without whose inspiration and support this effort would never have materialized or been completed, Judith Wolf-Nevid and Lois Fichner-Rathus. Beverly Greene would like to extend her appreciation to Robert and Jennifer Pasley for the ways they continue to amaze and inspire her.

J.S.N
New York, New York

S.A.R.
Short Hills, New Jersey
SRathus@aol.com

B.A.G
Brooklyn, New York

Jeffrey S. Nevid is Professor of Psychology at St. John's University in New York, where he directs the Doctoral Program in Clinical Psychology, teaches graduate courses in research methods and behavior therapy, and supervises doctoral trainees in psychotherapy. He earned his Ph.D. in Clinical Psychology from the State University of New York at Albany and was awarded a National Insititue of Mental Health Post-Doctoral Fellowship in Mental Health Evaluation Research at Northwestern University. He has published numerous articles in such areas as clinical and community psychology, health psychology, training models in clinical psychology, and methodological issues in clinical research. He formerly taught at Hofstra University before joining the faculty at St. John's. He holds a Diplomate in Clinical Psychology from the American Board of Professional Psychology, is a Fellow of the Academy of Clinical Psychology (FAClinP), has served on the editorial board of the *Journal of Consulting and Clinical Psychology,* has coauthored several books with Spencer Rathus, and is author of the books, *A Student's Guide to AIDS* and *Other Sexually Transmitted Diseases* and *Choices: Sex in the Age of STDs.* His recent research on the development of a culturally-specific smoking cessation program for Hispanic smokers was supported by a grant from the National Heart, Lung, and Blood Institute of the National Institutes of Health.

Spencer A. Rathus received his Ph.D. from the State University of New York at Albany in 1972. He is on the faculty of Montclair State University in New Jersey. His areas of interest include psychological assessment, cognitive behavior therapy, and deviant behavior. He is the originator of the Rathus Assertiveness Schedule and has authored several books, including *Psychology in the New Millennium, Essentials of Psychology,* and *The World of Children.* He has coauthored *Making the Most of*

College with Lois Fichner-Rathus; *AIDS: What Every Student Needs to Know* with Susan Boughn; and *Behavior Therapy, Adjustment and Growth, Human Sexuality in a World of Diversity,* and *Health in the New Millennium* with Jeffrey S. Nevid.

Beverly A. Greene is Professor of Psychology at St. John's University and a licensed psychologist in private practice in New York City. She is a Fellow of the American Psychological Association, the Academy of Clinical Psychology, and the American Orthopsychiatric Association. She received her doctorate in clinical psychology from Adelphi University and holds a Diplomate in Clinical Psychology (ABPP). She has served on the editorial boards of the journals *Violence Against Women, Journal of Cultural Diversity and Ethnic Minority Psychology, Women & Therapy,* and *Journal of Feminist Family Therapy.* She was also the founding co-editor of *Psychological Perspectives on Lesbian, Gay and Bisexual Issues.* She is currently co-editing (with Leslie Jackson), *Psychotherapy with African American Women: Psychodynamic Perspectives* (Guilford Press).

Dr. Greene is the recipient of numerous national awards for her contributions to issues relating to diversity in professional psychology. She was the recipient of the Women of Color Psychologies Publication Award (1991), the Distinguished Humanitarian Award from the American Association of Applied and Preventive Psychology (1994), and the Psychotherapy with Women Research Award from the APA Division of Psychology of Women (1995, 1996). Her co-edited book, *Women of Color: Integrating Ethnic and Gender Identities in Psychotherapy,* was honored with the 1995 Distinguished Publication Award and the 1995 Women of Color Psychologies Publication Award, sponsored by the Association for Women in Psychology. She was also the recipient of a 1996 Outstanding Achievement Award from the APA Committee on Lesbian, Gay and Bisexual Concerns for pioneering scholarship and training efforts relating to the interaction of gender, ethnicity, and sexual orientation in contemporary psychology.

© Diana Ong
Grey Clowns

CHAPTER

Perspectives on Abnormal Psychology

TRUTH *or* FICTION?

1.1 Psychological disorders affect relatively few of us.

1.2 Behavior deemed abnormal in one society may be perceived as perfectly normal in another.

1.3 The modern medical model of abnormal behavior can be traced to the work of a Greek physician some 2,500 years ago.

1.4 Innocent people were drowned in medieval times as a way of certifying they were not possessed by the devil.

1.5 A night on the town in London a few hundred years ago may have included peering at the inmates at the local asylum.

1.6 Recent discoveries have shown that genetic factors account for a large number of psychological disorders.

1.7 Freud likened the mind to an immense iceberg, with only the tip rising into conscious awareness.

1.8 A survey of 1,500 Americans may provide a more accurate reflection of voting preferences and attitudes of the American public than one based on millions of participants.

1.9 Case studies have been conducted on people who have been dead for hundreds of years.

*When you have completed your study of
Chapter 1, you should be able to:*

1. Discuss six criteria used to define abnormal behavior.

2. Discuss relationships between cultural beliefs and norms and the labeling of behavior as normal or abnormal.

3. Recount the history of beliefs about disturbed behavior and treatment of people deemed "mad" or mentally ill.

4. Discuss the following contemporary perspectives on abnormal behavior: biological, psychodynamic, learning-based, humanistic, cognitive, and sociocultural.

5. Discuss the steps involved in the scientific method.

6. Discuss the various methods used to study abnormal behavior, including the naturalistic-observation method, the correlational method, the experimental method, kinship studies, the epidemiological method, and the case study method.

7. Explain the differences between three types of experimental validity and the ways in which experimenters control for subjects' and researchers' expectations.

Abnormal behavior might seem the concern of a few. After all, only a minority of the population will ever be admitted to a psychiatric hospital. Most people never seek the help of a **psychologist** or **psychiatrist.** Only a few people plead not guilty to crimes on grounds of insanity. Many of us have an "eccentric" relative, but few of us have relatives we would consider truly bizarre.

The truth of the matter is that abnormal behavior affects everyone in one way or another. Abnormal behavior patterns are conceptualized as disturbances of mental health and are classified as psychological disorders (also called mental disorders). These disorders involve deviations from normal psychological functioning. If we confine our definition of abnormal behavior to diagnosable mental disorders, such as anxiety disorders, mood disorders, schizophrenia, sexual dysfunctions, alcohol or drug abuse, and the like, perhaps 1 in 2 of us have been directly affected (R. C. Kessler, 1994). If we include the mental health problems of our family members, friends, and co-workers, and take into account those who foot the bill for treatment in the form of taxes and health insurance premiums, then perhaps none of us remains unaffected.

TRUTH *or* **FICTION** REVISITED

1.1 *False.* Psychological disorders affect virtually all of us in one way or another.

Abnormal psychology is the branch of the science of psychology that addresses the description, causes, and treatment of patterns of abnormal behavior. Let us pause for a moment to consider our use of terms. We prefer to use the term *psychological disorder* when referring to abnormal behavior patterns, rather than *mental disorder.* There are several reasons why we have adopted this approach. First, the term *psychological disorder* puts the study of abnormal behavior squarely within the purview of the field of psychology. Another reason is that the term *mental disorder* is generally associated with the **medical model** perspective that considers abnormal behavior patterns to be "symptoms" of underlying mental illnesses or disorders. Although the medical model remains a prominent perspective for understanding abnormal behavior patterns, we shall see that other perspectives, including psychological and sociocultural perspectives, also inform our understanding of abnormal behavior. Another reason is that the term mental disorder reinforces the traditional distinction between mental and physical phenomena. As we'll see, there is increasing awareness of the interrelationships between the body and the mind that calls into question this distinction.

In this chapter we first address the task of defining abnormal behavior. We see that throughout history, and even in the preceding prehistory, abnormal behavior has been viewed from different perspectives, or models. We chronicle the development of concepts of abnormal behavior and its treatment. We see that, historically speaking, "treatment" usually referred to what was done *to,* rather than *for,* people with abnormal behavior. Finally, we describe the ways in which psychologists and other scholars study abnormal behavior today.

WHAT IS ABNORMAL BEHAVIOR?

There are diverse patterns of abnormal behavior. Some involve anxiety or depression, but most of us become anxious or depressed from time to time, and our behavior is not deemed abnormal. It is normal to become anxious in anticipation of an important job interview or a final examination. It is appropriate to feel depressed when you have lost someone close to you or when you have failed at a test or on the job.

When are emotions such as anxiety and depression thus judged abnormal? One answer is that these feelings may be appraised as abnormal when they are not appropriate to the situation. It is normal to feel blue because of failure on a test, but not when one's grades are good or excellent. It is normal to feel anxious during a college admissions interview, but not whenever one enters a department store or boards a crowded elevator.

Abnormal behavior may also be suggested by the magnitude of the problem. Although some anxiety is normal enough before a job interview, feeling that one's heart is hammering away so relentlessly that it might leap from one's chest—and consequently canceling the interview—are not. Nor is it normal to feel so anxious in this situation that your clothing becomes soaked with perspiration.

Psychologists generally concur that behavior may be deemed abnormal when it meets some combination of these criteria:

1. *Behavior is unusual.* Behavior that is unusual is often considered abnormal. Only a few of us report seeing or hearing things that are not really there; "seeing things" and "hearing things" are almost always considered abnormal in our culture, except, perhaps, in cases of religious experience (see Chapter 12). Yet hallucinations are not deemed unusual in some non-Western cultures. Becoming overcome with feelings of panic when entering a department store or when standing in a crowded elevator is also uncommon and considered abnormal. But uncommon behavior is not in itself abnormal. Only one person can hold the record for swimming or running the fastest 100 meters. The record-holding athlete differs from the rest of us but, again, is not considered abnormal.

Thus, rarity or statistical deviance is not a sufficient basis for labeling behavior abnormal; nevertheless, it is one yardstick often used to judge abnormality.

2. *Behavior is socially unacceptable or violates social norms.* All societies have norms (standards) that define the kinds of behaviors that are acceptable in given contexts. In our society, standing on a soapbox in a park and repeatedly shouting "Kill!" to passersby would be labeled abnormal; shouting "Kill!" in the grandstands at an important football game is usually within normal bounds, however tasteless it may seem. Although the use of norms remains one of the important standards for defining abnormal behavior, we should be aware of some limitations of this definition.

One implication of basing the definition of abnormal behavior on social norms is that norms reflect relative standards, not universal truths. What is normal in one culture may be abnormal in another. For example, Americans who assume strangers are devious and try to take advantage are usually regarded as distrustful, perhaps even **paranoid.** But such suspicions were justified among the Mundugumor, a tribe of cannibals studied by anthropologist Margaret Mead (1935). Within that culture, male strangers, even the male members of one's own family, *were* typically malevolent toward others.

TRUTH *or* FICTION REVISITED

1.2 *True.* Behavior that is deemed normal in one culture may be viewed as abnormal in another.

Clinicians need to weigh cultural differences in determining what is normal and abnormal. In the case of the Mundugumor, this need is more or less obvious. Sometimes, however, differences are more subtle. For example, what is seen as normal, outspoken behavior by most American women might be interpreted as brazen behavior when viewed in the context of another, more traditional culture. Moreover, what strikes one generation as abnormal may be considered by others to fall within the normal spectrum. For example, until the mid-1970s homosexuality was classified as a mental disorder by the psychiatric profession (see Chapter 11). Today, however, the psychiatric profession no longer considers homosexuality a mental disorder, and many people argue that contemporary societal norms should include homosexuality as a normal variation in behavior.

When is anxiety abnormal? Negative emotions such as anxiety are considered abnormal when they are judged to be excessive or inappropriate to the situation. Anxiety is generally regarded as normal when it is experienced during a job interview (A), so long as it is not so severe that it prevents the interviewee from performing adequately. Anxiety is deemed to be abnormal if it is experienced whenever one boards an elevator (B).

Is this abnormal? One of the criteria used to determine whether behavior is abnormal is whether it deviates from acceptable standards of conduct or social norms. The behavior and attire of these men might be considered abnormal in the context of a classroom or workplace, but perhaps not at a football game.

Another implication of basing normality on compliance with social norms is the tendency to brand nonconformists as mentally disturbed. We may come to brand behavior we do not like or understand as "sick," rather than accept that behavior may be normal even if it offends or puzzles us.

3. *Perception or interpretation of reality is faulty.* Normally speaking, our sensory systems and cognitive processes permit us to form accurate mental representations of the environment. But seeing things and hearing voices that are not present are considered **hallucinations,** which in our culture are often taken as signs of an underlying disorder. Similarly, holding unfounded ideas or **delusions,** such as **ideas of persecution** that the CIA or the Mafia are out to get one, may be regarded as signs of mental disturbance—unless, of course, they *are.* (A former secretary of state is credited with having remarked that he might, indeed, be paranoid; his paranoia, however, did not mean he was without enemies.)

It is normal in the United States to say that one "talks" to God through prayer. If, however, a person claims to have literally seen God or heard the voice of God—as opposed to, say, being divinely inspired—we may come to regard her or him as mentally disturbed.

4. *The person is in significant personal distress.* States of personal distress caused by troublesome emotions, such as anxiety, fear, or depression, may be considered abnormal. As we noted earlier, however, anxiety and depression are sometimes appropriate responses to one's situation. Real threats and losses occur from time to time, and *lack* of an emotional response to them would be regarded as abnormal. Appropriate feelings of distress are not considered abnormal unless they become prolonged or persist long after the source of

anguish has been removed (after most people would have adjusted) or if they are so intense that they impair the individual's ability to function.

5. *Behavior is maladaptive or self-defeating.* Behavior that leads to unhappiness rather than self-fulfillment can be regarded as abnormal. Behavior that limits our ability to function in expected roles, or to adapt to our environments, may also be considered abnormal. According to these criteria, heavy alcohol consumption that impairs one's health or social and occupational functioning may be viewed as abnormal. **Agoraphobic** behavior, characterized by intense fear of venturing into public places, may be considered abnormal in that it is both uncommon and also maladaptive because it impairs the individual's ability to fulfill work and family responsibilities.

6. *Behavior is dangerous.* Behavior that is dangerous to oneself or other people may be considered abnormal. Here, too, the social context is crucial. In wartime, people who sacrifice themselves or charge the enemy with little apparent concern for their own safety may be characterized as courageous, heroic, and patriotic. But people who threaten or attempt suicide because of the pressures of civilian life are usually considered abnormal.

Abnormal behavior thus has multiple definitions. Depending on the case, some criteria may be weighted more heavily than others. But in most cases, a combination of these criteria is used to define abnormality.

It is one thing to recognize and label behavior as abnormal; it is another to understand and explain it. Philosophers, physicians, natural scientists, and psychologists have used various approaches, or **models,** in the effort to explain abnormal behavior. Some approaches have been based on superstition; others have invoked religious explanations. Some current views are predominantly biological; others, psychological. We consider various historical and contemporary approaches to understanding abnormal behavior. First, let us look further at the importance of cultural beliefs and expectations in determining which behavior patterns are deemed abnormal. Let us also consider what the results of a recent national survey tell us about the mental health of Americans (see "A Closer Look").

CULTURAL BASES OF ABNORMAL BEHAVIOR

Behavior that is considered normal in one culture may be deemed abnormal in another. Hallucinating (hearing voices or seeing things that are not in fact present) is a common experience among Australian aborigines (D. J. Spencer, 1983) but is generally taken as a sign of abnormality in our culture. Aborigines also believe they can communicate with the spirits of their ancestors and that dreams are shared among people, especially close relatives. Such beliefs may be regarded in Western culture as delusions (fixed false beliefs). Hallucinations and delusions are taken to be common features of schizophrenia in Western culture. Should we thus conclude that aborigines are seriously disturbed or have schizophrenia? What standards should be applied in judging abnormal behavior in other cultures? Even aborigines perceive "madness" in some members of their community, although the criteria used to label someone as mentally disturbed may differ from those used by health professionals in Western society.

Kleinman (1987) offers an example of "hearing voices" among Native Americans to underscore the ways in which judgments about abnormal behavior are embedded within a cultural context:

> Ten psychiatrists trained in the same assessment technique and diagnostic criteria who are asked to examine 100 American Indians shortly after the latter have experienced the death of a spouse, a parent or a child may determine with close to 100% consistency that those individuals report hearing, in the first month of grieving, the voice of the dead person calling to them as the spirit ascends to the afterworld. [While such judgments may be consistent across observers] the determination of whether such reports are a sign of an abnormal mental state is an interpretation based on knowledge of this group's behavioural norms and range of normal experiences of bereavement. (p. 453)

To many Native Americans, bereaved people who report hearing the spirits of the deceased calling to them as they ascend to the afterlife are regarded as normal. Kleinman's example leads us to recognize that behavior should not be considered abnormal when it is normative within the cultural setting in which it occurs. Concepts of health and illness may also have different meanings in different cultures. Many traditional Native American cultures distinguish between illnesses that are believed to arise from influences outside the culture, called "White man's sicknesses," such as alcoholism and drug addiction, from those that emanate from a lack of harmony with traditional tribal life and thought, which are called "Indian sicknesses" (Trimble, 1991). Traditional healers, shamans, and medicine men and women are called on to treat and cure "Indian sickness." When the problem is thought to have its cause outside the community, help may be sought from "White man's medicine."

The very words that Western cultures use to describe psychological disorders—words such as depression or even mental health—may have very different meanings in other cultures or no equivalent meaning at all. In many non-Western societies, depression may be closer in meaning to the concept of "soul loss" than to Western concepts involving a sense of loss of purpose and meaning in life (Shweder, 1985).

Abnormal behavior patterns may also take different forms in different cultures. Westerners may experience anxiety, for example, in the form of excessive worrying about paying the mortgage, losing a job, and so on. Yet "[I]n a number of African cultures, anxiety is expressed as fears of failure in procreation, in dreams and complaints about witchcraft" (Kleinman, 1987). Some Australian aborigines develop intense fears of sorcery, which may be accompanied by the belief that one is in mortal danger from evil spirits (D. J. Spencer, 1983).

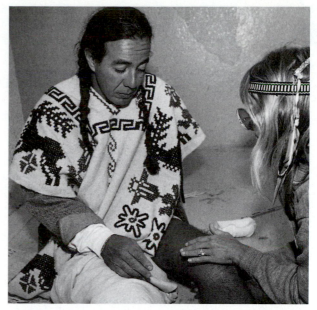

A traditional Native-American healer. Many traditional Native Americans distinguish between illnesses that are believed to arise from influences external to their own culture ("White man's sicknesses") and those that emanate from a lack of harmony with traditional tribal life and thought ("Indian sicknesses"). Traditional healers such as the one shown here may be called on to treat "Indian sickness," whereas "White man's medicine" may be sought to help people deal with problems whose causes are seen as lying outside the community, such as alcoholism and drug addiction.

Depression may also be expressed differently in different cultures (Bebbington, 1993). In some Eastern cultures, depression is experienced largely in terms of physical symptoms such as headaches, fatigue, or weakness, rather than by feelings of guilt or sadness that are common in Western cultures (APA, 1994). The fact that cultural differences exist does not mean the diagnostic categories we use to classify depression or other abnormal behavior patterns have no relevance in other cultures. Yet we need to determine that our concepts of abnormal behavior are recognizable and valid when applied to other cultures (Bebbington, 1993; Kleinman, 1987). The reverse is equally true. The concept of "soul loss" may characterize psychological distress in some non-Western societies but have little or no relevance to middle class North Americans.

Evidence from multinational studies conducted by the World Health Organization (WHO) in the 1960s and 1970s showed that the behavior pattern we characterize as schizophrenia exists in countries as far flung as Colombia, India, China, Denmark, Nigeria, and the former Soviet Union, among others (Jablensky et al., 1992). Rates of schizophrenia and its general features were actually quite similar among the countries studied. However, differences have also been observed in the features of schizophrenia across cultures (Thakker & Ward, 1998).

We also find evidence based on a study of medical patients in some 14 different countries, including Germany, the Netherlands, India, Turkey, Nigeria, Japan, China, and Brazil, that diagnosable mental health disorders such as

The Mental Health of Americans

The fact that abnormal behavior patterns are not a problem affecting only relatively few in our society is underscored by the results of the most comprehensive study to date of the mental health of Americans. The National Comorbidity Survey (NCS) represents the first survey of its kind to use a structured psychiatric interview administered to a nationally representative sample of adults in the United States (R. C. Kessler, 1994; R. C. Kessler et al., 1993, 1994; Regier et al., 1998).[1] The term comorbidity refers to the co-occurrence of two or more disorders.

How common are psychological disorders? Very common. Nearly half (48%) of the people surveyed had a diagnosable psychological disorder at some point in their lives, and nearly one in three (30%) had experienced a diagnosable disorder during the past year. More than half of the people who had any psychological disorder during their lives had at least two disorders. Though critics of the survey argue that the rates may be somewhat overstated (D. L. Newman et al., 1996), it is clear that psychological disorders affect a large proportion of the population.

Figure 1.1 shows the lifetime and past-year prevalences of several major classes of psychological disorders in the NCS survey. The rates of particular disorders varied in relation to such factors as age, gender, region, social class, and ethnicity. Psychological disorders were most common among people in the 25- to 32-year age range and declined with increasing age. Anxiety and

depression were more common among women. Alcohol and substance abuse problems more commonly affected men. People living in urban areas were as likely as people in rural communities to have experienced psychological disorders during the previous year or in the course of their lifetimes. Yet people from the lower socioeconomic levels were more likely than more affluent people to have experienced a psychological disorder. The South had the lowest rates of psychological disorders. The East had the greatest number of people with a history of three or more disorders. Later in the chapter we focus on differences across ethnic groups.

The results of the NCS survey illustrate not only how common psychological disorders are but also how often these disorders go untreated. Overall, only about 1 in 5 people with a diagnosable psychological disorder during the past year reported receiving any professional help for the problem, and fewer than 1 in 8 received help from a mental health professional. Even among people with three or more disorders in the past year, only 1 in 3 received any professional treatment during that time, and only about 1 in 5 received treatment from a mental health professional. Though many of the diagnosable disorders reported in the NCS survey involve milder conditions that do not require treatment (Spitzer, 1998; Dubovsky, 1998), it is clear that a great many people with severe psychological disorders that could benefit from treatment go untreated.

Psychiatric disorders and related problems such as days lost from work because of mental health problems

---

[1]To be precise, the NCS was not quite national, as the sample was limited to people residing in the 48 states in the U.S. mainland.

---

depression and anxiety disorders were common, although prevalence rates did vary across countries (Ormel et al., 1994). Still, depression may be experienced differently across cultures (Thakker & Ward, 1998). This doesn't mean that depression doesn't exist in other cultures. Rather, it suggests we need to consider how people in different cultures experience states of emotional distress, including depression and anxiety, rather than imposing our perspectives on their experiences.

Societal views of abnormal behavior also vary across cultures. In our culture, models based on medical disease and psychological factors have achieved prominence in explaining abnormal behavior. "In traditional cultures, mental disorder is frequently perceived in terms of supernatural causation or possession" (Lefley, 1990). The notion of su-

pernatural causation, or **demonology,** held prominence in Western society until the Age of Enlightenment.

HISTORICAL PERSPECTIVES ON ABNORMAL BEHAVIOR

Throughout the history of Western culture, concepts of abnormal behavior have been shaped, to some degree, by the prevailing **worldview** of the time. Throughout much of history, beliefs in supernatural forces, demons, and evil spirits held sway. Abnormal behavior was often taken as a sign of **possession.** In more modern times, the predominant—but by no means universal!—worldview has shifted toward beliefs in science and reason. Abnormal behavior has come to

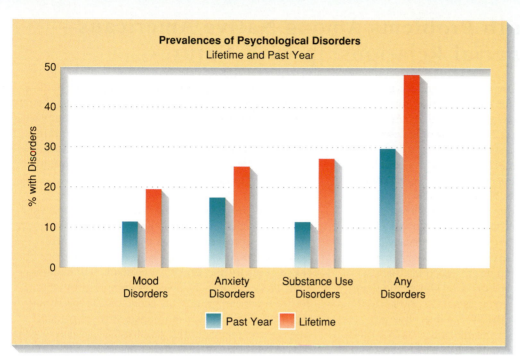

FIGURE 1.1 *Lifetime and past year prevalences of psychological disorders.*
This graph shows the percentages of adults in the U.S. in the 15–49-year-old age range who show evidence of having diagnosable psychological disorders in either the past year or lifetime. The data are shown for several major diagnostic categories. The category of mood disorders includes major depressive episode, manic episode, and dysthymia (discussed in Chapter 7). Anxiety disorders includes panic disorder, agoraphobia without panic disorder, social phobia, specific phobia, and generalized anxiety disorder (discussed in Chapter 5). Substance use disorders include abuse or dependence disorders involving alcohol or other drugs (discussed in Chapter 9).

Source: National Comorbidity Survey; Kessler et al. (1994).

are more prevalent in the United States than in the Canadian province of Ontario (R. C. Kessler et al., 1997a). The reasons for this difference are unclear, but two possibilities are worth exploring: U.S. residents (1) face greater stress in their lives or (2) have less access to supportive social networks.

be viewed in our culture as the product of physical and psychosocial factors, not demonic possession.

The Demonological Model

Let us begin our journey with an example from prehistory. Archaeologists have unearthed human skeletons from the Stone Age with egg-sized cavities in the skull. One interpretation of these holes is that our prehistoric ancestors believed abnormal behavior reflected the invasion of evil spirits. Perhaps they used the harsh method—called **trephining**—of creating a pathway through the skull to provide an outlet for those irascible spirits. Fresh bone growth indicates that some people managed to survive the ordeal.

Threat of trephining may have persuaded people to comply with group or tribal norms to the best of their abilities. Because no written records or accounts of the purposes of trephination exist, other explanations are possible. Perhaps trephination was used as a primitive form of surgery to remove shattered pieces of bone or blood clots that resulted from head injuries (Maher & Maher, 1985).

Explanation of abnormal behavior in terms of supernatural or divine causes is termed the *demonological model*. The ancients explained natural forces in terms of divine will and spirits. The ancient Babylonians believed the movements of the stars and the planets were fashioned by the adventures and conflicts of the gods. The ancient Greeks believed their gods toyed with humans; when aroused to wrath, they could unleash forces of nature to wreak havoc

Mental Health Problems Among Native Americans— Loss of a Special Relationship with Nature?

Native Americans—American Indians and Alaskan Natives—constitute one of the smallest ethnic minority groups in the United States (Trimble, 1991). According to the 1990 census, nearly 2 million people describe themselves as either American Indian or Alaskan Native (Aleut Eskimo, or Indian). Native American populations are found in virtually every state but are largely concentrated in states west of the Mississippi River. On the whole, the Native American population is among the most impoverished ethnic groups in the country. Like other groups who are socially and economically disadvantaged, Native Americans suffer from a disproportionate incidence of mental health problems, such as alcoholism, depression, suicide, drug abuse, and delinquency (T. J. Young & French, 1996). In one study, the death rate for cirrhosis of the liver (a liver disease caused primarily by chronic alcoholism) was four times greater among Native Alaskans (Indians, Eskimos,

Aleuts) than among White Alaskans (Kraus & Buffler, 1979). In a study of an American Indian village, the rate of diagnosable mood disorders was about four times greater than the rate in the general population (Kinzie, Leung, Boehntein, & Matsunaga, 1992). The death rate due to suicide among Native Alaskans was found to be three times the national average (Kraus & Buffler, 1979).

When you envision hula dancing, luaus, and wide tropical beaches, you may assume Native Hawaiians are a carefree people. Reality paints a different picture, however. One reason for studying the relationships between ethnicity and abnormal behavior is to debunk erroneous stereotypes. Native Hawaiians, like other Native American groups, are economically disadvantaged and suffer a disproportionate share of physical diseases and mental health problems. The death rate for Native Hawaiians is 34% higher than that of the general

---

on disrespectful or arrogant humans, even cloud their minds with madness.

In ancient Greece, people who behaved abnormally were often sent to temples dedicated to Aesculapius, the god of healing. Priests believed Aesculapius would visit the afflicted persons while they slept in the temple and offer them restorative advice through dreams. Rest, a nutritious diet, and exercise were also believed to contribute to treatment. Incurables might be driven from the temple by stoning.

Origins of the Medical Model: In "Ill Humor"

Not all ancient Greeks believed in the demonological model. The seeds of naturalistic explanations of abnormal behavior were sown by Hippocrates and developed by other physicians in the ancient world, especially Galen.

Hippocrates (ca. 460–377 B.C.), the celebrated physician of the Golden Age of Greece, challenged the prevailing beliefs of his time by arguing that illnesses of the body and mind were the result of natural causes, not possession by supernatural spirits. He believed the health of the body and mind depended on the balance of **humors** or vital fluids in the body: phlegm, black bile, blood, and yellow bile. An imbalance of humors, he thought, accounted for abnormal behavior. A lethargic or sluggish person was believed to have an excess of phlegm, from which we derive the word **phleg-**

matic. An overabundance of black bile was believed to cause depression, or **melancholia.** An excess of blood created a **sanguine** disposition: cheerful, confident, and optimistic. An excess of yellow bile made people "bilious" and **choleric**—quick-tempered, that is.

Though we no longer subscribe to Hippocrates's theory of bodily humors, his theory is of historical importance because of its break from demonology. It is also foreshadowed the development of the modern medical model, the view that abnormal behavior results from underlying biological processes.

TRUTH ⊕ FICTION REVISITED

1.3 *True.* The foundations of the modern medical model can be traced to the Greek physician Hippocrates who lived some 2,500 years ago.

Hippocrates made many contributions to modern thought and, indeed, to modern medical practice. Hippocrates had even begun to classify abnormal behavior patterns, using three main categories that find some equivalents today: *melancholia* to characterize excessive depression, *mania* to refer to exceptional excitement, and *phrenitis* (from the Greek, "inflammation of the brain") to characterize the bizarre kinds of behavior that might today typify schizophrenia. Medical schools continue to pay homage to Hippocrates by having new physicians swear the Hippocratic oath in his honor.

U.S. population, largely because of an increased rate of serious diseases including cancer and heart disease (Mokuau, 1990). Native Hawaiians also have a 5- to 10-year lower life expectancy than other groups in Hawaii (Hammond, 1988). Compared to other Hawaiians, Native Hawaiians have experienced higher rates of mental health problems, including higher suicide rates among males, higher rates of alcoholism and drug abuse, and higher rates of antisocial disorders (Mokuau, 1990). Researchers have linked depression and associated feelings of despair and a sense of hopelessness to suicide attempts among native Hawaiian adolescents (Yuen et al., 1996).

Mental health problems among Native Americans and Native Hawaiians may at least partly reflect alienation and disenfranchisement from the land and a way of life that resulted from colonization by European cultures. Native peoples often attribute mental health problems, especially depression and alcoholism, to the collapse of their traditional culture brought about by colonization (Timpson et al., 1988). Here some researchers recount how a Native Canadian elder in northwestern Ontario explained depression in his people (Timpson et al., 1988, p. 6.):

Before the White Man came into our world we had our own way of worshipping the Creator. We had our own church and rituals. When hunting was good, people would gather together to give gratitude. This gave us close contact with the Creator. There were many different rituals depending on the tribe. People would dance in the hills and play drums to give recognition to the Great Spirit. It was like talking to the Creator and living daily with its spirit. Now people have lost this. They can't use these methods and have lost conscious contact with this high power. The more distant we are from the Creator the more complex things are because we have no sense of direction. We don't recognize where life is from.

The depression so common among indigenous or native peoples apparently reflects the loss of a relationship with the world that was based on maintaining harmony with nature (Timpson et al., 1988). The description of the loss of this special relationship reminds one of the Western concept of alienation.

Galen (ca. A.D. 130–200), a Greek physician who attended Roman emperor-philosopher Marcus Aurelius, adopted and expanded on the teachings of Hippocrates. Among Galen's contributions was the discovery that arteries carried blood, not air, as had been formerly believed.

Medieval Times

The Middle Ages, or medieval times, cover the millennium of European history from about A.D. 476 through A.D. 1450. After the passing of Galen, belief in supernatural causes, especially the doctrine of possession, increased in influence and eventually dominated medieval thought. The doctrine of possession held that abnormal behaviors were a sign of possession by evil spirits or the devil. This belief was embodied within the teachings of the Roman Catholic church, which became the unifying force in western Europe following the decline of the Roman Empire. Although belief in possession antedated the Church and is found in ancient Egyptian and Greek writings, the Church revitalized it. The treatment of choice for abnormal behavior was **exorcism.** Exorcists were employed to persuade evil spirits that the bodies of their intended victims were basically uninhabitable. Methods included prayer, waving a cross at the victim, beating and flogging, even starving the victim. If the victim still displayed unseemly behavior, there were yet more powerful remedies, such as the rack, a device of torture. It seems clear that recipients of these "remedies" would be motivated to conform their behavior to social expectations as best they could.

The Renaissance—the great European revival in learning, art, and literature—began in Italy in the 1400s and spread gradually throughout Europe. The Renaissance is considered the transition from the medieval world to the modern. Therefore, it is ironic that fear of witches also reached its height during the Renaissance.

Witchcraft

The late 15th through the late 17th centuries were especially dangerous times to be unpopular with your neighbors. These were times of massive persecutions of people, particularly women, who were accused of witchcraft. Officials of the Roman Catholic church believed witches made pacts with the devil, practiced satanic rituals, and committed heinous acts, such as eating babies and poisoning crops. In 1484, Pope Innocent VIII decreed that witches be executed. Two Dominican priests compiled a manual for witch-hunting, called the *Malleus Maleficarum* ("The Witches' Hammer"), to help inquisitors identify suspected witches. Over 100,000 accused witches were killed in the next two centuries.

There were also creative "diagnostic" tests for detecting possession and witchcraft. One was a water-float test. It was

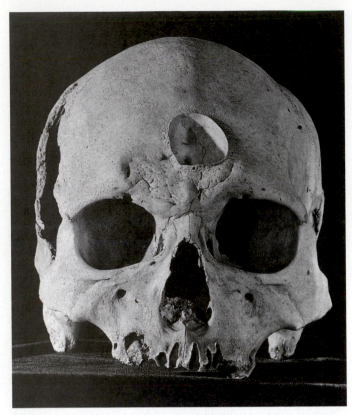

Trephining. Trephining refers to a practice of some prehistoric cultures by which a hole was chipped into a person's skull. Some investigators speculate that the practice represented an ancient form of surgery. Perhaps trephining was intended to release demons that were believed responsible for abnormal behavior.

Exorcism. This medieval woodcut illustrates the practice of exorcism, which was used to expel evil spirits who were believed to have possessed people.

based on the principle that pure metals settle to the bottom during smelting, whereas impurities bob up to the surface. Suspects who sank and were drowned were ruled pure. Suspects who were able to keep their heads above water were regarded as being in league with the devil. Then they were in "real" trouble. This trial is the source of the phrase, "Damned if you do and damned if you don't."

TRUTH *or* FICTION REVISITED

1.4 *True.* Innocent people were drowned in medieval times as a way of certifying they were not possessed by the devil.

Modern scholars once believed the "witches" of the Middle Ages and the Renaissance were actually people who were mentally disturbed. They were believed to be persecuted because their abnormal behavior was taken as evidence they were in league with the devil. It is true that many suspected witches confessed to impossible behaviors, such as flying or engaging in sexual intercourse with the devil. At face value such confessions might suggest disturbances in thinking and perception that are consistent with a modern diagnosis of a psychological disorder, such as schizophrenia. Most of these confessions can be discounted, however, because they were extracted under torture by inquisitors who were bent on finding evidence to support accusations of

witchcraft (Spanos, 1978). In other cases, the threat of torture and other forms of intimidation were sufficient to extract false confessions. Although some of those who were persecuted as witches probably did show abnormal behavior patterns, most did not (Schoenman, 1984). Rather, accusations of witchcraft appeared to be a convenient means of disposing of social nuisances and political rivals, of seizing property, and of suppressing heresy (Spanos, 1978). In English villages, many of the accused were poor, unmarried elderly women who were forced to beg their neighbors for food. If misfortune befell people who declined to help, the beggar might be accused of causing the misery by having cast a curse on the uncharitable family (Spanos, 1978). If the woman was generally unpopular, accusations of witchcraft were more likely to be followed up.

Although demons were believed to play roles both in abnormal behavior and witchcraft, there was a difference between the two. Victims of possession may have been perceived to have been afflicted as retribution for wrongdoing, but it was allowed that some people who showed abnormal behavior might be totally innocent victims of demonic possession. Witches, on the other hand, were believed to have voluntarily entered into a pact with the devil and renounced God. Witches were generally seen as more deserving of torture and execution (Spanos, 1978).

Historical trends do not follow straight lines. Although the demonological model held sway during the Middle Ages and much of the Renaissance, it did not universally supplant belief in naturalistic causes (Schoenman, 1984). In medieval England, for example, demonic possession was only rarely invoked as the cause of abnormal behavior in cases in which

The water-float test. This test was one way in which medieval authorities sought to detect possession and witchcraft. Managing to float above the water line was deemed a sign of impurity. In the lower right-hand corner, you can see the bound hands and feet of one poor unfortunate who failed to remain afloat, but whose drowning would have cleared any suspicions of possession.

a person was held to be insane by legal authorities (Neugebauer, 1979). Most explanations involved natural causes for unusual behavior, such as illness or trauma to the brain. In England, in fact, some disturbed people were kept in hospitals until they were restored to sanity (Alldheridge, 1979). The Renaissance Belgian physician Johann Weyer (1515–1588) also took up the cause of Hippocrates and Galen by arguing that abnormal behavior and thought patterns were caused by physical problems.

Asylums By the late 15th and early 16th centuries, **asylums,** or "madhouses," began to crop up throughout Europe. Many were former leprosariums, which were no longer needed because of a decline in leprosy that occurred during the late Middle Ages. Asylums often gave refuge to beggars as well as the disturbed, and conditions were generally appalling. Residents were often chained to their beds and left to lie in their own waste or wander about unassisted. Some asylums became public spectacles. In one asylum in London, Bethlehem Hospital—from which the word *bedlam* is derived—the public could buy tickets to observe the bizarre antics of the inmates, much as they would view a sideshow in a circus or animals at a zoo.

"Bedlam." The bizarre antics of the patients at Bethlehem Hospital in London in the 18th century were a source of entertainment for the well-heeled gentry of the town, such as the two well-dressed women in the middle of the painting. The word *bedlam* derives from the name of this hospital.

TRUTH _or_ FICTION REVISITED

1.5 True. A night on the town for the gentry of London may have included a visit to a local asylum, Bethlehem Hospital.

The Reform Movement and Moral Therapy

The modern era of treatment can be traced to the efforts of individuals such as the Frenchmen Jean-Baptiste Pussin and Philippe Pinel in the late 18th and early 19th centuries. They argued that people who behaved abnormally suffered from diseases and should be treated humanely. This view was not popular at the time. Deranged people were generally regarded by the public as threats to society, not as sick people in need of treatment.

From 1784 to 1802, Pussin, a layman, was placed in charge of a ward for people considered "incurably insane" at La Bicêtre, a large mental hospital in Paris. Although Pinel is often credited with freeing the inmates of La Bicêtre from their chains, Pussin was actually the first official to unchain a group of the "incurably insane." These unfortunates had been considered too dangerous and unpredictable to be left unchained. But Pussin believed that if they were treated with kindness, there would be no need for chains. As he predicted, most of the shut-ins became manageable and calm when their chains were removed. They could walk the hospital grounds and take in fresh air. Pussin also forbade the staff from treating the residents harshly, and he discharged employees who disregarded his directives.

Pinel (1745–1826) became medical director for the incurables' ward at La Bicêtre in 1793 and continued the humane treatment Pussin had begun. He stopped harsh practices, such as bleeding and purging, and moved patients from darkened dungeons to well-ventilated, sunny rooms.

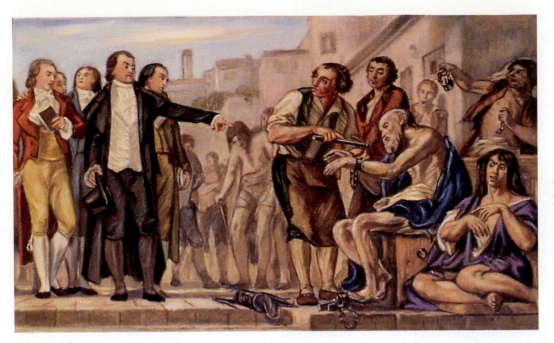

The unchaining of inmates at La Bicêtre by 18th-century French reformer Philippe Pinel. Continuing the work of Jean-Baptiste Pussin, Pinel stopped harsh practices, such as bleeding and purging, and moved inmates from darkened dungeons to sunny, airy rooms. Pinel also took the time to converse with inmates, in the belief that understanding and concern would help restore them to normal functioning.

Pinel also spent hours talking to inmates, in the belief that showing understanding and concern would help restore them to normal functioning.

The philosophy of treatment that emerged from these efforts was labeled **moral therapy.** It was based on the belief that functioning could be restored by providing humane treatment in a relaxed and decent environment. Similar reforms were instituted at about this time in England by William Tuke and later in the United States by Dorothea Dix. Another influential figure was the American physician Benjamin Rush (1745–1813)—also a signatory to the Declaration of Independence and an early leader of the antislavery movement (Farr, 1994). Rush, considered the "father of American psychiatry," penned the first American textbook on psychiatry in 1812: *Medical Inquiries and Observations upon the Diseases of the Mind.* He believed that madness was caused by engorgement of the blood vessels of the brain. To relieve pressure, he recommended bloodletting and other harsh treatments such as purging and ice-cold baths. On the other hand, he advanced humane treatment by encouraging the staff of his Philadelphia Hospital to treat patients with kindness, respect, and understanding. He also favored the therapeutic use of occupational therapy, music, and travel (Farr, 1994). His hospital became the first in the United States to admit patients for psychological disorders.

Dorothea Dix (1802–1887), a Boston schoolteacher, traveled about the country decrying the deplorable conditions in the jails and almshouses where deranged people were often placed. As a direct result of her efforts, 32 mental hospitals were established throughout the United States.

A Step Backward In the latter half of the 19th century, however, the belief that abnormal behaviors could be successfully treated or cured by moral therapy fell into disfavor. A period of apathy ensued in which patterns of abnormal behavior were deemed incurable (Grob, 1983). Mental institutions in the United States grew in size and came to provide little more than custodial care. Conditions deteriorated. Mental hospitals became frightening places. It was not uncommon to find residents "wallowing in their own excrements," in the words of a New York State official of the time (Grob, 1983). Straitjackets, handcuffs, cribs, straps, and other devices were used to restrain excitable or violent patients.

Deplorable hospital conditions remained commonplace through the middle of the 20th century. By the mid-1950s, the population in mental hospitals had risen to half a million patients. Although some good state hospitals provided decent and humane care (Grob, 1983), many were described as little more than "human snakepits." Residents were crowded into wards that lacked even rudimentary sanitation. Inhabitants were literally locked up for indefinite stays and received little more than custodial care. By the mid-20th century, the appalling conditions that many mental patients were forced to endure led to increasing calls for reforms of the mental health system.

The Contemporary Exodus from State Hospitals Two major factors led to a mass exodus from mental hospitals in the post-World War II era: the advent of a new class of drugs—the *phenothiazines*—and the Community Mental-Health Centers Act of 1963. The **phenothiazines,** a group of antipsychotic drugs that helped quell the most flagrant behavior patterns associated with schizophrenia, were introduced in the 1950s. They reduced the need for indefinite hospital stays and permitted many people with schizophrenia to be discharged to less restrictive living arrangements in the community, such as halfway houses, group homes, and independent living.

In response to the growing call for reform of the mental-health system, Congress established in 1963 a nationwide system of community mental-health centers that was intended to offer continuing support and care to former hospital residents. It was hoped these centers would help patients return to their communities and assume more independent and fulfilling lives. This policy of **deinstitutionalization** caused a steady decline in the mental hospital census. The mental hospital population across the United States declined from more than 550,000 in 1955 to fewer than 130,000 by the late 1980s (D. Braddock, 1992; Kiesler & Sibulkin, 1987). Some mental hospitals were closed entirely (Salokangas & Saarinen, 1998). Although deplorable conditions may persist in some institutions, most contemporary mental hospitals are better managed and provide more humane care than those of the 19th and early 20th centuries.

Critics contend that the exodus from state hospitals abandoned tens of thousands of marginally functioning people to communities that lacked adequate housing and other forms of support. Many of the homeless people we see wandering city streets and sleeping in bus terminals and train stations are discharged mental patients (see Chapter 3).

Pathways to the Present

By the late 17th century, society at large began to turn from religious dogma to reason and science to explain natural phenomena and human behavior. The nascent sciences of biology, chemistry, physics, and astronomy offered promise that knowledge could be derived from scientific methods of observation and experimentation. The 18th and 19th centuries witnessed rapid developments in medical science. Scientific discoveries uncovered the microbial causes of some kinds of diseases and gave rise to preventive measures. Against this backdrop the German physician Wilhelm Griesinger (1817–1868) argued that abnormal behavior was rooted in diseases of the brain. Griesinger's views influenced another German physician, Emil Kraepelin (1856–1926), who wrote an influential textbook on psychiatry in 1883 in which he likened mental disorders to physical diseases. Griesinger and Kraepelin paved the way for the development of the modern medical model, which attempts to explain abnormal behavior on the basis of underlying biological defects or abnormalities, not evil spirits. According to the medical model, people behaving abnormally suffer from mental illnesses or disorders that can be classified, like physical illnesses, according to their distinctive causes and symptoms. Not all adopters of the medical model believe every pattern of abnormal behavior is a product of defective biology, but they maintain that patterns of abnormal behavior can be likened to physical illnesses in that their features can be conceptualized as symptoms of underlying disorders, whatever their cause.

Emil Kraepelin and the Development of the Medical Model
Kraepelin specified two main groups of mental disorders or diseases: **dementia praecox** (from roots meaning "precocious [premature] insanity"), which we now call schizophrenia, and manic-depressive psychosis,

which is now labeled **bipolar disorder.** Kraepelin believed that dementia praecox was caused by a biochemical imbalance and manic-depressive psychosis by an abnormality in body metabolism. But his major contribution was the development of a classification system that forms the cornerstone for current diagnostic systems.

The medical model was supported by evidence that a form of derangement called **general paresis** represented an advanced stage of syphilis in which the syphilis bacterium directly invaded brain tissue. Scientists grew optimistic that other biological causes, and, as important, treatments, would soon be discovered for other so-called mental disorders. This early optimism has remained largely unfulfilled because the causes of most patterns of abnormal behavior remain obscure.

Much of the terminology in current use reflects the influence of the medical model. Because of the medical model, many professionals and laypeople speak of people whose behavior is deemed abnormal as being mentally *ill*. It is because of the medical model that so many speak of the *symptoms* of abnormal behavior, rather than the features or characteristics of abnormal behavior. Other terms spawned by the medical model include *mental health, syndrome, diagnosis, patient, mental patient, mental hospital, prognosis, treatment, therapy, cure, relapse,* and *remission.*[2]

The medical model is a major advance over demonology. It inspired the idea that abnormal behavior should be treated by learned professionals and not be punished. Compassion supplanted hatred, fear, and persecution.

Development of Psychological Models
Although the medical model was gaining influence in the 19th century, there were those who believed organic factors alone could not explain the many forms of abnormal behavior. The contributions of a French neurologist, Jean-Martin Charcot (1825–1893), and a prominent Viennese physician, Joseph Breuer (1842–1925), excited the interest of a young Austrian physician, Sigmund Freud (1856–1939), who went on to develop the first major psychological theory of abnormal behavior. Before discussing Freud's contributions, we need to set the stage.

A highly respected neurologist in Paris, Jean-Martin Charcot, was experimenting at the time with the use of **hypnosis** in treating hysterics, people with physical symptoms, such as paralysis or numbness of the arms, that had no identifiable physical cause. Charcot demonstrated that it was possible to remove hysterical symptoms in patients or

---

[2]Because the medical model is not the only way of viewing abnormal behavior patterns, we adopt a more neutral language in this text in describing abnormal behavior patterns. For example, we often refer to "features" or "characteristics" of abnormal behavior patterns or psychological disorders, rather than "symptoms." But our adoption of nonmedical jargon is not an absolute rule. In some cases, there may be no handy substitutes for terms that derive from the medical model, such as the term *remission* or the reference to patients in mental hospitals as *mental patients.* In other cases we may use terms such as *disorder, therapy,* and *treatment* because they are commonly used by psychologists who "treat" "mental disorders" with psychological "therapies."

A teaching clinic held by the Parisian neurologist Jean-Martin Charcot. Here, Charcot presents a woman patient who exhibits the highly dramatic behavior associated with hysteria, such as becoming faint at a moment's notice. Charcot was an important influence on the young Sigmund Freud.

Bertha Pappenheim. Pappenheim (1859–1936) is known more widely in the psychological literature as "Anna O." Freud believed that her hysterical symptoms represented the transformation of blocked-up emotions into physical complaints.

even induce them in normal subjects simply through the use of hypnotic suggestions. Hypnotically induced hysterical behavior was indistinguishable from "genuine" hysterical behavior. Among those who attended Charcot's demonstrations was Sigmund Freud.

Charcot's work with hypnosis had a profound impact on Freud because it demonstrated that hysterical behavior—which could be treated or abolished by the suggestion of "ideas"—was psychological in origin (E. Jones, 1953). Freud was also influenced by his association with Joseph Breuer, 14 years Freud's senior. Breuer too had used hypnosis to treat a 21-year-old woman, Anna O., with hysterical complaints for which there was no apparent medical basis, such as paralysis in her limbs, numbness, and disturbances of vision and hearing (E. Jones, 1953). A "paralyzed" muscle

Sigmund Freud at about the age of 30.

in her neck prevented her from turning her head. Immobilization of the fingers of her left hand made it all but impossible for her to feed herself. Breuer believed there was a strong psychological component to the symptoms. He treated her by encouraging her to talk about them, sometimes under hypnosis. Recalling and talking about events connected with the appearance of the symptoms—especially events that evoked feelings of fear, anxiety, or guilt—appeared to provide symptom relief, at least for a time. Anna referred to the treatment as the "talking cure" or, when joking, as "chimney sweeping."

The hysterical symptoms were taken to represent the transformation of these blocked-up emotions, forgotten but not lost, into physical complaints. In Anna's case, the symptoms seemed to disappear once the emotions were brought to the surface and "discharged." Breuer labeled the therapeutic effect **catharsis,** a Greek term meaning purgation or purification of feelings. Cases of **hysteria,** such as that of Anna O., seem to have been a common occurrence in the later Victorian period but are relatively rare today (Spitzer, Gibbon, Skodol, Williams, & First, 1989).

CONTEMPORARY PERSPECTIVES ON ABNORMAL BEHAVIOR

We've seen that since earliest times humans have sought explanations for strange or deviant behavior. In ancient times and through the Middle Ages, beliefs about abnormal behavior centered on the role of demons and other supernatural forces. But even in ancient times, there were some scholars, such as Hippocrates and Galen, who sought natural explanations of abnormal behavior. In contemporary times, the understanding of abnormal behavior has been largely approached from biological, psychological, and sociocultural perspectives.

Biological Perspectives

The medical model, inspired by physicians from Hippocrates through Kraepelin, remains a powerful force in contemporary understanding of abnormal behavior. The medical model represents a biological perspective on abnormal behavior. We prefer to use the term *biological perspectives* rather than *medical model* to refer to approaches that emphasize the role of biological factors in explaining abnormal behavior and the use of biologically based treatments in treating psychological disorders. One can speak of biological perspectives without adopting the tenets of the medical model, which treats abnormal behavior patterns as *disorders* and their features as *symptoms*. For example, certain behavior patterns (shyness or a lack of musical ability) may have a strong genetic component but not be considered "symptoms" of underlying "disorders."

To lay a framework for discussing biological factors in abnormal behavior, we first need to describe some key biological structures and processes, beginning with the nervous system.

The Nervous System Perhaps you would not be nervous if you did not have a nervous system, but even calm people have nervous systems. The nervous system is made up of nerve cells called **neurons.** Neurons communicate with one another, or transmit "messages." These messages somehow account for events as diverse as sensing an itch from a bug bite; coordinating a figure skater's vision and muscles; composing a symphony; solving an architectural equation; and, in the case of hallucinations, hearing or seeing things that are not really there.

Every neuron has a cell body, or **soma,** dendrites, and an axon (see Figure 1.2). The cell body contains the nucleus of the cell and metabolizes oxygen to carry out the work of the cell. Short fibers called **dendrites** project from the cell body to receive messages from adjoining neurons. Each neuron has a single **axon** that projects trunklike from the cell body. They can extend as long as several feet if they are conveying messages between the toes and the spinal cord. Axons may branch and project in various directions. Axons terminate in small branching structures that are aptly termed **terminals.** Swellings called **knobs** occupy the tips of axon terminals. Neurons convey messages in one direction, from the dendrites or cell body along the axon to the axon terminals. The messages are then conveyed from terminal knobs to other neurons, muscles, or glands.

Neurons transmit messages to other neurons by means of chemical substances called **neurotransmitters.** Neurotransmitters induce chemical changes in receiving neurons. These changes cause axons to conduct the messages in electrical form.

The junction between a transmitting neuron and a receiving neuron is termed a **synapse.** A transmitting neuron is termed *presynaptic.* A receiving neuron is said to be *postsynaptic.* A synapse consists of an axon terminal from a transmitting neuron, a dendrite of a receiving neuron, and a small fluid-filled gap between the two that is called the *synaptic cleft.* The message does not jump the synaptic cleft like a spark. Instead, axon terminals release neurotransmitters into the cleft like myriad ships casting off into the seas (Figure 1.3).

Each kind of neurotransmitter has a distinctive chemical structure. It will fit only into one kind of harbor, or

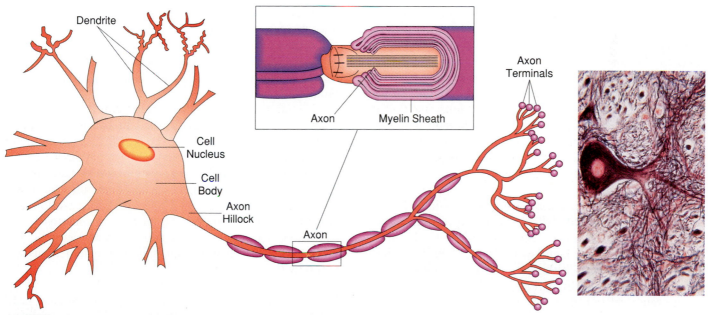

FIGURE 1.2 *Anatomy of a neuron.*
Neurons typically consist of cell bodies (or somas), dendrites, and one or more axons. The axon of this neuron is wrapped in a myelin sheath, which insulates it from the bodily fluids surrounding the neuron and facilitates transmission of neural impulses (messages that travel within the neuron).

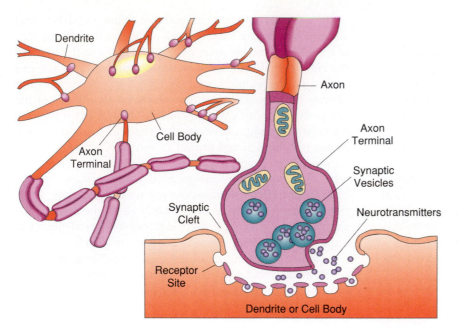

FIGURE 1.3 *Transmission of neural impulses across the synapse.* Neurons transmit messages or neural impulses across synapses, which consist of the axon terminal of the transmitting neuron, the gap or synaptic cleft between the neurons, and the dendrite of the receiving neuron. The "message" consists of neurotransmitters that are released by synaptic vesicles (sacs) into the synaptic cleft and taken up by receptor sites on the receiving neuron.

receptor site, on the receiving neuron. Consider the analogy of a lock and key. Only the right key (neurotransmitter) operates the lock, causing the postsynaptic neuron to forward the message.

Once released, some molecules of a neurotransmitter reach port at receptor sites of other neurons. "Loose" neurotransmitters may be broken down in the synaptic clefts by enzymes or be reabsorbed by the axon terminal (a process termed *reuptake*), so as to prevent the receiving cell from continuing to fire.

Excesses or deficiencies of neurotransmitters have been linked to various kinds of mental health problems. Excesses and deficiencies of the neurotransmitter **norepinephrine** have been connected with mood disorders (see Chapter 7). Alzheimer's disease, which involves the progressive loss of memory and cognitive functioning, is associated with reductions in the levels in the brain of the neurotransmitter **acetylcholine.** Irregularities involving the neurotransmitter **dopamine** appear to be involved in schizophrenia. People with schizophrenia may use more of the dopamine that is available in their brains than do nonschizophrenic individuals (see Chapter 12). The result may be hallucinations, incoherent speech, and delusional thinking. Antipsychotic drugs used to treat schizophrenia apparently work by blocking dopamine transmission.

Serotonin, another neurotransmitter, may be linked to various psychological disorders, including anxiety disorders, mood disorders, sleep disorders, and eating disorders (Lesch et al., 1996; J. J. Mann et al., 1996; McBride, Anderson, & Shapiro, 1996). Although neurotransmitters are believed to play a role in various psychological disorders, precise causal relationships have not been determined.

Parts of the Nervous System The nervous system consists of two major parts, the **central nervous system** and the **peripheral nervous system.** These parts are

further divided. The central nervous system consists of the brain and spinal cord. The peripheral nervous system is made up of nerves that (1) receive and transmit sensory messages (messages from sense organs such as the eyes and ears) to the brain and spinal cord; and (2) transmit messages from the brain or spinal cord to the muscles, causing them to contract, and to glands, causing them to secrete hormones.

We begin an overview of the parts of the nervous system with the back of the head, where the spinal cord meets the brain, and work forward (see Figure 1.4). The lower part of the brain, or hindbrain, consists of the medulla, pons, and cerebellum. Many nerves that link the spinal cord to higher brain levels pass through the **medulla.** The medulla plays roles in such vital functions as heart rate, respiration, and blood pressure, and also in sleep, sneezing, and coughing. The **pons** transmits information about body movement and is involved in functions related to attention, sleep, and respiration.

Behind the pons is the **cerebellum** (Latin for "little brain.") The cerebellum is involved in balance and motor (muscle) behavior. Injury to the cerebellum may impair motor coordination and cause stumbling and loss of muscle tone.

The **reticular activating system** (RAS) starts in the hindbrain and rises through the midbrain into the lower forebrain. The RAS plays vital roles in sleep, attention, and arousal. RAS injury may leave an animal **comatose.** RAS stimulation triggers messages that heighten alertness. Depressant drugs, such as alcohol, which dampen nervous system activity, lower RAS activity.

Important areas in the frontal part of the brain, or forebrain, are the thalamus, hypothalamus, limbic system, basal ganglia, and cerebrum. The **thalamus** relays sensory information, as from the eyes and ears, to higher brain regions for processing. The thalamus is also involved in sleep and attention.

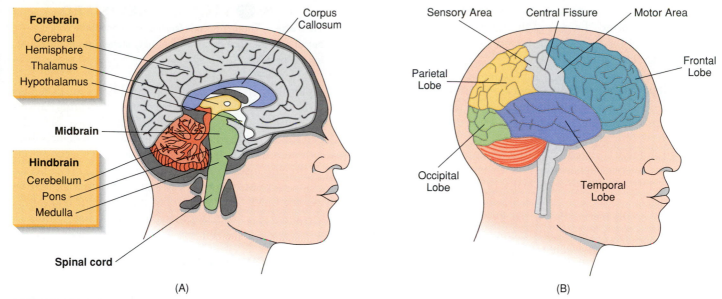

FIGURE 1.4 *The geography of the brain.*
Part A shows parts of the hindbrain, midbrain, and forebrain. Part b shows the four lobes of the cerebral cortex: frontal, parietal, temporal, and occipital. In part B, the sensory (tactile) and motor areas lie across the central fissure from one another. Researchers are investigating the potential relationships between various patterns of abnormal behavior and irregularities in the formation or functioning of the structures of the brain.

The **hypothalamus** is a tiny structure located between the thalamus and the pituitary gland. The hypothalamus is vital in regulating body temperature, concentration of fluids, storage of nutrients, and motivation and emotion. By implanting electrodes in parts of the hypothalamus of animals and observing the effects when a current is switched on, researchers have found that the hypothalamus is involved in a range of motivational drives and behaviors, including hunger, thirst, sex, parenting behaviors, and aggression.

The hypothalamus together with parts of the thalamus and other structures make up the **limbic system.** The limbic system plays a role in memory and in regulating the more basic drives involving hunger, thirst, and aggression. The **basal ganglia** lie under the cortex in front of the thalamus and help to regulate postural movements and coordination.

The **cerebrum** is the "crowning glory" and is responsible for the round shape of the human head. The surface of the cerebrum is convoluted with ridges and valleys. This surface is called the **cerebral cortex.** The hemispheres of the cerebral cortex are connected by the **corpus callosum,** a thick fiber bundle.

The peripheral nervous system connects the brain to the outer world. Without the peripheral nervous system, people could not perceive the world or act on it. The two main divisions of the peripheral nervous system are the somatic nervous system and the autonomic nervous system.

The **somatic nervous system** transmits messages about sights, sounds, smells, temperature, body position, and so on, to the brain. Messages from the brain and spinal cord to the somatic nervous system regulate intentional body movements such as raising an arm, winking, or walking; breathing; and subtle movements that maintain posture and balance.

Psychologists are particularly interested in the **autonomic nervous system** (ANS) because its activities are linked to emotional response. *Autonomic* means "automatic." The ANS regulates the glands and **involuntary** activities such as heart rate, breathing, digestion, and dilation of the pupils of the eyes, even when we are asleep.

The ANS has two branches, or subdivisions: the **sympathetic** and the **parasympathetic.** These branches have mostly opposing effects. Many organs and glands are served by both branches of the ANS. The sympathetic division is most involved in processes that draw body energy from stored reserves, which helps prepare the person to fend off threats or dangers (see Chapter 4). When we are afraid or anxious, the sympathetic branch of the ANS accelerates the heart rate. When we relax, the parasympathetic branch decelerates the heart rate. The parasympathetic division is most active during processes that replenish energy reserves, such as digestion.

The Cerebral Cortex The human activities of thought and language involve the two hemispheres of the cerebrum. Each hemisphere is divided into four parts, or lobes, as shown in Figure 1.4. The *occipital lobe* is primarily involved in vision, while the *temporal lobe* is involved in processing sounds or auditory stimuli. The *parietal lobe* is involved in determining our sense of body position. The *sensory area* of the parietal lobe receives messages from skin sensors all over the body. Neurons in the motor area (or *motor cortex*) of the *frontal lobe* are involved in controlling muscular responses, which enables us to move our limbs. The *prefrontal cortex* (the part of the frontal lobe that lies in front of the motor cortex) is involved in memory, speech, and language functions.

Heredity   Heredity plays a critical role in determining a wide range of traits. The structures we inherit make our behavior possible (humans can walk and run) and at the same time place limits on us (humans cannot fly without artificial equipment). Heredity plays a role not only in determining our physical characteristics (hair color, eye color, height, and the like) but also many of our psychological characteristics.

Genes are the basic building blocks of heredity. They are the structures that regulate the development of traits. Some traits, such as blood type, are transmitted by a single pair of genes, one of which is derived from each parent. Other traits, referred to as **polygenic,** are determined by complex combinations of genes. **Chromosomes** are the rod-shaped structures that house our genes and are found in the nuclei of the body's cells. Each consists of more than 1,000 genes. A normal human cell contains 46 chromosomes, which are organized into 23 pairs. Chromosomes consist of large complex molecules of deoxyribonucleic acid (DNA). Genes occupy various segments along the length of chromosomes. There are about 100,000 genes in every cell in our bodies.

The set of traits specified by our genetic code is referred to as our **genotype.** Our appearance and behavior are not determined by our genotype alone. We are also influenced by environmental factors such as nutrition, exercise, accident and illness, learning, and culture. The constellation of our actual or expressed traits is called our **phenotype.** Our phenotype represents the interaction of genetic and environmental influences. People who possess genotypes for particular psychological disorders are said to have a *genetic predisposition* that makes them more likely to develop the disorder in response to stress or other factors, such as physical or psychological trauma.

Evaluating Biological Perspectives   There is no question that biological structures and processes are involved in many patterns of abnormal behavior, as we see in later chapters. For some disorders, such as Alzheimer's disease, biological processes play the direct causative role. Even then, however, the precise causes remain unknown. In other cases, such as with schizophrenia, biological factors, especially genetics, appear to interact with stressful environmental factors in the development of the disorder.

Genetic influences are implicated in a wide range of psychological disorders, including schizophrenia, bipolar (manic-depressive) disorder, major depression, alcoholism, autism, Alzheimer's disease, anxiety disorders, dyslexia, and antisocial personality disorder (DiLalla, Carey, Gottesman, & Bouchard, 1996; Plomin, DeFries, McClearn, & Rutter, 1997). Yet genetic factors cannot account entirely for any of these psychological disorders (Carey & DiLalla, 1994). Environmental factors also play an important role.

TRUTH *or* FICTION REVISITED
1.6 *False.*   Though genetic factors may contribute to a number of psychological disorders, heredity alone does not account for any of them.

Biological perspectives on abnormal behavior have also led to the development of effective drugs for treating various psychological disorders. For example, drugs have been developed that quell the more flagrant features of schizophrenia, although they do not bring about a "cure." Drugs alone do not prepare institutionalized patients for reentry into society, however. Acquiring social and vocational skills that will permit them to assume more independent communal roles requires psychosocial or psychoeducational training.

Psychodynamic Perspectives

Psychodynamic theory is based on the contributions of Sigmund Freud and his followers. Drawing on his experience with Breuer and his own case experiences, Freud developed the belief that hysteria and other psychological problems are derived from unconscious conflicts, which can be traced to childhood. According to **psychoanalytic theory,** which he developed, these unconscious conflicts involve the opposition of primitive sexual and aggressive instincts or drives and the effort to keep these primitive impulses from being expressed in action or brought into direct awareness. Abnormal behavior patterns such as hysteria are "symptoms" of the dynamic struggle within the mind between these opposing psychic forces. In the case of hysteria, the "symptom" represented the *conversion* of an unconscious psychological conflict into a physical problem.

The Structure of the Mind   Freud's clinical experiences led him to conclude that the mind is like an iceberg (Figure 1.5). Only the tip of an iceberg is visible above the surface of the water. The great mass of the iceberg lies below the surface, darkening the deep. Freud came to believe that people, similarly, perceive but a few of the ideas, wishes, and impulses that dwell within them and determine their behavior. Freud held that the larger part of the mind, which includes our deepest wishes, fears, and instinctual urges, remains below the surface of consciousness. Freud labeled the region that corresponds to one's present awareness the **conscious** part of the mind. The regions that lie beneath the surface of awareness were labeled the *preconscious* and the *unconscious.*

TRUTH *or* FICTION REVISITED
1.7 *True.*   Freud likened the mind to a giant iceberg, with only the tip rising into conscious awareness.

In the **preconscious** mind are found memories of experience that are not in awareness but that can be brought into awareness by focusing on them. Your telephone number, for example, remains in the preconscious until you focus on it. The **unconscious** mind, the largest part of the mind,

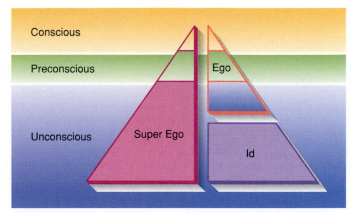

FIGURE 1.5 *The parts of the mind, according to Sigmund Freud.*
According to psychodynamic theory, the mind is akin to an iceberg in that only a small part of it rises to conscious awareness at any moment in time. Although material in the preconscious mind may be brought into consciousness by focusing our attention on it, the impulses and ideas in the unconscious tend to remain veiled in mystery.

Denial? Denial is a defense mechanism in which the ego fends off anxiety by preventing recognition of the true nature of a threat. Failing to take seriously the warnings of health risks from cigarette smoking can be considered a form of denial.

remains shrouded in mystery. Its contents can only be brought to awareness with great difficulty, if at all. Freud believed that the unconscious is the repository of biological drives, or instincts, such as sex and aggression.

The Structure of Personality According to Freud's **structural hypothesis**, the personality is divided into three mental entities, or **psychic** structures: the *id, ego,* and *superego.* Psychic structures cannot be seen or measured directly, but their presence is suggested by observable behavior and expressed in thoughts and emotions.

The **id** is the only psychic structure present at birth. It is the repository of our baser drives and instinctual impulses, including hunger, thirst, sex, and aggression. The id, which operates completely in the unconscious, was described by Freud as "a chaos, a cauldron of seething excitations" (1933/1964, p. 73). The id follows the **pleasure principle.** It demands instant gratification of instincts without consideration of social rules or customs or the needs of others. It operates by **primary process thinking,** which is a mode of relating to the world through imagination and fantasy. This enables the id to achieve gratification by conjuring up the mental image of the object of desire.

During the first year of life, the child discovers its every demand is not instantly gratified. It must learn to cope with delay of gratification. The **ego** develops during this first year to organize reasonable ways of coping with frustration. Standing for "reason and good sense" (Freud, 1964, p. 76), the ego seeks to curb the demands of the id and to direct behavior that is in keeping with social customs and expectations. Gratification can thus be achieved, but not at the expense of social disapproval. The id floods your consciousness with hunger pangs. Were it to have its way, the id might also prompt you to wolf down any food at hand or even to swipe someone else's plate. But the ego creates the ideas of walking to the refrigerator, making yourself a sandwich, and pouring a glass of milk.

The ego is governed by the **reality principle.** It considers what is practical and possible, as well as the urgings of the id. The ego engages in **secondary process thinking**—the remembering, planning, and weighing of circumstances that permit a compromise between the fantasies of the id and the realities of the world outside. The ego lays the groundwork for the development of the conscious sense of the **self.**

During middle childhood, the **superego** develops. The moral standards and values of parents and other key people become internalized through **identification.** The superego operates according to the **moral principle**; it demands strict adherence to moral standards. The superego represents the moral values of an ideal self, called the **ego ideal.** It also serves as a conscience, or internal moral guardian, that monitors the ego and passes judgment on right and wrong. It metes out punishment in the form of guilt and shame when it finds that ego has failed to adhere to superego's moral standards. Ego stands between the id and the superego. It endeavors to satisfy the cravings of the id without offending the moral standards of the superego.

Defense Mechanisms Although part of the ego rises to consciousness, some of its activity is carried out unconsciously. In the unconscious, the ego serves as a kind of watchdog, or censor, that screens impulses from the id. It uses psychological defenses to prevent socially unacceptable impulses from rising into consciousness. If it were not for these defenses, or defense mechanisms, the darkest sins of our childhoods, the primitive demands of our ids, and the censures of our superegos might disable us psychologically. Repression is considered the most basic of the defense mechanisms. Others are described in Table 1.1.

A dynamic unconscious struggle thus takes place between the id and the ego. It pits biological drives that strive for expression (the id) against the ego, which seeks to restrain them or channel them into socially acceptable outlets.

TABLE 1.1

Some Defense Mechanisms of the Ego, According to Psychodynamic Theory

Defense Mechanism	Definition	Examples
Repression	The ejection of anxiety-evoking ideas from awareness.	A student forgets a difficult term paper is due. A patient in therapy forgets an appointment when anxiety-evoking material is to be discussed.
Regression	The return, under stress, to a form of behavior characteristic of an earlier stage of development.	An adolescent cries when forbidden to use the family car. An adult becomes highly dependent on his parents following the breakup of his marriage.
Rationalization	The use of self-deceiving justifications for unacceptable behavior.	A student blames her cheating on her teacher's leaving the room during a test. A man explains his cheating on his income tax by saying, "Everyone does it."
Displacement	The transfer of ideas and impulses from threatening or unsuitable objects onto less threatening objects.	A worker picks a fight with her spouse after being criticized sharply by her supervisor.
Projection	The thrusting of one's own unacceptable impulses onto others so that others are assumed to harbor them.	A hostile person perceives the world as being a dangerous place. A sexually frustrated person interprets innocent gestures of others as sexual advances.
Reaction formation	Assumption of behavior in opposition to one's genuine impulses in order to keep impulses repressed.	A person who is angry with a relative behaves in a "sickly sweet" manner toward that relative. A sadistic individual becomes a physician.
Denial	Refusal to accept the true nature of a threat.	Belief that one will not contract cancer or heart disease although one smokes heavily ("It can't happen to me.")
Sublimation	The channeling of primitive impulses into positive, constructive efforts.	A person paints nudes for the sake of "beauty" and "art." A hostile person directs aggressive energies into competitive sports.

Source: S. A. Rathus. (1996). *Psychology*, 6th edition. Ft. Worth: Harcourt Brace College Publishers, p. 443. Reprinted with permission.

The conflict can give rise to psychological disorders and behavioral problems. Because we cannot view the unconscious mind directly, Freud developed a method of mental detective work called **psychoanalysis**, which is described in Chapter 3.

The use of defense mechanisms to cope with feelings such as anxiety, guilt, and shame is considered normal. These mechanisms enable us to constrain impulses from the id as we go about our daily business. In his work *The Psychopathology of Everyday Life,* Freud noted that slips of the tongue and ordinary forgetfulness can represent hidden motives that are kept out of consciousness by repression. If a friend means to say, "I hear what you're saying," but it comes out, "I hate what you're saying," perhaps the friend is expressing a repressed emotion. If a lover storms out in anger but forgets his umbrella, perhaps he is unconsciously creating an excuse for returning. Defense mechanisms may also give rise to abnormal behavior, however. The person who regresses to an infantile state under pressures of enormous stress is clearly not acting adaptively to the situation.

Stages of Psychosexual Development Freud aroused heated controversy by arguing that sexual drives are the dominant factors in the development of personality, even among children. Freud believed that the child's basic relationship to the world in its first several years of life is organized in terms of its pursuit of sexual pleasures that take different forms as the child matures. In Freud's view, all activities that are physically pleasurable, such as eating or moving one's bowels, are in essence "sexual." The word *sensuality* is probably closer in present-day meaning to what Freud meant by *sexuality*.

The drive for sexual pleasure represents, in Freud's view, the expression of a major life instinct, which he called **Eros**— the basic drive to preserve and perpetuate life. The energy contained in Eros that allows it to fulfill its function was termed **libido,** or sexual energy. Freud believed that libidinal energy is expressed through sexual pleasure in different body parts, called **erogenous zones,** as the child matures. In Freud's view, the stages of human development are **psychosexual** in nature, because they correspond to the transfer of libidinal energy from one erogenous zone to another. Freud proposed the existence of five psychosexual stages of development: oral, anal, phallic, latency, and genital.

In the first year of life, the **oral stage,** infants achieve sexual pleasure by sucking their mothers' breasts and by

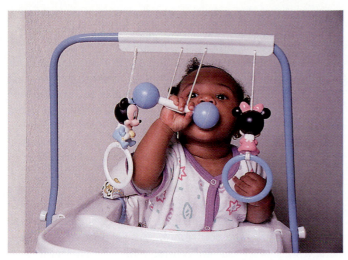

The oral stage of psychosexual development? According to Freud, the child's early encounters with the world are largely experienced through the mouth.

mouthing anything that happens to be nearby. Oral stimulation, in the form of sucking and biting, is a source of both sexual gratification and nourishment.

One of Freud's central beliefs is that the child may encounter conflict during each of the psychosexual stages of development. Conflict during the oral stage centers around the issue of whether or not the infant receives adequate oral gratification. Too much gratification could lead the infant to expect that everything in life is given with little or no effort on its part. In contrast, early **weaning** might lead to frustration. Too little or too much gratification at any stage could lead to **fixation** in that stage, which leads to the development of personality traits characteristic of that stage. Oral fixations could include an exaggerated desire for "oral activities," which could become expressed in later life in smoking, alcohol abuse, overeating, and nail-biting. Like the infant who depends on the mother's breast for survival and gratification of oral pleasure, orally fixated adults may also become clinging and dependent in their interpersonal relationships.

During the **anal stage** of psychosexual development, the child experiences sexual gratification through contraction and relaxation of the sphincter muscles that control elimination of bodily waste. Although elimination had been controlled reflexively during much of the first year of life, the child now learns she or he is able, though perhaps not reliably at first, to exercise voluntary muscular control over elimination.

Now the child begins to learn she or he can delay gratification of the need to eliminate when the urge is felt. During toilet training, the issue of self-control may become a source of conflict between the parent and the child. **Anal fixations** that derive from this conflict are associated with two sets of traits. Harsh toilet training may lead to the development of **anal retentive** traits, which involve excessive needs for self-control. These include perfectionism and extreme needs for orderliness, cleanliness, and neatness. By contrast, excessive gratification during the anal period

might lead to **anal expulsive** traits, which include carelessness and messiness.

The next stage of psychosexual development, the **phallic stage,** generally begins during the third year of life. The major erogenous zone during the stage is the phallic region (the penis in boys, the clitoris in girls). Conflict between parent and child may occur over masturbation—the rubbing of the phallic areas for sexual pleasure—which parents may react to with threats and punishments. Perhaps the most controversial of Freud's beliefs was his suggestion that phallic-stage children develop incestuous wishes for the parent of the opposite gender and begin to view the parent of the same sex as a rival. Freud dubbed this conflict the **Oedipus complex,** after the legendary Greek king Oedipus who unwittingly slew his father and married his mother. The female version of the Oedipus complex has been named by some followers (though not by Freud himself) the **Electra complex,** after the character of Electra, who, according to Greek legend, avenged the death of her father, King Agamemnon, by slaying her father's murderers—her own mother and her mother's lover.

Freud believed the Oedipus conflict represents a central psychological conflict of early childhood, the resolution of which has far-reaching consequences in later development and in determining the acquisition of **gender roles.** He also believed that **castration anxiety** played an important role in resolving the complex for boys. Adults sometimes threaten boys with castration to try to get them to stop touching themselves. Freud documented such castration threats from parents or nurses in several case studies. At some point boys discover that girls are different—they do not have penises. Freud conjectured that boys might imagine that girls had lost their penises as a form of punishment. Going further, Freud hypothesized that boys develop castration anxiety, based on the fantasy that their rivals for their mother's affections, namely their fathers, would seek to punish them for their incestuous wishes by removing the organ that has become connected with sexual pleasure. To prevent castration, Freud argued, boys repress their incestuous wishes for their mothers and identify with their fathers. Keep in mind that Freudian theory posits that these developments (incestuous wishes and castration anxiety) are largely unconscious and are part and parcel of normal development. Successful resolution of the Oedipus complex involves the boy repressing his incestuous wishes for his mother and identifying with his father. This identification leads to development of the aggressive, independent characteristics associated with the traditional masculine gender role.

The Oedipus complex in girls is somewhat of a mirror image of the one in boys. Freud believed little girls naturally become envious of boys' penises. This jealousy leads them to become resentful toward their mothers, whom they blame for bringing them into the world so "ill-equipped." Girls come to desire to possess their fathers, in a way substituting their fathers' penises for their own missing ones. But the rivalry with their mothers for their fathers' affection places them in peril of losing their mothers' love and protection.

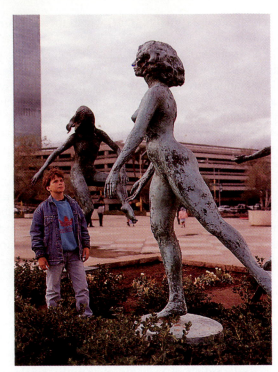

Are young children interested in sex? According to Freud, even young children have sexual impulses. Freud's view of childhood sexuality shocked the scientific establishment of his day, and many of Freud's own followers believe that Freud placed too much emphasis on sexual motivation.

Successful resolution of the complex for the girl involves repression of the incestuous wishes for her father and identification with her mother, leading to the acquisition of the more passive, dependent characteristics traditionally associated with the feminine sex role. Eventually the wish for a penis is transformed into the desire to marry a man and bear children, which represents the ultimate adjustment of surrendering the wish "to be a man" by accepting a baby as a form of penis substitute. Freud hypothesized that, in adulthood, women who retain the wish for a penis of their own ("to be a man") can become maladjusted and develop masculine-typed characteristics such as competitiveness and dominance and even a lesbian sexual orientation.

The Oedipus complex comes to a point of resolution, whether fully resolved or not, by about the age of 5 or 6. From the identification with the parent of the same gender comes the internalization of parental values in the form of the superego. Children then enter the **latency stage** of psychosexual development, a period of late childhood during which sexual impulses remain in a latent state. Interests become directed toward school and play activities. But sexual drives are once again aroused with the **genital stage**, beginning with puberty, which reaches fruition in mature sexuality, marriage, and the bearing of children. The sexual feelings toward the parent of the opposite gender that had remained repressed during the latency period emerge during adolescence but are displaced, or transferred, onto socially appropriate members of the opposite gender. Boys might still look for girls "just like the girl that married dear old dad." And girls might still be attracted to boys who resemble their "dear old dads."

In Freud's view, successful adjustment during the genital stage involves the attainment of sexual gratification through sexual intercourse with someone of the opposite gender, presumably within the context of marriage. Other forms of sexual expression, such as oral or anal stimulation, masturbation, and homosexual activity, are considered **pregenital** fixations, or immature forms of sexual conduct.

Other Psychodynamic Theorists Freud left a rich intellectual legacy that has stimulated the thinking of many theorists. Psychodynamic theory has been shaped over the years by the contributions of psychodynamic theorists who shared certain central tenets in common with Freud, such as the belief that behavior reflects unconscious motivation, inner conflict, and the operation of defensive responses to anxiety. They tended to deemphasize the roles of basic instincts such as sex and aggression, however, and to place greater emphasis on roles for conscious choice, self-direction, and creativity. These theorists also differed from each other in various ways.

One of the most prominent of the early psychodynamic theorists was Carl Jung (1875–1961), a Swiss psychiatrist who was formerly a member of Freud's inner circle. His break with Freud came when he developed his own psychodynamic theory, which he called **analytical psychology.** Like Freud, Jung believed that unconscious processes are important in explaining behavior. Jung believed that an understanding of human behavior must incorporate the facts of self-awareness and self-direction as well as the impulses of the id and the mechanisms of defense. He believed that not only do we have a *personal* unconscious, a repository of repressed memories and impulses, but we also inherit a **collective unconscious.** To Jung, the collective unconscious represents the accumulated experience of humankind, which he believed is passed down genetically through the generations. The collective unconscious is believed to contain primitive images, or **archetypes,** which reflect upon the history of our species, including vague, mysterious mythical images such as the all-powerful God, the fertile and nurturing mother, the young hero, the wise old man, and themes of rebirth or resurrection. Although archetypes remain unconscious, in Jung's view, they influence our thoughts, dreams, and emotions and render us responsive to cultural themes in stories and films.

Alfred Adler (1870–1937), like Jung, had held a place in Freud's inner circle but broke away as he developed his own beliefs that people are basically driven by an **inferiority complex,** not by the sexual instinct as Freud had maintained. For some people, feelings of inferiority are based on physical problems and the resulting need to compensate for them. But all of us, because of our small size during childhood, encounter feelings of inferiority to some degree. These feelings lead to a powerful **drive for superiority,** which motivates us to achieve prominence and social dominance. In the healthy personality, however, strivings for dominance are tempered by devotion to helping other people.

Adler, like Jung, believed self-awareness plays a major role in the formation of personality. Adler spoke of a **creative self,** a self-aware aspect of personality that strives to overcome obstacles and develop the individual's potential. With the hypothesis of the creative self, Adler shifted the emphasis of psychodynamic theory from the id to the ego. Because our potentials are uniquely individual, Adler's views have been termed **individual psychology.**

Many other psychodynamic models have arisen with the work of Freud's followers, who are sometimes referred to collectively as **neo-Freudians.** Some psychodynamic theorists, such as Karen Horney and Harry Stack Sullivan (1892–1949), focused on the social context of psychological problems and stressed the importance of child-parent relationships in determining the nature of later interpersonal relationships. Sullivan, for example, maintained that children of rejecting parents tend to become self-doubting and anxious. These personality features persist and impede the development of close relationships in adult life.

More recent psychodynamic models also place a greater emphasis on the self or the ego and less emphasis on the sexual instinct than Freud. Today, most psychoanalysts see people as motivated on two tiers: by the growth-oriented, conscious pursuits of the ego as well as by the more primitive, conflict-ridden drives of the id. Heinz Hartmann (1894–1970) was one of the originators of **ego psychology,** which posits that the ego has energy and motives of its own. Freud, remember, believed ego functions are fueled by the id, are largely defensive, and are perpetually threatened by the irrational. Hartmann and other ego analysts find Freud's views of the ego—and of people in general—too pessimistic and ignoble. Hartmann argued that the cognitive functions of the ego could be free of conflict. The choices to seek an education, dedicate oneself to art and poetry, and further humanity are not merely defensive forms of sublimation, as Freud had seen them.

Another ego analyst, Erik Erikson (1902–1994), attributed more importance to children's social relationships than to unconscious processes. Whereas Freud's developmental theory ends with the genital stage, beginning in early adolescence, Erikson focused on developmental processes that he believed continued throughout adulthood. The goal of adolescence, in Erikson's view, is not genital sexuality, but rather the attainment of **ego identity.** Adolescents who achieve ego identity develop a clearly defined and firm sense of who they are and what they believe in. Adolescents who drift without purpose or clarity of self remain in a state of **role diffusion** and are especially subject to negative peer influences.

One popular contemporary psychodynamic approach is termed **object-relations theory,** which focuses on how children come to develop symbolic representations of important others in their lives, especially their parents. One of the major contributors to object-relations theory was Margaret

Mahler (1897–1985), who saw the process of separating from the mother during the first 3 years of life as crucial to personality development (discussed further in Chapter 8).

According to psychodynamic theory, we **introject,** or incorporate, into our own personalities, elements of major figures in our lives. Introjection is more powerful when we fear losing others to death or rejection of us. Thus, we might be particularly apt to incorporate elements of people who *disapprove* of us or who see things differently.

In Mahler's view, these symbolic representations, which are formed from images and memories of others, come to influence our perceptions and behavior. We experience internal conflict as the attitudes of introjected people battle with our own. Some of our perceptions may be distorted or seem unreal to us. Some of our impulses and behavior may seem unlike us, as if they come out of the blue. With such conflict, we may not be able to tell where the influences of other people end and our "real selves" begin. The aim of Mahler's therapeutic approach was to help clients separate their own ideas and feelings from those of the introjected objects so they could develop as individuals—as their own persons.

Psychodynamic Perspectives on Normality and Abnormality Freud believed there is a thin line between the normal and the abnormal. Normal as well as abnormal people are motivated or driven by the irrational drives of the id. The difference between normal and abnormal people may be largely a matter of degree. Normality is a matter of the balance of energy among the psychic structures of id ego, and superego. In normal people, the ego has the strength to control the instincts of the id and to withstand the condemnation of the superego. The presence of acceptable outlets for the expression of some primitive impulses, such as the expression of mature sexuality in marriage, decreases the pressures within the id and, at the same time, lessens the burdens of the ego in repressing the remaining impulses. Being reared by reasonably tolerant parents might prevent the superego from becoming overly harsh and condemnatory.

In psychological disorders, the balance of energy is lopsided. Some unconscious impulses may "leak," producing anxiety or leading to the development of **neuroses,** such as hysteria and phobias. The neurotic symptom—a fear of knives, for example—serves a purpose of shielding the self from awareness of these threatening unconscious impulses. So long as the symptom is maintained (the person avoids knives), the murderous or suicidal impulses are kept at bay. If the superego becomes overly powerful, it may create excessive feelings of guilt and lead to depression. An underdeveloped superego is believed to play a role in explaining the antisocial tendencies of people who intentionally hurt others without feelings of guilt.

Freud believed that the underlying conflicts in neuroses have childhood origins that are buried in the depths of the unconscious. Through psychoanalysis, he sought to help people uncover and learn to deal with these underlying

Margaret Mahler.

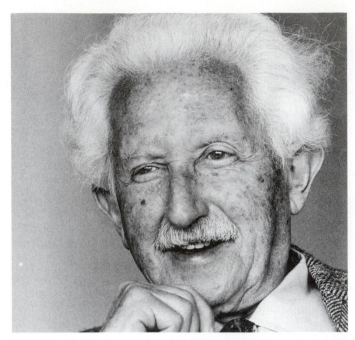

Erik Erikson.

conflicts to free themselves of the need to maintain the overt symptom.

Perpetual vigilance and defense takes its toll. The ego can weaken and, in extreme cases, lose the ability to keep a lid on the id. **Psychosis** results when the urges of the id spill forth, untempered by an ego that either has been weakened or is underdeveloped. The fortress of the ego is overrun, and the person loses the ability to distinguish between fantasy and reality. Behavior becomes detached from reality. Primary process thinking and bizarre behavior rule the day. Psychoses are characterized, in general, by more severe disturbances of functioning than neuroses, by the appearance of bizarre behavior and thoughts, and by faulty perceptions of reality, such as hallucinations ("hearing voices" or seeing things that are not present). Speech may become incoherent, and there may be bizarre posturing and gestures. The most prominent form of psychosis is schizophrenia, discussed in Chapter 12.

Freud equated psychological health with the *abilities to love and to work*. The normal person can care deeply for other people, find sexual gratification in an intimate relationship, and engage in productive work. To accomplish these ends, there must be an opportunity for sexual impulses to be expressed in a relationship with a partner of the opposite gender. Other impulses must be channeled (sublimated) into socially productive pursuits, such as work, enjoyment of art or music, or creative expression. When some impulses are expressed directly and others are sublimated, the ego has a relatively easy time of it repressing those that remain in the boiling cauldron.

Other psychodynamic theorists, such as Jung and Adler, emphasized the need to develop a differentiated self—the unifying force that provides direction to behavior and helps develop a person's potential. Adler also believed that psy-

chological health involves efforts to compensate for feelings of inferiority by striving to excel in one or more of the arenas of human endeavor. For Mahler, similarly, abnormal behavior derives from failure to separate ourselves from those we have psychologically brought within us. The notion of a guiding self provides bridges between psychodynamic theories and other theories, such as humanistic-existential theories (which also speak of a self and the fulfillment of inner potential) and social-cognitive theory (which speaks in terms of self-regulatory processes).

Evaluating Psychodynamic Perspectives Psychodynamic theory has had a pervasive influence, not only on concepts of abnormal behavior but more broadly on art, literature, philosophy, and the general culture. It has focused attention on our inner lives—our dreams, our fantasies, our hidden motives. People unschooled in Freud per se nevertheless look for the symbolic meanings of each other's slips of the tongue and assume that abnormalities can be traced to early childhood. Terms like *ego* and *repression* have become commonplace, although their everyday meanings do not fully overlap with those intended by Freud.

One of the major contributions of the psychodynamic model was the increased awareness that people may be motivated by hidden drives and impulses of a sexual or aggressive nature. Freud's beliefs about childhood sexuality were both illuminating and controversial. Before Freud, children were perceived as *pure innocents*, free of sexual desire. Freud recognized, however, that young children, even infants, seek pleasure through stimulation of the oral and anal cavities and the phallic region. Yet his beliefs that primitive drives give rise to incestuous desires, intrafamily rivalries and conflicts, and castration anxiety and penis envy remain sources of controversy, even within psychodynamic circles.

Karen Horney.

For one thing, these processes are deemed to occur largely if not entirely at an unconscious level and so are difficult if not impossible to study, let alone validate, by scientific means. For another, there is little evidence to support even the existence of the Oedipus complex, let alone its universality (Kupfersmid, 1995).

Freud's views of female psychosexual development have been roundly attacked by women and by modern-day psychoanalysts. One of the most prominent critics, the psychoanalyst Karen Horney (1885–1952), for example, argued that evidence of penis envy was not confirmed by observations of children and that Freud's view reflected the cultural prejudice in Western society against women. To Horney, cultural expectations played a greater role in shaping women's self-images than penis envy. In fairness to Freud, we should note that his theories should be viewed in the context of his day and time. In Freud's day, motherhood and family life were, by and large, the only socially proper avenues of fulfillment for women. Today, the choices available to women are more varied, and normality is not conceptualized in terms of rigidly defined gender roles.

Many critics, including some of Freud's followers, believe he placed too much emphasis on sexual and aggressive impulses and underemphasized social relationships. Critics have also argued that the psychic structures—the id, ego, and superego—may be little more than useful fictions, poetic ways to represent inner conflict. Sir Karl Popper (1985) argued that Freud's hypothetical mental processes are not scientific concepts because they cannot be directly observed or tested. Therapists can speculate, for example, that a client "forgot" about an appointment because "unconsciously" she or he did not want to attend the session. Such unconscious motivation is not subject to scientific verification, however. Popper held that Freud's propositions about mental structures are unscientific because no imaginable evidence can disprove them. Any behavior (e.g., showing up or not showing up for an appointment) can be explained in terms of the interactions of these hypothesized (but unobservable) mental structures.

Freud formulated his views of normal development on the basis of case studies of troubled people in Victorian Vienna, mostly White, upper-middle-class women aged 20 to 44 (S. Fisher & Greenberg, 1978). How can they be said to represent African Americans in Detroit, Hispanic Americans in Dade County, Native Americans in the Southwest, Asian Americans in Silicon Valley, or contemporary American non-Hispanic White suburbanites? Persons seeking psychotherapy are also unlikely to represent the general population. (They are likely to have more psychological problems than the population at large.) Freud carried out his work in an era of culturally repressed sexuality but nevertheless concluded that all people undergo similar sexual conflicts. Can his findings generalize to contemporary young people who have been repeatedly exposed to sexually provocative films and TV programs?

Also, as the philosopher Adolph Grünbaum (1985) took note, Freud's method of gathering evidence from the therapy session may be suspect. Freud based his views of childhood on the recollections of his clients, not on direct observation. Therapists may influence their clients in subtle ways to produce material they expect to find. Therapists may also be negligent in separating the information reported by their clients from their own interpretations.

Learning Perspectives

Psychodynamic models of Freud and his followers were the first major psychological theories of abnormal behavior, but other relevant psychologies were also taking shape early in the 20th century. Among the most important was the behavioral perspective, which is identified with contributions by the Russian physiologist Ivan Pavlov (1849–1936), the discoverer of the conditioned reflex, and the American psychologist John B. Watson (1878–1958), the father of **behaviorism.** The behavioral perspective focuses on the role of learning in explaining both normal and abnormal behavior. From the behavioral perspective, abnormal behavior represents the learning of inappropriate, maladaptive behaviors.

From the medical and psychodynamic perspectives, abnormal behavior is *symptomatic,* respectively, of underlying biological or psychological problems. From the behavioral perspective, however, abnormal behavior need not be symptomatic of anything. The abnormal behavior itself is the problem. Abnormal behavior is regarded as learned in much the same way as normal behavior. Why, then, do some people behave abnormally? One reason is found in situational factors: Their learning histories, that is, might differ from most people's. For example, harsh punishment for early exploratory behavior, such as childhood sexual exploration in the form of masturbation, might give rise to adult anxieties over autonomy or sexuality. Inconsistent discipline, as shown

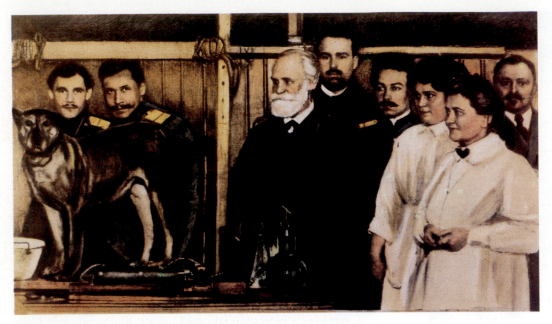

Ivan Pavlov. Here Russian physiologist Ivan Pavlov (the bearded man in the center) demonstrates his apparatus for classical conditioning to students. How might the principles of classical conditioning explain the acquisition of excessive irrational fears that we refer to as phobias?

in haphazard rewards for good behavior and capricious punishment of misconduct, might give rise to antisocial behavior. Then, too, children with abusive or neglectful parents might learn to pay more attention to inner fantasies than to the world outside, giving rise, at worst, to difficulty in separating reality from fantasy. The behavioral perspective has given rise to a treatment approach called **behavior therapy,** which applies principles of learning to help people overcome psychological problems and develop more effective behaviors.

Watson and other behaviorists, such as Harvard University psychologist B.F. Skinner (1904–1990), believed that human behavior is basically the product of genetic endowment and environmental or situational influences. Like Freud, Watson and Skinner discarded concepts of personal freedom, choice, and self-direction. But whereas Freud saw us as driven by irrational forces, behaviorists see us as products of environmental influences that shape and manipulate our behavior. To Watson and Skinner, even the belief that we have free will is determined by the environment just as surely as is our learning to raise our hands in class before speaking. Behaviorists focus on the roles of classical conditioning and operant conditioning in the development of abnormal behavior.

Role of Classical Conditioning   Pavlov discovered the conditioned reflex (now called a *conditioned response*) quite by accident. In his laboratory, he harnessed dogs to an apparatus like that in Figure 1.6 to study their salivary response to food. Yet he observed that the animals would start salivating and secreting gastric juices even before they started eating. These responses appeared to be elicited by the sounds made by his laboratory assistants when they wheeled in the food cart. So Pavlov undertook a clever experimental program that showed that animals could learn to salivate to other stimuli, such as the sound of a bell, if these stimuli were *associated* with feeding.

Since dogs don't normally salivate to the sound of bells, Pavlov reasoned that they had acquired this response, called a **conditioned response** (CR), or conditioned reflex, because it had been paired with an **unconditioned stimulus** (US)—in this case, food, which naturally elicits salivation (see Figure 1.7). The salivation to food, an unlearned response, is called the **unconditioned response** (UR), and the bell, a previously neutral stimulus, is called the **conditioned stimulus** (CS).

Can you recognize classical conditioning in your everyday life? Do you flinch in the waiting room at the sound of

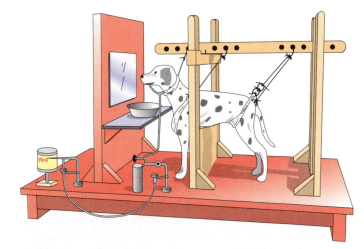

FIGURE 1.6   *The apparatus use in Ivan Pavlov's experiments on conditioning.*
Pavlov used an apparatus such as this to demonstrate the process of conditioning. To the left is a two-way mirror, behind which a researcher rings a bell. After ringing the bell, meat is placed on the dog's tongue. Following several pairings of the bell and the meat, the dog learns to salivate in response to the bell. The animal's saliva passes through the tube to a vial, where its quantity may be taken as a measure of the strength of the conditioned response.

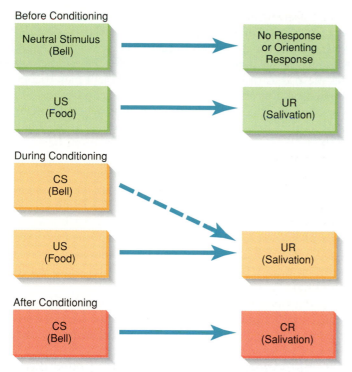

Before Conditioning

Neutral Stimulus (Bell) → No Response or Orienting Response

US (Food) → UR (Salivation)

During Conditioning

CS (Bell) ⤏

US (Food) → UR (Salivation)

After Conditioning

CS (Bell) → CR (Salivation)

FIGURE 1.7 *Schematic diagram of the process of classical conditioning.* Before conditioning, food (an unconditioned stimulus, or US) that is placed on a dog's tongue will naturally elicit salivation (an unconditioned response, or UR). The bell, however, is a neutral stimulus that may elicit an orienting response but not salivation. During conditioning, the bell (the conditioned stimulus, CS) is rung while food (the US) is placed on the dog's tongue. After several conditioning trials have occurred, the bell (the CS) will elicit salivation (the conditioned response, or CR) when it is rung, even though it is not accompanied by food (the US). The dog is said to have been conditioned, or to have learned, to display the conditioned response (CR) in response to the conditioned stimulus (CS). Learning theorists have suggested that irrational excessive fears of harmless stimuli may be acquired through principles of classical conditioning.

Role of Operant Conditioning Operant conditioning involves the acquisition of behaviors, called *operant behaviors,* that are emitted by the organism and that operate upon, or manipulate, the environment to produce certain effects. Skinner (1938) showed that food-deprived pigeons will learn to peck buttons when food pellets drop into their cages as a result. It takes a while for the birds to happen on the first peck, but after a few repetitions of the button-pecking–food association, pecking behavior, an operant responses, becomes fast and furious until the pigeons have had their fill.

In operant conditioning, organisms acquire responses or skills that lead to **reinforcement.** Reinforcers are changes in the environment (stimuli) that increase the frequency of the preceding behavior. A **reward** is a *pleasant* stimulus that increases the frequency of behavior, and so it is a type of reinforcer. But Skinner found the concept of reinforcement to be preferable to that of reward because it is defined in terms of relationships between observed behaviors and environmental effects. In contrast to *reward,* the meaning of reinforcement does not depend on "mentalistic" conjectures about what is pleasant to another person or lower animal. Many psychologists use the words *reinforcement* and *reward* interchangeably, however.

Positive reinforcers boost the frequency of behavior when they are presented. Food, money, social approval, and the opportunity to mate are examples of positive reinforcers. **Negative reinforcers** increase the frequency of behavior when they are removed. Fear, pain, and social disapproval are examples of negative reinforcers. We usually learn to do what leads to their removal.

Adaptive, normal behavior involves learning responses or skills that permit us to obtain positive reinforcers and avoid or remove negative reinforcers. Adaptive behavior involves developing skills that permit us to obtain money,

the dentist's drill? The drill sounds may be conditioned stimuli for conditioned responses of fear and muscle tension.

Phobias or excessive fears may be acquired by classical conditioning. For instance, a person may develop a phobia for riding on elevators following a traumatic experience while riding on an elevator. In this example, a previously neutral stimulus (elevator) becomes paired or associated with an aversive stimuli (trauma), which leads to the conditioned response (phobia).

From the behaviorist perspective, normal behavior involves responding adaptively to stimuli—including conditioned stimuli. After all, if we do not learn to be afraid of drawing our hand too close to a hot stove after one or two experiences of being burned or nearly burned, we might suffer unnecessary burns. On the other hand, acquiring inappropriate and maladaptive fears on the basis of conditioning may cripple our efforts to function in the world. Chapter 5 explains how conditioning may help to explain anxiety disorders such as phobias and **posttraumatic stress disorder.**

B. F. Skinner.

food, and social approval, and to avoid fear, pain, and social condemnation. But if our early learning environments do not provide opportunities for learning new skills, we might be hampered in our efforts to obtain reinforcers. A lack of social skills can also reduce opportunities for social reinforcement, especially when a person withdraws from social situations, leading perhaps to depression and social isolation.

Inadequate levels of reinforcement may be involved in explaining abnormal behavior patterns. In Chapter 7, we explore learning models that relate changes in the level of reinforcement to the development of depression. Inappropriate reinforcement from deviant peer groups, such as gangs, can become an impetus to criminal or delinquent behavior, especially among adolescents (see Chapter 15).

We can also differentiate primary and secondary, or conditioned, reinforcers. **Primary reinforcers** influence behavior because they satisfy basic physical needs. We do not learn to respond to these basic reinforcers; we are born with that capacity. Food, water, sexual stimulation, and escape from pain are examples of primary reinforcers. **Secondary reinforcers** influence behavior through their association with established reinforcers. Thus, we learn to respond to secondary reinforcers. People learn to seek money—a secondary reinforcer—because it can be exchanged for primary reinforcers such as food and heat (or air conditioning).

Punishments are aversive stimuli that decrease or suppress the frequency of the preceding behavior when they are applied. Negative reinforcers, by contrast, increase the frequency of the preceding behavior when they are removed. A loud noise, for example, can be either a punishment (if its introduction reduces the rate of the preceding behavior) or a negative reinforcer (if, by its removal, the rate of the preceding behavior increases).

Punishment, especially physical punishment, may suppress but not eliminate undesirable behavior. The behavior may return when the punishment is withdrawn. One limitation of punishment is that it does not lead to the development of more desirable alternative behaviors. Another is that it may also encourage people to withdraw from such learning situations. Punished children may cut classes, drop out of school, or run away. Punishment may generate anger and hostility, rather than constructive learning. Finally, because people also learn by observation, punishment may become imitated as a means for solving interpersonal problems.

Rewarding desirable behavior is thus generally preferable to punishing misbehavior. But rewarding good behavior requires paying attention to it, not just to misbehavior. Some children who develop conduct problems can gain the attention of other people only by misbehaving. They learn that by acting out others will pay attention to them. To them punishment may actually serve as a positive reinforcer, increasing the rate of response of the behavior it follows. Learning theorists point out that it is not sufficient to expect good conduct from children. Instead, adults need to teach children proper behavior and regularly reinforce them for emitting it.

Let us now consider a contemporary model of learning called social-cognitive theory (formerly called social-learning theory), which broadens the focus of traditional learning theory.

Social-Cognitive Theory Social-cognitive theory represents the contributions of theorists such as Albert Bandura, Julian B. Rotter, and Walter Mischel. Social-cognitive theorists emphasize the roles of thinking or cognition and of learning by observation, or **modeling**, in human behavior. For example, social-cognitive theorists suggest that phobias may be learned *vicariously*, by observing the fearful reactions of others in real life or shown on television or in the movies.

Social-cognitive theorists view people as impacting upon their environments, just as the environment impacts upon them. They see people as self-aware and purposeful learners who seek information about their environments, who do not just respond automatically to the stimuli that impinge upon them. Social-cognitive theorists concur with more traditional behaviorists that theories of human nature should be tied to observable behavior. They assert, however,

Observational learning. According to social-cognitive theory, much human behavior is acquired through modeling, or observational learning. In contrast to operant conditioning, observational learning can occur even when the observer does not engage in the behavior or is not directly reinforced for doing so.

that factors *within* the person should also be considered in explaining human behavior. Rotter (1972), for example, argues that behavior cannot be predicted from situational factors alone. Whether or not people behave in certain ways also depends on certain cognitive factors, such as the person's **expectancies** about the outcomes of behavior. For example, we shall see in Chapter 9 that people who hold more positive expectancies about the outcomes of using drugs are more likely to use them and to use them in larger quantities.

Evaluating the Learning Perspectives One of the principal values of learning models, in contrast to psychodynamic approaches, is their emphasis on observable behavior and environmental factors, such as rewards and punishments, that can be systematically manipulated to observe their effects on behavior. Behavioral approaches to therapy have made major advances in treating phobias, sexual dysfunctions, depression, and other abnormal behavior patterns (see Chapter 3). Reinforcement-based programs are now widely used in helping parents learn better parenting skills and helping children learn in the classroom.

Critics contend that behaviorism cannot explain the richness of human behavior and that human experience cannot be reduced to observable responses. Many learning theorists, too—especially social-cognitive theorists—have been dissatisfied with the strict behavioristic view that environmental conditions mechanically control our behavior. Humans experience thoughts and dreams and formulate goals and aspirations; behaviorism seems not to address much of what it means to be human. Social-cognitive theorists have broadened the scope of traditional behaviorism, but critics claim that social-cognitive theory places too little emphasis on genetic contributions to behavior and has failed to provide a meaningful account of self-awareness.

Humanistic-Existential Perspectives

A "third force" in modern psychology emerged during the mid-20th century—humanistic psychology. Humanistic theorists such as American psychologists Carl Rogers (1902–1987) and Abraham Maslow (1908–1970) believed human behavior was a product neither of unconscious conflicts nor of simple conditioning. Rejecting the determinism implicit in these theories, they saw people as *actors* in the drama of life, not *reactors* to instinctual or environmental pressures. Humanistic psychology is closely linked with the school of European philosophy called *existentialism*. The existentialists, notably the philosophers Martin Heidegger (1889–1976) and Jean-Paul Sartre (1905–1980), focused on the search for meaning and the importance of choice in human existence. Existentialists believe our humanness makes us responsible for the directions our lives will take.

The humanists maintain that people have an inborn tendency toward *self-actualization*—to strive to become all they are capable of being. Each of us possesses a singular cluster of traits and talents that gives rise to an individual set of feelings and needs and grants us a unique perspective on life. Despite the finality of death, we can each imbue our lives with meaning and purpose if we recognize and accept our genuine needs and feelings. By being true to ourselves, we live *authentically*. We may not decide to act out every wish and fancy, but self-awareness of authentic feelings and subjective experiences can help us to make more meaningful choices.

To understand abnormal behavior, in the humanist's view, we need to understand the roadblocks that people encounter in striving for self-actualization and authenticity. To accomplish this, psychologists must learn to view the world from clients' own perspectives because their views of their

Carl Rogers (A) and Abraham Maslow (B), two of the principal forces in humanistic psychology.

world lead them to interpret and evaluate their experiences in self-enhancing or self-defeating ways. The humanistic-existential viewpoint is sometimes called the *phenomenological* perspective because it involves the attempt to understand the subjective or phenomenological experience of others, the experience people have of "being in the world."

Concepts of Abnormal Behavior   Rogers developed the most influential humanistic account of abnormal behavior (C. R. Rogers, 1951). His central belief was that abnormal behavior results from the development of a distorted concept of the self. When parents show children **conditional positive regard**—accept them only when they behave in an approved manner—the children may learn to disown the thoughts, feelings, and behaviors their parents have rejected. With conditional positive regard, children may learn to develop **conditions of worth,** to think of themselves as worthwhile only if they behave in certain approved ways. For example, children who are valued by their parents only when they are compliant may deny to themselves ever having feelings of anger. Children in some families learn it is unacceptable to hold their own ideas, lest they depart from their parents' views. Parental disapproval causes them to see themselves as rebels and their feelings as wrong, selfish, or evil. If they wish to retain self-esteem, they may have to deny many or most of their genuine feelings, or disown parts of themselves. In this way their self-concepts, or views of themselves, also grow distorted, and they can become strangers to themselves.

Rogers believed that anxiety may arise from the partial perception of feelings and ideas that are inconsistent with one's distorted self-concept. Because anxiety is unpleasant, we may deny to ourselves that these feelings and ideas even exist. And so the actualization of our authentic self is bridled by the denial of important ideas and emotions. Psychological energy is channeled toward continued denial and self-defense, not growth. Under such conditions, we cannot hope to perceive our genuine values or personal talents, leading to frustration and setting the stage for abnormal behavior.

So we cannot fulfill all of the wishes of others and remain true to ourselves. This does not mean that self-actualization invariably leads to conflict. Rogers was more optimistic about human nature than Freud. Rogers believed that people hurt one another or become antisocial in their behavior only when they are frustrated in their endeavors to reach their unique potentials. But when parents and others treat children with love and tolerance for their differences, children, too, grow to be loving—even if some of their values and preferences differ from their parents'.

In Rogers's view, the pathway to self-actualization involves a process of self-discovery and self-awareness, of getting in touch with our true feelings, accepting them as our own, and acting in ways that genuinely reflect them. These are the goals of Rogers's method of psychotherapy, called *person-centered therapy.*

Self-Actualization.   Humanistic theorists believe that there exists in each of us a drive toward self-actualization—to become all that we are capable of being. In the humanistic view, each of us, like artist Faith Ringgold—is unique. No two people follow quite the same pathway toward self-actualization.

Evaluating Humanistic-Existential Perspectives   The strengths of humanistic-existential perspectives to the understanding of abnormal behavior lie largely in their focus on conscious experience and their innovation of therapy methods that assist people along pathways of self-discovery and self-acceptance. The humanistic-existential movement put concepts of free choice, inherent goodness, responsibility, and authenticity back on center stage and brought them into modern psychology. Ironically, the primary strength of the humanistic-existential approaches—their focus on conscious experience—may also be their primary weakness. Conscious experience is private and subjective. Therefore, the validity of formulating theories in terms of consciousness has been questioned. How can psychologists be certain they are accurately perceiving the world through the eyes of their clients?

Nor can the concept of self-actualization—which is so basic to Maslow and Rogers—be proved or disproved. Like a psychic structure, a self-actualizing force is not directly measurable or observable. It is inferred from its supposed effects. Self-actualization also yields circular explanations for behavior. When someone is observed engaging in striving, what do we learn by attributing striving to a self-actualizing tendency? The source of the tendency remains a mystery. And when someone is observed not to be striving, what do we gain by attributing the lack of endeavor to a blocked or frustrated self-actualizing tendency? We must still determine the source of frustration or blockage.

Cognitive Perspectives

The word *cognitive* derives from the Latin *cognitio,* meaning "knowledge." Cognitive theorists study the cognitions—the thoughts, beliefs, expectations, and attitudes—that accom-

The power of unconditional positive regard. Rogers believed that parents can help their children develop self-esteem and set them on the road toward self-actualization by showing them unconditional positive regard—prizing them on the basis of their inner worth, regardless of their behavior of the moment.

pany and may underlie abnormal behavior. They focus on how reality is colored by our expectations, attitudes, and so forth, and how inaccurate or biased processing of information about the world—and our places within it—can give rise to abnormal behavior. Cognitive theorists believe that our interpretations of the events in our lives, and not the events themselves, determine our emotional states.

Information Processing Approaches Many cognitive psychologists are influenced by concepts of computer science. Computers process information to solve problems. Information is fed into the computer (encoded so it can be accepted by the computer as input). Then it is placed in *memory* while it is manipulated. You can also place the information permanently in *storage,* on a floppy disk, a hard disk, or another device. Information-processing theorists thus think in terms such as the *input* (based on perception), *storage, retrieval, manipulation,* and *output* of information. They view psychological disorders as disturbances in these processes. Disturbances might be caused by the blocking or distortion of input or by faulty storage, retrieval, or manipulation of information. Any of these can lead to lack of output or distorted output (e.g., bizarre behavior). People with schizophrenia, for example, frequently jump from topic to topic in a disorganized fashion, which may reflect problems in retrieving and manipulating information.

They also seem to have difficulty focusing their attention and filtering out extraneous stimuli, such as distracting noises. This may represent problems relating to initial processing of input from their senses.

Information processing may also be distorted by what cognitive therapists call *cognitive distortions,* or errors in thinking. For example, people who are depressed tend to develop an unduly negative view of their personal situation by exaggerating the importance of unfortunate events they experience (Meichenbaum, 1993). Cognitive theorists such as Albert Ellis and Aaron Beck have postulated that distorted or irrational thinking patterns can lead to emotional problems and maladaptive behavior.

Social-cognitive theorists, who share much in common with the cognitive theorists, focus on the ways in which social information is encoded. Aggressive boys and adolescents are likely to incorrectly encode other people's behavior as threatening (see Chapter 13). They assume other people intend them ill when they do not. Aggressive children and adults may behave in ways that elicit coercive or hostile behavior from others, which serves to confirm their aggressive expectations (Meichenbaum, 1993). Rapists, especially date rapists, may misread a woman's expressed wishes. They may wrongly assume, for example, that the woman who says "no" really means yes and is merely playing "hard to get."

Albert Ellis Psychologist Albert Ellis (1977a, 1987), a prominent cognitive theorist, believes that troubling events in themselves do not lead to anxiety, depression, or disturbed behavior. Rather, it is the irrational beliefs about unfortunate experiences that foster negative emotions and maladaptive behavior. Consider someone who loses a job and becomes anxious and despondent about it. It may seem that being fired is the direct cause of the person's misery, but the misery actually stems from the person's beliefs about the loss and not directly from the loss itself.

Ellis uses an "A→B→C approach" to explain the causes of the misery. Being fired is an *activating event* (A). The ultimate outcome, or *consequence* (C), is emotional distress. But the activating event (A) and the consequences (C) are mediated by various *beliefs* (B). Some of these beliefs might include "That job was the major thing in my life," "What a useless washout I am," "My family will go hungry," "I'll never be able to find another job as good," "I can't do a thing about it." These exaggerated and irrational beliefs compound depression, nurture helplessness, and distract us from evaluating what to do. For instance, the beliefs "I can't do a thing about it" and "What a useless washout I am" promote helplessness.

The situation can be diagrammed like this:

Activating events → Beliefs → Consequences

Ellis points out that apprehension about the future and feelings of disappointment are perfectly normal when people face losses. However, the adoption of irrational beliefs leads people to **catastrophize** the magnitude of losses, leading to

Albert Ellis and Aaron Beck, two of the leading cognitive theorists.

profound distress and states of depression. By intensifying emotional responses and nurturing feelings of helplessness, such beliefs impair coping ability. Other examples of irrational beliefs include the following: "I must have love and approval nearly all the time from people who are important to me," and "I must be competent in everything I do." Ellis notes that the desire for others' approval is understandable, but it is irrational to assume you cannot survive without it. It would be marvelous to excel in everything we do, but it's absurd to demand it of oneself. Sure, in tennis it would be great to serve and volley like a pro, but most people haven't the leisure or aptitude to perfect the game. Insisting on perfection deters people from playing simply for fun.

Ellis has developed a model of therapy, called *rational-emotive behavior therapy* (REBT), to help people dispute these irrational beliefs and substitute more rational ones. Ellis admits that childhood experiences are involved in the origins of irrational beliefs, but cognitive appraisal—the here and now—causes people misery. For most people who are anxious and depressed, the ticket to greater happiness does not lie in discovering and liberating deep-seated conflicts but in recognizing and modifying irrational self-demands.

Aaron Beck Another prominent cognitive theorist, psychiatrist Aaron Beck, proposes that depression may result from "cognitive errors" such as judging oneself entirely on the basis of one's flaws or failures, and interpreting events in a negative light (as though wearing blue-colored glasses) (A. T. Beck, Rush, Shaw, & Emery, 1979). Beck stresses the pervasive roles of four basic types of cognitive errors that contribute to emotional distress:

1. *Selective abstraction.* People may *selectively abstract* the parts of their experiences that reflect upon their flaws and ignore evidence of their competencies.

2. *Overgeneralization.* People may *overgeneralize* from a few isolated experiences. For example, they may see their futures as hopeless because they were laid off or believe they will never marry because they were rejected by a dating partner.

3. *Magnification.* People may blow out of proportion, or *magnify,* the importance of unfortunate events. Students may catastrophize a bad test grade by jumping to the conclusion that they will flunk out of college and their lives will be ruined.

4. *Absolutist thinking.* Absolutist thinking is seeing the world in black and white terms, rather than in shades of gray. Absolutist thinkers may assume that any grade less than a perfect "A," or a work evaluation less than a rave, is a total failure.

Evaluating the Cognitive Perspectives As we'll see in later chapters, cognitive theorists have had an enormous impact on our understanding of abnormal behavior patterns and development of therapeutic approaches. The overlap between the learning-based and cognitive approaches is best represented by the emergence of cognitive-behavior therapy (CBT), a form of therapy that focuses on modifying self-defeating beliefs in addition to overt behaviors (see Chapter 3).

A major issue concerning cognitive perspectives is their range of applicability. Cognitive therapists have largely focused on emotional disorders relating to anxiety and depression but have had less impact on the development of treatment approaches, or conceptual models, of more severe forms of disturbed behavior, such as schizophrenia. Moreover, in the case of depression, it remains unclear, as we see in Chapter 7, whether distorted thinking patterns are causes of depression or merely effects of depression.

Sociocultural Perspectives

Sociocultural theorists look for the causes of abnormal behavior in the failures of society, rather than in the person. They believe that psychological problems are often rooted in the social ills of society, such as poverty, social decay, racial and gender discrimination, and lack of economic opportunity.

According to the more radical sociocultural theorists, such as the psychiatrist Thomas Szasz, mental illness is no more than a myth—a label used to stigmatize and subjugate people whose behavior is socially deviant (T. S. Szasz, 1961). Szasz argues that so-called mental illnesses are really "problems in living," not diseases in the sense that influenza, hypertension, and cancer are diseases. Szasz argues that people who offend others or engage in socially deviant behavior are perceived as threats by the establishment. Labeling them as sick allows others to deny the validity of their problems and to put them away in institutions.

Sociocultural theorists maintain that once the label of "mental illness" is applied, it is very difficult to remove. The label also affects other people's responses to the "patient." Mental patients are stigmatized and socially degraded. Job opportunities may be denied, friendships may dissolve, and the "patient" may become increasingly alienated from society. Szasz argues that treating people as mentally ill strips them of their dignity because it denies them responsibility for their own behavior and choices. He claims that troubled people should be encouraged to take more responsibility for managing their lives and solving their problems.

Evaluating Sociocultural Perspectives Lending support to the linkage between social class and psychological disturbance, classic research in New Haven, CT, showed that people from the lower socioeconomic classes were more likely to be institutionalized for psychiatric problems (Hollingshead & Redlich, 1958). One reason perhaps is that the poor have less access to private outpatient care.

An alternative view is that people from the lower socioeconomic groups may be at greater risk of severe behavior problems because living in poverty subjects them to a greater level of social stress than that faced by the more well-to-do. Yet another view, the *downward drift* hypothesis, suggests that problem behaviors, such as alcoholism, may lead

Roots of abnormal behavior? Sociocultural theorists believe that the roots of abnormal behavior are found not in the individual but in the social ills of society, such as poverty, social decay, racial and gender discrimination, and lack of economic opportunity.

people to drift downward in social status, thereby explaining the linkage between low socioeconomic status and severe behavior problems.

Certainly it is desirable for social critics such as Szasz to rivet our attention on the political implications of our responses to deviance. The views of Szasz and other critics of the mental health establishment have been influential in bringing about much needed changes to protect the rights of mental patients in psychiatric institutions better. Many professionals, however, believe the more radical sociocultural theorists such as Szasz go too far in arguing that mental illness is merely a fabrication invented by society to stigmatize social deviants.

The sociocultural theorists have focused much needed attention on the social stressors that may lead to abnormal behavior. Throughout the text we examine relationships between abnormal behavior patterns and sociocultural factors such as gender, ethnicity, and socioeconomic status, beginning with the accompanying *Focus on Diversity* feature, "Ethnicity and Mental Health."

TYING IT TOGETHER

We have seen that there are several models or perspectives for understanding and treating psychological disorders. The fact that there are different ways of looking at the same phenomenon doesn't mean that one model must be right and the others wrong.

No one theoretical perspective can account for the complex forms of abnormal behavior that we shall encounter in this text. Each of the major perspectives we have discussed—the psychological, biological, and sociocultural frameworks—contributes something to our understanding, but none offers a complete view. We are only beginning to ferret out the subtle and often complex interactions involving the multitude of factors that give rise to abnormal behavior patterns.

Levels of Analysis Different models or perspectives approach the same subject matter from different vantage points or *levels of analysis.* The biological perspective adopts a physiological level of analysis. It examines the role that biochemical processes, such as imbalances in brain chemistry, may play in the development of psychological disorders. The learning perspective adopts a behavioral level of analysis. It focuses on how our behavior is shaped by learning experiences. The humanistic-existential perspective adopts a phenomenological vantage point. It explores people's subjective experiences. The cognitive perspective focuses on the role of dysfunctional cognitions or thinking patterns in psychological disorders, such as irrational beliefs and errors in thinking. The psychodynamic perspective probes the unconscious motives and conflicts that are believed to underlie psychological disorders. Sociocultural theory adopts a much broader level of analysis. It examines psychological disorders in the context of the larger society.

Some perspectives offer more to our understanding of certain psychological disorders than others. For instance, certain forms of mental retardation have identifiable biological causes, such as chromosomal abnormalities (see Chapter 12) or maternal alcohol consumption during pregnancy (see Chapter 9). We know that some phobias are learned reactions to the association or pairing of an object or event with a traumatic or painful experience (see Chapter 5). Most psychological disorders appear to involve a complex interplay of biological, psychological, and sociocultural factors that we are only beginning to ferret out. No one factor or cause can fully explain them.

The Diathesis-Stress Model: An Interactionist View

Many theorists today adopt an interactionist view. They believe we need to take into account the interaction of multiple factors in explaining many abnormal behaviors. The most prominent interactionist model today is the **diathesis-stress** model.

The diathesis-stress model holds that psychological disorders result from the combination or interaction of a **diathesis** (vulnerability or predisposition) with stress (see Figure 1.9). The model proposes that some people possess a vulnerability or diathesis, usually genetic in nature, that increases their risk of developing a particular disorder. Yet whether they develop the disorder depends on the kinds and level of stress they experience. Stress may take the form of biological events such as prenatal trauma, birth complications, and physical illness; psychosocial events such as childhood sexual or physical abuse and family conflict; and negative life events, such as prolonged unemployment and loss of loved ones.

In some cases, people with a diathesis for a particular disorder may remain free of the disorder or develop a milder form of the disorder if the level of stress in their lives remains low or they develop effective coping responses for handling the stress they encounter. However, the stronger the diathesis, the less stress is generally needed to produce the disorder. In some cases the diathesis may be so strong that the disorder develops even under the most benign life circumstances.

The diathesis–stress hypothesis was originally developed as an explanatory framework for understanding the development of schizophrenia (see Chapter 12). It has since been applied to other psychological disorders, such as depression. Although the term *diathesis* generally refers to an inherited predisposition, a diathesis may involve psychological factors such as dysfunctional thinking patterns or personality traits. For example, a dysfunctional pattern of thinking may put individuals at greater risk of developing depression in the face of upsetting or stressful life events such as prolonged unemployment or divorce (see Chapter 7).

The diathesis-stress model is not the only interactionist account of how abnormal behavior patterns develop. We will also consider other interactionist models, such as the cognitive model of panic disorder (see Chapter 5). Throughout the text we will find that many forms of abnormal behavior involve a complex interplay of multiple influences that include psychological, biological, and/or sociocultural factors.

Models of psychological disorders provide a framework not only for explanation but also for treatment (see Chapter 3). They also lead to the formulation of predictions, or *hypotheses*, that guide research. The medical model, for example, fosters inquiry into genetic and biochemical research. Learning models encourage inquiries into the situational determinants of psychological disorders. In the following sections we consider the research methods used by investigators in the field of abnormal psychology.

RESEARCH METHODS IN ABNORMAL PSYCHOLOGY

Abnormal psychology is a branch of the scientific discipline of psychology, which means the pursuit of knowledge in the field is based on the application of the scientific method. Here we examine how researchers apply the scientific method in investigating abnormal behavior.

Let us begin by asking you to imagine you are a brand-new graduate student in psychology and are sitting in your research methods course on the first day of the term. The professor, a distinguished woman of about 50, enters the class. She is carrying a small wire-mesh cage with a white rat. She smiles and sets the cage on her desk.

The professor removes the rat from the cage and places it on the desk. She asks the class to observe its behavior. As a serious student, you attend closely. The animal moves to the edge of the desk, pauses, peers over the edge, and seems to jiggle its whiskers at the floor below. It maneuvers along the edge of the desk, tracking the perimeter. Now and then

FIGURE 1.9 *The diathesis-stress model.*

it pauses and vibrates its whiskers downward in the direction of the floor.

The professor picks up the rat and returns it to the cage. She asks the class to describe the animal's *behavior*.

A student responds, "The rat seems to be looking for a way to escape."

Another student: "It is reconnoitering its environment, examining it." Reconnoitering? you think. That student has seen too many war movies.

The professor writes each response on the blackboard. Another student raises her hand. "The rat is making a visual search of the environment," she says. "Maybe it's looking for food."

The professor prompts other students for their descriptions.

"It's looking around," says one.

"Trying to escape," says another.

Your turn arrives. Trying to be scientific, you say, "We can't say what its motivation might be. All we know is that it's scanning its environment."

"How so?" the professor asks.

"Visually," you reply, confidently.

The professor writes the response and then turns to the class, shaking her head. "Each of you observed the rat," she said, "but none of you described its *behavior*. Each of you made certain *inferences*, that the rat was 'looking for a way down' or 'scanning its environment' or 'looking for food,' and the like. These are not unreasonable inferences, but they are inferences, not descriptions. They also happen to be wrong. You see, the rat is blind. It's been blind since birth. It couldn't possibly be looking around, at least not in a visual sense."

Description, Explanation, Prediction, and Control: The Objectives of Science

Description is one of the primary objectives of science. To understand abnormal behavior, we must first learn to describe it. Description allows us to recognize abnormal behavior and provides the basis for explaining it.

Descriptions should be clear, unbiased, and based on careful observation. Our anecdote about the blind rat illustrates the point that our observations and our attempts to describe them can be influenced by our expectations, or biased. Our expectations reflect our models of behavior, and they may incline us to perceive events—such as the rat's movements and other people's behavior—in certain ways. Describing the rat in the classroom as "scanning" and "looking" for something is an **inference** or conclusion we draw from our observations that is based on our model of how animals explore their environments. Description would involve a precise accounting of the animal's movements around the desk, measuring how far in each direction it moves, how long it pauses, how it bobs its head from side to side, and so on.

Inference is also important in science, however. Inference allows us to jump from the particular to the general—

to suggest laws and principles of behavior that can be woven into models and **theories** of behavior, such as psychodynamic and learning models. Without a way of organizing our descriptions of phenomena in terms of models and theories, we would be left with a buzzing confusion of unconnected observations. The crucial issue is to distinguish between description and inference—to recognize when one jumps from a description of events to an inference based on an interpretation of events. For example, one does not *describe* a person's behavior as "schizophrenic," but rather one *interprets* behavior as schizophrenic on the basis of one's model of schizophrenia. To do otherwise, we would affix ourselves to a given label or model and lose the intellectual flexibility that is needed to revise our inferences in the light of new evidence or ways of conceptualizing information.

Theories help scientists explain puzzling behavior and predict future behavior. Prediction entails the discovery of factors that anticipate the occurrence of events. Geology, for example, seeks clues in the forces affecting the earth that can forecast natural events such as earthquakes and volcanic eruptions. Scientists who study abnormal behavior seek clues in overt behavior, biological processes, family interactions, and so forth, to predict the development of abnormal behaviors as well as factors that might predict response to various treatments. It is not sufficient for theoretical models such as psychodynamic or learning models to help us explain or make sense of events or behaviors that have already occurred. Useful theories must allow us to predict the occurrence of particular behaviors.

The idea of controlling human behavior—especially the behavior of people with serious problems—is controversial. The history of societal response to abnormal behaviors, including abuses such as exorcism and cruel forms of physical restraint, render the idea particularly distressing. Within science, however, the word *control* need not imply that people are coerced into doing the bidding of others, like puppets dangling on strings. Psychologists, for example, are committed to the dignity of the individual, and the concept of human dignity requires that people be free to make decisions and exercise choices. Within this context, *controlling behavior* means using scientific knowledge to help people shape their own goals and more efficiently use their resources to accomplish them. Today, in the United States, even when helping professionals restrain people who are violently disturbed, their goal is to assist them to overcome their agitation and regain the ability to exercise meaningful choices in their lives.[3] Ethical standards prohibit the use of injurious techniques in research or practice.

Psychologists and other scientists use the *scientific method* to advance the description, explanation, prediction, and control of abnormal behavior.

---

[3]Here we are talking about violently confused and disordered behavior, not criminal behavior. Criminals and disturbed people may both be dangerous to others, but with criminals the intention of restraint is usually limited to protecting society.

Ethnicity² and Mental Health

When Europeans first arrived on America's shores, the land was populated solely by Native Americans. By the time the United States achieved nationhood, the numbers of people of European descent were approaching those of Native Americans. During the 19th century, the nation became predominantly populated by White people. Although non-Hispanic White Americans (also called European Americans) remain in the majority today, the nation is becoming increasingly ethnically diverse, as a result of both an excess of births over deaths among various U.S. ethnic groups and contemporary trends in immigration.

Figure 1.8 shows the ethnic composition of the U.S. population. The term *minority group* is becoming something of a misnomer when applied to non-white populations. If present trends continue, non-Hispanic White Americans will be in the minority in the state of California by the year 2000 or shortly thereafter. And, if present trends continue, European Americans (non-Hispanic White Americans) will become a minority in the United States before this century is over.

Given the increasing ethnic diversity of the U.S. population, researchers have turned to study ethnic group differences in the prevalences of psychological disorders. Knowing a disorder disproportionately affects one group or another can help planners direct prevention and treatment programs to the groups that are most in need. Researchers recognize that income level or socioeconomic status needs to be considered when comparing rates of a given diagnosis across ethnic groups. We also need to account for differences among ethnic subgroups, such as among the various subgroups that comprise the Hispanic American and Asian American populations. We find, for example, higher levels of depression among Hispanic immigrants to the United

---

²The word ethnicity is derived from the Greek word *ethnikos,* meaning people or nation.

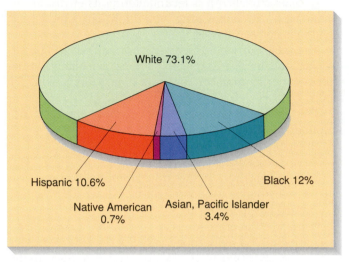

FIGURE 1.8   *Ethnic composition of the United States.*

States from Central America than from Mexico, even when considering differences in educational backgrounds (Salgado de Snyder, Cervantes, & Padilla, 1990).

Some ethnic groups have been underrepresented in previous research. For example, no nationwide surveys of the prevalence of psychological disorders among Asian Americans have been reported (Sue et al., 1995). However, the available evidence indicates that psychological disorders are not significantly lower among Asian Americans than other ethnic groups, which stands in contrast to the popular perception of Asian Americans as a group generally free of mental health problems (Sue et al., 1995; Zane & Sue, 1991).

The major source of evidence relating ethnicity and mental health comes from two large-scale surveys that involved the administration of structured psychiatric interviews. The National Comorbidity Survey (NCS), which we described earlier, was based on a representa-

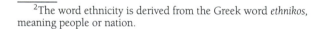

The Scientific Method

The scientific method involves systematic attempts to test our assumptions and theories about the world through gathering objective evidence. Various means are used in applying the scientific method, including observational and experimental methods. Here let us focus on the basic steps involved in using the scientific method in experimentation:

1. *Formulating a research question.*   Scientists derive research questions from their observations and theories of events and behavior. For instance, based on their clinical observations and understandings of the underlying mechanisms in depression, they may formulate questions about whether certain experimental drugs or particular types of psychotherapy can help people overcome depression.

2. *Framing the research question in the form of a hypothesis.*   A **hypothesis** is a precise prediction about behavior

tive sample of more than 8,000 people from across the United States (R. C. Kessler, 1994; Kessler et al., 1993, 1994). Another major study, the National Institute of Mental Health's Epidemiologic Catchment Area (ECA) Study, involved interviews of nearly 20,000 residents in five U.S. communities (New Haven, CT; Baltimore, MD; St. Louis, MO; Durham, NC; and Los Angeles, CA) (Robins & Regier, 1991). We should caution that the sites selected for the ECA study, and the participants in each site, were not randomly drawn. Thus, the prevalences reported are not necessarily representative of the U.S. population at large. By contrast, the NCS was constructed to mirror the general population. There were also some differences in methodology between the two surveys, such as in terms of how questions were worded or how deeply interviewers probed, so the results may not be directly comparable.

The ECA study found no differences in the rates of schizophrenia between African Americans and non-Hispanic White Americans while controlling for socio-economic factors and other factors such as age and marital status (Keith, Regier, & Rea, 1991). However, Hispanic Americans had lower rates of schizophrenia, especially among men, than either non-Hispanic White Americans or African Americans. A different picture emerges when one looks at diagnoses in ordinary clinical practice, however. Researchers find that schizophrenia is often overdiagnosed in members of traditionally disadvantaged minority groups (Coleman & Baker, 1994; Loring & Powell, 1988), perhaps because of the stereotyping of minority group members as "out of control" by mental health professionals.

Despite stereotypes that mental health problems are more common among ethnic minorities, NCS researchers found no disorder occurring more frequently among African Americans than among non-Hispanic Whites when differences in income and educational level were taken into account (R. C. Kessler et al., 1994). To the contrary, African Americans had lower rates of psychological disorders overall, and lower rates of mood disorders and substance abuse disorders in particular, than did non-Hispanic Whites.

Hispanics were no more likely to have anxiety disorders or alcohol-related disorders than European Americans but were more likely to show evidence of a current mood disorder. Data on Asian Americans or Native Americans were not reported in either of the two major surveys. Researchers also used the ECA data to examine differences between religious groups. Comparisons between Jews and non-Jews showed no difference in the rates of psychological disorders overall, but Jews showed higher rates of depression and lower rates of alcohol abuse than did Catholics and Protestants (Yeung & Greenwald, 1992).

We should be cautious—and think critically—when interpreting ethnic group differences in rates of diagnoses of psychological disorders. Might differences reflect differential vulnerabilities to particular patterns of abnormal behaviors? Would such vulnerabilities reflect genetic factors, sociocultural factors, or an interaction of these and other factors? Might diagnostic patterns in actual practice reflect a bias on the part of diagnosticians to assign diagnoses on the basis of racial and ethnic stereotypes? Consider evidence showing that African Americans and Hispanics are more likely to be diagnosed with schizophrenia even when independent evidence shows that a diagnosis of schizophrenia is unjustified (Garb, 1997).

Whatever the underlying differences in psychopathology between ethnic groups may be, some ethnic minorities, such as Mexican Americans (Griffith, 1985; Hough et al., 1987) and Asian Americans (Zane & Sue, 1991), underutilize mental health services in relation to non-Hispanic White Americans. Those who do seek services are more likely to drop out prematurely from treatment. In Chapter 3 we consider barriers that limit the utilization of mental health services by various ethnic minority groups in our society.

that is examined through research. For example, scientists might hypothesize that people who are clinically depressed will show greater improvement on measures of depression if they are given an experimental drug than if they receive an inert placebo ("sugar pill").

3. *Testing the hypothesis.* Scientists test hypotheses through carefully controlled observation and experimentation. They might test the hypothesis about the experimental drug by setting up an experiment in which one group of people with depression is given the experimental drug and another group is given the placebo. They would then administer tests to see if the people who received the active drug showed greater improvement over a period of time than those who received the placebo.

4. *Drawing conclusions about the hypothesis.* In the final step, scientists draw conclusions from their findings about the correctness of their hypotheses. Psychologists use statistical methods to determine the likelihood that differences

between groups are **significant** as opposed to chance fluctuations. Psychologists are reasonably confident that group differences are significant—that is, not due to chance—when the probability that chance alone can explain the difference is less than 5%. When well-designed research findings fail to bear out hypotheses, scientists can modify the theories from which the hypotheses are derived. Research findings often lead to modifications in theory, new hypotheses, and, in turn, subsequent research.

Let us consider the major research methods used by psychologists and others to study abnormal behavior: the naturalistic-observation, correlational, experimental, epidemiological, kinship, and case-study methods. Before we do so, however, let us consider some of the principles that guide ethical conduct in research.

Ethics in Research

Ethical principles are designed to promote the dignity of the individual, protect human welfare, and preserve scientific integrity. Psychologists are prohibited by the ethical standards of their profession from using methods that cause psychological or physical harm to subjects or clients (American Psychological Association [APA], 1992). Psychologists also must follow ethical guidelines that protect animal subjects in research.

Institutions such as universities and hospitals have review committees, called *institutional review boards* (IRBs) that review proposed research studies in light of ethical guidelines. Investigators must receive IRB approval before they

are permitted to begin their studies. Two of the major principles upon which ethical guidelines are based are (1) *informed consent* and (2) *confidentiality*.

The principle of **informed consent** requires that people be free to choose whether they wish to participate in research studies. They must be given sufficient information in advance about the study's purposes and methods, and its risks and benefits, to allow them to make an informed decision about their participation. Subjects must also be free to withdraw from a study at any time without penalty. In some cases, researchers may withhold certain information until all the data are collected. For instance, subjects in placebo control studies of experimental drugs are told that they may receive an inert placebo rather than the active drug. After the study is concluded, participants who received the placebo would be given the option of receiving the active treatment. In studies in which information was withheld or deception was used, subjects must be **debriefed** afterwards. That is, they must receive an explanation of the true methods and purposes of the study and why it was necessary to keep them in the dark.

Subjects also have a right to expect that their identities will not be revealed. Investigators are required to protect their **confidentiality** by keeping the records of their participation secure and by not disclosing their identities to others.

The Naturalistic-Observation Method

The **naturalistic-observation method** is used to observe behavior in the field, where it happens. Anthropologists have lived in preliterate societies in order to study human diversity. Sociologists have followed the activities of adolescent gangs in inner cities. Psychologists have spent weeks observing the behavior of homeless people in train stations and bus terminals. They have even observed the eating habits of slender and overweight people in fast-food restaurants, searching for clues to obesity.

Scientists take every precaution to ensure their naturalistic observations are **unobtrusive,** so as to prevent any interference with the behavior they observe. Otherwise, the presence of the observer may distort the behavior that is observed. Over the years naturalistic observers have sometimes found themselves in controversial situations. For example, they have allowed sick or injured apes to die when medicine could have saved them. Observers of substance abuse and other criminal behavior have allowed illicit behavior to go unreported to authorities. In such cases, the ethical trade-off is that unobtrusive observation can yield information that will be of benefit to all.

Naturalistic observation provides a good deal of information as to how subjects behave, but it does not necessarily reveal why they do so. Men who frequent bars and drink, for example, are more likely to get into fights than men who do not. But such observations do not show that alcohol *causes* aggression. As we see in the following pages, questions of cause and effect are best approached by means of controlled experiments.

Naturalistic observation. Anthropologists learn about other cultures by observing how members of these other societies live from day to day, in some cases actually living for a time in the societies they study. Here an American anthropologist is shown sitting among members of an African pygmy tribe.

Correlation

Correlation is a statistical measure of the relationships between two factors or **variables.** In the naturalistic-observation study that occurred in the fast-food restaurant, eating behaviors were related—or correlated—to patrons' weights. They were not directly manipulated. In other words, the investigators did not manipulate the weights or eating rates of their subjects but merely measured the two variables in some fashion and examined whether they were statistically related to each other. When one variable (weight level) increases as the second variable (rate of eating) increases, there is a **positive correlation** between them. If one variable decreases as the other increases, the correlation between the variables is said to be a **negative correlation.**

Although correlational research reveals whether or not there is a statistical relationship between variables, it does not prove that the variables are causally related. Causal connections sometimes work in unexpected directions, and sometimes there is no causal connection between variables that are merely correlated. There are correlations between depression and negative thoughts, and it may seem logical that depression is caused by such thoughts. However, it is also possible that feelings of depression give rise to negative thoughts. Perhaps the direction of causality works both ways, with negative thinking contributing to depression and depression in turn influencing negative thinking. Moreover, depression and negative thinking may both reflect a common causative factor, such as stress, and not be causally related to each other at all.

Although correlational research does not reveal cause and effect, it can be used to serve the scientific objective of prediction. When two variables are correlated, we can use one to predict the other. Knowledge of correlations among alcoholism, family history, and attitudes toward drinking helps us predict which adolescents are at great risk of developing problems with alcohol, although causal connections are complex and somewhat nebulous. But knowing which factors predict future problems may help us direct preventive efforts toward these high-risk groups to help prevent these problems from developing.

The Longitudinal Study One type of correlational study is the *longitudinal study,* in which subjects are studied at periodic intervals over lengthy periods, perhaps for decades. By studying people over time, researchers can investigate the events associated with the onset of abnormal behavior and, perhaps, learn to identify factors that predict the development of such behavior. However, such research is time consuming and costly. It requires a commitment that may literally outlive the original investigators. Therefore, long-term longitudinal studies are relatively uncommon. In Chapter 12 we examine one of the best known longitudinal studies, the Danish high-risk study that has tracked since 1962 the development of a group of children whose mothers had schizophrenia and so were at increased risk of developing the disorder (Mednick & Schulsinger, 1965).

Prediction is based on the *correlation* between events or factors that are separated in time. As in other forms of correlational research, we must be careful not to infer *causation* from *correlation.* A **causal relationship** between two events involves a time-ordered relationship in which the second event is the direct result of the first. We need to meet two strict conditions to posit a causal relationship between two factors:

1. The effect must follow the cause in a time-ordered sequence of events.
2. Other plausible causes of the observed effects (rival hypotheses) must be eliminated.

Through the experimental method, scientists seek to demonstrate causal relationships by first manipulating the causal factor and then measuring its effects under controlled conditions that minimize the risk of possible rival hypotheses.

The Experimental Method

The term *experiment* can cause some confusion. Broadly speaking, an "experiment" is a trial or test of a hypothesis. From this vantage point, any method that actually seeks to test a hypothesis could be considered "experimental"—including naturalistic observation and correlational studies. But investigators usually limit the use of the term **experimental method** to refer to studies in which researchers seek to uncover cause-and-effect relationships by manipulating possible causal factors directly.

The factors or variables hypothesized to play a causal role are manipulated or controlled by the investigator in experimental research. These are called the **independent variables.** The observed effects are labeled **dependent variables,** because changes in them are believed to depend on the independent or manipulated variable. Dependent variables are observed and measured, not manipulated, by the experimenter. Examples of independent and dependent variables of interest to investigators of abnormal behavior are shown in Table 1.2.

In an experiment, subjects are exposed to an *independent variable,* for example, the type of beverage (alcoholic vs. nonalcoholic) they consume in a laboratory setting. They are then observed or examined to determine whether the independent variable makes a difference in their behavior, or, more precisely, whether the independent variable affects the dependent variable—in this case, whether they behave more aggressively if they consume alcohol.

Experimental and Control Subjects Well-controlled experiments assign subjects to experimental and control groups at random. **Experimental subjects** are given the experimental treatment. **Control subjects** are not. Care is taken to hold other conditions constant for each group. By using random assignment and holding other conditions constant, experimenters can be reasonably confident that the experimental treatment, and not uncontrolled factors such as room temperature or differences between the types

TABLE 1.2

Examples of Independent and Dependent Variables in Experimental Research

Independent Variables	Dependent Variables
Type of treatment: for example, different types of drug treatments or psychological treatments	Behavioral variables: for example, measures of adjustment, activity levels, eating behavior, smoking behavior
Treatment factors: for example, brief vs. long-term treatment, inpatient vs. outpatient treatment	Physiological variables: for example, measures of physiological responses such as heart rate, blood pressure, and brain wave activity
Experimental manipulations: for example, types of beverage consumed (alcoholic vs. nonalcoholic)	Self-report variables: for example, measures of anxiety, mood, or marital or life satisfaction

of subjects in the experimental and control groups, brought about the differences in outcome between the experimental and control groups.

Random Assignment Why should experimenters assign subjects to experimental and control groups at random? Consider a study intended to investigate the effects of alcohol on behavior. If we allowed subjects to decide whether or not they wanted to be in a group that drank alcohol, a **selection factor,** rather than the independent variable, might be responsible for the results. In this example, subjects who chose to drink might differ in important ways from those who preferred not to drink. One of their differences might lie in their aggressiveness. Therefore, we would not know whether the experimental manipulation (giving them or not giving them alcohol) or the selection factor was ultimately responsible for observed differences in behavior. Moreover, knowledge of which treatment they were receiving might also affect the experimental outcome—in this case by shaping subjects' expectations.

Controlling for Subjects' Expectations Apparent treatment effects may stem from subjects' expectations regarding their effects rather than from treatments themselves. Thus, researchers also try to control for subjects' expectations about the treatments. In order to do so, they may have to render subjects **blind** as to what treatment they are receiving. For example, the taste of an alcoholic beverage such as vodka may be masked by mixing it with tonic water in certain amounts, so as to keep subjects blind as to whether the drinks they receive contain alcohol or tonic water only.

Placebo-Control Studies Drug treatment studies are often designed to control for subjects' expectations by keeping subjects in the dark as to whether they are receiving the experimental drug or an *inert placebo* control. The term **placebo** derives from the Latin meaning "I shall please," referring to the fact that belief in the effectiveness of a treatment (its pleasing qualities) may inspire hopeful expectations that help people mobilize themselves to overcome

their problems—regardless of whether the substance they receive is chemically active or inert. In medical research on chemotherapy, a placebo—also referred to as a "sugar pill"—is an inert substance that physically resembles an active drug. By comparing the effects of the active drug with those of the placebo, the experimenter can determine whether or not the drug has specific effects beyond those accounted for by expectations.

In a *single-blind placebo-control study,* subjects are randomly assigned to treatment conditions in which they receive an active drug (experimental condition) or a placebo (placebo-control condition), but they are kept blind, or uninformed, about which drug they are receiving. It is also helpful to keep the dispensing researchers blind as to which substances the subjects are receiving, lest the researchers' expectations come to affect the results. So in the case of a *double-blind placebo design,* neither the researcher nor the subject is told whether an active drug or a placebo is being administered. Of course, this approach assumes that the subjects and the experimenters cannot "see through" the blind. In some cases, however, telltale side effects or obvious drug effects may break the blind (Basoglu et al., 1997). Still, the double-blind placebo control is among the strongest and most popular experimental designs, especially in drug treatment research.

Placebo-control groups have also been used in psychotherapy research in order to control for subject expectancies. For example, an *attention-placebo* control group design may be used to separate the effects of a particular form of psychotherapy from placebo effects. In an attention-placebo group, subjects are exposed to a believable or credible treatment that contains the nonspecific factors that therapies share—such as the attention and emotional support of a therapist—but not the specific ingredients of therapy represented in the active treatment. Attention-placebo treatments commonly substitute general discussions of participants' problems for the specific ingredients of therapy contained in the experimental treatment. Unfortunately, although attention-placebo subjects may be kept blind as to whether or not they are receiving the experimental treatment, the therapists themselves are generally aware of which treatment is being administered. Therefore, the attention-placebo method may not control for therapists' expectations.

Experimental Validity Experimental studies are judged as to whether or not they are valid, or sound. The concept of experimental validity has multiple meanings, and we consider three of them: *internal validity, external validity,* and *construct validity.* We see in Chapter 2 that the term *validity* is also applied in the context of tests and measures to refer to the degree to which these instruments measure what they purport to measure.

Experiments are said to have **internal validity** when the observed changes in the dependent variable(s) can be causally related to the independent or treatment variable. Assume a group of depressed subjects is treated with a new antidepressant medication (the independent variable), and changes in their mood and behavior (the dependent variables) are tracked over time. After several weeks of treatment, the researcher finds most subjects have improved and claims the new drug is an effective treatment for depression. "Not so fast," you think to yourself, "how does the experimenter know that the independent variable and not some other factor was causally responsible for the improvement? Perhaps the subjects improved naturally as time passed, or perhaps they were exposed to other events that were responsible for their improvement." Experiments lack internal validity to the extent they fail to control for other factors (called *confounds*, or threats to validity) that might pose rival hypotheses for the results.

Experimenters randomly assign subjects to treatment and control groups to help control for such rival hypotheses. Random assignment helps ensure that subjects' attributes—intelligence, motivation, age, race, and so on—and presumably the life events they experience are randomly distributed across the groups and are not likely to favor one group over the other. Through the random assignment to groups, researchers can be reasonably confident that significant differences between the treatment and control groups reflect the effects of independent (treatment) variables and not confounding selection factors.

External validity refers to the generalizability or applicability of the results of an experimental study to other subjects and settings, and at other times. In most cases, researchers are interested in generalizing the results of a specific study (for example, effects of a new antidepressant medication on a sample of people who are depressed) to a larger population (people in general who are depressed). The external validity of a study is strengthened to the degree the **sample** is representative of the target population. In studying the problems of the urban homeless, it is essential to make the effort to recruit a representative sample of the homeless population, for example, rather than focusing on a few homeless people who happen to be available.

Analogue Studies One method of research that gives rise to many questions of external validity is the **analogue**

study. Analogue studies usually take place in laboratory settings that are designed to simulate **in vivo** (real-life) behaviors or events. In the laboratory, however, the experimenter has the ability to investigate the behavior of interest under more tightly controlled conditions. In Chapter 5 we see that people who experience repeated panic attacks in their daily lives are more likely than others to report panicky feelings when they were administered certain chemical substances in the laboratory. Because it may not be feasible to monitor panic attacks in the natural setting, the induction of panicky sensations under laboratory conditions allows researchers to explore the factors that may give rise to attacks in the natural environment.

To the extent that experimental arrangements for analogue studies are reasonable counterparts of natural settings, we can have confidence in their applicability to real-life settings. To the extent that we share physiological processes with other species, animal experiments may have much to teach us about ourselves. We should be careful, however, in conjecturing about whether or not animals can become "depressed" or "anxious" or suffer loss of problem-solving ability in ways that mirror these experiences among humans.

Construct validity represents a conceptually higher level of validity—the degree to which treatment effects can be accounted for by the theoretical mechanisms or constructs that are represented in the independent variables. A drug, for example, may have predictable effects but not for the theoretical reasons claimed by the researchers.

Consider a hypothetical experimental study of a new antidepressant medication. The research may have internal validity in the form of solid controls and external validity in the form of generalizability across samples of seriously depressed people. However, it may lack construct validity if the drug does not work for the reasons proposed by the researchers. Perhaps the researchers assumed that the drug would work by raising the levels of certain chemicals in the nervous system, whereas the drug actually works by increasing the sensitivity of receptors for those chemicals. So what? you may think. After all, the drug still works. True enough—in terms of immediate clinical applications. However, a better understanding of why the drug works can advance theoretical knowledge of depression and give rise to the development of yet more effective treatments.

We can never be certain about the construct validity of research. Scientists recognize that their current theories about why their results occurred may eventually be toppled by other theories that better account for the findings.

Epidemiological Method

The **epidemiological method** studies the rates of occurrence of abnormal behavior in various settings or population groups. One type of epidemiological study is the **survey** method, which relies on interviews or questionnaires. Surveys are used to ascertain the rates of occurrence of various disorders in the population as a whole and in various subgroups classified according to such factors as race, ethnicity, gender, or social class. Rates of occurrence of a given disorder are expressed in terms of **incidence,** or the number of new cases of a disorder occurring during a specific period of time, and **prevalence,** which refers to the overall number of cases of a disorder existing in the population during a given period of time. Prevalence rates, then, include both new and continuing cases. The ECA and NCS studies discussed previously are the most comprehensive epidemiological surveys on the prevalences of psychological disorders in the United States to date.

Samples and Populations   In the best of possible worlds, we would conduct surveys in which every member of the **population** of interest would participate. In that way, we could be sure the survey results accurately represent the population we wish to study. In reality, unless the population of interest is rather narrowly defined (say, for example, designating the population of interest as the students living on your dormitory floor), chances are it is extremely difficult, if not impossible, to survey every member of a given population. Even census takers can't count every head in the general population. Consequently, most surveys are based on a sample, or subset, of the population. Researchers take steps when constructing a sample to ensure that it *represents* the target population. A researcher who sets out to study smoking rates in a local community by interviewing people drinking coffee in late-night cafés will probably overestimate its true prevalence.

One method of obtaining a representative sample is random sampling. A **random sample** is drawn in such a way that each member of the population of interest has an equal probability of selection. Epidemiologists sometimes construct random samples by surveying at random a given number of households within a target community. By repeating this process in a random sample of U.S. communities, the overall sample can approximate the general U.S. population.

Scientists use randomly drawn nationwide samples of about 1,500 people to gain an accurate picture of the voting patterns of the general U.S. population. But a sample of several million that was haphazardly drawn might not provide an accurate picture.

TRUTH *or* FICTION REVISITED

1.8 *True.* A representative nationwide sample of about 1,500 people may be more accurate than a haphazard sample of millions.

Epidemiological studies may point to potential causal factors in illnesses and disorders, even though they lack the power of experiments. By finding that illnesses or disorders "cluster" in certain groups or locations, researchers may be able to identify certain distinguishing characteristics that place these groups or regions at higher risk. Yet such epidemiological studies cannot control for selection factors—that is, they cannot rule out rival hypotheses that other unrecognized factors might play a causal role in putting a certain group at greater risk. Therefore, they must be considered suggestive of possible causal influences that must be tested further in experimental studies.

Kinship Studies

Kinship studies attempt to disentangle the roles of heredity and environment in determining behavior. The more closely people are related, the more genes they have in common. Children receive half their genes from each parent. There is thus a 50% overlap in genetic heritage between each parent and his or her offspring. Siblings (brothers and sisters) similarly share half their genetic heritage. Aunts and uncles who are related by blood to their nephews and nieces have a 25% overlap; first cousins, a 12.5% overlap (see Figure 1.10).

In order to determine whether a pattern of abnormal behavior has a genetic basis, researchers locate one case of a person with the disorder and then study how the disorder is distributed among the person's family members. The case first diagnosed is referred to as the index case or **proband.** If the distribution of the disorder among family members of the proband approximates their degree of kinship, there may be a genetic involvement in the disorder. However, the closer their kinship, the more likely people also are to share environmental backgrounds. For this reason, twin and adoptee studies are of particular value.

Twin Studies   Sometimes a fertilized egg cell (or zygote) divides into two cells that separate, so each develops into a separate person. In such cases, there is a 100% overlap in genetic makeup, and the couple are known as identical twins, or **monozygotic (MZ) twins.** Sometimes a woman releases two egg cells, or ova, in the same month,

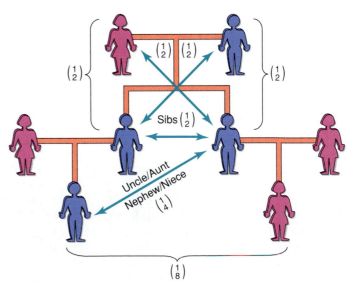

FIGURE 1.10   *A family tree showing the proportion of shared inheritance among relatives.*
The more closely people are related, the more genes they have in common. Kinship studies, including twin studies and adoptee studies, afford researchers insight into the heritability of various patterns of abnormal behavior.

and they are both fertilized. In such cases, the zygotes (fertilized egg cells) develop into fraternal twins, or **dizygotic (DZ) twins.** DZ twins overlap 50% in their genetic heritage, just as other siblings do.

Identical, or MZ, twins are important in the study of the relative influences of heredity and environment because differences between MZ twins are the result of environmental rather than genetic influences. MZ twins look more alike and are closer in height than DZ twins. In twin studies, researchers identify probands for a given disorder who are members of MZ or DZ twin pairs and then study the other twins in the pairs. A role for genetic factors is suggested when MZ twins are significantly more likely than DZ twins to share a disorder. Differences in the rates of **concordance** for MZ versus DZ twins are found for some forms of abnormal behavior, such as schizophrenia and bipolar disorder. Even among MZ twins, though, environmental influences cannot be ruled out. Parents and teachers, for example, often encourage MZ twins to behave in similar ways. Put it another way: If one twin does X, everyone expects the other to do X also. Expectations have a way of influencing behavior and making for self-fulfilling prophecies. We should also note that twins may not be typical of the general population, so we need to be cautious when generalizing the results of twin studies to the larger population. Twins tend to have had shorter gestational periods, lower birth weights, and a greater frequency of congenital malformations than nontwins (Kendler, 1994). Perhaps differences in prenatal experiences influence their later development in ways that set them apart from nontwins.

Adoptee Studies Adoptee studies can provide powerful arguments for or against genetic factors in the appearance of psychological traits and disorders. Assume that children are reared by adoptive parents from a very early age—perhaps from birth. The children share environmental backgrounds with their adoptive parents but not their genetic heritages. Then assume we compare the traits and behavior patterns of these children to those of their biological parents and their adoptive parents. If the children show a greater similarity to their biological parents than their adoptive parents on certain traits or disorders, we have strong evidence indeed for genetic factors in these traits and disorders.

Although adoptee studies may represent the strongest source of evidence for genetic factors in explaining abnormal behavior patterns, we should recognize that adoptees, like twins, may not be typical of the general population. In later chapters we explore the role that adoptee and other kinship studies play in ferreting out genetic and environmental influences in many psychological disorders.

The Case-Study Method

Case studies have been important influences in the development of theories and treatment of abnormal behavior. Psychodynamic theory, originated by Sigmund Freud, was developed primarily on the basis of case studies, such as that of Anna O. Case studies have also been reported by therapists representing other theoretical viewpoints.

Types of Case Studies Case studies involve intensive studies of individuals. Some case studies are based on historical material, involving subjects who have been dead for hundreds of years. Freud, for example, conducted a case study of the Renaissance artist and inventor Leonardo da Vinci. More commonly, case studies reflect an in-depth analysis of an individual's course of treatment. They typically include detailed histories of the subject's background and response to treatment. The therapist attempts to glean information from a particular client's experience in therapy that may be of help to other therapists treating similar clients.

TRUTH or FICTION REVISITED

1.9 True. Case studies have been conducted on people who have been dead for hundreds of years, such as Freud's study of Leonardo. Such studies rely on historical records rather than interviews.

Despite the richness of clinical material that case studies can provide, they are much less rigorous as research designs than experiments. There are bound to be distortions or gaps in memory or when people discuss historical events, especially those of their childhoods. Some people may intentionally color events in such a way as to make a favorable impression on the interviewer; others aim to shock the interviewer with exaggerated or fabricated recollections. Interviewers themselves may unintentionally guide subjects into slanting the histories they report in ways that are compatible with their own theoretical perspectives.

Case reports of treatment effectiveness also have certain problems. The individual subject or small number of subjects are hardly representative of the general population. Another weakness is the lack of a control group. In the absence of a control group, it is difficult to tell whether beneficial changes in behavior that are observed over the course of treatment are due to

1. Specific treatment techniques,
2. Nonspecific therapeutic factors such as raising clients' expectations or giving them time to talk about their problems with a supportive therapist,
3. Naturally occurring ("spontaneous") improvement over time, or
4. External factors such as advice from loved ones, winning the lottery, and so forth.

Like many of us, therapists sometimes engage in self-serving explanations of therapy outcomes: They tend to accept credit for treatment successes but to blame treatment failures on other factors, such as lack of full cooperation on the part of the client.

FIGURE 1.11 *Diagram of an A-B-A-B reversal design.*

Single-Case Experimental Designs The lack of control available in the traditional case study method led researchers to develop more sophisticated methods, called **single-case experimental designs**, in which subjects are used as their own controls. One of the most common forms of the single-case experimental design is the A-B-A-B, or so-called *reversal design* (see Figure 1.11). The reversal design consists of the repeated measurement of clients' behavior across four successive phases:

1. A baseline phase (A). The baseline phase occurs prior to the inception of treatment and is characterized by repeated measurement of the target problem behaviors at periodic intervals. This measurement allows the experimenter to establish a baseline rate for the behavior before treatment begins;

2. A treatment phase (B). Now the target behaviors are measured as the client undergoes treatment;

3. A second baseline phase (A, again). Treatment is now temporarily withdrawn or suspended. This is the reversal in the reversal design, and it is expected the positive ef-

fects of treatment should now be reversed because the treatment has been withdrawn; and

4. A second treatment phase (B, again). Treatment is reinstated, and the target behaviors are assessed yet again.

Clients' target behaviors or response patterns are compared from one phase to the next in order to determine the effects of treatment. The experimenter looks for evidence of a correspondence between the subject's behavior and the particular phase of the design to determine whether or not the independent variable (that is, the treatment) has produced the intended effects. If the behavior improves whenever treatment is introduced (during the first and second treatment phases) but returns (or is reversed) to baseline levels during the reversal phase, the experimenter can be reasonably confident the treatment had the intended effect.

The method is illustrated by a case in which Azrin and Peterson (1989) used a controlled blinking treatment to eliminate a severe eye tic—a form of squinting in which her eyes shut tightly for a fraction of a second—in a 9-year-old girl. The tic occurred about 20 times a minute when the girl was at home. In the clinic, the rate of eye tics or squinting

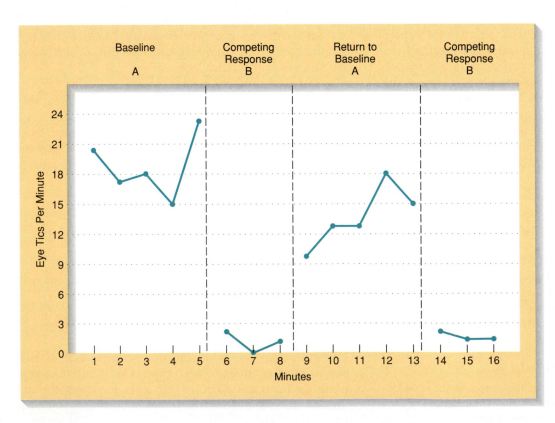

FIGURE 1.12 *Treatment results from the Azrin and Peterson study.* Notice how the target response, eye tics per minute, decreased when the competing response was introduced in the first "B" phase. It then increased to near baseline levels when the competing response was withdrawn during the second "A" phase. It decreased again when the competing response was reinstated in the second "B" phase.

was measured for 5 minutes during a baseline period (A). Then the girl was prompted to blink her eyes softly every 5 seconds (B). The experimenters reasoned that voluntary "soft" blinking would activate motor (muscle) responses that were incompatible with those producing the tic, thereby suppressing the tic. As you can see in Figure 1.12, the tic was virtually eliminated in but a few minutes of practicing the incompatible, or competing, response ("soft" blinking) but returned to near baseline levels during the reversal phase (A) when the competing response was withdrawn. The positive effects were quickly reinstated during the second treatment period (B). The child was also taught to practice the blinking response at home during scheduled 3-minute practice periods and whenever the tic occurred or she felt an urge to squint. The tic was completely eliminated during the first 6 weeks of the treatment program and remained absent at a follow-up evaluation 2 years later.

Although reversal designs offer better controls than traditional treatment case studies, it is not always possible or ethical to reverse certain behaviors or treatment effects. Participants in a stop-smoking program who reduce or quit smoking during treatment may not revert to their baseline smoking rates when treatment is temporarily withdrawn during a reversal phase.

The *multiple-baseline design* is a type of single-case experimental design that does not require a reversal phase. In a multiple-baseline design *across behaviors,* treatment is applied, in turn, to two or more behaviors following a baseline period. A treatment effect is inferred if changes in each of these behaviors corresponded to the time at which each was subjected to treatment. Because no reversal phase is required, many of the ethical and practical problems associated with reversal designs are avoided.

A multiple-baseline design was used to evaluate the effects of a social skills training program in the treatment of the case of a shy, unassertive 7-year-old girl named Jane (Bornstein, Bellack, & Hersen, 1977). The program taught Jane to maintain eye contact, speak more loudly, and make requests of other people through **modeling** (therapist demonstration of the target behavior), **rehearsal** (practice), and therapist **feedback** regarding the effectiveness of practice. However, the behaviors were taught sequentially, not simultaneously. Measurement of each behavior and an overall rating of assertiveness were obtained during a baseline period from observations of Jane's role playing of social situations with other children, such as playing social games at school and conversing in class. As shown in Figure 1.13, Jane's performance of each behavior improved following treatment. The rating of overall assertiveness showed more gradual improvement as the number of behaviors included in the program increased. Treatment gains were generally maintained at a follow-up evaluation.

To show a clear-cut treatment effect, changes in target behaviors should occur only when they are subjected to treatment. In some cases, however, changes in the treated behaviors may lead to changes in the yet untreated behav-

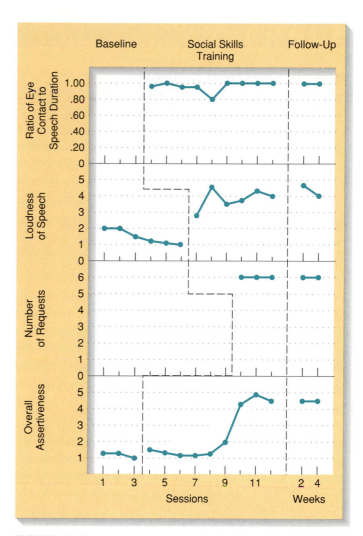

FIGURE 1.13   *Treatment results from the study by Bornstein, Bellack, and Hersen.*

The red dotted line shows the point at which social skills training was applied to each of the targeted behaviors. Here we see that the targeted behaviors (eye contact, loudness of speech, and number of requests) improved only when they were subject to the treatment approach (social skills training). We thus have evidence that the treatment—and not another, unidentified factor—accounted for the results. The section on the bottom shows ratings of Jane's overall level of assertiveness during the baseline assessment period, the social skills training program, and the follow-up period.

iors, apparently because of generalization of the effect. Fortunately, though, generalization effects have tended to be the exception, rather than the rule, in experimental research (Kazdin, 1992).

No matter how tightly controlled the design, or how impressive the results, single-case designs suffer from weak external validity because they do not show whether a treatment that is effective for one person is effective for others. Replication with other individuals can help strengthen external validity. If these results prove encouraging, they may lead to controlled experiments to provide even more convincing evidence of treatment effectiveness.

What Is Abnormal Behavior?

Various criteria are used to define abnormal behavior. Psychologists generally consider behavior abnormal when it meets some combination of the following criteria: (1) unusual or statistically infrequent; (2) socially unacceptable or in violation of social norms; (3) fraught with misperceptions or misinterpretations of reality; (4) associated with states of severe personal distress; (5) maladaptive or self-defeating; or (6) dangerous.

Cultural Bases of Abnormal Behavior

The determination of which behavior patterns are deemed abnormal depends on cultural beliefs and expectations. Concepts of health and illness may also have different meanings in different cultures. Abnormal behavior patterns may take different forms in different cultures, and societal views of abnormal behavior vary across cultures.

Historical Perspectives on Abnormal Behavior

Ancient societies attributed abnormal behavior to divine or supernatural forces. In medieval times, belief in possession held sway, and exorcists were used to rid people who behaved abnormally of the evil spirits that were believed to possess them. There were some authorities in ancient times, such as the Greek physicians Hippocrates and Galen, who believed that abnormal behavior reflected natural causes. The 19th-century German physician Wilhelm Griesinger argued that abnormal behavior was caused by diseases of the brain. He, along with another German physician who followed him, Emil Kraepelin, were influential in the development of the modern medical model, which likens abnormal behavior patterns to physical illnesses.

Asylums, or "madhouses," began to crop up throughout Europe in the late 15th and early 16th centuries, often on the site of former leprosariums. Conditions in these asylums were dreadful and in some, such as Bethlehem Hospital in England, a circus atmosphere prevailed. With the rise of moral therapy in the 19th century, largely spearheaded by the Frenchmen Jean-Baptiste Pussin and Philippe Pinel, conditions in mental hospitals improved. Proponents of moral therapy believed that mental patients could be restored to functioning if they were treated with dignity and understanding. The decline of moral therapy in the latter part of the 19th century led to a period of apathy and to the belief the "insane" could not be successfully treated. Conditions in mental hospitals deteriorated, and they offered little more than custodial care.

Not until the middle of the 20th century did public outrage and concern about the plight of mental patients mobilize legislative efforts toward the development of community mental health centers as alternatives to long-term hospitalization. This movement toward deinstitutionalization was spurred by the introduction of psychoactive drugs, called phenothiazines, which curbed the more flagrant features of schizophrenia.

Contemporary Perspectives on Abnormal Behavior

Abnormal behavior may be viewed from various contemporary perspectives. The medical model conceptualizes abnormal behavior patterns, like physical diseases, in terms of clusters of symptoms, called syndromes, which have distinctive causes that are presumed to be biological in nature. Biological perspectives incorporate the medical model but refer more broadly to approaches that relate abnormal behavior to biological processes and apply biologically based treatments. Psychodynamic perspectives reflect the views of Freud and his followers, who believed that abnormal behavior stemmed from psychological causes involving underlying psychic forces. Freud developed psychoanalysis as a means of uncovering the unconscious conflicts dating back to childhood that he believed were at the root of mental disorders such as hysteria. Learning theorists posit that the principles of learning can be used to explain both abnormal and normal behavior. Behavior therapy is an outgrowth of the learning model. Humanistic-existential perspectives reject the determinism of psychodynamic theory and behaviorism. Humanistic and existential theorists believe that it is important to understand the obstacles that people encounter as they strive toward self-actualization and authenticity. Cognitive theorists focus on the role of distorted and self-defeating thinking in explaining abnormal behavior. Sociocultural theorists believe that abnormal behavior is rooted in social ills, such as poverty, not in the individual. Today, many theorists believe that multiple factors interacting in complex ways are involved in the development of abnormal behavior patterns. The leading interactionist model, the diathesis-stress model, posits that some people have predispositions (diathesis) for particular disorders, but whether these disorders actually develop depends upon the type and severity of the stressors they experience.

Research Methods in Abnormal Psychology

The scientific approach focuses on four general objectives: description, explanation, prediction, and control. There are four steps to the scientific method: formulating a research question, framing the research question in the form of a hypothesis, testing the hypothesis, and drawing conclusions about the correctness of the hypotheses. Psychologists follow the ethical principles that govern research with human and nonhuman subjects. Two of the key ethical provisions in research with humans are informed consent and confidentiality.

Research samples need to be representative of the target population. The naturalistic-observation method allows scientists to measure behavior under naturally occurring conditions. Correlational research explores the relationship between variables, which may help predict future behavior and suggest possible underlying causes of behavior. But correlational research does not directly test cause-and-effect relationships. Longitudinal research is a type of correlational design that involves the study of selected subjects at periodic intervals over long periods of times, sometimes spanning decades.

In the experimental method, the investigator directly controls or manipulates the independent variable under controlled conditions in order to demonstrate cause-and-effect relationships. Experiments use random assignment as the basis for determining which subjects (called experimental subjects) receive an experimental treatment and which others (called control subjects) do not. Researchers use various methods to attempt to control for subjects' and researchers' expectations, including *single-blind placebo-control studies, double-blind placebo-control studies,* and *attention placebo* control studies.

Experiments are evaluated in terms of their experimental validity. Internal validity refers to the ability of an experi-

mental study to justify a cause-and-effect relationship between the independent variable and dependent variables. External validity refers to the degree to which experimental results can be generalized to other subjects, settings, and at other times. Construct validity refers to the degree to which treatment effects can be accounted for by the theoretical mechanisms or constructs that are represented by the independent variables.

The epidemiological method examines the rates of occurrence of abnormal behavior in various population groups or settings. Evidence of how disorders cluster in certain groups or geographic areas may reveal underlying causes. Kinship studies attempt to disentangle the contributions of environment and heredity.

Case-study methods can provide a richness of clinical material, but they are limited by difficulties of obtaining accurate and unbiased client histories, by possible therapist biases, and by the lack of control groups. Single-case experimental designs are intended to help researchers overcome some of the limitations of the case-study method.

REVIEW QUESTIONS

1. What do we mean by the term "abnormal behavior"? How is it defined? What different criteria are used to determine whether behavior is considered abnormal?

2. How do judgments about abnormal behavior reflect the cultural context in which they are made? How do abnormal behavior patterns vary across cultures?

3. What were the major models that have been used to account for abnormal behavior through the course of history until the present time? What changes occurred in how society treated people deemed to be "mad" or mentally disturbed?

4. How do the following perspectives attempt to account for the development of abnormal behavior: biological perspectives, psychodynamic perspectives, learning perspectives, humanistic-existential perspectives, cognitive perspectives, and sociocultural perspectives? Why is it necessary to consider multiple perspectives in explaining abnormal behavior?

5. How is the nervous system organized? What is the structure of the neuron? How are nervous impulses transmitted through the nervous system? How is the brain structured? What roles do the following parts or structures of the brain perform: medulla, cerebellum, RAS, thalamus, limbic system, basal ganglia, and cerebral cortex? What are the four lobes of the cerebral cortex and the functions they perform? What is the difference between a phenotype and a genotype?

6. What is the diathesis-stress model? How does it represent an interactionist approach to explaining abnormal behavior?

7. What are the major research methods used by investigators to study abnormal behavior? How are they used? What are their limitations?

© **Jean Dubuffet**
Ontogenese, 1975

Classification and Assessment of Abnormal Behavior

TRUTH or FICTION?

2.1 Some men in India develop a psychological disorder involving excessive concerns or anxiety over losing semen.

2.2 A psychological test must be valid in order to be reliable.

2.3 Researchers find that people report more personal problems when interviewed by human interviewers than impersonal computers.

2.4 The most widely used personality inventory consists of items that were answered in the same direction by people with psychological disorders and normal groups.

2.5 Some clinicians examine how people interpret inkblots to reveal aspects of their underlying personalities.

2.6 One of the first reported uses of behavioral assessment was by one of the founding fathers of the United States.

2.7 Despite advances in technology, physicians today still need to perform surgery to study the workings of the brain.

Systems of classification of abnormal behavior date to ancient times. Hippocrates classified abnormal behaviors on the basis of his theory of humors. Although his theory proved to be flawed, he arrived at some diagnostic categories that generally correspond to those in modern diagnostic systems. His description of melancholia, for example, is similar to present conceptions of depression. During the Middle Ages some "authorities" classified abnormal behaviors according to those that represented possession and those that represented natural causes. The 19th-century German psychiatrist Emil Kraepelin is generally considered the first modern theorist to develop a comprehensive model of classification based on the distinctive features, or "symptoms," associated with abnormal behavior patterns. The most commonly used classification system today is largely an outgrowth and extension of Kraepelin's work: the *Diagnostic and Statistical Manual of Mental Disorders* (DSM), which is published by the American Psychiatric Association. The DSM system classifies abnormal behavior patterns as mental disorders on the basis of specified diagnostic criteria.

Why is it important to classify abnormal behavior? For one thing, classification is the core of science. Without labeling and organizing patterns of abnormal behavior, researchers could not communicate with one another, and progress toward understanding these disorders would come to a halt. Moreover, important decisions are made on the basis of classification. Certain psychological disorders respond better to one therapy than another or to one drug than another. Classification also helps clinicians predict behavior. Some patterns of abnormal behavior, such as schizophrenia, follow more or less predictable courses of development. Classification also helps researchers identify populations with similar patterns of abnormal behavior. By classifying groups of people as depressed, for example, researchers might be able to identify common factors that help explain the origins of depression.

This chapter reviews the classification and assessment of abnormal behavior. First we examine the DSM system. We then consider the basic requirements for methods of assessment—that they be reliable and valid. Next we explore methods of assessment that clinicians use to arrive at diagnostic impressions, including interviews, psychological testing, self-report questionnaires, behavioral measures, and physiological measures. The role of assessment, however, goes further than classification. A careful assessment provides a wealth of information about clients' personalities and cognitive functioning. This information helps clinicians acquire a broader understanding of their clients' problems and recommend appropriate treatment.

CLASSIFICATION OF ABNORMAL BEHAVIOR

The DSM was introduced in 1952 and has been revised several times. The present version, the fourth edition, is called the DSM–IV. Another common system of classification, published by the World Health Organization, is used mainly for compiling statistics on the worldwide occurrence of disorders: the *International Classification of Diseases* (ICD), which is now in its tenth revision (the ICD-10). The DSM was designed to be compatible with the ICD, so that DSM diagnoses could be coded in the ICD system as well. This allows users of the two systems to share information about the prevalences and characteristics of particular disorders. However, the two systems are not perfectly compatible, which means users of the DSM in the United States sometimes have difficulties communicating with their counterparts in other parts of the world who use the ICD. Compatibility remains a problem, even though the latest version of the DSM, the DSM-IV, made a substantial effort and achieved some success in bringing the DSM system more in line with the ICD (Nathan, 1994).

We focus on the DSM because of its widespread adoption by mental health professionals. However, many psychologists and other professionals criticize the DSM on several grounds, such as relying too strongly on the medical model. Our focus on the DSM reflects recognition of its widespread use, not an endorsement.

In the DSM, people are regarded as exhibiting *psychopathology* or abnormal behavior patterns—or, in the medical jargon of the manual, as having "mental disorders"—if they experience emotional distress or show significant impairment in psychological functioning. Impaired functioning involves difficulties in meeting responsibilities at work, within the family, or within society at large. It also includes behavior that places people at risk for personal suffering, pain, or death.

Diagnosis of mental disorders within the DSM system requires that the behavior pattern not represent an expected or culturally appropriate response to a stressful event, such as the loss of a loved one. People who show signs of bereavement or grief following the death of loved ones are not considered disordered, even if their behavior is significantly impaired. If their behavior remains significantly impaired over an extended period of time, however, a diagnosis of a mental disorder might become appropriate.

The DSM and Models of Abnormal Behavior

The DSM system adheres in some important respects to the medical model. It treats abnormal behaviors as signs or symptoms of underlying pathologies called mental disorders. Unlike the strictest form of the medical model, however, the manual does not assume abnormal behaviors necessarily reflect biological causes or defects. It recognizes that the causes of most mental disorders remain uncertain. Some disorders may have purely biological causes. Some may have psychological causes. Still others are likely to reflect a multifactorial model that reflects the interaction of biological, psychological, social (socioeconomic, sociocultural, and ethnic), and physical environmental factors.

Nor does the DSM subscribe to a particular theory of abnormal behavior. With the introduction in 1980 of the third edition of the DSM, the DSM-III, terms linked to specific theories (such as *neurosis,* which was originally a psychoanalytic term) were deemphasized in favor of atheoretical descriptive terms such as "anxiety disorders" and "mood disorders." Disorders are classified on the basis of their clinical features and behavior patterns, not on the basis of inferences about underlying theoretical mechanisms. Because the DSM does not endorse particular theoretical models unless evidence of causal factors is overwhelming, it can be used by practitioners of diverse theoretical persuasions, who can agree on the criteria for diagnosing various disorders, even if they disagree on their causes and proper treat-

ments. Yet critics contend the DSM is something of a hodgepodge of disorders that are grouped together in various clusters without a consistent conceptual framework (Kutchins & Kirk, 1995).

The authors of the DSM recognize that their use of the term *mental disorder* is problematic because it perpetuates a long-standing but dubious distinction between mental and physical disorders (APA, 1994). They point out that there is much that is "physical" in "mental" disorders and much that is "mental" in "physical" disorders. The diagnostic manual continues to use the term *mental disorder* because its developers have not been able to agree on an appropriate substitute. In this text we use the term *psychological disorder* in place of *mental disorder* because we feel it is more appropriate to place the study of abnormal behavior more squarely within a psychological context. Moreover, the term *psychological* has the advantage of encompassing behavioral patterns as well as strictly "mental" experiences such as emotions, thoughts, beliefs, and attitudes.

J. C. Wakefield (1992a, 1992b, 1997) proposed that the term *disorder* be conceptualized as "harmful dysfunction." A harmful dysfunction represents a failure of a mental or physical system to perform its natural function, resulting in negative consequences or harm to the individual. By this definition, dysfunction alone is not enough to constitute a disorder. For example, even though the body was naturally designed to have two kidneys, and it would be dysfunctional to have but one, a failure of one kidney to function properly (or even the loss of a kidney) may not be harmful to the individual's well being. By contrast, a dysfunction involving a breakdown in the brain's ability to store or retrieve information would constitute a disorder if it leads to harmful consequences such as memory deficits that make it difficult for the person to function effectively. We find Wakefield's conceptualization of disorders as harmful dysfunctions to be instructive to our approach to this text, although we recognize not all psychologists share his point of view (see Lilienfeld & Marino, 1995). One problem is that we may lack agreement on what constitutes the "natural function" of mental systems (Bergner, 1997).

Finally, we should recognize that the DSM is used to classify disorders, not people. This is an important distinction that has a bearing on the terminology we use to describe people who display abnormal behavior patterns. Rather than classify someone as a *schizophrenic* or a *depressive,* we refer to them as *an individual with schizophrenia* or *a person with major depression.* This difference in terminology is not simply a matter of semantics. To label someone a schizophrenic carries an unfortunate and stigmatizing implication that a person's identity is defined in terms of a disorder he or she may have or exhibit.

Features of the DSM

The DSM is descriptive, not explanatory. It describes the diagnostic features—or, in medical terms, symptoms—of abnormal behaviors rather than attempting to explain their origins. Let us consider a number of features of the DSM classification system.

Specific diagnostic criteria are used. The clinician arrives at a diagnosis by matching clients' behaviors with the criteria that define particular patterns of abnormal behavior ("mental disorders"). Diagnostic categories are described in terms of *essential features* (criteria that must be present for the diagnosis to be made) and *associated features* (criteria often associated with the disorder but not essential to making a diagnosis). An example of diagnostic criteria for Conduct Disorder, a disorder of childhood or adolescence, is shown in Table 2.1.

Abnormal behavior patterns that share clinical features are grouped together. Abnormal behavior patterns are categorized according to their shared clinical features, not theoretical speculation about their causes. Abnormal behavior patterns chiefly characterized by anxiety are classified as anxiety disorders. Behaviors chiefly characterized by disruptions in mood are categorized as mood disorders.

The system is "multiaxial." The DSM employs a multiaxial, or multidimensional, system of assessment that provides a broad range of information about the individual's functioning, not just a diagnosis (see Table 2.2). The system contains the following axes:

1. *Axis I includes a classification of Clinical* **Syndromes,** which incorporates a wide range of diagnostic classes such as anxiety disorders; mood disorders; schizophrenia and other psychotic disorders; adjustment disorders; and disorders usually first diagnosed during infancy, childhood, or adolescence (except for mental retardation, which is coded on Axis II). Axis I also includes a classification of *Other Conditions That May Be a Focus of Clinical Attention.* These are conditions or problems that may be the focus of diagnosis and treatment, such as relationship problems, academic or occupational problems, or bereavement, but do not in themselves constitute definable psychological disorders.

These conditions also include a category of psychological factors that affect medical conditions, such as anxiety that exacerbates an asthmatic condition, or depressive symptoms that delay recovery from surgery.

2. *Axis II, Personality Disorders,* includes the more enduring and rigid patterns of maladaptive behavior that generally impair interpersonal relationships and social adaptation, including antisocial, paranoid, narcissistic, and borderline personality disorders. Mental retardation is also coded on Axis II.

Separating the diagnostic categories into two axes provides greater flexibility in reaching diagnostic impressions. People may be given either Axis I or Axis II diagnoses, or a combination of the two when both apply. A person may receive a diagnosis of an anxiety disorder (Axis I) and a second diagnosis of a personality disorder (Axis II) if the diagnostic criteria for both are met, for example. When multiple diagnoses are given, the *principal diagnosis* is the condition that apparently precipitated the evaluation and in most cases is the main focus of treatment. Clients may also receive multiple diagnoses within axes. For example, they may be given Axis I diagnoses for a substance abuse disorder and a mood disorder, if both apply.

3. *Axis III, General Medical Conditions,* lists medical conditions and diseases that may be important to the understanding or treatment of the individual's mental disorder. For example, if **hypothyroidism** is a direct cause of an individual's mood disorder (such as major depression), it would be coded under Axis III. Medical conditions that affect the understanding or treatment of a mental disorder but are not direct causes of the disorder are also listed on Axis III. For instance, the presence of a heart condition may determine whether a particular course of pharmacotherapy would be used with a depressed person.

4. *Axis IV, Psychosocial and Environmental Problems,* lists psychosocial and environmental problems that are

---

TABLE 2.1

Sample Diagnostic Criteria for Conduct Disorder

A.   A persistent and repeated pattern of disturbed conduct involving behaviors that violate others' basic rights or social norms and rules appropriate to the individual's age, lasting for at least 6 months, which is characterized by at least three behaviors from a listing of 15 behaviors that include the following:

 1. Bullying, threatening, or intimidating others

 2. Starting physical fights

 3. Using a weapon, such as a bat, gun, or knife, that could harm others

 4. Stealing with confrontation of the victim, as in a mugging, purse-snatching, armed robbery, or extortion

 5. Showing physical cruelty to people

 6. Showing physical cruelty to animals

 7. Forcing another person into sexual activity with him- or herself

 8. Frequent lying or breaking of promises in the attempt to "con" others to acquire desired goods or favors or to avoid fulfilling obligations

 9. Frequent violation of parental prohibitions about staying out at night, beginning before age 13

10. Stealing property without actually confronting the victim, such as by shoplifting, burglary, or forgery

B.   If age 18 or older, person does not meet diagnostic criteria for Antisocial Personality Disorder.

Source: Adapted from the DSM-IV (APA, 1994).

TABLE 2.2

The Multiaxial Classification System of the DSM-IV

Axis	Type of Information	Brief Description
Axis I	Clinical Syndromes	The patterns of abnormal behavior ("mental disorders") that impair functioning and are stressful to the individual
	Other Conditions That May Be a Focus of Clinical Attention	Other problems that may be the focus of diagnosis or treatment but do not constitute mental disorders, such as academic, vocational, or social problems, and psychological factors that affect medical conditions (such as delayed recovery from surgery due to depressive symptoms)
Axis II	Personality Disorders Mental Retardation	Personality disorders involve excessively rigid, enduring, and maladaptive ways of relating to others and adjusting to external demands. Mental retardation involves a delay or impairment in the development of intellectual and adaptive abilities.
Axis III	General Medical Conditions	Chronic and acute illnesses and medical conditions that are important to the understanding or treatment of the psychological disorder or that play a direct role in causing the psychological disorder
Axis IV	Psychosocial and Environmental Problems	Problems in the social or physical environment that affect the diagnosis, treatment, and outcome of psychological disorders
Axis V	Global Assessment of Functioning	Overall judgment of current functioning with respect to psychological, social, and occupational functioning; the clinician may also rate the highest level of functioning occurring for at least a few months during the past year

Source: Adapted from the DSM-IV (APA, 1994).

believed to affect the diagnosis, treatment, or outcome of a mental disorder. Psychosocial and environmental problems include negative life events (such as a job termination or a marital separation or divorce), homelessness or inadequate housing, lack of social support, the death or loss of a friend, or exposure to war or disasters. Some positive life events may also be listed, such as a job promotion, but only when they create problems for the individual, such as difficulties adapting to a new job. A listing of these types of problems is found in Table 2.3.

TABLE 2.3

Psychosocial and Environmental Problems

Problem Categories	Examples
Problems with Primary Support Group	Death of family members; health problems of family members; marital disruption in the form of separation, divorce, or estrangement; sexual or physical abuse within the family; child neglect; birth of a sibling
Problems Related to the Social Environment	Death or loss of a friend; social isolation or living alone; difficulties adjusting to a new culture (acculturation); discrimination; adjustment to transitions occurring during the life cycle, such as retirement
Educational Problems	Illiteracy; academic difficulties; problems with teachers or classmates; inadequate or impoverished school environment
Occupational Problems	Work-related problems including stressful work loads and problems with bosses or co-workers; changes in employment; job dissatisfaction; threat of loss of job; unemployment
Housing Problems	Inadequate housing or homelessness; living in an unsafe neighborhood; problems with neighbors or landlord
Economic Problems	Financial hardships or extreme poverty; inadequate welfare support
Problems with Access to Health Care Services	Inadequate health care services or availability of health insurance; difficulties with transportation to health care facilities
Problems Related to Interaction with the Legal System/Crime	Arrest or imprisonment; becoming involved in a lawsuit or trial; being a victim of crime
Other Psychosocial Problems	Natural or human-made disasters; war or other hostilities; problems with caregivers outside the family, such as counselors, social workers, and physicians; lack of availability of social service agencies

Source: Adapted from the DSM-IV (APA, 1994).

TABLE 2.4

Global Assessment of Functioning (GAF) Scale

Code	Severity of Symptoms	Examples
91–100	Superior functioning across a wide variety of activities of daily life	Lacks symptoms Handles life problems without them "getting out of hand"
81–90	Absent or minimal symptoms, no more than everyday problems or concerns	Mild anxiety before exams Occasional argument with family members
71–80	Transient and predictable reactions to stressful events, OR no more than slight impairment in functioning	Difficulty concentrating after argument with family Temporarily falls behind in schoolwork
61–70	Some mild symptoms, OR some difficulty in social, occupational, or school functioning, but functioning pretty well	Feels down, mild insomnia Occasional truancy or theft within household
51–60	Moderate symptoms, OR moderate difficulties in social, occupational, or school functioning	Occasional panic attacks Few friends, conflicts with co-workers
41–50	Serious symptoms, OR any serious impairment in social, occupational, or school functioning	Suicidal thoughts, frequent shoplifting Unable to hold job, has no friends
31–40	Some impairment in reality testing or communication, OR major impairment in several areas	Speech illogical Depressed man unable to work, neglects family, and avoids friends
21–30	Strong influence on behavior of delusions or hallucinations, OR serious impairment in communication or judgment, OR inability to function in almost all areas	Grossly inappropriate behavior, speech sometimes incoherent Stays in bed all day; no job, home, or friends
11–20	Some danger of hurting self or others, OR occasionally fails to maintain personal hygiene, OR gross impairment in communication	Suicidal gestures, frequently violent Smears feces
1–10	Persistent danger of severely hurting self or others, OR, persistent inability to maintain minimal personal hygiene, OR seriously suicidal act	Largely incoherent or mute Serious suicidal attempt, recurrent violence

Source: Adapted from the DSM–IV (APA, 1994).

---

5. *Axis V, Global Assessment of Functioning,* refers to the clinician's overall judgment of clients' psychological, social, and occupational functioning. Using a scale similar to that shown in Table 2.4, the clinician rates the client's current level of functioning and may also indicate the highest level of functioning achieved for at least a few months during the preceding year. The level of current functioning is taken to indicate the current need for treatment or intensity of care. The level of highest functioning is suggestive of the level of functioning that might be restored.

An example of a diagnosis in the *DSM-IV* multiaxial system is shown in Table 2.5.

The DSM-IV The DSM-IV is generally recognized as an improvement over past DSM versions. For one thing, the DSM-IV places a much greater emphasis than did previous editions on the role of cultural factors in diagnosis (DeAngelis, 1994b; Nathan, 1994). Each disorder now carries a section describing issues relating to culture, age, and gender that should be taken into account when using the diagnosis. These sections also contain information concerning differences in the prevalence of the disorder among groupings based on culture, age, and gender. The manual contains a

new appendix, *Outline for Cultural Formulation and Glossary of Culture-Bound Syndromes,* that helps guide users to take into account the individual's cultural background when formulating a diagnostic impression. A glossary of culture-bound syndromes is now included, which lists psychological disorders found in certain cultures but only infrequently, if at all, in others.

The DSM-IV was also more strongly based on empirical evidence than were earlier versions. Changes in the diagnostic criteria incorporated into the DSM-IV had to be based on a clear rationale and consistent evidence from empirical

TABLE 2.5

Example of a Diagnosis in the Multiaxial DSM–IV System

Axis I	Generalized Anxiety Disorder
Axis II	Dependent Personality Disorder
Axis III	Hypertension
Axis IV	Problem with Primary Support Group (marital separation); Occupational Problem (unemployment)
Axis V	GAF = 62

studies that supported the proposed changes (Nathan, 1994). A lengthy process of field testing was undertaken to determine whether the changes in diagnostic criteria improved the validity of the diagnostic categories (Widiger, 1994).

Although the DSM-IV may well be an improvement over its predecessors, it represents more of a refinement of the diagnostic system than a wholesale change in the process of classifying abnormal behavior patterns. Some of the fundamental questions concerning the reliability and validity of the DSM remain (Kutchins & Kirk, 1995; Thakker & Ward, 1998).

Evaluation of the DSM System

Two basic criteria used in evaluating the value of a diagnostic system such as the DSM are its reliability and validity. A diagnostic system may be considered **reliable,** or consistent, if various diagnosticians using the system are likely to arrive at the same diagnoses when they evaluate the same cases. Versions of the DSM system that preceded the 1980 introduction of the DSM-III generally suffered from poor reliability. Skilled diagnosticians often disagreed on the correct diagnoses for clients, largely because the diagnostic criteria were often fuzzy or ambiguous.

The DSM-III was based on more specific ("tighter") diagnostic criteria than the DSM-II and showed greater interrater reliability (i.e., agreement among diagnosticians). The DSM-III showed weak reliability in the diagnosis of Axis II personality disorders, however (Drake & Vaillant, 1985). Early evidence shows greater reliability of the diagnostic criteria in the DSM-IV than the DSM-III for some diagnostic categories, such as oppositional defiant disorder and conduct disorder in children and adolescents (Lahey et al., 1994). We await further evidence to determine whether the DSM-IV shows greater reliability for diagnosing personality disorders.

The issue of **validity,** or accuracy, of diagnostic categories is more complex. How are we to know whether a diagnosis is valid or accurate? A physician may seek to confirm the validity of a diagnosis of a physical disorder through a laboratory test. If blood samples are taken and the suspected microbe is found, the diagnosis may be confirmed. No such laboratory tests exist for psychological disorders.

The most appropriate test of the validity of a diagnostic system for psychological disorders is its correspondence with behavioral observations. Researchers generally approach the question of validity in terms of whether or not the behavior of people who are given particular diagnoses differs in predictable ways from that of people given other diagnoses. Certain DSM classes, such as anxiety disorders, appear to have generally good validity in terms of grouping people with similar behaviors (S. M. Turner, McCann, Beidel, & Mezzich, 1986b). The validity of some other diagnostic classes, such as personality disorders, remains to be demonstrated.

The predictive validity of the DSM system may be tested by determining whether or not it is useful in *predicting* the course the disorder is likely to follow or its response to treatment. Evidence is accumulating that persons classified in certain categories respond better to certain types of medication. Persons with bipolar disorder, for example, respond reasonably well to lithium (see Chapter 7). Specific forms of psychological treatment may also be more effective with certain diagnostic groupings. For example, persons who have *specific phobias* (such as fear of height) are generally highly responsive to behavioral techniques for reducing fears (see Chapter 5).

Another yardstick by which a diagnostic system is evaluated is its degree of coverage, or its ability to place cases of abnormal behavior into suitable categories (Blashfield & Draguns, 1976). A system with low coverage essentially "dumps" or sweeps aside a large number of cases that don't

Assessment of level of functioning. The assessment of functioning takes into account the individual's ability to manage the responsibilities of daily living. Here we see a group home for people with mental retardation. The residents assume responsibility for household functions.

precisely fit existing categories into a catchall, or so-called wastebasket, category such as "unspecified disorder." Attempts to increase the coverage of the system may occur at the expense of reducing the "purity" of the diagnostic categories, however. Think of it this way: The more cases with slightly varying patterns you try to squeeze into a given category, the less similar the cases assigned to the particular category are likely to be.

The DSM-III contained tighter diagnostic criteria than its predecessors, thereby increasing the diagnostic purity of the categories but at the expense of reduced coverage. We still can't say how diagnostic coverage and purity will be affected under the DSM-IV.

Advantages and Disadvantages of the DSM System

Many consider the major advantage of the DSM to be its designation of specific diagnostic criteria. The DSM permits the clinician to readily match a client's complaints and associated features with specific standards to see which diagnosis fits the case. The multiaxial system paints a comprehensive picture of clients by integrating information concerning abnormal behaviors, medical conditions that affect abnormal behaviors, psychosocial and environmental problems that may be stressful to the individual, and level of functioning. The possibility of multiple diagnoses prompts clinicians to consider presenting problems (Axis I) along with the relatively long-standing personality problems (Axis II) that may contribute to them.

Criticisms have also been leveled against the DSM system. Questions remain about the system's reliability and validity. Some critics challenge specific diagnostic criteria, such as the requirement that major depression be present for 2 weeks before diagnosis (Kendler & Gardner, 1998). Others challenge the reliance on the medical model. In the DSM system, problem behaviors are viewed as symptoms of underlying psychological disorders in much the same way that physical symptoms are signs of underlying physical disorders. The very use of the term *diagnosis* presumes the medical model is an appropriate basis for classifying abnormal behaviors. Some clinicians feel that behavior, abnormal or otherwise, is too complex and meaningful to be treated merely as symptomatic. They assert the medical model focuses too much on what may happen within the individual and not enough on external influences on behavior, such as social factors (socioeconomic, sociocultural, and ethnic) and physical environmental factors.

Another concern is that the medical model focuses on categorizing psychological (or mental) disorders rather than describing people's behavioral strengths and weaknesses. Nor does the DSM attempt to place behavior within a contextual framework that examines the settings, situations, and cultural contexts in which behavior occurs (Follette & Houts, 1996; Wulfert, Greenway, & Dougher, 1996). To behaviorally oriented psychologists, the understanding of behavior, abnormal or otherwise, is best approached by ex-

amining the interaction between the person and the environment. The DSM aims to determine what "disorders" people "have"—not what they can "do" in particular situations. An alternative model of assessment, the behavioral model, focuses more on behaviors than on underlying processes—more on what people "do" than on what they "are" or "have." Behaviorists and behavior therapists also use the DSM, of course, in part because mental-health centers and health-insurance carriers require the use of a diagnostic code, in part because they want to communicate in a common language with practitioners of other theoretical persuasions. Many behavior therapists view the DSM diagnostic code as a convenient means of labeling patterns of abnormal behavior, a shorthand for a more extensive behavioral analysis of the problem.

Another concern about the DSM system is the potential for stigmatization of people labeled with psychiatric diagnoses. There is a strong negative bias in our society against people who are labeled as mentally ill. They are often shunned by others, including even family members in many cases, and are frequently subjected to discrimination in housing and employment. The negative stereotyping of people who are identified as mentally ill is labeled **sanism** (Perlin, 1994), the counterpart to other forms of prejudice and discrimination that exist in our society such as racism, sexism, and ageism.

The potential for stigmatization is at the heart of an ongoing debate about whether women who suffer intense emotional distress preceding their menstrual periods should be classified as suffering from a mental disorder labeled *premenstrual dysphoric disorder*. This diagnosis is included in the appendix of the DSM-IV as a potential diagnosis requiring further study. One of the problems lies in determining the boundary between normal and abnormal fluctuations in mood that precede or accompany menstruation. Proponents of the diagnosis argue it applies to the relatively small percentage of women who experience such intense premenstrual distress and negative emotions that they feel overwhelmed and might benefit from psychiatric treatment (Goleman, 1994c). However, opponents are concerned it might stigmatize women with severe premenstrual symptoms by giving them a psychiatric diagnosis.

Some critics argue that recent editions of the DSM have been overzealous in the removal of concepts of abnormal behavior that are derived from particular theories, such as the concept of neurosis. Some would like to see a return to a diagnostic system that focuses more on the causes of abnormal behaviors. Description alone, such critics claim, is too superficial. Many critics likewise claim the DSM focuses too much on current behaviors and not enough on history or childhood experiences.

The DSM system, despite its critics, has become part and parcel of the everyday practice of most U.S. mental-health professionals. It may be the one reference manual found on the bookshelves of nearly all professionals and dog-eared from repeated use. Perhaps the DSM is best considered a work in progress, not a final product.

Sociocultural Factors in the Classification of Abnormal Behavior

The DSM aims to be atheoretical, but just designating behaviors as normal or abnormal rests on cultural and professional assumptions. Many observers (e.g., Eisenbruch, 1992; Fabrega, 1992) have argued that the DSM should become more sensitive to diversity in culture and ethnicity. The behaviors included as diagnostic criteria in the DSM are determined by consensus of mostly U.S.-trained psychiatrists, psychologists, and social workers. Had the American Psychiatric Association asked Asian-trained or Latin American–trained professionals to develop their diagnostic manual, for example, there might have been some different or some revised diagnostic categories.

In fairness to the DSM, however, the latest edition—the DSM-IV—does place greater emphasis than did earlier editions on weighing cultural factors when assessing abnormal behavior. It recognizes that clinicians who are unfamiliar with an individual's cultural background may incorrectly classify the individual's behavior as abnormal when it in fact falls within the normal spectrum in the individual's culture. In Chapter 1 we noted the same behavior may be deemed normal in one culture but abnormal in another. The DSM specifies that for a diagnosis of a mental disorder to be made, the behavior in question must not merely represent a culturally expectable and sanctioned response to a particular event, even though it may seem odd in light of the examiner's own cultural standards. The DSM-IV also recognizes abnormal behaviors may take different forms in different cultures, and some abnormal behavior patterns are culturally specific (see nearby feature, "Culture-Bound Syndromes").

To explore cultural variations in diagnostic practices, Baskin (1984) asked mental-health professionals in Europe, Asia, Oceania, and North America to indicate whether the people described in several case vignettes were mentally ill and, if so, to fix an appropriate diagnosis. His results showed wide variation among respondents from country to country and within countries in terms of whether or not behavior patterns were considered normal or abnormal, and in terms of the diagnostic categories that were used to classify people deemed abnormal. If a diagnostic system is to be used with people from other cultures than the one in which it was developed, evidence should be gathered that it too is reliable and valid within the culture to which it is applied. Some categories in the DSM may be valid in other cultures; others may not.

Psychological distress may also be experienced differently in different cultures. For example, researchers in Puerto Rico have examined a culture-bound or locally identified syndrome—*ataque de nervios* ("attack of nerves") (Guarnaccia, 1993; Guarnaccia, Rubio-Stipec, & Canino, 1989). Although these "attacks" have some similar features to what the DSM system classifies as a panic attack (described in Chapter 5), such as dizziness, fear of going crazy, fear of losing control, and fear of dying, other features are different, such as screaming, hitting oneself or others, break-

ing things, and becoming hysterical (Liebowitz et al., 1994). Also, unlike panic attacks, *ataques* do not seem to come out of the blue but rather tend to follow stressful events, such as the death of a loved one, natural disasters, or arguments with family members (Guarnaccia, 1993).

Now let us consider various ways of assessing abnormal behavior. We begin with a discussion of the characteristics of useful methods of assessment: reliability and validity.

CHARACTERISTICS OF METHODS OF ASSESSMENT

Important decisions are made on the basis of classification and assessment. For example, recommendations for specific treatment techniques vary according to our assessment of the problems that clients exhibit. Therefore, methods of assessment, like diagnostic categories, must be *reliable* and *valid*.

Reliability

The reliability of a method of assessment, like that of a diagnostic system, refers to its consistency. A gauge of height would be unreliable if people looked taller or shorter at every measurement. A reliable measure of abnormal behavior must also yield comparable results on different occasions. Also, different people should be able to check the yardstick and agree on the measured height of the subject. A yardstick that shrinks and expands markedly with the slightest change in temperature will be unreliable. So will one that is difficult to read.

There are three main approaches for demonstrating the reliability of assessment techniques.

Internal Consistency Correlational techniques are used to show whether the different parts or items of an assessment instrument, such as a personality scale or test, yield results that are consistent with one another and with the instrument on the whole. **Internal consistency** is crucial for tests that are intended to measure single traits or construct dimensions. When the individual items or parts of a test are highly correlated with each other, we can assume they are measuring a common trait or construct. For example, if responses to a set of items on a depression scale are not highly correlated with each other, there is no basis for assuming the items measure a single common dimension or construct—in this case, depression.

One commonly used method of assessing internal consistency, **coefficient alpha,** is based on a statistical computation of the average intercorrelations (interrelationships) of all the items making up the particular test. The higher the coefficient alpha, the greater the internal consistency of the test.

Some tests are multidimensional in content. They contain subscales or factors that measure different construct dimensions. One such test is the Minnesota Multiphasic Personality Inventory (MMPI), which assesses various dimensions of abnormal behavior. In such cases, subscales within the test intended to measure individual traits, such as

Culture-Bound Syndromes

Some patterns of psychological distress are limited to just one, or a few, cultures. These **culture-bound** disorders are believed to be a manifestation, however exaggerated, of common superstitions and belief patterns within the particular culture or cultures. For example, the psychiatric syndrome **taijin-kyofu-sho,** (TKS), is common in Japan but rare elsewhere. TKS is characterized by excessive fear that one may behave in ways that will embarrass or offend other people (McNally, Cassiday, & Calamari, 1990). People with TKS may dread blushing in front of others for fear of causing them embarrassment, not for fear of embarrassing themselves. In our culture, an excessive fear of social embarrassment is called a *social phobia* (see Chapter 5). Unlike people with TKS, however, people with social phobias have excessive concerns they will be rejected by, or embarrassed in front of, others, not that they will embarrass other people. People with TKS may also fear mumbling thoughts aloud, lest they inadvertently offend others (R. Prince & Tcheng-Laroche, 1987). The syndrome primarily affects young Japanese men and is believed to

be related to an emphasis in Japanese culture on not embarrassing others as well as deep concerns about issues of shame (McNally et al., 1990; Spitzer et al., 1994). S. C. Chang (1984) reports that TKS is diagnosed in 7% to 36% of the people who are treated by psychiatrists in Japan. Table 2.6 lists some other culture-bound syndromes identified in the DSM-IV.

We generally think of culture-bound syndromes as abnormal behavior patterns associated with folk cultures in non-Western societies. Yet some disorders, such as anorexia nervosa (discussed in Chapter 10) and dissociative identity disorder (formerly called *multiple personality disorder*; discussed in Chapter 6), are recognized as culture-bound syndromes that are specific to industrialized or technological societies, such as our own. They occur rarely if at all in other societies.

TRUTH or FICTION REVISITED

2.1 *True.* Some men in India develop a psychological disorder, called *dhat syndrome*, that is characterized by excessive fears over loss of semen.

Taijin-Kyofu-Sho. TKS is a culture-related syndrome that is common in Japan. It is characterized by excessive fear that one may embarrass or offend other people. The syndrome primarily affects young Japanese men and is apparently connected with the Japanese cultural emphasis on avoiding embarrassing other people.

TABLE 2.6

Examples of Culture-Bound Syndromes

Culture-Bound Syndrome	Description
amok	A disorder principally occurring in men in southeastern Asian and Pacific island cultures, as well as in traditional Puerto Rican and Navajo cultures in the West, it describes a type of dissociative episode (a sudden change in consciousness or self-identity) marked by a violent or aggressive outburst following a period of brooding. These episodes are usually precipitated by a perceived slight or insult. During the episode the person may experience amnesia or have a sense of acting automatically, as if robotic. Violence may be directed at people or objects and is often accompanied by perceptions of persecution. A return to the person's usual state of functioning follows the episode. In the West, we use the expression "running amuck" to refer to an episode of losing oneself and running around in a violent frenzy. The word *amuck* is derived from the Malaysian word *amoq*, meaning "engaging furiously in battle."
ataque de nervios ("attack of nerves")	A way of describing states of emotional distress among Latin American and Latin Mediterranean groups, it most commonly involves features such as shouting uncontrollably, fits of crying, trembling, feelings of warmth or heat rising from the chest to the head, and aggressive verbal or physical behavior. These episodes are usually precipitated by a stressful event affecting the family (e.g., receiving news of the death of a family member) and are accompanied by feelings of being out of control. After the attack, the person returns quickly to his or her usual level of functioning, although there may be amnesia for events that occurred during the episode.
bouffée délirante	A French term used to describe a syndrome occurring in West Africa and Haiti that is characterized by a sudden change in behavior, in which the person becomes highly agitated or aggressive, confused, and experiences a speeding up of body movements. Auditory or visual hallucinations and paranoid thinking may be present.
dhat syndrome	A disorder (described further in Chapter 6) affecting males found principally in India that involves intense fear or anxiety over the loss of semen through nocturnal emissions, ejaculations, or through excretion with urine (despite the folk belief, semen doesn't actually mix with urine). In Indian culture, there is a popular belief that loss of semen depletes the man of his vital natural energy.
falling out or *blacking out*	Occurring principally among southern U.S. and Caribbean groups, the disorder involves an episode of sudden collapsing or fainting. The attack may occur without warning or be preceded by dizziness or feelings of "swimming" in the head. Although the eyes remain open, the individual reports an inability to see. The person can hear what others are saying and understands what is occurring but feels powerless to move.
ghost sickness	A disorder occurring among American Indian groups, it involves a preoccupation with death and with the "spirits" of the deceased. Symptoms associated with the condition include bad dreams, feelings of weakness, loss of appetite, fear, anxiety, and a sense of foreboding. Hallucinations, loss of consciousness, and states of confusion may also be present, among other symptoms.
koro	Found primarily in China and some other South and East Asian countries, the syndrome (also discussed further in Chapter 6) refers to an episode of acute anxiety involving the fear that one's genitals (the penis in men and the vulva and nipples in women) are shrinking and retracting into the body and that death may result.
zar	A term used in a number of countries in North Africa and the Middle East to describe the experience of spirit possession. Possession by spirits is often used in these cultures to explain dissociative episodes (sudden changes in consciousness or identity) that may be characterized by periods of shouting, banging of the head against the wall, laughing, singing, or crying. Affected people may seem apathetic or withdrawn or refuse to eat or carry out their usual responsibilities.

Adapted from the DSM-IV (APA, 1994) and other sources.

the hypochondriasis and depression subscales, are expected to show internal consistency. Subscales need not correlate with each other, however, unless the traits they are presumed to measure are interrelated.

Temporal Stability Reliable methods of assessment have **temporal stability** (stability over time). They yield similar results on separate occasions. We would not trust a bathroom scale that yielded different results each time we weighed ourselves—unless we had stuffed or starved ourselves between weighings. The same principle applies to methods of psychological assessment. Temporal stability is measured by means of **test-retest reliability,** which represents the correlation between two administrations of the test separated by a period of time. The higher the correlation, the greater the temporal stability or test-retest reliability of the test.

Assessment of test-retest reliability is most important in the measurement of traits assumed to remain stable over time, such as intelligence and aptitude. Yet measures of test-retest reliability on intelligence and aptitude tests can be compromised because of a "warm-up effect"; that is, scores can improve due to familiarity with the test.

Interrater Reliability Interrater reliability—also referred to as **interjudge reliability**—is usually of greatest importance in making diagnostic decisions and for measures requiring ratings of behavior. A diagnostic system is not reliable unless expert raters agree as to their diagnoses on the basis of the system. Two teachers may be asked to use a behavioral rating scale to evaluate a child's aggressiveness, hyperactivity, and sociability. The level of agreement between the raters would be an index of the reliability of the scale.

Validity

The validity of assessment techniques or measures refers to the degree to which the instruments in question measure what they are intended to measure. There are various kinds of validity, such as *content, construct,* and *criterion validity.*

Content Validity The **content validity** of an assessment technique is the degree to which its content covers a representative sample of the behaviors associated with the construct dimension or trait in question. For example, depression includes features such as sadness and lack of participation in previously enjoyed activities. To have content validity, techniques assessing depression should thus have features or items that address these areas. One type of content validity, called **face validity,** is the degree to which questions or test items bear an apparent relationship to the constructs or traits they purport to measure. A face-valid item on a test of assertiveness could be, "I have little difficulty standing up for my rights." An item that lacks face validity as a measure of assertiveness could read, "I usually subscribe to magazines that contain features about world events."

The limitation of face validity is its reliance on subjective judgment in determining whether or not the test measures what it is supposed to measure. The apparent or face validity of an assessment technique is not sufficient to establish its scientific value. A scientific test may also be valid if its results relate to some standard or criterion, even though the items themselves do not have high face validity. This brings us to criterion validity.

Criterion Validity **Criterion validity** represents the degree to which the assessment technique correlates with an independent, external criterion (standard) of what the technique is intended to assess. There are two general types of criterion validity: concurrent validity and predictive validity.

Concurrent validity is the degree to which test responses predict scores on criterion measures taken at about the same time. Most psychologists presume intelligence is in part responsible for academic success. The concurrent validity of intelligence test scores is thus frequently studied by correlating test scores with criteria such as school grades and teacher ratings of academic abilities.

A test of depression might be validated in terms of its ability to identify people who meet diagnostic criteria for depression. Two related concepts are important here: **sensitivity** and **specificity.** Sensitivity refers to the degree to which a test correctly identifies people who have the disorder the test is intended to detect. Tests that lack sensitivity produce a high number of "false negatives"—individuals identified as not having the disorder who truly have the disorder. Specificity refers to the degree to which the test avoids classifying people as having a particular disorder who truly do not have the disorder. Tests that lack specificity produce a high number of "false positives"—people identified as having the disorder who truly do not have the disorder. By taking into account sensitivity and specificity of a given test, we can determine the ability of a test to classify individuals correctly.

Predictive validity refers to the ability of a test to predict future behavior. A test of academic aptitude may be validated in terms of its ability to predict school performance in that particular area.

Construct Validity **Construct validity** is the degree to which a test corresponds to the theoretical model of the underlying construct or trait it purports to measure. Consider a test that purports to measure anxiety. Anxiety is not a concrete object or phenomenon. It can't be measured directly, counted, weighed, or touched. Anxiety is a theoretical construct that helps to explain phenomena like a pounding heart or sudden inability to speak when you ask an attractive person out on a date. Anxiety may be indirectly measured by such means as self-report (rating one's own level of anxiety) and physiological techniques (measuring the level of sweat on the palms of one's hands).

The construct validity of a test of anxiety requires that the results of the test predict other behaviors which would be expected given your theoretical model of anxiety. Assume that your theoretical model predicts that anxious college students would experience greater difficulties than calmer students in speaking coherently when asking someone for a date, but not when they are merely rehearsing the invitation in private. If the speech behavior of high and low scorers on a test purported to measure test anxiety fit these predicted patterns, we can say that the evidence supports the construct validity of the test. Construct validity involves a continuing process of testing relationships among variables that are predicted from a theoretical framework. We can never claim to have proven the construct validity of a test because it is always possible to come up with an alternative theoretical account of these relationships.

Assessment techniques, including psychological tests, can be highly reliable yet also invalid. A test of musical aptitude might have excellent reliability but be invalid as a measure of general intelligence. Nineteenth-century **phrenologists** believed they could gauge people's personalities by measuring the bumps on their heads. Their calipers provided reliable measures of their subjects' bumps and protrusions; the measurements, however, did not provide valid estimates of subjects' psychological traits. The phrenologists were bumping in the dark, so to speak.

TRUTH *or* FICTION REVISITED

2.2 *False.* A test may be reliable (give you consistent responses) but still not measure what it purports to measure.

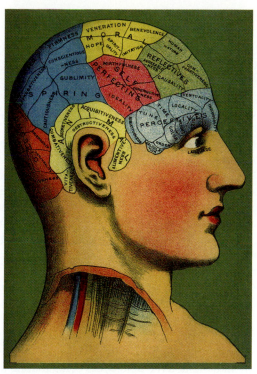

Phrenology. In the 19th century, some people believed that mental faculties and abilities were based in certain parts of the brain and that people's acumen in such faculties could be assessed by gauging the protrusions and indentations of the skull.

Sociocultural and Ethnic Factors in the Assessment of Abnormal Behavior

Researchers and clinicians also need to be aware of sociocultural and ethnic factors when they assess personality traits and psychological disorders. Assessment techniques may be reliable and valid within one culture but not within another, even when they are translated accurately (Kleinman, 1987). In one study, Chan (1991) administered a Chinese-language version of the Beck Depression Inventory (BDI), a widely used inventory of depression in the United States, to a sample of Chinese students and psychiatric patients in Hong Kong. The Chinese BDI met tests of reliability, as judged by internal consistency, and of validity, as judged by its ability to distinguish people with depression from nondepressives among a small sample of Chinese psychiatric patients. Yet other investigators found that Chinese people in both Hong Kong and the People's Republic of China tended to achieve higher scores on a subscale of the Chinese MMPI that is suggestive of deviant responses (F. Cheung, Song, & Butcher, 1991). These higher-scores subjects appeared to reflect cultural differences, however, rather than greater psychopathology (F. Cheung et al., 1991; F. M. Cheung & Ho, 1997).

A recent study in our own culture put the recently revised MMPI, called the MMPI-2, under a cultural microscope. Researchers found the test was as accurate in making predictions of the psychological adjustment of African Americans as of non-Hispanic White Americans (Timbrook & Graham, 1994). Moreover, researchers found small differ-

ences in the average test scores of African Americans and non-Hispanic White Americans when factors such as age, education, and income were taken into account. Another study found no evidence of cultural bias on the MMPI-2 between African American and Caucasian clients at a mental health center (McNulty et al., 1997).

Other investigators found a greater prevalence of depression among Mexican Americans than among non-Hispanic White Americans in Los Angeles, as measured by the CES-D, a commonly used measure of depression (Garcia & Marks, 1989). Here again the meaning of this difference was unclear. The difference may have reflected semantic or sociocultural factors rather than differences in the prevalences of depression (Fabrega, 1992). Researchers thus need to disentangle psychopathology from sociocultural factors.

A review of widely used diagnostic instruments for assessing abnormal behavior revealed that most (8 of 11) made references to cultural factors in helping evaluators make diagnostic judgments (López & Núñez, 1987). For example, 6 of 10 instruments for diagnosing schizophrenia require the user to determine that beliefs and perceptions which may be judged as delusional or hallucinatory are not shared by other members of the person's cultural group. In some Native American cultures, hallucinations during tribal rituals are common and not indicative of schizophrenia. Similarly, speech or thought patterns deemed abnormal within our culture might be considered normal in others. As an example, pressured speech (speaking so fast it seems as if the brain is racing ahead of the person's ability to form words) may be taken as a sign of manic behavior in the United States at large, but may represent normative speaking patterns among certain sociocultural groups, such as the Amish (Egeland et al., 1983).

Most diagnostic schedules consider culture to some degree, but researchers believe that they fail to provide adequate norms for different cultural and ethnic groups. Translations of instruments should not only translate words; they should also provide instructions that encourage examiners to address the importance of cultural beliefs, norms, and values, so diagnosticians and interviewers will be prompted to consider the individual's background seriously when making assessments of abnormal behavior patterns.

Interviewers need also to be sensitized to problems that can arise when interviews are conducted in a language other than the client's mother tongue. Hispanics, for example, often are judged more disturbed when interviewed in English (Fabrega, 1990). Problems can also arise when interviewers who use a second language fail to appreciate the idioms and subtleties of the language. The first author recalls a case in a U.S. mental hospital in which the interviewer, a foreign-born and -trained psychiatrist, reported that a patient exhibited the delusional belief that he was outside his body. This assessment was based on the patient's response to a question posed by the psychiatrist. The psychiatrist had asked the patient if he was feeling anxious and the patient replied, "Yes, Doc, I feel like I'm jumping out of my skin at times."

THE CLINICAL INTERVIEW

The interview is the most widely used means of assessment. It is employed by all helping professionals and paraprofessionals. The interview, moreover, is usually the client's first face-to-face contact with a clinician.

The interview is usually initiated by a phone call made by the client or someone who is concerned about the client's behavior, perhaps a family member, a member of the clergy, or a social service agency. A telephone screening might be used to determine whether it seems appropriate to schedule the client for a face-to-face interview, or whether another agency might be better suited to evaluate the problem.

A client who would apparently profit from the services offered by the agency is scheduled for an **intake interview.** The intake provides an opportunity to learn more about the client's **presenting problem** and history. On the basis of this information, the interviewer may arrive at an initial diagnostic impression and recommend treatment or further evaluation.

Clinicians often begin by asking clients to describe the presenting complaint in their own words. They may say something like, "Can you describe to me the problems you've been having lately?" (Therapists learn not to ask, "What brings you here?" to avoid receiving such answers as, "A car," "A bus," or "My social worker.") The clinician will then usually probe aspects of the presenting complaint, such as behavioral abnormalities and feelings of discomfort, the cir-

cumstances regarding the onset of the problem, history of past episodes, and how the problem affects the client's daily functioning. The clinician may explore possible precipitating events, such as changes in life circumstances, social relationships, employment, or schooling. The interviewer encourages the client to describe the problem in her or his own words in order to understand it from the client's point of view.

Although the format of the intake process may vary from clinician to clinician, most interviews cover topics such as these:

1. *Identifying Data.* Information regarding the client's sociodemographic characteristics: address and telephone number, marital status, age, gender, racial/ethnic characteristics, religion, employment, family composition, and so on.

2. *Description of the Presenting Problem(s).* How does the client perceive the problem? What troubling behaviors, thoughts, or feelings are reported? How do they affect the client's functioning? When did they begin?

3. *Psychosocial History.* Information describing the client's developmental history: educational, social, and occupational history; early family relationships.

4. *Medical/Psychiatric History.* History of medical and psychiatric treatment and hospitalizations. Is the present problem a recurrent episode of a previous problem? How was the problem handled in the past? Was treatment successful? Why or why not?

5. *Medical Problems/Medication.* Description of present medical problems and present treatment, including medication. The clinician is alert to ways in which medical problems may affect the presenting psychological problem. For example, drugs for certain medical conditions can affect people's moods and general levels of arousal.

Differences in Theoretical Approaches

Each interviewer is guided by his or her own theoretical approach. A behaviorally oriented interviewer might seek detailed information about the events that precede and follow the occurrence of the problem behavior—searching for stimuli that trigger the problem behavior and for reinforcements that maintain it.

Consider the case of Pamela:

A young woman of 19, Pamela, is seen for an initial evaluation. She complains of fear of driving her car across a bridge on a route that she must take to attend college. She reports that she fears "freezing up" at the wheel and causing an accident if she were to drive across the bridge. Upon interview, she reports that the problem began 6 months earlier, shortly after she experienced intense anxiety driving across a different bridge. It nearly caused her to lose control of the car. Now she takes three buses to make the trip, increasing her commutation by more than an hour each way. But she has heard that the bus company may terminate her route,

A behavioral interviewer might try to determine the stimulus cues that evoke Pamela's fear. For example, is the fear greater or lesser depending on the height of the bridge? The depth of the ground or water below? The steepness of the incline? The narrowing of the road? Can the client quantify the fear she encounters at the inclines, overpasses, and bridges in the roadways she uses? Such information might help the therapist map out a strategy of gradual exposure to these stimuli (see Chapter 5).

The psychodynamically oriented interviewer might focus on Pamela's early childhood experiences, seeking clues as to how her fear of driving over bridges may symbolize unconscious conflicts. Might the crossing of a bridge symbolically represent separation from her parents and signify conflict concerning issues of independence and separation? Did Pamela experience separation anxiety as a child that might be reactivated in her current travel? Does her travel phobia protect her from facing adult challenges that require more independence and self-confidence than she can muster—such as attending a college outside her immediate community and pursuing the more demanding career opportunities the college offers?

Whatever the theoretical orientation of the interviewer, interviewing skills and techniques have some features in common. Psychologists and other professionals are trained to establish **rapport** and feelings of trust with the client. These feelings help put the client at ease and encourage candid communication. Effective interviewers do not pressure clients to disclose sensitive information. Clients are generally more willing to disclose their personal feelings and experiences to someone who shows concern and understanding, someone they feel they can trust. When the interviewer is skillful, clients are less likely to fear they will be criticized or judged for revealing sensitive information.

Interview Formats

There are three general types of clinical interviews: **unstructured interviews, semi-structured interviews,** and **structured interviews.** In an unstructured interview, the clinician adopts his or her own style of questioning rather than following any standard format. In a semi-structured interview, the clinician follows a general outline of questions designed to gather essential information but is free to ask the questions in any particular order and to branch off into other directions in order to follow up clinically important information. In a structured interview, the interviews follow a preset series of questions in a particular order.

The major advantage of the unstructured interview is its spontaneity and conversational style. There is an active give-and-take between the interviewer and the client as the interviewer is not bound to follow any specific set of questions. The major disadvantage is the lack of standardization. Different interviewers may ask questions in different ways. For example, one interviewer might ask, "How have your moods been lately?" while another might pose the question, "Have you had any periods of crying or tearfulness during the past week or two?" The clients responses may depend to a certain extent on how the questions were asked. Another drawback is that the conversational flow of the interview may fail to touch upon important clinical information needed to form a diagnostic information. A semi-structured interview provides more structure and uniformity, but at the possible expense of spontaneity. Clinicians may seek to strike a balance by conducting a semi-structured interview in which they follow a general outline of questions but allow themselves the flexibility to depart from the interview protocol to pursue issues that seem important to them.

Structured interviews (also called *standardized interviews*) provide the highest level of reliability and consistency in reaching diagnostic judgments, which is why they are used frequently in research settings. Yet many clinicians prefer using a semi-structured approach because of its greater flexibility. Two examples of structured interview protocols are the National Institute of Mental Health's Diagnostic Interview Schedule (DIS) and the Structured Clinical Interview for the DSM (SCID).

The DIS uses a prearranged set of questions that must be asked in a precise order. It can be administered by a clinician or a lay interviewer (L. N. Robins, Helzer, Croughan, & Ratcliff, 1981) (see Table 2.7). The interview responses are fed into a computer that determines the most appropriate diagnostic category. In addition to specifying the behaviors exhibited and reported by the client, the DIS outlines the history of the problems and the life experiences associated with them.

The clinician or layperson must be well trained in administering the interview. The DIS shows high interjudge reliability; it produces high rates of agreement in diagnostic judgments among professional clinicians (Helzer et al., 1985). Evidence is mixed concerning the reliability of information attained by nonprofessional interviewers, however, even when they are well trained (Erdman et al., 1987).

Although the DIS provides information a computer can analyze to make diagnoses, it more closely resembles a symptom checklist or questionnaire than an interview, which is why it can be administered by a lay interviewer. The SCID, on the other hand, is intended for professionals who are experienced interviewers and familiar with the DSM system. The SCID includes **closed-ended questions** to determine the presence of behavior patterns that suggest specific diagnostic categories and **open-ended questions** that allow clients to elaborate their problems and feelings. The SCID guides the clinician in testing diagnostic hypotheses

TABLE 2.7

A Section of the DIS Relevant to Panic Disorder

61. Have you ever considered yourself a nervous person?
62. Have you ever had a spell or attack when all of a sudden you felt frightened, anxious, or very uneasy in situations when most people would not be afraid?

    For those answering yes to Q. 62, the following questions would be asked. If the answer is no, the interviewer skips to the next series of questions.

A. During one of your worst spells of suddenly feeling frightened or anxious or uneasy, did you ever notice that you had any of the following problems?

    During this spell—
    (1) were you short of breath—having trouble catching your breath?
    (2) did your heart pound?
    (3) were you dizzy or light-headed?
    (4) did your fingers or face tingle?
    (5) did you have tightness or pain in your chest?
    (6) did you feel like you were choking or smothering?
    (7) did you feel faint?
    (8) did you sweat?
    (9) did you tremble or shake?
    (10) did you feel hot or cold flashes?
    (11) did things around you seem unreal?
    (12) were you afraid either that you might die or that you might act in a crazy way?

B. How old were you the first time you had one of these sudden spells of feeling frightened or anxious? Age _____

    Whole Life = code 02
    If don't know and age under 40, code 01
    If don't know and age 40 or more, ask: "Would you say it was before or after you were 40?"

C. Have you ever had 3 spells like this close together—say within a 3-week period?

D. Have spells like this occurred during at least 6 different weeks of your life?

E. Have you had a spell like this within the last 2 weeks?

Note: A panic disorder is a type of anxiety disorder characterized by recurrent panic attacks (see Chapter 5).
Source: Robins, L. N., Helzer, J. E., Croughan, J., & Ratcliff, K. S. (1981). National Institute of Mental Health: Diagnostic Interview Schedule.
Archives of General Psychiatry, 41, 949-958. Copyright 1981, American Medical Association.

---

as the interview progresses. Recent research supports the reliability of the SCID across various clinical settings (J. B. Williams et al., 1992).

In the course of the interview, the clinician may also conduct a more formal assessment of the client's cognitive functioning by administering a **mental status examination.** A diagnostic impression is usually based on an assessment of the client's presenting problems, history, and cognitive functioning.

Mental Status Examination

The mental status examination is based on observation of the client's behavior and self-presentation and the client's response to questions that probe various aspects of cognitive functioning. The specifics of the mental status exam may vary from clinician to clinician, but the following factors are usually assessed:

    1. *Appearance.*   The examiner describes the appropriateness of the client's general appearance, grooming, and dress or attire.

    2. *Behavioral Observations.*   The examiner notes signs of psychological disturbance in the client's verbal and nonverbal behavior. Does the client maintain eye contact? (Avoidance can indicate shyness, depression, or other problems.) Do facial expressions or general posture suggest underlying emotional states? How does the client relate to the interviewer? Is she or he cooperative and friendly, or hostile and evasive? Are there signs of serious disturbance, such as bizarre behavior, inappropriate laughter, or giggling? Is the client's manner of speech pressured, controlled, or hesitant?

Nonverbal cues are interpreted according to their context. Grimacing and clenching jaws throughout an interview may express general discomfort or anxiety. If these behaviors occur only in response to questions about one's spouse, they may reflect more specific feelings. The tone of voice and style of speech are important sources of information. Pressured or rapid speech may suggest stress or a manic episode. Slow, halting speech is more characteristic of depression or brain damage.

The client's body movement and posture, facial expressions, and gestures are clues to the client's emotions. The interviewer looks for subtle changes in the client's nonverbal

Nonverbal behavior. Interviewers need to be aware of how their clients' nonverbal behaviors may indicate their underlying emotional states. What emotions are reflected in this woman's posture and facial expression?

the external world, perhaps due to brain damage. Clinicians may write that the client's "sensorium is clear" to indicate apparently accurate sensing of the external world.

6. *Perceptual Processes.* Perception is a psychological process by which people interpret the information provided by the senses. Sometimes, as in the case of hallucinations, perceptions may occur in the absence of external sensory input, and the client may not be able to distinguish them from reality. The clinician notes whether or not the client appears to be responding to hallucinations, such as attending to voices or seeing things that are not there. In the case of schizophrenia, the senses may be flooded with false perceptions (hallucinations).

7. *Mood and Affect.* These terms are often used interchangeably but have a slightly different meaning. The noun **affect** (pronounced AFF-ect) refers to the emotions or feelings the client attaches to objects or ideas, such as anger, joy, or sadness. The central issue is whether or not the affect is *appropriate* to the client's life situation and the ideas being expressed. Inappropriateness of affect (such as laughing while discussing tragic events) or impoverished emotional reactivity (described as blunted or flat affect) is often connected with severe problems such as schizophrenia. **Mood** refers to the prevailing emotions displayed during the interview.

8. *Intelligence.* The clinician usually judges the client's general level of intellectual functioning on the basis of the client's speech (level of vocabulary and ability to formulate and express ideas clearly), apparent level of sophistication (general knowledge), and achieved socioeconomic status (educational and employment history). If questions arise as to the client's cognitive abilities, the interviewer may direct questions that test the client's ability to interpret proverbs, to name officeholders such as the local mayor or governor, or to compute simple arithmetic tasks—questions that assess the client's capacities for acquiring and manipulating information.

9. *Thought Processes.* This category refers to the form and content of thought. Concerning the form of thought, the clinician notes whether or not the client's thought processes appear logical and coherent. Is there perhaps a loosening of associations—an apparent stringing together of loosely connected or disconnected thoughts or ideas suggestive of disordered thinking processes that often occur in schizophrenia? Is there evidence of thought blocking—a gap or pause in the client's speech when a troubling topic is touched on? Is there evidence of flight of ideas—a tendency to jump from topic to topic that may prevent the examiner from following the connections, as might occur during manic episodes? Does the client speak very little, perhaps because of impoverishment of thought? Description of the client's thought content touches on any evidence of troubling belief patterns such as delusional beliefs (false ideas) or obsessions (nagging, repetitious thoughts).

10. *Insight.* Does the client recognize a problem exists? Has the client developed a reasonable understanding of the factors that might account for the problem? Does the client deny the existence of the problem or blame others for it, as may occur in personality disorders?

behavior throughout the interview, connecting nonverbal cues that accompany discussion of particular topics to become better aware of the emotions these issues may evoke.

3. *Orientation.* Normally speaking, we know who we and our relations are, where we are, and what time it is—although your authors are usually off by a day or two. The clinician notes whether the client shows lapses in *orientation* and, if there is any doubt, questions the client about who she or he is, who other people present are, where they are (where the interview is taking place), and what time it is (year, day, time of day). An elderly woman who had suffered brain damage told the authors her hospital room was "some kind of spaceship" and "Nixon" was president (at the time, Ronald Reagan was president). Disorientation may be associated with problems such as degeneration of the brain, drug intoxication, or schizophrenia.

4. *Memory.* Is the client's memory intact for recent events and remote events? Can the client recall last night's dinner (recent memory) or when and where she or he was married (remote memory)? In some conditions associated with advanced age, people can recall events 30 years in the past but have difficulty forming new memories. As a result, they may not be able to recall the name of a new grandchild or whether they have taken their medication.

5. *Sensorium.* **Sensorium** derives from the Latin *sensus,* meaning "sense," and *-ium,* a suffix used to form the names of biological structures. The term *sensorium* is defined as the individual's entire sensory apparatus and is used by clinicians to refer to the client's focusing of attention, capacity for concentration, and level of awareness of the world. Clients whose attention or concentration drifts in and out during the interview, or who are generally unresponsive, may have difficulties processing information from

A CLOSER LOOK

Would You Tell Your Problems to a Computer?

Picture yourself seated before a computer screen in the not-too-distant future. The message on the screen asks you to type in your name and press the return key. Not wanting to offend, you comply. This message then comes on the screen: "Hello, my name is Sigmund. I'm programmed to ask you a set of questions to learn more about you. May I begin?" You nod your head yes, momentarily forgetting the computer can only "perceive" key strokes. You type "yes" and the interview begins.

The future, as the saying goes, is now. Computerized clinical interviews have been used for more than 25 years. Computers offer some advantages over us traditional human interviewers (Farrell, Camplair, & McCullough, 1987):

1. Computers can be programmed to ask a specific set of questions in a predetermined order, whereas human beings may omit critical items or steer the interview toward less important topics.

2. The client may be less embarrassed about relating personal matters to the computer because computers do not show emotional responses to clients' responses.

3. Computerized interviews can free clinicians to spend more time providing direct clinical services.

Consider a computerized interview system named CASPER. Interview questions and response options, such as the following, are presented on the screen:

"About how many days in the past month did you have difficulty falling asleep, staying asleep, or waking too early (include sleep disturbed by bad dreams)?"

"During the past month, how have you been getting along with your spouse/partner? (1) Very satisfactory; (2) Mostly satisfactory; (3) Sometimes satisfactory, sometimes unsatisfactory; (4) Mostly unsatisfactory; (5) Very unsatisfactory."

FARRELL ET AL., 1987, P. 692

The subject presses a numeric key to respond to each item. CASPER is a branching program that follows up on problems suggested by the clients' responses. For example, if the client indicates difficulty in falling or remaining asleep, CASPER asks whether or not sleep has become a major problem—"something causing you great personal distress or interfering with your daily functioning" (Farrell, p. 693). If the client indicates yes, the computer will return to the problem after other items have been presented and ask the client to rate the duration and intensity of the problem. Clients may also add or drop complaints—change their minds, that is.

A recent study found that a brief diagnostic interview conducted over the phone by a computer equipped with voice response technology achieved similar results as a human interviewer using a more intensive interview protocol, the SCID (Kobak et al., 1997). Moreover, it appeared that clients reported a greater

---

The interviewer takes note of any apparent discrepancies between the client's verbal and nonverbal behavior. Nonverbal cues may be more accurate reflections of emotional state than verbal reports. Clients may lack insight into feelings of anger toward their parents but raise their voices when they discuss them. Clients may deny problems at work but tightly grasp the arms of their chairs when they talk about their jobs.

11. *Judgment.* Does the client apply sound and reasonable judgments in making life decisions? Does the client approach problems thoughtfully and rationally? Or does the client act in a rash or impulsive manner, failing to consider the consequences of his or her actions, as may happen, for example, in manic episodes, personality disorders, or substance abuse?

PSYCHOLOGICAL TESTS

Psychological tests are structured methods of assessment used to evaluate reasonably stable traits such as intelligence

and personality. Tests are usually standardized on large numbers of subjects and provide norms that compare clients' scores with the average. By comparing test results from samples of people who are free of psychological disorders with those of people who have diagnosable psychological disorders, we may gain some insights into the types of response patterns that are indicative of abnormal behavior.

INTELLIGENCE TESTS

The assessment of abnormal behavior often includes an evaluation of intelligence. Formal tests of intelligence are used to help diagnose mental retardation. They evaluate the intellectual impairment that may be caused by other disorders, such as organic mental disorders caused by damage to the brain. They also provide a profile of the client's intellectual strengths and weaknesses to help develop a treatment plan suited to the client's competencies.

Intelligence is a controversial concept in psychology, however. Even attempts at definition stir debate. David

number of problems to CASPER than to a flesh-and-blood clinician. Perhaps the computer interview is especially helpful in identifying problems the client is embarrassed or unwilling to report to a human. Perhaps the computer seems more willing to take the time to note all complaints.

TRUTH *or* FICTION REVISITED

2.3 *False*. Evidence shows that people generally reveal more personal problems when interviewed by computers than by humans. Perhaps people are less concerned about being "judged" by computers.

Reviews of research suggests that computer programs are as capable as skilled clinicians at obtaining information from clients and reaching an accurate diagnosis, and are less expensive and more time-efficient (B. L. Bloom, 1992; Kobak et al., 1996). It seems that most of the resistance to using computer interviews for this purpose comes from clinicians rather than clients.

Computer-assisted treatments for mental health problems have also become available, including systems designed to help people overcome phobias and test anxiety. Almost all of these are aids to therapy, not substitutes for a live therapist (I. Marks et al., 1998a). But with the rapid pace of technological developments today, there may well come a day when computerized programs with interactive voice technology will be used as stand-alone "therapists."

Interview by computer. Would you be more likely, or less likely, to tell your problems to a computer than to a person? Computerized clinical interviews have been used for more than 20 years, and some research suggests that the computer may be more sensitive than its human counterpart in teasing out problems.

Wechsler, the originator of a widely used series of intelligence tests, defined intelligence as "capacity . . . to understand the world . . . and . . . resourcefulness to cope with its challenges" (1975). From his perspective, intelligence has to do with the ways in which we (1) mentally represent the world, and (2) adapt to its demands. There are various intelligence tests, including group tests and those that are administered individually, such as the Stanford-Binet and Wechsler scales. Individual tests allow examiners to observe the behavior of the respondent as well as record answers. Examiners can thus gain insight as to whether factors such as testing conditions, language problems, illness, or level of motivation contribute to a given test performance.

The Stanford-Binet Intelligence Scale (SBIS)

The SBIS was originated by the Frenchmen Alfred Binet and Theodore Simon in 1905 in response to the French public

school system's quest for a test that could identify children who might profit from special education. The initial Binet-Simon scale yielded a score called a **mental age** (MA) that represented the child's overall level of intellectual functioning. The child who received an MA of 8 was functioning like the typical 8-year-old. Children received "months" of credit for correct answers, and their MAs were determined by adding them up.

Louis Terman of Stanford University adapted the Binet-Simon test for American children in 1916, which is why it is now called the *Stanford*-Binet Intelligence Scale (SBIS). The SBIS also yielded an **intelligence quotient** (IQ), not an MA, which reflected the relationship between a child's MA and chronological age (CA), according to this formula:

$$IQ = \frac{MA}{CA} \times 100$$

Examination of this formula shows that children who received identical mental-age scores might differ markedly in IQ, with the younger child attaining the higher IQ.

Binet assumed that intelligence grew as children developed, so older children would obtain more correct answers. He thus age-graded his questions and arranged them according to difficulty level, a practice carried over into the Stanford-Binet, as shown in Table 2.8.

Today the SBIS is used with children and adults, and test takers' IQ scores are based on their deviation from the norms of their age group. A score of 100 is defined as the mean. People who answer more items correctly than the average obtain IQ scores above 100; those who answer fewer items correctly obtain scores of less than 100.

The so-called **deviation IQ** was developed by psychologist David Wechsler, who also originated various intelligence tests of his own.

The Wechsler Scales

Wechsler developed several intelligence scales for children and adults. The Wechsler scales group questions into subtests like those shown in Table 2.9, each of which measures a different intellectual task. The Wechsler scales are thus designed to offer insight into respondents' relative strengths and weaknesses, and not simply yield an overall score.

Wechsler's scales describe so-called *verbal* and *performance* subtests. Verbal subtests generally require knowledge of verbal concepts; performance subtests rely more on spatial relations skills. (Figure 2.1 shows items like those on performance scales of the Wechsler scales.) Wechsler's scales allow for computation of verbal and performance IQs.

Students from various backgrounds yield different profiles. College students, generally speaking, perform better on verbal subtests than on performance subtests. Australian Aboriginal children outperform white Australian children on performance-type tasks that involve visual-spatial skills (Kearins, 1981). Such skills are likely to foster survival in the harsh Australian outback. Intellectual attainments, like psychological adjustment, are connected with the demands of particular sociocultural and physical environmental settings.

Wechsler IQ scores are based on how respondents' answers deviate from those attained by their age-mates. The mean whole test score at any age is defined as 100. Wechsler distributed IQ scores so 50% of the scores of the population would lie within a "broad average" range of 90 to 110.

Most IQ scores cluster around the mean (see Figure 2.2). Just 5% of them are above 130 or below 70. Wechsler labeled people who attained scores of 130 or above as "very superior," those with scores below 70 as "intellectually deficient." IQ scores below 70 are one of the criteria used in diagnosing mental retardation.

PERSONALITY TESTS

Clinicians use various formal tests to assess personality. We consider two types of personality tests: *self-report* and *projective* tests. Some self-report tests or personality scales are intended to measure a particular trait or construct, such as anxiety or depression. The Beck Depression Inventory, (BDI;

TABLE 2.8

Items Similar to Those on the Stanford-Binet Intelligence Scale

Level (Years)	Item
2 years	1. Children show knowledge of basic vocabulary words by identifying parts of a doll such as the mouth, ears, and hair. 2. Children show counting and spatial skills along with visual-motor coordination by building a tower of four blocks to match a model.
4 years	1. Children show word fluency and categorical thinking by filling in the missing words when they are asked questions such as: "Father is a man; mother is a _____?" "Hamburgers are hot; ice cream is _____?" 2. Children show comprehension by answering correctly when they are asked questions such as: "Why do people have automobiles?" "Why do people have medicine?"
9 years	1. Children can point out verbal absurdities, as in this question: "In an old cemetery, scientists unearthed a skull which they think was that of George Washington when he was only five years of age. What is silly about that?" 2. Children show fluency with words, as shown by answering the questions: "Can you tell me a number that rhymes with snore?" "Can you tell me a color that rhymes with glue?"
Adult	1. Adults show knowledge of the meanings of words and conceptual thinking by correctly explaining the differences between word pairs like "sickness and misery," "house and home," and "integrity and prestige." 2. Adults show spatial skills by correctly answering questions like "If a car turned to the right to head north, in what direction was it heading before it turned?"

Source: S.A. Rathus (1996). *Psychology* (6th ed.). Ft. Worth: Harcourt Brace College Publishers, p. 336.

TABLE 2.9

Examples of Subtests from the Wechsler Adult Intelligence Scale

Verbal Subtest	Performance Subtest
1. *Information:* "What is the capital of the United States?"	7. *Digit Symbol:* Learning and drawing meaningless figures that are associated with numbers.
2. *Comprehension:* "Why do we have zip codes?" "What does 'A stitch in time saves 9' mean?"	8. *Picture Completion:* Pointing to the missing part of a picture.
3. *Arithmetic:* "If 3 candy bars cost 25 cents, how much will 18 candy bars cost?"	9. *Block Design:* Copying pictures of geometric designs using multicolored blocks.
4. *Similarities:* "How are good and bad alike?" "How are peanut butter and jelly alike?"	10. *Picture Arrangement:* Arranging cartoon pictures in sequence so that they tell a meaningful story.
5. *Digit Span:* Repeating a series of numbers forward and backward.	11. *Object Assembly:* Putting pieces of a puzzle together so that they form a meaningful object.
6. *Vocabulary:* "What does canal mean?"	

Items for verbal subtests 1, 2, 3, 4, and 6 are similar but not identical to actual test items on the WAIS.

Source: S.A. Rathus (1996). *Psychology* (6th ed.). Ft. Worth: Harcourt Brace College Publishers, p. 337.

Picture Arrangement
These pictures tell a story but they are in the wrong order. Put them in the right order so that they tell a story.

Picture Completion
What part is missing from this picture?

Block Design
Put the blocks together to make this picture.

Object Assembly
Put the pieces together as quickly as you can.

FIGURE 2.1 *Items similar to those found on the performance subtests of the Wechsler Intelligence Scales.*
The Wechsler scales yield verbal and performance IQs that are based on the extent to which an individual's test scores deviate from the norm for her or his age group.

Source: Copyright © 1981 by the Psychological Corporation. Reproduced by permission. All rights reserved.

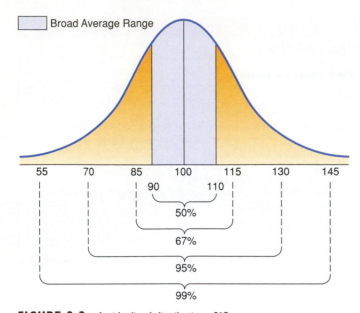

FIGURE 2.2 *An idealized distribution of IQ scores.*
The distribution of IQ scores is based on a bell-shaped curve, which is referred to by psychologists as a *normal curve*. Wechsler defined the deviation IQ in such a way that 50% of the scores fall within the broad average range of 90 to 110.

A. T. Beck, Ward, Mendelson, Mock, & Erbaugh, 1961), for instance, is a widely used measure of depression. In many clinic sites, such as the training clinic where the first author supervises clinical psychology students, the BDI is used routinely to screen new clients for depression. Here our focus is on multidimensional self-report personality tests or inventories, with particular emphasis on the most widely used of these instruments, the Minnesota Multiphasic Personality Inventory (MMPI).

Self-Report Personality Inventories

Do you like automobile magazines? Are you easily startled by noises in the night? Are you bothered by periods of anxiety or shakiness? Self-report inventories use structured items, similar to these, to measure personality traits such as anxiety, depression, emotionality, hypomania, masculinity-femininity, and introversion. Comparison of clients' responses on scales measuring these traits to those of a normative sample reveals their relative standing.

Self-report personality inventories are also called **objective tests.** They are objective in that the range of possible responses to items is limited. Empirical objective standards—rather than psychological theory—are also used to derive test items. Tests might ask respondents to check adjectives that apply to them, to mark statements as true or false, to select preferred activities from lists, or to indicate whether items apply to them "always," "sometimes," or "never." Tests with **forced-choice formats** require respondents to mark which of a group of statements is truest for them, or to select their most preferred activity from a list. They cannot answer "none of the above." Forced-choice

formats are commonly used in interest inventories, as in this item:

I would rather

a. be a forester.
b. work in an office setting.
c. play in a band.

With objective personality tests, items are selected according to some empirical standard. With the Minnesota Multiphasic Personality Inventory (MMPI), the standard was whether or not items differentiated clinical diagnostic groups from normal comparison groups.

Minnesota Multiphasic Personality Inventory (MMPI) The MMPI contains more than 500 true-false statements that assess interest patterns, habits, family relationships, somatic complaints, attitudes, beliefs, and behaviors characteristic of psychological disorders. It is widely used as a test of personality as well as assisting in the diagnosis of abnormal behavior patterns.

In the 1930s, the developers of the MMPI—Starke Hathaway, a psychologist, and Charles McKinley, a psychiatrist—constructed the MMPI scales on the basis of clinical data. This was an innovation because most personality tests at the time were based on a theoretical approach, in which the developer derives test items according to her or his theoretical belief that a given item measures a certain psychological attribute (Graham, 1993). Items were assigned to particular MMPI scales if they tended to be answered differently by members of carefully selected diagnostic groups, such as patients diagnosed with schizophrenia or depression, than by members of normal comparison groups that were composed primarily of relatives and visitors of patients in the University of Minnesota hospitals.

TRUTH *or* FICTION REVISITED
2.4 *False.* The MMPI, the most widely used personality test, consists of items that discriminated between clinical and normal groups.

Consider a hypothetical item: "I often read detective novels." If groups of depressed people tended to answer the item in a direction different from normal groups, the item would be placed on the depression scale—regardless of whether or not the item had face validity. Many items that discriminate normal people from clinical groups are transparent in meaning, such as "I feel down much of the time." Some items are more subtle in meaning or bear no obvious relationship to the measured trait.

Derivation of scales on the basis of their ability to distinguish the response patterns of comparison groups such as clinical and normal groups is called the **contrasted groups approach.** The contrasted groups technique establishes concurrent validity; group membership is the criterion by which the validity of the test is measured.

Eight clinical scales were derived through the contrasted groups approach. Two additional clinical scales were developed by using nonclinical comparison groups: a scale measuring masculine–feminine interest patterns and one measuring social introversion. The clinical scales are described in Table 2.10. The MMPI also has **validity scales** that assess tendencies to distort test responses in a favorable ("faking good") or unfavorable ("faking bad") direction.

The respondent's raw score for each of the clinical scales on the MMPI scale is simply the number of items scored in a clinical direction. Raw scores are converted into **standard scores** with a mean of 50 and a standard deviation of 10. A standard score of 65 or higher on a particular scale places an individual at approximately the 92nd percentile or higher of the revised normative sample, and is considered to be clinically significant.

The MMPI is interpreted according to individual scale elevations and interrelationships among scales. For example, a "2–7 profile," commonly found among people seeking therapy, refers to a test pattern in which scores for scales 2 ("Depression") and 7 ("Psychasthenia") are clinically elevated. Clinicians may refer to "atlases," or descriptions, of people who usually attain various profiles.

MMPI scales are regarded as reflecting continua of personality traits associated with the diagnostic categories represented by the test. For example, a high score on *psychopathic deviation* suggests the respondent holds a higher-than-average number of nonconformist beliefs and may be rebellious, which are characteristics often found in people with antisocial personality disorder. However, because it is

TABLE 2.10

Clinical Scales of the MMPI

Scale Number	Scale Label	Items Similar to Those Found on MMPI Scale	Sample Traits of High Scorers
1	Hypochondriasis	My stomach frequently bothers me. At times, my body seems to ache all over.	Many physical complaints, cynical defeatist attitudes, often perceived as whiny, demanding
2	Depression	Nothing seems to interest me anymore. My sleep is often disturbed by worrisome thoughts.	Depressed mood; pessimistic, worrisome, despondent, lethargic
3	Hysteria	I sometimes become flushed for no apparent reason. I tend to take people at their word when they're trying to be nice to me.	Naive, egocentric, little insight into problems, immature; develops physical complaints in response to stress
4	Psychopathic Deviate	My parents often disliked my friends. My behavior sometimes got me into trouble at school.	Difficulties incorporating values of society, rebellious, impulsive, antisocial tendencies; strained family relationships; poor work and school history
5	Masculinity-Femininity	I like reading about electronics. (M) I would like to work in the theater. (F)	Males endorsing feminine attributes: have cultural and artistic interests, effeminate, sensitive, passive Females endorsing male interests: Aggressive, masculine, self-confident, active, assertive, vigorous
6	Paranoia	I would have been more successful in life but people didn't give me a fair break. It's not safe to trust anyone these days.	Suspicious, guarded, blames others, resentful, aloof, may have paranoid delusions
7	Psychasthenia	I'm one of those people who have to have something to worry about. I seem to have more fears than most people I know.	Anxious, fearful, tense, worried, insecure, difficulties concentrating, obsessional, self-doubting
8	Schizophrenia	Things seem unreal to me at times. I sometimes hear things that other people can't hear.	Confused and illogical thinking, feels alienated and misunderstood, socially isolated or withdrawn, may have blatant psychotic symptoms such as hallucinations or delusional beliefs, or may lead detached, schizoid lifestyle
9	Hypomania	I sometimes take on more tasks than I can possibly get done. People have noticed that my speech is sometimes pressured or rushed.	Energetic, possibly manic, impulsive, optimistic, sociable, active, flighty, irritable, may have overly inflated or grandiose self-image or unrealistic plans
10	Social introversion	I don't like loud parties. I was not very active in school activities.	Shy, inhibited, withdrawn, introverted, lacks self-confidence, reserved, anxious in social situations

not tied specifically to DSM criteria, it cannot be used to establish a diagnosis of antisocial personality disorder or any other psychological disorder. Perhaps it is unfair to expect that the MMPI, which was developed under a largely outmoded diagnostic system, should provide diagnostic judgments that are consistent with the current version of the DSM system. Even so, MMPI profiles may suggest possible diagnoses that can be considered in the light of other evidence. Moreover, many clinicians use the MMPI to gain general information about respondents' personality traits and attributes that may underlie their psychological problems, rather than a diagnosis per se.

The MMPI has been revised and restandardized. The new version, the MMPI-2, was renormed on a nationwide sample of some 2,600 normal adults (Graham, 1993), including a proportionate number of African Americans (the original normative group was all white). The revised scale also contains additional validity scales and a new set of scales, called *content scales,* which measure an individual's specific complaints and concerns, such as anxiety, anger, family problems, and problems of low self-esteem. There is also a new adolescent version.

The validity of the original MMPI is supported by a large body of research demonstrating its ability to discriminate between control and psychiatric samples and between groups composed of people with different types of psychological disorders, such as anxiety vs. depressive disorders (Zalewski & Gottesman, 1991). Evidence is mounting supporting the validity of the MMPI-2 as well (e.g., Keiller & Graham, 1993; Finn, 1996). Moreover, the content scales of the MMPI-2 provide additional information to that provided by the clinical scales, which can help clinicians learn more about the client's specific problems (Ben-Porath et al., 1991, 1993; Graham, 1993).

The Millon Clinical Multiaxial Inventory (MCMI)

The MCMI (Millon, 1982) was developed to help the clinician make diagnostic judgments within the multiaxial DSM system, especially in the personality disorders found on Axis II. The MCMI consists of 175 true-false items that yield scores for 20 clinical scales associated with DSM categories.

The MCMI is the only objective personality test that focuses on personality style and disorders (Antoni, Levine, Tischer, Green, & Millon, 1986). The MMPI, in contrast, focuses on personality patterns associated with Axis I diagnoses, such as mood disorders, anxiety disorders, and schizophrenic disorders. Using the MCMI and MMPI in combination may help the clinician make more subtle diagnostic distinctions than are possible with either test alone because they assess different patterns of psychopathology (Antoni, Tischer, Levine, Green, & Millon, 1985; Antoni et al., 1986). However, the relationship between the MCMI and the personality disorders defined in the DSM system remains unclear (Chick et al., 1993; Wetzler, 1990). Researchers find that the MCMI produces too many false positives (i.e., findings of personality disorders that are not confirmed by structured diagnostic interviews) (Guthrie & Mobley, 1994). Other researchers report that among the 11 personality scales on the MCMI that are paired with particular personality disorders in the DSM system, only one, the schizotypal scale, was significantly related to the DSM disorder with which it is matched (i.e., schizotypal personality disorder; discussed in Chapter 8) (Chick et al., 1993). It appears that although the MCMI measures some aspects of personality that are related to personality disorders, it may have only limited value as a diagnostic instrument.

Evaluation of Self-Report Inventories Self-report tests have the benefits of relative ease and economy of administration. Once the examiner has read the instructions to clients, and ascertained they can read and comprehend the items, clients can complete the tests unattended. Because the tests permit limited response options, such as marking items either true or false, they can be scored with high interrater reliability. Moreover, the accumulation of research findings on respondents provides a quantified basis for interpreting test responses. Such tests often reveal information that might not be revealed during a clinical interview or by observing the person's behavior.

A disadvantage of self-rating tests is that they rely on clients as the source of data. Test responses may therefore reflect underlying response biases, such as tendencies to answer items in a socially desirable direction, rather than accurate self-perceptions. For this reason, self-report inventories like the MMPI contain validity scales to help ferret out response biases. Yet even these validity scales may not detect all sources of bias (Nicholson et al., 1997). Examiners may also look for corroborating information, such as interviewing others who are familiar with the client's behavior.

Tests are also only as valid as the criteria that were used to validate them. The original MMPI was limited in its role as a diagnostic instrument by virtue of the obsolete diagnostic categories that were used to classify the original clinical groups. Moreover, if a test does nothing more than identify people who are likely to belong to a particular diagnostic category, its utility is usurped by more economical means of arriving at diagnoses, such as the structured clinical interview. We expect more from personality tests than diagnostic classification, and the MMPI has shown its value in showing personality characteristics associated with people with certain response patterns. Psychodynamically oriented critics suggest that self-report instruments tell us little about possible unconscious processes. The use of such tests may also be limited to relatively high functioning individuals who can read well, respond to verbal material, and focus on a potentially tedious task. Clients who are disorganized, unstable, or confused may not be able to complete tests.

Projective Personality Tests

Projective tests, unlike objective tests, offer no clear, specified answers. Clients are presented with ambiguous stimuli, such as vague drawings or inkblots, and are usually asked to describe what the stimuli look like or to relate stories about them. The tests are called projective because they were derived from the psychodynamic *projective hypothesis,* the belief that people impose, or "project," their psychological needs, drives, and motives, much of which may lie in the unconscious, onto their interpretations of unstructured or ambiguous stimuli.

The psychodynamic model holds that potentially disturbing impulses and wishes, often of a sexual or aggressive nature, are often hidden from consciousness by defense mechanisms. Defense mechanisms may thwart direct probing of threatening material. Indirect methods of assessment, however, such as projective tests, may offer clues to unconscious processes. More behaviorally oriented critics contend, however, that the results of projective tests are based more on clinicians' subjective interpretations of test responses than on empirical evidence.

The two most prominent projective techniques are the Rorschach inkblot test and the Thematic Apperception Test (TAT).

Rorschach Inkblot Test
The Renaissance artist and inventor Leonardo da Vinci suggested that individual differences could be studied by means of people's interpretations of cloud formations. A century later, Shakespeare's Hamlet toyed with Polonius by suggesting alternately that a cloud formation resembled a camel, a hunched weasel, or a whale. Polonius showed more political savvy than integrity because he agreed with each suggestion. Hamlet saw through him, of course. Today, some clinicians use a psychological test—the Rorschach—in which a person's response to inkblots is used to form diagnostic impressions.

Hermann Rorschach (1884–1922), a Swiss psychiatrist, also believed ambiguous figures could be used to help clinicians "see through"—or better understand—people with psychological problems. Rorschach turned to inkblots and not clouds, however. As a child, Rorschach was intrigued by the game of dripping ink on paper and folding the paper to make symmetrical figures. He noted that people saw different things in the same blot, and he believed their "percepts" reflected their personalities as well as the stimulus cues provided by the blot. In high school his fellows gave him the nickname *Klecks,* which means "inkblot" in German. As a psychiatrist, Rorschach experimented with hundreds of blots to identify those that could help in the diagnosis of psychological problems. He finally found a group of 15 blots that seemed to do the job and could be administered in a single session. Ten blots are used today because Rorschach's publisher did not have the funds to reproduce all 15 blots in the first edition of the text on the subject. Rorschach never had the opportunity to learn how popular

FIGURE 2.3 *An inkblot similar to those found on the Rorschach Inkblot Test.*
What does the blot look like to you? What could it be? Rorschach assumed that people project their personalities into their responses to ambiguous inkblots as well as respond to the stimulus characteristics of the blot.

and influential his inkblot test would become. The year following its publication, at the age of 38, he died of complications from a ruptured appendix.

Five of the inkblots are black and white and the other five have color (see Figure 2.3). Each inkblot is printed on a separate card, which is handed to subjects in sequence. Subjects are asked to tell the examiner what the blot might be or what it reminds them of.

Most systems for scoring responses refer to the *location, determinants, content,* and *form level* of responses. After the subject has responded to all cards, the examiner conducts an **inquiry** to clarify which aspects of the blot gave rise to the responses.

The location is the area of the blot selected—the whole card or a prominent or minor detail. **Determinants** include properties of the blot such as form, shading, texture, or color that inspire the response, and features of the percept the respondent imposes upon, or reads into, the blot, such as **movement**—perceiving figures as animated, as running, dancing, or flying. The content is the *what* of the percept, for instance a winged creature, a jack-o'-lantern, or a torso. **Form level** signifies (1) the consistency of a response with the shape of the blot and (2) the complexity of the response.

Clinicians who use the Rorschach tend to interpret responses in the following ways. Clients who use the entire blot in their responses show ability to perceive part-whole relationships and integrate events in meaningful ways. People whose responses are based solely on minor details may have obsessive-compulsive tendencies that, in psychodynamic theory, protect them from having to cope with the larger issues in their lives. Clients who respond to the negative (white) spaces tend to see things in their own way, suggestive of negativism or stubbornness.

Relationships between form and color are suggestive of clients' capacity to control impulses. When clients use color but are primarily guided by the form of the blots, they are believed capable of feeling deeply but also of holding their feelings in check. When color predominates—as in perceiving any reddened area as "blood"—clients may not be able to exercise control over impulses. A response consistent with the form or contours of the blot is suggestive of adequate **reality testing**. People who see movement in the blots may be revealing intelligence and creativity. Content analysis may shed light on underlying conflicts. For example, adult clients who see animals but no people may have problems relating to people. Clients who appear confused about whether or not percepts of people are male or female may, according to psychodynamic theory, be in conflict over their own gender.

Evaluation of the Rorschach The validity of the Rorschach has been the subject of extensive debate. One problem was the lack of a standard scoring procedure. Interpretation of clients' responses is not objective; it depends to some degree on the subjective judgment of the examiner. Two examiners may interpret the same Rorschach response differently. Recent attempts to develop a comprehensive scoring approach, such as the Exner system (Exner, 1991, 1993), have advanced the effort to standardize scoring of responses. But the debate over the reliability of the Rorschach, including the Exner system, continues (see G. J. Meyer, 1997; Wood, Nezworski, & Stejskal, 1996, 1997). Yet even if a Rorschach response can be scored reliably, the interpretation of the response—what it means—remains an open question.

Critics and even some proponents of the Rorschach technique such as Hertz (1986) recognize that evidence is lacking to support the interpretation of some particular responses. Though evidence supporting the validity of various aspects of the Rorschach has accumulated (see K. C. H. Parker, Hanson, & Hinsley, 1988; G. J. Meyer & Handler, 1997; Shontz & Green, 1992; Ornberg & Zalewski, 1994; Leavitt & Labott, 1997; R. F. Bornstein, 1996; I. B. Weiner, 1996, 1997), the validity of the test continues to be hotly debated among psychologists (e.g., Wood et al., 1996). Perhaps the Rorschach should be thought of more as a method for gathering information about the ways in which individuals construct meaning from unstructured or ambiguous situations (Blatt, 1986) than as a formal personality test per se (I. B. Weiner, 1994).

The Thematic Apperception Test (TAT)
The Thematic Apperception Test (TAT) was developed by psychologist Henry Murray (1943) at Harvard University in the 1930s. *Apperception* is from a French word that can be translated as "interpreting (new ideas or impressions) on the basis of existing ideas (cognitive structures) and past experience." The TAT consists of a series of cards, like that shown in Figure 2.4, each of which depicts an ambiguous scene.

FIGURE 2.4 *A drawing similar to those found on the Thematic Apperception Test (TAT).*
Psychologists ask test-takers to provide their impressions of what is happening in the scene depicted in the drawing. They ask test-takers what led up to the scene and how it will turn out. How might your responses reveal aspects of your own personality?

Respondents are asked to construct stories about the cards. It is assumed their tales reflect their experiences and outlooks on life—and, perhaps, also shed light on deep-seated needs and conflicts.

Respondents are asked to describe what is happening in each scene, what led up to it, what the characters are thinking and feeling, and what will happen next. Psychodynamically oriented clinicians assume that respondents identify with the protagonists in their stories and project their psychological needs and conflicts into the events they *apperceive*. On a more superficial level, the stories also suggest how respondents might interpret or behave in similar situations in their own lives. TAT results are also suggestive of clients' attitudes toward others, particularly family members and lovers.

The TAT has been used extensively in research on motivation as well as in clinical practice. For example, psychologist David McClelland (e.g., McClelland, Alexander, & Marks, 1982) helped pioneer the TAT assessment of social motives such as the needs for achievement and power. The rationales for this research are that we are likely to be somewhat preoccupied with our needs, and our needs are projected into our reactions to ambiguous stimuli and situations.

Evaluation of the TAT   One criticism of the TAT is that the stimulus properties of some of the cards, such as cues depicting sadness or anger, may exert too strong a "stimulus pull" on the subject. The pictures themselves may pull for certain types of stories. If so, clients' responses may represent reactions to the stimulus cues rather than projections of their personalities (Murstein & Mathes, 1996). The TAT, like the Rorschach, is open to criticism that the scoring and interpretation of responses largely depends on the clinician's subjective impressions. The validity of the TAT in eliciting deep-seated material or tapping underlying psychopathology also remains to be demonstrated.

One general problem with the projective instruments such as the TAT and Rorschach is the more healthy test-takers talk or see in response to projective instruments, the more likely they will be judged as having psychological problems (Murstein & Mathes, 1996). Proponents of projective testing argue that in skilled hands, tests like the TAT and the Rorschach can yield meaningful material that might not be revealed in interviews or by self-rating inventories. Moreover, allowing subjects freedom of expression through projective testing reduces the tendency of individuals to offer socially desirable responses. Despite the lack of direct evidence for the projective hypothesis, the appeal of projective tests among clinicians remains high (Lubin, Larsen, & Makarazzo, 1984; Lubin, Larsen, Makarazzo, & Seever, 1985).

NEUROPSYCHOLOGICAL ASSESSMENT

Neuropsychological assessment is used to evaluate whether or not psychological problems reflect underlying neurological damage or brain defects. When neurological impairment is suspected, a neurological evaluation may be requested from a *neurologist*—a medical doctor who specializes in disorders of the nervous system. A clinical *neuropsychologist* may also be consulted to administer neuropsychological assessment techniques, such as behavioral observation and psychological testing, to reveal signs of possible brain damage. Neuropsychological tests not only suggest whether or not clients are suffering from brain damage but may also suggest which parts of the brain may be involved.

The Bender Visual Motor Gestalt Test

One of the first neuropsychological tests to be developed was the Bender Visual Motor Gestalt test (Bender, 1938). "The Bender" consists of geometric figures that illustrate various Gestalt principles of perception. The client is asked to copy nine geometric designs (see Figure 2.5). Signs of possible brain damage include rotation of the figures, distortions in shape, and incorrect sizing of the figures in relation to

one another. The examiner then asks the client to reproduce the designs from memory because neurological damage can impair memory functioning.

Although the Bender remains a convenient and economical means of uncovering possible organic impairment, it has been criticized for producing too many **false negatives**—that is, persons with neurological impairment who make satisfactory drawings (Bigler & Erhenfurth, 1981). In recent years, more sophisticated tests have been developed.

The Halstead-Reitan Neuropsychological Battery

The Halstead-Reitan Neuropsychological Battery may be the most widely used neuropsychological battery. Psychologist Ralph Reitan developed the battery by adapting tests used by his mentor, Ward Halstead, an experimental psychologist, to study brain-behavior relationships among organically impaired individuals. The battery contains tests that measure perceptual, intellectual, and motor skills and performance. A battery of tests permits the psychologist to observe patterns of results, and various patterns of performance deficits are suggestive of certain kinds of organic defects. The tests in the battery include the following:

1. *The Category Test.*   This test measures abstract thinking ability, as indicated by the individual's proficiency at forming principles or categories that relate different stimuli to one another. A series of groups of stimuli that vary in shape, size, location, color, and other characteristics are flashed on a screen. The subject's task is to discern the principle that links them, such as shape or size, and to indicate which stimuli in each grouping represent the correct category by pressing a key. By analyzing the patterns of correct and incorrect choices, the subject normally learns to identify the principles that determine the correct choice. Performance on the test is believed to reflect functioning in the frontal lobe of the brain.

2. *The Rhythm Test.*   This is a test of concentration and attention. The subject listens to 30 pairs of tape-recorded rhythmic beats and indicates whether the beats in each pair are the same or different. Performance deficits are associated with damage to the right temporal area of the brain.

3. *The Tactual Performance Test.*   This test requires the blindfolded subject to fit wooden blocks of different shapes into corresponding depressions on a form board. Afterward, the subject draws the board from memory as a measure of visual memory.

The Luria Nebraska Test Battery

The Luria Nebraska Test Battery is based on the work of the Russian neuropsychologist A. R. Luria and was developed by psychologists at the University of Nebraska (C. J. Golden, Hammeke, & Purisch, 1980). Like the Halstead-Reitan, the Luria Nebraska reveals patterns of skill deficits that are

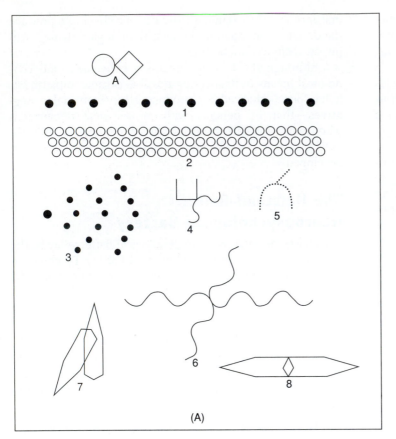

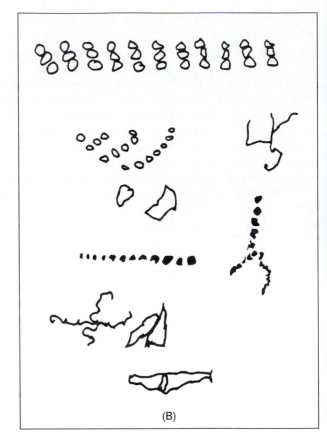

FIGURE 2.5 *The Bender Gestalt Test.*
The Bender is intended to assess organic impairment. Part A shows the series of figures respondents are asked to copy. Part B shows the drawings of a person who is known to be brain-damaged.

suggestive of particular sites of brain damage. The Luria Nebraska is more efficiently administered than the Halstead-Reitan, requiring about one third of the time to complete.

A wide range of skills is assessed. Tests measure tactile, kinesthetic, and spatial skills; complex motor skills; auditory skills; receptive and expressive speech skills; reading, writing, and arithmetic skills; and general intelligence and memory functioning. Although the Luria Nebraska is promising, more research is needed to substantiate its reliability and validity.

Neuropsychological tests attempt to reveal brain dysfunctions without surgical procedures. We later consider other contemporary techniques that figuratively and literally allow us to see inside the brain without surgery.

BEHAVIORAL ASSESSMENT

The traditional model of assessment, or **psychometric approach,** holds that psychological tests reveal *signs* of reasonably stable traits or dispositions that largely determine people's behavior. The psychometric approach aims to classify people in terms of personality types according to traits such as anxiety, introversion-extraversion, obsessiveness, hostility, impulsivity, and aggressiveness. This model inspired de-

velopment of trait-based tests such as the Rorschach, TAT, and the MMPI.

The alternative model of **behavioral assessment** treats test results as samples of behavior that occur in specific situations rather than signs of underlying personality types or traits. According to the behavioral approach, behavior is primarily determined by environmental or situational factors, such as stimulus cues and reinforcements.

The behavioral model has inspired the development of techniques that aim to sample an individual's behavior in settings as similar as possible to the real-life situation, thus maximizing the relationship between the testing situation and the criterion. Behavior may be observed and measured in such settings as the home, school, or work environment. The examiner may also try to simulate situations in the clinic or laboratory that serve as analogues of the problems the individual confronts in daily life.

The examiner may conduct a **functional analysis** of the problem behavior—relating it to the *antecedents,* or stimulus cues that trigger it, and the *consequences,* or reinforcements that maintain it. Knowledge of the environmental conditions in which a problem behavior occurs may help the therapist work with the client and the family to change the conditions that trigger and maintain it.

Consider the case of Kerry:

> *A 7-year-old boy, Kerry, is brought by his parents for evaluation. His mother describes him as a "royal terror." His father complains he won't listen to anyone. Kerry throws temper tantrums in the supermarket, screaming and stomping his feet if his parents refuse to buy him what he wants. At home, he breaks his toys by throwing them against the wall and demands new ones. Sometimes, though, he appears sullen and won't talk to anyone for hours. At school he appears inhibited and has difficulty concentrating. His progress at school is slow and he has difficulty reading. His teachers complain he has a limited attention span and doesn't seem motivated.*
>
> THE AUTHORS' FILES

The psychologist may use direct home observation to assess the interactions between Kerry and his parents. Alternatively, the psychologist may observe Kerry and his parents through a one-way mirror in the clinic. Such observations may suggest interactions that explain the child's noncompliance. For example, Kerry's noncompliance may follow parental requests that are vague (e.g., a parent says, "Play nicely now," and Kerry responds by throwing toys) or inconsistent (e.g., a parent says, "Go play with your toys but don't make a mess," to which Kerry responds by scattering the toys). Observation may suggest ways in which Kerry's parents can improve communication and cue and reinforce desirable behaviors.

Clinicians may directly observe children's school behavior in the classroom or ask teachers to complete behavior rating scales that highlight problem behaviors that can be targeted for treatment. Clinicians can also observe children in the clinic performing school tasks, such as math problems, so as to evaluate their approach to problem solving and possible deficits in attention or concentration.

Behavioral clinicians may supplement behavioral observations with traditional forms of assessment, such as the MMPI, or perhaps even with projective tests, such as the Rorschach or TAT. However, they are likely to interpret test data as samples of clients' behavior at a particular point in time, and not as signs of stable traits. Trait-oriented clinicians may similarly employ behavioral assessment to learn how personality "traits" are "revealed" in different settings and to see how particular traits affect clients' daily functioning.

Let us consider some of the techniques of behavioral assessment.

The Behavioral Interview

The **behavioral interview** poses questions to learn more about the history and situational aspects of problem behavior. Like other interviewers, the behavioral interviewer establishes rapport with clients and evaluates clients' nonverbal behaviors. But the behavioral interview focuses more on the situational factors that relate to the problem behavior than is typically the case in the standard interview. If a client seeks help because of panic attacks, the behavioral interviewer might ask how the client experiences these attacks—when, where, how often, under what circumstances. The interviewer looks for precipitating cues, such as thought patterns (e.g., thoughts of dying or losing control) or situational factors (e.g., entering a department store) that may provoke an attack. The interviewer also seeks information about reinforcers that may maintain the panic. Does the client flee the situation when an attack occurs? Is escape reinforced by relief from anxiety? Has the client learned to lessen anticipatory anxiety by avoiding exposure to situations in which attacks have occurred?

How have other aspects of the client's life been affected by the problem behavior? Do family members treat the client differently? (Have they changed patterns of reinforcement?) For example, have family members assumed added responsibilities to relieve the client of stress, thereby reinforcing dependent behavior? Does the client possess behavioral competencies or skills—such as self-relaxation skills—for coping with the problem? Do skill deficits such as communication or social skills deficits impede progress in coping?

The behavioral interviewer may also assess cognitive factors that affect the problem behavior. The interviewer may ask the client to relate any thoughts she or he can associate with an attack. The interviewer might probe the client's attitudes and beliefs to ascertain whether dysfunctional beliefs (such as mislabeling a minor bodily sensation as a sign of an impending heart attack) are present in the chain of events that led to a panic attack.

Self-Monitoring

Training clients to record or monitor the problem behavior in their daily lives is a direct method of relating problem behavior to the settings in which it occurs. In **self-monitoring**, clients assume the primary responsibility for assessing the problem behavior.

An early example of self-monitoring was described by Benjamin Franklin, one of the founding fathers of the United States and a signer of the Declaration of Independence. In his effort to improve his behavior, he kept records of the daily frequency of faulty behaviors that reflected on 13 "virtues":

> I made a book, in which I allotted a page for each of the virtues. I ruled each page with red ink, so as to have seven columns, one for each day of the week, marking each column with a letter for the day. I crossed these columns with thirteen red lines, marking the beginning of each line with the first letter of one of the virtues, on which line, and in its proper column, I might mark by a little black spot every fault I found upon examination to have been committed respecting that virtue upon that day. (Cited in Thoresen & Mahoney, 1974, p. 41)

Benjamin Franklin. An early example of self-recording is found in the diaries kept by Benjamin Franklin, one of our country's founding fathers. In an attempt to improve his behavior, Franklin kept a daily record of his faulty behaviors.

Franklin's diary is akin to contemporary self-monitoring of "nonvirtuous" behaviors such as cigarette smoking or overeating. Self-monitoring permits direct measurement of the problem behavior when and where it occurs. Behaviors that can be easily counted, such as food intake, cigarette smoking, nail-biting, hair pulling, study periods, or social activities are well suited for self-monitoring. Clients are usually best aware of the frequency of these behaviors and their situational contexts. Self-monitoring can also produce highly accurate measurement because the behavior is recorded as it occurs, not reconstructed from memory.

TRUTH or FICTION REVISITED

2.6 True. Benjamin Franklin made use of a self-recording or diary method for keeping track of his faulty behaviors.

There are various devices for keeping track of the targeted behavior. A behavioral diary or log, like Franklin's, is a handy way to record calories ingested or cigarettes smoked. Such logs are organized in columns and rows to track the frequency of occurrence of the problem behavior and the

situations in which it occurs (time, setting, feeling state, etc.). A record of eating may include entries for the type of food eaten, the number of calories, the location in which the eating occurred, the feeling states associated with eating, and the consequences of eating (e.g., how the client felt afterward). In reviewing an eating diary with the clinician, a client can identify problematic eating patterns, such as eating when feeling bored or in response to TV food commercials, and devise better ways of handling these cues.

Behavioral diaries can also help clients increase desirable but low-frequency behaviors, such as assertive behavior and dating behavior. Unassertive clients might track occasions that seem to warrant an assertive response and jot down their actual responses to each occasion. Clients and clinicians then review the log to highlight problematic situations and rehearse assertive responses. A client who is anxious about dating might record social contacts with the opposite gender. To measure the effects of treatment, clinicians may encourage clients to engage in a baseline period of self-monitoring before treatment is begun.

Self-monitoring, though, is not without its disadvantages. Some clients are unreliable and do not keep accurate records. They become forgetful or sloppy, or they underreport undesirable behaviors, such as overeating or smoking, because of embarrassment or fear of criticism. To offset these biases, clinicians may, with clients' consent, corroborate the accuracy of self-monitoring by gathering information from other parties, such as clients' spouses. Private behaviors such as eating or smoking alone cannot be corroborated in this way, however. Sometimes other means of corroboration, such as physiological measures, are available. For example, biochemical analysis of the carbon monoxide in clients' breath samples or of nicotine metabolites in their saliva or blood can be used to corroborate reports of abstinence from smoking.

Another issue in self-monitoring is *reactivity,* or changes in measured behavior that stem from the act of measurement. Some clients may change undesirable behaviors merely as a consequence of focusing on them or recording them. When reactivity leads to more adaptive behavior, it renders the measurement process an effective therapeutic tool, although it can make it difficult to tease out the effects due to measurement from those due to treatment.

Self-monitoring may actually be an important, perhaps even necessary feature of some behavior change programs, such as weight management programs. A recent study showed that the more consistently participants monitored what they ate, the more weight they lost (Baker & Kirschenbaum, 1993). This is not to imply that self-monitoring alone is sufficient to produce a desired behavior change. Motivation to change and skills needed to make behavior changes are also important.

Analogue or Contrived Measures

Analogue or contrived measures are intended to simulate the setting in which the behavior naturally takes place but

Behavioral approach task. One form of behavioral assessment of phobia involves measurement of the degree to which the person can approach or interact with the phobic stimulus. Here we see a woman with a snake phobia tentatively reaching out to touch the phobic object. Other people with snake phobias would not be able to touch the snake or even remain in its presence unless it was securely caged.

are carried out in laboratory or controlled settings. Role-playing exercises are common analogue measures. Clinicians cannot follow clients who have difficulty expressing dissatisfaction to authority figures throughout the day. Instead, clinicians may rely on role-playing exercises, such as having the clients enact challenging an unfair grade. A scene might be described to the client as follows: "You've worked very hard on a term paper and received a very poor grade, say a D or an F. You approach the professor, who asks, 'Is there some problem?' What do you do now?" The client's enactment of the scene may reveal deficits in self-expression that can be addressed in therapy or assertiveness training.

The Behavioral Approach Task, or BAT, is a popular analogue measure of a phobic person's approach to a feared object, such as a snake. Approach behavior is broken down into levels of response, such as looking in the direction of the snake from about 20 feet, touching the box holding the snake, and touching the snake. The BAT provides direct measurement of a response to a stimulus in a controlled situation. The subject's approach behavior can be quantified by assigning a score to each level of approach.

Direct Observation

Direct observation, or behavioral observation, is the hallmark of behavioral assessment. Through behavioral observation, clinicians can observe and quantify problem behavior. Observations may be videotaped to permit subsequent analysis of behavioral patterns. Observers are trained to identify and record targeted patterns of behavior. Behav-

ior coding systems have been developed that enhance the reliability of recording.

There are advantages and disadvantages to direct observation. One advantage is that direct observation does not rely on the client's self-reports, which may be distorted by efforts to make a favorable or unfavorable impression. In addition to providing accurate measurements of problem behavior, behavioral observation can suggest strategies for intervention. A mother might report that her son is so hyperactive he cannot sit still long enough to complete homework assignments. By using a one-way mirror, the clinician may discover the boy becomes restless only when he encounters a problem he cannot solve right away. The child may thus be helped by being taught ways of coping with frustration and of solving certain kinds of academic problems.

Direct observation also has its drawbacks. One issue is the possible lack of consensus in defining problems in behavioral terms. In coding the child's behavior for hyperactivity, clinicians must agree on which aspects of the child's behavior represent hyperactivity. Another potential problem is a lack of reliability, or inconsistency, of measurement across time or between observers. Reliability is reduced when an observer is inconsistent in the coding of specific behaviors or when two or more observers code behavior inconsistently.

Observers may also show response biases. An observer who has been sensitized to expect that a child is hyperactive may perceive normal variations in behavior as subtle cues of hyperactivity and erroneously record them as instances of hyperactive behavior. Such expectations are less likely to affect behavioral ratings when the target behaviors are defined concretely (S. L. Foster & Cone, 1986).

People may also put their best feet forward when they know they are being observed. This tendency may be reduced by using covert observation techniques, such as hidden cameras or one-way mirrors. Covert observation may not be feasible, however, because of ethical concerns or practical constraints. Another approach is to accustom subjects to observation by watching them a number of times before collecting data (S. L. Foster & Cone, 1986).

Another potential problem is *observer drift*—the tendency of observers, or groups of raters, to deviate from the coding system in which they were trained as time elapses. One suggestion to help control this problem is to regularly retrain observers to ensure continued compliance with the coding system (Kazdin, 1992). As time elapses, observers may also become fatigued or distracted. It may be helpful to limit the duration of observations and to provide frequent breaks.

Behavioral observation is limited to measuring overt behaviors. Many clinicians also wish to assess subjective or private experiences—for example, feelings of depression and anxiety or distorted thought patterns. Such clinicians may combine direct observation with forms of assessment that permit clients to reveal internal experiences. Staunch behavioral clinicians tend to consider self-reports unreliable and to limit their data to direct observation.

Behavioral Rating Scales

A **behavioral rating scale** is a checklist that provides information about the frequency, intensity, and range of problem behaviors. Behavioral rating scales differ from self-report personality inventories, in that items assess specific behaviors rather than personality characteristics, interests, or attitudes.

Behavioral rating scales are often used by parents to assess children's problem behaviors. The Child Behavior Problem Checklist (CBCL) (Achenbach, 1978; Achenbach & Edelbrock, 1979), for example, asks parents to rate their children on more than 100 specific problem behaviors, including the following:

_____ refuses to eat
_____ is disobedient
_____ hits
_____ is uncooperative
_____ destroys own things

The scale yields an overall problem behavior score and subscale scores on dimensions such as delinquency, aggressiveness, and physical problems. The clinician can compare the child's score on these dimensions with norms based on samples of age-mates.

COGNITIVE ASSESSMENT

Cognitive assessment involves the measurement of cognitions—thoughts, beliefs, and attitudes. Cognitive therapists believe that people who hold self-defeating or dysfunctional cognitions are at greater risk of developing emotional problems, such as depression, in the face of stressful or disappointing life experiences. They help clients replace dysfunctional thinking patterns with self-enhancing, rational thought patterns.

Several methods of cognitive assessment have been developed. One of the most straightforward is the thought record or diary. Depressed clients may carry such diaries to record dysfunctional thoughts as they arise. Aaron Beck (A. T. Beck, Rush, Shaw, and Emery, 1979) designed a thought diary or "Daily Record of Dysfunctional Thoughts" to help clients identify thought patterns that are connected with troubling emotional states. Each time the client experiences a negative emotion such as anger or sadness, entries are made to identify

1. The situation in which the emotional state occurred,
2. The automatic or disruptive thoughts that passed through the client's mind,
3. The type or category of disordered thinking that the automatic thought(s) represented (e.g., selective abstraction, overgeneralization, magnification, or absolutist thinking—see Chapter 1),
4. A rational response to the troublesome thought,
5. The emotional outcome or final emotional response.

A thought diary can become part of a treatment program in which the client learns to replace dysfunctional thoughts with rational alternative thoughts.

Cognitive assessment of Pamela's travel phobia (see p. 64) might involve asking her to describe the thoughts that pass through her mind when she imagines herself approaching the fearful situation. Pamela might also be asked to keep a diary of the thoughts she experiences while preparing for a drive, or while driving toward a phobic stimulus such as a bridge or an overpass. By examining her imagined and **in vivo** thoughts, the therapist can help Pamela identify styles of thinking that are linked to phobic episodes, such as catastrophizing ("I'm going to lose control of the car") and self-deprecation ("I'm just a jerk. I can't handle anything"). Several more formal methods of assessing cognitions assessment have been developed, including those described next.

Methods of Cognitive Assessment

The Automatic Thoughts Questionnaire (ATQ-30; Hollon & Kendall, 1980) has clients rate the weekly frequency and degree of conviction associated with 30 automatic negative thoughts. (Automatic thoughts are thoughts that seem to just pop into our minds.) Sample items include the following:

I don't think I can go on.
I hate myself.
I've let people down.

A total score is obtained by summing the frequencies of occurrence of each item. Higher scores are considered typical of depressive thought patterns. The scale discriminates between college students who attain high or low scores on the Beck Depression Inventory (Hollon & Kendall, 1980) and among depressed psychiatric outpatients, nondepressed psychiatric patients, and nondepressed people (Harrel & Ryon, 1983). The 30-item ATQ has been statistically sorted into four categories or factors of related thoughts (Hollon & Kendall, 1980; see Table 2.11).

A similar measure, the 26-item Cognition Checklist (CCL), contains a listing of 26 anxious or depressing thoughts of a type similar to such items as "I'm a failure," and "I feel like something terrible is going to happen to me" (Beck et al., 1987). Clients rate the frequency of occurrence of these thoughts to give clinicians a sense of whether they are troubled by the kinds of disruptive thoughts that people with anxiety and depressive disorders frequently encounter (Steer et al., 1994).

Another cognitive measure, the Dysfunctional Attitudes Scale (DAS; A. T. Beck et al., 1991; A. N. Weissman & Beck, 1978), consists of an inventory of beliefs or attitudes believed to measure vulnerability to depression. Examples include "I feel like I'm nothing if someone I love doesn't love me back." Subjects use a 7-point scale to rate the degree to which they endorse each belief. Recent evidence suggests that the DAS may actually be measuring depression itself, rather than vulnerability to depression (Calhoon, 1996).

TABLE 2.11

Items Defining Factors on the Automatic Thoughts Questionnaire

Factor 1: Personal Maladjustment and Desire for Change	Something has to change. What's the matter with me? I wish I were a better person. What's wrong with me? I'm so disappointed in myself.
Factor 2: Negative Self-Concept and Negative Expectations	My future is bleak. I'm a failure. I'll never make it. My life's not going the way I wanted it to. I'm a loser. Why can't I ever succeed? I'm no good.
Factor 3: Low Self-Esteem	I'm worthless. I hate myself.
Factor 4: Giving Up/Helplessness	I can't finish anything. It's just not worth it.

Source: Adapted from Hollon & Kendall (1980).

Whatever the case, it clearly taps into a style of thinking associated with depression.

Evaluation of Cognitive Assessment   Cognitive assessment opens a new domain to the psychologist in understanding how disruptive thoughts are related to abnormal behavior. Only in the past two decades or so have cognitive and cognitive-behavioral therapists begun to explore what Skinner labeled the "black box"—people's internal states—to learn how thoughts and attitudes influence emotional states and behavior.

The behavioral objection to cognitive techniques is that clinicians have no direct means of verifying clients' subjective experiences, their thoughts and beliefs. These are private experiences that can be reported but not observed and measured directly. Even though thoughts remain private experiences, reports of cognitions in the form of rating scales or checklists can be quantified and validated by reference to external criteria.

PHYSIOLOGICAL MEASUREMENT

We can also learn about abnormal behavior by studying people's physiological responses. Anxiety, for example, is associated with arousal of the sympathetic division of the autonomic nervous system (see Chapter 1). Anxious people therefore show elevated heart rates and blood pressure, which can be measured directly by means of the pulse and a blood pressure cuff. People also sweat more heavily when they are anxious. When we sweat, our skin becomes wet, increasing its ability to conduct electricity. Sweating can be measured by means of the **electrodermal response** or **galvanic skin response** (GSR). (*Electrodermal* contains the Greek word *derma,* meaning "skin." *Galvanic* is named after

the Italian physicist and physician, Luigi Galvani, who was a pioneer in research in electricity.) Measures of the GSR assess the amount of electricity that passes through two points on the skin, usually of the hand. We assume the person's anxiety level correlates with the amount of electricity conducted across the skin.

The GSR is just one example of a physiological response that is measured through probes or sensors connected to the body. Another example is the **electroencephalograph** (EEG), which measures brain waves by attaching electrodes to the scalp.

Changes in muscle tension are also often associated with states of anxiety or tension. They can be detected through the **electromyograph** (EMG), which monitors muscle tension through sensors attached to targeted muscle groups. (*Myo-* derives from the Greek *mys,* meaning "mouse" or "muscle." The Greeks observed that muscles moved mouselike beneath the skin.) Placement of EMG probes on the forehead can indicate muscle tension associated with tension headaches. Other probes are used to assess sexual arousal (see Chapter 11).

Ambulatory blood pressure devices allow clinicians to monitor clients' blood pressure at intervals throughout the day. Clients may log their concurrent activities or feeling states to reveal how changes in blood pressure are connected with stress.

Response Systems

P. J. Lang (1968) suggested that fear or anxiety consists of three different response systems: behavioral, physiological, and verbal. The behavioral response is avoidance of fear-inducing objects or situations. The physiological response can be measured in terms of changes in heart rate, GSR, or other bodily responses. The verbal system involves measurement of the subjective experience of anxiety. These response systems may act independently, however, so changes in one may not generalize to another. For example, people may report they feel progressively less anxious when they confront a fearful situation, but their hearts may continue to pound. Or people may be able to approach a phobic situation though they report lingering feelings of anxiety or fear. Because response systems can be independent, most researchers recommend that investigations include multiple measures of anxiety or fear across response domains, such as self-report of subjective feelings, behavioral approach measures, and physiological measurement.

Probing the Workings of the Brain

Researchers and clinicians use various techniques to study the structure and function of the brain without the need for surgery. One of the most common is the electroencephalograph (EEG), which is a record of the electrical activity of the brain (Figure 2.6). The EEG detects minute amounts of electrical activity in the brain, or brain waves, that are conducted between electrodes. Certain brain wave patterns are associated with mental states such as relaxation and with the different stages of sleep. The EEG is used to examine brain wave patterns associated with psychological disorders, such as schizophrenia, and with brain damage. It is also used to study various abnormal behavior patterns. The EEG is also used by medical personnel to reveal brain abnormalities such as tumors.

Brain-imaging techniques generate images that reflect the structure and functioning of the brain. In **computed tomography** (the CT scan), a narrow X-ray beam is aimed at the head (Figure 2.7). The radiation that passes through is measured from multiple angles. The CT scan reveals abnormalities in shape and structure that may be suggestive of lesions, blood clots, or tumors. The computer enables scientists to integrate the measurements into a three-dimensional picture of the brain. Evidence of brain damage that was once detectable only by surgery may now be displayed on a monitor.

Another imaging method, **positron emission tomography** (the PET scan), is used to study the functioning of various parts of the brain (Figure 2.8). In this method, a small amount of a radioactive compound or tracer is mixed with glucose and injected into the bloodstream. When it reaches the brain, patterns of neural activity are revealed by measurement of the positrons—positively charged particles—emitted by the tracer. The glucose metabolized by parts of the brain generates a computer image of neural activity. Areas of greater activity metabolize more glucose. The PET

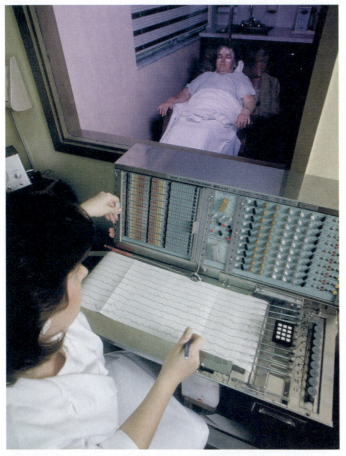

FIGURE 2.6 *The Electroencephalogram (EEG).*
The EEG is a record of brain wave activity as recorded by an electro-encephalograph. The EEG can be used to study differences in brain waves between groups of normal people and people with problems such as schizophrenia or organic brain damage.

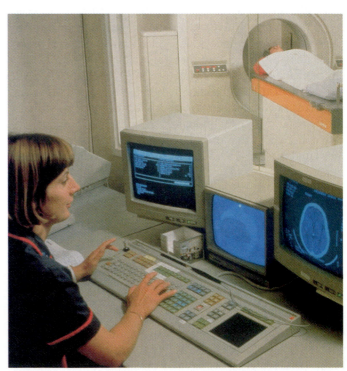

FIGURE 2.7 *The computerized axial tomography (CT) scan.*
The CT scan aims a narrow X-ray beam at the head, and the resultant radiation is measured from multiple angles as it passes through. The computer enables researchers to consolidate the measurements into a three-dimensional image of the brain. The CT scan reveals structural abnormalities in the brain that may be implicated in various patterns of abnormal behavior.

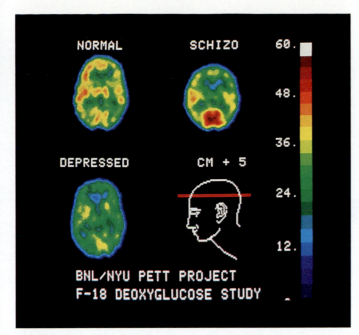

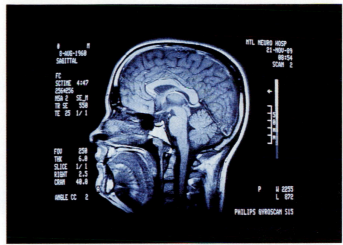

FIGURE 2.9 *Magnetic resonance imaging (MRI).*
In MRI, the person is placed in a donut-shaped tunnel that generates a strong magnetic field. Radio waves are directed at the brain, which emit signals that are measured from several angles and integrated into a computer-generated image of the brain.

FIGURE 2.8 *The positron emission tomography (PET) scan.*
In the PET scan, a small amount of a radioactive tracer is mixed with glucose and injected into the bloodstream. When it reaches the brain, patterns of neural activity are revealed by measurement of the positively charged particles that are emitted by the tracer. The glucose metabolized by parts of the brain generates a computer image of neural activity. Areas of greater activity metabolize more glucose. These PET scan images suggest differences in the metabolic processes of the brains of people with depression, schizophrenia, and controls who are free of psychological disorders.

scan has been used to learn which parts of the brain are most active (metabolize more glucose) when we are listening to music, solving a math problem, or using language. It can also be used to reveal differences in brain activity in people with schizophrenia (see Chapter 12).

A third imaging technique is **magnetic resonance imaging** (MRI) (Figure 2.9). In MRI, the person is placed in a donut-shaped tunnel that generates a strong magnetic field. Radio waves of certain frequencies are directed at the head. As a result, parts of the brain emit signals that can be measured from several angles. As with the CT scan, the signals are integrated into a computer-generated image of the brain which can be used to investigate brain abnormalities associated with schizophrenia (see Chapter 12) and other disorders, such as obsessive-compulsive disorder (Breiter et al., 1996; Jenike et al., 1996).

Brain electrical activity mapping (BEAM), a sophisticated type of EEG, uses the computer to analyze brain wave patterns and reveal areas of relative activity and inactivity from moment to moment (Figure 2.10) (F. H. Duffy, 1994). Twenty or more electrodes are attached to the scalp and simultaneously feed information about brain activity to a computer. The computer analyzes the signals and displays the pattern of brain activity on a color monitor, providing a vivid image of the electrical activity of the brain at work. BEAM and other similar techniques have been helpful in

studying the brain activity of people with schizophrenia (see Chapter 12) and other physical and psychological disorders. In later chapters we see how modern imaging techniques are furthering our understanding of various patterns of abnormal behavior.

TRUTH or FICTION REVISITED

2.7 False. Advances in medical technology such as the CT scan, the PET scan, MRI, and BEAM allow us to form inner images of the brain without surgery.

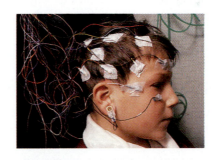

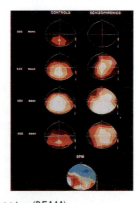

FIGURE 2.10 *Brain electrical activity mapping (BEAM).*
BEAM is a type of EEG in which electrodes are attached to the scalp (Part A) to measure electrical activity in various regions of the brain. The left column of Part B shows the average level of electrical activity in the brains of 10 normal people ("controls") at 4 time intervals. The column to the right shows the average level of activity of subjects with schizophrenia during the same intervals. Higher activity levels are represented in increasing order by yellows, reds, and whites. The computer-generated image in the bottom center summarizes differences in activity levels between the brains of normal subjects and those with schizophrenia. Areas of the brain depicted in blue show small differences between the groups. White areas represent larger differences.

In conclusion, people's psychological problems, which are no less complex than people themselves, are thus assessed in many ways. Clients are generally asked to explain their problems as best they can, and sometimes a computer does the asking. Psychologists can also draw on batteries of tests that assess intelligence, personality, and neuropsychological integrity. Many psychologists prefer to observe people's behavior directly when possible, and sometimes the observations are recorded by devices that assess physiological markers of emotional states, such as changes in blood pressure. Modern technology has provided several means of studying the structure and function of the brain. The methods of assessment selected by clinicians reflect the problems of their clients, the clinicians' theoretical orientations, and the clinicians' mastery of specialized technologies.

SUMMARY

Classification of Abnormal Behavior

Diagnostic classification may be traced as far back as Hippocrates but was ushered into the modern era by Kraepelin in the late 19th century. His classification system influenced the development of the *Diagnostic and Statistical Manual of Mental Disorders* (DSM), which is the most widely accepted diagnostic system, now in its fourth edition.

The DSM uses specific diagnostic criteria to group patterns of abnormal behaviors that share common clinical features and a multiaxial system of evaluation. Strengths of the DSM include its use of specified diagnostic criteria and a multiaxial system to provide a comprehensive picture of the person's functioning. Weaknesses include questions about reliability and validity and about the medical model framework.

Characteristics of Methods of Assessment

Methods of assessment must be reliable and valid. Reliability of assessment techniques is shown in various ways, including internal consistency, temporal stability, and interrater reliability. Validity is measured by means of content validity, criterion validity, and construct validity.

The Clinical Interview

The most widely used method of assessment, the clinical interview involves the use of a set of questions designed to elicit relevant information from people seeking treatment. Clinicians generally use a structured interview, which consists of a fairly standard series of questions, to gather a wide range of information concerning presenting problems or complaints, present circumstances, and history.

Psychological Tests

Psychological tests are structured methods of assessment that are used to evaluate reasonably stable traits such as intelligence and personality.

Intelligence Tests

Tests of intelligence, such as the Stanford-Binet and the Wechsler scales, are used for various purposes in clinical assessment, including determining evidence of mental retardation or cognitive impairment, and assessing strengths and weaknesses. Intelligence is expressed in the form of an intelligence quotient (IQ).

Personality Tests

Self-report personality inventories, such as the MMPI and MCMI, use structured items to measure various personality traits, such as anxiety, depression, and masculinity-femininity. These tests are considered *objective* in the sense that they make use of a limited range of possible responses to items and an empirical, or objective, method of test construction.

Projective personality tests, such as the Rorschach and TAT, ask subjects to interpret ambiguous stimuli in the belief their answers may shed light on their unconscious processes. Concerns persist about the validity of these tests, however.

Neuropsychological Assessment

Methods of neuropsychological assessment help determine organic bases for impaired behavior and psychological functioning. The Bender Visual Motor Gestalt Test requires subjects to reproduce nine geometric designs on a piece of paper. The Halstead-Reitan Neuropsychological Battery and Luria Nebraska Test Battery are more sophisticated batteries of tests measuring various perceptual, intellectual, and motor skills and performance.

Behavioral Assessment

In behavioral assessment, test responses are taken as samples of behavior rather than as signs of underlying traits or dispositions. The behavioral examiner may conduct a functional assessment, which relates the problem behavior to its antecedents and consequents. Methods of behavioral assessment include behavioral interviewing, self-monitoring, use of analogue or contrived measures, direct observation, and behavioral rating scales.

Cognitive Assessment

Cognitive assessment focuses on the measurement of thoughts, beliefs, and attitudes in order to help identify distorted thinking patterns. Specific methods of assessment include the use of a thought record or diary and the use of rating scales such as the Automatic Thoughts Questionnaire (ATQ), the Cognition Checklist (CCL), and the Dysfunctional Attitudes Scale (DAS).

Physiological Measurement

Measures of physiological function include heart rate, blood pressure, galvanic skin response (GSR), muscle tension, and brain wave activity. Brain-imaging techniques such as EEG, CT scans, PET scans, MRI, and BEAM probe the inner workings and structures of the brain.

REVIEW QUESTIONS

1. What is the DSM system? How is it used to classify abnormal behavior patterns? How is it a "multiaxial" system?

2. Why is it important for clinicians to take cultural factors into account when diagnosing psychological or mental disorders?

3. How do investigators determine the reliability and validity of the methods of assessment they use?

4. What are the various ways that mental health professionals assess abnormal behavior patterns? What are their basic features and limitations?

5. What are the differences between projective and objective personality tests?

6. Jamie complains of feeling depressed since the death of her brother in a car accident last year. What methods of assessment might a psychologist use to evaluate her mental status?

© **Paul Brach**
Ahola #6, 1991

Methods of Therapy and Treatment

TRUTH *or* FICTION?

3.1 In some states, anyone can set up shop as a psychotherapist.

3.2 Some psychologists have been trained to prescribe drugs.

3.3 In classical psychoanalysis, you are asked to express whatever thought happens to come to mind.

3.4 More psychotherapists identify with an eclectic approach than with any specific school of therapy.

3.5 The average client who receives psychotherapy is no better off than control clients who go without it.

3.6 A psychotic Haitian man responded positively to a form of therapy that included the lifting of a curse by a *vodou* priest.

3.7 Despite beliefs that it is a wonder drug, the antidepressant Prozac appears to be no more effective than the earlier generation of antidepressants.

3.8 Severely depressed people who have failed to respond to other treatments may be helped dramatically by treatments in which they have jolts of electricity passed through their heads.

3.9 Virtually all community mental health centers in the United States are providing the basic services they are mandated to provide.

Carla, a 19-year-old college sophomore, had been crying more or less continuously for several days. She felt her life was falling apart, that her college aspirations were in a shambles and she was a disappointment to her parents. The thought of suicide had crossed her mind. She could not seem to drag herself out of bed in the morning and had withdrawn from her friends. Her misery had seemed to descend on her from nowhere, although she could pinpoint some pressures in her life: a couple of poor grades at school, a recent breakup with a boyfriend, some adjustment problems with roommates.

The psychologist who examined her arrived at a diagnosis of major depressive disorder. Had she broken her leg, her treatment from a qualified professional would have followed a fairly standard course. Yet the treatment that Carla or someone else with a psychological disorder receives is likely to vary not only with the type of disorder involved but also with the therapeutic orientation and professional background of the helping professional. A psychiatrist might recommend a course of antidepressant medication, perhaps in combination with some form of psychotherapy. A cognitively oriented psychologist might suggest a program of cognitive therapy to help Carla identify dysfunctional thoughts that may underlie her depression, whereas a psychodynamic therapist might recommend she begin psychoanalytically oriented therapy to uncover inner conflicts originating in childhood that may lie at the root of her depression.

This chapter focuses on ways of treating psychological disorders. In later chapters we see how these treatment approaches are applied to particular disorders. Here we focus on the treatments themselves. Each of the major psychological models of abnormal behavior we discussed in Chapter 1—the psychodynamic, behavioral, humanistic-existential, and cognitive—has spawned corresponding psychological approaches to treatment, or models of **psychotherapy**. Although most approaches to psychotherapy focus on individual treatment, we will see that some approaches extend the therapeutic focus to the group, as in group, family, and marital therapy. We also review biological approaches to treatment—the use of **psychotropic** (or psychotherapeutic) drugs, electroconvulsive therapy (ECT), and psychosurgery. We conclude by examining the roles of the hospital and the community mental health center in the contemporary mental health system and the changes brought about by the policy of deinstitutionalization.

PSYCHOTHERAPY

Psychotherapy is a systematic interaction between a client and a therapist that incorporates psychological principles to help bring about changes in the client's behaviors, thoughts, and feelings in order to help the client overcome abnormal behavior, solve problems in living, or develop as an individual. Let us take a closer look at these features of psychotherapy:

1. *Systematic interaction.* The process of psychotherapy involves systematic interactions between clients and therapists. "Systematic" means that therapists structure these interactions with plans and purposes that reflect their theoretical points of view.

2. *Psychological principles.* Psychotherapists draw on psychological principles, research, and theory in their practice.

3. *Behavior, thoughts, and feelings.* Psychotherapy may be directed at behavioral, cognitive, and emotional domains to help clients overcome psychological problems and lead more satisfying lives.

4. *Abnormal behavior, problem solving, and personal growth.* At least three groups of people are assisted by psychotherapy. First are people with abnormal behavior problems such as mood disorders, anxiety disorders, or

schizophrenia. Second are people who seek help for personal problems that are not regarded as abnormal, such as social shyness or confusion about career choices. Third are people who seek personal growth. For them, psychotherapy is a means of self-discovery that may help them reach their potentials as, for example, parents, creative artists, performers, or athletes.

Psychotherapies share other features as well. For one, psychotherapies involve verbal interactions. Psychotherapies are "talking therapies," forms of interchange between clients and therapists that involve talking or conversation. In some cases, there is much verbal discussion between clients and therapists. In others, such as traditional psychoanalysis, clients do most of the talking. In each case, skillful therapists are attentive listeners. Attentive listening is an active, not a passive, activity. Therapists listen carefully to what clients are saying in order to understand as clearly as possible what they are experiencing and attempting to convey. Skillful therapists are also sensitive to clients' nonverbal cues, such as gestures that may indicate underlying feelings or conflicts. Therapists also seek to convey empathy through words as well as nonverbal gestures, such as establishing eye contact and leaning forward to indicate interest in what the client is saying. Therapist empathy is a consistent predictor of therapy outcome. Clients of therapists who are perceived as warmer and more empathic tend to show greater improvement than clients of other therapists, whether the therapists are psychodynamic (Luborsky et al., 1988) or cognitive-behavioral (Burns & Nolen-Hoeksema, 1992) in their therapeutic approach.

Another common feature of psychotherapies is the instilling in clients of a sense of hope of improvement (Bandura, 1986). Clients generally enter therapy with expectations of receiving help to overcome their problems. Responsible therapists do not promise results or guarantee cures. They do instill hope, however, that they can help clients deal with their problems. Positive expectancies can become a type of self-fulfilling prophecy by leading clients to mobilize their efforts toward overcoming their problems. Responses to positive expectancies are termed *placebo effects* or *expectancy effects*.

The common features of psychotherapy that are not specific to any one form of therapy, such as the encouragement of hope and the display of empathy and attentiveness on the part of the therapist, are often referred to as **nonspecific treatment factors.** Nonspecific factors may have therapeutic benefits in addition to the specific benefits of particular forms of therapy.

Major Types of Mental Health Professionals

The three major groups of mental health professionals are clinical psychologists, psychiatrists, and psychiatric social workers. Unfortunately, many states do not limit the use of the titles *therapist* or *psychotherapist* to trained professionals.

In such states, anyone can set up shop as a psychotherapist and practice "therapy" without a license. Thus, people seeking help are advised to inquire about the training and licensure of helping professionals. The public is also confused about the differences in qualifications and training of the various types of mental health providers (Farberman, 1997).

TRUTH *or* FICTION REVISITED

3.1 *True.* In some states anyone can set up shop as a psychotherapist.

Clinical Psychologists A clinical psychologist is a psychologist trained in the assessment, diagnosis, and treatment of psychological problems. All psychologists, including clinical psychologists, must have at least a master's degree. In most states, they must have a doctoral degree (PhD, EdD, or PsyD) to be licensed to practice psychology. Psychologists use various techniques to diagnose psychological problems, including clinical interviews, psychological tests, and behavioral observations. They also use psychotherapy as a means of treating these problems. Psychologists often receive extensive training in research, which helps them conduct studies in clinical settings and critically evaluate the clinical literature. If you or someone you know should decide to consult a psychologist, how would you find one? The nearby feature, "How Do I Find a Psychologist?," offers some suggestions.

Psychiatrists Psychiatrists are licensed physicians who have earned medical degrees such as the MD (Doctor of Medicine) or DO (Doctor of Osteopathy). They have also completed a postdoctoral residency program in psychiatry that provides specialized training in diagnosing and treating psychological problems. Like psychologists, psychiatrists conduct psychotherapy and conduct diagnostic interviews. Unlike psychologists,[1] they can prescribe drugs and administer other biological treatments, such as ECT. Psychiatrists may rely on psychologists for psychological testing to help determine a diagnosis or course of treatment.

Psychiatric Social Workers Psychiatric social workers earn a graduate degree in social work at the master's level (Master of Social Work; MSW) or doctoral level (Doctor of Social Work; DSW). They receive supervised training in helping people adjust and utilize social support services and community agencies. Many psychiatric social workers conduct psychotherapy or specialize in marital or family therapy.

We now consider the major types of psychotherapy and their relationships to the theoretical models from which they derive.

---

[1]However, some psychologists are being trained in specialized postdoctoral programs to prescribe psychotropic medications (Sammons & Brown, 1997; Seppa, 1997). The issue of prescription privileges for psychologists continues to be hotly debated among psychologists and between psychologists and psychiatrists (see Cullen & Newman, 1997; Evans & Murphy, 1997; Gutierrez & Silk, 1998; also Ax, Forbes, & Thompson, 1997; DeLeon et al., 1997).

How Do I Find a Psychologist?

To find a psychologist, ask your physician or another health professional. Call your local or state psychological association. Consult a local university or college department of psychology. Ask family and friends. Contact your area community mental health center. Inquire at your church or synagogue.

What to Consider When Making the Choice. . .

Psychologists and clients work together. The right match is important. Most psychologists agree that an important factor in determining whether or not to work with a particular psychologist, once that psychologist's credentials and competence are established, is your level of personal comfort with that psychologist. A good rapport with your psychologist is critical. Choose a psychologist with whom you feel comfortable and at ease.

Questions to Ask. . .

- Are you a licensed psychologist? How many years have you been practicing psychology?
- I have been feeling (anxious, tense, depressed, etc.), and I'm having problems (with my job, my mar-

riage, eating, sleeping, etc.). What experience do you have helping people with these types of problems?

- What are your areas of expertise—for example, working with children and families?
- What kinds of treatments do you use, and have they been proven effective for dealing with my kind of problem or issue?
- What are your fees? (Fees are usually based on a 45- to 50-minute session.) Do you have a sliding-scale fee policy? How much therapy would you recommend?
- What types of insurance do you accept? Will you accept direct billing to/payment from my insurance company? Are you affiliated with any managed care organizations? Do you accept Medicare/Medicaid insurance?

Finances. . .

Many insurance companies provide coverage for mental health services. If you have private health insurance coverage (typically through an employer), check with your insurance company to see if mental health services

---

TRUTH or FICTION REVISITED

3.2 *True.* Some psychologists have been trained in an experimental program to prescribe psychotropic medications.

PSYCHODYNAMIC THERAPIES

Psychoanalysis is the form of psychodynamic therapy originated by Sigmund Freud. Practitioners of psychoanalysis, or *psychoanalysts,* view psychological problems as rooted in early childhood experiences and unconscious conflicts. Although they have much in common with traditional psychoanalysis, more recent *psychoanalytic* or *psychodynamic* therapies tend to be briefer, to focus more on issues concerning present relationships, and to follow a somewhat different format (Strupp, 1992).

Traditional Psychoanalysis

Freud used psychoanalysis to help clients gain insight into, and resolve, unconscious conflicts. Working through these conflicts, the ego would be freed of the need to maintain defensive behaviors—such as phobias, obsessive-compulsive behaviors, hysterical complaints, and the like—that shield it from recognition of inner turmoil.

Freud summed up the goal of psychoanalysis by saying, "Where id was, there shall ego be." This meant, in part, that psychoanalysis could help shed the light of awareness, represented by the conscious ego, on the inner workings of the id. But Freud did not expect, or intend, that clients should seek to become conscious of all repressed material—of all their impulses, wishes, fears, and memories. The aim, rather, was to replace defensive behavior with more adaptive behavior. By so doing, clients could find gratification without incurring social or self-condemnation.

Through this process a man with a phobia of knives might become aware he had been repressing impulses to vent a murderous rage against his father. His phobia keeps him from having contact with knives, thereby serving a hidden purpose of keeping his homicidal impulses in check. Another man might come to realize that unresolved anger toward his dominating or rejecting mother has sabotaged his intimate relationships with women during his adulthood. A woman with a loss of sensation in her hand that could not be explained medically might come to see she harbored guilt over urges to masturbate. The loss of sensation may have prevented her from acting on these urges. Through confronting hidden impulses and the conflicts they produce, clients learn to sort out their feelings and find more constructive and

are covered and, if so, how you may obtain these benefits. This also applies to persons enrolled in HMOs and other types of managed care plans. Find out how much the insurance company will reimburse for mental health services and what limitations on the use of benefits may apply.

If you are not covered by a private health insurance plan or employee assistance program, you may decide to pay for psychological services out of pocket. Some psychologists operate on a sliding-scale fee policy, where the amount you pay depends on your income.

Another potential source of mental health services involves government-sponsored health care programs—including Medicare for individuals age 65 or older, as well as health insurance plans for government employees, military personnel, and their dependents. Community mental health centers throughout the country are another possible alternative for receiving mental health services. And some state Medicaid programs for economically disadvantaged individuals provide for limited mental health services from psychologists.

Credentials to Look For. . .
After graduation from college, psychologists spend an average of seven years in graduate education training and research before receiving a doctoral degree. As part of their professional training, they must complete a supervised clinical internship in a hospital or organized health setting and at least one year of postdoctoral supervised experience before they can practice independently in any health-care arena. It's this combination of doctoral-level training and clinical internship that distinguishes psychologists from many other mental health care providers.

Psychologists must be licensed by the state or jurisdiction in which they practice. Licensure laws are intended to protect the public by limiting licensure to those persons qualified to practice psychology as defined by state law. In most states, renewal of this license depends upon the demonstration of continued competence and requires continuing education. In addition, members of the American Psychological Association (APA) adhere to a strict code of professional ethics.

socially acceptable ways of handling their impulses and wishes. The ego is then freed to focus on more constructive interests.

The major methods that Freud used to accomplish these goals were free association, dream analysis, and analysis of the transference relationship.

Free Association You are asked to lie down on a couch and to say anything that enters your mind. The psychoanalyst (or *analyst* for short) sits in a chair behind you, out of direct view. For the next 45 or 50 minutes, you let your mind wander, saying whatever pops in, or saying nothing at all. The analyst remains silent most of the time, prompting you occasionally to utter whatever crosses your mind, no matter how seemingly trivial, no matter how personal. This process continues, typically for three or four sessions a week, for a period of several years. At certain points in the process, the analyst offers an **interpretation,** drawing your attention to connections between your disclosures and unconscious conflicts.

TRUTH or FICTION REVISITED

3.3 True. In classical psychoanalysis, clients are asked to report any thought that comes to mind. The technique is called free association.

Free association is the process of uttering uncensored thoughts as they come to mind. Free association is believed to gradually break down the defenses that block awareness of unconscious processes. Clients are told not to censor or screen out thoughts, but to let their minds wander "freely" from thought to thought. Psychoanalysts do not believe that the process of free association is truly free. Repressed impulses press for expression or release, leading to a **compulsion to utter.** Although free association may begin with small talk, the compulsion to utter eventually leads the client to disclose more meaningful material.

The ego, however, continues to try to avert the disclosure of threatening impulses and conflicts. Consequently, clients may show **resistance,** an unwillingness or inability to recall or discuss disturbing or threatening material. Clients might report that their minds suddenly go blank when they venture into sensitive areas. They might switch topics abruptly, or accuse the analyst of trying to pry into material that is too personal or embarrassing to talk about. Or they might conveniently "forget" the next appointment after a session in which sensitive material is touched upon. The analyst monitors the dynamic conflict between the "compulsion to utter" and resistance. Signs of resistance are often suggestive of meaningful material. Now and then, the

Freud's consulting room in London. Here we see the couch used by Freud for psychoanalysis after his arrival in London.

analyst brings interpretations of this material to the attention of the client to help the client gain better **insight** into deep-seated feelings and conflicts.

Dream Analysis   To Freud, dreams represented the "royal road to the unconscious." During sleep, the ego's defenses are lowered and unacceptable impulses find some form of expression in dreams. Because the defenses are not completely eliminated, the impulses take a disguised or symbolized form in dreams. In psychoanalytic theory, dreams have two levels of content:

1. **Manifest content:** the material of the dream the dreamer experiences and reports, and

2. **Latent content:** the unconscious material the dream symbolizes or represents.

A man might dream of flying in an airplane. Flying is the apparent or manifest content of the dream. Freud believed that flying may symbolize erection, so perhaps the latent content of the dream reflects unconscious issues related to fears of impotence. Such symbols may vary from person to person. Analysts therefore ask clients to free associate to the manifest content of the dream to provide clues to the latent content.

Transference   Freud found that clients responded to him not only as an individual but also in ways that reflected their feelings and attitudes toward other important people in their lives. A young female client might respond to him as a father figure, **displacing,** or transferring, onto Freud her feelings toward her own father. A man might also view him as a father figure, responding to him as a rival in a manner Freud believed might reflect the man's unresolved Oedipal complex.

The process of analyzing and working through the **transference relationship** is considered an essential component of psychoanalysis. Freud believed the transference

Dream analysis. Freud believed that dreams represent the "royal road to the unconscious." Dream interpretation was one of the principal techniques that Freud used to uncover unconscious material.

relationship provides a vehicle for the reenactment of childhood conflicts with parents. Clients may react to the analyst with the same feelings of anger, love, or jealousy they felt toward their own parents. Freud termed the enactment of these childhood conflicts the *transference neurosis.* This "neurosis" had to be successfully analyzed and worked through for clients to succeed in psychoanalysis.

Childhood conflicts usually involve unresolved feelings of anger or rejection, or needs for love. For example, a client may interpret any slight criticism by the therapist as a devastating blow, transferring feelings of self-loathing that the client had repressed from childhood experiences of parental rejection. Transferences may also distort or color the client's relationships with others, such as a spouse or employer. Clients might relate to their spouses as they had to their parents, perhaps demanding too much from them or unjustly accusing them of being insensitive or uncaring. Or they might not give new friends or lovers the benefit of a fair chance, if they had been mistreated by others who played similar roles in their past. The analyst helps the client recognize transference relationships, especially the therapy transference, and to work through the residues of childhood feelings and conflicts that led to self-defeating behavior in the present.

According to Freud, transference is a two-way street. Freud felt he transferred his feelings onto his clients, perhaps viewing a young man as a competitor or a woman as a rejecting love interest. Freud referred to the feelings that he projected onto clients as **countertransference**. Psychoanalysts in training are expected to undergo psychoanalysis themselves to help them uncover motives that might lead to countertransferences in their therapeutic relationships. In their therapeutic training, psychoanalysts learn to monitor their own reactions in therapy, so as to become better aware of when and how countertransferences intrude on the therapy process.

Although the analysis of the therapy transference is a crucial element of psychoanalytic therapy, it generally takes months or years for a transference relationship to develop and be resolved. This is one reason why psychoanalysis is typically a lengthy process.

Modern Psychodynamic Approaches

Although some psychoanalysts continue to practice traditional psychoanalysis in much the same manner as Freud, briefer and less intensive forms of psychodynamic treatment have emerged that focus more on issues concerning present relationships (Strupp, 1992). These newer approaches are often referred to as "psychoanalytic psychotherapy," "psychoanalytically oriented" therapy, or "psychodynamic therapy." They are able to reach clients who are seeking briefer and less costly forms of treatment, perhaps once or twice a week.

Modern psychodynamic psychotherapy. Modern psychodynamic therapists engage in more direct, face-to-face interactions with clients than do traditional Freudian psychoanalysts. Modern psychodynamic approaches are also generally briefer and focus more on the direct exploration of clients' defenses and transference relationships.

Like Freudian psychoanalysis, the newer psychodynamic approaches aim to uncover unconscious motives and break down resistances and psychological defenses. Yet they focus more on the client's present relationships and encourage the client to make adaptive behavior changes. Because of the briefer format, therapy may entail a more open and direct exploration of the client's defenses and transference relationships than was traditionally the case. Unlike the traditional approach, the client and therapist generally sit facing each other. Rather than offer an occasional interpretation, the therapist engages in more frequent verbal give-and-take with the client, as in the following vignette. Note how the therapist uses interpretation to help the client, Mr. Arianes, achieve insight into how his relationship with his wife involves a transference of his childhood relationship with his mother:

Mr. Arianes: I think you've got it there, Doc. We weren't communicating. I wouldn't tell her [his wife] what was wrong or what I wanted from her. Maybe I expected her to understand me without saying anything.

Therapist: Like the expectations a child has of its mother.

Mr. Arianes: Not my mother!

Therapist: Oh?

Mr. Arianes: No, I always thought she had too many troubles of her own to pay attention to mine. I remember once I got hurt on my bike and came to her all bloodied up. When she saw me she got mad and yelled at me for making more trouble for her when she already had her hands full with my father.

Therapist: Do you remember how you felt then?

Mr. Arianes: I can't remember, but I know that after that I never brought my troubles to her again.

Therapist: How old were you?

Mr. Arianes: Nine, I know that because I got that bike for my ninth birthday. It was a little too big for me still, that's why I got hurt on it.

Therapist: Perhaps you carried this attitude into your marriage.

Mr. Arianes: What attitude?

Therapist: The feeling that your wife, like your mother, would be unsympathetic to your difficulties. That there was no point in telling her about your experiences because she was too preoccupied or too busy to care.

Mr. Arianes: But she's so different from my mother. I come first with her.

Therapist: On one level you know that. On another, deeper level there may well be the fear that people—or maybe only women, or maybe only women you're close to—are all the same, and you can't take a chance at being rejected again in your need.

Mr. Arianes: Maybe you're right, Doc, but all that was so long ago, and I should be over that by now.

Therapist: That's not the way the mind works. If a shock, or a disappointment is strong enough it can permanently freeze our picture of ourselves and our expectations of the world. The rest of us grows up—that is, we let ourselves learn about life from experience and from what we see, hear, or read of the experiences of others, but that one area where we really got hurt stays unchanged. So what I mean when I say you might be carrying that attitude into your relationship with your wife is that when it comes to your hopes of being understood and catered to when you feel hurt or abused by life, you still feel very much like that nine-year-old boy who was rebuffed in his need and gave up hope that anyone would or could respond to him.

SOURCE: BASCH, 1980, PP. 29–30.
REPRINTED WITH PERMISSION.

Some modern psychodynamic therapies focus more on the role of the ego and less on the role of the id. Therapists adopting this view believe Freud placed too much emphasis on the sexual and aggressive impulses and underplayed the importance of the ego. These therapists, such as Heinz Hartmann, are generally described as **ego analysts.** Other modern psychoanalysts, such as Melanie Klein and Margaret Mahler, are identified with object-relations approaches to psychodynamic therapy. **Object-relations** therapists focus on helping people separate their own ideas and feelings from the elements of others they have incorporated or introjected within themselves. They can then develop more as individuals—as their own persons.

HUMANISTIC-EXISTENTIAL THERAPIES

Psychodynamic therapies tend to focus on unconscious processes, such as internal conflicts. By contrast, humanistic-existential therapies focus on clients' subjective, conscious experiences. Humanistic-existential therapies also focus more on what clients are experiencing in the present—the here and now—rather than on the past. But there are also similarities between the psychodynamic and the humanistic-existential therapies. Both assume the past affects present behavior and feelings and both seek to expand clients' self-insight.

Person-Centered Therapy

Carl Rogers (1951), a humanistic psychologist who was the developer of **person-centered therapy** (formerly called **client-centered therapy**), believed people have natural motivational tendencies toward growth, fulfillment, and health. In Rogers's view, psychological disorders develop largely from the roadblocks that others place in the journey toward self-actualization. When others are selective in their approval of our childhood feelings and behavior, we may come to disown the criticized parts of ourselves. To earn social approval, we may don social masks or facades. We learn "to be seen and not heard" and may become deaf even to our own inner voices. Over time, we may develop distorted self-concepts that are consistent with others' views of us but are not of our own making and design. As a result, we may become poorly adjusted, unhappy, and confused as to who and what we are.

Well-adjusted people make choices and take actions that are consistent with their personal values and needs. *Person-centered therapy* creates conditions of warmth and acceptance in the therapeutic relationship that help clients become more aware and accepting of their true selves. Rogers was a major shaper of contemporary psychotherapy and was rated the single most influential psychotherapist in a survey of therapists (D. Smith, 1982). Rogers did not believe that therapists should impose their own goals or values on their clients. His focus of therapy, as the name implies, is centered on the person.

Person-centered therapy is *nondirective*. The client, not the therapist, takes the lead and directs the course of therapy. The therapist reflects back or paraphrases the client's expressed feelings without interpreting them or passing judgment on them. This encourages the client to further explore his or her feelings and get in touch with deeper feelings and parts of the self that had become disowned because of social condemnation.

Rogers stressed the importance of creating a warm therapeutic relationship that would encourage the client to engage in self-exploration and self-expression. The effective person-centered therapist should possess four basic qualities or attributes: *unconditional positive regard, empathy, genuineness,* and *congruence.* First, the therapist must be able to express **unconditional positive regard** for clients. In contrast to the conditional approval the client may have received from parents and others in the past, the therapist must be unconditionally accepting of the client as a person, even if the therapist sometimes objects to the client's choices or behaviors. Unconditional positive regard provides clients with a sense of security that encourages them to explore their feelings without fear of disapproval. As clients feel accepted or prized for themselves, they are encouraged to accept themselves in turn. To Rogers, every human being has intrinsic worth and value. Traditional psychodynamic theory holds that people are basically motivated by primitive forces, such as sexual and aggressive impulses. Rogers believed, however, that people are basically good and are motivated to pursue *pro* social goals.

Therapists who display **empathy** are able to reflect or mirror accurately their clients' experiences and feelings. Therapists try to see the world through their clients' eyes or frames of reference. They listen actively to clients and set aside their own judgments and interpretations of events. Empathic understanding encourages clients to get in touch with feelings of which they may be only dimly aware.

Genuineness is the ability to be open about one's feelings. Rogers admitted he had negative feelings at times during therapy sessions, typically boredom, but he attempted to express these feelings openly rather than hide them (Bennett, 1985).

Congruence refers to the fit between one's thoughts, feelings, and behavior. The congruent person is one whose behavior, thoughts, and feelings are integrated and consistent. Congruent therapists serve as models of psychological integrity to their clients.

In this vignette, Rogers (C.R.) uses reflection to help a client, Jill, focus more deeply on her feelings:

Jill: I'm having a lot of problems dealing with my daughter. She's 20 years old; she's in college; I'm having a lot of trouble letting her go. . . And I have a lot of guilt feelings about her; I have a real need to hang on to her.

C.R.: A need to hang on so you can kind of make up for the things you feel guilty about. Is that part of it?

Jill: There's a lot of that. . . Also, she's been a real friend to me, and filled my life. . . And it's very hard. . . a lot of empty places now that she's not with me.

C.R.: The old vacuum, sort of, when she's not there.

Jill: Yes. Yes. I also would like to be the kind of mother that could be strong and say, you know, "Go and have a good life," and this is really hard for me, to do that.

C.R.: It's very hard to give up something that's been so precious in your life, but also something that I guess has caused you pain when you mentioned guilt.

Jill: Yeah. And I'm aware that I have some anger toward her that I don't always get what I want. I have needs that are not met. And, uh, I don't feel I have a right to those needs. You know. . . she's a daughter; she's not my mother. Though sometimes I feel as if I'd like her to mother me . . . it's very difficult for me to ask for that and have a right to it.

C.R.: So, it may be unreasonable, but still, when she doesn't meet your needs, it makes you mad.

Jill: Yeah I get very angry, very angry with her.

C.R.: (Pause) You're also feeling a little tension at this point, I guess.

Jill: Yeah. Yeah. A lot of conflict. . . (C.R.: M-hm.). A lot of pain.

C.R.: A lot of pain. Can you say anything more about what that's about?

SOURCE: FARBER, BRINK & RASKIN, 1996, PP. 74-75.
REPRINTED WITH PERMISSION.

Existential Therapies

Existential therapists and humanistic therapists such as Rogers share an emphasis on helping clients become more aware of their conscious experiences and make personal choices that give their lives meaning and a sense of fulfillment. They also emphasize the uniqueness of the individual. Some of the more prominent existential therapists

Rollo May.

include the Swiss psychiatrists Ludwig Binswanger and Medard Boss, the Viennese psychiatrist Victor Frankl, and the American psychologist Rollo May.

Many existential therapists, especially those who trained or practiced in Europe, also incorporate psychodynamic concepts in their approach to therapy, such as the analysis of defenses that people use to distort their feelings and experiences. Whereas Rogerian therapists emphasize acceptance and empathetic understanding of the client, existential therapists stress the importance of coming to terms with the fundamental questions of existence, of recognizing the finality of life and of one's personal responsibility for making choices that give life meaning and purpose.

COGNITIVE THERAPIES

There is nothing either good or bad, but thinking makes it so.

SHAKESPEARE, *HAMLET*

In these words, Shakespeare did not mean to imply that misfortunes or ailments are painless or easy to manage. His point, rather, is that the ways in which we evaluate upsetting events can heighten our discomfort and impair our ability to cope. Several hundred years later, cognitive therapists adopted this simple but elegant expression as a kind of motto for their approach to therapy.

Cognitive therapists focus on helping clients identify and correct maladaptive beliefs, automatic types of thinking, and self-defeating attitudes that create or compound emotional problems. They believe that negative emotions such as anxiety and depression are caused by the interpretations we place on troubling events, not on the events themselves. Here we focus on the contributions of two prominent types of cognitive therapy: Albert Ellis's rational-emotive behavior therapy and Aaron Beck's cognitive therapy.

Rational-Emotive Behavior Therapy

Albert Ellis (1977b, 1993) believes the adoption of irrational, self-defeating beliefs gives rise to psychological problems and negative feelings. A salient irrational belief is that one must almost always have the love and approval of the important people in one's life. Ellis finds it understandable to want other people's approval and love, but he argues that it is irrational to believe one cannot survive without it. Another irrational belief is that one must be thoroughly competent and achieving in everything one seeks to accomplish. We are usually doomed to fall short of these irrational expectations. When we do fall short, such expectations engender negative emotional consequences, such as depression and lowered self-esteem. Emotional difficulties such as anxiety and depression are not directly caused by negative events, but rather by viewing them through the dark-colored glasses of irrational beliefs. Thinking irrationally transforms challenging events, such as forthcoming examinations, into looming disasters. Ellis's rational-emotive behavior therapy (REBT) (formerly called *rational-emotive therapy*) seeks to free people from such irrational beliefs and their consequences. In REBT, therapists actively *dispute* irrational beliefs and their premises and assist clients to develop more rational, adaptive beliefs.

Ellis and Dryden (1987) describe the case of a 27-year-old woman, Jane, who was socially inhibited and shy, particularly with attractive men. Through REBT, Jane identified some of her underlying irrational beliefs, such as "I must speak well to people I find attractive" and "When I don't speak well and impress people as I should, I'm a stupid, inadequate person!" (p. 68). REBT helped Jane discriminate between these irrational beliefs and rational alternatives, such as "If people do reject me for showing them how anxious I am, that will be most unfortunate, but I can stand it" (p. 68). REBT encouraged Jane to debate or dispute irrational beliefs by posing challenging questions to herself: (1) "*Why* must I speak well to people I find attractive?" and, (2) "When I don't speak well and impress people, how does that make me a *stupid and inadequate person?*" (p. 69). Jane learned to form rational responses to her self-questioning, for example, (1) "There is no reason I must speak well to people I find attractive, but it would be desirable if I do so, so I shall make an effort—but not kill myself—to do so," and, (2) "When I speak poorly and fail to impress people, that only makes me a *person who* spoke unimpressively this time—not a *totally stupid or inadequate person*" (p. 69).

Jane also rehearsed more rational ideas several times a day. Examples included, "I would like to speak well, but I never *have to,*" and, "When people I favor reject me, it often reveals more about them and their tastes than about me" (pp. 69–70). After 9 months of REBT, Jane was able to talk comfortably to men she found attractive and was preparing to take a job as a teacher, a position she had previously avoided due to fear of facing a class.

Ellis recognizes that irrational beliefs may be formed on the basis of early childhood experiences. Changing them requires finding rational alternatives in the here and now, however. REBT therapists also help clients substitute more effective interpersonal behavior for self-defeating or maladaptive behavior. Ellis often gives clients specific tasks or homework assignments, like disagreeing with an overbearing relative or asking someone for a date. He assists them in practicing or rehearsing adaptive behaviors.

Beck's Cognitive Therapy

As formulated by psychiatrist Aaron Beck and his colleagues (Beck, 1976; Beck et al., 1979; Beck, Freeman, & Associates, 1990), cognitive therapy, like REBT, focuses on clients' maladaptive cognitions. Cognitive therapists encourage clients to recognize and change errors in their thinking, called *cognitive distortions,* that affect their moods and impair their behavior, such as tendencies to magnify negative events and minimize personal accomplishments.

Cognitive therapists utilize homework assignments, which require clients to record the thoughts that are prompted by upsetting events and to connect them with their emotional responses. Therapists also use behavioral homework assignments, such as encouraging depressed clients to fill their free time with structured activities, such as gardening or completing work around the house. Carrying out such tasks serves to counteract the apathy and loss of motivation that tend to characterize depression and may also provide concrete evidence of competence, which helps combat self-perceptions of helplessness and inadequacy.

Another type of homework assignment involves reality testing. Clients are asked to test out their negative beliefs in the light of reality. For example, a depressed client who feels unwanted by everyone might be asked to call two or three friends on the phone to gather data about the friends' reactions to the calls. The therapist might then ask the client to report on the assignment: "Did they immediately hang up the phone? Did they seem pleased you called? Did they express any interest at all in talking to you again or getting together sometime? Does the evidence support the conclusion that *no one* has any interest in you?" Such exercises help clients replace distorted beliefs with rational alternatives.

Consider this case in which a depressed man was encouraged to test his belief he was about to be fired from his job. The case also illustrates several cognitive distortions or errors in thinking, such as selectively perceiving only one's flaws (in this case, self-perceptions of laziness) and expecting the worst (expectations of being fired):

A 35-year-old man, a frozen foods distributor, had suffered from chronic depression since his divorce six years earlier. During the past year the depression had worsened and he found it increasingly difficult to call upon customers or go to the office. Each day that he avoided working made it more difficult for him to go to the office and face his boss. He was convinced that he was in imminent danger of being fired since he had not made any sales calls for more than a month. Since he had not earned any commissions in a while, he felt he was not adequately supporting his two daughters and was concerned that he wouldn't have the money to send them to college. He was convinced that his basic problem was laziness, not depression. His therapist pointed out the illogic in his thinking. First of all, there was no real evidence that his boss was about to fire him. His boss had actually encouraged him to get help and was paying for part of the treatment. His therapist also pointed out that judging himself as lazy was unfair because it overlooked the fact that he had been an industrious, successful salesman before he became depressed. While not fully persuaded, the client agreed to a homework assignment in which he was to call his boss and also make a sales call to one of his former customers. His boss expressed support and reassured him that his job was secure. The customer ribbed him about "being on vacation" during the preceding six weeks but placed a small order. The client discovered that the small unpleasantness he experienced in facing the customer and being teased paled in comparison to the intense depression he felt at home while he was avoiding work. Within the next several weeks he gradually worked himself back to a normal routine, calling upon customers and making future plans. This process of viewing himself and the world from a fresh perspective led to a general improvement in his mood and behavior.

ADAPTED FROM BURNS AND BECK, 1978, PP. 124–126

REBT and Beck's cognitive therapy have much in common, especially the focus on helping clients replace self-defeating thoughts and beliefs with more rational ones. Perhaps the major difference between the two approaches is one of therapeutic style. REBT therapists tend to be more confrontational and forceful in their approach to disputing client's irrational beliefs (Dryden, 1984; A. Ellis, Young, & Lockwood, 1989). Cognitive therapists tend to adopt a more gentle, collaborative approach in helping clients discover the distortions in their thinking.

BEHAVIOR THERAPY

Behavior therapy, which is also referred to as *behavior modification,* employs techniques derived from learning theories to assist clients to make adaptive behavioral changes. Behavior therapists focus on helping clients make overt changes in their behavior. They also frequently use cognitive techniques to modify clients' cognitive distortions and self-defeating beliefs. Many common behavioral techniques, in fact, such as systematic desensitization, make use of cognitive processes such as visual imagery (e.g., mentally picturing oneself approaching the phobic object). Behavior therapists insist that therapeutic outcomes be assessed in terms of behavioral changes that can be observed and measured, however, such as the ability to approach a phobic stimulus that had previously been avoided.

Like the humanistic-existential and cognitive schools of therapy, behavior therapists focus on the here and now. They also seek to foster client self-insight in the sense of helping clients gain a better awareness of the circumstances in which their problem behaviors occur and the early learning experiences that may have led to their development. Because the focus is on changing behavior—not on personality change or deep probing into the past—behavior therapy is relatively brief, lasting typically from a few weeks to a few months. Behavior therapists, like other therapists, seek to develop warm therapeutic relationships with clients, but they believe the special efficacy of behavior therapy derives from the learning-based techniques rather than from the nature of the therapeutic relationship. Let us consider several of the major behavior therapy techniques.

Methods of Fear Reduction

Behavior therapy first gained widespread attention as a means of helping people overcome fears and phobias, problems that had proved resistant to insight-oriented therapies. Among these methods are systematic desensitization, gradual exposure, and modeling.

Systematic Desensitization   **Systematic desensitization** involves a therapeutic program of exposure (in imagination or by means of pictures or slides) to progressively more fearful stimuli while one remains deeply relaxed. First the person uses a relaxation technique, such as progressive muscle relaxation (discussed in Chapter 4), to become deeply relaxed. The client is then instructed to imagine (or perhaps view, as through a series of slides) progressively more anxiety-arousing scenes. If fear is evoked, the client focuses on restoring relaxation. The process is repeated until the scene can be tolerated without anxiety. The client then progresses to the next scene in the *fear-stimulus hierarchy*. The procedure is continued until the person can remain relaxed while imagining the most distressing scene in the hierarchy.

Gradual Exposure   In **gradual exposure** (also called *in vivo,* meaning "in life," exposure), people who are troubled by phobias purposely expose themselves to the stimuli that evoke their fear. Like systematic desensitization, the person progresses at his or her own pace through a hierarchy of progressively more anxiety-evoking stimuli. The person with a fear of snakes, for example, might first look at a harmless, caged snake from across the room and then gradually approach and interact with the snake in a step-by-step process, progressing to each new step only when feeling completely calm at the prior step. Gradual exposure is often combined with cognitive techniques that focus on replacing anxiety-arousing irrational thoughts with calming rational thoughts.

Modeling Modeling is a form of observational learning in which clients first observe and then imitate others who approach or interact with fear-evoking situations or objects. After observing the model, the client may be assisted or guided by the therapist or the model in performing the target behavior. The client receives ample reinforcement from the therapist for each attempt. Modeling approaches were pioneered by Albert Bandura and his colleagues, who had remarkable success using modeling techniques to treat various phobias, especially fears of animals, such as snakes and dogs (Bandura, Blanchard, & Ritter, 1969; Bandura, Jeffery, & Wright, 1974).

Aversive Conditioning

Whereas fear-reduction methods instill *approach* behaviors, **aversive conditioning** leads to the development of *avoidance* behaviors. Aversive conditioning involves the pairing of painful or aversive stimuli with unwanted behaviors, such as cigarette smoking, problem drinking, or deviant sexual responses. For example, to help problem drinkers control their intake of alcohol, the tastes of alcoholic beverages can

Modeling. Modeling techniques are often used to help people overcome phobic behaviors. Here a woman models approaching and petting a dog to a phobic child. As the phobic child observes the woman harmlessly engage in the desired behavior, he is more likely to imitate the behavior.

be paired with electric shock or with drugs that induce nausea or vomiting. Smokers have been treated with some success with a form of aversive conditioning called *rapid smoking,* in which the rate of puffing is increased to the point that smoking becomes a noxious event (see Chapter 9). Some success has also been reported with the use of aversive conditioning for treating self-injurious behaviors in children with autism (see Chapter 13). It may seem paradoxical that aversive stimulation in the form of electric shock can sometimes stop such self-injurious behaviors as repeated head-banging. Perhaps the head-banging is reinforced by the stimulation it provides, or by attention from others, and not because of the physical pain it induces. The long-term results of aversive conditioning are frequently disappointing, however, especially with people seeking to overcome substance abuse problems. Unless alternative behaviors are learned that become reinforcing in themselves, the problem behavior often returns when the individual is no longer faced with the immediate aversive consequences.

Operant Conditioning

Operant conditioning is based on the assumption that what happens after a response is emitted is more important than what precedes the response (Delprato & Midgley, 1992; S. S. Glenn, Ellis, & Greenspoon, 1992). Thus, operant conditioning approaches focus on the use of reinforcement to foster acquisition of adaptive responses and the withdrawal of reinforcement to extinguish maladaptive responses. Operant conditioning techniques have a wide range of applications. For example, parents and teachers may be trained to systematically reinforce children for appropriate behavior by showing appreciation and to extinguish inappropriate behavior by ignoring it. In institutional settings, **token economy** systems seek to increase adaptive behavior by allowing patients to earn tokens for performing appropriate behaviors, such as self-grooming and making their beds. The tokens can eventually be exchanged for desired rewards. Token systems have also been used to treat children with conduct disorder problems. In the following case example, a token reinforcement program was used to improve a child's academic functioning in a classroom setting:

The child was a third-grade student who was inattentive to her teacher's instructions and refused to complete school assignments or participate with her classmates in school projects. Most of her time at school was spent dawdling or daydreaming. Her parents reported that she had few friends and lacked social skills. A token reinforcement program was designed that rewarded her for "on task" behavior at school—following her teacher's instructions, completing assignments, and cooperating in class projects. The measure of outcome was the number of reading units the child completed. During a baseline period, the child completed zero reading units. Beans were then used as tokens that the child

Social Skills Training

Social skills training is used to help people develop more effective social skills (such as conversational skills and assertiveness skills) and overcome social anxieties. Social skills training also has been used to help adolescents with anger control problems handle interpersonal conflicts without "flying off the handle" or acting out aggressively. People with schizophrenia have participated in social skills training to learn to relate more effectively to others, which can help them in their efforts to adjust to the demands of community living. A type of social skills training called **assertiveness training** helps unassertive people speak up for their rights and communicate their feelings, needs, and interests.

Social skills training usually includes such techniques as self-monitoring, coaching, modeling, practice or behavior rehearsal, and feedback. In *self-monitoring,* clients are instructed to keep a running diary of upsetting social interactions in order to identify examples of social avoidance and awkward behavior. The therapist may then *coach* (provide instruction in) more effective social behavior or *model* (demonstrate) more effective behavior. The client then practices (engages in *behavior rehearsal* of) the behavior in role-playing exercises as the therapist provides constructive *feedback*. The therapist is attentive not only to what the client says and does in the practice opportunities but also to the client's posture, tone of voice, and facial expressions.

Social skills training is often conducted in a group treatment setting. In the role-play enactments, group members take the parts of important people in each other's lives, such as parents, spouses, employers, or potential dates. Homework assignments are used to provide clients with opportunities to practice newly acquired behaviors in real-life settings.

Self-Control Techniques

Whereas insight-oriented therapists have traditionally encouraged clients to uncover the "meanings" of problem habits such as smoking or excessive drinking, behavior therapists directly train people in self-control or self-management skills. Self-control training can be used for a wide range of problem behaviors such as nail-biting, inadequate study habits, overeating, and substance abuse.

Self-control strategies involve changing the A's, or stimulus antecedents, which trigger the problem behavior; the B's, or problem behaviors themselves; and the C's, or reinforcement consequences that follow. Smokers, for example, may be instructed to reduce their contact with smoking-related cues (the A's), stretch the chain of behaviors that leads to smoking a cigarette (the B's), and reward or punish themselves (the C's) for meeting or exceeding their smoking reduction goals. Examples of the ABC's of weight control are provided in Chapter 10. The ABC's of substance abuse are provided in Chapter 9.

Self-control training often begins with a **functional analysis** of the problem behavior, that is, a systematic study of the antecedent stimuli or cues that trigger it and the reinforcers that maintain it. For example, smokers may be asked to track each cigarette smoked, jotting down the time of day it was smoked, the presence of any cues that may have triggered the urge, including internal cues (for example, negative emotions, sensations of hunger) and external cues (seeing someone else smoking), and the reinforcement consequences (feelings of pleasure, relief from anxiety, relaxation, and so forth). A functional analysis can reveal stimulus and reinforcement patterns that can be modified to foster self control. For example, a smoker may find that smoking occurs most often in response to feelings of boredom or loneliness and is maintained by the stimulation it provides. By filling in unstructured time with stimulating activities, preferably in nonsmoking environments, the smoker may be able to cut down substantially the number of cigarettes smoked.

Cognitive-Behavioral Therapy

The parallel interest in the development of cognitive psychology and information processing in the 1970s and 1980s focused attention on the role of cognitions in psychopathology and the treatment of psychological disorders. Cognitive-behavioral therapy developed from the attempt to integrate therapeutic techniques that focus not only on overt behavior but also on dysfunctional thoughts and cognitions. Cognitive-behavioral therapy draws on the assumptions that cognitions and information processing play important roles in the genesis and maintenance of maladaptive behavior and that the impact of external events is mediated by cognitive processes (Beidel & Turner, 1986). Despite its recent development, cognitive-behavioral therapy has become the most widely emphasized therapeutic orientation in doctoral training programs in clinical psychology in the United States (Nevid, Lavid, & Primavera, 1986, 1987).

Cognitive-behavioral therapists use an assortment of behavioral and cognitive techniques in therapy. The following case illustration shows how behavioral techniques (exposure to fearful situations) and cognitive techniques (changing maladaptive thoughts) were used in the treatment of **agoraphobia,** a type of anxiety disorder characterized by excessive fears of venturing out in public:

Mrs. X was a 41-year-old woman with a 12-year history of agoraphobia. She feared venturing into public places alone and required her husband or children to accompany her from place to place. In vivo (actual) exposure sessions were arranged in a series of progressively more fearful encounters—a fear-stimulus hierarchy. The first step in the hierarchy, for example, involved taking a shopping trip while accompanied by the therapist. After accomplishing this task, she gradually moved upwards in the hierarchy. By the third week of treatment, she was able to complete the last step in her hierarchy—shopping by herself in a crowded supermarket. Cognitive restructuring was conducted along with the exposure training. Mrs. X was asked to imagine herself in various fearful situations and to report the self-statements (self-talk) she experienced. The therapist helped her identify disruptive self-statements, such as "I am going to make a fool of myself." This particular self-statement was challenged by questioning whether it was realistic to believe that she would actually lose control, and, secondly, by disputing the belief that the consequences of losing control, were it to happen, would truly be disastrous. She progressed rapidly with treatment and became capable of functioning more independently. But she still harbored concerns about relapsing in the future. The therapist focused at this point on deeper cognitive structures involving her fears of abandonment by the people she loved if she were to relapse and be unable to attend to their needs. In challenging these beliefs, the therapist helped her realize that she was not as helpless as she perceived herself to be and that she was loved for other reasons than her ability to serve others. She also explored the question, "Who am I improving for?" She realized that she needed to find reasons to overcome her phobia that were related to meeting her own personal needs, not simply the needs of her loved ones. At a follow-up interview nine months after treatment, she was functioning independently, which allowed her to pursue her own interests, such as taking night courses and seeking a job.

ADAPTED FROM BIRAN, 1988, PP. 173–176

It could be argued that any behavioral method involving imagination or mental imagery, such as systematic desensitization, bridges behavioral and cognitive domains. Cognitive therapies such as Ellis's rational-emotive therapy and Beck's cognitive therapy might also be regarded as forms of cognitive behavioral therapy because they incorporate cognitive and behavioral treatment methods. The dividing lines between the psychotherapies may not be as clearly drawn as authors of textbooks—who are given the task of classifying them—might desire. Not only are traditional boundaries between the cognitive and behavioral therapies blurring, but many therapists adopt an eclectic or integrative approach in which they incorporate principles and techniques derived from different schools of therapy.

TYING IT TOGETHER: ECLECTIC MODELS OF PSYCHOTHERAPY

Each of the major psychological models of abnormal behavior—the psychodynamic, learning theory, humanistic-existentialist, and cognitive approaches—has spawned its own approaches to psychotherapy. Though many therapists identify with one or another of these schools of therapy, an increasing number of therapists identify with an **eclectic** approach, which draws upon techniques and teachings of different therapeutic approaches. Eclectic therapists look beyond the theoretical barriers that divide one school of psychotherapy from another in an effort to define what is common among the schools of therapy and what is useful in each of them. They seek to enhance their therapeutic effectiveness by incorporating principles and techniques from different therapeutic orientations (B. E. Wolfe & Goldfried, 1988). An eclectic therapist might use behavior therapy techniques to help a client change specific maladaptive behaviors, for example, along with psychodynamic techniques to help the client gain insight into the childhood roots of the problem.

During the 1940s and 1950s, psychotherapy was virtually synonymous with psychodynamic therapy. Few other psychotherapy approaches had much impact on psychotherapists or on public awareness (Garfield, 1982). During the 1970s and 1980s, however, surveys of therapists consistently showed that the largest single group of psychologists and other psychotherapists (ranging from around one third to more than half of those sampled) identified with an eclectic therapeutic orientation (Garfield, 1994). Researchers find that therapists who adopt an eclectic approach tend to be older and more experienced (Beitman, Goldfried, & Norecorss 1989). Perhaps they have learned through experience of the value of drawing on diverse contributions to the practice of therapy.

TRUTH *or* FICTION REVISITED

3.4 *True.* Leading surveys show that more psychotherapists endorse an eclectic therapeutic orientation than any other orientation.

Types of Eclecticism

Eclecticism has different meanings for different therapists. Some therapists are *technical eclectics*. They draw on techniques from different schools of therapy without necessarily adopting the theoretical positions that spawned the techniques (Lazarus et al., 1992). They assume a pragmatic approach—using techniques from different therapeutic approaches that they believe are most likely to work with a given client. The therapist attempts to match the therapeutic approach to the particular characteristics of the client, rather than apply the same therapeutic approach to all clients presenting with a given diagnosis or type of problem. Thus, the eclectic therapy offered to one client will be different than the eclectic therapy offered to another (Beutler, 1995).

Other eclectic therapists are *integrative eclectics.* They attempt to synthesize and integrate diverse theoretical approaches—to stitch together different therapeutic elements from diverse approaches so that they result in a seamless psychotherapy.

The development of a truly integrative psychotherapy largely remains more of an aspiration than a reality (Wachtel, 1991). Various approaches to integrative psychotherapy have been proposed, but there is as yet no clear agreement as to the principles and practices that constitute therapeutic integration (Freedheim, 1994; Garfield, 1994). Perhaps multiple approaches are needed (Safran & Messer, 1997). Nor has research reached a stage of development that would permit us to demonstrate how different psychotherapies may be integrated to best advantage in order to maximize therapeutic effectiveness (Wolfe & Goldfried, 1988).

Not all therapists subscribe to the view that therapeutic integration is a desirable or achievable goal. They believe that combining elements of different therapeutic approaches will lead to a hodgepodge of techniques that lack a cohesive conceptual framework. Still, interest in the professional community in therapeutic integration is growing, and we expect to see new models emerging that aim at tying together the contributions of different approaches.

We next consider forms of therapy in which the focus of therapy extends to groups of people, families, and married couples.

GROUP THERAPY

Group therapy has several advantages over individual treatment. For one, group therapy is less costly because several clients are treated at the same time. Many clinicians also believe group therapy may be more effective in treating groups of clients who have similar problems, such as complaints relating to anxiety, depression, lack of social skills, or adjustment to divorce or other life stresses. The group format provides clients with the opportunity to learn how people with similar problems cope with them and provides the social support of the group as well as the therapist. The particular approach to treatment reflects the theoretical orientation of the therapist or group leader. In psychoanalytic groups, for example, an emphasis may be placed on interpretations and working through transferences that emerge between group members or between group members and the therapist. Person-centered groups seek to create an accepting atmosphere for clients to explore their deeper feelings without fears of social criticism. In behavior therapy groups, people with similar problems may be treated in a group administration of techniques such as systematic desensitization and social skills training.

All in all, group therapy has certain advantages over individual treatment, including the following:

1. *Group therapy is less costly.*
2. *Group therapy allows greater access to limited therapist*

Group therapy. What are some of the advantages of group therapy over individual therapy? What are some of its disadvantages?

resources. Therapists may not have the time to see all the people who request assistance in a one-to-one treatment format.

3. *Group therapy may increase the fund of information and experience that clients can draw on.* Group members can share their life experiences, providing information on ways of solving one another's problems.

4. *Group therapy provides group support for appropriate behavior.* Clients may expect therapists to be supportive toward them, but an outpouring of support from one's peers may have greater impact on increasing self-esteem and self-confidence.

5. *Group therapy helps clients recognize their problems are not unique (and therefore they are not alone).* People who experience psychological difficulties often feel they are different than other people, and perhaps inferior. Group members are often reassured to learn others have made similar mistakes, experienced similar failures, and had similar self-doubts.

6. *Group members who improve provide a source of hope for other members.* Seeing other people progress may bolster hope of improvement in others.

7. *Group therapy provides opportunities for learning to deal more effectively with other people.* Many people seek help for difficulties relating to others or for reasons of social inhibition. Group therapy provides members with opportunities to work through their problems in relating to others. For example, the therapist or other members may point out to a particular member when he or she acts in a bossy manner or tends to withdraw when criticized, patterns of behavior that may mirror the behavior the client shows in relationships with others outside the group. Group members may also rehearse social skills with one another in a

supportive atmosphere. Members may role-play important people in each other's lives to hone interpersonal skills.

Despite these advantages, clients may prefer individual therapy for various reasons. For one, clients might not wish to disclose their problems to others in a group. Some clients prefer the individual attention of the therapist. Others are too socially inhibited to feel comfortable in a group setting, even though they might be the ones who could most profit from a group experience. Because of such concerns, group therapists require that group disclosures be kept confidential, that group members relate to each other supportively and nondestructively, and that group members receive the attention they need.

FAMILY AND MARITAL THERAPY

In **family therapy,** it is the family, not the individual, that is the unit of treatment. Family therapy aims to help troubled families resolve their conflicts and problems so the family functions better as a unit and individual family members are subjected to less stress from family conflicts.

Faulty patterns of communications within the family often contribute to family problems. In family therapy, family members learn to communicate more effectively and to air their disagreements constructively. Family conflicts often emerge at transitional points in the life cycle when family patterns are altered by changes in one or more members. Conflicts between parents and children, for example, often emerge when adolescent children seek greater independence or autonomy. Family members with low self-esteem may be unable to tolerate different attitudes or behaviors from other members of the family and may resist their efforts to change or become more independent. Family therapists work with families to resolve these conflicts and help them adjust to life changes among family members.

Family therapists are sensitive to tendencies of families to scapegoat one family member as the source of the problem, or the "identified client." Disturbed families seem to adopt a sort of myth: Change the identified client, the "bad apple," and the "barrel," or family, will once again become functional. Family therapists encourage families to work together to resolve their disputes and conflicts, instead of resorting to scapegoating.

One widely adopted approach to family therapy, called *conjoint family therapy,* was developed by Virginia Satir (1967). Satir conceptualized the family in terms of a pattern or *system* of communications and interactions that needs to be studied and changed to enhance family functioning as well as the growth of individual family members.

Another prominent approach to family therapy is **structural family therapy** (Minuchin, 1974). This approach also adopts a family systems model of abnormal behavior. It conceptualizes problem behaviors of individual members of the family as arising from dysfunctional relationship patterns within the family system, rather than as problems involving only the individuals themselves. Family members may develop psychological or physical problems in response to stressful role relationships in the family. The family system

Family therapy. In family therapy, the family, not the individual, is the unit of treatment. Family therapists help family members communicate more effectively with one another, for example, to air their disagreements in ways that are not hurtful to individual members. Family therapists also try to prevent one member of the family from becoming the scapegoat for the family's problems.

usually resists efforts of individual members to change these role relationships, no matter how distorted or dysfunctional they become. Structural family therapists analyze the family roles played by individual members and help families restructure themselves in ways that are more supportive of the members. For example, a child may feel in competition with other siblings for a parent's attention and develop enuresis, or bed-wetting, as a means of securing attention. The structural family therapist would help the family understand the hidden messages in the child's behavior and assist the family to make changes in their relationships to meet the child's needs more adequately. In so doing, the therapist shows the family how the member with the identified problem (enuresis) is responding to wider problems in the family.

Marital therapy may be considered a subtype of family therapy, in which the family unit is the marital couple. Like other forms of family therapy, marital therapy focuses on improving communication and analyzing role relationships in order to improve the marital relationship. For example, one partner may play a dominant role and resist any request to share power with the other. The marital therapist would help bring these role relationships into the open, so alternative ways of relating to one another could be explored that would lead to a more satisfying relationship.

EVALUATING THE EFFECTIVENESS OF PSYCHOTHERAPY

Does psychotherapy work? Are some forms of therapy more effective than others? Are some forms of therapy more effective for some types of clients or for some types of problems than for others?

The effectiveness of psychotherapy receives strong support from the research literature. Reviews of the scientific literature often utilize a statistical technique called **meta-analysis,** which averages the results of a large number of studies in order to determine an overall level of effectiveness.

In the most frequently cited meta-analysis of psychotherapy research, M. L. Smith and Glass (1977) analyzed the results of some 375 controlled studies comparing various types of therapies (psychodynamic, behavioral, humanistic, etc.) against control groups. The results of their analyses showed the average psychotherapy client in these studies was better off than 75% of the clients who remained untreated. In 1980, Smith and Glass and their colleague Miller reported the results of a larger analysis based on 475 controlled outcome studies, which showed the average person who received therapy was better off at the end of treatment than 80% of those who did not (M. L. Smith et al., 1980).

Other meta-analyses also show positive outcomes for psychotherapy, including analyses of both behavioral approaches (Bowers & Clum, 1988) and brief psychodynamic approaches (E. M. Anderson & Lambert, 1995; Crits-Christoph, 1992) and psychotherapy with children (Weisz et al., 1995). A recent meta-analysis of meta-analyses (a compilation of more than 300 meta-analyses) provided yet further evidence that well-developed psychological interventions are generally effective (Lipsey & Wilson, 1993, 1995). Evidence indicates that psychotherapy is effective not only in the confines of clinical research centers but also in settings that are more typical of ordinary clinical practice (Shadish et al., 1997). Although not all researchers endorse the use of meta-analysis as a methodological tool, the technique has achieved widespread acceptance within psychology and has provided some of the strongest evidence to date supporting the effectiveness of psychotherapy.

Evidence also shows that the greatest gains in psychotherapy are typically achieved in the first several months of treatment (Barkham, et al., 1996; Howard, Kopta, Krause, & Orlinksy, 1986). Gains tend to be lasting (Nicholson & Berman, 1983). Researchers find that about 75% of clients in psychotherapy show some improvement by the end of 6 months of once-weekly therapy and about 75% experience a remission of their presenting complaints sufficient to restore them to normal levels of functioning after about 1 year of therapy (Howard et al., 1986; S. M. Kopta et al., 1994).

Other evidence supporting the effectiveness of psychotherapy comes from a recent survey of subscribers to the consumer magazine, *Consumer Reports* (Consumer Reports, 1995; Seligman, 1995). Of the nearly 3,000 respondents who reported seeking treatment from a mental health professional, most reported considerable improvement from the care they had received. Respondents who consulted a mental health professional for their problems reported more long-term improvement than those who sought care from their family physicians. Similar progress was reported whether people saw psychologists, psychiatrists, or social workers. Yet those who stayed in treatment for longer periods of time reported greater improvement than those who received briefer treatment. And those whose choice of therapists or duration of treatment was limited by their insurance coverages reported poorer results than others with more flexible coverage.

We should bear in mind, however, that the fact the average client can expect to benefit from psychotherapy does not mean every client benefits. Negative outcomes do occur. Some clients experience little if any benefit; still others deteriorate (Mohr, 1995; Ogles, Lambert, & Sawyer, 1995; Scogin et al., 1996). We know little about the types of patients or types of interventions that are likely to produce ineffective or even harmful outcomes (Matt & Navarro, 1997). The issue of whether psychotherapy actually causes deterioration or simply fails to prevent deterioration from occurring has been a subject of debate (Mohr, 1995). People who receive other types of intervention, such as drug therapy or electroconvulsive therapy (ECT), may also fail to respond positively or may experience adverse effects.

Research evidence also provides strong support for the efficacy of both marital and family therapy (Baucom et al., 1998; Bray & Jouriles, 1995; Shadish & Ragsdale, 1996). A recent meta-analysis showed a significant level of benefit, with the average client who receives these forms of therapy achieving better results at the termination of treatment than 70% of control subjects who receive no treatment (Shadish et al., 1993). What we don't yet know is whether there are differences in the levels of effectiveness among the various forms of family and marital therapy.

Evidence from controlled studies examining the effectiveness of group therapy remains lacking. One review of the group therapy literature showed results that favored group therapy over placebo or no treatment conditions, for example, but the studies comprising the analysis tended to be plagued by poor methodologies (Kaul & Bednar, 1986). Moreover, there is a lack of evidence that directly compares each form of group therapy with a comparable form of individual therapy.

Comparing Different Therapeutic Approaches

There are major methodological problems in comparing therapies directly, such as a direct comparison of behavioral and psychodynamic approaches. Among the problems are possible differences in the types of therapists who practice one form of therapy or the other and the types of problems treated, and difficulties obtaining consent from clients and clinic administrators to permit random assignment to different therapies. Not surprisingly, few head-to-head comparisons between different approaches to therapy have been reported in the research literature. As an alternative to direct comparisons, investigators have turned to the use of meta-analysis to compare the relative level of effectiveness of different therapies when each is compared against control groups.

Meta-analyses show only negligible differences, overall, in outcomes among the various therapies when such therapies are compared to control groups (Crits-Christoph, 1992; M. L. Smith et al., 1980; Wampold et al., 1997a, 1997b). Such minor differences suggest that the effectiveness of psychotherapy may have more to do with the features they share in common than with the specific techniques that set them apart (M. J. Lambert & Bergin, 1994). These common features are called *nonspecific treatment factors*. Nonspecific or common factors in psychotherapy stem largely from the therapist-client relationship. These factors include the following: (1) empathy, support, and attention shown by the therapist; (2) *therapeutic alliance,* or attachment the client develops toward the therapist and the therapy process; and (3) the *working alliance,* or the development of an effective working relationship in which the therapist and client strive jointly and constructively toward identifying and confronting the important issues and problems the client faces (J. L. Binder & Strupp, 1997; Connors et al., 1997; M. J. Lambert & Okiishi, 1997; J. Weinberger, 1995).

Does this necessarily mean that different therapeutic approaches are about equally effective? One possibility is that different therapies have about equal effects overall but may not have equal effectiveness with every patient (Wampold et al., 1997a). That is, a given therapy may be more effective for a particular patient or for a particular type of problem.

Nonspecific factors. Are the benefits of psychotherapy due to nonspecific factors that various psychotherapists share in common, such as the mobilization of hope, the attention and support provided by the therapist, and the development of a good working alliance between the client and therapist? It appears that both specific and nonspecific factors are involved in accounting for therapeutic change.

It is thus insufficient to ask which therapy works best. We must ask, Which therapy works best for which type of problem? Which clients are best suited for which type of therapy? What are the advantages and limitations of particular therapies? Behavior therapy, for example, has shown impressive results in treating various types of anxiety disorders, sleep disorders, and sexual dysfunctions, and in improving the adaptive functioning of people with schizophrenia and with mental retardation. Psychodynamic and humanistic-existential approaches may be more effective in fostering self-insight and personality growth. Cognitive therapy has demonstrated impressive results in treating depression and anxiety disorders. By and large, however, the process of determining which treatment, practiced by whom, and under what conditions is most effective for a given client remains a challenge.

All in all, psychotherapies appear to be complex processes that incorporate common features along with specific techniques that foster adaptive change. The therapeutic alliance may well be a stronger determinant of positive outcomes in therapy than the particular treatment method used (Castonguay et al., 1996; Krupnick et al., 1996). Yet evidence shows that gains from cognitive-behavioral and brief psychodynamic therapy are not simply accounted for by nonspecific factors alone (Borkovec & Costello, 1993; Oei & Shuttlewood, 1996; Grissom, 1996). Presently we lack theories and models that consider all the relevant factors and processes that account for therapeutic change (Arkowitz, 1995). In the final analysis, accounting for therapeutic change may well involve both specific and nonspecific factors, as well as their interaction (Ilardi & Craighead, 1994).

Empirically Validated Treatments   Another approach to the question of determining which therapies are effective for which types of problems was undertaken by a task force commissioned by the Clinical Psychology Division of the American Psychological Association. The task force concluded that enough evidence now exists from controlled trials to support the therapeutic efficacy of various psychological interventions (listed in Table 3.1) for specific psychological problems or disorders (Chambless et al., 1998; Chambless & Hollon, 1998). To be considered effective, the task force required that a given treatment must have met either one or both of the following criteria: (1) been demonstrated in at least two independent studies to be more effective than a drug or psychological placebo condition or an alternative treatment, or to be equivalent to already well-established treatments; or (2) been demonstrated to be effective on the basis of a large series of well-designed, experimental single-subject design studies in which the treatment was compared to another treatment or placebo condition.

Other treatment interventions may be added to the list of empirically validated treatments as scientific evidence attesting to their effectiveness becomes available. We should caution you not to infer that the inclusion of a particular

TABLE 3.1

Examples of Empirically Validated Psychological Treatments

Treatment	Well-Established Treatments (Chapter in text where treatment is discussed is shown in parentheses.)
Cognitive therapy	Depression (Ch. 7)
Behavior modification or behavior therapy	Depression (Ch. 7) Persons with developmental disabilities (Ch. 13) Enuresis (Ch. 13) Headache (Ch. 4)
Cognitive-behavior-therapy	Panic disorder with and without agoraphobia (Ch. 5) Generalized anxiety disorder (Ch. 5) Bulimia (Ch. 10) Smoking cessation (Ch. 9)
Exposure treatment	Agoraphobia and specific phobia (Ch. 5)
Exposure and response prevention	Obsessive-compulsive disorder (Ch. 5)
Interpersonal psychotherapy	Depression (Ch. 7)
Parent training programs	Children with oppositional behavior (Ch. 13)

Source: Adapted from Chambless et al., 1998

treatment guarantees it is effective in every case. Nor does it mean the treatment alone is *sufficient* to achieve a maximum benefit. For example, family education or intervention programs may be helpful in the treatment of schizophrenia (see Chapter 12) but are usually a part of a multifaceted approach involving drug therapy, psychosocial rehabilitation, and other treatment components.

The effort to develop a listing of empirically validated treatments comes at a time when health-care professionals are facing increasing pressure to demonstrate the effectiveness of the treatments they use. As task force member William Sanderson (Task Force, 1995) said , "More than ever before, psychologists—and all health-care providers—are being called on to show the efficacy of their interventions. Society wants proof that a treatment works—whether it be medication, surgery or psychotherapy—before it is administered" (p. 5).

Managed Care or Managed Costs? This is an appropriate juncture to note that the practice of psychotherapy has been influenced by changes in the general health care environment in recent years, especially the increasing role of managed care systems such as health maintenance organizations (HMOs). Managed care systems typically impose limits on the number of treatment sessions they will approve for payment and the fees they will allow for reimbursement. Consequently, there is greater emphasis today on briefer, more direct forms of treatment, including cognitive-behavioral therapy and shorter-term psychodynamic therapies. Traditional long-term psychodynamic psychotherapy is likely to become a luxury that is available to only a very few (Strupp, 1992). Moreover, managed care has curbed

costly inpatient mental health treatment, primarily through limiting the lengths of stay of patients in psychiatric hospitals (Wickizer, Lessler, & Travis, 1996). Whether costs can be managed without sacrificing quality of care remains to be seen.

Though health-care providers understand the need to curtail the spiraling costs of care, they are understandably concerned that the cost-cutting emphasis of managed care

"IT'S YOUR INSURANCE COMPANY, THEY SAY YOU'RE CURED."

Managed Care or Managed Costs?

plans may discourage needful people with identifiable psychological disorders from seeking help or receiving an adequate level of care (Landerman et al., 1994). Overzealous cost-cutting policies may also be financially short-sighted because the failure to provide adequate mental health care when problems arise may lead to an increased need for more expensive care at some later point. Evidence shows that for people with severe psychological disorders, such as schizophrenia, bipolar disorder, and borderline personality disorder, psychotherapy actually reduces health care costs by reducing the need for hospitalization and reducing work impairment (Fraser, 1996; Gabbard et al., 1997).

MULTICULTURAL ISSUES IN PSYCHOTHERAPY

In our evaluation of the effectiveness of psychotherapy, we noted we must not only consider whether clients who receive therapy, generally speaking, are better off than those who do not. We must also consider what kind of therapy is most effective for what kind of client and for what kind of problem. Part of that appraisal involves considering how cultural and ethnic factors relate to the therapeutic process.

Despite a growing body of evidence supporting the effectiveness of various forms of psychotherapy, members of ethnic minority groups have been underrepresented in psychotherapy research. Consider, for example, that we have considerable evidence attesting to the effectiveness of behavior therapy in treating anxiety disorders in the majority White population, but know little about the effectiveness of these techniques with African Americans (S. M. Turner, 1992). For that matter, we know little about the effectiveness of psychotherapy in general with people of color (Matt & Navarro, 1997).

The pendulum is beginning to swing in the other direction, however. Evidence is emerging that shows psychotherapy to be helpful in treating low-income groups and people of color, especially when treatment is offered in a culturally sensitive context. In one recent example, researchers obtained promising results using a cognitive-behavioral approach in treating depression in low-income, medical outpatients, most of whom were Hispanic American or African American women (Organista, Munoz, & Gonzales, 1994). The therapy program was offered in a culturally competent context, utilizing bilingual and bicultural staff members and offering Spanish-language therapy and translation of measures as they were needed. Participants achieved significant reductions in depression, although not to the extent typically found in other treatment outcome studies.

We should note, however, that cultural mistrust can impact negatively on the therapeutic process. Research with a sample of African American students from a predominantly White, southern university showed that those who held a deeper level of cultural mistrust had more negative expectancies toward receiving help from White therapists than did other African American students with lower levels of cultural mistrust (Nickerson, Helms, & Terrell, 1994). Therapists who address racial issues early in therapy may be more effective in overcoming cultural mistrust than those who ignore issues of race.

In this section, we consider some of the specific issues involved in treating African Americans, Asian Americans, Hispanic Americans, and Native Americans. It is clear that clinicians must avoid stereotypes and be sensitive to the values, languages, and cultural beliefs of members of minority groups they treat in psychotherapy (Comas-Diaz & Griffith, 1988; Lee & Richardson, 1991).

African Americans

The cultural history of African Americans must be understood in the context of a history of extreme racial discrimination (Boyd-Franklin, 1989; Greene, 1990). African Americans have needed to develop coping mechanisms for managing the racism they encounter in such areas as employment, housing, education, and access to health care (Greene, 1993a, 1993b). For example, the sensitivity of many African Americans to the potential for maltreatment and exploitation has been a survival tool that may take the form of a heightened level of suspiciousness or reserve (Greene, 1986). Therapists need to be aware of the tendency of African American clients to minimize their vulnerability by being less self disclosing, especially in earlier stages of therapy (Ridley, 1984). Therapists should not confuse such suspiciousness with paranoia, however (Boyd-Franklin, 1989; Greene, 1986; Grier & Cobbs, 1968).

In addition to whatever psychological problems an African American client may present, the therapist often needs to help the client develop coping mechanisms to deal with societal racial barriers. Therapists also need to be attuned to tendencies of some African Americans to internalize within their self concepts the negative stereotypes about Blacks that are perpetuated in the dominant culture (Greene, 1985, 1992b, 1992c; Pinderhughes, 1989; Nickerson, Helms, & Terrell, 1994).

To be culturally competent, therapists not only must develop a better awareness of the cultural traditions and languages of the groups with which they work, but must also come to an understanding of their own racial and ethnic attitudes and how their underlying attitudes affect their clinical practice (Greene, 1985, 1992b, 1992c; Nickerson, Helms, & Terrell, 1994; Pinderhughes, 1989). Therapists are exposed to the same negative stereotypes about African Americans as other people in society and must recognize how the incorporation of these stereotypes, if left unexamined, can become destructive to the therapeutic relationships they form with African American clients. In effect, therapists must be willing to confront their own racism and prejudices and work to replace these attitudes with more realistic appraisals of African Americans (Mays, 1985).

Therapists must also be aware of the cultural characteristics associated with African American families, such as strong kinship bonds between family members, often

Ethnic Matching of Clients and Therapists

The great majority of psychotherapists in the United States are non-Hispanic White Americans whose primary language is English. Are such therapists as effective in treating minority clients as therapists from the clients' own ethnic group?

The so-called *cultural responsivenessness hypothesis* suggests clients will respond better to therapy when the therapist is similar to them in ethnic and language background. Although clients who identify strongly with their own culture tend to prefer ethnically similar counselors (Coleman, Wampold, & Casali, 1995), evidence is mixed on whether or not ethnic matching increases therapeutic benefits. A recent large-scale study of the mental health system in Los Angeles County found at least partial support for the cultural responsiveness hypothesis (Sue et al., 1991). On the one hand, therapist-client matching was associated with lower rates of premature termination (dropping out after only one session) and greater length of treatment for all groups (African, Mexican, non-Hispanic White, and Asian Americans). Ethnic matching, however, was unrelated to treatment outcome, except for Mexican Americans. It thus appears from this study that ethnic matching had a greater effect in general on retaining clients in therapy than it did on eventual outcome. For Mexican Americans and Asian Americans who did not speak English as their primary language, however, ethnic and language matching was associated with both retention in therapy and outcome. Other researchers find ethnic matching to be associated with lower treatment dropout rates with Hispanic clients (O'Sullivan & Lasso, 1992), Black clients (Rosencheck, Fontana, & Cottrol, 1995), and Asian and Pacific Islander clients (Takeuchi, Mokuau, & Chun, 1992). Language match-

ing as well as ethnic matching may be of greater value to clients who are not native English speakers.

Whatever the benefits of matching therapists to clients on the basis of ethnicity might be, it is important to recognize that ethnicity alone is not a sole determinant of therapeutic effectiveness. Therapists' sensitivity and ability to establish rapport are likely to be critical factors in determining therapeutic effectiveness, whether one is treating clients of the same or different ethnicity (Sue, 1988).

Must the ethnic backgrounds of therapists and clients match? The cultural responsiveness hypothesis suggests that clients will respond better to therapy if therapists are similar to them in ethnicity and language. The available evidence indicates that ethnic matching may have more of an effect on retaining clients in therapy than on eventual outcome. It is clear that clients who are not fluent in English do profit from having therapists who can conduct therapy in their own languages.

including people who are not biologically related (for example, a close friend of a parent may have some parenting role and may be addressed as an "aunt"); strong religious and spiritual orientation; multigenerational households; adaptibility and flexibility of gender roles (African American women have a long history of working outside the home); and distribution of child-care responsibilities among different family members (Boyd-Franklin, 1989; Ferguson-Peters, 1985; Greene, 1990). For example, grandmothers often assume significant parenting responsibilities and may be referred to by the children as "mother." A therapist who is unfamiliar with this cultural tradition may find it confusing that the child experiences the grandmother as the psychological parent.

Among African Americans, there is often the assumption that one is supposed to be able at all times to manage one's problems and be strong in the face of stress. Any sign of emotional weakness carries such a strong negative stigma that people who encounter anxieties, feelings of depression, or even normal reactions to stress may perceive themselves as having a "nervous breakdown" (Boyd-Franklin, 1989; Childs, 1990; Greene, 1993b). Yet the cultural expectation that they should just "get over it" on their own often delays their seeking help until the problem becomes serious. In times of stress, African Americans are more likely to seek religious support than mental health services. For example, in the aftermath of Hurricane Andrew in 1992, Black residents of the affected area were more likely to use religion to help them cope, whereas Whites were more likely to use therapy (West et al., 1995). Interestingly, however, the use of either coping resource—religion or therapy—was equally effective in reducing psychological distress for both Blacks and Whites.

Asian Americans

Zane and Sue (1991) explain various ways in which cultural influences affect the utilization and effectiveness of mental health services for Asian Americans. Mental health problems carry a severe social stigma among Asian Americans, which may deter them from recognizing problems and seeking help to deal with them. Asian Americans, especially recent immigrants, may also have little understanding of, or faith in, Western models of psychotherapy. The emphasis in Western psychotherapy on the open expression of feelings may conflict with traditional Asian tendencies to refrain from public displays of emotion. Asians may also prefer structured, unambiguous approaches to solving problems, which may conflict with the open-ended, unstructured, and often ambiguous style of Western insight-oriented psychotherapies. Asians, that is, may regard the therapist as an authority figure who should give them direct advice to help them solve their problems, whereas the traditional Western therapist may prefer to help clients clarify their feelings and reach their own decisions, rather than tell them what to do. Moreover, Asian Americans may have a different conception of mental health. They may believe mental health arises from turning one's thoughts away from painful experiences or "morbid" thoughts, whereas traditional Western psychotherapy focuses on getting in touch with painful thoughts and feelings. For these and other reasons, many Asian Americans may find Western psychotherapy to be incompatible with their values and beliefs.

Clinicians also note that Asians often express psychological complaints in terms of physical symptoms. The tendency to somaticize emotional problems may be attributed in part to differences in communication styles (Zane & Sue, 1991). That is, Asians may use somatic terms to convey emotional distress.

Culturally sensitive therapists not only understand the beliefs and values of other cultures but also integrate this knowledge within the therapy process. Such therapists need to assess the client's willingness and ability to express personal feelings and to tailor therapy to match the client's cultural expectations. Consider the therapeutic relationship between therapists and Japanese clients. Generally speaking, Asian cultures, including Japanese culture, value restraint in talking about oneself and one's feelings. Therapists thus need to be patient and not expect instant self-disclosures from Japanese American clients (Henkin, 1985). Public expression of affect is also discouraged in Asian cultures. Suppression of emotions, especially negative emotions, is valued, and failure to keep one's feelings to oneself is believed to reflect poorly on one's upbringing (L. H. Huang, 1994). Asian clients who appear emotionally restrained or constricted when judged by Western standards may be responding in ways that are culturally appropriate.

In some cases, there may also be inherent role conflicts between the goals of therapy and the values of a particular culture. The individual centeredness of American society, which becomes expressed in therapeutic interventions in Western society that focus on development of the self, also contrasts sharply with the group- and family-centered values of Asian cultures (L. H. Huang, 1994). Therapeutic approaches that emphasize the importance of individuality and self-determination may be inappropriate when applied to Asian clients who adhere strongly to traditional Asian cultural values, which emphasize the importance of the group over the individual (Ching et al., 1995; Henkin, 1985).

Respect for cultural differences is a keynote feature of culturally sensitive therapies. Training in multicultural therapy is becoming more widely integrated into training programs for therapists (e.g., Neville et al., 1996). Culturally sensitive therapies adopt a respectful attitude that encourages people to tell their own personal story as well as the story of their culture (Coronado & Peake, 1992).

Hispanic Americans

Although Hispanic American subcultures differ in various respects, many of them share certain cultural values and beliefs, such as adherence to a strong patriarchal (male-dominated) family structure and strong kinship ties. De la Cancela and Guzman (1991) identify some other values shared by many Hispanic Americans:

> One's identity is in part determined by one's role in the family. The male, or *macho,* is the head of the family, the provider, the protector of the family honor, and the final decision maker. The woman's role (*marianismo*) is to care for the family and the children. Obviously, these roles are changing, with women entering the work force and achieving greater educational opportunities. Cultural values of *respeto* (respect), *confianza* (trust), *dignidad* (dignity), and *personalismo* (personalism) are highly esteemed and are important factors in working with many [Hispanic Americans]. (p. 60)

Therapists need to be sensitive to these cultural factors, if they are to be successful in developing effective interventions with Hispanic American clients. They need to recognize, for example, value conflicts that may occur between the traditional Hispanic American value of interdependency on the family with the values of independence and self-reliance, which are stressed in the mainstream U.S. culture (De la Cancela & Guzman, 1991). Psychotherapeutic interventions should respect differences in values rather than attempt to impose values of majority cultures on people from ethnic minority groups. Therapists should also be trained to reach beyond the confines of their offices to work within the Hispanic American community itself, in settings that impact on the daily lives of Hispanic Americans, such as social clubs, *bodegas* (neighborhood groceries), and neighborhood beauty and barber shops.

Although many therapists recognize the importance of cultural factors in psychotherapy, some therapists have gone further by developing culturally sensitive approaches to therapy. For example, Malgady and his colleagues (Malgady, Rogher, & Constantino, 1990) describe several forms of culturally specific psychotherapy in providing mental health services to Hispanic Americans. Malgady and his colleagues cite the cultural distance between the typically lower socio-economic class Hispanic American client and the typically middle-class, non-Hispanic White therapist as the root of the difficulty in treating Hispanic American clients. Malgady and his colleagues outline some therapeutic approaches that they believe might close the gap between mental health service providers and Hispanic American clients:

1. Recruiting bicultural/bilingual staff and creating a therapeutic atmosphere that is accepting of Hispanic American cultural values (Guarnaccia & Rodriguez, 1996).

2. Using treatment methods that are in keeping with Hispanic American clients' cultural values. One might, for example, adopt Ruiz's (1981) recommendation to tailor the type of treatment to the client's level of acculturation.

3. Incorporating clients' cultural values in therapy. An example of integrating cultural values directly into psychotherapy is found in the use of *cuento therapy* with Puerto Rican children by Malgady and his colleagues (see Chapter 13). *Cuento therapy* is a storytelling technique that adapts Hispanic folktales, or cuentos, to model therapeutic themes or morals. The child characters in the folktales embody socially desirable beliefs, values, and behaviors.

Your first author and colleagues (Nevid, 1997; Nevid & Javier, 1997; Nevid, Javier, & Moulton, 1996) adapted a form of *cuento therapy* within a smoking cessation program for Hispanic American smokers. They developed a series of videotaped vignettes featuring Hispanic American actors in scenes that conveyed culturally laden values intended to promote antismoking messages and encourage smoking cessation (see Chapter 9).

Native Americans

Among all the ethnic minority groups in the United States, Native Americans may be most in need of effective mental health treatment. Native Americans suffer disproportionately from various mental health problems and related physical problems, such as cirrhosis of the liver (caused by chronic alcoholism), alcohol and tobacco dependence, depression, and developmental disabilities. Estimates indicate that the lifetime prevalence of psychological disorders may exceed 50% of the population of some Native American tribes (Trimble, 1991). Despite the need, Native Americans remain severely underserved by mental health professionals, in part because of the cultural gap that exists between providers and recipients of these services.

Kahn (1982) argues that if mental health professionals are to be successful in helping Native Americans, they must do so within a context that is relevant and sensitive to Native Americans' customs, culture, and values. For instance, Native American speakers tend to pause for longer intervals when engaged in a back-and-forth conversation than non-natives (Renfrey, 1992). The therapist who is unaware of this cultural difference may interrupt the Native American speaker or fail to give the speaker enough time to formulate a response to questions. Moreover, many Native Americans expect the therapist will do most of the talking and they will play a passive role in treatment. These expectations are in keeping with the traditional healer role but may conflict with the client-focused approach of many forms of conventional therapy. There may yet be other differences in gestures, eye contact, facial expression, and other modes of nonverbal expression that can impede effective communication between therapist and client (Renfrey, 1992).

To be effective, therapists need to use techniques that are culturally congruent with the clients they serve and respectful of cultural differences (E. E. Williams & Ellison, 1996). More directive forms of treatment, such as cognitive-behavioral therapy, may work better with Native Americans than other approaches that focus on exploration of the client's feelings (Renfrey, 1992). Even directive therapies need to be adjusted to the cultural realities of Native Americans.

Prevention efforts should focus on strengthening cultural cohesion, identity, and ethnic pride and helping Native American peoples regain a sense of mastery over the world in which they live. In some cases, language and cultural differences create so great a gap between Native American peoples and the dominant culture that only trained Native American mental health counselors may be effective as service providers. Among the Papago Indians in Arizona, utilization of mental health services was virtually nil until culturally sensitive programs with indigenous counselors were developed (Kahn, 1982).

Therapists can use indigenous ceremonies that are part of the client's cultural or religious traditions. To do so, mental health professionals need to become knowledgeable about traditional Native cultures as well as their own and attempt to integrate the two (Timpson et al., 1988). Lefley (1990) notes that purification and cleansing rites are therapeutic for many Native American peoples in the United States and elsewhere, as among the African Cuban *santeria,* the Brazilian *umbanda,* and the Haitian *vodou.* Cleansing rites are often sought by people who believe their problems are caused by failure to placate malevolent spirits or to perform mandatory rituals (Lefley, 1990).

Lifting the Curse from Technical Eclecticism?

Lefley (1990) recounts the case of a hospitalized psychotic Haitian man who remained acutely psychotic after 10 days of hospital treatment. According to his own belief system, the patient's problems were due to a curse that had to be lifted. In a cross-cultural example of technical eclecticism, a *vodou* priest (called a *boungan*) was invited to perform curative

Feminist Therapy

Feminist psychotherapy has its theoretical origins in feminist political theory, philosophy, and ethics. Feminist ideology challenges the validity of gender-role stereotypes and expectations, which have traditionally maintained patterns of male dominance and female subordination (Greene, 1997; Greene & Sanchez, 1997). Feminist therapy emerged as a response to male dominance of mental health professions and institutions and to the role of the mental health establishment in maintaining social inequities between men and women and between members of the majority culture and those of visible ethnic minority groups. Although feminist therapists use a variety of therapeutic techniques, they are guided by the commitment to political, economic, and social equality for men and women and between the client and therapist (M. Butler, 1985).

Feminist therapists argue that social inequality, rather than individual psychopathology, has a prominent role in creating and maintaining many of the problems presented by clients in psychotherapy, particularly when those clients are members of traditionally oppressed groups (Brown, 1992). They validate their client's realistic experience of social mistreatment and assist them, when appropriate, in understanding that many of their problems are a function of social inequities rather than their own personal problems or deficiencies (L. S. Brown, 1992; Dutton-Douglas & Walker, 1988). In this framework, distinctions are made between reactions and behavior. Negative reactions to mistreatment, such as anger and suspiciousness toward people who oppress or abuse them, are deemed healthy and appropriate. The task of the therapist is to help the client make conscious choices in developing assertive strategies or behaviors to address mistreatment, not simply accept it. Recent expansions and revisions of feminist principles extend these principles to working with members of ethnic and racial minority groups (Brown & Root, 1990; Greene, 1997).

Recognition of the need for change in social systems and institutions, and not just within the client, and a commitment to making social changes are the core features of feminist therapy that distinguish it from traditional psychotherapies (M. Butler, 1985). Feminist therapy criticizes traditional approaches for their failure to challenge or label as abnormal the behaviors of dominant group members that are destructive to nondominant group members. For example, feminist therapists would view racist, sexist, or heterosexist behavior as pathological and would not see the negative reactions of the victims of such behavior as pathological.

Feminist therapy also demands that therapists explore and understand their own social biases and the role of those biases in their work as therapists. Feminist therapy further challenges therapists to pay greater attention to the differences in power between members of the male-dominated culture and women, members of ethnic minority groups, economically disadvantaged persons, and gay men and lesbians and the expression of those power differences in psychological theories of diagnosis and treatment. A feminist criticism of the traditional psychotherapies is the tendency to label as normal those attributes identified with the male-dominated mainstream and to label as abnormal those attributes associated with femininity and with minority cultures.

---

rituals. The patient calmed down at once, was stabilized on medications, and soon sent home.

TRUTH *or* FICTION REVISITED

3.6 *True.* A psychotic Haitian man responded positively to a form of therapy that included the lifting of a curse by a *vodou* priest.

BIOLOGICAL THERAPIES

There is a growing emphasis in American psychiatry on the biological bases of abnormal behavior, or **biological psychiatry.** Biological psychiatry seeks to understand the biological underpinnings of abnormal behavior and emphasizes the use of biological approaches to treatment, such as drugs and electroconvulsive shock therapy (ECT). The trend toward biological psychiatry has been spurred by recent scientific advancements—for example, the development of sophisticated brain-imaging techniques such as MRI. Knowledge is also expanding concerning the role of neurotransmitters in abnormal behaviors and in the development of new drugs to correct specific types of neurotransmitter imbalances. In experimental work that a few years ago would have seemed science fiction, researchers are attempting to repair damaged or destroyed brain tissue by implanting neurotransmitter-producing brain cells in the hopes these cells might proliferate and replenish depleted levels of neurotransmitters. Such research may potentially be of benefit in treating such disor-

For example, women who acted assertively were often perceived by traditional psychoanalysts as suffering from unresolved penis envy, while assertive men were deemed to be appropriately masculinized. Feminist therapists object to the use of such gender-role stereotypes to support cultural beliefs in male superiority and female inferiority. Similarly, they object to using cultural differences, such as differences in child-rearing practices, as a basis for characterizing minority cultural groups as inferior to majority cultural groups.

Feminist therapy practices encourage a more respectful appreciation of cultural and gender differences and recognize that the existence of differences between groups does not imply that one is inferior or superior to another. Despite this, feminist therapy theory has been appropriately criticized for its tendency to speak of women's issues and problems predominantly from the perspective of White, middle-class, and well-educated women (Greene, 1997; Greene & Sanchez, 1997). This often led them to assume that gender was a primary locus of societal disadvantage for all women. For example, for many White middle- and upper-class women, working outside the home represented the key to their liberation. Many ethnic minority and poor White women did not share the history of being unable to work outside the home. For them, the opportunity to remain home with their children would be a welcome relief to demands that they work to bring much needed money into their families. While issues relevant to a more culturally diverse group of women tend to be underrepresented in the feminist literature, they are still represented to a much greater degree than in the traditional psychotherapy literature (R. L. Hall & Greene, 1996).

How does feminist therapy challenge traditional psychotherapies? Feminist therapy challenges the validity of gender-role stereotypes and traditional inequalities of power between men and women, and between people who represent the dominant culture and ethnic minority groups. Feminist therapists argue that the traditional mental health establishment has a tendency to label forms of behavior that run counter to the interests of the dominant culture as pathological. For example, do women who act assertively suffer from unresolved penis envy?

ders as Alzheimer's disease and Parkinson's disease (see Chapter 14) in which brain cells that produce certain types of neurotransmitters are destroyed. Molecular geneticists are also mapping out the genes that may be associated with various psychological disorders. One day it may become common practice to repair or replace problematic genes.

Current biological approaches to the treatment of abnormal behaviors include drug therapy, ECT, and psychosurgery.

Although the biological or medical approaches have had dramatic success in treating some forms of abnormal behavior, they also have their limitations. For one, biological therapies may have unwelcome or dangerous side effects. There is also the potential for abuse. One of the most com-

monly prescribed minor tranquilizers, Valium, has become a major drug of abuse among people who become psychologically and physiologically dependent on it. Psychosurgery has been all but eliminated as a form of treatment because of serious harmful effects of earlier procedures.

Drug Therapy

Different classes of psychotropic drugs are used in the treatment of various types of mental health problems.

Antianxiety Drugs Antianxiety drugs (also called *anxiolytics,* from the Greek *anxietas,* meaning anxiety, and *lysis,* meaning "bringing to an end") are drugs that combat anxiety and reduce states of muscle tension. They include mild tranquilizers, such as *diazepam* (Valium), *chlordiazepoxide* (Librium), *alprazolam* (Xanax); barbiturates, such as *meprobamate* (Miltown); and hypnotic-sedatives, such as *triazolam* (Halcion) and *flurazepam* (Dalmane). For many years, Valium was the most widely prescribed drug in the world. Valium, a member of the *benzodiazepine* family of antianxiety drugs, is often prescribed for treatment of anxiety, insomnia, and tension.

About 6% of the general adult population have used antianxiety agents for relief of anxiety or insomnia in their lifetimes; 2% have used such drugs within the past year (APA, 1994). These drugs depress the level of activity in certain parts of the central nervous system (CNS). In turn, the CNS decreases the level of sympathetic nervous system activity, reducing the respiration rate and heart rate, and lessening states of anxiety and tension. Minor tranquilizers such as Valium grew in popularity when physicians became concerned about the use of more potent sedatives, such as barbiturates, which are highly addictive and extremely dangerous when taken in overdoses or mixed with alcohol. Unfortunately, it has become clear that the minor tranquilizers also can, and often do, lead to physiological dependence (addiction). People who are dependent on Valium may go into convulsions when they abruptly stop taking it. Deaths have been reported among people who mix mild tranquilizers with alcohol or who are unusually sensitive to them. There are other less severe side effects, such as fatigue, drowsiness, and impaired motor coordination, that might nonetheless impair the ability to function or to operate an automobile. Regular usage of benzodiazepines can also produce **tolerance,** a physiological sign of dependence, which refers to the need over time for increasing dosages of a drug to achieve the same effect. Quite commonly, patients become involved in tugs of war with their physicians as they demand increased dosages despite their physicians' concerns about the potential for abuse and dependence.

When used on a short-term basis, antianxiety drugs can be safe and effective in treating anxiety and insomnia. Yet drugs by themselves do not teach people more adaptive ways of solving their problems and may encourage them to rely on a chemical agent to cope with stress rather than develop active means of coping. Drug therapy is thus often combined with psychotherapy to help people with anxiety complaints deal with the psychological and situational bases of their problems. However, combining drug therapy and psychotherapy may present special problems and challenges. For one, drug-induced relief from anxiety may reduce clients' motivation to try to solve their problems. For another, medicated clients who develop skills for coping with stress in psychotherapy may fail to retain what they have learned once the tranquilizers are discontinued or find themselves too tense to employ their newly acquired skills.

Rebound anxiety is another problem associated with regular use of minor tranquilizers. Many people who regularly use antianxiety drugs report that anxiety or insomnia returns in a more severe form once they discontinue them.

For some, this may represent a fear of not having the drugs to depend on. For others, rebound anxiety might reflect changes in biochemical processes that are not well understood at present.

Antipsychotic Drugs   Antipsychotic drugs, also called **major tranquilizers** or **neuroleptics,** are commonly used to treat the more flagrant features of schizophrenia or other psychotic disorders, such as hallucinations, delusions, and states of confusion. Many of these drugs, including *chlorpromazine* (Thorazine), *thioridazine* (Mellaril), and *fluphenazine* (Prolixin) belong to the **phenothiazine** class of chemicals. Phenothiazines appear to control psychotic features by blocking the action of the neurotransmitter dopamine at receptor sites in the brain. Although the underlying causes of schizophrenia remain unknown, researchers suspect a dysregulation of the dopamine system in the brain may be involved (see Chapter 12). Clozapine (brand name Clozaril), a neuroleptic of a different chemical class than the phenothiazines, has been shown to be effective in treating many people with schizophrenia whose symptoms were unresponsive to other neuroleptics (A. I. Green & Salzman, 1990; Naber & Hippius, 1990; P. J. Perry et al., 1991; Pickar et al., 1992). The use of clozapine must be carefully monitored, however, because of potentially dangerous side effects (also discussed in Chapter 12).

Antipsychotics have reduced the need for more restrictive forms of treatment for severely disturbed patients, such as physical restraints and confinement in padded cells, and have lessened the need for long-term hospitalization. The introduction of major tranquilizers in the mid 1950s was one of the major factors that led to the massive exodus of chronic mental patients from state institutions that has occurred in the intervening years. Many ex-hospitalized patients have been able to resume family life and hold jobs while continuing to take their medications.

Antipsychotics are not without their problems, including potential side effects such as muscular rigidity and tremors. Although these side effects are generally controllable by use of other drugs, long-term use of antipsychotic drugs (possibly excepting clozapine) can produce a potentially irreversible and disabling motor disorder called *tardive dyskinesia* (see Chapter 12), which is characterized by uncontrollable eye blinking, facial grimaces, lip smacking, and other involuntary movements of the mouth, eyes, and limbs. Researchers are experimenting with lowered dosages, intermittent drug regimens, and use of new medications to reduce the risk of such complications.

Antidepressants   Three major classes of **antidepressants** are used in treating depression: **tricyclics, monoamine oxidase (MAO) inhibitors,** and **selective serotonin-reuptake inhibitors (SSRIs).** Although they work in different ways (see Chapter 7), the first two kinds of antidepressants, tricyclics and MAO inhibitors, increase the availability of the neurotransmitters norepinephrine and serotonin in the brain. Some of the more common tricyclics are *imipramine* (Tofranil), *amitriptyline* (Elavil), and *doxepin*

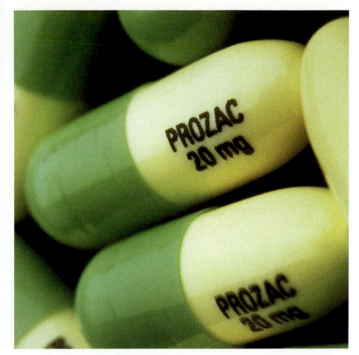

Drug therapy. Drug therapy is the most common biological treatment of abnormal behavior problems. Among the many different types of psychotropic drugs are minor tranquilizers, major tranquilizers (neuroleptics), antidepressants, and stimulants, such as Ritalin, used in the treatment of attention-deficit/hyperactivity disorder (ADHD). The drug Prozac (shown here) has become the most widely used antidepressant.

(Sinequan). The MAO inhibitors include such drugs as *phenelzine* (Nardil) and *tranylcypromine* (Parnate). Tricyclic antidepressants (TCAs) are more commonly favored over MAO inhibitors because of potentially serious side effects associated with MAO inhibitors.

The third class of antidepressants, selective serotonin-reuptake inhibitors, or SSRIs, have more specific effects on serotonin function in the brain. Drugs in this class include *fluoxetine* (Prozac), now the most widely prescribed antidepressant on the market, and *sertraline* (Zoloft). They increase the availability of serotonin in the brain by interfering with its reuptake by the transmitting neuron.

By the latest estimates, it appears that slightly more than half of the people with clinically significant depression who are treated with antidepressants of the tricyclic class will respond favorably (Depression Guideline Panel, 1993b). A favorable response to treatment does not mean depression is relieved, however. Overall, the effects of tricyclic antidepressants (TCAs) appear to be modest (Greenberg, Bornstein, Greenberg, & Fisher, 1992). Nor does any particular antidepressant appear to be clearly more effective than any other (Depression Guideline Panel, 1993b). Even Prozac, which was hailed by some as a "wonder drug," appears on the basis of present evidence to be no more effective than the TCAs (Greenberg et al., 1994). Prozac and other SSRIs may be preferred, however, because they are associated with fewer side effects, such as weight gain, and have a lower risk of lethal overdoses than the older tricyclics (Depression Guideline Panel, 1993b).

We shall see that antidepressants also have beneficial effects in treating a wide range of psychological disorders, including panic disorder (see Chapter 5), obsessive-compulsive disorder (see Chapter 5), and eating disorders (see Chapter 10). As research into the underlying causes of these disorders continues, we may find that dysregulation of neurotransmitters plays a key role in their development.

Lithium Lithium carbonate, a salt of the metal lithium in tablet form, has demonstrated remarkable effectiveness in stabilizing the dramatic mood swings associated with bipolar disorder (formerly manic depression) (see Chapter 7). Because of its potential toxicity, the blood levels of patients maintained on lithium must be carefully monitored. Like people with diabetes who must take insulin through their lifetimes to control their disease, people with bipolar disorder may have to continue using lithium indefinitely to control the disorder. Table 3.2 lists psychotropic drugs according to their drug class and category.

Electroconvulsive Therapy

In 1939, the Italian psychiatrist Ugo Cerletti introduced the technique of **electroconvulsive therapy** (ECT) in psychiatric treatment. Cerletti had observed the practice in some slaughterhouses of using electric shock to render animals unconscious. He observed that the shocks also produced convulsions. Cerletti incorrectly believed, as did other researchers in Europe at the time, that convulsions of the type found in epilepsy were incompatible with schizophrenia and a method of inducing convulsions might be used to cure schizophrenia.

After the introduction of the phenothiazines in the 1950s, the use of ECT became generally limited to the treatment of severe depression. The introduction of antidepressants has limited the use of ECT even further today. However, evidence indicates that about 50% of people with major depression who fail to respond to antidepressants show significant improvement following ECT (Sackheim, Prudic, & Devanand, 1990).

ECT remains a source of controversy for several reasons. First, many people, including many professionals, are uncomfortable about the idea of passing an electric shock through a person's head, even if the level of shock is closely regulated and the convulsions are controlled by drugs. Second are the potential side effects. ECT often produces dramatic relief from severe depression, but concerns remain about its potential for inducing cognitive deficits, such as memory loss. A recent review of the evidence, however, finds memory losses following ECT to be temporary, except perhaps for some persistent loss of memory for events transpiring immediately around the time of the procedure itself

TABLE 3.2
Psychotropic Drugs

Category	Drug Class	Generic Name	Trade Name
Antianxiety agents (also called minor tranquilizers or anxiolytics)	Benzodiazepines	Diazepam	Valium
		Chlordiazepoxide	Librium
		Clorazepate	Tranxene
		Oxazepam	Serax
		Lorazepam	Ativan
		Alprazolam	Xanax
	Barbiturates	Meprobamate	Miltown
			Equanil
	Hypnotics	Flurazepam	Dalmane
		Triazolam	Halcion
		Zolpidem	Ambien
	Other anxiolytics	Busipirone	Buspar
Antipsychotic drugs (also called neuroleptics or major tranquilizers)	Phenothiazines	Chlorpromazine	Thorazine
		Thioridazine	Mellaril
		Mesoridazine	Serentil
		Perphenazine	Trilafon
		Trifluoperazine	Stelazine
		Fluphenazine	Prolixin
	Thioxanthenes	Thiothixene	Navane
	Butyrophenones	Haloperidol	Haldol
	Dibenzoxazepines	Loxapine	Loxitane
	Dibenzodiazepine	Clozapine	Clozaril
Antidepressants	Tricyclic antidepressants (TCAs)	Imipramine	Tofranil
		Desipramine	Norpramin
		Amitriptyline	Elavil
		Doxepin	Sinequan
		Clomipramine	Anafranil
		Nortriptyline	Pamelor
		Protriptyline	Vivactil
		Trimipramine	Surmontil
	MAO inhibitors (MAOIs)	Phenelzine	Nardil
		Tranylcypromine	Parnate
	Selective serotonin reuptake inhibitors (SSRIs)	Fluoxetine	Prozac
		Sertraline	Zoloft
		Paroxetine	Paxil
		Fluvoxamine	Luvox
	Azapirones	Buproprion	Wellbutrin
Antimanic Agents		Lithium carbonate	Eskalith
		Carbamazapine	Tegretol
		Divalproex	Depakote
		Valproate	Depakene
Stimulants		Methylphenidate	Ritalin
		Pemoline	Cylert

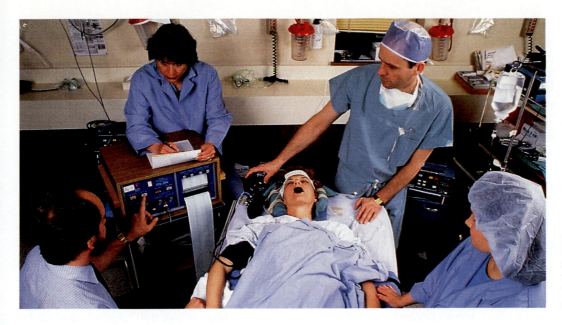

Electroconvulsive therapy (ECT). ECT is helpful in many cases of severe or prolonged depression that do not respond to other forms of treatment. Still, its use remains controversial.

(Devanand et al., 1994). Third are questions of relative efficacy. The relative effectiveness of ECT as compared to antidepressant drugs, to sham (simulated) ECT, and to cognitive-behavioral therapy remains under study. Fourth, no one yet knows why ECT works, although it is suspected it might help correct neurotransmitter imbalances in the brain.

Although controversies concerning the use of ECT persist, increasing evidence indicates its effectiveness in helping people overcome severe depression that might not be responsive to psychotherapy or antidepressant medication (Sackheim et al., 1990). Moreover, ECT may help reduce the risk of suicide among severely depressed people (R. L. Martin et al., 1985). However, ECT is usually considered a treatment of last resort, after less intrusive methods have been tried.

TRUTH *or* **FICTION** **REVISITED**

3.8 *True.* ECT is actually helpful in many cases of severe depression that do not respond to other forms of treatment.

Psychosurgery

Psychosurgery is yet more controversial than ECT and is rarely practiced today. Although no longer performed, the most widely used form of psychosurgery was the **prefrontal lobotomy,** in which the nerve pathways linking the thalamus to the prefrontal lobes of the brain are surgically severed. The operation was based on the theory that extremely disturbed patients suffer from overexcitation of emotional impulses that emanate from the lower brain centers, such as the thalamus and hypothalamus. It was believed that by severing the connections between the thalamus and the higher brain centers in the frontal lobe of the cerebral cortex, the patient's violent or aggressive tendencies could be controlled. The prefrontal lobotomy was developed by the

Portuguese neurologist António Egas Moniz and was introduced to the United States in the 1930s. More than 1,000 mental patients received the operation by 1950. Although the operation did reduce violent and agitated behavior in many cases, it was not always successful. In a cruel ironic twist, one of Moniz's treatment failures later shot him, leaving him paralyzed from a bullet that lodged in his spine.

Many distressing side effects are associated with the prefrontal lobotomy, including hyperactivity, impaired learning ability and reduced creativity, distractibility, apathy, overeating, withdrawal, epileptic-type seizures, and even death. The occurrence of these side effects, combined with the introduction of the phenothiazines, led to the elimination of the operation.

Several more sophisticated psychosurgery techniques have been introduced in more recent years for various purposes. Generally speaking, they are limited to smaller parts of the brain and produce less damage than the prefrontal lobotomy. These operations have been performed to treat such problems as intractable aggression, depression, and psychotic behavior; chronic pain; some forms of epilepsy; and persistent obsessive-compulsive disorder (Irle et al., 1998; Sachdev & Hay, 1996). Follow-up studies of such procedures have shown marked improvement in about one quarter to one half of cases. Concerns about possible complications of these procedures, including decrements in intellectual functioning (Irle et al., 1998), have greatly limited their use.

Ethnic Differences in Response to Psychotropic Medication

Cultural or ethnic differences may play a role in responsiveness to psychotropic medications (Lefley, 1990; Lesser, 1992). African Americans, for example, tend to show a better response to antidepressants and phenothiazines than other groups. Hispanic Americans tend to show lower effective dosage levels (Lawson, 1986). Some clinical evidence indicates that African Americans, as compared to non-Hispanic White Americans, show a quicker response to tricyclic antidepressants but may encounter more side effects (Lesser, 1992). Cultural differences may also play a role in determining acceptability of medication or even the preferred method of drug administration (Lefley, 1990). For example, evidence from several samples shows greater resistance to taking pills among African Americans (Page et al., 1983). Sharing of medications within the family is a common practice among Hispanic Americans in New York.

Evaluation of Biological Approaches

There is little doubt that the use of psychotropic drugs has helped many people with severe psychological problems. Many thousands of people with schizophrenia who were formerly hospitalized are able to function more effectively in the community because of antipsychotic drugs. Antidepressant drugs have helped relieve depression in many cases and have shown therapeutic benefits in treating other disorders, such as panic disorder, obsessive-compulsive disorder, and eating disorders. ECT is helpful in relieving depression in many people who have been unresponsive to other treatments.

On the other hand, in the case of depression, it may be that some forms of psychotherapy are as effective as drug therapy. Moreover, problems persist with respect to the side effects of various psychotropic drugs. In addition, minor tranquilizers have often become drugs of abuse among people who become dependent on them for relieving the effects of stress rather than seeking more adaptive ways of solving their problems. Medical practitioners have often been too quick to use their prescription pads to help people with anxiety complaints, rather than to help them examine their lives or refer them for psychological treatment. Physicians often feel pressured, of course, by patients who seek a chemical solution to their life problems.

While we continue to learn more about the biological foundations of abnormal behavior patterns, the interface between biology and behavior can be construed as a two-way street. Researchers have uncovered links between psychological factors and many physical disorders and conditions (see Chapter 4). Researchers are also investigating whether the combination of psychological and drug treatments for such problems as depression, anxiety disorders, and substance abuse disorders, among others, may increase the therapeutic benefits of either of the two approaches alone. Although American psychiatry has become increasingly "medicalized" in recent years, some within the psychiatric community have warned their colleagues not to overlook the role of psychological factors in explaining and treating mental health problems (van Praag, 1988).

HOSPITALIZATION AND COMMUNITY-BASED CARE

People receive mental health services within various settings, including hospitals, outpatient clinics, community mental health centers, and private practices. In this section we explore the purposes of hospitalization and the movement toward community-based care. Due to *deinstitutionalization*—the policy of shifting the burden of care from the state hospitals to the community—an exodus has taken place from state mental hospitals. We will see that deinstitutionalization has had a profound impact on the delivery of mental health services as well as on the larger community.

Ethnic Group Differences in Use of Mental Health Services

African Americans are more likely than non-Hispanic White Americans to be admitted to mental hospitals and to be committed to such institutions involuntarily (Lindsey & Paul, 1989). The question is, why?

Relationships between ethnicity and prevalence of mental disorders are complex, to say the least. Results from the National Comorbidity Survey (NCS) show that when controlling for socioeconomic factors, African Americans as a group are no more likely to develop schizophrenia, a severe psychological disorder that often leads to hospitalization, than are White Americans (see Chapter 1). Yet African Americans are overrepresented among the lower socioeconomic groups in our society, and the lower strata on the socioeconomic ladder do tend to have higher prevalences of severe psychological disorders. Thus, socioeconomic factors may come into play in explaining ethnic/racial differences in rates of psychiatric hospitalization. So too might ethnic stereotyping by mental health professionals, especially of the poor, which may contribute to an overdiagnosis of severe psychological problems requiring hospitalization.

The other side of the coin is the underutilization of outpatient-based mental health services by ethnic minorities (Wallen, 1992). For example, African Americans tend to receive fewer aftercare services in the community upon discharge from mental hospitals than non-Hispanic White Americans. Nor are mental health clinics the first places where African Americans typically go for help for emotional problems. African Americans seeking mental health interventions turn most often to the church and second to the emergency room of the local general hospital (Lewis-Hall, 1992). The National Survey of African Americans found that slightly more than half (54%) of those who reported experiencing feelings of a "nervous breakdown" failed to consult any type of professional for help with their problems (Neighbors, 1992). Another recent study found that only about 1 in 10 African Americans in a community-based sample who experienced major depression consulted a mental health professional (D. R. Brown, Ahmed, Gary, & Milburn, 1995).

Asian American/Pacific Islanders (Breaux, Matsuoka, & Ryujin, 1995) and Hispanic Americans (Hough et al., 1987) also tend to underutilize mental health services. Cultural insensitivity and outright discrimination may play a role in determining underutilization of mental health services by ethnic minorities (Sanchez & Mohl, 1992). If ethnic minority clients perceive majority therapists and the institutions in which they work to be cold and insensitive, they are less likely to place their trust in them.

Researchers report that Hispanic Americans who encounter emotional problems are more likely to seek assistance from friends and relatives, or from spiritualists, than to reach out to mental health facilities, which they perceive as cold and impersonal institutions (De La Cancela & Guzman, 1991). Hispanic people are also more likely to seek assistance for emotional problems from primary care physicians than from psychologists or psychiatrists.

Cheung (1991) notes several barriers that may help to explain the low rates of utilization of outpatient mental health services by ethnic minorities, including the following:

1. *Institutional or structural barriers.* People from minority groups often fail to use mental health services because they believe such services will be unresponsive to their needs. Facilities may be inaccessible to minority group members because they are located at a considerable distance from their homes or because of lack of public transportation. Most facilities only operate during daytime work hours, which means they are inaccessible to minority group members who are unable to take time off. Moreover, minority group members feel staff members often make them feel stupid for not being familiar with clinic procedures and their requests for assistance often become tangled in red tape.

2. *Cultural barriers.* Many recent immigrants, especially those from Southeast Asian countries, have had little, if any, previous contact with mental health professionals. They may hold different conceptions of mental health problems or view mental health problems as less severe than physical problems. In some ethnic minority subcultures, the family is expected to take care of members who have psychological problems and may resist seeking outside assistance because of guilt engendered by the belief that seeking outside help would represent rejection of the family member and would embarrass the family. Other cultural barriers include cultural differences between typically lower socioeconomic strata minority group members and mostly White, middle-class staff members and incongruence between the cultural practices of minority group members and techniques used by mental health professionals. For example, Asian immigrants may find little value in talking about their problems or may be uncomfortable expressing their feelings to strangers. In many ethnic minority groups, personal and interpersonal problems are brought to trusted elders in the family or religious leaders, not to outside professionals.

3. *Language barriers.* Differences in language make it difficult for minority group members to describe their problems or obtain needed services. Many mental health services do not have staff members who can communicate in the languages used by ethnic minority residents in their communities.

4. *Economic barriers.* Minority group members often live in economically distressed areas and have limited resources. Studies show that communities with more limited resources are unable to provide the range and accessibility of services available to the public of wealthier communities, which have more resources available. A recent review of the literature on the use of mental health services by Hispanic Americans showed that financial barriers were a major determinant of underutilization of these services (Woodward, Dwinell, & Arons, 1992).

Cheung (1991) concludes that greater utilization of mental health services will depend to a great extent on the ability of the mental health system to develop programs that consider these cultural factors and build staffs that consist of culturally sensitive providers, including minority mental health professionals and paraprofessionals. Changes in traditional patterns of underutilization may be in the offing. For example, investigators in a recent study in Texas failed to find differences in dropout rates in psychotherapy or in length of treatment between Mexican American and non-Hispanic White American clients (Sanchez & Mohl, 1992).

Roles for Hospitalization

Different types of hospitals provide different types of mental health treatment. Municipal and community-based hospitals tend to focus on short-term care for people with serious psychological problems who need a structured hospital environment to help them through an acute crisis. In such cases, psychotropic drugs and other biological treatments, such as ECT for severe cases of depression, are often used in combination with short-term psychotherapy. Hospitalization may be followed by outpatient treatment. Many private care hospitals provide longer-term care or are specialized to help people withdraw safely from alcohol or drugs.

The state mental hospital system has traditionally served as the bastion of long-term residential care. Unfortunately, state hospitals have historically failed to provide decent living conditions and the structured treatment needed to restore chronic mental patients to community life. This failure sparked the shift toward community-based care earlier in this century. Prior to deinstitutionalization, mental patients in back wards were essentially *warehoused*. That is, they were left to live out their lives with little hope or expectation of recovery or return to the community. Many received little professional care and were abused by poorly trained and supervised staffs.

Preventing Psychological Disorders

"An ounce of prevention is worth a pound of cure"—so goes the saying. Today we stockpile vital supplies such as grain and oil to lessen the effects of shortages. In medical science, the development of vaccines has helped protect people from contracting such diseases as smallpox and polio. In the mental health system, however, resources are generally directed toward treating mental health problems rather than attempting to prevent them from developing. A recent report mandated by the prestigious Institute of Medicine (IOM) called for increased funding support for prevention research focusing on identifying factors that increase or lessen the risk of mental disorders and developing effective programs to promote psychological well-being and mental health (Muñoz, Mrazek, & Haggerty, 1996).

Traditionally, the term *prevention* has been applied to interventions that run the gamut from programs designed to prevent the onset of mental disorders to those that attempt to reduce the impact of disorders once they

develop. The IOM report, which was initiated by the U.S. Congress, limits the term *prevention* to interventions that occur before the onset of a diagnosable disorder (Muñoz, Mrazek, & Haggerty, 1996). Interventions focusing on lessening the impact of already developed disorders are classified as *treatment interventions* rather than prevention.

The IOM report conceptualizes a mental health spectrum of interventions ranging from prevention efforts through treatment and maintenance interventions (see Figure 3.1). Three categories of prevention programs are identified: universal, selective, and indicated.

Universal preventive interventions are targeted toward the whole population or general public, such as programs designed to enhance prenatal health or childhood nutrition. *Selective preventive interventions* are targeted toward individuals or groups known to be at higher than average risk of developing mental disorders, such as children of schizophrenic parents. *Indicated pre-*

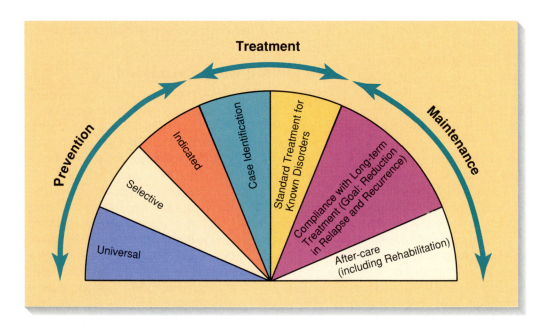

FIGURE 3.1 *The mental health intervention spectrum for mental disorders.* Reprinted with permission from "Reducing Risks for Mental Disorders: Frontiers for Preventive Intervention Research." Copyright 1994 by the National Academy of Sciences. Courtesy of the National Academy Press, Washington, D.C.

Most state hospitals today are better managed and provide more humane care than those of the 19th and early 20th centuries, but here and there deplorable conditions persist. Today's state hospital is generally more treatment-oriented and focuses on preparing residents to return to community living. State hospitals today often function, under deinstitu-

tionalization, as part of an integrated, comprehensive approach to treatment. They provide the structured environment that is needed for people who are unable to function in a less restrictive community setting. When hospitalization restores patients to a higher level of functioning, the patients are reintegrated in the community and provided with follow-

ventive interventions are directed toward individuals with early signs or symptoms that foreshadow the development of a mental disorder but who don't yet meet diagnostic criteria for the designated disorder. Preventive interventions may be successful in "nipping in the bud" the development of clinically diagnosable disorders. For example, preventive programs aimed at changing the drinking habits of high-risk drinkers or early problem drinkers may forestall the onset of more severe alcohol-related problems or alcohol dependence (Botelho & Richmond, 1996; Kivlahan, Marlatt, Fromme, Coppel, & Williams, 1990; Marlatt et al., 1998).

We have had some success in the health arena in developing effective prevention programs for reducing the risks of teenage pregnancies, sexually transmitted diseases, and some forms of drug use (e.g., Blackman, 1996; Stover et al., 1996). Psychologist Martin Seligman and his colleagues have shown that teaching cognitive skills involved in disputing catastrophic, negative thoughts reduced the risk of depression in both college students and school-age children (Gilham, Reivich, Jaycox, & Seligman, 1994; Seligman, 1998). Still, we have much to learn about developing effective prevention programs to prevent psychological disorders. The development of effective preventive programs rests in large part on expanding our knowledge base about the underlying causes of these disorders and mounting controlled investigations that examine ways of preventing them (Muñoz, Mrazek, & Haggerty, 1996).

Some prevention proponents believe that society must address social problems such as poverty, discrimination, lack of economic opportunity, inadequate housing, and chronic joblessness that may contribute to psychological disorders. This approach—a *systems-level strategy*—focuses on changing society rather than changing individuals (Cowen, 1985). However, implementation of major societal changes can represent momentous undertakings. Obstacles include differences in opinions concerning what changes are needed, the costs of such changes, and the time that would be required to implement such changes. An alternative approached, called the *person-centered approach,* focuses on helping

"An Ounce of Prevention." Obtaining good prenatal care can help prevent health problems affecting both the mother-to-be and fetus. Psychologists too are exploring ways of preventing mental health problems or "nipping in the bud" developing problems.

individuals cope more effectively with the life stressors they face (Cowen, 1985). For example, counseling and other support services provided to families undergoing a divorce may help them to cope with the financial and emotional consequences of divorce and perhaps prevent the development of psychological disorders.

The challenge of preventing psychological disorders is before us. The question is whether the nation can muster the political will and financial resolve to meet the challenge (Muñoz, Mrazek, & Haggerty, 1996).

up care and transitional residences, if needed, to help them adjust to community living. Patients may be rehospitalized as needed in a state hospital if a community-based hospital is not available or if they require more extensive care than a community hospital can provide. For younger and less intensely disturbed people, the state hospital stay is typically briefer than it was in the past, lasting only until their condition allows them to reenter society. Older chronic patients may be unprepared to handle the most rudimentary tasks (shopping, cooking, cleaning, and so on) of independent life, however—in part because the state hospital may be the only home such patients have known as adults.

The Community Mental Health Center

Community mental health centers (CMHCs) perform many functions in the effort to reduce the need for hospitalization of new patients and rehospitalization of formerly hospitalized patients. A primary function of the CMHC is to help discharged mental patients adjust to the community by providing continuing care and closely monitoring their progress. Unfortunately, not enough CMHCs have been established to serve the needs of the hundreds of thousands of ex-hospitalized patients and to try to prevent the need for hospitalization of new patients by providing intervention services and alternatives to full hospitalization, such as day hospital programs. Patients in day hospitals attend structured therapy and vocational rehabilitation programs in a hospital setting during the day but are returned to their families or homes at night. Many CMHCs also administer transitional treatment facilities in the community, such as halfway houses, which provide a sheltered living environment to help discharged mental patients gradually adjust to the community as well as to provide people in crisis with an alternative to hospitalization. CMHCs also serve in consultative roles to other professionals in the community, such as training police officers to handle disturbed people.

We shall take a closer look at the issue of deinstitutionalization. Has the policy of deinstitutionalization achieved its goal of successfully reintegrating mental patients into society, or does it remain a promise that is largely unfulfilled? In the nearby "Closer Look" feature we examine a broader question that confronts not only mental health professionals but the larger society as well, the question of whether we can prevent mental disorders from developing in the first place.

The Movement Toward Deinstitutionalization

By the mid-20th century, the deplorable conditions that existed in many public mental hospitals led to calls for reform of the mental health system. Understaffed and underfunded, many institutions at the time provided only minimal attention to the needs of patients.

In 1961, a congressional commission issued a report that was sharply critical of existing psychiatric hospitals and called for sweeping reforms (Joint Commission on Mental Illness and Health, 1961). This report spearheaded the movement that would eventually be called *deinstitutionalization*. The thrust of the commission's report was to promote reintegration of mental patients in the community.

The call for reform of the mental health system led to the creation of a nationwide system of community mental health centers (CMHCs) by an act of Congress in 1963. By 1980, over 700 CMHCs had been established (Kiesler & Sibulkin, 1987), providing alternatives to hospitalization to many people in need of care. The advent of phenothiazines in the 1950s provided a second impetus toward deinstitu-

tionalization. As we noted in Chapter 1, the policy of deinstitutionalization led to a dramatic decline in the mental hospital population nationwide. In 1955, more than 550,000 people were hospitalized in mental hospitals in the United States. By the late 1980s, the count had been reduced to fewer than 130,000 (Braddock, 1992; Kiesler & Sibulkin, 1987).

Many other factors played a role in the exodus of mental patients from the institution to the community. Civil libertarians and patients' rights advocates brought the dehumanizing conditions in many psychiatric hospitals into closer public scrutiny (Grob, 1983). Community-based care was promoted as a more humane alternative to long-term hospitalization. Increased attention to patients' rights led to landmark court cases that established minimal standards of care that state institutions must provide (see Chapter 16). Given these standards, which would have raised hospital care costs significantly, state legislators who were eager to reduce costs to taxpayers may have found it more expedient to release large numbers of patients to the community (Grob, 1983).

Other economic factors also contributed to deinstitutionalization. Many CMHCs were seeded by federal funding, for example, whereas the large state institutions largely depended on state funding (Grob, 1983). Moreover, the introduction of federal disability subsidies in the 1960s, such as the Supplemental Security Income (SSI) disability program, provided a source of revenue that could be passed along to nursing home and group care ("board-and-care") home operators in the community. Community providers could thus offer alternative residential treatment to formerly hospitalized patients and others who might have been hospitalized in earlier times (Shadish, Lurigio, & Lewis, 1989).

Evaluation of Deinstitutionalization

Deinstitutionalization has often been criticized for failing to live up to its expectations. The criticism seems to be well founded. Among the most frequent criticisms is the charge that many hospital patients were merely dumped into the community and not provided with the community-based services they needed to adjust to demands of community living.

A 1991 government report found that 249 of the 600 community mental health centers across the United States that had received federal funds had failed to provide even the basic services, such as emergency care and outpatient clinics, which they were required to offer (Hilts, 1991). Failure to provide such services is seen by experts in the mental health field as one of the "reasons for the growing number of homeless mentally ill people now wandering the streets of American cities untreated" (Hilts, 1991) (see "A Closer Look" section). Although the agency responsible for overseeing the community mental health system, the National Institute of Mental Health, felt the problems were not as widespread as the government report alleged, it is clear that many centers fail to provide adequate services to severely disturbed or formerly institutionalized clients.

Deinstitutionalization and the Psychiatric Homeless Population

Most people are homeless because of adverse life circumstances such as prolonged unemployment, family dissolution, or the lack of affordable housing, not because they suffer from psychological disorders (DeAngelis, 1994a). The groups most at risk of becoming homeless are veterans, young adults, and poor single mothers with children. Yet nearly one third of the homeless people in the United States have severe psychological disorders (Center for Mental Health Services, 1994). Many are ex-hospitalized mental patients who were discharged under the policy of deinstitutionalization. Many homeless people who are psychiatrically disturbed suffer from alcohol- or drug-related problems.

Many ex-hospitalized mental patients were essentially dumped into local communities following discharge and left with little if any support. Lacking adequate support, they often face more dehumanizing conditions on the street, under deinstitutionalization, than they did in the hospital. Many compound their problems by turning to illegal street drugs such as crack (Dugger, 1995). Also, some of the younger psychiatric homeless population might have been hospitalized in earlier times but are now, in the wake of deinstitutionalization, directed toward community support programs, when they are available. The lack of available housing and transitional care facilities and effective case management plays an important role in accounting for homelessness among people with psychiatric problems (T. Golden, 1990b; H. R. Lamb & Lamb, 1990). Some homeless people with severe psychiatric problems are repeatedly hospitalized for brief stays in community-based hospitals during acute episodes. They move back and forth between the hospital and the community as though caught in a revolving door. Frequently, they are released from the hospital with inadequate arrangements for housing and community care. Some are left essentially to fend for themselves. Problems of homelessness are especially compounded for children in homeless families. Not surprisingly, homeless children tend to have more behavior problems than housed children (Schteingart et al., 1995). The problem of psychiatric homelessness is not limited to urban areas, although it is on our city streets that the problem is most visible. The pattern in rural areas tends to be one of inconsistent housing and unstable living arrangements, rather than outright homelessness (Drake et al., 1991).

The functional deficits associated with psychological disorders are also seen as contributing factors, such as disorganized thinking and actions, depression, poor problem-solving skills, and severe paranoia that prevents the individual from accepting help from others (H. R. Lamb & Lamb, 1990). As a vicious cycle, the stresses of homelessness may worsen the individual's mental condition, which in turn makes it more difficult for the person to extricate him- or herself from prolonged homelessness. Then, too, substance abuse often plays an important role in the mounting problems the psychiatric homeless face.

Facing the Challenge of Psychiatric Homelessness

The mental health system alone does not have the resources to resolve the multifaceted problems faced by the psychiatric homeless population. Helping the psychiatric homeless escape from homelessness requires an integrated effort involving mental health and alcohol and drug abuse programs; access to decent, affordable housing; and provision of other social services (Dennis

Psychiatric homeless. A multifaceted effort is needed to meet the needs of the psychiatric homeless population, including access to affordable housing and to medical, drug and alcohol, and mental health treatment, and other social services. Far too often, homeless people with severe psychological problems fall through the cracks of the mental health and social service systems, and are left largely to fend for themselves.

box continues on following page

Deinstitutionalization and the Psychiatric Homeless Population

et al., 1991; Dixon et al., 1997). Mental health systems also need better means for tracking ex-hospital patients and providing them with follow-up care. Many discharged patients are left to wander city streets and have no fixed addresses.

The psychiatric homeless population lacks secure, affordable housing in addition to continuity of care. Mental health agencies may be able to overcome community resistance to accepting discharged mental patients by demonstrating that mental patients are not simply dumped in the community but are closely monitored in supervised residences. The psychiatric homeless population also needs social services, medical services, and drug and alcohol treatment services. These services are likely to be more effective if they are integrated within a single treatment facility near where homeless people congregate than if spread out all over town (Frances & Goldfinger, 1986). Drug- and alcohol-free homes and residences can also play important roles in the process of drug and alcohol rehabilitation (McCarty et al., 1991).

Another difficulty is that homeless people with severe psychological problems typically do not seek out mental health services (Arana, 1990). Aggressive outreach services are often needed to reach them. Programs involving mobile outreach, more intensive case management, drop-in centers, and shelter-based programs, among other approaches, have been developed (Dennis et al., 1991). More intensive outreach efforts that focus on helping homeless people connect with the types of services they needed produce better outcomes than standard treatment with respect to housing, level of stressful life events, medication compliance, and general mental health (Dixon et al., 1997; Lehman et al., 1997; Shern et al., 1997; Toro et al., 1997). If deinstitutionalization is eventually to succeed for all patients, patients must be provided with continuing care and afforded opportunities for decent housing, gainful employment, and training in social and vocational skills (Lurigio & Lewis, 1989).

Although the numbers of specialized programs for the psychiatric homeless population have greatly increased in recent years, they still reach only a small fraction of those in need (Dennis et al., 1991).

TRUTH _or_ FICTION REVISITED

3.9 _False._ Unfortunately, a large number of community mental health centers are failing to provide even the basic services required of them, according to a recent government report.

Deinstitutionalization: A Promise as Yet Unfulfilled

Many factors contribute to the failure of deinstitutionalization to have fulfilled its promises, including the following:

1. _Lack of community support services._ Federal funding support never reached the levels that were promised when the deinstitutionalization movement was ushered in during the early 1960s. In addition, insufficient funds were shifted from state hospitals to community services. State governments were unable or unwilling to commit additional funds to develop community care facilities, such as **halfway houses** and group homes. Savings from shifting patients from hospital to community care often disappeared into the general state coffers rather than being directed toward opening group homes or providing community support services (Dugger, 1995). Patients were thus frequently left unsupervised.

2. _Community resistance._ The "not-in-my-backyard" (NIMBY) syndrome prevented the establishment of community care facilities and group homes in many communities. Many people are willing to support the establishment of community services for the mentally ill—in someone else's community, that is.

3. _Lack of public housing._ Many of the homeless in our urban centers are ex-hospital patients or people with psychiatric disturbances who might have been hospitalized in earlier times, but who now wander from place to place for lack of decent affordable housing and community support services.

4. _Limits of psychotropic drugs._ Psychotropic drugs did not help restore the deficits in social and occupational functioning of many people coping with chronic schizophrenia (Shadish et al., 1989).

A study of ex-hospital patients in Chicago (Lurigio & Lewis, 1989) places the problems of deinstitutionalization in perspective. The study found that the overwhelming majority of discharged mental patients were poor, unemployed, and on welfare. They lacked job skills and close family ties. A substantial number were homeless. Aftercare services were generally inadequate. The researchers saw little hope that these people could escape from poverty and despair to lead more productive lives. Most eventually returned to the state hospitals, which had provided the only stable environment and source of support they had known.

All in all, deinstitutionalization has failed to restore a reasonable quality of life to vast numbers of discharged patients. Nor has it decreased their dependency on mental health services or helped them meet their basic needs (Shadish et al., 1989). Many remain in custodial-type nursing homes that resemble the back wards of the institutions from which they were released. Many others are homeless.

New, promising services exist to improve community-based care for people with chronic psychological disorders—for example, psychosocial rehabilitation centers, family psychoeducational groups, supported housing and work programs, and social skills training (Anthony, Cohen, & Kennard, 1990). Unfortunately, too few of these services exist to meet the needs of the hundreds of thousands of people who might benefit from them. The community mental health movement continues to need expanded community support and adequate financial resources if it is to succeed in fulfilling its original promise.

SUMMARY

Psychotherapy

Psychotherapy involves a systematic interaction between a therapist and clients that incorporates psychological principles to help clients overcome abnormal behavior, solve problems in living, or develop as individuals. The various approaches to psychotherapy employ theory-based specific treatment factors and nonspecific factors such as the quality of the therapeutic relationship and the instillation of hope.

Psychodynamic Therapies

Psychodynamic therapies originated with psychoanalysis, the approach to treatment developed by Freud. Psychoanalysts use techniques such as free association and dream analysis to help people gain insight into their unconscious conflicts and work them through in the light of their adult personalities. More recent psychoanalytic therapies are generally briefer and less intensive.

Humanistic-Existential Therapies

Humanistic-existential approaches focus on the client's subjective, conscious experience in the here and now. Rogers's person-centered therapy helps people increase their awareness and acceptance of inner feelings that had met with social condemnation and been disowned. The effective person-centered therapist possesses the qualities of unconditional positive regard, empathetic understanding, genuineness, and congruence. Existential therapies focus on helping clients get in touch with their subjective experiences and make personal choices that will imbue life with meaning and a sense of purpose.

Cognitive Therapies

Cognitive therapies focus on modifying the maladaptive cognitions that are believed to underlie emotional problems and self-defeating behavior. Ellis's rational-emotive therapy focuses on disputing the irrational beliefs that occasion emotional distress and substituting adaptive behavior for maladaptive behavior. Beck's cognitive therapy focuses on helping clients identify, challenge, and replace distorted cognitions, such as tendencies to magnify negative events and minimize personal accomplishments.

Behavior Therapy

Behavior therapy applies the principles of learning to help people make adaptive behavioral changes. Behavior therapy techniques include systematic desensitization, gradual exposure, modeling, aversive conditioning, operant conditioning approaches, social skills training, self-control techniques, and relaxation techniques. Cognitive-behavioral therapy integrates the behavioral and cognitive approaches.

Tying It Together: Eclectic Models of Psychotherapy

Eclectic therapists make use of multiple models of psychotherapy. In technical eclecticism, therapists use techniques from different approaches without necessarily adopting the theoretical models on which they were based. In integrative eclecticism, therapists attempt to synthesize and integrate diverse theoretical models.

Group Therapy

Group therapy has several advantages over individual treatment, such as reduced costs, opportunities for shared learning experiences and mutual support, and increased utilization of scarce therapist resources. The particular approach to group therapy depends on the orientation of the therapist.

Family and Marital Therapy

Family therapists work with conflicted families to help them resolve their differences. Family therapists focus on clarifying family communications, resolving role conflicts, guarding against scapegoating individual members, and helping members develop greater autonomy. Marital therapists focus on helping couples improve their communications and resolve their differences.

Evaluating the Effectiveness of Psychotherapy

Psychotherapy researchers have generated encouraging evidence of the effectiveness of psychotherapy. Although there are few well-designed head-to-head comparative treatment studies, the results of meta-analyses of research studies that compare psychotherapy with control groups support the efficacy of various approaches to psychotherapy.

Multicultural Issues in Psychotherapy

Therapists need to take cultural factors into account in determining the appropriateness of Western forms of psychotherapy for different cultural groups. Some groups may, for example, have different views of the importance of the autonomy of the individual, or may place more value on spiritual than psychotherapeutic interventions.

Biological Therapies

Biological approaches include drug therapy, electroconvulsive shock therapy (ECT), and psychosurgery. Minor tranquilizers such as Valium may relieve short-term anxiety but do not directly help people solve their problems. Neuroleptics help relieve flagrant psychotic features, but regular use of most antipsychotic drugs has been associated with a risk of disabling side effects. Antidepressants have been shown to be effective in treating depressive disorders, and lithium has been shown to be effective in treating bipolar disorder. ECT is often associated with dramatic relief from severe depression. Psychosurgery is conducted only rarely because of adverse consequences.

Hospitalization and Community-Based Care

The mental hospital provides a structured treatment environment for people in acute crisis and for those who are unable to adapt to community living. The mental hospital today aims to restore patients to community functioning and incorporates treatment approaches such as biological therapies, psychotherapies, structured living environments, and drug and alcohol rehabilitation. Deinstitutionalization has greatly reduced the population of state mental hospitals but has not yet fulfilled its promise to restore mental patients to a reasonable quality of life in the community. Community mental health centers provide continuing care to ex-hospitalized patients, crisis intervention, partial hospitalization and halfway house programs, and community consultation. Many homeless people have severe psychological problems but are not receiving adequate care in the community.

1. What are the basic features of psychotherapy?

2. What are the major types of mental health professionals? How do they differ in their training and the types of roles they perform?

3. What are the goals and techniques used by psychodynamic therapists, humanistic-existential therapists, cognitive therapists, and behavior therapists?

4. Is psychotherapy effective? What evidence exists to support the efficacy of psychotherapy?

5. What cultural issues do therapists need to consider when working with members of diverse cultural and racial groups?

6. What are the major types of drugs used in the treatment of psychological disorders? What are the benefits and risks associated with them?

7. What are the roles of the community mental health center and mental hospitals?

8. What is the policy of deinstitutionalization? How successful has it been? What steps are needed to help fulfill the promise of deinstitutionalization?

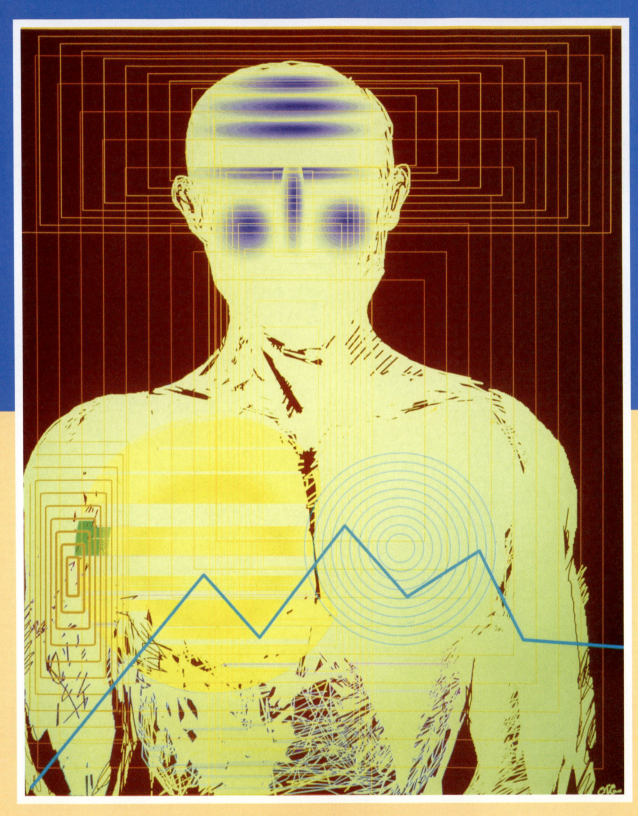

© **Diana Ong**
Medicine Man

Stress, Psychological Factors, and Health

4.1 If you have been having trouble concentrating on your schoolwork because of the breakup of a recent romance, you could be experiencing a psychological disorder.

4.2 As you read this page, millions of microscopic warriors in your body are engaged in search-and-destroy missions against invading hordes.

4.3 Investigators report a surprising finding that stress can reduce susceptibility to dental cavities and the common cold.

4.4 Talking or writing about your feelings can be good for your physical and emotional health.

4.5 Optimistic people recover more rapidly than pessimistic people from coronary artery bypass surgery.

4.6 People with a good sense of humor are more susceptible to the effects of stress.

4.7 Immigrants who become highly acculturated to their host culture are better off psychologically than those who maintain an identity with their original culture.

4.8 People can relieve the pain of migraine headaches by raising the temperature in a finger.

4.9 Cancer patients who maintain a "fighting spirit" experience better outcomes than those who resign themselves to their illness.

When you have completed your study of Chapter 4, you should be able to:

1. Describe the features of adjustment disorders.

2. Explain how labeling an adjustment disorder a "mental disorder" may blur the line between what is normal and what is abnormal.

3. Explain what is meant by a multifactorial view of health and illness.

4. Explain the significance of biological factors in health and illness, paying special attention to the role of the immune system.

5. Explain the significance of psychological factors in health and illness.

6. Explain the significance of socioeconomic, sociocultural, and ethnic factors in health and illness.

7. Explain the significance of natural environmental and technological factors in health and illness.

8. Discuss roles of psychological factors in the origins and treatment of physical disorders including headaches, cardiovascular disorders, asthma, cancer, and AIDS.

An age-old debate concerns the relationships between the mind and the body. Mental functioning certainly depends on the brain, but because the workings of the mind are of a different quality than biological processes, there is continuing temptation to regard them separately. The 17th-century French philosopher René Descartes (1596–1650) influenced modern thinking with his belief in *dualism,* or separateness, between the mind and body. Today, scientists and clinicians have come to recognize that mind and body are more closely intertwined than would be suggested by a dualistic model—that psychological factors both influence, and are influenced by, physical functioning. Psychologists who study the interrelationships between psychology and physical health are called **health psychologists.**

We begin this chapter by focusing on the role of stress in both mental and physical functioning. The term *stress* refers to pressure or force placed upon a body. In the physical world, tons of rocks that crash to the ground in a landslide cause stress upon impact, causing indentations or craters to form in the roadbed or ground upon which they land. In psychology, we use the term **stress** to refer to the pressure or demand that is placed upon an organism to adapt or adjust. A **stressor** is a source of stress. Stressors (or stresses) include psychosocial factors, such as examinations in school and problems in social relationships; life changes, such as the death of a loved one, divorce, or a job termination; and physical environmental factors, such as exposure to extreme temperatures or noise levels. The term *stress* should be distinguished from **distress,** which refers to a state of physical or mental pain or suffering. Some degree of stress is probably necessary to keep us active and alert. But stress that is prolonged or intense can overtax our coping ability and lead to emotional distress, such as states of anxiety or depression or physical complaints such as fatigue and headaches.

Stress is implicated in a range of physical and psychological problems. We begin our study of the effects of stress by discussing a category of psychological disorders called *adjustment disorders,* which involve maladaptive reactions to stress. We then consider the role of stress and other psychological and sociocultural factors in various physical disorders.

ADJUSTMENT DISORDERS

Adjustment disorders are the first psychological disorders we discuss in this book, and they are among the mildest. An adjustment disorder is a maladaptive reaction to an identified stressor that develops within a few months of the onset of the stressor. The maladaptive reaction is characterized by significant impairment in social, occupational, or academic functioning, or by states of emotional distress that exceed those normally induced by the stressor. For the diagnosis to apply, the stress-related reaction must not be sufficient to meet the diagnostic criteria for other clinical syndromes, such as anxiety disorders or mood disorders. The maladaptive reaction may be resolved if the stressor is removed or the individual learns to cope with it. If the maladaptive reaction lasts for more than 6 months after the stressor (or its consequences) have been removed, the diagnosis may be changed.

If your relationship with someone comes to an end (an identified stressor) and your grades are falling off because you are unable to keep your mind on schoolwork, you may fit the bill for an adjustment disorder. If Uncle Harry has been feeling down and pessimistic since his divorce from Aunt Jane, he too may be diagnosed with an adjustment disorder. So too might Cousin Billy if he has been cutting classes and spraying obscene words on the school walls or showing other signs of disturbed conduct. There are several subtypes of adjustment disorders that vary in terms of the type of maladaptive reaction (see Table 4.1).

TABLE 4.1

Subtypes of Adjustment Disorders

Disorder	Chief Features
Adjustment Disorder with Depressed Mood	The chief features are sadness, crying, and feelings of hopelessness.
Adjustment Disorder with Anxiety	The chief features are worrying, nervousness, and jitters (or in children, separation fears from primary attachment figures).
Adjustment Disorder with Mixed Anxiety and Depressed Mood	The chief feature involves a combination of anxiety and depression.
Adjustment Disorder with Disturbance of Conduct	The chief feature is violation of the rights of others or violation of social norms appropriate for one's age. Sample behaviors include vandalism, truancy, fighting, reckless driving, and defaulting on legal obligations (e.g., stopping alimony payments).
Adjustment Disorder with Mixed Disturbance of Emotions and Conduct	The predominant feature involves both emotional disturbance, such as depression or anxiety, and conduct disturbance (as described above).
Adjustment Disorder Unspecified	A residual category that applies to cases not classifiable in one of the other subtypes.

Source: Adapted from the *DSM-IV* (APA, 1994).

The concept of "adjustment disorder" as a *mental disorder* highlights some of the difficulties in attempting to define what is normal and what is not. When something important goes wrong in life, we should feel bad about it. If there is a crisis in business, if we are victimized by a crime, if there is a flood or a devastating hurricane, it is understandable that we might become anxious or depressed. There might, in fact, be something more seriously wrong with us if we did not react in a "maladaptive" way, at least temporarily. However, if our emotional reaction exceeds an expectable response, or our ability to function is impaired (e.g., avoidance of social interactions, difficulty getting out of bed, or falling behind in our schoolwork), then a diagnosis of adjustment disorder may be indicated. Thus, if you are having trouble concentrating on your schoolwork because of the break up of a recent romance, you may be suffering from a diagnosable mental disorder called an *adjustment disorder*. In some cases of adjustment disorder, the stressor is severe enough to distress most people, such as receiving a diagnosis of a serious disease. Yet the diagnosis is justified because the distress experienced impairs the person's ability to meet usual occupational or social responsibilities.

TRUTH *or* FICTION REVISITED

4.1 True. If you are having trouble concentrating on your schoolwork following the breakup of a romantic relationship, you may have a mild type of psychological disorder called an adjustment disorder.

Stress and Illness

Stressful life events may not only diminish our capacity for adjustment, they may also have detrimental effects on our health. Upwards of 70% of all doctor visits can be traced to stress-related illness (NBC Nightly News, 1996). Stress increases the risk of various types of physical illness, ranging from digestive disorders to heart disease (S. Cohen, Tyrell, & Smith, 1993).

The field of **psychoneuroimmunology** studies relationships between psychological factors, especially stress, and the workings of the endocrine system, the immune system, and the nervous system (Kiecolt-Glaser & Glaser, 1992; S. F. Maier, Watkins, & Fleshner, 1994). Before we consider these linkages, let's take a closer look at the workings of the endocrine system and immune system.

The Endocrine System The body has two kinds of glands: glands that carry their secretions to specific locations by means of ducts, and ductless glands that pour their secretions directly into the bloodstream. Saliva, tears, and sweat reach their destinations by way of a system of ducts. Psychologists are particularly interested in the chemicals secreted by ductless glands because of their behavioral effects. The ductless glands make up the **endocrine system,** and they secrete chemicals called **hormones.**

Although they are discharged into the bloodstream and circulate throughout the body, hormones act on receptors in specific locations. Certain hormones released by the hypothalamus influence the pituitary gland, for example. Some hormones secreted by the pituitary affect the adrenal cortex, others affect the testes and ovaries, and so on. Some endocrine glands are shown in Figure 4.1.

The hypothalamus produces various releasing hormones, or "factors," that induce the pituitary gland to release corresponding hormones. The pituitary gland is so vital that it has been referred to as the "master gland." The anterior (front) and posterior (back) lobes of the pituitary secrete many hormones. Growth hormone regulates development of muscles, bones, and glands. Prolactin, another pituitary hormone, regulates maternal behavior in lower

Difficulty in concentrating or adjustment disorder? An adjustment disorder is a maladaptive reaction to a stressful event that may take the form of impaired functioning at school or at work, such as having difficulties keeping one's mind on one's studies.

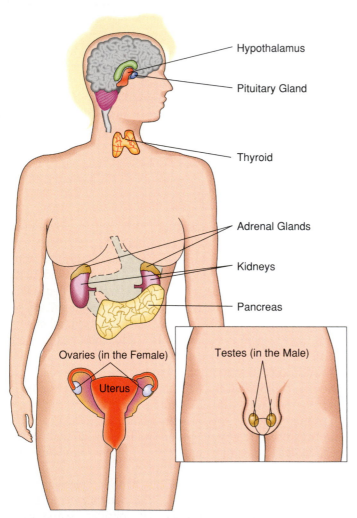

FIGURE 4.1 *Major glands of the endocrine system.*
The glands of the endocrine pour their secretions—called *hormones*—directly into the bloodstream. Although hormones may travel throughout the body, they act only upon specific receptor sites. Many hormones are implicated in stress reactions and various patterns of abnormal behavior.

mammals, such as rats, and stimulates milk production in women.

The adrenal glands, situated above the kidneys, have an exterior layer, or cortex, and an interior core, or medulla. The adrenal cortex is regulated by adrenocorticotrophic hormone (ACTH), a pituitary hormone that causes the adrenal cortex to release several cortical **steroids** (cortisol is one) or **corticosteroids** (a class of steroidal hormones produced by the adrenal cortex). Cortical steroids boost resistance to stress; foster muscle development; and induce the liver to release sugar, providing energy for emergencies. They may bolster self-esteem, stimulate the sex drive, and increase one's energy level.

The pancreas regulates the blood sugar level through the hormones insulin and glucagon. Diabetes mellitus is a disease characterized by excess sugar in the blood (hyperglycemia) and urine; it can cause coma and death. Diabetes is caused by deficient secretion or utilization of insulin, a hormone that is essential for the metabolism of blood sugar (glucose) and regulation of the blood sugar level. **Hypoglycemia** is characterized by a deficient blood sugar level. Symptoms of hypoglycemia include shakiness, lack of energy, and dizziness, a syndrome easily mistaken for anxiety. Many people seek help for anxiety and learn by means of blood tests that they actually have hypoglycemia. Hypoglycemia is usually controlled by diet.

The thyroid gland produces **thyroxin,** which affects the metabolic rate. Thyroxin deficiency can cause **cretinism** in children, a disorder characterized by mental retardation and stunted growth. Adults deficient in thyroxin are said to have **hypothyroidism.** They may feel sluggish and put on weight. Excess thyroxin can cause **hyperthyroidism,** which is characterized by excitability, insomnia, and weight loss.

The **catecholamines** epinephrine (also called adrenaline) and norepinephrine (also called noradrenaline) are released by the adrenal medulla. Epinephrine is secreted solely by the adrenal glands. Norepinephrine, however, is also manufactured elsewhere in the body. Under stress, the sympathetic branch of the autonomic nervous system (ANS) prompts the adrenal medulla to secrete a mixture of epinephrine and norepinephrine that prepares the body to cope. Norepinephrine raises the blood pressure. In the nervous system, it functions as a neurotransmitter.

The male sex hormone **testosterone** is produced by the testes. A few weeks following conception, testosterone prompts prenatal development of male sex organs. During puberty it fosters growth of muscle and bone and the ripening of **primary** and **secondary sex characteristics.** Primary sex characteristics differentiate females from males and are directly involved in reproduction. The sex organs are prime examples. Secondary sex characteristics, such as deepening of the voice and growth of the beard, also differentiate males and females but are not directly involved in reproduction.

The ovaries secrete **estrogen** and **progesterone.** Estrogen is a collective name for numerous female sex hormones that spur development of female reproductive capacity and secondary sex characteristics. They account for accumulation of fatty deposits in the breasts and hips. Progesterone also has many functions. It induces growth of the female reproductive organs and preserves pregnancy.

The Immune System

Given the intricacies of the human body and the rapid advance of scientific knowledge, we tend to consider ourselves dependent on highly trained medical specialists to contend with illness. Actually we cope with most diseases by ourselves, through the functioning of our immune systems.

The **immune system** is the body's system of defense against disease. It combats disease in a number of ways. Your body is constantly engaged in search-and-destroy missions against invading microbes, even as you're reading this page. The "troops" involved in these missions are called **leukocytes** (white blood cells), and they form the basis for the body's immune response, systematically enveloping and killing **pathogens** such as bacteria, viruses, and fungi; worn-out body cells; and cells that have become cancerous.

TRUTH or FICTION REVISITED

4.2 True. Millions of white blood cells, or leukocytes, in your body are continually engaged in microscopic warfare against invading microbes.

Leukocytes recognize invading pathogens by their surface fragments, called **antigens,** literally *antibody generators.* Some leukocytes produce **antibodies,** kinds of specialized proteins, that attach to these foreign bodies, inactivate them, and mark them for destruction.

Special "memory lymphocytes" (lymphocytes are a type of leukocyte) are held in reserve, rather than marking foreign bodies for destruction or going to war against them. They can remain in the bloodstream for years and form the basis for a quick immune response to an invader the second time around.

White blood cells attacking and engulfing pathogens. White blood cells—or *leukocytes*—form part of the body's immune system.

Stress and the Immune System Researchers are particularly interested in how stress may affect the immune system, the body's line of defense against disease-causing organisms and disease-ridden cells, such as cancer cells. A weakened immune system can make us more vulnerable to common illnesses, such as colds and the flu, and may increase our risks of developing chronic diseases, including cancer.

Exposure to physical sources of stress such as cold or loud noise, especially when intense or prolonged, can suppress immunological functioning. So too can various psychological stressors ranging from sleep deprivation to final examinations (Maier, Watkins, & Fleshner, 1994). Traumatic stress, such as exposure to earthquakes, hurricanes, or other natural or technological disasters or to violence, can hamper immunological functioning (G. F. Solomon et al., 1997; Ironson et al., 1997). Life stressors such as divorce and chronic unemployment can also take a toll on the immune system (A. O'Leary, 1990). Chronic stress may make it take longer for wounds to heal (Kiecolt-Glaser et al., 1995).

In one study with dental students (Jemmott et al., 1983), saliva levels of an antibody, immunoglobulin A, were measured during stressful school periods and right after relaxing vacations. Immunoglobulin A is involved in protecting the body against infectious agents such as the common cold virus and bacteria that cause dental cavities. The students showed lower levels of immunoglobulin A, a sign of a weaker immune response, during stressful school periods. Thus stress can increase our susceptibility to both dental cavities and the common cold.

TRUTH or FICTION REVISITED

4.3 False. Stress can contribute to dental cavities by suppressing levels of antibodies which fight the bacteria that cause cavities.

Medical students, similarly, show poorer immune functioning during exam time than they do a month before

Stress and the immune system. Students show evidence of a poorer immunological response during times of stress. Loneliness too may be associated with a weaker immune system response.

exams, when their lives are relatively less stressful (Glaser et al., 1987). Medical and dental students with larger numbers of friends show better immune functioning than students with fewer friends (Jemmott et al., 1983; Kiecolt-Glaser, Speicher, Holliday, & Glaser, 1984). Social support thus appears to moderate the stresses of school life as well as other stresses. Along these lines, consider that lonely students show a greater suppression of the immune response than do students with greater social support (Glaser, Kiecolt-Glaser, Speicher, & Holliday, 1985). Newly separated and divorced people also show evidence of suppressed immune response, especially those who remain more attached to their ex-partners (Kiecolt-Glaser et al., 1987b, 1988).

Can stress make us sick? Evidence suggests that it can. In one study, people who reported higher levels of daily stress, such as pressures at work, showed lower levels in their bloodstreams of antibodies that fend off cold viruses (A. A. Stone et al., 1994). In another study, exposure to severe chronic stress lasting a month or longer, of the type associated with underemployment, unemployment, and interpersonal problems with family members or friends, was associated with an increased risk of developing a common cold after exposure to cold viruses (O. J. Cohen et al., 1998).

Stress may have more general effects that can lead to illness. Stress stimulates the release of various hormones, including adrenaline and cortisol (discussed later in the chapter). These hormones help the body prepare to cope with an impending threat or stressor. Once the stressor has passed, the body returns to a normal state. During states of chronic stress, however, the body may continue to pump out these stress hormones, which can have effects through-

out the body, including suppressing the ability of the immune system to protect us from various infections and disease ("Can stress make you sick?," 1998).

Other researchers have shown that immune system control over the Epstein-Barr virus is compromised in college students during examination periods, another indication that stress can impair immunological functioning (Glaser et

Hassles. One of the major sources of stress in everyday life are common hassles like traffic jams.

"You Gotta Have Friends"

Having many different types of social relationships might be good for your physical health as well as your mental health. In a recent study, 276 healthy adult volunteers agreed to be exposed to cold viruses and then were quarantined in a hotel for 5 days (S. Cohen et al., 1997; S. Gilbert, 1997b). The idea was to see if the likelihood of contacting a cold was related to the person's social ties. It turned out that people who had more types of active social relationships—with spouses, children, other relatives, friends, colleagues, members of organizations and religious groups, etc.—were less likely to come down with a cold. And when they did get sick, they tended to develop milder symptoms. Interestingly, the total number of people in one's social network had no bearing on the likelihood of getting sick. What mattered was the breadth of one's social network—how many different types of relationships one regularly maintains by either visiting or phone contact. The lead investigator on the study, Dr. Sheldon Cohen of Carnegie-Mellon Institute, believes that having a more diverse social network may help ward off colds by buffering a person's response to stress (cited in S. Gilbert, 1997b).

There may be some tradeoff in having lots of friends, since the more social contacts one has, the greater the odds of contracting a cold virus. Still, researchers suspect, exposure to lots of germs may bolster one's immunological defenses over time, perhaps enough to thwart the cold bug.

al., 1991, 1993; Glaser, Pearl, Kiecolt-Glaser, & Malarkey, 1994). The Epstein-Barr virus is a pathogen linked to a chronic fatigue state.

We should caution that much of the research in the field of psychoneuroimmunology is largely correlational. Researchers examine immunological functioning in relation to different indices of stress, but do not (nor would they!) directly manipulate stress to observe its effect on subjects' health. Correlational research helps researchers understand relationships between variables but does not in itself demonstrate causal connections.

On the other hand, there is evidence that psychological interventions can play a causal role in boosting immune functioning. One experiment with older adults demonstrated that a combination of relaxation training and training in coping skills *enhanced* the functioning of the immune system (Kiecolt-Glaser et al., 1985). These findings are especially significant in light of two factors: (1) immunological functioning declines with age; and (2) stress may have even more damaging effects on older adults by accelerating the process of wearing down the immune system that occurs with aging, which might increase the risks of developing cancer and other chronic diseases (Esterling et al., 1994a). Efforts to help improve immune function in older people could potentially increase their resistance to disease and prolong life. In another study, a broad-based psychological intervention consisting of stress management techniques (such as relaxation training) and psychological support led to improved immunological response in (postsurgical) patients with malignant skin cancer (Fawzy et al., 1990).

Stress and Life Changes

Another way in which researchers have investigated the stress-illness connection is by quantifying life stress in terms of **life changes.** T. H. Holmes and Rahe (1967) assembled a scale to gauge the effect of life changes. They calibrated the scale by assigning marriage a weight of 50 "life-change units." (Both positive events, such as marriage, and negative events, such as a job termination, can be stressful because the changes they involve impose demands on us to adjust.) Then, using marriage as a reference point, subjects from various walks of life assigned units to additional life changes. Most changes were considered less stressful than marriage. A few, however, were rated as more stressful, including death of a spouse (100 units) and divorce (73 units). Other items are listed in Table 4.2.

Researchers have investigated links between life changes and proneness to illness. Holmes and Rahe (1967) reported that about 80% of the people who chalked up 300 or more life-change units during a year developed medical problems. By contrast, only about 30% of those who "earned" fewer than 150 units within a year developed medical difficulties. Other investigators have also reported linkages between life stressors, such as life changes and daily hassles, with physical illness, and even with sports injuries (A. D. Kanner, Coyne, Schaefer, & Lazarus, 1981; R. E. Smith, Smoll, & Ptacek, 1990; Stewart et al., 1994; Thoits, 1983).

Negative life changes are also predictive of poorer psychological adjustment in children with asthma (MacLean et al., 1992). Lastly, researchers find that people undergoing

A CLOSER LOOK

Writing as Therapy

Evidence is accumulating that talking about your feelings or writing them down may be good for your emotional and physical health. Researchers find that writing about traumatic events strengthens the immune system, the body's defense against invading microbes and diseased cells (Pennebaker, Kiecolt-Glaser, & Glaser, 1988; Smyth, 1998). In another recent study, investigators followed 122 students entering college (Cameron & Nicholls, 1998). The students were first asked to complete a scale that classified them as either optimists or pessimists. They were then assigned to one of three conditions: (1) a *self-regulation condition* in which they were asked to write about their thoughts and feelings about entering college and develop coping plans, (2) a *disclosure condition* consisting of writing about their thoughts and feelings only, or (3) a *control task* (writing about trivial topics). The writing assignments were completed in three weekly sessions. The results showed that the self-regulation and disclosure conditions, which both involved writing about thoughts and feel-

ings, produced fewer illness-related visits to the campus clinic visits during the following month. Among the pessimists, however, only the self-regulation condition, which combined expressing thoughts and feelings with developing coping strategies, reduced the number of clinic visits.

Keeping your thoughts and feelings about traumatic events hidden may place a stressful burden on the ANS, which may in turn weaken the immune system and so contribute to the development of stress-related disorders. Facing the trauma directly by talking or writing about it frees one from having to keep these thoughts and feelings under wraps. It may also help one come to terms with the emotional consequences of traumatic experiences.

TRUTH *or* FICTION REVISITED

4.4 *True.* Talking or writing about your feelings may be good for your emotional and physical health.

---

heart surgery who had fewer life changes preoperatively had better postoperative recoveries than those with a greater number of preoperative life change events (C. D. Jenkins et al., 1994).

Despite these findings, we need to be cautious in our interpretations. For one thing, the links are correlational and not experimental. In other words, researchers did not (and

would not!) assign subjects to conditions in which they would be exposed to either high or low levels of hassles and life changes to see what effects these conditions might have on the subjects' health over time. Rather, the existing data are based on observations of relationships between hassles and life changes, on the one hand, and psychological and physical problems on the other. These relationships are

For better or for worse. Life changes such as marriage and the death of loved ones are sources of stress that require adjustment. People identified the death of a spouse as the most stressful life change on Holmes and Rahe's scale of life-change units.

TABLE 4.2

Scale of Life-Change Units

Life Event	Life-Change Units
Death of one's spouse	100
Divorce	73
Marital separation	65
Jail term	63
Death of a close family member	63
Personal injury or illness	53
Marriage	50
Being fired at work	47
Marital reconciliation	45
Retirement	45
Change in the health of a family member	44
Pregnancy	40
Sex difficulties	39
Gain of a new family member	39
Business readjustment	39
Change in one's financial state	38
Death of a close friend	37
Change to a different line of work	36
Change in number of arguments with one's spouse	35
Mortgage over $10,000*	31
Foreclosure of a mortgage or loan	30
Change in responsibilities at work	29
Son or daughter leaving home	29
Trouble with in-laws	29
Outstanding personal achievement	28
Wife beginning or stopping work	26
Beginning or ending school	26
Change in living conditions	25
Revision of personal habits	24
Trouble with one's boss	23
Change in work hours or conditions	20
Change in residence	20
Change in schools	20
Change in recreation	19
Change in church activities	19
Change in social activities	18
Mortgage or loan of less than $10,000	17
Change in sleeping habits	16
Change in number of family get-togethers	15
Change in eating habits	15
Vacation	13
Christmas	12
Minor violations of the law	11

*This figure seemed appropriate in 1967, when the scale was constructed. Today, inflation and advances in real estate prices probably balloon this figure to at least $100,000.

Source: Holmes, T. H., & Rahe, R. H. (1967). The social readjustment rating scale. *Journal of Psychosomatic Research*, 11, 213–218.

quarrels with one's family, changes in housing and sleeping patterns, and so forth. Hence, in many cases the causal direction may be reversed: Physical and psychological problems may give rise to, rather than stem from, daily hassles and life changes. There has been little research to date to tease out the possible cause-and-effect relationships (Suls, Wan, & Blanchard, 1994).

Although both positive and negative life changes can be stressful, positive life changes seem to be less disruptive than daily hassles and negative life changes (Thoits, 1983). In other words, marriage tends to be less stressful than divorce or separation. Or to put it another way: A change for the better may be a change, but it is less of a hassle. Let us also note that "eventlessness" (i.e., the absence of life changes) may be just as stressful and indicative of the risk of illness as negative life events (Theorell, 1992).

The General Adaptation Syndrome Stress researcher Hans Selye (1976) coined the term **general adaptation syndrome (GAS)** to describe a common biological response pattern to prolonged or excessive stress. Selye pointed out that our bodies respond similarly to many kinds of stressors, whether the source of stress is an invasion of microscopic disease organisms, a divorce, or the aftermath of a flood. The GAS model suggests that our bodies, under stress, are like clocks with alarm systems that do not shut off until their energy is perilously depleted.

The GAS includes three stages: the alarm reaction, the resistance stage, and the exhaustion stage. Perception of an immediate stressor (for example, a car that swerves in front of your own on the highway) triggers the **alarm reaction.** The alarm reaction mobilizes the body for defense. It is initiated by the brain and regulated by the endocrine system and the sympathetic branch of the ANS. In 1929, Harvard University physiologist Walter Cannon called the initial mobilization of the body's defenses the **fight-or-flight reaction.**

The fight-or-flight reaction most probably helped our early ancestors cope with the many perils they faced. The reaction may have been provoked by the sight of a predator or by a rustling sound in the undergrowth. But our ancestors usually did not experience prolonged activation of the alarm reaction. Once a threat is eliminated, the body reinstates a lower level of arousal. Our ancestors fought off predators or they fled quickly; if not, they failed to contribute their genes to the genetic pools of their groups. In short, they died. Sensitive alarm reactions bestowed survival. Yet our ancestors did not invest years in the academic grind, struggle to balance the budget each month, or face any of the myriad persistent stressors that contemporary men and women endure. Modern stressors can excite our alarm systems for hours, days, or weeks at a time or longer.

If the alarm reaction is aroused and the stressor persists, we progress to the **resistance stage,** or adaptation stage, of the GAS. Endocrine and sympathetic activities remain at high levels, but not quite as high as during the alarm reaction. During this stage the body tries to renew spent energy and repair damage. When stressors continue to persist, we

open to other interpretations. It could be that physical symptoms or psychological difficulties are sources of stress in themselves and may lead to the accumulation of more daily hassles or life-change units. Physical illness may lead to life disruptions involving hassles and life changes, such as

may advance to the final, or **exhaustion stage** of the GAS. Although there are individual differences in capacity to resist stress, all of us will eventually exhaust or deplete our bodily resources. The exhaustion stage is characterized by dominance of the parasympathetic branch of the ANS. Consequently, our heart and respiration rates decelerate. Do we benefit from the respite? Not necessarily. If the source of stress persists, we may develop what Selye termed "diseases of adaptation." These range from allergic reactions to coronary heart disease—and, at times, even death.

Stress has a domino effect on the endocrine system. First, the hypothalamus secretes corticotrophin-releasing hormone (CRH), which causes the pituitary gland to secrete adrenocorticotrophic hormone (ACTH). ACTH, in turn, stimulates the adrenal cortex to release cortisol and other corticosteroids. Corticosteroids—steroidal hormones produced by the adrenal cortex—help defend the body by fighting allergic reactions (such as difficulty breathing) and inflammation.

The sympathetic branch of the ANS also activates the adrenal medulla, causing the release of a mixture of **catecholamines**—epinephrine (adrenaline) and norepinephrine (noradrenaline). The mixture mobilizes the body by accelerating the heart rate and stimulating the liver to release stored glucose (sugar), making more energy available where it can be of use. Table 4.3 summarizes the bodily changes in response to stress that characterize the alarm reaction.

Cortical steroids are perhaps one reason that persistent stress eventually exhausts our capacities to cope. Although cortical steroids in some ways help the body cope with stress, persistent secretion of these steroids actually suppresses the activity of the immune system. Cortical steroids have negligible effects when they are only periodically released. Continuous secretion, however, decreases inflammation and weakens the immune system by disrupting the production of antibodies. As a result, we grow more vulnerable to various diseases, even the common cold (S. Cohen, Tyrell, & Smith, 1991).

Although Selye's model speaks to the general response pattern of the body under stress, different biological processes may be involved in response to particular kinds of stressors. For example, persistent exposure to excessive noise may invoke different bodily processes than other sources of stress, such as overcrowding, or psychological sources of stress, such as divorce or separation.

Individuals, too, may react differently to stress depending on psychological factors such as cognitive appraisal. For example, the impact of a stressful event reflects the individual's appraisal of the event in terms of its positive and negative features. For example, whether pregnancy is a positive or negative life change depends on a couple's desire for a child and their readiness to care for a child. We cognitively evaluate hassles and life changes (Lazarus, De Longis, Folkman, & Gruen, 1985). The same event is less taxing for people who appraise it as meaningful and believe they can cope with it. Other psychological factors, such as hardiness and humor, may also mediate or buffer the effects of stress.

A MULTIFACTORIAL VIEW OF HEALTH AND ILLNESS

Although some people inherit predispositions toward certain illnesses, health professionals no longer see people as simply "lucky" enough to have rugged constitutions, or as "unlucky" enough to have certain disorders run in their families. Many factors interact to determine whether or not people will develop various physical disorders (Stokols, 1992). Biological variables such as family history of an illness, exposure to disease-causing agents (pathogens), the ability of the immune system to fight them off, and inoculations or vaccinations may strike us as the most likely causes or deterrents of physical illnesses. Yet, as shown in Table 4.4, the causes of physical illness are best viewed as *multifactorial*. Psychological, social, technological, and natural environmental factors are also involved. Even though our heredity may work against us in certain ways, biology may not be destiny and we may be able to change other factors to maintain or restore health. In later chapters we see that a multifactorial approach may also best explain the origins of many psychological disorders.

A multifactorial view of health and illness provides insight into causation and also suggests multiple pathways of prevention and treatment involving psychosocial and medical approaches. Let us consider some of the multiple factors that are connected with physical health and illness.

TABLE 4.3

Stress-Related Changes in the Body Associated with the Alarm Reaction

Corticosteroids are released	Blood shifts from the internal organs to the skeletal muscles
Epinephrine and norepinephrine are released	Digestion is inhibited
Heart rate, respiration rate, and blood pressure increase	Sugar is released by the liver
Muscles tense	Increased blood clotting ability

Stress triggers the alarm reaction. The reaction is defined by secretion of corticosteroids, catecholamines, and activity of the sympathetic branch of the ANS. The alarm reaction mobilizes the body for combat or flight.

TABLE 4.4

Factors in Health and Illness: Biological, Psychological, Social, Technological, and Natural Environment

Biological	Psychological		Social: Socioeconomic, Sociocultural, and Ethnic	Technological	Natural Environmental
	Personality	Behavioral			
Family history of illness	Self-efficacy expectancies	Diet (intake of calories, fats, fiber, vitamins, etc.)	Socioeconomic status	Adequacy of available health care	Natural disasters (earthquakes, floods, hurricanes, drought, extremes of temperature, tornados)
Exposure to infectious pathogens (e.g., bacteria and viruses)	Psychological hardiness	Consumption of alcohol	Availability and use of social support	Vehicular safety	Radon
Functioning of the immune system	Health locus of control (belief that one is in charge of one's own health)	Cigarette smoking	Social climate in the home environment and in the workplace	Architectural features (e.g., injury-resistant design, nontoxic construction materials, aesthetic design, air quality, noise insulation)	
Inoculations	Optimism/pessimism	Level of physical activity			
Medication history	Sense of humor	Sleep patterns	Major life changes such as death of a spouse or divorce	Aesthetics of residential, workplace, and communal architecture and landscape architecture	
Congenital disabilities	Attributional style (how one explains one's failures to oneself)	Safety practices (e.g., driving with seat belts; careful driving; practice of sexual abstinence, monogamy, or "safe sex"; attaining of comprehensive prenatal care)	Health-related cultural and religious beliefs and practices		
Physiological conditions (e.g., obesity, hypertension, serum cholesterol level)	Introversion/ extraversion		Major economic changes (e.g., taking out a large mortgage, losing one's job)	Water quality	
Reactivity of the cardiovascular system (e.g., "hot reactor")	Coronary-prone (Type A) personality	Health-care utilization (e.g., regular medical and dental checkups)	Health promotion programs in the workplace or the community	Solid waste treatment and sanitation	
Age	Depression/anxiety	Compliance with medical and dental advice	Ethnicity	Pollution	
Gender	Hostility/ suspiciousness	Interpersonal/ social skills	Prejudice and discrimination	Radiation	
	Tendencies to express or deny feelings of frustration and anger	Type A behavior pattern (TABP)	Health-related legislation	Global warming	
			Availability of health insurance	Ozone depletion	

Source: Adapted from Stokols (1992).

A CLOSER LOOK

Styles of Coping with Illness

What do you do when faced with a serious problem? Do you pretend that it does not exist? Like Scarlett O'Hara in *Gone with the Wind,* do you say to yourself "I'll think about it tomorrow" and then banish it from your mind? Or do you take charge and confront it squarely?

Pretending that problems do not exist is a form of denial. Denial is an example of **emotion-focused coping** (Lazarus & Folkman, 1984). In emotion-focused coping, people take measures that immediately reduce the impact of the stressor, such as denying its existence or withdrawing from the situation. Emotion-focused coping, however, does not eliminate the stressor or help the individual develop better ways of managing the stressor. In **problem-focused coping**, by contrast, people examine the stressors they face and do what they can to change them or modify their own reactions to render stressors less harmful. These basic styles of coping—emotion focused and problem focused—have been applied to ways in which people respond to illness.

Emotion-Focused Coping: Reducing Awareness of Physical Trauma

Denial is one of the principal ways of passively coping with illness. It can take various forms, including the following:

1. Failure to recognize the seriousness of the illness,

2. Minimization of the emotional distress the illness causes,

3. Misattribution of symptoms to other causes (for example, assuming the appearance of blood in the stool represents nothing more than a local abrasion), and

4. Ignoring of threatening information about the illness (J. Levine et al., 1987).

Denial can be dangerous to your health, especially if it leads to avoidance of, or noncompliance with, needed medical treatment. Avoidance is another form of emotion-based coping. In a recent study, people who had a more avoidant style of coping with cancer (for example, by trying not to think or talk about it) showed greater disease progression when evaluated a year later than did people who more directly confronted the illness (Epping-Jordan, Compas, & Howell, 1994). Like denial, avoidance may deter people from complying with medical

Problem-focused coping. Unlike emotion-focused coping in which people attempt to psychologically distance themselves from sources of stress by use of denial or avoidance, people who use problem-focused coping attempt to meet stressors head-on. When it comes to serious medical problems, problem-focused strategies such as seeking information and maintaining a hopeful outlook may be adaptive and improve the chances of recovery.

treatments, which can lead to a worsening of their medical condition. It's also possible that avoidance may contribute to heightened emotional distress and arousal, which may impair immunological functioning.

Another form of emotion-focused coping, the use of wish-fulfillment fantasies, has also been linked to poorer adjustment in coping with serious illness. Examples of wish-fulfillment fantasies include ruminating about what might have been had the illness not occurred and longing for better times. Wish-fulfillment fantasy offers the patient no means of coping with life's difficulties other than an imaginary escape.

Does this mean that people are invariably better off when they know all the facts concerning their illnesses? Not necessarily. Whether or not you will be better off knowing all the facts may depend on your preferred style of coping. A mismatch between the individual's style of coping and the amount of information provided may hamper recovery. In one study, cardiac patients with a repressive style of coping (relying on denial) who received information about their condition showed a higher incidence of medical complications than repressors who were largely kept in the dark (R. Shaw, Cohen, Doyle, & Palesky, 1985). Sometimes ignorance helps people manage stress—at least temporarily.

Problem-Focused Coping: Confronting the Trauma of Serious Illness

Problem-focused coping involves strategies to deal directly with the source of stress, such as seeking information about the illness through self-study and medical consultation. Information seeking may help the individual maintain a more optimistic frame of mind by creating an expectancy that the information will prove to be useful.

The ways in which we come to terms with serious illness affect our emotional adjustment and, perhaps, our survival. In one study, positive expectations prior to heart transplantation predicted better health outcomes 6 months after the operation (Leedham et al., 1995). This finding supports the belief that confronting a health problem with a positive outlook, even a catastrophic health problem, is ultimately adaptive. The finding held up even when the patient's preoperative health and adherence to medical directions after the procedure were taken into account.

Finding a silver lining in a dark cloud may also be healthful. One study interviewed heart attack survivors 7 weeks after they were stricken. Survivors who were able to cite benefits of their attacks were less likely to suffer recurrent attacks and were more likely to have survived at an 8-year follow-up than those who were unable to recognize any benefits associated with the attack (Affleck, Tennen, Croog, & Levine, 1987). The types of benefits connected with subsequent health are shown in Table 4.5. Blaming others for the initial heart attacks and attributing them to stress responses (for example, excessive worrying or anxiety) were associated with increased mortality at the 8-year follow-up. Patients who saw their heart attacks as caused by factors they could control, such as diet and smoking, more often followed through on behavioral programs that modified these risk behaviors.

TABLE 4.5

Examples of Perceived Benefits Following Heart Attacks Associated with Increased Rates of Survival

Type of Perceived Benefit	Life Changes Associated with Perceived Benefits
Helped victim recognize the benefits of preventative health behaviors	Smoking cessation Regular exercise Proper diet
Helped lead or expected it would lead to positive life changes	Taking life easier Taking more vacations Slowing down the pace of daily life
Helped produce changes in "philosophy of life," personal values, and religious view.	Becoming more content with accepting one's lot in life Taking each day as it comes Valuing home life more Renewing religious faith

Source: Adapted from Affleck et al. (1987).

Biological Factors

Biology plays key roles in health and illness. We are generally healthier when we are younger, when we receive inoculations for common illnesses, and when we control physiological conditions such as hypertension and blood cholesterol levels. It has been clearly established that people with family histories of some disorders, such as cardiovascular disease and certain types of cancer, are at greater risk of developing these problems. In some cases the genetic predisposition may be so powerful that prevention and treatment efforts are either futile or can only forestall the inevitable. In other cases, such as obesity (Brownell & Wadden, 1992) and many cases of cancer (Andersen, 1992; Pyeritz, 1997), genetic predispositions interact with lifestyle factors, such as dietary practices, to either increase or decrease the risk of developing the disorder.

Psychological Factors

Psychological factors include our behavior patterns and personalities. Our behavior patterns are fundamental factors in health and illness. For example, diet and exercise are two facets of behavior that figure prominently in proneness to health problems such as obesity and coronary heart disease. Personality refers to the reasonably stable patterns of emotions, motives, attitudes, and psychological traits that distinguish people from one another (Prigatano, 1992). Many personality features, such as self-efficacy expectancies, psychological hardiness, optimism, and a sense of humor, are believed to have positive effects on our health, by means of buffering the effects of stress. The so-called Type A personality and chronic feelings of hostility may increase our susceptibility to coronary heart disease, however. Our style of coping with illness may also play a large role in recovery, as we explore in the feature "Styles of Coping with Illness."

Self-Efficacy Expectancies Self-efficacy expectancies refer to our expectations regarding our abilities to cope with the challenges we face, to perform certain behaviors skillfully, and to effect change in our lives (Bandura, 1982, 1986). We may be better able to manage stress if we feel confident (have higher self-efficacy expectancies) in our ability to cope effectively. A forthcoming exam may be more or less stressful depending on your confidence in your ability to achieve a good grade. Researchers find that spider-phobic women show high levels of the stress hormones epinephrine and norepinephrine when they interact with the phobic object, such as by allowing a spider to crawl on their laps (Bandura, Barr-Taylor, Williams, Mefford, & Barchas, 1985). As their confidence or self-efficacy expectancies for coping with these tasks increased, the levels of these hormones declined. Epinephrine and norepinephrine arouse the body by way of the sympathetic branch of the ANS. As a consequence, we are likely to feel shaky, to have "butterflies in the stomach" and general feelings of nervousness. Because high self-efficacy expectancies appear to be associated with lower secretion of catecholamines, people who believe they can cope with their problems may be less likely to feel nervous.

Psychological Hardiness Psychological hardiness refers to a cluster of traits that may help people manage stress. For research on the subject, we are largely indebted to Suzanne Kobasa (1979) and her colleagues who investigated business executives who resisted illness despite heavy burdens of stress. Three key traits distinguished the psychologically hardy executives (Kobasa, Maddi, & Kahn, 1982, pp. 169–170):

1. The hardy executives were high in *commitment*. Rather than feeling alienated from their tasks and situations, they involved themselves fully. That is, they believed in what they were doing.

2. The hardy executives were high in *challenge*. They believed change was the normal state of things, not sterile sameness or stability for the sake of stability.

3. The hardy executives were also high in perceived *control* over their lives (Maddi & Kobasa, 1984). They believed and acted as though they were effectual rather than powerless in controlling the rewards and punishments of life. In terms suggested by social-learning theorist Julian Rotter (1966), psychologically hardy individuals have an internal **locus of control**.

People who are psychologically hardy appear to cope more adaptively with stress, such as by using more active, problem-solving approaches (P. G. Williams, Wiebe, &

Psychological hardiness. Psychological hardiness is a psychological factor that moderates the effects of stress. Psychologically hardy business executives resist illness despite heavy stress loads. Psychologically hardy executives are committed to their work (they believe in what they are doing), seek challenges, and perceive themselves to be in control of their lives.

Smith, 1992). Psychological hardiness also appears to be positively related to other indices of mental health and recovery from posttraumatic stress disorder (PTSD) (L. A. King et al., 1998; Maddi & Khoshaba, 1994). Other evidence shows a relationship between proneness to illness and psychological hardiness in people with behavior patterns that may place them at risk of cardiovascular illness, such as the **Type A behavior pattern** (TABP). Type A people are highly driven, impatient, competitive, and hostile. Psychologically hardy Type A people have been shown to be more resistant to coronary heart disease than nonhardy Type A people (e.g., Booth-Kewley & Friedman, 1987; Kobasa, Maddi, & Zola, 1983). Kobasa and co-workers suggest that hardy people are better able to handle stress because they perceive themselves as *choosing* their stress-creating situations. They encode stress as rendering life interesting, not as intensifying the pressures on them. A sense of control is a key factor in psychological hardiness.

Optimism   Research suggests that seeing the glass as half full is healthier than seeing it as half empty (M. F. Scheier & Carver, 1992). In one study on the relationships between optimism and health, Scheier and Carver (1985) administered a measure of optimism, the Life Orientation Test (LOT), to college students. The students also tracked their physical symptoms for 1 month. It turned out that students who received higher optimism scores reported fewer symptoms such as fatigue, dizziness, muscle soreness, and blurry vision. (Subjects' symptoms at the beginning of the study were statistically taken into account, so it could not be argued that the study simply shows healthier people are more optimistic.)

Optimism is related to a number of health issues. Pain patients who expressed more pessimisitic thoughts during flare-ups of pain also reported more severe pain and distress (Gil et al., 1990). The pessimistic thoughts included, "I can no longer do anything," "No one cares about my pain," and "It isn't fair I have to live this way." In a study of first-year law school students, optimism was associated with better mood and better immune system responses (Segerstrom et al., 1998). In another study, optimistic women were less likely than pessimistic women to experience postpartum depression (depression experienced following childbirth) (Carver & Gaines, 1987). Optimistic cardiac patients even recover relatively more rapidly from coronary artery bypass surgery (M. F. Scheier et al., 1989). The optimistic patients are up and about their rooms more rapidly after surgery. They have fewer postoperative complications and return sooner to their preoperative routines (including their work and exercise routines).

TRUTH *or* FICTION REVISITED
4.5 True.   Optimistic people tend to recover more rapidly than pessimistic people from coronary artery bypass surgery.

Research to date shows only correlational links between optimism and health. Perhaps we shall soon find out whether learning to alter one's attitude—to learn to see the glass as half-filled—plays a causal role in maintaining or restoring health.

You can complete the nearby Life Orientation Test to evaluate your own level of optimism.

Humor: Does "A Merry Heart Doeth Good Like a Medicine?"   The notion that humor eases the burdens of the day has been with humankind for millennia (Lefcourt & Martin, 1986). Ponder the biblical adage, "A merry heart doeth good like a medicine" (Proverbs 17:22).

Research evidence buttresses the biblical maxim by suggesting that humor may indeed play a stress-buffering role and perhaps more. In one study, negative life events had less of a depressing effect on students who had a better sense of humor and those who were better able to produce humor under conditions of stress (R. A. Martin & Lefcourt, 1983). Moreover, higher levels of humor are associated with a more positive self-concept and higher self-esteem and the experiencing of positive emotions during times of both positive and negative life events (N. A. Kuiper & Martin, 1993; R. A. Martin et al., 1993). This line of research suggests that humor may not only serve as a buffer against stress but actually enhance enjoyment of positive life events and good times (R. A. Martin et al., 1993). But we should be careful about drawing causal inferences from such correlational relationships. Persons with a better developed sense of humor may also possess other qualities that buffer the impact of stress.

TRUTH *or* FICTION REVISITED
4.6 False.   A sense of humor may buffer or moderate the impact of stress, but more research is needed to determine whether it plays a causal role.

Socioeconomic, Sociocultural, and Ethnic Factors

Social factors in health include economic and cultural issues, and ethnic and racial characteristics. One economic factor is that many poor people do not have access to health insurance or cannot afford to carry health insurance on their own. They thus have more limited access to health care, which can jeopardize their health by preventing them from receiving the care they need. There is also an interaction between health-care utilization and cultural values. Within some groups, as among Christian Scientists and some native peoples, mainstream health-care utilization may be essentially nil because of preference for religious or spiritual practices.

Health problems have differential impacts on various cultural and ethnic groups around the world and within the United States. In some cases, genetic factors may interact with cultural and ethnic factors. In others, poverty, prejudice and discrimination, lack of education, and lack of

The Life Orientation Test

Do you see the glass as half full or half empty? Do you expect bad things to happen or do you find the silver lining in every cloud? The Life Orientation Test can afford you insight as to how optimistic or pessimistic you are.

Directions: Indicate whether or not each of the items represents your feelings by writing a number in the black space according to the following code. Then turn to the scoring key at the end of the chapter.

4 = strongly agree
3 = agree
2 = neutral
1 = *disagree*
0 = strongly *disagree*

_____ 1. In uncertain times, I usually expect the best.
_____ 2. It's easy for me to relax.
_____ 3. If something can go wrong for me, it will.
_____ 4. I always look on the bright side of things.
_____ 5. I'm always optimistic about my future.
_____ 6. I enjoy my friends a lot.
_____ 7. It's important for me to keep busy.
_____ 8. I hardly ever expect things to go my way.
_____ 9. Things never work out the way I want them to.
_____ 10. I don't get upset too easily.
_____ 11. I'm a believer in the idea that "every cloud has a silver lining."
_____ 12. I rarely count on good things happening to me.

Source: Scheier, M. F., & Carver, C. S. (1985)

accessibility of health care may play the predominant roles. Consider the following examples:

- African Americans are nearly one third more likely to develop **hypertension** than non-Hispanic White Americans (American Heart Association, 1990). They are also more apt to have hypertension than Black Africans are, which leads many health professionals to conclude that the life experiences of Blacks in the United States, especially stress due to racial discrimination and poor economic conditions, as well as unhealthful diets, high levels of smoking (among men), and low levels of regular exercise may interact with genetic vulnerability to increase the risk of hypertension (Gillum, 1996; Krieger & Sidney, 1996; Livingston, 1993).

- Cases of severe uncontrolled hypertension among African Americans and Hispanic Americans are found predominantly among those with lower levels of education and limited access to medical care (S. Shea et al., 1992).

- The incidence of most kinds of cancer is also higher among African Americans than non-Hispanic White Americans. The overall cancer rate in the United States declined from 1990 to 1995 for both men and women of every racial group except one: Black males (Stolberg, 1998a). Male and female African Americans also have lower cancer survival rates than non-Hispanic White Americans, in large part because they tend to be diagnosed later in the progression of the disease and have

more limited access to quality medical care (Leary, 1995b; Stolberg, 1998a).

- Death rates from cancer are higher in nations where the population consumes large quantities of fat, such as England, the Netherlands, Denmark, the United States, and Canada (L. A. Cohen, 1987). Cancer takes fewer lives in nations such as Thailand, the Philippines, and Japan, where people consume lower levels of dietary fat.

- Ingestion of fatty foods is also connected with obesity. Japanese American men who reside in California and Hawaii are two to three times more likely than Japanese men who reside in Japan to become obese (Curb & Marcus, 1991). Why? Because many Japanese Americans have adopted the typical American diet which is richer in dietary fat than the traditional Japanese diet.

- Hispanic Americans utilize health care less regularly than do African Americans and non-Hispanic White Americans, largely because of lack of health insurance, language obstacles, qualms about medical intervention, and—for illegal aliens—concern about possible deportation (Perez-Stable, 1991; L. Thompson, 1991).

- Poor people are more likely to suffer stress-related illnesses. For one thing, they are more likely to encounter stressful life situations, such as financial problems, overcrowded housing, and neighborhood crime. For another, they are less likely to have access to resources

Mediators of Stress Among African Americans

African Americans are at greater risk than non-Hispanic White Americans of developing health problems such as obesity (Van Italie, 1985), hypertension (American Heart Association, 1990), heart disease, diabetes, and certain types of cancer (L. P. Anderson, 1991). Researchers suspect the particular stressors that African Americans in our society often face, such as racism, poverty, violence, and overcrowded living conditions, may play an important role in explaining the heightened health risks they face (Anderson, 1991).

There is no one-to-one connection between stress and such disorders among African Americans, however. Factors such as the availability of social support from family and friends, beliefs in one's ability to handle stress (self-efficacy), coping skills, and awareness of one's ethnic identity may mediate the effects of stress. Yet African Americans who may be in the greatest need of support, such as older adults and single parents, are often the most reluctant to seek support from family members (Anderson, 1991).

Among African Americans, as among other groups, self-esteem is tied to racial or ethnic identity. Acquiring and maintaining pride in one's racial identity and cultural heritage may help African Americans—and other ethnic minorities—withstand the stresses imposed by racism. Although more research is needed to elucidate the links between racial identity, self-esteem, and toler-

ance of stress, the available evidence shows that African Americans who become alienated from their culture develop more negative self-images and stand a greater risk of developing not only physical and psychological disorders but also academic underachievement and marital conflicts (Anderson, 1991).

Ethnic pride as a moderator of the effects of stress. Pride in one's racial or ethnic identity may help one withstand the stress imposed by racism and intolerance.

to help them deal with stress or to receive health education messages stressing the importance of early medical intervention when symptoms develop (N. E. Adler et al., 1994).

Social Support Social support has a positive impact on health and may help buffer the impact of stress (Uchino, Cacioppo, & Keicolt-Glaser, 1996). People with more social support may actually live longer, as suggested by studies of Alameda County, California (Berkman & Breslow, 1983; Berkman & Syme, 1979) and Tecumseh, Michigan (House, Robbins, & Metzner, 1982), and in a more recent study conducted in Sweden (Goleman, 1993a). In the Swedish study, researchers followed middle-aged men who had experienced a high level of emotional stress due to such factors as financial trouble or serious problems with a family member. Men who were highly stressed but lacked social support were three times more likely to die within a period of 7 years as were those

whose lives were low in stress (Goleman, 1993a). Yet men with highly stressed lives who had ample amounts of emotional support in their lives showed no increased rate of mortality. Having other people available may help people find alternative ways of coping with stressors or simply provide them with the emotional support they need during difficult times.

Social support also appears to buffer the psychological effects of coping with serious illness. In a recent study of people with heart disease, higher levels of social support were associated with fewer depressive symptoms when measured a year later (Holahan et al., 1995).

Natural Environmental Factors

Hurricanes, blizzards, monsoons, floods, tornadoes, windstorms, ice storms, earthquakes, avalanches, mudslides, and volcanic eruptions provide a sampling of the natural disasters humankind has faced. Sometimes we are warned of

Making it in America: Acculturative Stress and Psychological Adjustment

Should Hindu women who emigrate to the United States give up the sari in favor of California casuals? Should Soviet immigrants continue to teach their children Russian in the home? Should African American children be acquainted with the music and art of African peoples? Should women from traditional Islamic societies remove the veil and enter the competitive workplace? How do the stresses of acculturation affect the psychological well-being of immigrants and their families?

Sociocultural theorists have alerted us to the importance of accounting for social stressors in explaining abnormal behavior. One of the primary sources of stress imposed on immigrant groups, or on native groups adapting to living in the larger mainstream culture, is the need to adapt to a new culture. The term **acculturation** refers to the process of adaptation in which immigrants and native groups identify with the new culture through making behavioral and attitudinal changes (Rogler, Cortes, & Malgady, 1991).

Consider the challenges faced by Hispanic Americans. There are two general theories of the relationships between acculturation and adjustment (Griffith, 1983). One theory, dubbed the *melting pot theory,* holds that acculturation helps people adjust to living in the host culture. From this perspective, Hispanic Americans might adjust better by replacing Spanish with English and adopting the values and customs associated with mainstream American culture. A competing theory, the *bicultural theory,* holds that psychosocial adjustment is fostered by identification with both traditional and host cultures. That is, ability to adapt to the ways of the new society combined with a supportive cultural tradition and a sense of ethnic identity may predict good adjustment. From a bicultural perspective, immigrants maintain their ethnic identity and traditional values while learning to adapt to the language and customs of the host culture.

We first must be able to measure acculturation if we are to investigate its relationship to mental health among immigrant and native groups. Measures of acculturation vary. In assessing acculturation among Hispanic Americans, for example, researchers assess variables such as the degree to which people favor English or Spanish in social situations, when reading, or watching media such as TV; preferences for types of food and styles of clothing; and self-perceptions of ethnic identity. Using such measures, the relationships between acculturation and adjustment are complex.

How does acculturation affect the psychological well-being of immigrant groups? The melting pot theory holds that acculturation helps people adjust to living in the host culture. From this perspective, Hispanic Americans might adjust better by replacing Spanish with English and adopting the values and customs of the mainstream U.S. culture. According to bicultural theory, adjustment is fostered by identification with both traditional and host cultures—that is, maintaining a supportive cultural tradition while adapting to the ways of the new society.

Let us summarize some of the findings concerning the relationships between acculturation and psychological disorders among Hispanic Americans:

- Highly acculturated Hispanic American women in a large national survey were nine times more likely than relatively unacculturated women to be heavy drinkers (Caetano, 1987). In Latin American cultures, men tend to drink much more alcohol than women, largely because gender-based cultural prohibitions against drinking constrain alcohol use among women. These constraints appear to have loosened among Hispanic American women who adopt "mainstream" U.S. attitudes and values.

- Third-generation Mexican American male adolescents—who are more likely to be acculturated than first- or second-generation Mexican Americans—were at higher risk of delinquency (Buriel, Calzada, & Vazquez, 1982).

- Highly acculturated Hispanic American high school girls were more likely than their less acculturated counterparts to show test scores associated with anorexia (an eating disorder characterized by excessive weight loss and fears of becoming fat—see Chapter 10) on an eating attitudes questionnaire (Pumariega, 1986). Acculturation apparently made these girls more vulnerable to the demands of striving toward the contemporary American ideal of the (very!) slender woman.

- Despite these associations of acculturation with mental health problems, studies have also found that Mexican Americans who are *less* proficient in English show *more* signs of depression and anxiety than those who are more proficient (Salgado de Snyder, 1987; Warheit, Vega, Auth, & Meinhardt, 1985). Are these Mexican Americans depressed because they remain more invested in Mexican culture, because they have lower language proficiency, or because other factors—such as economic problems—can be connected both to acculturation and language proficiency? Mexican American women who remain more invested in Mexican culture also show generally lower levels of self-esteem and encounter more stress in adapting to living in the United States (Salgado de Snyder, 1987). Other researchers find significantly higher levels of depression among the least acculturated Mexican American men relative to European American men (Neff & Hoppe, 1993).

We can see that evidence relating acculturation status to mental health outcomes is mixed. Inconsistencies in research results may partly reflect differences in the indices by which mental health is measured (problem drinking vs. depression, for example) and the complexities of acculturative processes. Adjustment to a host society may depend on such factors as economic opportunity, language proficiency, and the availability of a supportive network of acculturated individuals of similar cultural background. Still, a general pattern is emerging that points to a linkage between low acculturation and mental health problems, especially depression. In a study of Mexican American elders, those who were minimally acculturated showed higher levels of depression than did those who were either acculturated or bicultural (Zamanian et al., 1992). The bicultural and highly acculturated groups were similar in their levels of depression. Thus, evidence indicates that low acculturation status, at least among Hispanic Americans, is linked to a greater risk of depression. However,

holding a bicultural identity in which one maintains an identification with one's original culture while adapting to the new culture is not associated with any greater vulnerability to depression.

Low acculturation status is often a marker for low socioeconomic status (SES). People who are minimally acculturated often face economic hardship. Financial difficulties add to the stress of adapting to the host culture, which can increase the risk of depression and other psychological problems. Reflecting the importance of economic and social stress, a national study of more than 1,000 Puerto Rican, Mexican, and Cuban American adults showed that levels of depression were lowest among those who were married and employed and highest among those who were unmarried and unemployed (Guarnaccia, Angel, & Worobey, 1991). A more recent study of Hispanic college students showed that low SES, not ethnicity or acculturation per se, was associated with a heightened risk of depression (Cuéllar & Roberts, 1997). Yet SES isn't the only, or necessarily the most important, determinant of mental health in immigrant groups. In a Northern California sample, researchers found better mental health profiles among Mexican immigrants than people of Mexican descent born in the United States, despite the socioeconomic disadvantages faced by the immigrant group (Vega et al., 1998). Acculturation and "Americanization" may have damaging effects on mental health of Mexican Americans, while retention of cultural traditions may have a protective or "buffer" effect (Escobar, 1998).

Studies are also pointing to the benefits of adapting to the host culture while maintaining ties to the traditional culture. Among Asian Americans, establishing contacts with the majority culture while maintaining one's ethnic identity appears to generate less stress than withdrawal and separation from the host culture (L. H. Huang, 1994; Phinney, Lochner, & Murphy, 1990). Withdrawal fails to prepare the individual to make the adjustments necessary to function in a multicultural society, which often results in maladjustment. Maintaining one's ethnic identity also seems to hold a psychological benefit. Studies with Asian American adolescents show that those who have achieved an ethnic identity are better psychologically adjusted and have higher self-esteem

box continues on following page

Making it in America: Acculturative Stress and Psychological Adjustment

(L. H. Huang, 1994; Phinney, 1989). A recent study of immigrant Chinese children showed more adjustment problems among those living in more stressful situations (Short & Johnston, 1997).

Moreover, some outcomes need careful interpretation. For example, does the finding that highly acculturated Hispanic American women are more likely to drink heavily argue in favor of the placing of greater social constraints on women? The point would seem to be that a loosening of restraint is a double-edged sword, and that all people—male and female, Hispanic and non-Hispanic—may encounter adjustment problems when they gain new freedoms.

Other research appears to bear out this point. There is a strong relationship in Hispanic immigrants between the stress of adapting to a new culture and environment and states of psychological distress. In one study, female immigrants showed higher levels of depression than male immigrants (Salgado de Snyder, Cervantes, & Padilla, 1990). The depression may be linked to the greater level of stress women encountered in adjusting to changes in family and personal issues, such as the greater freedom of gender roles for men and women in U.S. society. Because they were reared in cultures in which men are expected to be breadwinners and women homemakers, immigrant women may encounter more family and internal conflict when they enter the work force, regardless of whether their entry results from economic necessity or personal choice. Given these factors, we shouldn't be surprised by recent findings that greater marital distress was reported by wives in more acculturated Mexican-American couples (Negy & Snyder, 1997).

natural disasters. We may be aware of living in earthquake- or flood-prone areas. When warned, we may be able to evade or avert disaster. Otherwise, we are dazed by the abruptness of a disaster and left numb.

Natural disasters are dangerous as they occur and also create lingering problems. Like the 1988 Armenian earthquake (Goenjian et al., 1996), and Hurricane Andrew, which ripped the Florida and Louisiana coastlines in 1992, they can kill our loved ones, destroy our property, and disrupt our communities. They are thus among the most stressful types of experiences. Electric power, water, and other services that had been taken for granted may be disrupted. The earthquake that hit the Los Angeles area in 1994 lasted only 10 seconds but killed 38 people, caused billions of dollars in damage, and left thousands homeless (Blakeslee, 1994a; Gross, 1994a; Weinraub, 1994). Hurricane Andrew left 250,000 Floridians homeless and disrupted electric power to some communities for weeks. Disasters, whether natural or human-made, can deprive us of our sense of control over things, compromising our psychological hardiness.

Technological Factors

We owe our dominion over nature to technological advances. Through technology we build and power our communication, transportation, and other systems. Advances in medical technology have enabled us to overcome many of the health problems posed by nature.

Sometimes technology fails, however, or fails to reach all those who need it. Many people, especially those from cultural and ethnic minorities, do not have available access to the latest technological advances in health care. Sometimes technology leads to disaster. Consider the leakage of poisonous gas at Bhopal, India, in 1984; the collapse of a bridge along the Connecticut Turnpike in 1983; the nuclear accident at Three Mile Island in 1979; the Buffalo Creek dam collapse in 1976; the fire at the Beverly Hills Supper Club in 1977; the Exxon *Valdez* oil spill in 1989; blackouts, airplane disasters, and the leakage of toxic wastes. These are but a sampling of the human-made disasters that befall us and can have profound effects on the psychological and physical functioning of survivors.

The 1976 Buffalo Creek dam collapse inundated the town of Saunders, West Virginia, with thousands of tons of water. The flood lasted 15 minutes but killed 125 people and left over 5,000 homeless. Reactions included anxiety, emotional numbness, depression, physical complaints, unfocused feelings of anger, regression among children, and sleep disturbances, including nightmares (Gleser, Green, & Winget, 1981). Many victims experienced **survivor guilt** that they had been spared the deluge while family members and friends had drowned.

TYING IT TOGETHER: ULCERS AND STRESS

About one American in ten suffers from *peptic ulcers,* or open sores on the lining of the stomach or small intestine. For many years, the peptic ulcer was classified as a **psychosomatic disorder** because it was assumed that stress plays a causative role (Levenstein et al., 1999). The general line of thinking was that peptic ulcers arise in people with a genetic vulnerability who encounter significant life stress. However, many people came to reject this conceptualization when it was discovered that the great majority of peptic ulcers were caused by a bacterium, Helicobacter (*H. pylori*) (Boren, Faulk, Larson, & Normack, 1993; Mason, 1994). The bacterium damages the protective lining of the stomach or intestines. Fortunately, treatment with a regimen of antibiotics can help cure peptic ulcers by attacking the bacterium directly (Altman, 1994a). Now that the peptic ulcer has taken its place in the pantheon of infectious diseases, belief in a psychological component has fallen by the wayside or has come to be regarded as a popular superstition. Yet there's a twist to the story. It turns out that the great majority of people infected with the bacterium do not develop peptic ulcers. We don't yet know why some people with *H. pylori* develop ulcers and others don't. Investigators believe it is conceivable that psychological stress may be involved, as might other behavioral factors, such as alcohol abuse, smoking, and even lack of sleep (Levenstein et al., 1999). Though evidence remains inconclusive, it is possible that stress may increase the risk of peptic ulcers by stimulating release of stomach acid, which in combination with *H. pylori* may lead to ulcers forming on the lining of the stomach or small intestine. Psychological stress might also promote the growth of *H. pylori*. Multiple causal pathways may be involved, with stress playing a role in some cases but not in others. The peptic ulcer is an excellent example of the dangers of thinking in terms of single causes to complex phenomena. The lesson here is to recognize that most physical and psychological disorders involve multiple factors interacting in complex ways.

PSYCHOLOGICAL FACTORS AND PHYSICAL DISORDERS

We noted at the start of the chapter that psychological factors can influence physical functioning; physical factors can also influence mental functioning. In these next sections we take a look at the role of psychological factors in various physical disorders. Physical disorders in which psychological factors are believed to play a causal or contributing role have traditionally been termed *psychosomatic* or **psychophysiological.** These disorders include certain cardiovascular disorders, asthma, and headaches.

The field of psychosomatic medicine was developed to explore the possible health-related connections between the mind and the body. The term *psychosomatic* is derived from the Greek roots *psyche,* meaning "soul" or "intellect," and *soma,* which means "body." Today, evidence points to the importance of psychological factors in a much wider range of physical disorders than those traditionally identified as psychosomatic. In this section we discuss several of the traditionally identified psychosomatic disorders as well as two other diseases in which psychological factors may play a role in the course or treatment of the disease—cancer and AIDS.

Headaches

Headaches are symptomatic of many medical disorders. When they occur in the absence of other symptoms, however, they may be classified as stress related. By far the most frequent kind of headache is the tension headache (Mark, 1998). Persistent stress can lead to persistent contractions of the muscles of the scalp, face, neck, and shoulders, giving rise to periodic or chronic tension headaches. Such headaches develop gradually and are generally characterized by dull, steady pain on both sides of the head and feelings of pressure or tightness. A survey in the Baltimore area showed that 38% of respondents complained of occasional tension headaches, with women reporting a 16% higher rate of these headaches than men (B. S. Schwartz et al., 1998).

Most other headaches, including the severe migraine headache, are believed to involve changes in the blood flow to the brain. Migraine headaches affect perhaps as many as 18 million Americans (J. E. Brody, 1988b). Typical migraines last for hours or days. They may occur as often as daily or as seldom as every other month. Piercing or throbbing sensations may become so intense that they seem intolerable. Sleep, mood, and thinking processes may be affected as the individual's mental state becomes dominated by the misery of a brutal migraine. Migraine attacks usually last from 4 to 72 hours. There are two major types of migraines: migraine without aura (formerly called *common migraine*) and migraine with aura (formerly called *classic migraine*) (Olesen, 1994). An aura is a cluster of warning sensations that precedes the attack. Auras are typified by perceptual distortions, such as flashing lights, bizarre images, or blind spots. These sensations are apparently connected with fluctuations in the levels of serotonin and norepinephrine in the brain. About 1 in 5 migraine sufferers experiences auras. Other than the presence or absence of the aura, the two types of migraine are the same.

Theoretical Perspectives Why, under stress, do some people develop tension headaches? One possible answer is found in the principle of **individual response specificity,** which holds that people may respond to a stressor in idiosyncratic ways. Differences in response may reflect a combination of genetic influences, histories of learning, and ways of encoding experience. In classic research, Malmo and Shagass (1949) induced pain in patients with muscular complaints (backaches) and patients with hypertension. The

Psychological Resilience in Marginalized Groups

Psychology has begun to conduct explorations of cultural difference and diversity from more affirmative rather than deficit perspectives. At one time, ethnic and cultural groups whose beliefs and practices did not fit the characteristics of middle-class White Americans, who were deemed the norm, were labeled abnormal, pathological, or defective depending on the degree of their deviance. We acknowledge that social adversity can have harmful effects on the mental health of socially disadvantaged groups, such as ethnic minority group members, lesbians, and gay men (F. Jones, 1997). The need to grapple continually with prejudice and discrimination can require a great expense of psychological resources that may eventually take its toll on one's psychological adjustment. Yet despite these stresses, many members of traditionally marginalized groups display amazing strength and coping skills. Just as social adversity can contribute to psychological vulnerability, it can also facilitate the development of **psychological resilience.**

Ferdinand Jones (1997) of Brown University observes that a key component of psychological resilience in members of marginalized groups is *psychological independence.* In this context, psychological independence refers to the capacity or ability to take a step back and assess one's circumstances from a wider range of perspectives rather than passively accept the validity about what one is told about one's self or others. People who develop this form of independence have the capacity to distance themselves psychologically from people who intend them harm or treat them unfairly. They can also interact with malevolent others without internalizing the negative things they say or feel that they deserve the ill treatment they receive. Psychological independence is nurtured by loving caregivers who provide support and encouragement. It is also fostered by the strengthening of the sense of personal effectiveness that may develop through opportunities in the social environment for employment, education, and training.

---

hypertensive patients responded to the stimulus with larger changes in the heart rate, whereas the backache group showed greater muscle contractions. Tension-headache sufferers may thus be more likely to respond to stress by tensing the muscles of the forehead, shoulders, and neck.

Investigators suspect that migraines are due to an imbalance, probably genetic in origin, in the levels of the brain chemical serotonin (Edelson, 1998; "Unlocking the secrets of serotonin," 1996). These imbalances lead blood vessels in the brain to contract (narrow) and then dilate (expand). This stretching stimulates nerve endings that give rise to the throbbing, piercing sensations associated with migraine.

Given a genetic predisposition to migraines, many factors may trigger migraine attacks. These include stress; stimuli such as bright lights; changes in barometric pressure; pollen; certain drugs; the chemical monosodium glutamate (MSG), which is often used to enhance the flavor of food; red wine—even hunger (P. R. Martin & Seneviratne, 1997). Hormonal changes of the sort that affect women prior to and during menstruation can also trigger attacks, and the incidence of migraines among women is about twice that among men.

Treatment   Commonly available pain relievers, such as aspirin, ibuprofen, and acetaminophen, may reduce or eliminate pain associated with tension headaches. A recent study reported that a combination of acetaminophen, aspirin, and caffeine (the ingredients in the over-the-counter pain reliever *Excedrin*) produced greater relief from the pain of migraine headaches than a placebo control (Lipton et al., 1998). Drugs that help regulate levels of serotonin in the brain can also help relieve migraine headache pain (Edelson, 1998).

Psychological treatment can also help relieve tension or migraine headache pain in many cases. These treatments include biofeedback, relaxation training, coping skills training, and some forms of cognitive therapy (E. B. Blanchard & Diamond, 1996; Gauthier, Ivers, & Carrier, 1996). Psychological interventions appear to have long-lasting effects that are comparable in magnitude to those obtained by use of pain medications (Gauthier, Ivers, & Carrier, 1996). However, we need to learn more about treating the 20% to 40% of clients who fail to respond to psychological intervention ("Biofeedback Applications as Central or Adjunctive Treatment," 1997). We also need to learn whether combining drug and psychological approaches produces a greater benefit than either approach alone.

Biofeedback training (BFT) is becoming more widely used in treating headaches. BFT helps people gain control over various bodily functions, such as muscle tension and brain waves, by giving them information (feedback) about these functions in the form of auditory signals (e.g., "bleeps") or visual displays. People learn to attend to ways of making the signal change in the desired direction. Training people to use relaxation skills combined with biofeedback has also been shown to be effective.

In Jones's view, the individual's connections with the larger community can also help foster psychological resilience. Over 100 years of racial segregation created separate and segregated racial communities that are still a reality in many parts of the United States. African and White Americans generally lived, worshiped, attended schools, shopped, played, and often worked in completely separate worlds. While segregation resulted in inequities for African Americans in access to the mainstream culture, it may have offered them something less tangible. Distinctive African American communities developed in isolation from the dominant White American culture. These isolated communities often permitted the development of self-images that were healthy alternatives to, and a respite from, the demeaning stereotypes used to depict African Americans in the dominant culture. Jones observes that in segregated communities, African Americans were often socialized to mentally challenge White versions of the truth and to develop a healthy view of themselves that helped them remain resilient in the face of oppression and prejudice.

Elaine Pinderhughes (1989) of Boston College observes that practice in confronting societal obstacles helps people from marginalized groups learn important survival and preparedness skills. She views the development of the skills needed to negotiate social adversity as an important aspect of their resilience.

While many individuals from marginalized groups do internalize negative stereotypes about themselves that are generated by the dominant culture, many do not passively accept the negative stereotypes and labels that others, particularly dominant group members, apply to them. The development of a healthy self-image allows members of disparaged groups to recognize that these negative images are social creations of the dominant culture, not a reflection of their own personal defects. This awareness may be seen as a key ingredient in psychological resilience and can play a major role in fostering mental health.

Electromyographic (EMG) biofeedback is a form of BFT that involves relaying information about muscle tension in the forehead. EMG biofeedback thus heightens awareness of muscle tension in this region and helps people learn to reduce it.

Some people have relieved the pain of migraine headaches by raising the temperature in a finger. This biofeedback technique, called *thermal BFT*, modifies patterns of blood flow throughout the body, including blood flow to the brain, which helps to control migraine headaches (E. B. Blanchard et al., 1990; Gauthier, Ivers, & Carrier, 1996). One way of providing thermal feedback is by attaching a **thermistor** to a finger. A console "bleeps" more slowly[1] as the temperature rises. The temperature rises because more blood is flowing into the limb—away from the head. The client can imagine the finger growing warmer to facilitate the change in the body's distribution of blood. Regular home practice appears to enhance the effects of thermal BFT for migraine headaches (Gauthier, Coté, & French, 1994).

TRUTH *or* **FICTION** REVISITED

4.8 True. Some people have relieved migraine headaches by raising the temperature in a finger. This biofeedback technique modifies patterns of blood flow throughout the body.

---
[1]Or more rapidly. The choice of direction is decided by the therapist or therapist and client.

Cardiovascular Disease

Cardiovascular disease (heart and artery disease) is the leading cause of death in the United States, claiming about 1 million lives annually and accounting for more than 4 in 10 deaths, most often as the result of heart attacks or strokes.

Coronary heart disease (CHD) is the major form of cardiovascular disease, accounting for about 700,000 deaths annually according to recent reports, mostly resulting from heart attacks (National Center for Health Statistics [NCHS], 1996b). About 10% of the population, some 22 million Americans, have CHD. In coronary heart disease, the flow of blood to the heart is insufficient to meet its needs. The underlying disease process in CHD is **arteriosclerosis,** or "hardening of the arteries," a condition in which artery walls become thicker, harder, and less elastic, which makes it more difficult for blood to flow freely. The major cause of arteriosclerosis is **atherosclerosis,** a process involving a build-up of fatty deposits along artery walls, leading to the formation of artery-clogging plaque. If a blood clot should form in an artery narrowed by plaque, it may nearly or completely block the flow of blood to the heart. The result is a heart attack (also called **myocardial infarction**), a life-threatening condition in which heart tissue dies due to a lack of oxygen-rich blood. If a blood clot chokes off the supply of blood in an artery serving the brain, a **stroke** may occur, leading to death of brain tissue that can result in loss of function controlled by that part of the brain or even death.

Psychological Methods for Lowering Arousal

Stress induces bodily responses such as excessive levels of sympathetic nervous system arousal, which if persistent may impair our ability to function optimally and possibly increase the risk of stress-related illnesses. Psychological treatments have been shown to lower states of bodily arousal that may be prompted by stress. In this feature, we consider two widely used psychological methods of lowering arousal: meditation and progressive relaxation.

Meditation

Meditation comprises several ways of narrowing consciousness to moderate the stressors of the outer world. Yogis study the design on a vase or a mandala. The ancient Egyptians riveted their attention on an oil-burning lamp, which is the inspiration for the tale of Aladdin's lamp. Islamic mystics of Turkey, so-called whirling dervishes, fix on their movements and the cadences of their breathing.

There are many meditation methods, but they share the common thread of narrowing one's attention by focusing on repetitive stimuli. Through passive observation, the regular person-environment connection is transformed. Problem solving, worry, planning, and routine concerns are suspended, and consequently, levels of sympathetic arousal are reduced.

Going with the flow. Meditation is a popular method of managing the stresses of the outside world by reducing states of bodily arousal. This young woman practices yoga, a form of meditation. She "goes with the flow," allowing the distractions of her environment to sort of "pass through." Contrast her meditative state with the apparently stressful features of the young man sitting behind her.

Thousands of Americans regularly practice **transcendental meditation** (TM), a simplified kind of Indian meditation brought to the United States in 1959 by Maharishi Mahesh Yogi. Practitioners of TM repeat **mantras**—relaxing sounds such as *ieng* and *om*.

Benson (1975) studied TM practitioners aged 17 to 41—students, businesspeople, artists. His subjects included relative novices and veterans of 9 years of practice. Benson found that TM yields a so-called relaxation response in many people. The relaxation response is characterized by reductions in the body's metabolic rate and by a reduction in blood pressure in people who have hypertension (high blood pressure) (Benson, Manzetter, & Rozuer, 1973; J. E. Brody, 1996a). Meditators also produced more alpha waves, brain waves connected with relaxation.

Other researchers concur that meditation lowers arousal but contend that similar effects can be attained by other relaxing activities (M. A. West, 1985) or simply by resting silently for an equal amount of time (Holmes, Solomon, Cappo, & Greenberg, 1983). The Holmes group reported no differences between veteran meditators and subjects who simply sat quietly in heart or respiration rate, blood pressure, and galvanic skin response (GSR). Critics of meditation do not hold that meditation is without value; they suggest, instead, that meditation may have no distinct effects when compared to a restful break from a stressful routine.

Although there are differences among meditative techniques, the following suggestions illustrate some general guidelines:

1. Try meditation once or twice a day for 10 to 20 minutes at a time.

2. Keep in mind that when you're meditating, what you *don't* do is more important than what you do. So embrace a passive attitude: Tell yourself, "What happens, happens." In meditation, you take what you get. You don't *strive* for more. Striving of any kind hinders meditation.

3. Place yourself in a hushed, calming environment. For example, don't face a light directly.

4. Avoid eating for an hour before you meditate. Avoid caffeine (found in coffee, tea, many soft drinks, and chocolate) for at least 2 hours.

5. Get into a relaxed position. Modify it as needed. You can scratch or yawn if you feel the urge.

6. For a focusing device, you can concentrate on your breathing or sit in front of a serene object such as a plant or incense. Benson suggests "perceiving" (not

"mentally saying") the word *one* each time you breathe out. That is, think the word, but "less actively" than you normally would. Other researchers suggest thinking the word *in* as you breathe in and *out,* or *ah-h-h,* as you breathe out. They also suggest mantras such as *ah-nam, rah-mah,* and *shi-rim.*

7. When preparing for meditation, repeat your mantra aloud many times—if you're using a mantra. Enjoy it. Then say it progressively more softly. Close your eyes. Focus on the mantra. Allow thinking the mantra to become more and more "passive" so you "perceive" rather than think it. Again, embrace your "what happens, happens" attitude. Keep on focusing on the mantra. It may become softer or louder, or fade and then reappear.

8. If unsettling thoughts drift while you're meditating, allow them to sort of "pass through." Don't worry about squelching them, or you may become tense.

9. Remember to take what comes. Meditation and relaxation cannot be forced. You cannot force the relaxing effects of meditation. Like sleep, you can only set the stage for it and then permit it to happen.

10. Let yourself drift. (You won't get lost.) What happens, happens.

Progressive Relaxation

Progressive relaxation was originated by University of Chicago physician Edmund Jacobson in 1938. Jacobson noticed that people tense their muscles under stress, intensifying their uneasiness. They tend to be unaware of these contractions, however. Jacobson reasoned that if muscle contractions contributed to tension, muscle relaxation might reduce tension. But clients who were asked to focus on relaxing muscles often had no idea what to do.

Jacobson's method of progressive relaxation teaches people how to monitor muscle tension and relaxation. With this method, people first tense, then relax, selected muscle groups in the arms; facial area; the chest, stomach, and lower back muscles; the hips, thighs, and calves; and so on. The sequence heightens awareness of muscle tensions and helps people differentiate feelings of tension from relaxation. The method is progressive in that people progress from one group of muscles to another in practicing the technique. Since the 1930s, progressive relaxation has been used by a number of behavior therapists, including Joseph Wolpe and Arnold Lazarus (1966).

The following instructions from Wolpe and Lazarus (1966, pp. 177–178) illustrate how the technique is applied to relaxing the arms. Relaxation should be practiced in a favorable setting. Settle back on a recliner, couch, or a bed with a pillow. Select a place and time when you're unlikely to be disturbed. Make the room warm and comfortable. Dim sources of light. Loosen tight clothing. Tighten muscles about two thirds as hard as you could if you were trying your hardest. If you sense that a muscle could have a spasm, you are tightening too much. After tensing, let go of tensions completely.

Relaxation of Arms (time: 4–5 minutes) Settle back as comfortably as you can. Let yourself relax to the best of your ability . . . Now, as you relax like that, clench your right fist, just clench your fist tighter and tighter, and study the tension as you do so. Keep it clenched and feel the tension in your right fist, hand, forearm . . . and now relax. Let the fingers of your right hand become loose, and observe the contrast in your feelings . . . Now, let yourself go and try to become more relaxed all over . . . Once more, clench your right fist really tight . . . hold it, and notice the tension again . . . Now let go, relax; your fingers straighten out, and you notice the difference once more . . . Now repeat that with your left fist. Clench your left fist while the rest of your body relaxes; clench that fist tighter and feel the tension . . . and now relax. Again enjoy the contrast . . . Repeat that once more, clench the left fist, tight and tense. . . . Now do the opposite of tension—relax and feel the difference. Continue relaxing like that for a while . . . Clench both fists tighter and together, both fists tense, forearms tense, study the sensations . . . and relax; straighten out your fingers and feel that relaxation. Continue relaxing your hands and forearms more and more . . . Now bend your elbows and tense your biceps, tense them harder and study the tension feelings . . . all right, straighten out your arms, let them relax and feel that difference again. Let the relaxation develop . . . Once more, tense your biceps; hold the tension and observe it carefully . . . Straighten the arms and relax; relax to the best of your ability . . . Each time, pay close attention to your feelings when you tense up and when you relax. Now straighten your arms, straighten them so that you feel most tension in the triceps muscles along the back of your arms; stretch your arms and feel that tension . . . And now relax. Get your arms back into a comfortable position. Let the relaxation proceed on its own. The arms should feel comfortably heavy as you allow them to relax . . . Straighten the arms once more so that you feel the tension in the triceps muscles; straighten them. Feel that tension . . . and relax. Now let's concentrate on pure relaxation in the arms without any tension. Get your arms comfortable and let them relax further and further. Continue relaxing your arms even further. Even when your arms seem fully relaxed, try to go that extra bit further; try to achieve deeper and deeper levels of relaxation.

Let us now examine a number of risk factors for CHD.

Age   The risk of CHD increases sharply with age from about 40 upward. For men, the rate of increase is steady. For women, it is slow until menopause and then increases rapidly (U.S. Department of Health and Human Services [USDHHS], 1991b).

Gender   Men develop CHD about twice as frequently as women (C. D. Jenkins, 1988). The mortality rate among women approximates that of men about 10 years younger (J. E. Brody, 1993a), so the average 60-year-old woman has about the same risk as the average 50-year-old man (Brody, 1993a). By age 65, however, the risks are about the same.

Family History   People whose families show a history of CHD are more likely to develop CHD themselves.

Socioeconomic Status (SES)   Persons of low SES are at greater risk for CHD than those higher in SES. People at lower SES levels, who also tend to be less well educated, are more likely to smoke, less likely to watch their diets, and more likely to encounter various life stresses, all of which may contribute to CHD (C. D. Jenkins, 1988). Health promotion efforts targeting disease prevention through adoption of healthier eating and dietary habits have also been less successful in reaching poorer, less educated people.

Obesity   Obesity is a major risk factor for CHD and stroke (Brownell & Wadden, 1992; Rexrode et al., 1997). Obesity is associated with higher circulating cholesterol, which contributes to atherosclerosis, and high blood pressure (USDHHS, 1991b).

Hypertension   Blood pressure (BP) is the pressure that blood exerts on the walls of blood vessels. Hypertension (high blood pressure) increases the risk of CHD, heart attacks, and strokes. Because elevated blood pressure can damage the cardiovascular system for years without noticeable symptoms, it is crucial to have one's blood pressure checked periodically. Stressors such as high levels of noise can raise blood pressure.

The prevailing psychodynamic perspective on hypertension has been that hypertensive people have difficulty expressing pent-up anger (F. Alexander, 1939). Pent-up feelings somehow "press" against a biological barrier—the walls of blood vessels—increasing blood pressure. Research supporting the anger-hypertension connection is mixed, with evidence from a longitudinal study of some 5,000 people in Framingham, Massachusetts, failing to show any connection between the ways in which people cope with anger (for example, holding anger in or expressing it) and their later risk of developing hypertension (J. H. Markovitz et al., 1993). We shouldn't shut the lid on a possible role of anger in hypertension. The Framingham results were based on a middle-aged, White sample. It is possible that anger plays a

Risk.   What's wrong with this picture? How many risk factors for cardiovascular disorders can you identify in this photograph?

more important role in younger people and in non-White populations.

High BP is generally controllable by medication. Unfortunately, because of lack of symptoms, many patients do not take medication reliably. Obesity and dietary factors such as sodium (salt) intake can elevate the BP. Dietary restrictions and weight management are therefore part of the usual treatment program for people with hypertension. Behavioral techniques such as meditation and relaxation training have been shown to be of value in supplementing the medical treatment of high BP (e.g., Hoelscher, Lichstein, Fischer, & Hegarty, 1987). These techniques may also prove helpful in the nonpharmacological approach to treating mild hypertension (J. H. Markovitz et al., 1993; Yung & Keltner, 1996). This should come as no surprise because men who are highly anxious are about twice as likely as their more relaxed counterparts to develop hypertension (J. H. Markovitz et al., 1993).

Cholesterol Levels   High blood cholesterol levels are linked to greater risk of heart disease. The culprit seems to be LDL (low-density **lipoprotein**) cholesterol, a type of cholesterol that sticks to the artery walls, forming fatty deposits or placques that can clog arterial passageways and eventually lead to a heart attack or stroke (Avins & Browner, 1998; Grover, Coupal, & Hu, 1995). The body converts dietary cholesterol and saturated fats found in animal fats and dairy products into LDL cholesterol. Even cholesterol-free vegetable matter can raise LDL levels if it contains high levels of saturated fat, such as products containing coconut and palm oils. Another form of cholesterol, HDL (high-density lipoprotein) cholesterol, is dubbed "good cholesterol" because it actually sweeps away fatty deposits from artery walls, which lowers the risk of CHD.

Patterns of Consumption   Certain patterns of consumption, such as heavy drinking, smoking, overeating, and eating food high in cholesterol or saturated fats, are linked to increased risk of CHD and premature death (Lichtenstein & Glasgow, 1992; Stamler et al., 1986). Smoking alone is believed responsible for more than 20% of deaths from CHD (National Cancer Institute, 1991). Adopting healthy habits, such as lowering intake of dietary cholesterol and saturated fat, avoiding smoking, maintaining a healthy weight, and avoiding excessive intake of alcohol, can substantially reduce your risk of CHD.

Type A Behavior Pattern

The Type A behavior pattern, a style of behavior that characterizes people who are hard-driving, ambitious, impatient, and highly competitive, has been associated with a modestly higher risk of CHD (T. Q. Miller et al., 1991). Evidence indicates that psychological interventions focused on helping people reduce their Type A behavior substantially reduce the risk of subsequent heart attacks in people who have already suffered one (J. E. Brody, 1996c; M. Friedman et al., 1986). Perhaps there is a lesson in this for us all.

The questionnaire, "Are You Type A?," on page 160 helps you assess whether or not you fit the Type A behavior profile (TABP). If you would like to begin modifying Type A behavior, a good place to start is with lessening your sense of time urgency. Here are some suggestions (M. Friedman & Ulmer, 1984):

1. Increase social activity with family and friends.
2. Each day, spend a few minutes recalling distant events. Peruse photos of family and old friends.
3. Read books—biographies, literature, drama, politics, nature, science, science fiction. (Books on business and on climbing the corporate ladder are not recommended!)
4. Visit art galleries and museums. Consider works for their aesthetic value, not their prices.
5. Go to the movies, theater, concerts, ballet.
6. Write letters to family and old friends.
7. Take an art course; start violin or piano lessons.
8. Keep in mind that life is by nature unfinished. You needn't have all your projects finished by a certain date.
9. Ask family members what they did during the day. *Listen* to the answer.

Hostility—quickness to anger—is the key element of the TABP that has been linked most closely to cardiovascular risk (J. E. Brody, 1996c) (see nearby "Closer Look" section). People with TABP tend to have "short fuses" and are prone to get angry easily. Some researchers believe hostility is the most harmful feature of the TABP. To reduce anger and hostility, Type A experts recommend the following (J. E. Brody, 1996c; M. Friedman & Ulmer, 1984):

1. Tell your family that you love them.
2. Make new friends.
3. Let friends know you are available to help them.
4. Get a pet and care for it.

5. Don't get involved in discussions that you know lead to pointless arguments.
6. When others do things that disappoint you, consider situational factors such as education and cultural background that affect their behavior. Don't jump to the conclusion that they intend to get you upset.
7. Focus on the beauty and pleasure in things.
8. Don't curse as much.
9. Express appreciation to people for their support and assistance.
10. Play to lose, at least occasionally.
11. Say "Good morning" cheerfully.
12. Check out your face in the mirror from time to time. Look for signs of anger and aggravation; ask yourself if you really need to look like that.
13. Don't sweat the small stuff. Let it go. Avoid grudges and let bygones be bygones.

Social Environmental Stress

Social environmental stress also appears to heighten the risk of CHD (D. S. Krantz et al., 1988). Overtime work, assembly-line labor, and exposure to conflicting demands appear to contribute to raising the CHD risk (C. D. Jenkins, 1988).

The stress-CHD connection is not straightforward, however. For example, the effects of demanding occupations are apparently moderated by factors such as psychological hardiness and whether or not people find their work meaningful (D. S. Krantz, Contrada, Hills, & Friedler, 1988).

One model relates the demands of an occupation to the degree of control afforded the individual worker. As suggested by Figure 4.2, waiters and waitresses, store managers, and firefighters have highly demanding jobs. Architects, scientists, physicians, and some others have occupations in which they exert a good deal of control over their job-related activity. **High-strain** jobs are high in demand and low in the amount of personal control they afford. High-strain jobs apparently place workers at highest risk for CHD (D. S. Krantz et al., 1988; R. B. Williams et al., 1997). Workers in high-strain occupations have been found to have about 1.5 times the risk of CHD as workers in low-strain occupations (LaCroix & Haynes, 1987). Working women in general do not have higher risks of CHD than homemakers or men. Yet, women who are working in high strain jobs—those involving repetitive jobs with nonsupportive bosses in which they are not allowed to make decisions on their own and are given too much work and too little time to complete it—are at greater risk for CHD or for risk factors associated with CHD (such as hostility and anxiety) (D. S. Krantz et al., 1988; R. B. Williams et al., 1997).

Sedentary Lifestyle

Even moderate levels of physical activity, such as walking a half hour a day at a 3 or 4 mile an hour rate, can reduce the risk of cardiovascular disease if practiced regularly (C. Bouchard, Shephard, & Stephens, 1993; "How Hard Do You Really Need to Exercise?," 1995;

FIGURE 4.2 *The job strain model.*
The job strain model shows the relationship of various occupations to two dimensions of job strain: decision control and psychological demand. Occupations that are characterized by both *low* control and *high* demand (the lower right quadrant) have been associated with greater risk of cardiovascular disease.

Source: "Bosses Face Less Risk Than the Bossed," April 3, 1983. *The New York Times.* Copyright © 1983 by the New York Times. Reprinted by permission.

Pate et al., 1995). In a recent study of twins, investigators found that people who exercised the equivalent of at least six, brisk half-hour walks per month had a 44% lower rate of death than their sedentary twins ("A Few Brisk Walks a Month Are Linked to Living Longer," 1998). Unfortunately, too few of us get enough physical activity or exercise.

Ethnicity and CHD

The death rate from heart disease for African American adults aged 45 to 64 is about 75% higher than for non-Hispanic White Americans. Within the same age range, the death rate from heart disease for Native Americans is slightly higher (8% higher) than the rate for non-Hispanic White Americans. The comparable death rate for Hispanic Americans is about 23% lower than the rate for non-Hispanic White Americans, and the rate for Asian Americans is lowest, about half that of non-Hispanic White Americans (USDHHS, 1991b).

Ethnic differences in prevalences of CHD reflect underlying differences in risk factors (Winkleby et al., 1998). Consider hypertension, a major risk factor. About 20% of Americans have hypertension, or high blood pressure (USDHHS, 1991b). As shown in Figure 4.3, non-Hispanic Black Americans are more likely than non-Hispanic White Americans to have hypertension. African Americans are also less likely than White Americans to receive aggressive and often life-saving treatments for CHD, such as coronary artery bypass surgery

and balloon angioplasty (a surgical procedure in which a tiny balloon is threaded into a clogged artery and inflated to widen the artery) (E. D. Peterson et al., 1997). This dual standard of care is believed to involve discrimination as well as cultural factors that impede access to care, such as the cultural mistrust of African Americans toward the medical establishment.

Possible genetic differences in sodium (salt) sensitivities may also be involved in racial differences in hypertension. Interestingly, African Americans are more likely to have high blood pressure than groups with common ancestry, such as Black Africans. This suggests that factors *other* than a common genetic ancestry are involved. Dietary patterns and life experiences of African Americans, especially the stresses of racial discrimination and economic hardship, high-fat diets, and high levels of smoking (among men), may mix in with genetic vulnerability to increase the risk of hypertension and other cardiovascular problems. Inadequate health care access is yet another factor. Fewer than half of African American men with hypertension receive treatment. Lack of regular exercise may be yet another factor.

Because African Americans are more likely than non-Hispanic White Americans to suffer from hypertension, some researchers suggest that cardiovascular responsiveness to stress may have genetic origins. If so, African Americans of darker skin color should be more prone to hypertension because they have a higher percentage of Black ancestors. However, the shade-of-skin–hypertension connection holds only for African Americans of lower socioeconomic status.

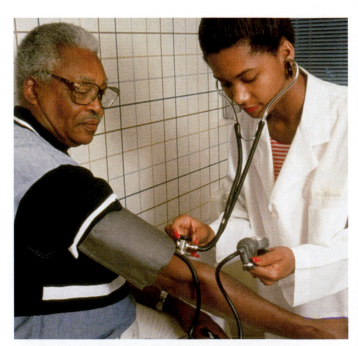

Do you know your BP? About 20% of Americans are reported to have hypertension, or high blood pressure. African Americans suffer disproportionately from hypertension, but it is unclear whether genetic factors or stress play more crucial causal roles. Because we cannot directly sense our own blood pressure, it is advisable to have it checked regularly through means such as the blood pressure cuff.

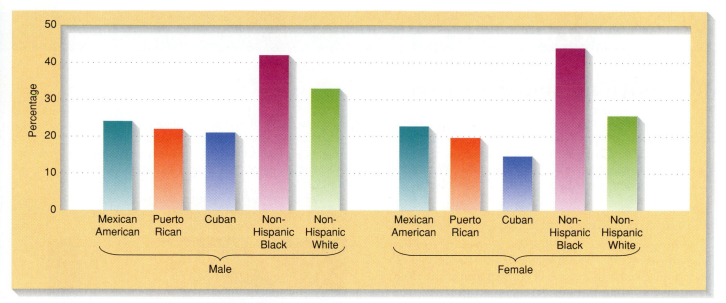

FIGURE 4.3 *Hypertension among people aged 20 to 74, according to race ethnicity.*
Non-Hispanic African Americans are more likely than non-Hispanic White Americans to have high blood pressure, and non-Hispanic White Americans are more likely to have high blood pressure than Hispanic Americans. Except in the case of non-Hispanic African Americans, men aged 20 to 74 are more likely than women in the same age group to have high blood pressure.

Source: USDHHS, Public Health Service (1991), *Health United States 1990.* DHHS Pub. No. (PHS) 91-1232.

For this reason, Klag (1991) suggests that stress is the key culprit. He argues that African Americans of darker color are subjected to greater discrimination—a socioeconomic and sociocultural stressor.

Non-Hispanic White Americans are more likely to have hypertension than Hispanic Americans (USDHHSb, 1991). Nevertheless, Mexican Americans, who constitute the largest group of Hispanic Americans, are more likely to suffer CHD than non-Hispanic White Americans, in part because health promotion efforts focusing on the need to adopt lower fat diets and regular exercise have been less successful in reaching them ("Heart Disease Higher in Mexican-Americans," 1997; Winkleby et al., 1998).

We finish this section with encouraging news. Americans are taking better care of their health. The incidence of CHD and deaths from heart disease has been declining steadily during the past 50 years, thanks largely to reductions in smoking, to improved treatment of heart patients, and perhaps also to other changes in lifestyle, such as reduced intake of dietary fat (J. E. Brody, 1993a, 1994a; P. G. McGovern et al., 1996; Traven et al., 1995). Better educated people are also more likely to modify unhealthful behavior patterns and reap the benefits of change. Is there a message in there for you?

Asthma

Asthma is a respiratory disorder in which the main tubes of the windpipe—the bronchi—constrict and become inflamed and large amounts of mucus are secreted. During asthma attacks, people wheeze, cough, and struggle to breathe in enough air. They may feel as though they are suffocating.

Asthma affects about 13 million people in the United States, including nearly 5 million children. About one third of the sufferers are children under 16. Asthma has been rising rapidly, with a jump of nearly 50% in prevalence from the mid-1980s to the mid-90s (Homer, 1997; Lemanske & Busse, 1997). Attacks can last from a few minutes to several hours and vary notably in intensity. Series of attacks can harm the bronchial system, causing mucus to collect and muscles to lose their elasticity. Sometimes the bronchial system is weakened to the point where a subsequent attack is lethal. Fortunately, few sufferers die from asthma, however ("Study Finds Few Sufferers Die of Asthma," 1994).

Theoretical Perspectives Many causes are implicated in asthma, including allergic reactions; exposure to environmental pollutants, including cigarette smoke and smog; and genetic factors (Cookson & Moffatt, 1997). Asthmatic reactions in susceptible people can be triggered by exposure to allergens such as pollen, mold spores, and animal dander; by cold, dry air; and by emotional responses such as anger or even laughing too hard (J. E. Brody, 1988). Some researchers suggest there are two kinds of asthma: allergic and nonallergic. In the allergic form, the body's immune system overresponds to harmless substances, such as pollen, by producing antibodies that bind to receptors in the airways of the nose and chest. This leads to a chain reaction that produces the sneezing and runny noses associated with

Emotions and the Heart

Might your emotions be putting you at risk of developing coronary heart disease? It appears so. Evidence has accumulated that points to emotional stress in the form of persistent negative emotions, especially anxiety and anger, as a major risk factor for CHD and other heart problems.

The Anxious Heart

Investigators have linked phobic anxiety, the type of anxiety characterized by unfounded fears and panicky feelings, to a greater risk of death in men as the result of irregular heart rhythms. A study of some 34,000 men, none of whom were diagnosed at the outset of the study with CHD, showed those scoring at the high end of an index of phobic anxiety were six times more likely to suffer sudden coronary death over a 2-year period than were less anxious men (Hilchey, 1994; Kawachi et al., 1994). The researchers suspect that persistent, high levels of anxiety may produce "electrical storms" in the heart, resulting in irregular heart rhythms that may lead to sudden coronary death. Fortunately, the number of cardiac-related deaths during the 2-year study period was relatively small (only 16 among 34,000).

Other investigators have linked states of anxiety and tension with an increased risk of coronary symptoms and death in people with established coronary heart disease (Denollet et al., 1996; Gullette et al., 1997). In other recent research, people exposed to mental stress, like the kind experienced when we are required to work under pressure, can induce episodes of restricted blood flow to the heart (called *ischemic*

events) in people with CHD. Moreover, people who experienced ischemic events in response to mental stress were more likely to later experience a heart attack or other cardiac events than were nonresponders (Jian et al., 1996).

Researchers in the Framingham study found a connection between anxiety in middle-age men and the

Emotions and the heart. Emotional stress in the form of persistent negative emotions, such as anxiety and anger, has emerged as a major risk factor in heart-related disorders.

allergies and, in some cases, the wheezing and coughing associated with asthma. Scientists have discovered a gene that appears to be linked to forms of asthma stemming from allergic reactions ("Scientists Say Gene is Linked to Asthma," 1994). Nonallergic types could stem from a variety of causes, including respiratory infections such as bronchitis and pneumonia (A. B. Alexander, 1981) and maternal smoking during pregnancy (Martinez, Cline, & Burrows, 1992).

Psychological factors, such as emotional stress, loss of loved ones, and intense disappointment, appear to increase susceptibility to asthmatic attacks (Moran, 1991). Asthma, moreover, has psychological consequences. Some sufferers avoid strenuous activity, including exercise, for fear of increasing their demand for oxygen and tripping attacks.

Treatment   Though asthma cannot be cured, it can be controlled by reducing exposure to allergens, by desensitization therapy ("allergy shots") to help the body acquire more resistance to allergens, by use of inhalers, and by drugs that open bronchial passages during asthma attacks (called *bronchodilators*) and others (called *anti-inflammatories*) that reduce future attacks by helping to keep bronchial tubes open.

Recent reports also point to a role for psychological treatment by showing that asthma sufferers can improve their breathing by muscle relaxation training (P. M. Lehrer, Sargunaraj, & Hochron, 1992; M. Lehrer et al., 1994), biofeedback that focuses on relaxing facial muscles (Klotses et al., 1991), and family therapy that reduces the stresses on asthmatic children (P. M. Lehrer et al., 1992).

later risk of developing hypertension, a major risk factor for CHD (J. H. Markovitz et al., 1993). Highly anxious men were about twice as likely as their more relaxed counterparts to develop hypertension. We don't yet know whether this relationship also applies to women.

Anger and Hostility

Occasional feelings of anger may not damage the heart in healthy people, but chronic anger—the type of anger you see in people who seem angry all of the time—may be as dangerous a risk factor in CHD as smoking, obesity, family history, or a high-fat diet (J. E. Brody, 1996c; "Coronary Disease: Taking Emotions to Heart," 1996; T. Q. Miller et al., 1996; Talan, 1996a).

We may define hostility as an attitude of perceiving others and the world in a negative, blaming manner (Eckhardt, Barbour, & Stuart, 1997; Eckhardt & Deffenbacher, 1995). Anger is a strongly felt emotion of displeasure toward others whom we believe have treated us unfairly. Hostile people are quick to anger and become angry more often and more intensely than other people when they feel they have been mistreated. Though hostility may not be a direct cause of heart disease, it can aggravate the disease and precipitate heart attacks in vulnerable people (J. E. Brody, 1996c). Researchers find that among people with heart disease, the risk of suffering a heart attack doubles in the few hours following times when they feel angry as compared to other times (Talan, 1996a).

Linking Emotions and the Heart

Though more research is needed to better understand the mechanism that links negative emotions to heart disease (Marzuk & Barchas, 1997), it is believed that the stress hormones epinephrine and norepinephrine play a significant role. Emotional arousal in the form of anxiety or anger is accompanied by the release of these stress hormones by the adrenal glands. These hormones mobilize the body's resources to deal with threatening situations. They increase the heart rate, breathing rate, and blood pressure, which increases the flow of oxygen-rich blood to the muscles to prepare for defensive action—to fight or to flee—in the face of a threatening stressor. When people are persistently or repeatedly anxious or angry, the body may remain overaroused for long periods of time, continuing to pump out these stress hormones, which eventually may have damaging effects on the heart and blood vessels. Stress hormones also appear to increase the stickiness of the clotting factors in blood, which might increase the chances that potentially dangerous blood clots may form ("Fizzle Anger," 1996).

Investigators continue to explore relationships between heart disease and emotional states. At the same time, cognitive behavior therapists are focusing on ways of helping chronically anxious and angry people learn to control their emotional responses in anxiety-provoking or angering situations. By helping people to remain calm in these situations, psychological treatment may prove to have beneficial effects on the heart as well as the mind. In Chapter 15 we examine further cognitive-behavioral approaches to anger management that can help people reduce high levels of hostility that may predispose them to coronary heart disease (Gidron & Davidson, 1996).

Cancer

The word *cancer* is arguably the most feared word in the language and rightly so: One of every four deaths in the United States is caused by cancer (Stolberg, 1998a). Cancer claims more than a half million lives in the United States annually. Men have a 1 in 2 chance of developing cancer at some point in their lives; for women the odds are 1 in 3. Yet there is good news to report: The number of new cancer cases and deaths from cancer are declining. Cancer cases are on the decline due largely to reductions in smoking, while the declining death rate is attributed largely to increased screening and better treatments (Stolberg, 1998a).

Cancer involves the development of aberrant, or mutant, cells that form growths (tumors) that spread to healthy tissue. Cancerous cells can take root anywhere—the blood, the bones, lungs, digestive tract, and genital organs. When they are not contained early, cancer may metastasize, or establish colonies throughout the body, leading to death.

Risk Factors Genetics plays a role in at least some forms of cancer, including breast cancer (USDHHS, 1991a). Cancer risks also generally increase with age and vary across ethnic groups. African American men have greater risks of contracting lung cancer and prostate cancer than other U.S. men (Stolberg, 1998b). Japanese Americans and non-Hispanic White Americans have relatively high rates of colorectal cancer, which is apparently connected with a higher intake of dietary fat. Non-Hispanic White women have relatively higher incidences of breast cancer than women from

Are You Type A?

People with the Type A behavior pattern are impatient, competitive, and aggressive. They feel rushed, under pressure; they keep one eye glued to the clock. They are prompt and often arrive early for appointments. They walk, talk, and eat rapidly. They grow restless when others work slowly.

Type A people don't just stroll out on the tennis court to bat the ball around. They scrutinize their form, polish their strokes, and demand consistent self-improvement.

Are you Type A? The following questionnaire may afford you insight.

Directions: Write a checkmark under the Yes if the behavior pattern described is typical of you. Place one under the No if it is not. Work rapidly and answer all items. Then check the scoring key at the end of the chapter.

DO YOU: YES   NO

1. Strongly emphasize important words in your ordinary speech? ___ ___
2. Walk briskly from place to place or meeting to meeting? ___ ___
3. Think that life is by nature dog-eat-dog? ___ ___
4. Get fidgety when you see someone complete a job slowly? ___ ___
5. Urge others to complete what they're trying to express? ___ ___
6. Find it exceptionally annoying to get stuck in line? ___ ___
7. Envision all the things you have to do even when someone is talking to you? ___ ___
8. Eat while you're getting dressed, or jot notes down while you're driving? ___ ___
9. Catch up on work during vacations? ___ ___
10. Direct the conversation to things that interest you? ___ ___
11. Feel as if things are going to pot because you're relaxing for a few minutes? ___ ___
12. Get so wrapped up in your work that you fail to notice beautiful scenery passing by? ___ ___

YES   NO

13. Get so wrapped up in money, promotions, and awards that you neglect expressing your creativity? ___ ___
14. Schedule appointments and meetings back to back? ___ ___
15. Arrive early for appointments and meetings? ___ ___
16. Make fists or clench your jaws to drill home your views? ___ ___
17. Think that you have achieved what you have because of your ability to work fast? ___ ___
18. Have the feeling that uncompleted work must be done *now* and fast? ___ ___
19. Try to find more efficient ways to get things done? ___ ___
20. Struggle always to win games instead of having fun? ___ ___
21. Interrupt people who are talking? ___ ___
22. Lose patience with people who are late for appointments and meetings? ___ ___
23. Get back to work right after lunch? ___ ___
24. Find that there's never enough time? ___ ___
25. Believe that you're getting too little done, even when other people tell you that you're doing fine? ___ ___

other ethnic groups. Non-Hispanic White and Asian Americans have higher 5-year survival rates for cancers of the lung, colon, rectum, and prostate than African Americans, Native Americans, and Mexican Americans, apparently because of earlier detection and treatment. Consider that while non-Hispanic White women are more likely to develop breast cancer, Black women are more likely to die from the disease (USDHHS, 1996).

Many behavior patterns increase the risk for cancer, including dietary practices (high fat intake), heavy alcohol consumption, smoking, and sunbathing (ultraviolet light causes skin cancer). On the other hand, regular intake of a

Reducing Type A behavior. Slowing down the pace of your daily life and making time for loved ones are among the ways of reducing Type A behavior. Can you think of other ways that can help you decrease Type A behavior?

healthy daily supply of fruits and vegetables may lower the risk of some forms of cancer. Death rates from cancer are lower in Japan than in the United States, where people ingest more fat, especially animal fat. The difference is not genetic or racial, however, because Japanese Americans whose fat intake approximates that of other Americans show similar death rates from cancer.

Personality, Stress, and Cancer A weakened or compromised immune system may increase susceptibility to cancer. We've seen that psychological factors, such as exposure to stress, may affect the immune system. Research with animals has shown that exposure to stress can hasten the onset of a virus-induced cancer (Riley, 1981). Might exposure to stress in humans increase the risk of cancer? Several studies show an increased incidence of stressful life events, such as the loss of loved ones, preceding the development of some forms of cancer (Levenson & Bemis, 1991). However, as other studies show no linkage between stress and cancer onset, the question remains open to further inquiry.

Psychological Factors in Treatment and Recovery Cancer is a physical disease that is treated medically by means of surgery, radiation, and chemotherapy. Yet psychologists and mental health professionals may play a key role in helping cancer patients deal with the emotional consequences of coping with the disease. Feelings of hopelessness and helplessness are common reactions to receiving a cancer diagnosis, but such feelings may hinder recovery (Andersen, 1992), perhaps by depressing the patient's immune system.

Evidence also shows that cancer patients who maintain a "fighting spirit" experience better outcomes than those who resign themselves to their illness (O'Leary, 1990). For example, a 10-year follow-up of breast cancer patients found that patients who met their diagnosis with anger and a fighting spirit rather than stoic acceptance showed significantly higher survival rates (Pettingale et al., 1985). The will to fight the illness may help to increase survival.

TRUTH *or* **FICTION** REVISITED

4.9 *True.* Investigators found in a sample of breast cancer patients that those who maintained a "fighting spirit" had higher survival rates than those who became resigned to their illness.

Social support may also be of help. Women with metastatic breast cancer who participated in a group support program survived a year and half longer on the average than women assigned to a no-treatment control group (D. Spiegel et al., 1989). How psychological approaches affect the course of cancer is unclear, however. One possible mode of action is enhancement of the immune system (Andersen, 1992).

Investigators have examined the value of training cancer patients to use coping skills, such as relaxation, stress management, and restructuring maladaptive cognitions, to relieve the stress and pain of coping with cancer. These interventions may also help cancer patients cope with the anticipatory side effects of chemotherapy. Cues associated with chemotherapy, such as the hospital environment itself, become conditioned stimuli that elicit nausea and vomiting even before the drugs are administered (Redd, 1995). By pairing relaxation, pleasant imagery, and attentional distraction with these cues, investigators find that nausea and vomiting can be lessened (Redd, 1995). Playing video games as a form of distraction has helped lessen the discomfort of chemotherapy in children with cancer (Kolko & Rickard-Figueroa, 1985).

Psychosocial interventions have had positive effects on emotional and behavioral adjustment in adult cancer patients, as well as reducing symptomatic distress arising from the disease and from chemotherapy treatment (Compas et al., 1998; T. J. Meyer & Mark, 1995). Although it is too early to tell with certainty whether psychosocial techniques actually prolong life in cancer patients, preliminary evidence indicates that it may (Fawzy & Fawzy, 1994; Kogon et al., 1997). Other investigators find relaxation training to have a beneficial effect on reducing negative mood states, such as tension, depression, and anger, in cancer patients undergoing radiation therapy (Decker, Cline-Elsen, & Gallagher, 1992). Psychological treatment also leads to improved quality of life of cancer patients and reduces emotional distress, as well as imparting more effective coping skills (Andersen, 1997).

Learning to modify expectations is also important. Cancer patients who are able to maintain or restore their psychological well-being appear to be able to do so by readjusting their expectations of themselves in line with their present capabilities (Heidrich, Forsthoff, & Ward, 1994).

Acquired Immunodeficiency Syndrome (AIDS)

Lily was not supposed to get AIDS. She was an heiress to a cosmetics fortune. She had received her bachelor's degree from Wellesley and had been enrolled in a graduate program in art history when she came down with intractable flu-like symptoms and was eventually diagnosed as having AIDS.

"No one believed it," she said. "I was never a gay male in San Francisco. I never shot up crack in the alleys of The Bronx. My boyfriends didn't shoot up either. There was just Matthew . . ." Now Lily was 24. At 17, in her senior year in high school, she had had a brief affair with Matthew. Later she learned that Matthew was bisexual. Five years ago, Matthew died from AIDS.

"I haven't exactly been a whore," Lily said ironically. "You can count my boyfriends on the fingers of one hand. None of them caught it from me; I guess I was just lucky." Her face twisted in anger. "You may think this is awful," she said, "but there are times when I wish Jerry and Russ had gotten it from me. Why should they get off?"

Lily's family was fully supportive, emotionally and, of course, financially. Lily had been to fine clinics. Physicians from Europe had been brought in. She was

on a regimen of three medicines: two antiviral drugs, which singly and in combination had shown some ability to slow the progress of AIDS, and an antibiotic intended to prevent bacterial infections from taking hold. She took some vitamins—not megavitamin therapy. She exercised almost daily when she felt up to it, and she was doing reasonably well. In fact, there were times when she thought she might get over her illness.

"Sometimes I find myself thinking about children or grandchildren. Or sometimes I find myself looking at all these old pictures [of grandparents and other relatives] and thinking that I'll have silver in my hair, too. Sometimes I really think this is the day the doctors will call me about the new wonder drug that's been discovered in France or Germany."

"I want to tell you about Russ," she said once. "After we found out about me, he went for testing, and he was clear [of antibodies indicative of infection by the AIDS virus]. He stayed with me, you know. When I wanted to do it, we used condoms. A couple of months later, he went for a second test and he was still clear. Then maybe he had second thoughts, because he became impotent—with me. We'd try, but he couldn't do anything. Still he stayed with me, but I felt us drifting apart. After a while, he was just doing the right thing by staying with me, and I'll be damned if anyone is going to be with me because he's doing the right thing."

Lily looked the [interviewer] directly in the eye. "What sane man wants to play Russian roulette with AIDS for the sake of looking like a caring person? And I'll tell you why I eventually sent him away," she added, tears welling, "the one thing I've learned is that you die alone. I don't even feel that close to my parents anymore. Everyone loves you and wishes they could trade places with you, but they can't. You're suddenly older than everyone around you and you're going to go alone. I can't tell you how many times I thought about killing myself, just so that I could be the one who determines exactly where and when I die—how I would be dressed and how I would feel on the final day."

Lily died in 1992.

THE AUTHORS' FILES

Acquired immunodeficiency syndrome—AIDS—is a lethal viral condition caused by the **human immunodeficiency virus** (HIV). HIV attacks the person's immune system, leaving it helpless to fend off diseases that it normally would hold in check.

HIV is transmitted by sexual contact (vaginal and anal intercourse; oral-genital contact); direct infusion of contaminated blood, as from transfusions of contaminated blood, accidental pricks from needles used previously on an infected person, or needle sharing among injecting drug users; and from an infected mother to a child during pregnancy or childbirth or through breast-feeding (USDHHS, 1991a). HIV is not contracted by donating blood; by airborne germs; by insects; or by casual contact, such as using public toilets, holding or hugging infected people, sharing eating utensils with them, or living or going to school with them. Routine screening of the blood supplies for HIV have reduced the risk of infection from blood transfusions to virtually nil.

HIV infection and AIDS cut across all boundaries of race, ethnicity, income level, gender, sexual orientation, and drug use classification. You needn't be a sexually active gay male or an IV-drug user to get infected, as the case of Lily sadly illustrates.

There is no cure or vaccine for AIDS, but recent advances in treatment with a combination of antiviral drugs (the so-called drug cocktail) has brought hope that the disease may be controlled (Chartrand, 1996; Hogg et al., 1998). Whether the beneficial effects of antiviral therapy are long-lasting remains an open question as of this writing. Concerns have been raised about the potential rise of strains of HIV that may be resistant to any of the presently available drugs (O. J. Cohen & Fauci, 1998). Moreover, many patients cannot afford the expensive drug regimen, and many others in routine clinical practice fail to benefit from the new treatment regimen (Zuger, 1998).

The lack of a cure or effective vaccine means that prevention programs focusing on reducing or eliminating risky sexual and injection practices represent our best hope for controlling the epidemic. Psychologists have become involved in the fight against AIDS because behavior is the major determinant of the risk of contracting the deadly virus and because AIDS, like cancer, has devastating psychological effects on persons affected by the disease, their families and friends, and society at large.

Adjustment of People with HIV and AIDS

Given the nature of the disease and the stigma suffered by people with HIV and AIDS, it is not surprising that many people with HIV, though certainly not all, develop psychological problems, most commonly anxiety and depression (W. C. Holmes et al., 1997; Kelly et al., 1998; Lyketsos et al., 1996; Rabkin et al., 1997). Other frequently occurring psychological problems include poor self-esteem, guilt, increased suicidal risk, and anger. Guilt is often related to self-blame for having contracted the disease and concerns about possibly infecting others (Kalichman & Sikkema, 1994). Anger is often directed against the medical establishment for failing to find a cure and at people whom they believe have discriminated against them because of their infection.

Psychological factors also affect AIDS progression. These include negative expectancies about the future of one's health, a psychological response to coping with the disease based on denial and avoidance, and sensitivity to rejection (Cole, Kemeny & Taylor, 1997; Solano et al., 1993).

Psychological and Psychopharmacological Interventions

Behavior change programs focus on reducing risky sexual and injection practices (J. A. Kelly &

Kalichman, 1995; Kelly et al., 1998). These training programs have been shown to be effective with groups of sexually active gay men (J. A. Kelly, Brasfield, & St. Lawrence, 1991) and with adolescents, including substance-dependent adolescents (St. Lawrence et al., 1995a,1995b).

Psychological treatment, typically in the form of support groups, self-help groups, and organized therapy groups, have also been used to provide psychological assistance to people with HIV/AIDS, their families, and friends. Treatment may incorporate training in active coping skills, such as stress management techniques like self-relaxation and positive mental imagery, and cognitive strategies to control intrusive negative thoughts and preoccupations. Coping skills training and cognitive-behavioral therapy have been shown to help improve psychological functioning and ability to handle stress in people with HIV or AIDS and to reduce feelings of depression and anxiety in these groups (Lutgendorf et al., 1997). Antidepressant medication has also been found to be helpful in treating depression in people with HIV (Elliott et al., 1998; Ferrando et al., 1997; Grasssi et al., 1997; J. C. Markowitz et al., 1998). Whether treatment of depression or coping skills training for handling stress can improve immunological functioning or prolong life in people with HIV and AIDS remains an open question. Reducing alcohol and illicit drugs and following a proper diet and sensible exercise program may well help the immune system ward off opportunistic infections.

The advent of AIDS presents the mental health community with an unparalleled challenge to help prevent the spread of AIDS and to treat people who have been infected with HIV and who have developed AIDS. As frightening as AIDS may be, it is preventable, as noted in the feature "Preventing AIDS."

AIDS support group. AIDS support groups offer emotional support and assistance to people with HIV/AIDS, their families and friends.

Preventing AIDS

For the first time, a generation of college students is coming of age at a time when the threat of AIDS hangs over every sexual encounter. People may decrease the risk of being infected by HIV and other sexually transmitted diseases (STDs) by taking the following measures. Only the first two are sure paths to avoiding the sexual transmission of HIV. The others reduce the risk of infection but cannot be certified as perfectly safe. If we are going to be sexually active without knowing (not guessing) whether we or our partners are infected with HIV or some other STD, we can speak only of safe(r) sex—not of perfectly safe sex.

1. Maintaining lifelong celibacy.

2. Remaining in a lifelong monogamous relationship with an uninfected person who is doing the same thing. Although these first two sexual career paths guarantee safety, they are not followed by the majority of students or other Americans.

3. *Being discerning in one's choice of sex partners.* Get to know another person before engaging in sexual activity. Still, getting to know a person is no guarantee the person is uninfected with HIV. Avoid contact with multiple partners or with people who are likely to have multiple partners.

4. *Being assertive with sex partners.* It is important to communicate concerns about AIDS clearly and assertively with sex partners.

5. *Inspecting one's partner's sex organs.* There are no obvious signs of HIV infection, but people who are infected with HIV are often infected by other STDs as well. It may be feasible to visually inspect your partner's sex organs for rashes, chancres, blisters, discharges, warts, and lice during foreplay. Consider any disagreeable odor a warning sign.

6. *Using latex condoms.* Condoms protect men from infected vaginal fluids and stop infected semen from entering women. All condoms (including so-called natural condoms made of animal intestines or "skins") act as barriers to sperm, but only latex condoms can prevent transmission of HIV.

7. *Using spermicides.* Spermicides containing the ingredient nonoyxnol-9 kill HIV as well as sperm. Spermicides should be used along with latex condoms, not as a substitute for condoms.

8. *Consulting a physician following suspected exposure to an STD.* Antibiotics following unprotected sex may guard against bacterial STDs, but they are of no use against viral STDs such as genital herpes and HIV/AIDS. Consult with a physician before using any medications, including medications you may have stored away in your medicine cabinet.

9. *Seeking regular medical checkups.* Checkups and appropriate laboratory tests enable you to learn about and treat disorders that might have gone unnoticed.

10. *Avoiding sexual activity if there are doubts about safety.* None of the safer sex practices listed guarantees protection. Why not avoid sexual activity when doubts of safety exist?

We end this section on a sobering note. Researchers find that information about risk reduction alone is not sufficient to induce widespread changes in sexual behavior (Geringer et al., 1993; J. A. Kelly et al., 1995; Klepinger et al., 1993). People need to know not only about the dangers of unsafe sexual practices but also how to change their behavior (e.g., learning how to refuse invitations to engage in unsafe sex and how to communicate effectively with one's partner(s) about safer sex), and they must be motivated to change their risk behavior (J. D. Fisher et al., 1994; J. D. Fisher & Fisher, 1992). Other factors not to be overlooked in prevention efforts are drug and alcohol use and peer group norms. The likelihood of people engaging in safer sex practices is linked to the avoidance of alcohol and drugs before sex and to the perception that safer sex practices are the social norm within one's peer group.

SUMMARY

In this chapter we focused on relationships between stress and health, and on the psychological factors involved in health. Psychology has much to offer to the understanding and treatment of physical disorders. Psychological approaches may help in the treatment of such physical disorders as headaches, hypertension, and coronary heart disease. Psychologists also help people reduce the risks of contracting health problems such as cardiovascular disorders, cancer, and AIDS. Emerging fields like psychoneuroimmunology promise to further enhance our knowledge of the intricate relationships between mind and body.

Adjustment Disorders

Adjustment disorders are maladaptive reactions to identified stressors. Impairment usually takes the form of problems at work or in social relationships or activities, or by signs of personal distress that are greater than expected given the circumstances.

A Multifactorial View of Health and Illness

Many factors interact to determine physical health and illness. Health is not a matter of luck. Biological variables such as family history of an illness, exposure to pathogens, the ability of the immune system to fight them off, and inoculations are common causes or deterrents of physical illnesses. The immune system combats disease by producing white blood cells that systematically envelop and kill pathogens, worn-out body cells, and cancerous cells.

Psychological factors that affect our health include our personalities and our behavior patterns. Many personality features, such as self-efficacy expectancies, psychological hardiness, optimism, and a sense of humor, are believed to have positive effects on our health. The stress imposed by social, biological, and physical environmental factors reflects people's psychological appraisal of these factors. Persistent stress eventually exhausts our capacities to cope by compromising our immune systems.

Social factors that affect our health include economic realities, cultural issues, and ethnic variables. Health problems have differential impacts on diverse cultural and ethnic groups. Social support helps buffer the impact of stress. Natural and technological disasters are dangerous as they occur and also create lingering problems in adjustment.

Psychological Factors and Physical Disorders

Psychological factors are involved in the origins, course, and treatment of many physical health problems. The principle of individual response specificity holds that people respond to stress in idiosyncratic ways, giving rise to particular health problems. The most common headache is the muscle-tension headache, which is often stress related. Behavioral methods of relaxation training and biofeedback are of help in treating headaches. Risk factors in coronary heart disease include age, gender, family history, socioeconomic status, obesity, hypertension, blood cholesterol, patterns of consumption, Type A behavior, anger, phobic anxiety, stress, and a sedentary lifestyle.

Asthma attacks can be tripped by allergic reactions; cold, dry air; emotional responses such as anger; and stress. Treatment for asthma often consists of medications, including bronchodilators, but asthma sufferers can improve their breathing by muscle relaxation training and family therapy that reduces the stresses on asthmatic children.

Risk factors for cancer include family history, dietary practices (especially high fat intake), heavy alcohol use, smoking, and sunbathing. Research shows that a fighting spirit may help people recover from cancer. Psychological interventions help cancer patients cope better with the symptoms of the disease and its treatment.

Our behavior patterns influence our risk for contracting AIDS. Psychologists have become involved in the prevention and treatment of AIDS because AIDS, like cancer, has devastating psychological effects on victims, their families and friends, and society at large, and because AIDS can be prevented through reducing risky behavior.

Scoring Key for "The Life Orientation Test"

In order to arrive at your total score for the test, first *reverse* your score on items 3, 8, 9, and 12. That is,

4 is changed to 0
3 is changed to 1
2 remains the same
1 is changed to 3
0 is changed to 4

Now add the numbers of items 1, 3, 4, 5, 8, 9, 11, and 12. (Items 2, 6, 7, and 10 are "fillers"; that is, your responses are not scored as part of the test.) Your total score can vary from 0 to 32.

Scheier and Carver (1985) provide the following norms for the test, based on administration to 357 undergraduate men and 267 undergraduate women. The average (mean) score for men was 21.03 (standard deviation = 4.56), and the mean score for women was 21.41 (standard deviation = 5.22). All in all, approximately 2 out of 3 undergraduates obtained scores between 16 and 26. Scores above 26 may be considered quite optimistic, and scores below 16, quite pessimistic. Scores between 16 and 26 are within a broad average range, and higher scores within this range are relatively more optimistic.

Answer Key for "Are You Type A?"

Yesses are suggestive of the Type A behavior pattern (TABP). In appraising whether or not you show the TABP, you need not be concerned with the precise number of "yes" answers. We have no normative data for you. As Friedman and Rosenman (1974, p. 85) note, however, you should have little trouble spotting yourself as "hard core" or "moderately afflicted"—that is, if you are honest with yourself.

1. What are adjustment disorders? How do clinicians distinguish between adjustment disorders and other types of psychological problems?

2. How does the body's immune system help protect us from disease? What are the relationships between psychological factors, especially stress, and the functioning of the immune system?

3. What physical response patterns are associated with each of the phases of the general adaptation syndrome?

4. What factors are represented within the multifactorial model that can help account for physical health and illness?

5. What psychological factors are implicated in physical disorders and diseases such as headaches, cardiovascular disorders, asthma, cancer, and AIDS?

6. What role do psychological techniques play in the treatment of physical health disorders and conditions?

© **Miriam Schapiro**
Free Fall, 1985

5

Anxiety Disorders

TRUTH or FICTION?

5.1 Some people who experience panic attacks believe they are having a heart attack, even though there is nothing wrong with their heart.

5.2 Some people are so fearful of leaving their homes they are unable to venture outside even to mail a letter.

5.3 It may take an hour or more for people with obsessive-compulsive disorder to leave the house.

5.4 Men are more than twice as likely as women to develop posttraumatic stress disorder (PTSD).

5.5 Some theorists believe we are genetically programmed to more readily acquire fears of some classes of stimuli, including snakes.

5.6 Catastrophic misinterpretations of bodily sensations may set into motion a spiraling cycle of anxiety that culminates in full-fledged panic attacks.

5.7 The same drugs used to treat schizophrenia are also used to control panic attacks.

5.8 Peering over a virtual ledge 20 stories up has helped some people overcome their fear of actual heights.

Anxiety is a generalized state of apprehension or foreboding. There is much to be anxious about—our health, social relationships, examinations, careers, international relations, and the condition of the environment are but a few sources of possible concern. It is normal, even adaptive, to be somewhat anxious about these aspects of life. Anxiety serves us when it prompts us to seek regular medical checkups or motivates us to study for tests. Anxiety is an appropriate response to threats, but anxiety can be abnormal when its level is out of proportion to a threat, or when it seems to come out of the blue—that is, when it is not in response to environmental changes. In extreme forms, anxiety can impair our daily functioning. Consider the case of Dick:

Slowly the trains snake their way through the maze of tunnels that lie beneath the city, carrying the Dashing Dans and Danielles on their way to work each morning. Most commuters pass the time by reading the morning newspapers, sipping coffee, or catching a few last winks. For Dick, the morning commute was an exercise in terror on an ordinary day in July. At first, Dick noticed the perspiration clinging to his shirt. The air conditioning seemed to be working fine, for a change. How then was he to account for the sweat? As the train entered the tunnel and darkness shrouded the windows, Dick was gripped by sheer terror. He sensed his heart beating faster, the muscles in his neck tightening. Queasiness soured his stomach. He felt as though he might pass out. Other commuters, engrossed in their morning papers or their private thoughts, paid no heed to Dick, nor did they seem concerned about the darkness that enveloped the train.

Dick had known these feelings all too well before. But now the terror was worse. Other days he could bear it. This time, it seemed to start earlier than usual, before the train entered the tunnel. "Just don't think about it," he told himself, hoping it would pass. "I must think of something to distract myself." He tried humming a song, but the panic grew worse. He tried telling himself that it would be all right, that at any moment the train would enter the station and the doors would open. Not this day, however. On this day, the train came to a screeching halt. The conductor announced a "signaling problem." Dick tried to calm himself: "It's only a short delay. We'll be moving soon." But the train did not start moving soon. More apologies from the conductor. A train had broken down further ahead in the tunnel. Dick realized it could be a long delay, hours perhaps. Suddenly he felt the urgent desire to escape. But how? he wondered. There was barely room for a crawlspace outside the train. Then again, could he even break the window and crawl out of the train, if he had to?

He felt like he was losing control. Wild imaginings flooded his mind. He saw himself bolting down the aisles in a futile attempt to escape, bowling people over, trying vainly to pry open the doors. He was charged with a sense of doom. Something terrible was about to happen to him. "Is this the first sign of a heart attack?" he wondered anxiously. By now, the perspiration had soaked his clothes. His once neat tie hung awry. He felt his breathing become heavy and labored, drawing attention from other passengers. "What do they think of me?" he thought. "Will they help me if I need them?"

The train jerked into motion. He realized he would soon be free. "I'm going to be okay," he told himself, "the feelings will pass. I'm going to be myself again." The train pulled slowly into the station, twenty minutes late. The doors opened and the passengers hurried off. Stepping out himself, Dick adjusted his tie and readied himself to start the day. He felt as though he'd been in combat. Nothing that his boss could dish out could hold a candle to what he had experienced on the 7:30 train.

THE AUTHORS' FILES

Dick had suffered a panic attack, one of many he had experienced before seeking treatment. The attacks varied in frequency. Sometimes they occurred daily, sometimes once a week or so. He never knew whether an attack would occur on a particular day. He knew, however, that he couldn't go on living like this. He feared that one day he would suffer a heart attack on the train. He pictured some passengers trying vainly to revive him while others stared at him in the detached distant way that people stare at traffic accidents. He pictured emergency workers rushing to the train, bearing him on a stretcher through the dismal tunnels to an ambulance.

For a while he considered changing jobs, accepting a less remunerative job closer to home, one that would free him from the train. He also considered driving to work, but the roads were too thick with traffic. No choice, he figured; either commute by train or switch jobs. His wife, Jill, was unaware of his panic attacks. She wondered why his shirts were heavily stained with perspiration and why Dick was talking about changing jobs. She worried about making ends meet on a lower income. She had no idea it was the train ride, and not his job, that Dick was desperate to avoid.

Panic attacks, like that suffered by Dick, are a feature of **panic disorder,** a type of **anxiety disorder.** During a panic attack, one's level of anxiety can rise to the level of sheer terror. Panic attacks are an extreme form of anxiety. Anxiety encompasses a myriad of physical features, cognitions, and behaviors as shown in Table 5.1. Although anxious people do not often experience all of them, it is easy to see why anxiety is distressing.

HISTORIC PERSPECTIVES ON ANXIETY DISORDERS

The anxiety disorders, along with dissociative disorders and somatoform disorders (see Chapter 6), were classified as neuroses throughout most of the 19th century. The term *neurosis* derives from roots meaning "an abnormal or diseased condition of the nervous system." It was coined by the Scottish physician William Cullen in the 18th century. As the derivation implies, it was assumed neurosis had biological origins. It was seen as an affliction of the nervous system.

At the beginning of the 20th century, Cullen's organic assumptions were largely replaced by Sigmund Freud's psychodynamic views. Freud maintained that neurotic behavior stems from the threatened emergence of unacceptable anxiety-evoking ideas into conscious awareness. Various neurotic behavior patterns—anxiety disorders, somatoform disorders, and dissociative disorders—might look different enough on the surface. According to Freud, however, they all represent ways in which the ego attempts to defend itself against anxiety. Freud's **etiological** assumption, in other words, united the disorders as neuroses. Freud's concepts were so widely accepted in the early 1900s that they formed the basis for the classification systems found in the first two editions of the *Diagnostic and Statistical Manual of Mental Disorders* (DSM).

Since 1980, the DSM has not contained a category termed *neuroses.* The current DSM (DSM-IV) is based on

TABLE 5.1
Some Features of Anxiety

Physical Features of Anxiety
Jumpiness, jitteriness
Trembling or shaking of the hands or limbs
Sensations of a tight band around the forehead
Tightness in the pit of the stomach or chest
Heavy perspiration
Sweaty palms
Light-headedness or faintness
Dryness in the mouth or throat
Difficulty talking
Difficulty catching one's breath
Shortness of breath or shallow breathing
Heart pounding or racing
Tremulousness in one's voice
Cold fingers or limbs
Dizziness
Weakness or numbness
Difficulty swallowing
A "lump in the throat"
Stiffness of the neck or back
Choking or smothering sensations
Cold, clammy hands
Upset stomach or nausea
Hot or cold spells
Frequent urination
Feeling flushed
Diarrhea
Feeling irritable or "on edge"

Behavioral Features of Anxiety
Avoidance behavior
Clinging, dependent behavior
Agitated behavior

Cognitive Features of Anxiety
Worrying about something
A nagging sense of dread or apprehension about the future
Belief that something dreadful is going to happen, with no clear cause
Preoccupation with bodily sensations
Keen awareness of bodily sensations
Feeling threatened by people or events that are normally of little or no concern
Fear of losing control
Fear of inability to cope with one's problems
Thinking the world is caving in
Thinking things are getting out of hand
Thinking things are swimming by too rapidly to take charge of them
Worrying about every little thing
Thinking the same disturbing thought over and over
Thinking that one must flee crowded places or else pass out
Finding one's thoughts jumbled or confused
Not being able to shake off nagging thoughts
Thinking that one is going to die, even when one's doctor finds nothing medically wrong
Worrying that one is going to be left alone
Difficulty concentrating or focusing one's thoughts

similarities in observable behavior and distinctive features rather than on causal assumptions. Many clinicians continue to use the terms *neurosis* and *neurotic* in the manner in which Freud described them, however. Some clinicians use "neuroses" as a convenient means of grouping milder behavioral problems in which people maintain relatively good contact with reality. "Psychoses," such as schizophrenia, are typified by loss of touch with reality, and by the appearance of bizarre behavior, beliefs, and hallucinations. Anxiety is not limited to the diagnostic categories traditionally termed "neuroses," moreover. People with adjustment problems, depression, and psychotic disorders may also encounter problems with anxiety.

In this chapter we review the specific types of anxiety disorders: panic disorder; phobic disorders such as specific phobia, social phobia, and agoraphobia; generalized anxiety disorder; obsessive-compulsive disorder; and acute and posttraumatic stress disorders. Table 5.2 lists the diagnostic features of anxiety disorders. The anxiety disorders are not mutually exclusive. People frequently meet diagnostic criteria for more than one of them.

PANIC DISORDER

The essential diagnostic feature of a panic disorder is the occurrence of repeated, unexpected panic attacks. There is a stronger bodily component to panic attacks than to other forms of anxiety. Panic attacks involve intense anxiety reactions that are accompanied by physical symptoms such as a pounding heart; rapid respiration, shortness of breath, or difficulty breathing; heavy perspiration; and weakness or dizziness. The attacks are accompanied by feelings of sheer terror and a sense of imminent danger or impending doom and by an urge to escape the situation. They are usually accompanied by thoughts of losing control, going crazy, or

dying. People who experience panic attacks tend to be keenly aware of changes in their heart rates (Ehlers & Breuer, 1992; Richards, Edgar, & Gibbon, 1996). They often believe they are having a heart attack even though there is nothing wrong with their hearts.

TRUTH _or_ FICTION REVISITED

5.1 _True._ People experiencing a panic attack may believe they are having a heart attack, even though their hearts are perfectly healthy.

Panic attacks occur suddenly and quickly reach a peak of intensity, usually in 10 minutes or less (APA, 1994). They usually last for several minutes, but can extend to hours and are associated with a strong sense of uncontrollability. The first attacks occur spontaneously or unexpectedly. Over time they may become associated with certain situations or cues, such as entering a crowded department store, or, like Dick, riding on a train, which can lead to avoidance of these situations in the hope of preventing a recurrent attack. For a diagnosis of panic disorder to be made, there must be the presence of recurrent unexpected panic attacks—attacks that are not triggered by specific objects or situations. They seem to come out of the blue.

It remains unclear whether cued (situationally bound) panic attacks differ in kind from uncued attacks. The only difference may be the presence or absence of an identifiable cue (Craske, 1991). Yet it may be difficult to distinguish between cued and uncued attacks. Panic sufferers may be unaware of the more subtle changes in their bodily sensations

---

TABLE 5.2

Diagnostic Features of Anxiety Disorders

Agoraphobia	Fear and avoidance of places or situations in which it would be difficult or embarrassing to escape, or in which help might be unavailable in the event of a panic attack or panic-type symptoms.
Panic Disorder Without Agoraphobia	Occurrence of recurrent, unexpected panic attacks in which there is persistent concern about them but without accompanying agoraphobia.
Panic Disorder with Agoraphobia	Occurrence of recurrent, unexpected panic attacks in which there is persistent concern about them and accompanying agoraphobia.
Generalized Anxiety Disorder	Persistent and excessive levels of anxiety and worry that are not tied to any particular object, situation, or activity.
Specific Phobia	Clinically significant anxiety relating to exposure to specific objects or situations, often accompanied by avoidance of these stimuli.
Social Phobia	Clinically significant anxiety relating to exposure to social situations or performance situations, often accompanied by avoidance of these situations.
Obsessive-Compulsive Disorder	Recurrent obsessions and/or compulsions.
Posttraumatic Stress Disorder	The reexperiencing of a highly traumatic event accompanied by heightened arousal and avoidance of stimuli associated with the event.
Acute Stress Disorder	Features similar to those of posttraumatic stress disorder but limited to the days and weeks following exposure to the trauma.

Note: All of these disorders are coded on Axis I in the DSM-IV.
Source: Adapted from _DSM-IV_ (APA, 1994).

Panic. Panic attacks have stronger physical components—especially cardiovascular symptoms—than other types of anxiety reactions.

my head and my ears; I thought that my heart was going to stop. I could see black and yellow lights. I could hear the voices of the people but from a long way off. I could not think of anything except the way that I was feeling and how I had to get out and run quickly or I would die. I must escape and get into fresh air. Outside it subsided a little but I felt limp and weak; my legs were like jelly as though I had run a race and lost; I had a lump in my throat like a golf ball. The incident seemed to me to have lasted hours. I was absolutely drained when I got home and I just broke down and cried; it took until the next day to feel normal again."

ADAPTED FROM HAWKRIGG, 1975, PP. 1280–1282

People often describe panic attacks as the worst experiences of their lives. Their coping abilities are overwhelmed. They may feel they must flee. If flight seems useless, they may freeze. There is a tendency to cling to others for help or support. Some people with panic attacks fear going out alone. Recurrent panic attacks may become so difficult to cope with that sufferers may become suicidal. A study of community residents who suffered panic attacks found that 12% had attempted suicide (M. M. Weissman et al., 1989).

Table 5.3 lists the diagnostic features of panic attacks. Not all of these features need to be present. A diagnosis of panic disorder is based on the following criteria: (1) encountering repeated (at least two) unexpected panic attacks; and (2) at least one of the attacks is followed by at least a month of persistent fear of subsequent attacks, or worry about the implications or consequences of the attack (e.g., fear of losing one's mind, or "going crazy," or having a heart attack), or significant change in behavior (e.g., refusing

that may precipitate an attack, and so the panic may be perceived as spontaneous because these underlying changes are not detected. If panic sufferers are unable to identify the actual triggers, they may attribute their sensations to more serious causes, such as an impending heart attack or break with reality ("going crazy").

In many cases, people who experience panic attacks limit their activities to avoid places in which they fear attacks may occur or they are cut off from their usual supports (B. J. Cox et al., 1992). Panic disorder is thus often associated with agoraphobia—fear of being in public places. After a panic attack, the person may feel exhausted, as if he or she has survived a truly traumatic experience, as in the following case:

"I was inside a very busy shopping precinct and all of a sudden it happened; in a matter of seconds I was like a mad woman. It was like a nightmare, only I was awake; everything went black and sweat poured out of me—my body, my hands, and even my hair got wet through. All of the blood seemed to drain out of me; I went white as a ghost. I felt as if I was going to collapse; it was as if I had no control over my limbs; my back and legs were very weak and I felt as though it were impossible to move. It was as if I had been taken over by some stronger force. I saw all of the people looking at me—just faces, no bodies; all merged into one. My heart started pounding in

---

TABLE 5.3
Features of Panic Attacks

A panic attack involves an episode of intense fear or discomfort in which at least four of the following features develop suddenly and reach a peak within 10 minutes:

1. Heart palpitations, pounding heart, tachycardia (rapid heart rate)
2. Sweating
3. Trembling or shaking
4. Shortness of breath or smothering sensations
5. Choking sensations
6. Chest pains or discomfort
7. Feelings of nausea or other signs of abdominal distress
8. Feelings of dizziness, unsteadiness, light-headedness, or faintness
9. Feelings of strangeness or unreality about one's surroundings (derealization) or detachment from oneself (depersonalization)
10. Fear of losing control or going crazy
11. Fear of dying
12. Numbness or tingling sensations
13. Chills or hot flushes

Source: Adapted from the *DSM-IV* (APA, 1994).

to leave the house or venture into public for fear of having another attack) (APA, 1994).

People with other types of phobias may experience panic attacks when they are exposed to fear-evoking stimuli. People with claustrophobia (persons with fears of enclosed spaces) may experience panic when they are confined to a crowded elevator. A person with social phobia may panic when asking someone for a date.

Estimates based on a nationally representative survey of Americans ranging from 15 to 54 years of age, the National Comorbidity Survey (NCS), indicate that about 15% of the general population have experienced at least one panic attack in their lifetimes (Eaton et al., 1994). About 3% of the population in this age range report experiencing a panic attack during the past month. About 1% can be diagnosed with panic disorder at any given time, and about 3.5% have experienced panic disorder at some point in their lives. About half of the people with panic disorder do not report accompanying agoraphobia.

Panic disorder usually begins in late adolescence or the early twenties. Women are two to three times more likely than men to develop panic disorder (Eaton et al., 1994) (Fig. 5.1). What little we know about the long-term course of panic disorder suggests that it tends to follow a chronic course that waxes and wanes in severity over time (Ehlers, 1995). In one recent study, 92% of a sample of 39 people

with panic disorder continued to experience panic attacks when evaluated a year later (Ehlers, 1995).

Although reports of panic attacks are common among college samples and other nonclinical samples, these "panic attacks" tend to be milder than those experienced by people with diagnosable panic disorder (K. G. Wilson et al., 1992). Yet, in one college sample of more than 1,600 students, 7% to 8% of the respondents reported experiencing panic attacks that were similar in severity to those experienced by people with diagnosable panic disorder (K. G. Wilson et al., 1992).

GENERALIZED ANXIETY DISORDER

Generalized anxiety disorder (GAD) is characterized by persistent feelings of anxiety that are not triggered by any specific object, situation, or activity, but rather seem to be what Freud labeled "free floating." People with GAD are chronic worriers, and excessive worrying is considered the keynote feature of the disorder (Rapee, 1991). They may be excessively worried about life circumstances such as finances, the well-being of their children, or social relationships. According to one study, 9 out of 10 of them, report worrying excessively about even minor things (Sanderson & Barlow, 1990). Children with generalized anxiety are more likely to be worried about academics, athletics, and other social aspects of school life. Other related features include restlessness, feeling tense, "keyed up" or "on edge," becoming easily fatigued, having difficulty concentrating or finding one's mind going blank, irritability, muscle tension, and disturbances of sleep (such as difficulty falling asleep, staying asleep, or having restless and unsatisfying sleep) (APA, 1994). The features of generalized anxiety—anxiety, worry, and physical symptoms—cause a significant level of emotional distress or impaired functioning (APA, 1994).

GAD tends to be a stable disorder that initially arises in the mid-teens to mid-twenties and then follows a lifelong course (Rapee, 1991). The lifetime prevalence of GAD in the general U.S. population is estimated to be about 5% (APA, 1994; Wittchen et al., 1994). The disorder is believed to be twice as common in women as in men.

Although GAD typically involves less intense physiological responses than panic disorder, the emotional distress associated with GAD is severe enough to substantially interfere with the person's daily life (Wittchen et al., 1994). GAD frequently occurs together (comorbidly) with other disorders, such as depression or other anxiety disorders like agoraphobia and obsessive-compulsive disorder. Although about 90% of people with GAD have experienced some other diagnosable psychological disorder in their lifetime, evidence supports the view that GAD represents a distinct clinical syndrome (Brawman-Mintzer et al., 1993; Wittchen et al., 1994).

In the following case example we find a number of features of generalized anxiety disorder:

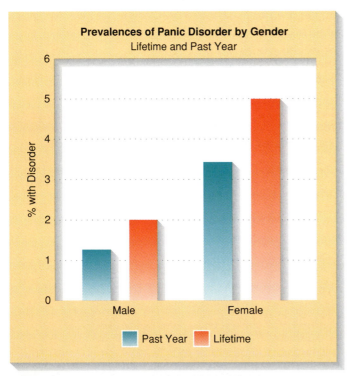

FIGURE 5.1 *Prevalences of panic disorder by gender.*
Panic disorder affects about two to three times as many women as men.

Source: National Comorbidity Survey; Kessler et al. (1994).

Earl was a 52-year-old supervisor at the automobile plant. His hands trembled as he spoke. His cheeks were pale. His face was somewhat boyish, making his hair seem grayed with worry.

He was reasonably successful in his work, although he noted that he was not a "star." His marriage of nearly three decades was in "reasonably good shape," although sexual relations were "less than exciting—I shake so much that it isn't easy to get involved." The mortgage on the house was not a burden and would be paid off within 5 years, but "I don't know what it is; I think about money all the time." The three children were doing well. One was employed, one was in college, and one was in high school. But "With everything going on these days, how can you help worrying about them? I'm up for hours worrying about them."

"But it's the strangest thing," Earl shook his head. "I swear I'll find myself worrying when there's nothing in my head. I don't know how to describe it. It's like I'm worrying first and then there's something in my head to worry about. It's not like I start thinking about this or that and I see it's bad and then I worry. And then the shakes come, and then, of course, I'm worrying about worrying, if you know what I mean. I want to run away; I don't want anyone to see me. You can't direct workers when you're shaking."

Going to work had become a major chore. "I can't stand the noises of the assembly lines. I just feel jumpy all the time. It's like I expect something awful to happen. When it gets bad like that I'll be out of work for a day or two with shakes."

Earl had been worked up "for everything; my doctor took blood, saliva, urine, you name it. He listened to everything, he put things inside me. He had other people look at me. He told me to stay away from coffee and alcohol. Then from tea. Then from chocolate and Coca-Cola, because there's a little bit of caffeine [in them]. He gave me Valium [a minor tranquilizer] and I thought I was in heaven for a while. Then it stopped working, and he switched me to something else. Then that stopped working, and he switched me back. Then he said he was 'out of chemical miracles' and I better see a shrink or something. Maybe it was something from my childhood."

THE AUTHORS' FILES

PHOBIC DISORDERS

The word *phobia* derives from the Greek *phobos*, meaning "fear." The concepts of fear and anxiety are closely related. **Fear** is the feeling of anxiety and agitation in response to a threat. Phobic disorders are persistent fears of objects or situations that are disproportionate to the threat posed by them. The experience of gripping fear when one's car is about to go out of control is normal because there is an objective basis to the fear. In phobic disorders, however, the fear exceeds any reasonable appraisal of danger. People with a driving phobia, for example, might become fearful even when they are driving well below the speed limit on a sunny, uncrowded highway. Or they might be so afraid they will not drive or even ride in a car. People with phobic disorders are not out of touch with reality; they generally recognize their fears are excessive or unreasonable.

A curious thing about phobias is that they usually involve fears of the ordinary events in life, not the extraordinary. People with phobias become fearful of ordinary experiences that most people take for granted, such as taking an elevator or driving on a highway. Phobias can become disabling when they interfere with daily tasks such as taking buses, planes, or trains; driving; shopping; or leaving the house.

Phobias are quite common. The Epidemiologic Catchment Area (ECA) study found that phobic disorders affect about 1 in 7 adults (14.3%) at some point in their lives (L. N. Robins, Locke, & Reiger, 1991). Lifetime prevalences are estimated to be 5.7% for agoraphobia, 13.3% for social phobia, and 11.3% for specific phobia (Magee et al., 1996).

Different kinds of phobias tend to appear at different ages, as noted in Table 5.4. The ages of onset appear to reflect factors such as cognitive development and life experiences. Animals are frequent subjects of children's fantasies, for example. The kinds of experiences that may relate to fears of leaving the house, as in agoraphobia, may follow the development of panic attacks that begin in early adulthood.

Phobic disorders are classified within the DSM system as *specific phobia, social phobia,* or *agoraphobia.*

Specific Phobias

Specific phobias are persistent, excessive fears of specific objects or situations, such as fear of heights (**acrophobia**), fear of enclosed spaces (**claustrophobia**), or fear of small animals such as mice or snakes and various other "creepy-crawlies." The fear is associated with high levels of physiological arousal when the person encounters the feared

TABLE 5.4
Typical Age of Onset for Various Phobias

	No. of Cases	Mean Age of Onset
Animal phobia	50	7
Blood phobia	40	9
Injection phobia	59	8
Dental phobia	60	12
Social phobia	80	16
Claustrophobia	40	20
Agoraphobia	100	28

Source: Adapted from Öst (1987, 1992).

stimulus. The fear and the unpleasant arousal evoke strong tendencies to escape or avoid the feared stimulus. A diagnosis of specific phobia is indicated only if the phobia significantly impacts a person's lifestyle or functioning or causes marked distress. You may have a fear of snakes, but unless your fear interferes with your daily life or causes you significant emotional distress, it would not merit a diagnosis of a phobic disorder.

Specific phobias often begin in childhood. Many children develop passing fears of specific objects or situations. Some, however, go on to develop chronic fears or phobias (Merckelbach et al., 1996). Claustrophobia seems to develop later than most other specific phobias, with a mean age of onset of 20 years (see Table 5.4).

The *DSM-IV* groups specific phobias within five subtypes (APA, 1994):

1. *Animal Type.*   This subtype, which usually has an onset during childhood, includes fears of animals or insects.

2. *Natural Environment Type.*   This subtype, which also generally develops during childhood, involves phobias that are cued by environmental factors, such as heights, storms, or water.

3. *Blood-Injection-Injury Type.*   This subtype, which apparently has a strong familial connection, refers to phobias evoked by seeing blood or receiving injections or other invasive medical procedures.

4. *Situational Type.*   The phobias included in this subtype are triggered by exposure to specific situations, such as fears of driving over bridges or through tunnels, taking an elevator ride or flying, or being in enclosed places. These phobias typically develop either in childhood or in the mid-twenties.

5. *Other Type.*   This category includes phobias such as fear of choking, vomiting, or contracting an illness; "space phobias" (fears of falling down if standing away from a wall or a person used for support); and various fears occurring in children, such as fear of loud noises or costumed characters.

Although more than one subtype may be present, the most frequently occurring subtypes are *situational*, followed by *natural environment, blood-injection-injury,* and *animal*. Specific phobias are among the most common types of psychological disorders, affecting approximately 1 in 10 people at some point in their lives (APA, 1994). They occur more frequently in women than men (Merckelbach et al., 1996), perhaps because of cultural factors that socialize women to be dependent on men for protection from threatening objects in the environment. Examiners also need to be aware of cultural factors when making diagnostic judgments. Fears of magic or spirits are common in some cultures and should not be considered a sign of a phobic disorder, unless the fear is excessive in light of the cultural context in which it occurs and leads to significant emotional distress or impaired functioning (APA, 1994).

One specific phobia that often has significant behavioral consequences is fear of riding on elevators. Some people with phobias will not enter elevators despite hardships such as walking six or more flights of stairs. True, the cable *could* break. Yes, the ventilation *could* fail. One *could* get caught in midair waiting for repairs. These calamities are uncommon, however, and most people would find it unreasonable to walk up many flights of stairs to avoid them, or to reject an attractive job offer because the office is located on an upper floor. Persons with a blood-injection-injury type of phobia may similarly refuse injections or to have their blood drawn for analysis, even when their health suffers as a result. Although medical procedures may involve some degree of pain, the person might be willing to endure equally painful pinches in the arm if they would improve their health, as suggested by the case of a 28-year-old high school English teacher:

"This will sound crazy, but I wouldn't get married because I couldn't stand the idea of getting the blood test. [Blood tests for syphilis were required at the time.] I finally worked up the courage to ask my doctor if he would put me out with ether or barbiturates—taken by pills—so that I could have the blood test. At first he was incredulous. Then he became sort of sympathetic but said that he couldn't risk putting me under any kind of general anesthesia just to draw some blood. I asked him if he would consider faking the report, but he said that 'administrative procedures' made that impossible.

"Then he got me really going. He said that getting tested for marriage was likely to be one of my small life problems. He told me about minor medical problems that could arise and make it necessary for blood to be drawn, or to have an IV in my arm, so his message was I should try to come to grips with my fear. I nearly fainted while he was talking about these things, so he gave it up.

"The story has half a happy ending. We finally got married in [a state] where we found out they no longer insisted on blood tests. But if I develop one of those problems the doctor was talking about, or if I need a blood test for some other reason, even if it's life-threatening, I really don't know what I'll do. But maybe if I faint when they're going to [draw blood], I won't know about it anyway, right? . . .

"People have me wrong, you know. They think I'm scared of the pain. I don't like pain—I'm not a masochist—but pain has nothing to do with it. You could pinch my arm till I turned black and blue and I'd tolerate it. I wouldn't like it, but I wouldn't start shaking and sweating and faint on you. But even if I didn't feel the needle at all—just the knowledge that it was in me is what I couldn't take."

THE AUTHORS' FILES

Social Phobia

Many of us experience some trepidation in social situations such as dating, attending parties or social gatherings, or giving a talk or presentation to a class or group. A person with **social phobia** has such an intense fear of social situations that he or she may avoid them altogether or endure them with great distress. Social phobias arise from excessive concerns of being judged negatively by others. People with social phobias have a persistent fear of doing something humiliating or embarrassing. They may feel as if a thousand eyes are scrutinizing them. They tend to be overly critical of their own performance, are overly focused on themselves when speaking to others, fear negative evaluations by other people, and experience excessive bodily arousal in social interactions (Turner, Beidel, Dancu, & Keys, 1986a; Woody, 1996).

Some even experienced full-fledged panic attacks in social situations. Stage fright and speech anxiety are common social phobias. A random sample of some 500 residents of Winnipeg, Manitoba, found that about 1 in 3 had experienced excessive anxiety when speaking to a large audience that was significant enough to have had a detrimental impact on their lives (M. B. Stein, Walker, & Forde, 1996).

People with social phobias may find excuses for declining social invitations. They may lunch at their desks to avoid socializing with co-workers. Or they may find themselves in social situations and attempt a quick escape at the first sign of anxiety. Escape behavior is reinforced by relief from anxiety, but escape prevents people with phobias from learning to cope with fear-evoking situations more adaptively. Leaving the scene before the anxiety dissipates only strengthens the association between the social situation and anxiety. Some people with social phobia are unable to order food in a restaurant for fear the server or their companions might make fun of the foods they order or how they pronounce them. Others fear meeting new people and dating.

Social phobias may prevent people from completing educational goals, advancing in their careers, or even holding a job in which they need to interact with others (Liebowitz, Gorman, Fyer, & Klein, 1985b). People with social phobias often turn to tranquilizers or try to "medicate" themselves with alcohol when preparing for social interactions (see Figure 5.2). In extreme cases, they may become so fearful of interacting with others that they become essentially housebound (S. M. Turner & Beidel, 1989).

Some anxiety in unfamiliar social situations is normal and adaptive. It prompts us to pay some attention to what we wear, say, and do. Simple shyness also occurs often enough. Although people who are shy and those who have social phobia may share such features in common as fear of criticism, people with social phobia are more likely to develop difficulties in daily functioning, such as avoiding social contacts. Yet it remains unclear whether social phobia is an extreme form of shyness or a qualitatively different phenomenon (S. M. Turner, Beidel, & Townsley, 1990).

Estimates of the lifetime prevalence of social phobia range from 3% to 13%. The disorder is apparently more common among women than men (APA, 1994), perhaps because of the greater social or cultural pressures placed on young women to please others and earn their approval.

The roots of social phobia may begin in childhood. People with social phobia typically report they were shy as children (Stemberger et al., 1995). Consistent with the *diathesis-stress model,* shyness may represent a diathesis or predisposition that makes one more vulnerable to develop social phobia in the face of stressful experiences, such as traumatic social encounters (e.g., being embarrassed in front of others). Social phobia tends to begin in adolescence and typically follows a chronic and persistent course in life (Liebowitz et al., 1985b).

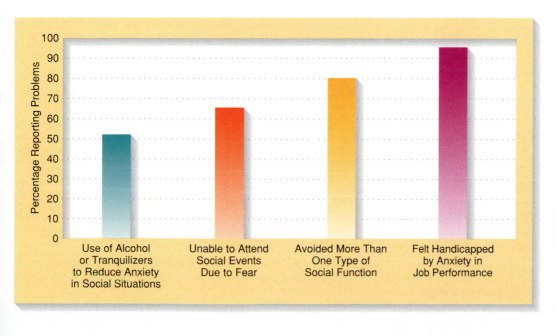

FIGURE 5.2 *Percentages of people with social phobia reporting specific difficulties associated with their fears of social situations.* More than 90% of people with social phobia feel handicapped by anxiety in their jobs.

Source: Adapted from Turner & Beidel (1989).

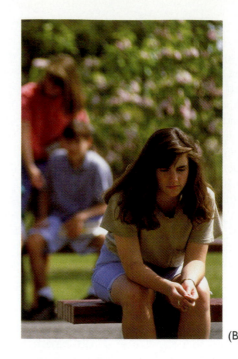

(A)

(B)

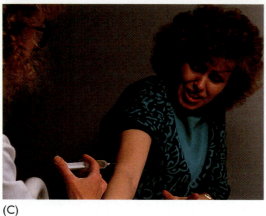

(C)

Three types of phobic disorders. The woman in photo A has such severe agoraphobia that she resists leaving her house. The young woman in photo B would like to join others, but keeps to herself because of social phobia, an intense fear of social criticism and rejection. The woman in photo C has a specific phobia for injections. She does not fear the potential pain of the injection; rather, she cannot tolerate the idea of the needle sticking her.

Agoraphobia

The word *agoraphobia* is derived from Greek words meaning "fear of the marketplace," which is suggestive of a fear of being out in open, busy areas. Agoraphobia involves fear of places and situations from which it might be difficult or embarrassing to escape in the event of panicky symptoms or a full-fledged panic attack; or of situations in which help may be unavailable if such problems should occur. People with agoraphobia may fear shopping in crowded stores; walking through crowded streets; crossing a bridge; traveling on a bus, train, or car; eating in restaurants; or even leaving the house. They may structure their lives around avoiding exposure to fearful situations and in some cases become housebound for months or even years, making agoraphobia potentially the most incapacitating type of phobia.

TRUTH *or* FICTION REVISITED

5.2 *True.* Some people with agoraphobia become literally housebound and unable to venture outside even to mail a letter.

Agoraphobia is more common in women than men (M. H. J. Bekker, 1996; Eaton et al., 1994; Gater et al., 1998; Yonkers et al., 1998). It frequently begins in late adolescence or early adulthood. The ECA study found that 5.6% of adult Americans had experienced agoraphobia at some point during their lifetimes (Eaton, Dryman, & Weissman, 1991). Agoraphobia may occur with or without an accompanying panic disorder. In panic disorder with agoraphobia, the person may live in fear of recurrent attacks and avoid public places where attacks have occurred or might occur. Because panic attacks can descend from nowhere, some people restrict their activities for fear of making public spectacles of themselves or finding themselves without help (Amering et al., 1997). Others venture outside only with a companion. Still others forge ahead despite intense anxiety.

People who have agoraphobia but no history of panic disorder may experience milder episodes of panicky symptoms, such as dizziness, that leads them to avoid venturing away from places where they feel safe or secure. They too tend to become dependent on others for support. There is some evidence that people with agoraphobia without a history of panic disorder tend to function more poorly than people with panic disorder with agoraphobia (Goisman et al., 1994). The following case of agoraphobia without a history of panic disorder illustrates the dependencies often associated with agoraphobia:

> *Helen, a 59-year-old widow, became increasingly agoraphobic after the death of her husband 3 years earlier. By the time she came for treatment, she was essentially housebound, refusing to leave her home except under the strongest urging of her daughter, Mary, age 32, and only if Mary accompanied her. Her daughter and 36-year-old son, Pete, did her shopping for her and took care of her other needs as best they could. Yet the burden of caring for their mother, on top of their other responsibilities, was becoming too great for them to bear. They insisted that Helen begin treatment and Helen begrudgingly acceded to their demands.*
>
> *Helen was accompanied to her evaluation session by Mary. She was a frail-looking woman who entered the office clutching Mary's arm and insisted that Mary stay throughout the interview. Helen recounted that she had lost her husband and mother within 3 months of one another; her father had died 20 years earlier. Although she had never experienced a panic attack, she always considered herself an insecure, fearful person. Even so, she had been able to function in meeting the needs of her family until the deaths of her husband and mother left her feeling abandoned and alone. She had now become afraid of "just about everything" and was terrified of being out on her own, lest something bad would happen and she wouldn't be able to cope with it. Even at home, she was fearful that she might lose Mary and Pete. She needed constant reassurance from them that they too wouldn't abandon her.*
>
> THE AUTHORS' FILES

OBSESSIVE-COMPULSIVE DISORDER (OCD)

An **obsession** is an intrusive and recurrent thought, idea, or urge that seems beyond the person's ability to control (Foa, 1990). Obsessions can be potent and persistent enough to interfere with daily life and can engender significant distress and anxiety. They include doubts, impulses, and mental images. One may wonder endlessly whether or not one has locked the doors and shut the windows, for example. One may be obsessed with the impulse to do harm to one's spouse. One can harbor images, such as one mother's recurrent fantasy that her children had been run over by traffic on the way home from school.

A **compulsion** is a repetitive behavior (such as handwashing or checking door locks) or mental acts (such as praying, repeating certain words, or counting) that the person feels compelled or driven to perform (APA, 1994).

Compulsions often occur in response to obsessional thoughts and are frequent and forceful enough to interfere with daily life or cause significant distress. Corinne, a compulsive hand-washer, engaged in elaborate hand-washing rituals. She spent 3 to 4 hours daily at the sink and complained, "My hands look like lobster claws." Some people literally take hours checking and rechecking that all the appliances are off before they leave home, and then doubts still remain.

TRUTH *or* FICTION REVISITED

5.3 *True.* People with OCD may be delayed in leaving the house for an hour or more as they carry out their checking rituals.

Most compulsions fall into two categories: checking rituals and cleaning rituals. Rituals can become the focal point of life. Checking rituals, like repeatedly checking that the gas jets are turned off or the doors are securely locked before leaving the house, cause delays and annoy companions; cleaning can occupy several hours a day. Table 5.5 shows some relatively common obsessions and compulsions.

Compulsions often accompany obsessions and appear to at least partially relieve the anxiety created by obsessional thinking (Steketee & Foa, 1985). The person may believe the compulsive act will help prevent some dreaded event from occurring, even though there is no realistic basis to the belief or the behavior far exceeds what is reasonable under

An obsessive thought? One type of obsession involves recurrent, intrusive images of a calamity occurring as the result of one's carelessness. For example, a person may not be able to shake the image of his or her house catching fire due to an electrical short in an appliance inadvertently left on.

TABLE 5.5

Examples of Obsessive Thoughts and Compulsive Behaviors

Obsessive Thought Patterns	Compulsive Behavior Patterns
Thinking that one's hands remain dirty despite repeated washing.	Rechecking one's work time and time again.
Difficulty shaking the thought that a loved one has been hurt or killed.	Rechecking the doors or gas jets before leaving home.
Repeatedly thinking that one has left the door to the house unlocked.	Constantly washing one's hands to keep them clean and germ free.
Worrying constantly that the gas jets in the house were not turned off.	
Repeatedly thinking that one has done terrible things to loved ones.	

the circumstances. By washing one's hands 40 or 50 times in a row each time a public doorknob is touched, the compulsive hand-washer may experience some relief from the anxiety engendered by the obsessive thought that germs or dirt still linger in the folds of skin. Compulsive rituals apparently also reduce the anxiety that would occur if they were prevented from being carried out (Foa, 1990).

OCD affects between 2% and 3% of adults in the United States and in other countries during their lifetimes (APA, 1994; S. Taylor, 1995; M. M. Weissman et al., 1994). The disorder seems to affect women and men in about equal numbers (Karno et al., 1988). The DSM diagnoses obsessive-compulsive disorder when people are troubled by recurrent obsessions, compulsions, or both such that they cause marked distress, occupy more than an hour a day, or significantly interfere with normal routines or occupational or social functioning (APA, 1994; L. M. Koran, Thienemann, & Davenport, 1996).

The line between obsessions and the firmly held but patently false beliefs that are called **delusions,** which are found in schizophrenia, is sometimes less than clear. Obsessions, such as the belief that one is contaminating other people, can, like delusions, become almost unshakable. Although adults with OCD may be uncertain at a given time about whether their obsessions or compulsions are unreasonable or excessive (Foa & Kozak, 1995), they will eventually concede their concerns are groundless or excessive (APA, 1994). True delusions fail to be shaken. Children with OCD may not come to recognize their concerns are groundless, however.

The case of Jack illustrates a checking compulsion:

Jack, a successful chemical engineer, was urged by his wife Mary, a pharmacist, to seek help for "his little behavioral quirks," which she had found increasingly annoying. Jack was a compulsive checker. When they left the apartment, he would insist on returning to check that the lights or gas jets were off, or that the refrigera-

tor doors were shut. Sometimes he would apologize at the elevator and return to the apartment to carry out his rituals. Sometimes the compulsion to check struck him in the garage. He would return to the apartment, leaving Mary fuming. Going on vacation was especially difficult for Jack. The rituals occupied the better part of the morning of their departure. Even then, he remained plagued by doubts.

Mary had also tried to adjust to Jack's nightly routine of bolting out of bed to recheck the doors and windows. Her patience was running thin. Jack realized his behavior was impairing their relationship as well as causing himself distress. Yet he was reluctant to enter treatment. He gave lip service to wanting to be rid of his compulsive habits. However, he also feared that surrendering his compulsions would leave him defenseless against the anxieties they helped ease.

THE AUTHORS' FILES

ACUTE AND POSTTRAUMATIC STRESS DISORDERS

In adjustment disorders (discussed in Chapter 4), people have difficulty adjusting to life stressors—business or marital problems, chronic illness, or bereavement over a loss. Here we focus on stress-related disorders that arise from exposure to *traumatic* events. Exposure to traumatic events can produce both acute or prolonged stress-related disorders that are labeled, respectively, **acute stress disorder** (ASD) and **posttraumatic stress disorder** (PTSD).

In these disorders, the traumatic event involves either actual or threatened death or serious physical injury, or threat to one's own or another's physical safety (APA, 1994). The person's response to the threat involves feelings of intense fear, helplessness, or a sense of horror. Children with PTSD may have experienced the threat differently, such as by showing disorganized or agitated behavior. Both types of stress disorders have occurred among soldiers exposed to combat, rape survivors, and people who have witnessed the destruction of their homes and communities by natural disasters such as floods, earthquakes, or tornadoes or technological disasters such as railroad or airplane crashes.

Exposure to horrific trauma can have profound psychological effects. After a terrorist attack on a van of Hasidic Jews on the Brooklyn Bridge, 4 of 11 survivors later developed both PTSD and major depression, one developed major depression, and two developed adjustment disorders (Trappler & Friedman, 1996). A study of 63 men and 73 women who were survivors of a 1991 mass killing in a Killeen, Texas, cafeteria by a lone gunman in which 24 people were killed (including the gunman, who fatally shot himself when police cornered him) showed that 1 in 5 of the men and about 1 in 3 of the women later developed PTSD (North, Smith, & Spitznagel, 1994). About 60% of survivors of an earthquake in rural India suffered from a diagnosable mental disorder, most commonly PTSD (23%) (Sharan et al., 1996).

Exposure to trauma is quite common in the general population ("What Is PTSD?," 1996). A recent random sample of Americans showed that 72% reported some traumatic experience, such as exposure to natural disasters; death of a child; serious motor vehicle accidents; witnessing violence; or experiencing physical assault, rape, or physical or sexual abuse (Elliott, 1997). But not everyone who experiences trauma develops traumatic stress reactions, of course. Vulnerability depends on many factors, including differences in neurobiological responsivity to traumatic experiences, the severity of the trauma and degree of exposure, the use of passive rather than active coping responses, availability of social support, and perhaps perceptions of helplessness and left-over emotional effects, such as guilt and depression. The ability to find a sense of purpose or meaning in the traumatic experience, such as participation in a war the person believes is just, may also be involved in bolstering the person's ability to cope with the stressful circumstances and help avert the development of traumatic stress reactions (Sutker et al., 1995).

Though men more often encounter traumatic experiences, women are more likely to develop PTSD in response to trauma (Breslau et al., 1997b; Ehlers, Mayou, & Bryant, 1998). Overall, women are about twice as likely to develop the disorder during their lifetimes than are men. PTSD in women is also linked to a history of battering in marriage and to childhood sexual abuse (Astin et al., 1995; Rodriguez et al., 1997). Researchers find women who develop PTSD to also have an increased risk of suffering major depression and alcohol use disorders (Breslau et al., 1997a).

TRUTH *or* FICTION REVISITED

5.4 *False.* Women are about twice as likely as men to develop PTSD.

The National Comorbidity Survey (NCS) reported a lifetime prevalence of PTSD among adults in the United States of 7.8%, and a current (1-month) prevalence rate of 2.3%

(R. C. Kessler et al.,1995). The diagnostic category of acute stress disorder was introduced recently with the publication of the DSM-IV, and we know little about its prevalence.

The DSM-IV loosened the criteria for PTSD to include reactions to a wider range of traumatic stressors, including receiving a diagnosis of a life-threatening illness. In breast cancer survivors, PTSD symptoms appear to be more common than would be expected in the general population (Cordova et al., 1995). PTSD symptoms may also develop in children exposed to violence or other traumatic experiences, such as hurricanes and other natural disasters (LaGreca et al., 1996).

Features of Traumatic Stress Reactions

Some of the basic features of traumatic stress reactions are the reexperiencing of the traumatic event; avoidance of cues or stimuli connected with the event; a numbing of general or emotional responsiveness; heightened states of bodily arousal; and significant emotional distress or impairment of functioning. In the case of an acute stress reaction, there may be an inability to perform necessary tasks, such as obtaining needed medical or legal assistance, or a failure to mobilize one's resources to obtain support from family as the result of not informing family members about the traumatic experience (APA, 1994). ASD is further characterized by extreme anxiety and by *dissociation,* or feelings of detachment from oneself or one's environment. People with an acute stress disorder may feel they are "in a daze" or the world seems unreal.

The diagnosis of ASD is applied to a stress reaction that occurs during the days and weeks immediately following a traumatic experience. Many people with ASD go on to develop persistent stress-related problems that lead to a diagnosis of PTSD (Bryant & Harvey, 1997, 1998). A recent study showed that about 3 out of 4 motor vehicle accident survivors were found to have PTSD when evaluated 6 months after the trauma (Bryant & Harvey, 1998). By contrast to ASD, PTSD may persist for months, years, or even decades and may not develop until many months or years after exposure to the stressor.

Acute stress disorders frequently occur in the context of combat or exposure to natural or technological disasters. A soldier may come through a horrific battle not remembering important features of the battle, and feeling numb and detached from the environment. People who are injured or who nearly lose their lives in a hurricane may walk around "in a fog" for days or weeks afterward; be bothered by intrusive images, flashbacks, and dreams of the disaster; or relive the experience as though it were happening again. Feelings of being disconnected from one's surroundings shortly following the traumatic incident also increase the risk of developing PTSD (Shalev et al., 1996).

In acute and posttraumatic stress disorders, the traumatic event may be reexperienced in various ways. There can be intrusive memories, recurrent disturbing dreams, and the feeling the event is indeed recurring (as in "flashbacks" to the event). Exposure to events that resemble the traumatic experience can cause intense psychological distress. People with traumatic stress reactions tend to avoid stimuli that evoke recollections of the trauma. For example, they may not be able to handle a television account of it or a friend's wish to talk about it. They may have feelings of detachment or estrangement from other people. They may show less responsiveness to the external world after the traumatic event, losing the ability to enjoy previously preferred activities or to have loving feelings (Litz, 1992).

Have you ever been awakened by a nightmare and been reluctant to return to sleep for fear of reentering the orb of the dream? Nightmares in traumatic stress reactions often involve the reexperiencing of the traumatic event, which can lead to abrupt awakenings and difficulty falling back to sleep—because of fear associated with the nightmare and elevated levels of arousal. Other features of heightened arousal include difficulty falling or staying asleep, irritability or anger outbursts, hypervigilance (being continuously on guard), difficulty concentrating, and an exaggerated startle response (jumping in response to sudden noises or other stimuli) (APA, 1994; C. A. Morgan et al., 1997; Orr et al., 1995).

Though PTSD may wax and wane over time, it can last for years, even decades (Bremmer et al., 1996; Falk, Hersen, & Van Hasselt, 1994; R. C. Kessler et al., 1995). Many World War II and Korean War veterans, for example, are found to meet diagnostic criteria for PTSD when evaluated four or five decades after their combat experience ended (Engdahl et al., 1997). Some elderly Holocaust survivors continued to suffer PTSD 50 or more years after their traumatic exposure (Yehuda et al., 1996). Yet there is some good news to report: People who obtain treatment for PTSD typically recover sooner from the symptoms of PTSD than those who do not (R. C. Kessler et al., 1995). We can't say whether treatment shortens the duration of PTSD symptoms because it is possible that people who seek out treatment may differ in important ways from those who do not. Still, it suggests treatment has a positive influence.

PTSD Among Combat Veterans

Combat and psychological distress go hand in hand. Soldiers (and local civilians) can face numerous brushes with death. Civilians may witness the annihilation of their neighborhoods and ways of life. Soldiers may face cold, rain, and filth, along with the constant threat of death. Even if they escape personal harm, their fellows may be killed and wounded. Combat veterans are at greater risk for developing PTSD in civilian life than are nonveterans or veterans who did not see combat.

PTSD entered the popular vocabulary after the Vietnam conflict. Numerous studies have illuminated the plight of the Vietnam veteran (e.g., Hendin & Haas, 1991; J. Wolfe et al., 1994). All in all, PTSD has been estimated to have affected about 470,000 male Vietnam veterans, or 15% of the 3.14 million men who served there (Gelman, 1988). PTSD in veterans of the Vietnam War and other wars is not limited to men, however. More than a quarter of the women in a Boston sample composed of 109 female veterans of the Vietnam War met criteria for PTSD (J. Wolfe et al., 1994).

Nor did combat-related PTSD begin or end with the Vietnam War, of course. Veterans from earlier conflicts, including World War II and the Korean conflict, show evidence of PTSD, as do American soldiers who served in the Somalian conflict (Ehlich et al., 1997; Litz et al., 1996,

Combat trauma. The stresses of combat can lead to intense anxiety and impaired functioning. Stress-related problems may not develop until long after the cannons of battle have been silenced, but may linger for years afterwards in the form of posttraumatic stress disorder (PTSD).

1997a, 1997b) and in the Persian Gulf war (Schmitt, 1995; Southwick et al., 1995; Sutker et al., 1995).

It remains unclear why some soldiers are affected by the disorder and others are not. The nature of the wartime experience certainly plays a role. Based on a sample of male and female Vietnam war veterans, researchers examined four types of wartime stressors: exposure to traditional combat; exposure to atrocities or extreme abusive violence; the sense of threat; and the experience of living in a harsh, stressful, and unpleasant environment (D. W. King et al., 1995). Interestingly, for men, traditional combat held the weakest relationship with the development of PTSD symptomatology; for women, the weakest predictor of PTSD was exposure to atrocities/abusive violence. For both men and women, the degree to which the environment was perceived as malevolent (harsh, hassled, unpleasant, and stressful) had the strongest relationship to later PTSD. This suggests that PTSD may be linked more strongly to exposure to the daily muck and mire of combat than to the brutalities of combat.

Precombat and postcombat factors also play a role. Precombat exposure to trauma (accidents, assaults, and natural disasters) and lower intelligence are associated with a greater risk of developing PTSD symptoms following combat (D. W. King et al., 1996; Macklin et al.,1998). Having a supportive social network following military service appears to lessen the impact of combat experiences (Stretch, 1987). The incidence of PTSD in Vietnam veterans was thus greater among combat veterans who lived alone (whether divorced, separated, or never married), as compared to married veterans (Card, 1987), and among those who lacked support from family and friends upon returning home (Fontana & Rosenheck, 1994).

The problems of combat veterans with PTSD extend well beyond the signs and symptoms of the disorder itself (Zatzic et al., 1997). Many veterans with PTSD abuse alcohol and drugs and become violent or socially withdrawn (Sutker, Uddo-Crane, & Allain, 1991). They also have high rates of other psychological disorders, including major depression, panic disorder, and social phobias (Orsillo et al., 1996). They are also more likely to commit suicide (Bullman & Kang, 1994). Anger management problems and violent behavior are also common features of veterans with PTSD (Chemtob et al., 1997). Their children are also more likely to have behavioral problems than are children of veterans without PTSD.

Veterans with PTSD continue to suffer in other ways. A high prevalence of criminal behavior, psychiatric problems, unemployment, drug- and alcohol-related problems, homelessness, as well as marital and job-related stress has been reported among Vietnam veterans (Card, 1987; Rosenheck & Fontana, 1994; Zatzic et al., 1997).

THEORETICAL PERSPECTIVES

The anxiety disorders offer something of a theoretical laboratory. Many theories of abnormal behavior were developed with these disorders in mind. Classic case studies and experiments have been carried out to affirm or disprove various points of view.

Civilian trauma. ASD and PTSD are not limited to combat veterans. Survivors of disasters and catastrophes, like the Oklahoma City bombing, may also develop traumatic stress disorders.

Psychodynamic Perspectives

From the psychodynamic perspective, anxiety disorders are viewed as neuroses. The anxiety experienced in neuroses reflects (1) the efforts of unacceptable, repressed impulses to break into consciousness, and (2) fear as to what might happen if they do. Feelings of anxiety represent danger signals that threatening impulses are nearing the level of awareness. To fend off these threatening impulses, the ego tries to stem or divert the tide through defense mechanisms.

Phobias develop through the use of the defense mechanisms of **projection** and **displacement**. A phobic reaction is believed to represent the projection of the person's own threatening impulses onto the phobic object. For instance, persons who are excessively fearful of knives and other sharp instruments may harbor unconscious impulses to use these implements on themselves or others. Avoiding contact with sharp instruments prevents these destructive wishes from becoming consciously realized or acted upon. Similarly, people with acrophobia may harbor unconscious wishes to jump that are controlled by avoiding heights. Freud believed that phobias help both to contain threatening impulses and to keep them out of awareness by motivating the person to keep away from the phobic object or situation. The phobic object or situation symbolizes or represents these unconscious wishes or desires. The person is aware of the phobia but not of the unconscious impulses that it symbolizes.

Do phobias represent the operation of unconscious defense mechanisms?
Psychodynamic theorists suggest that phobias represent the operation of unconscious defense mechanisms such as projection and displacement. In their view, a fear of heights, or acrophobia, may represent the ego's attempt to defend itself against the emergence of threatening self-destructive impulses, such as an impulse to jump from a dangerous height. By avoiding heights, the person can maintain a safe distance from such threatening impulses. Because this process occurs unconsciously, the person may be only aware of the phobia, not of the unconscious impulses that it symbolizes.

Freud's (1909/1959a) historic case of "Little Hans," a 5-year-old boy who feared he would be bitten by a horse if he left his house, illustrates his principle of displacement. Freud hypothesized that Hans's fear of horses represented the displacement of an unconscious fear of his father. According to Freud's conception of the Oedipus complex, boys have unconscious incestuous desires to possess their mothers and fears of retribution from their fathers, whom they see as rivals in love. Hans's fear of being bitten by horses thus symbolized an underlying fear of castration.

Learning theorists view Hans's childhood fears as a case of classical conditioning (Wolpe & Rachman, 1960). They argue that Hans's fear had been learned from his being frightened by an accident involving a horse and a transport vehicle, which generalized to fears of horses. The story of Little Hans has sparked a spirited debate in the psychological annals.

Applying the psychodynamic model to other anxiety disorders, we might hypothesize that in generalized anxiety disorder, unconscious conflicts remain hidden, but anxiety leaks through to the level of awareness. The person is unable to account for the anxiety because its source remains shrouded in unconsciousness, however. In panic disorder, unacceptable sexual or aggressive impulses approach the boundaries of consciousness and the ego strives desperately to repress them, generating high levels of conflict that bring on a full-fledged panic attack. Panic dissipates when the impulse has been safely repressed.

Obsessions are believed to represent the leakage of unconscious impulses into consciousness, and compulsions are acts that help keep these impulses repressed. Obsessive thoughts about contamination by dirt or germs may represent the threatened emergence of unconscious infantile wishes to soil oneself and play with feces. The compulsion (in this case, cleanliness rituals) helps keep such wishes at bay or partly repressed.

People who become obsessed with thoughts of harming the people they love may harbor unconscious aggressive impulses that intrude into consciousness. The aggressive impulses may be clearly expressed, as in the case of a man who becomes obsessed with thoughts of killing his wife. The aggressive impulses may also be indirectly expressed, in the form of obsessions or repeated fantasies of one's children or spouse being struck by a car or involved in a terrible accident. Consider, for example, the case of Bonnie:

Bonnie, 29, complained of being obsessed by fantasies that her 8- and 11-year-old children were run over on their way home from school. It was April and the fantasies had begun in September, gradually occupying more time during the day.

"I'm usually all right for most of the morning," she explained. "But after lunch the pictures come back to me. There's nothing I can do about it. The pictures are in my head. I see them walking home and crossing the street, and I know what's going to happen and I think 'Why can't I do something to stop it?' but I can't. They're walking into the street and a car is coming along speeding, or a truck, and then it happens again, and they're lying there, and it's a horrible mess." She broke into tears. "And I can't function. I can't do anything. I can't get it out of my head.

"Then sometimes it bothers me at night and [my husband] says 'What's wrong?' He says I'm shaking and white as a ghost and 'What's wrong?' I can't tell him what's going on because he'll think I'm crazy. And then I'm in and out of [the children's] bedrooms, checking that they're all right, tucking them in, kissing them, making sure I can see that they're breathing. And sometimes I wake [the 11-year-old] up with my kissing and he says 'Mommy' and I start crying as soon as I get out of the room."

Through discussions with the psychologist, it appeared that Bonnie was generally dissatisfied with her life. She had gotten married at a young age because of an unplanned pregnancy and had remained largely housebound. Her daytime companion was her television set. Her husband was generally good to her, but he did not understand why Bonnie might be unhappy, "especially when so many women have to work these days to make ends meet." Within a few weeks Bonnie came to the conclusion that it was "all right" for her to feel

Bonnie's case is of the type that may lend support to psychodynamic views. It suggests that obsessions and other anxious behavior patterns can reflect hostilities that we (psychologically) "sweep under the rug" or do not think about (that is, no "good mother" should have hostile feelings toward her children). On the other hand, Bonnie's case does not offer direct evidence of the existence of such unconscious impulses or conflicts.

Learning Perspectives

From the behavioral perspective, anxiety disorders are acquired through conditioning. According to O. Hobart Mowrer's (1948) classic **two-factor model,** both classical and operant conditioning are involved in phobias. The fear component of phobia is assumed to be acquired by means of classical conditioning. It is assumed that neutral objects and situations gain the capacity to evoke fear by being paired with aversive stimuli. A child who is frightened by a barking dog may acquire a phobia for dogs. A child who receives a painful injection may develop a phobia for hypodermic syringes. Evidence shows that many cases of acrophobia, claustrophobia, and blood and injection phobias involve earlier aversive experiences with the phobic object (e.g., Kendler et al., 1992c; Merckelbach, Arntz, & de Jong, 1991; Merckelbach et al., 1996).

Learning theorists have also noted the role of observational learning in acquiring fears. Modeling (observing parents or others react fearfully to a stimulus) and receiving negative information (hearing from others or reading that a particular stimulus—spiders for example—are fearful or disgusting) may also lead to phobias (Merckelbach et al., 1996). In one study of 42 people with severe phobias for spiders, observational learning apparently played a more prominent role in fear acquisition than did conditioning (Merckelbach et al., 1991).

However phobias may develop, the avoidance component of phobias is acquired and maintained by operant conditioning. That is, avoiding fear-inducing stimuli is negatively reinforced by relief from anxiety. The person with an elevator phobia learns to avoid anxiety over taking the elevator by opting for the stairs instead. Avoiding the phobic stimulus thus lessens anxiety, which negatively reinforces the avoidance behavior. Yet there is a significant cost to avoiding the phobic stimulus. The person is not able to unlearn the fear (through **extinction**) via exposure to the phobic stimulus in the absence of any aversive consequences.

From the behavioral perspective, generalized anxiety is precisely that: a product of stimulus generalization. People who are concerned about broad life themes, such as finances, health, and family matters, are likely to experience their apprehensions in a variety of settings. Anxiety would thus become connected with almost any environment or situation. Similarly, agoraphobia would represent a kind of generalized anxiety. Anxiety would become triggered by cues associated with various social or vocational situations outside of the home in which the individual is expected to perform independently, as in traveling, going to work, even shopping. Some learning theorists similarly assume that panic attacks that appear to descend out of nowhere are triggered by cues that are subtle and not readily identified.

There are many challenges to these behaviorist notions. For example, many people with phobias insist they cannot recall painful exposures to the dreaded stimuli. Behaviorists may assume such memory failures are understandable because many phobias are acquired in early childhood. Yet many phobias, such as social phobias and agoraphobia, develop at later ages and appear to reflect cognitive processes relating to an exaggerated appraisal of threat in social situations (excessive fears of embarrassment or criticism) or public places (perceptions of helplessness or fears of panic attacks).

Reinforcement of Obsessive-Compulsive Behavior From the learning perspective, compulsive behaviors are operant responses that are negatively reinforced by relief of the anxiety that is engendered by obsessional thoughts. If a person obsesses that other people's hands are contaminated by dirt or foreign bodies, shaking hands or turning a doorknob may evoke powerful anxiety. Compulsive hand washing following exposure to a possible contaminant provides some relief from anxiety. They thus become more likely to repeat the obsessive-compulsive cycle the next time they are exposed to anxiety-evoking cues, such as shaking hands or touching doorknobs.

The question remains as to why some people develop obsessive thoughts whereas others do not. Some theorists look to an interaction of learning and biological factors for answers. Perhaps people who develop obsessive-compulsive disorder are physiologically sensitized to overreact to minor cues of danger (Steketee & Foa, 1985).

Prepared Conditioning Some investigators suggest that people may be genetically prepared to acquire phobic responses to certain classes of stimuli (McNally, 1987; Mineka, 1991; Seligman & Rosenhan, 1984). For this reason, this model is often referred to as **prepared conditioning.** The model suggests that evolutionary forces would have favored the survival of human ancestors who were genetically predisposed to acquire fears of large animals, snakes and other "creepy-crawlies," heights, enclosed spaces, and strangers. Humans who were not so genetically endowed, and who did not readily acquire these fears, would have been less likely to survive and to pass along their genetic dispositions. Therefore, people may have inherited a tendency to develop phobias that had survival value in the past, even if they no longer do today.

Experimental studies indicate that subjects appear more *prepared* to acquire and maintain fear responses to stimuli such as snakes and spiders (e.g., Hugdahl & Ohman, 1977; McNally, 1987; Ohman, Fredrikson, Hugdahl, & Rimmo, 1976). These experiments do not demonstrate that the subjects are *genetically* prepared to develop their fear responses, however. Keep in mind that subjects were reared in a society in which many people react negatively to these creepy-crawlies. People might therefore be culturally and cognitively prepared—not genetically prepared—to acquire fear responses to snakes, spiders, and other stimuli generally perceived as repugnant in our society.

Generalized Anxiety Disorder: A Safety Perspective

Woody & Rachman (1994) have proposed a safety perspective for understanding GAD. They maintain that people with GAD see the world as a highly threatening place and perceive very few safe places to turn where they can feel secure. The loss of available sources of safety (such as a supportive partner) increases anxiety and worry and provokes a search for other safety resources. Finding a new source of safety may temporarily diminish generalized anxiety but is unlikely to be a strong enough safety signal to eliminate anxiety and hypervigilance for good. Woody and Rachman speculate that if the safety perspective has merit, there may be therapeutic value in teaching people with GAD how to search and acquire safety resources, such as by developing a plan of action in the case of an emergency. The therapist needs to learn what makes people with GAD feel safe and help them develop ways of increasing the availability or accessibility of these safety resources.

A Conditioning Model of Posttraumatic Stress Disorder

From a classical conditioning perspective, traumatic experiences function as unconditioned stimuli that become paired with neutral (conditioned) stimuli such as the sights, sounds, and smells associated with the trauma scene—for example, the battlefield or the neighborhood in which a person has been raped or assaulted (Foy, Resnick, Sipprele, & Carroll, 1987). Subsequent exposures to similar stimuli evoke the anxiety (a conditioned emotional response) associated with PTSD. The conditioned stimuli that reactivate the conditioned response include memories or dream images of the trauma, or visits to the scene of the trauma. Research supporting the conditioning model of PTSD shows that PTSD subjects whose problems are combat related show greater arousal (as measured by heart rate and GSR) than control subjects do when they are exposed to slides or recordings of the sounds of combat (e.g., Blanchard, Kalb, Pallmeyer, & Gerardi, 1982).

PTSD is likely to persist when sufferers avoid exposure to conditioned stimuli—as in refusing to think or talk about painful memories (Foy et al., 1987). Avoidance of combat- or assault-related stimuli can be viewed as an operant response that is reinforced by reduction of the anxiety produced by the stimuli. Avoidance prolongs PTSD because sufferers do not have the opportunity to learn to manage their conditioned reactions. Extinction of conditioned anxiety may only occur when conditioned stimuli (e.g., the cues related to combat or the traumatic setting) are presented in the absence of the troubling unconditioned stimuli. That is, the fear may extinguish when the person is able to gradually encounter the conditioned stimuli without incident.

Cognitive Perspectives

Cognitive theorists and researchers have identified various patterns of thinking, or cognitive factors, that are associated with anxiety disorders.

Overprediction of Fear

People with anxiety disorders often overpredict the amount of fear or anxiety they will experience when exposed to anxiety-evoking stimuli (Rachman, 1994). The person with a snake phobia, for example, may expect to tremble upon exposure to a snake but finds the actual exposure to be far less terrifying than expected. A single unexpected panic attack can sharply increase the likelihood of overpredicting the level of fear the person expects to experience when exposed again to the same situation.

Overprediction of fear may have survival value because it encourages people to keep their distance from fear-evoking situations (Rachman & Bichard, 1988). However, avoidance of fear-inducing situations prevents people from gaining experience that can promote a less threatening appraisal of the situation. Researchers find that fearful subjects become more accurate in predicting their level of fear following actual exposure to the fearful situation (Rachman & Bichard, 1988). A clinical implication is that with repeated exposure people with anxiety disorders may come to anticipate their responses to fear-inducing stimuli more accurately, leading to reductions of fear expectancies. This in turn may reduce avoidance behavior.

The overprediction of fear has also been extended to a common phobia, fear of dental visits (M. Marks & De Silva, 1994). People with dental phobia often overpredict how much pain they expect to experience. In this case, the cost involved in overpredicting fear may involve postponed or canceled dental visits and eventual tooth decay.

Self-Defeating or Irrational Beliefs

Self-defeating thoughts can heighten and perpetuate anxiety and phobic disorders. When faced with fear-evoking stimuli, the person may think, "I've got to get out of here," or "My heart is going to leap out of my chest" (Meichenbaum & Deffenbacher, 1988). Thoughts such as these intensify autonomic arousal, disrupt planning, magnify the aversiveness of stimuli, prompt avoidance behavior, and decrease self-efficacy expectancies concerning capacity to control the situation.

People with phobias also tend to hold more of the sorts of irrational beliefs catalogued by Albert Ellis than nonfearful people do. Such beliefs often center around exaggerated needs to be approved of by everyone one meets and to avoid any situation in which problems might arise (Mizes, Landolf-Fritsche, & Grossman-McKee, 1987). Consider these beliefs: "I couldn't stand it if people saw me having an attack. What would they think of me? They might think I was crazy. I couldn't stand it if they looked at me that way." In one study, 65% of the anxious subjects, as compared to only 2% of nonanxious subjects, endorsed the belief that one must be loved by, and earn the approval of, practically everyone (Newmark, Frerking, Cook, & Newmark, 1973). Results of another study may hit closer to home: College men who believe it is awful to be turned down when requesting a date show more social anxiety than men who are less likely to catastrophize rejection (Gormally, Sipps, Raphael, Edwin, & Varvil-Weld, 1981).

Cognitive theorists relate obsessive-compulsive disorder to tendencies to exaggerate the risk of negative outcomes and to adopt irrational beliefs, especially perfectionistic beliefs (Steketee & Foa, 1985). Because they expect bad things to happen, people with OCD engage in rituals to prevent them. An accountant who imagines terrible consequences for slight mistakes on a client's tax forms may feel compelled to repeatedly check her or his work. The perfectionist exaggerates the consequences of turning in less than perfect work and may feel compelled to redo his or her efforts until every detail is flawless.

Oversensitivity to Threats An oversensitivity to threatening cues is a central characteristic of anxiety disorders (A. T. Beck & Clark, 1997). People with phobias may perceive danger in situations that most people consider safe. Magnifying the importance of threatening events may determine whether an event is experienced as traumatic, which may set the stage for PTSD (Creamer, Burgess, & Patterson, 1992). Generally speaking, anxious people appear to pay special attention to threatening cues and to construe unclear events in an ominous way (Mathews, 1990; Rapee, 1991).

Oversensitivity to threats often reflects exaggerated perceptions of external dangers (as in, "The bridge might collapse," or "The elevator cables may break"). They may refer to internal cues that function as signs of danger (as in "I think I'm going to fall apart," or "I feel like I'm about to lose control"). Sometimes the cognitions involve themes of social embarrassment or rejection (as in "What if they think I'm stupid? That would be awful," or "I'm afraid of making a scene"). People with phobic disorders may dwell on various combinations of self-defeating cognitions. Fear of flying may involve perceptions of the plane as unsafe ("What's that vi-

bration? It feels like the plane is about to come apart"), perceptions of personal vulnerability ("What if I have an anxiety attack? There's no escape at 35,000 feet!"), and threats of social embarrassment ("Everybody will notice I'm shaking. They'll think I'm a fool").

An internal alarm system that is sensitive to cues of threat may have evolutionary advantages by optimizing the chances of survival (A. T. Beck & Clark, 1997). In other words, humans and other animals that respond quickly to potential threats—such as a rustling sound in the bush that might indicate the presence of a lurking predator—may have been better prepared to take defensive action (to fight or flee) than were those with a less sensitive alarm system. Feelings of fear may have motivated our ancestors to take defensive action, which helped them survive in a hostile world. In today's world, however, an overly sensitive internal alarm may prove maladaptive. Rather than helping us cope effectively with threats, it may lead to the development of inappropriate anxiety reactions to a wide range of cues that pose no objective danger.

Anxiety Sensitivity Anxiety sensitivity, or fear of fear, refers to the extent to which a person believes that their own internal emotions or bodily arousal will lead to harmful consequences (Reiss et al., 1986; K. E. Williams, Chambless, & Ahrens, 1997). People with a high degree of anxiety sensitivity may be prone to panic when they experience bodily signs of anxiety, such as a racing heart or shortness or breath, because they take these symptoms to be signs of an impending heart attack or loss of control.

Evidence is mounting that anxiety sensitivity is an important risk factor for panic disorder (Lilienfeld, 1997). In one study, researchers used an anxiety sensitivity measure to predict which military recruits would be most likely to panic during a highly stressful period of basic training (Schmidt, Lerew, & Jackson, 1997). One in five recruits who scored in the top 10% on a measure of anxiety sensitivity experienced a panic attack, as compared with only 6% of the other recruits.

Misattributions for Panic Sensations Cognitive models of panic disorder generally assume that panic attacks involve catastrophic misinterpretations of bodily sensations, such as heart palpitations, dizziness, or light-headedness (Acierno, Hersen, & Van Hasselt, 1993; D. M. Clark, 1986; van den Hout, Arntz, & Hoekstra, 1994; Zoellner, Craske, & Rapee, 1996). Panic-prone people may believe that changes in bodily sensations signal an impending heart attack or other threatening events, such as a loss of control or "going crazy." Changes in bodily sensations in otherwise healthy individuals may be induced by various factors such as unrecognized hyperventilation, temperature changes, or reactions to certain drugs or medications. Or they may be fleeting, normally occurring changes in bodily states that typically go unnoticed by most people.

A cognitive model of panic disorder involving an interaction of cognitive and physiological factors is depicted in

Figure 5.3. The model picks up on the idea that people with a proneness to panic disorder perceive certain internal bodily cues or external stimuli as threatening or dangerous, perhaps because they are overly sensitive to these cues or have associated these cues with earlier panic attacks. The sense of threat induces anxiety or apprehension, which is accompanied by sympathetic nervous system activation, leading to the release of epinephrine (adrenaline) (Wilkinson et al., 1998). The release of epinephrine intensifies physical sensations by producing an accelerated heart rate, rapid breathing, and sweating, among other bodily symptoms. These changes in bodily sensations, in turn, are interpreted as signs of an impending panic attack or worse, an imminent catastrophe ("My God, I'm having a heart attack!"), which in either case reinforces perceptions of threat, which further heightens anxiety, leading to yet more anxiety-related bodily symptoms, and so on, in a vicious cycle that can quickly spiral to a full-fledged panic attack. Thus, catastrophic misinterpretations of bodily cues may set into motion a vicious cycle that brings on panic attacks in some people.

TRUTH ⓞ FICTION REVISITED

5.6 *True.* According to cognitive theorists, catastrophic misinterpretations of bodily cues may set into motion a vicious cycle that brings on panic attacks.

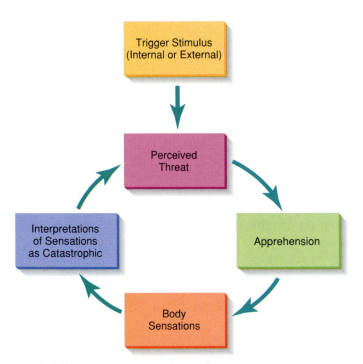

FIGURE 5.3 *A cognitive model of panic disorder.*
This model involves the interaction of cognitive and physiological factors. In panic-prone people, perceptions of threat from internal or external cues lead to feelings of apprehension or anxiety, which lead to changes in body sensations (for example, cardiovascular symptoms). These changes lead, in turn, to catastrophic interpretations, thereby intensifying the perception of threat, which further heightens anxiety, and so on in a vicious circle that may culminate in a full-blown panic attack.

Source: Adapted from Clark (1986).

Low Self-Efficacy Expectancies

Low levels of self-efficacy for handling threats (e.g., beliefs that one will fall apart or be unable to cope) tend to heighten anxiety (Bandura et al., 1985). When people feel capable of performing a task—playing the piano, giving a speech in public, riding on a train without panicking, or touching a small rodent or insect—they are less likely to be troubled by anxiety or fear when they attempt it.

On the other hand, when people rivet their attention on their perceived inadequacies, they may fail to seek out personal resources that might be used to cope with stressful situations, as in the case of Brenda:

> *Brenda, a 19-year-old sophomore, was plagued by anxiety almost from the moment she began her college studies. She had enrolled in a college several hundred miles away from home. While she had been away from home before—at sleep-away camp and on a teen tour through Europe—college life presented various challenges and stresses which she felt a lack of ability to handle. She seemed to be most anxious when meeting new friends and when sitting in class, especially the small seminar classes in which she expected to be called on by the professor. She found herself becoming tongue tied and dripping with perspiration whenever she confronted these situations. What was more surprising and perplexing to her was that she had never had any trouble before either making new friends or talking in class.*

How do self-doubts affect our performance? According to the self-efficacy model, we are likely to feel more anxious in situations in which we doubt our ability to perform competently. Anxiety may hamper our performance, making it more difficult for us to perform successfully. Even accomplished athletes may be seized with anxiety when they are under extreme pressure, as during slumps or when competing in championship games.

In both situations, Brenda lost confidence in her ability to express herself. The ideas she wished to express were blocked by anxiety, which impaired her ability to think and speak clearly. The anxiety was maintained by an erroneous perception of herself as incapable of saying the right thing when called upon in class or when meeting new people. Brenda reported that she hadn't had any problems in high school either speaking up in class or making new friends. College, however, was a different experience. At college there were people she hadn't grow up with, and there were professors who had no tolerance, or so she believed, for any student who wasn't a budding genius. Her whole mental set had shifted into a defensive attitude in which self-doubts replaced self-confidence.

Brenda's history of social and academic success couldn't shield her from the nagging self-doubts she began to experience as she confronted the more demanding stresses of college life. She was not any less capable of coping with these challenges in college than she was in high school. She didn't suddenly lose her wits or her social skills when she entered college. What was different was that she began to perceive herself as unable to cope with the demands of a new environment that seemed both unsupportive and threatening. Appraising herself this way, it was little wonder that she experienced anxiety in class and social situations, which impaired her efforts to speak clearly. She then interpreted her speech difficulties as evidence of her inadequacies, feeding the vicious cycle of anxiety in which self-doubt leads to anxiety, which hampers performance, which occasions more self-doubts and anxiety, and so on.

THE AUTHORS' FILES

Evidence supporting cognitive formulations of anxiety disorders is mounting. For example, recent work shows that people with panic disorder have a greater tendency to misinterpret bodily sensations as signs of impending catastrophe than do people with other anxiety disorders or nonpatient controls (D. M. Clark et al., 1997). Studies also show that panic-prone people tend to have greater awareness of, and sensitivity to, their internal physiological cues, such as heart palpitations (Pauli et al., 1997; Richards, Edgar, & Gibbon, 1996; Schmidt, Lerew, & Jackson, 1997). Still, we lack direct evidence that these cognitive factors play a causal role in the development of panic disorder.

Biological Perspectives

Biological factors play roles in anxiety disorders. Many questions remain concerning the interactions of biological and other factors, however.

Genetic Factors Various anxiety disorders such as social phobia, specific phobia, obsessive-compulsive disorder, and panic disorder tend to run in families (APA, 1994; Fredrikson, Annas, & Wik, 1997; R. B. Goldstein et al., 1994). Familial association does not necessarily mean a disorder is genetic in origin because families share common environments as well as genes. Twin studies can help tease out environmental and genetic influences. The results of one carefully thought out study examined the monozygotic (MZ) and dizygotic (DZ) twins of people identified as having anxiety disorders (Torgersen, 1983). Overall, the concordance rate (i.e., the percentage of co-twins who had an anxiety disorder) was twice as high for MZ twins (34%) as for DZ twins (17%). This 2 to 1 ratio supports a genetic contribution because MZ twins share twice as many (100%) of their genes as DZ twins, who share 50%.

Another twin study based on female twin pairs showed genetic factors to be most prominent in agoraphobia, modestly prominent in generalized anxiety disorder, and least prominent in specific phobias (Kendler et al., 1992c). We also have evidence of higher concordance rates for obsessive-compulsive disorder and panic disorder in MZ twins than DZ twins (APA, 1994; Torgersen, 1983). Still, we should caution that MZ twins may share more common environments (i.e., they may be treated more alike) than DZ twins. We await studies of adopted-away children to help sort out environmental from genetic factors in anxiety disorders.

In 1996, researchers reported finding a gene linked to **neuroticism** (Begley, 1998). Neuroticism is characterized by anxiety, a sense of foreboding, and the tendency to avoid fear-inducing stimuli. Earlier, Sandra Scarr and her colleagues (1981) compared the neuroticism test scores of adopted adolescents to those of their natural and adoptive parents. The scores of parents and their biological children correlated more highly than those of parents and adopted children. Researchers estimate that about half of the variability among people on this underlying trait is due to genetic factors, with environmental factors accounting for the rest (Plomin, Owen, & McGuffin, 1994).

Genetics may play a lesser role in specific phobias than in agoraphobia, perhaps because aversive experiences are more likely to contribute to the development of specific phobias, such as nearly falling out of a window or being locked in a closet (Kendler et al., 1992c). Researchers recently linked a specific gene to OCD, although it is believed that several genes may be involved in the disorder (Begley, 1998).

Neurotransmitters The neurotransmitter **gamma-aminobutyric acid (GABA)** is implicated in anxiety. GABA is an *inhibitory* neurotransmitter found throughout the gray matter of the central nervous system. That is, GABA regulates nervous activity by preventing neurons from overly exciting their neighbors. When the action of GABA is inadequate, neurons can fire excessively, possibly bringing about seizures. In less dramatic cases, inadequate action of GABA apparently contributes to anxiety. This view of the role of GABA is supported by the action of the family of antianxiety drugs referred to as **benzodiazepines,** which include the well-known Valium and Librium. Benzodiazepines make

GABA receptors more sensitive, thus enhancing GABA's calming (inhibitory) effects (Zorumski & Isenberg, 1991).

Oversensitivity of serotonin or norepinephrine receptors in the brain has also been implicated in anxiety disorders (Southwick et al., 1997). This may explain why antidepressant drugs that affect the availability of these neurotransmitters in the brain often have beneficial effects in treating some types of anxiety disorder, especially panic disorder. Investigators also suspect that genes involved in regulation of serotonin may play a role in determining anxiety-related traits (Angier, 1996; Lesch et al., 1996).

Biological Aspects of Panic Disorder The strong physical components of panic disorder have led some theorists to speculate that panic attacks have biological underpinnings, perhaps involving an underlying brain dysfunction (Barlow, Brown, & Craske, 1994). Donald Klein (D. F. Klein, 1993, 1994; Talan, 1994) proposed that a defect in brain systems that respond to cues of suffocation may be involved. He speculates that for people with an unusually sensitive suffocation-alarm system, even rising levels of carbon dioxide in the blood can trigger a respiratory alarm, producing the cascading sensations that characterize the classic panic attack: shortness of breath, smothering sensations, dizziness, faintness, increased heart rate or palpitations, trembling, sensations of hot or cold flashes, and feelings of nausea. Klein's intriguing proposal has met with some support in the professional community (McNally et al., 1995; Taylor & Rachman, 1994), as well as some dissenting voices (Ley, 1996, 1997; Schmidt, Telch, & Jaimez, 1996; Schmidt, Trakowski, & Staab, 1997). Other researchers report that episodes of traumatic suffocation (near-drownings or near-chokings) may play a role in the development of panic disorder in some patients (Bouwer & Stein, 1997).

Support for a biological basis of panic disorder is found in studies showing that people with panic disorder are more likely than nonpanic control subjects to experience panicky symptoms in response to certain biological challenges, such as infusion of the chemical sodium lactate or manipulation of carbon dioxide (CO_2) levels in the blood either by intentional **hyperventilation** (which reduces levels of CO_2 in the blood) or inhalation of carbon dioxide (which increases CO_2 levels) (Antony, Brown, & Barlow, 1997; Papp et al., 1997; Perna et al., 1996; Schmidt, Trakowski, & Staab, 1997).

Cognitive theorists propose that cognitive factors may be involved in explaining these sensitivities. They point out that biological challenges produce intense physical sensations that may be catastrophically misinterpreted by panic-prone people as signs of an impending heart attack or loss of control (McNally & Eke, 1996; Schmidt, Trakowski, & Staab, 1997). Perhaps these misinterpretations—not underlying biological sensitivities—may in turn induce panic.

Supportive evidence for the cognitivist perspective comes from a recent study showing that cognitive behavior therapy that focused on changing faulty interpretations of bodily sensations eliminated CO_2-induced panic in a majority of panic disorder patients (Schmidt, Trakowski, & Staab, 1997). Results of yet another study showed that panic patients who underwent the CO_2 infusion with a safe person present did not show more panicky symptoms than controls (M. M. Carter et al., 1995). Having a supportive person available may lead the person to cognitively appraise the situation as less threatening, which may avert the spiraling of anxiety that can lead to panic attacks.

The fact that panic attacks often seem to come out of the blue also seems to support the belief that the attacks are biologically triggered. However, it is possible the cues that set off many panic attacks may be internal, involving changes in bodily sensations, rather than external. As we noted in our discussion of cognitive factors, people with a proneness to develop panic disorder may overreact to slight changes in their physical sensations by misattributing them to dire causes, such as an impending heart attack. Changes in physical cues, combined with catastrophic thinking, may lead to a spiraling of anxiety that culminates in a full-blown panic attack.

Biological Aspects of Obsessive-Compulsive Disorder One biological model receiving attention is the belief that obsessive-compulsive disorder may involve heightened arousal in a so-called *worry circuit,* a neural network in the brain involved in signaling danger. According to this view, the brain may be constantly sending messages that something is wrong and requires immediate attention, leading to obsessional worrisome thoughts and repetitive compulsive behaviors. The compulsive aspects of OCD may involve disturbances in other brain circuits that usually inhibit repetitive behaviors, leading people to feel like they are "stuck in gear" (Begley, 1998; D. R. Rosenberg et al., 1997b). Normally, the frontal cortex controls the lower movement centers of the brain located in the brain stem. It is possible that a disruption in these neural pathways may be involved in the failure to inhibit the repetitive hand-washing and compulsive checking behaviors seen in people with OCD. Evidence also points to structural differences in the brains of people with OCD than in nonpatient controls (Grachev et al., 1998; D. R. Rosenberg et al., 1997a; Wu et al., 1997). The significance of these structural differences in explaining OCD remains unclear, however.

TYING IT TOGETHER: CAUSAL PATHWAYS IN ANXIETY DISORDERS

Unraveling the complex interactions of environmental, physiological, and psychological factors in explaining how anxiety disorders develop remains a challenge (see Figure 5.4). There may be different causal pathways at work. To illustrate, let us offer some possible causal pathways involved in phobic disorders and panic disorder.

FOCUS ON DIVERSITY

Ethnicity and Anxiety Disorders

Although anxiety disorders have been the subject of extensive study, little attention has been directed toward examining ethnic differences in the prevalences of these disorders (Neal & Turner, 1991). Are anxiety disorders more common in certain racial/ethnic groups? We might think that the stressors that African Americans in our society are more likely to encounter, such as racism and economic hardship, might contribute to a greater prevalence of anxiety disorders in this population group (Neal & Turner, 1991). On the other hand, it is possible that African Americans, by dint of having to cope with these hardships in early life, may have developed a resiliency in the face of stress that shields them from anxiety disorders.

Evidence relating anxiety disorders to ethnicity remains mixed. The Epidemiologic Catchment Area (ECA) study of five different communities in the United States found anxiety disorders overall to be more prevalent among African Americans than among other groups (Robins et al., 1984). Overall rates may mask differences in the rates of specific disorders, however. Both African Americans and Hispanic Americans were more likely than their non-Hispanic White counterparts to develop phobic disorders yet were less likely to develop panic disorder (Eaton et al., 1991).

The samples of African Americans in the ECA study contained overrepresentations of poor, elderly, and female respondents, which restricts our ability to generalize more broadly. Differences between groups may relate more closely to socioeconomic status (SES), age, and gender than to race or ethnicity per se. The National Comorbidity Survey (NCS), which was based on a sample that more closely represented the general U.S. adult population, found that anxiety disorders overall and specific anxiety disorders in particular were no more common among African Americans than among non-Hispanic White Americans (Eaton et al., 1994). Moreover, supporting the ECA findings, NCS researchers

found a lower prevalence of panic disorder among African Americans than non-Hispanic White Americans, but only among people in the 45- to 54-year age group. Panic disorder was also less common among Hispanics than non-Hispanic Whites among people in the 35- to 44-year age range. Trivial differences were found among younger people across racial/ethnic lines.

Anxiety disorders are not unique to our culture. Panic disorder, for example, is known to occur in many countries in the world, perhaps even universally (Amering & Katschnig, 1990). A multinational study of more than 40,000 people in 10 countries (United States, Canada, Puerto Rico, France, West Germany, Italy, Lebanon, Taiwan, Korea, and New Zealand) showed that rates of panic disorder were relatively consistent, ranging between 1% and 3% in all of these countries except Taiwan, where the rate was under 1%. However, the specific features of panic attacks, such as shortness of breath or fear of dying, may vary from culture to culture (Amering & Katschnig, 1990). There are also some culture-bound syndromes that have features similar to panic attacks but also some differences, such as *ataques de nervios* (see Chapter 2).

PTSD is also found in other cultures. Investigators report high rates of PTSD in a Southwestern U.S. Indian tribe and among Khmer refugees who had survived the "killing fields" of the Pol Pot War in Cambodia from 1975 to 1979 (W. H. Sack et al., 1994; W. H. Sack, Clarke, & Seeley, 1996). Cultural factors may play a role in determining how people manage and cope with trauma as well as their vulnerability to traumatic stress reactions and the specific form such a disorder might take (de Silva, 1993). There may also be cross-cultural similarities in the features of traumatic stress reactions. In another study of Cambodian war refugees, researchers found a similar symptom picture to that found among U.S. trauma survivors (E. B. Carlson & Rosser-Hogan, 1994).

Some people may develop phobias by way of classical conditioning—the pairing of a previously neutral stimulus with an unpleasant or traumatic experience. A person may develop a fear of small animals because of experiences in which they were bitten or nearly bitten. A fear of riding in elevators, as we shall see in the cases of Kevin and Phyllis discussed in a later section of this chapter, may arise from experiences of being trapped in elevators or other enclosed spaces.

Bear in mind that not all people who have traumatic experiences develop related phobias. Perhaps some people

have a genetic predisposition that sensitizes them to acquire more readily conditioned responses to stimuli associated with aversive situations. Or perhaps people are more sensitized to these experiences because of an inherited predisposition to respond with greater negative arousal to aversive situations. Whatever the factors involved in the acquisition of the phobia, people with persistent phobias may be those who have learned to avoid any further contact with the object and so do not avail themselves of opportunities to extinguish the phobia through repeated uneventful contacts

Anxiety Disorders **191**

Social-Environmental Factors
Threatening or Traumatic Events
Observing Fear Responses in Others
Challenging Demands in New Situations
Cultural Factors Leading to Socialization
    in Passive or Dependent Roles
Lack of Social Support

Biological Factors
Genetic Predisposition
Disturbances in Neurotransmitter Activity
    or Suffocation Alarm System
Abnormalities in Brain Circuits Involved
    in Signaling Danger or Inhibiting
    Repetitive Behaviors

Behavioral Factors
Conditioning Experiences
Lack of Extinction Opportunities

Emotional and Cognitive Factors
Unresolved Psychological Conflicts
    (Freudian or Psychodynamic)
Cognitive Factors (anxiety sensitivity, self-
    defeating or irrational thinking,
    catastrophic misinterpretations of bodily
    cues, over-sensitivity to threats, low
    self-efficacy)

FIGURE 5.4 *Multiple factors in anxiety disorders.*

with the object or situation. Then there are people who acquire phobias without prior aversive experiences with the phobic stimulus, or at least none they can recall. We can conjecture that cognitive factors, such as observing other people's aversive responses, may play a contributing role in these cases.

Possible causal pathways in panic disorder highlight roles for biological, cognitive, and environmental factors. Some people may inherit a genetic predisposition, or *diathesis,* that makes them more likely to panic in response to changes in bodily sensations. This genetic predisposition may involve an overly sensitive suffocation alarm system that is triggered by mild fluctuations in blood levels of carbon dioxide, perhaps resulting from unrecognized hyperventilation. Cues associated with changing carbon dioxide levels, such as dizziness, tingling, or numbness, may be misconstrued as signs of an impending disaster—suffocation, a heart attack, or loss of control. This in turn may lead, like dominoes falling in line, to an anxiety reaction that quickly spirals into a full-fledged panic attack. Whether the anxiety reaction spirals into a state of panic may depend on another vulnerability factor, the individual's level of anxiety sensitiv-

ity. People with a high level of anxiety sensitivity (extreme fear of their own bodily sensations) may be more likely to panic in response to changes in their physical sensations. In some cases, anxiety sensitivity may be so high that panic ensues even in individuals without a genetic predisposition. Environmental factors may come into play as panic attacks come to be triggered by specific environmental cues, such as stimuli associated with situations (boarding a train or elevator) in which attacks have occurred in the past.

TREATMENT OF ANXIETY DISORDERS

Each of the major theoretical perspectives has spawned approaches for treating anxiety disorders. Psychological approaches may differ from one another in their techniques and expressed aims, but they seem to have one thing in common: In one way or another, they encourage clients to face rather than avoid the sources of their anxieties. The biological perspective, by contrast, has focused largely on drugs that quell anxiety.

Psychodynamic Approaches

From the psychodynamic perspective, anxieties reflect the energies attached to early childhood conflicts and the ego's efforts to keep them repressed. Traditional psychoanalysis fosters awareness of how clients' anxiety disorders symbolize their inner conflicts, so the ego can be freed from expending its energy on repression. The ego can thus attend to more creative and enhancing tasks.

More modern psychodynamic therapies also foster clients' awareness of inner sources of conflict. They focus more so than traditional approaches on exploring sources of anxiety that arise from current rather than past relationships, however, and they encourage clients to assume more adaptive behavior. Such therapies are briefer and more directive than traditional psychoanalysis.

Humanistic-Existential Approaches

Humanistic-existential theories posit that many of our anxieties stem from social repression of our genuine selves. Anxiety occurs when the incongruity between one's true inner self and one's social facade draws closer to the level of awareness. The person senses something bad will happen, but is unable to say what it is because the disowned parts of oneself are not directly expressed in consciousness. Because of the disapproval of others, people may fail to develop their individual talents and recognize their authentic feelings. Humanistic-existential therapies thus aim at helping people get in touch with and express their genuine talents and feelings. As a result, clients become free to discover and accept their true selves, rather than reacting with anxiety whenever their true feelings and needs begin to surface.

Biological Approaches

Pharmaceutical houses earn large shares of their income from minor tranquilizers, the drugs most often used to treat tension and anxiety. For many years, the benzodiazepine Valium (generic name, *diazepam*) was the most widely prescribed drug in the world. Other commonly used benzodiazepines include Tranxene (*clorazepate*), Librium (*chlordiazepoxide*), and Xanax (*alprazolam*).

Although the therapeutic use of benzodiazepines is usually limited to 60 days, an American Psychiatric Association (1991) task force estimates that as many as 2 million Americans have taken them for many years because of chronic insomnia, lingering depression, or other long-standing problems. Physical dependence (addiction) can develop with chronic use of benzodiazepines, however, leading to withdrawal symptoms when use of the drugs is stopped abruptly. Withdrawal symptoms include rebound anxiety, insomnia, and restlessness (Shader & Greenblatt, 1993; Shapiro et al., 1993). These symptoms prompt many patients to return to using the drugs.

Antidepressant drugs have also proven helpful in treating panic disorder as well as depression (Broocks et al., 1998; Roy-Byrne & Cowley, 1998; van Balkom et al., 1997).

Some antidepressants in common use for treating panic disorder include the tricyclics *imipramine* (brand name Tofranil) and *clomipramine* (brand name Anafranil) and the selective serotonin-reuptake inhibitors (SSRIs) *paroxetine* (brand name Paxil) and *sertraline* (brand name Zoloft). However, troublesome side effects may occur, such as heavy sweating and heart palpitations, which leads many patients to stop using the drugs prematurely. The high-potency tranquilizer *alprazolam* (Xanax), which is a type of benzodiazepine, is also helpful in treating panic disorder and social phobia (Gould et al., 1997; Lydiard, Brawman-Mintzer, & Ballenger, 1996; van Balkom et al., 1997). However, drugs have not been shown to be effective in treating specific phobias (Roy-Byrne & Cowley, 1998).

TRUTH *or* FICTION REVISITED

5.7 *False.* Drugs used to treat schizophrenia are not used in the treatment of panic disorder. But antidepressants have shown therapeutic benefits in helping to control panic attacks.

A potential problem with drug therapy is that patients may attribute clinical improvement to the drugs and not their own resources. Nor do such drugs effect cures. Relapses are common after patients discontinue the medication (D. A. Spiegel & Bruce, 1997). Reemergence of panic is likely unless cognitive-behavioral treatment is provided to help panic patients modify their overreactions to their bodily sensations (D. M. Clark, 1986). Drug therapy is sometimes combined with cognitive-behavioral therapy. Evidence suggests that drug therapy does not interfere with the effectiveness of the cognitive-behavioral treatment (Bruce, 1996; Hegel, Ravaris, & Ahles, 1994).

Antidepressants may also be helpful in treating other anxiety disorders, including agoraphobia accompanying panic disorder, social phobia, PTSD, obsessive-compulsive disorder, and generalized anxiety disorder (Gould et al., 1997; Roy-Byrne & Cowley, 1998; M. B. Stein et al., 1998; Yehuda, Marshall, & Giller, 1998). Other research suggests that alprazolam may also be helpful in treating social phobia and generalized anxiety disorder (Gould et al., 1997; Lydiard, Brawman-Mintzer, & Ballenger, 1996).

Obsessive-compulsive disorder (OCD) appears to be especially responsive to SSRI-type antidepressants—drugs such as *fluoxetine* (Prozac) and *clomipramine* (brand name Anafranil) that work specifically on increasing the availability in the brain of the neurotransmitter serotonin (Jenike et al., 1997; Koran et al., 1996, 1997; Lydiard, Brawman-Mintzer, & Ballenger, 1996). The effectiveness of these drugs leads researchers to suspect that a problem with serotonin transmission in the brain may be involved in the development of OCD in at least some people with the disorder (Hollander et al., 1992). Still, drugs that affect serotonin levels tend to have more of a therapeutic effect on compulsions than obsessions (Michels & Marzuk, 1993). Moreover, some patients fail to respond to these drugs, and among those who do respond, a complete remission of symptoms is uncommon (DeVeaugh-Geiss, 1994).

Learning-Based Approaches

Behavioral treatments based on learning approaches include a variety of techniques aimed at helping individuals confront the objects or situations that elicit their fears and anxieties.

Systematic Desensitization

Adam has a phobia for receiving injections. His behavior therapist treats him as he reclines in a comfortable padded chair. In a state of deep muscle relaxation, Adam observes slides projected on a screen. A slide of a nurse holding a needle has just been shown three times, 30 seconds at a time. Each time Adam has shown no anxiety. So now a slightly more discomforting slide is shown: one of the nurse aiming the needle toward someone's bare arm. After 15 seconds, our armchair adventurer notices twinges of discomfort and raises a finger as a signal (speaking might disturb his relaxation). The projector operator turns off the light, and Adam spends two minutes imagining his "safe scene"—lying on a beach beneath the tropical sun. Then the slide is shown again. This time Adam views it for 30 seconds before feeling anxiety.

SOURCE: RATHUS, 1996

Adam is undergoing systematic desensitization, a fear-reduction procedure originated by psychiatrist Joseph Wolpe (1958) in the 1950s. Systematic desensitization is a gradual process. Clients learn to handle progressively more disturbing stimuli while they remain relaxed. About 10 to 20 stimuli are arranged in a sequence, or hierarchy—called a **fear-stimulus hierarchy**—according to their capacity to evoke anxiety. By using their imagination or by viewing photos, clients are exposed to the items in the hierarchy, gradually imagining themselves approaching the target behavior—be it ability to receive an injection or remain in an enclosed room or elevator—without undue anxiety.

Joseph Wolpe developed systematic desensitization on the assumption that maladaptive anxiety responses, like other behaviors, are learned or conditioned. He assumed they can be unlearned by counterconditioning. In counterconditioning, a response incompatible with anxiety is made to appear under conditions that usually elicit anxiety. Muscle relaxation is generally used as the incompatible response, and followers of Wolpe usually use the method of progressive relaxation (described in Chapter 4) to help clients acquire relaxation skills. For this reason Adam's therapist is teaching Adam to experience relaxation in the presence of (otherwise) anxiety-evoking slides of needles.

Behaviorally oriented therapists, such as Wolpe, explain the benefits of systematic desensitization and similar therapies in terms of principles of counterconditioning, or extinction. Cognitively oriented therapists note, however, that remaining in the presence of phobic imagery, rather than running from it, is also likely to enhance self-efficacy ex-

pectancies (i.e., self-perceptions of being able to manage the phobic stimuli without anxiety) (Galassi, 1988). Positive self-efficacy expectancies are negatively (inversely) correlated with catecholamine levels in the bloodstream (Bandura et al., 1985). A treatment that raises clients' self-efficacy expectancies may thus lower their catecholamine levels, which may counteract feelings of nervousness and relieve the physical aspects of anxiety.

Gradual Exposure This method helps people overcome phobias through a stepwise approach of actual exposure to the phobic stimuli. The effectiveness of exposure therapy is well-established, making it the treatment of choice for specific phobias (Barlow, Esler, & Vitali, 1998; G. T. Wilson, 1997). Here exposure therapy was used in treating a case of claustrophobia:

Claustrophobia (fear of enclosed spaces) is not very unusual, though Kevin's case certainly was. Kevin's claustrophobia took the form of a fear of riding on elevators. What made his case so unusual was his occupation: He worked as an elevator mechanic. Kevin spent his work days repairing elevators. Unless it was absolutely necessary, however, Kevin managed to complete the repairs without riding in the elevator. He would climb the stairs to the floor where an elevator was stuck, make repairs, and hit the down button. He would then race downstairs to see that the elevator had operated correctly. When his work required an elevator ride, panic would seize him as the doors closed. Kevin tried to cope by praying for divine intervention to prevent him from passing out before the doors opened.

Kevin related the origin of his phobia to an accident three years earlier in which he had been pinned in his overturned car for nearly an hour. He remembered feelings of helplessness and suffocation. Kevin developed claustrophobia—a fear of situations from which he could not escape, such as flying on an airplane, driving through a tunnel, taking public transportation, and, of course, riding in an elevator. Kevin's fear had become so incapacitating that he was seriously considering switching careers, although the change would require considerable financial sacrifice. Each night he lay awake wondering whether he would be able to cope the next day if he were required to test-ride an elevator.

Kevin's therapy involved gradual exposure. Gradual exposure, like systematic desensitization, is a step-by-step procedure that involves a fear-stimulus hierarchy. In gradual exposure, however, the target behavior is approached in actuality rather than symbolically. Moreover, the individual is active rather than relaxed in a recliner.

A typical hierarchy for overcoming a fear of riding on an elevator might include the following steps:
1. *Standing outside the elevator.*
2. *Standing in the elevator with the door open.*

Gradual exposure. In gradual exposure, the client is exposed to a fear-stimulus hierarchy in real life situations, often with a therapist or companion serving in a supportive role. The therapist or companion gradually withdraws direct support, so as to encourage the person to accomplish the exposure tasks increasingly on his or her own. Gradual exposure is often combined with cognitive techniques that focus on helping the client replace anxiety-producing thoughts and beliefs with calming, rational alternatives.

3. Standing in the elevator with the door closed.
4. Taking the elevator down one floor.
5. Taking the elevator up one floor.
6. Taking the elevator down two floors.
7. Taking the elevator up two floors.
8. Taking the elevator down two floors and then up two floors.
9. Taking the elevator down to the basement.
10. Taking the elevator up to the highest floor.
11. Taking the elevator all the way down and then all the way up.

Clients begin at step 1 and do not progress to step 2 until they are able to remain calm on the first. If they become bothered by anxiety, they remove themselves from the situation and regain calmness by muscle relaxation or focusing on soothing mental imagery. The encounter is then repeated as often as necessary to reach and sustain feelings of calmness. They then proceed to the next step, repeating the process.

Kevin was also trained to practice self-relaxation and talk calmly and rationally to himself to help himself remain calm during his exposure trials. Whenever he began to feel even slightly anxious, he would tell himself to calm down and relax. He was able to counter the disruptive belief that he was going to fall apart if he was trapped in an elevator with rational self-statements such as "Just relax. I may experience some anxiety, but it's nothing that I haven't been through before. In a few moments I'll feel relieved."

Kevin gradually overcame his phobia but still occasionally experienced some anxiety, which he interpreted as a reminder of his former phobia. He did not exaggerate the importance of these feelings. Now and then it dawned on him that an elevator he was servicing had once occasioned fear. One day following his treatment, Kevin was repairing an elevator which serviced a bank vault 100 feet underground. The experience of moving deeper and deeper underground aroused fear, but Kevin did not panic. He repeated to himself, "It's only a couple of seconds and I'll be out." By the time he took his second trip down, he was much calmer.

THE AUTHORS' FILES

Cognitive Techniques

Through his rational-emotive approach, Ellis might show people with social phobias how irrational needs for social approval and perfectionism engender unnecessary anxiety in social interactions. Lessening exaggerated needs for social approval of people with social phobias is apparently a key therapeutic factor (G. Butler, 1989). Through his cognitive-therapy methods, Beck might point out how cognitive errors such as dwelling on perceived weaknesses, catastrophizing disappointments, and anticipating failure in all social endeavors give rise to social fears and avoidance (A. T. Beck, Emery, & Greenberg, 1985).

Beck's cognitive therapy seeks to identify and correct dysfunctional or distorted beliefs. For example, people with social phobias might think no one at a party will want to talk with them and that they will wind up lonely and isolated for the rest of their lives (G. Butler, 1989). Cognitive therapists help clients recognize the logical flaws in their thinking and assist them in viewing situations rationally. Clients may be asked to gather evidence to test out their

Virtual Therapy

Virtual reality, the computer-generated simulated environment, has now become a therapeutic tool. By donning a specialized helmet and gloves that are connected to a computer, a person with a fear of heights, for example, can encounter frightening stimuli in this virtual world, such as riding a glass-enclosed elevator to the 49th floor, peering over a railing on a balcony on the 20th floor, or crossing a virtual Golden Gate Bridge (Goleman, 1995d; Steven, 1995). By a process of exposure to a series of increasingly more frightening virtual stimuli, while progressing only when fears at each preceding step diminish, people learn to overcome fears in much the same way they would had they followed a program of graduated exposure to phobic stimuli in real-life situations. The advantage of virtual reality is that it provides an opportunity to experience situations that might be difficult or impossible to arrange in reality. In order for virtual therapy to be effective, says psychologist Barbara Rothbaum, who found the technique to produce significant reductions in acrophobia in a recent controlled study (Rothbaum et al., 1995), the person must become immersed in the experience and believe at some level it is real and not like watching a videotape (cited in Goleman, 1995d). "If the first person had put the helmet on and said, 'This isn't scary,' it wouldn't have worked," Dr. Rothbaum said. "But you get the same physiological changes—the racing heart, the sweat—that you would in the actual place" (Goleman, 1995d, p. C11).

TRUTH *or* FICTION REVISITED

5.8 *True.* Virtual therapy has been used successfully in helping people overcome phobias, including fears of heights.

We have only begun to explore the potential therapeutic uses of this new technology. Therapists are experimenting with virtual therapy to help people overcome other types of fears, such as fear of public speaking and agoraphobia. It has been used as a form of group therapy in which a group of people who are actually in different places can don virtual reality gear, log on to their computers at the same time, and meet electronically in a simulated therapy office. The virtual group members can see simulated faces of each other and communicate by typing messages directed at the group at large or to individual members (Goleman, 1995d). In other applications, virtual therapy may help clients work through unresolved conflicts with significant figures in their lives by allowing them to confront these "people" in a virtual environment. A family therapist envisions virtual family sessions in which participants can see things from the emotional and physical vantage points of each other member of the family (Steven, 1995). Other potential uses of virtual therapy include treating people with depression, social phobias, and obsessive-compulsive disorder, children with attention-deficit disorders, adults with fears of intimacy or sexual aversion, and people who have problems controlling their anger or aggressive behavior (K. Glantz et al., 1996; Steven, 1995). Self-help "therapy" modules, consisting of compact disks and virtual reality helmets and gloves, may even begin to appear on the shelves of your neighborhood computer software store in the not-too-distant future. With these self-help modules, people may be able in their own living rooms to confront objects or situations they fear, or learn to stop smoking or lose weight, all with the

beliefs, which may lead them to alter beliefs they find are not grounded in reality. Therapists may encourage clients with social phobias to test their beliefs that they are bound to be ignored, rejected, or ridiculed by others in social gatherings by attending a party, initiating conversations, and monitoring other people's reactions. Therapists may also help clients develop social skills to improve their interpersonal effectiveness and teach them how to handle social rejection, if it should occur, without catastrophizing.

One example of cognitive techniques is **cognitive restructuring** (also called *rational restructuring*). This involves a process in which therapists help clients pinpoint their self-defeating thoughts and generate rational alternatives so they learn to cope with anxiety-provoking situations. Kevin learned to replace self-defeating thoughts with rational alter-

natives and to practice speaking rationally and calmly to himself during his exposure trials. Consider the case of Phyllis, who also suffered from an elevator phobia:

Phyllis, a 32-year-old writer and mother of two sons, had not been on an elevator in 16 years. Her life revolved around finding ways to avoid appointments and social events on high floors. She had suffered from fear of elevators since the age of 8, when she had been stuck between floors with her grandmother.

To help overcome her fear of elevators, Phyllis imagined herself getting stuck in an elevator and countering the self-defeating thoughts she might experience with rational statements. She closed her eyes and re-

help and guidance of a "virtual therapist." Virtual therapy has recently been successfully extended to fear of spiders (Carlin, Hoffman, & Weghorst, 1997) and to fear of flying, in which the virtual environment simulates the experience of sitting in an airplane during take-off and flight (Rothbaum, 1996).

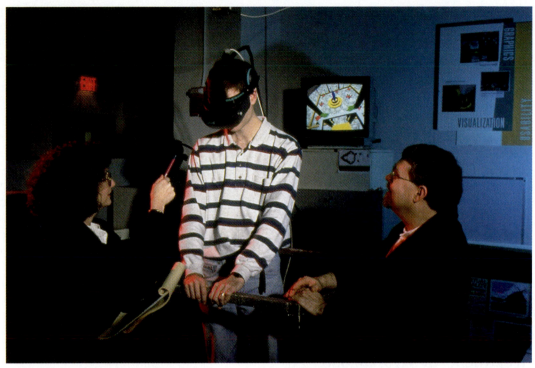

Overcoming fears with virtual reality. Virtual reality is now being used to help people overcome phobias. Using this technique, a person with a fear of heights, as pictured here, can learn to handle exposure to progressively more frightening stimuli presented in virtual reality. Hopefully, this learning will transfer to real-life exposure to such stimuli.

ported the thoughts that would come to mind. The psychologist encouraged her to create a rational counterpoint to each of them. She then repeated the exercise in imagination and practiced replacing the self-defeating thoughts with rational alternatives, as in the following examples:

Self-Defeating Thought	*Rational Alternative*
Oh, oh, I'm stuck. I'm going to lose control.	*Relax. Just think coolly, what do I have to do next?*
I can't take it. I'm going to pass out.	*Okay, practice your deep breathing. Help will be coming shortly.*
I'm having a panic attack. I can't stand it.	*You've experienced all these feelings before. Just let them pass through.*
If it takes hours, that would be horrible.	*That would be annoying, but it wouldn't necessarily be horrible. I've gotten stuck in traffic longer than that.*
I've got to get out of here.	*Stay calm. There's no real danger. I can just sit down and imagine I'm somewhere else until someone comes to help.*

THE AUTHORS' FILES

Behavioral Treatment of Social Phobia

Exposure has emerged as an effective form of treatment of social phobia as well as specific phobia (Barlow, Esler, & Vitali, 1998; DeRubeis & Crits-Christoph, 1998; Feske & Chambless, 1996; Gould et al., 1997; Scholing & Emmelkamp, 1996; Turner, 1996). In exposure therapy, clients are instructed to enter increasingly stressful social situations and to remain in those situations until the urge to escape has lessened. The therapist may help guide them during exposure trials, gradually withdrawing direct support so clients become capable of handling the situations on their own. Exposure treatment is often combined with cognitive techniques that assist clients in replacing maladaptive anxiety-inducing thoughts with more rational alternatives and with behavioral technique, such as social skills training, that helps them sharpen their conversational skills (Feske & Chambless, 1996; Gould et al., 1997). The gains achieved from cognitive-behavioral treatment of social phobia appear to be durable (Gould et al., 1997; Turner, 1996).

Flooding is a type of exposure therapy in which subjects are exposed to intensely anxiety-provoking situations. Why? The belief is that anxiety that has been conditioned to a phobic stimulus should extinguish if the individual remains in the phobic situation for a long enough period of time and nothing traumatic occurs. Typically the phobic individual either avoids the phobic stimulus or beats a hasty retreat at the first opportunity for escape. Thus, no opportunity for unlearning (extinguishing) the fear response occurs. In one example, 9 of 10 people with social phobia achieved at least moderate improvement through a flooding procedure in which they were directly exposed to highly anxiety-evoking situations, such as giving a talk before an expert audience (Turner, Beidel, & Jacob, 1994).

Behavioral Treatment of Agoraphobia

Evidence shows gradual exposure to fear-inducing stimuli to be more effective than control conditions in reducing avoidance behavior in people with agoraphobia (DeRubeis & Crits-Christoph, 1998; Mueser & Liberman, 1995). Treatment is stepwise and gradually exposes the phobic individual to increasingly fearful stimulus situations, such as walking through congested streets or shopping in department stores. A trusted companion or perhaps the therapist may accompany the person during the exposure trials. The eventual goal is for the person to be able to handle each situation alone and without discomfort or an urge to escape. Involving the spouse in treatment can provide social support and convert a spouse from a sideline critic into a helpmate (Fokias & Tyler, 1995). The benefits of gradual exposure are typically enduring. Overall, researchers find that about 6 in 10 people with agoraphobia show clinically meaningful improvement following exposure-based treatment (Jacobson, Wilson, & Tupper, 1988). Fewer than 1 in 3, however, are no longer agoraphobic by the end of treatment.

Behavioral Treatment of Posttraumatic Stress Disorder

Exposure therapy has achieved good results in reducing symptoms of PTSD in controlled studies (DeRubeis & Crits-Christoph, 1998; Foa & Meadows, 1997; Keane & Kaloupek, 1996; Keane, 1998). Exposure to cues associated with the trauma may involve talking about the trauma, reexperiencing the trauma in imagination, viewing related slides or films, or visiting the scene of the event. For combat-related PTSD, homework assignments may involve visiting war memorials or viewing war movies (Frueh et al., 1996). The person comes to gradually reexperience the traumatic event and accompanying anxiety in a safe setting that is free of negative consequences, which allows extinction to take its course. Exposure therapy is often supplemented with cognitive restructuring, which focuses on replacing dysfunctional thoughts with rational alternatives (I. Marks et al., 1998b). Training in stress management skills, such as self-relaxation, may help enhance the client's ability to cope with the troubling features of PTSD, such as heightened arousal and the desire to run away from trauma-related stimuli. Training in anger management skills may also be helpful, especially with combat veterans with PTSD (Frueh et al., 1996).

Behavioral Treatment of Obsessive-Compulsive Disorder

Behavior therapy has achieved impressive results in treating obsessive-compulsive disorder with a combination of exposure with response prevention within intensive, carefully monitored programs (Franklin & Foa, 1998; G. T. Wilson, 1997). Overall, about 4 of 5 people undergoing this therapy show significant improvement (Abramowitz, 1996; Foa, 1996; Fals-Stewart, Marks, & Schafer, 1993). Exposure involves purposefully placing oneself in situations that evoke obsessive thoughts. For many

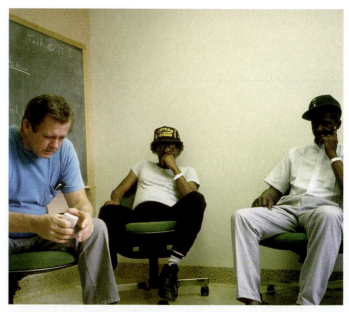

Counseling veterans with posttraumatic stress disorder. Storefront counseling centers have been established across the country to provide supportive services to combat veterans suffering from PTSD.

EMDR: A Fad or a Find?

A new and controversial technique has emerged in the treatment of PTSD—eye movement desensitization and reprocessing (EMDR) treatment (F. Shapiro, 1989, 1995). In EMDR, the client is asked to visualize an image associated with the trauma while the therapist rapidly moves a finger back and forth in front of the client's eyes for about 15 to 20 seconds. While holding the image in mind, the client is asked to move his or her eyes to follow the therapist's finger. The client then relates to the therapist the images, feelings, and thoughts that were experienced during the procedure. The procedure is then repeated until the client becomes desensitized to the emotional impact of this disturbing material. The technique remains controversial, largely because the reasons underlying its effectiveness are not understood. Some evidence exists supporting the therapeutic benefits of EMDR in treating PTSD (e.g., DeBell, & Jones, 1997a; R. Greenwald, 1996; Wilson, Becker, & Tinker, 1995, 1997) and of the extension of the technique to the treatment of panic disorder (Feske & Goldstein, 1997). Yet more research is needed to establish the efficacy of the technique for PTSD (Feske, 1998; Foa & Meadows, 1997; Keane, 1998). Questions also remain about whether the effects are due to the induction of rapid eye movements or, as seems possible, to the exposure component (imaginal presentation of the traumatic image) (DeRubeis & Crits-Christoph, 1998). EMDR may turn out to be just a novel way of conducting exposure-based therapy.

---

people, such situations are hard to avoid. Leaving the house, for example, can trigger obsessional thoughts about whether or not the gas jets are turned off or the windows and doors are locked. Response prevention involves the effort to physically prevent the compulsive behavior from occurring. Through exposure with response prevention, people with OCD learn to tolerate the anxiety triggered by their obsessive thoughts while they are prevented from performing their compulsive rituals. With repeated exposure, the anxiety eventually subsides and the person feels less compelled to perform the ritual. Extinction, or the weakening of the anxiety response following repeated presentation of the obsessional cues in the absence of any aversive consequences, is believed to underlie the treatment effect.

Consider the example of people with a germ obsession who feel compelled to repeatedly wash their hands. They may be instructed to dig in the dirt with their bare hands but are not permitted to wash immediately afterwards. Clients with checking rituals may be exposed to situations in which they experience checking urges, such as when leaving their homes, but are prevented from rechecking the appliances or the door lock. Exposure trials are usually structured in a hierarchy of increasingly stressful situations. In an early study, exposure and response prevention resulted in improvement in 65% to 75% of approximately 200 people with OCD (Steketee & Foa, 1985). Cognitive therapy is often combined with exposure therapy. The therapist focuses on helping the person correct cognitive distortions, such as tendencies to overestimate the likelihood and severity of feared consequences (Freeston et al., 1997).

Behavior therapy appears to be at least as effective as drug therapy (use of SSRI-type antidepressants) and may produce more lasting results (Rauch & Jenike, 1998; Stanley & Turner, 1995). Yet it remains to be seen whether a combination of drugs and behavior therapy is more effective than either approach alone (Franklin & Foa, 1998).

Behavioral therapy may also change brain function as well as behavior. A recent study of nine people with obsessive-compulsive disorder who received cognitive-behavioral therapy showed changes in their brain functioning, as measured by the PET scan (Goleman, 1996a; J. M. Schwartz et al., 1996). A part of the brain that is unusually active in persons with OCD showed a lessening of activity, the same kind of change seen when OCD is treated with the antidepressant Prozac.

Cognitive-Behavioral Treatment of Generalized Anxiety Cognitive-behavior therapists use a combination of techniques to treat generalized anxiety disorder, including relaxation training; substitution of adaptive thoughts for intrusive, anxiety-inducing thoughts; and de-catastrophizing (avoiding tendencies to think the worst). Cognitive-behavioral approaches have been shown to produce greater benefits than either control conditions or alternative therapies (Barlow, Esler, & Vitali, 1998; DeRubeis & Crits-Christoph, 1998; Newman & Borkovec, 1995).

Cognitive-Behavioral Therapy for Panic Disorder According to the cognitive model of panic, people who are susceptible to panic disorder are likely to overreact to changes in bodily sensations as signs that a catastrophe, perhaps a heart attack, is about to happen. By exaggerating the consequences of their physical sensations, panic sufferers set the stage for a vicious cycle in which anxiety spirals to the point that a full-blown panic attack ensues. Cognitive behavior therapists help them think differently about their bodily cues, such as passing sensations of dizziness or heart palpitations. Receiving corrective information that these sensations will subside naturally and are not signs of an impending catastrophe helps clients learn to cope with them without panicking (A. T. Beck et al., 1992; Salkovskis, Clark, & Hackmann, 1991). (Persons who complain of cardiovascular symptoms should also be evaluated medically to ensure they are physically healthy.) On a cognitive level, clients are taught to replace catastrophizing thoughts and self-statements ("I'm having a heart attack") with calming, rational alternatives ("Calm down. These are panicky feelings that will soon pass.").

Breathing retraining may also be used (Garssen, de Ruiter, & Van Dyck, 1992; Ley, 1991). This technique aims at restoring a normal level of carbon dioxide in the blood by having clients breathe slowly and deeply from the abdomen, so as to avoid the shallow, rapid breathing (hyperventilation) that leads to breathing off too much carbon dioxide (Garssen et al., 1992). In some treatment programs, people with panic disorder purposefully hyperventilate in the controlled setting of the treatment clinic in order to discover for themselves the relationship between breathing off too much carbon dioxide and cardiovascular sensations. Through these firsthand experiences, they learn to calm themselves down and cope with these sensations rather than overreacting. Some of the common elements of cognitive-behavioral therapy (CBT) for panic are shown in Table 5.6.

The efficacy of CBT in treating panic disorder is well established (for example, see Arntz & van den Hout, 1996; DeRubeis & Crits-Christoph, 1998; Jacobson & Hollon, 1996; S. Taylor et al., 1996; van Balkom et al., 1997;

Williams & Falbo, 1996). Investigators find that from about two thirds to about four fifths of panic patients treated with CBT become panic-free by the end of treatment (M. G. Newman et al., 1997; Wade, Treat, & Stuart, 1998). Despite the common belief that panic disorder is best treated with psychotherapeutic drugs, CBT appears to produce even better results than drug treatment with imipramine or benzodiazepines (Clum, Clum, & Surls, 1993; Gould, Otto, & Pollack, 1995). Treatment gains from CBT appear to be long-lasting (Barlow, 1994; Sharp et al., 1996).

CBT has emerged as the treatment of choice for panic disorder (Michelson & Marchione, 1991; Wilson, 1997). The treatment components in CBT for panic disorder include training in skills relating to handling panic attacks without catastrophizing, breathing retraining, exposure to bodily cues associated with panic, and training in relaxation. For panic disorder with agoraphobia, some form of gradual exposure to anxiety-evoking situations in real-life settings, perhaps assisted by the therapist, is usually advised and may even be critical to success (Michelson & Marchione, 1991; Michelson et al., 1996; van den Hout, Arntz, & Hoekstra, 1994). The effectiveness of cognitive-behavior therapy in some cases may be enhanced by the addition of antidepressant drugs (Sharp et al., 1996; van Balkom et al., 1997).

All in all, cognitive-behavioral techniques have been shown to be effective in treating various types of anxiety disorder (Chambless & Gillis, 1993; Barlow & Lehman, 1996). However, it is no panacea, as participants often improve to varying degrees but fall short of complete resolution of the problems that prompted treatment. More effective treatments may be needed, perhaps involving a combination of treatments tailored to the individual client.

In this chapter we have explored the diagnostic class of anxiety disorders. In the next chapter we examine dissociative and somatoform disorders, which have been historically linked to the anxiety disorders as neuroses.

TABLE 5.6

Elements of Cognitive-Behavioral Programs for Treatment of Panic Disorder

Self-Monitoring	Keeping a log of panic attacks to help determine situational stimuli that might trigger them.
Exposure	A program of gradual exposure to situations in which panic attacks have occurred. During exposure trials, the person engages in self-relaxation and rational self-talk to prevent anxiety from spiraling out of control. In some programs, participants learn to tolerate changes in bodily sensations associated with panic attacks by experiencing these sensations within a controlled setting of the treatment clinic. The person may be spun around in a chair to induce feelings of dizziness, learning in the process that such sensations are not dangerous or signs of imminent harm.
Development of Coping Responses	Developing coping skills to interrupt the vicious cycle in which overreactions to anxiety cues or cardiovascular sensations culminate in panic attacks. Behavioral methods focus on deep, regular breathing and relaxation training. Cognitive methods focus on modifying catastrophic misinterpretations of bodily sensations. Breathing retraining may be used to help the individual avoid hyperventilation during panic attacks.

Sources: Adapted from Craske, Brown & Barlow, 1991; Rapee, 1987; Turovsky & Barlow, 1995, and other sources.

A CLOSER LOOK

Coping with a Panic Attack

People who have panic attacks usually feel their hearts pounding such that they are overwhelmed and unable to cope. They typically feel an urge to flee the situation as quickly as possible. If escape is impossible, they may become immobilized and "freeze" until the attack dissipates. What can you do if you suffer a panic attack or an intense anxiety reaction? Let us suggest a few coping responses:

- Don't let your breathing get out of hand. Breathe slowly and deeply.
- Try breathing into a paper bag. The carbon dioxide in the bag may help you calm down by restoring a more optimal balance between oxygen and carbon dioxide.
- "Talk yourself down." Tell yourself to relax. Tell yourself you're not going to die. Tell yourself no matter how painful the attack is, it is likely to pass soon.

- Find someone to help you through the attack. Telephone someone you know and trust. Talk about anything at all until you regain control.
- Don't fall into the trap of making yourself housebound to avert future attacks.
- If you are uncertain as to whether or not sensations such as pain or tightness in the chest have physical causes, seek immediate medical assistance. Even if you suspect your attack may "only" be one of anxiety, it is safer to have a medical evaluation than to diagnose yourself.

You need not suffer recurrent panic attacks and fears about loss of control. If attacks are persistent or frightening, consult a professional. When in doubt, see a professional.

SUMMARY

Anxiety, a generalized sense of apprehension or fear, is normal and desirable under some conditions, but it can become abnormal when it is excessive or inappropriate. Anxiety may be experienced with a range of physical features, cognitions, and behaviors.

Historic Perspectives on Anxiety Disorders

Disorders involving anxiety were historically classified as neuroses, which were originally believed to be organic in nature. Psychodynamic theory posited that the origins of neurosis lie in psychological factors, that neuroses reflect the threat of the conscious emergence of repressed unacceptable impulses. Freud believed the different kinds of neuroses reflect the different ways in which the ego defends itself from anxiety. This etiological hypothesis united what we now conceptualize as anxiety, dissociative, and somatoform disorders as neuroses.

Panic Disorder

Panic disorder is characterized by repeated panic attacks, which involve intense physical features, notably cardiovascular symptoms, that may be accompanied by sheer terror and fears of losing control, losing one's mind, or dying. Etiological speculation focuses on biological causes or interactions between biological and cognitive factors. Panic attack sufferers often limit their outside activity in fear of recurrent attacks. This can lead to agoraphobia, the fear of venturing into public places.

Generalized Anxiety Disorder

Generalized anxiety disorder involves persistent anxiety that seems to be "free floating."

Phobic Disorders

Phobias are excessive irrational fears of specific objects or situations. Phobias involve a behavioral component, avoidance of the phobic stimulus, in addition to physical and cognitive features. Specific phobias are excessive fears of particular objects or situations, such as mice, spiders, tight places, or heights. Social phobia involves an intense fear of being judged negatively by others. Agoraphobia involves fears of venturing into public places. Agoraphobia may occur with or in the absence of panic disorder.

Obsessive-Compulsive Disorder

Obsessive-compulsive disorder involves recurrent patterns of obsessions, compulsions, or a combination of the two.

Obsessions are nagging, persistent thoughts that create anxiety and seem beyond the person's ability to control. Compulsions are apparently irresistible repetitious urges to perform certain behaviors, such as repeated elaborate washing after using the bathroom.

Acute and Posttraumatic Stress Disorders

In acute and posttraumatic stress disorders (PTSD), people develop stress reactions that follow exposure to traumatic events. Acute stress disorder occurs in the days and weeks following exposure to a traumatic event. Posttraumatic stress disorder persists for months or even years or decades after the traumatic experience and may not begin until months or years after the event.

Theoretical Perspectives

Psychodynamic theorists view anxiety disorders as attempts by the ego to control the conscious emergence of threatening impulses. Feelings of anxiety are warning signals that threatening impulses are nearing awareness. The ego mobilizes defense mechanisms to divert the impulses, thus leading to different anxiety disorders. Phobic objects symbolize aspects of unconscious conflicts, for example.

Learning theorists explain anxiety disorders through conditioning and observational learning. Mowrer's two-factor model incorporates classical and operant conditioning in the explanation of phobias. Phobias, however, appear to be moderated by cognitive factors, such as self-efficacy expectancies. The principles of reinforcement may help explain patterns of obsessive-compulsive behavior. People may be genetically predisposed to acquire certain types of phobias that may have had survival value for our prehistoric ancestors. Cognitive factors may also play a role in the anxiety disorders, such as overpredictions of fear, irrational beliefs, self-efficacy expectancies, self-defeating thoughts, and attributions for panic attacks.

Biological perspectives have sought explanations of anxiety disorders on the basis of studies of genetic factors, neurotransmitters, and the induction of panic by biological means.

Treatment of Anxiety Disorders

Each theoretical perspective is connected with methods of treating anxiety disorders. Traditional psychoanalysis helps people work through unconscious conflicts that are thought to underlie anxiety disorders. Modern psychodynamic approaches also focus on current disturbed relationships and encourage clients to assume more adaptive behavior patterns. The biological perspectives have spawned the development of various drugs to treat anxiety.

Learning perspectives encompass a broad range of behavioral and cognitive-behavioral techniques to help people overcome anxiety-related problems. Exposure methods help people with phobias overcome their fears through gradual exposure to the phobic stimuli. Cognitive restructuring helps clients pinpoint self-defeating thoughts and substitute rational alternatives. Obsessive-compulsive disorder is often treated with a combination of exposure and response prevention. Relaxation training is often used to help people with generalized anxiety learn skills of self-relaxation. Behavioral treatment of PTSD incorporates progressive exposure to trauma-related cues and training in stress management skills, such as self-relaxation.

Cognitive approaches, such as rational-emotive therapy and cognitive therapy, help people identify and correct cognitive errors that give rise to or maintain anxiety disorders. Cognitive-behavioral approaches to the treatment of panic disorder help people with a proneness to panic disorder learn to cope more effectively with cardiovascular and other bodily sensations.

1. What physical, psychological, and behavioral features are associated with anxiety?

2. Under what conditions is anxiety considered to be normal or abnormal?

3. What are the distinguishing features of each of the anxiety disorders discussed in the text?

4. How are anxiety disorders conceptualized within psychodynamic, humanistic-existential, biological, and learning-based perspectives?

5. What techniques are used to treat the specific types of anxiety disorders? What evidence exists to support their efficacy?

6. John has been experiencing sudden panic attacks on and off for the past few months. During the attacks, he has difficulty breathing and fears that his heart is racing out of control. His personal physician checked him out and told him the problem is with his nerves, not his heart. What treatment alternatives are available that might be of benefit to John?

© **Naoki Okamoto**
Untitled

Dissociative and Somatoform Disorders

TRUTH or FICTION?

6.1 Each personality in people with multiple personalities may have its own allergies and eyeglass prescriptions.

6.2 The term *split personality* refers to schizophrenia.

6.3 Very few of us have episodes of feeling detached from our bodies or thought processes.

6.4 Despite some sensationalistic cases in the media, the great majority of people with multiple personalities were not physically or sexually abused as children.

6.5 Some people who have lost their ability to see or move their legs become strangely indifferent toward their physical condition.

6.6 There was an epidemic in China in the 1980s affecting more than 2,000 people who fell prey to the belief that their genitals were shrinking and retracting into their bodies.

6.7 Some people show up repeatedly at hospital emergency rooms, feigning illness and seeking treatment for no apparent reason.

When you have completed your study of Chapter 6, you should be able to:

1. Distinguish the dissociative and somatoform disorders from the anxiety disorders in terms of the theorized role of anxiety and discuss historical changes in the classification of these diagnostic classes.

2. Describe the major features of dissociative identity disorder, dissociative amnesia, dissociative fugue, and depersonalization disorder.

3. Explain why inclusion of depersonalization disorder as a dissociative disorder generates controversy.

4. Discuss problems in differentiating dissociative disorders from malingering.

5. Recount various theoretical perspectives on the dissociative disorders.

6. Describe various methods for treating dissociative disorders.

7. Describe the features of conversion disorder, hypochondriasis, and somatization disorder.

8. Discuss theoretical perspectives on somatoform disorders.

9. Distinguish somatoform disorders from malingering.

10. Describe the features of Münchausen syndrome and theoretical accounts of its origins.

In the Middle Ages, the clergy exorcised the possessed to bring forth demons. Curious incantations were heard during the contests for victims' souls.

Curious phrasings were also heard recently in 20th-century Los Angeles. They were intended to evoke another sort of demon from Kenneth Bianchi, a suspect in a police inquest.

At one point, the question was put to Bianchi, "Part, are you the same thing as Ken or are you different?" The question was styled not by the clergy but by a police psychiatrist. The interviewee had been dubbed the "Hillside strangler" by the press. He had terrorized the city, leaving prostitutes dead in the mountains that bank the metropolis.

Under hypnosis—not religious incantations—Bianchi claimed that a hidden personality or "part" named "Steve" had committed the murders. "Ken" knew nothing of them. Bianchi claimed to be suffering from multiple personality disorder (now called dissociative identity disorder), one of the intriguing but perplexing diagnostic categories we explore in this chapter.

In Chapter 5, we reviewed the anxiety disorders, which were classified as neuroses in the first and second editions of the *Diagnostic and Statistical Manual* (DSM) and conceptualized according to the psychodynamic model. In this chapter, we focus on two classes of disorders, the dissociative and somatoform disorders, which were also categorized as neuroses in early editions of the DSM. They were related to anxiety in theory, however, not in terms of observable behavior. Unlike the other forms of neuroses, the role of anxiety in the dissociative and somatoform disorders was inferred rather than expressed in behavior. Persons with *dissociative disorders* may show no signs of overt anxiety. However, they manifest other psychological problems, such as loss of memory or changes in identity, that are theorized within the psychodynamic model to serve the purpose of keeping the underlying sources of anxiety out of awareness. Persons with *somatoform disorders* complain of physical symptoms that have no apparent organic basis. They often manifest a queer indifference to physical ailments that would concern most of us. Here, too, it is theorized the "symptoms" mask unconscious sources of anxiety. Some theorists interpret indifference to symptoms to mean there is an underlying benefit to them; that is, they help prevent anxiety from intruding into consciousness.

The DSM now separates the anxiety disorders from the other categories of neuroses—the dissociative and somatoform disorders—with which they were historically linked. Yet many practitioners continue to use the broad conceptualization of neuroses as a useful framework for classifying the anxiety, dissociative, and somatoform disorders.

DISSOCIATIVE DISORDERS

The key feature of the **dissociative disorders** is a change or disturbance in the functions of self-identity, memory, or consciousness that make the personality whole. Normally speaking, we know who we are. We may not be certain of ourselves in an existential, philosophical sense, but we know our names, where we live, and what we do for a living. We also tend to remember the salient events of our lives. We may not recall every detail, and we may confuse what we ate for dinner on Tuesday with what we had on Monday, but we generally know what we have been doing for the past days, weeks, and years. Normally speaking, there is a unity to consciousness that gives rise to a sense of self. We perceive ourselves as progressing through space and time. In the dissociative disorders, one or more of these aspects of daily living is disturbed—sometimes bizarrely so.

The major dissociative disorders include *dissociative identity disorder, dissociative amnesia, dissociative fugue,* and *depersonalization disorder.* In each case there is a disruption or dissociation ("splitting off") of the functions of identity, memory, or consciousness that normally make us whole. Reseachers estimate the prevalence of dissociative disorders in the general populations falls between 5% and 10% (C. A. Ross, Joshi, & Currie, 1990).

Dissociative Identity Disorder

The Ohio State campus dwelled in terror as four college women were seized, coerced to cash checks or get money from automatic teller machines, then raped. A cryptic phone call led to the capture of Billy Milligan, a 23-year-old drifter who had been dishonorably discharged from the Navy.

Billy wasn't quite the boy next door.

He tried twice to commit suicide while he was awaiting trial, so his lawyers requested a psychiatric evaluation. The psychologists and psychiatrists who examined Billy deduced that ten personalities dwelled inside of him. Eight were male and two were female. Billy's personality had been fractured by a brutal childhood. The personalities displayed diverse facial expressions, memories, and vocal patterns. They performed in dissimilar ways on personality and intelligence tests.

Arthur, a sensible but phlegmatic personality, conversed with a British accent. Danny, 14, was a painter of still lifes. Christopher, 13, was normal enough, but somewhat anxious. A 3-year-old English girl went by the name of Christine. Tommy, a 16-year-old, was an antisocial personality and escape artist. It was Tommy who had enlisted in the Navy. Allen was an 18-year-old con artist. Allen also smoked. Adelena was a 19-year-old introverted lesbian. It was she who had committed the rapes. It was probably David who had made the mysterious phone call. David was an anxious 9-year-old who wore the anguish of early childhood trauma on his sleeve. After his second suicide attempt, Billy had been placed in a straitjacket. When the guards checked his cell, however, he was sleeping with the straitjacket as a pillow. Tommy later explained that he had effected Billy's escape.

The defense argued that Billy was afflicted with multiple personality disorder. Several alternate personalities resided within him. The alternate personalities knew about Billy, but Billy was unaware of them. Billy, the core or dominant personality, had learned as a child that he could sleep as a way of avoiding the sexual and physical abuse of his father. A psychiatrist claimed that Billy had likewise been "asleep"—in a sort of "psychological coma"—when the crimes were committed. Therefore, Billy should be judged innocent by reason of insanity.

Billy was decreed not guilty by reason of insanity. He was committed to a mental institution. In the insti-

tution, 14 additional personalities emerged. Thirteen were rebellious and labeled "undesirables" by Arthur. The fourteenth was the "Teacher," who was competent and supposedly represented the integration of all the other personalities. Billy was released six years later.

ADAPTED FROM KEYES, 1982

Billy was adjudged to be suffering from multiple personality disorder, which is now called **dissociative identity disorder.** In dissociative identity disorder, sometimes referred to as "split personality," two or more personalities—each with well-defined traits and memories—"occupy" one person. They may or may not be aware of one another. Some case materials show various personalities may even show different EEG records, allergic reactions, responses to medication, and even different eyeglass prescriptions and pupil sizes (Birnbaum, Martin, & Thomann, 1997; S. D. Miller et al., 1991). Or one personality may be color blind, whereas others are not (Braun, 1986). If such patterns stand up to further scientific scrutiny, they would offer a remarkable illustration of the diversity of perceptions and somatic patterns that are possible within the same person.

TRUTH *or* FICTION REVISITED

6.1 *True.* Some evidence indicates that each personality in people with multiple personalities may have their own allergies and eyeglass prescriptions.

Celebrated cases of multiple personality have been depicted in the popular media. One became the subject of the film *The Three Faces of Eve.* In the film, Eve White is a timid housewife who harbors two other personalities: Eve Black, a libidinous antisocial personality; and Jane, a balanced, developing personality who could accept her primitive urges but still engage in socially appropriate behavior (see Figure 6.1). The three faces eventually merged into one—Jane, providing a "happy ending." In real life, however, Eve was Chris Sizemore. After Sizemore's personality was apparently integrated, it reportedly split into 22 subsequent personalities. A second well-known case is that of Sybil. Sybil was played by Sally Field in the film of the same name and reportedly had 16 personalities.

In one of the largest studies on multiple personality to date, Ross and his colleagues (1989) collected 236 case reports of people with the disorder from 203 health professionals in Canada. Unlike reports of multiple personality in the 19th and early 20th centuries, in which most cases involved dual personalities, cases in the Canadian sample averaged 15 to 16 alter personalities each (C. A. Ross, Norton, & Wozney, 1989).

There are many variations. Sometimes two personalities vie for control of the person. Sometimes there is one dominant or core personality and several subordinate personalities. Some of the more common alternate personalities (or "alter personalities") include children of various ages, including one whose emotions were shaped by parental

(A)   (B)   (C)

FIGURE 6.1 *The Three Faces of Eve.*
In the film *The Three Faces of Eve*, a timid housewife, Eve White (A), harbors two alter personalities: Eve Black (B), a libidinous antisocial personality; and Jane (C), an integrated personality who can accept her sexual and aggressive urges but still engage in socially appropriate behavior. In real life, however, the person depicted in the film reportedly split into 22 personalities later in life.

abuse; adolescents of the opposite gender; prostitutes; and gay males and lesbians. In the Canadian study of 236 cases of multiple personality, a child personality was present in 86% of cases, a personality of a different age in 85% of cases, a protector personality in 84%, and a persecutor personality, also in 84% of cases (Ross et al., 1989). Some of the personalities may appear psychotic.

All in all, the clusters of alter personalities serve as something of a microcosm of conflicting urges and cultural themes. Themes of sexual ambivalence and ambiguity are particularly common. It is as if conflicting internal impulses cannot coexist or achieve dominance. As a result, each is expressed as the cardinal or steering trait of an alternate personality. The clinician can sometimes elicit alternate personalities by inviting them to make themselves known, as in asking, "Is there another part of you that wants to say something to me?"

The case of Margaret illustrates the emergence of an alternate personality:

> *[Margaret explained that] she often "heard a voice telling her to say things and do things." It was, she said, "a terrible voice" that sometimes threatened to "take over completely." When it was finally suggested to [Margaret] that she let the voice "take over," she closed her eyes, clenched her fists, and grimaced for a few moments during which she was out of contact with those around her. Suddenly she opened her eyes and one was in the presence of another person. Her name, she said, was "Harriet." Whereas Margaret had been paralyzed,*

> *and complained of fatigue, headache and backache, Harriet felt well, and she at once proceeded to walk unaided around the interviewing room. She spoke scornfully of Margaret's religiousness, her invalidism, and her puritanical life, professing that she herself liked to drink and "go partying" but that Margaret was always going to church and reading the Bible. "But," she said impishly and proudly, "I make her miserable—I make her say and do things she doesn't want to." At length, at the interviewer's suggestion, Harriet reluctantly agreed to "bring Margaret back," and after more grimacing and fist clenching, Margaret reappeared, paralyzed, complaining of her headache and backache, and completely amnesiac for the brief period of Harriet's release from prison.*

> NEMIAH, 1978, PP. 179–180

As with Billy Milligan, Chris Sizemore, and Margaret, the dominant personality is often unaware of the existence of the alternate personalities. It thus seems that the mechanism of dissociation is controlled by unconscious processes. Although the dominant personality lacks insight into the existence of the other personalities, she or he may vaguely sense that something is amiss. There may even be "interpersonality rivalry" in which one personality aspires to do away with another, usually in blissful ignorance of the fact that conferring the *coup de grace* on an alternate would result in the death of all.

Although the majority of cases of multiple personality have involved women (Kluft, 1984a; Ross et al., 1989; D. W. Schafer, 1986), the proportion of males diagnosed with the disorder has been on the rise (Goff & Summs, 1993). The numbers of reported alternates has also been rising. During the 1980s, an average of 12 alternates was reported per case, as compared to an average of 3 in earlier cases. Women with the disorder tend to have more alternate identities, averaging 15 or more, than do men, who average about 8 identities (American Psychiatric Association [APA], 1994). The reasons for this difference remain unknown.

The diagnostic features of dissociative identity disorder are listed in Table 6.1.

Although multiple personality is generally considered to be rare, its prevalence and even its existence continues to be a topic of debate in the field. It is difficult to acquire reliable information about how frequently it occurs. The first case was reported in 1817 (Boor, 1982). Only a handful of cases worldwide were reported from 1920 to 1970, but since then the number of reported cases has skyrocketed into the thousands (Spanos, 1994). This has led some practitioners to suggest that multiple personality may be more common than was earlier believed (Bliss & Jeppsen, 1985; D. W. Schafer, 1986). Others, however, are not so sure. The DSM cautions that the disorder has lately become overdiagnosed in people who are highly suggestible (compliant with suggestions) (APA, 1994). Increased public attention paid to the disorder in recent years may also account for the perception that its prevalence is greater than was commonly believed.

The disorder does appear to be culture bound and largely restricted to North America (Spanos, 1994). Very few cases have been reported elsewhere, even in such Western countries as Great Britain and France. A recent survey in Japan failed to find even one case, and in Switzerland, 90% of the psychiatrists polled had never seen a case of the disorder (Modestin, 1992; Spanos, 1994). Even in North America, few psychologists and psychiatrists have ever encountered a case of multiple personality. Most cases of multiple personality are reported by a relatively small number of investigators and clinicians who are strong adherents to the belief in the disorder. Could it be they are helping to manufacture that which they are seeking?

TABLE 6.1

Diagnostic Features of Dissociative Identity Disorder (Formerly Multiple Personality Disorder)

1. At least two distinct personalities exist within the person, with each having a relatively enduring and distinct pattern of perceiving, thinking about, and relating to the environment and the self.

2. Two or more of these personalities repeatedly take complete control of the individual's behavior.

3. There is a failure to recall important personal information too substantial to be accounted for by ordinary forgetfulness.

4. The disorder cannot be accounted for by the effects of a psychoactive substance or a general medical condition.

Source: Adapted from the *DSM-IV* (APA, 1994).

Some leading authorities, such as the late psychologist Nicholas Spanos, believe so. Spanos and others have questioned the existence of dissociative identity (multiple personality) disorder (Reisner, 1994; Spanos, 1994). To Spanos, multiple personality is a form of role playing in which individuals come to construe themselves as having multiples selves and then act in accordance with this self-construction to the point that it becomes a reality to them. Perhaps their therapists or counselors, maybe unwittingly, plant the idea in their minds that their confusing welter of emotions and behaviors may represent different personalities at work. Therapists may also provide direct information or more subtle cues to clients about the features of multiple personality, enough so the client can convincingly enact the role.

Many reinforcers may become contingent on the enactment of the role of a multiple personality: Receiving attention from others and evading accountability for unacceptable behavior are two (Spanos, Weekes, & Bertrand, 1985). According to Nicholas Spanos and his colleagues (1985), films and TV shows such as *The Three Faces of Eve* and *Sybil* have given the public detailed examples of the behaviors that characterize multiple personalities. That is, people may learn how to enact the role of persons with the disorder by watching others enacting the role on television and in the movies.

This is not to suggest that people with multiple personalities are "faking" any more than it would be to suggest you are faking your behavior when you perform daily roles as student, spouse, or worker. You may enact the role of a student (e.g., sitting attentively in class, raising your hand when you wish to talk) because you have learned to organize your behavior according to the nature of the role and because you have been rewarded for doing so. People with multiple personalities may have come to identify so closely with the role that it becomes real for them.

In support of his belief that multiple personality represents a form of role playing, Spanos and his colleagues had shown that with proper cues, college students in a laboratory simulation of the Bianchi-type interrogation could easily enact a multiple personality role, even attributing the blame to an alternate personality for a murder they were accused of committing (Spanos et al., 1985). Perhaps the manner in which the Bianchi interrogation was conducted had cued Bianchi to enact the multiple personality role.

Relatively few cases of people with multiple personalities involve criminal behavior, in which enactment of the multiple personality role may be connected with clear expectations of gain. But even in more typical cases, there may be subtle incentives for enacting the role of a multiple personality. Such incentives include the therapist's expression of interest and excitement at the possibility of discovering a multiple personality. People who seek help for problems may be ready to accept their clinicians' interpretations of their distressing behavior patterns—even when unusual possibilities such as multiple personality are raised. People with multiple personalities were often highly imaginative during childhood. Accustomed to playing games of "make-believe," they may readily adopt alternate identities—especially if

Kenneth Bianchi, the so-called Hillside Strangler. Did the police psychiatrist who interviewed Bianchi suggest to him that he could role play a person with multiple personalities?

they learn how to enact the multiple personality role and there are external sources of validation—such as a clinician's interest and concern.

The social reinforcement model may help to explain why some clinicians seem to "discover" many more cases of multiple personality than others. These clinicians may be "multiple personality magnets." They may unknowingly cue clients to enact the multiple personality role and reinforce the performance with extra attention and concern. With the right set of cues, certain clients may adopt the role of a multiple personality to please their clinicians. The role-playing model has been challenged (e.g., Gleaves, 1996), and it remains to be seen how many cases of the disorder in clinical practice can be explained by the model.

Whether multiple personality is a real phenomenon or a form of role playing, there is no question that people who display this behavior have serious emotional and behavioral difficulties. Moreover, the diagnosis may not be all that unusual among some subgroups in the population, such as among psychiatric inpatients. In one study of 484 adult psychiatric inpatients, at least 5% showed evidence of multiple personality (C. A. Ross et al., 1991). Your authors have noted a tendency for *claims* of multiple personality to spread on inpatient units. In one case, Susan, a prostitute admitted for depression

and suicidal thoughts, claimed she could only exchange sex for money when "another person" inside her emerged and took control. (Suicidal behavior is common among people with multiple personalities. Seventy-two percent of the cases in the Canadian study [C. A. Ross et al., 1989] had attempted suicide, and about 2% had succeeded.) Upon hearing this, another woman, Ginny—a child abuser who had been admitted for depression after her daughter had been removed from her home by social services—later claimed that she only abused her daughter when another person inside of her assumed control of her personality. Susan's chart recommended that she be evaluated further for multiple personality disorder (the term used at the time to refer to the disorder), but Ginny was diagnosed with a depressive disorder and a personality disorder, not with multiple personality disorder.

Multiple personality, which often is called "split personality" by laypeople, should not be confused with schizophrenia. Schizophrenia (which comes from roots that mean "split brain") occurs much more commonly than multiple personality and involves the "splitting" of cognition, affect, and behavior. There may thus be little agreement between the thoughts and the emotions, or between the individual's perception of reality and what is truly happening. The person with schizophrenia may become giddy when told of disturbing events, or may experience hallucinations or delusions. In people with multiple personalities, the personality apparently divides into two or more personalities, but each of them usually shows more integrated functioning on cognitive, affective, and behavioral levels than is true of people with schizophrenia.

TRUTH *or* FICTION REVISITED

6.2 *False.* The term split personality refers to multiple personality, not schizophrenia.

Clouding the issue of diagnosis, however, is the finding that some people with multiple personalities also show behaviors associated with schizophrenia, such as auditory and visual hallucinations (Kluft, 1987). Although dissociative identity disorder is not considered a form of schizophrenia, the dominant personalities of people with the disorder may report auditory hallucinations such as two voices arguing about them. One of the voices may be threatening and the other protective. Another common auditory hallucination involves voices that provide a running commentary on the dominant personality's behavior, often derogatory. (The subordinate personalities typically comment on the dominant personality.) People with dissociative identity disorder also frequently present with coexisting mood disorders and other psychological disorders such as substance abuse disorders and personality disorders.

Some people with the disorder complain of being "possessed" but may be experiencing the influence of an alter personality. Many clinicians, however, are likely to take a claim of being possessed as a type of schizophrenic delusion. Perhaps more cases of dissociative identity disorder would be diagnosed if the competing diagnosis of schizophrenia were not so common (Putnam, Guroff, Silberman, Barban, & Post, 1986). Clinicians may also be reluctant to report a case of multiple personality for fear others might believe they had been duped by clients who faked their symptoms. Some clinicians have been accused of being in collusion with their clients to protect them from, say, criminal charges, by providing them with a basis for a pleading of "not guilty by reason of insanity."

Clinicians may also be reluctant to make a diagnosis of dissociative identity disorder because it is considered rare and its features can overlap those of other diagnoses. People with the disorder may thus go unrecognized or receive other diagnoses for years after their initial evaluations (D. W. Schafer, 1986). In a study of 100 persons with multiple personalities, the mean length of time between initial assessment and ultimate diagnosis of the disorder was nearly 7 years (Putnam et al., 1986). These people averaged 3.6 alternative diagnoses in the process. These alternative diagnoses may also reflect the finding that persons with multiple personalities display a wide range of abnormal behaviors, including physical complaints with no known organic basis; amnesia; depression and suicidal behavior; anxiety and panic attacks; and other disturbances in states of consciousness, such as depersonalization and **derealization** (Bliss, 1984).

Several features may alert the clinician to the possible presence of a multiple personality:

1. Amnesic periods ("blackouts") in the dominant personality (D. W. Schafer, 1986).
2. Severe physical or sexual abuse in childhood.
3. A stormy or turbulent history of psychiatric or psychological treatment (Schafer, 1986).
4. A nickname that does not fit the individual's dominant personality. Perhaps an alter personality is known by that name to others (Schafer, 1986).
5. High hypnotizability (ability to be hypnotized) and suggestibility to hypnotic suggestions (Bliss, 1984; Goff, 1993). Braun (1986) suggests that hypnotizability may be used as a diagnostic criterion when it is necessary to distinguish between various diagnostic possibilities.

Some persons with multiple personalities lead surprisingly accomplished lives, in fact. Three such cases, two physicians and a research scientist, were recently reported (Kluft, 1986). High-functioning people with multiple personalities often elude diagnosis because clinicians are not likely to probe for evidence of the disorder among functional clients. Accomplished people with multiple personalities also may have developed elaborate strategies to cloak their alter personalities. Sometimes alter personalities apparently cooperate with the effort to keep them out of the limelight. The careers of such individuals are stabilizing influences, and they may maintain a veneer of normality for fear of losing them.

Dissociative Amnesia

Dissociative amnesia is considered the most common type of dissociative disorder (Maldonado, Butler, & Speigel, 1998). *Amnesia* derives from the Greek roots *a-,* meaning "not," and *mnasthai,* meaning "to remember." In **dissociative amnesia** (formerly called *psychogenic amnesia*), the person becomes unable to recall important personal information usually involving material relating to traumatic or stressful experiences that cannot be accounted for by simple forgetfulness. Nor can the memory loss be attributed to a particular organic cause, such as a blow to the head or a particular medical condition, or to the direct effects of drugs or alcohol. Unlike some progressive forms of memory impairment (such as dementia associated with Alzheimer's disease; see Chapter 14), the memory loss in dissociative amnesia is reversible, although it may last for days, weeks, or even years. Recall of dissociated memories may occur gradually but often occurs suddenly and spontaneously, as when the soldier who has no recall of a battle for several days afterward suddenly recalls the experience after being transported to a hospital away from the battlefield.

There are five types of dissociative amnesia: localized, selective, generalized, continuous, and systematized (APA, 1994).

1. *Localized amnesia.* In this most common type of amnesia, events that occur during a specific time period are lost to memory. For example, the person cannot recall events for a number of hours or days after a stressful or traumatic incident, as in warfare or as in the case of the uninjured survivor of an accident.

2. *Selective amnesia.* In this form of amnesia, people forget only the disturbing particulars that take place during a certain time period. A person may recall the period of life during which he conducted an extramarital affair, but not the guilt-arousing affair itself. The soldier may recall most of the battle, but not the death of his buddy.

3. *Generalized amnesia.* In generalized amnesia, people forget their entire lives—who they are, what they do, where they live, whom they live with. This form of amnesia is rare, although you wouldn't think so if you watched daytime soap operas. Persons with generalized amnesia cannot recall personal information, but they tend to retain their habits, tastes, and skills. If you had generalized amnesia, you would still know how to read, although you would not recall your elementary school teachers. You would still prefer french fries to baked potatoes—or vice versa.

4. *Continuous amnesia.* In this form of amnesia, people forget all events that take place after the problem begins. Everything from that time through to the present is lost, and, of course, the present keeps moving ahead. If you had continuous amnesia since the time you began college, all of your college experiences would be lost to you. You would not be able to recall what you are reading; all new information would go in one ear and out the other. Continuous amnesia is a rare form of dissociative amnesia.

5. *Systematized amnesia.* A rare form of dissociative amnesia in which memories relating to specific categories of information are lost, such as memories of one's college experiences, family, or specific people in one's life. The person with systematized amnesia may have no memory of an ex-lover or spouse.

Although only one type of dissociative amnesia is labeled selective, most instances of amnesia are selective. That is, people usually forget events or periods of life that were traumatic—that generated strong negative emotions such as horror or guilt. Consider the case of Rutger:

> *He was brought to the emergency room of a hospital by a stranger. He was dazed and claimed not to know who he was or where he lived, and the stranger had found him wandering in the streets. Despite his confusion, it did not appear that he had been drinking or abusing drugs or that his amnesia could be attributed to physical trauma. After staying in the hospital for a few days, he awoke in distress. His memory had returned. His name was Rutger and he had urgent business to attend to. He wanted to know why he had been hospitalized and demanded to leave. At time of admission, Rutger appeared to be suffering from generalized amnesia: He could not recall his identity or the personal events of his life. But now that he was requesting discharge, Rutger showed localized amnesia for the period between entering the emergency room and the morning he regained his memory for prior events.*
>
> *Rutger provided information about the events prior to his hospitalization that was confirmed by the police. On the day when his amnesia began, Rutger had killed a pedestrian with his automobile. There had been witnesses, and the police had voiced the opinion that Rutger—although emotionally devastated—was blameless in the incident. Rutger was instructed, however, to fill out an accident report and to appear at the inquest. Still nonplussed, Rutger filled out the form at a friend's home. He accidentally left his wallet and his identification there. After placing the form in a mailbox, Rutger became dazed and lost his memory.*
>
> *Although Rutger was not responsible for the accident, he felt awful about the pedestrian's death. His amnesia was probably connected with feelings of guilt, the stress of the accident, and concerns about the inquest.*
>
> ADAPTED FROM CAMERON, 1963, PP. 355–356

People with dissociative amnesia seem less concerned about their memory problems than do their family, friends, and the people who are trying to help them. This relative lack of concern has inspired hypotheses that the memory loss serves the adaptive function of relieving anxiety or some other kind of psychological pain associated with past trauma. Sometimes the painful circumstances can be recalled under hypnosis.

People sometimes claim they cannot recall certain events of their lives: engaging in socially unacceptable behavior, making promises, and so forth. Falsely claiming amnesia as a way of escaping responsibility is **malingering**, an attempt to fabricate symptoms or make false claims for personal gain. Current research methods cannot guarantee that we can ferret out all people who engage in malingering. But experienced clinicians can make reasonably well-educated guesses.

Dissociative Fugue

Fugue derives from the Latin *fugere,* meaning "flight." The word *fugitive* has the same origin. Fugue is like amnesia "on the run." In **dissociative fugue** (formerly called *psychogenic fugue*), the person travels suddenly and unexpectedly from his or her home or place of work, is unable to recall past personal information, and either becomes confused about his or her identity or assumes a new identity (either partially or completely) (APA, 1994). Despite these odd behaviors, the person may appear "normal" and show no other signs of mental disturbance (Maldonado, Butler, & Speigel, 1998). The person may not think about the past, or may report a past filled with bogus memories that are not recognized as false.

Whereas people with amnesia appear to wander aimlessly, people in a fugue state act more purposefully. Some stick close to home. They spend the afternoon in the park or in a theater, or they spend the night at a hotel under another name, usually having little if any contact with others during the fugue state. But the new identity is incomplete and fleeting, and the individual's former sense of self soon returns in a matter of hours or a few days. Less common is a pattern in which the fugue state lasts for months or years and involves travel to distant cities or foreign lands and assumption of a new identity. These individuals may assume an identity that is more spontaneous and sociable than their former selves, which were typically "quiet" and "ordinary." They may establish new families and successful businesses. Although these events may sound rather bizarre, the fugue state is not considered psychotic because people with the disorder can think and behave quite normally—in their new lives, that is. Then one day, quite suddenly, their awareness of their past identity returns to them, and they are flooded with old memories. Now they typically do not recall the events that occurred during the fugue state. The new identity, the new life—including all its involvements and responsibilities—vanish from memory.

Fugue, like amnesia, is relatively rare and is believed to affect about 2 people in 1,000 among the general population (APA, 1994). It is most likely to occur in wartime (Loewenstein, 1991) or in the wake of another kind of disaster or extremely stressful event. The underlying notion is that dissociation in the fugue state protects one from traumatic memories or other sources of emotionally painful experiences or conflict (Maldonado, Butler, & Speigel, 1998).

Fugue can also be difficult to distinguish from malingering. That is, a number of persons who were dissatisfied with their former lives could claim to be amnesic when they are uncovered in their new locations and new identities.

Consider the following case, in which the evidence supports a diagnosis of dissociative fugue (Spitzer et al., 1994):

> *The man told the police that his name was Burt Tate. "Burt," a 42-year-old white male, had gotten into a fight at the diner where he worked. When the police arrived, they found that he carried no identification. He told them he had drifted into town a few weeks earlier, but could not recall where he had lived or worked before arriving in town. While no charges were pressed against him, the police prevailed upon him to come to the emergency room for evaluation. "Burt" knew the town he was in and the current date, and recognized that it was somewhat unusual that he couldn't remember his past, but didn't seem to be concerned about it. There was no evidence of any physical injuries or head trauma, or of drug or alcohol abuse. The police made some inquiries and discovered that "Burt" fit the profile of a missing person, Gene Saunders, who had disappeared a month earlier from a city some 2,000 miles away. Mrs. Saunders was called in and confirmed that "Burt" was indeed her husband. She reported that her husband, who had worked in middle-level management in a manufacturing company, had been having difficulty at work before his disappearance. He was passed over for promotion and his supervisor was highly critical of his work. The job stress apparently affected his behavior at home. Once easygoing and sociable, he withdrew into himself and began to criticize his wife and children. Then, just before his disappearance, he had a violent argument with his 18-year-old son. His son called him a "failure" and stormed out the door. Two days later, the man disappeared. When he came face to face with his wife again, he claimed he didn't recognize her, but appeared visibly nervous.*
>
> ADAPTED FROM SPITZER ET AL., 1994, PP. 254–255

Although the presenting evidence supported a diagnosis of dissociative fugue, clinicians can find it difficult to distinguish true amnesia from amnesia that is faked to allow a person to get a new start in life.

Depersonalization Disorder

Depersonalization involves a temporary loss or change in the usual sense of our own reality. In a state of depersonalization, people may feel detached from their minds or bodies. They may have the sense of living in a dream or a movie, or acting like a robot (Maldonado, Butler, & Speigel, 1998).

Derealization—a sense of unreality about the external world involving strange changes in perception of surroundings, or in the sense of the passage of time—may also be present. People and objects may seem to change in size or shape; they may sound different. All these feelings can be associated with feelings of anxiety, including dizziness and fears of going insane, or with depression.

Although these sensations are strange, people with depersonalization maintain contact with reality. They can distinguish reality from unreality, even during the depersonalization episode. In contrast to generalized amnesia and fugue, they know who they are. Their memories are intact and they know where they are—even if they do not like their present state. Feelings of depersonalization usually come on suddenly and fade gradually.

What is even more unusual about all this is that we have thus far described *only normal* feelings of depersonalization. According to the DSM, single brief episodes of depersonalization are experienced by about half of all adults, usually during times of extreme stress..

TRUTH *or* FICTION REVISITED

6.3 False. About half of all adults, according to the DSM, will at some time experience an episode in which they feel detached from their own bodies or mental processes.

Consider Richie's experience:

> *"We went to Orlando with the children after school let out. I had also been driving myself hard, and it was time to let go. We spent three days 'doing' Disneyworld, and it got to the point where we were all wearing shirts with mice and ducks on them and singing Disney songs like 'Yo ho, yo ho, a pirate's life for me.' On the third day I began to feel unreal and ill at ease while we were watching these middle-American Ivory-soap teenagers singing and dancing in front of Cinderella's Castle. The day was finally cooling down, but I broke into a sweat. I became shaky and dizzy and sat down on the cement next to the 4-year-old's stroller without giving [my wife] an explanation. There were strollers and kids and [adults'] legs all around me, and for some strange reason I became fixated on the pieces of popcorn strewn on the ground. All of a sudden it was like the people around me were all silly mechanical creatures, like the dolls in the 'It's a Small World' [exhibit] or the animals on the 'Jungle Cruise.' Things sort of seemed to slow down, the way they do when you've smoked marijuana, and there was this invisible wall of cotton between me and everyone else.*
>
> *"Then the concert was over and my wife was like 'What's the matter?' and did I want to stay for the Electrical Parade and the fireworks or was I sick? Now I was beginning to wonder if I was going crazy and I said I was sick, that my wife would have to take me by the hand and drive us back to the Sonesta Village [motel]. Somehow we got back to the monorail and turned in the strollers. I waited in the herd [of people] at the station like a dead person, my eyes glazed over, looking out over kids with Mickey Mouse ears and Mickey Mouse balloons. The mechanical voice on the monorail almost did me in and I got really shaky.*
>
> *"I refused to go back to the Magic Kingdom. I went with the family to Sea World, and on another day I*

Depersonalization. Episodes of depersonalization are characterized by feelings of detachment from oneself. During an episode, it may feel as if one were walking through a dream or observing the environment or oneself from outside one's body.

dropped [my wife] and the kids off at the Magic Kingdom and picked them up that night. My wife thought I was goldbricking or something, and we had a helluva fight about it, but we had a life to get back to and my sanity had to come first."

THE AUTHORS' FILES

Richie's depersonalization experience was limited to the one episode and would not qualify for a diagnosis of **depersonalization disorder**. Depersonalization disorder is diagnosed only when such experiences are persistent or recurrent and cause marked distress (M. Steinberg, 1991). The DSM diagnoses depersonalization disorder according

---

TABLE 6.2

Diagnostic Features of Depersonalization Disorder

1. Recurrent or persistent experiences of depersonalization, which are characterized by feelings of detachment from one's mental processes or body, as if one were an outside observer of oneself. The experience may have a dreamlike quality.

2. The individual is able to maintain reality testing (i.e., distinguish reality from unreality) during the depersonalization state.

3. The depersonalization experiences cause significant personal distress or impairment in one or more important areas of functioning, such as social or occupational functioning.

4. Depersonalization experiences cannot be attributed to other disorders or to the direct effects of drugs, alcohol, or medical conditions.

Source: Adapted from the *DSM-IV* (APA, 1994).

---

to the criteria shown in Table 6.2. Note the following case example:

A 20-year-old college student feared that he was going insane. For two years, he had increasingly frequent experiences of feeling "outside" himself. During these episodes, he experienced a sense of "deadness" in his body, and felt wobbly, frequently bumping into furniture. He was more apt to lose his balance during episodes which occurred when he was out in public, especially when he was feeling anxious. During these episodes, his thoughts seemed "foggy," reminding him of his state of mind when he was given shots of a painkilling drug for an appendectomy five years earlier. He tried to fight off these episodes when they occurred, by saying "stop" to himself and by shaking his head. This would temporarily clear his head, but the feeling of being outside himself and the sense of deadness would shortly return. The disturbing feelings would gradually fade away over a period of hours. By the time he sought treatment, he was experiencing these episodes about twice a week, each one lasting from three to four hours. His grades remained unimpaired, and had even improved in the past several months, since he was spending more time studying. However, his girlfriend, in whom he had confided his problem, felt that he had become totally absorbed in himself and threatened to break off their relationship if he didn't change. She had also begun to date other men.

ADAPTED FROM SPITZER ET AL., 1994, PP. 270–271

Inclusion of depersonalization disorder as a dissociative disorder is controversial. One reason is that in contrast to the other three major dissociative disorders, there is no disturbance in memory. Another is that in multiple personality, amnesia, and fugue, dissociation seems to *protect* the individual from anxiety. In depersonalization, however, dissociation—and the resultant sense that things are unreal—frequently *generates* anxiety. Note, too, that depersonalization involves some cardiovascular sensations (e.g., dizziness) that can be blown out of proportion and generate further cycles of anxiety. Richie, for example, was motivated to avoid another visit to the Magic Kingdom at Disneyworld. He also arranged to be elsewhere when the children watched the Disney Channel.

In terms of observable behavior and associated features, depersonalization may be more closely related to disorders such as phobias and panic than to dissociative disorders. Unlike other forms of dissociative disorders that seem to protect the self from anxiety, depersonalization can lead to anxiety and in turn to avoidance behavior, as we saw in the case of Richie. For now, depersonalization disorder remains grouped with the other dissociative disorders, although it may involve different causal pathways. Depersonalization disorder tends to follow a chronic course and is associated with significant distress and problems in interpersonal functioning.

Theoretical Perspectives

The dissociative disorders are fascinating and perplexing phenomena. How can one's sense of personal identity become so distorted that one develops multiple personalities, blots out large chunks of personal memory, or develops a new self-identity? Though these disorders remain in many ways mysterious, clues have emerged that provide insights into their origins.

Psychodynamic theorists believe that dissociative disorders involve the massive use of repression, which leads to the "splitting off" from consciousness of unacceptable impulses and painful memories. In dissociative amnesia and fugue, the ego protects itself from becoming flooded with anxiety by blotting out disturbing memories or dissociating threatening impulses. In multiple personality, people may express unacceptable impulses through alternate personalities. In depersonalization, people stand outside themselves—safely distanced from the turmoil within.

Learning and cognitive theorists view dissociation as a learned response that involves *not thinking* about disturbing acts or thoughts in order to avoid feelings of guilt and shame evoked by such experiences. The habit of *not thinking about these matters* is negatively reinforced by relief from anxiety or by removal of feelings of guilt or shame. Some social learning theorists, including the late Nicholas Spanos, believe that dissociative identity disorder is a form of role playing that is acquired by means of observational learning and reinforcement. This is not quite the same as pretending or malingering; people can honestly come to organize their behavior patterns according to particular roles they have observed. They might also become so absorbed in role playing that they "forget" they are enacting a role.

 TYING IT TOGETHER: TRAUMA AND DISSOCIATIVE DISORDERS

There is compelling evidence that exposure to childhood trauma, usually by a relative or caretaker, is involved in the development of dissociative disorders, especially dissociative identity disorder. The great majority of people with multiple personalities report being physically or sexually abused as children (Coons, 1994; D. O. Lewis et al., 1997; Scroppo, Drob, Weinberger, & Eagle, 1998; Weaver & Clum, 1995). In one sample, 83% of people with dissociative identity disorder reported a history of childhood sexual abuse and 2 of 3 reported both physical and sexual abuse (Putnam et al., 1986). In other samples, rates of childhood physical or sexual abuse ranged from 76% to 95% of cases (Ross et al., 1990; Scroppo et al., 1998). Evidence of cross-cultural similarity comes from a study in Turkey, which showed that more than 3 of 4 of 35 dissociative identity disorder patients reported sexual or physical abuse in childhood (Sar et al., 1996). Traumatic abuse in childhood is also reported more often in cases of dissociative amnesia and depersonalization disorder than in control groups (Coons, Bowman, & Pellow, 1989; Simeon et al., 1997).

TRUTH or FICTION REVISITED

6.4 False. The great majority of people with multiple personalities do in fact report being physically or sexually abused as children.

Childhood abuse is not the only source of trauma linked to dissociative disorders. Exposure to the trauma of warfare among both civilians and soldiers plays a part in dissociative fugue and dissociative amnesia in some cases. In fugue, the stress of combat and the secondary gain of leaving the battlefield seem to be important contributors (Loewenstein, 1991). The stress of coping with severe financial problems and the wish to avert punishment for socially unacceptable behavior are other possible antecedents to episodes of fugue (Riether & Stoudemire, 1988). Exposure to high levels of stress may also be linked to depersonalization disorder (Kluft, 1988).

The most widely held view of dissociative identity disorder is that it represents a means of coping with and surviving childhood abuse (J. B. Murray, 1994a; Ross et al., 1990). Some severely abused children may retreat into alter personalities as a psychological defense against unbearable abuse. The construction of alter personalities allows these children to psychologically escape or distance themselves from their suffering. In the face of repeated abuse, these alter personalities may become stabilized, making it difficult for the person to maintain a unified personality. In adulthood, people with multiple personalities may use their alter personalities to block out traumatic childhood memories and their emotional reactions to them—wiping the slate clean and beginning life anew in the guise of alter personalities

The Dissociative Experiences Scale

Many of us experience brief dissociative experiences from time to time, such as transient feelings of depersonalization. Recently, researchers randomly sampled 1,055 adults in Winnipeg, Canada, and found that dissociative experiences were quite common in the general population, although they tended to decline with age (C. A. Ross et al., 1990). Dissociative disorders, by comparison, involve the occurrence of more persistent and severe dissociative experiences. Other researchers have developed a measure, the Dissociative Experiences Scale (DES), to offer clinicians a way of measuring dissociative experiences that occur in both the general population and among people with dissociative disorders (E. M. Bernstein & Putnam, 1986; Putnam & Carlson, 1994; B. Sanders & Green, 1995; Sar et al., 1996). Fleeting dissociative experiences are quite common, but those reported by people with dissociative disorders are more frequent and problematic than those in the general population (Waller & Ross, 1997).

The following is a listing of some of the types of dissociative experiences drawn from the DES that many people encounter from time to time. Bear in mind that transient experiences like these are reported by both normal and abnormal groups in varying frequencies. Let us also suggest that if these experiences become persistent or commonplace, or cause you concern or distress, then it might be worthwhile to discuss them with a professional.

Have You Ever Experienced the Following?

1. Suddenly realizing, when you are driving the car, that you don't remember what has happened during all or part of the trip.
2. Suddenly realizing, when you are listening to someone talk, that you did not hear part or all of what the person said.
3. Finding yourself in a place and having no idea how you got there.
4. Finding yourself dressed in clothes that you don't remember putting on.
5. Experiencing a feeling that seemed as if you were standing next to yourself or watching yourself do something and actually seeing yourself as if you were looking at another person.
6. Looking in a mirror and not recognizing yourself.
7. Feeling sometimes that other people, objects, and the world around you are not real.
8. Remembering a past event so vividly that it seems like you are reliving it in the present.
9. Having the experience of being in a familiar place but finding it strange and unfamiliar.
10. Becoming so absorbed in watching television or a movie that you are unaware of other events happening around you.
11. Becoming so absorbed in a fantasy or daydream that it feels as though it were really happening to you.
12. Talking out loud to yourself when you are alone.
13. Finding that you act so differently in a particular situation compared with another that it feels almost as if you were two different people.
14. Finding that you cannot remember whether or not you have just done something or perhaps had just thought about doing it (for example, not knowing whether you have just mailed a letter or have just thought about mailing it).
15. Feeling sometimes as if you were looking at the world through a fog such that people and objects appear faraway or unclear.

Source: Bernstein, E. M., & Putnam, F. W. (1986). Development, reliability, and validity of a dissociation scale. *Journal of Nervous and Mental Disease, 174,* 727–735. Copyright © Williams & Wilkins, 1986.

(D. W. Schafer, 1986). The alter identities or personalities may also serve as a way of coping with stressful situations or of expressing deep-seated resentments that the individual is unable to integrate within his or her primary personality (Spanos, 1994).

Dissociative Identity Disorder—A Diathesis-Stress Model Despite widespread evidence of childhood trauma in cases of dissociative identity disorder, only a precious few abused children develop multiple personalities, even among those who suffer severe abuse. Consistent with the *diathesis-stress model,* certain personality traits, such as fantasy proneness, high hypnotizability, and openness to altered states of consciousness, may predispose individuals to develop dissociative experiences in the face of extreme stress in the form of traumatic abuse. These traits themselves do not lead to dissociative disorders (Rauschenberger & Lynn, 1995). They are actually quite common in the population. However, they may increase the risk that people who experience severe trauma will develop dissociative phenomena as a

Imaginary Friends? Like the child in the photo, it is normal for children to have imaginary playmates. In the case of many multiple personalities, however, games of "make believe" and the invention of imaginary play-mates may be used as psychological defenses against abuse. Research suggests that most people who de-velop multiple personalities were abused as children.

survival mechanism (L. D. Butler et al., 1996). People who are low in hypnotizability or fantasy proneness may experi-ence the kinds of anxious, intrusive thoughts characteristic of posttraumatic stress disorder (PTSD), rather than dissocia-tive experiences (Kirmayer, Robbins, & Paris, 1994).

People with multiple personalities typically showed evi-dence of a rich fantasy life in childhood, including inventing imaginary playmates (Spanos et al., 1985). Adults with mul-tiple personalities are found to be highly hypnotizable, which suggests they possess a knack for disconnecting or dissociating various aspects of consciousness from others (Bliss, 1984; Wilbur, 1986). Perhaps exposure to childhood trauma produces a hypnotic state in susceptible individuals that leads to the development of alter personalities (Braun, 1990). There may also be a link between self-hypnosis and multiple personality. People who exhibit multiple personali-ties may be hypnotizing themselves into trancelike states when they enact their alter personalities (Bliss, 1984).

Because of their dissociative capacities, people who de-velop multiple personalities may handle the intense anger and hatred generated by abuse by forming alter personalities to express their negative feelings. The core or dominant per-sonality thus finds it easier to keep such feelings repressed, easing the burden of the ego to censor them. Wilbur (1986) notes that sometimes during therapy, an angry, violent subor-dinate personality may emerge who threatens or attacks the analyst. Persons with multiple personalities may also have phobic reactions to stimuli that are connected with early traumatic experiences. Alter personalities may emerge who can confront and manage these phobic objects and situations.

Kluft (1984b) accounts for the development of multiple personality through four integrated factors:

- *Factor 1:* The internal capacity to dissociate from one's surroundings. This capacity may be genetic in origin.

- *Factor 2:* The occurrence of overwhelming trauma, such as physical or sexual abuse perpetrated by a par-ent, which prompts the use of dissociation as a defense mechanism. Braun (1986) notes that abused children are generally placed in a bind because they are discour-aged from discussing the abuse both by the perpetrator and by the other parent, who usually does not want to hear about it.

- *Factor 3:* The development of the personality around an imaginary companion, ego states, or other such phe-nomena, which prevents the personality from achiev-ing a cohesive self.

- *Factor 4:* The failure of other people to protect the child from further trauma or to provide nurturance that might help the child endure the trauma and develop normally. For example, a daughter who tells her mother that her father is sexually abusing her may be accused of lying and told she is bad for making such outlandish accusations. The child may adapt to this bind by adopting two conflicting personalities—the dependent child who is eager to please, and the hostile, noncom-pliant child (Braun, 1986).

Some cases of multiple personality may involve role-playing. The role of the "multiple personality" is learned from enactments in books, films, or on TV. It may be subtly encouraged or reinforced by therapists. Over time, the person may become so identified with playing these "multiples" that they become incorporated as alternate identities.

Despite its rarity, much theoretical attention has been paid to multiple personality—partly because the phenomenon is fascinating, partly because it serves as a sort of inspiration to theorists of various persuasions. Early theoretical work by Janet (1889) and M. Prince (1906) outlined psychological mechanisms believed responsible for splitting the personality. They also connected the fracturing of consciousness with childhood trauma.

Perhaps most of us can divide our consciousness so we become unaware of—at least temporarily—those events we normally focus on. Perhaps most of us can thrust the unpleasant from our minds and enact various roles—parent, child, lover, businessperson, soldier—that help us meet the requirements of our situations. Perhaps the marvel is *not* that attention can be splintered but that human consciousness is normally integrated into a meaningful whole.

Treatment of Dissociative Disorders

Dissociative amnesia and fugue are usually transient and terminate abruptly. Episodes of depersonalization can be recurrent and persistent, and they are most likely to occur when people are undergoing periods of mild anxiety or depression. In such cases, clinicians usually focus on managing the anxiety or the depression.

We lack systematic, controlled studies of treatment approaches to dissociative amnesia, dissociative identity disorder, and depersonalization disorder (Maldonado, Butler, & Speigel, 1998). Nonetheless, theorists and clinicians have developed some interesting approaches to treatment of these disorders, especially dissociative identity disorder, which is the focus of this section.

Psychodynamic Approaches Traditional psychoanalysis aims at helping people with dissociative identity disorder uncover and learn to cope with early childhood traumas. Wilbur (1986) offers some variations on the theme in her discussion of the psychoanalytic treatment of people with multiple personalities.

First, Wilbur points out that the analyst can work with whatever personality is in ascendance during the therapy session. Any and all personalities can be asked to talk about their memories and dreams as best they can. Any and all personalities can be assured the therapist will help them make sense of their anxieties and to safely "relive" traumatic experiences so they can be made conscious and they can free the psychic energy trapped by them. Wilbur enjoins therapists to keep in mind that anxiety experienced during a therapy session may lead to a switch in personalities because alternate personalities were presumably developed as a means to cope with intense anxiety. Eventually, however, sufficient early experience may be brought to light so that reintegration of the personality becomes possible.

Wilbur describes the formation of another treatment goal in the case of a woman with a multiple personality:

A 45-year-old woman had suffered from a multiple personality disorder throughout her life. Her dominant personality was timid and self-conscious, rather reticent about herself. But soon after she entered treatment, a group of "little ones" emerged, who cried profusely. The therapist asked to speak with someone in the personality system who could clarify the personalities that were present. It turned out that they included several children, all of whom were under 9 years of age and had suffered severe, painful sexual abuse at the hands of an uncle, a great-aunt, and a grandmother. The great-aunt was a lesbian with several voyeuristic lesbian friends. They would watch the sexual abuse, generating fear, pain, rage, humiliation, and shame.

It was essential in therapy for the "children" to come to understand that they should not feel ashamed because they had been helpless to resist the abuse.

ADAPTED FROM WILBUR, 1986, PP. 138–139

Reports of the effectiveness of psychoanalytic psychotherapy or of other forms of treatment, such as behavior therapy, rely on uncontrolled case studies. Controlled studies of treatments of dissociative identity disorder have yet to be reported (Maldonado, Butler, & Spiegel, 1998). The relative infrequency of the disorder has hampered efforts to conduct controlled experiments that compare different forms of treatment with each other and with control groups.

In one example of the case study approach, Coons (1986) followed 20 "multiples" aged from 14 to 47 at time of intake for an average of $3\frac{1}{4}$ years. They were treated primarily by means of psychoanalytically oriented psychotherapy and hypnosis. Only five of the subjects showed a complete reintegration of their personalities. Therapy was reportedly hampered by continuation of mechanisms of repression and denial and the use of secrecy, a pattern that had begun during childhood. Reflecting the difficulties in working therapeutically with such clients, therapists often reported feelings of anger, emotional exhaustion, and exasperation. Other therapists find significant symptom improvement in measures of dissociative symptoms and depressive symptoms in treated patients, even in those who failed to achieve integration. However, greater symptom improvement was reported for those who achieved integration (Ellason & Ross, 1997).

Biological Approaches No drugs have been developed to integrate alter personalities. However, persons with multiple personalities frequently suffer from depression, anxiety, and other problems that may be treated with drugs such as antidepressants and antianxiety agents. Drugs tend to be most readily prescribed when the different personalities "agree" in the problems they present—whether anxiety, depression, or other problems (Barkin, Braun, & Kluft,

The Recovered Memory Controversy

A business executive's comfortable life fell apart one day when his 19-year-old daughter accused him of having repeatedly molested her throughout her childhood. The man lost his marriage as well as his $400,000-a-year job as a wine executive. But he fought back against the allegations, which he insisted were untrue. He sued his daughter's therapists who had assisted her in recovering these memories. A jury sided with him, awarding him $500,000 in damages from the two therapists.

This case is but one of many involving allegations made by adults who claim to have only recently become aware of memories of being sexually abused during childhood. Hundreds of people throughout the country have been brought to trial on the basis of recovered memories of childhood abuse, with many of these cases resulting in convictions and long jail sentences, even in the absence of any corroborating evidence. Recovered memories of sexual abuse in childhood often occur following suggestive probing by a therapist or hypnotist (Loftus, 1993; Loftus & Ketcham, 1994). The issue of recovered memories continues to be debated in psychology and the broader community. At the heart of the debate is the question, "Are recovered memories believable?" No one doubts that child sexual abuse is a major problem confronting our society. But should recovered memories be taken at face value?

Several lines of evidence lead us to question the validity of recovered memories. Experiments have shown that under some circumstances people who are given plausible but false information about their childhoods may come to believe the information is true (Loftus, 1996; Loftus & Ketcham, 1994). Moreover, while people who have experienced actual abuse in childhood may be somewhat sketchy on the details, total amnesia concerning the trauma is rare (H. Wakefield & Underwager, 1996). A leading memory expert, psychologist Elizabeth Loftus (1996, p. 356), writes of the dangers of taking recovered memories at face value:

> After developing false memories, innumerable "patients" have torn their families apart, and more than a few innocent people have been sent to prison. . . This is not to say that people cannot forget horrible things that have happened to them; most certainly they can. But there is virtually no support for the idea that clients presenting for therapy routinely have extensive histories of abuse of which they are completely unaware, and that they can be helped only if the alleged abuse is resurrected from their unconscious.

Should we conclude, then, that recovered memories are bogus? Not necessarily. It is possible for people in adulthood to recover memories of childhood (Melchert, 1996), perhaps even memories of abuse. Some recovered memories may be true; others may not be (L. S. Brown, 1997; Reisner, 1996; Rubin, 1996; Scheflin & Brown, 1996). Unfortunately we don't have the tools to distinguish the true memory from the false one (Loftus, 1993).

We shouldn't think of the brain as a kind of mental camera that stores snapshots of events as they actually happened in the form of memories. Memory is more of a reconstructive process in which bits of information are pieced together in a way that can sometimes lead to a distorted version of events, even though the person may be convinced the memory is accurate.

1986). Some evidence exists showing selective serotonin-reuptake inhibitors such as Prozac to have some modest benefits in treating depersonalization disorder (Simeon et al., 1997). However, more research is needed to investigate biological approaches that may help clinicians foster integration of the various personalities.

Behavioral Approaches   Behavioral techniques have been applied to the treatment of people with multiple personalities. Here as well, we are limited to the isolated case study. Kohlenberg (1973), for example, reported a case in which token reinforcers (poker chips that could be exchanged for tangible rewards) were used to increase the frequency of response of the best adjusted of three alternate personalities in a 51-year-old institutionalized person. Any time the preferred personality emitted a response, the subject earned a token and a pat on the hand. During reinforced trials, the preferred personality "appeared" significantly more often. During extinction trials, however, when reinforcement was withheld, the preferred personality dropped to a response level below the original baseline, and alternate personalities spent more time out in the open.

Kohlenberg concluded that multiple personality is a learned response pattern whose performance is connected with reinforcement contingencies. In the case of multiple personality, as noted by Spanos and his colleagues (1985), reinforcement can take the form of extra attention from therapists who consider cases of multiple personality to be glamorous and exotic. There is too little evidence to conclude that people with multiple personalities will generally

The Truth Is out There

The *X-Files* was one of television's most popular shows during the 1990s. It featured two FBI agents, Fox Mulder and Dana Scully, who were charged with investigating mysterious phenomena. One of the running themes in the show was the belief in alien abductions. The show picked up on the claims of hundreds or thousands of real people who said they had been abducted by space aliens. Though details of alien abductions vary, they usually involve reports of being spirited away to an alien spaceship, whereupon various medical procedures or experiments are performed on them before they are returned to Earth. What are we to make of these reports? Some reports may be fabrications, concocted for publicity or in hopes of achieving fame or securing a lucrative Hollywood contract for their stories. Yet many of these claims are difficult to ascribe to either lying or insanity (L. S. Newman & Baumeister 1996).

These reports have not been subjected to formal scientific study, so our beliefs about them rest largely on theoretical speculation. Some psychologists view them as false memories derived from sleep-related hallucinations or nightmares that are pieced together under hypnosis and reinforced by a popular culture that gives credence to alien sightings (S. E. Clark & Loftus, 1996; L. S. Newman & Baumeister, 1996). Memory is a reconstructive process, not a photographic rendering of events. A number of experiments have shown that under the right circumstances people can be led to believe that they experienced events which did not actually take place (S. E. Clark & Loftus, 1996). Hypnosis is believed to play a part, as memories of alien abductions often develop after hypnosis (Orne et al., 1996). However, we cannot simply ascribe memories of alien abductions to effects of hypnotic suggestion on reconstructed memories. Hypnosis doesn't play a part in many cases; in still others, hypnosis was used to fill in some details after the person made a report of an alien abduction (R. L. Hall, 1996).

Others suggest that memories of alien abductions are individual delusions—false but strongly held beliefs that anyone can develop in the attempt to explain unusual events that happen to them (Banaji & Kihlstrom, 1996). Other avenues of speculation treat alien abduction phenomena as (1) forms of mass delusion supported by a social network of people holding such deviant beliefs (R. L. Hall, 1996), (2) types of dissociative experiences or splitting of consciousness in response to extreme stress (Fisman & Takhar, 1996; Shopper, 1996), or (3) attempts to escape from the self (L. S. Newman & Baumeister 1996). Though speculation abounds, we lack a solid foundation of research evidence on which to judge these theoretical accounts (Arndt & Greenberg, 1996). Perhaps we will learn more as research on this intriguing phenomenon continues. Or perhaps reports of alien abductions will shortly disappear into the trash heap of discarded cultural trends. There is yet another, however unlikely, explanation. Perhaps these people were truly abducted by space aliens. On this account, we'd best leave the investigation to the likes of Mulder and Scully.

In the *X-Files,* F.B.I. agents Fox Mulder and Dana Scully, played by actors David Duchovny and Gillian Anderson, investigate mysterious phenomena, including reports of abductions by space aliens. How have psychologists attempted to explain these experiences?

respond to selective reinforcement of the most adaptive personality. This form of therapy also raises the ethical issue as to whether or not therapists have the right to determine which personality should be selectively reinforced.

SOMATOFORM DISORDERS

The word *somatoform* derives from the Greek *soma,* meaning "body." In the **somatoform disorders,** people have physical symptoms suggestive of physical disorders, but no organic abnormalities can be found to account for them. Moreover, there is evidence, or some reason to believe, that the symptoms reflect psychological factors or conflict. Some people complain of problems in breathing or swallowing, or of a "lump in the throat." Problems such as these can reflect overactivity of the sympathetic branch of the autonomic nervous system, which can be related to anxiety. Sometimes the symptoms take more unusual forms, as in a "paralysis" of a hand or leg that is inconsistent with the workings of the nervous system. In yet other cases, people are preoccupied with the belief that they have a serious disease, yet no evidence of a physical abnormality can be found. We consider several forms of somatoform disorders, including *conversion disorder, hypochondriasis,* and *somatization disorder.* We also consider *Münchausen's syndrome,* which is a form of feigned illness, or **factitious disorder,** that seems to be motivated by a desire to be hospitalized and treated for a faked illness.

Conversion Disorder

Conversion disorder is characterized by a major change in or loss of physical functioning, although there are no medical findings to support the physical symptoms or deficits (see Table 6.3). The symptoms are not intentionally produced. The person is not malingering. The physical symptoms usually come on suddenly in stressful situations. A soldier's hand may become "paralyzed" during intense combat, for example. The fact that conversion symptoms first appear in the context of, or are aggravated by, conflicts or stressors the individual encounters gives credence to the view that they relate to psychological factors (APA, 1994).

Conversion disorder is so named because of the psychodynamic belief that it represents the channeling or *conversion* of repressed sexual or aggressive energies into physical symptoms. Conversion disorder was formerly called *hysteria* or *hysterical neurosis.* Investigations of cases of hysterical neurosis played a prominent role in the development of psychoanalysis. In one of the classic cases in the annals of abnormal behavior, Anna O., a young woman who complained of numerous physical problems that fit the pattern of conversion disorder, received psychoanalytic treatment. Hysterical or conversion disorders seem to have been more common in Freud's day but are relatively rare today.

According to the DSM, conversion symptoms mimic neurological or general medical conditions involving problems with voluntary motor (movement) or sensory functions.

TABLE 6.3
Diagnostic Features of Conversion Disorder

1. At least one symptom or deficit involving voluntary motor or sensory functions that suggests the presence of a physical disorder.

2. Psychological factors are judged to be associated with the disorder because the onset or exacerbation of the physical symptom is linked to the occurrence of psychosocial stressors or conflict situations.

3. The person does not purposefully produce or fake the physical symptom.

4. The symptom cannot be explained as a cultural ritual or response pattern, nor can it be explained by any known physical disorder on the basis of appropriate testing.

5. The symptom causes significant emotional distress, impairment in one or more important areas of functioning, such as social or occupational functioning, or is sufficient to warrant medical attention.

6. The symptom is not restricted to complaints of pain or problems in sexual functioning, nor can it be accounted for by another mental disorder.

Source: Adapted from the DSM-IV (APA, 1994).

Some of the "classic" symptom patterns involve paralysis, epilepsy, problems in coordination, blindness and tunnel vision, loss of the sense of hearing or of smell, or loss of feeling in a limb (anesthesia). The bodily symptoms found in conversion disorders often do not match the medical conditions they suggest. For example, conversion epileptics, unlike true epileptic patients, may maintain control over their bladders during an attack. People whose vision is supposedly impaired may wend their ways through the physician's office without bumping into the furniture. People who become "incapable" of standing or walking may nevertheless perform other leg movements normally.

If you suddenly lost your vision, or if could no longer move your legs, you would probably show understandable concern. But some people with conversion disorders, like those with dissociative amnesia, show a remarkable indifference to their symptoms, a phenomenon termed **la belle indifférence** ("beautiful indifference"). The DSM advises against relying on indifference to symptoms in making the diagnosis, however, because many people cope with real physical disorders by denying their pain or concern, which provides the semblance of indifference and relieves anxieties—at least temporarily.

TRUTH *or* FICTION REVISITED

6.5 True. Some people with conversion disorder show a remarkable lack of concern about their symptoms (*la belle indifférence*).

Labels of hysteria or conversion disorder are now and then erroneously applied to people with underlying medical conditions that go unrecognized and untreated, as in the case of Gladys:

> Gladys was a 57-year-old housewife who complained to her physician of a "lump in the throat." The physician found no organic basis for the complaint and referred her to a psychiatrist who informed her that her symptom was a common neurotic symptom and probably reflected her unwillingness to "swallow" her lot in life, now that the children were grown and she sat alone in the house much of the day. Several months later, the symptom persisted and Gladys visited a psychologist at a community mental-health center. Before treating the "hysterical symptom," the psychologist referred her to medical specialists in Boston so that an organic basis for the disorder could be ruled out. Throat cancer was diagnosed, but the cancer had metastasized and it was too late to save Gladys's life.
>
> THE AUTHORS' FILES

Gladys's case is not unique. Investigators find that many patients presenting with unusual or initially unexplained medical symptoms who are given a diagnosis of conversion disorder actually have underlying organic causes of their symptoms (Fishbain & Goldberg, 1991). A study of neurological patients who had documented neurological disorders showed that most presented with features of conversion disorder such as *la belle indifférence* and sensory losses that were inconsistent with recognized organic patterns of pathology (Gould, Miller, Goldberg, & Benson, 1986). In the opinion of these researchers, certain classes of people, including women and gay men, are at greater risk of being misdiagnosed as hysterical because of stereotypes held by clinicians that they are more prone to such disorders. Perhaps as many as 80% of individuals given the diagnosis of conversion disorder have real neurological problems that go undiagnosed (Gould et al., 1986).

Hypochondriasis

The term **hypochondriasis** is derived from the Greek *hypochondrion*, which refers to the abdomen, the soft part of the body below (*hypo-*) the cartilage (*chondrion*) of the breastbone. This area is the site of many—but not all—of the physical complaints. Based on their interpretation of bodily signs (for example, sores) or sensations (for example, "heaviness in the chest"), people who are diagnosed with hypochondriasis are preoccupied with the fear that their symptoms are due to an underlying serious illness, such as cancer or a heart defect. No organic basis can be found that fully accounts for their complaints or justifies their fears of having a serious disease, however. Fear of serious illness persists despite medical reassurance that their fears are groundless (see Table 6.4).

People who develop hypochondriasis are not consciously faking their symptoms. They believe they have or

TABLE 6.4
Diagnostic Features of Hypochondriasis

1. The person is preoccupied with a fear of having a serious illness, or with the belief that one has a serious illness. The person interprets bodily sensations or physical signs as evidence of physical illness.

2. Fears of physical illness, or beliefs of having a physical illness, persist despite medical reassurances.

3. The preoccupations are not of a delusional intensity (the person recognizes the possibility that these fears and beliefs may be exaggerated or unfounded) and are not restricted to concerns about appearance.

4. The preoccupations cause significant emotional distress or interfere with one or more important areas of functioning, such as social or occupational functioning.

5. The disturbance has persisted for 6 months or longer.

6. The preoccupations do not occur exclusively within the context of another mental disorder.

Source: Adapted from the DSM-IV (APA, 1994).

fear they have a serious disease. They genuinely experience their reported discomfort. Unlike conversion disorder, hypochondriasis does not involve the loss or distortion of physical function. Unlike the attitude of indifference toward one's symptoms that is sometimes found in conversion disorders, people who develop hypochondriasis express grave concern about their symptoms. The disorder is about equally common in men and women and most often begins

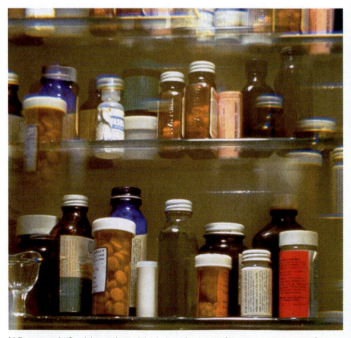

What to take? Hypochondriasis involves persistent concerns or fears that one is seriously ill, although no organic basis can be found to account for one's physical complaints. People with this disorder frequently medicate themselves with over-the-counter medications and find little if any reassurance in doctor's assertions that their health is not in jeopardy.

between the ages of 20 and 30, although it can begin at any age. The prevalence of hypochondriasis remains unknown.

People who develop hypochondriasis have more health worries, more psychiatric symptoms, and perceive their health as worse than do other people (Noyes et al., 1993). They are also more likely than other psychiatric patients to report being sick as children, having missed school because of health reasons, and having experienced childhood trauma, such as sexual abuse or physical violence (Barsky et al., 1994). According to recent studies, most people who meet diagnostic criteria for hypochondriasis continue to show evidence of the disorder when re-interviewed 5 years later (Barsky et al., 1998). Most also have other psychological disorders, especially major depression and anxiety disorders (Barsky, Wyshak, & Klerman, 1992; Noyes et al., 1993).

People who develop hypochondriasis may focus on slight changes in heartbeat and minor aches and pains. Anxiety about one's physical status produces its own physical sensations, however—for example, heavy sweating, dizziness, even fainting. People who develop hypochondriasis may be incredulous and resentful when the doctor explains how their own fears may be plaguing them. They frequently go "doctor shopping" in the hope that a competent and sympathetic physician will heed them before it is too late. Physicians, too, can develop hypochondriasis, as we see in the following case example:

A 38-year-old radiologist has just returned from a 10-day stay at a famous diagnostic center where he has undergone extensive testing of his entire gastrointestinal tract. The evaluation proved negative for any significant physical illness, but rather than feel relieved, the radiologist appeared resentful and disappointed with the findings. The radiologist has been bothered for several months with various physical symptoms, which he describes as symptoms of mild abdominal pain, feelings of "fullness," "bowel rumblings," and a feeling of a "firm abdominal mass." He has become convinced that his symptoms are due to colon cancer and has become accustomed to testing his stool for blood on a weekly basis and carefully palpating his abdomen for "masses" while lying in bed every several days. He has also secretly performed X-ray studies on himself after regular hours. There is a history of a heart murmur that was detected when he was 13 and his younger brother died of congenital heart disease in early childhood. When the evaluation of his murmur proved to be benign, he nonetheless began to worry that something might have been overlooked. He developed a fear that something was actually wrong with his heart, and while the fear eventually subsided, it has never entirely left him. In medical school he worried about the diseases that he learned about in pathology. Since graduating, he has repeatedly experienced concerns about his health that follow a typical pattern: noticing certain symptoms, becoming preoccupied with what the symptoms might

mean, and undergoing physical evaluations that proved negative. His decision to seek a psychiatric consultation was prompted by an incident with his 9-year-old son. His son accidentally walked in on him while he was palpating his abdomen and asked, "What do you think it is this time, Dad?" He becomes tearful as he relates this incident, describing his feelings of shame and anger— mostly at himself.

ADAPTED FROM SPITZER ET AL., 1994, PP. 88–90.

Hypochondriasis is generally considered to be more common among elderly people. As noted by Paul Costa and Robert McCrae (1985) of the National Institute on Aging, however, authentic age-related health changes do occur, and most "hypochondriacal" complaints probably reflect these changes.

Somatization Disorder

Somatization disorder, formerly known as Briquet's syndrome, is characterized by multiple and recurrent somatic complaints that began prior to the age of 30 (but usually during the teen years), have persisted for at least several years, and result in the seeking of medical attention or significant impairment in fulfilling social or occupational roles. Complaints usually involve different organ systems (Spitzer et al., 1989). Seldom a year passes without some physical complaint that prompts a trip to the doctor. People with somatization disorder are heavy users of medical services (G. R. Smith, 1994). Community surveys show that virtually all (95%) of the people with somatization disorder had visited a doctor during the past year, and nearly half (45%) had been hospitalized (Swartz et al., 1991). The complaints cannot be explained by physical causes or exceed what would be expected from a known physical problem. Complaints seem vague or exaggerated, and the person frequently receives medical care from a number of physicians, sometimes at the same time.

Somatization disorder usually begins in adolescence or young adulthood and appears to be a lifelong disorder involving major disability (Kirmayer, Robbins, & Paris, 1994; G. R. Smith, 1994). The DSM provides groups of symptoms and specifies that the diagnosis of somatization disorder requires the individual to have a history of complaints involving four separate symptom groups (APA, 1994). The groups of symptoms are categorized as pain involving multiple sites (e.g., head, abdomen, back, or joints) or functions (e.g. during sexual intercourse, menstruation, or urination); gastrointestinal (e.g., vomiting or diarrhea); sexual other than pain (e.g., loss of sexual interest, erectile or ejaculatory problems, excessive menstrual bleeding, or irregular menses); and pseudoneurological (e.g., symptoms suggesting a neurological disorder such as conversion symptoms such as blindness, difficulty swallowing, blurry vision, paralysis, or weakness, or dissociative symptoms such as loss of memory for personal events).

Koro and Dhat Syndromes: Far Eastern Somatoform Disorders?

In the United States, it is common for people who develop hypochondriasis to be troubled by the idea that they have serious illnesses, such as cancer. The Koro and Dhat syndromes of the Far East share some clinical features with hypochondriasis. Although these syndromes may seem, well, foreign to most American readers, they are each connected with folklore within their Far Eastern cultures.

Koro Syndrome

Koro syndrome is a culture-bound syndrome found primarily in China and some other Far Eastern countries (Sheung-Tak, 1996). People with Koro syndrome fear their genitals are shrinking and retracting into the body, which they believe will result in death (Fabian, 1991; Goetz & Price, 1994; Tseng et al., 1992). Koro is considered a culture-bound syndrome, although some cases have been reported outside China and the Far East (Chowdhury, 1996; Tobin, 1996). The syndrome has been identified mainly in young men, although some cases have also been reported in women (Tseng et al., 1992). Koro syndrome tends to be short-lived and to involve episodes of acute anxiety that one's genitals are retracting. Physiological signs of anxiety that approach panic proportions are common, including profuse sweating, breathlessness, and heart palpitations (Tseng et al., 1992). Men who suffer from Koro have been known to use mechanical devices, such as chopsticks, to try to prevent the penis from retracting into the body (Devan, 1987).

Koro syndrome has been traced within Chinese culture as far back as 3000 B.C. (Devan, 1987). Epidemics involving hundreds or thousands of people have been reported in parts of Asia such as China, Singapore, Thailand, and India (Tseng et al., 1992). In Guangdong Province in China, an epidemic involving more than 2,000 persons occurred during the 1980s (Tseng et al.,

1992). Guangdong residents who did not fall victim to Koro tended to be less superstitious, higher in intelligence, and less accepting of Koro-related folk beliefs (such as the belief that shrinkage of the penis will be lethal) than those who fell victim to the epidemic (Tseng et al., 1992). Medical reassurance that such fears are unfounded often quell Koro episodes (Devan, 1987). Medical reassurance generally fails to dent the concerns of Westerners who develop hypochondriasis, however. Koro episodes among those who do not receive corrective information tend to pass with time but may recur.

Dhat syndrome. Found principally in India, Dhat syndrome describes men with an intense fear or anxiety over the loss of semen.

The Epidemiologic Catchment Area (ECA) study revealed that somatization disorder was relatively uncommon, affecting about 1 American in 1,000 (Swartz et al., 1991). The ECA study found the disorder was 10 times more likely to occur among women than men and 4 times more likely to occur among African Americans than other ethnic or racial groups (Swartz et al., 1991). Moreover, the ECA study revealed that somatization disorder tends to occur within the context of other abnormal behavior patterns. All of the people with somatization disorder experienced at least one

other psychiatric disorder at some point in their lives, most commonly phobic disorders (69%) or major depression (55%) (Swartz et al., 1991). Personality disorders, including avoidant personality disorder and antisocial personality disorder (discussed in Chapter 8), are also common (Rost, Akins, Brown, & Smith, 1992; G. R. Smith et al., 1991). Although not much is known of the childhood backgrounds of people with somatization disorder, one study found that women with the disorder were significantly more likely to report sexual molestation in childhood than a matched

A number of investigators (R. L. Bernstein & Gaw, 1990; Fishbain, 1991) would like to see the Koro syndrome incorporated into the DSM as a somatoform disorder.

Dhat Syndrome

Dhat (loosely translated as the elixir of life) syndrome is found among young Asian Indian males and involves excessive fears over the loss of seminal fluid during nocturnal emissions (S. Akhtar, 1988). Some men with this syndrome also believe (incorrectly) that semen mixes with urine and is excreted through urination. Men with Dhat syndrome may roam from physician to physician seeking help to prevent nocturnal emissions or the (imagined) loss of semen mixed with excreted urine. There is a widespread belief within Indian culture (and other Near and Far Eastern cultures) that the loss of semen is harmful because it depletes the body of physical and mental energy (Chadda & Ahuja, 1990). Like other culture-bound syndromes, Dhat must be understood within its cultural context:

> In India, attitudes toward semen and its loss constitute an organized, deep-seated belief system that can be traced back to the scriptures of the land . . . [even as far back as the classic Indian sex manual, the Kama Sutra, which was believed to be written by the sage Vatsayana between the third and fifth centuries A.D.]. . . . Semen is considered to be the elixir of life, in both a physical and mystical sense. Its preservation is supposed to guarantee health and longevity.
>
> S. AKHTAR, 1988, P. 71

It is a commonly held Hindu belief that it takes "forty meals to form one drop of blood; forty drops of blood to fuse and form one drop of bone marrow, and forty drops of this produce one drop of semen" (S. Akhtar, 1988, p. 71). Based on the cultural belief in the life-preserving nature of semen, it is not surprising that some Indian males experience extreme anxiety over the involuntary loss of the fluid through nocturnal emissions (S. Akhtar, 1988). *Dhat* syndrome has also been associated with difficulty in achieving or maintaining erection, apparently due to excessive concern about loss of seminal fluid through ejaculation (Singh, 1985).

Culture-Bound Dissociative Conditions

Commonalities also exist between the Western concept of dissociative disorders and certain culture-bound syndromes found in other parts of the world. For example, *amok* is a culture-bound syndrome occurring primarily in southeast Asian and Pacific island cultures that describes a trancelike state in which a person suddenly becomes highly excited and violently attacks other people or destroys objects (see Chapter 2). People who "run amuck" may later claim to have no memory of the episode or recall feeling as if they were acting like a robot. Another example is *zar*, a term used in countries in North Africa and the Middle East to describe spirit possession in people who experience dissociative states during which they engage in unusual behavior ranging from shouting to banging their heads against the wall. The behavior itself is not deemed abnormal, since it is believed to be controlled by spirits.

The DSM-IV includes a proposed diagnostic category called *dissociative trance disorder,* intended to classify trancelike states that involve changes in consciousness or personal identity that cannot be explained as part of the accepted social or religious customs or practices within the culture and that cause significant distress or difficulties in normal functioning. Although the diagnostic category is exploratory, it will hopefully stimulate interest in examining the various forms in which dissociative experiences are expressed and understood in different cultures.

---

comparison group of women with mood disorders (J. Morrison, 1989).

The essential feature of hypochondriasis is fear of disease, of what bodily symptoms may portend. Persons with somatization disorder, by contrast, are pestered by the symptoms themselves. Both diagnoses may be given to the same individual if the diagnostic criteria for both disorders are met. Somatization disorder is rarely diagnosed in males, whereas hypochondriasis is believed to affect women and men equally.

Emil Kraepelin, one of the founders of modern psychiatry, presented a case in the 19th century that closely parallels somatization disorder (Spitzer et al., 1989). It involved a 30-year-old woman who complained of many physical problems that dated to adolescence and for which no physical cause could be determined: seizures, difficulty walking, muscle weakness, abdominal pain, diarrhea, menstrual problems, chest pain, and urinary problems, among others. Like many others with the disorder, the woman also presented with genuine physical problems, but her physical condition could not account for the range of complaints. Every type of treatment available at the time was tried, but with temporary benefits or none. They included therapeutic baths, stays on the Riviera and in the country, even mild electric currents.

Theoretical Perspectives

Conversion disorder, or "hysteria," was known to Hippocrates, who attributed the strange bodily symptoms to a wandering uterus, which created internal chaos. The term *hysterical* derives from the Greek *hystera,* meaning "uterus." Hippocrates noticed that these complaints were less common among married women. He prescribed marriage as a "cure" on the basis of these observations, and also on the theoretical assumption that pregnancy would satisfy uterine needs and fix the organ in place. Pregnancy fosters hormonal and structural changes that are of benefit to some women with menstrual complaints, but Hippocrates's belief in the "wandering uterus" has contributed to degrading interpretations of complaints by women of physical problems throughout the centuries. Despite Hippocrates's belief that hysteria was exclusively a female concern, it also occurs in men.

Modern theoretical accounts of the somatoform disorders, like those of the dissociative disorders, have most often sprung from psychodynamic and learning theories. Although not much is known about biological underpinnings of somatoform disorders, evidence indicates that somatization disorder tends to run in families, primarily among female members (Guze, 1993). This is suggestive of a genetic linkage, although we cannot rule out the possibility that family influences play a part in explaining this familial association.

Hysterical disorders provided an arena for some of the debate between the psychological and biological theories of the 19th century. The alleviation—albeit often temporarily—of hysterical symptoms through hypnosis by Charcot, Breuer, and Freud contributed to the belief that hysteria was rooted in psychological rather than physical causes and led Freud to the development of a theory of the unconscious mind. Freud held that the ego manages to control unacceptable or threatening sexual and aggressive impulses arising from the id through defense mechanisms such as repression. Such control prevents the outbreak of anxiety that would occur if the person were to become aware of them. In some cases, the leftover emotion or energy that is "strangulated," or cut off, from the threatening impulses becomes *converted* into a physical symptom, such as hysterical paralysis or blindness. Although the early psychodynamic formulation of hysteria is still widely held, empirical evidence has been lacking (E. Miller, 1987). One problem with the Freudian view is that it does not explain how energies left over from unconscious conflicts become transformed into physical symptoms (E. Miller, 1987).

According to psychodynamic theory, hysterical symptoms are functional: They allow the person to achieve **primary gains** and **secondary gains.** The primary gains consist of allowing the individual to keep internal conflicts repressed. The person is aware of the physical symptom, but not of the conflict it represents. In such cases, the "symptom" is symbolic of, and provides the person with a "partial solution" of, the underlying conflict. For example, the hysterical paralysis of an arm might symbolize and also prevent the individual from acting on repressed unacceptable sexual (e.g., masturbatory) or aggressive (e.g., murderous) impulses. Repression occurs automatically, so the individual remains unaware of the underlying conflicts. *La belle indifférence,* first noted by Charcot, is believed to occur because the physical symptoms help relieve rather than cause anxiety. From the psychodynamic perspective, conversion disorders, like dissociative disorders, serve a purpose.

Secondary gains may allow the individual to avoid burdensome responsibilities and to gain the support—rather than condemnation—of those around them. For example, soldiers sometimes experience sudden "paralysis" of their hands, which prevents them from firing their guns in battle. They may then be sent to recuperate at a hospital, rather than face enemy fire. The symptoms in such cases are not considered contrived, as would be the case in malingering. A number of bomber pilots during World War II suffered hysterical "night blindness" that prevented them from carrying out dangerous nighttime missions. In the psychodynamic view, their "blindness" may have achieved a primary gain of shielding them from guilt associated with dropping bombs on civilian areas. It may also have achieved a secondary purpose of helping them avoid dangerous missions.

Psychodynamic theory and learning theory concur that the symptoms in conversion disorders relieve anxiety. Psychodynamic theorists, however, seek the causes of anxiety in unconscious conflicts. Learning theorists focus on the more direct reinforcing properties of the symptom and its secondary role in helping the individual avoid or escape uncomfortable or anxiety-evoking situations.

From the learning perspective, the symptoms in conversion and other somatoform disorders may also carry the benefits, or reinforcing properties of, the "sick role" (Kendell, 1983). Persons with conversion disorders may be relieved of chores and responsibilities such as going to work or performing household tasks (E. Miller, 1987). Being sick also usually earns sympathy and support. People who received such reinforcers during past illnesses are likely to learn to adopt a sick role even when they are not ill (Kendell, 1983).

Differences in learning experiences may explain why conversion disorders were historically more often reported among women. It may be that women in our culture have been socialized, more so than men, to react to stress by enacting a sick role (E. Miller, 1987). We are not suggesting that people with conversion disorders are fakers. We are merely pointing out that people may learn to adopt roles that lead to reinforcing consequences, regardless of whether or not they deliberately seek to enact these roles.

Most theorists distinguish between *malingering,* or consciously making false claims to achieve various gains, and conversion disorder, in which the symptoms are not seen as

B-29 bombers on a bombing mission over Japan during World War II. Some World War II pilots were reported to have suffered from hysterical night blindness, which prevented them from carrying out dangerous nighttime missions. Their night blindness may have served the psychological purpose of shielding them from guilt over dropping bombs on civilian areas—a type of primary gain. It may also have served the secondary purpose of helping them avoid dangerous combat missions.

being consciously directed (E. Miller, 1987). People who engage in malingering do fake or exaggerate symptoms to obtain external rewards or incentives, such as avoiding military service or obtaining better living conditions. If persons with conversion disorders fake their symptoms, they do not appear to be consciously aware of it. One might even say they are deceiving *themselves* as well as others about the legitimacy of their complaints.

Some learning theorists see a close relationship between hypochondriasis and obsessive-compulsive disorder (OCD) (Barsky et al., 1992; Salkovskis & Warwick, 1986). People who develop hypochondriasis are bothered by obsessive, anxiety-inducing thoughts about their health. The urge to run from doctor to doctor may be seen as a form of compulsive behavior reinforced by the temporary, partial relief from anxiety they experience when they are reassured by their doctors that their fears are unwarranted. The troublesome thoughts eventually return, prompting repeated consultations. The cycle then repeats.

Cognitive theorists have speculated that some cases of hypochondriasis may represent a type of self-handicapping strategy, a way of blaming poor performance on failing health (T. W. Smith, Snyder, & Perkins, 1983). In other cases, diverting attention to physical complaints can serve as a means of avoiding thinking about other life problems.

Another cognitive explanation focuses on the role of distorted thinking. People who develop hypochondriasis have a tendency to "make mountains out of molehills" by exaggerating the importance of their physical complaints.

They misinterpret relatively minor physical complaints as signs of a serious illness, creating anxiety and leading them to chase down one doctor after another in an attempt to uncover the dreaded disease they fear they have. The anxiety itself may lead to unpleasant physical symptoms, which are likewise exaggerated in importance, leading to more worrisome cognitions.

Cognitive theorists have recently speculated that hypochondriasis and panic disorder, with which it often occurs concurrently, may share a common cause, namely a cognitive bias to misinterpret changes in bodily cues or sensations as signs of catastrophic harm (Salkovskis & Clark, 1993). Differences between the two disorders may hinge on whether the misinterpretation of bodily cues carries a perception of imminent threat leading to a rapid spiraling of anxiety (panic disorder) or of a longer range threat in the form of an underlying disease process (hypochondriasis). Research into cognitive processes involved in hypochondriasis deserves further study. Given the linkages that may exist between hypochondriasis and anxiety disorders such as panic disorder and OCD, it remains unclear whether hypochondriasis should be classified as a somatoform disorder or an anxiety disorder (Barsky et al., 1992).

Treatment of Somatoform Disorders

The treatment approach that Freud pioneered, psychoanalysis, began with the treatment of hysteria, which is now termed *conversion disorder.* Psychoanalysis seeks to uncover and bring unconscious conflicts that originated in childhood into conscious awareness. Once the conflict is aired and worked through, the symptom is no longer needed as a "partial solution" to the conflict and should disappear. The psychoanalytic method is supported by case studies, some reported by Freud and others by his followers. However, the infrequency of conversion disorders in contemporary times has made it difficult to mount controlled studies of the psychoanalytic technique.

The behavioral approach to treating conversion disorders, and other somatoform disorders, may focus on removing sources of secondary reinforcement (or secondary gain) that may become connected with physical complaints. Individuals with somatization disorder, for example, are often perceived by family members and others as sickly and infirm, as incapable of carrying normal responsibilities. Other people may be unaware of how they reinforce dependent and complaining behaviors when they relieve the sick person of responsibilities. The behavior therapist may teach family members to reward attempts to assume responsibility and ignore nagging and complaining. The behavior therapist may also work more directly with the person with a somatoform disorder, helping the person learn more adaptive ways of handling stress or anxiety through relaxation and cognitive restructuring, for example. Here again, the absence of controlled studies in the treatment of somatoform disorders prevents a fair assessment of relative efficacy of different approaches.

Attention has recently turned to the use of antidepressants, especially fluoxetine (Prozac), in treating some types of

Münchausen Syndrome

A woman staggered into the emergency room of a New York City hospital bleeding from the mouth, clutching her stomach, and wailing with pain. It was some entrance. Even in that setting, forever serving bleeders and clutchers and wailers, there was something about her, some terrible star quality that held stage center. Her pain was larger than life.

> She told a harrowing story: A man had seduced her, then tied her up, beaten her, forced her to surrender money and jewelry on threat of death. She had severe pain in her lower left side, and an unbearable headache.
>
> She was admitted, and exhaustively tested. Nothing could be found; no reason for the bleeding or the pain; the specialists were left scratching their heads.
>
> Then, one day, a hospital aide came upon these items in her bedside table: a needle, syringe, and a blood thinner called heparin. Eureka. Inject yourself with enough blood thinner and you, too, can take stage center in an emergency room.
>
> Confronted, she denied all charges. The stuff was not hers; someone was trying to frame her; if nobody believed her, she would check out of the place and find doctors who really cared. And off she went. Later, it was learned that she had recently been in two other hospitals: The same story, same symptom and same sequence of events.
>
> Diagnosis: Münchausen syndrome.
>
> LEAR, 1988, P. 21. COPYRIGHT © 1988 BY THE NEW YORK TIMES. REPRINTED BY PERMISSION.

Münchausen Syndrome

Münchausen syndrome was named after Baron Karl von Münchausen, one of history's great fibbers. The good baron, an 18th-century German army officer, entertained friends with tales of outrageous adventures. In the vernacular, *Münchausenism* describes tellers of tall tales. In clinical terms, **Münchausen syndrome** refers to patients who tell tall tales or outrageous lies to their doctors. The baron did not have the disorder that carries his name and was by all accounts a jolly man, yet the people who today carry his name as a diagnostic label usually suffer deep anguish as they bounce from hospital to hospital and subject themselves to unnecessary, painful, and, sometimes, risky medical treatments, even surgery.

TRUTH **or** FICTION REVISITED

6.7 True. People with Münchausen syndrome may show up repeatedly at emergency rooms, feigning illness and demanding treatment. Their motives remain a mystery.

Tall tales. The Baron Münchausen, who regaled his friends with tales of his incredible feats. In one of his tall tales, depicted here, he claimed that he had fallen asleep inside a cannon and was inadvertently shot across the Thames River.

Factitious Disorders

Although there may be gains in having physical symptoms, individuals with somatoform disorders do not purposefully produce them. Even if there is no medical basis to their symptoms, they do not set out to deceive others. Thus, Münchausen syndrome is not a somatoform disorder. It is a kind of factitious disorder. Factitious disorders involve the deliberate fabrication of physical or psychological complaints. Münchausen syndrome, in particular, refers to a chronic pattern of deliberate fabrication of seemingly plausible physical complaints.

In factitious disorders, as with malingering (faking), physical or psychological symptoms are consciously and deliberately produced. People who engage in malingering also invent a complaint, but for obvious gain. Perhaps they wish to be relieved of military or jury duty or just want to take a day off. Because malingering is motivated by external incentives, it is not considered a mental disorder, according to the DSM. In factitious disorders, the symptoms are not connected with obvious gains. The absence of external incentives suggests that factitious disorder serves a psychological need; hence, it is considered a mental disorder. Factitious disorders are maladaptive. Persons with factitious disorders seem compelled to feign illness, even though their fakery may subject them to painful or dangerous medical procedures (Schretlen, 1988). Persons with Münchausen syndrome may travel widely, visiting emergency rooms in one city after another, where they present themselves as suffering from acute, dramatic symptoms.

People with Münchausen syndrome weave tales of illness for no apparent reason other than gaining admission to the hospital. The syndrome may be seen as a form of compulsive behavior, perhaps even a form of "addiction" to hospitals, in which people crave opportunities to perform the sick role (Lear, 1988). They may go to great lengths to seek a confirmatory diagnosis, such as agreeing to exploratory surgery. Some inject themselves with certain drugs to produce symptoms such as skin rashes. When confronted with evidence of their deception, they may turn nasty and stick to their guns. They are also skillful enough actors to convince others that their complaints are genuine (A. J. Sutherland & Rodin, 1990). Unlike people who engage in malingering, people with Münchausen disorders are often unaware of the motives for their behavior (Schoenfeld, Margolin, & Baum, 1987).

Why Fake Symptoms?

The psychological needs served by Münchausen syndrome are conjectural. It has been suggested that people with Münchausen disorder may be trying to expunge guilt for felt misdeeds by subjecting themselves to painful medical procedures. Perhaps they hold grudges against doctors or hospitals for perceived injustices at the hands of the medical establishment (Lear, 1988) and delight in their ability to "put one over on the doctors." Methods of inducing symptoms can be dangerous and have sometimes been interpreted as expressing suicidal wishes (Schoenfeld et al., 1987).

Some conjectures focus on the early childhood experiences of Münchausen patients. Perhaps they learned to garner attention from parents by "playing sick," and this childhood pattern is reactivated when they need attention as adults (Lear, 1988). Their childhoods were often characterized by parental rejection or deprivation, traumatic events, family instability and foster homes, parental illness, or childhood hospitalizations (Schoenfeld et al., 1987; Trask & Sigmon, 1997). Somehow they learn what being sick means. Perhaps enacting the sick role in the protected hospital environment provides a sense of security that was lacking in childhood. Perhaps the hospital becomes a stage on which they can act out resentments against doctors and parents that have been brewing since childhood. Perhaps they are trying to identify with a parent who was often sick. Or perhaps they learned to enact a sick role in childhood to escape from repeated sexual abuse or other traumatic experiences and continue to enact the role to escape stressors in their adult lives (Trask & Sigmon, 1997).

Münchausen Syndrome by Proxy: A New Disorder?

Writers and health professionals have speculated that a new psychological disorder might have recently emerged, one in which people induce symptoms *in others* rather than themselves—"Münchausen syndrome by proxy"

Whereas people who have Münchausen syndrome itself may appropriately elicit our sympathy and concern, Münchausen syndrome by proxy is a form of child abuse associated with heinous crimes against children—with as many as 200 cases of child abuse since 1977 (Balleza, 1992; J. B. Murray, 1997; Polledri, 1996). Parents or caregivers induce illnesses in their children or foster children, perhaps to gain the sympathy of outsiders or to experience the sense of control made possible by attending to a sick child. In a California case, a foster mother is alleged to have brought about the deaths of three children by giving them overdoses of medicines containing potassium and sodium. The chemicals induced suffocation or heart attacks. An FBI bulletin carried articles that noted that cases of Münchausen syndrome by proxy may be suggested by mysterious high fevers in children, seizures of unknown origin, and similar symptoms. Doctors typically find the illnesses to be unusual, prolonged, and unexplained (Balleza, 1992). They require some medical sophistication on the part of the perpetrator.

All in all, Münchausen syndrome remains a mysterious and intriguing disorder with little known about its origins (J. B. Murray, 1997; Trask & Sigmon, 1997).

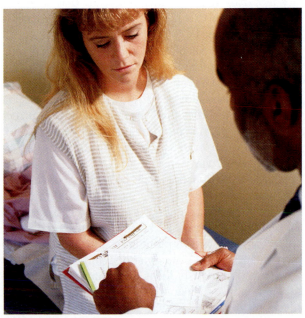

Is this patient telling the truth? Münchausen syndrome is characterized by the fabrication of medical complaints for no other apparent purpose than to gain admission to hospitals. Some Münchausen patients may produce life-threatening symptoms in their attempts to deceive doctors.

somatoform disorder. Though we lack specific drug therapies for conversion disorder (Simon, 1998), a study involving 16 patients with hypochondriasis with no coexisting major depression showed significant reductions in hypochondriacal complaints over the course of a 12-week trial with Prozac (B. A. Fallon et al., 1993). Here, too, the lack of controlled drug-placebo studies prevents firm conclusions regarding the efficacy of drug therapy. We also lack any systematic studies of approaches to treating factitious disorder (Münchausen's syndrome) and are limited to a few isolated case examples (Simon, 1998).

The dissociative and somatoform disorders remain among the most intriguing and least well understood patterns of abnormal behavior.

SUMMARY

The dissociative and somatoform disorders were historically linked with the anxiety disorders as forms of neuroses. Anxiety is expressed directly in different forms in the anxiety disorders, but its role in the dissociative and somatoform disorders is inferred.

Dissociative Disorders

Dissociative disorders involve changes or disturbance in identity, memory, or consciousness that affect the ability to maintain an integrated sense of self. Dissociative disorders include dissociative identity disorder, dissociative amnesia, dissociative fugue, and depersonalization disorder.

In dissociative identity disorder, two or more distinct personalities, each possessing well-defined traits and memories, exist within the person and repeatedly take control of the person's behavior. Dissociative amnesia involves loss of memory for personal information. There are five types of dissociative amnesia: localized, selective, generalized, continuous, and systematized. In dissociative fugue, the person travels suddenly away from home or place of work, shows a loss of memory for his or her personal past, and experiences identity confusion or takes on a new identity. Depersonalization disorders involve persistent or recurrent episodes of depersonalization that are of sufficient severity to cause significant distress or impairment in functioning.

Psychodynamic theorists view dissociative experiences as a form of psychological defense by which the ego defends itself against troubling memories and unacceptable impulses by blotting them out of consciousness. There is increasing documentation of a link between dissociative disorders and early childhood trauma, which lends support to the view that dissociation may serve to protect the self from troubling memories.

To learning and cognitive theorists, dissociative experiences involve ways of learning not to think about certain troubling behaviors or thoughts that might lead to feelings of guilt or shame. Relief from anxiety negatively reinforces this pattern of dissociation. Social-learning theorists and cognitive theorists suggest that multiple personality may represent a form of role-playing behavior. Some dissociative states, such as dissociative amnesia and fugue, may be transient and terminate abruptly. Psychodynamic approaches help the person with dissociative identity disorder uncover and cope with dissociated painful experiences from childhood. Within the diathesis-stress model, dissociative identity disorder may be explained in terms of a diathesis consisting of psychological traits such as a rich inner fantasy life and high levels of hypnotizability interacting with traumatic stress in the form of severe childhood abuse.

Biological approaches focus on the use of drugs to treat the anxiety and depression often associated with the disorder, but drugs have not been able to bring about reintegration of the personality. Learning perspectives focus on the use of behavioral methods of reinforcement of the most well-adjusted personality.

Somatoform Disorders

In somatoform disorders, there are physical complaints that cannot be accounted for by organic causes. Thus, the symptoms are theorized to reflect psychological rather than organic factors. Three types of somatoform disorders are considered: conversion disorder, hypochondriasis, and somatization disorder.

In conversion disorder, symptoms or deficits in voluntary motor or sensory functions occur that suggest an underlying physical disorder, but no apparent medical basis for the condition can be found. Hypochondriasis is a preoccupation with the fear of having, or the belief that one has, a serious medical illness, but no medical basis for the complaints can be found and fears of illness persist despite medical reassurances. Formerly known as Briquet's syndrome, somatization disorder involves multiple and recurrent complaints of physical symptoms that have persisted for many years and began prior to the age of 30, but most typically during adolescence.

The psychodynamic view holds that conversion disorders represent the conversion into physical symptoms of the leftover emotion or energy cut off from unacceptable or threatening impulses that the ego has prevented from reaching awareness. The symptom is functional, allowing the person to achieve both primary and secondary gains.

Learning theorists focus on reinforcements that are associated with conversion disorders, such as the reinforcing effects of adopting a "sick role." A learning theory view likens hypochondriasis to obsessive-compulsive behavior. Cognitive factors in hypochondriasis include possible self-handicapping strategies and cognitive distortions.

Münchausen syndrome is a form of factitious disorder involving the conscious fabrication of medical complaints for no apparent cause other than to gain admission to a hospital.

Malingering, by contrast, involves the fabrication of physical or psychological symptoms for obvious external gain.

Psychoanalysis seeks to uncover and bring to the level of awareness the unconscious conflicts, originating in childhood, that are believed to be at the root of the problem. Once the conflict is uncovered and worked through, the hysterical symptom should disappear because it is no longer needed as a partial solution to the underlying conflict. Behavioral approaches focus on removing sources of reinforcement that may be maintaining the abnormal behavior pattern. Behavior therapists may also work more directly to help people with somatoform disorders learn to handle stressful or anxiety-arousing situations more effectively.

REVIEW QUESTIONS

1. What is the hypothesized role of anxiety in the dissociative and somatoform disorders?

2. What features are associated with dissociative identity disorder, dissociative amnesia, dissociative fugue, and depersonalization disorder?

3. What psychological formulations have been proposed to explain the development of dissociative disorders?

4. What role is childhood physical and sexual abuse believed to play in dissociative disorders? What evidence supports relationships between prior abuse and the development of dissociative disorders?

5. Why does the diagnosis of dissociative identity disorder remain controversial?

6. What are the major features associated with conversion disorder, hypochondriasis, and somatization disorder?

7. What role did somatoform disorders play in the development of psychological models of treating abnormal behavior patterns?

8. How are dissociative and somatoform disorders distinguished from malingering? What difficulties arise in trying to make these determinations?

© **Edvard Minch**
Melancholy, 1894–1895

Mood Disorders and Suicide

TRUTH *or* FICTION?

7.1 It is abnormal to feel depressed.

7.2 Most people who experience a major depressive episode never go on to have another one.

7.3 The bleak light of winter casts some people into a diagnosable state of depression.

7.4 Some people ride an emotional roller coaster, swinging from the heights of elation to the depths of depression without external cause.

7.5 In some ways, many "mentally healthy" people see things *less* realistically than people who are depressed.

7.6 The most widely used remedy for depression in Germany is not a drug, but an herb.

7.7 The ancient Greeks and Romans used a chemical to curb turbulent mood swings that is still used today.

7.8 People who threaten suicide are only seeking attention.

1. Distinguish between normally and abnormally depressed moods and define the term "mood disorder."

2. Describe the features of major depressive disorder and dysthymic disorder and distinguish between them.

3. Discuss seasonal affective disorder and postpartum depression.

4. Discuss the prevalence of major depressive disorder, with particular attention to ethnic and gender differences and changes in prevalence rates worldwide.

5. Differentiate between reactive and endogenous depression.

6. Describe the features of bipolar disorder and cyclothymic disorder and distinguish between them.

7. Discuss the relationships between stress and mood disorders.

8. Discuss psychodynamic, behavioral, cognitive, and biological perspectives on the origins and treatment of mood disorders.

9. Discuss integrative models for understanding depression.

10. Discuss the incidence of suicide and theoretical perspectives on its causes.

Life has its ups and downs. Most of us feel elated when we have earned high grades, a promotion, or the affections of Ms. or Mr. Right. Most of us feel down or depressed when we are rejected by a date, flunk a test, or suffer financial reverses. It is normal and appropriate to be happy about uplifting events. It is just as normal, just as appropriate, to feel depressed by dismal events. It might very well be "abnormal" if one were *not* depressed by life's miseries.

TRUTH *or* FICTION REVISITED

7.1 *False.* Feeling depressed is not abnormal in the context of depressing events or circumstances.

Personal ups and downs are appropriate responses to the ups and downs of life. Some people, however, experience emotional extremes in mood that seem divorced from external events or are unusually prolonged or profound. Illness or the loss of a loved one may trigger periods of depression that are considered abnormal because of their severity or duration. Some people become severely depressed even when things appear to be going well, or when they encounter mildly upsetting events that others take in stride. Still others experience extreme mood swings. They ride an emotional roller coaster with dizzying heights and abysmal depths when the world around them remains largely on an even keel.

MOOD DISORDERS

Our **moods** are enduring states of feeling that color our psychological lives. When we are in a "good mood," many of the insults of daily life roll off our backs. When our moods are depressed, however, even delightful events may do little to cheer us. **Mood disorders** are disturbances in mood that are unusually severe or prolonged and impair our ability to function.

In this chapter we focus on several mood disorders, including two kinds of depressive disorders, major depressive disorder and dysthymic disorder, and two kinds of disorders that involve mood swings, bipolar disorder and cyclothymic disorder (see Table 7.1). Table 7.2 lists some of the common features of depression. The depressive disorders are considered **unipolar** because the disturbance lies in only one emotional direction or pole. Disorders that involve mood swings are **bipolar.** They involve excesses of both depression and elation, usually in an alternating pattern.

MAJOR DEPRESSIVE DISORDER

Many of us, probably most of us, have periods of sadness from time to time. We may feel down in the dumps, cry, lose interest in things, find it hard to concentrate, expect the worst to happen, or even consider suicide. A recent survey of a sample of college students at the University of North Iowa showed that about 30% of the students reported feeling at least mildly depressed (Wong & Whitaker, 1993). Downcast mood was greater among freshman than seniors or graduate students, which may be a reflection of the difficulties that many freshman have adjusting to college life.

For most of us, mood changes pass quickly or are not severe enough to interfere with our lifestyle or ability to function. Among people experiencing a **major depressive disorder,** however, mood changes are more severe and affect daily functioning. Such people may also have poor appetite, lose or gain substantial amounts of weight, and become physically agitated or—at the other extreme—show a marked slowing down in their motor activity. They may lose interest in most of their usual activities and pursuits, have difficulty concentrating and making decisions, and have pressing

TABLE 7.1
Types of Mood Disorders

Depressive Disorders (Unipolar Disorders)

Major Depressive Disorder	Occurrence of one or more periods or episodes of depression (called major depressive episodes) without a history of naturally occurring manic or hypomanic episodes. People may have one major depressive episode, followed by a return to their usual state of functioning. The majority of people with a major depressive episode have recurrences that are separated by periods of normal or perhaps somewhat impaired functioning.
Dysthymic Disorder	A pattern of mild depression (but perhaps an irritable mood in children or adolescents) that occurs for an extended period of time—in adults, typically for many years.

Bipolar Disorders

Bipolar Disorder	Disorders with one or more manic or hypomanic episodes (episodes of inflated mood and hyperactivity in which judgment and behavior are often impaired). Manic or hypomanic episodes often alternate with major depressive episodes with intervening periods of normal mood.
Cyclothymic Disorder	A chronic mood disturbance involving numerous hypomanic episodes (episodes with manic features of a lesser degree of severity than manic episodes) and numerous periods of depressed mood or loss of interest or pleasure in activities, but not of the severity to meet the criteria for a major depressive episode.

Source: Adapted from the *DSM-IV* (APA, 1994).

thoughts of death or attempt suicide. Although depression is a diagnosable psychological disorder, more than 40% of Americans polled in recent surveys perceive it to be a sign of a personal weakness (Brody, 1992b). Many people don't seem to understand that people who are clinically depressed can't simply "shake it off" or "snap out of it." This attitude may explain why, despite the availability of safe and effective treatments, most people who are clinically depressed remain undiagnosed and untreated (S. Gilbert, 1997a; Hirschfield et al., 1997; Howard, et al., 1996). Many people with un-treated depression believe they can handle the problem themselves (Blumenthal & Endioctt, 1997). Even for those who receive treatment, the great majority receive inadequate treatment (Hirschfield et al., 1997).

The diagnosis of *major depressive disorder* is based on the occurrence of one or more *major depressive episodes* in the absence of a history of **manic** or **hypomanic** episodes. In a major depressive episode, the person experiences either a depressed mood (feeling sad, hopeless, or "down in the dumps") or loss of interest or pleasure in all or virtually all activities for a period of at least 2 weeks (APA, 1994). The diagnostic features of a major depressive episode are listed

TABLE 7.2
Common Features of Depression

Changes in Emotional States	Changes in mood (persistent periods of feeling down, depressed, sad, or blue) Tearfulness or crying Increased irritability, jumpiness, or loss of temper
Changes in Motivation	Feeling unmotivated, or having difficulty getting going in the morning or even getting out of bed Reduced level of social participation or interest in social activities Loss of enjoyment or interest in pleasurable activities Reduced interest in sex Failure to respond to praise or rewards
Changes in Functioning and Motor Behavior	Moving about or talking more slowly than usual Changes in sleep habits (sleeping too much or too little, awakening earlier than usual and having trouble getting back to sleep in early morning hours—so-called early morning awakening) Changes in appetite (eating too much or too little) Changes in weight (gaining or losing weight) Functioning less effectively than usual at work or school
Cognitive Changes	Difficulty concentrating or thinking clearly Thinking negatively about oneself and one's future Feeling guilty or remorseful about past misdeeds Lack of self-esteem or feelings of inadequacy Thinking of death or suicide

When are changes in mood considered abnormal? Although changes in mood in response to the ups and downs of everyday life may be quite normal, persistent or severe changes in mood, or cycles of extreme elation and depression, may suggest the presence of a mood disorder.

in Table 7.3. People who are clinically depressed may also be unable to find pleasure in activities and events enjoyed by others. An ebbing capacity for pleasure (**anhedonia**) discourages them from participating in normally pleasant activities, such as sports or family barbecues. To be diagnosed, a major depressive disorder cannot be accounted for by another psychologcial disorder, an organic factor, such as tumor or other physical illness, or by the use of drugs or medications. Nor can it represent a normal grief reaction to the death of a loved one—that is, bereavement.

Problems of anxiety and depression often occur together and have overlapping symptoms. A recently proposed model, the *tripartite* (meaning "three-part") *model,* groups the respective symptoms of anxiety and depression in terms of three dimensions or factors (L. A. Clark & Watson, 1991; D. Watson et al., 1995a, 1995b): (1) a factor of general emotional distress, labeled *negative,* that is common to both anxiety and depression; (2) a set of symptoms characterized by states of bodily tension and physiological arousal that is relatively unique to anxiety; and (3) a third factor specific to depression involving anhedonia (lack of pleasure). Although the tripartite model may need some refining, evidence is mounting that supports the central tenet of the model: that anxiety and depression share a common factor (negative affect) while also having some distinctive features (hyperarousal in anxiety; lack of pleasure in depression) (J. A. Brown, Chorpita, & Barlow, 1998; Joiner, Catanzaro, & Laurent, 1996; Steer et al., 1995; Watson et al., 1995a).

TABLE 7.3
Diagnostic Features of a Major Depressive Episode

A major depressive episode is denoted by the occurrence of five or more of the following features or symptoms during a 2-week period, which represents a change from previous functioning. At least one of the features must involve either (1) depressed mood, or (2) loss of interest or pleasure in activities. Moreover, the symptoms must cause either clinically significant levels of distress or impairment in at least one important area of functioning, such as social or occupational functioning, and must not be due directly to the use of drugs or medications, or to a medical condition, or accounted for by another psychological disorder. *Nor can it represent a normal grief reaction to the death of a loved one—that is, **bereavement.**

1. Depressed mood during most of the day, nearly every day. Can be irritable mood in children or adolescents.

2. Greatly reduced sense of pleasure or interest in all or almost all activities, nearly every day for most of the day.

3. A significant loss or gain of weight (more than 5% of body weight in a month) without any attempt to diet, or an increase or decrease in appetite.

4. Daily (or nearly daily) insomnia or hypersomnia.

5. Excessive agitation or slowing down of movement responses nearly every day.

6. Feelings of fatigue or loss of energy nearly every day.

7. Feelings of worthlessness or misplaced or excessive or inappropriate guilt nearly very day.

8. Reduced ability to concentrate or think clearly or make decisions nearly every day.

9. Recurrent thoughts of death or suicide without a specific plan, or occurrence of a suicidal attempt or specific plan for committing suicide.

*The DSM includes separate diagnostic categories for mood disorders due to medical conditions or use of substances such as drugs of abuse.
Source: Adapted from the *DSM-IV* (APA, 1994).

Major depression versus bereavement. Major depression is distinguished from a normal grief reaction to the death of a loved one, which is termed *bereavement.* But major depression may occur in people whose bereavement becomes prolonged or seriously interferes with normal functioning.

Major depressive disorder is the most common type of diagnosable mood disorder, affecting nearly 1 in 5 adults (17%) in the United States at some point in their lives (Blazer et al., 1994). About 1 in 20 people can be diagnosed with major depression at any given time. Depression is so common that it has been dubbed the "common cold" of psychological problems (M. E. P. Seligman, 1973). Effective treatment for depression is available and leads not only to psychological improvement but also leads to increased income as people are able to return to a more productive level of functioning (Sturm & Wells, 1995).

Major depression in some cases, particularly in more severe episodes, is accompanied by psychotic features, such as delusions of unworthiness or guilt for assumed wrongdoings, or delusions that one's body is rotting from illness (Coryell, 1996; Coryell et al., 1996). People with severe depression may also experience hallucinations, such as "hearing" the voices of others, or of demons, condemning one for perceived misdeeds.

The following case illustrates the range of features connected with major depressive disorder:

A 38-year-old female clerical worker has suffered from recurrent bouts of depression since she was about 13 years of age. Most recently, she has been troubled by crying spells at work, sometimes occurring so suddenly she wouldn't have enough time to run to the ladies room to hide her tears from others. She has difficulty concentrating at work and feels a lack of enjoyment from work

she used to enjoy. She harbors severe pessimistic and angry feelings, which have been more severe lately since she has been recently putting on weight and has been neglectful in taking care of her diabetes. She feels guilty that she may be slowly killing herself by not taking better care of her health. She sometimes feels that she deserves to be dead. She has been bothered by excessive sleepiness for the past year and a half, and her driving license has been suspended due to an incident the previous month in which she fell asleep while driving, causing her car to hit a telephone pole. She wakes up most days feeling groggy and just "out of it," and remains sleepy throughout the day. She has never had a steady boyfriend, and lives quietly at home with her mother, with no close friends outside of her family. During the interview, she cried frequently and answered questions in a low monotone, staring downward continuously.

ADAPTED FROM SPITZER ET AL., 1989, PP. 59–62

A major depressive disorder, if left untreated, usually lasts for 6 months or longer and possibly even 2 or more years (APA, 1994) . Some people experience a single episode with a full return to previous levels of functioning. However, the great majority of people with major depression, perhaps as many as 80%, have repeated occurrences (Judd, 1997; Simpson, Nee, & Endicott, 1997; D. A. Solomon et al., 1997). The average person with major depression can expect to have four episodes, each of about 20 weeks in duration, during his or her lifetime (Judd, 1997). Many people with major depression show continuing symptoms that fluctuate in severity for years (Judd et al., 1998). Given a pattern of repeated occurrences of major depressive episodes and prolonged symptomatology, many professionals have come to view major depression as a chronic, indeed lifelong, disorder.

TRUTH *or* FICTION REVISITED

7.2 *False.* Most people who experience a major depressive episode have recurrences.

Identified Risk Factors for Major Depression

Factors that place people at greater risk of developing major depression include the following: age (initial onset is more common among younger adults than older adults); socioeconomic status (people on the lower rungs of the socioeconomic ladder are at greater risk than those who are better off); and marital status (people who are separated or divorced have higher rates than married or never-married people).

Women are nearly twice as likely as men to develop major depression (Blazer et al., 1994; Gater et al., 1998; R. C. Kessler et al., 1994) (see Figure 7.1). The difference in relative risk between males and females begins in early

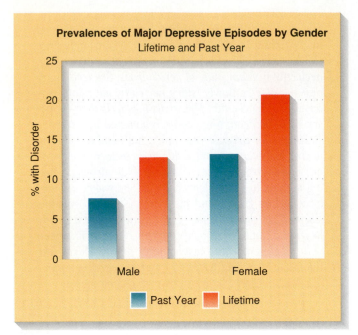

FIGURE 7.1 *Prevalences of major depressive episodes by gender.*
Major depressive episodes affect about twice as many women as men.

Source: National Comorbidity Survey; Kessler et al. (1994).

adolescence and persists through at least the mid-fifties (R. C. Kessler et al., 1993). The nearby "Focus on Diversity" section discusses several possible reasons for the gender difference in depression. Despite the gender difference in prevalence, the course of major depression is similar for both genders, as men and women with the disorder do not differ significantly in the likelihood of having recurrences, the frequency of recurrences, the severity or duration of recurrences, or the time to first recurrence (Eaton et al., 1997; Simpson, Nee, & Endicott, 1997).

Rates of major depression are highest among young adults (twenties and thirties) (APA, 1994; Karel, 1997). Major depression may even affect young children, though the risks are very low through age 14 (Lewinsohn, Duncan, Stanton, & Hautzinger, 1986).

Sociocultural Factors in Depression

Rates of diagnosable depression vary across ethnic groups in the United States. The multisite Epidemiologic Catchment Area (ECA) study found lifetime prevalences of major depressive disorder to be lower among African Americans than non-Hispanic White Americans or Hispanic Americans (Weissman et al., 1991). The National Comorbidity Survey (NCS), the largest and most representative national survey to date, confirmed that African Americans, at least in most age groups, were less likely than non-Hispanic Whites and Hispanics to experience major depression (Blazer et al., 1994). Interestingly, African Americans tend to report more depressive complaints, perhaps because they encounter greater life stress, but are less likely to suffer from major de-

pressive disorder (Somervell et al., 1989; Weissman et al., 1991). Somehow, for reasons that remain unclear, feelings of depressed mood among African Americans may be less likely to progress to the level of severity associated with clinical depression.

Multinational Study of Depression The results of a multinational study show that rates of major depression have been rising in the United States and worldwide (Cross-National Collaborative Group, 1992). Investigators used similar methods and criteria for diagnosing depression in nine countries in North America (United States and Canada), the Caribbean basin (Puerto Rico), western Europe (Italy, France, Germany), the Middle East (Lebanon), and Asia and the Pacific Rim (Taiwan and New Zealand). By comparing people born at different times, investigators were able to show that depression had increased among successive generations in all sites, although there were variations in the rate of increase across countries. In some countries, young people born after 1955 stood about three times greater likelihood of suffering a major depression than did their grandparents when they were the same age (Goleman, 1992c). The greatest increases were found in Florence, Italy; the least in Christchurch, New Zealand.

Rates of depression varied widely across countries. The lowest rate, 1.5 cases/100 adults, was obtained in Taiwan; the highest, 19 cases/100 adults, was found in Beirut, Lebanon, a city which had endured decades of internal warfare (Weissman et al., 1996). Interestingly, the rates for bipolar disorder did not vary widely among the participating countries. In all countries, rates for depression were higher among women than men.

No one knows why depression has been on the rise in many cultures, but speculation centers on social and environmental changes, such as increasing urbanization and fragmentation of families, exposure to wars, and increased incidence of violent crimes, as well as possible exposure to toxins or infectious agents in the environment that might affect mental as well as physical health (Cross-National Collaborative Group, 1992). One example is the dramatic increase in depression that occurred in the period 1950 to 1960 in Beirut, Lebanon. This was a period of chaotic political and demographic changes in the country. Depression dropped sharply in the following period, 1960 to 1970, a time of relative prosperity and stability in the country, but increased again between 1970 and 1980 during a time of social upheaval and internal warfare.

Reactive vs. Endogenous Depression

Some depressive episodes are apparently connected with external events or stressors, such as the loss of a loved one or failure to achieve a professional goal. Changes that affect intimate relationships are prominently connected with depression, especially "exit events," which involve the departure or loss of significant others through death, divorce, or academic or military obligations.

We expect people to feel down or depressed following the loss of a loved one. Major depressive disorder persists beyond what is considered a normal time period or is significantly more intense than "uncomplicated" bereavement or grief. In contrast to uncomplicated bereavement, major depressive disorder may entail feelings of worthlessness, suicidal thoughts, profound impairment in functioning, or a slowing down of mental and physical functioning (**psychomotor retardation**) (Sobin & Sackeim, 1997).

Depressive episodes that are linked to negative events are often called *reactive* depressions. It is believed they are responsive to external precipitants. Many depressive episodes seem to occur in the absence of clear external events, however. Such depressive episodes are often labeled **endogenous** (deriving from Greek roots meaning "born" from "within"). Endogenous depression (also called *melancholic depression*) is often seen as biologically based because its occurrence is presumably linked to inner causes rather than to external changes (Heiby et al., 1987). In contrast, reactive depressions (also referred to as neurotic or *exogenous* depressions) are more likely to reflect psychological, social, and physical environmental factors.

There are problems in distinguishing reactive from endogenous depressions on the basis of precipitants, however. For one, people who are depressed may be forgetful or confused and be unable to recall external precipitants. Their friends and loved ones may also be unaware of precipitating factors. They may also report problems that actually occur coincidentally with the onset of the depressive episode rather than causing it. Our clinical experience has suggested that it is nearly always possible to find some apparent precipitant of a depressive episode, even when things are apparently going well in general. Researchers also find stressful life events occurring prior to the onset of the disorder to be about as common in cases of endogenous depression as nonendogenous depression (G. W. Brown et al., 1994). It is useful to remain cautious in labeling events as precipitants of depression, as it is useful to remain cautious in any endeavor that attempts to ferret out cause and effect.

Because of such problems, the distinction between reactive and endogenous depressions typically rests more on manifest behaviors than on the presence or absence of potential precipitants. Depressions labeled endogenous are more likely to be characterized by the "vegetative" physical features of depression, such as loss of weight or appetite, early morning awakening (waking up hours earlier than usual and being unable to fall back asleep), loss of pleasure, apathy, and psychomotor retardation. These physical features appear to be less prominent in reactive depressions. Melancholic depression appears to be a more severe subtype of major depression than nonmelancholic depression.

Seasonal Affective Disorder

Are you glum on gloomy days? Is your temper short during the brief days of winter? Are you dismal during the dark of long winter nights? Are you up when the sun is high in the sky?

SAD in winter? Some people complain of depression during the fall and winter seasons but bounce back during the spring and summer. This pattern of depression has been called seasonal affective disorder—SAD—and is associated with changes in climate, especially seasonal changes in the amount of sunlight.

Many people report that their moods vary with the weather. For some people, the changing of the seasons from summer into fall and winter leads to a type of depression called *seasonal affective (mood) disorder*—SAD.[1]

TRUTH *or* **FICTION** REVISITED

7.3 *True.* The changing of the seasons apparently does produce a depressive disorder in some people.

The features of SAD include fatigue, excessive sleep, craving for carbohydrates, and weight gain. SAD tends to lift with the early buds of spring. It affects women more often than men and is most common among young adults. Nearly half of those who are affected report that SAD episodes began during childhood or adolescence (J. B. Murray, 1989b).

Although the causes of SAD remain unknown, one possibility drawing attention today is that internal body rhythms that fluctuate with seasonal changes in light-dark cycles may be involved (T. M. C. Lee et al., 1998; Teicher et al., 1997). Another possibility is that some parts of the central nervous system may have deficiencies in transmission of the mood-regulating neurotransmitter, serotonin, during the winter months (P. J. Schwartz, 1997). Whatever the underlying cause, a trial of phototherapy consisting of exposure to

---

[1]Seasonal affective disorder is not classified as a diagnostic category in its own right in the *DSM-IV* but is designated as a specifier of mood disorders in which major depressive episodes occur. For example, major depressive disorder that occurs seasonally would be given a diagnosis of major depressive disorder *with seasonal pattern*.

Gender Differences in Depression

Women are nearly twice as likely as men to develop major depression. The reasons for this difference remain unclear. Although hormonal differences may be involved, a panel convened by the American Psychological Association (APA) attributed the gender difference largely to the greater amount of stress that women encounter in contemporary life (Goleman, 1990b; McGrath, Keita, Strickland, & Russo, 1990). In reviewing the relevant research, the panel concluded that women are more likely than men to encounter such stressful life factors as physical and sexual abuse, poverty, single parenthood, and sexism. The APA panel acknowledged that hormonal changes during the menstrual cycle, childbirth, and unhappy marriages may also contribute to increased rates of depression among women. Women are also more likely than men to be support givers, which may compound the stress they encounter by heaping additional caregiving burdens on them and by exposing them to the problems that others face (Shumaker & Hill, 1991). An APA panel member, Bonnie Strickland, expressed surprise that still greater numbers of women are not clinically depressed, given that they are treated as second-class citizens and are more likely than men to fall beneath the poverty line in socioeconomic status (Goleman, 1990c). Even in households with two working spouses, it is the woman who usually shoulders responsibility for household and childcare responsibilities. Working mothers typically put in a double shift—one on the job and a second one at home (Bianchi & Spain, 1997).

Role of Coping Styles

Differences in coping styles may also help explain women's greater proneness toward depression. Regardless of whether or not the initial precipitants of depression are biological, psychological, or social, one's coping responses may exacerbate or reduce the severity and duration of depressive episodes. Nolen-Hoeksema and her colleagues (1991; Nolen-Hoeksema, Morrow, & Fredrickson, 1993) propose that men are more likely to distract themselves when they are depressed, whereas women are more likely to amplify depression by ruminating about their feelings and their possible causes. Women may be more likely to sit at home when they are depressed and think about how they feel or try to understand the reasons they feel the way they do, whereas men may try to distract themselves by doing something they enjoy, such as by going to a favorite hangout to get their mind off their feelings. On the other hand, men often distract themselves by turning to alcohol as a form of self-medication, which can lead to another set of psychological and social problems (Nolen-Hoeksema et al., 1993).

Rumination is not limited to women, however. Men or women who ruminate more following the loss of loved ones or when feeling down or sad are more likely to become depressed and to suffer longer and more severe depression than those who ruminate less (N. Just & Alloy, 1997; Nolen-Hoeksema, McBride & Larson, 1997).

Role of Gender-Role Stereotypes

It is also important to attend to gender-role stereotypes and their effect on the client and therapist in the diagnosis of depressive disorders. Gender-role stereotypes are sociocultural beliefs about what women and men are like and the things they are supposed to do or want to do. Gender roles are often attributed to presumed natural or biological gender differences, but they are sociocultural constructs that often say more about cultural values than biology.

The mental-health professions are institutions of the dominant culture, and despite attempts at academic rigor, many gender-role stereotypes pervade apparently scientific definitions of mental-health as well as diagnosis and treatment. Adherence to gender-role stereotypes and cultural assumptions about psychological normalcy that accompany them can produce double standards in diagnosis of depression among women and men. In one study, investigators report that the gender and race of the therapist and the client affected the likelihood of making a diagnosis of depression, even when therapists were given clear diagnostic criteria that were free of gender biases (Loring & Powell, 1988).

Consider, too, that gender-role stereotypes of women may bear a closer similarity to symptoms of depression than that of men. People typically give descriptions of "healthy adults" in terms of such traits as assertiveness, competence, and rationality (Rothblum, 1983). Conversely, they generally describe "healthy women" as warm, emotionally expressive, dependent, and demure (that is, passive) (Rothblum, 1983). These expectations render the woman who conforms to these

Women and depression. Women are more likely to suffer from major depression than men. A panel convened by the American Psychological Association (APA) attributed the higher rates of depression among women to factors such as unhappy marriages, physical and sexual abuse, impoverishment, single parenthood, sexism, hormonal changes, childbirth, and excessive caregiving burdens. APA panel member Bonnie Strickland expressed surprise that even more women were not clinically depressed, since they are treated as second-class citizens.

traditional gender-role stereotypes closer in behavioral terms to a depressive pattern. Men, moreover, are expected, like cowboys, to be rugged and independent, which are traits that run counter to a depressive pattern.

Expectations placed on men to be strong and self-reliant may also discourage them from seeking help if they do become depressed (Basow, 1992; Brody, 1997b). The reason that men are more likely than women to respond to emotional pain by turning to alcohol or other drugs, or by aggressive acting out, may also have a lot to do with gender-role stereotypes. These stereotypical response patterns to depression (that depression is "unmanly") may lead to an underreporting of the disorder in men, because some men who are primarily depressed may receive a diagnosis of substance abuse or antisocial personality if they are brought to the attention of mental-health professionals. Women, however, who are expected to be emotionally expressive and dependent, are likely to be more comfortable in admitting to depressive symptoms and seeking help for them.

Role of Gender Biases

Gender biases on the part of mental-health professionals may lead to and reinforce social inequalities between women and men. These biases may lead mental-health professionals to encourage clients to conform to cultural stereotypes as part and parcel of coping with their problems (Basow, 1992). Women may be encouraged by their therapists, perhaps in subtle ways, to become more dependent, which further restricts their options, and may help maintain a depressive state. Even so, evidence does not show that depressed women respond better to female therapists than to male therapists (Zlotnick, Elkin, & Shea, 1998).

Recent research points to a possible biological explanation of the gender gap in depression. The brain chemical serotonin is believed to be involved in regulating mood states and other psychological functions, including pain perception and aggressive and impulsive behavior (Rivas-Vazquez & Blais, 1997). Some preliminary evidence based on 15 subjects indicates that men's brains synthesize serotonin at a faster rate than do women's brains (Nishizawa et al., 1997). Whether this finding holds up in subsequent research remains to be seen. Moreover, we don't know whether these differences have any bearing on women's greater vulnerability to depression.

Though the gender gap in depression continues, the gap appears to be closing as more men are coming forward seeking help for depression. The male ego also seems to be battered by assaults from corporate downsizing to growing financial insecurity. Though long viewed by men as a sign of personal weakness, the stigma associated with depression show signs of lessening, though not disappearing (NBC Nightly News, 1996).

Light therapy. Exposure to bright artificial light for a few hours a day during the fall and winter months can often bring relief from seasonal affective disorder.

2 to 3 hours of bright artificial light a day produces relief from depressive symptoms in many cases (e.g., Kogan & Guilford, 1998; P. J. Schwartz et al., 1996; Sato, 1997). The artificial light apparently supplements the meager sunlight these people otherwise receive. Patients usually carry out some of their daily activities (for example, eating, reading, writing) during their phototherapy sessions. Improvement generally occurs within several days of phototherapy, but treatment is apparently required throughout the course of the winter season. Light directed at the eyes tends to be more successful than light directed at the skin (Sato, 1997). Time of day in which the light is given does not appear to affect the efficacy of treatment, however (Wirz-Justice et al., 1993).

We still don't know how phototherapy works (M. A. Hill, 1992). However, mobilizing expectations of improvement (a placebo effect) may be involved in explaining part, though probably not all, of the therapeutic benefit (Sato, 1997). Phototherapy does not help all people with SAD, especially those who are more severely affected (Schwartz et al., 1996). Efforts are now focused on identifying factors that predict which patients are likely to benefit from the procedure (Terman et al., 1996).

Postpartum Depression

Many, perhaps most, new mothers experience mood changes, periods of tearfulness, and irritability following the birth of a child. These mood changes may affect the majority of new mothers (Harding, 1989) and are commonly called the "maternity blues," "postpartum blues," or "baby blues." The "blues" usually last for a couple of days and are believed to be a normal response to hormonal changes that attend childbirth. Given these turbulent hormonal shifts, it would be "abnormal" for most women *not* to experience some changes in feeling states shortly following childbirth.

Some mothers, however, undergo severe mood changes that may persist for months or even a year or more. These problems in mood are referred to as **postpartum depression** (PPD). *Postpartum* derives from the Latin roots *post,* meaning "after," and *papere,* meaning "to bring forth." PPD is often accompanied by disturbances in appetite and sleep, low self-esteem, and difficulties in maintaining concentration or attention. Between 8% and 15% of mothers experience a diagnosable postpartum depressive disorder of at least moderate severity (S. B. Campbell & Cohn, 1991; Gitlin & Pasnau, 1989). Postpartum depression is not unique to the United States; evidence from a study in an urban area in Portugal reported a similar prevalence rate (13%) (Augusto et al., 1996).

Women who suffer a miscarriage also stand an increased risk of developing a subsequent major depression, especially women who are childless or have a prior history of major depression (Janssen et al., 1997; Neugebauer et al., 1997).

The *DSM-IV* does not classify postpartum depression separately from other mood disorders. Rather, it instructs clinicians to specify a major depressive episode (or other mood disorder) that develops within 4 weeks of childbirth as occurring "with postpartum onset" (APA, 1994). This basis of classification is in keeping with the belief that postpartum depression is not a unique form of depression (Whiffen, 1992; Whiffen & Gotlib, 1993). Some cases of mild depression may involve a type of adjustment disorder that affects women (especially first-time mothers) who encounter difficulties adapting to the demands of caring for a new baby as well as a consequence of the birth itself (Whiffen, 1992).

Postpartum depression typically falls in a mild range of severity and tends to resolve more quickly than other depressive episodes (Whiffen & Gotlib, 1993). Yet some suicides are linked to postpartum depression (McQuiston, 1997). Although it may involve chemical or hormonal imbalances brought on by childbirth, psychosocial factors such as financial problems, a troubled marriage, lack of social or emotional support from the partner, a history of depression, or an unwanted or sick baby all increase a woman's vulnerability to PPD (Gotlib et al., 1991; Leathers, Kelley, & Richman, 1997; O'Hara et al., 1991). PPD also appears to increase the risk of future depressive episodes (L. H. Philipps & O'Hara, 1991). Mothers who appear to be most at risk of PPD include first-time mothers, single mothers, and mothers who lack social support from their partners or other family members (Gitlin & Pasnau, 1989).

Exposure to stress and use of passive coping strategies (wishful thinking) are also related to the risk of postpartum depression (Terry, Mayocchi, & Hynes, 1996). A study of 124 women carrying their firstborns showed that PPD could be predicted on the basis of such factors as depressed mood and marital stress during pregnancy (Whiffen, 1988). PPD was also related to the mother's perceptions of the infant as temperamentally difficult and as crying excessively. Caring for a difficult, temperamental infant heightens the mother's level of stress and can contribute to feelings of maternal inadequacy, both of which may, in turn, contribute to depression.

DYSTHYMIC DISORDER

Major depressive disorder is severe and marked by a relatively abrupt change from one's preexisting state. A milder form of depression seems to follow a chronic course of development that often begins in childhood or adolescence (D. N. Klein, Taylor, Dickstein, & Harding, 1988). Earlier diagnostic formulations of this type of chronic sadness were labeled "depressive neurosis" or "depressive personality" (Brody, 1995a). It was so labeled in an effort to account for several features that are traditionally connected with neurosis, such as early childhood origins, a chronic course, and generally mild levels of severity. The DSM labels this form of depression **dysthymia** (from Greek roots *dys-,* meaning "bad" or "hard" and *thymos,* meaning "spirit").

Persons with dysthymic disorder do feel "bad spirited" or "down in the dumps" most of the time and for most of the day, but they are not so severely depressed as those with major depressive disorder. Dysthymic disorder can generally be distinguished from major depression on the basis of an earlier age of onset and more gradual onset, a lesser severity of symptoms, and a longer duration (McCullough et al., 1996). Dysthymic disorder may develop in childhood, adolescence, or adulthood. Whereas major depressive disorder tends to be severe and time limited, dysthymic disorder is relatively mild and nagging, typically lasting for years (D. N. Klein et al., 1998). The average duration of dysthymic disorder is estimated to be about 5 years (Keller, 1990).

Dysthymic disorder affects about 3% of the adult population in the United States at some point in their lives (McGonagle et al., in press). More than 7 million people in the United States have been affected (Brody, 1995a). Like major depressive disorder, dysthymic disorder is more common in women than men (see Figure 7.2).

In dysthymic disorder, complaints of depression may become such a fixture of people's lives that it seems to be intertwined with their personality structures (D. N. Klein et al., 1988). The persistence of complaints may lead others to perceive them as whining and complaining (Akiskal, 1983). Although dysthymic disorder is less severe than major depressive disorder, persistent depressed mood and low self-esteem can affect the person's occupational and social functioning, as we see in the following case:

The woman, a 28-year-old junior executive, complained of chronic feelings of depression since the age of 16 or 17. Despite doing well in college, she brooded about how other people were "genuinely intelligent." She felt she could never pursue a man she might be interested in dating because she felt inferior and intimi-

QUESTIONNAIRE

Are You Depressed?

This test, offered by the organizers of the National Depression Screening Day (October 8, 1992), can help you assess whether you are suffering from a serious depression. It is not intended for you to diagnose yourself, but rather to raise your awareness of concerns you may want to discuss with a professional.

YES   NO

—   —   1. I feel downhearted, blue, and sad.

—   —   2. I don't enjoy the things that I used to.

—   —   3. I feel that others would be better off if I were dead.

—   —   4. I feel that I am not useful or needed.

—   —   5. I notice that I am losing weight.

—   —   6. I have trouble sleeping through the night.

—   —   7. I am restless and can't keep still.

—   —   8. My mind isn't as clear as it used to be.

—   —   9. I get tired for no reason.

—   —   10. I feel hopeless about the future.

Rating your responses: If you agree with at least five of the statements, including either item 1 or 2, and if you have had these complaints for at least 2 weeks, professional help is strongly recommended. If you answered "yes" to statement 3, seek consultation with a professional immediately. If you don't know who to turn to, contact your college counseling center, neighborhood mental-health center, or health provider.

Source: J.E. Brody, "Myriad masks hide an epidemic of depression," *New York Times,* September 30, 1992, p. C12. Copyright 1992 by The New York Times. Reprinted by permission.

dated. While she had extensive therapy through college and graduate school, she could never recall a time during those years when she did not feel somewhat depressed. She got married shortly after college graduation to the man she was dating at the time, although she didn't think that he was anything "special." She just felt she needed to have a husband for companionship and he was available. But they soon began to quarrel and she's lately begun to feel that marrying him was a mistake.

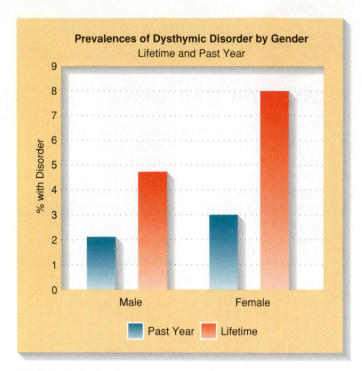

FIGURE 7.2 *Prevalences of dysthymic disorder by gender.*
Like major depression, dysthymic disorder occurs in about twice as many women as men.

Source: National Comorbidity Survey; Kessler et al. (1994).

> *She has had difficulties at work, turning in "slipshod" work and never seeking anything more than what was basically required of her and showing little initiative. While she dreams of acquiring status and money, she doesn't expect that she or her husband will rise in their professions because they lack "connections." Her social life is dominated by her husband's friends and their spouses and she doesn't think that other women would find her interesting or impressive. She lacks interest in life in general and expresses dissatisfaction with all facets of her life—her marriage, her job, her social life.*
>
> ADAPTED FROM SPITZER ET AL., 1994, PP. 110–112

People with dysthymic disorder may experience concurrent episodes of major depression as well. The term **double depression** applies to people who have a major depressive episode superimposed upon a dysthymic disorder (Keller, Hirschfeld, & Hanks, 1997). Major depressive episodes tend to occur more frequently and to be longer in duration in people with double depression than those with major depression alone (I. W. Miller & Norman, 1986).

BIPOLAR DISORDER

Most of us have our ups and downs. But some people ride an emotional roller coaster, swinging from the heights of elation to the depths of depression without external cause.

They are said to have bipolar disorder. The first episode may be either manic or depressive. Manic episodes, typically lasting from a few weeks to several months, are generally shorter in duration and end more abruptly than major depressive episodes. Some people with recurring bipolar disorder attempt suicide "on the way down" from the manic phase. They report that they would do nearly anything to escape the depths of depression they know lie ahead.

TRUTH *or* FICTION REVISITED

7.4 *True.* Some people with bipolar disorder do ride an emotional roller coaster between periods of extreme elation and periods of extreme depression, without external cause.

The DSM distinguishes between two general types of bipolar disorder, *bipolar I disorder* and *bipolar II disorder* (APA, 1994). The essential feature of bipolar I disorder is the occurrence of one or more manic episodes. A disorder can thus be labeled "bipolar" even if it consists of manic episodes without any past or present major depressive episodes. In such cases, it is possible that a major depressive disorder will eventually appear or has been overlooked. In a few cases of bipolar I disorder, called the mixed type, both a manic episode and a major depressive episode occur simultaneously. More frequently, though, cycles of elated and depressed mood states alternate with intervening periods of normal mood.

Bipolar II disorder is associated with a milder form of mania. In bipolar II disorder, the person has experienced one or more major depressive episodes and at least one hypomanic episode, but never a full-blown manic episode. Whether bipolar I and bipolar II disorders represent qualitatively different disorders or different points along a continuum of severity of bipolar disorder remains to be determined.

Bipolar disorders are relatively uncommon, with reported lifetime prevalence rates from community surveys of 0.4% to 1.6% for bipolar I disorder and 0.5% for bipolar II disorder (APA, 1994). Only about 1 in 3 people with bipolar disorder receives any treatment (Goleman, 1994b). Sadly, about 1 in 5 of the people who go untreated eventually commit suicide (Hilts, 1994).

Unlike major depression, rates of bipolar I disorder appear about equal in men and women. Gender differences in rates of bipolar II disorder are not well established. The typical age of onset of bipolar disorder is in the late twenties or early thirties (Coryell & Winokur, 1992), but the disorder may not appear until the forties or fifties. The onset of bipolar I disorder typically begins in men with a manic episode and in women with a major depressive episode. The underlying reason for this gender difference remains unknown.

Sometimes there are periods of "rapid cycling" in which the individual experiences two or more full cycles of mania and depression within a year without any intervening normal periods. Rapid cycling is relatively uncommon, but occurs more often among women than men (Leibenluft, 1996). It is usually limited to a year or less, but is associated with poorer vocational and social functioning (Coryell,

Patty Duke. The actress Patty Duke has highlighted her own struggles against bipolar disorder to focus public attention on the disorder and its treatment.

Endicott, & Keller, 1992b) and a higher rate of relapse (Keller et al., 1993).

Manic Episode

Manic episodes, or periods of mania, typically begin abruptly, gathering force within days. During a manic episode, the person experiences a sudden elevation or expansion of mood and feels unusually cheerful, euphoric, or optimistic. The person seems to have boundless energy and is extremely sociable, although perhaps to the point of becoming overly demanding and overbearing toward others. Other people recognize the sudden shift in mood to be excessive in light of the person's circumstances. It is one thing to feel elated if one has just won the state lottery. It is another to feel euphoric "because" it's Wednesday.

People in a manic episode or phase are excited and may strike others as silly, by carrying jokes too far, for example. They tend to show poor judgment and to become argumentative, sometimes going so far as destroying property. Roommates may find them abrasive and avoid them. They tend to speak very rapidly (with **pressured speech**). Their thoughts and speech may jump from topic to topic (in a **rapid flight of ideas**). Others find it difficult to get a word in edgewise. They may also become extremely generous and make large charitable contributions they can ill afford or give away costly possessions. They may not be able to sit still or sleep restfully. They almost always show less need for sleep. They tend to awaken early yet feel well rested and full of energy. They sometimes go for days without sleep and without feeling tired. Although they may have abundant stores of energy, they seem unable to organize their efforts constructively. Their elation impairs their ability to work and maintain normal relationships.

People in a manic episode generally experience an inflated sense of self-esteem that may range from extreme self-confidence to wholesale delusions of grandeur. They may feel capable of solving the world's problems or of composing symphonies, despite a lack of any special knowledge or talent. They may spout off about matters on which they know little, such as how to solve world hunger or create a new world order. It soon becomes clear that they are disorganized and incapable of completing their projects. They become highly distractible. Their attention is easily diverted by irrelevant stimuli such as the sounds of a ticking clock or of people talking in the next room. They tend to take on multiple tasks, biting off more than they can chew. They may suddenly quit their jobs to enroll in law school, wait tables at night, organize charity drives on weekends, and work on the great American novel in their "spare time." They tend to exercise poor judgment and fail to weigh the consequences of their actions. As a result, they may get into trouble as a result of lavish spending, reckless driving, or sexual escapades. In severe cases, they may experience disorders of thinking similar to those of people with schizophrenia. They may experience hallucinations or become grossly delusional, believing, for example, that they have a special relationship with God.

The following case provides a firsthand account of a manic episode. The early stages are dominated by euphoria, boundless energy, and an inflated sense of self. As mania intensifies, the individual may become confused:

When I start going into a high, I no longer feel like an ordinary housewife. Instead I feel organized and accomplished and I begin to feel I am my most creative self. I can write poetry easily. I can compose melodies without effort. I can paint. My mind feels facile and absorbs everything. I have countless ideas about improving the conditions of mentally retarded children, of how a hospital for these children should be run, what they should have around them to keep them happy and calm and unafraid. I see myself as being able to accomplish a great deal for the good of people. I have countless ideas about how the environment problem could inspire a crusade for the health and betterment of everyone. I feel able to accomplish a great deal for the good of my family and others. I feel pleasure, a sense of euphoria or elation. I want it to last forever. I don't seem to need much sleep. I've lost weight and feel healthy and I like myself. I've just bought six new dresses, in fact, and they look quite good on me. I feel sexy and men stare at me. Maybe I'll have an affair, or perhaps several. I feel capable of speaking and doing good in politics. I would like to help people with problems similar to mine so they won't feel hopeless.

It's wonderful when you feel like this. . . . The feeling of exhilaration—the high mood—makes me feel light and full of the joy of living. However, when I go beyond this stage, I become manic, and the creativeness becomes so magnified I begin to see things in my mind that aren't real. For instance, one night I created an entire movie, complete with cast, that I still think would be terrific. I saw the people as clearly as if watching them in real life. I also experienced complete terror, as if it were actually happening, when I knew that an assassination scene was about to take place. I cowered under the covers and became a complete shaking wreck. As you know, I went into a manic psychosis at that point. My screams awakened my husband, who tried to reassure me that we were in our bedroom and everything was the same. There was nothing to be afraid of. Nevertheless, I was admitted to the hospital the next day.

FIEVE, 1975, PP. 12–18

More than 90% of people who experience manic episodes eventually experience a recurrence (APA, 1994). Manic episodes are relatively uncommon, affecting but 8 persons in every 1,000 (0.8%), according to the Epidemiologic Catchment Area (ECA) survey (M. M. Weissman et al., 1991).

CYCLOTHYMIC DISORDER

Cyclothymia is derived from the Greek *kyklos,* which means "circle," and *thymos* ("spirit"). The notion of a circular-moving spirit is an apt description because this disorder involves a chronic cyclical pattern of mood disturbance characterized by mild mood swings of at least 2 years (1 year for children and adolescents). Cyclothymic disorder usually begins in late adolescence or early adulthood and persists for years. Few, if any, periods of normal mood last for more than a month or two. Neither the periods of elevated nor the depressed mood are severe enough to warrant a diagnosis of bipolar disorder, however. Estimates from community studies indicate lifetime prevalence rates for cyclothymic disorder of between 0.4% to 1% (4 to 10 people in a 1,000), with men and women about equally likely to be affected (APA, 1994).

The periods of elevated mood are called hypomanic episodes, from the Greek prefix *hypo-,* meaning "under" or "less than." *Hypo*manic episodes are less severe than manic episodes. People are more restless and irritable than normal during them, however. Hypomanic episodes also occur without the severe social or occupational problems that are engendered by full-blown manic episodes. People who experience hypomania may have an inflated sense of self-esteem and feel unusually charged with energy and alert. They may be able to work long hours with little fatigue or need for sleep. Their projects may be left unfinished when their moods reverse, however. Then they enter a mildly depressed mood state and find it difficult to summon the energy or interest to persevere. They feel lethargic and depressed, but not to the extent that is typical of a major depressive episode.

Social relationships may become strained by shifting moods, and work may suffer. Social invitations, eagerly sought during hypomanic periods, may be declined during depressed periods. Phone calls may not be returned as the mood slumps. Sexual interest waxes and wanes.

The boundaries between bipolar disorder and cyclothymic disorder are not yet clearly established. Some forms of cyclothymic disorder may represent a mild, early type of bipolar disorder. Perhaps as many as 50% of people with cyclothymia go on to develop full-fledged bipolar disorder. Others never develop bipolar disorder, nor do they respond to treatment with lithium carbonate (as people with bipolar disorder often do) or present with a family history of bipolar disorder (Howland & Thase, 1993). It appears that cyclothymic disorder is a heterogeneous disorder that may include some subtypes that are related to bipolar disorder and others that are not. We presently lack the ability to distinguish persons with cyclothymia who are likely to develop bipolar disorder eventually (Howland & Thase, 1993).

The following case presents an example of the mild mood swings that typify cyclothymic disorder:

The man, a 29-year-old car salesman, reports that since the age of 14 he has experienced alternating periods of "good times and bad times." During his "bad" periods, which generally last between 4 and 7 days, he sleeps excessively and feels a lack of confidence, energy, and motivation, as if he were "just vegetating." Then his moods abruptly shift for a period of three or four days, usually upon awakening in the morning, and he feels aflush with confidence and sharpened mental ability. During these "good periods" he engages in promiscuous sex and uses alcohol, in part to enhance his good feelings and in part to help him sleep at night. The good periods may last upwards of 7–10 days at times, before shifting back into the "bad" periods, generally following a hostile or irritable outburst.

ADAPTED FROM SPITZER ET AL., 1994, PP. 155–157

THEORETICAL PERSPECTIVES

Multiple factors—biological, psychological, social, and environmental—appear to be involved in the development of mood disorders (Cui & Vaillant, 1996). In this section we first consider the relationships between stress and the mood disorders. Then we consider psychological and biological perspectives on depression.

Stress and Mood Disorders

Investigators have long recognized that life stress plays a significant role in depression. Stressors such as the loss of a loved one, prolonged unemployment, physical illness, marital or relationship problems, economic hardship, pressure at work, or racism and discrimination may all contribute to the onset or maintenance of mood disorders, especially major depression. (Karel, 1997; J. M. Lewis, 1998; Lynch, Kaplan, & Shema, 1997; Stader & Hokanson, 1998). In community samples, about four of five cases of depression are preceded by stressful life events (Mazure, 1998). People are also more likely to become depressed when they hold themselves responsible for undesirable events, such as school problems, financial difficulties, unwanted pregnancy, interpersonal problems, and problems with the law (Hammen & de Mayo, 1982).

Yet the relationship between stress and depression may cut both ways: Stressful life events may contribute to depression, and depressive symptoms in themselves may be stressful or lead to additional stress, such as divorce or loss of a job (Cui & Vaillant, 1997; E. C. Chang, 1997; Daley et al., 1997). When you're depressed, for example, you may find it more difficult to keep up with your work at school or on the job, which can lead to more stress as your work backs up. The closer the stressful event taps the person's core concerns (failing at work or school, for instance), the more likely it is to precipitate a relapse in people with a history of depression (Z. V. Segal et al., 1992).

Stressful events also play an important role in time to recovery in episodes of bipolar disorder and to relapses, though it seems not necessarily to the onset of the disorder (Hammen & Gitlin, 1997; S. L. Johnson & Miller, 1997; S. L. Johnson & Roberts, 1995).

Coping Styles and Social Support: Resources for Handling Stress   Some people seem better able to

withstand stress or recover from losses than do others. Investigators find that psychosocial factors such as social support and coping styles may serve as buffers against depression in times of stress (Karel, 1997). For instance, major depressive disorder occurs twice as often among people who live alone than among people living with others. A strong marital relationship may provide a source of support during times of stress. Not surprisingly, people who are divorced or separated have higher rates of depression and suicide attempts than married people (M. M. Weissman et al., 1991).

Evidence also shows that people with depression are less likely to use active problem-solving strategies to alleviate stress than nondepressed people (e.g., J. R. Asarnow, Carlson, & Guthrie, 1987; A. M. Nezu & Ronan, 1985). People with major depression also show evidence of deficits in the skills needed to solve interpersonal problems they may have with their friends, co-workers, or supervisors (Marx, Williams, & Claridge, 1992). Taking an active approach to solving one's problems is also linked to better outcomes following a depressive episode (Sherbourne, Hays, & Wells, 1995).

Both higher levels of current social support and perceptions of one's parents as being warm and loving have been linked to a lesser risk of depression in women (Kendler et al., 1993b). Perhaps people who have a closer relationship with their parents are better able to develop mutually supportive relationships with others, which may provide them with a buffer against depression when faced with disturbing life events. The availability of social support is also associated with quicker recoveries and better outcomes in people with major depression (Lara, Leader, & Klein, 1997; Moos, Cronkite, & Moos, 1998). Research also shows that people

Social support as a buffer against depression.   Social support appears to buffer the effects of stress and may reduce the risk of depression. People who lack important relationships and who rarely join in social activities are more likely to suffer from depression.

with poorer social integration (lack of important relationships or social connections) are more likely to suffer depression, which again highlights the role that social support plays in proneness to depression (P. A. Barnett & Gotlib, 1988).

Psychodynamic Perspectives

The classic psychodynamic theory of depression of Freud (1957/1917) and his followers (e.g., Abraham, 1948/1916) holds that depression represents anger directed inward rather than against others. Anger may become directed against the self following the actual or threatened loss of important others.

Freud believed that **mourning,** or normal bereavement, is psychologically a healthy process by which one eventually comes to separate from a person who is lost through death, separation, divorce, or another avenue. Pathological mourning, however, does not promote separation and could foster lingering depression. Pathological mourning is likely to occur in people who hold powerful **ambivalent** feelings—a combination of positive (love) and negative (anger, hostility) feelings—toward the person who has departed or whose departure is feared. Freud theorized that when people lose, or even if they fear losing, an important figure about whom they are ambivalent, their feelings of anger toward the other person turn to rage. Yet rage triggers conscious and unconscious imagery of harm, producing guilt. Guilt, in turn, prevents the person from venting anger directly at the lost person (called an "object").

To preserve the lost object, people **introject,** or bring inward, their mental representations of the object. They thus incorporate the other person into their selves. Now anger is turned inward, against the part of the self that represents the inward representation of the lost person, producing self-loathing that leads to depression.

From the psychodynamic viewpoint, bipolar disorder represents shifting dominance of the individual's personality by the ego and superego. In the depressive phase, the superego is dominant, producing exaggerated notions of wrongdoing and flooding the individual with feelings of guilt and worthlessness. After a time, the ego rebounds and asserts supremacy, producing feelings of elation and self-confidence that come to characterize the manic phase. The excessive display of ego eventually triggers a return of guilt, once again plunging the individual into depression.

The Self-Focusing Model: An Integrative Psychodynamic-Cognitive Model More recent psychodynamic models, such as the self-focusing model, emphasize the effects of loss on the individual's sense of self-worth or self-esteem. According to the self-focusing model, depression may occur when an individual pursues love objects or goals it would be more adaptive to surrender (Pyszczynski & Greenberg, 1987). The self-focusing model considers how people allocate their attentional processes after the loss. Thus, it may be considered a type of integrative psychodynamic-cognitive model. According to the model, depression-prone people experience a period of intense self-examination or self-focusing following a major loss or disappointment. They focus their attention on the difference between what they are left with and what they want and are unable to surrender hope of regaining the lost object (loved one) or goal. Fruitless focus on restoring the lost object or goal triggers self-blame, diminishing self-esteem and depressing their mood. People may become so trapped in negative self-focusing that they cannot accept success experiences as reasons to reevaluate their self-concepts. They may attribute negative events to personal shortcomings but explain away positive events as "good fortune." They come to expect the worst in relationships, an expectation that may become a self-fulfilling prophecy.

Consider a person who must cope with the termination of a failed romantic relationship. It may be clear to all concerned that the relationship is beyond hope of revival. The self-focusing model proposes, however, that the depression-prone individual persists in focusing attention on restoring the relationship, rather than recognizing the futility of the effort and getting on with life. Moreover, the lost partner was someone who was a source of emotional support and whom the depression-prone individual had relied on to maintain feelings of self-esteem. Following the loss, the depression-prone individual feels stripped of hope and optimism because these positive feelings had depended on the other person, now lost. The loss of self-esteem and feelings of security, not of the relationship per se, precipitates depression. If depression-prone people peg their self-worth to a specific occupational goal, such as success in a modeling career, failure triggers self-focusing and consequent depression. Only by surrendering the object or lost goal and fostering alternative sources of identity and self-worth can the cycle be broken.

Research Evidence Psychodynamic theorists focus on the role of loss in depression. Research does show that the losses of significant others (through death or divorce, for example) are often associated with the onset of depression (Paykel, 1982). Such losses may also lead to other psychological disorders, however. There is yet a lack of research to support Freud's view that repressed anger toward the departed loved one is turned inward in depression.

Research on the utility of the self-focusing model has been mixed. On the one hand, people suffering from depression have been shown to engage in higher levels of self-focusing following failure experiences than do others, and in relatively lower levels of self-focusing following successes (Pyszczynski & Greenberg, 1985, 1986). On the other hand, self-focused attention has been linked to disorders other than depression, including anxiety disorders, alcoholism, mania, and schizophrenia (Ingram, 1990, 1991). The general linkage between self-focused attention and psychopathology may limit the model's value as an explanation of depression (Ingram, 1991).

Humanistic-Existential Perspectives

From the humanistic-existential perspective, people become depressed when they cannot imbue their existence with meaning and make authentic choices that lead to self-fulfillment. The world is then a drab place. People's search for meaning gives color and substance to their lives. Guilt may arise when people believe they have not lived up to their potentials. Humanistic psychologists challenge us to take a long hard look at our lives. Are they worthwhile and enriching? Or are they drab and routine? If the latter, it may be we have frustrated our needs for self-actualization. We may be settling, coasting through life. Settling can give rise to a sense of dreariness that becomes expressed in depressive behavior—lethargy, sullen mood, and withdrawal.

Like psychodynamic theorists, humanistic theorists also focus on the loss of self-esteem that can arise when people lose friends or family members or suffer occupational setbacks or losses. We tend to connect our personal identity and sense of self-worth with our social roles as parents, spouses, students, or workers. When these role identities are lost, through the death of a spouse, the departure of children to college, or loss of a job, our sense of purpose and self-worth can be shattered. Depression is a frequent consequence of such losses. It is especially likely when we base our self-esteem on our occupational role or success. The loss of a job, a demotion, or a failure to achieve a promotion are common precipitants of depression, especially when we are reared to value ourselves on the basis of occupational success.

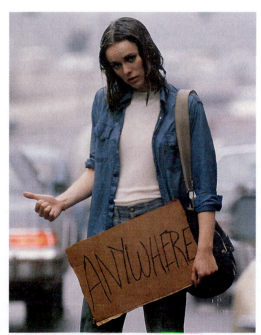

What happens when we lose our sense of direction? According to the humanistic-existential perspective, depression may result from the inability to find meaning and purpose in one's life.

Learning Perspectives

Whereas psychodynamic perspectives focus on inner, often unconscious, determinants of mood disorders, learning perspectives dwell more on situational factors, such as the loss of positive reinforcement. We perform best when levels of reinforcement are commensurate with our efforts. Changes in the frequency or effectiveness of reinforcement can shift the balance so that life becomes unrewarding.

Reinforcement and Depression Peter Lewinsohn (1974) suggested that depression may result when a person's behavior receives too little reinforcement from the environment. Lack of reinforcement can sap motivation and induce feelings of depression. A vicious cycle may ensue: Inactivity and social withdrawal deplete opportunities for reinforcement; lesser reinforcement exacerbates withdrawal. The low rate of activity that is typical of depression may also be a source of secondary gain or secondary reinforcement. Family members and other people may rally around people suffering from depression and release them from their responsibilities. Rather than help people who are struggling with depression regain normal levels of instrumental behavior, sympathy may thus backfire and maintain depressed behavior.

Reduction in reinforcement levels can occur for many reasons. A person who is recuperating at home from illness may find little that is reinforcing to do. Social reinforcement may plummet when people close to us, who were suppliers of reinforcement, die or leave us. People who suffer social losses are more likely to become depressed when they lack the social skills to form new relationships. Some first-year college students are homesick and depressed because they lack the skills to form rewarding new relationships. Widows and widowers may be at a loss as to how to ask someone for a date or start a new relationship.

Changes in life circumstances may also alter the balance of effort and reinforcement. A prolonged layoff may reduce financial reinforcements, which may in turn force painful cutbacks in lifestyle. A disability or an extended illness may also impair one's ability to ensure a steady flow of reinforcements.

Lewinsohn's model is supported by research findings that connect depression to a low level of positive reinforcement. For example, Lewinsohn and Libet (1972) noted a correspondence between depressed moods and lower rates of participation in potentially reinforcing activities. People with depressive disorders were also found to report fewer pleasant activities than nondepressed people (MacPhillamy & Lewinsohn, 1974). It remains unclear, however, whether depression precedes or follows a decline in the level of reinforcement (J. M. Williams, 1984). It may be that people who become depressed lose interest in pleasant activities or withdraw from potentially reinforcing social interactions, and not that inactivity leads to depression. Regardless of the causes of depression, behavioral treatment approaches that encourage people who become depressed to increase their

Does participation in pleasant events help keep our moods on an even keel? According to psychologist Peter Lewinsohn, participation in pleasant events or reinforcing activities contributes to feelings of happiness and well-being.

levels of pleasant activities and provide them with the skills to do so are often helpful in alleviating depression (DeRubeis & Crits-Christoph, 1998; Jacobson et al., 1996).

Interactional Theory The interactions between depressed persons and other people may help explain the former group's shortfall in positive reinforcement. Interactional theory, developed by James Coyne (1976), proposes that the adjustment to living with a depressed person can become so stressful that the partner or family member becomes progressively less reinforcing toward the depressed person.

Interactional theory is based on the concept of reciprocal interaction. People's behavior influences, and is influenced by, the behavior of others. The theory holds that depression-prone people react to stress by demanding greater social support and reassurance. At first people who become depressed may succeed in garnering support. Over time, however, their demands and behavior begin to elicit anger or annoyance. Although loved ones may keep their negative feelings to themselves, so as not to further upset the depressed person, the feelings may surface in subtle ways that spell rejection. Depressed people may react to rejection with deeper depression and greater demands, triggering a vicious cycle of further rejection and more profound depression. They may also feel guilty about distressing their family members, which can exacerbate negative feelings about themselves.

Evidence shows that people who become depressed do tend to encounter rejection in long-term relationships (D. K. Marcus & Nardone, 1992). Family members may find it stressful to adjust to the behavior of the person who is depressed, especially such behaviors as withdrawal, lethargy,

fretfulness, and despair. The links among depression, the seeking of reassurance, and social rejection may be moderated by traditional gender-role expectations. A study of mildly depressed college students supported Coyne's prediction that people who encounter depression seek reassurance from others (in this case, college roommates of the same gender) to relieve their doubts about whether others really care about them (Joiner, Malfano, & Metalsky, 1992). Men who were depressed, but not women, encountered rejection by roommates when they strongly sought such reassurance. Perhaps men who are depressed but "suffer in silence" and "take it like a man" are more valued by their peers. Women who are depressed may not be perceived as violating a gender stereotype when they seek emotional reassurance and may thus be less likely to be rejected.

All in all, research evidence generally supports Coyne's belief that people who suffer from depression elicit rejection from others, but there remains a lack of evidence to show this rejection is mediated by negative emotions that the depressed person induces in others (Segrin & Dillard, 1992). Rather, a growing body of literature shows that people who develop depression have social skills deficits which may account for the fact that others reject them (Segrin & Abramson, 1994). They tend to be unresponsive, uninvolved, and even impolite when they interact with others. For example, they tend to gaze very little at the other person, take an excessive amount of time to respond, show very little approval or validation of the other person, and dwell on their problems and negative feelings (Segrin & Abramson, 1994). They even dwell on negative feelings when interacting with strangers. In effect, they turn other people off, setting the stage for rejection.

Whether social skills deficits are a cause or a symptom of depression remains to be determined. Whatever the case, impaired social behavior likely may play an important role in determining the persistence or recurrence of depression. As we shall see, some psychological approaches to treating depression (i.e., interpersonal psychotherapy and Lewinsohn's social skills training approach—discussed later) focus on helping people with depression better understand and overcome their interpersonal problems. This may help, in turn, alleviate depression or perhaps prevent future recurrences.

Cognitive Perspectives

Cognitive theorists relate the origin and maintenance of depression to the ways in which people see themselves and the world around them.

Aaron Beck's Cognitive Theory One of the most influential cognitive theorists, psychiatrist Aaron Beck (Beck, 1976; Beck, Rush, Shaw, & Emery, 1979; Beck & Young, 1985), relates the development of depression to the adoption of a negatively biased or distorted way of thinking—the **cognitive triad of depression** (see Table 7.4). The cognitive triad includes negative beliefs about oneself (e.g., "I'm no good"), the environment or the world at large (e.g., "This school is awful"), and the future (e.g., "Nothing will ever

TABLE 7.4

The Cognitive Triad of Depression

Negative view of oneself	Perceiving oneself as worthless, deficient, inadequate, unlovable, and as lacking the skills necessary to achieve happiness.
Negative view of the environment	Perceiving the environment as imposing excessive demands and/or presenting obstacles that are impossible to overcome, leading continually to failure and loss.
Negative view of the future	Perceiving the future as hopeless and believing that one is powerless to change things for the better. All that one expects of the future is continuing failure and unrelenting misery and hardship.

According to Aaron Beck, depression-prone people adopt an habitual style of negative thinking—the so-called cognitive triad of depression.

Source: Adapted from Beck & Young, 1985; Beck et al., 1979.

turn out right for me"). Cognitive theory holds that people who adopt this negative way of thinking are at greater risk of becoming depressed in the face of stressful or disappointing life experiences, such as getting a poor grade or losing a job.

Beck views these negative concepts of the self and the world as mental templates or *cognitive schemes* that are adopted in childhood on the basis of early learning experiences. Children may find that nothing they do is good enough to please their parents or teachers. As a result, they may come to regard themselves as basically incompetent and to perceive their prospects as dim. These beliefs may sensitize them later in life to interpret any failure or disappointment as a reflection of something basically wrong or inadequate about themselves. Minor disappointments and personal shortcomings become "blown out of proportion." Even a minor disappointment becomes a crushing blow or a total defeat, which can lead to depression.

The tendency to magnify the importance of minor failures is an example of an error in thinking that Beck labels a *cognitive distortion*. He believes cognitive distortions can set the stage for depression in the face of negative life events. David Burns (1980) enumerated a number of the cognitive distortions associated with depression:

1. *All-or-Nothing Thinking.* Seeing events in black and white, as either all good or all bad. For example, one may perceive a relationship that ended in disappointment as a totally negative experience, despite any positive feelings or experiences that may have occurred along the way. Perfectionism is an example of all-or-nothing thinking. Perfectionists judge any outcome other than perfect success to be complete failure. They may consider a grade of B+ or even A− to be tantamount to an F. They may feel like abject failures if they fall a few dollars short of their sales quotas or receive a very fine (but less than perfect) performance evaluation. Perfectionism is connected with an increased vulnera-

bility to depression as well as poor outcomes in treatment, whether the treatment involves antidepressant medication or psychological approaches such as cognitive therapy or interpersonal psychotherapy (Blatt et al., 1995, 1998; Hewitt, Flett, & Ediger, 1996; Minarik & Ahrens, 1996).

2. *Overgeneralization.* Believing that if a negative event occurs, it is likely to recur in similar situations in the future. One thus interprets a single negative event as foreshadowing an endless series of negative events. For example, one receives a letter of rejection from a potential employer and assumes all other job applications will be rejected.

3. *Mental Filter.* Focusing only on negative details of events, thereby rejecting the positive features of one's experiences. Like a droplet of ink that spreads to discolor an entire beaker of water, focusing only on a single negative detail can darken one's vision of reality. Beck called this cognitive distortion **selective abstraction,** meaning the individual selectively abstracts the negative details from events and ignores their positive features. One thus bases one's self-esteem on perceived weaknesses and failures, rather than on positive features or on a balance of accomplishments and shortcomings. For example, one receives a job evaluation that contains positive and negative comments but focuses only on the negative.

4. *Disqualifying the Positive.* This refers to the tendency to snatch defeat from the jaws of victory by neutralizing or denying your accomplishments. An example is dismissal of congratulations for a job well done by thinking and saying, "Oh, it's no big deal. Anyone could have done it." By contrast, taking credit where credit is due may help people overcome depression by increasing their belief they can make changes that will lead to a positive future (Needles & Abramson, 1990).

5. *Jumping to Conclusions.* Forming a negative interpretation of events, despite a lack of evidence. Two examples of this style of thinking are "mind reading" and "the fortune teller error." In *mind reading,* you arbitrarily jump to the conclusion that others don't like or respect you, as in interpreting a friend's not calling for a while as a rejection. The *fortune teller error* involves the prediction that something bad is always about to happen to oneself. The person believes the prediction of calamity is factually based even though there is an absence of evidence to support it. For example, the person concludes that a passing tightness in the chest *must* be a sign of heart disease, discounting the possibility of more benign causes.

6. *Magnification and Minimization.* Magnification, or **catastrophizing,** refers to the tendency to make mountains out of molehills—to exaggerate the importance of negative events, personal flaws, fears, or mistakes. Minimization is the mirror image, a type of cognitive distortion in which one minimizes or underestimates one's good points.

7. *Emotional Reasoning.* Basing reasoning on emotions—thinking, for example, "If I feel guilty, it must be because I've done something really wrong." One interprets feelings and events on the basis of emotions rather than dispassionate evaluation of the evidence.

8. *Should Statements.* Creating personal imperatives or self-commandments— "shoulds" or "musts." For example, "I *should* always get my first serve in!" or, "I *must* make Chris like me!" By creating unrealistic expectations, **musterbation**—the label given this form of thinking by Albert Ellis—can lead one to become depressed when one falls short.

9. *Labeling and Mislabeling.* Explaining behavior by attaching negative labels to oneself and others. You may explain a poor grade on a test by thinking you were "lazy" or "stupid" rather than simply unprepared for the specific exam or, perhaps, ill. Labeling other people as "stupid" or "insensitive" can engender hostility toward them. Mislabeling involves the use of labels that are emotionally charged and inaccurate, such as calling yourself a "pig" because of a minor deviation from your usual diet.

10. *Personalization.* This refers to the tendency to assume you are responsible for other people's problems and behavior. You may assume your partner or spouse is crying because of something you have done (or not done), rather than recognizing that other causes may be involved.

Consider the errors in thinking illustrated in the following case:

Christie was a 33-year-old real estate sales agent who suffered from frequent episodes of depression. Whenever a deal fell through, she would blame herself: "If only I had worked harder . . . negotiated better . . . talked more persuasively . . . the deal would have been done." After several successive disappointments, each one followed by self-recriminations, she felt like quitting altogether. Her thinking became increasingly dominated by negative thoughts, which further depressed her mood and lowered her self-esteem: "I'm a loser . . . I'll never succeed . . . It's all my fault . . . I'm no good and I'm never going to succeed at anything."

Christie's thinking included cognitive errors such as the following: (1) personalization (believing herself to be the sole cause of negative events), (2) labeling and mislabeling (labeling herself to be a loser); (3) over-generalization (predicting a dismal future on the basis of a present disappointment); and (4) mental filter (judging her personality entirely on the basis of her disappointments). In therapy, Christie was helped to think more realistically about events and not to jump to conclusions that she was automatically at fault whenever a deal fell through, or to judge her whole personality on the basis of disappointments or perceived flaws within herself. In place of this self-defeating style of thinking, she began to think more realistically when disappointments occurred, like telling herself, "Okay, I'm disappointed. I'm frustrated. I feel lousy. So what? It doesn't mean I'll never succeed. Let me discover what went wrong and try to correct it the next time. I have to look ahead, not dwell on disappointments in the past."

The Authors' Files

Distorted thinking tends to be experienced as automatic, as if the thoughts had just popped into one's head. These **automatic thoughts** are likely to be accepted as statements of fact rather than opinions or habitual ways of interpreting events.

Beck and his colleagues formulated a **cognitive-specificity hypothesis**, which proposes that different disorders, anxiety disorders and depressive disorders in particular, are characterized by different types of automatic thoughts. The results of one study (Beck, Brown, Steer, Eidelson, & Riskind, 1987) showed some interesting differences in the types of automatic thoughts reported by people with depressive and anxiety disorders (see Table 7.5). People with diagnosable depression more often reported thoughts concerning themes of loss, self-deprecation, and pessimism. People with anxiety disorders more often reported thoughts concerning physical danger and other threats.

Research Evidence on Cognitions and Depression
Evidence shows that distorted cognitions and negative thinking are linked to depressive symptoms and clinical depression (D. A. Clark, Cook, & Snow, 1998; McDermut, Haaga, & Bilek, 1997; Stader & Hokanson, 1998; Wong & Whitaker, 1993). People who are depressed also tend to

TABLE 7.5

Automatic Thoughts Associated with Depression and Anxiety

Common Automatic Thoughts Associated with Depression:

1. I'm worthless.
2. I'm not worthy of other people's attention or affection.
3. I'll never be as good as other people are.
4. I'm a social failure.
5. I don't deserve to be loved.
6. People don't respect me anymore.
7. I will never overcome my problems.
8. I've lost the only friends I've had.
9. Life isn't worth living.
10. I'm worse off than they are.
11. There's no one left to help me.
12. No one cares whether I live or die.
13. Nothing ever works out for me anymore.
14. I have become physically unattractive.

Common Automatic Thoughts Associated with Anxiety:

1. What if I get sick and become an invalid?
2. I am going to be injured.
3. What if no one reaches me in time to help?
4. I might be trapped.
5. I am not a healthy person.
6. I'm going to have an accident.
7. Something will happen that will ruin my appearance.
8. I am going to have a heart attack.
9. Something awful is going to happen.
10. Something will happen to someone I care about.
11. I'm losing my mind.

Source: Adapted from Beck et al., 1987.

On Positive Illusions and Mental Health: Is It Adaptive to See Things as They Truly Are?

A common assumption exists that there is an objective reality "out there" and the ability to perceive reality accurately is a basic feature of psychological adjustment. Individuals who perceive the world for what it is may be better able to adapt to their physical and social environments and avoid harm (Colvin & Block, 1994). Yet might it be more adaptive under some circumstances to hold certain positive biases or optimistic illusions about oneself and one's place in the world? Although we usually equate mental-health with good reality testing, and mental illness with distorted perceptions and cognitions, the negative perceptions held by many people who experience depression don't appear to be distorted at all, but are rather quite realistic. Research suggests that "mentally healthy" people may in some ways view the world less realistically than people who are depressed. Many people with depression may be more accurate in their assessment of the extent to which they can actually exercise control over events (Alloy & Abramson, 1988). It may be the rest of us who are seeing the world through "rose-colored lenses" that cast a rosy tint on how we perceive our abilities and our likelihood of success. Might it be that optimistic illusions and biases are psychologically adaptive?

Perhaps people help keep themselves out of the dumps by maintaining optimistic illusions despite evidence to the contrary. Perhaps too we need to have some illusions if we are to maintain high self-esteem and belief in our own coping ability (Alloy & Clements, 1992). Such positive biases may reduce vulnerability to depression and other psychological disorders in the face of frustrating or disappointing experience. They may also help us keep our chins up and maintain expectancies of success in the future, rather than accept negative outcomes as somehow fated for us.

Researchers devised a research project to test this hypothesis. In essence, they created a laboratory situation in which subjects had no control over a laboratory task so they could assess which subjects nevertheless managed to maintain an *illusion of control*. The results showed that subjects who maintained an illusion of control showed less evidence of depression following exposure to stressful experiences afterward (Alloy & Clements, 1992). Perhaps the tendency to think we are in charge of our destinies reduces our susceptibility to depression, even if we are wrong. We should caution that more evidence is needed to support the link between positive illusions and psychological adjustment. Let us also note that holding extremely positive illusions, such as delusions of grandeur, is clearly associated with psychological problems such as mania and schizophrenia (S. E. Taylor & Brown, 1994).

TRUTH *or* FICTION REVISITED

7.5 *True.* Researchers find that "mentally healthy" people may in some ways view the world less realistically than people who are depressed. Many people with depression may be more accurate in their assessment of the extent to which they actually can exercise control over events.

Perhaps depressed people don't see the proverbial glass as half empty but as both half empty and half full, whereas nondepressed people tend to see the glass as only half full. In another study, researchers found depressed women attended equally to positive and negative stimuli in a laboratory task (the stimuli were either positive, neutral, or negative words presented on a computer display). Nondepressed women showed a positive bias by attending more to the positive or neutral stimuli (McCabe & Gotlib, 1995). This suggests that people who are depressed don't necessarily have an attentional bias toward perceiving only the negative. Rather, what seems to set them apart from nondepressed people is their failure to maintain a positive bias.

hold more pessimistic views of the future and are more critical of themselves and others (Glara et al., 1993). College students with more distorted thoughts are also at greater risk of becoming depressed in the face of negative life events, such as illness, relocation, or death of loved ones, than are students with healthier outlooks (E. H. Wise & Barnes, 1986).

The relationship between negative thinking and depression may depend more on the balance between negative and positive thoughts than on the presence of negative thoughts alone. Research using a thought-counting method showed that people who functioned well psychologically experienced both positive and negative thoughts, but the positive thoughts occurred one and a half to two times as often as the negative thoughts (R. M. Schwartz, 1986). People with a mild level of psychological dysfunction, by contrast, produced about equal numbers of positive and negative thoughts. Thinking positive thoughts may serve as a kind of buffer or shock absorber in helping people cope with negative life events without becoming depressed (Bruch, 1997; Lightsey, 1994a, 1994b).

All in all, there is broad research support for many aspects of the theory, including Beck's concept of the cognitive triad of depression and his view that people with depression think more negatively than nondepressed people about themselves, the future, and the world in general (Haaga, Dyck, & Ernst, 1991). Although dysfunctional cognitions (negative, distorted, or pessimistic thoughts) are more common among people who are depressed, the causal pathways remain unclear. We can't yet say whether dysfunctional or negative thinking causes depression or is merely a feature of depression. Thus, the central theme of cognitive theory, that negative, distorted thoughts are causally related to depression, remains unsubstantiated (Cole et al., 1998; Haaga et al., 1991; Stader & Hokanson, 1998).

Perhaps the causal linkages go both ways. Our thoughts may affect our moods and our moods may affect our thoughts (Kwon & Oei, 1994). Think in terms of a vicious cycle. People who feel depressed may begin thinking in more negative, distorted ways. The more negative and distorted their thinking becomes, the more depressed they feel, and the more depressed they feel, the more dysfunctional their thinking becomes. Alternatively, dysfunctional thinking may come first in the cycle, perhaps in response to a disappointing life experience, which then leads to a downcast mood, which in turn accentuates negative thinking, and so on. We are still faced with the old "chicken or the egg" dilemma of determining which comes first in the causal sequence, distorted thinking or depression. Future research may help tease out these causal pathways. Even if it should become clear that distorted cognitions play no direct causal role in the initial onset of depression, the reciprocal interaction between thoughts and moods may play a role in maintaining depression and in determining the likelihood of recurrence (Kwon & Oei, 1994). We know, for example, that people who recover from depression but continue to hold distorted cognitions tend to be at greater risk of recurrence of depression (Rush & Weissenberger, 1986). Fortunately, evidence shows that dysfunctional attitudes tend to decrease with effective treatment for depression (Fava et al., 1994).

Learned Helplessness (Attributional) Theory

The **learned helplessness** model proposes that people may become depressed because they learn to view themselves as helpless to control the reinforcements in their environments—or to change their lives for the better. The originator of the learned helplessness concept, Martin Seligman (1973, 1975), suggests that people learn to perceive themselves as helpless because of their experiences. The learned helplessness model thus straddles the behavioral and the cognitive: Situational factors foster attitudes that lead to depression.

The learned helplessness model is based on laboratory studies of animals by Seligman and his colleagues. In early studies, dogs exposed to an inescapable electric shock showed the "learned helplessness effect" by failing to learn

How could he have missed that tackle? This football player missed a crucial tackle and is rehashing it. He is putting himself down and telling himself that there is nothing he can do to improve his performance. Cognitive theorists believe that a person's self-defeating or distorted interpretations of negative events can set the stage for depression.

to escape when the shock was later made escapable (Overmier & Seligman, 1967; Seligman & Maier, 1967). Exposure to uncontrollable forces apparently taught the animals they were helpless to change their situation. Animals who developed learned helplessness showed behaviors that were similar to those of people with depression, including lethargy, lack of motivation, and difficulty acquiring new skills (Maier & Seligman, 1976).

Seligman (1975, 1991) proposed that some forms of depression in humans might result from exposure to apparently uncontrollable situations. Such experiences can instill the expectation that future reinforcements will also be beyond the individual's control. A cruel vicious cycle may come into play in many cases of depression. A few failures may produce feelings of helplessness and expectations of further failure. Perhaps you know people who have failed certain subjects, such as mathematics. They may come to believe themselves incapable of succeeding in math. They may thus decide that studying for the quantitative section of the Graduate Record Exam is a waste of time. They then do poorly, completing the self-fulfilling prophecy by confirming their expectations, which further intensifies feelings of helplessness, leading to lowered expectations, and so on, in a vicious cycle.

Although it stimulated much interest, Seligman's model failed to account for the low self-esteem typical of people who are depressed. Nor did it explain variations in the persistence of depression. Seligman and his colleagues (Abramson, Seligman, & Teasdale, 1978) offered a reformulation of the theory to meet such shortcomings. The revised theory held that perception of lack of control over reinforcement alone did not explain the persistence and severity of depres-

causes of negative events (such as failure in work, school, or romantic relationships) according to these three types of attributions are most vulnerable to depression:

1. Internal factors, or beliefs that failures reflect their personal inadequacies, rather than external factors, or beliefs that failures are caused by environmental factors;

2. Global factors, or beliefs that failures reflect sweeping flaws in personality rather than specific factors, or beliefs that failures reflect limited areas of functioning; and

3. Stable factors, or beliefs that failures reflect fixed personality factors rather than unstable factors, or beliefs that the factors leading to failures are changeable.

Let us illustrate these attributional styles with the example of a first-year student who goes on a disastrous date. Afterward he shakes his head in wonder and tries to make sense of his experience. An internal attribution for the calamity would involve self-blame, as in "I really messed it up." An external attribution would place the blame elsewhere, as in "Some couples just don't hit it off," or, "She must have been in a bad mood." A stable attribution would suggest a problem that cannot be changed, as in "It's my personality." An unstable attribution, on the other hand, would suggest a transient condition, as in "It was probably the head cold." A global attribution for failure magnifies the extent of the problem, as in "I really have no idea what I'm doing when I'm with people." A specific attribution, in contrast, chops the problem down to size, as in "My problem is how to make small talk to get a relationship going."

The revised theory holds that each attributional dimension makes a specific contribution to feelings of helplessness. Internal attributions are linked to diminished self-esteem. Stable attributions for negative events help explain the persistence—or, in medical terms, the chronicity—of helplessness cognitions. Global attributions are associated with the generality or pervasiveness of feelings of helplessness following negative events. Attributional style should be distinguished from negative thinking (Gotlib et al., 1993). You may think negatively (pessimistically) or positively (optimistically), but still hold yourself to blame for your perceived failures.

Research is generally but not completely supportive of the reformulated helplessness (attributional) model. There is widespread support for the belief that people who are depressed are more likely than others to attribute the causes of failures to internal, stable, and global factors (e.g., Heimberg et al., 1987; Pyszczynski & Greenberg, 1985; Seligman et al., 1988; P. D. Sweeney, Anderson, & Bailey, 1986). Depressive attributional styles have also been shown to predict response to antidepressant medication in depressed patients (Levitan, Rector & Bagby, 1998). People who change their depressive attributional style also tend to achieve better outcomes following cognitive therapy, as the model would predict (Hollon, Evans, & DeRubeis, 1990).

On the other hand, we still lack evidence to show that attributional style is a cause, rather than an effect, of

Is it me? According to reformulated helplessness theory, the kinds of attributions we make concerning negative events can make us more or less vulnerable to depression. Attributing the break-up of a relationship to internalizing ("It's me"), globalizing ("I'm totally worthless"), and stabilizing ("Things are always going to turn out badly for me") causes can lead to depression.

sion. It was also necessary to consider cognitive factors, especially the ways in which people explain their failures and disappointments to themselves.

Seligman and his colleagues recast helplessness theory in terms of the social psychology concept of **attributional style.** An attributional style is a personal style of explanation. When disappointments or failures occur, we may explain them in various characteristic ways. We may blame ourselves (an **internal attribution**) or our circumstances (an **external attribution**). We may see bad experiences as typical events (a **stable attribution**) or as isolated events (an **unstable attribution**). We may see them as evidence of broader problems (a **global attribution**) or as evidence of precise and limited shortcomings (a **specific attribution**). The revised helplessness theory—called the *reformulated helplessness theory*—holds that people who explain the

depression (Beidel & Turner, 1986; Clark, Watson, & Mineka, 1994). We also lack evidence demonstrating that the interaction of a depressive attributional style and negative life events predicts the development of depression (Clark, Watson, & Mineka, 1994). Moreover, it appears that attributional style may have a stronger relationship to depression in people who tend to think more about the causes of events (Haaga, 1995). Though attributional style is related to dysfunctional attitudes and beliefs, they do not appear to tap the same construct (Spangler et al., 1997). In fact, it appears that people who hold dysfunctional attitudes may be different than those who hold a depressive attributional style. These two cognitive vulnerabilities may describe two separate cognitive pathways to depression.

Biological Perspectives

Evidence is accumulating that points to the role of biological factors, especially genetic factors and neurotransmitter function, in the development of mood disorders. Recent investigations are examining the biological roots of depression at the neurotransmitter level and even at the genetic, molecular, and cellular level (e.g., Duman, Heninger, & Nestler, 1997).

Genetic Factors Growing evidence implicates genetic factors in mood disorders. For one thing, mood disorders tend to run in families. Families, however, share environmental similarities as well as genes. Family members may share blue eyes (an inherited attribute) but also a common religion (a cultural attribute). Yet strengthening the genetic link are findings showing the closer the genetic relationship one shares with a person with a major mood disorder such as major depression or bipolar disorder, the greater the likelihood that one will also suffer from a major mood disorder (Faraone, Kremen, & Tsuang, 1990).

Twin studies and adoptee studies provide additional evidence of a genetic contribution. A higher concordance rate among monozygotic (MZ) twins than dizygotic (DZ) twins for a given disorder is taken as supportive evidence of genetic factors. Both types of twins share common environments, but MZ twins share 100% of their genes as compared to 50% for DZ twins. The concordance rate for major mood disorders (unipolar and bipolar disorders) between MZ twins averages 70%, which is about triple the rate between DZ twins (Faraone et al., 1990; Kendler et al., 1992a, 1993b). This supports a significant genetic component but is short of the 100% concordance we would expect if genetics was solely responsible for these disorders. Adoptee studies, which might provide corroborating evidence of genetic factors in mood disorders, are sparse.

All in all, heredity appears to play a contributing role in major depression (Gatz et al., 1992; Kendler et al., 1993a, 1993b; 1996a; McGuffin et al., 1996). Genetic factors appear to be equally important in determining the risk of major depression in both men and women (Kendler &

Prescott, 1999). However, genetics isn't the only, nor is it even the major, determinant of risk of major depression. Environmental factors, such as stressful life events, appear to play an equal if not greater role than genetics in determining the risk of the disorder (Kendler et al., 1993a; Kendler & Prescott, 1999). Genetic factors may play a greater role in explaining bipolar disorder than unipolar (major depressive) disorder, with one estimate indicating that perhaps 80% or more of the risk of bipolar disorder is accounted for by genetic factors (Blackwood et al., 1996; R. Katz & McGuffin, 1993). Data from twin studies suggest that dysthymic disorder may be relatively less influenced by genetic factors than major depression or bipolar disorder (Torgersen, 1986).

Researchers are zeroing in on several chromosomes that may carry genes that increase susceptibility to bipolar disorder (Bellivier et al., 1998; Berrettini et al., 1997; Cohn, 1997; Freimer et al., 1996; Ginns et al., 1996); Papolos et al., 1996). Even though genetic factors are believed to create a predisposition for bipolar disorder, they do not, in themselves, determine whether it will occur. Psychological, social, and environmental stresses are also involved (Hirschfeld & Cross, 1982).

Biochemical Factors in Depression If there is a genetic component to depression, just what is inherited? Perhaps the genetic vulnerability expresses itself in abnormalities in neurotransmitter activity.

Neurotransmitters were first suspected of playing a role in depression back in the 1950s. Findings were reported then that hypertensive patients who were taking the drug *reserpine* often became depressed. Reserpine is known to reduce the supplies of various neurotransmitters in the brain, including norepinephrine and serotonin. Then came the discovery that drugs that increase the brain levels of neurotransmitters such as norepinephrine and serotonin also help relieve depression. These drugs, called antidepressants, consist of *tricyclics,* such as imipramine (trade name Tofranil) and amitriptyline (trade name Elavil); *monoamine oxidase (MAO) inhibitors,* such as phenelzine (trade name Nardil); and *selective serotonin-reuptake inhibitors* (SSRIs), such as fluoxetine (trade name Prozac).

But if neurotransmitters are involved in depression, what role do they play? Antidepressants increase the availability of neurotransmitters in the brain within hours, but typically don't relieve symptoms of depression until several weeks afterwards (Quitkin et al., 1996). Therefore, it is unlikely these drugs are effective simply by boosting levels of neurotransmitters in the brain (Duman, Heninger, & Nestler, 1997).

The present view is that depression may involve an overabundance or oversensitivity of receptor sites on postsynaptic (receiving) neurons where neurotransmitters dock. Antidepressants may work by gradually reducing the number and sensitivity of these receptors. It is also possible that there is more than one mechanism explaining how antidepressants work (Duman, Heninger, & Nestler, 1997).

Though early speculation focused on the role of norepinephrine in depression, investigators today believe that we need to take into account irregularities in other neurotransmitters as well, especially serotonin, in explaining depression (Larisch et al., 1997; Mann, 1996).

Another line of research uses brain imaging techniques such as the PET scan (to measure metabolic activity) and the MRI (to examine structural differences) to peer into the brains of the people with depression. It turns out that the metabolic activity and size of the *prefrontal cortex* (the area of the frontal lobes lying in front of the motor areas) is typically lower in clinically depressed groups than in healthy controls (Drevets et al., 1997; Damasio, 1997). The prefrontal cortex is involved in regulating neurotransmitters implicated in depression, including serotonin and norepinephrine, so it is not surprising that evidence points to irregularities in this region of the brain.

There is also evidence suggesting other biochemical pathways to depression, including roles for proteins that help nerve cells communicate (M. S. Kramer et al., 1998) and endocrine system activity, including possible thyroid gland problems (Marangell et al., 1997), and fluctuations of the female sex hormones estrogen and progesterone in women (Seeman, 1997). Yet the major focus of interest on endocrine activity involves the adrenal glands, the endocrine glands located above the kidneys that produce epinephrine and norepinephrine and a group of steroidal hormones, including cortisol. The body normally suppresses the release of cortisol from the adrenal glands for about 24 hours after the person is given a synthetic steroid called *dexamethasone*. More than 9 of 10 nondepressed people show this suppression effect, as compared to only one third to one half of people with major depression (APA, 1987b; Valdivieso et al., 1996). Nonsuppression of cortisol release following ingestion of dexamethasone may thus be a marker for some cases of depression, especially those involving depression with psychotic features (J. C. Nelson & Davis, 1997).

TYING IT TOGETHER: THE DIATHESIS-STRESS MODEL AND DEPRESSION

Depression and other mood disorders involve an interplay of multiple factors. Consistent with the *diathesis-stress model*, depression may reflect an interaction of biological factors (perhaps involving levels or actions of neurotransmitters), psychological factors (such as cognitive distortions or learned helplessness), and social and environmental stressors (such as divorce or loss of a job).

Let us consider a possible causal pathway based on the diathesis-stress model (see Figure 7.3). Stressful life events, such as prolonged unemployment or a divorce, may have a depressing effect by reducing neurotransmitter activity in the brain. These biochemical effects may be more likely to occur or be more pronounced in people with a certain genetic predisposition or *diathesis* for depression. However, a depressive disorder may not develop, or may develop in a milder form, in people with more effective coping resources for handling stressful situations. For example, people who receive emotional support from others may be better able to withstand the effects of stress than those who have to go it alone. So too for people who make active coping efforts to meet the challenges they face in life.

Sociocultural factors may be major sources of stress that impact upon the development of mood disorders. These factors include poverty; overcrowding; exposure to racism, sexism, and prejudice; violence in the home or community; unequal stressful burdens placed on women; and family disintegration. These factors may figure prominently in either precipitating mood disorders or accounting for their recurrence. Other sources of stress include negative life events such as the loss of a job, the development of a serious illness, the breakup of a romantic relationship, and the loss of a loved one.

The diathesis for depression may take the form of a psychological vulnerability involving a depressive thinking

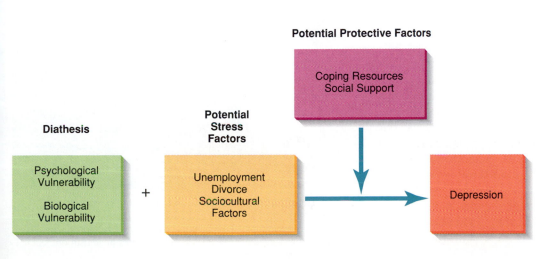

Potential Protective Factors

Coping Resources
Social Support

Diathesis

Psychological Vulnerability

Biological Vulnerability

+

Potential Stress Factors

Unemployment
Divorce
Sociocultural Factors

Depression

FIGURE 7.3 *Diathesis-stress model of depression.*

style, one characterized by tendencies to exaggerate the consequences of negative events, to heap blame on oneself, and to perceive oneself as helpless to effect positive change. This cognitive diathesis may increase the risk of depression in the face of negative life events. These cognitive influences may also interact with a genetically based diathesis to further increase the risk of depression following stressful life events. Then too, the availability of social support from others may help bolster a person's resistance to stress during difficult times. People with more effective social skills may be better able to garner and maintain social reinforcement from others and thus be better able to resist depression than people lacking social skills. But biochemical changes in the brain might make it more difficult for the person to cope effectively and bounce back from stressful life events. Lingering biochemical changes and feelings of depression may exacerbate feelings of helplessness, compound the effects of the initial stressor, and so on.

Gender-related differences in coping styles may also come into play. Men and women may respond differently to feelings of depression. According to Nolen-Hoeksema, women are more likely to ruminate when facing emotional problems, while men are more likely to seek refuge in a bottle. Differences in coping styles may propel women into longer and more severe bouts of depression while setting the stage for the development of alcohol-related problems in men. As you can see, a complex web of contributing factors may be involved in the development of mood disorders.

TREATMENT

Just as theoretical perspectives suggest that many factors may be involved in the development of mood disorders, there are various approaches to their treatment that derive from psychological and biological models. Here we focus on several of the leading contemporary approaches.

Psychodynamic Approaches

Traditional psychoanalysis aims to help people who become depressed understand their ambivalent feelings toward important people (objects) in their lives they have lost or whose loss was threatened. By working through feelings of anger toward these lost objects, they can turn anger outward—through verbal expression of feelings, for example—rather than leave it to fester and turn inward.

Traditional psychoanalysis can take years to uncover and deal with unconscious conflicts. Modern psychoanalytic approaches also focus on unconscious conflicts, but they are more direct, relatively brief, and focus on present as well as past conflicted relationships. A recent study supported the efficacy of structured, short-term dynamic therapy that focused on underlying transference conflicts in relation to depressive symptoms (Luborsky et al., 1996). Eclectic psychodynamic therapists may also use behavioral methods to help clients acquire the social skills they need to develop a broader social network.

Interpersonal Psychotherapy Newer models of psychotherapy for depression have emerged from the interpersonal school of psychodynamic therapy derived initially from the work of Harry Stack Sullivan (see Chapter 1) and other neo-Freudians, such as Karen Horney. One contemporary example is interpersonal psychotherapy (IPT) (Klerman, Weissman, Rounsaville, & Chevron, 1984). IPT is a brief form of therapy (usually no more than 9 to 12 months) that focuses on the client's current interpersonal relationships. The developers of ITP believe that depression occurs within an interpersonal context and that relationship issues need to be emphasized in treatment. IPT has been shown to be an effective treatment for major depression and shows promise in the treatment of other psychological disorders, including dysthymic disorder and bulimia (DeRubeis & Crits-Christoph, 1998; Frank, 1991; M. M. Weissman & Markowitz, 1994).

Although IPT shares some features with traditional psychodynamic approaches (principally the belief that early life experiences and persistent personality features are important issues in psychological adjustment), it differs from traditional psychodynamic therapy by focusing primarily on clients' current relationships, rather than helping them acquire insight into unconscious internal conflicts of childhood origins. Although unconscious factors and early childhood experiences are recognized, therapy focuses on the present—the here and now.

IPT helps clients deal with unresolved or delayed grief reactions following the death of a loved one as well as role conflicts in their present relationships (M. M. Weissman & Markowitz, 1994). The therapist helps clients express grief and their sense of loss while assisting them in developing new activities and relationships to make up for their loss. The therapist also help clients identify areas of conflict in their present relationships, understand the issues that underlie them, and consider ways of resolving them. If the

Interpersonal psychotherapy (IPT). IPT is a brief, psychodynamically-oriented therapy that focuses on issues in the person's current interpersonal relationships. Like traditional psychodynamic approaches, IPT assumes that early life experiences are key issues in adjustment, but IPT focuses on the present—the here and now.

problems in a relationship are beyond repair, the therapist helps the client consider ways of ending it and establishing new relationships.

In the case of Sal D., a 31-year-old TV repairman's assistant, depression was associated with marital conflict:

> Sal began to explore his marital problems in the fifth therapy session, becoming tearful as he recounted his difficulty expressing his feelings to his wife because of feelings of being "numb." He felt that he had been "holding on" to his feelings, which was causing him to become estranged from his wife. The next session zeroed in on the similarities between himself and his father, in particular how he was distancing himself from his wife in a similar way to how his father had kept a distance from him. By session 7, a turning point had been reached. Sal expressed how he and his wife had become "emotional" and closer to one another during the previous week and how he was able to talk more openly about his feelings, and how he and his wife had been able to make a joint decision concerning a financial matter that had been worrying them for some time. When later he was laid off from his job, he sought his wife's opinion, rather than picking a fight with her as a way of thrusting his job problems on her. To his surprise he found that his wife responded positively—not "violently" as he had expected—to times when he expressed his feelings. In his last therapy session (session 12), Sal expressed how therapy had led to a "reawakening" within himself with respect to the feelings he had been keeping to himself— an openness that he hoped to create in his relationship with his wife.
>
> ADAPTED FROM KLERMAN ET AL., 1984, PP. 111–113

Behavioral Approaches

Behavioral approaches to treatment presume that depressive behaviors are learned and can be unlearned. Behavior therapists aim to modify depressive behaviors directly rather than to foster client awareness of possible unconscious causes of these behaviors.

One illustrative behavioral program was developed by Lewinsohn and his colleagues (Lewinsohn, Antonuccio, Steinmetz, & Terry, 1984). It consists of a 12-session, 8-week group therapy program organized as a course—the *Coping With Depression (CWD) Course*. The course helps clients acquire relaxation skills, engage in pleasant activities, and build social skills that enable them to obtain social reinforcement. For example, students learn how to accept rather than deny compliments and how to ask friends to join them in activities to raise the frequency and quality of their social interactions. Participants are taught to generate a self-change plan, to think more constructively, and to develop a lifetime plan for maintaining treatment gains and preventing recurrent depression. The therapist is considered a teacher; the client, a student; the session, a class. Each participant is treated as a responsible adult who is capable of learning. The structure involves lectures, activities, and homework, and each session follows a structured lesson plan. The effectiveness of the CWD course has been demonstrated with both adolescents and adults (Antonuccio, 1998).

> Liz Foster, a 27-year-old woman diagnosed as suffering from major depressive disorder, participated in an eight-member Coping with Depression Course. Prior to therapy, Liz had been feeling depressed for two months, eating poorly, sleeping excessively, and experiencing suicidal thoughts. She had had similar bouts of depression during the previous eight years. When she was depressed, she would spend most of her time alone at home—watching TV, reading, or just sitting. She engaged in a low rate of pleasant activities.
>
> Liz had been laid off from work eleven months earlier and had few social contacts other than her boyfriend. She rarely saw her family, and two of her closest friends had moved away. Her remaining friends rarely visited, and she made no effort to see them.
>
> With the eight other women in her class, Liz learned to focus on behaviors that she could change to increase her level of pleasant activities. At first she complained, "I don't feel like doing anything." The group instructors acknowledged that it would be hard, at first, to select desired reinforcers. Group members were encouraged to try out activities they had formerly enjoyed to see if they still found pleasure in them. Group members were instructed to identify stressful situations or hassles that increased their level of daily stress and were trained in relaxation techniques that they could use to cope with these stresses. They were given Pleasant Events Schedules to complete and encouraged to increase their frequency of pleasant activities.
>
> Liz and the other group members plotted on a graph their level of pleasant activities from week to week and rated their mood levels on a daily basis. Most group members, including Liz, noticed a relationship between their moods and pleasant activities. Liz, whose initial rate of pleasant activities was about 8 per day, decided to increase her rate to 15–20 activities a day, and devised a plan to reinforce herself with rewards of 25 cents for each activity she completed over 13, pooling her rewards until she had earned $8.00, which she then used to buy a record album. Liz was able to increase her rate to 20 and noticed that her mood had improved.
>
> The course also exposed participants to various techniques for controlling their thoughts. Liz selected the technique of self-reward/self-punishment: She rewarded herself with money for positive thoughts and charged herself (a nickel a thought) for negative thoughts. In tracking her thoughts, Liz found that she was able to increase her daily average of positive thoughts from 6 to 11 and decrease her negative

thoughts from 7 to 2. By the eighth session, Liz was reporting that she was no longer depressed and felt more in control of her thoughts and feelings.

In later class sessions, group members learned assertive techniques for handling conflicts, such as dealing with aggressive salespeople, and for starting conversations with strangers. In later sessions, group members prepared life plans which they could use to deal with major life events and maintain the progress they had made. Liz recognized that she needed to maintain her frequency of pleasant activities at a high level, and she continued to monitor these activities to ensure that the frequency remained above a critical level. At a class-reunion six months following the course, she reported that she continued to use the techniques she had learned. Follow-up evaluations through a period of one and one half years showed that Liz had maintained her gains.

ADAPTED FROM LEWINSOHN, TERI, &
WASSERMAN, 1983, PP. 94–101

Behavioral therapy for depression has been shown to be produce substantial benefits in treating depression both in adults and adolescents (W. E. Craighead, Craighead, & Ilardi, 1998; Lewinsohn et al., 1991).

Cognitive Approaches

Cognitive theorists believe that distorted thinking plays a key role in the development of depression. Aaron Beck and his colleagues have developed a multicomponent treatment approach, called **cognitive therapy**, that focuses on helping people with depression learn to recognize and change their dysfunctional thinking patterns. People who develop depression tend to focus on their feelings of fatigue, lethargy, sadness, and hopelessness rather than on the thoughts that may give rise to them. That is, they usually pay more attention to how bad they feel than to the thoughts that may trigger or maintain their depressed moods.

Cognitive therapy, like behavior therapy, entails a relatively brief therapy format, frequently 14 to 16 weekly sessions (A. C. Butler & Beck, 1995). Therapy employs behavioral and cognitive techniques to help clients identify and change dysfunctional thoughts and develop more adaptive behavior.

To assist clients in connecting their thoughts patterns with their negative moods, they are taught to monitor their automatic negative thoughts through the use of a thought diary or daily record. They note when and where the thoughts occur and how they feel at the time. Once disruptive thoughts are identified, the therapist helps the client challenge the validity of these thoughts and replace them with more adaptive thoughts. The following case shows how a cognitive therapist helps a client dispute the validity of certain thoughts that represent the type of cognitive distortion called selective abstraction (the tendency to judge one-

self entirely on the basis of specific weaknesses or flaws in character). In this case, the client judged herself to be completely lacking in self-control because she ate a piece of candy while she was on a diet.

Client: I don't have any self-control at all.

Therapist: On what basis do you say that?

C: Somebody offered me candy and I couldn't refuse it.

T: Were you eating candy every day?

C: No, I just ate it this once.

T: Did you do anything constructive during the past week to adhere to your diet?

C: Well, I didn't give in to the temptation to buy candy every time I saw it at the store . . . Also, I did not eat any candy except that one time when it was offered to me and I felt I couldn't refuse it.

T: If you counted up the number of times you controlled yourself versus the number of times you gave in, what ratio would you get?

C: About 100 to 1.

T: So if you controlled yourself 100 times and did not control yourself just once, would that be a sign that you are weak through and through?

C: I guess not—not through and through (smiles).

ADAPTED FROM BECK ET AL., 1979, P. 68

Or consider the case of Cliff, a 22-year-old stock clerk who worked in an auto parts store:

Cliff became depressed in the course of a romantic relationship that followed a seesaw pattern of breakups and brief reconciliations. Most of the time a breakup would follow an incident in which Cliff had reacted excessively and angrily when he perceived—or rather misperceived—his girlfriend as acting distant or aloof, even in trivial matters such as how far away from him she sat in the front seat of the car. Cliff needed constant reassurance of love and was acutely sensitive to verbal criticism and nonverbal cues of emotional distance. His girlfriend would say to him, "You must really want this relationship, since you're always badgering me to tell you that I love you."

Cliff's thinking was patterned by a set of underlying beliefs that undermined his relationships. These beliefs included musterbation *("This relationship must work out . . . or else"),* personalizing *("If she's in a bad mood it's because she doesn't really love me"), and* catastrophizing *("I won't be able to survive if this relationship breaks up"). In therapy, Cliff began to see that his way of viewing himself and the world limited possibilities for growth. Cliff was a quick study and readily learned to monitor his thoughts and replace self-defeating thoughts with rational alternatives. Instead of responding automatically to a perception that his girlfriend was rejecting him, he stopped and asked himself, "Where's the evidence for that? Might there be another explanation for her behavior?" When she wasn't available to see him on a particular night, he was able to attribute it to her feeling fatigued rather than misconstrue it as a sign of rejection. When problems arose in the relationship, Cliff learned to distinguish disappointment from disaster. He began to ease his expectations, seeing the relationship less as a "do or die" situation and more as a growth experience.*

THE AUTHORS' FILES

Evidence supports the effectiveness of cognitive therapy in treating major depression (A. C. Butler & Beck, 1996; W. E. Craighead, Craighead, & Ilardi, 1998; Jacobson & Hollon, 1996a, 1996b; Persons, Thase, & Crits-Christoph, 1996). Depressive symptoms often lift within 8 to 12 sessions (A. C. Butler & Beck, 1995).

The benefits achieved from cognitive therapy or cognitive behavior therapy appear to be at least equal to those achieved from antidepressant medication in treating mild to moderate depression and is more effective in preventing relapse than use of medication alone (Beck, 1993; A. C. Butler & Beck, 1995, 1996; Clarkin, Pilkonis, & Magruder, 1996; Elkin et al., 1989; Hollon, Shelton, & Davis, 1993). Cognitive behavioral therapy and interpersonal psychotherapy appear to produce about the same level of benefit (Elkin et al., 1989; D. A. Shapiro et al., 1994, 1995). Little research has been reported on treatment of dysthymia, although techniques used for treating major depression, such as cognitive therapy and interpersonal psychotherapy, as well as antidepressant medication, have shown promising results (Kocsis et al., 1997; Thase, 1997a, 1997b; Thase et al., 1996).

Questions remain about how effective cognitive or cognitive-behavioral approaches may be in treating severe depression (Jacobson & Hollon, 1996b). The issue of whether the combination of cognitive and behavioral approaches is superior to behavioral treatment alone (e.g., increasing pleasant events and opportunities for reinforcement) also remains unsettled (Gortner et al., 1998). Questions also remain about whether cognitive changes occurring during cognitive therapy are responsible for its therapeutic effects. In one study, reductions in dysfunctional thinking early in cognitive therapy predicted alleviation of depression later in therapy, lending support to the view that cognitive change underlies the success of cognitive therapy (DeRubeis et al., 1990). Yet more research is needed to identify the responsible mechanisms for change.

Biological Approaches

The most common biological approaches to treating mood disorders involves the use of antidepressant drugs and elec-troconvulsive therapy for depression and lithium for bipolar disorder.

Antidepressant Drugs Drugs that are used to treat depression include several classes of antidepressants: tricylic antidepressants (TCAs); monoamine oxidase (MAO) inhibitors, and selective serotonin-reuptake inhibitors (SSRIs). All of these drugs increase brain levels and, perhaps, the actions of neurotransmitters. The increased availability of key neurotransmitters in the synaptic cleft may enhance the sensitivity of postsynaptic neurons to these chemical messengers. As we noted, antidepressants tend to have a delayed effect, typically requiring several weeks of treatment before a therapeutic benefit is achieved. SSRI's not only lift mood, but in many cases they eliminate the delusions that sometimes accompany severe depression (Zanardi et al., 1996).

The different classes of antidepressants increase the availability of neurotransmitters, but in different ways (see Figure 7.4). The tricyclics, which include imipramine (trade name Tofranil), amitriptyline (Elavil), desipramine (Norpramin), and doxepin (Sinequan), are so named because of their three-ringed molecular structure. They increase levels in the brain of the neurotransmitters norepinephrine and serotonin by interfering with the reuptake (reabsorption by the transmitting cell) of these chemical messengers. As a result, more of these neurotransmitters remain available in the synapse, which induces the receiving cell to continue to fire, prolonging the volley of nerve impulses traveling through the neural highway in the brain.

The SSRIs (fluoxextine, trade name Prozac, is one) work in a similar fashion but have more specific effects on raising the levels of serotonin in the brain. The MAO inhibitors increase the availability of neurotransmitters by inhibiting the action of monoamine oxidase, an enzyme that normally breaks down or degrades neurotransmitters in the synaptic cleft. Another antidepressant, buproprion (trade name Wellbutrin), inhibits the reuptake of the neurotransmitter dopamine to a certain extent.

The potential side effects of tricyclics and MAO inhibitors include dry mouth, psychomotor retardation, constipation, blurred vision, and, less frequently, urinary retention, paralytic ileus (a paralysis of the intestines, which impairs the passage of intestinal contents), confusion, delirium, and cardiovascular complications, such as reduced blood pressure. Tricyclics are highly toxic, moreover, raising the prospect of suicidal overdoses if the drugs are used without close supervision.

The SSRIs such as Prozac and Zoloft are about equal in effectiveness to the older generation of tricyclics. Yet because they hold two major advantages, they have largely replaced the earlier generation of tricyclic antidepressants or TCAs (Nemeroff & Schatzberg, 1998). They are less toxic and so are less dangerous in overdose and have fewer side effects (such as dry mouth, constipation, and weight gain) than the tricyclics or MAO inhibitors (P. E. Christiansen et al., 1996; Modell et al., 1997; Thase & Kupfer, 1996). Still, Prozac and other SSRIs may produce side effects such as upset

Correcting Cognitive Distortions with Rational Alternatives

Cognitive theorists suggest that cognitive errors can lead to depression if they are left to rummage around unchallenged in the individual's mind. They help assist clients to recognize cognitive distortions and replace them with more rational alternative thoughts.

TABLE 7.6

Cognitive Distortions and Rational Responses

Automatic Thought	Kind of Cognitive Distortion	Rational Response
I'm all alone in the world.	All-or-Nothing Thinking	It may feel like I'm all alone, but there are some people who care about me.
Nothing will ever work out for me.	Overgeneralization	No one can look into the future. Concentrate on the present.
My looks are hopeless.	Magnification	I may not be perfect looking, but I'm far from hopeless.
I'm falling apart. I can't handle this.	Magnification	Sometimes I just feel overwhelmed. But I've handled things like this before. Just take it a step at a time and I'll be okay.
I guess I'm just a born loser.	Labeling and Mislabeling	Nobody is destined to be loser. Stop talking yourself down.
I've only lost 8 pounds on this diet. I should just forget it. I can't succeed.	Minimization/Disqualifying the Positive/Jumping to Conclusions/All-or-Nothing Thinking	Eight pounds is a good start. I didn't gain all this weight overnight, and I have to expect that it will take time to lose it.
I know things must really be bad for me to feel this awful.	Emotional Reasoning	Feeling something doesn't make it so. If I'm not seeing things clearly, my emotions will be distorted too.
I know I'm going to flunk this course.	Fortune Teller Error	Give me a break! Just focus on getting through this course, not jumping to negative conclusions.
I know John's problems are really my fault.	Personalization	Stop blaming yourself for everyone else's problems. There are many reasons why John has these problems that have nothing to do with me.

stomach, headaches, agitation, insomnia, lack of sexual drive, and delayed orgasm.

MAO inhibitors were commonly used in the treatment of depression prior to the advent of the tricylics and fluoxetine. Some of the more popular MAO inhibitors include tranylcypromine (Parnate) and phenelzine (Nardil). Although they are generally about as effective as the tricyclics (Depression Guideline Panel, 1993b), they play a smaller role in treatment of depression today because of potentially serious interactions with certain foods and alcoholic bever-

ages. The most serious side effect of MAO inhibitors is a sudden, potentially life-threatening rise in blood pressure that can occur when a user consumes foods containing tyramine, which is found in cheeses, chocolate, beer, and red wines.

Antidepressant medication is clearly effective in helping relieve major depression in many cases. Moreover, we have evidence that antidepressant medication is helpful in treating dysthymia (Hellerstein et al., 1993; Thase & Kupfer, 1996).

Table 7.6 shows some common examples of automatic thoughts, the types of cognitive distortions they represent, and some rational alternative responses.

Automatic Thought	Kind of Cognitive Distortion	Rational Response
Someone my age should be doing better than I am.	Should Statements	Stop comparing yourself to others. All anyone can be expected to do is their best. What good does it do to compare myself to others? It only leads me to get down on myself, rather than get motivated.
I just don't have the brains for college.	Labeling and Mislabeling	Stop calling yourself names like stupid. I can accomplish a lot more than I give myself credit for.
Everything is my fault.	Personalization	There you go again. Stop playing this game of pointing blame at yourself. There's enough blame to go around. Better yet, forget placing blame and try to think through how to solve this problem.
It would be awful if Sue turns me down.	Magnification	It might be upsetting. But it needn't be awful unless I make it so.
If people really knew me, they would hate me.	Mind Reader	What evidence is there for that? More people who get to know me like me than don't like me.
If something doesn't get better soon, I'll go crazy.	Jumping to Conclusions/ Magnification	I've dealt with these problems this long without falling apart. I just have to hang in there. Things are not as bad as they seem.
I can't believe I got another pimple on my face. This is going to ruin my whole weekend.	Mental Filter	Take it easy. A pimple is not the end of the world. It doesn't have to spoil my whole weekend. Other people get pimples and seem to have a good time.

Though cognitive behavior therapy may be at least as effective as antidepressants in the treatment of depression overall (Antonuccio, Thomas, & Danton, 1998; Elkin et al., 1989; Hollon, Shelton, & Loosen, 1991), antidepressants may have the edge when it comes to treating more severe cases of depression (Elkin et al., 1995). A review of the available evidence also suggests that the combination of antidepressants and psychotherapy may hold no advantage over psychotherapy alone in treating milder depression, but the combination approach may be more effective in treating more severe cases (Thase et al., 1997b). Still, the question of whether a combination approach is preferred requires more study (Clarkin, Pilkonis, & Magruder, 1996; W. E. Craighead, Craighead, & Ilardi, 1998).

One issue we need to address in discussing drug therapy is the high rate of relapse following discontinuation of the medication. A review of drug withdrawal studies showed relapse rates of up to 69% when antidepressants were terminated within 2 months of a treatment response (Paykel & Hale, 1986). Long-term (maintenance) treatment

St. John's Wort—A Natural "Prozac"?

Might a humble herb be a remedy for depression? The herb, called St. John's wort, or *Hypericum perforatum*, has been used for centuries to help heal wounds. Now, people are using it to relieve depression (E. L. Andrews, 1997). Nowhere is it more popular than Germany, where high-strength versions of the herb are far and away the most widely used antidepressant on the market, outselling Prozac, its nearest competitor, by a margin of 4 to 1. Early small-scale studies in Europe provide preliminary support for the benefits of the St. John's wort, with few reported side effects, in cases of mild to moderate depression (B. Carey, 1998). The herb appears to increase the levels of serotonin in the brain by interfering with its reabsorption, the same mecha-

nism believed to account for Prozac's benefits. Yet we don't yet know whether it is effective in treating severe depression. Nor do we know about the herb's long-term safety or efficacy (Brody, 1997c). We also can't say whether it is as effective as established antidepressants. Though people seeking help for depression may be attracted to the idea of using a natural product such as St. John's wort, more definitive studies are needed to establish its safety and effectiveness.

TRUTH or FICTION REVISITED

7.6 *True*. The most widely used remedy for depression in Germany is a herb, St. John's wort. Clinical trials are underway to evaluate its effectiveness.

with antidepressants may also help reduce the rate of relapse (Kocsis et al., 1996). Psychologically based therapies may provide greater protection against a recurrence of depression following termination of treatment, presumably because the learning that occurs during therapy carries past the end of active treatment (A. C. Butler & Beck, 1995; Hollon, Shelton, & Davis, 1993). Cognitive-behavioral therapy also appears to be more cost-effective (costing less to produce similar levels of benefit) than antidepressant treatment (Prozac) (Antonuccio, Thomas, & Danton, 1997).

Overall, evidence shows that about 1 in 2 people with major depressive disorder will respond favorably to either cognitive behavior therapy or interpersonal psychotherapy, or to tricyclic antidepressants (Depression Guideline Panel, 1993b). Antidepressant medication may be most appropriate when psychotherapy alone fails or in treating people with severe depression (Elkin et al., 1995; Thase & Kupfer, 1996; Thase et al., 1997). Recognize, too, that some people who fail to respond to drug therapy may respond favorably to psychotherapy.

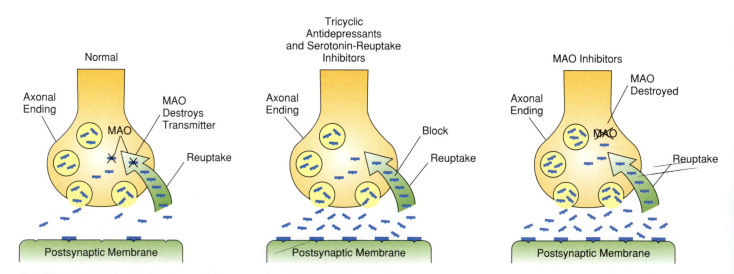

FIGURE 7.4 *The actions of various types of antidepressants at the synapse.*
Tricyclic antidepressants and serotonin-reuptake inhibitors both increase the availability of neurotransmitters by preventing their reuptake by the presynaptic neuron. Tricyclic antidepressants impede the reuptake of both norepinephrine and serotonin. MAO inhibitors work by inhibiting the action of monoamine oxidase, an enzyme that normally breaks down neurotransmitters in the synaptic cleft.

A CLOSER LOOK

Prozac Nation: Is This the Start of a New Drug Culture?

Prozac (fluoxetine) is the most widely prescribed anti-depressant drug in the United States. Another of the new generation of SSRI antidepressants, Zoloft (sertraline), is not far behind. Though these drugs are most commonly used to treat depression, their use has spread to people who are not clinically depressed or suffering from other psychological disorders. Some people are using these drugs to enhance their performance, to give them an "edge" in their work, or as a psychological "pick-me-upper" to help them cope with the ordinary ups and downs of daily life. Concerns have been raised that the wider use of these drugs might be creating a new legalized drug culture, revolving around the use of drugs whose long-term effects are not known (Cowley, 1994). Many, indeed probably most, physicians who prescribe Prozac to their patients are not psychiatrists who specialize in the treatment of people with mental-health problems but family physicians and internists in general practice. Family practitioners may be less likely than mental-health specialists to probe for the underlying reasons for people's general discontent with life before reaching for their prescription pads.

Some practitioners believe drugs such as Prozac do more than lift a person's mood and can actually lead to more fundamental changes in personality, making inhibited people more outgoing, popular, and self-confident, among other changes (P. Kramer, 1993). Psychiatrist Peter Kramer advanced the notion in his best-selling book, *Listening to Prozac,* that the drug not only alleviated depression but transformed the core personalities of his patients, making them more cheerful,

confident, and relaxed. It is not yet clear whether Prozac or similar drugs can alter one's personality. Is personality altered, or does Prozac, by alleviating depression, merely reveal the real person who was hidden beneath the veil of depression (Rimer, 1993)? What seems like a change in personality might merely reflect the brighter outlook and boost in self-confidence that results when the cobwebs of depression are swept away (Talan, 1993b). There are also additional concerns raised about the possible long-term risks of using drugs that alter brain chemistry.

Futurists have speculated that future drugs may even allow people to design their own personalities by giving them the means of chemically sculpting their brains. Although drugs such as Prozac do not create a "high" and so are not likely to become drugs of abuse, the expanding use of such drugs raises a host of questions with which we are only now beginning to grapple: Who should prescribe these drugs? For what conditions? Should psychoactive drugs be prescribed to people who are not clinically depressed but want a lift to help them function or perform better? Should drugs be prescribed to people seeking a chemical fix for what's wrong with their lives? Where should we draw the line between the legal and illegal use of psychotropic drugs? What do you think?

As the debate over these drugs continues, researchers report that Prozac did not boost mood or affect other psychological variables when given to normal, healthy individuals (Gelfin, Gorfine, & Lerer, 1998).

Lithium   The drug lithium carbonate, a powdered form of the metallic element lithium, is the most widely used and recommended treatment for bipolar disorder (Winokur et al., 1993; Schou, 1997). It could be said that the ancient Greeks and Romans were among the first to use lithium as a form of chemotherapy. They prescribed mineral water that contained lithium for people with turbulent mood swings.

TRUTH or FICTION REVISITED

7.7 *True.* The ancient Greeks and Romans did use a chemical substance to control mood swings, which is still widely used today. It is called lithium.

Lithium is effective in stabilizing moods in people with bipolar disorder and reducing recurrent episodes of mania and depression (Keck & McElroy, 1998; Thase & Kupfer 1996; Tondo et al., 1998). People with bipolar disorder may need to use lithium indefinitely to control their mood swings, just as diabetic patients use insulin continuously to control their illness. Lithium is given orally in the form of a natural mineral salt, lithium carbonate. Despite more than 40 years of use, we still can't say how lithium works (Price & Heninger, 1994).

Yet lithium treatment is not a panacea. At least 30% to 40% of patients with mania either fail to respond to the drug or cannot tolerate it (Bowden et al., 1994; A. Duffy et al.,

1998). Of those who do respond, about 6 in 10 eventually experience a relapse (Goleman, 1994b).

Lithium treatment must be closely monitored because of potential toxic effects and other side effects. Lithium can produce a mild impairment in memory (Price & Heninger, 1994), "the kind of thing that might make a productive person stop taking it," as one expert put it (Goleman, 1994b). The drug can also lead to weight gain, lethargy, and grogginess, and to a general slowing down of motor functioning. It can also produce gastrointestinal distress and lead to liver problems over the long term (Azar, 1994). For a number of reasons, many patients discontinue using lithium or fail to take it reliably (R. J. Johnson & McFarland, 1996).

Anticonvulsive drugs used in the treatment of epilepsy, such as *carbamazepine* (brand name Tegretol) and *valproate* (brand name Depakene) can also help stabilize moods and treat acute manic symptoms of people with bipolar disorder (Bowden et al., 1994, 1996; Keck & McElroy, 1998; McElroy, et al., 1996; Samara et al., 1997). In a recent controlled trial, valproate was as effective as lithium in treating mania, with both drugs showing better results than a placebo control (Bowden et al., 1994). Anticonvulsive drugs may be of benefit in treating people with bipolar disorder who either do not respond to lithium or cannot tolerate the drug because of side effects. Anticonvulsive drugs usually cause fewer or less severe side effects than lithium. Anticonvulsive drugs may also be more effective than lithium in treating the rapid cycling type of bipolar disorder and have more potent antidepressant effects in treating bipolar patients (Bowden et al., 1994; Dilsaver et al., 1996). However, some patients have only a partial response to lithium or anticonvulsive drugs, and some fail to respond at all (Keck & McElroy, 1998). Thus, there remains an need for alternative treatments or drug strategies to be developed, perhaps involving a combination of these or other drugs (Denicoff et al., 1997; Keck & McElroy, 1998).

Electroconvulsive Therapy   Electroconvulsive therapy (ECT), more commonly called shock therapy, continues to evoke controversy. The idea of passing an electric current through someone's brain may seem barbaric. Yet ECT is a generally safe and effective treatment of severe depression and can help relieve depression in many cases in which alternative treatments have failed.

ECT involves the administration of an electrical current to the head. A current of between 70 to 130 volts is used to induce a convulsion that is similar to a grand mal epileptic seizure. ECT is usually administered in a series of 6 to 12 treatments over a period of several weeks. The patient is put to sleep with a brief-acting general anesthetic and given a muscle relaxant to avoid wild convulsions that might result in injury. As a result, spasms may be barely perceptible to onlookers. The patient awakens soon after the procedure and generally remembers nothing. Although ECT had earlier been used in the treatment of a wide variety of psychological disorders, including schizophrenia and bipolar disorder, the American Psychiatric Association recommended in 1990 that ECT be used only to treat major depressive disorder in people who do not respond to antidepressant medication.

ECT leads to significant improvement in at least 80% of people with major depression (Coffey & Weiner, 1990) and in about 50% to 60% of people with major depression who have failed to respond to antidepressant medication (Prudic et al., 1996; Sackheim et al., 1990;). ECT also results in shorter and less costly hospitalizations (Olfson et al., 1998). Although it often leads to dramatic relief from severe depression, no one knows exactly how ECT works. ECT produces such mammoth chemical and electrical changes in the body that it is difficult to pinpoint the mechanism of therapeutic action. It is suspected, however, that ECT may work by normalizing brain levels of certain neurotransmitters (Coffey & Weiner, 1990). Although ECT can be an effective short-term treatment of severe depression, it too is no panacea. Depression often returns at some later point, even among people who continue to be treated with antidepressant medication (Sackheim et al., 1994).

ECT may be administered either to both sides of the head (*bilateral ECT*) or to only one side of the head (*unilateral ECT*) (Sackheim et al., 1996). Unilateral ECT is applied to the nondominant hemisphere of the brain, which, for most people, is the right side. Bilateral ECT tends to produce a somewhat greater clinical benefit than unilateral ECT, but also greater short-term memory impairment (Sackheim et al., 1994).

There is an understandable concern among patients, relatives, and professionals themselves concerning the possible risk of brain damage from ECT (W. Z. Potter & Rudorfer, 1993). Much of this concern has focused on potential memory loss. A recent review concluded that ECT does not result in structural damage to the brain, and any memory losses suffered as the result of treatment are temporary except for events occurring shortly before or after ECT administration (Devanand et al., 1994). Earlier memories or those formed weeks after ECT do not appear to be affected (W. Z. Potter & Rudorfer, 1993). Still, many professionals view ECT as a treatment of last resort, which is to be used only after other treatment approaches have been tried and failed.

In summing up, let us note that a government-sponsored expert panel in 1993 issued a set of clinical practice guidelines for depression. The guidelines were based on evidence from controlled studies showing the following treatments to be effective in treating depression (Depression Guideline Panel, 1993b):

- Antidepressant medication (tricyclics or selective serotonin-reuptake inhibitors)
- Three specific forms of psychotherapy: cognitive therapy, behavior therapy, and interpersonal psychotherapy
- A combination of one of the recommended forms of psychotherapy and antidepressant medication
- Other specified forms of treatment, including ECT and phototherapy for seasonal depression.

SUICIDE

Suicidal thoughts are common enough. Under great stress, many, if not most, people have considered suicide. More than half (54%) of one sample of 694 college first-year students reported they had contemplated suicide on at least one occasion (Meehan et al., 1991). In a large sample of adolescents in Oregon, nearly 1 in 5 (19%) reported having suicidal thoughts at some point in their lives (Lewinsohn, Rohde, & Seeley, 1996). It is fortunate that most people who entertain such thoughts do not act on them. Among the college first-year students who had considered suicide, fewer than 1 in 5 had attempted suicide (Meehan et al., 1991). Still, nearly one quarter of a million Americans try to commit suicide each year (S. J. Blumenthal, 1985). About 30,000 of them succeed, accounting for 1% of all deaths in the United States (Gelman, 1994). In the adolescent sample, one in 10 girls and one in 25 boys had attempted suicide.

Suicide ranks as the eighth leading cause of death in the United States and the third leading cause of death among young people in the 15 to 24 age range (Belluck, 1998). However, despite the increased attention on the problem of suicide in recent years, the actual rate of suicide has remained stable in the United States since the end of World War II (Gelman, 1994), although among adolescents, the suicide rate has quadrupled since 1950 (Weller, 1997).

Who Commits Suicide

The problem of teenage suicide often grabs the headlines, but suicide rates are highest among older adults, especially older White males (Karel, 1997) (see Figure 7.5). The suicide rate among older Americans, now at nearly twice the national rate, jumped 9% from 1980 to 1992, reversing the trend of a half century of decline ("Elderly's suicide rate is up 9% over 12 years,"1996; Gelman, 1994). The suicide rate among White teenagers has leveled off, but it is rising sharply among Black youths (Belluck, 1998). Though the suicide rate among teenagers has traditionally been much higher among Whites than Blacks, the racial gap has been narrowing.

Perhaps the rise in suicides among the elderly occurred as the result of medical advances increasing the life span but not necessarily the quality of life. Despite life-extending advances in medical care, some older adults may find the quality of their lives is less than satisfactory. With longer life, older people are more susceptible to diseases such as cancer and Alzheimer's, which can leave them with feelings of helplessness and hopelessness, which can give rise to suicidal thinking. Many older adults also suffer a mounting accumulation of losses of friends and loved ones as time progresses, leading to social isolation. These losses, as well as the loss of good health and of a responsible role in the community, may wear down the will to live. Not surprisingly, the highest suicide rates in older men are among those who are widowed or lead socially isolated lives. Society's increased acceptance of suicide in older people may also play a part. Whatever the causes, suicide has become an increased risk for elderly people (Szanto et al., 1996). Perhaps society should focus its attention as much on the quality of life that is afforded our elderly as on simply providing them the medical care that helps make longer life possible.

Overall, Whites are about twice as likely as Blacks to commit suicide. Although more women than men, by a ratio of 3 to 1, attempt suicide, men are four times more likely to

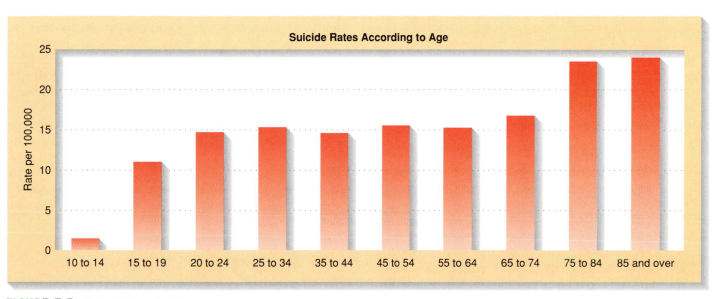

FIGURE 7.5 *Suicide rates according to age.*
Although adolescent suicides may be more highly publicized, adults, especially older adults, have significantly higher suicide rates.

Source: U. S. Bureau of the Census (1994). *Statistical Abstract of the United States: 1994* (114th ed.). Washington, D.C.: U. S. Government Printing Office.

"succeed" (Gelman, 1994; M. T. Tsuang, Simpson, & Fleming, 1992). More males succeed, at least in part, because they choose quicker acting and more lethal means (G. A. Carlson & Miller, 1981). A study of 204 San Diego County suicides that took place in the early 1980s found that men who committed suicide were more likely to use guns (60% of the male suicides versus 28% of the female suicides) (Rich, Fowler, Fogarty, & Young, 1988). Women who committed suicide more often used drugs or poisons than did men (44% versus 11%, respectively).

Gender differences in suicide risk may mask underlying factors. The common finding that men are more likely to take their own lives may be due to the fact that men are also more likely to have a history of alcohol and drug abuse and less likely to have children in the home. When these two factors were taken into account in a recent study, gender differences in suicide risk disappeared (M. A. Young et al., 1994).

Why Do People Commit Suicide?

To many lay observers, suicide seems so extreme an act that they believe only "insane" people (meaning people who are out of touch with reality) would commit suicide. However, suicidal thinking does not necessarily imply loss of touch with reality, deep-seated unconscious conflict, or a personality disorder. The contemplation of suicide, instead, generally reflects a narrowing of the range of options people think are available to them (Rotheram-Borus, Traukman, Dopkins, & Schrout, 1990; Schotte, Cools, & Payvar, 1990). That is, they are discouraged by their problems and see no other way out.

Most suicides are associated with major depression or bipolar disorder (Strakowski et al., 1996), which is why we include the topic in this chapter. Attempted or completed suicide is also connected with other psychological disorders such as alcoholism and drug dependence, schizophrenia, panic disorder, and personality disorders, including antisocial personality disorder and borderline personality disorder (Amador et al., 1998; Fenton et al., 1997; Heikkinen et al., 1997; Isometsä et al., 1996). Suicide is the leading cause of premature death among people with schizophrenia (Fenton et al., 1997). More than half the suicide attempters in a recent study had two or more psychiatric disorders (Beautrais et al., 1996).

Stress is also implicated in many suicides. Suicide attempts often occur following highly stressful life events, especially "exit events" such as the death of a spouse, close friend, or relative; divorce or separation; a family member leaving home; or the loss of a close friend. People who consider taking their lives in response to stressful events have poorer problem-solving skills than those who do not consider suicide (Schotte & Clum, 1987). People who consider suicide in times of stress may be less able to find alternative ways of coping with the stressors they face. Underscoring the psychological impact of severe stress, researchers find suicides to be more common among survivors of natural disasters, especially severe floods (Krug et al., 1998).

Theoretical Perspectives on Suicide

The classic psychodynamic model views depression as the turning inward of anger against the internal representation of a lost love object. Suicide then represents inward-directed anger that turns murderous. Suicidal people, then, do not seek to destroy themselves. Instead, they seek to vent their rage against the internalized representation of the love object. In so doing, they destroy themselves as well, of course. In his later writings, Freud speculated that suicide may be motivated by the "death instinct," a tendency to return to the tension-free state that preceded birth. Existential and humanistic theorists relate suicide to the perception that life is meaningless and hopeless. Suicidal people report they find life duller, emptier, and more boring than nonsuicidal people (Mehrabian & Weinstein, 1985).

The 19th-century social thinker Emile Durkheim noted that people who experienced *anomie*—who felt lost, without identity, rootless—were more likely to commit suicide (Durkheim, 1958). Sociocultural theorists likewise believe that alienation in today's society may play a role in suicide. In our modern, mobile society, people frequently move hundreds or thousands of miles to school and jobs. Executives and their families may be relocated every 2 years or so. Military personnel and their families may be shifted about yet more rapidly. Many people are thus socially isolated or cut off from their support groups. Moreover, city dwellers tend to limit or discourage informal social contacts because of crowding, overstimulation, and fear of crime. It is thus understandable that many people find few sources of support in times of crisis. In some cases, the availability of family support may not be helpful. Family members may be perceived as part of the problem, not part of the solution.

Learning theorists point to the reinforcing effects of prior suicide threats and attempts and to the effects of stress, especially when combined with inability to solve personal problems. According to Shneidman (1985), suicide attempters usually wish to escape unbearable psychological pain. People who threaten or attempt suicide may also receive sympathy and support from loved ones and others, perhaps making future—and more lethal—attempts more likely. This is not to suggest that suicide attempts or gestures should be ignored. It is *not* true that people who threaten to commit suicide are only seeking attention. People who commit suicide often tell others of their intentions or leave clues beforehand (Cordes, 1985). Moreover, many people make aborted suicide attempts in which they stop just before inflicting harm on themselves before they go on to make actual suicide attempts (M. E. Barber et al., 1998).

TRUTH *or* FICTION REVISITED

7.8 *False*. It is not the case that people who threaten suicide are merely seeking attention. Though people who threaten suicide may not carry out the act, their threats should be taken seriously. Most people who do commit suicide had told others of their intentions or had left clues about.

Risk of Suicide Among Native American Youth

Native Americans are at greater than expected risk for suicide attempts and completed suicides. Among young people aged 15 to 24, for example, the suicide rate for Native Americans is nearly twice that for non-Hispanic White youth: 26 per 100,000 as compared with 14 per 100,000 (USDHHS, 1991b). The suicide rates for Hispanic, African, and Asian Americans of the same age group are 30% to 60% *lower* than that of non-Hispanic White youth (USDHHS, 1991b).

One in 6 Native American teenagers overall has attempted suicide, a rate four times higher than that of other U.S. teenagers (Resnick et al., 1992). A recent study of 83 Native American Zuni adolescents 15 to 16 years of age showed an even higher rate of suicide attempts—30%—as compared to rates of 4% to 13% reported in studies of adolescents in the general popula-

tion (Howard-Pitney et al., 1992). Native American girls were two to three times more likely than boys to have attempted suicide, a finding that mirrors that of the general population.

Hopelessness and exposure to other people who have attempted or completed suicide would appear to explain much of the risk of suicide among Native American youth. Native American youth at greatest risk tend to be reared in communities that are largely isolated from the benefits of U.S. society at large. They perceive themselves as having relatively few opportunities to gain the skills necessary to join the work force in the larger society and are also relatively more prone to substance abuse, including alcohol abuse. Knowledge that peers have attempted or completed suicide renders suicide a highly visible escape from psychological pain.

Social-cognitive theorists suggest that suicide may be motivated by positive expectancies and by approving attitudes toward suicide (D. Stein et al., 1998). People who kill themselves may expect they will be missed or eulogized after death, or that survivors will feel guilty for mistreating them. Suicidal psychiatric patients have been shown to hold more positive expectancies concerning suicide than nonsuicidal psychiatric patients. They more often expressed the belief that suicide would solve their problems, for example (Linehan, Camper, Chiles, Strosahl, & Shearin, 1987). Suicide may represent a desperate attempt to deal with one's problems in one fell swoop rather than piecemeal.

Social-cognitive theorists also focus on the potential modeling effects of observing suicidal behavior in others, especially among teenagers who feel overwhelmed by academic and social stressors. A *social contagion*, or spreading of suicide in a community, may occur in the wake of suicides that receive widespread publicity. Teenagers, who seem to be especially vulnerable to these modeling effects, may even romanticize the suicidal act as one of heroic courage. The incidence of suicide among teenagers sometimes rises markedly in the period following news reports about suicide (R. C. Kessler et al., 1990). In the Oregon study, suicidal behavior of a friend was a risk factor in suicide attempts among adolescents (Lewinsohn, Rohde, & Seeley, 1996). Copycat suicides may be more likely to occur when reports of suicides are sensationalized such that other teenagers expect their demises to have broad impacts on their communities (R. C. Kessler et al., 1990).

Biological factors also appear to be involved in suicide. Evidence shows reduced serotonin activity in people who attempt or commit suicide (Siever & Trestman, 1993; Ghanshyam et al., 1995; Mann & Malone, 1997; Talan, 1996b). Serotonin deficits have been implicated in depression, so the relationship with suicide is not surprising. Yet serotonin acts to curb or inhibit nervous system activity, so perhaps decreased serotonin function leads to a *disinhibition,* or release, of impulsive behavior that takes the form of a suicidal act in vulnerable individuals. Suicide also tends to run in families, which hints of genetic factors. Evidence from a recent twin study showed that among 9 twin pairs in which both twins committed suicide, 7 were MZ twins and 2 were DZ twins (Roy et al., 1991). All in all, about 1 suicide attempter in 4 has a family member who has committed suicide (Sorensen & Rutter, 1991).

The presence of various psychological disorders among family members is also apparently connected with suicide (Sorensen & Rutter, 1991). But what are the causal connections? Do people who attempt suicide inherit vulnerabilities to disorders that are connected with suicide? Does the family atmosphere subject its members to feelings of hopelessness? Does the suicide of one family member give others the idea of doing the same thing? Does one suicide create the impression that other family members are destined to kill themselves?

Suicide is connected with a complex web of factors, and its prediction is no simpler. Yet it is clear that many suicides could be prevented if people with suicidal feelings would receive treatment for the disorders that underlie suicidal

A CLOSER LOOK

Suicide Prevention

Imagine yourself having an intimate conversation with a close campus friend, Chris. You know that things have not been good. Chris's grandfather died 6 weeks ago, and the two were very close. Chris's grades have been going downhill, and Chris's romantic relationship also seems to be coming apart at the seams. Still, you are unprepared when Chris says very deliberately, "I just can't take it anymore. Life is just too painful. I don't feel like I want to live anymore. I've decided that the only thing I can do is to kill myself."

When somebody discloses that he or she is contemplating suicide, you may feel bewildered and frightened, as if a great burden has been placed on your shoulders. It has. If someone confides suicidal thoughts to you, your goal should be to persuade him or her to see a professional, or to get the advice of a professional yourself as soon as you can. But if the suicidal person declines to talk to another person and you sense you can't break away for such a conference, there are some things you can do then and there:

1. Draw the person out. Shneidman advises framing questions like, "What's going on?" "Where do you hurt?" "What would you like to see happen?" (Shneidman, 1985, p. 11). Such questions may prompt people to verbalize thwarted psychological needs and offer some relief. They also grant you the time to appraise the risk and contemplate your next move.

2. Be sympathetic. Show that you fathom how troubled the person is. Don't say something like, "You're just being silly."

3. Suggest that means other than suicide can be discovered to work out the person's problems, even if they are not apparent at the time. Shneidman (1985) notes that suicidal people can usually see only two solutions to their predicaments—either suicide or some kind of magical resolution. Professionals try to broaden the available alternatives of people who are suicidal.

4. Inquire as to *how* the person expects to commit suicide. People with explicit methods who also possess the means (for example, a gun or drugs) are at greater risk. Ask if you may hold on to the gun,

drugs, or whatever, for a while. Sometimes the person agrees.

5. Propose that the person accompany you to consult a professional right *now*. Many campuses have hot lines that you or the suicidal individual can call. Many towns and cities have such hot lines and they can be called anonymously. Other possibilities include the emergency room of a general hospital, a campus health center or counseling center, or the campus or local police. If you are unable to maintain contact with the suicidal person, get professional assistance as soon as you separate.

6. Don't say something like "You're talking crazy." Such comments are degrading and injurious to the individual's self-esteem. Don't press the suicidal person to contact specific people, such as parents or a spouse. Conflict with them may have given rise to the suicidal thoughts.

Above all, keep in mind that your primary goal is to confer with a helping professional. Don't go it alone any longer than you have to.

A suicide hot line. Suicide hot lines have been established on many college campuses and in most communities. If you or someone you know is experiencing suicidal thoughts, why not speak to a mental health professional or call a suicide hot line for advice?

Teen suicide. Suicidal teenagers may see no other way of handling their life problems. The availability of counseling and support services may help prevent suicide by assisting troubled teens in learning alternate ways of reducing stress and resolving conflicts with others.

behavior, including depression, schizophrenia, and alcohol and substance abuse ("Many Suicides Can Still Be Prevented" 1997).

Predicting Suicide

"I don't believe it. I just saw him last week and he looked fine."

"She sat here just the other day, laughing with the rest of us. How were we to know what was going on inside her?"

"I knew he was depressed, but I never thought he'd do something like this. I didn't have a clue."

"Why didn't she just call me?"

Friends and family members often respond to news of a suicide with disbelief or guilt that they failed to pick up signs of the impending act. Yet even trained professionals find it difficult to predict who is likely to commit suicide.

Evidence points to the pivotal role of hopelessness in predicting suicidal thinking and behavior (Joiner, Rudd, & Rajab, 1997; M. A. Young et al., 1996). In one study, psychiatric outpatients with hopelessness scores above a certain cutoff were 11 times more likely to commit suicide than those with scores below the cutoff (A. T. Beck et al., 1990). But *when* does hopelessness lead to suicide?

People who commit suicide tend to signal their intentions, often quite explicitly, such as by telling others about their suicidal thoughts (Denneby et al., 1996). Some attempt to cloak their intentions. Behavioral clues may still reveal suicidal intent, however. Edwin Shneidman, a leading researcher on suicide, found that 90% of the people who committed suicide had left clear cues, such as disposing of their possessions (Gelman, 1994). People contemplating suicide may also suddenly try to sort out their affairs, as in drafting a will or buying a cemetery plot. They may purchase guns despite lack of prior interest in firearms. When troubled people decide to commit suicide, they may seem to be suddenly at peace; they feel relieved of having to contend with life problems. This sudden calm may be misinterpreted as a sign of hope.

The prediction of suicide is not an exact science, even for experienced professionals. Many observable factors, such as hopelessness, do seem to be connected with suicide, but we cannot predict *when* a hopeless person will attempt suicide, if at all.

SUMMARY

Mood Disorders

Mood disorders are disturbances in mood that are unusually prolonged or severe and serious enough to impair daily functioning. There are various kinds of mood disorders, including depressive (unipolar) disorders such as major depressive disorder and dysthymic disorder, and disorders involving mood swings, such as bipolar disorder and cyclothymic disorder.

Major Depressive Disorder

People with major depressive disorder experience profound changes in mood that impair their ability to function. There are many associated features of major depressive disorder, including depressed mood; changes in appetite; difficulty sleeping; reduced sense of pleasure in formerly enjoyable activities; feelings of fatigue or loss of energy; sense of worthlessness; excessive or misplaced guilt; difficulties concentrating, thinking clearly, or making decisions; repeated thoughts of death or suicide; attempts at suicide; and even psychotic behaviors (hallucinations and delusions).

About twice as many women as men seem to be affected by major depressive disorder, but the reasons for this gender difference remain unclear. Depression can begin or recur at any age, but the risk of initial onset of depression is age related. Major depression has been increasing worldwide.

Dysthymic Disorder

Dysthymic disorder is a form of chronic depression that is milder than major depressive disorder but may nevertheless be associated with impaired functioning in social and occupational roles.

Bipolar Disorder

There are two general types of bipolar disorders, bipolar I and bipolar II disorders. Bipolar I disorder is identified by the occurrence of one or more manic episodes, which generally but not necessarily occur in persons who have experienced major depressive episodes. In bipolar II disorder, depressive episodes occur along with hypomanic episodes, but without the occurrence of a full-blown manic episode. Manic episodes are characterized by sudden elevation or expansion of mood and sense of self-importance, feelings of almost boundless energy, hyperactivity, and extreme sociability, which often takes a demanding and overbearing form. People in manic episodes tend to exhibit pressured or rapid speech, rapid "flight of ideas," and decreased need for sleep.

Cyclothymic Disorder

Cyclothymic disorder is a type of bipolar disorder characterized by a chronic pattern of mild mood swings that sometimes progresses to bipolar disorder.

Theoretical Perspectives

In classic psychodynamic theory, depression is viewed in terms of inwardly directed anger. People who hold strongly ambivalent feelings toward people they have lost, or whose loss is threatened, may direct unresolved anger toward the inward representations of these people that they have incorporated or introjected within themselves, producing self-loathing and depression. Bipolar disorder is understood within psychodynamic theory in terms of the shifting balances between the ego and superego. More recent psychodynamic models, such as the self-focusing model, incorporate both psychodynamic and cognitive aspects in explaining depression in terms of the continued pursuit of lost love objects or goals that it would be more adaptive to surrender.

In the existential-humanistic framework, feelings of depression reflect the lack of meaning and authenticity in the person's life.

Learning perspectives focus on situational factors in explaining depression, such as changes in the level of reinforcement. When reinforcement is reduced, the person may feel unmotivated and depressed, which can occasion inactivity and further reduces opportunities for reinforcement. Coyne's interactional theory focuses on the negative family interactions that can lead the family members of people with depression to become less reinforcing toward them.

Beck's cognitive theory focuses on the role of negative or distorted thinking in depression. Depression-prone people hold negative beliefs toward themselves, the environment, and the future. This cognitive triad of depression leads to specific errors in thinking, or cognitive distortions, in response to negative events, that in turn lead to depression.

The learned helplessness model is based on the belief that people may become depressed when they come to view themselves as helpless to control the reinforcements in their environment or to change their lives for the better. A reformulated version of the theory holds that the ways in which people explain events—their attributions—determine their proneness toward depression in the face of negative events. The combination of internal, global, and stable attributions for negative events renders one most vulnerable to depression.

Genetics appears to play a role in mood disorders, especially in explaining major depressive disorder and bipolar disorder. Imbalances in the neurotransmitter activity in the brain appear to be involved in depression and mania. The diathesis-stress model is used as an explanatory framework to illustrate how biological or psychological diatheses may interact with stress in the development of depression.

Treatment

Psychodynamic treatment of depression has traditionally focused on helping the depressed person uncover and work through ambivalent feelings toward the lost object, thereby lessening the anger directed inward. Modern psychodynamic approaches tend to be more direct and briefer and focus on developing more adaptive means of achieving self-worth and resolving interpersonal conflicts. Learning theory approaches have focused on helping people with depression increase the frequency of reinforcement in their lives through such means as increasing the rates of pleasant activities in which they participate and assisting them in developing more effective social skills to increase their ability to obtain social reinforcements from others. Cognitive therapists focus on helping the person identify and correct distorted or dysfunctional thoughts and learn more adaptive behaviors. Biological approaches have focused on the use of antidepressant drugs and other biological treatments, such as electroconvulsive therapy (ECT). Antidepressant drugs appear to increase the levels of neurotransmitters in the brain. Bipolar disorder is commonly treated with lithium.

Suicide

Mood disorders are often linked to suicide. Although women are more likely to attempt suicide, more men actually succeed, probably because they select more lethal means. The elderly—not the young—are more likely to commit suicide, and the rate of suicide among the elderly appears to be increasing. People who attempt suicide are often depressed, but they are generally in touch with reality. They may, however, lack effective problem-solving skills and see no way to deal with their life stress other than by suicide.

1. How do clinicians distinguish between normal and abnormal variations in mood?

2. What are the major features of the following mood disorders—major depressive disorder, dysthmia, bipolar disorder, and cyclothymic disorder?

3. What is the difference between unipolar disorders and bipolar disorders?

4. How do clinicians distinguish between a manic episode and a hypomanic episode?

5. What are the features of seasonal affective disorder and postpartum depression?

6. How is depression conceptualized with psychodynamic, behavioral, cognitive, and biological perspectives?

7. What treatment alternatives are available to people suffering from mood disorders? What evidence supports their value?

8. Do you think that drugs like Prozac affect our personalities, not just our moods? Why or why not?

9. What factors are related to suicide and suicide prevention? What have you learned from your reading of the text that might be helpful to you if someone you knew was threatening suicide?

© **Paul Klee**
Beware of Red, 1940

8

Personality Disorders

TRUTH or FICTION?

8.1 Warning signs of personality disorders may begin appearing in early childhood.

8.2 Some people have deeper feelings for animals than they do for people.

8.3 People with psychopathic personalities inevitably run afoul of the law.

8.4 Many notable figures in history, from Lawrence of Arabia to Adolf Hitler and even Marilyn Monroe have been depicted as borderline personalities.

8.5 Some people with dependent personality disorder have such difficulty making independent decisions that they allow their parents to decide whom they will or will not marry.

8.6 It is often difficult to draw the line between normal variations in behavior and personality disorders.

8.7 The conceptualization of certain types of personality disorders may be sexist.

8.8 Despite a veneer of self-importance, people with narcissistic personalities may harbor deep feelings of insecurity.

8.9 People with antisocial personalities tend to remain unduly calm in the face of impending pain.

1. Define personality disorder.

2. Discuss controversies in diagnosing personality disorders.

3. Describe the features of paranoid, schizoid, and schizotypal personality disorders.

4. Describe the features of antisocial, borderline, histrionic, and narcissistic personality disorders.

5. Describe the features of avoidant, dependent, and obsessive-compulsive personality disorders.

6. Discuss problems in the classification of personality disorders, including their reliability and validity, and sexist biases.

7. Discuss theoretical perspectives on the personality disorders.

8. Discuss the special problems in treating personality disorders.

A ll of us have particular styles of behavior and ways of relating to others. Some of us are orderly, others sloppy. Some of us prefer solitary pursuits, others are more social. Some of us are followers; others, leaders. Some of us seem immune to rejection by others, whereas others avoid social initiatives for fear of getting shot down. When behavior patterns become so inflexible or maladaptive that they cause significant personal distress or impair people's social or occupational functioning, they may be diagnosed as personality disorders.

PERSONALITY DISORDERS

In most of us by the age of thirty, the character has set like plaster, and will never soften again.

WILLIAM JAMES

Personality disorders are excessively rigid patterns of behavior or ways of relating to others. Their rigidity prevents people from adjusting to external demands; thus, they ultimately become self-defeating. The disordered personality traits become evident by adolescence or early adulthood and continue through much of adult life, becoming so deeply ingrained that they are highly resistant to change. The warning signs of personality disorders may be detected during childhood, even in the troubled behavior of preschoolers. Children with childhood behavior problems such as conduct disorder, depression, anxiety, and immaturity are at greater than average risk of developing personality disorders during adolescence (D. P. Bernstein et al., 1996).

TRUTH *or* FICTION REVISITED

8.1 *True.* Warning signs of personality disorder may be found in problem behaviors observed in young children, even preschoolers.

Despite the self-defeating consequences of their behavior, people with personality disorders do not generally perceive a need to change. Using psychodynamic terms, the DSM notes that people with personality disorders tend to perceive their traits as **ego syntonic**—as natural parts of themselves. As a result, persons with personality disorders are more likely to be brought to the attention of mental-health professionals by others than to seek services themselves. In contrast, persons with anxiety disorders or mood disorders tend to view their disturbed behaviors as **ego dystonic**. They do not see their behaviors as parts of their self-identities and are thus more likely to seek help to relieve the distress caused by them.

The DSM groups clinical syndromes on Axis I and personality disorders on Axis II. Both clinical syndromes and personality disorders may thus be diagnosed in clients whose behavior meets the criteria for both classes of disorders. For example, a person may have an Axis I mood disorder, such as major depression, and also show the more enduring characteristics associated with an Axis II personality disorder.

Types of Personality Disorders

The DSM groups personality disorders into three clusters:

Cluster A: People who are perceived as odd or eccentric. This cluster includes paranoid, schizoid, and schizotypal personality disorders.

Cluster B: People whose behavior is overly dramatic, emotional, or erratic. This grouping consists of antisocial, borderline, histrionic, and narcissistic personality disorders.

Cluster C: People who often appear anxious or fearful. This cluster includes avoidant, dependent, and obsessive-compulsive personality disorders.

PERSONALITY DISORDERS CHARACTERIZED BY ODD OR ECCENTRIC BEHAVIOR

This group of personality disorders includes paranoid, schizoid, and schizotypal disorders. People with these disorders often have difficulty relating to others, or they may show little or no interest in developing social relationships.

Paranoid Personality Disorder

The defining trait of the **paranoid personality disorder** is pervasive suspiciousness—the tendency to interpret other people's behavior as deliberately threatening or demeaning. People with the disorder are excessively mistrustful of others, and their relationships suffer for it. They may be suspicious of co-workers and supervisors but can generally maintain employment.

The following case illustrates the unwarranted suspicion and reluctance to confide in others that typifies people with paranoid personalities:

An 85-year-old retired businessman was interviewed by a social worker to determine the health care needs for himself and his infirm wife. The man had no history of treatment for a mental disorder. He appeared to be in good health and mentally alert. He and his wife had been married for 60 years, and it appeared that his wife was the only person he'd ever really trusted. He had always been suspicious of others. He would not reveal personal information to anyone but his wife, believing that others were out to take advantage of him. He had refused offers of help from other acquaintances because he suspected their motives. When called on the telephone, he would refuse to give out his name until he determined the nature of the caller's business. He'd always involved himself in "useful work" to occupy his time, even during the 20 years of his retirement. He spends a good deal of time monitoring his investments and has had altercations with his stock broker when errors on his monthly statement prompted suspicion that his broker was attempting to cover up fraudulent transactions.

ADAPTED FROM SPITZER ET AL., 1994, PP. 211–213

People who have paranoid personalities tend to be overly sensitive to criticism, whether real or imagined. They take offense at the smallest slight. They are readily angered and hold grudges when they think they have been mistreated. They are unlikely to confide in others because they believe that personal information may be used against them. They question the sincerity and trustworthiness of friends and associates. A smile or a glance may be viewed with suspicion. As a result, they have few friends and intimate relationships. When they do form an intimate relationship, they may suspect infidelity, although there is no evidence to back up their suspicions. They tend to remain hypervigilant, as if they must be on the lookout against harm. They deny blame for misdeeds, even when warranted, and are perceived by others as cold, aloof, scheming, devious, and humorless. They tend to be argumentative and may launch repeated lawsuits against those who they believe have mistreated them.

Clinicians need to weigh cultural and sociopolitical factors when arriving at a diagnosis. They may find members of immigrant or ethnic minority groups, political refugees, or people from other cultures to be guarded or defensive in their behavior. This behavior may reflect unfamiliarity with the language, customs, or rules and regulations of the majority culture or reflect a cultural mistrust arising from a history of neglect or oppression of the majority culture against the individual's cultural or ethnic group. Such behavior should not be confused with paranoid personality disorder (APA, 1994).

Although the suspicions of people with paranoid personality disorder are exaggerated and unwarranted, there is an absence of the outright paranoid delusions that characterize the thought patterns of people with paranoid schizophrenia (for example, believing the FBI is out to get them). People who have paranoid personalities are unlikely to seek treatment for themselves; they see others as causing their problems. The reported prevalence of paranoid personality disorder in the general population ranges from 0.5% to 2.5%. The disorder is diagnosed in clinical samples more often in men than women (APA, 1994).

Schizoid Personality Disorder

Social isolation is the cardinal feature of **schizoid personality disorder.** Often described as a loner or an eccentric, the person with a schizoid personality lacks interest in social relationships. The emotions of persons with schizoid personalities appear shallow or blunted, but not to the degree found in schizophrenia (see Chapter 12). People with this disorder seem rarely, if ever, to experience strong anger, joy, or sadness. They look distant and aloof. Their faces tend to show no emotional expression, and they rarely exchange social smiles or nods. They seem indifferent to criticism or praise and appear to be wrapped up in abstract ideas rather than in thoughts about people. Although they prefer to remain distant from others, they maintain better contact with

Schizoid personality.   It is normal to be reserved about displaying one's feelings, especially when one is among strangers. But people with schizoid personalities rarely express emotions and are distant and aloof. Yet the emotions of people with schizoid personalities are not as shallow or blunted as they are in people with schizophrenia.

reality than people with schizophrenia do. The prevalence of the disorder in the general population remains unknown.

The schizoid personality pattern is usually recognized by early adulthood. Men with this disorder rarely date or marry. Women with the disorder are more likely to passively accept romantic advances and marry, but they seldom initiate relationships or develop strong attachments to their partners.

Akhtar (1987) claims there may be discrepancies between outer appearances and the inner lives of people with schizoid personalities. Although they may appear to have little appetite for sex, for example, they may harbor voyeuristic wishes and become attracted to pornography. Akhtar also suggests that the distance and social aloofness of people with schizoid personalities may be somewhat superficial. They may also harbor exquisite sensitivity, deep curiosities about people, and wishes for love that they cannot express. In some cases, sensitivity is expressed in deep feelings for animals rather than people:

> John, a 50-year-old retired police officer, sought treatment a few weeks after his dog was hit by a car and died. Since the dog's death, John has felt sad and tired. He has had difficulty concentrating and sleeping. John lives alone and prefers to be by himself, limiting his contacts with others to a passing "Hello" or "How are you?" He feels that social conversation is a waste of time and feels awkward when others try to initiate a friendship. Although he avidly reads newspapers and keeps abreast of current events, he has no real interest in people. He works as a security guard and is described by his co-workers as a "loner" and a "cold fish." The only relationship he had was with his dog, with whom he felt he could exchange more sensitive and loving feelings than he could share with people. At Christmas, he would "exchange gifts" with his dog, buying presents for the dog and wrapping a bottle of Scotch for himself as a gift from

> the animal. The only event that ever saddened him was the loss of his dog. In contrast, the loss of his parents failed to evoke an emotional response. He considers himself to be different from other people and is bewildered by the displays of emotionality that he sees in others.
>
> ADAPTED FROM SPITZER ET AL., 1989, PP. 249–250

TRUTH *or* FICTION REVISITED

8.2 *True.* People with a schizoid personality may show little or no interest in people but develop strong feelings for animals.

Schizotypal Personality Disorder

Schizotypal personality disorder usually becomes evident by early adulthood. The diagnosis applies to people who have difficulties forming close relationships and whose behavior, mannerisms, and thought patterns are peculiar or odd but not disturbed enough to merit a diagnosis of schizophrenia. They may be especially anxious in social situations, even when interacting with familiar people. Their social anxieties seem to be associated with paranoid thinking (e.g., fears that others mean them harm) rather than concerns about being rejected or evaluated negatively by others (APA, 1994). In the DSM-II, the behavior pattern was considered a type of schizophrenia, labeled *simple schizophrenia*. Simple schizophrenia was characterized by persistent oddities in behavior that did not include the gross disorganization that typified other types of schizophrenia. With the advent of the DSM-III in 1980, the label of *schizotypal* personality disorder was introduced to help distinguish between schizophrenic disorders and behavior patterns that were similar and persistent but not as severe.

Schizotypal personality disorder is believed to be slightly more common in males and to affect about 3% of the general population (APA, 1994). Clinicians need to be careful not to label as schizotypal certain behavior patterns that reflect culturally determined beliefs or religious rituals, such as beliefs in voodoo and other magical beliefs (APA, 1994).

The eccentricity associated with the schizoid personality is limited to a lack of interest in social relationships. Schizotypal personality disorder refers to a wider range of odd behaviors, beliefs, and perceptions. Persons with the disorder may experience unusual perceptions or illusions, such as feeling the presence of a deceased family member in the room. They realize, however, that the person is not actually there. They may become unduly suspicious of others or paranoid in their thinking. They may develop **ideas of reference**, such as the belief that other people are talking about them. They may engage in "magical thinking," such as believing they possess a "sixth sense" (i.e., can foretell the future) or that others can sense their feelings. They may attach unusual meanings to words. Their own speech may be vague or unusually abstract but not so it becomes incoherent or filled with the loose associations that characterize schizophrenia. They may appear unkempt, display unusual mannerisms, and engage in unusual behaviors such as talking to themselves in the presence of others. Their faces may register little emotion. Like people with schizoid personalities, they may fail to exchange smiles with, or nod at, others. Or they may appear silly and smile and laugh at the wrong times. They tend to be socially withdrawn and aloof, with few if any close friends or confidants. They seem to be especially anxious around unfamiliar people.

Some of these features are found in the case of Jonathan:

> *Jonathan, a 27-year-old auto mechanic, had few friends and preferred science fiction novels to socializing with other people. He seldom joined in conversations. At times, he seemed to be lost in his thoughts, and his co-workers would have to whistle to get his attention when he was working on a car. He often showed a "queer" expression on his face. Perhaps the most unusual feature of his behavior was his reported intermittent experience of "feeling" his deceased mother standing nearby. These illusions were reassuring to him, and he looked forward to their occurrence. Jonathan realized they were not real. He never tried to reach out to touch the apparition, knowing it would disappear as soon as he drew closer. It was enough, he said, to feel her presence.*
>
> THE AUTHORS' FILES

Despite the DSM's grouping of "schizotypal" behaviors with personality disorders, the schizotypal behavior pattern may fall within a spectrum of schizophrenia-related disorders that also includes paranoid and schizoid personality disorders, as well as schizoaffective disorder (discussed in Chapter 12) and schizophrenia itself. Schizotypal personality disorder may actually share a common genetic basis with schizophrenia (Battaglia et al., 1995; Kendler & Walsh, 1995; Nigg & Goldsmith, 1994). Biological relatives of people with schizotypal personality disorder are more likely than relatives of people with nonschizophrenic-related personality disorders (for example, histrionic, borderline, or narcissistic disorders) to be diagnosed as suffering from a schizophrenia-spectrum disorder (Siever et al., 1990).

Let us note, however, that schizotypal personality disorder tends to follow a chronic course, and relatively few people diagnosed with the disorder go on to develop schizophrenia or other psychotic disorders (APA, 1994). Perhaps the emergence of schizophrenia in persons with this shared genetic predisposition is determined by such factors as stressful early family relationships.

PERSONALITY DISORDERS CHARACTERIZED BY DRAMATIC, EMOTIONAL, OR ERRATIC BEHAVIOR

This cluster of personality disorders includes the antisocial, borderline, histrionic, and narcissistic types. The behavior patterns of these types are excessive, unpredictable, or self-centered. People with these disorders have difficulty forming and maintaining relationships.

Antisocial Personality Disorder

People with **antisocial personality disorder** persistently violate the rights of others and often break the law. They disregard social norms and conventions, are impulsive, and fail to live up to interpersonal and vocational commitments. Cleckley (1976) notes that these people often show a superficial charm and are at least average in intelligence. Perhaps the features that are most striking about them are their low levels of anxiety in threatening situations and lack of guilt following wrongdoing. Punishment seems to have little if any effect on their behavior. Although they have usually been punished by parents and others for their misdeeds, they persist in leading irresponsible and impulsive lives.

Although women are more likely than men to develop anxiety and depressive disorders, men are more likely to receive diagnoses of antisocial personality disorder (Robins, Tipp, & Przybeck, 1991; Russo, 1990). The prevalence rates for the disorder, based on the National Comorbidity Survey (NCS), are about 6% in men and about 1% in women (R. C. Kessler et al., 1994) (see Figure 8.1). Though the prevalence of the disorder has been rising for both genders in recent years, it has been climbing even more sharply among women (APA, 1994).

For the diagnosis of antisocial personality disorder to be applied, the person must be at least 18 years of age. The alternative diagnosis of conduct disorder is used with younger

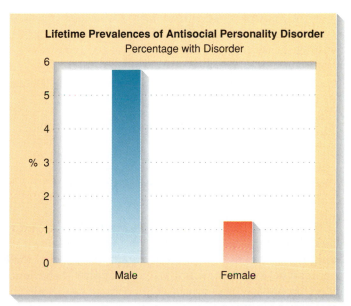

FIGURE 8.1 *Lifetime prevalences of antisocial personality disorder by gender.*
Antisocial personality disorder is more than five times as common among men than women. However, the disorder has been rising more rapidly among women in recent years.

Source: National Comorbidity Survey; Kessler et al. (1994).

people (see Chapter 13). Many children with conduct disorders do not continue to show antisocial behavior as adults.

We once used terms such as *psychopath* and *sociopath* to refer to the type of people who today are classified as having antisocial personalities, people whose behavior is amoral and asocial, impulsive, and lacking in remorse and shame. Some clinicians continue to use these terms interchangeably with antisocial personality. The roots of the word *psychopath* focus on the idea that there is something amiss (pathological) in the individual's psychological functioning. The roots of *sociopath* center on the person's social deviance. As we will see, the use of these terms reflected popular beliefs of the times in which they arose.

The pattern of behavior that characterizes antisocial personality disorder begins in childhood or adolescence and extends into adulthood. However, the antisocial and criminal behavior associated with the disorder tends to decline with age and may actually disappear by the time the person reaches the age of 40. Not so for the underlying personality traits associated with the disorder—traits such as egocentricity; manipulativeness; lack of empathy, guilt, or remorse; and callousness toward others. These appear to be relatively stable, even with increasing age (Harpur & Hare, 1994).

Much of our attention in this chapter focuses on antisocial personality disorder. Historically it is the personality disorder that has been most extensively studied by scholars and researchers.

Historical Perspectives on Antisocial Personality

In the 18th century, some thinkers proposed that moral depravity might represent mental defects that impaired the person's ability to conform to common standards of decency. The French reformer Philippe Pinel, who called for more humane treatment of mental patients, regarded moral depravity as a form of mania *without* insanity. In 1835, the English psychiatrist J. R. Prichard reconceptualized the disorder as "moral insanity." He considered the problem to be a form of mental derangement in which the intellectual functions remained relatively intact but the

> . . . moral and active principles of the mind were strongly perverted or depraved . . . and the individual is found to be incapable not of talking or reasoning on any subject proposed to him, but of conducting himself with decency and propriety in the business of his life (Prichard, 1835, p. 15).

Pinel argued that people with abnormal behavior need a kind and gentle form of treatment, which became known as moral therapy. Moral therapy was based on the belief that abnormal behaviors, including morally depraved behaviors, reflect oppressive or deprived childhoods. It was hoped a nurturant and supportive therapeutic environment would steer depraved people in the right direction.

Later in the 19th century, discoveries of the causes of various physical diseases and some abnormal behavior patterns (e.g., general paresis) inspired hope that organic causes would eventually be discovered for all abnormal behaviors, including antisocial behavior. The medical model suggested that psychopaths—as they were labeled at the time—suffered from a biological defect, presumably hereditary, that predisposed them to criminal or antisocial conduct.

The rise of interest in sociology and social work in the early and mid-20th century led to the view that deviant behavior is rooted in the person's alienation from society. Recognition that social problems such as poverty, unemployment, and exposure to antisocial models are related to deviant behavior led many to substitute the label of sociopathy for psychopathy. Remember a delinquent's discovery in the classic musical *West Side Story*: "Hey, I've got a social disease!"

Sociocultural Factors and Antisocial Personality Disorder

The disorder is more common among people in the lower socioeconomic strata (SES). One explanation is that that people with antisocial personality disorder may drift downward occupationally, perhaps because their antisocial behavior makes it difficult for them to hold steady jobs or progress upwards. It is possible too that people from lower SES levels were more likely to have been reared by parents who themselves modeled antisocial behavior. However, it is also possible that the diagnosis is misapplied to people living in hard-pressed communities who may engage in seemingly antisocial behaviors as a type of defense strategy in order to survive (APA, 1994).

The Epidemiologic Catchment Area (ECA) survey found no ethnic differences in the rates of antisocial personality disorder (Robins et al., 1991). Kosson and his colleagues (Kosson, Smith, & Newman, 1990) compared African Americans and non-Hispanic White Americans with antisocial personality disorder. Prison inmates of both ethnic groups with antisocial personality disorder had histories of greater criminality than other inmates in these ethnic groups. Moreover, the measures used to classify antisocial personality disorder among non-Hispanic White Americans appeared to be generalizable to African Americans.

Antisocial Behavior and Criminality

We may tend to think of antisocial behavior as synonymous with criminal behavior. Though there is a strong relationship between the two, not all people with psychopathic or antisocial behavior become criminals (Lilienfeld & Andrews, 1996). Many are law-abiding and quite successful in their chosen occupations. Yet they possess a personality style characterized by a callous disregard of the interests and feelings of others.

TRUTH or FICTION REVISITED

8.3 *False*. Not all criminals show signs of psychopathy, and not all people with psychopathic personalities become criminals.

Investigators have begun to view psychopathic personality as composed of two, somewhat independent dimensions.

The first is a personality dimension. It consists of such traits as superficial charm, selfishness, lack of empathy, and callous and remorseless use of others and disregard of their feelings and welfare. This type of psychopathic personality applies to people who have these kinds of psychopathic traits but don't become law-breakers.

The second dimension is considered a behavioral dimension. It is characterized by the adoption of an unstable and antisocial lifestyle, including frequent problems with the law, poor employment history, and unstable relationships (S. L. Brown & Forth, 1997; D. J. Cooke & Michie, 1997; Hare, Hart, & Harpur, 1991). These two dimensions are not entirely separate, as many psychopathic individuals show evidence of both sets of traits.

We should also note that people may become criminals or delinquents not because of a disordered personality but because they were reared in environments or subcultures that encouraged and rewarded criminal behavior (Hare, 1986). The criminal behavior of the professional thief or drug pusher, although antisocial, does not in itself justify a diagnosis of antisocial personality disorder. Criminal and aggressive behavior has multiple causes and represents many personality styles (L. J. Siegel, 1992). Although the behavior of criminals is deviant to society at large, it may be normal by the standards of their subcultures. We should also recognize that lack of remorse, which is a cardinal feature of antisocial personality disorder, does not characterize all criminals. Some criminals regret their crimes, and evidence of remorse is considered when sentence is passed.

Only about half of prison inmates could be diagnosed with antisocial personality disorder (Robins et al., 1991).

Conversely, fewer than half of the people with antisocial personality disorder run afoul of the law (Robins et al., 1991)—many fewer still fit (thankfully!) the stereotype of the psychopathic killer popularized in such films as *The Silence of the Lambs*.

Hervey Cleckley (1941) showed that the characteristics defining the psychopathic (antisocial) personality—self-centeredness, irresponsibility, impulsivity, and insensitivity to the needs of others—exist not only among criminals but also among many respected members of the community including doctors, lawyers, politicians, and business executives.

Profile of Antisocial Personality Disorder

Common features of people with antisocial personality disorder include failure to conform to social norms, irresponsibility, aimlessness and lack of long-term goals or plans, impulsive behavior, outright lawlessness, violence, chronic unemployment, marital problems, lack of remorse or empathy, substance abuse, a history of alcoholism, and a disregard for the truth and for the feelings and needs of others (Patrick, Cuthbert, & Lang, 1994; Robins et al., 1991; S. S. Smith & Newman, 1990). Irresponsibility may be seen in a personal history dotted by repeated, unexplained absences from work, abandonment of jobs without having other job opportunities to fall back on, or long stretches of unemployment despite available job opportunities. Irresponsibility extends to financial matters, where there may be repeated failure to repay debts, to pay child support, or to meet other financial responsibilities to one's family and dependents. The diagnostic features of antisocial personality disorder, as defined in the DSM, are shown in Table 8.1.

TABLE 8.1

Diagnostic Features of Antisocial Personality Disorder

(a) The person is at least 18 years old.

(b) There is evidence of a conduct disorder prior to the age of 15 as shown by such behavior patterns as truancy, running away, initiating physical fights, use of weapons, forcing someone into sexual activities, physical cruelty to people or animals, deliberate destruction of property or fire setting, lying, stealing, or mugging.

(c) Since the age of 15, there has been general indifference to and violation of the rights of other people, as shown by several of the following:

   (1) Lack of conformity to social norms and legal codes, as shown by law-breaking behavior that may or may not result in arrest, such as destruction of property, engaging in unlawful occupations, stealing, or harrassing others

   (2) Aggressive and highly irritable style of relating to others, as shown by repeated physical fights and assaults with others, possibly involving abuse of one's spouse or children

   (3) Consistent irresponsibility, as shown by failure to maintain employment due to chronic absences, lateness, abandonment of job opportunities or extended periods of unemployment despite available work; and/or by failure to honor financial obligations, such as failing to maintain child support or defaulting on debts; and/or by lack of a sustained monogamous relationship

   (4) Failure to plan ahead or impulsivity, as shown by traveling around without prearranged employment or clear goals

   (5) Disregard for the truth, evidenced by repeated lying, conning others, or use of aliases for personal gain or pleasure

   (6) Recklessness with regard to personal safety or the safety of other people, as shown by driving while intoxicated or repeated speeding

   (7) Lack of remorse for misdeeds, as shown by indifference to the harm done to others, and/or by rationalizing that harm.

Source: Adapted from the DSM-IV (APA, 1994).

Antisocial personality. Serial killer Ted Bundy, shown here shortly before his execution, killed without feeling or remorse but also displayed some of the superficial charm seen in some people with antisocial personality disorder.

The following case represents a number of antisocial characteristics:

> *The 19-year-old male is brought by ambulance to the hospital emergency room in a state of cocaine intoxication. He's wearing a T-shirt with the imprint "Twisted Sister" on the front, and he sports a punk-style haircut. His mother is called and sounds groggy and confused on the phone; the doctors must coax her to come to the hospital. She later tells the doctors that her son has arrests for shoplifting and for driving while intoxicated. She suspects that he takes drugs, although she has no direct evidence. She believes that he is performing fairly well at school and has been a star member of the basketball team.*
>
> *It turns out that her son has been lying to her. In actuality, he never completed high school and never played on the basketball team. A day later, his head cleared, the patient tells his doctors, almost boastfully, that his drug and alcohol use started at the age of 13, and that by the time he was 17, he was regularly using a variety of psychoactive substances, including alcohol, speed, marijuana, and cocaine. Lately, however, he has preferred cocaine. He and his friends frequently participate in drug and alcohol binges. At times they each drink a case of beer in a day along with downing other drugs. He steals car radios from parked cars and money from his mother to support his drug habit, which he justifies by adopting a (partial) "Robin Hood" attitude—that is, taking money only from people who have lots of it.*
>
> ADAPTED FROM SPITZER ET AL., 1994, PP. 81-83

Although this case is suggestive of antisocial personality disorder, the diagnosis was maintained as provisional because the interviewer could not determine that the deviant behavior (lying, stealing, skipping school) began before the age of 15.

We base our profile of the antisocial personality on the criteria listed by Cleckley in describing this personality type in his classic book *The Mask of Sanity,* which was first published in 1941 and has continued, in subsequent editions, to influence conceptions of the disorder. Although there is much overlap between Cleckley's characterization and the DSM concept of antisocial personality disorder, we should note some differences. The DSM places a greater emphasis on specific undesirable behaviors, such as a history of lying or criminal behavior, or inability to maintain steady employment or meet family or financial responsibilities. Although he recognized specific antisocial behaviors as part of his overall profile, Cleckley emphasized the personality traits and interpersonal and subjective aspects of the disorder (called psychopathy at the time), such as superficial charm and lack of capacity for love, along with inability to profit from experience. By focusing more on behavior, the DSM may improve the reliability of diagnostic judgments of antisocial personality. Cleckley's clinical profile, however, provides researchers and clinicians a richer understanding of the psychological features of people with antisocial personalities:

1. *Superficial charm and intelligence.* People with antisocial personalities may be superficially charming, even while committing cruel or murderous actions. They may appear friendly and easy to talk to, giving no impression of being fraudulent or manipulative.

2. *Absence of anxiety in stressful situations.* They may be poised and cool under pressure, not displaying nervousness in stressful situations that might cause others to feel embarrassed or anxious. This lack of fearfulness or anxiety proneness under stressful conditions does not mean they are necessarily free of anxiety altogether. Some individuals with antisocial personality may experience high levels of anxiety relating to the legal and social difficulties they find themselves in by virtue of their excessive risk-taking behavior (Lilienfeld, 1994; Sher & Trull, 1994).

3. *Insincerity and lack of truthfulness.* They are often able to speak convincingly of feelings toward loved ones and appear to be sensitive to the needs of others, even while taking advantage.

4. *Lack of remorse and shame.* They may feel no pangs of guilt or remorse, no feelings of shame for misdeeds and injurious behavior.

5. *Inability to experience love or genuine emotion.* Although they may profess feelings of love, often convincingly so, the feelings are not genuine. They are egocentric, exploitive and manipulative, and lack the capacity to love, and often wind up hurting the purported objects of love. Lack of empathy and deep feelings may facilitate the callous mistreatment of "loved ones."

6. *Unreliability and irresponsibility.* They lack a sense of obligation, duty, or responsibility. They may walk away from jobs or desert their families, leaving a pile of unpaid bills.

7. *Impulsivity and disregard for socially acceptable behavior.* They tend to act on the spur of the moment. They drift from place to place without concrete goals or destinations in mind. They may commit impulsive antisocial acts with little or no planning, such as stealing a car because they "felt like it," using illicit drugs, or passing bad checks when money runs out. The aimlessness with which they break the law often separates them from committed criminals whose crimes are planned and rehearsed. They seem unable to tolerate frustration or delay gratification. They demand to have (or take) what they want when they want it, even if it means stealing or otherwise breaking the law.

8. *Absence of delusions or irrational thinking.* They seem to be clearheaded. Others may perceive them as holding firm rational convictions and being capable of warm responses toward their families and loved ones.

9. *Inability to profit from experience.* They may commit the same misdeeds repeatedly, despite a history of punishment. Punishment has little effect on their behavior; despite promises to "go straight," they eventually return to impulsive antisocial behavior. They may have difficulty avoiding punishments because they may be overresponsive to immediate, tangible goals that are right before them (Kosson, 1996).

10. *Lack of insight.* They are unable to see themselves as others do. They are more likely to blame others for their difficulties than to recognize that they have brought their problems on themselves.

Borderline Personality Disorder

Borderline personality disorder (BPD) is characterized primarily by a pervasive pattern of instability in relationships, self-image, and mood and by a lack of control over impulses. People with borderline personality disorder tend to be uncertain about their values, goals, loyalties, careers, choices of friends, perhaps even their sexual orientations. This instability in self-image or identity leaves them with persistent feelings of emptiness and boredom. They cannot tolerate being alone and will make desperate attempts to avoid feelings of abandonment (Gunderson, 1996). Fear of abandonment renders them clinging and demanding in their social relationships, but their clinging often pushes away the people on whom they depend. Signs of rejection

Borderline personality. In the movie *Fatal Attraction*, the actress Glenn Close played a character that had many of the characteristics associated with borderline personality disorder, including impulsivity, extreme mood swings, and unstable relationships.

may enrage them, straining their relationships further. Their feelings toward others are consequently intense and shifting. They alternate between extremes of adulation (when their needs are met) and loathing (when they feel scorned). They tend to view other people as all good or all bad, shifting abruptly from one extreme to the other. As a result, they may flit from partner to partner in a series of brief and stormy relationships. People whom they had idealized are treated with contempt when relationships end or when they feel the other person fails to meet their needs (Gunderson & Singer, 1986).

The label of borderline personality has been applied to people as diverse as Marilyn Monroe, Lawrence of Arabia, Adolf Hitler, and the philosopher Sören Kierkegaard (Sass, 1982). Some theorists believe we live in highly fragmented and alienating times, which tend to create the problems in forming cohesive identities and stable relationships that characterize people with borderline personalities (Sass, 1982). "Living on the edge," or border, can be seen as a metaphor for an unstable society. Borderline personality disorder is believed to occur in about 2% of the general population (APA, 1994). Although it is diagnosed more often (about 75% of the time) in women, gender differences in prevalence rates for BPD in the general population remain undetermined.

TRUTH *or* **FICTION** **REVISITED**

8.4 *True.* Many notable figures have been described as having personality features associated with borderline personality disorder.

A CLOSER LOOK

The Pause That Reflects

People with antisocial personality disorder are notoriously undeterred by punishment. They may repeatedly engage in self-defeating patterns of behavior, such as gambling or coming in late to work, despite negative consequences. Perhaps one reason they fail to profit from experience is they find it difficult to switch gears (change their behavior) in the face of changing reinforcement contingencies. They may once have won at gambling or been able to sneak late into work without getting caught. But gambling losses eventually exceed winnings, and latenesses eventually put them on the unemployment line. Nonetheless, they may get stuck in maladaptive patterns of behavior, a response deficit that psychologists label **perseveration.**

Perseveration (and what might be done about it) was demonstrated in a card-playing experiment with persons with antisocial personality disorder and normal control subjects (J. P. Newman, Patterson, & Kosson, 1987). Subjects could win or lose money by playing repeated hands of cards. The odds of winning were stacked, however, so subjects were likely to win in the early rounds and lose in the later rounds. Subjects were free to stop playing at any time. The people from the normal control group tended to play as long as they were winning and to quit when they started to lose as frequently as they won. They apparently recognized that the odds had turned against them and chose to take their winnings and leave. By contrast, people with antisocial personality disorder tended to play on when their "luck" changed, until they lost all their money or were out of cards.

In another experimental condition, a forced delay of a few seconds was introduced between rounds. The people with antisocial personality disorder who had to pause terminated their playing when the odds changed just as the subjects in the normal control group did. Giving them time to think about punishment apparently disrupted their perseveration and helped them benefit from experience. Perhaps antisocial individuals would benefit from other treatments that focus on teaching them to stop and think about the consequences before they act.

The term *borderline personality* was originally used to refer to individuals whose behavior appeared on the border between neuroses and psychoses. People with borderline personality disorder generally maintain better contact with reality than people with psychoses, although they may show transient psychotic behaviors during times of stress. Generally speaking, they seem to be more severely impaired than most people with neuroses but not as dysfunctional as those with psychotic disorders.

Borderline personality disorder may lie closer to the mood disorders than psychotic disorders. Some researchers find that nearly half of those diagnosed with borderline personality disorder also meet diagnostic criteria for major depression or bipolar disorder (H. G. Pope, Jones, Hudson, Cohen, & Gunderson, 1983). Others find a weaker link between borderline personality and depression, however, so connections remain somewhat muddled (Gunderson & Phillips, 1991). Many people with borderline personality disorder also meet criteria for other personality disorders, such as histrionic, narcissistic, and antisocial personality disorders. Although questions remain about the diagnostic category, the evidence supports the belief that borderline personality is a distinct disorder (Zalewski & Archer, 1991).

Instability of moods is a central characteristic of borderline personality disorder. Moods run the gamut from anger and irritability to depression and anxiety, with each lasting from a few hours to a few days. People with BPD have difficulty controlling anger and are prone to fights or smashing things. They often act on impulse, like eloping with someone they have just met. This impulsive and unpredictable behavior is often self-destructive and linked to a risk of suicidal attempts and gestures (Brodsky et al., 1997). It may also involve spending sprees, gambling, drug abuse, engaging in unsafe sexual activity, reckless driving, binge eating, or shoplifting. Impulsive acts of self-mutilation, such as scratching their wrists or burning cigarettes on their arms, may also occur, as in the following case:

CLIENT: *I've got such repressed anger in me; what happens is . . . I can't feel it; I get anxiety attacks. I get very nervous, smoke too many cigarettes. So what happens to me is I tend to explode. Into tears or hurting myself or whatever . . . because I don't know how to contend with all those mixed up feelings.*
INTERVIEWER: *What was the more recent example of such an "explosion"?*
CLIENT: *I was alone at home a few months ago; I was frightened! I was trying to get in touch with my boyfriend and I couldn't . . . He was nowhere to be*

> *found. All my friends seemed to be busy that night and I had no one to talk to . . . I just got more and more nervous and more and more agitated. Finally, bang!—I took out a cigarette and lit it and stuck it into my forearm. I don't know why I did it because I didn't really care for him all that much. I guess I felt I had to do something dramatic . . ."*
>
> ADAPTED FROM STONE, 1980, P. 400

Self-mutilation is sometimes carried out as an expression of anger or a means of manipulating others. Such acts may be intended to counteract self-reported feelings of "numbness," particularly in times of stress. Not surprisingly, among people with BPD, frequent self-mutilation is associated with an increased risk of suicidal thinking (Dulit et al., 1994).

Individuals with BPD tend to have very troubled relationships with their families of origin and others. They tend to view their relationships as rife with hostility and to perceive others as rejecting and abandoning (Benjamin & Wonderlich, 1994). They also tend to be difficult to work with in psychotherapy, demanding a great deal of support from therapists and calling them at all hours or acting suicidally to elicit support. They tend to drop out early from psychotherapy, and those who improve seem more the exception than the rule (T. A. Aronson, 1989), except for those who have a coexisting mood disorder that is more amenable to treatment (H. G. Pope et al., 1983). Their feelings toward therapists, as toward other people, undergo rapid alterations between idealization and outrage. These abrupt shifts in feelings are interpreted by psychoanalysts as signs of "splitting," or inability to reconcile the positive and negative aspects of one's experience of oneself and others. From the modern psychodynamic perspective, borderline individuals cannot synthesize positive and negative elements of personality into complete wholes. They therefore fail to achieve fixed self-identities or images of others. Rather than viewing important figures in their lives as sometimes loving and as sometimes rejecting, they shift back and forth between viewing them as all good or all bad, between idealization and abhorrence. The psychoanalyst Otto Kernberg, a leading authority on borderline personality, tells of a woman in her thirties whose attitude toward him vacillated in such a way:

> In one session, the patient may experience me as the most helpful, loving, understanding human being and may feel totally relieved and happy, and all the problems are solved. Three sessions later, she may berate me as the most ruthless, indifferent, manipulative person she has ever met. Total unhappiness about the treatment, ready to drop it and never come back. (Cited in Sass, 1982, p. 15. Copyright © 1982 by The New York Times. Reprinted by permission.)

Borderline personality disorder remains in many ways a perplexing and frustrating problem.

Histrionic Personality Disorder

Histrionic personality disorder refers to individuals with excessive emotionality and needs to be the center of attention. The term is derived from the Latin *histrio,* which means "actor." People with histrionic personality disorder tend to be dramatic and emotional, but their emotions seem shallow, exaggerated, and volatile. The disorder was formerly called *hysterical* personality. The supplanting of *hysterical* with *histrionic* and the associated exchange of the roots *hystera* (meaning "uterus") and *histrio* allow professionals to distance themselves from the notion that the disorder is intricately bound up with being female. The disorder is diagnosed more frequently in women than men, however (Hartung & Widiger, 1998; Pfohl, 1991), although some studies using structured interview methods find similar rates of occurrence among men and women (APA, 1994). Whether the gender discrepancy in clinical practice reflects true differences in the prevalence of the disorder, diagnostic biases, or other factors remains something of an open question (Corbitt & Widiger, 1995).

Despite a long-standing belief among clinicians that histrionic personality is closely related to conversion disorder, research has not borne out this connection (Kellner, 1992). People with conversion disorder are actually more likely to show features of dependent personality disorder than histrionic personality disorder.

People with histrionic personalities may become unusually upset by news of a sad event and cancel plans for the evening, inconveniencing their friends. They may exude exaggerated delight when they meet someone or become enraged when someone fails to notice their new hairstyle. They may faint at the sight of blood or blush at a slight faux pax. They tend to demand that others meet their needs for attention and play the victim when others fall short. If they feel a touch of fever, they may insist that others drop everything to rush them to the doctor. They tend to be self-centered and intolerant of delays of gratification; they want what they want when they want it. They grow quickly restless with routine and crave novelty and stimulation. They are drawn to fads. Others may see them as putting on airs or playacting, although they may evince a certain charm. They may enter a room with a flourish. They embellish their experiences with flair. When pressed for details, however, they fail to color in the specifics of their tales. They tend to be flirtatious and seductive but are too wrapped up in themselves to develop intimate relationships or have deep feelings toward others. As a result, their associations tend be stormy and ultimately ungratifying. They tend to use their physical appearance as a means of drawing attention to themselves. Men with the disorder may act and dress in an overly "macho" manner to draw attention to themselves; women may choose very frilly, feminine clothing. Glitter supercedes substance.

People with histrionic personalities may be attracted to professions such as modeling or acting, where they can hog the spotlight. Despite outward successes, they may lack self-esteem and strive to impress others to boost their self-worth. If they suffer setbacks or lose their place in the limelight, depressing inner doubts may emerge.

The case of Marcella shows some of these features:

> Marcella was a 36-year-old, attractive, but overly made up woman who was dressed in tight pants and high heels. Her hair was in a bird's nest of the type that had been popular when she was a teenager. Her social life seemed to bounce from relationship to relationship, from crisis to crisis. Marcella sought help from the psychologist at this time because her 17-year-old daughter, Nancy, had just been hospitalized for cutting her wrists. Nancy lived with Marcella and Marcella's current boyfriend, Morris, and there were constant arguments in the apartment. Marcella recounted the disputes that took place with high drama, waving her hands, clanging the bangles that hung from her bracelets, and then clutching her breast. It was difficult having Nancy live at home, because Nancy had expensive tastes, was "always looking for attention," and flirted with Morris as a way of "flaunting her youth." Marcella saw herself as a doting mother and denied any possibility that she was in competition with her daughter.
>
> Marcella came for a handful of sessions during which she basically ventilated her feelings and was encouraged to make decisions that might lead to a reduction of some of the pressures on her and her daughter. At the end of each session she said, "I feel so much better" and thanked the psychologist profusely. At termination of "therapy," she took the psychologist's hand and squeezed it endearingly. "Thank you so much, doctor," she said and made her exit.
>
> THE AUTHORS' FILES

Marcella also showed a number of features of narcissism, which we discuss next.

Narcissistic Personality Disorder

Narkissos was a handsome youth who, according to Greek myth, fell in love with his reflection in a spring. Because of his excessive self-love, in one version of the myth, he was transformed by the gods into the flower we know as the narcissus.

Persons with **narcissistic personality disorder** have an inflated or grandiose sense of themselves and an extreme need for admiration. They brag about their accomplishments and expect others to shower them with praise. They expect others to notice their special qualities, even when their accomplishments are ordinary, and they enjoy basking in the light of adulation. They are self-absorbed and lack empathy for others. Although they share certain features with histrionic personalities, such as demanding to be the center of attention, they have a much more inflated view of

Narkissos. According to one version of the Greek myth, Narkissos fell in love with his reflection in a spring. Because of his excessive self-love, the gods transformed him into a flower—the narcissus.

themselves and are less melodramatic than people with histrionic personality disorder. The label of borderline personality disorder (BPD) is sometimes applied to them, but people with narcissistic personality disorder are generally better able to organize their thoughts and actions. They tend to be more successful in their careers, better able to rise to positions of status and power. Their relationships also tend to be more stable than those of people with BPD.

Narcissistic personality disorder is believed to occur in less than 1% of the general population (APA, 1994). Although more than half of the people diagnosed with the disorder are men, we cannot say whether there is an underlying gender difference in prevalence rates in the general population. A certain degree of narcissism or self-aggrandizement may represent a healthful adjustment to insecurity, a shield from criticism and failure, or a motive for achievement (Goleman, 1988b). Excessive narcissistic qualities can become unhealthful, especially when cravings for adulation are insatiable. Table 8.2 compares "normal" self-interest with self-defeating extremes of narcissism. Up to a point, self-interest fosters success and happiness. In more extreme cases, as with narcissism, it can compromise relationships and careers.

People with narcissitic personalities tend to be preoccupied with fantasies of success and power, ideal love, or recognition for brilliance or beauty. They, like people with

TABLE 8.2

Features of Normal Self-Interest as Compared to Self-Defeating Narcissism

Normal Self-Interest	Self-Defeating Narcissism
Appreciating acclaim, but not requiring it in order to maintain self-esteem.	Craving adoration insatiably; requiring acclaim in order to feel momentarily good about oneself.
Being temporarily wounded by criticism.	Being inflamed or crushed by criticism and brooding about it extensively.
Feeling unhappy but not worthless following failure.	Having enduring feelings of mortification and worthlessness triggered by failure.
Feeling "special" or uncommonly talented in some way.	Feeling incomparably better than other people, and insisting upon acknowledgment of that preeminence.
Feeling good about oneself, even when other people are being critical.	Needing constant support from other people in order to maintain one's feelings of well-being.
Being reasonably accepting of life's setbacks, even though they can be painful and temporarily destabilizing.	Responding to life's wounds with depression or fury.
Maintaining self-esteem in the face of disapproval or denigration.	Responding to disapproval or denigration with loss of self-esteem.
Maintaining emotional equilibrium despite lack of special treatment.	Feeling entitled to special treatment and becoming terribly upset when one is treated in an ordinary manner.
Being empathic and caring about the feelings of others.	Being insensitive to other people's needs and feelings; exploiting others until they become fed up.

Source: Based on Goleman, 1988b, p. C1.

A person with a narcissistic personality? People with narcissistic personalities are often preoccupied with fantasies of success and power, ideal love, or recognition for their brilliance or beauty. They may pursue careers that provide opportunities for public recognition and adulation, such as acting, modeling, or politics. They may become deeply wounded by the slightest hint that they are not as special as they believe themselves to be.

histrionic personalities, may gravitate toward careers in which they can receive adulation, such as modeling, acting, or politics. Although they tend to exaggerate their accomplishments and abilities, many people with narcissistic personalities are quite successful in their occupations. But they envy those who achieve even greater success. Insatiable ambition may prompt them to devote themselves tirelessly to work. They are driven to succeed, not so much for money as for the adulation that attends success.

Interpersonal relationships are invariably strained by the demands they impose on others and by their lack of empathy with, and concern for, other people. They seek the company of flatterers and are often superficially charming and friendly and able to draw people to them. But their interest in people is one-sided: They seek people who will serve their interests and nourish their sense of self-importance (Goleman, 1988b). They have feelings of entitlement that lead them to exploit others. They treat sex partners as devices for their own pleasure or to brace their self-esteem.

The case of Bill illustrates several features of the narcissistic personality:

Most people agreed that Bill, a 35-year-old investment banker, had a certain charm. He was bright, articulate, and attractive. He possessed a keen sense of humor that drew people to him at social gatherings. He would always position himself in the middle of the room, where he could be the center of attention. The topics of conversation invariably focused on his "deals," the "rich and famous" people he had met, and his outmaneuvering of opponents. His next project was always bigger and more daring than the last. Bill loved an audience. His face would light up when others responded to him with praise or admiration for his business successes, which were always inflated beyond their true measure. But when the conversation shifted to other people, he would lose interest and excuse himself to make a drink or to call his answering machine. When hosting a party, he would urge guests to stay late and feel hurt if they had to leave early; he showed no sensitivity to, or awareness of, the needs of his friends.

The few friends he had maintained over the years had come to accept Bill on his own terms. They recognized that he needed to have his ego fed or that he would become cool and detached.

Bill had also had a series of romantic relationships with women who were willing to play the adoring admirer and make the sacrifices that he demanded—for a time. But they inevitably tired of the one-sided relationship or grew frustrated by Bill's inability to make a commitment or feel deeply toward them. Lacking empathy, Bill was unable to recognize other people's feelings and needs. His demands for constant attention from willing admirers did not derive from selfishness, but from a need to ward off underlying feelings of inadequacy and diminished self-esteem. It was sad, his friends thought, that Bill needed so much attention and adulation from others and that his many achievements were never enough to calm his inner doubts.

THE AUTHORS' FILES

PERSONALITY DISORDERS CHARACTERIZED BY ANXIOUS OR FEARFUL BEHAVIOR

This cluster of personality disorders includes the avoidant, dependent, and obsessive-compulsive types. Although the features of these disorders differ, they share a component of fear or anxiety.

Avoidant Personality Disorder

Persons with **avoidant personality disorder** are so terrified of rejection and criticism that they are generally unwilling to enter relationships without ardent reassurances of acceptance. As a result, they may have few close relationships outside their immediate families. They also tend to avoid group occupational or recreational activities for fear of rejection. They prefer to lunch alone at their desks. They shun company picnics and parties, unless they are perfectly sure of acceptance. Avoidant personality disorder, which appears to be equally common in men and women, is be-

A person with an avoidant personality? People with avoidant personalities often keep to themselves because of fear of rejection.

lieved to affect between 0.5% and 1.0% of the general population (APA, 1994).

Unlike people with schizoid qualities, with whom they share the feature of social withdrawal, individuals with avoidant personalities have interest in, and feelings of warmth toward, other people. However, fear of rejection prevents them from striving to meet their needs for affection and acceptance. In social situations, they tend to hug the walls and avoid conversing with others. They fear public embarrassment, the thought that others might see them blush, cry, or act nervously. They tend to stick to their routines and exaggerate the risks or effort involved in trying new things. They may refuse to attend a party that is an hour away on the pretext the late drive home would be too taxing.

The case of Harold illustrates several of the features of the avoidant personality:

Harold, a 24-year-old accounting clerk, had dated but a few women, and he had met them through family introductions. He never felt confident enough to approach a woman on his own. Perhaps it was his shyness that first attracted Stacy. Stacy, a 22-year-old secretary, worked alongside Harold and asked him if he would like to get together sometime after work. At first Harold declined, claiming some excuse, but when Stacy asked again a week later, Harold agreed, thinking she must really like him if she were willing to pursue him. The relationship developed quickly, and soon they were dating virtually every night. The relationship was strained, however. Harold interpreted any slight hesitation in her voice as a

There is a good deal of overlap between avoidant personality disorder and social phobia, particularly with a severe subtype of social phobia that involves a generalized pattern of social phobia (excessive, irrational fear of most social situations) (Herbert, Hope, & Bellack, 1992; S. M. Turner, Beidel, & Townsley, 1992; Widiger, 1992). Although research evidence shows that many cases of generalized social phobia occur in the absence of avoidant personality disorder (Holt, Heimberg, & Hope, 1992), relatively fewer cases of avoidant personality occur in the absence of generalized social phobia (Widiger, 1992). Thus, avoidant personality disorder may represent a more severe form of social phobia (S. G. Hoffman et al., 1995). Still, the scientific jury is still out on the question of whether avoidant personality disorder should be considered a severe form of generalized social phobia or a distinct diagnostic category as it is presently classified.

Dependent Personality Disorder

Dependent personality disorder describes people who have an excessive need to be taken care of by others. This leads them to be overly submissive and clinging in their relationships and extremely fearful of separation. People with this disorder find it very difficult to do things on their own. They seek advice in making even the smallest decision. Children or adolescents with the problem may look to their parents to select their clothes, diets, schools or colleges, even their friends. Adults with the disorder allow others to make important decisions for them. Sometimes they even permit others to make marital decisions, as in the case of Matthew:

TRUTH or FICTION REVISITED
8.5 *True.* People with dependent personality disorder may be so dependent on others for making decisions that they allow their parents to determine whom they will or will not marry.

After marriage, people with dependent personality disorder may rely on their spouses to make decisions such as where they should live, which neighbors they should cultivate, how they should discipline the children, what jobs they should take, how they should budget money, and where they should vacation. Like Matthew, individuals with dependent personality disorder avoid positions of responsibility. They turn down challenges and promotions and work beneath their potentials. They tend to be overly sensitive to criticism and are preoccupied with fears of rejection and abandonment. They may be devastated by the end of a close relationship or by the prospect of living on their own. Because of fear of rejection, they often subordinate their wants and needs to those of others. They may agree with outlandish statements about themselves and do degrading things in order to please others.

Although dependent personality disorder is diagnosed more frequently in women (R. F. Bornstein, 1996b, 1997; Loranger, 1996), it is not clear that there is an underlying difference in the prevalence of the disorder between men and women (Corbitt & Widiger, 1995). The diagnosis is often applied to women who, for fear of abandonment, tolerate husbands who openly cheat on them, abuse them, or gamble away the family's resources. Underlying feelings of inadequacy and helplessness discourage them from taking effective action. In a vicious cycle, their passivity encourages further abuse, leading them to feel yet more inadequate and helpless. The diagnosis of women with this pattern is controversial and may be seen as unfairly "blaming the victim" because women in our society are often socialized into more dependent roles. A panel convened by the American Psychological Association noted that women also encounter greater stress than men in contemporary life (Goleman, 1990b). Women are more likely than men to be subjected to second-class citizenship, which may set the stage for dependency.

Dependent personality disorder has been linked to other psychological disorders, including major depression, bipolar disorder, and social phobia (Loranger, 1996; Reich, 1996; Skodol, Gallaher, & Oldham, 1996), and to physical problems such as hypertension, cancer, and gastrointestinal disorders such as ulcers and colitis (Greenberg & Bornstein, 1988a). There also appears to be a link between dependent personality and what psychodynamic theorists refer to as "oral" behavior problems, such as smoking, eating disorders, and alcoholism (Greenberg & Bornstein, 1988b). Psychodynamic writers trace dependent behaviors to the utter dependence of the newborn baby and the baby's seeking of nourishment through oral means (suckling). From infancy, they suggest, people associate provision of food with love. Food may come to symbolize love, and persons with dependent personalities may overeat to symbolically ingest love (Greenberg & Bornstein, 1988b).

Research shows that people with dependent personalities are more reliant on other people for support and guidance than is the average person (Greenberg & Bornstein, 1988a). People with dependent personalities often attribute their problems to physical rather than emotional causes and seek support and advice from medical experts rather than psychologists or counselors (Greenberg & Bornstein, 1988b).

Obsessive-Compulsive Personality Disorder

The defining features of **obsessive-compulsive personality disorder** involve an excessive degree of orderliness, perfectionism, rigidity, difficulty coping with ambiguity, difficulties expressing feelings, and meticulousness in work habits. About 1% of people in community samples are diagnosed with the disorder (APA, 1994). The disorder is about twice as common in men than women. Unlike obsessive-compulsive anxiety disorder, people with obsessive-compulsive personality disorder do not necessarily experience outright obsessions or compulsions. If they do, both diagnoses may be deemed appropriate.

Persons with obsessive-compulsive personality disorder are so preoccupied with perfection that they cannot complete things in a timely fashion. Their efforts inevitably fall short of their expectations, and they force themselves to redo their work. Or they may ruminate about how to prioritize their assignments rather than get started. They focus on details that others perceive as trivial. As the saying goes, they often fail to see the forest for the trees. Their rigidity impairs their social relationships; they insist on doing things their way rather than compromising. Their zeal for work keeps them from participating in, or enjoying, social and leisure activities. They tend to be stingy with money. They find it difficult to make decisions; they postpone or avoid them for fear of making the wrong choice. They tend to be rigid in issues of morality and ethics because of inflexibility in personality rather than deep-seated convictions. They tend to be

"A place for everything, and everything in its place?" People with obsessive-compulsive personalities may have invented this maxim. Many such people have excessive needs for orderliness in their environment.

overly formal in relationships and find it difficult to express feelings. It is hard for them to relax and enjoy pleasant activities; they worry about the costs of such diversions.

Consider the case of Jerry:

Jerry, a 34-year-old systems analyst, was perfectionistic, overly concerned with details, and rigid in his behavior. Jerry was married to Marcia, a graphics artist. He insisted on scheduling their free time hour by hour and became unnerved when they deviated from his agenda. He would circle a parking lot repeatedly in search of just the right parking spot to ensure that his car would not be scraped by another. He refused to have the apartment painted for over a year because he couldn't decide on the color. He had arranged all the books in their bookshelf alphabetically and insisted that every book be placed in its proper position.

Jerry never seemed to be able to relax. Even on vacation, he was bothered by thoughts of work that he had left behind and by fears that he might lose his job. He couldn't understand how people could lie on the beach and let all their worries evaporate in the summer air. Something can always go wrong, he figured, so how can people let themselves go?

THE AUTHORS' FILES

PROBLEMS WITH THE CLASSIFICATION OF PERSONALITY DISORDERS

Questions remain about the reliability and validity of the diagnostic categories for personality disorders. There may be too much overlap among the diagnoses to justify so many different categories. Agreement between raters on personality disorder diagnoses remains modest at best (Coolidge & Segal, 1998). The classification system also seems to blur the distinctions between normal and abnormal variations in personality. Some categories of personality disorder, moreover, may be based on sexist presumptions. Finally, there is concern that the diagnoses may confuse labels with explanations.

Undetermined Reliability and Validity

The present DSM system sought to clarify the ambiguities in the diagnostic criteria of earlier editions by providing descriptive criteria that more tightly define particular disorders. The reliability and validity of the definitions used in the *DSM-IV* remain to be fully tested, however.

Problems Distinguishing Axis I from Axis II Disorders

Some commentators on the DSM system question whether there is sufficient justification for placing personality disorders and clinical syndromes on separate axes—Axis I and Axis II, respectively (Livesley et al., 1994). Livesley and his colleagues question the assumption that personality disorders are discriminable on the basis that, unlike clinical syndromes such as anxiety or depressive disorders, personality disorders reflect underlying personality traits. As an example, they suggest the clinical syndrome of generalized anxiety disorder may arise in people who possess a low threshold for anxiety, which can be conceptualized as a trait of anxiety vulnerability. Secondly, clinical syndromes are believed to be variable over time, whereas personality disorders are held to be generally more enduring patterns of disturbance. Yet evidence indicates that features of personality disorders may vary over time with changes in circumstances. On the other hand, some Axis I clinical syndromes (dysthymia, for example) follow a more or less chronic course.

Overlap Among Disorders

There is also a high degree of overlap among the personality disorders (S. A. Ball et al., 1997; Morgenstern et al., 1997; Skodol, Gallaher, & Oldham, 1996). Overlap undermines the DSM's conceptual clarity or purity by increasing the number of cases that seem to fit two or more diagnostic categories (Livesley, 1985; Livesley, West, & Tanney, 1986). Although some personality disorders have distinct features, many appear to share common traits. For example, the same person may have traits suggestive of dependent personality disorder (inability to make decisions or initiate activities independently) and of avoidant personality disorder (extreme social anxiety and heightened sensitivity to criticism).

This degree of overlap suggests the possibility that the DSM class of personality disorders contains too many categories (Livesley, West, & Tanney, 1985; Widiger & Costa, 1994). One study found that as many as 25% of people with schizoid personality disorders could also be diagnosed as having avoidant personality disorder, for example (Reich & Noyes, 1986). Another reported that in a sample of people with borderline personality disorder, about 1 in 4 (23%) also met criteria for antisocial personality disorder (Hudziak et al., 1996). Even higher percentages were diagnosed with Axis I diagnoses of major depression (87%), generalized anxiety disorder (55%), or panic disorder (51%).

Overall, about 2 in 3 people with personality disorders meet diagnostic criteria for more than one type of personality disorder (Widiger, 1991). Some "disorders" may thus represent different aspects of the same disorder, not separate diagnostic categories. It has been argued, for example, that the schizoid, avoidant, and schizotypal personality disorders should be regarded as different aspects of a schizoid personality (Livesley et al., 1985).

Difficulty in Distinguishing Between Variations in Normal Behavior and Abnormal Behavior

Another problem with the diagnosis of personality disorders is that they involve traits which, in lesser degrees, describe the behavior of most normal individuals. Feeling suspicious now and then does not mean you have a paranoid personality disorder. The tendency to exaggerate your own importance does not mean you are narcissistic. You may avoid social interactions for fear of embarrassment or rejection without having an avoidant personality disorder, and you may be especially conscientious in your work without having an obsessive-compulsive personality disorder. Because the defining attributes of these disorders are commonly occurring personality traits, clinicians should apply these diagnostic labels only when the patterns are so pervasive that they interfere with the individual's functioning or cause significant personal distress. Knowing where to draw the line, however, remains a problem. We continue to lack data to determine the point at which a trait becomes sufficiently inflexible or maladaptive to justify a personality disorder diagnosis (Widiger & Costa, 1994).

TRUTH *or* FICTION REVISITED

8.6 *True.* It can be difficult to draw the line between normal variations in behavior and personality disorders.

Sexist Biases

The construction of certain personality disorders may be sexist. For example, diagnostic criteria for personality disorders

Are there sexist biases in the conception of personality disorders? The concept of the *histrionic personality disorder* seems to be a caricature of the highly stereotyped feminine personality. Why, then, is there not also something akin to a *macho male personality disorder*, which caricatures the highly stereotyped masculine personality?

label stereotypical feminine behaviors as pathological with greater frequency than is the case with stereotypical masculine behaviors. The concept of the histrionic personality, for example, seems a caricature of the traditional stereotype of the feminine personality: flighty, emotional, shallow, seductive, attention-seeking. But if the feminine stereotype corresponds to a mental disorder, shouldn't we also have a diagnostic category that reflects the masculine stereotype of the "macho male"? It may be possible to show that overly masculinized traits are associated with significant distress or impairment in social or occupational functioning in certain males: Highly masculinized males often get into fights and experience difficulties working for female bosses. There is no personality disorder that corresponds to the "macho male" stereotype, however.

The diagnosis of dependent personality disorder may also unfairly stigmatize women who have been socialized into dependent roles as showing a "mental disorder." Women may be at greater risk of receiving diagnoses of histrionic or dependent personality disorders because clinicians perceive these patterns as existing more commonly among women or because women are more likely than men to be socialized into these behavior patterns.

TRUTH *or* FICTION REVISITED

8.7 *True*. The concepts of histrionic and dependent personality disorders may be sexist. It could be argued that the descriptions of these disorders are parodies of the traditional feminine gender-role stereotype.

Clinicians may also be biased in favor of perceiving women as having histrionic personality disorder and men as having antisocial personality disorder even when they do not differ in symptomatology (Garb, 1997). Clinicians may also have a gender bias when it comes to diagnosing borderline personality disorder. In one study, researchers presented a hypothetical case example to a sample of 311 psychologists, social workers, and psychiatrists (D. Becker & Lamb, 1994). Half of the sample was presented with a case identified as a female; the other half read the identical case except it was identified as a male. Clinicians more often diagnosed the case identified as female as having borderline personality disorder.

Confusing Labels with Explanations

It may seem obvious that we should not confuse diagnostic labels with explanations, but in practice the distinction is sometimes clouded. If we confuse labeling with explanation, we may fall into the trap of circular reasoning. For example, what is wrong with the logic of the following statements?

1. John's behavior is antisocial.
2. Therefore, John has an antisocial personality disorder.
3. John's behavior is antisocial because he has an antisocial personality disorder.

The statements are circular in reasoning because they (1) use behavior to make a diagnosis, and then (2) use the diagnosis as an explanation for the behavior. We may be guilty of circular reasoning in our everyday speech. Consider: "John never gets his work in on time; therefore, he is lazy. John doesn't get his work in because he's lazy." The label allows for general conversation but lacks scientific rigor. In order for a construct such as laziness to have scientific rigor, we need to understand the causes of laziness and the factors that help maintain it. We should not confuse the label we attach to behavior with the cause of the behavior.

Moreover, the tendency to label people with disturbing behavior as personality disordered tends to overlook the social and environmental contexts in which the behavior occurs. We need to attend to the impact of specific traumatic life events, which may occur with a greater range or intensity among members of one gender or cultural group, as important factors underlying patterns of maladaptive behavior. The conceptual underpinnings of the personality disorders lack such a perspective. Moreover, conceptualizations of personality disorders fail to account for the social inequalities in society and the differences in power between the genders or between dominant and minority cultures that may give rise to the types of problems identified as personality disorders. For example, L. S. Brown (1992) and L. E. Walker (1988) document the significant prevalence of a history of childhood physical and sexual abuse among women diagnosed with personality disorders. The ways in which people cope with abuse may come to be viewed as flaws in their character, rather than viewed in terms of dysfunctional societal factors that underlie abusive relationships.

Brown (1992) argues in favor of a new category, labeled *abuse and oppression artifact disorders*, which would describe a group of disorders that are more situationally determined than the traditional personality disorders and perhaps more amenable to change. Such disorders would be characterized by a history or current experience of trauma of a repetitive nature. The stressors accompanying sexism, racism, and other forms of societal oppression are examples of such trauma. Feminist theorists, such as Brown (1992), strongly urge that greater attention be focused on the societal contexts underlying maladaptive behavior, which would include attending to the power differentials in the dominant culture with respect to race, gender, ethnicity, sexual orientation, and so on, and the ways that cultural biases may creep into diagnostic conceptualizations and treatment interventions.

All in all, personality disorders are convenient labels for identifying common patterns of ineffective and ultimately self-defeating behavior, but labels do not explain their causes. Still, the development of an accurate descriptive system is an important step toward scientific explanation. The establishment of reliable diagnostic categories sets the stage for valid research into causation and treatment.

THEORETICAL PERSPECTIVES

In this section we consider theoretical perspectives on the personality disorders. Many of the theoretical accounts of disturbed personality derive from the psychodynamic model. We thus begin with a review of traditional and modern psychodynamic models.

Psychodynamic Perspectives

Traditional Freudian theory focused on problems arising from the Oedipus complex as the foundation for many abnormal behaviors, including personality disorders. Freud believed that children normally resolve the Oedipus complex by forsaking incestuous wishes for the parent of the same gender and identifying with the parent of the opposite gender. As a result, they incorporate the parent's moral principles in the form of a personality structure called the superego. Many factors may interfere with appropriate identification, however, such as having a weak or absent father or an antisocial parent. These factors may sidetrack the normal developmental process, preventing children from developing the moral constraints that prevent antisocial behavior and the feelings of guilt or remorse that normally follow behavior that is hurtful to others. Freud's account of moral development focused mainly on the development of males. He has been criticized for failing to account for the moral development of females.

More recent psychodynamic theories have generally focused on the earlier, pre-Oedipal period of about 18 months to 3 years, during which infants are theorized to begin to develop their identities as separate from those of their parents. These recent advances in psychodynamic theory focus on the development of the sense of self in explaining such disorders as narcissistic and borderline personality disorders.

Hans Kohut One of the principal shapers of modern psychodynamic concepts is Hans Kohut, whose views are labeled **self psychology.** Kohut focused much of his attention on the development of the narcissistic personality.

Kohut (1966) believed a self-image riddled with feelings of insecurity lay beneath the inflated veneers of people with narcissistic personality disorders. The narcissist's self-esteem is like a reservoir that needs to be constantly replenished lest it run dry. A steady stream of praise and attention prevents the narcissist from withering with insecurity. A sense of grandiosity helps people with a narcissistic personality mask their underlying feelings of worthlessness. Failures or disappointments threaten to expose these feelings and drive the person into a state of depression. As a defense against despair, the person attempts to diminish the importance of disappointments or failures. Such people may become enraged by others whom they perceive have failed to protect them from disappointment or have declined to shower them with reassurance, praise, and admiration. They may become infuriated by even the slight criticism, no matter how well intentioned. They may mask feelings of rage and humiliation by adopting a facade of cool indifference. They can make difficult psychotherapy clients because they may become enraged when therapists puncture their inflated self-images to help them develop more realistic self-concepts.

TRUTH or FICTION REVISITED

8.8 *True.* Theorists such as Hans Kohut believe people who have narcissistic personalities may mount a facade of self-importance to cover up deep feelings of inadequacy.

Kohut believed early childhood is characterized by a normal stage of "healthful narcissism." Infants feel powerful, as though the world revolves around them. Infants also normally perceive older people, especially parents, as idealized towers of strength and wish to be one with them to share their power. Empathic parents reflect their children's inflated perceptions by making them feel that anything is possible and by nourishing their self-esteem (e.g., telling them how terrific and precious they are). Even empathic parents are critical from time to time, however, and puncture their children's grandiose sense of self. Or they fail to measure up to their children's idealized views of them. Gradually, unrealistic expectations dissolve and are replaced by more realistic appraisals. This process of childhood narcissism eventually giving way to more realistic appraisals of self and others is perfectly normal. Earlier grandiose self-images form the basis for assertiveness later in childhood and set the stage for ambitious striving in adulthood. In adolescence, childhood idealization is transformed into realistic admiration for parents, teachers, and friends. In adulthood, these ideas develop into a set of internal ideals, values, and goals.

Lack of parental empathy and support, however, sets the stage for pathological narcissism in adulthood. Children who are not prized by parents may fail to develop a sturdy sense of self-esteem and be unable to tolerate even slight blows to their self-worth. They develop damaged self-concepts and feel incapable of being loved and admired because of perceived inadequacies or flaws. Pathological narcissism involves the construction of a grandiose facade of self-perfection that is merely a shell to cloak perceived inadequacies. The facade always remains on the brink of crumbling, however, and must be continually shored up by a constant flow of reassurance that one is special and unique. This leaves the person vulnerable to painful blows to self-esteem following failure to achieve social or occupational goals. So needy of constant approval, the person with a narcissistic personality may fly into a rage when he or she feels slighted in any way.

Kohut's approach to therapy provides clients who have a narcissistic personality an initial opportunity to express their grandiose self-images and to idealize the therapist. Over time, however, the therapist helps them explore the childhood roots of their narcissism and gently points out imperfections in both client and therapist to encourage clients to form more realistic images of the self and others.

Otto Kernberg   Modern psychodynamic views of the borderline personality also trace the disorder to difficulties in self-development in early childhood. Kernberg (1975), a leading psychodynamic theorist, views borderline personality in terms of a pre-Oedipal failure to develop a sense of constancy and unity in one's image of the self and others. Kernberg proposes that childhood failure to synthesize these contradictory images of good and bad results in a failure to develop a consistent self-image and in tendencies toward **splitting**—shifting back and forth between viewing oneself and other people as "all good" or "all bad."

In Kernberg's view, parents, even excellent parents, invariably fail to meet all their children's needs. Infants therefore face the early developmental challenge of reconciling images of the nurturing, comforting "good mother" with those of the withholding, frustrating "bad mother." Failure to reconcile these opposing images into a realistic unified and stable parental image may fixate children in the pre-Oedipal period. As adults, then, they may retain these rapidly shifting attitudes toward their therapists and others.

Margaret Mahler   Mahler, another influential modern psychodynamic theorist, explained borderline personality disorder in terms of childhood separation from the mother figure. Mahler and her colleagues (Mahler, Pine, & Bergman, 1975; Mahler & Kaplan, 1977) believed that during the first year the infant develops a **symbiotic** attachment to its mother. *Symbiosis* is a biological term derived from Greek roots meaning "to live together" and describes life patterns in which two species lead interdependent lives. In psychology, symbiosis is likened to a state of oneness in which the child's identity is fused with the mother's. Nor-mally, children gradually differentiate their own identities or senses of self from their mothers. The process is called **separation-individuation.** Separation is development of a separate psychological and biological identity from the mother. Individuation involves the recognition of the personal characteristics that define one's self-identity. Separation-individuation may be a stormy process. Children may vacillate between seeking greater independence and moving closer to, or "shadowing," the mother, which is seen as a wish for reunion. The mother may disrupt normal separation-individuation by refusing to let go of the child or by pushing the child too quickly toward independence. The tendencies of people with borderline personalities to react to others with ambivalence, to alternate between love and hate, is suggestive to Mahler of earlier ambivalences during the separation-individuation process. Borderline personality disorder may arise from the failure to master this developmental challenge.

All in all, psychodynamic theory provides a rich theoretical mine for the understanding of the development of several personality disorders. But some critics contend that theories of such disorders as borderline personality disorder and narcissistic personality disorder are based largely on inferences drawn from behavior and retrospective accounts of adults, rather than on observations of children (Sass, 1982). Mahler's theory has been challenged by evidence that even infants show a certain degree of psychological differentiation from others (M. Klein, 1981). We may also question whether direct comparisons should be made between normal childhood experiences and abnormal behaviors in adulthood. For example, the ambivalences that characterize the adult borderline personality may bear only a superficial relationship, if any at all, to children's vacillations between closeness and separation with maternal figures during separation-individuation.

Separation-Individuation.   According to psychodynamic theorist Margaret Mahler, young children undergo a process of separation-individuation by which they learn to differentiate their own identities from their mothers.' She believed that a failure to successfully master this developmental challenge may lead to the development of a borderline personality.

Attachment Theory Attachment theory straddles the psychoanalytic and cognitive domains. It examines how infants come to develop attachments to parents and other caregivers. In research with children and their mothers, Mary Ainsworth and her colleagues (e.g., Ainsworth et al., 1978) have identified various styles of attachment in infants and young children. An infant with a *secure style* of attachment uses its mother as "safe base" and explores its environment when mother is about. The infant will cry when mother departs the room and will warmly greet her when she returns. The insecurely attached infant shows either an *insecure-avoidant style* (generally ignoring mother when she is in the room or returns, showing little distress when she leaves), or an *insecure-resistant style* (shows ambivalence toward mother, alternating between clinging to her and pulling away). Attachment styles measured in infancy have been found to predict psychosocial adjustment in children and adolescents. For example, researchers find that adolescents who were securely attached in infancy have better peer relationships, fewer adjustment problems, and do better in school than their peers with insecure attachments in infancy (Azar, 1995).

Might an insecure style of attachment in infancy or childhood predict later difficulties in developing adult attachments that are typical of many people with personality disorders? We lack sufficient data to draw any firm conclusions, but it stands to reason that attachment patterns formed in childhood may be enduring. One proving ground for a linkage between attachment theory and personality disorders is likely to be borderline personality disorder (BPD). People with BPD have impaired attachment relationships. Though they are able to form attachments, these relationships tend to be short-lived, chaotic, and volatile. It remains to be seen whether the attachment styles of BPD patients differ from those of other personality disordered groups. One ongoing study in England has failed thus far to find such differences, but research is continuing (Fonagy et al., 1995).

Let us also underscore the role of childhood maltreatment and abuse. The linkages between child abuse and the later development of personality disorders suggests that failure to form close-bonding relationships with parental caretakers in childhood plays a critical role in the development of the maladaptive personality patterns classified as personality disorders.

Learning Perspectives

Learning theorists tend to focus more on the acquisition of behaviors than on the notion of enduring personality traits. Similarly, they think more in terms of maladaptive behaviors than of disorders of "personality." Personality traits are theorized to steer behavior—to provide consistent behavior in diverse situations. Many critics (e.g., Mischel, 1979), however, argue that behavior is actually not as consistent across situations as traits theorists would suggest. Behavior may depend more on situational demands than on inherent traits. For example, we may describe a person as lazy and unmotivated. But is this person always lazy and unmotivated? Are there not some situations in which the person may be energetic and ambitious? What differences in these situations may explain differences in behavior? Learning theorists are generally interested in defining the learning histories and circumstances that give rise to maladaptive behaviors and the reinforcers that maintain them.

Learning theorists suggest it is in childhood that many salient experiences occur that contribute to the development of the maladaptive habits of relating to others, which constitute personality disorders. Repeated punishment of, or lack of reward for, childhood assertiveness and exploratory behavior may result in a dependent personality behavior pattern, for example. Obsessive-compulsive personality disorder may be connected with excessive parental discipline or overcontrol in childhood. Social-learning theorist Theodore Millon (1981) suggests that children whose behavior is rigidly controlled and punished by parents, even for slight transgressions, may develop inflexible, perfectionistic standards. As such children mature, they may strive to develop in an area in which they excel, such as schoolwork or athletics, as a way of avoiding parental criticism or punishment. Overattention to a single area of development may prevent them from becoming well rounded. They may thus squelch spontaneity, avoid new challenges or risks, and develop other behaviors associated with the obsessive-compulsive personality pattern.

Millon suggests that histrionic personality disorder may be rooted in childhood experiences in which social reinforcers, such as parental attention, are connected to the child's appearance and willingness to perform for others, especially in cases where reinforcers are dispensed inconsistently. Inconsistent attention teaches children not to take approval for granted and to strive for it continually. People with histrionic personalities may also have identified with parents who are dramatic, emotional, and attention-seeking. Extreme sibling rivalry would further heighten motivation to perform for attention from others.

Social-learning theories emphasize the role of reinforcement in explaining the origins of antisocial behaviors. Ullmann and Krasner (1975) proposed, for example, that people with antisocial personalities fail to respond to other people as potential reinforcers. Most children learn to treat others as reinforcing agents because others reinforce them with praise when they behave appropriately and punish them for misbehavior. Reinforcement and punishment provide feedback (information about social expectations) that helps children modify their behavior to maximize the chances of future rewards and minimize the risks of future punishment. As a consequence, children become socialized. They become sensitive to the demands of powerful others, usually parents and teachers, and learn to regulate their behavior accordingly. They thus adapt to social expectations. They learn what to do and what to say, how to dress and how to act to obtain social reinforcement or approval from others.

People with antisocial personalities, by contrast, may not have become socialized because their early learning

What are the origins of antisocial personality disorder? Here we see a group of young men in Brooklyn showing their gang sign. Are youth who develop antisocial personalities largely unsocialized because early learning experiences lack the consistency and predictability that help other children connect their behavior with rewards and punishments? Or are they very "socialized"—but socialized to imitate the behavior of other antisocial youth? Are we confusing antisocial behavior with antisocial personality disorder? To what extent does criminal behavior or membership in gangs overlap with antisocial personality disorder? Can environmental factors explain how people with antisocial personality disorder maintain their composure (their relatively low levels of arousal) under circumstances that would induce anxiety in most of us?

experiences lacked the consistency and predictability that helped other children connect their behavior with rewards and punishments. Perhaps they were sometimes rewarded for doing the "right thing," but just as often not. They may have borne the brunt of harsh physical punishments that depended more on parental whims than on their own conduct. As adults they may not place much value on what other people expect because there was no clear connection between their own behavior and reinforcement in childhood. They may have learned as children that there was little they could do to prevent punishment and so perhaps lost the motivation to try. Although Ullmann and Krasner's views may account for some features of antisocial personality disorder, they may not adequately address the development of the "charming" type of antisocial personality, which describes people who are skillful at reading social cues produced by other people and using them for personal advantage.

Social-cognitive theorist Albert Bandura (1973, 1986) has studied the role of observational learning in aggressive behavior, which is one of the common components of antisocial behavior. He and his colleagues (e.g., Bandura, Ross, & Ross, 1963) have shown that children acquire skills, including aggressive skills, by observing the behavior of others. Exposure to aggression may come from watching violent television programs or observing parents who act violently toward each other. Bandura does not believe children and adults display aggressive behaviors in a mechanical way, however. Rather, people usually do not imitate aggressive behaviors unless they are provoked and believe they are more likely to be rewarded than punished for it. When models get their way with others by acting aggressively, children may be more likely to imitate them. Children may also acquire antisocial behaviors such as cheating, bullying, or lying by direct reinforcement if they find such behaviors help them avoid blame or manipulate others.

All in all, learning approaches to personality disorders, like psychodynamic approaches, have their limitations. They are grounded in theory rather than in observations of family interactions that presage the development of personality disorders. Research remains to be conducted to determine whether childhood experiences proposed by psychodynamic and learning theorists actually lead to the hypothesized disorders.

Family Perspectives

Many theorists have argued that disturbances in family relationships underlie the development of personality disorders. Consistent with psychodynamic formulations, researchers find that people with borderline personality disorder (BPD) *remember* their parents as having been more controlling and less caring than do reference subjects with other psychological disorders (Zweig-Frank & Paris, 1991). When people with BPD recall their earliest memories, they are more likely than other people to paint significant others as malevolent or evil. They portray their parents and others close to them as having been more likely to injure them deliberately or to have failed to help them escape injuries by others (Nigg et al., 1992).

Investigators find a high frequency of childhood trauma, including emotional, physical, and sexual abuse, in the backgrounds of adults with BPD (e.g., Laporte & Guttman, 1996; Weaver & Clum, 1995; Zanarini et al., 1997). Perhaps the "splitting" that is observed in people with the disorder is a function of having learned to cope with unpredictable and harsh behavior from parental figures or other caregivers. Not all cases of BPD show evidence of physical abuse; some cases are characterized more by parental neglect than physical abuse (Zanarini et al., 1997). We should also note that much of the evidence relating childhood trauma to BPD rests on recollections of childhood experiences. The accuracy of such memories and reports of childhood trauma remains an open question. We should also note that the linkages between childhood trauma and BPD are correlational and do not prove a causal relationship. Yet we can't ignore the fact that childhood trauma is often a prelude to the development of BPD and may in fact play a role in its development, at least in some cases.

Again consistent with psychodynamic theory, family factors such as parental overprotection and authoritarianism have been implicated in the development of dependent personality traits that may hamper the development of independent behavior (R. F. Bornstein, 1992). Extreme fears of abandonment may also be involved, perhaps resulting from a failure to develop secure bonds with parental attachment figures in childhood due to parental neglect, rejection, or death. Subsequently, a chronic fear of being abandoned by other people with whom one has close relationships may develop, leading to the clinginess that typifies dependent personality disorder. Theorists also suggest that obsessive-compulsive personality disorder may emerge within a strongly moralistic and rigid family environment, which does not permit even minor deviations from expected roles or behavior (e.g., Oldham, 1994).

As in the case of BPD, researchers find that childhood abuse or neglect is a risk factor in the development of antisocial personality disorder (APD) in adulthood (Luntz & Widom, 1994). In a view that straddles the psychodynamic and learning theories, the McCords (McCord & McCord, 1964) focus on the role of parental rejection or neglect in the development of APD. They suggest that children normally learn to associate parental approval with conformity to parental practices and values, and disapproval with disobedience. When tempted to transgress, children feel anxious for fear of losing parental love. Anxiety serves as a signal that encourages the child to inhibit antisocial behavior. Eventually, the child identifies with the parents and internalizes these social controls in the form of a conscience. When parents do not show love for their children, this identification does not occur. Children do not fear loss of love because they have never had it. The anxiety that might have served to restrain antisocial and criminal behavior is absent.

Children who are rejected or neglected by their parents may not develop warm feelings of attachment to others. They may lack the ability to empathize with the feelings and needs of others, developing instead an attitude of indifference toward others. Or perhaps they still retain a wish to develop loving relationships but lack the ability to experience genuine feelings.

The McCords cite their own research, which shows a strong connection between early childhood emotional deprivation and subsequent delinquency. They write that frequent harsh, physical punishments may temporarily force children into obedience. When the threat of punishment is removed, however, children lack inner restraints or "residues of conscience" to inhibit antisocial behavior. Although lack of love does not invariably cause antisocial behavior or sociopathy, the more severe the parental rejection, the more likely the child will become aggressive and lack the capacity for guilt or remorse. In the McCords' view, less severe forms of parental rejection may also interact with other factors to give rise to antisocial behavior, such as modeling effects provided by an antisocial parent.

The McCords' views may apply to some children, but certainly not to all. Although family factors may be implicated in some cases of antisocial personality disorder, many neglected children do not later show antisocial or other abnormal behaviors. We are left to develop other explanations to predict which deprived children will develop antisocial personalities or other abnormal behaviors, and which will not.

Cognitive Perspectives

Cognitively oriented psychologists have shown that the ways in which people with personality disorders interpret their social experiences influence their behavior. Antisocial adolescents, for example, tend to erroneously interpret other people's behavior as threatening (K. A. Dodge, 1985). Perhaps because of their family and community experiences, they tend to presume that others intend them ill when they do not. In a promising cognitive therapy method based on such findings, **problem-solving therapy,** antisocial adolescent boys have been encouraged to reconceptualize their social interactions as problems to be solved rather than as threats to their "manhood" (Lochman, 1992). They then generate nonviolent solutions to social confrontations and, like scientists, test out the most promising ones. In the section on biological perspectives we also see that the antisocial personality's failure to profit from punishment is connected with a cognitive factor: the *meaning* of the aversive stimulus.

Biological Perspectives

Little is known about biological factors in most personality disorders. Although many theorists see personality disorders as the expression of maladaptive personality traits, the potential biological facets of such traits remain for the most part unknown.

Genetic Factors   We have little direct evidence of genetic transmission of personality disorders (G. Carey & DiLalla, 1994). We do have suggestive evidence of genetic factors based in part on findings that the first-degree biological relatives (parents and siblings) of people with certain personality disorders, especially antisocial, schizotypal, and borderline types, are more likely to be diagnosed with these disorders than are members of the general population (APA, 1994; Battaglia et al., 1995; Nigg & Goldsmith, 1994). As we noted earlier, schizotypal personality disorder is also more common among the close biological relatives of people with schizophrenia than among the general population, which is suggestive of a possible genetic continuity with schizophrenia.

Studies of familial transmission are limited because family members share common environments as well as genes. Hence, researchers have turned to twin and adoptee studies to tease out genetic and environmental effects. Evidence from twin studies suggests that dimensions of personality associated with particular personality disorders may have an inherited component (Livesley et al., 1993). Researchers examined the genetic contribution to 18 dimensions that underlie various personality disorders, including callousness, identity problems, anxiousness, insecure attachment, narcissism, social avoidance, self-harm, and oppositionality (negativity) (Livesley et al., 1993). Genetic influences were suggested by findings of greater correlations on a given trait among identical (monozygotic, or MZ) twins than among fraternal (dizygotic, or DZ) twins. A statistical measure of heritability, reflecting the percentage of variability on a given trait that is accounted for by genetics, was computed for each personality dimension. The results showed that 12 of the 18 dimensions had heritabilities in the 40% to 60% range, indicating a substantial genetic contribution to these characteristics. The highest heritabilities were for narcissism (64%) and identity problems (59%), and the lowest for conduct problems (0%) and submissiveness (25%). Bear in mind that these twins were selected from the general population, not from a sample of people with diagnosed personality disorders. Therefore, the results may not be generalizable to people with diagnosable disorders. Still, the findings suggest that genetics plays a role in varying degrees to the development of traits that underlie personality disorders. Certainly not all people possessing these traits develop personality disorders. It is possible, however, that people with a genetic predisposition for these traits may be more vulnerable to develop personality disorders if they encounter certain environmental influences, such as being reared in a dysfunctional family.

Evidence from adoption studies shows that the biological and adopted children of people with antisocial personality disorder are more likely to develop the disorder themselves, which is consistent with the view that both genetics and environment play a role in its development (APA, 1994). Consistent with a genetic contribution, evidence shows striking similarities among identical twins reared apart on some personality dimensions, including a psychopathic personality dimension (DiLalla et al., 1996). A Danish study found four to five times greater incidence of psychopathy among the biological relatives of antisocial adoptees than among the adoptive relatives (F. Schulsinger, 1972). However, the size of the genetic contribution was relatively small. Environmental influences also contribute to antisocial behavior. Evidence from adoption studies also links criminal behavior to genetics, although environmental factors also play a role (G. Carey, 1992; G. Carey & DiLalla, 1994; DiLalla & Gottesman, 1991; Mednick, Moffitt, & Stack, 1987).

Lack of Emotional Responsiveness According to Cleckley (1976), people with antisocial personalities can maintain their composure in stressful situations that would induce anxiety in most people. Lack of anxiety in response to threatening situations may help explain the failure of punishment to induce antisocial people to relinquish antisocial behavior. For must of us, the fear of getting caught and being punished is sufficient to inhibit antisocial impulses. People with antisocial personalities, however, often fail to inhibit behavior that has led to punishment in the past (Arnett, Smith, & Newman, 1997). They may not learn to inhibit antisocial or aggressive behavior because they experience little if any fear or anticipatory anxiety about being caught and punished.

In an early classic study, Lykken (1957) showed that prison inmates with antisocial personalities performed more poorly than normal controls on a shock-avoidance task, although their general learning ability did not differ from that of normal individuals. The shock-avoidance task involved learning responses that averted the presentation of the aversive stimulus (electric shock). Lykken reasoned that the inmates who had antisocial personalities were less able to learn avoidance responses because they experienced unusually low levels of anxiety in anticipation of the shock.

Schachter and Latané (1964) found that prisoners with antisocial personalities performed significantly better on the Lykken avoidance-learning task when they were administered epinephrine (adrenaline), a hormone that increases heart rate and other indices of arousal of the autonomic nervous system. Their performance apparently improved because the epinephrine had heightened their anticipatory anxiety. Other researchers (Chesno & Kilmann, 1975) showed similar results after raising antisocial subjects' levels of autonomic arousal through bursts of aversive noise rather than injections of epinephrine.

Cognitive theorists can point to research showing that the effects of aversive stimuli on people with antisocial personality disorder may depend on the *meaning* or *value* of the stimuli. Anticipation of aversive stimulation in the form of electric shock may not foster avoidance learning in persons with antisocial personalities, but the threat of punishment in the form of loss of money may do so. In another classic study, Schmauk (1970) had subjects perform a maze-learning task under three different forms of punishment for incorrect responses: electric shock, loss of money (losing a quarter for each error from an initial "bankroll" of 40 quarters), and social disapproval (the experimenter said "Wrong" following each incorrect response). Under the shock and social punishment conditions, people with antisocial personalities performed more poorly than normal controls. They outperformed normal controls, however, when they were threatened with forfeiture of money. Although people with antisocial personalities may not be deterred from misconduct by the threat of physical punishment, they may be keenly sensitive to the loss of money. Perhaps they learn better from their mistakes when the cost is meaningful to them.

Autonomic Nervous System Reactivity When people get anxious, their palms tend to sweat. This skin response, called the **galvanic skin response** (GSR), is a sign of activation of the sympathetic branch of the autonomic nervous system (ANS). In an early study, Hare (1965) showed that people with antisocial personalities had lower GSR levels when they were expecting painful stimuli than did normal controls. Apparently their autonomic nervous systems were less responsive to the threat of impending pain. Some theorists have suggested that the ANSs of people with antisocial personalities are generally underresponsive to stressful stimuli. This may account for their "immunity" to guilt and their failure to show any anxiety in the face of possible punishment.

In a later study, Hare, Frazelle, and Cox (1978) warned subjects to expect a blast of noise (an aversive stimulus) following a 12-second countdown. Nonsociopathic prisoners showed high levels of skin conductance, indicative of greater ANS reactivity, 3 seconds into the countdown, but sociopathic prisoners failed to react until just before the blast. Even then, they showed a relatively weak GSR response, which is suggestive of minimal levels of anxiety or fear.

Hare's findings of a weaker GSR response in sociopathic inmates in anticipation of an aversive stimulus has been replicated a number of times (Arnett, 1997; Patrick, Cuthbert, & Lang, 1994). Other research generally supports the view that people with antisocial personalities are generally less aroused than others both at times of rest and in situations in which they are faced with stress (Fowles, 1993). This lack of emotional responsivity may help explain why the threat of punishment seems to have so little effect on deterring their antisocial behavior.

The Craving-for-Stimulation Model Other investigators have attempted to explain the antisocial personality's lack of emotional response in terms of the levels of stimulation necessary to maintain an **optimum level of arousal.** Our optimum levels of arousal are the degrees of arousal at which we feel best and function most efficiently.

Psychopathic individuals appear to have exaggerated cravings for stimulation (Arnett, Smith, & Newman, 1997). Perhaps they require a higher-than-normal threshold of stimulation to maintain an optimum state of arousal (Quay, 1965). That is, they may need more stimulation than other people to function normally.

A need for higher levels of stimulation may explain why people with psychopathic traits tend to become bored more easily than other people and more often gravitate to more stimulating but potentially dangerous activities, such as use of drugs or alcohol, motorcycling, skydiving, high-stakes gambling, or sexual adventures. A higher-than-normal threshold for stimulation would not directly cause antisocial or criminal behavior; after all, part of the "right stuff" of the nation's respected astronauts includes sensation seeking. However, threat of boredom and inability to tolerate monotony may influence some sensation seekers to drift into crime or reckless behavior (R. J. Smith, 1978).

Lack of Restraint on Impulsivity Other recent research on brain wave functions shows lower levels of activity in the frontal lobes of the **cerebral cortex** in men with antisocial personality disorder (Deckel, Hesselbrock, & Bauer, 1996). The frontal cortex plays a key role in inhibiting impulsive behavior, which may help explain why people with antisocial personalities have difficulty controlling impulsive or aggressive behavior. Some theorists have speculated that the cerebral cortex may mature more slowly in people with antisocial personalities (W. J. Reid, 1986). Still, we need more direct evidence tying a brain dysfunction to impulsivity and lack of inhibition in antisocial individuals (Sher & Trull, 1994).

Sociocultural Views

The sociocultural perspective leads us to examine the social conditions that may contribute to the development of the behavior patterns identified as personality disorders. Since antisocial personality disorder is reported more frequently among people from lower socioeconomic classes, we might examine the role that particular stresses encountered by disadvantaged families may play in the development of these behavior patterns. Many inner-city neighborhoods are beset by social problems such as alcohol and drug abuse, teenage pregnancy, and disorganized and disintegrating families. These stresses are associated with an increased likelihood of child abuse and neglect, which may in turn contribute to lower self-esteem and breed feelings of anger and resentment in children. Neglect and abuse may become translated into the lack of empathy and a callous disregard for the welfare of others that are associated with antisocial personalities.

Children reared in poverty are also more likely to be exposed to deviant role models, such as neighborhood drug dealers. Maladjustment in school may lead to alienation and frustration with the larger society, leading to antisocial behavior (L. J. Siegel, 1992). Addressing the problem of antisocial personality may involve attempts at a societal level to redress social injustice and ameliorate deprivation.

Little information is available about the prevalences of personality disorders in other cultures. A recent initiative in this direction involved a joint program sponsored by the World Health Organization (WHO) and the Alcohol, Drug Abuse, and Mental Health Administration (ADAMHA) of the U.S. government. The goal of the program was to develop and standardize diagnostic instruments that could be used to arrive at psychiatric diagnoses worldwide. One result of this effort was the development of the International Personality Disorder Examination (IPDE), a semistructured interview protocol for diagnosing personality disorders (Loranger et al., 1994). The IPDE was pilot-tested by psychiatrists and clinical psychologists in 11 different countries (India, Switzerland, the Netherlands, Great Britain, Luxembourg, Germany, Kenya, Norway, Japan, Austria, and the United States). The interview protocol had reasonably good reliability for diagnosing personality disorders among the different languages and cultures that were sampled. Although more research is needed to determine the worldwide prevalences of various personality disorders, investigators found the borderline and avoidant personality disorders

The Sensation-Seeking Scale

Do you crave stimulation or seek sensation? Are you satisfied by reading or watching TV, or must you ride the big wave or bounce your motorbike over desert dunes? Zuckerman and his colleagues (1978) have found that four factors are related to sensation seeking: (1) pursuit of thrill and adventure, (2) disinhibition (that is, proclivity to express impulses), (3) pursuit of experience, and (4) susceptibility to boredom. Although some sensation seekers get involved with drugs or encounter trouble with the law, many are law abiding and limit their sensation seeking to sanctioned activities. Thus, sensation seeking should not be interpreted as criminal or antisocial in itself.

Zuckerman (1980) developed several sensation-seeking scales that assess the levels of stimulation people seek to feel at their best and function efficiently. A brief form of one of them follows. To assess your own sensation-seeking tendencies, pick the choice, A or B, that best depicts you. Then compare your responses to those in the key at the end of the chapter.

1. A. I would like a job that requires a lot of traveling.
   B. I would prefer a job in one location.
2. A. I am invigorated by a brisk, cold day.
   B. I can't wait to get indoors on a cold day.
3. A. I get bored seeing the same old faces.
   B. I like the comfortable familiarity of everyday friends.
4. A. I would prefer living in an ideal society in which everyone is safe, secure, and happy.
   B. I would have preferred living in the unsettled days of our history.
5. A. I sometimes like to do things that are a little frightening.
   B. A sensible person avoids activities that are dangerous.
6. A. I would not like to be hypnotized.
   B. I would like to have the experience of being hypnotized.
7. A. The most important goal in life is to live it to the fullest and experience as much as possible.
   B. The most important goal in life is to find peace and happiness.
8. A. I would like to try parachute jumping.
   B. I would never want to try jumping out of a plane, with or without a parachute.

9. A. I enter cold water gradually, giving myself time to get used to it.
   B. I like to dive or jump right into the ocean or a cold pool.
10. A. When I go on a vacation, I prefer the change of camping out.
    B. When I go on a vacation, I prefer the comfort of a good room and bed.
11. A. I prefer people who are emotionally expressive even if they are a bit unstable.
    B. I prefer people who are calm and even-tempered.
12. A. A good painting should shock or jolt the senses.
    B. A good painting should give one a feeling of peace and security.
13. A. People who ride motorcycles must have some kind of unconscious need to hurt themselves.
    B. I would like to drive or ride a motorcycle.

Source: Zuckerman, M. (1980). Sensation seeking. In H. London & J. Exner (eds.), *Dimensions of personality.* New York: John Wiley & Sons. Copyright © John Wiley & Sons. Reprinted by permission of John Wiley & Sons, Inc.

Sensation! Is there a connection between sensation seeking and antisocial personality disorder? Not all people who crave excitement have antisocial personalities. Yet people with antisocial personalities may have an excessive need for stimulation that makes them more likely to engage in antisocial or reckless behavior.

were the most frequently diagnosed types. Perhaps the characteristics associated with these types reflect some dimensions of personality disturbance that are commonly encountered throughout the world.

TREATMENT

We began the chapter with a quote from the eminent psychologist William James, who suggested that people's personalities seem to be "set in plaster" by a certain age. His view may seem to be especially applicable to many people with personality disorders, who are typically highly resistant to change.

People with personality disorders usually see their behaviors, even maladaptive, self-defeating behaviors, as natural parts of themselves. Although they may be unhappy and distressed, they are unlikely to perceive their own behavior as causative. Like Marcella, whom we described as showing features of a histrionic personality disorder, they may condemn others for their problems and believe others, not they, need to change. Thus, they usually do not seek help on their own. Or they begrudgingly acquiesce to treatment at the urging of others but drop out or fail to cooperate with the therapist. Or they may go for help when they feel overwhelmed by anxiety or depression and terminate treatment as soon as they find some relief rather than probe more deeply for the underlying causes of their problems. People with personality disorders also tend to respond more poorly to treatment of problems such as depression than do others, perhaps because of the negative influence of their maladaptive behavioral patterns (M. T. Shea, Widiger, & Klein, 1992).

Psychodynamic Approaches

Psychodynamic approaches are often used to help people with personality disorders become more aware of the roots of their self-defeating behavior patterns and learn more adaptive ways of relating to others. Progress in therapy may be hampered by difficulties in working therapeutically with people with personality disorders, especially clients with borderline and narcissistic personality disorders. Psychodynamic therapists often report that people with borderline personality disorder tend to have turbulent relationships with them, sometimes idealizing them, sometimes denouncing them as uncaring. Case studies suggest that therapists feel manipulated and exploited by borderline clients' needs to test their approval, such as calling them at all hours or threatening suicide. Such clients can be exhausting and frustrating, although some successes have been reported among therapists who can handle clients' demands.

Some theorists have expressed the belief that people with antisocial personality disorder are beyond the reach of psychotherapy (e.g., Cleckley, 1976). Although this view might be too broad to be accurate, it seems that people with antisocial personalities have not responded well to psychodynamic treatment, apparently for several reasons

(R. J. Smith, 1978). One reason is that they rarely seek treatment voluntarily and are not usually motivated to change their behavior. Another reason is that they usually mistrust others, including therapists, making it difficult to establish effective therapeutic relationships. Despite problems in treating people with personality disorders in psychotherapy, some promising results have been reported based on a brief, structured form of psychodynamic therapy pioneered at New York's Beth Israel Medical Center (Winston et al., 1991). There, researchers reported that a relatively brief form of psychodynamically oriented psychotherapy that averaged 40 weeks of treatment resulted in significant improvement in symptom complaints and social adjustment of people with personality disorders (Winston et al., 1994). The treatment emphasized interpersonal behavior and used a more active, confrontational style in addressing the client's defenses than is the case in traditional psychoanalysis.

Behavioral Approaches

Behavior therapists see their task as changing clients' behaviors rather than their personality structures. Many behavioral theorists do not think in terms of clients' "personalities" at all, but rather in terms of acquired maladaptive behaviors that are maintained by reinforcement contingencies. Behavior therapists therefore focus on attempting to replace maladaptive behaviors with adaptive behaviors through techniques such as extinction, modeling, and reinforcement. If clients are taught behaviors that are likely to be reinforced by other people, the new behaviors are likely to be maintained.

Behavioral marital therapists, for example, may encourage clients not to reinforce their spouses' histrionic behaviors. Techniques for treating social phobia, such as those described in Chapter 5, have also been of benefit in treating people with avoidant personality disorder (Renneberg et al., 1990). This may include social skills training to help clients function more effectively in social situations, such as dating and meeting new people. Cognitive methods may be incorporated to help socially avoidant individuals offset catastrophizing beliefs, such as the exaggerated fear of being shot down or rejected by dates.

Despite difficulties in treating borderline personality disorder (BPD), two groups of therapists headed by Aaron Beck (e.g., A. T. Beck, Freeman, & Associates, 1990; Arntz, 1994) and Marsha Linehan (Linehan, 1993; Linehan et al., 1991, 1994) report promising results using cognitive-behavioral techniques specifically adapted to the problems encountered in working with clients with BPD. Beck's approach focuses on helping the individual correct cognitive distortions that underlie tendencies to see oneself and others as either all good or all bad. Marsha Linehan's technique, called *dialectical behavior therapy* (DBT), combines behavior therapy and supportive psychotherapy. Behavioral techniques are used to help clients develop more effective social skills and problem-solving skills, which can help improve their relationships with others and ability to cope with negative events. Because people with BPD tend to be overly sensitive to even the slightest cues of rejection, therapists provide continuing acceptance and support, even when clients push the limits by becoming manipulative or overly demanding. In a recent clinical trial, DBT was compared with a usual treatment approach in treating people with borderline personality disorder who suffered from chronic suicidal thinking. Clients treated with DBT showed lower therapy dropout rates, fewer days of psychiatric hospitalization, fewer suicide attempts, and improved interpersonal functioning (Linehan et al., 1991, 1994).

Some antisocial adolescents have been placed, often by court order, in residential and foster-care programs that contain numerous behavioral elements (W. H. Reid & Balis, 1987). These residential programs have concrete rules and clear rewards for obeying them. At Achievement Place, for example, which was founded in Kansas in the 1960s and has been reproduced elsewhere, prosocial behaviors such as completing homework are systematically reinforced; antisocial behaviors, such as using profanity, are extinguished (E. L. Phillips, Phillips, Fixsen, & Wolf, 1971). Some residential programs rely on **token economies,** in which prosocial behaviors are rewarded with tokens such as plastic chips that can be exchanged for privileges. Although participants in such programs may show improved behavior, it remains unclear whether such programs reduce the risk that adolescent antisocial behavior will continue into adulthood.

Biological Approaches

Drug therapy does not directly treat personality disorders. Antidepressants or antianxiety drugs are sometimes used to treat the emotional distress that individuals with personality disorders may encounter, however. Drugs do not alter the long-standing patterns of maladaptive behavior that may give rise to distress. However, a study indicates that the antidepressant Prozac can reduce aggressive behavior and irritability in impulsive and aggressive individuals with personality disorders (Coccaro & Kavoussi, 1997). Researchers suspect that impulsive aggressive behavior may be related to serotonin deficiencies (discussed further in Chapter 15). Prozac and similar drugs act to increase the availability of serotonin.

Much remains to be learned about working with people who have personality disorders. The major challenges involve recruiting people who do not see themselves as being disordered into treatment and prompting them to develop insight into their self-defeating or injurious behaviors. Current efforts to help such people are too often reminiscent of the old couplet:

> He that complies against his will,
> Is of his own opinion still.
>
> SAMUEL BUTLER, HUDIBRAS

In this chapter we have considered a number of problems in which people act out on maladaptive impulses yet fail to see how their behaviors are disrupting their lives. In the next chapter we explore other maladaptive behaviors that are frequently connected with lack of self-insight: behaviors involving substance abuse.

SUMMARY

Personality Disorders

Maladaptive or rigid behavior patterns or personality traits associated with states of personal distress or that impair the person's ability to function in social or occupational roles are called personality disorders. People with personality disorders do not generally recognize a need to change themselves. Personality disorders may be organized into three clusters, as follows.

Personality Disorders Characterized by Odd or Eccentric Behavior

People with paranoid personality disorder are unduly suspicious and mistrustful of others, to the point that their relationships suffer. But they do not hold the more flagrant paranoid delusions typical of schizophrenia. Schizoid personality disorder describes people who have little if any interest in social relationships, show a restricted range of emotional expression, and appear distant and aloof. People with schizotypal personalities appear odd or eccentric in their thoughts, mannerisms, and behavior, but not to the degree found in schizophrenia.

Personality Disorders Characterized by Dramatic, Emotional, or Erratic Behavior

Antisocial personality disorder describes people who persistently engage in behavior that violates social norms and the rights of others and who tend to show no remorse for their misdeeds. Borderline personality disorder is defined in terms of instability in self-image, relationships, and mood. People with borderline personality disorder often engage in impulsive acts, which are frequently self-destructive. People with histrionic personality disorder tend to be highly dramatic and emotional in their behavior, whereas people diagnosed with narcissistic personality disorder have inflated or grandiose senses of themselves and, like those with histrionic personalities, demand to be the center of attention.

Personality Disorders Characterized by Anxious or Fearful Behavior

Avoidant personality disorder describes people who are so terrified of rejection and criticism that they are generally unwilling to enter relationships without unusually strong reassurances of acceptance. People with dependent personality disorder are overly dependent on others and have extreme difficulty acting independently or making even the smallest decisions on their own. People with obsessive-compulsive personality disorder have various traits such as orderliness, perfectionism, rigidity, and overattention to detail but are without the true obsessions and compulsions associated with obsessive-compulsive (anxiety) disorder.

Problems with the Classification of Personality Disorders

Various controversies and problems attend the classification of personality disorders, including lack of demonstrated reliability and validity, too much overlap among the categories, difficulty in distinguishing between variations in normal behavior and abnormal behavior, underlying sexist biases in certain categories, and confusion of labels with explanations.

Theoretical Perspectives

Traditional Freudian theory focused on unresolved Oedipal conflicts in explaining normal and abnormal personality development. More recent psychodynamic theorists have focused on the pre-Oedipal period in explaining the development of such personality disorders as narcissistic and borderline personality.

Learning theorists view personality disorders in terms of maladaptive patterns of behavior, rather than personality traits. Learning theorists seek to identify the early learning experiences and present reinforcers that may explain the development and maintenance of personality disorders.

Many theorists have argued that disturbed family relationships play roles in the development of many personality disorders. Antisocial personality disorder is connected with parental rejection or neglect and parental modeling of anti-social behavior. Cognitive theorists have focused on the role of encoding strategies in explaining tendencies of antisocial adolescents to presume that others mean them ill.

Research on biological perspectives has shown familial links in various personality disorders that are consistent with, but do not prove, genetic means of transmission. Some research evidence shows that people with antisocial personalities not only lack emotional responsiveness to physically threatening stimuli but also have reduced levels of autonomic reactivity. People with antisocial personalities may also require higher levels of stimulation to maintain optimal levels of arousal.

Sociocultural theorists focus on the adverse social conditions that may contribute to the development of personality disorders, especially antisocial personality. The effects of poverty, urban blight, and drug abuse can lead to family disorganization and disintegration, making it less likely that children will receive the nurturance and support they need to develop more socially adaptive behavior patterns.

Treatment

Therapists from different schools of therapy try to assist people with personality disorders to gain better awareness of their self-defeating behavior patterns and learn more adaptive ways of relating to others. Despite the difficulties in working therapeutically with these clients, promising results are emerging from the use of relatively short-term psychodynamic therapy and cognitive-behavioral treatment approaches.

Key for Sensation-Seeking Scale

Because this is an abbreviated version of a questionnaire, no norms are applicable. However, answers that agree with the following key are suggestive of sensation seeking:

1. A	8. A
2. A	9. B
3. A	10. A
4. B	11. A
5. A	12. A
6. B	13. B
7. A	

REVIEW QUESTIONS

1. What are personality disorders? How are they classified in the DSM system?

2. What particular features are associated with the various types of personality disorders?

3. Why does the classification of personality disorders remain a source of controversy?

4. What theoretical formulations have been proposed to account for the development of personality disorders?

5. How is antisocial personality disorder distinguished from criminal behavior?

6. How is psychopathic behavior different than psychotic behavior?

7. What treatment approaches are used in treating personality disorders? What problems do they encounter in treating individuals with these disorders?

© **Christopher Richard Wynne Nevinson**
A Bursting Shell, 1915

Substance Abuse and Dependence

TRUTH *or* FICTION?

9.1 Most deaths linked to use of psychoactive substances involve narcotic drugs such as heroin.

9.2 In order to become psychologically dependent on a drug, you must first develop a physiological dependence.

9.3 Alcohol "goes to women's heads" more rapidly than to men's.

9.4 Alcohol use at any level is associated with a higher risk of heart attacks.

9.5 Heroin was developed during a search for a nonaddictive drug that would relieve pain as effectively as morphine.

9.6 Coca-Cola originally contained cocaine.

9.7 Habitual smoking is a bad habit, not a physical addiction.

9.8 Breast cancer is the leading cause of cancer deaths among U.S. women.

9.9 Being able to "hold your liquor" better than most people helps prevent the development of problem drinking.

9.10 A widely used treatment for heroin addiction involves the substitution of another addictive drug.

1. Distinguish between substance abuse, substance dependence, substance intoxication, and substance withdrawal.

2. Distinguish between psychological dependence and physiological dependence.

3. Describe physical and psychological effects of alcohol, opioids, amphetamines, cocaine, nicotine, PCP, LSD, and marijuana.

4. Discuss biological, psychodynamic, learning, cognitive, and sociocultural approaches to understanding substance abuse and dependence.

5. Discuss approaches to treating substance abuse and dependence disorders by professionals and lay organizations.

6. Discuss the need for, and methods of, relapse-prevention training.

7. Discuss the controversies concerning controlled social drinking programs.

8. Discuss problems in evaluating the effectiveness of drug treatment programs.

The planet is a supermarket of **psychoactive** chemicals, or drugs. The United States is flooded with substances that alter the mood and twist perceptions—substances that lift you up, cool you down, and turn you upside down. Many people use these substances because their friends do. Adolescents often use them because their parents and authority figures tell them not to. Some users are seeking pleasure. Others are searching for inner truth.

The old standby alcohol is the most popular drug on campus—whether the campus is a high school or college campus (L. D. Johnston, Bachman, & O'Malley, 1992). In fact, nearly 9 of 10 college students report using alcohol within the past year, as compared to 1 student in 3 who report using any illicit drug. Under certain conditions, the use of substances that affect mood and behavior is normal enough, at least as gauged by statistical frequency and social standards. It is normal to start the day with caffeine in the form of coffee or tea, to take wine or coffee with meals, to meet friends for a drink after work, and to end the day with a nightcap. Many of us take prescription drugs that calm us down or ease our pain. Flooding the bloodstream with nicotine by smoking is normal in the sense that about 1 in 4 Americans are smokers. Some psychoactive substances are illegal and are used illicitly, such as cocaine, marijuana, and heroin. Others, such as minor tranquilizers and amphetamines, are available by prescription. Still others are available without prescription or over the counter, for instance, tobacco (which contains the stimulant nicotine) and alcohol (which is a depressant). Ironically, the most widely and easily accessible substances–tobacco and alcohol—cause more deaths through sickness and accidents than all illicit drugs combined.

TRUTH *or* FICTION REVISITED

9.1 *False.* Two legally available substances, alcohol and tobacco, cause more deaths than all illicit drugs combined.

Thirteen percent of Americans age 12 or older report using illicit substances in the past year; more than 1 in 3 have at some time used illicit drugs (USDHHS, 1993). By the time young people get to their senior year in high school, about half have used an illicit drug (L. D. Johnston, O'Malley, & Bachman, 1996); 2 in 5 have tried marijuana. Among college students, about 1 in 2 have smoked marijuana at least once. Nearly 3 in 10 eighth graders have tried an illicit drug, most usually marijuana (Wren, 1997b). After falling steadily during the 1980s, illicit drug use among adolescents rose sharply during the early 1990s before leveling off by 1997 (USDHHS, 1997).

Speculation abounds about the underlying reasons for the recent upturn in illicit drug use. A leading drug researcher, Lloyd Johnston of the University of Michigan, attributes the rise to exposure to music and films that portray drug use as acceptable behavior.

Table 9.1 shows some results from a continuing government survey of young people in the United States, including high school seniors, college students, and young adults aged 18 to 30. The table highlights results for college students. Respondents are asked whether they have ever used a substance or used it during the past year, the past 30 days, or on a daily basis. Note the marked decline in the use of cocaine and other types of stimulants. Post-month use of marijuana, however, began to climb in the early 1990s, reversing a decade-long decline. Also of concern is the recent rise in LSD use. LSD use is now more popular among college students than at any time since the peak years of the 1970s.

The mainstays of the drug scene on campus, alcohol and cigarettes, remain popular, although current (past-month) use of alcohol declined

TABLE 9.1

Trends in Drug Use Among College Students During Lifetime and During Last 30 Days (in Percents)

Drug	Used ...	1980	1982	1984	1986	1988	1990	1992	1994
Marijuana	Ever	65.0	60.5	59.0	57.9	51.3	49.1	44.1	42.2
	Last 30 days	34.0	26.8	23.0	22.3	16.3	14.0	14.6	15.1
Inhalants	Ever	10.2	10.6	10.4	11.0	12.6	13.9	14.2	12.0
	Last 30 days	1.5	0.8	0.7	1.1	1.3	1.0	1.1	0.6
Hallucinogens (includes LSD)	Ever	15.0	15.0	12.9	11.2	10.2	11.2	12.0	10.0
	Last 30 days	2.7	2.6	1.8	2.2	1.7	1.4	2.3	2.1
Cocaine (includes Crack)	Ever	22.0	22.4	21.7	23.3	15.8	11.4	7.9	5.0
	Last 30 days	6.9	7.9	7.6	7.0	4.2	1.2	1.0	0.6
MDMA ("Ecstasy")	Ever	NA	NA	NA	NA	NA	3.9	2.9	2.1
	Last 30 days	NA	NA	NA	NA	NA	0.6	0.4	0.2
Heroin	Ever	0.9	0.5	0.5	0.4	0.3	0.3	0.5	0.1
	Last 30 days	0.3	0.0	0.0	0.0	0.1	0.0	0.0	0.0
Stimulants (other than cocaine)	Ever	NA	30.1	27.8	22.3	17.7	13.2	10.5	9.2
	Last 30 days	NA	9.9	5.5	3.7	1.8	1.4	1.1	1.5
Barbiturates	Ever	8.1	8.2	6.4	5.4	3.6	3.8	3.8	3.2
	Last 30 days	0.9	1.0	0.7	0.6	0.5	0.2	0.7	0.4
Alcohol	Ever	94.3	95.2	94.2	94.9	9.49	9.31	91.8	88.1
	Last 30 days	81.8	82.8	79.1	79.7	77.0	74.5	71.4	67.5
Cigarettes	Ever	NA	NA	NA	NA	NA	NA	NA	NA
	Last 30 days	25.8	24.4	21.5	22.4	22.6	21.5	23.5	23.5

Source: L. D. Johnston, P. M. O'Malley, and J. G. Bachman, *National Survey Results on Drug Use from The Monitoring the Future Study, 1975–1994. Volume II. College Students and Young Adults.* U. S. Department of Health and Human Services, Public Health Service, National Institutes of Health: National Institute on Drug Abuse, 1996, Tables 23 (p. 160) and 25 (p. 162).

slowly but steadily through much of the 1980s and early 1990s. Not so for cigarette smoking, which after declining modestly during the 1980s, turned upward in the 1990s.

Despite declines in overall alcohol consumption, problem drinking, especially binge drinking, remains widespread on college campuses. One national survey of college students found that 50% of the men and 39% of the women were binge drinkers (Adler, 1994; H. Wechsler et al., 1994). A binge drinker is someone who reports consuming five or more drinks (for men) or four or more drinks (for women) on one occasion during the preceding 2-week period. More than one third of freshmen in colleges known for heavy student drinking report binge drinking during their first week of school, which in many cases means they start binge drinking even before they have finished buying their books ("Study finds pattern in college binge drinking," 1995). Perhaps it comes as no surprise, but both college men and women involved in fraternities or sororities are more likely to engage in binge drinking than those with no affiliation (Arenson, 1997). More than 8 of 10 (84%) fraternity/sorority members report binge drinking, as compared to 40% living in off-campus housing (J. K. McCormick & Kalb, 1998). Nationally, alcohol dependence has been on the rise, due largely to increases in adolescent alcohol abuse leading eventually to outright dependence (Nelson, Heath, & Kessler, 1998).

Most binge drinkers do not consider themselves to have a drinking problem. Their beliefs belie the fact that binge drinking can lead to more regular, heavy drinking, which may set the stage for alcoholism. It is also a contributing factor to alcohol-related problems, such as motor vehicle accidents, physical injuries, violent or destructive behavior, and unsafe sexual practices that can lead to unwanted pregnancies or transmission of sexually transmitted diseases (Wechsler et al., 1994). As one AIDS prevention advertisement put it, "First you get drunk, then you get stupid, then you get AIDS."

CLASSIFICATION OF SUBSTANCE-RELATED DISORDERS

The *DSM-IV* classifies substance-related disorders into two major categories; **substance use disorders** and **substance-induced disorders.** Substance use disorders refer to patterns of maladaptive behavior involving the use of psychoactive substances. These include substance abuse and substance dependence. Substance-induced disorders refer to the many kinds of disorders that can be induced by the use of psychoactive substances, such as states of intoxication, withdrawal syndromes, mood disorders, delirium, dementia, amnesia, psychotic disorders, anxiety disorders, sexual dysfunctions, and sleep disorders. Different substances have different effects, so some of these disorders may apply to one, to a few, or to nearly all substances. For example, *substance intoxication* can result from use of alcohol, cocaine, or heroin, among other drugs, but not from nicotine, the mild stimulant found in tobacco. *Delirium* and *psychotic disorders* may be induced during states of intoxication from use of alcohol or cocaine but not, for instance, from use of caffeine or nicotine.

Substance Abuse and Dependence

Where does substance use end and abuse begin? From a legal standpoint, the answer is simple. For example, it is illegal in all states for people under the age of 21 to drink alcohol. It is also illegal to dispense prescribed drugs without prescriptions. When, however, does legal *use* of, say, alcohol cross the line and wax into *abuse*? According to the *DSM,* substance abuse involves a pattern of recurrent use that leads to damaging consequences. Damaging consequences may involve failure to meet one's major role responsibilities (e.g., as student, worker, or parent), putting oneself in situations where substance use is physically dangerous (e.g., mixing driving and substance use), encountering repeated problems with the law arising from substance use (e.g., multiple arrests for substance-related behavior), or having recurring social or interpersonal problems because of substance use (e.g., repeatedly getting into fights when drinking).

When people repeatedly miss school or work because they are drunk, or "sleeping it off," their behavior may fit the definition of **substance abuse.** A single incident of excessive drinking at a friend's wedding would not qualify. Nor would regular consumption of low to moderate amounts of alcohol be considered abusive so long as it is not connected with any impairment in functioning. Neither the amount nor the type of drug ingested, nor whether or not the drug is illicit, is the key to defining substance abuse according to the DSM. Rather, the determining feature of substance abuse is whether a pattern of drug-using behavior becomes repeatedly linked to damaging consequences.

Substance abuse is more likely to occur in individuals who have only recently begun to use a particular substance (APA, 1994). Substance abuse may continue for a long period of time or progress to **substance dependence,** a more severe type of substance use disorder characterized by the development of physiological signs of dependence (tolerance or withdrawal) or by compulsive use of a substance. People who become compulsive users lack control over their drug use. They may be aware of how their drug use is disrupting their lives or damaging their health but feel helpless or powerless to stop using drugs, even though they may want to. By the time they become dependent on a given drug, they've given over much of their lives to obtaining and using it. The diagnostic features associated with substance dependence are listed in Table 9.2.

Substance dependence often involves physiological features associated with chemical dependence. Repeated use of the substance may alter the body's physiological reactions, leading to the development of tolerance or a physical **withdrawal syndrome** (see Table 9.2). **Tolerance** is a state of physical habituation to a drug such that with frequent usage, higher doses are needed to achieve the same effect. A withdrawal syndrome (also called an **abstinence syndrome**) involves a characteristic cluster of withdrawal symptoms that occur when the person abruptly stops using a particular substance following a period of heavy, prolonged use.

Tolerance and withdrawal syndromes are often, although not always, associated with substance dependence.

Two of the many faces of alcohol use—and abuse.   Alcohol is our most widely used—and abused—drug. Many people use alcohol to celebrate achievements and happy occasions, as in the photograph on the left. Unfortunately, like the man in the photograph on the right, some people use alcohol to drown their sorrows, which may only compound their problems. Where does substance use end and abuse begin? According to the DSM, use becomes abuse when it leads to damaging consequences.

In some cases, substance dependence involves a pattern of compulsive use without the development of the physiological features of dependence (tolerance and/or a withdrawal syndrome). For example, people may become compulsive users of marijuana, especially when they rely on the drug to help them cope with the stresses of daily life, but not require larger amounts of the substance to get "high" or encounter significant withdrawal symptoms when they cease using it. In most cases, however, substance dependence involves the development of tolerance and/or a withdrawal syndrome, the primary physiological features of dependence.

Drugs associated with either substance abuse or substance dependence disorders include alcohol, opioids, stimulants such as amphetamines and cocaine, sedatives and barbiturates, prescription tranquilizers, and various psychedelic or **hallucinogenic** drugs such as LSD, PCP, and mari-

Going without . . .   The movie, *Rush,* starring Jason Patric and Jennifer Jason Leigh, examines the throes of drug dependency.

TABLE 9.2

Diagnostic Features of Substance Dependence

Substance dependence is defined as a maladaptive pattern of use that results in "significant impairment or distress," as typified by the following features occurring within the same year:

(1) Tolerance for the substance, as shown by either
    (a) the need for increased amounts of the substance to achieve the desired effect or intoxication, or
    (b) marked reduction in the effects of continuing to ingest the same amounts.

(2) Withdrawal symptoms, as shown by either
    (a) the withdrawal syndrome that is considered characteristic for the substance, or
    (b) the taking of the same substance (or a closely related substance, as when methadone is substituted for heroin) to relieve or to prevent withdrawal symptoms.

(3) Taking larger amounts of the substance, or for longer periods of time than the individual intended (e.g., person had desired to take only one drink, but after taking the first, continues drinking until severely intoxicated).

(4) Persistent desire to cut down or control intake of substance, or lack of success in trying to exercise self-control.

(5) Spending a good deal of time in activities directed toward obtaining the substance (for example, visiting several physicians to obtain prescriptions or engaging in theft), in actually ingesting the substance, or in recovering from its use. In severe cases, the individual's daily life revolves around substance use.

(6) The individual has reduced or given up important social, occupational, or recreational activities due to substance use (e.g., person withdraws from family events in order to indulge in drug use)

(7) Substance use is continued despite evidence of persistent or recurrent psychological or physical problems either caused or exacerbated by its use (e.g., repeated arrests for driving while intoxicated).

Note: Not all of these features need be present for a diagnosis to be made.
Source: Adapted from the *DSM-IV* (APA, 1994).

---

juana. Nicotine ingestion through smoking or chewing tobacco may lead to substance dependence but is not associated with substance abuse alone, because it is virtually unknown for someone to abuse nicotine without also having become dependent on it. Despite the fact that the DSM considers substance abuse and dependence to be distinct diagnostic categories, the borderline between the two is not always clear (Helzer & Schuckit, 1990).

The National Comorbidity Survey (NCS) shows how widespread the problems of substance dependence are in our society (Anthony, Warner, & Kessler, 1994; Warner et al., 1995). About 1 in 7 (14%) adults have a history of alcohol dependence. About 1 in 4 have developed nicotine dependence through the repeated use of tobacco products, most usually cigarettes. About 1 in 13 (7.5%) have developed a dependence on an illicit drug, inhalant, or nonprescription use of tranquilizers or other psychotropic drugs. Figure 9.1 gives the lifetime prevalences of drug dependence for various types of drugs.

Alcohol and drug dependence are more common among men than women with the exceptions of tobacco (nicotine) dependence, in which the gender ratio is relatively balanced, and dependence on depressants, such as sedatives and antianxiety drugs (minor tranquilizers like Valium), which occurs more frequently among women. The cigarette advertising slogan, "You've come a long way, baby," underscores the fact that women have virtually caught up with men in their use of tobacco and, sadly, in the incidence of diseases and premature deaths caused by cigarette smoking. The gender gap also appears to be narrowing with respect to alcohol abuse and dependence, at least among the

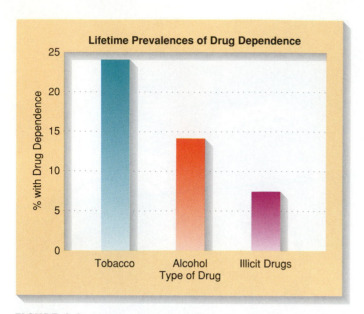

FIGURE 9.1 *Lifetime prevalences of drug dependence by type of drug.* One in four adults in the U.S. suffer from tobacco dependence at some point in their lives. About one in seven experience alcohol dependence and about one in thirteen develop a drug dependence on an illicit drug.

Source: National Comorbidity Survey; Anthony, Warner & Kessler (1994).

non-Black population (B. F. Grant et al., 1994; Nelson, Heath, & Kessler, 1998).

People may abuse or become dependent on more than one psychoactive substance at the same time. People who abuse or become dependent on heroin, for instance, may also abuse or become dependent on other drugs, such as alcohol, cocaine, stimulants, or other drugs—simultaneously or successively. People who engage in polydrug abuse encounter special problems. Ingestion of multiple drugs increases the potential for harmful overdoses, and "successful" treatment of one form of abuse may not affect abuse of other drugs, or in some cases may even exacerbate it.

Who's Most at Risk The NCS survey shows substance dependence to be more common among people at the lower income and educational levels, among the unemployed, among those living alone, and among those having no religious preference (Anthony, Warner, & Kessler, 1994). Despite the popular stereotype that problems of alcohol and drug dependence are more frequent among ethnic minorities, evidence from the NCS survey and other sources paints an entirely different picture. The NCS shows that dependence on alcohol and illicit drugs was actually less common among African Americans than non-Hispanic White Americans and was no more common among Hispanic Americans than among non-Hispanic White Americans. Other large-scale studies show similar results, with Blacks having about a 30% lower prevalence of alcohol abuse and dependence disorders than non-Blacks during the past year (B. F. Grant et al., 1994). There is also additional evidence based on a

1988 national survey that use of crack cocaine was not significantly different among African Americans, Hispanic Americans, and non-Hispanic White Americans living in the same neighborhoods (Lillie-Blanton, Anthony, & Schuster, 1993).

Addiction, Physiological Dependence, and Psychological Dependence

The *DSM* uses the terms *substance abuse* and *substance dependence* to classify people whose use of these substances impairs their functioning. It does not use the term *addiction* to describe these problems. Yet the concept of addiction is widespread among professionals and laypeople alike. But what is meant by addiction?

People define addiction in different ways. For our purposes, we define **addiction** as the habitual or compulsive use of a drug accompanied by evidence of physiological dependence. **Physiological dependence** means that one's body has changed as a result of the regular use of a psychoactive drug in such a way that tolerance and/or a withdrawal syndrome develop. By contrast, **psychological dependence** involves a pattern of compulsive use associated with impaired control over the use of a drug.

Although physical addiction is generally associated with substance dependence, you can develop a substance dependence disorder without becoming addicted. Substance dependence in some cases involves a compulsive style of drug-using behavior without the physical signs of addiction. People with a substance dependence disorder may be psychologically dependent on a drug even though they are not physiologically dependent or addicted. For example, habitual marijuana users may find it difficult to control their use of drug, even though they do not develop tolerance or show a withdrawal syndrome when they stop using it. Drugs that are associated with psychological dependence but have not been shown to produce physiological dependence include PCP as well as cannabis (marijuana).

TRUTH *or* FICTION REVISITED

9.2 False.   You can become psychologically dependent on a drug without developing a physiological dependence.

On the other hand, people may become physiologically dependent on a drug but not become a compulsive user or psychologically dependent. For example, people recuperating from surgery are often given narcotics derived from opium as painkillers. Some may develop signs of dependence, such as tolerance and a withdrawal syndrome, but do not develop into habitual users or show a lack of control over the use of these drugs.

In recent years, the concept of addiction has also extended beyond the abuse of chemical substances to apply to many habitual forms of maladaptive behavior, such as pathological gambling (see accompanying "A Closer Look" feature). In the vernacular, we hear of people being addicted to love or shopping or perhaps to almost anything, perhaps even the Internet. Yet these other "addictions" do not involve physiological dependence on a chemical substance. We limit the term *addiction* to habitual use of substances that produce physiological dependence.

Pathways to Drug Dependence

Though the progression to substance dependence varies from person to person, there are some common pathways that can be described according to the following stages (R. D. Weiss & Mirin ,1987):

1. *Experimentation.* During the stage of experimentation, or occasional use, the drug temporarily makes users feel good, even euphoric. Users feel in control and believe they can stop at any time.

2. *Routine use.* During the next stage, a period of routine use, people begin to structure their lives around the pursuit and use of drugs. Denial plays a major role at this stage, as users mask the negative consequences of their behavior to themselves and others. Values change. What had formerly been important, such as family and work, comes to matter less than the drugs.

The following clinical interview illustrates how denial can mask reality. The drug user, a 48-year-old executive, was brought for a consultation by his wife. She complained his once-successful business was jeopardized by his erratic behavior, he was grouchy and moody, and he had spent $7,000 in the previous month on cocaine.

Clinician:	Have you missed many days at work recently?
Executive:	Yes, but I can afford to, since I own the business. Nobody checks up on me.
Clinician:	It sounds like that's precisely the problem. When you don't go to work, the company stays open, but it doesn't do very well.
Executive:	My employees are well trained. They can run the company without me.
Clinician:	But that's not happening.
Executive:	Then there's something wrong with them. I'll have to look into it.
Clinician:	It sounds as if there's something wrong with you, but you don't want to look into it.
Executive:	Now you're on my case. I don't know why you listen to everything my wife says.
Clinician:	How many days of work did you miss in the last two months?
Executive:	A couple.
Clinician:	Are you saying that you missed only two days of work?
Executive:	Maybe a few.
Clinician:	Only three or four days?
Executive:	Maybe a little more.

Clinician:	Ten? Fifteen?
Executive:	Fifteen.
Clinician:	All because of cocaine?
Executive:	No.
Clinician:	How many were because of cocaine?
Executive:	Less than fifteen.
Clinician:	Fourteen? Thirteen?
Executive:	Maybe thirteen.
Clinician:	So you missed thirteen days of work in the last two months because of cocaine. That's almost two days a week.
Executive:	That sounds like a lot but it's no big deal. Like I say, the company can run itself.
Clinician:	How long have you been using cocaine?
Executive:	About three years.
Clinician:	Did you ever use drugs or alcohol before that in any kind of quantity?
Executive:	No.
Clinician:	Then let's think back five years. Five years ago, if you had imagined yourself missing over a third of your workdays because of a drug, and if you had imagined yourself spending the equivalent of $84,000 a year on that same drug, and if you saw your once-successful business collapsing all around you, wouldn't you have thought that that was indicative of a pretty serious problem?
Executive:	Yes, I would have.
Clinician:	So what's different now?
Executive:	I guess I just don't want to think about it.

SOURCE: WEISS & MIRIN, 1987, PP. 79–80

As routine drug use continues, problems mount. Users devote more of their resources to their drugs. Family bank accounts are ravaged, "temporary" loans are sought from friends and family for trumped-up reasons, family heirlooms and jewelry are sold to pawnbrokers for a fraction of their value. Lying and manipulation become a way of life to cover up the drug use. The husband sells the TV set to a pawnbroker and forces the front door open to make it look like a burglary. The wife claims to have been robbed at knifepoint to explain the disappearance of a gold chain or engagement ring. Family relationships become strained as the mask of denial shatters and the consequences of drug abuse become apparent: days lost from work, unexplained absences from home, rapid mood shifts, depletion of family finances, failure to pay bills, stealing from family members, and missing family gatherings or children's birthday parties.

3. *Addiction or dependence.* Routine use becomes addiction or dependence when users feel powerless to resist drugs, either because they want to experience their effects or to avoid the consequences of withdrawal. Little or nothing else matters at this stage, as seen in the case of Eugene, a 41-year-old architect, who related the following conversation with his wife:

Pathological Gambling

Gambling has never have been more popular in the United States. Twenty years ago there were only two states, Nevada and New Jersey, where some forms of legalized gambling were available. Today, legalized gambling is available in all but two states, Utah and Hawaii (Public Broadcasting Service, 1997). Legalized gambling is spreading in the form of state lotteries, offtrack betting (OTB) parlors, casino nights sponsored by religious and fraternal organizations, casinos on Indian reservations, and legalized gambling meccas, such as Atlantic City and Las Vegas. Americans lose more than $30 billion annually on legalized betting (O'Brien, 1998). Casinos alone take in more than 25 billion dollars annually, which is more than the amount spent on tickets to movies, plays, and music concerts combined (Sterngold, 1995). Illegal betting on sporting events is also growing. Most people who gamble maintain their self-control and can stop whenever they wish. Others, like the man in the following case, fall into a pattern of **pathological gambling.**

> *Twenty-eight years after his first two-bit bet at the race track, the double life of lies and deception caught up with an insurance executive whose gambling debts had climbed into the hundreds of thousands of dollars. The business he had built went bankrupt. His marriage ended in bitter divorce. Often, he considered killing himself.*
>
> *The former executive does not look like an addict, a liar, a manipulator or someone who would ignore his two young daughters, but he admits to having been all of these.*
>
> *Gambling," he said, dragging hard on a cigarette, "took me from a good man, which I basically am, to a person I didn't know. I was only happy when I was in action and I felt most at home when I was in action. The more I won, the more I gambled. The more I lost, the more I gambled. It was a no-win situation.*
>
> GATELY, 1989, P. 31. COPYRIGHT © 1989 BY THE NEW YORK TIMES COMPANY. REPRINTED BY PERMISSION.

By the time he sought treatment, he had lost more than $1 million. Many pathological gamblers (also called *compulsive gamblers*) seek treatment only during a financial or emotional crisis, such as bankruptcy or divorce. According to the DSM, pathological gambling is a disorder involving a pattern of repeated failure to resist the urge to gamble that affects one's ability to function in meeting personal, family, or occupational roles. Compulsive or pathological gamblers often report they had experienced a big win, or a series of winnings, early in their gambling careers. Eventually their losses began to mount, and they felt driven to bet with increasing desperation to reverse their luck and recoup them. Sometimes losses begin with the first bet, and pathological gamblers become trapped in a negative spiral of betting more frequently to recover earlier losses even as new losses and debts multiply. Pathological gambling is a progressive problem that, uncorrected, leads to rising debts, problems at work and home, and, sometimes, suicide. The link between gambling and suicide is suggested by findings that suicide rates in cities with legalized gambling (Atlantic City, Reno, Las Vegas) are four times higher than in comparably sized cities elsewhere in the United States (Blakeslee, 1997b). Family relationships can also become strained and even crack because of the time and resources channeled into gambling. There is often little money left for family vacations, school tuition, or monthly bills. Pathological gamblers often borrow from friends and family. When these sources dry up, they may turn to finance companies or illegal and potentially dangerous sources such as loan sharks and bookies. Pathological gamblers may attempt to reduce the stress of mounting debts by gambling yet more frequently, hoping for the "big score" that will put them "into the black."

Pathological gambling is classified in the DSM system as a type of **impulse-control disorder.** Impulse-control disorders involve the failure to resist impulses, temptations, or drives that lead to harmful consequences to oneself or others. **Kleptomania,** or compulsive stealing, is another type of impulse disorder. People with these disorders experience a rising level of tension or arousal just prior to the act, followed by a sense of relief or release when the act is completed.

Compulsive gambling is estimated to affect about 1.3% of adults in the United States and Canada, a prevalence rate that is up sharply during the past 20 years as legalized casinos and lotteries have proliferated (Pulley, 1997). The prevalence rate among teenagers is especially high—nearly 4%. Researchers have identified two distinct subgroups of compulsive gamblers, a higher income group composed largely of non-Hispanic White males with relatively higher levels of education and a lower income group composed largely of men of color with lower educational levels (Volberg & Steadman, 1992).

Pathological gambling is often likened to a form of nonchemical addiction. Like addictive disorders, compulsive gambling is characterized by a loss of control over the behavior, by a kind of physical high experienced when the behavior is performed, and by withdrawal symptoms, such as headaches, insomnia, and loss of appetite, when attempts are made to cut back or stop the compulsive behavior (Marriott, 1992; R. J. Rosenthal, 1992). Personality characteristics of pathological gamblers and chemical abusers also overlap, with the psychological test profiles of both groups showing traits such as self-centeredness, anxiety, low tolerance for frustration, impulsivity, and manipulativeness (Ciarrocchi, Kirschner, & Fallik, 1991; R. A. McCormick, Taber, Kruedelbach, & Russo, 1987; Vitaro, Arseneault, & Tremblay, 1997). Many people with substance abuse problems, especially alcoholism, also have problems with compulsive gambling, and vice versa (J. B. Murray, 1993a; Smelson, & Lindeken, 1996; Pulley, 1997). Gamblers Anonymous, a self-help organization for compulsive gamblers, is modeled after programs like Alcoholics Anonymous in which the addictive aspects of the problem are highlighted. However, compulsive gamblers are not a homogeneous group. The addiction model may apply more to some compulsive gamblers than others. Some forms of pathological gambling may be more closely related to depressive disorders or to obsessive-compulsive disorder than to substance use disorders.

Gamblers also tend to show cognitive biases, or errors in thinking, that contribute to their problems. These include biased evaluations of past gambling (crediting themselves for their wins and explaining away their losses), illusions of control (beliefs that they can control gambling outcomes that are actually governed by chance), the gambler's fallacy (belief that over time gambling wins and losses will even out), and overestimating the probability of success of the particular team or number on the Roulette table they are betting on

Gambling, American style? Gambling is big business in the United States. Although most gamblers can stop gambling whenever they want to do so, people with a pathological gambling disorder are unable to resist the urge to gamble. They may seek help only when their losses throw them into a financial or emotional crisis, such as bankruptcy or divorce.

(Gibson, Sanbonmatsu, & Posavac, 1997; Ladouceur & Walker, 1996; "Researchers Identify Cognitive Process That Contributes To Gambling Behavior," 1997).

Treatment of pathological gambling remains a challenge. With pathological gambling, as with personality disorders and substance use disorders, helping professionals face an uphill battle in working with individuals who make maladaptive choices and show little insight into the causes of their problems. Such clients commonly resist efforts to help them. Yet some successful treatments efforts have been reported, including cognitive-behavioral programs that focused on helping gamblers correct cognitive biases (e.g., beliefs that "if I lose four times in a row, I will win for sure the next time") (López Viets, & Miller, 1997; Sylvain, Ladouceur, & Boisvert, 1997). Some hospital-based treatment programs have also shown promising results (e.g., Lesieur & Blume, 1991).

She had just caught me with cocaine again after I had managed to convince her that I hadn't used in over a month. Of course I had been tooting (snorting) almost every day, but I had managed to cover my tracks a little better than usual. So she said to me that I was going to have to make a choice—either cocaine or her. Before she finished the sentence, I knew what was coming, so I told her to think carefully about what she was going to say. It was clear to me that there wasn't a choice. I love my wife, but I'm not going to choose anything over cocaine. It's sick, but that's what things have come to. Nothing and nobody comes before my coke.

WEISS & MIRIN, 1987, P. 55

Intoxication

Psychoactive substances can induce physiological effects identified with states of **intoxication**—also referred to as drunkenness or being high. Substance intoxication largely reflects the chemical actions of the psychoactive substances. The particular features of intoxication depend on which drug is ingested, the dose, the user's biological reactivity, and—to some degree—the user's expectations. Psychoactive substances that can cause intoxication include alcohol, opioids, barbiturates, antianxiety agents (minor tranquilizers), cocaine, caffeine, and hallucinogens (such as marijuana, LSD, and phencyclidine [PCP]).

Signs of intoxication often include confusion, belligerence, impaired judgment, inattention, and impaired motor and spatial skills. Extreme intoxication from use of alcohol, cocaine, opioids, and PCP can even result in death (yes, you can die from alcohol overdoses), either because of the substance's biochemical effects or because of behavior patterns—such as suicide—that are connected with psychological pain or impaired judgment brought on by use of the drug.

Withdrawal Syndromes

A withdrawal syndrome may develop after drug use stops abruptly following a period of heavy and prolonged use (APA, 1994). People who experience a withdrawal syndrome often return to using the substance in order to relieve the discomfort associated with withdrawal, which serves to maintain the addictive pattern. Substances that may lead to withdrawal syndromes include alcohol, opiates, cocaine, amphetamines, sedatives and barbiturates, nicotine, and antianxiety agents (minor tranquilizers). Marijuana and hallucinogens such as LSD are not recognized as producing a withdrawal syndrome because of a lack of evidence that abrupt withdrawal from these substances reliably produces clinically significant withdrawal effects (APA, 1994).

Caffeine, the psychoactive substance found in coffee, tea, and many kinds of chocolate and soda, may also be connected with a characteristic withdrawal syndrome, as shown in a double-blind study of 62 adults who drank about 2.5 cups of coffee per day. The subjects were switched to pills that contained either caffeine or a placebo. Coffee drinkers who took the placebo rather than caffeine were more likely to report such withdrawal symptoms as depression, anxiety, fatigue, and headache (Silverman, Evans, Strain, & Griffiths, 1992). Because evidence of a withdrawal syndrome for caffeine is not definitive, the *DSM-IV* places caffeine withdrawal in a category of proposed diagnostic criteria sets that require further study.

Withdrawal symptoms vary with the particular type of drug. The withdrawal syndrome associated with alcohol dependence may include dryness in the mouth, nausea or vomiting, weakness, **tachycardia**, anxiety and depression, headaches, insomnia, elevated blood pressure, and fleeting hallucinations. In some cases of chronic alcoholism, withdrawal produces a state of **delirium tremens**, or DTs. The DTs are usually limited to chronic, heavy users of alcohol who dramatically lower their intake of alcohol after many years of heavy drinking. The DTs involve intense autonomic hyperactivity (profuse sweating and tachycardia) and **delirium**—a state of mental confusion characterized by incoherent speech, **disorientation**, and extreme restlessness. Terrifying hallucinations—frequently of creepy, crawling animals—may also be present.

DEPRESSANTS

A **depressant** is a drug that slows down or curbs the activity of the central nervous system. By so doing, it reduces feelings of tension and anxiety, causes our movements to become sluggish, and impairs our cognitive processes. In high doses, depressants can arrest vital functions and cause death. Alcohol in large quantities usually kills by depressing respiration (breathing). There are other effects that are specific to the particular kind of depressant. For example, some depressants, such as heroin, produce a "rush" of pleasure.

Alcohol

You may not have thought of alcohol as a drug, perhaps because it is so popular or perhaps because it is ingested by drinking rather than by smoking or injection. But alcoholic beverages—wine, beer, and hard liquor—contain a depressant called *ethyl alcohol* (or *ethanol*). The concentration of the drug varies with the type of beverage (wine and beer have less pure alcohol per ounce than distilled spirits such as rye, gin, or vodka). Alcohol is classified as a depressant drug because it has biochemical effects similar to those of a class of minor tranquilizers, the benzodiazepines, which includes the well-known drugs *diazepam* (Valium) and *chlordiazepoxide* (Librium). We can think of alcohol as a type of over-the-counter tranquilizer.

Alcohol is used in many ways. It is our mealtime relaxant, our party social facilitator, our bedtime sedative. We observe holy days, laud our achievements, and express joyful wishes with alcohol. Adolescents assert their maturity with alcohol. Pediatricians have swabbed the painful gums of teething babies with alcohol. Alcohol even deals the death blow to germs on surface wounds and is the active ingredient in antiseptic mouthwashes.

Most American adults drink alcohol at least occasionally. Most people who drink do so in moderation, but about 1 in 10 people have a significant problem with alcohol (Leary, 1996b; W. R. Miller & Brown, 1997). Alcohol is the most widely abused substance in the United States and worldwide. Alcoholism affects an estimated 14 million Americans (Cable News Network [CNN], 1998a).

The National Comorbidity Survey (NCS) reported lifetime prevalence rates of 14% for alcohol dependence and 9% for alcohol abuse without dependence (R. C. Kessler et al., 1994). About 7% of the U.S. adult population could be classified as suffering from alcohol dependence during the past year and between 2% and 3% show evidence of alcohol abuse without dependence within the past year (B. F. Grant et al., 1994).

The personal and social costs of alcoholism exceed those of all illicit drugs combined. The economic costs of alcoholism—based on days lost from work, health problems associated with alcoholism, and costs resulting from motor vehicle accidents involving alcohol use—are staggering, amounting to more than $136 billion annually according to a recent estimate (T. Maier, 1995). Alcohol abuse is connected with lower productivity, loss of jobs, and downward movement in socioeconomic status. Estimates are that perhaps 30% to 40% of homeless people in the United States suffer from alcoholism (McCarty et al., 1991). Alcohol also plays a part in about 1 in 3 suicides in this country (Desmond, 1987). *More teenagers die from alcohol-related motor vehicle accidents than from any other cause of death* (National Highway Traffic Safety Administration, 1988).

Alcohol, not cocaine or other drugs, is the drug of choice among young people today and the leading drug of abuse (Johnston et al., 1992). Drinking has become so integrated into college life that it has become essentially normative, as much a part of the college experience as attending a weekend football or basketball game. Although use of cocaine has become less socially acceptable, peer approval for alcohol use among teens remains high (L. D. Johnston, O'Malley, & Bachman, 1991).

Alcoholism and Alcohol Use Disorders

The DSM classifies alcohol use disorders as either alcohol abuse or alcohol dependence. The term **alcoholism** is not used for purposes of classification. Yet many lay and professional people use the term *alcoholism* to refer to these problems. Although definitions of alcoholism vary, we use the term to refer to a state of physical dependence on, or addiction to, alcohol that is characterized by impaired control over the use of the drug.

Despite the popular image of the person who develops alcoholism as a skid-row drunk, only a small minority of people with alcoholism fit the stereotype. The great majority of people with alcoholism are the type of people you're likely to see every day—your neighbors, co-workers, friends, and members of your own family. They are found in all walks of life and from every social and economic class. Many have families, hold good jobs, and live fairly comfortably. Yet alcoholism can have just as devastating an effect on the well-to-do as on the indigent, leading to wrecked careers and marriages, to motor vehicle and other accidents, and to severe, life-threatening physical disorders, as well as exacting an enormous emotional toll. No one drinking pattern is exclusively associated with alcoholism. Some people with alcoholism drink heavily every day; others binge only on weekends. Others can abstain for lengthy periods of time but periodically "go off the wagon" and engage in episodes of binge drinking that may last for weeks or months.

Researchers have noted some gender differences in alcoholic drinking patterns. Men who develop alcoholism tend to alternate between periods of heavy drinking and periods of abstinence; women, apparently more stable than their male counterparts, are more likely to drink steadily but less likely to binge (S. Y. Hill, 1980).

Risk Factors for Alcoholism Investigators have identified a number of factors that place people at increased risk for developing alcoholism and alcohol-related problems. These include the following:

1. *Gender.* Alcohol dependence is more common in men than women (B. F. Grant, 1997). Recent estimates indicate that men are more than twice as likely (20% vs. 8%, respectively) to develop an alcohol dependence disorder (Kessler et al., 1997a). One possible reason for this gender difference is sociocultural; perhaps tighter cultural constraints are placed on women. Yet it may also be that alcohol hits women harder, and not only because women usually weigh less than men. Alcohol seems to "go to women's heads" more rapidly than men's. This is apparently because women metabolize less alcohol in the stomach than men do. Why? It appears that women have less of an enzyme that metabolizes alcohol in the stomach than men do (Lieber, 1990). Alcohol then reaches women's circulatory systems and brains relatively intact. It is almost as if women were injecting alcohol intravenously. It is not a substance to be trifled with.

TRUTH or FICTION REVISITED

9.3. *True.* Women metabolize less alcohol in the stomach than do men, which means that ounce for ounce women drinkers absorb more alcohol into their bloodstreams than do their male counterparts.

Researchers speculate that alcoholism may become more prevalent among women in the future (Helzer, Burnam, & McEvoy, 1991; Kendler, 1992d)—in part because social drinking has become more acceptable for women and

How Do You Know If You Are Hooked?

Are you dependent on alcohol? If you shake and shiver and undergo the tortures of the darned (our editor insisted on changing this word to maintain the decorum of a textbook) when you go without a drink for a while, the answer is clear enough. Sometimes the clues are more subtle, however.

The following items, adapted from the National Council on Alcoholism's self-test, can shed some light on the question. Simply place a check mark in the yes or no column for each item. Then check the key at the end of the chapter.

	YES	NO
1. Do you sometimes go on drinking binges?	—	—
2. Do you tend to keep away from your family or friends when you are drinking?	—	—
3. Do you become irritated when your family or friends talk about your drinking?	—	—
4. Do you feel guilty now and then about your drinking?	—	—
5. Do you often regret the things you have said or done when you have been drinking?	—	—
6. Do you find that you fail to keep the promises you make about controlling or cutting down on your drinking?	—	—
7. Do you eat irregularly or not at all when you are drinking?	—	—
8. Do you feel low after drinking?	—	—
9. Do you sometimes miss work or appointments because of drinking?	—	—
10. Do you use more and more to get drunk or high?	—	—

Source: Adapted from *Newsweek,* February 20, 1989, p. 52.

Women and alcohol. Women are less likely to develop alcoholism, in part because of greater cultural constraints on excessive drinking by women and perhaps because women metabolize more pure alcohol than men, leading them to become more affected by alcohol than men who drink the same amount.

dence develop before age 40. Although alcohol use disorders tend to develop somewhat later in women than in men, women who develop these problems experience similar health, social, and occupational problems by middle age as their male counterparts.

3. Antisocial personality disorder. Antisocial behavior in adolescence or adulthood increases the risk of later alcoholism. On the other hand, many people with alcoholism showed no antisocial tendencies in adolescence, and many antisocial adolescents do not abuse alcohol or other drugs as adults (Nathan, 1988).

4. Family History. The best predictor of problem drinking in adulthood appears to be a family history of alcohol abuse. Family members who drink may act as models ("set a poor example"). Moreover, the biological relatives of people with alcohol dependence may also inherit a predisposition that makes them more likely to develop problems with alcohol.

5. Sociodemographic Factors. A lifetime history of alcohol dependence is more common among people of lower income and educational levels, and among people living alone (Anthony, Warner, & Kessler, 1994). Ethnic group differences are discussed in the nearby "Focus on Diversity" feature.

Alcoholism: Disease, Moral Defect, or Behavior Pattern? According to the medical perspective, alcoholism is a disease. E. M. Jellinek (1960) set forth the axioms of this model. To Jellinek, alcoholism was a permanent, irreversible condition. Once a person who develops alcoholism takes a drink, the biochemical effects of the drug on the brain create an irresistible physical craving for more. Jellinek's ideas have contributed to the view that can be expressed "Once an alcoholic, always an alcoholic." Alcoholics Anonymous (AA), which has adopted Jellinek's concepts,

because the gap between men and women in the prevalence of alcoholism is the narrowest in the youngest age group (J. C. Anthony & Helzer, 1991).

2. Age. The age of onset of alcohol dependence peaks in the twenties and thirties (APA, 1994; Langenbucher & Chung, 1995). The great majority of cases of alcohol depen-

views people who suffer from alcoholism as either drinking or "recovering." In other words, alcoholism is never cured. People who suffer from alcoholism and are able to abstain are perceived as "recovering," never cured. Jellinek's concepts have also supported the idea that "just one drink" will cause the person with alcoholism to "fall off the wagon." In this view, the sole path to recovery is abstinence.

Although the disease model has achieved prominence and wide public acceptance, the nature of alcoholism continues to be debated. For most of history, immoderate drinking was seen as a moral defect. Alcoholism was only first labeled a disease by the American Medical Association in 1966 (Desmond, 1987). Since that time, the campaign to instill this view has been so pervasive that most Americans now endorse this view (Desmond, 1987).

Yet some investigators regard alcoholism not as a disease, in the medical sense of the term, but as a label to describe a harmful pattern of alcohol ingestion and related behaviors (e.g., Rohan, 1982). To them, for example, the "just-one-drink" hypothesis is not a biochemical inevitability. It is, instead, a common self-fulfilling prophecy, as we see later in the chapter.

Psychological Effects of Alcohol

The effects of alcohol or other drugs vary from person to person. By and large they reflect the interaction of (1) the physiological effects of the substances, and (2) our interpretations of those effects. What do most people expect from alcohol? People frequently hold stereotypical expectations that alcohol will reduce states of tension, enhance pleasurable experiences, wash away their worries, and enhance their social skills. But what *does* alcohol actually do?

At a physiological level, alcohol, like the benzodiazepines, appears to heighten the sensitivity of **GABA** receptor sites (Suzdak, Glowa, Crawley, & Schwartz, 1986). Because GABA is an inhibitory neurotransmitter, increasing the action of GABA serves to diminish overall nervous system activity, which produces feelings of relaxation. As people drink, their senses become clouded, and balance and coordination suffer. Still higher doses act on the medulla and spinal cord, which regulate involuntary vital functions such as heart rate, respiration rate, and body temperature.

People may do many things when drinking that they would not do when sober, in part because of expectations concerning the drug, in part because of the drug's effects on the brain. For example, they may become more flirtatious or sexually aggressive or say or do things they later regret. Their behavior may reflect their expectation that alcohol has liberating effects and provides an external excuse for questionable behavior. Later, they can claim, "It was the alcohol, not me." The drug may impair the brain's ability to curb impulsive behavior, perhaps by interfering with information-processing functions (Steele & Southwick, 1985). Though alcohol may make them feel more relaxed and self-confident, it may prevent them from exercising good judgment, which can lead them to make choices they would ordinarily reject, such as engaging in risky sex (C. M. Gordon & Carey, 1996). One of the lures of alcohol is that it induces short-term feelings of euphoria and elation that can drown self-doubts and self-criticism. Alcohol may also make people less capable of perceiving the unfortunate consequences of their behavior.

Frequent use over a year or more may deepen feelings of depression, however. Alcohol in increasing amounts can also dampen sexual arousal or excitement and impair our ability to perform sexually. As an intoxicant, alcohol also impairs intellectual functioning, interferes with judgment, hampers coordination and motor ability, and slurs speech. These effects help explain why alcohol use is implicated in nearly 50% of the nation's fatal auto accidents, about 25% of fatal falls, and 30% to 50% of fatal fires and drownings (see Figure 9.2; also *Alcohol and Health,* 1987; W. R. Miller & Brown, 1997).

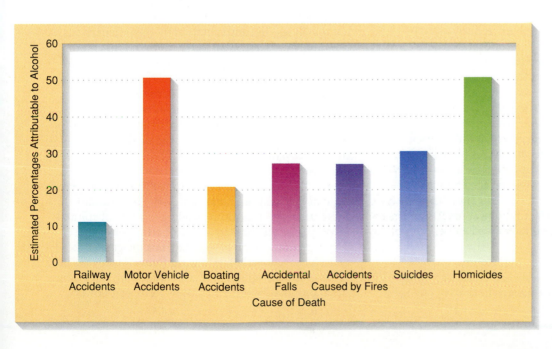

FIGURE 9.2 *Estimated percentages of deaths from various causes connected with use of alcohol.*
Alcohol use is apparently involved in half of the U.S. deaths due to motor vehicle accidents and homicide.

Source: Adapted from Ravenholt (1984).

Ethnicity and Alcohol Abuse

Native Americans and Irish Americans have the highest incidences of alcoholism in the United States (Lex, 1987; Moncher, Holden, & Trimble, 1990). Jewish Americans have relatively low incidences of alcoholism (Yeung & Greenwald, 1992), perhaps because Jews tend to expose children to the ritual use of wine within a religious context and to impose strong cultural restraints on excessive and underage drinking. Let us consider some other ethnic differences in alcohol abuse and the damage caused by excessive drinking.

Asian Americans

Asian Americans tend to drink less heavily than most other Americans, in part because of strong cultural constraints on excessive drinking and perhaps partly for biological reasons. Asian Americans are more likely than African, Hispanic, and non-Hispanic White Americans to show a flushing response to alcohol. Approximately 30% to 50% of Asians show this response, which involves perceptible redness and feelings of warmth on the face, and, at higher doses, nausea, rapid heart rate, dizziness, and headaches (Ellickson, Hays, & Bell, 1992; Newlin, 1989). Flushing may help curb excessive alcohol intake and reduce the risk of alcoholism among Asian Americans. Researchers find, for instance, that Asians (Koreans, Taiwanese, Japanese Americans, and Hawaiian Asians) who show a more marked flushing response tend to consume less alcohol than those who show less flushing (Park et al., 1984; Nakawatase, Yamamoto, & Saaso, 1993).

Hispanic Americans

Hispanic American men are about as likely as non-Hispanic White men to drink alcohol and to develop alcohol use disorders and alcohol-related physical problems (Caetano, 1987, 1991; R. C. Kessler et al., 1994). Hispanic American women, however, are much less likely to use alcohol and to develop alcohol use disorders than non-Hispanic White women. Why this difference? An important factor may be cultural expectations. Traditional Hispanic American cultures place severe restrictions on use of alcohol by women, especially heavy drinking. However, with increasing acculturation, Hispanic American women in the United States apparently are becoming more similar to European American women with respect to alcohol use and abuse.

African Americans

Alcohol abuse is taking a heavy toll on African Americans. The prevalence of *cirrhosis of the liver,* a potentially fatal liver disease, is nearly twice as high in African Americans as in non-Hispanic White Americans. African Americans are also much more likely to develop alcohol-related coronary heart disease and oral and throat cancers (Rogan, 1986). Alcohol is also implicated in almost half of homicides that involve African Americans (M. Williams, 1985). Yet African Americans are much less likely than non-Hispanic White Americans to develop alcohol abuse or dependence (Anthony, Warner, & Kessler, 1994; B. F. Grant et al., 1994). Why, then, do African Americans suffer more from alcohol-related problems?

Socioeconomic factors may help explain these differences. African Americans are more likely to encounter the stresses of unemployment and economic hardship, and stress may compound the damage to the body caused by heavy alcohol consumption. African Americans also tend to have poorer access to medical services and may be less likely to receive early treatment for the medical problems caused by alcohol abuse. Violence linked to alcohol abuse is also more common in economically disadvantaged and drug-ravaged communities that contain a disproportionate number of people of color.

Native Americans

Native Americans are the American ethnic group that has suffered the most from alcohol-related problems. Native Americans have more than four times the overall U.S. death rate due to alcohol-related cirrhosis of the liver (Beauvais & LaBoueff, 1985) and are the U.S. ethnic group most at risk of alcohol-related diabetes, fetal abnormalities, and automobile and other accident fatalities (Moncher et al., 1990). One death in four among Native American women is caused by alcohol-related cirrhosis of the liver. This figure is 37 times higher than the rate among White women (F. Moss et al., 1985). The prevalence of **fetal alcohol syndrome (FAS)** is more than 10 per 1,000 live births among some Native American tribes. This incidence is more than three times the overall U.S. incidence of FAS.

Many writers see the prevalence of alcoholism among Native Americans as a consequence of the forced attempt by European American society to eradicate tribal language and culture, leading to a loss of cultural identity that sets the stage for alcoholism, drug abuse, and depression. Kahn (1982) explains the greater incidence of psychopathology among Native Americans in terms of the disruption in traditional culture caused by the appropriation of their lands by European powers

Alcohol and ethnic diversity. The damage effects of alcohol abuse appear to be taking the heaviest toll on African Americans and Native Americans. The prevalence of alcohol-related cirrhosis of the liver is nearly twice as high among African Americans than among White Americans, even though African Americans are less likely to develop alcohol abuse or dependence disorders. Jewish Americans have relatively low incidences of alcohol-related problems, perhaps because they tend to expose children to the ritual use of wine in childhood and impose strong cultural restraints on excessive drinking. Asian Americans tend to drink less heavily than most other Americans, in part because of cultural constraints and possibly because they have less biological tolerance of alcohol, as shown by a greater flushing response to alcohol.

and the attempts to sever them from their cultural traditions while denying them full access to the dominant Western culture. Native peoples have since lived in severe cultural and social disorganization, which has resulted in high rates of psychopathology and substance abuse. Beset by such problems, Native American adults

are prone to child abuse and neglect. Abuse and neglect contribute to feelings of hopelessness and depression among adolescents, who then seek to escape their feelings through alcohol and other drugs (Berlin, 1987).

Research into the acculturation hypothesis suggests that alcohol and drug abuse is greatest among Native

(box continues on following page)

Ethnicity and Alcohol Abuse

American youths who identify least closely with traditional Native American values (that is, those who are more acculturated to the larger U.S. society). Next in level of use, however, came youth who were most closely identified with traditional Native American values. Bicultural youth, consisting of those who felt comfortable within Native American culture and the larger culture, showed the lowest abuse of alcohol and other drugs. These findings would suggest that the best adjustment (meaning the lowest levels of culture-related stress) is found among youth who have adapted to both cultures. Other factors, such as the poverty faced by many Native Americans who live on reservations, may also contribute to stress and alcohol and drug abuse.

Physical Health and Alcohol Chronic, heavy alcohol use affects virtually every organ and body system either directly or indirectly. Heavy alcohol use is linked to a higher risk of various forms of cancer, such as cancer of the throat, esophagus, larynx, stomach, colon, liver, and possibly of the bowels and breasts (e.g., Fuchs et al., 1995; Kruger & Jerrells, 1992; Reichman, 1994). Heavy drinking is also linked to coronary heart disease, ulcers, hypertension, gout, and pancreatitis (painful inflammation of the pancreas) (USDHHS, 1991a, 1991c). The linkages noted here are based on a statistical association or correlation between heavy drinking, on the one hand, and health problems on the other. These linkages are strongly suggestive of the damaging effects of heavy drinking; however, because they are based on correlational evidence, we cannot conclude they are necessarily causal.

Heavy drinking clearly does damage the liver, the organ that serves as the primary site of alcohol metabolism. Chronic, heavy consumption of alcohol is the single most important cause of illness and death from liver disease in the United States (USDHHS, 1991a, 1991c). Two of the major forms of alcohol-related liver disease are *alcoholic hepatitis,* which involves a serious and potentially life-threatening inflammation of the liver, and *cirrhosis of the liver.* Alcoholic hepatitis may be reversed following cessation of alcohol use, but cirrhosis is irreversible, although stopping the use of alcohol may prevent further deterioration of liver cells and possibly prolong life. Liver disease is the ninth leading killer in the United States and can to a large extent be prevented, as nearly half of all deaths due to chronic liver disease are due to alcohol consumption. To a great extent, the health risks of alcohol consumption depend on the amount and duration of use. Some people may also be genetically more susceptible to the harmful effects of heavy alcohol use than others.

Alcohol is fattening, yet habitual drinkers may be malnourished. Although it is high in calories, alcohol lacks vital nutrients such as vitamins and proteins. Alcohol also impedes the body's absorption of various vitamins, including thiamine, or vitamin B1. Chronic drinking can thus result in disorders that have been related to protein and vitamin deficiencies, including cirrhosis of the liver (linked to protein deficiency) and **alcohol-induced persisting amnestic disorder** (connected with vitamin B deficiency). Alcohol-induced persisting amnestic disorder (also known as **Korsakoff's syndrome**) is characterized by glaring confusion and disorientation, memory loss for recent events, and abnormalities in eye movements (see Chapter 14).

All told, about 100,000 deaths annually in the United States result from various alcohol-related diseases and motor vehicle and other accidents (J. D. Potter, 1997). After tobacco, alcohol is the next leading cause of premature death in our society. Men who drink heavily stand nearly twice the risk of dying before the age of 65 as men who abstain; women who drink heavily are more than three times as likely to die before age 65 as are women who abstain ("NIAAA report links drinking and early death," 1990).

Mothers who drink during pregnancy place their fetuses at risk for infant mortality, birth defects, central nervous system dysfunctions, and academic problems later on (Shaywitz, Cohen, & Shaywitz, 1980). Many children whose mothers drink during pregnancy develop fetal alcohol syndrome (FAS), a syndrome characterized by facial features such as a flattened nose, widely spaced eyes, and underdeveloped upper jaw and mental retardation. FAS affects between 1 and 3 children of every 1,000 live births (Niccols, 1994) and is among the most common known causes of mental retardation. Although the physical features of people with FAS may become more similar to those of nonaffected people during adolescence and adulthood, the mental retardation that affects a high percentage of children with FAS tends to be stable over time (Steinhausen et al., 1993; Streissguth, 1994). Children with FAS are also at increased risk of hyperactivity, serious behavior problems, and emotional disorders in childhood and adolescence (Steinhausen et al., 1993; B. F. Williams et al., 1994).

We don't know whether there is a minimum amount of alcohol needed to produce FAS (Niccols, 1994; Spohr, Willms, & Steinhausen, 1993). FAS has been found among children of mothers who drink as little as 2 ounces of alcohol a day during the first trimester (Astley et al., 1992).

Although the question of whether there is any safe dose of alcohol during pregnancy continues to be debated, the fact remains that FAS is an entirely preventable birth defect. The safest course for women who know or suspect they are pregnant is not to drink. Period.

Moderate Drinking: Is There a Health Benefit? Despite this list of adverse effects associated with heavy drinking, there is growing evidence linking light to moderate use of alcohol to reduced risks of heart attacks and lower death rates ("Alcohol and the Heart: Consensus Emerges" 1996; Grady, 1997c; Thun et al., 1997). Researchers suspect that alcohol may help prevent blood clots from forming that can clog arteries and lead to heart attacks. Alcohol also appears to increase the levels of HDL cholesterol, the so-called good cholesterol that sweeps away fatty deposits along artery walls (Ochs, 1998). Although light to moderate use of alcohol (about one drink per day) may have a protective effect on the heart, public health officials caution that promoting the possible health benefits of alcohol may backfire by increasing the risks of alcohol abuse and dependence (J. E. Brody, 1994d). Alcohol use is also linked to an increased risk of some forms of cancer, including breast cancer (Smith-Warner et al., 1998). Heavy drinking is clearly damaging to the heart and other organs, and any level of alcohol intake by a pregnant woman may be harmful to the developing fetus. Health promotion efforts might be better directed toward finding safer ways of achieving the health benefits associated with moderate drinking than by encouraging alcohol consumption, such as by quitting smoking, lowering dietary fat and cholesterol, and exercising more regularly (Gaziano et al., 1993).

TRUTH *or* FICTION REVISITED

9.4 *False.* Findings from recent studies show that light to moderate intake of alcohol is associated with a lower risk of heart attacks and lower death rates.

Sedatives, Hypnotics, and Antianxiety Drugs

Estimates indicate that about 1% of the adult population meet criteria for a substance abuse or dependence disorder involving sedatives, hypnotics, or antianxiety agents at some point in their lives (Anthony & Helzer, 1991). **Barbiturates** such as amobarbital, pentobarbital, phenobarbital, and secobarbital are depressants or **sedatives** with several medical uses, including alleviation of anxiety and tension, anesthetizing of pain, treatment of epilepsy and high blood pressure, and short-term treatment of insomnia. Barbiturates rapidly create psychological dependence and physiological dependence in the form of tolerance and development of a withdrawal syndrome.

In contrast to the profiles of young narcotics abusers, most barbiturate addicts are middle-aged people who used sedatives initially to combat anxiety or insomnia and then got hooked. Because of concerns about abuse, physicians today prescribe other drugs for the temporary relief of anxiety and tension, such as the minor tranquilizers Valium and Librium. However, it is now recognized that minor tranquilizers as well can create physiological dependence. Moreover, regular use of these drugs fails to help people alter the sources of stress in their lives.

Barbiturates are also popular street drugs because they are relaxing and produce a mild state of euphoria, or "high." High doses of barbiturates, like alcohol, produce drowsiness, slurred speech, motor impairment, irritability, and poor judgment—a particularly deadly combination of effects when their use is combined with operation of a motor vehicle. The effects of barbiturates last from 3 to 6 hours.

Because of synergistic effects, a mixture of barbiturates and alcohol is about four times as powerful as either drug used by itself (Combs, Hales, & Williams, 1980). A combination of barbiturates and alcohol is implicated in the deaths of the entertainers Marilyn Monroe and Judy Garland. Even such widely used antianxiety drugs as Valium and Librium, which have a wide margin of safety when used alone, can be dangerous and lead to overdoses when their use is combined with alcohol (APA, 1994).

Physiologically dependent people need to be withdrawn carefully, and only under medical supervision, from sedatives, barbiturates, and antianxiety agents. Abrupt withdrawal can produce states of delirium that can be life threatening (APA, 1994). Delirium may involve visual, tactile, or auditory hallucinations and disturbances in thinking processes and consciousness. The longer the period of use and the higher the doses used, the greater the risk of severe withdrawal effects. Epileptic (grand mal) seizures and even death may occur if the individual undergoes untreated, abrupt withdrawal.

Opioids

Opioids are **narcotics**, a term used for addictive drugs that have pain-relieving and sleep-inducing properties. Opioids include both naturally occurring opiates (morphine, heroin, codeine) derived from the juice of the poppy plant or synthetic drugs (Demerol, Percodan, Darvon) manufactured in the laboratory to have opiate-like effects. The ancient Sumerians named the poppy plant "opium," meaning "plant of joy." The major medical application of opioids is the relief of pain, or **analgesia.** Opioids produce a "rush" or intense feelings of pleasure, which is the primary reason for their popularity as street drugs. They also dull awareness of one's personal problems, which is attractive to people seeking a mental escape from stress.

Medical use of opioids is carefully regulated because overdoses can lead to coma and even death. Street use of these drugs is associated with many fatal overdoses and accidents. According to the ECA study, 0.7% of the adult population (7 people in 1,000) currently have or have had an opioid abuse or dependence disorder (Anthony & Helzer, 1991). Once dependence sets in, it usually follows a chronic course, although periods of temporary abstinence are frequent (APA, 1994).

Opioids produce pleasurable effects apparently because they stimulate brain centers that regulate sensations of pleasure and pain (Ling et al., 1984; USDHSS, 1986a). It appears the brain has its own natural opioid system. Two revealing discoveries were made in the 1970s. One was that neurons in the brain had receptor sites into which opioids fit—like a key in a lock. The second was that the human body produces substances similar to opioids in chemical structure that dock at the same receptor sites (A. Goldstein, 1976). Some of these natural substances are labeled **endorphins,** which is short for "endogenous morphine"—that is, morphine coming from within. Endorphins appear to play a role in regulating states of pleasure and pain. Opioids mimic the actions of endorphins by docking at receptor sites intended for them, which in turn stimulates the brain centers that produce pleasurable sensations.

Morphine Morphine—which receives its name from Morpheus, the Greek god of dreams—was introduced at about the time of the U.S. Civil War. Morphine, a powerful opium derivative, was used liberally to deaden pain from wounds. Physiological dependence on morphine became known as the "soldier's disease." There was little stigma attached to dependence until morphine became a restricted substance.

Heroin Ironically, **heroin** was so named because, when it was derived, it was purported to make people feel "heroic." It was also hailed as the "hero" that would cure physiological dependence on morphine. Heroin was developed in 1875 during a search for a drug that would relieve pain as effectively as morphine, but without causing addiction. Chemist Heinrich Dreser transformed morphine into a new and stronger miracle drug, heroin, by means of a minor chemical change. He believed, erroneously, that heroin did not create physiological dependence.

TRUTH *or* **FICTION** REVISITED

9.5 True. Heroin was developed during a search for a drug that would relieve pain as effectively as morphine, but without causing physical addiction.

Heroin, like the other opioids, is a powerful depressant that can provide a euphoric rush. Users of heroin claim it is so pleasurable it can eradicate any thought of food or sex. Soon after its initial appearance, heroin was used to treat so many problems that it became known as GOM ("God's own medicine").

By the 1990s, 1.3% of the U.S. population aged 12 and over, or nearly 3 million people, had used heroin in their lifetimes and at least 700,000 had used it during the past year (USDHHS, 1991c; 1993). These estimates may be on the low side because they are based on surveys of households, and heroin users may not be household members.

Heroin is usually injected either directly beneath the skin (skin popping) or into a vein (mainlining). The positive effects are immediate. There is a powerful rush that lasts

Shooting up. Heroin users often inject the substance directly into their veins. Heroin is a powerful depressant that provides a euphoric rush. Users often claim that heroin is so pleasurable that it obliterates any thought of food or sex. At the turn of the century, heroin was used to treat so many problems that it was often referred to as G.O.M. ("God's own medicine").

from 5 to 15 minutes and a state of satisfaction, euphoria, and well-being that lasts from 3 to 5 hours. In this state, all positive drives seem satisfied. All negative feelings of guilt, tension, and anxiety disappear. With prolonged usage, addiction can develop. Many physiologically dependent people support their habits through dealing (selling heroin), prostitution, or selling stolen goods. Heroin is a depressant, however, and its chemical effects do not directly stimulate criminal or aggressive behavior.

The withdrawal syndrome associated with dependence on opioids can be severe. It begins within 4 to 6 hours of the last dose. Flulike symptoms are accompanied by anxiety, feelings of restlessness, irritability, and cravings for the drug. Within a few days, symptoms progress to rapid pulse, high blood pressure, cramps, tremors, hot and cold flashes, fever, vomiting, insomnia, and diarrhea, among other symptoms. Although these symptoms can be uncomfortable, they are usually not devastating, especially when other drugs are prescribed to relieve them. Moreover, unlike withdrawal from barbiturates, the withdrawal syndrome rarely results in death.

STIMULANTS

Stimulants such as amphetamines and cocaine are psychoactive substances that increase the activity of the nervous system. Effects vary somewhat from drug to drug, but some stimulants contribute to feelings of euphoria and self-confidence. Stimulants such as amphetamines, cocaine, and even caffeine (the stimulant found in coffee) increase the availability in the brain of the neurotransmitters norepinephrine and dopamine. High levels of these neurotransmitters therefore remain available to the nervous system, causing continuous states of high arousal.

Amphetamines

The **amphetamines** are a class of synthetic stimulants. They produce high states of arousal by stimulating the release of the neurotransmitters norepinephrine and dopamine and by interfering with their reuptake. Street names for stimulants include speed, uppers, bennies (for *amphetamine sulfate;* trade name Benzedrine), "meth" (for *methamphetamine;* trade name Methedrine), and dexies (for *dextroamphetamine;* trade name Dexedrine). Slightly less than 2% of the adult population surveyed in the multisite Epidemiologic Catchment Area (ECA) study had an amphetamine abuse or dependence disorder during their lifetimes (Anthony & Helzer, 1991).

Amphetamines are used in high doses for their euphoric rush. The stimulant methylphenidate (trade name Ritalin), used in the treatment of childhood hyperactivity, is a chemical cousin of the amphetamines. Amphetamines are often taken in pill form or smoked in a relatively pure form called "ice" or "crystal meth." The most potent form of amphetamine, liquid methamphetamine, is injected directly into the veins and produces an intense and immediate rush. Some users inject methamphetamine for days on end to maintain an extended high. Eventually such highs come to an end. People who have been on extended highs sometimes "crash" and fall into a deep sleep or depression. Some people commit suicide on the way down. High doses can cause restlessness, irritability, hallucinations, paranoid delusions, loss of appetite, and insomnia.

Physical dependence leads to the development of an abstinence syndrome characterized most often by depression and fatigue, as well as by unpleasant, vivid dreams, insomnia or hypersomnia (excessive sleeping), increased appetite, and either a slowing down of motor behavior or agitation (APA, 1994). Psychological dependence is seen most often among people who use amphetamines as a way of coping with stress or depression.

Violent behavior may occur in the context of an amphetamine dependence, especially when the drug is smoked or injected intravenously (APA, 1994). The hallucinations and delusions of the **amphetamine psychosis** mimic the features of paranoid schizophrenia, which has encouraged researchers to study the chemical changes induced by amphetamines as possible causes of schizophrenia.

Cocaine

Do you remember the Coca-Cola commercials proclaiming that "Coke adds life"? Because of its sugar and caffeine content, Coca-Cola should grant quite a boost. But "Coke"—Coca-Cola, that is—has not been "the real thing" since 1906. In that year the company withdrew **cocaine** from its secret formula. Coca-Cola was first brewed by a pharmacist, John Styth Pemberton, in 1886. Pemberton described his product as a "brain tonic and intellectual beverage," in part because of its cocaine content. Cocaine is a natural stimulant extracted from the leaves of the coca plant—the plant from which the soft drink obtained its name. Coca-Cola is still flavored with an extract from the coca plant, one that is not known to be psychoactive.

TRUTH **or** FICTION REVISITED

9.6. True. The original formula for *Coca-Cola* contained an extract of cocaine.

Ingestion of coca leaves has a long history among the peoples of the coca-growing regions of South America. The Inca Indians used coca to help them endure physical labor with little sleep or food (R. D. Weiss & Mirin, 1987). Europeans began to experiment with cocaine following the extraction of the drug from coca leaves in the mid-19th century. One of the prominent early advocates of cocaine, at least initially, was Sigmund Freud. As did the Incas, he found that cocaine enabled people to work longer without sleep or food. In addition to enhancing performance, cocaine heightens vigilance and bolsters confidence, properties that have made it popular among professional athletes.

Freud's recognition of cocaine's analgesic qualities blazed the path to its use as the first local anesthetic. Freud changed his views on cocaine when he learned it was powerfully habit forming. Other notables of the late 19th and early 20th centuries who also endorsed cocaine included H. G. Wells, Thomas Edison, and Jules Verne, as well as kings, queens, and even two popes (R. D. Weiss & Mirin, 1987). Societal attitudes, like Freud's views, shifted in the early 20th century against cocaine use, based on increasing awareness of its habit-forming properties.

It was long believed that cocaine was not physically addicting. However, evidence now points to the addictive properties of the drug in producing a tolerance effect and an identifiable withdrawal syndrome, consisting of depression, inability to experience pleasure, and intense cravings for the drug (APA, 1994; Gawin & Ellinwood, 1988). Withdrawal symptoms are usually brief in duration and may involve a "crash," or period of intense depression and exhaustion following a cocaine binge.

Cocaine is brewed from coca leaves as a "tea," breathed in ("snorted") in powder form, and injected ("shot up") in liquid form. The rise in the use of **crack,** a hardened form of cocaine suitable for smoking that may contain more than 75% pure cocaine, has made cocaine—once the toy of the well-to-do—available to adolescents. Crack "rocks"—so called because they look like small white pebbles—are available in small ready-to-smoke amounts and considered to be the most habit-forming street drug available (R. D. Weiss & Mirin, 1987). Crack produces a prompt and potent rush that wears off in a few minutes. The rush from snorting is milder and takes a while to develop, but it tends to linger longer than the rush of crack.

Freebasing also intensifies the effects of cocaine. Cocaine in powder form is heated with ether, freeing the psychoactive

Crack. Crack "rocks" resemble small, white pebbles. Crack produces a powerful, prompt rush when smoked. Small, ready-to-smoke doses are available at prices that have made them affordable to adolescents.

chemical base of the drug, and then smoked. Ether, however, is highly flammable.

Next to marijuana, cocaine is the most widely used illicit drug in the United States. By 1991, more than 1 in 10 Americans had tried cocaine and about 1% were current users. Males were about twice as likely to be current users as females (USDHHS, 1993). Nearly 3% (2.7%) of adults in the United States in the 15- to 54-year age range have a history of dependence on cocaine (Anthony, Warner, & Kessler, 1994). Cocaine abuse is characterized by periodic binges lasting perhaps 12 to 36 hours, which are then followed by 2 to 5 days of abstinence, during which time the abuser may experience cravings that prompt another binge (Gawin et al., 1989). According to one estimate, between 10% and 15% of people who try snorting cocaine eventually develop cocaine abuse or dependence (Gawin, 1991).

The cocaine epidemic may have peaked in some respects (see Table 9.1, showing declining use among college students). Although the numbers of casual users of cocaine appear to be declining, there has been no corresponding reduction in the numbers of hard-core users.

The change in casual cocaine use is so dramatic that some officials have even suggested the crack and cocaine epidemics are over, at least for middle-class youth. However, use of illicit drugs, including cocaine, among high school dropouts is more entrenched (Gfroerer, Greenblatt, & Wright, 1997).

Effects of Cocaine Cocaine increases the availability in the brain of the neurotransmitter dopamine, producing a

pleasurable "high" (Volkow et al., 1997). Cocaine stimulates an abrupt rise in blood pressure, constriction of blood vessels (with associated reduction of the oxygen supply to the heart), and acceleration of heart rate. Overdoses can produce restlessness, insomnia, headaches, nausea, convulsions, tremors, hallucinations, delusions, and even sudden death. Death may result from respiratory or cardiovascular collapse. Although intravenous use of cocaine carries the greatest risk of a lethal overdose, other forms of use can also cause fatal overdoses. Table 9.3 summarizes a number of the health risks of cocaine use.

Repeated and high-dose use of cocaine can also give rise to depression and anxiety (Weiss & Mirin, 1987). Depression may be severe enough to prompt suicidal behavior. Both initial and routine users report episodes of "crashing" (feelings of depression after a binge), although crashing is more common among long-term high-dose users. Psychotic behaviors, which can be induced by cocaine use as well as by use of amphetamines, tend to become more severe with continued use. Cocaine psychosis is usually preceded by a period of heightened suspiciousness, depressed mood, compulsive behavior, fault finding, irritability, and increasing paranoia (Weiss & Mirin, 1987). The psychosis may include visual and auditory hallucinations and delusions of persecution, as described in the following case:

> *After a while, I was convinced that there were people trying to break into my house. I didn't know who they were, but I was sure that people were after me. There was probably some reality to it too, since I really was scared that the police would come in and bust me. The only way that I felt that I could protect myself was by getting a knife. So I started sleeping with a butcher knife next to me. That didn't work for long, though, because I still felt insecure. So I felt that I had to get a gun. Every night, I went to bed with a gun on one side of me and a butcher knife on the other side. I was just waiting for someone to come in the house so that I could blow his brains out. God knows what I was going to do with the knife. I swear, I was a maniac. It wouldn't have mattered who had come to the door. If someone had come to my door at the wrong time to borrow a cup of sugar, I can tell you with 100 percent certainty, he would have been dead.*
>
> R. D. WEISS AND MIRIN, 1987, P. 39

Violence may occur as self-defense against delusional persecutors. Tactile hallucinations, for example, of bugs crawling under the skin, may cause the user to pick at the skin until scabs form. The risk of cocaine-induced psychosis increases with chronicity and dosage levels.

Nicotine

Habitual smoking is not just a bad habit. It is also a form of physical addiction to a stimulant drug, nicotine, found in

TABLE 9.3
Health Risks of Cocaine Use

Physical Effects and Risks

Effects	Risks
1. Increased heart rate	Accelerated heart rate may give rise to heart irregularities that can be fatal, such as ventricular tachycardia (extremely rapid contractions) or ventricular fibrillation (irregular, weakened contractions).
2. Increased blood pressure	Rapid or large changes in blood pressure may place too much stress on a weak-walled blood vessel in the brain, which can cause it to burst, producing cerebral hemorrhage or stroke.
3. Increased body temperature	Can be dangerous to some individuals.
4. Possible grand mal seizures (epileptic convulsions)	Some grand mal seizures are fatal, particularly when they occur in rapid succession or while driving a car.
5. Respiratory effects	Overdoses can produce gasping or shallow irregular breathing that can lead to respiratory arrest.
6. Dangerous effects in special populations	Various special populations are at greater risk from cocaine use or overdose. People with coronary heart disease have died because their heart muscles were taxed beyond the capacity of their arteries to supply oxygen.

Medical Complications of Cocaine Use

Nasal Problems	When cocaine is administered intranasally (snorted), it constricts the blood vessels serving the nose, decreasing the supply of oxygen to these tissues, leading to irritation and inflammation of the mucous membranes, ulcers in the nostrils, frequent nosebleeds, and chronic sneezing and nasal congestion. Chronic use may lead to tissue death of the nasal septum, the part of the nose that separates the nostrils, requiring plastic surgery.
Lung Problems	Freebase smoking may lead to serious lung problems within 3 months of initial use.
Malnutrition	Cocaine suppresses the appetite so that weight loss, malnutrition, and vitamin deficiencies may accompany regular use.
Seizures	Grand mal seizures, typical of epileptics, may occur due to irregularities in the electrical activity of the brain. Repeated use may lower the seizure threshold, described as a type of "kindling" effect.
Sexual Problems	Despite the popular belief that cocaine is an aphrodisiac, frequent use can lead to sexual dysfunctions, such as impotence and failure to ejaculate among males, and decreased sexual interest in both sexes. Although some people report initial increased sexual pleasure with cocaine use, they may become dependent on cocaine for sexual arousal or lose the ability to enjoy sex for extended periods following long-term use.
Other Effects	Cocaine use may increase the risk of miscarriage among pregnant women. Sharing of infected needles is associated with transmission of hepatitis, endocarditis (infection of the heart valve), and HIV. Repeated injections often lead to skin infections as bacteria are introduced into the deeper levels of the skin.

Source: Adapted from R. D. Weiss & Mirin, 1987.

tobacco products including cigarettes, cigars and smokeless tobacco (D. A. Kessler et al., 1997). Smoking (or other tobacco uses) are the means of administering the drug to the body.

TRUTH *or* FICTION REVISITED

9.7 *False.* Habitual smoking leads to the development of a physical addiction to nicotine, a stimulant drug found in tobacco.

More than 400,000 lives in the United States are lost each year from smoking-related causes, mostly from lung cancer, cardiovascular disease, and chronic obstructive lung disease (Darnton, 1994; Fried et al., 1998; USDHHS, 1982, 1991a). This figure is nearly eight times the number who die from motor vehicle accidents and is about equal to the population of a city the size of Atlanta, Georgia. Smoking is implicated in 1 in 3 cancer deaths, including more than 100,000 deaths due to lung cancer (Boyle, 1993). Smokers overall stand double the risk of dying from cancer as nonsmokers; among heavy smokers, the risk is four times as great (Bartecchi, MacKenzie, & Schrier, 1994).

The World Health Organization estimates that 1 billion people across the world smoke, while more than 3 million

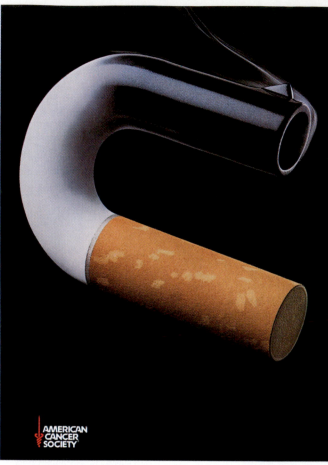

Changing times. Only a couple of generations ago, cigarette advertisements featured medical doctors recommending the beneficial effects of certain brands. Today, of course, the powerful links between smoking, cancer, and other physical disorders have become widely publicized, as suggested by the American Cancer Society poster. Camels used to advertise, "I'd walk a mile for a Camel." Many heavy smokers, sad to say, wish they felt well enough to walk a mile.

die annually from smoking-related causes ("As smoking goes passé in U.S.," 1997). Smoking is expected to become the world's leading cause of death by the year 2020 ("Smoking Will Be World's Biggest Killer," 1996).

We are losing the battle against teenage smoking. From 1991 to 1997, smoking rates among high school students jumped by a third (B. J. Feder, 1996; Stolberg, 1998b). The greatest increase in teenage cigarette smoking was among African Americans, up by 80%. Overall, about 40% of White male and female teens in 1997 reported smoking, as compared to 28% of Black males and 17% of Black females, and about 35% of Hispanic males and 33% of Hispanic females. It is estimated that about 3,000 American youngsters begin smoking each day. One in three of them will eventually die of a smoking-related cause.

Cigarette smoking causes cancer of the larynx, oral cavity, esophagus, and lungs and may contribute to cancer of the bladder, pancreas, and kidneys. Pregnant women who smoke risk miscarriage, premature birth, and birth defects in their offspring. Smokers stand twice the risk of developing Alzheimer's disease and other forms of dementia as non-smokers ("Extinguishing Alzheimer's," 1998). Lung cancer, which is caused in perhaps 90% of cases by smoking, has now surpassed breast cancer as the leading killer of women. Although quitting smoking clearly has health benefits, it unfortunately does not reduce the risks to normal (nonsmoking) levels. The lesson is clear: If you don't smoke, don't start. But if you do smoke, quit. **Passive smoking**, or secondhand smoking, is also associated with increased risks of respiratory illnesses, heart attacks, and other health problems in nonsmokers (USDHHS, 1991a).

TRUTH *or* FICTION REVISITED

9.8 *False.* Lung cancer has surpassed breast cancer as the leading cancer killer among women. It is also the leading cancer killer among men. Cigarette smoking is the culprit in the great majority of cases.

Largely because of health concerns, the percentage of Americans who smoke declined from 42% in 1966 to about 25% today (W. R. Miller & Brown, 1997). By the mid-1990s, however, smoking rates in the United States had leveled off in the general population but, as noted, had risen sharply among teenagers, reversing an earlier decline (Hilts, 1995; USDHHS, 1994). Cigarette advertising in magazines that appeal to young people may be a contributing factor to teen smoking (C. King et al., 1998).

Though the gap is narrowing, smoking rates among Black teens remain lower than among their White counterparts (Hilts, 1995; Meier, 1997). For adults, however, the prevalence of smoking is higher among African Americans—about 32% (see Figure 9.3)—than Hispanic Americans (28%), non-Hispanic Whites (27%), or Asian/Pacific Islanders (27%). The highest prevalence among men, however, is among Native Americans (36%). With the exception of Native Americans, women in each ethnic group are less likely to smoke than their male counterparts (Figure 9.3).

A profile of smokers is found in Figure 9.4. Smoking is becoming increasingly concentrated among the poorer and less well-educated segments of the population.

Components of Tobacco Smoke

When you light up a cigarette, you set off a chemical reaction that releases more than 4,000 chemical compounds into your body, including many that are carcinogenic (cancer causing). Several of the constituents of tobacco smoke are *carbon monoxide, hydrocarbons* (or *"tars"*), and *nicotine*.

Oxygen is transported through the bloodstream by **hemoglobin**. When carbon monoxide combines with hemoglobin, however, it lessens the blood's capacity to supply oxygen to the body, which can deprive vital body organs, including the heart, of the oxygen they require and lead to shortness of breath. **Hydrocarbons,** a thick sticky residue in tobacco smoke, contains hundreds of chemical compounds that blacken the lungs and can lead to cancerous growths.

Nicotine is a stimulant drug found in tobacco. It increases alertness but can give rise to cold, clammy skin, nausea and vomiting, dizziness and faintness, and diarrhea—all of which account for the discomforts of novice smokers. Nicotine also induces a discharge of epinephrine, which generates a rush of autonomic activity including rapid heartbeat and release of stores of sugar into the blood. Nicotine quells the appetite and provides a sort of psychological "kick" (Grunberg, 1991). Nicotine also leads to the release of endorphins, the opiate-like hormones produced in the brain. This may account for the pleasurable feelings associated with tobacco use.

Nicotine Dependence

Each puff of a cigarette or use of another tobacco product (such as pipe or cigar smoking, or smokeless tobacco) introduces a highly addictive drug, nicotine, into the bloodstream. Habitual use of nicotine leads to a physiological dependence on the drug (Lichtenstein & Glasgow, 1992). Nicotine dependence is associated with both tolerance (intake rises to a level of a pack or two a day before leveling off) and a characteristic withdrawal syndrome. The withdrawal syndrome for nicotine includes such features as lack of energy, depressed mood, irritability, frustration, nervousness, impaired concentration,

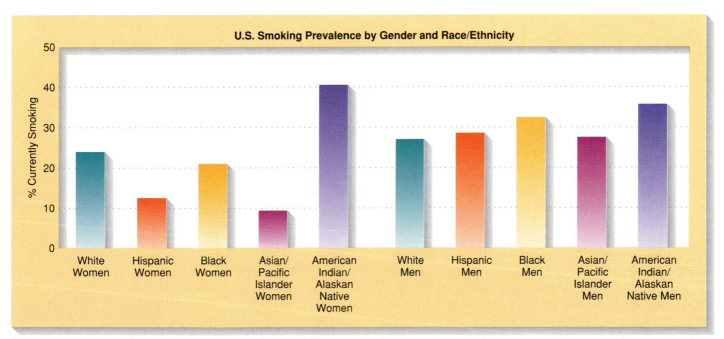

FIGURE 9.3 *Current U.S. cigarette smokers among people 18 years of age and above, according to gender and race ethnicity.*
The prevalences of smoking are highest for Native American men and women. Women in each ethnic group (with the exception of Native Americans) are less likely to smoke than their male counterparts. The rates for non-Hispanic White American men and women are comparable.

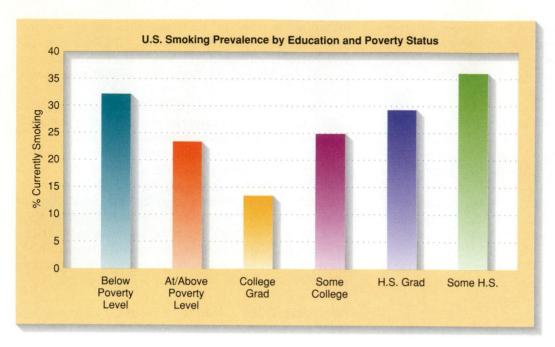

U.S. Smoking Prevalence by Education and Poverty Status

FIGURE 9.4 *Cigarette smokers in the United States, according to poverty status and level of education.*
Smoking is becoming increasingly more prevalent among the poorer and less educated members of society.

Source: Centers for Disease Control (1994). Cigarette smoking among adults—United States, 1993. *Morbidity and Mortality Weekly Report, 43,* 925-930.

light-headedness and dizziness, drowsiness, headaches, fatigue, irregular bowels, insomnia, cramps, lowered heart rate, heart palpitations, increased appetite, weight gain, sweating, tremors, and craving for cigarettes (APA, 1994; Klesges et al. 1997). It is nicotine dependence, not cigarette smoking per se, that is classifiable as a mental disorder in the DSM system. Although not all smokers become addicted to nicotine, between 50% and 80% of smokers are believed to meet diagnostic criteria for nicotine dependence (APA, 1994).

HALLUCINOGENS

Hallucinogens, also known as **psychedelics,** are a class of drugs that produce sensory distortions or hallucinations. There are major alterations in color perception and hearing. Various hallucinogenics may also have additional effects, such as relaxation and euphoria, or, in some cases, panic.

The hallucinogenics include such drugs as lysergic acid diethylamide (LSD), psilocybin, and mescaline. Psychoactive substances that are similar in effect to psychedelic drugs are marijuana (cannabis) and phencyclidine (PCP). Mescaline is derived from the peyote cactus and has been used for centuries by Native Americans in the Southwest, Mexico, and Central America in religious ceremonies, as has psilocybin, which is derived from certain mushrooms. LSD, PCP, and marijuana are more commonly used in North America.

Although tolerance to hallucinogens may develop, we lack evidence of a consistent or characteristic withdrawal syndrome associated with their use (APA, 1994). Cravings following withdrawal may occur, however. The lifetime prevalence of hallucinogen use disorders (hallucinogen abuse or dependence) was found to be 0.4% (4 people in 1,000) in the adult population, according to the ECA multisite survey (Anthony & Helzer, 1991).

LSD

LSD is the acronym for lysergic acid diethylamide, a synthetic hallucinogenic drug that was discovered by the Swiss chemist Albert Hoffman in 1938. Hoffman penned his initial experience with LSD as follows:

> I was forced to stop my work in the laboratory . . . and to go home, as I was seized by a particular restlessness associated with the sensation of mild dizziness. On arriving home, I lay down and sank into a kind of drunkenness which was not unpleasant and which was characterized by extreme activity of imagination. As I lay in a dazed condition with my eyes closed (I experienced daylight as disagreeably bright) there surged upon me an uninterrupted stream of fantastic images of extraordinary plasticity and vividness and accompanied by an intense, kaleidoscope-like play of colours. This condition gradually passed off after about two hours. (Hoffman, 1971, p. 23)

In addition to the vivid parade of colors and visual distortions produced by LSD, users have claimed it "expands consciousness" and opens new worlds—as if they were looking into some reality beyond the usual reality. Sometimes they believe they have achieved great insights during the LSD "trip," but when it wears off they usually cannot implement or even summon up these discoveries.

LSD apparently decreases the action of serotonin, a neurotransmitter that inhibits neural firing. LSD may also increase utilization of dopamine. Because LSD curbs the action of an inhibiting neurotransmitter and increases dopamine activity, brain activity escalates, in this case giving rise to a flurry of colorful sensations or hallucinations.

The effects of LSD are unpredictable and depend on the amount taken as well as the user's expectations, personality, mood, and surroundings (USDHHS, 1992). The user's prior

An LSD "trip." LSD is an hallucinogenic drug that gives rise to a vivid parade of colors and visual distortions. Some users have claimed to have achieved great insights while "tripping," but when the drug wears off, they usually cannot summon up or make use of these "insights."

experiences with the drug may also play a role, as users who have learned to handle the effects of the drug through past experience may be better prepared than new users.

Some users have unpleasant experiences with the drug, or "bad trips." Feelings of intense fear or panic may occur (USDHHS, 1992). Users may fear losing control or sanity. Some experience terrifying fears of death. Fatal accidents have sometimes occurred during LSD trips. **Flashbacks,** typically involving a reexperiencing of some of the perceptual distortions of the "trip," may occur days, weeks, or even years afterward. Flashbacks tend to occur suddenly and often without warning. They may stem from chemical changes in the brain caused by the prior use of the drug. Triggers for flashbacks include entry into darkened environments, use of various drugs, anxiety or fatigue states, or stress (APA, 1994). Psychological factors, such as underlying personality problems, may also be involved in explaining why some users experience flashbacks. In some cases, a flashback may involve an imaginal reenactment of the LSD experience (Matefy, 1980).

Phencyclidine (PCP)

PCP—referred to as "angel dust" on the streets—was developed as an anesthetic in the 1950s but was discontinued as such when the hallucinatory side effects of the drug were discovered. A smokable form of PCP became popular as a street drug in the 1970s because it was readily manufactured and relatively inexpensive. By the mid-1980s, more than 1 in 5 young people aged 18 to 25 years had used PCP (USDHHS, 1986c). However, its popularity has since waned, largely because of its unpredictable effects.

The effects of PCP, like most drugs, are dose related. In addition to causing hallucinations, PCP accelerates the heart rate and blood pressure and causes sweating, flushing, and numbness. PCP is classified as a *deliriant*—a drug capable of producing states of delirium. It also has dissociating effects, causing users to feel as if there is some sort of invisible barrier or wall between themselves and their environments. Dissociation can be experienced as pleasant, engrossing, or frightening, depending on the user's expectations, mood, setting, and so on. Overdoses can give rise to drowsiness and a blank stare, convulsions, and, now and then, coma; paranoia and aggressive behavior; and tragic accidents resulting from perceptual distortion or impaired judgment during states of intoxication.

Marijuana

Marijuana is produced from the *Cannabis sativa* plant. Marijuana helps some people to relax; others to elevate their moods. Marijuana sometimes produces mild hallucinations, so it is regarded as a minor hallucinogenic. The psychoactive substance in marijuana is **delta-9-tetrahydrocannabinol,** or THC. THC is found in branches and leaves of the plant but is highly concentrated in the resin of the female plant. **Hashish,** or "hash," is also derived from the resin. Although it is more potent than marijuana, hashish has similar effects.

Use of marijuana exploded throughout the so-called swinging sixties and the 1970s, but the drug then lost some (but not all) of its cachet. The numbers of people using the drug declined by more than a third during the 1980s (Treaster, 1991b). Still, marijuana remains our most widely used illegal drug, although its prevalence doesn't compare with alcohol's. Approximately 33% of people in the United States age 12 or older, nearly 70 million people, have tried marijuana at least once in their lives, and 5% are current users (USDHHS, 1993).

Marijuana dependence is the most common form of dependence on illicit drugs in the United States, affecting an estimated 4.2% of the adult population at some point in their lives (Anthony, Warner, & Kessler, 1994). Males are more likely than females to develop a marijuana use disorder (either abuse or dependence), and the prevalences of these disorders is greatest among young people age 18 to 30 (APA, 1994).

Psychoactive Effects of Marijuana Low doses of the drug can produce relaxing feelings similar to drinking a highball of liquor. Some users report that at low doses the drug makes them feel more comfortable in social gatherings. Higher doses, however, often lead users to withdraw into themselves. Some users believe the drug increases their capacity for self-insight or creative thinking, although the insights achieved under its influence may not seem so insightful once the drug's effects have passed. People may turn to marijuana, as to other drugs, to help them cope with life problems or to help them function when they are under stress. Strongly intoxicated people perceive time as passing more slowly. A song of a few minutes may seem to last an hour. There is increased awareness of bodily sensations, such as heartbeat. Smokers also report that strong intoxication heightens sexual sensations. Visual hallucinations may occur.

Strong intoxication can cause smokers to become disoriented. If their moods are euphoric, disorientation may be construed as harmony with the universe. Yet some smokers find strong intoxication disturbing. An accelerated heart rate and sharpened awareness of bodily sensations cause some smokers to fear their hearts will "run away" with them. Some smokers are frightened by disorientation and fear they will not "come back." High levels of intoxication now and then induce nausea and vomiting.

Marijuana dependence is associated more with patterns of compulsive use or psychological dependence than with physiological dependence. Although tolerance to many of the drug's effects may occur with chronic use, some users report reverse tolerance or sensitization. A withdrawal syndrome has not been reliably demonstrated (APA, 1994). However, new research with animals points to some disturbing similarities between marijuana and addictive drugs such as heroin and cocaine (Wickelgren, 1997). In one study researchers found that withdrawal from marijuana activated the same brain circuits involved in withdrawal from opiates, alcohol, and cocaine (Rodríguez de Fonseca et al., 1997). These brain circuits are also involved in producing feelings of anxiety when an animal or person is under stress (Blakeslee, 1997a). In another study, researchers determined that marijuana activated the same reward circuits in the brain as heroin (Tanda, Pontieri, & Di Chiara, 1997). Although these studies were conducted with animals, researchers believe that the underlying biological mechanisms may apply to humans as well (Blakeslee, 1997a).

College students who are heavy users of marijuana show evidence of cognitive impairment, including diminished ability in tasks requiring attention, abstraction, and mental flexibility (H. G. Pope & Yurgelun-Todd, 1996). However, it is unclear whether these deficits are due to the drug or to characteristics of people who become heavy users (T. H. Lee, 1996). We do know that marijuana impairs perception and motor coordination and thus makes driving and the operation of other machines dangerous. It also impairs short-term memory and retards learning ability. Although it induces positive mood changes in many users, some people report anxiety and confusion; there are also occasional reports of psychotic reactions. Marijuana elevates the heart rate to about 140 to 150 beats per minute and, in some people, raises the blood pressure. These changes are particularly taxing to people with hypertension and heart disease. Finally, marijuana smoke contains high amounts of cancer-causing substances.

THEORETICAL PERSPECTIVES

People begin using psychoactive substances for various reasons. Some adolescents start using drugs because of peer pressure or because they believe that drugs make them seem more sophisticated or grown up. Some use drugs as a way of rebelling against their parents or society at large. Regardless of why people get started with drugs, they continue to use them because they produce pleasurable effects or because they find it difficult to stop. For example, most adolescents drink alcohol to "get high," not to establish that they are adults. Many people smoke cigarettes for the pleasure they provide. Others smoke to help them relax when they are tense and, paradoxically, to give them a kick or a lift when they are tired. Yet many would like to quit but find it difficult to break their addiction.

People who are anxious about their jobs or social lives may be drawn to the calming effects of alcohol, marijuana (in certain doses), tranquilizers, and sedatives. People with low self-confidence and self-esteem may be drawn to the ego-bolstering effects of amphetamines and cocaine. Many poor young people attempt to escape the poverty, anguish, and tedium of inner-city life through heroin and similar drugs. More well-to-do adolescents may rely on drugs to manage the transition from dependence to independence and major life changes concerning jobs, college, and lifestyles.

In the next sections we consider several major theoretical perspectives on substance abuse and dependence.

Biological Perspectives

We are beginning to learn more about the biological underpinnings of addiction. Much of the recent research has focused on neurotransmitters, especially dopamine, and on the role of genetic factors.

Neurotransmitters   There appears to be a common pathway in the brain involving the neurotransmitter dopamine that may explain the pleasure-inducing effects of many drugs. Researchers suspect that drugs such as nicotine, alcohol, heroin, cocaine, and even marijuana produce pleasurable effects by increasing the levels of the neurotransmitter dopamine—the brain's "reward and reinforcing" agent (O'Brien & McLellan, 1997; Maldonado et al., 1997; Marzuk & Barchas, 1997; Michels & Marzuk, 1993; Volkow et al., 1997).

We know that laboratory rats will work for injections of cocaine by repetitively pressing a lever. They will continue to work for cocaine injections even if the neural pathways that use norepinephrine are destroyed. Their work effort plummets when the neural pathways for dopamine are destroyed (R. D. Weiss & Mirin, 1987). With repeated drug use over time, the brain's ability to make dopamine on its own can diminish, leading to cravings for drugs that will provide a steady supply of dopamine (Blakeslee, 1997a). This may explain the intense cravings and anxiety that accompany drug withdrawal and the difficulty people with chemical dependencies have maintaining abstinence.

Other neurotransmitters are also believed to be involved in drug use and abuse. Evidence points to the neurotransmitter serotonin playing a role in activating the brain's pleasure or reward circuits in response to use of cocaine and other drugs (Blakeslee, 1998; Rocha et al., 1998). We also know that endorphins, a group of neurotransmitters, have pain-blocking properties similar to opiates such as heroin. Endorphins and opiates dock at the same receptor sites in the brain. Normally, the brain produces a certain level of endorphins, which maintains a sort of psychological steady state of comfort and potential to experience pleasure. However, when the body becomes habituated to a supply of opiates, it may stop producing endorphins. This makes the user dependent on opiates for feelings of comfort, relief from pain, and feelings of pleasure. When the habitual user stops using heroin or other opiates, feelings of discomfort and little aches and pains may be magnified until the body resumes adequate production of endorphins. The discomfort this produces might underlie part of the withdrawal syndrome for opiates. This model remains speculative, as more research is needed to document direct relationships between endorphin production and withdrawal symptoms.

Genetic Factors Substance use disorders involving alcohol, opioids, cocaine, and even marijuana run in families (Bierut et al., 1998; Merikangas et al., 1998). For example, people with a family history of alcoholism are about three or four times more likely to develop alcohol abuse or dependence than others (APA, 1994; Schuckit & Smith, 1996). The closer the genetic relationship, the greater the risk of alcoholism. Familial patterns provide only suggestive evidence of genetic factors since families share common environment as well as common genes. More definitive evidence comes from twin and adoptee studies.

Monozygotic (MZ) twins have identical genes, whereas fraternal or dizygotic (DZ) twins share only half of their genes. If genetic factors are involved, we would expect MZ twins to have higher concordance (agreement) rates for alcoholism than DZ twins. The evidence for higher concordance rates for alcoholism among MZ twins than DZ twins is stronger for male twin pairs than female twin pairs, which indicates the genetic factors may be more strongly involved in alcoholism in males than females (Kendler et al., 1992d, 1994; Prescott et al., 1994; Svikis, Velez, & Pickens, 1994). Future research may help clarify these apparent gender differences.

Consistent with a genetic contribution, studies show that male adoptees whose biological parents suffered from alcoholism have an increased risk of developing alcoholism even if they are raised in nondrinking homes (Gordis, 1995; Schuckit, 1987). Among women, however, the rate of alcoholism in adopted-away daughters of parents with alco-

holism is only slightly higher than that for adopted-away daughters of nonalcoholics, thus casting doubt on a strong genetic linkage to alcoholism in women (Svikis, Velez, & Pickens, 1994). All in all, genetic factors are believed to play a moderate role in male alcoholism and a modest role in female alcoholism (McGue, 1993).

Other research on twin pairs shows genetic contributions to a wide range of substance abuse problems, including heroin, marijuana, and stimulant abuse (Tsuang et al., 1998). Whatever the role of heredity in substance use disorders may be, genes alone do not determine whether someone will develop an addictive disorder (Goldman & Bergen, 1998). Even among people with the same genes (identical twins), one may develop an alcohol or drug abuse or dependence disorder while the other may not. Genes interact with environmental factors, including peer pressure and modeling influences, in determining the risk of addictive disorders.

If alcoholism or other forms of substance abuse and dependence are influenced by genetic factors, what is it that is inherited? Some clues have begun to emerge. Researchers have linked alcoholism and opiate addiction to genes involved in determining the structure of dopamine receptors in the brain (Kotler, 1997). Dopamine is involved in regulating states of pleasure, so researchers suspect that genetic factors may enhance the pleasure derived from alcohol and hence increase cravings for the drug (Altman, 1990a). In all likelihood there is no one "alcoholism gene" but a set of genes that interact with each other and with environmental factors to increase the risk of alcoholism (CNN, 1998a; Devor, 1994). Other evidence suggests that a genetic vulnerability to alcoholism may involve a combination of reaping greater pleasure from alcohol and a capacity for greater biological tolerance for the drug (Pihl, Peterson, & Finn, 1990; Pollock, 1992). Recent evidence also points to a genetic role in the likelihood of smoking and development of nicotine dependence (Carmelli, Swan, Robinette, & Fabstitz, 1992; Lerman et al., 1999; Sabol et al., 1999). Again, genes involving dopamine are implicated, which may be involved in producing a greater sensitivity in some people to the pleasurable effects or reward value of nicotine.

Men who have immediate biological relatives (parents or siblings) with a history of alcoholism tend to metabolize alcohol more rapidly than do men without a history of alcoholism in their immediate families (Schuckit & Rayses, 1979). People who metabolize alcohol relatively quickly can tolerate larger doses and are less likely to develop upset stomachs, dizziness, and headaches when they drink. Unfortunately, a lower sensitivity to the unpleasant effects of alcohol may make it difficult to know when to say when. Thus, people who are better able to "hold their liquor" may be at greater risk of developing drinking problems. They may need to rely on other cues, such as counting their drinks, to learn to limit their drinking. People whose bodies more readily "put the brakes" on excess drinking may be less likely to develop problems in moderating their drinking than those with better tolerance.

TRUTH *or* **FICTION** REVISITED

9.9 False. Being able to "hold your liquor" may encourage you to drink more, which may set the stage for the development of problem drinking.

Learning Perspectives

Learning theorists propose that substance-related behaviors are largely learned and can, in principle, be unlearned. They focus on the roles of operant and classical conditioning and observational learning. Substance abuse problems are not regarded as symptoms of diseases but rather as problem habits. Although learning theorists do not deny that genetic or biological factors may be involved in the genesis of substance abuse problems, they place a greater emphasis on the role of learning in the development and maintenance of these problem behaviors (McCrady, 1993, 1994).

Operant Conditioning   Drug use may become habitual because of the pleasure or positive reinforcement that drugs produce. In the case of drugs such as cocaine, which appear capable of directly stimulating pleasure mechanisms in the brain, the reinforcement is direct and powerful (R. A. Wise, 1988). In animal studies, injection of psychoactive drugs such as cocaine has been made contingent on the performance of various tasks, such as pressing a lever (Weiss & Mirin, 1987). Laboratory animals will learn to press the lever repeatedly for cocaine. When cocaine reinforcement is then made intermittent, they will "work longer and harder" to attain it.

Researchers can estimate the reinforcing power of drugs by comparing the rates at which animals perform operant responses such as pressing a lever to receive them. Animals will perform to receive a wide range of drugs, including amphetamines, nicotine, barbiturates, opioids, alcohol, and PCP. Performance rates are most dramatic for cocaine, however. *Rhesus monkeys will work continuously for cocaine until they die* (Weiss & Mirin, 1987).

People may initially use a drug because of social influence, trial and error, or social observation. In the case of alcohol, they learn the drug can produce euphoria, reduce anxiety and tension, and release behavioral inhibitions. Alcohol can thus be reinforcing when it is used to combat depression (by producing euphoric feelings, even if short-lived), to combat tension (by functioning as a tranquilizer), or to help people sidestep moral conflicts (for example, by dulling awareness of moral prohibitions against sexual behavior or aggression). Social reinforcers are also made available by substance abuse, such as the approval of drug-abusing companions and, in the cases of depressants and stimulants, the (temporary) overcoming of social shyness.

Alcohol and Tension Reduction   Learning theorists have long maintained that one of the primary reinforcers for using alcohol is relief from states of tension. The tension-reduction theory proposes that the more often one drinks to reduce tension or anxiety, the stronger or more ha-

Self-medication?   People who turn to alcohol or drugs as a form of self-medication for anxiety or depression may wind-up only compounding their problems by developing a substance use disorder.

bitual the habit becomes. Viewed in this way, alcohol use can be likened to a form of self-medication, a way of easing psychological pain, at least temporarily.

Drugs, including nicotine from cigarette smoking, may also be used as a form of self-medication for depression (Breslau et al., 1998). Stimulants like nicotine temporarily elevate the mood, whereas depressants like alcohol quell anxiety. Although nicotine, alcohol, and other drugs may temporarily alleviate emotional distress, they cannot resolve underlying personal or emotional problems. Rather than learning to resolve these problems, people who use drugs as forms of self-medication often find themselves facing additional substance-related problems.

The tension-reduction theory of alcohol predicts that people who turn to alcohol to reduce tension will likely drink more as the level of stress in their lives mounts. Research suggests that the relationship between stress and alcohol may be moderated by psychological factors such as styles of coping and alcohol expectancies and by gender. One random survey of more than 1,000 adult drinkers revealed that drinking increased in relation to the level of stress among one group: men who tend to use avoidant forms of coping with stress and who have positive expectations about the effects of alcohol (M. L. Cooper et al., 1992). Avoidant coping involves the attempt to deny negative emotions or to try not to think about them. Positive alcohol expectancies involve beliefs that alcohol produces pleasure;

reduces anxiety and tension; and makes one more powerful, aggressive, and self-expressive. Men who had less positive expectations of alcohol and who were willing to face their negative feelings and cope with them more directly were actually *less* likely to drink under stress. Drinking in women was unrelated to stress, regardless of their style of coping or expectancies about alcohol.

Negative Reinforcement and Withdrawal

Once people become physiologically dependent, **negative reinforcement** comes into play in maintaining the drug habit. Resumption of drug use is negatively reinforced by relief from unpleasant withdrawal symptoms that occur when the person stops using the drug. The addicted smoker who quits cold turkey may shortly return to smoking to fend off the discomfort of withdrawal. Smokers who are able to quit and maintain abstinence are occasionally bothered by urges to smoke but have learned to manage them.

The Conditioning Model of Craving   Principles of classical conditioning may also help explain the cravings for drugs experienced by people with drug dependencies. Repeated exposure to the cues associated with drug use (such as the sight or aroma of an alcoholic beverage or the sight of a needle and syringe) can elicit conditioned responses in the form of alcohol or drug cravings (Drummond & Glautier, 1994). Cravings can be seen as conditioned responses rather than reflections of chemical deficiencies. They may be triggered by a wide range of cues (conditioned stimuli) that were previously associated with use of the substance. For example, socializing with certain companions ("drinking buddies") or even passing a liquor store may elicit conditioned cravings for alcohol. Sensations of anxiety or depression that were paired with use of alcohol or drugs may also elicit cravings. The following case illustrates conditioned cravings to environmental cues:

> A 29-year-old man was hospitalized for the treatment of heroin addiction. After four weeks of treatment, he returned to his former job, which required him to ride the subway past the stop at which he had previously bought his drugs. Each day, when the subway doors opened at this location, [he] experienced enormous craving for heroin, accompanied by tearing, a runny nose, abdominal cramps, and gooseflesh. After the doors closed, his symptoms disappeared, and he went on to work.
>
> WEISS & MIRIN, 1987, P. 71

Similarly, some people are primarily "stimulus smokers." They reach for a cigarette in the presence of smoking-related stimuli such as seeing someone smoke or smelling smoke. Smoking becomes a strongly conditioned habit because it is paired repeatedly with many situational cues—watching TV, finishing dinner, driving in the car, studying, drinking or socializing with friends, sex, and, for some, using the bathroom.

The conditioning model of craving is strengthened by research that shows that people who develop alcoholism tend to salivate more than others to the sight and smell of alcohol (Monti et al., 1987). In Pavlov's classic experiment, a salivation response was conditioned in dogs by repeatedly pairing the sound of a bell (a neutral or conditioned stimulus) with the presentation of food powder (an unconditioned stimulus). Salivation among people who develop alcoholism can also be viewed as a conditioned response to alcohol-related cues. Whereas salivating to a bell may be harmless, salivating at a bottle of Scotch, or at a picture of a bottle in a magazine ad, can throw the person who suffers from alcoholism and is trying to remain abstinent into a tailspin. People with drinking problems who show the greatest salivary response to alcohol cues may be at highest risk of relapse. They may also profit from treatments designed to extinguish their responses to alcohol-related cues.

One such treatment, called *cue exposure training,* holds promise in the treatment of alcohol dependence and other forms of addictive behavior (Drummond & Glautier, 1994; Monti et al., 1994). In cue exposure treatment, the person is repeatedly seated in front of the drug- or alcohol-related cues, such as open alcoholic beverages, while prevented from using the drug. This pairing of the cue (alcohol bottle) with nonreinforcement (by dint of preventing drinking) may lead to extinction of the conditioned craving. Cue exposure treatment may be combined with coping skills training to help people with substance abuse problems learn to cope with drug use urges without resorting to drug use (Monti et al., 1994). It has also been applied to helping nondependent problem drinkers learn to stop drinking after two or three drinks (Sitharthan et al., 1997).

Observational Learning   The role of modeling or observational learning may in part explain the increased risk of alcoholism among people with a family history of alcoholism. In one study, young men from families with a history of alcoholism were more strongly affected by exposure to others who modeled excessive drinking than were men without familial alcoholism (Chipperfield & Vogel-Sprott, 1988). Perhaps their parents had modeled excessive drinking, and they learned to regulate their own intake by observing the drinking behavior of others. When their drinking companions drink to excess, they may be more likely to follow their lead.

Cognitive Perspectives

Evidence supports the role of various cognitive factors in substance abuse and dependence, including expectancies, attitudes, beliefs, decision-making processes, and self-awareness.

Outcome Expectancies, Decision Making, and Substance Abuse   The beliefs and expectancies you hold concerning the effects of alcohol and other drugs clearly influence your decision to use them or not. People who hold positive expectancies about the effects of a drug

Peer pressure and drug use among peers is a major influence on adolescent drug use.

Outcome expectancies and alcohol abuse. People who hold more positive expectancies about the effects of alcohol may be at greater risk of developing a drinking problem. Positive expectancies include beliefs that alcohol enhances social skills, reduces worries, enhances sexual pleasure and performance, induces feelings of relaxation, and provides needed stimulation. What do the people in this picture expect from alcohol?

are not only more likely to use the drug (J.Schafer & Brown, 1991) but are also more likely to use larger quantities of the drug (Baldwin, Oei, & Young, 1994). One of the key factors in predicting problem alcohol use in adolescents is the degree to which their friends hold positive attitudes towards alcohol use (L. M. Scheier, Botvin, & Baker, 1997). Similarly, fifth and seventh graders who hold more positive impressions of smokers (for example, as cool, independent, or good looking) are more likely to become smokers by the time they reach the ninth grade than their peers (Dinh et al., 1995). Smoking prevention programs may need to focus on changing the image that young people hold of smokers long before they ever light up a cigarette themselves. Positive alcohol expectancies also appear in children even before drinking begins.

Among the most widely held expectancies concerning alcohol is that it reduces tension, helps divert attention from one's problems, heightens pleasure, and makes one more socially adept. In one study, alcohol expectancies were stronger predictors of the likelihood of drinking among adolescents than was family drinking history (B. A. Christiansen & Goldman, 1983). The belief that alcohol helps make a person more socially adept (more relaxed, outgoing, assertive, and carefree in social interactions) appears to be an especially important factor in prompting adolescent drinking (G. T. Smith et al., 1995). Expectancies that alcohol reduces states of tension are also linked to problem drinking in college students (S. A. Brown, 1985a, 1985b).

From a decision-making perspective, people choose whether or not to use drugs according to their weighing of the expected positive and negative consequences. Consider people with drinking problems who face the choice to drink or not to drink every day. They may be aware of the eventual

negative consequences of drinking (e.g., getting fired or divorced), but expectations of immediate relief from anxiety and feelings of pleasure may be more prominent at a given moment (Cox & Klinger, 1988). They thus decide to drink. The person with a drinking problem may or may not be aware of such decisions or of decisions to engage in the chain of behaviors that lead to problem drinking—such as whether or not to take a route from work that runs past a favorite watering hole.

Self-Efficacy Expectancies Part of the appeal of substances such as alcohol lies in their ability to enhance self-efficacy expectancies (beliefs in our ability to accomplish tasks) either directly (by enhancing feelings of energy, power, and well-being) or indirectly (by reducing stressful states of arousal, such as anxiety) (G. T. Wilson, 1987). Cocaine also enhances self-efficacy expectancies, an outcome sought in particular by performance-conscious athletes. People may therefore come to rely on substances in challenging situations where they doubt their abilities. Alcohol can also help protect one's sense of self-efficacy by shunting criticism for socially unacceptable behavior from the self to the alcohol. People who "screw up" while drinking can maintain their self-esteem by attributing their shortcomings to the alcohol.

Does One Slip Cause People with Substance Abuse or Dependence to Go on Binges? Perhaps What You Believe Is What You Get According to the disease model of alcoholism, abstainers who binge after just one drink do so largely for biochemical reasons. Experimental research, however, suggests that cognitive factors may be more important. In fact, the one-drink hypothesis may be explained by the drinker's expectancies rather than the biochemical properties of alcohol.

Studies of the one-drink hypothesis, like many other studies on alcohol, are made possible by the fact that the taste of vodka can be cloaked by tonic water. In a classic study by Marlatt, Demming, and Reid (1973), subjects were led to believe they were participating in a taste test. Alcohol-dependent subjects and social drinkers who were informed they were sampling an alcoholic beverage (vodka) drank significantly more than counterparts who were informed they were sampling a nonalcoholic beverage. The expectations of the alcohol-dependent subjects and the social drinkers alike turned out to be the crucial factors that predicted the amount consumed (see Figure 9.5). *The actual content of the beverages was immaterial.*

Marlatt (1978) explains the one-drink effect as a self-fulfilling prophecy. If people with alcohol-related problems believe just one drink will cause a loss of control, they perceive the outcome as predetermined when they drink. Their drinking—even taking one drink—may thus escalate into a binge. When individuals who were formerly physiologically dependent on alcohol share this belief—which is propounded by many groups, including AA—they may interpret "just one drink" as "falling off the wagon." Marlatt's point is that the "mechanism" of falling off the wagon due to one drink is cognitive, reflecting one's expectations about the effects of the drink, and not physiological. This expectation is an example of what Aaron Beck refers to as *absolutist thinking*. When we insist on seeing the world in black and white rather than shades of gray, we may interpret one bite of dessert as proof we are off our diets, or one cigarette as proof we are hooked again. Rather than telling ourselves, "Okay, I goofed, but that's it. I don't have to have more," we encode our lapses as catastrophes and transform them into relapses. Still, alcohol-dependent people who believe they may go on a drinking binge if they have just one drink are well advised to abstain rather than place themselves in a situation they feel they may not be able to manage.

Psychodynamic Perspectives

According to traditional psychodynamic theory, alcoholism reflects certain features of the oral-dependent personality. Alcoholism is, by definition, an oral behavior pattern. Psychodynamic theory connects immoderate drinking with other oral traits, such as dependence and depression, and

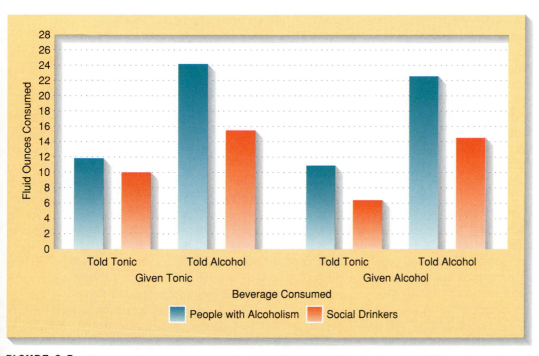

FIGURE 9.5 *Must people who develop alcoholism fall off the wagon if they have one drink?*
It is widely believed that people who develop alcoholism will lose control if they have just one drink. Will they? If so, why? Laboratory research by Marlatt and his colleagues suggests that the tendency of people who suffer from alcoholism to drink to excess following a first drink may be the result of a self-fulfilling prophecy rather than a craving. Like the dieter who eats a piece of chocolate, people who develop alcoholism may assume that they have lost control because they have fallen off the wagon and then go on a binge. This figure shows that people with alcoholism who participated in the Marlatt study drank more when they were led to believe that the beverage contained alcohol, regardless of its actual content. It remains unclear, however, whether binge drinking by people with alcohol-related problems in real-life settings can be explained as a self-fulfilling prophecy.

Source: Adapted from Marlatt et al. (1973).

traces the origins of these traits to fixation in the oral stage of psychosexual development. Excessive drinking in adulthood symbolizes efforts to attain oral gratification.

Psychodynamic theorists also view smoking as an oral fixation, although they have not been able to predict who will or will not smoke. Sigmund Freud smoked upward of 20 cigars a day despite several vain attempts to desist. Although he contracted oral cancer and had to have his jaw replaced, he would still not surrender his "oral fixation." He eventually succumbed to cancer of the mouth in 1939 at the age of 83, after years of agony.

Research support for these psychodynamic concepts is mixed. Although people who develop alcoholism often show dependent traits, it is unclear whether dependence contributes to or stems from problem drinking. Chronic drinking, for example, is connected with loss of employment and downward movement in social status, both of which would render drinkers more reliant on others for support. Moreover, an empirical connection between dependence and alcoholism does not establish that alcoholism represents an oral fixation due to unconscious childhood conflict.

Also, many—but certainly not all—people who suffer from alcoholism have antisocial personalities characterized by independence seeking as expressed through rebelliousness and rejection of social and legal codes (Graham & Strenger, 1988). All in all, there doesn't appear to be a single alcoholic personality (Sher & Trull, 1994).

Some theorists believe there are at least two subtypes of alcoholism: an anxious or neurotic subtype and an antisocial subtype (Sher & Trull, 1994). Cloninger (1987; Cloninger, Sigvardsson, & Bohman, 1996) labels these Type 1 and Type 2, respectively. Type 1 describes a type of alcoholism associated with an anxious or neurotic personality profile. People with this type become psychologically dependent on alcohol as a crutch to help them deal with stress or to calm their nerves. They tend to feel guilty about their drinking and are unlikely to get into fights because of their drinking or be arrested for alcohol-related offenses. The Type 2 profile describes people with alcoholism who fit an antisocial personality type. Found mainly among sons of men with alcoholism, people with this type of alcoholism are likely to be impulsive and become rowdy or aggressive when drinking. Though Type 1 and Type 2 alcoholism appear to be distinct forms of alcoholism, there appears to be a high degree of overlap between the two subtypes (Sigvardsson, Bohman, & Cloninger, 1996; Anthenelli et al., 1994; S. W. Glenn & Nixon, 1991). The Type 1–Type 2 distinction has also been extended to other substance use disorders such as cocaine abuse (S. A. Ball et al., 1995).

Sociocultural Perspectives

Cultural and religious factors are also related to consumption of alcohol and drugs. Rates of alcohol abuse vary across ethnic and religious groups (see earlier "Focus on Diversity" section). Let us note some other sociocultural factors. Church attendance, for example, is generally connected with abstinence from alcohol. Perhaps people who are more willing to engage in culturally sanctioned activities, such as churchgoing, are also more likely to adopt culturally sanctioned prohibitions against excessive drinking. Rates of alcohol use also vary across cultures. For example, alcohol use is greater in Germany than in the United States, apparently because of a cultural tradition that makes the consumption of alcohol, especially beer, normative within German society (Cockerham, Kuntz, & Lueschen, 1989).

Use of alcohol and drugs often occurs within a group or social setting. We go drinking with friends or entertain over drinks at home. A good wine list is a sign of class in a restaurant. Drinking is determined, in part, by where we live, whom we worship with, and by the social or cultural norms that regulate our behavior. Cultural attitudes can encourage or discourage problem drinking.

Peer pressure and peer drug use play important roles in use of alcohol and drugs among adolescents (Curran, Stice, & Chassin, 1997; Farrell & White, 1998). In a survey of 563 eleventh and twelfth graders from two southwestern communities, association with peers who used drugs was the single greatest predictor of drug usage (Swaim, Oetting, Edwards, & Beauvais, 1989). Yet studies of Hispanic and African American adolescents show that support from family members can reduce the negative influence of drug-using peers on adolescent's use of tobacco and other drugs (Farrell & White, 1998; Frauenglass et al., 1997).

TYING IT TOGETHER: FACTORS IN SUBSTANCE ABUSE AND DEPENDENCE

Substance abuse and dependence are complex patterns of behavior that involve an interplay of biological, psychological, and environmental factors. Genetic factors and the early home environment may give rise to predispositions (diatheses) to abuse and dependence. In adolescence and adulthood, positive expectations concerning drug use, together with social pressures and a lack of cultural constraints, affect drug use decisions and tendencies toward abuse. When physiological dependence occurs, people may use a substance to avoid withdrawal symptoms.

Genetic factors may create an inborn tolerance for certain drugs, such as alcohol, which can make it difficult to regulate usage, to know "when to say when." Some individuals may have genetic tendencies that lead them to become unusually tense or anxious. Perhaps they turn to alcohol or other drugs to quell their nervousness. Genetic predispositions may interact with environmental factors that increase the potential for drug abuse and dependence—factors such as pressure from peers to use drugs, parental modeling of excessive drinking or drug use, and family disruption that results in a lack of effective guidance or support. Cognitive factors, especially positive drug expectancies (e.g., beliefs that using drugs will enhance one's social skills or sexual prowess), may also raise the potential for alcohol or drug problems.

Sociocultural factors need to be taken into account in this matrix of factors, such as the availability of alcohol and other drugs, presence or absence of cultural constraints that might curb excessive or underage drinking, the glamorizing of drug use in popular media, and inborn tendencies (such as among Asians) to flush more readily following alcohol intake.

Learning factors also play important roles. Drug use may be *positively* reinforced by the pleasurable effects associated with the use of the drug (mediated perhaps by release of dopamine in the brain or by activation of endorphin receptors). It may also be *negatively* reinforced by the reduction of states of tension and anxiety that depressant drugs such as alcohol, heroin, and tranquilizers can produce. In a sad but ironic twist, people who become dependent on drugs may continue to use them solely because of the relief from withdrawal symptoms and cravings they encounter when they go without the drug.

Problems of substance abuse and dependence are best approached by investigating the distinctive constellation of factors that apply to each individual case. No single model or set of factors will explain each case, which is why we need to understand each individual's unique characteristics and personal history.

TREATMENT

There have been and remain a vast variety of nonprofessional, biological, and psychological approaches to substance abuse and dependence. However, treatment has been a frustrating endeavor. In many, perhaps most, cases, people with drug dependencies really do not want to discontinue the substances they are abusing. Most people who abuse cocaine, for example, like most abusers of alcohol and other drugs, do not seek treatment on their own (Carroll & Rounsaville, 1992). Those who do not seek treatment tend to be heavy abusers who deny the negative impact of cocaine on their lives and dwell within a social milieu that fails to encourage them to get help. When people do come for treatment, helping them through a withdrawal syndrome is usually straightforward enough, as we shall see. However, helping them pursue a life devoid of their preferred substances is more problematic. Moreover, treatment takes place in a setting—such as the therapist's office, a support group, a residential center, or a hospital—in which abstinence is valued and encouraged. Then the individual returns to the work, family, or street settings in which abuse and dependence were instigated and maintained. The problem of returning to abuse and dependence following treatment—that is, of *relapse*—can thus be more troublesome than the problems involved in initial treatment. For this reason, recent treatment efforts have focused on relapse prevention. Given the difficulties encountered in treating people with sub-

stance abuse problems, it is no wonder that there is a high degree of variability in the outcomes achieved in substance abuse treatment, regardless of the types of clients, treatments, or measures of outcome that are used (McLellan et al., 1994). One consistent finding that does emerge is that people with more severe alcohol and drug use problems preceding treatment tend to have poorer outcomes in controlling their substance use following treatment.

Another complication is that many people with substance abuse problems also have psychological disorders, and vice versa (McCrady & Langenbucher, 1996; Miller & Brown, 1997). Most clinics and treatment programs focus on the drug or alcohol problem, or the other psychological disorders, rather than treating all these problems simultaneously. This narrow focus results in poorer treatment outcomes, including more frequent rehospitalizations among those with these dual diagnoses. It has been estimated that 20% to 70% of people who have other psychological disorders—and 50% to 70% of the young adults with other psychological disorders—merit a dual diagnosis that includes substance abuse (Polcin, 1992).

Biological Approaches

There is an increasing range of biological approaches used in treating problems of substance abuse and dependence. For people with chemical dependencies, biological treatment typically begins with **detoxification**—that is, helping them through withdrawal from addictive substances.

Detoxification   Detoxification is often carried out in a hospital setting to provide the support needed to help the person withdraw safely from the addictive substance. In the case of addiction to alcohol or barbiturates, hospitalization allows medical personnel to monitor the development of potentially dangerous withdrawal symptoms, such as convulsions. The tranquilizing agents called *benzodiazepines*, such as Librium and Valium, may help block more severe withdrawal symptoms such as seizures and delirium tremens (Mayo-Smith et al., 1997). Behavioral treatment using monetary rewards for abstinent behavior (judged by clean urine samples) may help improve outcomes during detoxification from opiates (Bickel et al., 1997). Detoxification to alcohol takes about a week. When tranquilizers are used to cope with subsequent urges to drink, however, people can be caught up in a sort of game of "musical drugs."

Next we consider other drugs used to treat people with chemical dependencies.

Disulfiram   The drug disulfiram (brand name Antabuse) discourages alcohol consumption because the combination of the two produces a strong aversive reaction consisting of nausea, sweating, flushing, rapid heart rate, reduced blood pressure, and vomiting. In some extreme cases, drinking alcohol while taking disulfiram can lead to such a dramatic drop in blood pressure that the individual goes into a shock and may even die. Although disulfiram has been used widely in alcoholism treatment, its effectiveness is limited because many patients who want to continue drinking simply stop using the drug. Others stop taking the drug in the belief they can maintain abstinence without it. Unfortunately, many return to uncontrolled drinking. Another drawback is that the drug has toxic effects in people with liver disease, a frequent ailment of people who suffer from alcoholism. There is also little evidence supporting the efficacy of the drug in the long run (E. W. Larson et al., 1992; Schuckit, 1996).

Antidepressants Antidepressants have shown some promise in reducing cravings for cocaine following withdrawal from the drug. These drugs may stimulate neural processes that underlie feelings of pleasure in everyday experiences. If people with substance use disorders are more capable of deriving pleasure from nondrug-related activities, they may be less likely to return to cocaine to induce pleasurable feelings. However, antidepressants have thus far failed to produce consistent results in reducing relapse rates for cocaine dependence, so it is best to withhold judgment concerning their efficacy (O'Brien, 1996).

Researchers suspect that deficiencies of the neurotransmitter serotonin may underlie alcohol desires or cravings (Anton, 1994). Research is underway focusing on whether the appetite for alcohol can be curbed by using serotonin-reuptake inhibitors (Prozac is one) that increase the availability of serotonin in the brain. The use of these drugs in the early stages of abstinence may help people who are alcohol dependent to maintain sobriety and continue in treatment. In a recent clinical trial, Prozac improved the moods and reduced the drinking of people with coexisting (comorbid) alcohol dependence and depression (Cornelius et al., 1997). The actions of another neurotransmitter, dopamine, may account for the pleasurable or euphoric effects of alcohol. Drugs that mimic dopamine may be helpful in blocking the pleasurably reinforcing effects of alcohol.

Nicotine Replacement Therapy One promising development in the pharmacological treatment of cigarette smoking is nicotine replacement therapy in the form of prescription gum (brand name Nicorette), transdermal (skin) patches, and a recently approved nasal spray (Hurt et al., 1998). Many regular smokers, perhaps the great majority, are nicotine dependent. The use of nicotine replacements helps avert withdrawal symptoms following smoking cessation. After quitting smoking, ex-smokers can gradually wean themselves from the nicotine replacement.

Nicotine-chewing-gum treatment and the nicotine patch have been shown to be effective aids in quitting smoking (Joseph et al., 1996; O'Brien & McKay, 1998; Skaar et al., 1997; Tsoh et al., 1997). The jury is still out on nicotine nasal sprays. However, while nicotine patches and gum may help quell the physiological components of withdrawal, they have no effect on the behavioral components of the addiction, such as the habit of smoking while drinking alcohol

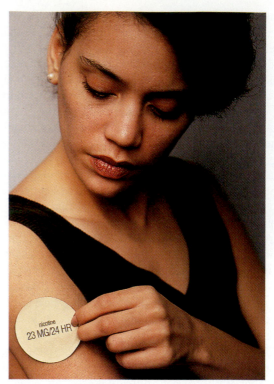

Is the path to abstinence from smoking skin deep? Forms of nicotine replacement therapy—such as nicotine transdermal (skin) patches and chewing gum that contains nicotine—allow people to continue to receive nicotine when they quit smoking. Though nicotine replacement therapy is more effective than a placebo in helping people quit smoking, it does not address the behavioral components of addiction to nicotine, such as the habit of smoking while drinking alcohol. For this reason, nicotine replacement therapy may be more effective if it is combined with behavior therapy that focuses on changing smoking habits.

(R. Weiss, 1992). As a result, nicotine replacement may be ineffective in promoting long-term changes unless it is combined with behavioral therapy that focuses on changing smoking habits ("Last Draw for Smokers," 1996). A study involving nearly 4,000 participants indicates that extended use of nicotine gum in the absence of acquiring coping skills for handling smoking temptations may even contribute to later relapse (Niles et al., 1995). In effect, the person may become too dependent on using the gum as a coping strategy. The combination of nicotine replacement therapy and behavioral counseling appears to be more effective than either approach alone (Cinciripini et al., 1996; Klesges, Ward, & DeBon, 1996).

In 1997, the government approved the use of the first non-nicotine-based antismoking drug, an antidepressant *bupropion* (trade name Zyban), which has been shown to be more effective than placebo in helping smokers quit ("FDA approves antidepressant to stop smoking," 1997; Hurt et al., 1997). This is the first drug that works on reducing cravings for nicotine, in much the same way that other antidepressants are being used to treat cocaine cravings.

Methadone-Maintenance Programs Methadone is a synthetic opiate that satisfies cravings for heroin and prevents the intense withdrawal symptoms that people addicted to heroin suffer upon withdrawal (O'Brien, 1996). Methadone does not produce the intense "high" or the stuperous state associated with heroin use, so people using it can hold jobs and perform complex tasks, such as teaching or practicing law or medicine (O'Brien & McKay, 1998). However, like other opiates, methadone is highly addictive. For this reason, people treated with methadone can be conceptualized as swapping dependence on one drug for dependence on another. Yet methadone programs are usually publicly financed and so relieve people who are addicted to heroin of the need to engage in criminal activity to support their dependence on methadone. Some 120,000 people in the United States participate in methadone programs. Though methadone can be taken indefinitely, individuals may be weaned from it without returning to using heroin.

TRUTH *or* FICTION REVISITED

9.10 True. Methadone, a synthetic narcotic, is widely used in treating heroin addiction.

For maximum effectiveness, methadone treatment must be combined with psychological counseling (O'Brien, 1996). Though methadone treatment produces clear benefits in improved daily functioning, not everyone succeeds with methadone, even with counseling (O'Brien & McKay, 1998). Some addicts turn to other drugs such as cocaine to get high or return to using heroin.

Naloxone and Naltrexone Naloxone and naltrexone are sister drugs that block the "high" produced by heroin and other opiates. By blocking the opioid's effects, they may be useful in helping addicts avoid relapsing following opiate withdrawal.

Naltrexone (brand name ReVia) blocks the high from alcohol as well as from opiates. In 1995, naltrexone became the first drug approved for treating alcoholism since disulfiram was introduced in 1948 (Croop, Faulkner, & Labriola, 1997; O'Brien & McLellan, 1997). In a double-blind placebo-control study, naltrexone in combination with behavioral treatment cut the relapse rates in people treated for alcoholism by more than half (Volpicelli et al., 1992, 1994). Naltrexone doesn't prevent the person from taking a drink but seems to blunt cravings for the drug (O'Brien & McKay, 1998; O'Malley et al., 1996). By blocking the pleasure produced by alcohol, the drug can help break the vicious cycle in which one drink creates a desire for another, leading to episodes of binge drinking. Naltrexone seems to work better in patients with stronger alcohol cravings (Jaffe et al., 1996), and, not surprisingly, with patients who complete treatment and take their medication (Volpicelli et al., 1997).

A nagging problem with drugs such as naltrexone, naloxone, disulfiram, and methadone is that people with substance abuse problems may simply stop using them and return to their substance-abusing behavior. Nor do such drugs provide alternative sources of positive reinforcement that can replace the pleasurable states produced by drugs of abuse. Drugs such as these are effective only in the context of a broader treatment program, consisting of psychological counseling and other treatment components, such as job training and stress management training—treatments designed to provide people with substance abuse problems the skills they need to embark on a life in the mainstream culture (W. R. Miller & Brown, 1997).

Culturally Sensitive Treatment of Alcoholism

Treatment programs for alcoholism involve common themes that cut across ethnic groups, such as recognizing the problem, increasing awareness of the reasons for drinking, and developing the motivation to refrain from drinking (F. Moss et al., 1985). Yet many members of ethnic minority groups resist traditional treatment approaches because they feel excluded from full participation in society (Westermeyer, 1984). Native American women, for example, tend to respond less favorably to traditional alcoholism counseling than White women (Rogan, 1986). G. Hurlburt and Gade (1984) attribute this difference to the resistance of Native American women to "White man's" authority. They suggest that the early stages of intervention might be more successful in overcoming this resistance if treatment was provided by Native American counselors.

The use of counselors from the client's own ethnic group is an example of a culturally sensitive treatment approach. Culturally sensitive approaches pay special attention to ethnic factors in alcoholism (Rogan, 1986). Culturally sensitive programs that address all facets of the human being, including racial and cultural identity, can

Culturally sensitive treatment for alcoholism. Culturally sensitive treatment of drinking problems address all aspects of the person, including ethnic factors and the nurturance of pride in one's cultural identity. Ethnic pride may help people resist the temptation to cope with stress through alcohol and other substances.

Multicultural Aspects of Smoking Cessation Interventions

Given the diversity of smoking patterns that exists in the United States in relation to such factors as ethnicity and socioeconomic level, health officials recognize that no one approach to smoking cessation is likely to be effective for all smokers (USDHHS, 1991a). Antismoking programs need to be specifically directed toward the groups they are intended to reach.

Your first author, together with colleague Rafael Javier, developed a culturally specific smoking cessation program for Hispanic American smokers in Queens, New York (Nevid, 1996; Nevid & Javier,1997; Nevid, Javier, & Moulton, 1996). Called the "SI, PUEDO" ("Yes, I Can") program, it was based on a behavioral group treatment approach that incorporated a series of videotaped vignettes featuring smoking-related themes. Culturally laden values such as *machismo* (masculinity), *familiarismo* (responsibility to family), and *respeto* (respect for self and others) were used in these vignettes to convey antismoking messages and encourage smoking cessation.

In another culturally sensitive program, the American Indian Health Care Association offered a smoking cessation program directed at Native Americans through Indian health clinics in the upper Midwest and Northwest (G.A.I.N.S. Project, 1990). At Ohio State University, a smoking cessation intervention was targeted toward Southeast Asian men, mostly recent immigrants from Vietnam and Cambodia, a group in which smoking rates are especially high (Chen, 1991).

Cigarette advertising has been increasingly directed at African Americans, which has created something of a backlash effect, with many community organizations in African American communities taking action to prevent the displays of cigarette advertisements on neighborhood billboards. In New York City and elsewhere, leading clergy and other community leaders have become involved in efforts to prohibit billboard advertising of cigarettes (in some cases, even "whitewashing" billboards) and ensure stricter enforcement of restrictions against selling cigarettes to minors. Other programs have recruited community residents from churches and community organizations to serve as volunteers in talking to their friends and neighbors about the dangers of cigarette smoking.

---

nurture pride that helps people resist the temptation to cope with stress through chemicals (Rogan, 1986).

Treatment providers may also be more successful if they recognize and incorporate indigenous forms of healing into the treatment process. For example, spirituality is an important aspect of traditional Native American culture, and spiritualists have played important roles as natural healers. Seeking the assistance of a spiritualist may help improve the counseling relationship. Likewise, given the importance of the church in African American and Hispanic American culture, counselors working with people with alcohol use disorders from these groups may be more successful when they draw on clergy and church members as resources in the treatment process.

Native American tribal leaders have attempted to deal with problems of alcohol abuse and dependence by emphasizing a return to traditional values and the development of industry to serve as sources of employment for Native American youth. Traditional values emphasize the importance of seeking to live in harmony with nature, respect for religious traditions, and the attainment of knowledge and wisdom. Knowledge is expected to be used wisely for the betterment of oneself and one's family, clan, and tribe (Edwards & Egbert-Edwards, 1990). More effective treatment and prevention programs are able to strengthen families, instill hope in the future, improve academic skills, and change peer relationships in the direction of discouraging drug use (Oetting, Beauvais, & Edwards, 1988). Several Native American communities have also developed specialized programs to teach young people parenting skills (Berlin, 1987). They also emphasize technical and scientific training to enable young people to bring new technology to the reservation and provide a new brand of tribal leadership. As Berlin notes, being a scientist does not mean "losing respect for tradition, for ceremony and ritual, and for the traditional healers and tribal leaders" (p. 304).

Nonprofessional Support Groups

Despite the complexity of the factors contributing to substance abuse and dependence, these problems are frequently handled by laypeople or nonprofessionals. Such people often have or had the problems themselves. For example, self-help group meetings are sponsored by organizations such as Alcoholics Anonymous (AA), Narcotics Anony-

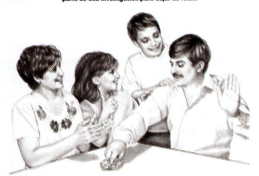

Culturally-specific smoking cessation intervention. Family responsibility is a central cultural value in Hispanic cultures, as it is in many other cultures. The Sí Puedo ("Yes, I Can") program, a culturally-specific smoking cessation program for Hispanic smokers, emphasized responsibility to self and family in its treatment approach, as represented here in this recruitment flyer.

Antismoking organizers have also made use of Black churches, recreational centers, and barbershops as settings for holding stop-smoking programs and distributing antismoking materials. In East Baltimore, Maryland, the *Heart, Body & Soul Project* involved a collaboration between Black clergymen and the Johns Hopkins Center for Health Promotion. The clergymen delivered smoking cessation messages as part of their regular sermons and sponsored health fairs and special programs for smoking cessation for their congregations (D. Levine et al., 1991).

Voluntary health organizations, such as the American Lung Association, the American Heart Association, and the American Cancer Society, have also become involved in spearheading stop-smoking initiatives targeting ethnic minority smokers. For example, the American Lung Association has developed a pamphlet, *Don't Let Your Dreams Go Up in Smoke,* that specifically addresses the problem of smoking in the Black community. With increasing attention focused on the problem of smoking throughout all segments of our society, "Joe Camel's" days may well be numbered.

mous, and Cocaine Anonymous. These groups promote abstinence and provide members an opportunity to discuss their feelings and experiences in a supportive group setting. More experienced group members (sponsors) support newer members during periods of crisis or potential relapse. The meetings are sustained by nominal voluntary contributions. We focus here on AA.

Alcoholics Anonymous Many laypeople and professionals consider **Alcoholics Anonymous** to provide the most effective treatment for alcoholism. AA, begun in the 1930s, is based on the belief that alcoholism is a disease, not a sin. AA assumes that people who suffer from alcoholism are never cured, regardless of how long they abstain from alcohol or how well they control their drinking. Instead of being "cured," people who suffer from alcoholism are seen as "recovering." It is also assumed that people who suffer from alcoholism cannot control their drinking and need help in order to stop drinking. There are more than 50,000 chapters of AA in North America ("Treatment of Drug Abuse and Addiction—Part 1," 1995). AA is so deeply embedded in the consciousness of helping professionals that many of them automatically refer newly detoxified people to AA as

the follow-up agency. About half of AA members have problems with illicit drugs as well as alcohol.

The AA experience is in part spiritual, in part group supportive, in part cognitive. AA follows a 12-step approach in which the beginning steps deal with acceptance of one's powerlessness over alcohol and turning one's will and life over to a higher power. This spiritual component may be helpful to some participants but not to others who prefer not to appeal for divine support. (Other lay organizations, such as Rational Recovery, do not adopt a spiritual approach.) The later steps focus on examining one's character flaws, admitting one's wrongdoings, being open to God's help to overcome one's character defects, making amends to others, and, at the 12th step, bringing the AA message to other people suffering from alcoholism (McCrady, 1994). Prayer and meditation are urged upon members to help them get in touch with their higher power. The meetings themselves provide group support. So does the buddy, or sponsoring, system, which encourages members to call each other for support when they feel tempted to drink.

AA claims to have a high success rate, one in the neighborhood of 75% (Wallace, 1985). Critics note that percentages this high are based on personal testimonies rather than

on careful surveys or experiments. Moreover, such estimates include only persons who attend meetings for extended periods. The drop-out rate is high, with as many as 70% of members dropping out within 10 meetings, according to one survey. Even AA estimates that 50% of members drop-out after 3 months (Treatment of Alcoholism—Part II, 1996). It has been difficult to conduct controlled studies because AA does not keep records of its members in order to protect their anonymity and also because of an inability to conduct randomized clinical trials in AA settings (McCaul & Furst, 1994). On the other hand, the greater involvement with AA, researchers find, the better the outcome in terms of days not drinking or using drugs (Morgenstern et al., 1997). Yet we can't say for certain whether regular participation in AA or personal motivation that may contribute to both use of AA and change in substance-use behavior is responsible for better outcomes. In all likelihood success is due to both factors. Nor can we say who is likely to succeed in AA and who is not.

Al-Anon, begun in 1951, is a spinoff of AA that supports the families and friends of people suffering from alcoholism. There are some 26,000 Al-Anon groups nationwide (Desmond, 1987). Another spinoff of AA, Alateen, provides support to children whose parents have alcoholism, helping them see they are not to blame for their parents' drinking and are thus undeserving of the guilt they may feel.

Residential Approaches

A residential approach to treatment involves a stay in a hospital or therapeutic residence. Hospitalization may be recommended when substance abusers cannot exercise self-control in their usual environments, or cannot tolerate withdrawal symptoms, and when their behavior is self-destructive or dangerous to others. Outpatient treatment is less costly and is often indicated when withdrawal symptoms are less severe, clients are committed to changing their behavior, and environmental support systems, such as families, strive to help clients make the transition to a drug-free lifestyle. The great majority (nearly 90%) of people treated for alcoholism are treated on an outpatient basis (McCaul & Furst, 1994).

When alcoholism was given disease status by the American Medical Association in 1966, only a few medically based treatment programs existed, such as the renowned Hazelden program in Minnesota, which was founded in 1949 and has since treated some 70,000 people (Karlen, 1995). Many other residential programs have come into being, with some facilities, such as the Betty Ford Clinic, receiving a great deal of media attention. Most inpatient programs use an extended 28-day detoxification, or drying-out, period, an approach initiated at Hazelden in 1949. Clients are helped through withdrawal symptoms in a few days. Then the emphasis shifts to counseling about the destructive effects of alcohol and combating distorted ideas or rationalizations. Consistent with the disease model, the goal of abstinence is urged (Desmond, 1987).

Despite the popularity of inpatient treatment, researchers find that most people with alcohol use disorders do not require hospitalization (some certainly do). Studies comparing outpatient and inpatient programs reveal no overall difference in relapse rates (McKay et al., 1995; W. R. Miller & Hester, 1986). However, medical insurance may not cover outpatient treatment, which may encourage many people who may benefit from outpatient treatment to admit themselves for inpatient treatment.

A number of residential therapeutic communities are also in use. Some of them have part- or full-time professional staffs. Others are run completely by lay people. One of the earliest communities was Synanon, which followed the disease model belief that people with substance abuse or dependence differ from other people in basic ways and must abstain completely from their habits. Participants were required to assume progressively more demanding responsibilities. They began by assuming responsibility for their personal hygiene, beds, and rooms and eventually worked toward contributing to community life in the residence. Lapses were directly confronted in group sessions. Members were also confronted about their excuses for failing to take responsibility for themselves and about their denial of the damage being done by their abuse. Members shared their life experiences to help each other develop productive ways of handling stress. Synanon has long since closed its doors, but its communal approach has served as a model for more than 500 therapeutic communities established in the United States ("Treatment of Drug Abuse and Addiction—Part I," 1995).

As with AA, we lack evidence from controlled studies demonstrating the efficacy of residential treatment programs. Also like AA, therapeutic communities have high numbers of early dropouts. Moreover, many former members of residential treatment programs who remain substance free during their time in residence relapse upon returning to the world outside. A recent study suggests that a day treatment therapeutic community may be as effective as a residential treatment facility (Guydish, et al, 1998).

Psychodynamic Approaches

Psychoanalysts view substance abuse and dependence as symptomatic of conflicts that are rooted in childhood experiences. Focusing on substance abuse or dependence per se is seen to offer, at most, a superficial type of therapy. It is assumed that if the underlying conflicts are resolved, abusive behavior will also subside as more mature forms of gratification are sought. Traditional psychoanalysts also assume that programs directed solely at abusive behavior will be of limited benefit because they fail to address the underlying psychological causes of abuse. Although there are many reports of successful psychodynamic case studies of people with substance abuse problems, there is a dearth of controlled and replicable research studies. The effectiveness of psycho-

dynamic methods for treating substance abuse and dependence thus remains unsubstantiated.

Behavioral Approaches

Behavioral approaches to substance abuse and dependence focus on modifying abusive and dependent behavior patterns. The issue to many behaviorally oriented therapists is not whether substance abuse and dependence are diseases but whether or not abusers can learn to change their behavior when they are faced with temptation.

Self-Control Strategies Self-control training focuses on helping abusers develop skills they can use to change their abusive behavior. Behavior therapists focus on three components of substance abuse:

1. The *antecedent* cues or stimuli (As) that prompt or trigger abuse,

2. The abusive *behaviors* (Bs) themselves, and

3. The reinforcing or punishing *consequences* (Cs) that maintain or discourage abuse.

Table 9.4 shows the kinds of strategies that are used to modify the "ABCs" of substance abuse.

Aversive Conditioning In **aversive conditioning,** painful or aversive stimuli are paired with substance abuse or abuse-related stimuli to make abuse less appealing. In the case of problem drinking, tastes of different alcoholic beverages are usually paired with chemically induced nausea and vomiting or with electric shock (G. T. Wilson, 1991). As a consequence, alcohol may come to elicit an aversive conditioned response, such as fear or nausea, that inhibits drinking. Avoidance of alcohol is then negatively reinforced by relief from aversive responses. **Covert sensitization** is based on the same principles but utilizes imagined aversive scenes. Evidence regarding the effectiveness of aversive therapies in the treatment of alcoholism remains mixed, however, and they have not achieved widespread use among treatment providers (Kadden, 1994). Moreover, aversive conditioned responses may be extinguished in real-life settings because alcohol use in these settings is not paired with aversive stimuli.

Aversive conditioning for smoking aims at making once pleasurable cigarette smoke aversive through some form of overexposure. In **rapid smoking,** for example, smokers puff at a faster than usual rate, about once every 6 seconds until they begin to feel nauseated. The nausea acts as an unconditioned stimulus that becomes paired with smoking-related conditioned stimuli such as the taste and aroma of cigarette smoke, the feel of the cigarette in the hand, and so on. After repeated pairings, cigarette smoke itself may become aversive, prompting avoidance of smoking. Taylor and Killen (1991) report an average quit rate across studies of rapid smoking at 1-year follow-ups of 25%. Interest in rapid

smoking appears to have waned, in part because questions persist about the safety of drawing so much nicotine and carbon monoxide into the body so quickly.

Social Skills Training Social skills training helps people develop effective interpersonal responses in social situations that prompt substance abuse. Assertiveness training, for example, may be used to teach people with alcohol-related problems how to fend off social pressures to drink. Behavioral marital therapy seeks to improve marital communication and a couple's problem-solving skills to relieve marital stresses that can trigger abuse. Couples may learn how to use written behavioral contracts. One such contract might stipulate that the person with a substance abuse problem agrees to abstain from drinking or to take Antabuse, while his or her spouse agrees to refrain from comments about past drinking and the probability of future lapses. The available evidence supports the utility of social skills training and behavioral marital therapy approaches in the treatment of alcoholism (Finney & Monahan, 1996; O'Farrell et al., 1996).

Relapse-Prevention Training

The word **relapse** derives from Latin roots meaning "to slide back." From 50% to 90% of people who are treated successfully for substance abuse problems eventually relapse (Leary, 1996b). Relapses often occur in response to negative mood states such as depression or anxiety, to interpersonal conflict, or to social pressures to resume drinking (Cooney et al., 1997). People with drinking problems who relapse are more likely than those who do not to have encountered stress, such as loss of a loved one or economic problems. They are also more likely than those who maintain sobriety to rely on avoidance methods of coping, such as denial. Successful abstainers from alcohol tend to have more social and family resources and support to draw upon in handling stress (Havassy, Hall, & Wasserman, 1991).

Because of the prevalence of relapse, behaviorally oriented therapists have devised a number of methods referred to as **relapse-prevention training.** Such training helps people with substance abuse problems cope with temptations and high-risk situations to prevent *lapses*—that is, slips—from becoming full-blown relapses (Marlatt & Gordon, 1985). High-risk situations include negative mood states, such as depression, anger, or anxiety; interpersonal conflict (e.g., marital problems or conflicts with employers); and socially conducive situations such as "the guys getting together." Participants learn to cope with these situations, for example, by learning self-relaxation skills to counter anxiety and learning to resist social pressures to resume use of the substance. Trainees are also taught to avoid practices that might prompt a relapse, such as keeping alcohol on hand for friends.

Although it contains many behavioral strategies, relapse-prevention training is a cognitive-behavioral technique in

TABLE 9.4

Self-Control Strategies for Modifying the "ABCs" of Substance Abuse

1. Controlling the As (Antecedents) of Substance Abuse:

People who abuse or become dependent on psychoactive substances become conditioned to a wide range of external (environmental) and internal stimuli (body states). They may begin to break these stimulus-response connections by:

- Removing drinking and smoking paraphernalia from the home—all alcoholic beverages, beer mugs, carafes, ashtrays, matches, cigarette packs, lighters, etc.

- Restricting the stimulus environment in which drinking or smoking is permitted. Use the substance only in a stimulus-deprived area of their homes, such as the garage, bathroom, or basement. All other stimuli that might be connected to using the substance are removed—there is no TV, reading materials, radio, or telephone. In this way, substance abuse becomes detached from many controlling stimuli.

- Not socializing with others with substance abuse problems, by avoiding situations linked to abuse— bars, the street, bowling alleys, etc.

- Frequenting substance-free environments—lectures or concerts, a gym, museums, evening classes. By socializing with nonabusers, sitting in nonsmoking cars of trains, eating in restaurants without liquor licenses.

- Managing the internal triggers for abuse. By practicing self-relaxation or meditation and not taking the substance when tense. By expressing angry feelings by writing them down or self-assertion, not by taking the substance. By seeking counseling for prolonged feelings of depression, not alcohol, pills, or cigarettes.

2. Controlling the Bs (Behaviors) of Substance Abuse:

People can prevent and interrupt substance abuse by:

- Using response prevention—breaking abusive habits by physically preventing them from occurring or making them more difficult. By not bringing alcohol home or cigarettes to the office.

- Using competing responses when tempted. By being prepared to handle substance-related situations with appropriate ammunition—mints, sugarless chewing gum, etc. By taking a bath or shower, walking the dog, walking around the block, taking a drive, calling a friend, spending time in a substance-free environment, practicing meditation or relaxation, or exercising when tempted, rather than using the substance.

- Making abuse more laborious—buying one can of beer at a time; storing matches, ashtrays, and cigarettes far apart; wrapping cigarettes in foil to make smoking more cumbersome; pausing for 10 minutes when struck by the urge to drink, smoke, or use another substance and asking oneself, "Do I really need *this* one?"

3. Controlling the Cs (Consequences) of Substance Abuse:

Substance abuse has immediate positive consequences such as pleasure, relief from anxiety and withdrawal symptoms, and stimulation. People can counter these intrinsic rewards and alter the balance of power in favor of nonabuse by:

- Rewarding themselves for nonabuse and punishing themselves for abuse.

- Switching to brands of beer and cigarettes they don't like.

- Setting gradual substance-reduction schedules and rewarding themselves for sticking to them.

- Punishing themselves for failing to meet substance-reduction goals. People with substance abuse problems can assess themselves, say, 10 cents for each slip and donate the cash to an unpalatable cause, such as a brother-in-law's birthday present.

- Rehearsing motivating thoughts or self-statements—such as writing reasons for quitting smoking on index cards. For example:

  > Each day I don't smoke adds another day to my life.
  > Quitting smoking will help me breathe deeply again.
  > Foods will smell and taste better when I quit smoking.
  > Think how much money I'll save by not smoking.
  > Think how much cleaner my teeth and fingers will be by not smoking.
  > I'll be proud to tell others that I kicked the habit.
  > My lungs will become clearer each and every day I don't smoke.

  > Smokers can carry a list of 20 to 25 such statements and read several of them at various times throughout the day. They can become parts of one's daily routine, a constant reminder of one's goals.

that it also focuses on the person's *interpretations* of any lapses or slips that may occur, such as smoking a first cigarette or taking a first drink following quitting. Clients are taught how to avoid the so-called **abstinence violation effect** (AVE)—the tendency to overreact to a lapse—by learning to reorient their thinking about lapses and slips. People who have a slip may be more likely to relapse if they attribute their slip to personal weakness, and experience shame and guilt, than if they attribute the slip to an external or transient event (Curry, Marlatt, & Gordon, 1987). For example, consider a skater who slips on the ice (Marlatt & Gordon, 1985). Whether or not the skater gets back up and

A CLOSER LOOK

The Controlled Social Drinking Controversy

The disease model of alcoholism contends that people who suffer from the disease who have just one drink will lose control and go on a binge. Some professionals, however, such as Linda and Mark Sobell, have argued that behavior modification self-control techniques can teach many people with alcohol abuse or dependence to engage in **controlled social drinking**—to have a drink or two without necessarily falling off the wagon.

The contention that people who develop alcoholism can learn to drink moderately remains controversial. The proponents of the disease model of alcoholism, who have wielded considerable political strength, stand strongly opposed to attempts to teach controlled social drinking.

To support their contention, the Sobells published the results of an experiment with 20 people who suffered from alcoholism who were taught to control their drinking. The Sobells (1973, 1976, 1984) reported that 85% of their subjects remained in control of their drinking at a 2-year follow-up. However, a research group critical of the Sobells (Pendery, Maltzman, & West, 1982) published its own follow-up of the Sobells' subjects. The group claimed that only one person had remained successful at controlled social drinking. Most had returned to uncontrolled drinking on many occasions, and four of the group had died from alcohol-related causes.

Yet other investigators have found that controlled social drinking is a reasonable treatment goal for younger people with problem drinking who are less alcohol dependent but are headed on the road toward chronic alcoholism (e.g., Miller & Muñoz, 1983; Sanchez-Craig, Annis, Bornet, & MacDonald, 1984; Sanchez-Craig & Wilkinson, 1986/1987). Evidence supporting controlled social drinking programs for people with chronic alcoholism, however, remains lacking. Interest in controlled social drinking programs has also waned, largely because of strong opposition from professionals and lay organizations committed to the abstinence model.

Controlled drinking programs may be best suited for the following: (1) younger persons with early-stage alcoholism or problem drinking, (2) those who reject goals of total abstinence or have failed in programs requiring abstinence, and (3) those who do not show severe withdrawal symptoms (Marlatt et al., 1993; H. Rosenberg, 1993; Sobell, Tonealtoo, & Sobell, 1990). Researchers also find that women tend to do better than men in controlled drinking programs (Marlatt et al., 1993). By offering moderation as a treatment goal, controlled drinking programs may also reach many people with alcohol use disorders who might otherwise go untreated because they refuse to participate in abstinence-only treatment programs (Marlatt et al., 1993). Controlled drinking programs may actually represent a pathway to abstinence for people who would not otherwise enter abstinence-only treatment programs (Marlatt et al., 1993). That is, treatment in a controlled drinking program may be the first step in the direction of giving up drinking completely. A large percentage (about 1 in 4 in one study; Miller et al., 1992) enter with the goal of achieving controlled drinking but become abstinent by the end of treatment. On the other hand, controlled social drinking may not be appropriate for people with established alcohol dependence and those who are taking medications that interact with alcohol or have other medical risks that might be aggravated by alcohol (Lawson, 1983; "Treatment of Alcoholism—Part II," 1996).

continues to perform depends largely on whether the skater sees the slip as an isolated and correctable event or as a sign of complete failure. Evidence shows that the best predictor of progression from a first to a second lapse among ex-smokers was the feeling of giving up after the first lapse (Shiffman et al, 1996). But those who responded to a first lapse by using coping strategies were more likely to succeed in averting a subsequent lapse on the same day.

In contrast to the disease model, which contends that people who suffer from alcoholism automatically lose control if they take a single drink, the relapse-prevention model assumes that whether or not a lapse becomes a relapse depends on the person's interpretation of the lapse (Marlatt & Gordon, 1985). Self-defeating attributions such as "What's the use? I'm just doomed to fail" trigger depression, resignation, and resumption of problem drinking. Participants in relapse-prevention training programs are encouraged to view lapses as temporary setbacks that provide opportunities to learn what kinds of situations lead to temptation and how they can avoid or cope with such situations. If they can learn to think, "Okay, I had a slip, but that doesn't mean all is lost unless I believe it is," they are less likely to catastrophize lapses and subsequently relapse. Other relapse-prevention techniques focus on training smokers' spouses or partners to be more helpful in maintaining abstinence. Social support appears to play a key role in determining relapse in abstinence-based programs for alcoholism, drug abuse, and cigarette smoking (Havassy et al., 1991; Niles et al., 1995). All in all, efforts to treat people with substance abuse and dependence problems have been mixed at best. Many abusers really do not want to discontinue use of these substances, although they would prefer, if possible, to avoid their negative consequences. The more effective substance abuse treatment programs involve intensive, multiple treatment approaches that address the wide range of problems that people with substance abuse disorders frequently present, including co-occurring (comorbid) psychiatric problems such as depression (R. A. Brown et al., 1997; Crits-Christoph & Siqueland 1996; Kessler et al., 1997b). Comorbidity of substance use disorders and other psychiatric disorders has become the rule in treatment facilities rather than the exception (Brems & Johnson, 1997). Substance abusers who have comorbid disorders typically fare more poorly in treatment for their drug or alcohol problems (Kranzler et al., 1996). For people with alcoholism and other substance abuse problems, a number of different therapies, including 12-step and cognitive-behavioral approaches, seem to work well if they are well delivered (Leary, 1996b; W. R. Miller & Brown, 1997; Ouimette, Finney, & Moos, 1997; Project MATCH Research Group, 1997).

The major problem is that as many as 80% of people in the United States with alcohol use disorders have no contact whatsoever with alcohol treatment programs or self-help organizations (Institute of Medicine, 1990). Clearly more needs to be done to help people whose use of alcohol and other drugs puts them at risk.

In the case of inner-city youth who have become trapped within a milieu of street drugs and hopelessness, the availability of culturally sensitive counseling and job training opportunities would be of considerable benefit in helping them assume more productive social roles. The challenge is clear: to develop cost-effective ways of helping people recognize the negative effects of substances and forgo the powerful and immediate reinforcements they provide.

SUMMARY

Classification of Substance-Related Disorders

According to the DSM, substance abuse disorders involve a pattern of recurrent use of a substance that repeatedly leads to damaging consequences. Substance dependence, which often includes features of physiological dependence, involves impaired control over use of a substance.

Depressants

Depressants include alcohol, sedatives and minor tranquilizers, and opioids. Effects of alcohol include intoxication, impaired coordination, slurred speech, and impaired intellectual functioning. Chronic alcohol abuse has been connected with disorders such as alcohol-induced persisting amnestic disorder (Korsakoff's syndrome), cirrhosis of the liver and other physical disorders, and fetal alcohol syndrome. Barbiturates are depressants or sedatives that have been used medically for relief of anxiety and short-term insomnia, among other uses. Opioids such as morphine and heroin are derived from the opium poppy. Others are synthesized. Used medically for relief of pain, they are strongly addictive.

Stimulants

Stimulants increase the activity of the nervous system. Amphetamines and cocaine increase the availability of neurotransmitters in the brain, heightening states of arousal and producing pleasurable feelings. High doses can produce an amphetamine psychosis, which mimics features of paranoid schizophrenia. Repeated use of nicotine, usually in the form of cigarette smoking, leads to physiological dependence.

Hallucinogens

The hallucinogens include LSD, psilocybin, and mescaline. Other drugs with similar effects are cannabis (marijuana) and phencyclidine (PCP). There is little evidence that these drugs induce physiological dependence, although psychological dependence may occur.

Theoretical Perspectives

Biological perspectives focus on uncovering the biological pathways that may explain mechanisms of physiological dependence. The disease model treats problems of substance abuse and dependence as disease processes. Learning theorists view substance abuse disorders as learned patterns of behavior. Cognitive perspectives focus on roles of attitudes, beliefs, and expectancies in accounting for substance use and abuse. Research suggests that the one-drink effect may be a self-fulfilling prophecy. Sociocultural perspectives have focused on the adoption of culturally sanctioned prohibitions against excessive drinking in explaining differences among various ethnic and religious groups in rates of alcoholism. Social factors, such as peer pressure and peer drug use, also influence the development of substance abuse. Psychodynamic theorists view problems of substance abuse, such as excessive drinking and habitual smoking, as signs of an oral fixation.

Treatment

Biological approaches to substance abuse disorders include detoxification; the use of drugs such as disulfiram, methadone, naloxone, naltrexone, and antidepressants; and nicotine replacement therapy. Residential treatment approaches include hospitals and therapeutic communities. Nonprofessional support groups, such as Alcoholics Anonymous, promote abstinence within a supportive group setting.

Psychodynamic therapists focus on uncovering the inner conflicts, originating in childhood, that are believed to be at the root of substance abuse problems. Behavior therapists focus on helping people with substance-related problems change problem behaviors through such techniques as self-control training, aversive conditioning, and skills training approaches. Regardless of the initial success of a treatment technique, relapse remains a pressing problem in treating people with substance abuse problems. Relapse-prevention training employs cognitive-behavioral techniques to help ex-abusers cope with high-risk situations and to prevent lapses from becoming relapses by helping participants interpret lapses in less damaging ways.

Key for "How Do You Know If You Are Hooked?" Questionnaire

Any "yes" answer suggests you may be dependent on alcohol. If you have answered any of these questions in the affirmative, we suggest you seriously examine what your drinking means to you.

REVIEW QUESTIONS

1. How do professionals distinguish between drug use and abuse? Between drug abuse and dependence?

2. What is the difference between psychological and physiological dependence?

3. What are the risk factors for alcoholism?

4. What are the effects of the various types of drugs discussed in the chapter—alcohol, sedatives and minor tranquilizers, opioids, amphetamines, cocaine, nicotine, PCP, LSD, and marijuana?

5. What is the disease model of alcoholism? What evidence supports biological factors in alcoholism and other substance use disorders?

6. How are behavioral and cognitive factors involved in alcoholism and other substance use disorders?

7. What treatment approaches are used in helping people with substance abuse and dependence disorders?

8. What is the controversy concerning controlled drinking? What does the research evidence suggest?

© K.N. Istomin
In Front of the Mirror

Eating Disorders, Obesity, and Sleep Disorders

TRUTH *or* FICTION?

10.1 Though others see them as but "skin and bones," young women with anorexia nervosa still see themselves as too fat.

10.2 Dieting represents an abnormal eating pattern among American women.

10.3 Bulimic women induce vomiting only after binges.

10.4 Drugs used to treat depression may also help curb bulimic binges.

10.5 The excess calories consumed by Americans each day could feed a country of 80 million people.

10.6 Obesity is mostly a cosmetic concern, not a health concern.

10.7 When you lose weight, your body starts putting the brakes on the rate at which it burns calories.

10.8 Obese people lose fat cells when they diet.

10.9 Most dieters eventually gain back the weight they lose.

10.10 Many of us suffer from sleep attacks in which we suddenly fall asleep without any warning.

10.11 Some people literally gasp for breath hundreds of times during sleep without realizing it.

Jessica was a 20-year-old communications major when she consulted a psychologist for the first time. For years she had kept a secret from everyone, including her fiancé Ken. She and Ken were planning to get married in three months. She had decided that now was the time she must finally confront the problem. She told the psychologist she didn't want to the bring the problem into the marriage with her, that it wouldn't be fair to Ken. She told the psychologist, "I don't want him to have to deal with this. I want to stop this before the marriage. I have to stop bingeing and throwing up." Jessica went on to describe her problem: "I would go on binges, and then throw it all up. It made me feel like I was in control, but really I wasn't." To conceal her secret, she would lock herself in the bathroom, run the water in the sink to mask the sounds, and induce vomiting. She would then clean up after herself and spray an air deodorant to mask any telltale odors. "The only one who suspects," she said with embarrassment, "is my dentist. He said my teeth were beginning to decay from stomach acid."

Jessica had **bulimia nervosa**, an eating disorder characterized by recurrent cycles of bingeing and purging. *Eating disorders* such as bulimia nervosa and anorexia nervosa often affect young people of high school or college age, especially young women. Though rates of diagnosable eating disorders in college students are not as high as you might think, chances are you have known people with anorexia or bulimia or with disturbed eating patterns that fall within a spectrum of eating-related disorders, such as repeated binge eating or excessive dieting. Another class of psychological disorders that commonly affects children and young adults are *sleep disorders*. The most common form of sleep disorder, chronic insomnia, affects many college students and young adults making their way in the world who tend to bring their worries and concerns to bed with them.

EATING DISORDERS

In a nation of plenty, some people literally starve themselves—sometimes to death. They are obsessed with their weight and desire to achieve an exaggerated image of thinness. Others engage in repeated cycles in which they binge on food and then attempt to purge their excess eating, as by inducing vomiting. These dysfunctional patterns are the two major types of **eating disorders**, *anorexia nervosa* and *bulimia nervosa*. Eating disorders are characterized by disturbed patterns of eating and maladaptive ways of controlling body weight. Like many other psychological disorders, anorexia and bulimia are often accompanied by other forms of psychopathology, including depression, anxiety disorders, and substance abuse disorders.

Anorexia nervosa and bulimia nervosa were once considered very rare but are becoming increasingly common in the United States and other developed countries. The great majority of cases occur among women, especially young women. Although these disorders may develop in middle or even late adulthood, they typically begin during adolescence or early adulthood when the pressures to be thin are the strongest (D. Beck, Casper, & Andersen, 1996). As these social pressures have increased, so too have the rates of eating disorders. Estimates are that between 1% and 2% of female adolescents in the United States today develop anorexia, and a similar percentage develop bulimia (French et al., 1995). Prevalences of both anorexia and bulimia in adolescent and young adult males are estimated at about 0.2% (2 in 1,000 individuals) (Carlat, Camargo, & Herzog, 1997).

A much larger percentage of young women show signs of bulimic behaviors (occasional bingeing and purging) or excessive dieting, but not to the point that they would warrant a diagnosis of an eating disorder. Studies of college women indicate that perhaps 1 in 2 have binged and purged at least once (Fairburn & Wilson, 1993).

Anorexia Nervosa

Karen was the 22-year-old daughter of a renowned English professor. She had begun her college career full of promise at the age of 17, but two years ago, after "social problems" occurred, she had returned to live at home and taken progressively lighter course loads at a local college. Karen had never been overweight, but about a year ago her mother noticed that she seemed to be gradually "turning into a skeleton."

Karen spent literally hours every day shopping at the supermarket, butcher, and bakeries conjuring up gourmet treats for her parents and younger siblings. Arguments over her lifestyle and eating habits had divided the family into two camps. The camp led by her father called for patience; that headed by her mother demanded confrontation. Her mother feared that Karen's father would "protect her right into her grave" and wanted Karen placed in residential treatment "for her own good." The parents finally compromised on an outpatient evaluation.

At an even 5 feet, Karen looked like a prepubescent 11-year-old. Her nose and cheekbones protruded crisply. Her lips were full, but the redness of the lipstick was unnatural, as if too much paint had been dabbed on a corpse for the funeral. Karen weighed only 78 pounds, but she had dressed in a stylish silk blouse, scarf, and baggy pants so that not one inch of her body was revealed.

Karen vehemently denied that she had a problem. Her figure was "just about where I want it to be" and she engaged in aerobic exercise daily. A deal was struck in which outpatient treatment would be tried as long as Karen lost no more weight and showed steady gains back to at least 90 pounds. Treatment included a day hospital with group therapy and two meals a day. But word came back that Karen was artfully toying with her food—cutting it up, sort of licking it, and moving it about her plate—rather than eating it. After 3 weeks Karen had lost another pound. At that point, her parents were able to persuade her to enter a residential treatment program, where her eating behavior could be more carefully monitored.

THE AUTHORS' FILES

Anorexia derives from the Greek roots *an-*, meaning "without," and *orexis*, meaning "a desire for." *Anorexia* thus means "without desire for [food]," which is something of a misnomer because loss of appetite among people with anorexia nervosa is rare. However, they may be repelled by food and refuse to eat more than is absolutely necessary to maintain a minimal weight for their ages and heights.

Anorexia Nervosa. Christy Heinrich, a champion gymnast, died from complications resulting from anorexia nervosa in 1994. She was pictured here with her boyfriend about a year before her death.

Often, they starve themselves to the point where they become dangerously emaciated. By and large, anorexia nervosa develops in early to late adolescence, between the ages of 12 and 18, although earlier and later onsets are sometimes found.

Anorexia is characterized by the clinical features listed in Table 10.1. Although reduced body weight is the most obvious sign, the most prominent clinical feature is an intense fear of obesity. One common pattern of anorexia begins after menarche when the girl notices added weight and insists it must come off. Extreme dieting and, often, excessive exercise continue unabated after the initial weight-loss goal is achieved, however—even after their families and others express concern. Another common pattern occurs among young women when they leave home to attend college and encounter difficulties adjusting to the demands of college life and independent living. Anorexia is also more common among young women involved in ballet or modeling, in which there is often a strong emphasis on maintaining an unrealistically thin body shape.

Though anorexia in women is far more common than in men, an increasing number of young men are presenting with anorexia. Many are involved in sporting activities, such

TABLE 10.1

Diagnostic Features of Anorexia Nervosa

A.   Refusal to maintain weight beyond the minimal normal weight for one's age and height; for example, a weight at least 15% below normal.

B.   Strong fear of putting on weight or becoming fat, despite being thin.

C.   A distorted body image in which one's body—or part of one's body—is perceived as fat, although others perceive the person as thin.

D.   In case of females who have had menarche, absence of three or more consecutive menstrual periods.

Source: Adapted from the *DSM-IV* (APA, 1994).

How do I see myself?   A distorted body image is a key component of eating disorders.

as wrestling, in which they have experienced pressure to maintain their weight in a lower weight classification.

Adolescent girls and women with anorexia almost always deny that they are losing too much weight or wasting away. They may argue that their ability to engage in stressful exercise demonstrates their fitness. Women with eating disorders are more likely than normal women to view themselves as heavier than they are (Horne, Van Vactor, & Emerson, 1991; Penner, Thompson, & Coovert, 1991). Whereas women like Karen may be little more than "skin and bones," they may see themselves as being too fat. Though they literally starve themselves, they may spend much of the day thinking and talking about food and even preparing elaborate meals for others (Rock & Curran-Celentano, 1996).

TRUTH *or* FICTION REVISITED

10.1 *True.*   Others may see them as nothing but "skin and bones," but anorexic women have a distorted body image and may still see themselves as too fat.

Subtypes of Anorexia   There are two general subtypes of anorexia, a *binge-eating/purging type* and a *restrictive type*. The first type is characterized by frequent episodes of binge eating and purging, while the second type is not. Though repeated cycles of binge eating and purging occur in bulimia, bulimic individuals do not reduce their weight to anorexic levels. The distinction between the subtypes of anorexia is supported by differences in personality patterns. Individuals with the eating/purging type tend to have problems relating to impulse control, which in addition to binge-eating episodes may involve substance abuse or stealing (Garner, 1993). They tend to alternate between periods of rigid control and impulsive behavior. Those with the restrictive type tend to be rigidly, even obsessively controlled about their diet and appearance.

Medical Complications of Anorexia   Anorexia can lead to serious medical complications, which in extreme cases can be fatal (Kaplan & Woodside, 1987). Weight losses of as much as 35% of body weight may occur, and

anemia may develop. Females suffering from anorexia are also likely to encounter dermatological problems such as dry, cracking skin; fine, downy hair; even a yellowish discoloration that may persist for years after weight is regained. Cardiovascular complications include heart irregularities, hypotension (low blood pressure), and associated dizziness upon standing, sometimes causing blackouts. Decreased food ingestion can cause gastrointestinal problems such as constipation, abdominal pain, and obstruction or paralysis of the bowels or intestines. Menstrual irregularities are common, and **amenorrhea** (absence or suppression of menstruation) is part and parcel of the clinical definition of anorexia in females. Muscular weakness and abnormal growth of bones may occur, causing loss of height and **osteoporosis**.

The death rate from anorexia is estimated at 5% to 8% over a 10-year period, with most deaths due to suicide or medical complications associated with severe weight loss (Goleman, 1995g).

Bulimia Nervosa

Nicole has only opened her eyes, but already she wishes it was time for bed. She dreads going through the day, which threatens to turn out like so many other days of her recent past. Each morning she wonders, is this the day that she will be able to get by without being obsessed by thoughts of food? Or will she "blow it again" and spend the day gorging herself? Today is the day she will get off to a new start, she promises herself. Today she will begin to live like a normal person. Yet she is not convinced that it is really up to her.

Nicole starts the day with eggs and toast. Then she goes to work on cookies; doughnuts; bagels smothered with butter, cream cheese, and jelly; granola; candy bars; and bowls of cereal and milk—all within 45 minutes. Then she cannot take in any more food and turns her attention to purging what she has eaten. She goes to the bathroom, ties back her hair, turns on the shower to mask any noise she will make, drinks a glass of water, and makes herself vomit. Afterward she vows, "Starting tomorrow, I'm going to change." But she suspects that tomorrow may be just another chapter of the same story.

ADAPTED FROM BOSKIND-WHITE & WHITE, 1983, P. 29

Nicole suffers from bulimia nervosa. *Bulimia* derives from the Greek roots *bous,* meaning "ox" or "cow," and *limos,* meaning "hunger." The unpretty picture inspired by the origin of the term is one of continuous eating, like a cow chewing its cud. Bulimia nervosa is an eating disorder characterized by recurrent episodes of gorging on large quantities of food followed by use of inappropriate ways to prevent weight gain, such as purging by means of self-induced vomiting or use of laxatives, diuretics, or enemas, or by fasting or engaging in excessive exercise (see Table 10.2). Two or more strategies may be used for purging, such as vomiting and use of laxatives (Tobin, Johnson, & Dennis, 1992). Though people with anorexia are extremely thin, bulimic individuals are usually of normal weight. However, they share an excessive concern about their shapes and weight.

Bulimic individuals typically gag themselves to induce vomiting. Most attempt to conceal their behavior. Fear of gaining weight is a constant factor. Although an overconcern with body shape and weight is a cardinal feature of bulimia and anorexia, bulimic individuals do not pursue the extreme thinness characteristic of anorexia. Their ideal weights are similar to those of women who do not suffer from eating disorders (Fairburn, Cooper, & Cooper, 1986).

The binge itself usually occurs in secret and involves consumption of forbidden foods that are generally sweet and rich in fat (Drewnowski, 1997). Binge eaters typically feel they lack control over their eating and may consume 5,000 to 10,000 calories at a sitting. One young woman described eating everything available in the refrigerator, even to the point of scooping out margarine from its container with her finger. The episode continues until the binger is spent or exhausted, suffers painful stomach distension, induces vomiting, or runs out of food. Drowsiness, guilt, and depression usually ensue, but bingeing is initially pleasant because of release from dietary constraints.

The average age for onset of bulimia is the late teens, when concerns about dieting and dissatisfaction with bodily shape or weight are at their greatest. Bulimia nervosa typically affects non-Hispanic White women in late adolescence or early adulthood (APA, 1994; Carlat & Camargo, 1991). Despite the widespread belief that eating disorders, especially anorexia nervosa, are more common among more affluent people, the available evidence shows no strong linkage between socioeconomic status and eating disorders (Gard & Freeman, 1996; Wakeling, 1996). Beliefs that eating disorders are associated with high socioeconomic status may reflect the tendency for more affluent patients to obtain treatment. Alternatively, it may be that the social pressures on young women to strive to achieve an ultrathin ideal have generalized across all socioeconomic levels.

Medical Complications of Bulimia   Bulimia is also associated with many medical complications (A. S. Kaplan & Woodside, 1987). Many of these stem from repeated vomiting. There may be irritations of the skin around the mouth due to frequent contact with stomach acid, blockage of salivary ducts, decay of tooth enamel, and dental cavities. The acid from the vomit may damage taste receptors on the palate, which might make the person less sensitive to the taste of vomit with repeated purgings (Rodin, Bartoshuck, Peterson, & Schank, 1990). Decreased sensitivity to the aversive taste of vomit may play a role in maintaining the purging behavior (Rodin et al., 1990). Cycles of bingeing and vomiting may cause abdominal pain, hiatus hernia, and other abdominal complaints. Stress on the pancreas may produce pancreatitis (inflammation), which is a medical emergency. Disturbed menstrual function is found in as many as 50% of normal-weight women with bulimia (Weltzin et al., 1994). Excessive use of laxatives may cause bloody diarrhea and laxative dependency, so the person cannot have normal bowel movements without laxatives. In the extreme, the bowel can lose its reflexive eliminatory response to pressure from waste material. Bingeing on large quantities of salty food may cause convulsions and swelling. Repeated vomiting or abuse of laxatives can lead to potassium deficiency, producing muscular weakness, cardiac irregularities, even sudden death—especially when diuretics are used. As with anorexia, menstruation may come to a halt.

TABLE 10.2

Diagnostic Features of Bulimia Nervosa

A.   Recurrent episodes of binge eating (gorging) as shown by both:

  (1) Eating an unusually high quantity of food during a 2-hour period, and

  (2) Sense of loss of control over food intake during the episode.

B.   Regular inappropriate behavior to prevent weight gain such as self-induced vomiting; abuse of laxatives, diuretics, or enemas; or by fasting or excessive exercise.

C.   A minimum average of two episodes a week of binge eating and inappropriate compensatory behavior to prevent weight gain over a period of at least 3 months.

D.   Persistent overconcern with the shape and weight of one's body.

Source: Adapted from the *DSM-IV* (APA, 1994).

Causes of Anorexia and Bulimia

Like other psychological disorders, anorexia and bulimia involve a complex interplay of factors. But most significant of all are the social pressures felt by young women that lead them to base their self-worth on their physical appearance, especially their weight.

Sociocultural Factors   Sociocultural theorists point to societal pressures and expectations placed on young women in our society as contributing to the development of eating disorders (Bemporad, 1996; Hsu, 1990; Stice, 1994). The pressure to achieve an unrealistic standard of thinness, combined with the importance attached to appearance in defining the female role in our society, can lead young women to strive toward an unrealistically thin ideal and to develop an overriding fear of gaining weight that can put them at risk of developing eating disorders.

The pressure to be thin falls most heavily on women. This pressure is so prevalent that dieting has become the normal eating pattern for American women. Four of five young women in the United States have gone on a diet by the time they reach their 18th birthdays. In actuality, the gender gap in obesity is quite small—27% of women versus 24% of men (see Figure 10.1). Moreover, gender differences in obesity do not arise until mid-life.

TRUTH *or* FICTION REVISITED

10.2 *False.* Dieting is so pervasive that it has essentially become a normative pattern of eating among American women.

In support of the sociocultural model, evidence shows that eating disorders are less common, even rare, in non-Western countries (Stice, 1994; Wakeling, 1996). Even in Western cultures, eating disorders are more prevalent in the weight-obsessed United States than in other countries where data are available, such as Greece and Spain, or in the most

The Barbie doll has long represented a symbol of the buxom but thin feminine form that has become idealized in our culture. If women were to be proportioned like the classic Barbie doll, they would resemble the woman in the photograph on the right. To achieve this idealized form, the average women would need to grow nearly a foot in height, reduce her waist by 5 inches, and add 4 inches to her bustline. What message do you think the Barbie-doll figure conveys to young girls?

technologically advanced nation in the Far East, Japan (Stice, 1994). The prevalences of disordered eating behaviors and eating disorders also vary in the United States among different ethnic groups, with higher rates found among White adolescents than African Americans and other ethnic minorities (Leon et al., 1995; Stice, 1994). Yet disordered eating behaviors that may give rise to eating disorders are more common among African American women who identify more closely with the dominant White culture (K. K. Abrams, Allen, & Gray, 1993). Disturbed eating behaviors may also be more common among Native American adolescents than is commonly believed (J. E. Smith & Krejci, 1991). Investigators also caution that body dissatisfaction may be more prevalent among Hispanic and Asian girls than is generally recognized and may set the stage for distorted eating behaviors in these groups (T. Robinson et al., 1996). There are also signs that suggest that eating disorders may increase in the future in developing countries (Grange, Telch, & Tibbs, 1998).

Psychosocial Factors   Though cultural pressures to conform to an ultrathin female ideal play a major role in eating disorders, the great majority of young women exposed to these pressures do not develop eating disorders. Other factors must be involved. Body dissatisfaction appears to be an important factor (Heatherton et al., 1997). Bulimic women spend significantly more time than other women thinking about food and their weight (Zotter & Crowther, 1991).

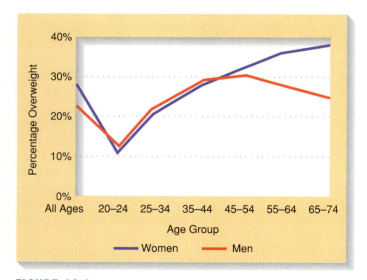

FIGURE 10.1   *Prevalence of overweight by gender & age.*

Source: National Heart, Lung, and Blood Institute (NHLBI), National Institutes of Health. March, 1993 Data Fact Sheet: Obesity and Cardiovascular Disease. Bethesda, MD: Author.

Thinness—A Cultural Obsession Takes its Toll

Perhaps many men have claimed that they were leafing through *Playboy* magazine to study cultural standards for beauty. Garner and his colleagues (1980) actually did so, however. Their aim was to document the increasing pressure on women to be slender. They compared pictures of Playboy centerfolds, Miss America contestants, and models from women's magazines over the past few decades. Sure enough, they found that the idealized models of the feminine form had become progressively thinner and more boyish over the years. In contrast to the large-breasted ideals of the 1950s, the models' busts and hips had become smaller in proportion to their waistlines.

We continue to be flooded with images of slender, often emaciated models. Glamour magazines and TV commercials idealize them as standards of health and beauty. This constant exposure puts pressure on young women to strive toward achieving an unrealistic standard of thinness. Consistent with the view that media depictions of the ultrathin female ideal play a part in the development of eating disorders, researchers find that college women who report a greater level of exposure to media containing a high concentration of ideal body images (for example, magazines on topics involving health and fitness, or beauty and fashion, as well as television shows) generally show more features of eating disorders than other women who report less exposure to these media sources (Stice et al., 1994).

The cultural emphasis on thinness affects our self-perceptions. Most American women believe that they are heavier than the physique men prefer, and heavier still than the feminine ideal (A. E. Fallon & Rozin, 1985). This plump self-concept is found in girls as young as 10 to 15 years of age (Cohn et al., 1987). In contrast, college men are generally more satisfied with their bodies. Generally, 10- to 15-year-old boys believe that the ideal male physique is heavier than their own. However, boys naturally gain muscle mass and become heavier as they mature. Thus the gap between their own shape and their ideal shape is likely to narrow. Girls, however, encounter a greater discrepancy between their own body shapes and the cultural ideal of thinness as they mature and their figures fill out.

As to preferences for body shape, both men and women are somewhat off-base in their estimates of the physiques that the other gender prefers (Fallon & Rozin, 1985). College men actually prefer women to be somewhat heavier than women think men want them to be. Ironically, women prefer men to be thinner than men imagine (see Figure 10.2).

Source: Adapted from Nevid et al., 1998.

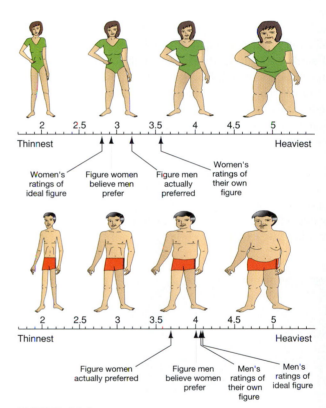

FIGURE 10.2
Mean ratings by men and women of their own figure, the figure they believe most preferred by the opposite sex, the figure of the opposite sex they most prefer, and the ideal figure for their own sex.

Source: Adapted from Fallon & Rozin, 1985.

Young women with anorexia often have perfectionistic attitudes and high achievement strivings. They tend to get down on themselves when they fail to meet the high standards they set for themselves, including their dieting standards. Their extreme dieting may give them a sense of control and independence that they may feel they lack in other aspects of their lives. Conflicts with parents over is-sues of autonomy are often implicated in the development of both anorexia nervosa and bulimia (Ratti, Humphrey & Lyons, 1996).

Psychodynamically oriented writers note that girls with anorexia often have difficulties separating from their families and consolidating separate, individuated identities (H. Bruch, 1973; Minuchin, Rosman, & Baker, 1978). Perhaps anorexia represents the girl's unconscious effort to remain a prepubescent child. By maintaining the veneer of childhood, pubescent girls may avoid dealing with such adult issues as increased independence and separation from their families, sexual maturation, and assumption of personal responsibilities. Because of the loss of fatty deposits, their breasts and hips flatten. Menstrual periods cease. In their fantasies, perhaps, they remain children, sexually undifferentiated.

Researchers have also noted linkages between bulimia and problems in interpersonal relationships. Women with bulimia tend to be shy and to have no close friends (Fairburn et al., 1997). One study of 21 college women with bulimia and a matched control group of 21 nonbulimic women found that those with bulimia had more social problems. They believed that less social support was available to them and reported more social conflict, especially with family members (Grissett & Norvell, 1992). They also rated themselves, and were judged by others, as less socially skillful than the control group. Although causal links between social skills and eating disorders remain to be elaborated, researchers wonder if enhancing the social skills of women with bulimia may increase the quality of their relationships and reduce their tendencies to use food in maladaptive ways.

Some learning theorists view anorexia as a type of weight phobia. Excessive, irrational fears of putting on weight may reflect the tendencies in our culture to idealize the slender female form. Learning theorists also suggest that purging may be a type of compulsive ritual that is reinforced by the reduction of the fear of gaining weight that follows a binge-eating episode, just as compulsive hand washing and checking in obsessive-compulsives may be reinforced by relief from the anxiety induced by obsessive thoughts (Leitenberg, Rosen, Gross, Nudelman, & Vara, 1988).

Rigid Dieting and Eating Disorders   There is a strong connection between rigid dieting and bulimia (Rock & Curran-Celentano, 1996). Bulimic women tend to have been slightly overweight preceding the development of bulimia, and the initiation of the binge-purge cycle usually follows a period of strict dieting to lose weight. In a typical scenario, the rigid dietary controls fail, which prompts initial bingeing. This sets in motion a chain reaction in which bingeing leads to fear of weight gain, which prompts self-induced vomiting or excessive exercise to reduce any added weight. Bulimic women may be so concerned about possible weight gain that they resort to vomiting to purge any weight gain from regular eating (Lowe, Glaves, & Murphy-Eberenz, 1998). Some induce vomiting after every meal. Purging is negatively reinforced by producing relief, or at least partial relief, from anxiety over gaining weight.

TRUTH _or_ FICTION REVISITED
10.3 _False._ Some bulimic women induce vomiting after every meal.

Though women who develop bulimia invariably have histories of dieting (Ruderman & Besbeas, 1992), dieting alone is not sufficient to explain the development of bulimia. Dieting is commonplace in our society, especially among young women, yet relatively few dieters go on to develop bulimia. Investigators have identified several characteristics that distinguish young women at increased risk of progressing from dieting to bulimia. For one thing, they tend to be extremely concerned about their body weight and shape (Fairburn, 1997). They typically engage in extreme dieting characterized by very strict rules about what they can eat, how much they can eat, and how often they can eat (Drewnowski et al., 1994). Their thinking tends to be both perfectionistic and dichotomous ("black-or-white") (Fairburn, 1997). Thus, they expect themselves to adhere perfectly to their rigid dietary rules and judge themselves as complete failures when they deviate. They also judge themselves harshly for episodes of binge eating and purging. These cognitive factors influence each other, as illustrated in Figure 10.3.

Another factor associated with an increased risk of bulimia is childhood sexual and physical abuse (S. L. Welch & Fairburn, 1996; Wonderlich et al., 1997). Bulimia may develop in some cases as an ineffective means of coping with abuse. In addition, women with bulimic tendencies tend to have a dysfunctional type of cognitive style that may lead to exaggerated beliefs about the negative consequences of gaining weight (Poulakis & Wertheim, 1993).

Young women with bulimia tend to have more psychological problems and lower self-esteem than other dieters (Fairburn, 1997; Ruderman & Besbeas, 1992). Bulimia often occurs together with many kinds of psychological disorders,

Bingeing.   People with bulimia nervosa may cram thousands of calories during a single binge and then attempt to purge what they have consumed by forcing themselves to vomit.

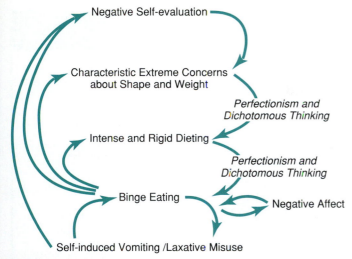

FIGURE 10.3 *A cognitive model of bulimia nervosa.*

Source: C.B. Fairburn, 1997, Eating disorders. In D.M. Clark & C.G. Fairburn (Eds.), *Science and Practice of Cognitive Behaviour Therapy.* Oxford: Oxford University Press. Reprinted by permission of Oxford University Press.

including alcoholism; major depression; and anxiety disorders such as panic disorder, phobia, and generalized anxiety disorder (Kendler et al., 1991). Perhaps some forms of binge eating involve attempts at self-medication for emotional problems. What we have gained from this research is the understanding that bulimia often develops within a context of extreme, rigid dieting overlaying psychological, interpersonal, and cognitive factors.

Biological Factors

Interest in the biological underpinnings of eating disorders, especially bulimia, has largely focused on the role of the neurotransmitter serotonin. Serotonin is involved in processes regulating moods and appetite, especially appetite for carbohydrates. Decreased serotonin activity or responsivity may be involved in prompting binge eating in bulimic individuals, especially carbohydrate bingeing (Levitan et al., 1997). This line of thinking is buttressed by evidence that antidepressant medication, such as Prozac, which increases serotonin activity, can decrease binge-eating episodes in patients with bulimia nervosa (Jimerson et al., 1997). We also know that many women with eating disorders are depressed or have a history of depression, and imbalances of serotonin are implicated in depressive disorders. It may be that bulimia is related to depression, perhaps at a genetic level.

TRUTH ⟨or⟩ FICTION REVISITED

10.4 *True.* Antidepressants have been shown to be helpful in curbing binge eating among bulimic women.

We do have evidence supporting a genetic contribution to bulimia. A large-scale study of more than 2,000 female twins showed a much higher concordance rate for the disorder, 23% versus 9%, among monozygotic (MZ) twins than among dizygotic (DZ) twins (Kendler et al., 1991). Greater concordance for anorexia is also found among MZ than DZ

twins, 50% vs. 5%, suggesting a role for genetics in anorexia as well (Holland, Sicotte, & Treasure, 1988). Eating disorders also tend to run in families, which is further suggestive of a genetic component. However, genetic factors cannot fully account for the development of eating disorders. Perhaps in the manner of the diathesis-stress model, a genetic predisposition involving a disregulation of neurotransmitter activity may interact with family, social, cultural, and environmental pressures in leading to the development of an eating disorder (Strober & Humphrey, 1987).

Family Factors and Eating Disorders Eating disorders frequently develop against a backdrop of family conflicts (Fairburn, 1997; Fairburn et al., 1997; Graber et al., 1994; Ratti, Humphrey, & Lyons, 1996; Wonderlich et al., 1997). Some theorists focus on the brutal effect that self-starvation has on parents. They suggest that some adolescents use refusal to eat to punish their parents for feelings of loneliness and alienation they experience in the home. One related study compared the mothers of adolescents with eating disorders to the mothers of other adolescents. Mothers of the adolescents with the eating disorders were more likely to be unhappy about their families' functioning, to have their own problems with eating and dieting, to believe that their daughters ought to lose weight, and to regard their daughters as unattractive (Pike & Rodin, 1991). Is binge eating, as suggested by Humphrey (1986), a metaphoric effort to gain the nurturance and comfort that the mother is denying her daughter? Does purging represent the symbolic upheaval of negative feelings toward the family?

Families of young women with eating disorders tend to be more often conflicted, while at the same time less cohesive and nurturing yet more overprotective and critical than those of reference groups (Fairburn et al., 1997; Ratti, Humphrey, & Lyons, 1996). The parents seem less capable of promoting independence in their daughters (Strober & Humphrey, 1987). Perhaps it is not surprising in this context that young women prone to develop eating disorders have difficulties relating to issues of control and autonomy. Yet it remains uncertain whether these family patterns contribute to the initiation of eating disorders, or whether eating disorders go on to disrupt family life. The truth probably lies in an interaction between the two.

From the **systems perspective**, families are systems that regulate themselves in ways that minimize the open expression of conflict and reduce the immediate need for overt change. Within this perspective, girls who develop anorexia may be seen as helping maintain the shaky balances and harmonies found in dysfunctional families by displacing attention from family conflicts and marital tensions onto themselves (Minuchin et al., 1978). The girl may become the *identified patient,* although the family unit is actually dysfunctional.

Regardless of the factors that initiate eating disorders, social reinforcers may maintain them. Children with eating disorders may quickly become the focus of attention of their

The Fear of Fat Scale

The fear of becoming fat is a prime factor underlying eating disorders such as anorexia and bulimia. The Goldfarb Fear of Fat scale (Goldfarb et al., 1985) measures the degree to which people fear becoming fat. The scale may help identify individuals at risk of developing eating disorders. It differentiates between anorexics and normal women, and between bulimic individuals and nonbulimics. Dieters, however, also score higher on the scale than nondieters.

To complete the Fear of Fat scale, read each of the following statements and write in the number that best represents your own feelings and beliefs. Then check the key at the end of the chapter.

1 = very untrue
2 = somewhat untrue
3 = somewhat true
4 = very true

_____ 1. My biggest fear is of becoming fat.
_____ 2. I am afraid to gain even a little weight.
_____ 3. I believe there is a real risk that I will become overweight someday.
_____ 4. I don't understand how overweight people can live with themselves.
_____ 5. Becoming fat would be the worst thing that could happen to me.
_____ 6. If I stopped concentrating on controlling my weight, chances are I would become very fat.
_____ 7. There is nothing that I can do to make the thought of gaining weight less painful and frightening.
_____ 8. I feel like all my energy goes into controlling my weight.
_____ 9. If I can eat even a little, I may lose control and not stop eating.
_____ 10. Staying hungry is the only way I can guard against losing control and becoming fat.

Source: Goldfarb L.A., Dynens, E.M., Gerrard, M. (1985). The Goldfarb fear of fat scale. *Journal of Personality Assessment, 49,* 329-332. Reprinted with permission.

---

families and receive attention from their parents that might otherwise be lacking.

Treatment of Anorexia Nervosa and Bulimia Nervosa

Eating disorders are difficult to treat. People with anorexia may be hospitalized, especially when weight loss is severe or body weight is falling rapidly. In the hospital they are usually placed on a closely monitored refeeding regimen. Behavior therapy is also commonly used, with rewards made contingent on adherence to the refeeding protocol (Rock & Curran-Celentano, 1996). Commonly used reinforcers include ward privileges and social opportunities.

Psychodynamic therapy is sometimes combined with behavior therapy to probe for deeper psychological conflicts. Family therapy may also be employed to help resolve underlying family conflicts. Behavior therapy has been shown to be effective in promoting weight gain of anorexic patients during hospitalization (W. G. Johnson, Tsoh, & Varnado, 1996). Individual or family therapy following hospitalization has also shown favorable long-term benefits (I. Eisler et al., 1997). However, recovery from anorexia tends to be a long process. A recent study of 88 German patients with anorexia showed that 50% of the patients did not recover sooner than 6 years after their first hospitalization

(W. Herzog, Schellberg, & Deter, 1997). The effectiveness of drug therapy (usually antidepressant medication, especially Prozac) appears promising but requires more study (Johnson, Tsoh, & Varnado, 1996).

Hospitalization may also be used to help break the binge-purge cycle in bulimia but appears to be necessary only in cases in which eating behaviors are clearly out of control and outpatient treatment has failed, or where there is evidence of severe medical complications, suicidality, or substance abuse (APA, 1994). Many people with bulimia hold rigid, distorted beliefs about which foods are good or bad, for example. They hold themselves to unrealistic, perfectionistic eating restrictions and engage in dichotomous (all or nothing) thinking that predisposes them to purge when they slip even a little from their rigid diets. They also tend to overemphasize their appearance in their evaluations of their self-worth.

Cognitive-behavioral therapy (CBT) is useful in helping bulimic individuals challenge these self-defeating cognitions and replace them with more adaptive thinking patterns. To eliminate self-induced vomiting, therapists may use the behavioral technique of exposure with response prevention that was developed for treatment of people with obsessive-compulsive disorder. In this technique, the bulimic patient is exposed to eating forbidden foods while the therapist stands by to prevent vomiting until the urge to purge passes.

Bulimic individuals thus learn to tolerate violations of their dietary rules without resorting to purging.

Cognitive-behavioral therapy (CBT) has emerged as an effective treatment for bulimia (Fairburn, 1997; Lewandowski et al., 1997; Walsh et al., 1997; Wilson & Fairburn, 1998). Another psychologically based treatment, interpersonal psychotherapy, has also shown good success and may be used as an alternative treatment in cases where CBT proves unsuccessful (P. J. Cooper & Steere, 1995; Wilson & Fairburn, 1998). Interpersonal therapy focuses on resolving interpersonal problems in the belief that more effective interpersonal functioning will lead to healthier food habits and attitudes.

Antidepressant drugs are also effective in treating bulimia (W. G. Johnson, Tsoh, & Varnado, 1996; Wilson & Fairburn, 1998). They are believed to work by decreasing the urge to binge through normalizing serotonin—the brain chemical involved in regulating appetite. However, the available evidence suggest that cognitive behavior therapy is more effective than antidepressant medication in treating bulimia nervosa and carries a lower rate of relapse (Compas et al., 1998; Johnson, Tsoh, & Varnado, 1996; Wilson & Fairburn, 1998). It appears that CBT should be the treatment of first choice for bulimia, followed by use of antidepressant medication if treatment is not successful (Compas et al., 1997; Wilson & Fairburn, 1998). Studies examining whether a combination CBT/medication treatment approach is more effective than either treatment component alone have thus far produced inconsistent results (Goldbloom et al., 1998; Johnson, Tsoh, & Varnado, 1996; Walsh et al., 1997).

Although progress has been made in treating eating disorders, there is considerable room for improvement (Compas et al., 1998). Even in CBT, about half of treated patients show continued evidence of bulimic behavior (Compas et al., 1998; Wilson & Fairburn, 1998). Eating disorders can be a tenacious and enduring problem, especially when excessive fears of body weight and distortions in body image are maintained. A recent study reported that 10 years after initial presentation with bulimia, approximately 30% of women showed either recurrent binge eating or purging behaviors (Keel, 1999).

If we are to make headway on the prevention front, we need to consider strategies that take into account the broader social context that gives rise to these problems. As suggested by Boskind-White and White (1986),

. . . if the toxic chain reaction of the terror of fat, fad diets, and eating disorders is to be broken, it is essential for the public to be properly informed regarding the dangers inherent in severe caloric deprivations. The media and fashion industry must take responsibility and introduce models who are womanly and fit rather than emaciated and unhealthy. Only then will women, young and old, begin to value themselves enough to reject inappropriate roles and implement more effective coping strategies with respect to food (pp. 363–364).

Binge Eating Disorder

People with **binge-eating disorder** (BED) have recurrent eating binges but do not purge themselves of the excess food afterwards. Binge-eating disorder is classified in the DSM manual as a potential disorder requiring further study. We presently know too little about the characteristics of people with BED to warrant its inclusion as an official diagnostic category. The criteria used for diagnosing the disorder also need further evaluation.

The available evidence indicates that, unlike bulimia, BED is more commonly found among obese individuals (Spitzer et al., 1992). It is frequently associated with depression and with a history of unsuccessful attempts at losing excess weight and keeping it off. People with BED tend to be older than those with anorexia or bulimia (Arnow, Kenardy, & Agras, 1992). Yet like other eating disorders it is found more frequently among women. Overall, about 2% of the population report frequent eating binges.

People with BED are often described as "compulsive overeaters." During a binge they feel a loss of control over their eating. BED may fall within a broader domain of compulsive behaviors characterized by impaired control over maladaptive behaviors, such as pathological gambling and substance abuse disorders. Cognitive-behavioral techniques have shown some success in treating binge-eating disorder (Agras et al., 1997; J. C. Carter & Fairburn, 1998; Wilson & Fairburn, 1998). Antidepressants, especially SSRIs such as Prozac, may also reduce the frequency of binge-eating episodes by helping to regulate serotonin levels in the brain.

OBESITY: A NATIONAL EPIDEMIC

There is no sincerer love than the love of food.

GEORGE BERNARD SHAW

The two biggest sellers in any bookstore are the cookbooks and the diet books. The cookbooks tell you how to prepare the food and the diet books tell you how not to eat any of it.

ANDY ROONEY

Food is essential to survival, but food means much more to many of us. It may symbolize family life and caring. We may connect it with the warmth of the parent-child relationship, with visits home on the holidays. Hosts offer food when we visit, and saying no can be construed as a personal rejection. Bacon and eggs, coffee and cream, red meat and potatoes mashed in butter—all seem inextricably interwoven with American values and agricultural abundance.

Yet many Americans are paying the price of plenty—**obesity.** Obesity has become a national epidemic. Consider some statistics:

- More than 1 in 3 adults in the United States are obese, and more than 1 in 2 (54%) are overweight (Hill &

Hazardous waist. Obesity is indeed a hazard—a hazard to health and longevity.

10.5 *True.* The excess calories consumed daily by Americans could feed a country of 80 million people. We, however, are paying the penalty of excess caloric intake in the form of obesity.

Why, in spite of all the money and effort expended on weight loss products and programs, are our collective waistlines getting larger? The answers are not completely clear but appear to involve a combination of eating more, eating ever larger portions ("Did someone say *supersize* it?"), and exercising less (Bouchard, 1997; Hill et al., 1998). The increased use of labor-saving devices (driving more, walking less) eventually translates into added inches to our waistlines (Bouchard, 1997). We are fast becoming a nation of couch potatoes and cyberslugs who are glued to the TV or computer screen.

In these next sections we examine the causes and treatment of obesity. Obesity is not classified as an eating disorder. It is considered a chronic medical disease, not a psychological disorder (Atkinson, 1997). Why, then, do we include the topic of obesity in an abnormal psychology textbook? There are at least five reasons:

1. Psychological factors may contribute to obesity or impair weight loss efforts. For example, negative emotions such as anxiety, anger, or depression may prompt overeating, even binge eating (Herman, Polivy, Lank, & Heatherton, 1987; Ruderman & Besbeas, 1992).

2. Obesity is a major risk factor for many health problems, including coronary heart disease, stroke, diabetes, and breast cancer, and may play a role in other cancers (Z. Huang et al., 1997; Kassirer & Angell, 1998; Rexrode et al., 1997; Trichopoulos, Li, & Hunter, 1996; Yong et al., 1996). Obesity increases the risk of premature death and contributes to an estimated 300,0000 deaths annually in the United States (McGinnis & Foege, 1993; J. Stevens et al., 1998). To put that figure in other terms, that's about equal to two jumbo jets crashing every day.

3. Obesity often has psychological effects, including problems with self-esteem and body image. Women, because they face greater social pressures to be thin, and people with severe obesity, because they encounter severe social stigmata associated with extreme obesity, may be most at risk of developing psychological problems relating to obesity (M. A. Friedman & Brownell, 1995).

4. Psychological approaches have been shown to be helpful to people seeking to take off excess weight and keep it off (Wadden, Foster, & Letizia, 1994).

5. Some people with obesity develop eating disorders, such as binge-eating disorder.

In these next sections we discuss the causes of obesity and ways of losing excess weight and keeping it off. First, however, let us consider the criteria used in classifying people as obese.

Peters, 1998; T. Meyer, 1997). More Americans today are overweight than at any time since the government started tracking obesity in the 1960s.

- Obesity in children and adolescents is also on the upswing; 1 in 4 children are either obese or overweight (Hill & Peters, 1998). Childhood obesity frequently sets the stage for a chronic course of lifelong obesity (Bouchard, 1997; Meyer, 1997).

- Americans consume 815 billion calories of food each day, which is 200 billion calories more than necessary to maintain their weight at moderate levels of activity (C. D. Jenkins, 1988). The extra calories are enough to sustain a country of 80 million people.

- Some 65 million Americans diet every year and use nearly 30,000 approaches (D. Blumenthal, 1988). As many as 1 in 4 Americans are on a diet on any given day (French & Jeffery, 1994).

- More than 90% of dieters fail to keep pounds off permanently (G. T. Wilson, 1994). Whether they drop 15 pounds or 50, most dieters put almost all the pounds back on within a year (J. E. Brody, 1992a).

- Although food can be expensive, the incidence of obesity is highest among people of lower socioeconomic status (Ernst & Harlan, 1991).

- The economic costs of obesity in the United States are estimated at $39 billion annually, which represents about 5% of all health-care costs in the nation (Colditz, 1992). As a nation, we spend in the pursuit of thinness between $30 and $50 billion dollars a year on diet programs, special foods, and over-the-counter diet remedies (Kassirer & Angell, 1998).

10.6 *False.* Obesity is a major health concern and is linked to such killers as heart disease, diabetes, stroke, and breast cancer.

Are You Obese?

The most widely used standard for determining obesity is the **body mass index,** or BMI. The BMI takes into account a person's body weight and height. It is calculated by dividing body weight (in kilograms) by the square of the person's height (in meters).

The National Institutes of Health has set a level of 25 as the cutoff for determining whether a person is overweight (see Figure 10.4) (J. E. Brody, 1998; L. Shapiro, 1998). This level is associated with a weight level about 20% above the recommended weight for a person's age and height. People in the range of 25 to 27 are considered slightly overweight. People with a BMI greater than 30 are considered obese.

The Body Mass Index

Federal health authorities are using this index to determine who is overweight. Under new guidelines, a body mass of **25** or more is considered overweight. To use the table, find the appropriate height in the left-hand column. Move across to a given weight. The number at the top of the column is the BMI at that height and weight. Pounds have been rounded off.

BMI

HEIGHT (inches)	19	20	21	22	23	24	25	26	27	28	29	30	31	32	33	34	35
								Body Weight (pounds)									
58	91	96	100	105	110	115	119	124	129	134	138	143	148	153	158	162	167
59	94	99	104	109	114	119	124	128	133	138	143	148	153	158	163	168	173
60	97	102	107	112	118	123	128	133	138	143	148	153	158	163	168	174	179
61	100	106	111	116	122	127	132	137	143	148	153	158	164	169	174	180	185
62	104	109	115	120	126	131	136	142	147	153	158	164	169	175	180	186	191
63	107	113	118	124	130	135	141	146	152	158	163	169	175	180	186	191	197
64	110	116	122	128	134	140	145	151	157	163	169	174	180	186	192	197	204
65	114	120	126	132	138	144	150	156	162	168	174	180	186	192	198	204	210
66	118	124	130	136	142	148	155	161	167	173	179	186	192	198	204	210	216
67	121	127	134	140	146	153	159	166	172	178	185	191	198	204	211	217	223
68	125	131	138	144	151	158	164	171	177	184	190	197	203	210	216	223	230
69	128	135	142	149	155	162	169	176	182	189	196	203	209	216	223	230	236
70	132	139	146	153	160	167	174	181	188	195	202	209	216	222	229	236	243
71	136	143	150	157	165	172	179	186	193	200	208	215	222	229	236	243	250
72	140	147	154	162	169	177	184	191	199	206	213	221	228	235	242	250	258
73	144	151	159	166	174	182	189	197	204	212	219	227	235	242	250	257	265
74	148	155	163	171	179	186	194	202	210	218	225	233	241	249	256	264	272
75	152	160	168	176	184	192	200	208	216	224	232	240	248	256	264	272	279
76	156	164	172	180	189	197	205	213	221	230	238	246	254	263	271	279	287

Sources: National Heart, Lung, and Blood Institute, 1998.

FIGURE 10.4 *The Body Mass Index.*

Source: Adapted from G.A. Bray & D.S. Gray (1998). Obesity. Part I-Pathogenesis. *Western Journal of Medicine, 149,* 429–441. Reprinted from "Clinical guidelines on the identification, evaluation, and treatment of overweight and obesity in adults." National Heart, Lung, and Blood Institute, 1998, Bethesda, MD.

There is some dispute about the level at which people need to be concerned about losing weight. Most health authorities agree that people with BMIs higher than 27, and especially those with BMIs greater than 30, should attempt to lose weight in order to reduce their risk of obesity-related health problems such as high blood pressure, heart disease, and Type II (adult-onset) diabetes. Yet the question of whether people in the 25 to 27 range would gain any health benefits from losing weight remains in dispute. Some authorities consider this range to represent a caution zone that should put people on notice to monitor their weight carefully and take steps to ensure it doesn't creep any further upwards (Shapiro, 1998). Yet even at a BMI level of 21 to 27, people who carry a greater amount of their weight around their middles ("apples") stand an increased health risk compared to people of the same weight who carry more of their weight in their buttocks and hips ("pears").

All in the family? Obesity tends to run in families. The question is, Why?

What Causes Obesity?

Body weight varies as a function of energy balance. When caloric intake exceeds energy output, the excess calories are stored in the body in the form of fat, which leads to obesity (Kuczmarksi et al., 1994). The key to preventing obesity is to bring energy expenditure in line with energy (caloric) intake. Unfortunately this prescription is easier said than done. Research suggests that a number of factors contribute to the imbalance between energy intake and expenditure that underlies obesity, including genetics, metabolic factors, lifestyle factors, and psychological factors.

Genetics: Is There a Fat Gene? Obesity clearly runs in families (Bouchard, 1997). The question is *why?*

It was once assumed that obese parents encouraged their children to become heavy by setting poor examples. A study of Scandinavian adoptees strongly suggests a key role for heredity, however (Stunkard et al., 1986). It revealed that children's weight is more closely related to the weight of their biological parents than to that of their adoptive parents. Perhaps the strongest evidence for the role of genetics comes from a study of identical twins, which showed that regardless of whether or not the twins were reared together or apart they wound up weighing virtually the same when they became adults (Stunkard et al., 1990). The researchers also studied fraternal (DZ) twins, who share only 50% genetic overlap, as compared with 100% genetic similarity among identical (MZ) twins. Consistent with the genetic hypothesis, fraternal twins varied much more in body weight (corrected for height) than MZ twins.

In 1994, a team of scientists reported they had discovered a gene in mice that is linked to obesity (Angier, 1994; Seligmann, 1994). Although human obesity appears more complicated than obesity in other animals, the gene, dubbed the *ob gene*, may also be a contributing factor in some cases of obesity in humans (Montague et al., 1997). The gene is involved in the process of signaling the brain when the body has had enough to eat, thereby producing feelings of satiety, or fullness. If the gene is defective, perhaps because of a mutation, it may fail to send the correct satiety signal, which can lead to overeating and weight gain. Another possibility gaining support is that while the ob gene in obese people may be normal, the brain may be insensitive to the hormone *leptin,* whose production it controls (Considine et al., 1996). It is leptin that signals the brain that the body has eaten enough. An insensitivity to leptin could lead to excessive eating.

The discovery of this gene may lead to the development of drugs that block the development of obesity, at least in some cases. Heredity may also influence body weight by affecting the body's **metabolic rate**, the speed at which food is processed, or "burned," in the body.

Does a genetic role in obesity mean biology is destiny? Not necessarily. Consider that the rate of obesity in the United States has risen sharply in just the past 10 or 15 years, which is much too short a time for genetic changes to wend their way through the population at large. The widening girth of Americans is primarily caused by lifestyle factors, not genetics (Brownell, 1994)—to a style of life dominated by high-fat diets, lack of regular exercise, and use of energy-saving equipment that reduces the need for calorie-burning physical exertion ("The Sedentary Society," 1996).

Metabolic Factors The body is a wondrous thing. It adjusts to all sorts of conditions, including deprivation. Sad to say, this capacity for adjustment can backfire on dieters. If you find it difficult to keep off the weight you lose, don't blame yourself.

When we lose weight, especially significant amounts of weight, our bodies react as if they were starving. The brain compensates by slowing the metabolic rate, the rate at which calories are burned (Kolata, 1995c; Leibel, Rosenbaum, & Hirsch, 1995). Some theorists believe that mechanisms in the brain control the body's metabolism to keep body weight around a genetically determined **set point** (Keesey, 1980).

10.7 *True.* Unfortunately, the body reacts to falling weight by slowing the metabolic rate, the rate at which it burns calories. This makes it difficult to continue losing more weight or even maintaining the weight loss.

By slowing the metabolic rate, the body preserves its stores of fat that might be needed for sustenance during times of famine. Thus, if you lose weight but continue to consume as many calories as you had before, you're likely to find your weight inching upwards. You may be able to offset this metabolic adjustment by following a more vigorous exercise regimen. Vigorous exercise burns calories directly and may increase the metabolic rate by replacing fat tissue with muscle, especially if the exercise program involves weight-bearing activity. Also, ounce for ounce, muscle burns more calories than fat. Before starting an exercise regimen, you should check with your physician to determine which types of activity are best suited to your overall health condition.

Fat Cells

The efforts of heavy people to keep a slender profile may be sabotaged by cells within their own bodies termed **fat cells.** No, fat cells are not corpulent cells. They are the cells that store fat. Fat cells compose the fatty tissue in the body (also called *adipose tissue*). Obese people have more fat cells (Brownell & Wadden, 1992). Severely obese people may have some 200 billion fat cells as compared to 25 or 30 billion in normal-weight individuals. Why does this matter? As time passes after eating, the blood sugar level declines, drawing out fat from these cells to supply more nourishment to the body. The hypothalamus in the brain detects the depletion of fat in these cells. The hypothalamus, in turn, signals the cerebral cortex, triggering the hunger drive, which motivates eating and thereby replenishes the fat cells.

People with more fatty tissue send more signals of depletion to the brain than people who are equal in weight but who have fewer fat cells. As a result, they feel food-deprived sooner. People who are markedly obese usually have more adipose tissue than people who are of normal weight or those with mild obesity. Sad to say, dieters do not expel fat cells; instead, they shrink them. Many dieters who are markedly obese, even successful dieters, thus complain they are constantly hungry as they struggle to maintain normal weights.

10.8 *False.* So far as we know people do not lose fat cells as they lose weight.

How is the number of fat cells in our bodies determined? Unfortunately, heredity seems to play a role. Excessive food intake in early childhood may also have an influence, however (Brownell & Wadden, 1992).

People with high levels of adipose tissue are doubly beset because adipose tissue metabolizes food more sluggishly than muscle. People with high fat-to-muscle ratios metabolize food more slowly than people of the same weight with lower fat-to-muscle ratios. As a result, they find it harder to lose weight and easier to gain weight at a given level of food consumption than people with lower fat-to-muscle ratios.

Lifestyle Factors Obese people are typically less physically active than people of normal weight (Brownell & Wadden, 1992; "The Sedentary Society," 1996). Although correlational evidence is insufficient to establish causality, it is reasonable to assume inactivity and overweight may interact with each other. In other words, inactivity may lead to weight gain, and gaining additional weight may lead people to become less active.

Other lifestyle factors such as adopting a high-fat diet and eating larger portions also contribute to obesity. Exposure to a constant bombardment of food-related cues in television commercials, print advertising, and the like may also play a part. Even though evidence does not show obese people to be more sensitive to food cues than normal-weight individuals, overresponsivity to these cues can lead to inappropriate food consumption in people of any weight class.

Psychological Factors According to psychodynamic theory, eating is the cardinal oral activity. Psychodynamic theorists believe that when people who were fixated in the oral stage by conflicts concerning dependence and independence are likely to regress in times of stress to excessive oral activities such as overeating.

Other psychological factors connected with overeating and obesity include low self-esteem, lack of self-efficacy expectancies, family conflicts, and negative emotions. Although the connections between these factors and obesity affect both genders, women most frequently seek assistance from professionals and diet centers, largely because of the pressures imposed on them by society to adhere to expectations of thinness. Consider the cases of Joan and Terry:

Joan was trapped in the yo-yo syndrome, repeatedly dropping 20 pounds, then regaining it. Whenever Joan got stuck at a certain weight plateau, or started to regain weight, her self-esteem plummeted. She'd hear herself muttering, "Who am I kidding? I'm not worthy of being thin. I should just accept being fat."

An incident with her mother revealed how her negative thinking was often triggered. Joan had lost 24 pounds from an original weight of 174 and was beginning to feel good about herself. Most other people reinforced her by complimenting her on her weight loss. She called her mother, who lived in another state, to share the good news. Instead of jumping on the bandwagon, her mother cautioned her not to expect too much from her success. After all, her mother pointed out, she had been repeatedly disappointed in the past. The message came through loud and clear: Don't get your hopes up because you will only be more disappointed in the end.

Joan's mother may have only meant to protect Joan from eventual disappointment, but the message she conveyed reinforced the negative view that Joan held of herself: You're a loser. Don't expect too much of yourself. Accept your reality. Don't try to change. You're a hopeless case.

As soon as she hung up the receiver, Joan rushed to the pantry. Without hesitation she devoured three packages of Famous Amos Chocolate Chip Cookies in a frenzied binge on the stairway. The next day she told her psychologist that the binge had reactivated memories of childhood bingeing on Oreos while hiding under the stairwell.

For years Terry's husband had scrutinized every morsel she consumed. "Haven't you had enough?" he would ask derisively. The more he harped on her weight, the more anger she felt, although she did not express her feelings directly. The criticism did not apply only to her weight. She also heard "You're not smart enough. . . . Why don't you take better care of yourself? . . . How come you're not sexy?" After years of assault on her self-esteem, Terry petitioned for divorce, convinced the single life could be no worse than her marriage.

While separated and awaiting the final divorce decree, Terry felt free to be herself for the first time in her adult life. However, she had not expected the effect freedom would have on her weight. She ballooned from 155 pounds to 186 pounds within a few months. She identified leftover resentment from her marriage as the driving factor. "There's no one to make me diet anymore," she said. Her overeating was like saying, "See, I can eat if I want to." Without her husband, she could express her anger and outrage toward him by eating to excess. Unfortunately, her mode of expressing anger was self-defeating. Terry's lingering resentments encouraged her to act spitefully rather than constructively.

THE AUTHORS' FILES

Treatment of Obesity

It is ironic that we live in a thinness-obsessed society that is getting fatter and fatter. The goal of weight-loss programs should be to help people who are overweight achieve and maintain a healthy weight, not a cosmetically desirable weight that is the product of a thinness-obsessed society (Brownell & Rodin, 1994; G. D. Foster & Kendall, 1994). Many people who seek help in losing weight may profit more from counseling that helps them recognize they are not as heavy as they think (Brownell, 1991). Yet, for people who are overweight, there are various treatment alternatives available to help them reduce excess weight. Even people whose heredity may work against them can control their weight within some broad limits through diet and exercise (G. D. Foster et al., 1997). A modest weight loss on the order of 10% or 15% of body weight can reduce the health risks associated with obesity (Lane, 1994).

Let us take a closer look at two of the most widely used methods for losing weight, behavior modification and appetite-suppressant drugs.

Behavior Modification Successful behavioral approaches to weight loss involve changes in lifestyle that include enhancing nutritional knowledge, adopting a sensible calorie reduction program, increasing exercise, and changing eating habits (Brownell & Wadden, 1992).

Behavior modification programs focus on helping participants alter their eating habits by changing the "ABCs" of eating. The As are the *antecedents* of eating—cues or stimuli that may "trigger" eating. These include environmental stimuli, such as the sight and aromas of food; internal stimuli, such as sensations of hunger; or emotional states, such as anxiety, fatigue, anger, depression, and boredom. Controlling the As of eating involves redesigning the environment so people are not continuously bombarded by food-related cues.

The Bs of eating refer to eating *behaviors* themselves. People who eat too quickly prevent their brains from "catching up" to their stomachs, because it takes about 15 minutes or so for feelings of satiety to register in the brain after food reaches the stomach. The Bs of eating extend to preparatory behaviors such as shopping, food storage habits, and so on.

The Cs of eating are the *consequences*. The immediate pleasure of overeating often overshadows the long-term negative consequences of obesity and risk to health. Food is also connected to other reward systems. Food can become a substitute friend or lover. When people feel depressed, they can lift their spirits with food, if only temporarily. Because food activates the parasympathetic branch of the autonomic nervous system (through digestive processes), food also acts as a natural sedative or tranquilizer, quelling feelings of anxiety or tension and helping people relax or get to sleep. In helping people cope with the Cs of eating, psychologists make the long-term benefits of sensible eating more immediate. Methods commonly used to address the ABCs of eating are shown in Table 10.3

A recent review of behavioral studies found that the average participant loses about 1.3 pounds a week, which works out to be nearly 21 pounds on the average through the course of a 16-week program or nearly 27 pounds in a 20-week program (Brownell & Wadden, 1992). About 60% to 70% of the weight loss, on the average, is maintained for at least a year following the treatment program. Another study reported 14% reductions from initial weight by the time of a 1-year follow-up (Wadden, Foster, & Letizia, 1994). Generally speaking, the longer the treatment and the greater number of therapy hours, the greater the weight loss.

Though behavior modification leads to modest weight losses that are generally well maintained through at least a year after treatment, a look at longer-term outcomes reveals a dimmer picture. As many as 90% to 95% of people who lose weight by dieting or behavior modification return to their baseline weight levels within 5 years (G. T. Wilson, 1994). The problem appears to be that the changes in diet, exercise

TABLE 10.3

Behavioral Techniques of Modifying the ABCs of Eating to Foster Weight Loss

Changing the As of Overeating

Changing the Environmental As	Avoid settings that trigger overeating. (Eat at The Celery Stalk, not The Chocolate Gourmet.) Don't leave tempting treats around the house. Serve food on smaller plates. Use a lunch plate rather than a dinner plate. Don't leave seconds on the table. Serve preplanned portions. Do not leave open casseroles on the table. Immediately freeze leftovers. Don't keep them warm on the stove. Avoid the kitchen as much as possible. Disconnect eating from other stimuli, such as watching television, talking on the telephone, or reading. Establish food-free zones in your home. Imagine there is a barrier at the entrance to your bedroom that prevents the passage of food.
Controlling the Internal As	Don't bury disturbing feelings in a box of cookies or a carton of mocha delight ice cream. Relabel feelings of hunger as signals that you're burning calories. Say to yourself, "It's okay to feel hungry. It doesn't mean I'm going to die or pass out. Each minute I delay eating, more calories are burned."

Changing the Bs of Overeating

Slow Down the Pace of Eating	Put down utensils between bites. Take smaller bites. Chew thoroughly. Savor each bite. Don't wolf bites down to make room for the next. Take a break during the meal. Put down your utensils and converse with your family or guests for a few minutes. (Give your rising blood sugar level a chance to signal your brain.) When you resume eating, ask yourself whether you need to finish every bite. Leave something over to be thrown away or enjoyed later.
Modify Shopping Behavior	Shop from a list. Don't browse through the supermarket. Shop quickly. Don't make shopping the high point of your day. Treat the supermarket like enemy territory. Avoid the aisles containing junk food and snacks. If you must walk down these aisles, put on mental blinders and look straight ahead. Never shop when hungry. Shop after meals, not before.
Practice Competing Responses	Substitute nonfood activities for food-related activities. When tempted to overeat, leave the house, take a bath, walk the dog, call a friend, or walk around the block. Substitute low-calorie foods for high-calorie foods. Keep lettuce, celery, or carrots in the middle of the refrigerator so they are available when you want a snack. Fill spare time with nonfood-related activities: volunteer at the local hospital, play golf or tennis, join exercise groups, read in the library (rather than the kitchen), take long walks.
Chain Breaking	Stretch the overeating chain. Before allowing yourself to snack, wait 10 minutes. Next time wait 15 minutes, etc. Break the eating chain at its weakest link. It's easier to interrupt the eating chain by taking a route home that bypasses the bakery than to exercise self-control when you're placing your order.

Changing the Cs of Overeating

Reward Yourself For Meeting Calorie/Diet Goals	One pound of body weight is equivalent to 3,500 calories. To lose 1 pound per week, you need to cut 3,500 calories per week, or 500 calories per day, from your typical calorie intake level, assuming your weight has been stable. Reward yourself for meeting weekly calorie goals. Reward yourself with gifts you would not otherwise purchase for yourself, such as a cashmere sweater or tickets to a show. Repeat the reward program from week to week. If during some weeks you miss your calorie goals, don't lose heart. Get back on track next week.
Use Self-Punishment	Charge yourself for deviating from your diet. Send one dollar to a political candidate you despise, or to a hated cause, each time the chocolate cake wins.

patterns, and eating habits that led to initial weight loss do not generally carry over into changes in lifestyles that would promote long-term maintenance of weight loss. Clearly, to maintain weight losses people need to make healthy changes in dietary and exercise patterns a part of their lifestyle.

Appetite-Suppressant Drugs Some people turn to drugs to curb their appetite. Recently, several diet drugs (*Redux* and *fenfluramine*, the "fen" in the popular diet drug combination "fen-phen") were removed from the market because of poentially serious side effects. These drugs curbed

Obesity in America: Why Are Some Groups at Greater Risk?

Obesity does not affect ethnic/racial groups in our society in equal proportions. It is more prevalent among people of color, especially African Americans, Hispanic Americans, and Native Americans, than among (non-Hispanic) White Americans (see Figure 10.5) (Burros, 1994; McMurtrie, 1994). These differences are most pronounced among women. The question is, why?

Socioeconomic Factors

Obesity is more prevalent among poorer people (Ernst & Harlan, 1991; Stunkard & Sørensen, 1993). Since people of color in our society are as a group lower in socioeconomic status than White Americans, it is not surprising that rates of obesity are higher among Blacks and Hispanics, at least among women.

Why are people on the lower rungs of the socioeconomic ladder at greater risk of obesity? For one thing, more affluent people have greater access to information about nutrition and health. They are more likely to take health education courses. They have greater access to health care providers. Poorer people also exercise less regularly than more affluent people do. The fitness boom has been largely limited to more affluent people. They have the time and income to participate in organized fitness programs. Many poor people in the inner city also turn to food as a way of coping with the stresses of poverty, discrimination, crowding, and crime.

A study in San Antonio, Texas, provided evidence of a clear link between socioeconomic status and obesity (Hazuda et al., 1991). Obesity was less prevalent among both Mexican Americans and non-Hispanic White Americans living in higher income neighborhoods than among those living in poorer neighborhoods. In other words, the link between socioeconomic level and obesity holds across ethnic groups.

Dietary Patterns

Cultural differences in dietary customs also contribute to excess body weight. African Americans, for example, are more likely than White Americans to consume high-fat, high-cholesterol foods.

Acculturation

Acculturation is the process by which immigrant or native groups adopt the cultural values, attitudes, and behaviors of the host or dominant society. Acculturation may help immigrant people to adapt more successfully to their new culture, but it can become a double-edged sword in terms of health if it involves adoption of unhealthful dietary practices of the host culture. Consider that Japanese-American men living in California and Hawaii eat a higher-fat diet than Japanese men do. Not surprisingly, *the prevalence of obesity is two to three times higher among Japanese-American men than among men living in Japan* (Curb & Marcus, 1991).

Acculturation may also contribute to high rates of obesity among Native Americans, who are more likely than White Americans to have diseases linked to obesity, such as cardiovascular disease and diabetes (Broussard et al., 1991; T. K. Young & Sevenhuysen, 1989). A study of several hundred Cree and Ojibwa Indians in Canada found that nearly 90% of the 45- to 54-year-old women were obese. The adoption of a high-fat Western-style diet, the destruction of physically demanding native industries, and chronic unemployment combined with low levels of physical activity are cited as factors contributing to obesity among Native Americans in the United States and Canada.

Metabolic Factors

Biological factors may also be involved. Researchers recently reported that Black women had lower resting meta-

appetite by increasing levels in the brain of the neurotransmitter serotonin. Serotonin plays a role in regulating feelings of satiety. The removal of these drugs created only a temporary vacuum, as another serotonergic agent designed to curb appetite, sibutramine (trade name *Meridia*) was approved in 1997 (Schwenk, 1998). Meridia can also produce potentially harmful side effects, such as increased blood pressure, and is not intended for use in people who are only modestly overweight (Chase, 1998).

Many people use over-the-counter diet drug such as *Dexatrim* and *Accutrim*. Unfortunately, their track record is not very promising. Though these diet aids may produce some modest benefits, most people find that any weight they lose returns when they stop using them (Kolata, 1992). The drugs may also have unpleasant side effects, especially dizziness and nausea. The long-term safety of using these drugs also remains unknown.

All in all, the effects of appetite suppressant medication for treating obesity are at best modest and temporary (L. W. Craighead & Agras, 1991; National Task Force on the Prevention and Treatment of Obesity, 1996). Moreover, taking a drug does not prepare users to make lifestyle changes in diet

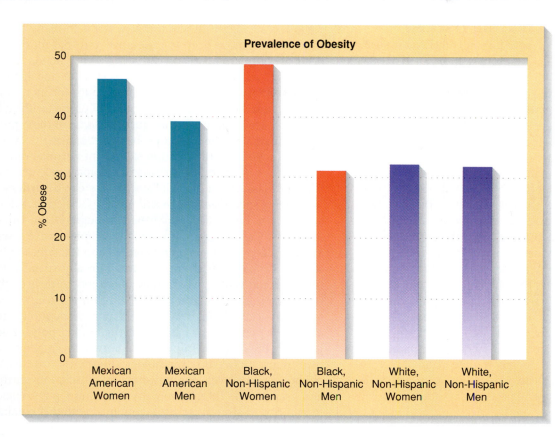

Prevalence of Obesity

(Y-axis: % Obese, values 0 to 50)

Bar categories: Mexican American Women; Mexican American Men; Black, Non-Hispanic Women; Black, Non-Hispanic Men; White, Non-Hispanic Women; White, Non-Hispanic Men

FIGURE 10.5
Obesity in the U.S. This figure shows the prevalences of obesity in the U.S. according to ethnic and gender groupings.

Source: National Heart, Lung, and Blood Institute (NHLBI), National Institutes of Health. March, 1993. *Data Fact Sheet: Obesity and Cardiovascular Disease.* Bethesda, MD: Author.

bolic rates (rate at which calories or food energy is burned while at rest) than did White women (J. E. Brody, 1997a).

Whatever the underlying reasons accounting for racial/ethnic differences in obesity, evidence shows that these differences may be narrowing. Though rates of obesity rose for men and women in all racial/ethnic groups during the 1980s, they rose most sharply among Whites (Burros, 1994, McMurtrie, 1994).

What Can Be Done?
Preventing obesity calls for strategies that apply regardless of ethnicity or income level, such as cutting back on fat intake and sugar consumption and adopting reg-

ular exercise habits. But certain health initiatives need to be specifically targeted toward the needs of the socially and economically disadvantaged groups, including the following (Jeffery, 1991):

- Increased access to health education;
- Requirements for health education curricula in all public schools;
- Guarantees of universal access to treatment of obesity;
- Increased access to healthful foods and recreational opportunities.

Source: Adapted from Nevid et al., 1998.

and exercise that promote lasting weight loss. People who use appetite suppressants may also attribute their initial weight loss to the drug rather than to their own efforts, so they may come to rely on medication rather than their own initiatives to lose weight and experience rebound weight gains whenever they discontinue the drug (Craighead, 1984).

Losing Weight and Keeping it Off: A Final Note
The more successful weight-control programs foster lifestyle changes in dietary patterns and physical exercise. They do not rely on "quickie" or "fad" diets that merely

encourage a cycle of *yo-yo dieting*. We have become a nation of dieters, but still our collective waistlines are increasing. The bottom line is that dieting alone doesn't work. More than 9 of 10 dieters fail to keep off the weight they lose (J. E. Brody, 1994c; Wilson, 1994), and 2 of 3 people who lose weight on a diet will regain every pound that they lost within a few years—and then some. The reason: Dieting offers a short-term strategy where a long-term approach is needed. Effective weight management comes from adopting a lifestyle that permits you to balance your energy input in the form of calories and energy output in the form of activity and exercise. Table 10.4 lists some suggestions for making changes in your daily lifestyle to help manage your weight.

TRUTH *or* FICTION REVISITED

10.9 *True.* Most dieters regain the weight they've lost—and then some.

Recent evidence highlights the importance of regular exercise in losing weight and keeping it off. For one thing, combining dieting and exercise is more effective in reducing weight than dieting alone (Brownell & Wadden, 1992; Dubbert, 1992). For another, regular exercise appears to be the key factor involved in maintaining weight (Klem et al., 1997; Tinker & Tucker, 1997; Wadden et al., 1997, 1998). In one study of men who had lost weight by dieting, those who increased their exercise level were more successful in keeping the weight off than those who either continued to count calories or made further attempts to reduce their calorie intake ("You Needn't Starve to Keep off Lost Pounds," 1990). Unfortunately, fewer than half of Americans exercise regularly, and many who start an exercise program drop out shortly afterward (M. Beck, 1994). Exercise programs that are likely to be the most successful are those that fit within the individual's lifestyle (Perri et al,. 1997). Perhaps we need to be thinking about how to incorporate regular physical activity (taking walks instead of driving, climbing stairs instead of taking elevators to low floors) into our daily routines.

PHYSIOLOGICAL AND PSYCHOLOGICAL FACTORS IN SLEEP DISORDERS

Sleep is a biological function that remains in many ways a mystery. We know sleep is restorative and that most of us need 6 hours or more of sleep a night to function at our best. Yet we cannot identify the specific biochemical changes occuring during sleep that account for its restorative function. We also know that many of us are troubled by sleep problems, although the causes of some of these problems remain obscure. Sleep problems of sufficient severity and frequency that they lead to significant personal distress or impaired functioning in social, occupational, or other roles are classified in the DSM system as **sleep disorders.**

Highly specialized diagnostic facilities, called *sleep disorders centers,* have been established throughout the United States and Canada to provide a more comprehensive assessment of sleep problems than is possible in the typical office setting. People with sleep disorders typically spend a few nights at the center, where they are wired to devices that track their physiological responses during sleep or attempted sleep—brain waves, heart and respiration rates, and so on. This form of assessment is termed **polysomnographic (PSG) recording,** because it involves simultaneous measurement of diverse physiological response patterns, including brain waves, eye movements, muscle movements, and respiration. Information obtained from physiological monitoring of sleep patterns is combined with that obtained

---

TABLE 10.4

Lifestyle Changes for Controlling Your Weight

- Reduce your intake of total dietary fat to less than 30%, and saturated fat to less than 10%, of your daily calorie intake. For 2,000 calorie per day diet, this means that total fat intake should not exceed 67 grams and saturated fat intake should not exceed 23 grams.

- Substitute low-fat for high-fat foods.

- Increase your intake of fruits and vegetables to at least 3-5 servings of vegetables and 2-4 servings of fruit a day.

- Control your portions: Don't supersize it!

- Slow down the pace of eating. It takes about 15 minutes for feelings of satiety to register in the brain. Give your brain a chance to catch up to your stomach.

- Beware of hidden calories. *For instance, fruit juices such as orange juice and grapefruit juice are loaded with calories—in fact more calories than regular Coca Cola.* Try diluting fruit juices with water or substitute the actual fruit itself.

- Become "food smart" when eating out. Stick to broiled or sauteed foods, not fried or coated, and hold the mayo! Skip high-fat toppings on salads, potatoes, and side dishes.

- Limit your sodium (salt) intake to 2,400 milligrams daily.

- Reduce your cholesterol intake to less than 300 mg per day.

- Make physical activity a part of your lifestyle. Health experts recommend 30 minutes a day of moderate physical activity—activity equivalent in strenuousness to walking at a brisk 3–4 mph pace (Pate et al., 1995). This doesn't mean you must work out at a gym every day or jog around the park. Taking a brisk walk from your car to your office or school, climbing stairs, or doing vigorous work around the house all can accumulate to reach your daily physical activity goals. Additional aerobic exercise in the form of working out on a treadmill, stationary skier, or stair-climber, or running, swimming, or taking aerobics classes may help even more.

from medical and psychological evaluations, subjective reports of sleep disturbance, and sleep diaries (i.e., daily logs compiled by the problem sleeper that track the length of time between retiring to bed and falling asleep, number of hours slept, nightly awakenings, daytime naps, and so on). Multidisciplinary teams of physicians and psychologists in these sleep centers sift through this information to arrive at a diagnosis and suggest treatment approaches to address the presenting problem.

The DSM groups sleep disorders within two major categories: **dyssomnias** and **parasomnias.**

Dyssomnias

Dyssomnias are characterized by disturbances in the amount, quality, or timing of sleep. There are five specific types of dyssomnias: primary insomnia, primary hypersomnia, narcolepsy, breathing-related sleep disorder, and circadian rhythm sleep disorder.

Insomnia   Insomnia derives from the Latin *in-,* meaning "not" or "without," and, of course, *somnus,* meaning "sleep." Occasional bouts of insomnia, especially during times of stress, are not abnormal. Survey evidence shows that between 9% and 15% of adults in the United States complain of chronic insomnia, with as many as 20% more reporting occasional difficulty sleeping (Morin & Wooten, 1996). However, about 1 in 3 adult Americans experience chronic or persistent insomnia in any given year (Gillin, 1991). Chronic insomnia affects more older than younger people and more women than men (Kupfer & Reynolds, 1997). Young people with insomnia usually complain it takes too long to get to sleep. Older people with insomnia are more likely to complain of waking frequently during the night, or of waking too early in the morning.

Chronic insomnia lasting a month or longer is often a sign of an underlying physical problem or a psychological disorder such as depression (Rakel, 1993). If the underlying problem is treated successfully, chances are that normal sleep patterns will be restored. Chronic insomnia that cannot be accounted for by another psychological or physical disorder, or by the effects of drugs or medications, is classified as a sleep disorder called *primary insomnia.* People with primary insomnia have persistent difficulty falling asleep or remaining asleep or achieving restorative sleep (sleep that leaves the person feeling refreshed and alert) for a period of a month or longer. The sleep disturbance or the associated daytime fatigue causes significant levels of personal distress or difficulties performing usual social, occupational, or other roles, such as impaired work performance or ability to carry out school assignments. Not surprisingly, there is a high rate of comorbidity (co-occurrence) between insomnia and other psychological problems, especially anxiety and depression (Breslau et al., 1996; Morin & Ware,1996). Although the prevalence of primary insomnia is unknown, it is considered the most common form of sleep disturbance.

Psychological factors play a prominent role in primary insomnia. People who are troubled by primary insomnia tend to bring their anxieties and worries to bed with them, which raises their bodily arousal to a level that prevents natural sleep. Then they worry about not getting enough sleep, which only compounds their sleep difficulties. They may try to force themselves to sleep, which tends to backfire by creating more anxiety and tension, making sleep even less likely to occur (Lacks & Morin, 1992). Sleep cannot be forced. We can only set the stage for sleep by retiring when we are tired and relaxed and allowing sleep to occur naturally.

Primary Hypersomnia   The word *hypersomnia* is derived from the Greek *hyper,* meaning "over" or "more than normal," and the Latin *somnus,* meaning sleep. Primary **hypersomnia** involves a pattern of excessive sleepiness during the day that continues for a period of a month or longer. The excessive sleepiness (sometimes referred to as "sleep drunkenness") may take the form of difficulty awakening following a prolonged sleep period (typically 8 to 12 hours of sleep). Or there may be a pattern of daytime sleep episodes occurring virtually every day in the form of intended or unintended napping (such as inadvertently falling asleep while watching TV). Despite the fact that daytime naps often last an hour or more, the person does not feel refreshed upon awakening. The disorder is considered primary because it cannot be accounted for by inadequate amounts of sleep during the night due to insomnia or other factors (such as loud neighbors keeping the person up), by another psychological or physical disorder, or by drug or medication use.

Although many of us feel sleepy during the day from time to time, and may even drift off occasionally while reading or watching TV, the person with primary hypersomnia has more persistent and severe periods of sleepiness that typically lead to difficulties in daily functioning, such as missing important meetings because of difficulty awakening. Although the prevalence of the disorder is unknown, surveys of the general population show complaints relating to daytime sleepiness affecting between 0.5% to 5% of the adult population (APA, 1994).

TRUTH *or* FICTION REVISITED

10.10 *False.*   Sleep attacks are relatively uncommon. They are characteristic of a disorder called narcolepsy, which affects between 2 and 16 persons in 10,000.

Narcolepsy   The word **narcolepsy** derives from the Greek *narke,* meaning "stupor" and *lepsis,* meaning "an attack." People with narcolepsy experience sleep attacks in which they suddenly fall asleep without any warning at various times during the day. They remain asleep for a period of about 15 minutes on the average. The person can be in the midst of a conversation at one moment and slump to the floor fast asleep a moment later. The diagnosis is made when sleep attacks occur daily for a period of 3 months or longer and are combined with the presence of one or both of the following conditions: (1) **cataplexy** (a sudden loss of muscular control); and (2) intrusions of **REM sleep** in the transitional state between wakefulness and sleep (APA, 1994). REM, or rapid eye movement, sleep is the stage of sleep associated with dreaming. It is so-named because the sleeper's eyes tend to dart about rapidly under the closed lids. Narcoleptic attacks are associated with an almost immediate transition into REM sleep from a state of wakefulness. In normal sleep, REM typically follows several stages of non-REM sleep.

Cataplexy typically follows a strong emotional reaction such as joy or anger. It can range from a mild weakness in the legs to a complete loss of muscle control that results in the person suddenly collapsing (Dahl, 1992). People with narcolepsy may also experience *sleep paralysis,* a temporary state following awakening in which the person feels incapable of moving or talking. The person may also report frightening hallucinations, called *hypnagogic hallucinations,* which occur just before the onset of sleep and tend to involve visual, auditory, tactile, and kinesthetic (body movement) sensations.

Narcolepsy affects men and women equally and is a relatively uncommon disorder, affecting an estimated 0.02% (2 in 10,000) to 0.16% (16 in 10,000) people within the general adult population (APA, 1994). Unlike hypersomnia in which daytime sleep episodes follow a period of increasing sleepiness, narcoleptic attacks occur abruptly and are experienced as refreshing upon awakening. The attacks can be dangerous and frightening, especially if they occur when the person is driving or using heavy equipment or sharp implements. About 2 of 3 people with narcolepsy have fallen asleep while driving, and 4 of 5 have fallen asleep on the job (Aldrich, 1992). Household accidents resulting from falls are also common (F. L. Cohen, Ferrans, & Eshler, 1992). Not surprisingly, the disorder is associated with a lower quality of life in terms of general health and daily functioning (Ferrans, Cohen, & Smith, 1992).

The cause of the disorder remains unknown, but a disturbance in the brain's regulation of REM sleep is suspected of playing a part (Aldrich, 1992; Tafti et al., 1992). Genetic factors may be involved, as the disorder occurs disproportionately among biological relatives of people with the disorder (APA, 1994).

Breathing-Related Sleep Disorder   People with a **breathing-related sleep disorder** experience repeated disruptions of sleep due to respiratory problems (APA, 1994). These frequent disruptions of sleep result in insomnia or excessive daytime sleepiness.

The subtypes of the disorder are distinguished in terms of the underlying causes of the breathing problem. The most common type is *obstructive sleep apnea,* which involves repeated episodes of either complete or partial obstruction of breathing during sleep. The word **apnea** derives from the Greek prefix *a-,* meaning "not, without," and *pneuma,* meaning "breath." The breathing difficulty results from the blockage of air flow in the upper airways, which is often due to a

Sleep apnea.   Loud snoring may be a sign of obstructive sleep apnea, a breathing-related sleep disorder in which the person may temporarily stop breathing as many times as 500 times during a night's sleep. Loud snoring, described by bed partners as reaching levels of industrial noise pollution, may alternate with momentary silences when breathing is suspended.

structural defect, such as an overly thick palate or enlarged tonsils or adenoids. In cases of complete obstruction, the sleeper may literally stop breathing for periods of from 15 to 90 seconds as many as 500 times during the night! When these lapses of breathing occur, the sleeper may suddenly sit up, gasp for air, take a few deep breaths, and fall back asleep without awakening or realizing that breathing was interrupted. The narrowing of the air passages also produces loud snoring, which alternates with these momentary silences when breathing is suspended (Phillipson, 1993). In some cases, only a partial obstruction of breathing occurs, resulting in unusually slow or shallow breathing but no outright cessation of breathing.

Although a biological reflex kicks in to force a gasping breath after these brief interruptions of breathing, the frequent disruptions of normal sleep resulting from apneas can leave people feeling sleepy the following day, making it more difficult for them to function effectively (Hilchey, 1995; Mitler, 1993). Obstructive sleep apnea is a relatively common problem, with estimates indicating the disorder affects approximately 1% to 10% of the adult population, perhaps as many as 20 million Americans (APA, 1994; Grady, 1997b). The disorder is more common in men, especially in middle-aged men. Though men with apnea outnumber women by about a 2:1 ratio, the disorder often goes undiagnosed in women (Young et al., 1996). It is also more common among people who are obese, apparently because of a narrowing of the upper airways due to an enlargement of soft tissue (APA, 1994; Partinen & Telakivi, 1992). Alcohol use before bedtime can also convert snoring due to a narrowing of the breathing passageways into outright blockages, resulting in sleep apneas (Phillipson, 1993).

People with sleep apnea may gasp for breath hundreds of times during the night without realizing it. They may only become aware of the problem when it is diagnosed or when their bed partners point it out to them. The person's bed partner is usually very aware of the problem because the loudness of the person's snoring can reach levels associated with industrial noise pollution. Bed partners commonly look for other sleeping places to obtain a good night's sleep. Not surprisingly, people who have sleep apnea report a poorer quality of life than unaffected people (Gall, Isaac, & Kryger, 1993).

TRUTH *or* FICTION REVISITED

10.11 *True.* People with sleep apnea may gasp for breath hundreds of times during the night without realizing it.

Sleep apnea is also associated with an increased risk of cardiovascular disease (Grady, 1997b; Strollo & Rogers, 1996). However, it is not clear whether apnea plays a causal role in these problems or may simply be a marker for cardiovascular problems through its association with aging and obesity (Marton, 1997; Wright et al., 1997).

Circadian Rhythm Sleep Disorder Most bodily functions follow a cycle or an internal rhythm—called a circadian rhythm—that lasts about 24 hours. Even when people are relieved of scheduled activities and work duties and placed in environments that screen the time of day, they usually follow relatively normal sleep-wake schedules.

In **circadian rhythm sleep disorder,** this rhythm becomes grossly disturbed because of a mismatch between the sleep schedule demands imposed on the person and the person's internal sleep-wake cycle. The disruption in normal sleep patterns caused by the mismatch can lead to insomnia or hypersomnia. Like other sleep disorders, the mismatch must be persistent and severe enough to cause significant

levels of distress or impair one's ability to function in social, occupational, or other roles. The "jet lag" that can accompany travel between time zones does not qualify because it is usually transient. However, frequent changes of time zones and frequent changes of work shifts (as encountered, for example, by nursing personnel) can induce more persistent or recurrent problems adjusting sleep patterns to scheduling demands, resulting in a circadian rhythm sleep disorder. Treatment may involve a program of making gradual adjustments in the sleep schedule to allow the person's circadian system to become aligned with changes in the sleep-wake schedule (Dahl, 1992).

Parasomnias

The parasomnias involve abnormal behaviors or physiological events taking place during sleep or at the threshold between wakefulness and sleep. Among the more common parasomnias are nightmare disorder, sleep terror disorder, and sleepwalking disorder.

Nightmare Disorder **Nightmare disorder** involves recurrent awakenings from sleep because of frightening dreams (nightmares). The nightmares typically involve lengthy storylike dreams that involve threats of imminent physical danger to the individual, such as being chased, attacked, or injured. The nightmare is usually recalled vividly upon awakening. Although alertness is regained quickly after awakening, anxiety and fear may linger and prevent a return to sleep. Perhaps half the adult population occasionally experiences nightmares, although the percentages of people having the intense, recurrent nightmares that produce the kind of emotional distress or difficulties in functioning that would lead to a diagnosis of nightmare disorder remains unknown (APA, 1994).

Nightmares are often associated with traumatic experiences and are generally more frequent when the individual is under stress. Supporting the general link between trauma and nightmares, researchers report that the incidence of nightmares was greater among survivors of the 1989 San Francisco earthquake in the weeks following the quake than among comparison groups (Wood et al., 1992). An increased frequency of nightmares was also observed among children who were exposed to the 1994 Los Angeles earthquake (Kolbert, 1994).

Nightmares generally occur during REM sleep. REM sleep tends to become longer and the dreams occurring during REM sleep more intense in the latter half of sleep, so nightmares usually occur late at night or toward morning. Although nightmares may contain great motor activity, as in fleeing from an assailant, dreamers show little muscle activity. The same biological processes that activate dreams—including nightmares—inhibit body movement, causing a type of paralysis. This is indeed fortunate, as it prevents the dreamer from jumping out of bed and running into a dresser or a wall in the attempt to elude the pursuing assailants from the dream.

Shift-Work. Frequent shifting of work schedules can play havoc with the body's natural circadian rhythms.

Sleep Terror Disorder   It typically begins with a loud, piercing cry or scream in the night. Even the most soundly asleep parent will be summoned to the child's bedroom as if shot from a cannon. The child (most cases involve children) may be sitting up, appearing frightened and showing signs of extreme arousal—profuse sweating with rapid heartbeat and respiration. The child may start talking incoherently or thrash about wildly but remain asleep. If the child awakens fully, he or she may not recognize the parent or may attempt to push the parent away. After a few minutes the child falls back into a deep sleep and, upon awakening in the morning, remembers nothing of the experience. These terrifying attacks, called *sleep terrors,* are more intense than ordinary nightmares. Unlike nightmares, sleep terrors tend to occur during the first third of nightly sleep and during deep, non-REM sleep (Dahl, 1992).

A **sleep terror disorder** involves repeated episodes of sleep terrors resulting in abrupt awakenings that begin with a panicky scream (APA, 1994). If awakening occurs during a sleep terror episode, the person will usually appear confused and disoriented for a few minutes. The person may feel a vague sense of terror and be able to report some fragmentary dream images, but not the sort of detailed dreams that are typical in the case of nightmares. Most of the time the person falls back asleep and remembers nothing of the experience the following morning.

Sleep terror disorder in children is typically outgrown during adolescence. More boys than girls are affected by the disorder, but among adults the gender ratio is about even. In adults, the disorder tends to follow a chronic course during which the frequency and intensity of the episodes waxes and wanes over time. Prevalence data on the disorder are lacking, but episodes of sleep terror are estimated to occur in 1% to 6% of children but in fewer than 1% of adults (APA, 1994). The cause of sleep terror disorder remains a mystery.

Sleepwalking Disorder   **Sleepwalking disorder** involves repeated episodes in which the sleeper arises from bed and walks about the house while remaining fully asleep. Because these episodes tend to occur during the deeper stages of sleep in which there is an absence of dreaming, it does not appear a sleepwalking episode involves the enactment of a dream. In sleepwalking disorder, the occurrence of repeated episodes of sleepwalking are of sufficient severity to cause significant levels of personal distress or impaired functioning. Sleepwalking disorder is more common in children, affecting between 1% and 5% of children according to some estimates (APA, 1994). Between 10% and 30% of children are believed to have had at least one episode of sleepwalking. The prevalence of the disorder among adults is unknown, as are its causes. However, perhaps as many as 7% of adults have experienced occasional sleepwalking episodes (APA, 1994). The causes of sleepwalking remain obscure, although both genetic and environmental factors are believed to be involved (Hublin et al., 1997).

Although sleepwalkers typically avoid walking into things, accidents occasionally happen. Sleepwalkers tend to have a blank stare on their faces during these episodes. They are generally unresponsive to others and difficult to awaken. When they do awaken the following morning, they typically have little if any recall of the experience. If they are awakened during the episode, they may be disoriented or confused for a few minutes (as is the case with sleep terrors), but full alertness is soon restored. There is no basis to the belief that it is harmful to sleepwalkers to awaken them during episodes. Isolated incidents of violent behavior have been associated with sleepwalking, but these are rare occurrences and may well involve other forms of psychopathology.

Treatment of Sleep Disorders

The most common method for treating sleep disorders in the United States is the use of sleep medications called **hypnotics.** However, because of problems associated with these drugs, nonpharmacological treatment approaches, principally cognitive-behavioral therapy, have come to the fore.

Biological Approaches   Various hypnotic (sleep-inducing) drugs are used to treat insomnia, including a class of minor tranquilizers called *benzodiazepines* (for example, Valium, Librium, Dalmane, Xanax, and Halcion). (These drugs are also widely used in treatment of anxiety disorders, as we saw in Chapter 5.) The most widely used hypnotic presently is a non-benzodiazepine called *zolpidem* (trade name Ambien) (Lobo & Greene, 1997). It appears to be about as effective as the benzodiazepines but may produce fewer side effects and possibly fewer withdrawal effects (Kupfer & Reynolds, 1997; Nowell et al., 1997). Nonetheless, all of these drugs can produce dependence if used regularly over time.

When used for the short-term treatment of insomnia, hypnotics are generally effective in reducing the time it takes to get to sleep, increasing total length of sleep, and reducing nightly awakenings (Nowell et al., 1998). They work by reducing states of arousal and inducing feelings of calmness, thereby making the person more receptive to sleep. However, as many as 10% of patients take sleeping pills for months or years despite a lack of evidence from controlled studies supporting their long-term efficacy (Roy-Byrne & Conley, 1998).

There are a number of problems with using drugs to combat insomnia (Murtagh & Greenwood, 1995). Sleep-inducing drugs tend to suppress REM sleep, which may interfere with some of the restorative functions of sleep. They can also lead to a carryover or "hangover" the following day, which is associated with daytime sleepiness and reduced performance. Rebound insomnia can also follow discontinuation of the drug, causing worse insomnia than was originally the case. Rebound insomnia may be lessened, however, by tapering off the drug rather than abruptly discontinuing it (Roehrs et al., 1992). These drugs quickly lose their effectiveness at a given dosage level, so progressively larger doses must be used to achieve the same effect. High doses can be dangerous, especially if they are mixed with alcoholic beverages at bedtime. Regular use can also lead to physical dependence (addiction). Once dependence is established, withdrawal symptoms following cessation of use may occur, including agitation, tremors, nausea, headaches, and, in severe cases, delusions or hallucinations.

Users can also become *psychologically* dependent on sleeping pills. That is, they can develop a psychological need for the medication and assume that they will not be able to get to sleep without them. Since worry about going without drugs heightens bodily arousal, such self-doubts are likely to become self-fulfilling prophecies. Moreover, users may attribute their success in falling asleep to the pill and not to themselves, which strengthens reliance on the drugs and makes it harder to forgo using them.

Not surprisingly, there is little evidence of long-term benefits of drug therapy after withdrawal (Morin & Wooten, 1996). Relying on sleeping pills does nothing to resolve the underlying cause of the problem or help the person learn more effective ways of coping with the problem. If hypnotic drugs such as benzodiazepines are to be prescribed at all for sleep problems, they should only be used for a brief period of time (a few weeks at most) and at the lowest possible dose (Dement, 1992; Kupfer & Reynolds, 1997). The aim should be to provide a temporary respite so the clinician can help the client find effective ways of handling the sources of stress and anxiety that contribute to insomnia.

Minor tranquilizers of the benzodiazepine family and tricyclic antidepressants are also used to treat the deep-sleep disorders—sleep terrors and sleepwalking. They seem to have a beneficial effect by decreasing the length of deep sleep and reducing partial arousals between sleep stages (Dahl, 1992). Use of sleep medications for these disorders, like primary insomnia, also incurs the risk of physiological and psychological dependence and thus should be used only in severe cases and only as a temporary means of "breaking the cycle." Other psychoactive drugs, such as stimulants, are sometimes used to help maintain wakefulness in people with narcolepsy and to combat daytime sleepiness in people with hypersomnia. Daily naps of 10 to 60 minutes, and coping support from mental health professionals or self-help groups, may also be of help to people with narcolepsy (Alaia, 1992; Aldrich, 1992). Sleep apnea is sometimes treated with drugs that act on brain centers that stimulate breathing. Surgery may also be used to widen the upper airways. Mechanical devices may help maintain breathing during sleep, such as a nose mask that exerts pressure to keep the upper airway passages open or a battery-powered device that continuously blows air through the nose to prevent the airways from collapsing (Hilchey, 1995; Marklund et al., 1998).

Psychological Approaches   Psychological approaches have by and large been limited to treatment of primary insomnia. Overall, cognitive-behavioral treatment approaches have produced substantial benefits in treating chronic insomnia, as measured by both reductions in sleep latency and improvement of perceived sleep quality (Kupfer & Reynolds, 1997; Morin & Wooten, 1996; Murtagh & Greenwood, 1995; Nowell et al., 1998). As many as 60% to 80%

Is your bed a cue for sleeping? People who use their beds for many other activities, including eating, reading, and watching television, may find that lying in bed loses its association with sleeping. Behavior therapists use stimulus control techniques to help people with insomnia create a stimulus environment associated with sleeping.

To Sleep, Perchance to Dream

From time to time, many of us have difficulty falling asleep or remaining asleep. Although sleep is a natural function and cannot be forced, we can develop more adaptive sleep habits that help us become more receptive to sleep. However, if insomnia or other sleep-related problems persist or become associated with difficulties functioning during the day, it would be worthwhile to have the problem checked out with a professional. Here are some techniques to help you acquire more adaptive sleep habits:

1. Retire to bed only when you feel sleepy.

2. Limit as much as possible your activities in bed to sleeping. Avoid watching TV or reading in bed.

3. If after 10 to 20 minutes of lying in bed you are unable to fall asleep, get out of bed, leave the bedroom, and put yourself in a relaxed mood by reading, listening to calming music, or practicing self-relaxation.

4. Establish a regular routine. Sleeping late to make up for lost sleep can throw off your body clock. Set your alarm for the same time each morning and get up, regardless of how many hours you have slept.

5. Avoid naps during the daytime. You'll feel less sleepy at bedtime if you catch z's during the afternoon.

6. Avoid ruminating in bed. Don't focus on solving your problems or organizing the rest of your life as you're attempting to sleep. Tell yourself that you'll think about tomorrow, tomorrow. Help yourself enter a more sleepful frame of mind by engaging in a mental fantasy or mind trip, or just let all thoughts slip away from consciousness. If an important idea comes to you, don't rehearse it in your mind. Jot it down on a handy pad so you won't lose it. But if thoughts persist, get up and follow them elsewhere.

7. Put yourself in a relaxed frame of mind before sleep. Some people unwind before bed by reading, while others prefer watching TV or just resting quietly. Do whatever you find most relaxing. You may

of patients respond favorably (Morin & Wooten, 1996). Still, only about a third become good sleepers (Lacks & Morin, 1992).

Cognitive-behavioral techniques are short term in emphasis and focus on directly lowering states of physiological arousal, modifying maladaptive sleeping habits, and changing dysfunctional thoughts (Lacks & Morin, 1992). Cognitive behavior therapists typically use a combination of techniques, including stimulus control, relaxation training, and rational restructuring. Stimulus control involves changing the stimulus environment associated with sleeping. Under normal conditions, we learn to associate stimuli relating to lying down in bed with sleeping, so that exposure to these stimuli comes to induce feelings of sleepiness. But when people use their beds for many other activities—such as eating, reading, and watching television—the bed may lose its association with sleepiness. Moreover, the longer the person with insomnia lies in bed tossing and turning, the more the bed becomes associated with cues related to anxiety and frustration. Stimulus control techniques attempt to strengthen the connection between the bed and sleep by restricting as much as possible the activities spent in bed to sleeping and by limiting the time spent in bed trying to fall

asleep to 10 or 20 minutes at a time. If sleep does not occur within the designated time period, the person is instructed to leave the bed and go to another room to restore a relaxed frame of mind before returning to bed, such as by sitting quietly, reading, watching TV, or practicing relaxation exercises. Relaxation techniques, such as the Jacobson progressive relaxation approach, may be practiced before bedtime to help reduce levels of physiological arousal. Biofeedback training may also be used as a way of teaching self-relaxation skills. Based on a meta-analysis of outcome studies, it does not appear that the combination of stimulus control and relaxation training produces any larger benefit than either approach alone (Murtagh & Greenwood, 1995).

Rational restructuring involves substituting rational alternatives for self-defeating, maladaptive thoughts or beliefs (see accompanying "Closer Look" section for examples). The belief that failing to get a good night's sleep will lead to unfortunate, even disastrous, consequences the next day reduces the chances of falling asleep because it raises the level of anxiety and can lead the person to try unsuccessfully to force sleep to happen. Most of us do reasonably well if we lose sleep or even miss a night of sleep, even though we might like more.

find it helpful to incorporate within your regular bedtime routine the techniques for lowering your level of arousal through meditation or progressive relaxation.

8. Establish a regular daytime exercise schedule. Regular exercise during the day (not directly before bedtime) can help induce sleepiness upon retiring.

9. Avoid use of caffeinated beverages, such as coffee and tea, in the evening or late afternoon. Also, avoid drinking alcoholic beverages. Alcohol can interfere with normal sleep patterns (reduced total sleep, REM sleep, and sleep efficiency) even when consumed six hours before bedtime (Landolt et al., 1996).

10. Practice rational restructuring with yourself. Substitute rational alternatives for self-defeating thoughts. Here are some examples:

Self-Defeating Thoughts

"I must fall asleep right now or I'll be a wreck tomorrow."

"What's the matter with me that I can't seem to fall asleep?"

"If I don't get to sleep right now, I won't be able to concentrate tomorrow on the exam (conference, meeting, etc.)."

Rational Alternatives

"I may feel tired, but I've been able to get by with little sleep before. I can make up for it tomorrow by getting to bed early."

"Stop blaming yourself. You can't control sleep. Just let whatever happens, happen."

"My concentration may be off a bit, but I'm not going to fall apart. There's no point blowing things out of proportion. I might as well get up for a while and watch a little TV rather than lie here ruminating."

SUMMARY

Eating Disorders

Two major types of eating disorders, anorexia nervosa and bulimia nervosa, tend to begin in adolescence. They affect many more females than males and involve preoccupations with weight control and maladaptive ways of trying to keep weight down. Anorexia nervosa involves maintenance of weight at least 15% below normal levels, intense fears of becoming overweight, distorted body image, and, in females, amenorrhea. Bulimia nervosa involves preoccupation with weight control and body shape, repeated binges, and regular purging to keep weight down.

Obesity

Obesity, a major health risk, is classified as a chronic disease, not a psychological disorder. Rates of obesity in the United States have been rising. The causes of obesity include genetic factors, metabolic factors, fat cells, lifestyle factors, and psychological factors. Treatment approaches to obesity include behavior modification (to alter problem eating habits) and appetite-suppressant drugs (to curb appetite). Long-term success depends on making lasting changes in dietary and exercise patterns.

Physiological and Psychological Factors in Sleep Disorders

Sleep disorders are classified in two major categories, dyssomnias and parasomnias. Dyssomnias involve disturbances in the amount, quality, or timing of sleep. They include five specific types: primary insomnia, primary hypersomnia, narcolepsy, breathing-related sleep disorder, and circadian rhythm sleep disorder. Parasomnias involve disturbed behaviors or abnormal physiological responses occurring either during sleep or at the threshold between wakefulness and sleep. They include three major types: nightmare disorder, sleep terror disorder, and sleepwalking disorder. The most common form of treatment of sleep disorders involves the use of hypnotic drugs. However, use of these drugs should be time limited because of the potential for psychological and/or physical dependence, among other problems associated with their use. Cognitive behavioral interventions have produced substantial benefits in helping people with chronic insomnia.

Norms for the Fear of Fat Scale

Comparative scores are available for women only. You may compare your own score on the Fear of Fat Scale to those obtained by the following groups:

Keep the following in mind as you interpret your score:

1. The Goldfarb samples are quite small
2. A score at a certain level does not place you in that group; it merely means that you report an equivalent fear of fat. In other words, a score of 33.00 does not indicate that you have bulimia or anorexia. It means that your self-reported fear of fat approximates those reported by bulimic and anorexic women in the Goldfarb study.

Group	N	Mean
Nondieting college women (women satisfied with their weight)	49	17.30
General female college population	73	18.33
College women who are dissatisfied with their weight and have been on three or more diets during the past year	40	23.90
Bulimic college women (actively bingeing and purging)	32	30.00
Anorexic women in treatment	7	35.00

Source: Goldfarb, L.A., Dykens, E.M., & Gerrard, M. (1985). The Goldfarb Fear of Fat Scale. *Journal of Personality Assessment, 49,* 329-332.

REVIEW QUESTIONS

1. What are the defining features of anorexia nervosa and bulimia nervosa?

2. What are the medical complications associated with anorexia and bulimia?

3. To what extent do cultural factors, family factors, and psychological factors play a part in the development of eating disorders?

4. What approaches are used in the treatment of eating disorders? How successful are they?

5. How is binge eating disorder different than bulimia?

6. Why is obesity considered a major health risk?

7. What sociocultural, biological, and psychological factors are involved in the development of obesity?

8. What roles can psychologists play in the treatment of obesity?

9. What are the features associated with the different types of sleep disorders? What do we know about the causal factors involved in each? How are these disorders treated?

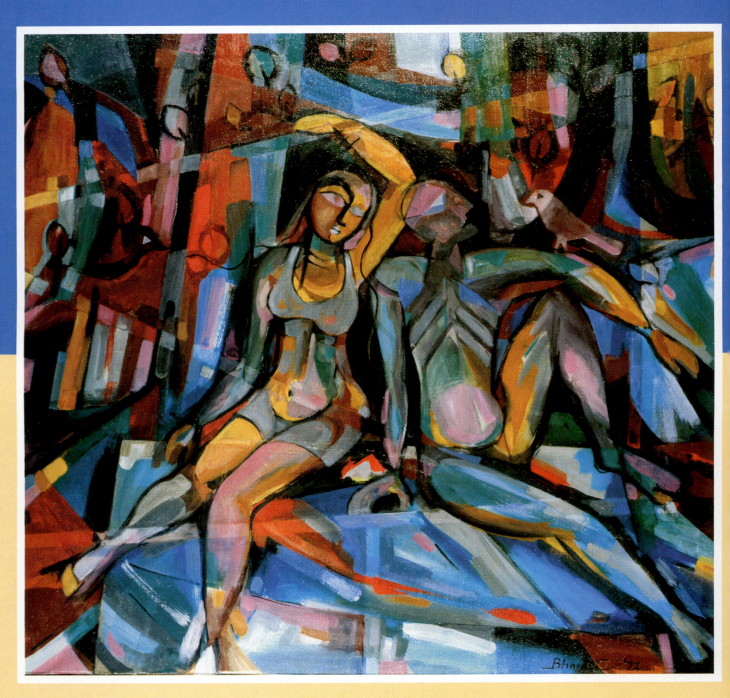

© **Bharati Chaudhuri**
Invisible Tension, 1992

Gender Identity Disorder, Paraphilias, and Sexual Dysfunctions

TRUTH *or* FICTION?

11.1 Gay males and lesbians have a gender identity of the opposite sex.

11.2 Homosexuality is classified as a mental disorder.

11.3 Professional strippers are considered exhibitionists according to clinical criteria.

11.4 Watching your partner disrobe or viewing an explicit movie are not forms of voyeurism.

11.5 Some people cannot become sexually aroused unless they are subjected to pain or humiliation by others.

11.6 Premature ejaculation is relatively uncommon, even among young men.

11.7 Orgasm is a reflex.

11.8 Only men produce testosterone in their bodies.

11.9 There is now a pill that can help men with erectile dysfunction achieve erections.

Off the fog-bound shore of Ireland lies the isle of Inis Beag.[1] From the air it is a verdant jewel, warm and enticing. From the ground, the perspective is different.

For example, the inhabitants of Inis Beag believe that normal women do not have orgasms and those who do must be deviant (Messenger, 1971). Premarital sex is virtually unknown. Women participate in sexual relations in order to conceive children and pacify their husbands' lustful urges. They need not be concerned about being called on for frequent performances because the men of Inis Beag believe, groundlessly, that sex saps their strength. Relations on Inis Beag take place in the dark—literally and figuratively, and with nightclothes on. Consistent with local standards of masculinity, the man ejaculates as quickly as he can. Then he rolls over and goes to sleep, without concern for his partner's satisfaction. Women do not complain, however, as they are reared to believe it is abnormal for them to experience sexual pleasure.

If Inis Beag is not your cup of tea, perhaps the ambience of Mangaia will strike you as more congenial. Mangaia is a Polynesian pearl. Languidly Mangaia lifts out of the azure waters of the Pacific. Inis Beag and Mangaia are on opposite sides of the world—literally and figuratively.

From childhood, Mangaian children are expected to explore their sexuality through masturbation (D. Marshall, 1971). Mangaian teenagers are encouraged by their elders to engage in sexual relations. They will be found on hidden beaches or beneath the sheltering fronds of palms, industriously practicing skills acquired from their elders. Mangaian women usually reach orgasm numerous times before their partners do. Young men vie to see who is more skillful in helping their partners attain multiple orgasms.

The inhabitants of Mangaia and Inis Beag have like anatomic features, and the same hormones pulse through their bodies. Their attitudes and cultural values about what is normal and abnormal differ vastly, however. Their attitudes affect their sexual behavior and the enjoyment they attain—or do not attain—from sex. In sex, as in other areas of behavior, the lines between the normal and the abnormal are not always drawn precisely. Sex, like eating, is a natural function. Yet this natural function has been profoundly affected by cultural, religious, and moral beliefs; custom, folklore; and superstition.

Even in the United States today, we find attitudes as diverse as those on Inis Beag and Mangaia. Some people feel guilty about any form of sexual activity and thus reap little if any pleasure from sex. Others, who see themselves as the children of the sexual revolution, may worry about whether they have become free enough or skillful enough in their sexual activity.

NORMAL AND ABNORMAL IN SEXUAL BEHAVIOR

In the realm of sexual behavior, our conceptions of what is normal and what is not are clearly influenced by sociocultural factors. Various patterns of sexual behavior that might be considered abnormal in Inis Beag, such as masturbation, premarital intercourse, and oral-genital sex, are normal in American society from the standpoint of statistical frequency. For example, a recent national survey, based on a representative sample of 3,432 males and females between the ages of 18 and 59, found that 63% of the adult men and 42% of the adult women surveyed reported that they had masturbated during the previous year (Laumann, Gagnon, Michael,

---

[1]Inis Beag is actually a pseudonym for an Irish folk community.

& Michaels, 1994). It is likely that many more practiced masturbation but were hesitant to admit so to interviewers.

Behavior is sometimes labeled as abnormal because it deviates from the norms of one's society. Yet consider a handful of the variations in sexual behavior and attitudes that we find around the world:

- Because women's breasts are eroticized in Western culture, Western laws and social codes require that they usually be shielded from public view. Yet the kinds of stimuli that are considered sexually arousing vary enormously from culture to culture. In some societies, breasts are considered of interest to nursing children only, and that is because the children connect them with food. Women in such societies often go barebreasted when the weather permits. Among the Abkhasian people in the southern part of the former Soviet Union, men are sexually aroused by women's armpits (Benet, 1974). Women's armpits may thus be seen by their husbands only (Kammeyer, 1990).

- The incest taboo is one of the few sexual beliefs found universally across the world. Even so, some societies believe men and women who eat together are engaging in a mild form of sexual activity. Societies with such beliefs thus forbid brothers and sisters from eating together (Kammeyer, Ritzer, & Yetman, 1990).

- Kissing is a highly popular form of mild petting in Western culture but is unknown among such cultures as the Siriono of Bolivia and the Thonga of Africa. The Thonga were shocked when they first observed European visitors kissing, and one man exclaimed, "Look at them—they eat each others' saliva and dirt."

- Sexual fidelity is highly valued nearly everywhere in the United States. Nevertheless, it is considered polite among the Native American Aleut people of Alaska for a husband to offer his wife to a visitor.

Sexual behavior may also be considered abnormal if it is self-defeating, harms others, or causes personal distress, among other criteria. The disorders we feature in this chapter—gender identity disorder, paraphilias, and sexual dysfunctions—meet one or more of these criteria. In exploring these disorders, we touch on questions that probe the boundaries between abnormality and normality. For example, is a gay male or lesbian sexual orientation a mental or psychological disorder? Are some instances of voyeurism or exhibitionism normal and others abnormal? When is it considered abnormal to have difficulty becoming sexually aroused or reaching orgasm?

GENDER IDENTITY DISORDER

Our **gender identity** is our sense of being male or being female. Gender identity is normally based on anatomic gender. In the normal run of things, our gender identity is consistent with our anatomic gender. In **gender identity disorder**, however, there is a conflict between one's anatomic gender and one's gender identity.

Gender identity disorder may begin in childhood. Children with the disorder find their anatomic genders to be sources of persistent and intense distress. The diagnosis is not used simply to label "tomboyish" girls and "sissyish" boys. It is applied to children who persistently repudiate their anatomic traits (girls might insist on urinating standing up or assert they do not want to grow breasts; boys may find their penis and testes revolting) or who are preoccupied with clothing or activities that are stereotypic of the other gender (see Table 11.1).

About five times as many boys as girls have gender identity disorder (Zucker & Green, 1992). The disorder takes many paths. It can come to an end or abate markedly by adolescence, with the child becoming more accepting of her or his gender identity. It may persist into adolescence or adulthood. The child may also develop a gay male or lesbian

What is normal and what is abnormal in the realm of sexual and sexually related behavior patterns? The cultural context must be considered in defining what is normal and what is abnormal. The people in these photographs—and the ways in which they cloak or expose their bodies—would be quite out of place in one another's societies.

TABLE 11.1

Clinical Features of Gender Identity Disorder

(a)   A strong, persistent identification with the other gender

At least four of the following features are required to make the diagnosis in children:

(1) Repeated expression of the desire to be a member of the other gender (or expression of the belief that the child does belong to the other gender)

(2) Preference for wearing clothing stereotypical of members of the other gender

(3) Presence of persistent fantasies about being a member of the other gender, or assumption of parts played by members of the other gender in make-believe play

(4) Desire to participate in leisure activities and games considered stereotypical of the other gender

(5) Strong preference for playmates who belong to the other gender (at ages when children typically prefer playmates of their own gender)

Adolescents and adults typically express the wish to be of the other gender, frequently "pass" as a member of the other gender, wish to live as a member of the other gender, or believe that their emotions and behavior typify the other gender

(b)   A strong, persistent sense of discomfort with one's anatomic gender or with the behaviors that typify the gender role of that gender

In children, these features are commonly present: Boys state that their external genitals are repugnant or that it would be better not to have them, show aversion to "masculine" toys, games, and rough-and-tumble play. Girls prefer not to urinate while sitting, express the wishes not to grow breasts or to menstruate, or show an aversion to "feminine" clothing

Adolescents and adults typically state that they were born the wrong gender and express the wish for medical intervention (e.g., hormone treatments or surgery) to rid them of their own sex characteristics and simulate the characteristics of the other gender

(c)   There is no "intersex condition," such as ambiguous sexual anatomy, that might give rise to such feelings

(d)   The features cause serious distress or impair key areas of occupational, social, or other functioning

Source: Adapted from the *DSM-IV* (APA, 1994).

---

sexual orientation at about the time of adolescence (Zucker & Green, 1992).

A number of cases of gender identity disorder among adults have been widely publicized. In 1953, for example, headlines were made by an ex-GI who journeyed to Denmark for a "sex-change operation." She then became known as Christine Jorgensen.

Earlier editions of the DSM used the diagnosis of *transsexualism* for people who have reached puberty, harbor persistent discomfort because of the belief their anatomic gender is wrong for them, and are preoccupied with transforming their sex characteristics to those of the other gender. Although the term transsexualism is still in widespread use, the *DSM-IV* uses the diagnostic category of *gender identity disorder* to describe both children and adults who psychologically perceive themselves to be members of the opposite gender and who show persistent discomfort with their anatomic gender. As noted in Table 11.1, however, the clinical features vary somewhat according to the age of the individual. Gender identity disorder should not be confused with a homosexual sexual orientation. Gay males and lesbians have erotic interests in members of their own gender but have a gender identity (their psychological sense of being male or female) that is consistent with their own anatomic gender. Nor do they desire to become members of the opposite gender. Unlike a gay male or lesbian sexual orientation, gender identity disorder is very rare.

TRUTH *or* **FICTION** REVISITED

11.1 *False.*   Gender identity should not be confused with sexual orientation. Gay males and lesbians have erotic interest in members of their own gender, but their gender identity is consistent with their anatomic sex.

Sexual attractions in themselves do not appear to be central in importance in gender identity disorder. Some people with gender identity disorder deny experiencing strong sexual feelings and are sexually attracted to neither males nor females. Others are sexually attracted to males, to females, or to both. People with gender identity disorder who are sexually attracted to members of their own anatomic gender are unlikely to consider themselves gay males or lesbians, however. Nature's gender assignment is a mistake in their eyes. From their perspective, they are trapped in the body of the wrong gender.

Gender Reassignment Surgery   As many as 6,000 to perhaps 11,000 gender reassignment surgeries have been performed in the United States (Selvin, 1993). One of the better known cases is that of the late tennis player Dr. Renée Richards, who was formerly Dr. Richard Raskin. Gender reassignment surgery does not transform one into a person of the opposite gender, if what is meant by gender reassignment is the implantation of the internal reproductive organs of the opposite gender. Rather, the surgery attempts to construct a likeness of the external genitalia of the opposite gender. The surgery is more precise in fashioning the external genitals in the male-to-female than female-to-male direction. People who have such operations can engage in sexual activity, even achieve orgasm, yet they are incapable of conceiving or bearing children.

The surgery is supplemented by a lifetime regimen of hormone treatments. For people who undergo male-to-female reassignment, estrogen, a female sex hormone, is taken to stoke the development of female secondary sex characteristics, which leads to the rounding of the hips, breast development, softening of the skin, and suppression of beard growth. In the case of female-to-male reassignment, male sex hormones (androgens) are taken to foster the development of male secondary sex characteristics, leading to the deepening of the voice, muscular development, a masculine pattern of hair growth, and a loss of fatty deposits in the breasts and hips.

Recent clinical studies shows generally favorable outcomes following gender reassignment surgery (e.g., R. Blanchard, Steiner, & Clemmensen, 1985; Cohen-Kettenis & van Goozen, 1997; Lief & Hubschman, 1993), especially when safeguards are taken to restrict surgical treatment to the most appropriate cases. Patients tend to be relatively well adjusted and satisfied with the procedure. In one recent study, 14 male-to-female and 5 female-to-male patients were found to be functioning well socially and psychologically postoperatively, with none expressing regrets about the procedure (Cohen-Kettenis & van Goozen, 1997).

Men seeking gender reassignment outnumber women applicants by perhaps 3 or 4 to 1, but outcomes are generally more favorable for female-to-male cases. One reason may be society's greater acceptance of women who desire to live as men (S. Abramowitz, 1986). Another reason appears to be that females with gender identity disorder are generally better adjusted than their male counterparts before surgery (Kockott & Fahrner, 1988). Male-to-female patients whose surgery left no telltale signs (such as scarring of the breasts or leftover erectile tissue) were found to be better adjusted than those whose surgery was less successful in allowing them to "pass" as women (M. Ross & Need, 1989).

A number of support groups and self-help programs across the United States aim to help people with cross-gender identities in the process of coming to terms with themselves and learning to cope with living in a society that does not make them feel welcome (Selvin, 1993). One example is the Gender Identity Project, a New York program that holds meetings where people with cross-gender identities can get together and share experiences and common concerns. These types of programs foster a feeling of community for individuals who feel alienated from the mainstream society.

Theoretical Perspectives   No one knows what causes gender identity disorder (Money, 1994). Psychodynamic theorists point to extremely close mother-son relationships, parents with empty relationships, fathers who were absent or detached (Stoller, 1969). These family circumstances may foster strong identification with the mother in young males, leading to a reversal of expected gender roles and identity. Girls with weak ineffectual mothers and strong masculine fathers may overly identify with their fathers and develop a psychological sense of themselves as "little men."

Learning theorists similarly point to father absence in the case of boys—to the unavailability of a strong male role

Changing identities.   High school physical education teacher Doris Richards (left) underwent hormonal treatments and surgery to become Steve Dain (right).

Gender Identity Disorder: A Disorder or Culture-Specific Creation?

Though our concept of gender, or maleness and femaleness, reflects the biological division of the sexes, it is also a social construction. It is a culturally based concept for designating the roles, attributes, responsibilities, privileges, and traits that a given culture assigns to men and women. Gender roles embody the behaviors a specific culture considers appropriate and fundamental to being a man or a woman. Gender identity, however is a psychological construct that reflects an individual's psychological sense of their own gender, of who and what they are.

Most of the assumptions we make about gender identity are based on the construction of gender as a dichotomous, mutually exclusive category in which we assume people are either male or female. We also assume that people's concept of their own gender should be consistent with their biological (anatomic) sex. People whose gender is at odds with their biological sex may be classified as having gender identity disorder. We assume people should be satisfied with the gender assigned by nature. As gender is also a social construction—a concept society creates and uses to assign people to different categories and statuses—it is also embedded in a socio-political context in which a person's gender not only defines them personally but also designates their place in a social hierarchy that determines their access to gender-based privileges. For example, men in our society have traditionally been accorded greater access than women to high prestige occupations in business, medicine, law, and engineering. Though

gender roles today are less rigid than they were a few generations ago, differences in social expectations continue. Certainly more women are working today, but by and large they earn less than men and are still expected to shoulder the lion's share of household and childcare responsibilities.

Just as traditional gender roles have been challenged, so too have traditional concepts of gender identity been challenged by people who are dissatisfied with their biological sex and/or who wish to adopt the gender roles of the other sex (Greene, in press). The assumptions we make about the fixed dichotomy of gender into maleness and femaleness are further challenged by cross-cultural studies that reveal the presence of cultures that have a socially sanctioned identity for persons who are regarded as neither male nor female. In these cultures, individuals who adopt the gender roles and identity of the other biological sex are not considered pathological or undesirable. They are simply regarded as having a third or other gender.

Into the late 1800s, the Plains Indians and many other Western tribes responded with understanding when a young member of the tribe crossed traditional gender roles (Wade & Tavris, 1994). Crossing traditional gender roles was not merely allowed but was accorded a respectable status in these societies. More than half of the surviving native languages have words that describe people who were neither male nor female but something else. Their presence and their roles are depicted in ways that indicated they were

model. Socialization patterns might have affected children who were reared by parents who had wanted children of the other gender and who strongly encouraged cross-gender dressing and patterns of play.

Nonetheless, the great majority of people with the types of family histories described by psychodynamic and learning theorists do not develop gender identity disorder. Perhaps these family factors play a role in combination with a biological predisposition. We know that people with gender identity disorder often show cross-gender preferences in toys, games, and clothing very early in childhood. If there are critical early learning experiences in gender identity disorder, they may occur very early in life. Prenatal hormonal imbalances may also be involved. Perhaps the brain is "masculinized" or "feminized" by sex hormones during certain stages of prenatal development. The brain could become

differentiated as to gender identity in one direction, while the genitals develop in the other direction (Money, 1987).

Intriguing findings suggestive of underlying biological differences were reported in 1995 by Dutch scientists who discovered that a part of the hypothalamus known to be smaller in women than in men was also smaller in transsexual men than other men (Angier, 1995). Whether these differences arise from prenatal factors or from influences occurring during childhood or adolescence remains unknown. We do know from research with other animals that this region of the hypothalamus is involved in controlling sexual behavior and that it plays a role in the release of reproductive hormones. Whether it plays a role in determining gender identity in humans remains unknown. Interestingly, the size of the area is no larger in gay men than in heterosexual men, so it does not appear that the region is

socially acceptable and even desirable members of the tribe. Native tribal members believed that human beings contained male and female elements. In many tribes, "two spirit" was the term used for persons who were believed to embody a higher level of integration of their male and female spirit. Sometimes a *two-spirit* person was a biological male who took on the tribe's female gender roles but was not considered a male or a female (Tafoya, 1996). On the other hand, a female could take on the role and behaviors associated with tribal males. She could be initiated into puberty as a male and could adopt male roles and activities thereafter, including marrying a female.

Native Americans are not the only cultural group who have categories for people who do not fit contemporary U.S. gender dichotomies. Their presence serves to highlight social contexts and cultures in which dichotomous categories of gender were not presumed to be the norm and in which inconsistencies between biological sex, gender identities, and gender roles were not considered a psychological problem. Given the variability of gender roles and identities that we observe across cultures, we may question the validity of the concept of what has been described as a "disorder."

Califia (1997) and others (Israel & Tarver, 1997; K. K. Wilson, 1997) argue that while people who are dissatisfied with their biological sex or who wish to adopt the gender role that is inconsistent with their biological sex are perhaps atypical, their conditions should neither constitute nor function as a marker of psychopathology. Rather, their dysphoria and distress can be attributed to living in a society that insists that people fit into either of two arbitrarily designated categories and subjects them to ill treatment if they do not.

Their plight may be compared to that of lesbians and gay men. We understand that the distress that lesbians and gay men often experience in reference to their sexual orientation is a function of the hostility and abuse they receive because of it. Their distress is not an inevitable consequence of their sexual orientation but rather an appropriate response to the negative treatment they receive. Still, at one time, the distress of lesbians and gay men resulting from prejudice against them was believed to be a direct response to their nontraditional sexual orientation. It could be argued that dissatisfaction with one's biological sex or an inconsistency between one's biological sex and desired gender role or identity is not a problem unless you live in a society that says it is and is intolerant of it. If the society you live in is intolerant of you for being different, it is understandable you would become distressed by it. The ill treatment that people with *transgender identities* (identities that cross traditional gender lines) in our society receive can be a significant source of personal distress (B. V. Reid & Whitehead, 1992). Looked at in this way, our concept of gender identity disorder may be understood as a social construction that reflects our culture's definition of gender and treatment of people who are different, rather than a diseased or disordered condition residing within the person. In other cultures in which concepts of mutually exclusive gender categories do not apply, the disorder is not held to exist. Just as beliefs about sexual orientation have changed over time, perhaps greater tolerance and a greater appreciation for the diversity of gender expression in human beings will lead us to conceptualize gender identity with greater flexibility.

---

involved in male sexual orientation. All in all, researchers suspect that gender identity disorders may develop as the result of an interaction in utero between the developing brain and the release of sex hormones (Zhou et al., 1995). But whatever the biological contributions to gender identity turn out to be, are people who are different by virtue of their gender identities necessarily suffering from a disease or disorder? The answer may depend on how the society or culture in which they live regards them, as we explore further in the accompanying *Focus on Diversity* feature.

PARAPHILIAS

The word *paraphilia* was coined from the Greek roots *para,* meaning "to the side of," and *philos,* meaning "loving." In the **paraphilias,** people show sexual arousal ("loving") in re-

sponse to atypical stimuli ("to the side of" normally arousing stimuli). According to the *DSM-IV,* paraphilias involve recurrent, powerful sexual urges and fantasies that center on either (1) nonhuman objects such as underwear, shoes, leather, or silk; (2) humiliation or experience of pain in oneself or one's partner; or (3) children and other persons who do not or cannot grant consent.

The diagnosis requires that the paraphilic urges are recurrent, powerful, and persistent over a period of at least 6 months. The person receiving the diagnosis must have acted out on the urges or must be distinctly distressed by them. The diagnosis can be made purely on the basis of the person's reported paraphilic fantasies, if they cause personal distress. Overt paraphilic behavior is not required.

Some persons who receive the diagnosis can function sexually in the absence of paraphilic stimuli or fantasies.

Homophobia: Social Prejudice or Personal Psychopathology?

Prior to 1973, **homosexuality** was classified as a mental disorder within the *Diagnostic and Statistical Manual of Mental Disorders*. The development of a lesbian or gay sexual orientation was presumed to represent a pathological outcome of psychosexual development. Treatment of lesbians and gay men was oriented toward altering their sexual orientation with the goal of making them heterosexual. In 1973, the American Psychiatric Association decided to drop homosexuality from its listing of mental disorders. Yet people who are persistently distressed or confused about their sexual orientation, whether they be gay, bisexual, or heterosexual, may continue to be diagnosed with a definable type of sexual disorder called "Sexual Disorder Not Otherwise Specified."[2] In practice, however, this diagnosis has been applied almost exclusively to people with a gay male, lesbian, or bisexual sexual orientation.

TRUTH *or* FICTION REVISITED

11.2 *False.* Homosexuality is no longer classified as a mental disorder.

Conceptions of abnormal behavior are societally constructed beliefs as to what behaviors are deemed normal or abnormal within a given culture and at a particular point in time. Mental-health professionals base judgments of abnormality on evidence showing that a particular pattern of behavior either causes personal distress or interferes significantly with a person's ability to function in meeting social and occupational roles. Yet

[2]In keeping with the suggestions of the American Psychological Association's (1991) Committee on Lesbian and Gay Concerns, we refer to *gay males* and *lesbians* rather than *homosexuals*. As noted by the Committee, there are several problems with the label *homosexual:* One, because it has been historically associated with concepts of deviance and mental illness, it may perpetuate negative stereotypes of gay men and lesbians. Two, the term is often used to refer to men only, thus rendering lesbians invisible. Third, it is often ambiguous in meaning—that is, does it refer to sexual behavior or sexual orientation?

evidence does not support the view that lesbians, gay males, and bisexuals are any more psychologically disturbed than comparison heterosexual groups, despite the ostracism, prejudice, and discrimination they face in society (E. Coleman, 1987; B. F. Reiss, 1980).

Though homosexuality per se is no longer considered a mental disorder, lesbians and gay men continue to be targets of extreme hostility, fear, and prejudice. The term **homophobia** describes the persistent, irrational

Is homosexuality a mental disorder? Gay males, lesbians, and bisexuals as a group are about as well adjusted as heterosexuals. Homosexuality is no longer considered a mental disorder within the DSM system.

Others resort to paraphilic stimuli under stress. Still others cannot become sexually aroused unless these stimuli are used, in actuality or in fantasy. For some individuals, the paraphilia is their exclusive means of attaining sexual gratification.

Some paraphilias are relatively harmless and victimless. Among these are fetishism and transvestic fetishism.

Others—exhibitionism, pedophilia, and some cases of sadism—have unwilling victims. A most harmful paraphilia is sexual sadism when acted out with a nonconsenting partner. Voyeurism falls somewhere in between because the "victim" does not typically know he or she is being watched.

fear of lesbians and gay men. Fear and anxiety about lesbians and gay men or lesbian/gay sexual orientations have been deemed irrational because such fears are usually based on beliefs that are of questionable validity or have been overwhelmingly disputed. Examples of false beliefs about lesbians and gay men are that gay men are more likely to become child molesters than heterosexual men; that lesbians and gay men wish to be members of the other gender; that they do not make good parents; that their children will become lesbian or gay; that they are sexually promiscuous or indiscriminate in their sexual attractions; that their relationships are transitory, based solely on sexual activity, and do not last long term; that they are responsible for the AIDS epidemic, etc. (Jenny, Roesler, & Poyer, 1994). Many people who hold these beliefs feel justified in engaging in prejudice against lesbians and gay men that may range from personal rudeness or hostility to vandalism, harassment, and even violent physical attacks (Freiberg, 1995; J. N. Katz, 1995).

As these attacks are commonplace in many parts of the United States, they create a climate of terror for lesbians and gay men and make their lives more difficult. The fact that these beliefs persist among many otherwise intelligent people, despite evidence to the contrary, and that they are often connected to expressions of violence that harm others makes their understanding an important social issue. It also raises important questions for behavioral scientists about what purpose they serve, what they mean to those who hold them, and how to alter them.

Many theoreticians use the term **heterosexism** (Herek, 1996) to describe a broader cultural ideology and resulting pattern of institutional discrimination against lesbians and gay men. They suggest that the anti-gay feelings of individuals are only a part of a broader institutional pattern that is embedded in our culture and is based on the cultural assumption that reproductive sexuality is the only outcome of psychosexual development that is psychologically healthy and morally correct. They go on to suggest that anti-gay sentiments are rewarded in our society more than they are punished and are not considered to be abnormal or pathological.

Still, others believe that homophobia represents a form of clinical pathology in that it is an irrational belief or belief system that persists in the face of evidence to the contrary. Marvin Kantor (1998) views homophobia as an emotional disorder in which the false beliefs about lesbians and gay men and the anxiety associated with them represents a symptom that is similar to that of a paranoid delusion. In this view, homophobic beliefs may represent people's underlying fears or anxieties about their own latent homosexual attractions or strivings or insecurity about their own masculinity or femininity.

Violent physical and verbal attacks against lesbians and gay men are referred to as *gay bashing* and are considered a form of hate crime. According to Kantor, many people who feel the need to bash lesbians and gay men and/or those who actually do so are really attempting to reassure themselves that they do not have such feelings or attractions. By punishing those who express these forbidden wishes, the gay basher may be seeking to prove to himself and others that he is not one of them.

Research on people who are homophobic suggests that they tend to have rigid personalities and are intolerant of anything that deviates from their personal view of appropriate behavior (Kantor, 1998). Other research suggests that they are people who have not, to their knowledge, had direct contact with lesbians or gay men (Herek, 1996). Despite the intensity of their belief, it is rarely based on information gathered in a personal relationship or interaction. Rather, it is selectively drawn from the culture which, in the United States, has historically put forth media images of lesbians and gay men that demean them by depicting them as dangerous, perverted, depressed, or so much the focus of comic relief that they would not be taken seriously. Ignorance about lesbians and gay men, maintained by their invisibility, fuels homophobic attitudes.

Because of the harm that homophobia and heterosexism do to lesbians and gay men and because of their adverse effects on their mental health, these phenomena are worthy of our serious attention and understanding. Do heterosexism and homophobia constitute some form of social or personal pathology, or both?

People with paraphilias usually do not consider themselves to be mentally disordered. They are generally seen by the mental-health system only when they get into conflict with their partners or with society. With the exceptions of sexual masochism and some isolated cases of other disorders, paraphilias are almost never diagnosed in women. Even with masochism, it is estimated that men receiving the diagnosis outnumber women by a ratio of 20 to 1 (APA, 1994).

Exhibitionism

Exhibitionism is the recurrent, powerful urge to expose one's genitals to an unsuspecting stranger in order to surprise, shock, or sexually arouse the victim. The person may masturbate while fantasizing about or actually exposing himself (almost all cases involve men; Freund & Blanchard, 1986). The victims are almost always females.

The person who is diagnosed with exhibitionism is typically not interested in actual sexual contact with the victim and is therefore not usually considered dangerous. Nevertheless, victims may believe themselves in great danger and may be traumatized by the act. Victims are probably best advised to show no reaction to people who expose themselves but to just continue on their way, if possible. It would be unwise to insult the person who exposed himself, lest it provoke a violent reaction. Although most people who engage in exhibitionism are not violent, 1 in 10 has considered or attempted rape (Gebhard, Gagnon, Pomeroy, & Christenson, 1965). Nor do we recommend an exaggerated show of shock or fear; it tends to reinforce the person for the act of exposing himself.

Some researchers view exhibitionism as a means of indirectly expressing hostility toward women, perhaps because of perceptions of having been wronged by women in the past or of not being noticed or taken seriously by them (Geer, Heiman, & Leitenberg, 1984). Men with this disorder tend to be shy, dependent, lacking in social and sexual skills, even socially inhibited (Dwyer, 1988). Some doubt their masculinity and hold feelings of inferiority (Blair & Lanyon, 1981). Their victims' revulsion or fear boosts their sense of mastery of the situation and heightens their sexual arousal.

Consider the case of Michael:

Michael was a 26-year-old, handsome, boyish-looking married male with a 3-year-old daughter. He had spent about one-quarter of his life in reform schools and in prison. As an adolescent he had been a fire-setter. As a young adult, he had begun to expose himself. He came to the clinic without his wife's knowledge because he was exposing himself more and more often—up to three

times a day—and he was afraid that he would eventually be arrested and thrown into prison again.

Michael said he liked sex with his wife, but it wasn't as exciting as exposing himself. He couldn't prevent his exhibitionism, especially now, when he was between jobs and worried about where the family's next month's rent was coming from. He loved his daughter more than anything and couldn't stand the thought of being separated from her.

Michael's method of operation was as follows: He would look for slender adolescent females, usually near the junior high school and the senior high school. He would take his penis out of his pants and play with it while he drove up to a girl or a small group of girls. He would lower the car window, continuing to play with himself, and ask them for directions. Sometimes the girls didn't see his penis. That was okay. Sometimes they saw it and didn't react. That was okay, too. When they saw it and became flustered and afraid, that was best of all. He would start to masturbate harder, and now and then he managed to ejaculate before the girls had departed.

Michael's history was unsettled. His father had left home before he was born, and his mother had drunk heavily. He was in and out of foster homes throughout his childhood, "all over" the capital district area of New York State. Before he was 10 years old he was involved in sexual activities with neighborhood boys. Now and then the boys also forced neighborhood girls into petting, and Michael had mixed feelings when the girls got upset. He felt bad for them, but he also enjoyed it. A couple of times girls seemed horrified at the sight of his penis, and it made him "really feel like a man. To see that look, you know, with a girl, not a woman, but a girl—a slender girl, that's what I'm after."

THE AUTHORS' FILES

Professional strippers do not typically meet the clinical criteria for exhibitionism. Nor do people who like to wear revealing swim suits. Although they may seek to show off the attractiveness of their bodies, they are generally not motivated by the desire to expose themselves to unsuspecting strangers in order to arouse them or shock them. The chief motive of the stripteaser, of course, may simply be to earn a living.

TRUTH *or* FICTION REVISITED

11.3 False. Wearing revealing bathing suits is not a form of exhibitionism in the clinical sense of the term. Virtually all people diagnosed with the disorder are men, and they are motivated by the wish to shock and dismay unsuspecting observers, not to show off the attractiveness of their bodies.

Fetishism

The French *fétiche* is thought to derive from the Portuguese *feitico*, referring to a "magic charm." In this case, the "magic" lies in the object's ability to sexually arouse. The chief

Exhibitionism. Exhibitionism is a type of paraphilia that characterizes people who seek sexual arousal or gratification through exposing themselves to unsuspecting victims. People with this disorder are usually not interested in actual sexual contact with their victims.

feature of **fetishism** is recurrent, powerful sexual urges and arousing fantasies involving inanimate objects, such as an article of clothing (bras, panties, hosiery, boots, shoes, leather, silk, and the like). It is normal for men to like the sight, feel, and smell of their lovers' undergarments. Men with fetishism, however, may prefer the object to the person and may not be able to become sexually aroused without it. They often experience sexual gratification by masturbating while fondling the object, rubbing it, or smelling it; or by having their partners wear it during sexual activity.

The origins of fetishisms may be traced to early childhood in many cases. Most individuals with a rubber fetish in one research sample were able to recall first experiencing a fetishistic attraction to rubber sometime between the age of 4 and 10 (Gosselin & Wilson, 1980).

Transvestic Fetishism

The chief feature of **transvestic fetishism** is recurrent, powerful urges and related fantasies involving cross-dressing for purposes of sexual arousal. Other people with fetishisms can be satisfied by handling objects such as women's clothing while they masturbate; people with transvestic fetishism want to wear them. They may wear full feminine attire and makeup or favor one particular article of clothing, such as women's stockings. Transvestic fetishism is reported only among heterosexual men. Typically, the man cross-dresses in private and imagines himself to be a woman who he is stroking as he masturbates. Some frequent transvestite clubs or become involved in a transvestic subculture.

Gay men may cross-dress to attract other men or because it is fashionable to masquerade as women in some social circles, not because they are sexually aroused by cross-dressing. Males with gender identity disorder cross-dress because of gender discomfort associated with wearing men's clothing. Because cross-dressing among gay men and men with gender identity disorder is performed for reasons other than sexual arousal or gratification, it is not considered a form of transvestic fetishism. Nor are female impersonators who cross-dress for theatrical purposes considered to have a form of transvestism. For reasons such as these, the diagnosis is limited to heterosexuals.

Most men with transvestism are married and engage in sexual activity with their wives, but they seek additional sexual gratification through dressing as women, as in the case of Archie:

Archie was a 55-year-old plumber who had been cross-dressing for many years. There was a time when he would go out in public as a woman, but as his prominence in the community grew, he became more afraid of being discovered in public. His wife Myrna knew of his "peccadillo," especially since he borrowed many of her clothes, and she also encouraged him to stay at home, offering to help him with his "weirdness." For many years his paraphilia had been restricted to the home.

The couple came to the clinic at the urging of the wife. Myrna described how Archie had imposed his will on her for 20 years. Archie would wear her undergarments and masturbate while she told him how disgusting he was. (The couple also regularly engaged in "normal" sexual intercourse, which Myrna enjoyed.) The cross-dressing situation had come to a head because a teenaged daughter had almost walked into the couple's bedroom while they were acting out Archie's fantasies.

With Myrna out of the consulting room, Archie explained how he grew up in a family with several older sisters. He described how underwear had been perpetually hanging all around the one bathroom to dry. As an adolescent Archie experimented with rubbing against articles of underwear, then with trying them on. On one occasion a sister walked in while he was modeling panties before the mirror. She told him he was a "dredge to society" and he straightaway experienced unparalleled sexual excitement. He masturbated when she left the room, and his orgasm was the strongest of his young life.

Archie did not think that there was anything wrong with wearing women's undergarments and masturbating. He was not about to give it up, regardless of whether his marriage was destroyed as a result. Myrna's main concern was finally separating herself from Archie's "sickness." She didn't care what he did anymore, so long as he did it by himself. "Enough is enough," she said.

That was the compromise the couple worked out in marital therapy. Archie would engage in his fantasies by himself. He would choose times when Myrna was not at home, and she would not be informed of his activities. He would also be very, very careful to choose times when the children would not be around.

Six months later the couple were together and content. Archie had replaced Myrna's input into his fantasies with transvestic-sadomasochistic magazines. Myrna said, "I see no evil, hear no evil, smell no evil." They continued to have sexual intercourse. After a while, Myrna even forgot to check to see which underwear had been used.

THE AUTHORS' FILES

Voyeurism

The chief feature of **voyeurism** is either acting upon or being strongly distressed by recurrent, powerful sexual urges and related fantasies involving watching unsuspecting people, generally strangers, who are undressed, disrobing, or engaging in sexual activity. The purpose of watching, or "peeping," is to attain sexual excitement. The person who engages in voyeurism does not typically seek sexual activity with the person or persons being observed.

Are the acts of watching one's partner disrobe or viewing sexually explicit films forms of voyeurism? The answer is no. The people who are observed know they are being observed by their partners or will be observed by film audiences. We should also note that feelings of sexual arousal while watching our partners undress or observing sex scenes in R- and X-rated films fall within the normal spectrum of human sexuality.

TRUTH *or* FICTION REVISITED

11.4 *True.* Watching and enjoying your sexual partner disrobe is not voyeurism. Voyeuristic acts involves watching unsuspecting persons disrobing or engaging in sexual activities.

During voyeuristic acts, the person usually masturbates while watching or while fantasizing about watching. Peeping may be the person's exclusive sexual outlet. Some people engage in voyeuristic acts in which they place themselves in risky situations. The prospects of being found out or injured apparently heighten the excitement.

Frotteurism

The French *frottage* refers to the artistic technique of making a drawing by placing paper over a raised object and rubbing the paper with chalk or pencil. The chief feature of the paraphilia of **frotteurism** is recurrent, powerful sexual urges and related fantasies involving rubbing against or touching a nonconsenting person. Frotteurism, or "mashing," generally occurs in crowded places, such as subway cars, buses, or elevators. It is the rubbing or touching, not the coercive aspect of the act, that is sexually arousing to the man. He may imagine himself enjoying an exclusive, affectionate sexual relationship with the victim. Because the physical contact is brief and furtive, people who commit frotteuristic acts stand only a small chance of being caught by authorities. Even the victims may not realize at the time what has happened or register much protest (Spitzer et al., 1989). In the following case example, a man victimized about 1,000 women over a period of years but was arrested only twice:

Charles, 45, was seen by a psychiatrist following his second arrest for rubbing against a woman in the subway. He would select as his target a woman in her 20s as she entered the subway station. He would then position himself behind her on the platform and wait for the train to arrive. He would then follow her into the subway car and when the doors closed would begin bumping against her buttocks, while fantasizing that they were enjoying having intercourse in a loving and consensual manner. About half of the time he would reach orgasm. He would then continue on his way to work. Sometimes when he hadn't reached orgasm, he would change trains and seek another victim. While he felt guilty for a time after each episode, he would soon become preoccupied with thoughts about his next encounter. He never gave any thought to the feelings his victims might have about what he had done to them. While he was married to the same woman for 25 years,

he appears to be rather socially inept and unassertive, especially with women.

ADAPTED FROM SPITZER ET AL., 1994, PP. 164–165; REPRINTED FROM NEVID, FICHNER-RATHUS, & RATHUS, 1995, P. 570

Pedophilia

Pedophilia derives from the Greek *paidos,* meaning "child." The chief feature of pedophilia is recurrent, powerful sexual urges and related fantasies that involve sexual activity with prepubescent children (typically 13 years old or younger). Molestation of children may or may not occur. To be diagnosed with pedophilia, individuals must be at least 16 years of age and at least 5 years older than the child or children they have victimized or to whom they are sexually attracted. In some cases of pedophilia, the person is attracted only to children; in other cases, the person is attracted to adults as well.

Although some persons with pedophilia restrict their pedophilic activity to looking at or undressing children, others engage in exhibitionism, kissing, fondling, oral sex, anal intercourse and, in the case of girls, vaginal intercourse (Knudsen, 1991). Not being worldly wise, children are often taken advantage of by molesters who inform them they are "educating" them, "showing them something," or doing something they will "like." Some men with pedophilia limit their sexual activity with children to incestuous relations with family members; others only molest children outside the family. Not all child molesters have pedophilia, however. The clinical definition of pedophilia is brought to bear only when sexual attraction to children is recurrent and persistent. Some molesters engage in pedophilic acts or experience such urges only occasionally or during times of opportunity.

Despite the stereotype, most cases of pedophilia do not involve "dirty old men" who hang around schoolyards in raincoats. Men with this disorder (virtually all cases involve men) are usually (otherwise) law-abiding, respected citizens in their thirties or forties. Most are married or divorced and have children of their own. They are usually well acquainted with their victims, who are typically either relatives or friends of the family. Many cases of pedophilia are not isolated incidents. They may be a series of acts that begin when children are very young and continue for many years until they are discovered or the relationship is broken off (Finkelhor, 1990).

The origins of pedophilia are complex and varied. Some cases fit the stereotype of the weak, shy, socially inept, and isolated man who is threatened by mature relationships and turns to children for sexual gratification because children are less critical and demanding (Ames & Houston, 1990; Overholser & Beck, 1986). In other cases, it may be that childhood sexual experiences with other children were so enjoyable that the man, as an adult, is attempting to recapture the excitement of earlier years. Or perhaps in some cases of pedophilia, men who were sexually abused in childhood by adults may now be reversing the situation in an effort to establish feelings of mastery. Men whose pedophilic acts involve incestuous relationships with their own children tend to fall at one extreme or the other on the dominance spectrum, being either very dominant or passive (Ames & Houston, 1990).

A recent study highlighted evidence of deviant sexual response patterns in male sexual offenders. Men who had sexually molested young girls showed a stronger penile response to stimuli depicting sexual interactions with female children than to consensual sexual interactions with adult women (Chaplin, Rice, & Harris, 1995). These men were not only aroused by female children but also by scenes containing brutal details of the harm experienced by the young victims.

Sexual Masochism

Sexual masochism derives its name from the Austrian novelist Ritter Leopold von Sacher Masoch (1835–1895), who wrote stories and novels about men who sought sexual gratification from women inflicting pain on them, often in the form of flagellation (being beaten or whipped). Some writers have attributed the desire to be flagellated to the practice of disciplining children with the rod, which was commonplace in the 19th century. But if such an origin was sufficient explanation, Reay Tannahill, author of *Sex in History* (1980), notes that the wish to be flagellated would have become "an international pandemic" (p. 382). It did not.

Sexual masochism involves strong, recurrent urges and related fantasies relating to sexual acts that involve being humiliated, bound, flogged, or made to suffer in other ways. The urges are either acted upon or cause significant personal

S&M paraphernalia. Some of the devices used by people who engage in sadomasochism.

distress. In some cases of sexual masochism, the person cannot attain sexual gratification in the absence of pain or humiliation.

TRUTH _or_ FICTION REVISITED

11.5 _True._ Some people with sexual masochism cannot become sexually aroused unless they are subjected to pain or humiliation by others.

In some cases, sexual masochism involves binding or mutilating oneself during masturbation or sexual fantasies. In others, a partner is engaged to restrain (bondage), blindfold (sensory bondage), paddle, or whip the person. Some partners are prostitutes; others are consensual partners who are asked to perform the sadistic role. In some cases, the person may desire, for purposes of sexual gratification, to be urinated or defecated upon or subjected to verbal abuse.

A most dangerous expression of masochism is **hypoxyphilia,** in which participants are sexually aroused by being deprived of oxygen—for example by using a noose, plastic bag, chemical, or pressure on the chest during a sexual act, such as masturbation. The oxygen deprivation is usually accompanied by fantasies of asphyxiating or being asphyxiated by a lover. People who engage in this activity generally discontinue it before they lose consciousness, but occasional deaths due to suffocation have resulted from miscalculations (R. Blanchard & Hucker, 1991; Cosgray et al., 1991).

Sexual Sadism

Sexual sadism is named after the infamous Marquis de Sade, the 18th-century Frenchman who wrote stories about the pleasures of achieving sexual gratification by inflicting pain or humiliation on others. Sexual sadism is the flip side of sexual masochism. It involves recurrent, powerful urges and related fantasies to engage in acts in which the person is sexually aroused by inflicting physical suffering or humiliation on another person. People with this paraphilia either act out their fantasies or are disturbed by them. They may recruit consenting partners, who may be lovers or wives with a masochistic streak, or prostitutes. Still others stalk and assault nonconsenting victims and become aroused by inflicting pain or suffering on their victims. Sadistic rapists fall into this last group. Most rapists, however, do not seek to become sexually aroused by inflicting pain on their victims; they may even lose sexual interest when they see their victims in pain.

Many people have occasional sadistic or masochistic fantasies or engage in sex play involving simulated or mild forms of **sadomasochism** with their partners. Sadomasochism describes a mutually gratifying sexual interaction involving both sadistic and masochistic acts. Simulation may take the form of using a feather brush to strike one's partner, so that no actual pain is administered. People who engage in sadomasochism frequently switch roles during their encounters or from one encounter to another. The clinical diagnosis of sexual masochism or sadism is not usually brought to bear unless such people become distressed by their behavior or fantasies, or act them out in ways that are harmful to themselves or others.

Other Paraphilias

There are many other paraphilias. These include making obscene phone calls ("telephone scatologia"), necrophilia (sexual urges or fantasies involving sexual contact with corpses), partialism (sole focus on part of the body), zoophilia (sexual urges or fantasies involving sexual contact with animals), and sexual arousal associated with feces (coprophilia), enemas (klismaphilia), and urine (urophilia).

Theoretical Perspectives

Psychodynamic theorists see many paraphilias as defenses against leftover castration anxiety from the Oedipal period. The thought of the penis disappearing within the vagina is unconsciously equated with castration. The man who develops a paraphilia may avoid this threat of castration anxiety by displacing sexual arousal into safer activities—for example, undergarments, children, or watching others. By sequestering his penis under women's clothes, the man with transvestic fetishism engages in a symbolic act of denial that women do not have penises, which eases castration anxiety by unconsciously providing evidence of women's (and his own) safety. The shock and dismay shown by the victim of a man who exposes himself provides unconscious reassurance that he does, after all, have a penis. Sadism involves an unconscious identification with the man's father—the "aggressor" of his Oedipal fantasies—and relieves anxiety by giving him the opportunity to enact the role of the castrator. Some psychoanalytic theorists see masochism as a way of coping with conflicting feelings about sex. Basically, the man feels guilty about sex but is able to enjoy it so long as he is being punished for it. Others view masochism as the redirection inward of aggressive impulses originally aimed at the powerful, threatening father. Like the child who is relieved when his inevitable punishment is over, the man gladly accepts bondage and flagellation in place of castration.

Learning theorists explain paraphilias in terms of conditioning and observational learning. Some object or activity becomes inadvertently associated with sexual arousal. The object or activity then gains the capacity to elicit sexual arousal. For example, a boy who glimpses his mother's stockings on the towel rack while he is masturbating may go on to develop a fetish for stockings (Breslow, 1989). Orgasm in the presence of the object reinforces the erotic connection, especially when it occurs repeatedly. Yet if fetishes were acquired by mechanical association, we would expect people to develop fetishes to stimuli that are inadvertently and repeatedly connected with sexual activity, such as bedsheets, pillows, even ceilings (Breslow, 1989). Yet such is not the case. The *meaning* of the stimulus also apparently plays a role. Perhaps the development of fetishes depends on people's ability to eroticize certain types of stimuli (like women's undergarments) and incorporate them within their erotic and masturbatory fantasies.

Fetishes can often be traced to early childhood. Consider the development of rubber fetishes. Reinisch (1990) speculates that the earliest awareness of sexual arousal or response (such as erection) may have been connected with rubber pants or diapers such that an association was made between the two, setting the stage for the development of the fetish.

Like other patterns of abnormal behavior, paraphilias may involve multiple biological, psychological, and sociocultural factors. Money and Lamacz (1990) hypothesize a multifactorial model that traces the development of paraphilias to childhood. They suggest that childhood experiences etch a pattern, or "lovemap," which can be likened to a software program in the brain that determines the kinds of stimuli and behaviors that come to sexually arouse people. In the case of paraphilias, lovemaps become "vandalized" by early traumatic experiences, such as incest, physical abuse, or neglect, and by excessively harsh antisexual child rearing. Yet not all children who undergo such experiences develop paraphilias. Nor do all people with paraphilias have such traumatic experiences. Perhaps some children are more vulnerable to developing distorted lovemaps than others. The precise nature of such a vulnerability remains to be defined.

Origins of fetishism? The conditioning model of the origins of fetishism suggests that men who develop fetishisms involving women's undergarments may have had experiences in childhood in which sexual arousal was repeatedly paired with exposure to their mother's undergarments. The developing fetish may have been strengthened by incorporating the object within the boy's erotic fantasies or masturbatory activity.

Treatment of Paraphilias

Therapists of various theoretical persuasions have attempted to treat clients with paraphilias. Psychoanalysts, for example, attempt to bring childhood sexual conflicts (typically of an Oedipal nature) into awareness so they can be resolved in the light of the individual's adult personality. Favorable results from individual case studies appear in the literature from time to time, but there is a dearth of controlled investigations to support the efficacy of psychodynamic treatment of paraphilias.

Behavior therapists have used aversive conditioning to induce a negative emotional reaction to paraphilic stimuli or fantasies. In aversive conditioning, the stimulus that elicits sexual arousal (for example, panties) is paired repeatedly with an aversive stimulus (for example, electric shock) in the belief the stimulus will acquire aversive properties. A basic limitation of aversive conditioning is that it does not help the individual acquire more adaptive behaviors in place of maladaptive response patterns. This may explain why researchers find that a broad-based, cognitive-behavioral program for treating exhibitionism, which emphasized the development of adaptive cognitions and the building of social skills and stress management skills, was more effective than an alternative program based on aversion therapy (Marshall, Eccles, & Barbaree, 1991).

Covert sensitization is a variation of aversive conditioning in which the pairing of an aversive stimulus and the problem behavior occurs in imagination. Covert sensitization has become the most common form of aversion therapy used to treat sex offenders in the United States (McConaghy, 1990). In an unusually broad-scale application, Maletzky (1980) used covert sensitization in the treatment of 38 cases of pedophilia and 62 cases of exhibitionism, more than half involving men who were court referred. Clients were instructed to fantasize pedophilic or exhibitionist scenes. Then:

> At a point . . . when sexual pleasure is aroused, aversive images are presented . . . Examples might include a pedophiliac fellating a child, but discovering a festering sore on the boy's penis; an exhibitionist exposing to a woman but then suddenly being discovered by his wife or the police; or a pedophiliac laying a young boy down in a field, only to lie next to him in a pile of dog feces.
>
> MALETZKY, 1980, P. 308

Maletzky used this treatment weekly for 6 months, then followed it with "booster sessions" every 3 months over a 3-year period. The procedure resulted in at least a 75% reduction of the deviant activities and fantasies for over 80% of the subjects at follow-up periods of up to 36 months. Treatment was equally effective for self- and court-referred clients.

Maletzky (1991, 1998) recently reported on the success rates of the largest treatment program study to date, which was based now on more than 7,000 cases of rapists and sex offenders with paraphilias. All were treated at a clinic at the University of Oregon Medical School that specialized in the treatment of sex offenders. Treatment procedures incorporated a variety of behavioral techniques, including aversive and nonaversive methods, that were tailored to the particular type of paraphilia. Success rates for various paraphilias are reported in Table 11.2. Several cautions are advised in interpreting these data, however. Criteria for success were at least partly dependent on self-reports of an absence of deviant sexual interests or behavior, and self-reports may be biased, especially in offender groups. Secondly, with the lack of a control group, we cannot discount the possibility that other factors, such as fears of legal consequences or nonspecific factors unrelated to the specific behavioral techniques used, influenced the outcome. Nonetheless, these data are among the strongest sources of evidence supporting the effectiveness of behavioral techniques in treating paraphilias.

Some promising results are also reported in using the antidepressant Prozac in treating voyeurism and fetishism (Lorefice, 1991; Perilstein, Lipper, & Friedman, 1991). Why Prozac? Prozac has been used effectively in treating obsessive-compulsive disorder (see Chapter 5). Researchers speculate that paraphilias may fall within an obsessive-compulsive spectrum (Kruesi et al., 1992). Many people with paraphilias report feeling compelled to carry out paraphilic acts, in much the same way that people with obsessive-compulsive disorder feel driven to perform compulsive acts. Paraphilias also tend to have an obsessional quality. The person experiences intrusive, repetitive urges to engage in paraphilic acts or thoughts that relate to the paraphilic object or situation. However, Maletzky (1998) cautions that these drugs may act to reduce sexual drives, rather than specifically target deviant sexual fantasies.

Whatever the form of therapy, treatment of paraphilias can be hampered by a number of factors, including the following:

1. People who engage in paraphilic behavior usually do not want or seek treatment, at least not voluntarily. They are generally seen by health professionals when forced to do so by a judge, their families, or their sex partners; or because of fear of exposure, prosecution, or humiliation (Spitzer et al., 1989).

2. Helping professionals may consider it unethical to serve at the behest of the judicial process to attempt to alter the behavior of remanded or incarcerated sex offenders who may not be in a position to render full, voluntary consent.

3. Therapy is usually unsuccessful when clients are resistant or recalcitrant.

4. Sex offenders usually insist they cannot control their impulses. Therapists usually find that accepting personal responsibility for one's actions is essential to change.

SEXUAL DYSFUNCTIONS

Sexual dysfunctions involve problems with sexual interest, arousal, or response. Because they are quite commonplace,

TABLE 11.2

Percentages of Sex Offenders Successfully Treated

Paraphilia	No. of Cases Treated	% of Cases Successfully Treated
Situational pedophilia (heterosexual)	3,012	95.6
Predatory pedophilia (heterosexual)	864	88.3
Situational pedophilia (homosexual)	717	91.8
Predatory pedophilia (homosexual)	596	80.1
Exhibitionism	1,130	95.4
Rape	543	75.5
Voyeurism	83	93.9
Public masturbation	77	94.8
Frotteurism	65	89.3
Fetishism	33	94.0
Transvestic fetishism	14	78.6
Obscene telephoning	29	93.1
Zoophilia	23	95.6

A treatment success was defined as an offender who completed all treatment sessions, reported no covert or overt deviant sexual behavior at the end of treatment or at any follow-up session, demonstrated no deviant sexual arousal at the end of treatment or at any follow-up session, and had no repeat legal charges for any sexual crime at the end of treatment or at any follow-up session.

Source: Maltezky, 1998. Reprinted with permission.

they may not be considered abnormal from the statistical perspective. What distinguishes them as psychological disorders is that they are a source of distress to oneself and/or one's sex partner. Although there are various types of sexual dysfunctions, they share some common features (see Table 11.3).

Accurate estimates of the prevalence of sexual dysfunctions are hard to come by. In the absence of a nationally representative sample, we have no clear basis for estimating the prevalences of sexual dysfunctions in the population at large. Even if such a sample were available, the hesitancy of many people to admit to sexual problems would probably lead to an underreporting of various problems. Even so, a review of available community surveys indicates a relatively high proportion of people reporting various types of sexual dysfunctions (Spector & Carey, 1990; see Table 11.4). More than 1 in 3 men report problems relating to premature (too rapid) ejaculation. Although somewhat less common, as

TABLE 11.3

Common Features of Sexual Dysfunctions

Fear of failure	Fears relating to failure to achieve or maintain erection or failure to reach orgasm.
Assumption of a spectator role rather than a performer role	Monitoring and evaluating your body's reactions during sex.
Diminished self-esteem	Thinking less of yourself for failure to meet your standard of normality.
Emotional effects	Guilt, shame, frustration, depression, anxiety.
Avoidance behavior	Avoiding sexual contacts for fear of failure to perform adequately; making excuses to your partner.

Source: Reprinted with permission from Nevid, Fichner-Rathus, and Rathus, 1995, p. 445.

TABLE 11.4	
Estimated Prevalence of Various Current Sexual Dysfunctions (percentage of respondents reporting any problem)	
Premature ejaculation	36–38
Erectile dysfunction	4–9
Male orgasmic disorder	4–10
Female orgasmic disorder	5–10

Source: Adapted from Spector, I. M., & Carey, M. P. (1990). Incidence and prevalence of the sexual dysfunctions: A critical review of the empirical evidence. *Archives of Sexual Behavior, 1,* 389–408. Reprinted with permission.

1. *Appetitive Phase.* This phase involves sexual fantasies and the desire to engage in sexual activity. The occurrence of sexual fantasies and desires are quite normal; the question is, "How much (or how little) sexual interest is normal?"

2. *Excitement Phase.* This phase involves the physical changes and feelings of pleasure that occur during the process of sexual arousal. In response to sexual stimulation, the heart rate, respiration rate, and blood pressure increase. Sexual excitement involves two essential sexual reflexes—erection in the man and vaginal lubrication ("wetness") in the woman. In men, erection occurs as blood vessels in chambers of loose tissue within the penis dilate to permit an increased blood flow to expand the tissues. In women, the breasts swell and the nipples become erect. Blood engorges the genitals, causing the clitoris to expand. The vagina lengthens and dilates, and lubrication appears as the engorgement of the blood vessels in the vagina forces moisture through capillary membranes.

3. *Orgasm Phase.* In both men and women, the building up of sexual tension reaches a peak and is released through involuntary rhythmic contractions of the pelvic muscles that are accompanied by feelings of pleasure. Orgasm, like erection and lubrication, is a reflex. In men, the contraction of the pelvic muscles forces semen to be expelled through the tip of the penis during ejaculation. In women, the pelvic muscles surrounding the outer third of the vagina contract reflexively. In men and women, the first contractions are strongest and spaced at 0.8-second intervals (five contractions in 4 seconds). Subsequent contractions are weaker and spread farther apart.

People cannot will or force an orgasm. Nor can they will or force other sexual reflexes, such as erection and vaginal lubrication. We can only set the stage for these sexual responses and let them happen. Setting the stage for orgasm involves receiving adequate sexual stimulation and having

many as 9% of men report difficulties achieving or maintaining erection (male erectile disorder) and as many as 10% of men and women report difficulty reaching orgasm (male or female orgasmic disorder). A Massachusetts study of more than 1,700 men in the 40- to 70-year-old age group reported a much higher percentage of men (52%) reporting some degree of male erectile disorder at some point in their lives (Altman, 1993b). Single people may be at greater risk of incurring sexual dysfunctions than married people, in part because singles may feel less secure in their sexual relationships and because they may lack familiarity with the sexual preferences of their partners.

TRUTH *or* FICTION REVISITED

11.6 *False.* Premature ejaculation is extremely common, affecting perhaps one in three men.

Some cases of sexual dysfunction have existed throughout the individual's lifetime and are thus labeled *lifelong dysfunctions.* In the case of *acquired dysfunctions,* the problem begins following a period (or at least one occurrence) of normal functioning. In the case of a *situational dysfunction,* the problem occurs in some situations (for example, with one's spouse), but not in others (for example, with a lover or when masturbating), or at some times but not others. In the case of a *generalized dysfunction,* the problem occurs in all situations and at all times the individual engages in sexual activity.

To provide perspective on the sexual dysfunctions, we first describe normal patterns of sexual response. Then we explore the various types of sexual dysfunctions and the methods used to treat them.

The Sexual Response Cycle

Sexual dysfunctions interfere with the initiation or completion of the sexual response cycle. Much of our understanding of the sexual response cycle is based on the pioneering work of sex researchers William Masters and Virginia Johnson. Elaborating upon their work and others, such as the late sex therapist Helen Singer Kaplan, the DSM describes the sexual response cycle in terms of four distinct phases:

When a source of pleasure becomes a source of anxiety. Sexual dysfunctions can be a source of intense personal distress and lead to friction between partners. Problems in communication can give rise to or exacerbate sexual dysfunctions.

an accepting attitude toward sexual pleasure. But trying to force an orgasm is likely to prevent it from happening.

TRUTH ◑ FICTION REVISITED

11.7 *True.* Orgasm is a reflex. People cannot will or force an orgasm. Nor can they will or force other sexual reflexes, such as erection and vaginal lubrication. However, they can set the stage for these sexual responses and let them happen naturally.

4. *Resolution Phase.* Relaxation and a sense of well-being occur. During this phase, men are physiologically incapable of reachieving erection and orgasm for a period of time. Women, however, may be able to maintain a high level of sexual excitement with continued stimulation and experience multiple orgasms in swift succession. During the sexual revolution of the 1960s and 1970s, awareness of this capacity for multiple orgasm caused some women to think they ought not be satisfied with just one orgasm. This is the flip side of the old saw that sexual enjoyment is appropriate for men only. In sex, as in other areas of life, oughts and shoulds are often arbitrary demands that elicit feelings of anxiety and inadequacy.

Types of Sexual Dysfunctions

The *DSM—IV* groups most sexual dysfunctions within the following categories:

1. Sexual desire disorders
2. Sexual arousal disorders
3. Orgasm disorders
4. Sexual pain disorders

The first three categories correspond to the first three phases of the sexual response cycle.

Sexual Desire Disorders   Disorders of sexual desire or appetite include hypoactive sexual desire disorder and sexual aversion disorder.

Hypoactive sexual desire disorder is characterized by the absence or lack of sexual interest or desire. Typically there is either a complete or virtual absence of sexual fantasies. However, clinicians have not reached any universally agreed-upon criteria for determining the level of sexual desire that is considered normal (J. G. Beck, 1995). Individual clinicians must weigh various factors in reaching a diagnosis in cases of low sexual desire, such as the client's lifestyle (the lack of sexual energy or interest in parents contending with the demands of infants or young children is to be expected), sociocultural factors (for example, culturally restrictive attitudes may restrain sexual desire or interest), the quality of the relationship between the client and her or his partner (declining sexual interest or activity may reflect relationship problems rather than diminished drive), and the client's age (desire normally declines but does not disappear with increasing age). Couples usually seek help when one or both partners recognize that the level of sexual activity in the rela-

tionship is deficient or has waned to the point that little desire or interest remains. Sometimes the lack of desire is limited to one partner. In other cases, both partners may feel sexual urges, but anger and conflict concerning other issues inhibit sexual interaction. Although problems in sexual desire were only first included in the DSM in 1980, the diagnosis of hypoactive sexual desire has become one of the most commonly diagnosed sexual dysfunctions today (Letourneau & O'Donohue, 1993).

Some problems that are categorized as problems in arousal or orgasm may actually involve an underlying lack of desire. Sex therapists usually advocate that couples who want different frequencies of sexual activity arrive at a compromise. They do not invariably encourage the less interested partner to meet all the needs of the other (Goleman, 1988a). Giving lie to the myth that men are always ready for sex, the numbers of men presenting with hypoactive sexual desire appears to be on the rise (Letourneau & O'Donohue, 1993; Spector & Carey, 1990).

People with **sexual aversion disorder** have a strong aversion to genital sexual contact and avoid all or nearly all genital contact with a partner. They may, however, desire and enjoy affectionate contact or nongenital sexual contact. Their aversion to genital contact may stem from childhood sexual abuse, rape, or other traumatic experiences. In other cases, deep-seated feelings of sexual guilt or shame may impair sexual response. In men, the diagnosis is often connected with a history of erectile failure (Spark, 1991). Such men may associate sexual opportunities with failure and shame. Their partners may also develop aversions to sexual contact because their sexual contacts have been so frustrating or emotionally painful.

Sexual Arousal Disorders   Disorders of sexual arousal involve an inability to achieve or maintain the physiological responses involved in sexual arousal or excitement—vaginal lubrication in the woman or penile erection in the man—that are needed to allow completion of sexual activity.

In women, sexual arousal is characterized by lubrication of the vaginal walls that makes entry by the penis possible. In men, sexual arousal is characterized by erection. Almost all women now and then have difficulty becoming or remaining lubricated. Almost all men have occasional difficulty attaining or maintaining an erection through intercourse. The diagnoses of **female sexual arousal disorder** and **male erectile disorder** (also called *sexual impotence* or erectile dysfunction) are reserved for persistent or recurrent problems in becoming genitally aroused.

Orgasm Disorders   There are three orgasm disorders: **female orgasmic disorder, male orgasmic disorder,** and **premature ejaculation.**

Orgasmic disorder refers to persistent or recurrent delay in reaching orgasm, or the absence of orgasm, following a normal phase of sexual excitement. The clinician needs to make a judgment about whether there is an "adequate" amount and type of stimulation to achieve an orgasmic response. There is a broad range of normal variation in sexual response that needs to be considered. Many women, for example, require direct clitoral stimulation (by means of manual stimulation by her own hand or her partner's) in order to achieve orgasm during vaginal intercourse. This should not be considered abnormal, since the clitoris, not the vagina, is the woman's most erotically sensitive organ.

In men, recurrent or persistent difficulty in achieving orgasm following a normal pattern of sexual interest and excitement is termed male orgasmic disorder. This disorder is relatively rare and has received very little attention in the clinical literature (Dekker, 1993; R. C. Rosen & Leiblum, 1995). Men with this problem can usually reach orgasm through masturbation but not through intercourse. Because of its infrequency, there are only a few isolated case studies on the problem (Dow, 1981; Rathus, 1978).

Premature ejaculation is defined as a recurrent or persistent pattern of ejaculation with minimal sexual stimulation. It can occur prior to, upon, or shortly after penetration, but before the man desires it. Note the subjective elements. In making the diagnosis, the clinician weighs the man's age, the novelty of the partner, and the frequency of sexual activity. Occasional experiences of rapid ejaculation, such as when the man is with a new partner, has had infrequent sexual contacts, or is very highly aroused, fall within the normal spectrum. More persistent patterns of premature ejaculation would occasion a diagnosis of the disorder.

Sexual Pain Disorders   In **dyspareunia**, sexual intercourse is associated with recurrent pain in the genital region. The pain cannot be explained fully by an underlying medical condition and so is believed to have a psychological component. However, many, perhaps even most, cases of coital pain are traceable to an underlying medical condition, such as insufficient lubrication or a urinary tract infection. The DSM classifies these cases under a different diagnostic label, "Sexual Dysfunction Due to Medical Condition."

Vaginismus involves an involuntary spasm of the muscles surrounding the vagina when vaginal penetration is attempted, making sexual intercourse painful or impossible.

Theoretical Perspectives

Like most psychological disorders, sexual dysfunctions reflect an interplay of biological, psychological, and other factors.

Biological Perspectives   Many cases of sexual dysfunction stem from biological factors or from a combination of biological and psychological factors (Carey, Wincze, & Meisler, 1998). Deficient testosterone production and thyroid overactivity or underactivity are among the many biological conditions that can lead to impaired sexual desire (Kresin, 1993). Medical conditions can also impair sexual arousal in both men and women (Graber, 1993). Diabetes, for instance, is the most common organic cause of erectile

dysfunction, with estimates indicating that half of diabetic men eventually suffer some degree of erectile dysfunction (Thomas & LoPiccolo, 1994). Diabetes may also impair sexual response in women, with decreased vaginal lubrication being the most common consequence.

Biological factors may play a more prominent role in erectile dysfunction than was formerly believed and may account for as many as 70% to 80% of cases (Brody, 1995b). Other biological factors that can impair sexual desire, arousal, and orgasm include nerve-damaging conditions such as multiple sclerosis, lung disorders, kidney disease, circulatory problems, damage caused by sexually transmitted diseases, and side effects of various drugs (Brody, 1995b; Segraves, 1988; Spark, 1991). Yet, even in cases of sexual dysfunction that are traced to physical causes, emotional problems, such as anxiety and depression, and marital conflict can compound the problem.

The male sex hormone testosterone plays a pivotal role in sexual interest and functioning in women as well as men (both genders produce testosterone in varying amounts) (Carani et al., 1990; Sherwin, Gelfand, & Brender, 1985). Men with deficient production of testosterone may lose sexual interest and the capacity for erections (Kresin, 1993; Spark, 1991). The adrenal glands and ovaries are the sites where testosterone is produced in women. Women who have these organs surgically removed because of invasive disease will no longer produce testosterone and may gradually lose sexual interest and the capacity for sexual response. Although hormonal deficiencies may play a role in sexual dysfunction in these types of cases, researchers find that most men and women with sexual dysfunctions have normal hormone levels (Schreiner-Engle et al., 1989; Spark, 1991; Stuart, Hammond, & Pett, 1987).

TRUTH _or_ FICTION REVISITED

11.8 _False._   Women also produce testosterone in their bodies, though in smaller amounts than men.

Many temporary physical conditions can lead to problems in desire, arousal, and orgasm—even to sexual pain. Fatigue impairs sexual response and can lead to genital pain if the couple persists in attempting intercourse. Depressants such as tranquilizers, alcohol, and narcotics can lessen sexual response (Schiavi, 1990; Segraves, 1988; Spark, 1991). These effects are normally isolated unless people do not recognize their causes and attach too much meaning to them. That is, if you are intoxicated and you do not know alcohol suppresses sexual response, you may wonder whether there is something wrong with you. Biological factors may thus interact with psychological factors in leading to the development of a persistent problem. Because of your concern, you may try to bear down during your next sexual opportunity, causing anxiety that may further interfere with normal sexual response. A second failure may strengthen self-doubts, which creates more anxiety, which stems performance, which leads to repeated failure experiences, and so on, in a vicious cycle.

When physical causes of erectile dysfunction are suspected, a physical examination and a round of laboratory tests (e.g., measures of testosterone levels) may be recommended to identify any underlying physical conditions. The man may also be evaluated in a sleep disorders center (see Chapter 10), where his erections during sleep can be physiologically measured through a technique called nocturnal penile **tumescence,** or NPT. For many years it has been known that men normally experience a number of erections while they are asleep, especially during rapid eye movement (REM) sleep. Lack of erections during sleep strongly suggests organic causes for erectile problems. NPT is usually carried out over three nights, during which time changes in tumescence are monitored continuously by devices such as the **penile strain gauge.** However, NPT has been criticized for producing too many false negatives (men with organic pathologies who produce normal NPT results) and false positives (men without organic problems who show abnormal NPT results) (LoPiccolo, 1985). The test is believed to lead to misleading findings in perhaps 1 in 5 cases (Meisler & Carey, 1990). All in all, the NPT test is considered suggestive of organic causes but not conclusive (Ackerman & Carey, 1995; Mohr & Beutler, 1990). A variation of the NPT technique for home use is now available that is more convenient and less expensive than a sleep center evaluation (Brody, 1995b). Physiological devices have also been developed to measure sexual arousal in women, but these efforts have lagged those undertaken for men (Conte, 1986).

Note, too, that objective (physiological) measures of sexual arousal do not necessarily correspond to subjective measures (the person's own reports). Perhaps objective and subjective measures of sexual arousal do not assess the same thing. Scientists may be tempted to assume that objective devices assess "the real thing," but without evidence we cannot conclude one measure is more valid than another (Conte, 1986). Assessing sexual arousal from multiple vantage points, including self-reports, physiological measures, and behavioral ratings, may increase the accuracy of diagnosis of sexual dysfunctions and lead to more appropriate treatment plans.

Psychodynamic Perspectives Psychodynamic hypotheses generally revolve around presumed conflicts of the phallic stage (Fenichel, 1945). Mature genital sexuality is believed to require successful resolution of the Oedipus and Electra complexes. Men with sexual dysfunctions are presumed to suffer from unconscious castration anxiety. Sexual intercourse elicits an unconscious fear of retaliation by the father, rendering the vagina unsafe. Erectile dysfunction "saves" the man from having to enter the vagina. Premature ejaculation allows him to "escape" rapidly and may also represent unconscious hatred of women (H. S. Kaplan, 1974). Orgasmic disorder prevents him from completing the act and unconsciously minimizes his guilt and fear. Rapid ejaculation serves the unconscious purpose of expressing hatred through soiling the woman and denying her sexual pleasure.

In women, enduring penis envy engenders hostility. The woman fixated in the phallic stage punishes her partner for bearing a penis and does not permit the organ to bring her pleasure, as in female sexual arousal disorder. The clamping down of the vaginal muscles in vaginismus may express an unconscious wish to castrate her partner (H. S. Kaplan, 1974). In orgasmic disorder, she has failed to overcome penis envy and to develop mature sexuality, which involves transferring erotic feelings from the clitoris to the vagina. She thus prevents orgasm from occurring through intercourse. It is difficult to test the validity of the psychoanalytic concepts because they involve unconscious conflicts, such as castration anxiety and penis envy, that cannot be scientifically observed. Evidence for these views relies on case studies that involve interpretation of patients' histories, but case study accounts are open to rival interpretations. We can say with certainty, however, that despite the traditional psychoanalytic conception, clitoral stimulation remains a key part of the woman's erotic response as she matures and is not a sign of an immature fixation.

Learning Perspectives Learning theorists focus on the role of conditioned anxiety in the development of sexual dysfunctions. The occurrence of physically or psychologically painful experiences associated with sexual activity may cause a person to respond to sexual encounters with anxiety that is strong enough to counteract sexual pleasure and performance. A history of sexual abuse or rape plays a role in many cases in women of sexual arousal disorder, sexual aversion disorder, orgasmic disorder, and vaginismus. People who have been sexually traumatized earlier in life may find it difficult to respond sexually when they develop intimate relationships. They may be flooded with feelings of helplessness, unresolved anger, or misplaced guilt, or experience flashbacks of the abusive experiences when they engage in sexual relations with their partners, preventing them from becoming sexually aroused or achieving orgasm.

Sexual fulfillment is also based on the learning of sexual competencies. Sexual competencies, like other competencies, involve the development of knowledge and skills. Knowledge and skills are acquired through opportunities for new learning. We learn about how our bodies and our partners' respond sexually in various ways, including trial and error with our partners, by learning about our own sexual response through self-exploration (as in masturbation), by reading about sexual techniques, and perhaps by talking to others or viewing sex films or videotapes. Yet children who are raised to feel guilty or anxious about sex may have lacked such opportunities to develop sexual knowledge and skills. Consequently, they may respond to sexual stimulation with their partners with feelings of anxiety and shame rather than arousal and pleasure.

Cognitive Perspectives Albert Ellis (1977b) points out that irrational beliefs and attitudes may contribute to sexual dysfunctions. Consider the irrational beliefs that we must have the approval at all times of everyone who is important to us and we must be thoroughly competent at everything we do. If we cannot abide the occasional disappointment of others, we may catastrophize the significance of a single frustrating sexual episode. If we insist that every sexual rendezvous be perfect, we set the stage for inevitable failure.

Helen Singer Kaplan (1974) noted problems that can occur with our ability to regulate our levels of sexual arousal. Men who ejaculate prematurely, for example, may have difficulty gauging their level of sexual arousal. As a consequence, they may not call upon self-control strategies, such as temporarily suspending stimulation, in time to delay ejaculation.

Most men respond to sexual arousal with positive emotions, such as joy and warmth. But for men with sexual dysfunctions, sexual arousal becomes disconnected from positive emotions (Rowland, Cooper, & Slob, 1996). Psychologist David Barlow (1986) proposed that anxiety may have inhibiting or arousing effects on sexual response, depending on the man's thought processes (see Figure 11.1). For men with sexual dysfunctions, anxiety has inhibiting effects. Perhaps because they expect to fail in sexual encounters, their thoughts are focused on anticipated feelings of shame and embarrassment rather than on erotic stimuli. Concerns about failing increase autonomic arousal or anxiety, which leads them to focus even more attention on the consequences of failure, which in turn leads to dysfunctional performance. Failure experiences in turn lead to avoidance of sexual encounters because these situations have become encoded as opportunities for repeated failure, frustration, and self-defeat. Functional men, by contrast, expect to succeed and focus their attention on erotic stimuli, not on fears of failure. Their erotic attentional focus increases autonomic arousal or anxiety, but not to the point that it interferes with their sexual response. Mild anxiety may actually enhance their sexual arousal. By focusing on erotic cues, functional men become more aroused, successfully engage in sexual activity, and heighten their expectations of future successful performance—all leading to increased approach tendencies.

The cognitive model formulated by Barlow highlights the role of interfering cognitions in sexual dysfunctions. Interfering cognitions include expectancies of failure that are evoked by performance demands. They heighten anxiety to the point of impairing sexual performance. In a vicious cycle, the more people focus on these interfering cognitions, the more difficult it will be for them to perform sexually—and the more likely they will be to focus on interfering cognitions in the future. Although the model was derived from research on men, Barlow believes it may also help explain sexual dysfunctions in women.

Problems in Relationships "It takes two to tango," to coin a phrase. Sexual relations are usually no better than other facets of relationships or marriages (Perlman &

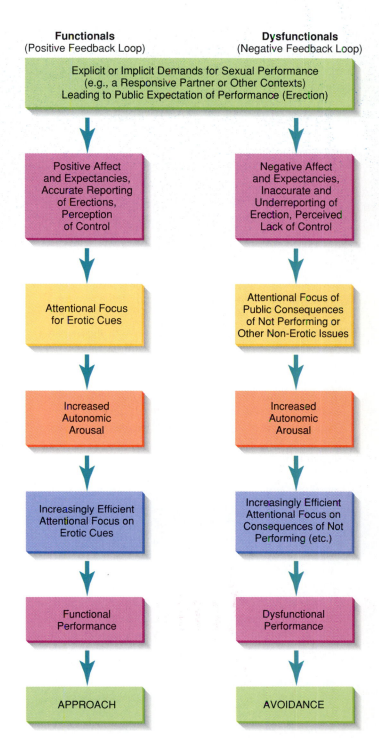

FIGURE 11.1 *Barlow's model of erectile dysfunction.*
In this model, past experience with erectile dysfunction leads men to expect that they will fail again. They consequently focus on anticipated feelings of shame and embarrassment when they engage in sexual relations, rather than on erotic stimuli. These concerns heighten their anxiety, impairing their performance and distracting them from erotic cues. Functional men, by contrast, expect to succeed and focus more of their attention on erotic stimuli, which heightens their sexual response. Though they too may experience anxiety, it is not severe enough to distract them from erotic cues or impair their performance.

Source: Barlow, 1986, p. 146.

Abramson, 1982). Couples who harbor resentments toward one another may choose the sexual arena for combat. Communication problems, moreover, are linked to general marital dissatisfaction. Couples who find it difficult to communicate their sexual desires may lack the means to help their partners become more effective lovers.

The following case illustrates how sexual arousal disorder may be connected with problems in the relationship:

> *After living together for six months, Paul and Petula are contemplating marriage. But a problem has brought them to a sex therapy clinic. As Petula puts it, "For the last two months he hasn't been able to keep his erection after he enters me." Paul is 26 years old, a lawyer; Petula, 24, is a buyer for a large department store. They both grew up in middle-class, surburban families, were introduced through mutual friends and began having intercourse, without difficulty, a few months into their relationship. At Petula's urging, Paul moved into her apartment, although he wasn't sure he was ready for such a step. A week later he began to have difficulty maintaining his erection during intercourse, although he felt strong desire for his partner. When his erection waned, he would try again, but would lose his desire and be unable to achieve another erection. After a few times like this, Petula would become so angry that she began striking Paul in the chest and screaming at him. Paul, who at 200 pounds weighed more than twice as much as Petula, would just walk away, which angered Petula even more. It became clear that sex was not the only trouble spot in their relationship. Petula complained that Paul preferred to spend time with his friends and go to baseball games than to spend time with her. When together at home, he would become absorbed in watching sports events on television, and showed no interest in activities she enjoyed—attending the theater, visiting museums, etc. Since there was no evidence that the sexual difficulty was due to either organic problems or depression, a diagnosis of male erectile disorder was given. Neither Paul or Petula was willing to discuss their nonsexual problems with a therapist. While the sexual problem was treated successfully with a form of sex therapy modeled after techniques developed by Masters and Johnson, and the couple later married, Paul's ambivalences continued, even well into their marriage, and there were future recurrences of sexual problems as well.*
>
> ADAPTED FROM SPITZER ET AL., 1994, PP. 198–200

Sociocultural Perspectives At the turn of the century, an Englishwoman said she would "close her eyes and think of England" when her husband approached her for sexual relations. This old-fashioned stereotype suggests how sexual pleasure was once considered exclusively a male preserve—that sex, for women, was primarily a duty. Mothers usually informed their daughters of the conjugal duties be-

fore the wedding, and girls encoded sex as just one of the ways in which women serviced the needs of others. Women who harbor such stereotypical attitudes toward female sexuality may be unlikely to become aware of their sexual potentials. In addition, sexual anxieties may transform negative expectations into self-fulfilling prophecies. Sexual dysfunctions in men, too, may be linked to severely restricted sociocultural beliefs and sexual taboos.

Modern psychodynamic theorists recognize that anger and other negative feelings that women may hold toward men can lead to sexual dysfunctions. Yet they believe that these negative emotions stem from sociocultural factors rather than from penis envy. Women in our society are often socialized to sacrifice for and submit to their husbands, which may engender rebellion that finds expression through sexual dysfunctions.

Javier (1993) notes, for example, the idealization within many Hispanic cultures of the *marianismo* stereotype, which derives its name from the Virgin Mary. From this sociocultural perspective, the ideal virtuous woman "suffers in silence" as she submerges her needs and desires to those of her husband and children. She is the provider of joy, even in the face of her own pain or frustration. It is not difficult to imagine that some women who adopt these stereotypical expectations may find it difficult to assert their own needs for sexual gratification or may express resistance to this cultural ideal by becoming sexually unresponsive.

Sociocultural factors play an important role in erectile dysfunction as well. Investigators find a greater incidence of erectile dysfunction in cultures with more restrictive sexual attitudes toward premarital sex among females, toward sex in marriage, and toward extramarital sex (M. R. Welch & Kartub, 1978). Men in these cultures may be prone to develop sexual anxiety or guilt that may interfere with sexual performance.

In India, cultural beliefs that link the loss of semen to a draining of the man's life energy underlie the development of Dhat syndrome, which involves an excessive fear of semen loss (see Chapter 6). Men with this condition sometimes develop erectile dysfunction because their fears about the risks of wasting precious seminal fluid interfere with their ability to perform sexually (Singh, 1985).

Psychological Factors Various psychological factors such as depression, anxiety, guilt, and low self-esteem can impair sexual interest or performance. One principal culprit is **performance anxiety**, a type of anxiety that involves an excessive concern about whether we will be able to perform successfully. People who are troubled by performance anxiety become spectators during sex, rather than performers. Their attention is focused on how their bodies are responding (or not responding) to sexual stimulation and on concerns they have about the negative consequences of failing to perform adequately, rather than absorbing themselves in their erotic experiences. Men with performance anxiety may have difficulty achieving or maintaining an erection or may ejaculate prematurely; women may fail to become adequately aroused or have difficulty achieving orgasm. A vicious cycle may ensue in which each failure experience instills deeper doubts, which leads to more anxiety during sexual encounters, which occasions repeated failure, and so on.

In Western cultures, the connection between a man's sexual performance and his sense of manhood is deeply ingrained. The man who repeatedly fails to perform sexually may suffer a loss of self-esteem, become depressed, or feel he is no longer a man (Carey, Wincze, & Meisler, 1998). He may see himself as a total failure, despite other accomplishments in life. Sexual opportunities are construed as tests of his manhood, and he may respond to them by bearing down and trying to will (force) an erection. Willing an erection may backfire because erection is a reflex that cannot be forced. With so much of his self-esteem riding on the line whenever he makes love, it is little wonder that anxiety about the quality of his performance—performance anxiety—may mount to a point that it inhibits erection. The erectile reflex is mediated by the parasympathetic branch of the autonomic nervous system. Activation of the sympathetic nervous system, which occurs when we are anxious, can block parasympathetic control, preventing the erectile reflex from occurring. Ejaculation, on the other hand, is under sympathetic nervous system control, so heightened levels of arousal, as in the case of performance anxiety, can trigger premature ejaculation.

One client who suffered erectile dysfunction described his feelings of sexual inadequacy this way:

I always felt inferior, like I was on probation, having to prove myself. I felt like I was up against the wall. You can't imagine how embarrassing this was. It's like you walk out in front of an audience that you think is a nudist convention and it turns out to be a tuxedo convention.

THE AUTHORS' FILES

Another man described how performance anxiety led him to prepare for sexual relations as though he were psyching himself up for a big game:

At work I have control over what I do. With sex, you don't have control over your sex organ. I know that my mind can control what my hands do. But the same is not true of my penis. I had begun to view sex as a basketball game. I used to play in college. When I would prepare for a game, I'd always be thinking, "Who was I guarding that night?" I'd try to psych myself up, sketching out in my mind how to play this guy, thinking through all possible moves and plays. I began to do the same thing with sex. If I was dating someone, I'd be thinking the whole evening about what might happen in bed. I'd always be preparing for the outcome. I'd sketch out in my mind how I was going to touch her, what I'd ask her to do. But all the time, right through dinner or the movies,

I'd be worrying that I wouldn't get it up. I kept picturing her face and how disappointed she'd be. By the time we did go to bed, I was paralyzed with anxiety.

THE AUTHORS' FILES

Women, too, may equate their self-esteem with their ability to reach frequent and intense orgasms. Yet when men and women try to bear down to will arousal or lubrication, or to force an orgasm, they may find that the harder they try, the more these responses elude them. Some 30 or 40 years ago the pressures concerning sex often revolved around the issue "Should I or shouldn't I?" Today, however, the pressures for both men and women are often based more on achieving performance goals relating to proficiency at reaching orgasm and satisfying one's partner's sexual needs.

Performance anxiety is not unique to our culture. We find, for example, reports of very high levels of performance anxiety in some cases of Arab men in Jordan who were treated for sexual dysfunction (Takriti, 1987). Among some newly married men, fear of sexual failure may have been aggravated by intense cultural pressures to deflower the bride and consummate the relationship. The groom who fails to perform sexually risks being disgraced by having his bride returned to her family home (Bhurgra & De Silva, 1993).

Sex Therapy

Until Masters and Johnson's work in the 1960s, there was no effective treatment for most sexual dysfunctions. Psychoanalytic forms of therapy approached sexual dysfunctions indirectly, for example. It was assumed that sexual dysfunctions represented underlying conflicts, and the dysfunctions might abate if the underlying conflicts—the presumed causes of the dysfunctions—were resolved through psychoanalysis. A lack of evidence that psychoanalytic approaches reversed sexual dysfunctions led clinicians and researchers to develop other approaches that focus more directly on the sexual problems themselves.

Most contemporary sex therapists assume sexual dysfunctions can be treated by directly modifying the couple's sexual interactions. Broadly speaking, sex therapy employs a variety of relatively brief, cognitive-behavioral techniques that center on enhancing self-efficacy expectancies, improving a couple's ability to communicate, fostering sexual competencies (sexual knowledge and skills), and reducing performance anxiety. Therapists may also work with couples to help them iron out problems in the relationship that may impede sexual functioning. When feasible, both sex partners are involved in therapy. In some cases, however, individual therapy may be preferable, as we shall see.

Significant changes have occurred in the treatment of sexual dysfunctions in the past 20 years. There is greater emphasis now on the role of biological or organic factors in the development of sexual problems and greater use of medical and surgical treatments, especially in treating male erectile dysfunction (Rosen & Leiblum, 1995). But even men whose erectile problems can be traced to physical causes can benefit from sex therapy along with medical intervention (Carey, Wincze, & Meisler, 1998).

The Masters and Johnson Approach

In the approach pioneered by Masters and Johnson (1970), the therapists are a female and male team that educates the couple and directs them through a sequence of homework assignments. Masters and Johnson employed an intensive 2-week therapy format in which couples would travel to their clinic, lodge in a local hotel, and focus entirely on their relationship during the treatment period. Anxieties and resentments usually surfaced in meetings between the couple and the therapists, and they were discussed. The focus was on behavioral change, however.

Most sex therapists do not demand that clients suspend all other responsibilities for a 2-week period. The necessity of the female and male team has also been questioned. In some instances, *bibliotherapy*—or self-treatment of dysfunctioning by following a written guide—has also been of help (see L. J. T. Dodge, Glasgow, & O'Neill, 1982).

The Helen Singer Kaplan Approach

Kaplan's (1974) approach is notable because it combines behavioral and psychodynamic methods. She attributed sexual dysfunctions to the interaction of immediate causes (poor technique, performance anxiety, marital conflict, and lack of communication) and remote causes (unresolved internal conflicts that predispose people to encounter anxiety in the expression of their sexual needs). Kaplan began therapy with a direct behavioral approach to sex therapy. She used brief insight-oriented (psychodynamic) therapy when remote causes apparently impeded client response to the behavioral approach. In this way, she brought to the surface any inner conflicts that may have impeded sexual interest or responsiveness.

Let us survey some of the more common sex therapy techniques that are used to treat sexual dysfunctions.

Sexual Desire Disorders

Sex therapists may try to help people with low sexual desire kindle their sexual appetite through the use of self-stimulation (masturbation) exercises together with erotic fantasies (LoPiccolo & Friedman, 1988). Or in working with couples, the therapist might prescribe mutual pleasuring exercises the couple could perform at home or encourage them to expand their sexual repertoire in order to add novelty and excitement to their sex life. When a lack of sexual desire is connected with depression, the treatment would probably focus on relieving the underlying depression in the hope that sexual interest would rebound when the depression lifts. When problems of low sexual desire or sexual aversion appear to be rooted in deep-seated causes, sex therapist H. S. Kaplan (1987) recommended the use of insight-oriented approaches to help uncover and resolve underlying issues. Some cases of hypoactive sexual desire involve hormonal deficiencies, especially lack of the male sex hormone testosterone (both men and women produce testosterone but in different amounts). Testosterone replacement is effective only in the relatively few cases in which testosterone production is truly deficient (Spark, 1991). A lack of sexual desire may also reflect relationship problems that may need to be addressed through couples therapy. Couples therapy might also be used when sexual aversion develops from problems in the relationship (Gold & Gold, 1993). In other cases of sexual aversion, a program of mutual pleasuring, beginning with partner stimulation in nongenital areas and gradually progressing to genital stimulation, may help desensitize fears about sexual contact.

Disorders of Arousal

Women who have difficulty becoming sexually aroused and men with erectile problems are first educated to the fact that they need not "do" anything to become aroused. As long as their problems are psychological, not organic, they need only experience sexual stimulation under relaxed, nonpressured conditions, so that disruptive cognitions and anxiety do not inhibit reflexive responses.

Masters and Johnson have the couple counter performance anxiety by engaging in **sensate focus exercises.** These are nondemand sexual contacts—sensuous exercises

Masters and Johnson. Sex therapists William Masters and Virginia Johnson.

that do not demand sexual arousal in the form of vaginal lubrication or erection. Partners begin by massaging one another without touching the genitals. The partners learn to "pleasure" each other and to "be pleasured" by following and giving verbal instructions and by guiding each other's hands. The method fosters both communication and sexual skills and countermands anxiety because there is no demand for sexual arousal. After several sessions, direct massage of the genitals is included in the pleasuring exercise. Even when obvious signs of sexual excitement are produced (lubrication or erection), the couple does not straightaway engage in intercourse, because intercourse might create performance demands. After excitement is achieved consistently, the couple engages in a relaxed sequence of other sexual activities, culminating eventually in intercourse.

A number of similar sex therapy methods were employed in the case of Victor P.

Victor P., a 44-year-old concert violinist, was eager to show the therapist reviews of his concert tour. A solo violinist with a distinguished orchestra, Victor's life revolved around practice, performances, and reviews. He dazzled audiences with his technique and the energy of his performance. As a concert musician, Victor had exquisite control over his body, especially his hands. Yet he could not control his erectile response in the same way. Since his divorce seven years earlier, Victor had been troubled by recurrent episodes of erectile failure. Time and time again he had become involved in a new relationship, only to find himself unable to perform sexually. Fearing repetition, he would sever the relationship. He was unable to face an audience of only one. For a while he dated casually, but then he met Michelle.

Michelle was a writer who loved music. They were a perfect match because Victor, the musician, loved literature. Michelle, a 35-year-old divorcée, was exciting, earthy, sensual, and accepting. The couple soon grew inseparable. He would practice while she would write— poetry mostly, but also short magazine pieces. Unlike some women Victor met who did not know Bach from Bartok, Michelle held her own in conversations with Victor's friends and fellow musicians over late night dinner at Sardi's. They kept their own apartments; Victor needed his own space and solitude for practice.

In the nine months of their relationship, Victor was unable to perform on the stage that mattered most to him—his canopied bed. It was just so frustrating, he said. "I would become erect and then just as I approach her to penetrate, pow! It collapses on me." Victor's history of nocturnal erections and erections during light petting suggested that he was basically suffering from performance anxiety. He was bearing down to force an erection, much as he might try to learn the fingering of a difficult violin piece. Each night became a command performance in which Victor served as his own severest critic. Victor became a spectator to his own perfor-

*mance, a role that Masters and Johnson refer to as **self-spectatoring**. Rather than focus on his partner, his attention was riveted on the size of his penis. As noted by the late great pianist Vladimir Horowitz, the worst thing a pianist can do is watch his fingers. Perhaps the worst thing a man with erectile problems can do is watch his penis.*

To break the vicious cycle of anxiety, erectile failure, and more anxiety, Victor and Michelle followed a sex therapy program (Rathus & Nevid, 1977) modeled after the Masters-and-Johnson-type treatment. The aim was to restore the pleasure of sexual activity, unfettered by anxiety. The couple was initially instructed to abstain from attempts at intercourse to free Victor from any pressure to perform. The couple progressed through a series of steps:

1. *Relaxing together in the nude without any touching, such as when reading or watching TV together.*
2. *Sensate focus exercises.*
3. *Genital stimulation of each other manually or orally to orgasm.*
4. *Nondemand intercourse (intercourse performed without any pressure on the man to satisfy his partner). The man may afterward help his partner achieve orgasm by using manual or oral stimulation.*
5. *Resumption of vigorous intercourse (intercourse involving more vigorous thrusting and use of alternative positions and techniques that focus on mutual satisfaction). The couple is instructed not to catastrophize occasional problems that may arise.*

The therapy program helped Victor overcome his erectile disorder. Victor was freed of the need to prove himself by achieving erection on command. He surrendered his post as critic. Once the spotlight was off the bed, he became a participant and not a spectator.

THE AUTHORS' FILES

Disorders of Orgasm Women with orgasmic disorder often harbor underlying beliefs that sex is dirty or sinful. They may have been taught not to touch themselves. They are often anxious about sex and have not learned, through trial and error, what kinds of sexual stimulation will arouse them and help them reach orgasm. Treatment in these cases includes modification of negative attitudes toward sex. When orgasmic disorder reflects the woman's feelings about or relationship with her partner, treatment requires working through these feelings or enhancing the relationship.

In either case, Masters and Johnson work with the couple and first use sensate focus exercises to lessen performance anxiety, open channels of communication, and help the couple acquire pleasuring skills. Then during genital massage and, later, during intercourse, the woman directs her partner in the caresses and techniques that stimulate her.

By taking charge the woman is also psychologically freed from the stereotype of the passive, submissive female role.

Many researchers find that a program of directed masturbation is most effective for helping preorgasmic women—women who have never achieved orgasm through any means (Baucom et al., 1998; Heiman & LoPiccolo, 1987; LoPiccolo & Stock, 1986). Even Masters and Johnson, who prefer a couples approach, reported in 1966 that masturbation is the most efficient way for women and men to reach orgasm. Masturbation provides people with a chance to learn about their own bodies and to give themselves pleasure without reliance on a partner. Directed masturbation programs educate women about their sexual anatomy and encourage them to experiment with self-caresses in the privacy of their own homes. Women proceed at their own pace and are encouraged to incorporate sexual fantasies and imagery during self-stimulation exercises to heighten their arousal. They are not distracted by external pressures to please a partner. Pleasure helps counter sexual anxiety, and women learn gradually to bring themselves to orgasm, sometimes with the help of an electric vibrator. Once women can masturbate to orgasm, additional couples treatment can facilitate, but does not guarantee, transference to orgasm with a partner (Heiman & LoPiccolo, 1987; LoPiccolo & Stock, 1986).

Although scant attention in the scientific literature has been focused on male orgasmic disorder, the standard treatment, barring any underlying organic problem, focuses on increasing sexual stimulation and reducing performance anxiety (LoPiccolo, 1990; LoPiccolo & Stock, 1986).

Masters and Johnson also use sensate focus exercises in treating premature ejaculation so that couples learn to give and take pleasure under nondemanding conditions. When the couple is ready to undertake sexual activity, they use the so-called *squeeze technique,* in which the tip of the penis is squeezed by the man's partner when the man is about to ejaculate and then released. The squeeze technique, which should be learned only through personal instruction, temporarily prevents ejaculation. Through repeating the procedure, the man gradually learns to extend intercourse without ejaculating.

In 1956, urologist James Semans suggested the so-called *stop-start* or *stop-and-go* technique for premature ejaculation. The man and his partner just suspend sexual activity when he is about to ejaculate and then resume stimulation when his sensations subside. Repeated practice enables him to regulate ejaculation by sensitizing him to the cues that precede the ejaculatory reflex (making him more aware of his "point of no return").

Although the *stop-and-go* or squeeze methods remain the predominant approaches to treatment, preliminary evidence indicates that antidepressant drugs may help delay ejaculation in men with premature ejaculation (Kim & Seo, 1998; Waldinger, Hengeveld, & Zwinderman, 1994). These drugs affect the availability of neurotransmitters that may play a role in the brain's regulation of the ejaculatory reflex.

Vaginismus and Dyspareunia Vaginismus is a conditioned reflex involving the involuntary constriction of the vaginal opening. It involves a psychologically based fear of penetration, rather than a physical defect or disorder (LoPiccolo & Stock, 1986). Treatment for vaginismus involves a combination of relaxation techniques and the use of vaginal dilators. The woman herself regulates the insertion in the vagina of dilators (rods) of increasing diameter, proceeding at her own pace to avoid discomfort (LoPiccolo & Stock, 1986). The method is generally successful as long as it is unhurried. Because women with vaginismus often have histories of sexual molestation or rape, psychotherapy for the psychological effects of such experiences may be part of the treatment program (LoPiccolo & Stock, 1986). For coital pain that occurs in dyspareunia or in sexual dysfunctions due to medical conditions, the treatment focuses on attempting to resolve the underlying psychological or medical conditions that give rise to the pain.

Evaluation of Sex Therapy Masters and Johnson (1970) claimed an overall success rate of 80% in treating sexual dysfunctions. Although Masters and Johnson's techniques were innovative, their evaluation of their own success has been criticized on numerous grounds. For example, they did not operationally define degrees of improvement, nor did they adequately follow up clients to see whether their treatment successes were maintained over time (Zilbergeld & Evans, 1980).

Success rates for sex therapy have been more impressive for some disorders than for others. High levels of success are reported in treating vaginismus in women and premature ejaculation in men (J. G. Beck, 1993; O'Donohue, Letourneau, & Geer, 1993). Reported success rates in treating vaginismus have ranged as high as 80% (Hawton & Catalan, 1990) to 100% (Masters & Johnson, 1970). Success rates in treating premature ejaculation with the stop-start or squeeze procedures as high as 95% have been reported, but relapse rates tend to be high (Segraves & Althof, 1998). Success rates in treating erectile dysfunction are more variable (R. C. Rosen, 1996), although some estimates indicate that as many as 7 in 10 men experience some improvement with treatment (Hawton, Catalan, & Fagg, 1992). However, relapses too are common (Segraves & Althof, 1998). Outcomes of treatment for male orgasmic disorder also vary and are often disappointing (Dekker, 1993).

Although some progress has been made in treating sexual desire disorders, we would benefit from new treatment techniques because present techniques often fail to resolve the problem (J. G. Beck, 1995; Hawton, 1991). Better results are generally reported from directed masturbation programs for preorgasmic women, with success rates (% of women achieving orgasm) reported in a range of 70% to 90% (R. C. Rosen & Leiblum, 1995). However, much lower rates are reported when measured in terms of percentages of women reporting orgasm during sexual intercourse with their partners (Segraves & Althof, 1998). Some researchers believe that the final determination of the effectiveness of directed masturbation as a treatment alternative remains to be made (O'Donohue, Dopke, & Swingen, 1997).

Biological Treatments of Male Sexual Disorders

Biological treatments of erectile disorder have included silicone implants, hormonal treatments, injections of muscle relaxants, vascular surgery, and now, a pill that promises to help men with erectile dysfunction achieve erections. The popularity of penile implants (semi-rigid or inflatable silicone rods) has fallen off in recent years because of its invasiveness and potential complications, and because less intrusive treatments are now available (Thomas & LoPiccolo, 1994; R. C. Rosen, 1996).

Muscle relaxants such as the drug alprostadil (*Caverject*) relax the muscles that surround the spongy tissues in the penis, allowing blood to flow more freely into the penis, which leads to an erection within a few minutes. A suppository form of the drug can be administered (painlessly for most men) by a tiny plunger inserted about an inch and a half into the tip of the penis (Blakeslee, 1995b). In 1998, the first drug was approved for treatment of erectile dysfunction (Morrow, 1998b). Called *Viagra,* the drug expands blood vessels in the penis, which increases the flow of blood to the penis, which in turn causes erection (I. Goldstein et al., 1998; Kolata, 1998). Taken about an hour before sexual relations, the drug has helped 70% to 80% of patients achieve erections. In the first few weeks following its release to the public, *Viagra* became the fastest selling new drug in history.

TRUTH *or* FICTION REVISITED

11.9 *True.* The pill is called *Viagra* and it quickly became the fastest selling new drug in history when it was introduced in 1998.

Hormone treatments may be helpful to men with abnormally low levels of male sex hormones but not those whose hormone levels are within normal limits (Carani et al., 1990; Spark, 1991). Because hormone treatments can have side effects, such as liver damage, they should not be undertaken lightly.

Viagra. Viagra, the first approved drug to treat erectile dysfunction, became the fastest selling new drug in history after its release in 1998. Former senator and presidential candidate, Bob Dole, appeared in advertisements raising public awareness about the problem of erectile disfunction.

Vascular surgery may be effective in rare cases in which blockage in the blood vessels prevents blood from swelling the penis, or in which the penis is structurally defective (LoPiccolo & Stock, 1986; Mohr & Beutler, 1990).

Several types of drugs, including the SSRI-type antidepressants clomipramine, paroxetine, and sertraline, have the effect of delaying ejaculation. The effectiveness of these drugs has been demonstrated in double-blind controlled studies (Segraves & Althof, 1998).

All in all, the success rates reported for treating sexual dysfunctions through psychological or biological approaches are quite encouraging, especially when we remember that only a generation or two ago there were no effective treatments available.

Normal and Abnormal in Sexual Behavior

Sexual behavior is largely influenced by sociocultural factors. What is considered normal in one culture may be considered abnormal in another.

Gender Identity Disorder

Gender identity disorder pertains to people who find their anatomic gender to be a source of persistent and intense distress. People with the disorder may seek to change their sex organs to resemble those of the opposite gender, and many undergo gender reassignment surgery to accomplish this purpose.

Paraphilias

Paraphilias are sexual deviations involving patterns of arousal to stimuli such as nonhuman objects (for example, shoes or clothes), humiliation or the experience of pain in oneself or one's partner, or children. Paraphilias include exhibitionism, fetishism, transvestic fetishism, voyeurism, frotteurism, pedophilia, sexual masochism, and sexual sadism. Although some paraphilias are essentially harmless (such as fetishism), others, such as pedophilia and sexual sadism, often harm nonconsenting victims. Paraphilias may be caused by the interaction of biological, psychological, and social factors. Efforts to treat paraphilias are compromised by the fact that most people with these disorders do not wish to change.

Sexual Dysfunctions

Sexual dysfunctions include sexual desire disorders (hypoactive sexual desire disorder and sexual aversion disorder), sexual arousal disorders (female sexual arousal disorder and male erectile disorder), orgasm disorders (female and male orgasmic disorders and premature ejaculation), and sexual pain disorders (dyspareunia and vaginismus). Sexual dysfunctions can stem from biological factors (such as disease or the effects of alcohol and other drugs), psychological factors (such as performance anxiety, unresolved conflicts, or lack of sexual competencies), and sociocultural factors (such as sexually restrictive cultural learning). Sex therapy focuses on directly modifying problematic sexual behavior by enhancing self-efficacy expectancies, teaching sexual competencies, improving sexual communication, and reducing performance anxiety.

1. Where should we draw the line between normal and abnormal sexual behavior? What criteria should we use?

2. How has the classification of homosexuality as a mental disorder changed over the years?

3. What is gender identity disorder? What is gender reassignment surgery? What outcomes of the surgery have researchers found?

4. What are the differences between a gay male or lesbian sexual orientation and transsexualism?

5. What are the various paraphilias, their distinguishing features, and their potential causes? What risks do they pose to others?

6. How do therapists treat paraphilias? What evidence do we have of their success?

7. What changes in the body occur during each of the phases of the sexual response cycle?

8. What are the various types of sexual dysfunctions, their distinguishing features, and the causal factors involved? How do therapists today treat these problems? How effective are these treatments?

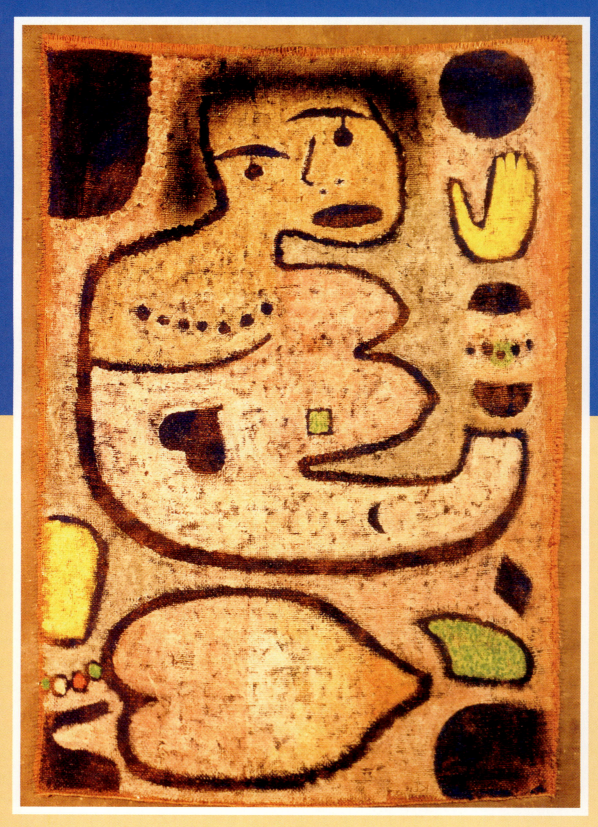

© Paul Klee
Love Song During The New Moon, 1939

Schizophrenia and Other Psychotic Disorders

TRUTH *or* FICTION?

12.1 People may show all the signs of schizophrenia for several months but still not be diagnosed with the disorder.

12.2 The syndrome we recognize as schizophrenia is experienced in virtually the same way in every culture that has been available for study.

12.3 We all experience hallucinations in one form or another.

12.4 Auditory hallucinations may be a form of inner speech.

12.5 Some people with schizophrenia sustain unusual, uncomfortable positions for hours and will not respond to questions or communicate during these periods.

12.6 A 54-year-old hospitalized woman diagnosed with schizophrenia was conditioned to cling to a broom by being given cigarettes as reinforcers.

12.7 If you have two parents with schizophrenia, it's nearly certain that you will develop schizophrenia yourself.

12.8 Living in a family that is hostile, critical, and unsupportive can increase the risk of relapse in people with schizophrenia.

12.9 Drugs developed in the past few years not only treat schizophrenia but can cure it in many cases.

12.10 Some people are deluded that they are loved by a famous person.

When you have completed your study of Chapter 12, you should be able to:

1. Discuss historical contributions of Emil Kraepelin, Eugen Bleuler, and Kurt Schneider to the concept of schizophrenia.

2. Describe the diagnostic features of schizophrenia, the phases occurring during the course of the disorder, and distinguish schizophrenia from brief psychotic disorder, schizophreniform disorder, and other disorders within the schizophrenic spectrum.

3. Review the disturbances in thought, speech, attention, perception, emotions, self-identity, volition, interpersonal behavior, and psychomotor behavior associated with schizophrenia.

4. Distinguish between the disorganized, catatonic, paranoid, undifferentiated, and residual types of schizophrenia.

5. Discuss the process-reactive dimension of schizophrenia, positive and negative symptoms of schizophrenia, and Type I and Type II schizophrenia.

6. Discuss theoretical perspectives on schizophrenia, including the diathesis-stress model, and evidence of supporting roles for biological and psychosocial factors in the development of schizophrenia.

7. Discuss biological, psychoanalytic, learning-based, psychosocial-rehabilitation, and family intervention treatments of schizophrenia.

8. Discuss research concerning the benefits and side effects of antipsychotic medication.

9. Discuss the features of delusional disorder and differentiate the disorder from paranoid schizophrenia and paranoid personality disorder.

Schizophrenia is perhaps the most puzzling and disabling clinical syndrome. It is the psychological disorder that best corresponds to popular conceptions of madness or lunacy. It often elicits fear, misunderstanding, and condemnation rather than sympathy and concern. Schizophrenia strikes at the heart of the person, stripping the mind of the intimate connections between thoughts and emotions and filling it with distorted perceptions, false ideas, and illogical conceptions, as in the case of Angela:

Angela, 19, was brought to the emergency room by her boyfriend Jaime because she had cut her wrists. When she was questioned, her attention wandered. She seemed transfixed by creatures in the air, or by something she might be hearing. It seemed as though she had an invisible earphone.

Angela explained that she had slit her wrists at the command of the "hellsmen." Then she became terrified. Later she related that the hellsmen had cautioned her not to disclose their existence. Angela had been fearful that the hellsmen would punish her for her indiscretion.

Jaime related that Angela and he had been living together for nearly a year. They had initially shared a modest apartment in town. But Angela did not like being around other people and persuaded Jaime to rent a cottage in the country. There Angela spent much of her days making fantastic sketches of goblins and monsters. She occasionally became agitated and behaved as though invisible beings were issuing directions. Her words would begin to become jumbled.

Jaime would try to persuade her to go for help, but she would resist. Then, about nine month's ago, the wrist-cutting began. Jaime believed that he had made the bungalow secure by removing all knives and blades. But Angela always found a sharp object.

Then he would bring Angela to the hospital against her protests. Stitches would be put in, she would be held under observation for a while, and she would be medicated. She would recount that she cut her wrists because the hellsmen had informed her that she was bad and had to die. After a few days in the hospital, she would disavow hearing the hellsmen and insist on discharge.

Jaime would take her home. The pattern would repeat itself.

THE AUTHORS' FILES

Schizophrenia touches every facet of the affected person's life. Acute episodes of schizophrenia are characterized by **delusions, hallucinations,** illogical thinking, incoherent speech, and bizarre behavior. Between acute episodes, people with schizophrenia may still be unable to think clearly and may lack an appropriate emotional response to the people and events in their lives. They may speak in a flat tone and show little, if any, facial expressiveness (Mandal, Pandey, & Prasad, 1998). Although researchers are immersed in probing the psychological and biological foundations of schizophrenia, the disorder remains in many ways a mystery. In this chapter, we examine how research has illuminated our understanding of schizophrenia. We also consider a number of other psychotic disorders, including brief psychotic disorder, schizophreniform disorder, schizoaffective disorder, and delusional disorder.

HISTORY OF THE CONCEPT OF SCHIZOPHRENIA

Although various forms of "madness" have afflicted people throughout the course of history, no one knows how long the behavior pattern we now label schizophrenia existed before it was first described as a medical syndrome by Emil Kraepelin in 1893. Modern conceptualizations of schizophrenia have been largely shaped by the contributions of Kraepelin, Eugen Bleuler, and Kurt Schneider.

Emil Kraepelin

Kraepelin (1856–1926), one of the fathers of modern psychiatry, called the disorder **dementia praecox.** The term derived from the Latin *dementis,* meaning "out" (*de-*) of one's "mind" (*mens*), and the roots that form the word *precocious,* meaning "before" one's level of "maturity." *Dementia praecox* thus refers to premature impairment of mental abilities. Kraepelin believed that dementia praecox was a disease process caused by specific, although unknown, pathology in the body.

Kraepelin wrote that dementia praecox involved the "loss of the inner unity of thought, feeling, and acting." The syndrome begins early in life, and the course of deterioration eventually results in complete "disintegration of the personality" (Kraepelin, 1909–1913, Vol. 2, p. 943). Kraepelin's description of dementia praecox includes behavior patterns such as delusions, hallucinations, and odd motor behaviors—the behavior patterns that typically characterize the disorder today.

Eugen Bleuler

In 1911, the Swiss psychiatrist Eugen Bleuler (1857–1939) renamed dementia praecox *schizophrenia,* from the Greek *schistos,* meaning "cut" or "split," and *phren,* meaning "brain." In doing so, Bleuler focused on the major characteristic of the syndrome, the splitting of the brain functions that give rise to cognition, feelings or affective responses, and behavior. A person with schizophrenia, for example, might giggle inappropriately when discussing an upsetting event or might show no emotional expressiveness in the face of tragedy.

Although the Greek roots of *schizophrenia* mean "split brain," schizophrenia should not be confused with dissocia-

Emil Kraepelin

Eugen Bleuler

tive identity disorder (formerly multiple personality disorder), which is frequently referred to as "split personality" by laypeople. People with dissociative identity disorder (see Chapter 6) exhibit two or more alter personalities, but the alter personalities typically show better integrated cognitive, affective, and behavioral functioning than is the case in schizophrenia. In schizophrenia, the splitting cleaves cognition, affect, and behavior. There may thus be little agreement between the thoughts and the emotions or between the individual's perceptions of reality and what is truly happening.

Although Bleuler accepted Kraepelin's description of the symptoms of schizophrenia, he did not accept Kraepelin's views that schizophrenia necessarily begins early in life and inevitably follows a deteriorating course. Bleuler proposed that schizophrenia follows a more variable course. In some cases, acute episodes occur intermittently. In others, there might be limited improvement rather than inevitable deterioration.

Bleuler believed that schizophrenia could be recognized on the basis of four primary features or symptoms. Today, we refer to them as the **four As:**

1. *Associations.* Associations or relationships among thoughts become disturbed. We now call this type of disturbance "thought disorder" or "looseness of associations." Looseness of associations means ideas are strung together with little or no relationship among them; nor does the speaker appear to be aware of the lack of connectedness. The person's speech appears to others to become rambling and confused.

2. *Affect.* Affect or emotional response becomes flattened or inappropriate. The individual may show a lack of response to upsetting events, or burst into laughter upon hearing that a family member or friend has died.

3. *Ambivalence.* People with schizophrenia hold ambivalent or conflicting feelings toward others, such as by loving and hating them at the same time.

4. *Autism.* Autism is withdrawal into a private fantasy world that is not bound by principles of logic.

In Bleuler's view, hallucinations and delusions represent "secondary symptoms," symptoms that accompany the primary symptoms but do not define the disorder. In more recent years, however, other theorists such as Kurt Schneider (1957) have proposed that hallucinations and delusions are key, or primary, features of schizophrenia. Bleuler was also strongly influenced by psychodynamic theory. He came to believe that the content of hallucinations and delusions could be explained by the attempt to replace the external world with a world of fantasy.

Bleuler's contributions led to the adoption of a broader definition of schizophrenia and brought the diagnostic category into more common use. Bleuler's ideas were especially influential in the United States. U.S.-trained professionals began to use the diagnosis more freely than their European counterparts, who were more influenced by Kraepelin's narrower definition of the disorder. The diagnosis of schizophrenia was broadened in the United States even beyond Bleuler's criteria to include people who showed combined features of schizophrenia and mood disorders. These cases are now generally classified separately from schizophrenia under the category of **schizoaffective disorder.**

Kurt Schneider

Another influential developer of modern concepts of schizophrenia was the German psychiatrist Kurt Schneider (1887–1967). Schneider believed Bleuler's criteria (his "four As") were too vague for diagnostic purposes and that they failed to distinguish schizophrenia adequately from other disorders. Schneider's (1957) most notable contribution was to discriminate between the features of schizophrenia that he believed are central to diagnosis, which he termed **first-rank symptoms,** and so-called **second-rank symptoms,** which he believed are found not only in schizophrenia but also in other psychoses and in some nonpsychotic disorders such as personality disorders. In Schneider's view, if first-rank symptoms are present and cannot be accounted for by organic factors, a diagnosis of schizophrenia is justified. Hallucinations and delusions are prominent first-rank symptoms. Disturbances in mood and confused thinking are considered second-rank symptoms. Although Schneider's ranking of disturbed behaviors helped distinguish schizophrenia from other disorders, we now know that first-rank symptoms are sometimes found among people with other disorders, especially bipolar disorder. Although first-rank symptoms are clearly associated with schizophrenia, they are not unique to it.

Contemporary Diagnostic Practices

The contributions of Kraepelin, Bleuler, and Schneider are expressed in modified form in the present DSM diagnostic system. Although the diagnostic code incorporates many of the features of schizophrenia identified by these early contributors, it is not limited, as Kraepelin had proposed, to cases in which there is a course of progressive deterioration. The narrower *DSM-IV* criteria for schizophrenia also place into other diagnostic categories persons with mood disorders complicated by psychotic behavior (for example, schizoaffective disorder) and people with schizophrenic-like thinking but without overt psychotic behavior (schizotypal personality disorder). The *DSM-IV* criteria for schizophrenia also require that psychotic behaviors be present at some point during the course of the disorder and that signs of the disorder be present for at least 6 months. People with briefer forms of psychosis are placed in diagnostic categories that may be connected with more favorable outcomes. Table 12.1 describes the major clinical criteria for schizophrenia.

TRUTH *or* **FICTION** REVISITED

12.1 *True.* A diagnosis of schizophrenia requires that the symptoms be present for at least 6 months.

PREVALENCE OF SCHIZOPHRENIA

Schizophrenia is a problem of enormous proportions. About 1% of the adult population in the United States is affected by schizophrenia, more than 2 million people in total (Keith, Regier, & Rae, 1991; Grady, 1997a). According to the results of the World Health Organization (WHO) multinational study reported in Chapter 1, the rate of schizophrenia appears to be similar in both developed and developing countries (Jablensky et al., 1992).

Nearly 1 million people in the United States receive treatment for schizophrenia each year, about a third of whom require hospitalization (Grady, 1997a). Schizophrenia

Hallucinations. According to Kurt Schneider, hallucinations and delusions are numbered among the first-rank symptoms of schizophrenia—that is, the symptoms of schizophrenia that are central to the diagnosis. So-called second-rank symptoms are found in other disorders as well. Schneider considered confusion and disturbances in mood to be second-rank symptoms.

TABLE 12.1

Major Clinical Features of Schizophrenia

A. Two or more of the following must be present for a significant portion of time over the course of a 1-month period:

   (1) delusions

   (2) hallucinations

   (3) speech that is either incoherent or characterized by marked loosening of associations

   (4) disorganized or catatonic behavior

   (5) negative features (e.g., flattened affect)

B. Functioning in such areas as social relations, work, or self-care during the course of the disorder is markedly below the level achieved prior to the onset of the disorder. If the onset develops during childhood or adolescence, there is a failure to achieve the expected level of social development.

C. Signs of the disorder have occurred continuously for a period of at least 6 months. This 6-month period must include an active phase lasting at least a month in which psychotic symptoms (listed in A) that are characteristic of schizophrenia occur.

D. Schizoaffective and mood disorders have been ruled out.

E. The disorder cannot be attributed to the effects of a substance (e.g., substance abuse or prescribed medication) or to a general medical condition.

Source: Adapted from the *DSM-IV* (APA, 1994).

---

accounts for 75% of all expenditures in the United States for mental-health treatment ("Schizophrenia Update—Part I," 1995).

Cross-cultural evidence shows that the course of the disorder and its symptoms vary across cultures (Thakker & Ward, 1998). For example, visual hallucinations appear to be more common in some non-Western cultures (Ndetei & Singh, 1983; Ndetei & Vadher, 1984). In a study conducted in an English hospital in Kenya, researchers found that people with schizophrenia of African, Asian, or Jamaican background were about twice as likely to experience visual hallucinations as those of European background (Ndetei & Vadher, 1984).

TRUTH *or* FICTION REVISITED

12.2 *False.* Both the course of schizophrenia and its features vary among cultures.

We still lack any firm conclusion on whether there is a gender difference in the rate of schizophrenia (APA, 1994). What is clear is that women tend to develop the disorder later and have a less severe course of the disorder than do men (Castle et al., 1995; Häfner et al., 1998). Women also tend to achieve a higher level of functioning before the onset of the disorder.

PHASES OF SCHIZOPHRENIA

Schizophrenia typically develops in late adolescence or early adulthood, at the very time that people are making their way from the family into the world outside (Kane, 1996). People who develop schizophrenia become increasingly disengaged from society. They fail to function in the expected roles of student, worker, or spouse, and their families and communities grow intolerant of their deviant behavior. The average (median) age of onset for the first schizophrenic episode falls in the early to mid-twenties in males and in the late twenties for females (APA, 1994). In about 3 of 4 cases, the first signs of schizophrenia appear by the age of 25 (Keith, Regier, & Rae, 1991).

In some cases, the onset of the disorder is acute. It occurs suddenly, within a few weeks or months. The individual may have been well adjusted and shown few, if any, signs of behavioral disturbance. Then a rapid transformation in personality and behavior leads to an acute psychotic episode.

In most cases, there is a slower, more gradual decline in functioning. It may take years before psychotic behaviors emerge, although early signs of deterioration may be observed. This period of deterioration is called the **prodromal phase.** It is characterized by waning interest in social activities and increasing difficulty in meeting the responsibilities of daily living. At first, such people seem to take less care of their appearance. They fail to bathe regularly or they wear the same clothes repeatedly. Over time, their behavior may become increasingly odd or eccentric. There are lapses in job performance or schoolwork. Their speech may become increasingly vague and rambling. At first these changes in personality may be so gradual they raise little concern among friends and families. They may be attributed to "a phase" that the person is passing through. But as behavior becomes more bizarre—such as hoarding food, collecting garbage, or talking to oneself on the street—the acute phase of the disorder begins. Frankly psychotic symptoms develop, such as wild hallucinations, delusions, and increasingly bizarre behavior.

Schizophrenia or *Nervios?* What's in a Name?—Quite a Lot, Apparently

The term *schizophrenia* is connected with a stigma in our society and with the expectation that the disorder is enduring (J. H. Jenkins & Karno, 1992). Yet to many Mexican Americans, a person with schizophrenia is perceived as suffering from *nervios* ("nerves"), a cultural label attached to a wide range of troubled behaviors, including anxiety, schizophrenia, and depression, and one that carries less stigma and more positive expectations than the label of schizophrenia (J. H. Jenkins, 1988; Jenkins & Karno, 1992). Researchers believe the label *nervios* may have the effect of *destigmatizing* the person with schizophrenia:

> *Since severe cases of* nervios *are not considered blame-worthy or under an individual's control, the person who suffers its effects is deserving of sympathy, support, and special treatment. Moreover, severe cases of* nervios *are potentially curable. It is interesting to note that Mexican-descent relatives do not adopt another possible cultural label for craziness,* loco. *As a loco, the individual would be much more severely stigmatized and considered to be out of control with little chance for recovery. . . .*
>
> *Defining the problem as* nervios, *a common condition that in its milder forms afflicts nearly everyone, provides them a way of identifying with and minimizing the problem by claiming that the ill relative is "just like me, only more so."*
>
> JENKINS & KARNO, 1992, PP. 17–18

Family members may respond differently to relatives who have schizophrenia if they ascribe aspects of their behavior to a temporary or curable condition, which they believe can be altered by willpower, than if they believe the behavior is caused by a permanent brain abnormality. The degree to which relatives perceive family members with schizophrenia as having control over their disorders may be a critical factor in understanding how they respond to them. Families may cope better with a family member with schizophrenia if they take a balanced view, believing on the one hand that people with schizophrenia can maintain some control over their behavior, while allowing that some of their odd or disruptive behavior is a product of their underlying disorder (Weisman et al., 1993). It remains to be seen whether these different ways in which family members conceptualize schizophrenia are connected with differences in the rates of recurrence of the disorder among affected family members.

Schizophrenia or an attack of nervios? Many Mexican Americans perceive people with schizophrenia to be suffering from *nervios* ("nerves"), a cultural label that is connected with problems such as anxiety, schizophrenia, and depression. The label *nervios* carries less stigma and more positive expectations than that of schizophrenia.

Following acute episodes, people who develop schizophrenia may enter the **residual phase,** in which their behavior returns to the level that was characteristic of the prodromal phase. Although flagrant psychotic behaviors may be absent during the residual phase, the person may continue to be impaired by a deep sense of apathy, by difficulties in thinking or speaking clearly, and by the harboring of unusual ideas, such as beliefs in telepathy or clairvoyance. Such patterns of behavior make it difficult to meet expected social roles as wage earners, marital partners, or students.

Full return to normal behavior is uncommon but may occur. More commonly, a chronic pattern characterized by occasional relapses and continued impairment between acute episodes develops (Wiersma et al., 1998).

BRIEFER FORMS OF PSYCHOSIS

Although we tend to link psychotic behavior with schizophrenia, some brief psychotic episodes do not progress to schizophrenia. The *DSM-IV* category of **brief psychotic disorder** applies to a psychotic disorder that lasts from a day to a month and is characterized by at least one of the following features: delusions, hallucinations, disorganized speech, or disorganized or catatonic behavior. Eventually there is a full return to the individual's prior level of functioning. Brief psychotic disorder is often linked to a significant stressor or stressors, such as the loss of a loved one or exposure to brutal traumas in wartime. Some cases in women involve a postpartum onset that begins within the first month after childbirth.

Schizophreniform disorder consists of abnormal behaviors identical to those in schizophrenia that have persisted for at least 1 month but less than 6 months. They thus do not yet justify the diagnosis of schizophrenia. Although some cases have good outcomes, in others the disorder persists beyond 6 months and may be reclassified as schizophrenia or perhaps another form of psychotic disorder, such as schizoaffective disorder. Questions remain about the validity of the diagnosis, however (Strakowski, 1994). It may be more appropriate to diagnose people who show psychotic features of recent origin with a classification such as *psychotic disorder of an unspecified type* until additional information clearly indicates the specific type of disorder involved.

SCHIZOPHRENIA-SPECTRUM DISORDERS

Some people have persistent patterns of unusual thinking or emotional responses that seem to lie within the broader spectrum of schizophrenic problems, but they may not fit the stringent definition of schizophrenia. The schizophrenia spectrum includes related disorders that vary in severity from milder personality disorders (schizoid, paranoid, and schizotypal types) to schizophrenia itself.

Also classified within the schizophrenia spectrum is **schizoaffective disorder,** which is characterized by a "mixed bag" of symptoms including psychotic features, such as hallucinations and delusions, together with major disturbances of mood, such as mania or major depression. Like schizophrenia, schizoaffective disorder tends to follow a chronic course that is characterized by persistent difficulties adjusting to the demands of adult life. A recent 8-year follow-up study showed the same general outcomes between schizophrenia and schizoaffective disorder (Tsuang & Coryell, 1993), underscoring the similar chronic course.

The distinction between schizophrenia and schizophrenia-spectrum disorders may be more a matter of degree than of kind. Differences in genetic vulnerability or environmental stress may lead to the development of milder or more severe forms of a common schizophrenic-type disorder (Andreasen, 1987a).

Some schizophrenia-spectrum disorders appear to share a common genetic link (Begley, 1998). Consistent with a common genetic basis, researchers find a greater than average incidence of schizoaffective disorders among the relatives of people with schizophrenia and a greater than average incidence of schizophrenia among the relatives of people with schizoaffective disorder (Kendler, Gruenberg, & Tsuang, 1985; Maj et al., 1991). Evidence also shows familial linkages between schizotypal personality disorder and schizophrenia. For example, researchers find that schizotypal personality disorder occurs more commonly in the biological relatives of people with schizophrenia than in those of nonschizophrenic controls (W. Maier et al., 1994; Torgersen et al., 1993). On the other hand, schizoid personality disorder occurs very rarely among the relatives of people with schizophrenia (Maier et al., 1994), which undercuts the belief in a shared genetic basis between these two disorders.

FEATURES OF SCHIZOPHRENIA

Schizophrenia is a pervasive disorder that affects a wide range of psychological processes involving cognition, affect, and behavior. Many people diagnosed with schizophrenia show only a few of the behavior patterns listed in Table 12.1. No one behavior pattern is unique to schizophrenia, nor is any one behavior pattern invariably present among people with schizophrenia. People with schizophrenia may exhibit delusions, problems with associative thinking, and hallucinations at one time or another, but not necessarily all at once. There are also different kinds or types of schizophrenia, characterized by different behavior patterns.

Men with schizophrenia appear to differ from women with the disorder in several ways. They tend to show an earlier age of onset, a poorer history of adjustment prior to exhibiting the disorder, more cognitive impairment, more behavioral deficits, and a poorer response to chemotherapy (M. J. Goldstein & Tsuang, 1990; Gorwood et al., 1995). These differences have led researchers to speculate that men and women may tend to develop different forms of schizophrenia. Perhaps schizophrenia affects different areas of the brain in men and women, which may explain differences in the form or features of the disorder between the genders.

Impaired Level of Functioning

In schizophrenia, there is a marked decline in occupational and social functioning. People with schizophrenia may have difficulty holding a conversation, forming friendships, holding a job, or taking care of their personal hygiene.

Disturbances in Thought and Speech

Schizophrenia is characterized by disturbances in thinking and in the conveyence of thoughts through coherent, meaningful speech. Disturbances in thinking may be expressed in terms of the content and the form of thought.

Disturbances in the Content of Thought   The most prominent disturbance in the content of thought involves **delusions,** or false beliefs that remain fixed in the person's mind despite their illogical bases and lack of evidence to support them. They tend to remain unshakable even in the face of disconfirming evidence. Delusions may take many forms, including *delusions of persecution* (e.g., "The CIA is out to get me"), *delusions of reference* ("People on the bus are talking about me," or "People on television are making fun of me"), *delusions of being controlled* (believing one's thoughts, feelings, impulses, or actions are controlled by external forces, such as agents of the devil), and *delusions of grandeur* (believing oneself to be Jesus or believing one is on a special mission, or having grand but illogical plans for saving the world). People with delusions of persecution may think they are being pursued by the Mafia, FBI, CIA, or some other group. A woman we treated who had delusions of reference believed television news correspondents were broadcasting coded information about her. A man with delusions of this type expressed the belief that the walls of his house had been bugged by his neighbors. Other delusions include beliefs that one has committed unpardonable sins, is rotting away from a horrible disease, or that the world or oneself do not really exist. Other commonly occurring delusions include *thought broadcasting* (believing one's thoughts are somehow transmitted to the external world so that others can overhear them), *thought insertion* (believing one's thoughts have been planted in one's mind by an external source), and *thought withdrawal* (believing that thoughts have been removed from one's mind).

Mellor (1970) offers the following examples of thought broadcasting, thought insertion, and thought withdrawal:

Thought Broadcasting: A 21-year-old student reported, "As I think, my thoughts leave my head on a type of mental ticker-tape. Everyone around has only to pass the tape through their mind and they know my thoughts" (p. 17).

Thought Insertion: A 29-year-old housewife reported that when she looks out of the window, she thinks, "The garden looks nice and the grass looks cool, but the thoughts of [a man's name] come into my mind. There are no other thoughts there, only his. . . . He treats my mind like a screen and flashes his thoughts on it like you flash a picture" (p. 17).

Thought Withdrawal: A 22-year-old woman experienced the following: "I am thinking about my mother, and suddenly my thoughts are sucked out of my mind by a phrenological vacuum extractor, and there is nothing in my mind, it is empty" (pp. 16–17).

Schizophrenia is not the only diagnostic category characterized by delusional thinking. People in a manic episode may experience delusions of grandeur. They may believe they hold a unique relationship to God or they have some special mission to fulfill. People with a "pure" delusional disorder (discussed later in the chapter) may hold delusions of jealousy or persecution that appear so convincing that others may accept them at face value. Psychotic behavior may also occur in major depression, usually in the form of delusions of guilt (beliefs that one is being persecuted because of some transgression) or somatic delusions (false, persistent beliefs that cancer is eating away at one's body).

Delusions in schizophrenia tend to be more bizarre and more often involve features of thought insertion and thought broadcasting than do delusions associated with mood or other mental disorders (Junginger, Barker, & Coe, 1992). In contrast, grandiose delusions (exaggerated perceptions of self-importance) tend to occur more commonly among people with bipolar or schizoaffective disorder.

Disturbances in the Form of Thought Unless we are engaged in daydreaming or purposefully letting our thoughts wander, our thoughts tend to be tightly knit together. The connections (or associations) between our thoughts tend to be logical and coherent. People with schizophrenia tend to think in a disorganized, illogical fashion, however. In schizophrenia, the form or structure of thought processes as well as their content is often disturbed. Clinicians label this type of disturbance a **thought disorder.**

Thought disorder is recognized by the breakdown in the organization, processing, and control of thoughts. Looseness of associations, which we now regard as a cardinal sign of thought disorder, was one of Bleuler's four As. The speech pattern of people with schizophrenia is often disorganized or jumbled, with parts of words combined incoherently or words strung together to make meaningless rhymes. Their speech may jump from one topic to another but show little interconnectivity between the ideas or thoughts that are expressed. People with thought disorder are usually unaware their thoughts and behavior appear abnormal. In severe cases their speech may become completely incoherent or incomprehensible.

Another common sign of thought disorder is poverty of content of speech (that is, speech that is coherent but lacks informational value because it is too vague, abstract, concrete, stereotypic, or repetitive). Less commonly occurring signs include **neologisms** (a word made up by the speaker that has little or no meaning to others), **perseveration** (inappropriate but persistent repetition of the same words or train of thought), **clanging** (stringing together of words or sounds on the basis of rhyming, such as, "I know who I am but I don't know Sam"), and **blocking** (involuntary abrupt interruption of speech or thought). Disconnected speech is more common and more severe among younger patients with schizophrenia than geriatric patients, while poverty of speech is found more often and is more severe among older patients (Harvey et al., 1997).

Many but not all people with schizophrenia show evidence of thought disorder. Some appear to think and speak coherently but have disordered content of thought, as seen by the presence of delusions. Nor is disordered thought unique to schizophrenia; it has even been found in milder form among people without psychological disorders (Andreasen & Grove, 1986), especially when they are tired or under stress. Disordered thought is also found among other diagnostic groups, such as persons with mania. Thought disorders in people experiencing a manic episode tend to be short-lived and reversible, however. In those with

Are people with schizophrenia overwhelmed by irrelevant stimulation that distracts them from useful information? People with schizophrenia appear to have difficulty filtering out extraneous information. This deficit impairs their ability to focus their attention and organize their thoughts. The deficit may reflect a neurological dysfunction that interferes with the allocation of attention and the filtering out of superfluous information.

schizophrenia, thought disorder tends to be more persistent or recurrent.

Thought disorder occurs most often during acute episodes but may linger into residual phases. Thought disorders that persist beyond acute episodes are connected with poorer prognoses, perhaps because lingering thought disorders reflect more severe disorders (Marengo & Harrow, 1987).

Deficits in Attention

To read this book you must screen out background noises and other environmental stimuli. The ability to focus on relevant stimuli is basic to learning and thinking. Kraepelin and Bleuler suggested that schizophrenia involves a breakdown in the processes of attention. People with schizophrenia appear to have difficulty filtering out irrelevant distracting stimuli, a deficit that makes it nearly impossible to focus their attention and organize their thoughts (R. F. Asarnow et al., 1991). People with schizophrenia may become easily distractible because of a brain abnormality that makes it difficult for them to allocate their attention to relevant tasks and filter out unessential information (Braff, 1993). Scientists have discovered a genetic defect tied to a brain abnormality that may explain this filtering deficit (Grady, 1997a). The mother of a son who had schizophrenia described her son's difficulties in filtering out extraneous sounds:

> . . . his hearing is different when he's ill. One of the first things we notice when he's deteriorating is his heightened sense of hearing. He cannot filter out anything. He hears each and every sound around him with equal intensity. He hears the sounds from the street, in the yard, and in the house, and they are all much louder than normal. (Anonymous, 1985, p. 1; cited in Freedman et al., 1987, p. 670)

People with schizophrenia appear to be *hypervigilant* or acutely sensitive to extraneous sounds, especially during the early stages of the disorder. During acute episodes, they may become flooded by these stimuli, overwhelming their ability to make sense of their environments. Through measuring the brain's involuntary brain wave responses to auditory stimuli, researchers find the brains of people with schizophrenia are less able than those of other people to inhibit or screen out responses to distracting sounds (Braff, 1993; Freedman et al., 1987).

Investigators suspect that attentional deficits associated with schizophrenia, including difficulty filtering out extraneous sounds and other distracting stimuli, is inherited to a certain extent (Finkelstein et al., 1997; Grady, 1997a). Though the underlying mechanism is not entirely clear, attentional deficits may be related to dysfunction in the subcortical parts of the brain that regulate attention to external stimuli, such as the basal ganglia (Cornblatt & Kelip, 1994). Scientists suspect there may be a "gating" mechanism in the brain responsible for filtering extraneous stimuli, much like closing a gate in a road can stem the flow of traffic (Freedman et al., 1987).

Cognitively oriented researchers have focused on the role of information processing in explaining deficits in attention. Information processing refers to the mechanisms by which the individual receives, stores, and processes information from the outside world. Experimental studies have shown that people with schizophrenia may have deficits in the early stages of information processing—that is, in transferring the immediate sensory impression, formed in the brain by external stimuli, such as light or sound, into short-term memory (Braff & Saccuzzo, 1985). People who have difficulty processing sensory information are handicapped indeed in their attempts to understand the outer world. Their environments may be perceived as confused and fragmentary.

Links between attentional deficits and schizophrenia are supported by various studies that focus on the psychophysiological aspects of attention (C. S. Carter et al., 1997). Let us briefly review some of the psychophysiological research pointing to underlying attentional dysfunctions in people with schizophrenia.

Deficiencies in Orienting Response When you are exposed to a stimulus, such as an auditory tone or a flash of light, you experience a pattern of automatic or involuntary psychophysiological responses, called the **orienting response** (OR), that alerts your brain to the presence of the stimulus. Orienting responses include pupil dilation, brain wave patterns connected with states of attention, and changes in the electrical conductivity of the skin—that is, galvanic skin response (GSR).

Studies conducted in the United States, Britain, and Germany (A. S. Bernstein, 1987) have shown that perhaps 40% to 50% of people with schizophrenia fail to demonstrate a normal OR, as measured by GSR, to auditory tones. Perhaps the attentional difficulties in at least some people with schizophrenia are related to failure of the brain mechanisms that normally allocate attention to incoming stimuli.

Eye Movement Dysfunction About half of the people with schizophrenia tested in one study showed evidence of an eye movement dysfunction (J. A. Sweeney et al., 1994). Eye movement dysfunction (also called eye tracking dysfunction) involves abnormal movements of the eyes as they track a target that moves across the field of vision (D. L. Levy et al., 1994). Rather than steadily tracking the target, the eyes fall back and then catch up in a kind of jerky movement ("Schizophrenia Update—Part I," 1995). Eye movement dysfunctions appear to involve a defect in the brain's involuntary attentional processes responsible for visual attention.

Eye movement dysfunctions are common among people with schizophrenia and among their first-degree relatives (parents and siblings), which suggests it might be a genetically transmitted trait, or **marker,** that is associated with genes involved in the development of schizophrenia (Holzman et al., 1997; Keefe et al., 1997; R. E. Litman et al, 1997).

The role of eye movement dysfunction as a biological marker for schizophrenia is clouded, however, because it is not unique to schizophrenia; many people with bipolar disorder show similar types of dysfunction (Sweeney et al., 1994). Research is needed to identify *markers* that are more specific to schizophrenia. We should also note that not all people with schizophrenia or their family members show eye movement dysfunctions. This suggests there may be different underlying genetic pathways associated with schizophrenia.

Deficiencies in Event-Related Potentials Researchers have also studied brain wave patterns, called event-related potentials, or ERPs, that occur in response to external stimuli. ERPs can be broken down into components that emerge at various intervals following the presentation of a stimulus such as a flash of light or an auditory tone. Early components (brain wave patterns occurring within the first 250 milliseconds [ms], or one quarter of a second, of exposure to a stimulus) may be involved in registering the stimulus in the brain. Later components such as the P300 component (a brain wave pattern that typically occurs about 300 ms, or three tenths of a second, after a stimulus) may be involved in focusing attention on the stimulus.

People with schizophrenia often have early ERP components (less than 250 ms) of greater than expected magnitude in response to touch (Holzman, 1987). This pattern of brain wave activity suggests that abnormally high levels of sensory information are reaching higher brain centers in people with schizophrenia, producing a condition called *sensory overload*. This may help explain the difficulty that people with schizophrenia have in filtering out distracting stimuli. We also have evidence of lower than expected levels of P300 brain wave patterns in response to auditory tones (D. Friedman & Squires-Wheeler, 1994; Salisbury et al., 1998). This evidence points to attentional deficits that may at least partly explain why people with schizophrenia have difficulty extracting meaningful information from stimuli (lights, sounds, touch) that impinge upon them. Studies of ERPs are thus consistent with the view that people with schizophrenia may be flooded with high levels of sensory information but have greater difficulty extracting useful information from it. As a result, they may be confused and find it difficult to filter out irrelevant stimuli such as extraneous noises. Although ERP research is promising, the meaning of ERP abnormalities in schizophrenia is not fully resolved (Tracy, Josiassen, & Bellack, 1995).

In sum, several lines of evidence point to underlying physiological deficits in the ability to attend to relevant stimuli and ignore distracting stimuli among people with schizophrenia (D. S. O'Leary et al, 1996). Although the search continues for biological markers for schizophrenia, no definitive marker (a biological pattern unique to schizophrenia) has yet been found (Szymanski, Kane, & Lieberman, 1991). Recent evidence indicates that training in attention skills may help reduce attentional deficits in schizophrenia patients (Medalia et al., 1998).

Perceptual Disturbances

Every so often during the interview, Sally would look over her right shoulder in the direction of the office door, and smile gently. When asked why she kept looking at the door, she said that the voices were talking about the two of us just outside the door and she wanted to hear what they were saying. "Why the

Hallucinations, the most common form of perceptual disturbance in schizophrenia, are images that are perceived in the absence of external stimulation. They are difficult to distinguish from reality. For Sally, the voices coming from outside the consulting room were real enough, even though no one was there. Hallucinations may involve any of the senses. Auditory hallucinations ("hearing voices") are most common. Tactile hallucinations (such as tingling, electrical, or burning sensations) and somatic hallucinations (feeling like snakes are crawling inside one's belly) are also common. Visual hallucinations (seeing things that are not there), gustatory hallucinations (tasting things), and olfactory hallucinations (sensing odors that are not present) are rarer.

Auditory hallucinations occur in about 70% of cases of schizophrenia (Cleghorn et al., 1992). In auditory hallucinations, the voices may be experienced as female or male and as originating inside or outside one's head (Asaad & Shapiro, 1986). Hallucinators may hear voices conversing about them in the third person, debating their virtues or faults.

Some people with schizophrenia experience *command hallucinations,* voices that instruct them to perform certain acts, such as harming themselves or others (Rogers et al., 1990). Angela, for example, was instructed by the "hellsmen" to commit suicide. People with schizophrenia who experience command hallucinations are often hospitalized for fear they may harm themselves or others. There is a good reason for this. A recent study found that 4 of 5 people with command hallucinations reported obeying them, with nearly half reporting they had obeyed commands to harm themselves during the past month (Kasper, Rogers, & Adams, 1996). Yet command hallucinations often go undetected by professionals because command hallucinators deny them or are unwilling to discuss them.

Hallucinations are not unique to schizophrenia. People with major depression and mania sometimes experience hallucinations. Nor are hallucinations invariably a sign of psychopathology. Cross-cultural evidence shows they are common and socially valued in some developing countries

(Bentall, 1990). Even in developed countries, studies show that about 10% of the people sampled report having experienced occasional hallucinations (Bentall, 1990). Hallucinations in people without psychiatric condition often are triggered by unusually low levels of sensory stimulation (lying in the dark in a soundproof room for extended time) or low levels of arousal (Teunisse et al,. 1996). Unlike psychotic individuals, these people realize that their hallucinations are not real.

People who are free of psychological disorders sometimes experience hallucinations during the course of a religious experience or ritual (Asaad & Shapiro, 1986). Participants in such experiences may report fleeting trance-like states with visions or other perceptual aberrations. We all experience hallucinations nightly in the form of dreams. Hallucinations may also occur in response to hallucinogenic drugs, such as LSD. Hallucinations may also occur during grief reactions, when images of the deceased may appear, and in other stressful conditions. In most cases, grief-induced hallucinations can be differentiated from psychotic

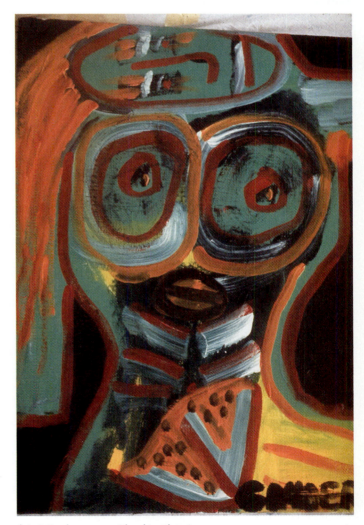

A painting by a man with schizophrenia.

hallucinations in that the individual can distinguish them from reality. Bentall (1990) views the hallucinations of psychiatric patients as involving the lack of ability to distinguish between real and imaginary events. They tend to confuse real and imaginary (hallucinations) events, that is.

TRUTH or FICTION REVISITED

12.3 *True.* All people hallucinate, if we include nocturnal hallucinations in the form of dreams. Hallucinations may also occur during religious experiences or grief reactions, or in response to hallucinogenic drugs.

Drug-induced hallucinations tend to be visual and often involve abstract shapes, such as circles or stars, or flashes of light. Schizophrenic hallucinations, in contrast, tend to be more fully formed and complex. Hallucinations (for example, of bugs crawling on one's skin) may also occur during delirium tremens (the DTs), which often occur as part of the withdrawal syndrome for chronic alcoholism. Hallucinations may also occur as side effects of medications or in neurological disorders, such as Parkinson's disease.

Causes of Hallucinations   The causes of psychotic hallucinations remain unknown, but speculations abound (Asaad & Shapiro, 1986). Disturbances in brain chemistry are suspected as playing a causal role. The neurotransmitter dopamine has been implicated because antipsychotic drugs that block dopamine activity also tend to reduce hallucinations. Conversely, drugs that lead to increased production of dopamine tend to induce hallucinations. Because hallucinations resemble dreamlike states, it is also possible that hallucinations are types of daytime dreams connected with a failure of brain mechanisms that normally prevent dream images from intruding on waking experiences.

Hallucinations may also represent a type of subvocal inner speech (Cleghorn et al., 1992). Many of us talk to ourselves from time to time, although we usually keep our mutterings beneath our breaths (subvocal) and recognize the voice as our own. Might auditory hallucinations that occur among people with schizophrenia be projections of their own internal voices, or self-speech, onto external sources? In one experiment, 14 of 18 hallucinators who suffered from schizophrenia reported the voices disappeared when they engaged in a procedure that prevented them from talking to themselves beneath their breaths (Bick & Kinsbourne, 1987). Similar results were obtained for 18 of 21 normal subjects who reportedly experienced hallucinations in response to hypnotic suggestions.

Auditory hallucinations may be a form of inner speech which, for unknown reasons, becomes misattributed to external sources. Researchers find that brain activity in Broca's area, a part of the brain involved in controlling speech, was greater in men with schizophrenia when they were hearing voices than at a later time when the men were no longer hallucinating (McGuire, Shah, & Murray, 1993). This same area is known to become active when people engage in inner speech (Paulesu, Frith, & Frackowisk, 1993). Re-

searchers also find evidence of similar electrical activity in the auditory cortex of the brain during auditory hallucinations and in response to hearing real sounds (Tiihonen et al., 1992). This evidence supports the view that auditory hallucinations may be a form of inner speech (silent self-talk), which for some unknown reason is attributed to external sources rather than to one's own thoughts (Goleman, 1993b; McGuire, Shah, & Murray, 1993).

TRUTH or FICTION REVISITED

12.4 *True.* Recent research suggests that auditory hallucinations may be a form of inner speech, which, for unknown reasons, becomes misattributed to external sources.

This line of research has led to treatment applications in which behavior therapists attempt to teach hallucinators to reattribute their voices to themselves (Bentall, Haddock, & Slade, 1994). Hallucinators are also trained to recognize the situational cues associated with their hallucinations. For example,

> *. . . one patient . . . recognized that her voices tended to become worse following family arguments. She became aware that the content of her voices reflected the things that she was feeling and thinking about her family but that she was unable to express. Specific targets and goals were then set to allow her to address these difficulties with her family, and techniques such as rehearsal, problem solving and cognitive restructuring were employed to help her work towards these goals.*
>
> BENTALL, HADDOCK, & SLADE, 1994, P. 58

Although research along these lines is still in its infancy, preliminary results show that the reattributional approach may be helpful in some cases in reducing the frequency of hallucinations and the severity of distress associated with hearing voices (Bentall, Haddock, & Slade, 1994). Even if theories linking subvocal speech to auditory hallucinations stand up to further scientific inquiry, however, they cannot account for hallucinations in other sensory modalities, such as visual, tactile, or olfactory hallucinations (Bentall, 1990).

Researchers using a PET scanner report finding brain circuits that are activated when patients with schizophrenia hallucinate (Goleman, 1995f; Silbersweig et al., 1995). The PET scan generates a computer image of neural activity in the brain. The parts of the brain that switched on during hallucinations included the thalamus and other structures located deep within the brain. The thalamus is involved in relaying sensory information to the higher interpretative regions of the brain and in mediating states of consciousness and sleep. Connections from the thalamus project into the auditory and visual areas of the cerebral cortex. A disturbance in the thalamus might lead to the kind of intrusive dreamlike images and sensory distortions people experience when they hallucinate. Other deep-brain structures that are involved in integrating present and past experience and connecting these experiences with emotions were also activated during hallucinations. These structures may give rise to the content (hearing a voice associated with someone from the past) and feeling tone (fear) connected with the hallucination. The brain mechanisms responsible for hallucinations are likely to involve a number of interconnected brain systems. One intriguing possibility is that defects in deeper brain structures may lead the brain to create its own reality, which goes unchecked because of a failure of the higher thinking centers in the brain, located in the frontal lobes, to perform a reality check on these images to determine whether they are real, imagined, or hallucinated (Begley, 1995). Consequently, people may misattribute their own internally generated voices to outside sources. As we'll see later, evidence accumulated from other brain-imaging studies points to abnormalities in the frontal lobes in people with schizophrenia.

Emotional Disturbances

Disturbances of affect or emotional response in schizophrenia are typified by blunted affect—also called *flat* affect—and by inappropriate affect. Flat affect is inferred from the absence of emotional expression in the face and voice. People with schizophrenia may speak in a monotone and maintain an expressionless face, or "mask." They may not experience a normal range of emotional responses to people and events. Or their emotional responses may be inappropriate, such as giggling at bad news.

It is not fully clear, however, whether emotional blunting in people with schizophrenia is a disturbance in their ability to express emotions, to report the presence of emotions, or to actually experience emotions (Berenbaum & Oltmanns, 1990). They may, in other words, experience emotions even if their experiences are not communicated to the world outside through such means as facial expression. Support along these lines is found in research showing that people with schizophrenia displayed less facial expression of positive and negative emotions when viewing emotion-eliciting films than did control subjects, but they reported experiencing as much positive or negative emotion (Kring et al., 1993). It may be that people with schizophrenia experience emotions internally but lack the capacity to express them outwardly (Kring & Neale, 1996).

Other Disturbances or Impairments

People who suffer from schizophrenia may become confused about their personal identities—the cluster of attributes and characteristics that define themselves as individuals and give meaning and direction to their lives. They may fail to recognize themselves as unique individuals and be unclear as to how much of what they experience is a part of themselves. In psychodynamic terms, this phenomenon is sometimes referred to as loss of *ego boundaries*. They may also have difficulty adopting a third-party perspective and fail to perceive their own behavior and verbalizations as socially inappropriate in a given situation because they are unable to see things from another person's point of view (Carini & Nevid, 1992).

Disturbances of volition are most often seen in the residual or chronic state and are characterized by loss of initiative to pursue goal-directed activities. People with schizophrenia may be unable to carry out plans and may lack interest or drive. Apparent ambivalence toward choosing courses of action may block goal-directed activities.

People with schizophrenia may show highly excited or wild behavior, or slow to a state of **stupor.** They may exhibit odd gestures and bizarre facial expressions, or become unresponsive and curtail spontaneous movement. In extreme cases, as in catatonic schizophrenia, the person may seem unaware of the environment or maintain a rigid posture. Or the person may move about in an excited but seemingly purposeless manner.

People with schizophrenia manifest significant impairment in their interpersonal relationships. They tend to withdraw from social interactions and become absorbed in private thoughts and fantasies. Or they cling so desperately to others that they make them uncomfortable. They may become so dominated by their own fantasies that they essentially lose touch with the outside world. They also tend to have been introverted and peculiar even before the appearance of psychotic behavior (Berenbaum & Fujita, 1994). These early signs may be associated with a vulnerability to schizophrenia, at least in people with a genetic risk of developing the disorder.

TYPES OF SCHIZOPHRENIA

There are various forms or types of schizophrenia. Kraepelin listed three types of schizophrenia: paranoid, catatonic, and hebephrenic (now called disorganized type). Bleuler included a fourth type, called **simple schizophrenia,** to describe a milder form of schizophrenia characterized by disorganized thinking, odd behavior, and excessively vague speech, but without active psychotic features such as hallucinations or delusions. Simple schizophrenia is no longer a diagnostic category in the DSM system. People who formerly may have received this diagnosis may fit the present criteria for *schizotypal personality disorder,* however—a form of personality disturbance that resembles a less severe form of schizophrenia.

The *DSM-IV* lists three specific types of schizophrenia: *disorganized, catatonic,* and *paranoid.* People with schizophrenia who display active psychotic features, such as hallucinations, delusions, incoherent speech, or confused or disorganized behavior, but who do not meet the specifications of the other types are considered to have an *undifferentiated type.* Others who have no prominent psychotic features at the time of evaluation but have some residual features (for example, social withdrawal, peculiar behavior, blunted or inappropriate affect, strange beliefs or thoughts) would be classified as having a *residual type* of schizophrenia.

A study of 200 people with schizophrenia showed that the disorganized subtype was associated with the earliest age

A person diagnosed with disorganized schizophrenia. One of the features of disorganized schizophrenia is grossly inappropriate affect, as shown by this young man who continuously giggles and laughs for no apparent reason.

of onset and the paranoid type with the latest age of onset (Beratis, Gabriel, & Hoidas, 1994). The average age of onset was 17 years for the disorganized subtype, 21 years for the catatonic type, 22 years for the residual and undifferentiated types, and 30 years for the paranoid type. The average age of onset across types was 25 years.

Disorganized Type

The **disorganized type** is associated with such features as confused behavior; incoherent speech; vivid, frequent hallucinations; flattened or inappropriate affect; and disorganized delusions that often involve sexual or religious themes. Social impairment is frequent among people with disorganized schizophrenia. They also display silliness and giddiness of mood, giggling and talking nonsensically. They often neglect their appearance and hygiene and lose control of their bladders and bowels.

Consider the case of Emilio:

A 40-year-old man who looks more like 30 is brought to the hospital by his mother, who reports that she is afraid of him. It is his twelfth hospitalization. He is dressed in a tattered overcoat, baseball cap, and bedroom slippers,

and sports several medals around his neck. His affect ranges from anger (hurling obscenities at his mother) to giggling. He speaks with a childlike quality and walks with exaggerated hip movements and seems to measure each step very carefully. Since stopping his medication about a month ago, his mother reports, he had been hearing voices and looking and acting more bizarrely. He tells the interviewer he has been "eating wires" and lighting fires. His speech is generally incoherent and frequently falls into rhyme and clanging associations. His history reveals a series of hospitalizations since the age of 16. Between hospitalizations, he lives with his mother, who is now elderly, and often disappears for months at a time, but is eventually picked up by the police for wandering in the streets.

ADAPTED FROM SPITZER ET AL., 1994, PP. 189–190

Catatonic Type

The **catatonic type** is a subtype of schizophrenia characterized by markedly impaired motor behavior and a slowing down of activity that progresses to a stupor but may switch abruptly into an agitated phase. People with catatonic schizophrenia may show unusual mannerisms or grimacing, or hold bizarre, apparently strenuous postures for hours, even as their limbs become stiff or swollen. A striking but less common feature is **waxy flexibility,** which involves the adoption of a fixed posture into which they have been positioned by others. They will not respond to questions or comments during these periods, which can last for hours. Later they may report they heard what others were saying at the time, however.

A 24-year-old man had been brooding about his life. He professed that he did not feel well, but could not explain his bad feelings. While hospitalized he initially sought contact with people, but a few days later was found in a statuesque position, his legs contorted in an awkward-looking position. He refused to talk to anyone and acted as if he couldn't see or hear anything. His face was an expressionless mask. A few days later, he began to talk, but in an echolalic or mimicking way. For example, he would respond to the question, "What is your name?" by saying, "What is your name?" He could not care for his needs and required to be fed by spoon.

ADAPTED FROM ARIETI, 1974, P. 40

Although catatonia is associated with schizophrenia, it may also occur in other physical and psychological disorders, including brain disorders, states of drug intoxication, metabolic disorders, and mood disorders ("What is catatonia?," 1995).

TRUTH *or* FICTION REVISITED

12.5 *True.* People with the catatonic subtype of schizophrenia may maintain unusual, uncomfortable positions in which others place them and will fail to respond to questions during these periods, which can last for hours.

A person diagnosed with catatonic schizophrenia. People with catatonic schizophrenia may remain in unusual, difficult positions for hours, even though their limbs become stiff or swollen. They may seem oblivious to their environment, even to people who are talking about them. Yet they may later say that they heard what was being said. Periods of stupor may alternate with periods of agitation.

On the run? People with paranoid schizophrenia hold systematized delusions that commonly involve themes of persecution and grandeur. They usually do not show the degree of confusion, disorganization, or disturbed motor behavior seen in people with disorganized or catatonic schizophrenia. Unless they are discussing the areas in which they are delusional, their thought processes may appear to be relatively intact.

Paranoid Type

The paranoid type is characterized by preoccupations with one or more delusions or with the presence of frequent auditory hallucinations (APA, 1994). The behavior and speech of someone with paranoid schizophrenia does not show the marked disorganization typical of the disorganized type, nor is there a prominent display of flattened or inappropriate affect or catatonic behavior. Their delusions often involve themes of grandeur, persecution, or jealousy. They may believe, for example, that their spouse or lover is unfaithful despite a lack of evidence. They may also become highly agitated, confused, and fearful.

Myra, a 25-year-old woman, was visibly frightened. She was shaking badly and had the look of someone who feared that she might be attacked at any moment. The night before she had been found cowering in a corner of the local bus station, mumbling to herself incoherently, having arrived in town minutes earlier on a bus from Philadelphia. The station manager had called the police, who took her to the hospital. She told the interviewer that she had to escape Philadelphia because the

Mafia was closing in on her. She was a schoolteacher, she explained, at least until the voices started bothering her. The voices would tell her she was bad and had to be punished. Sometimes the voices were in her head, sometimes they spoke to her through the electrical wires in her apartment. The voices told her how someone from the Mafia would come to kill her. She felt that one of her neighbors, a shy man who lived down the hall, was in league with the Mafia. She felt the only hope she had was to escape. To go somewhere, anywhere. So she hopped on the first bus leaving town, heading nowhere in particular, except away from home.

THE AUTHORS' FILES

DIMENSIONS OF SCHIZOPHRENIA

In addition to the various types of schizophrenia, researchers generally agree there are various dimensions of schizophrenia. Such dimensions include the process-reactive dimension, dimensions defined by positive and negative features or symptoms, and Type I–Type II schizophrenia.

The Process-Reactive Dimension

In some cases, schizophrenia appears to develop slowly or insidiously. No clearly identified stressor appears to evoke the changes in functioning. This pattern, called **process schizophrenia**, has traditionally been associated with more persistent impairment and less favorable outcomes than **reactive schizophrenia.** Reactive schizophrenia has a more sudden onset. It typically follows precipitating stressors such as moving away from home or the death of a parent.

Reactive schizophrenia is associated with a higher level of social, school, and vocational functioning before the acute phase of the disorder (called *premorbid adjustment*) than process schizophrenia. Many cases of reactive schizophrenia involve people who appeared normal before the abrupt onset of the disorder. Many had friends, held jobs, and did well at school. Process schizophrenia, by contrast, is associated with poorer social development, as evidenced by a failure to achieve an adequate social, educational, or occupational adjustment before the acute features of schizophrenia emerged.

The higher the level of premorbid adjustment, the better the eventual outcome or, in medical terminology, the **prognosis.** Several other factors also predict better outcomes, including a later age of onset, a more acute onset, the presence of precipitating events preceding the first psychotic episode, a briefer period of psychotic behavior during the active phase, a better level of functioning between episodes, and intact neurological functioning (APA, 1994).

Changes in diagnostic practices may have limited the prognostic value of the process-reactive distinction. Studies from the 1960s and 1970s generally showed that reactive schizophrenia was associated with better prognoses than process schizophrenia but were based on the broader conception of schizophrenia contained in the *DSM-II.* In 1980, the *DSM-III* adopted a narrower definition of schizophrenia, and many people with schizophrenic-type behavior were assigned to other categories, such as schizotypal personality disorder, schizoaffective disorder, brief reactive psychoses, and schizophreniform disorders. Studies conducted with subjects who meet the tighter DSM-III criteria for schizophrenia have generally failed to demonstrate the prognostic value of the process-reactive dimension. People with schizophrenia defined by *DSM-III* and *DSM-IV* criteria tend to be limited more to having the chronic process type. Yet the process-reactive dimension may still predict outcomes among the broader schizophrenia spectrum of disorders that includes schizotypal personality disorders and schizoaffective disorders, among others (Herron, 1987).

Positive and Negative Symptoms

The search for a classification system more in tune with present diagnostic practices has led to an attempt to distinguish two basic clusters of symptoms or features of schizophrenia: **negative symptoms** and **positive symptoms.**

Positive symptoms refer to the flagrant signs of psychosis, such as hallucinations, delusions, thought disorder, and bizarre behavior (Penn, 1998). Negative symptoms involve behavioral deficits or the absence of normal behaviors, such as low motivation, flat affect, loss of pleasure or interest in activities, limited production of thoughts and speech, a general slowing down of movement and psychological functioning (psychomotor retardation), and social isolation or withdrawal (Selten et al., 1998). Although we don't know very much about ethnic differences in symptom clusters, the available evidence indicates that African Americans with schizophrenia seem to exhibit fewer negative symptoms of schizophrenia than do their White counterparts (Fabrega, Mezzich, & Ulrich, 1988).

Positive symptoms may involve a defect in the inhibitory (blocking) mechanisms in the brain that would normally control excessive or distorted behaviors. Negative symptoms represent the more enduring or persistent characteristics of schizophrenia. The presence of negative symptoms of schizophrenia tends to be associated with the following characteristics (Earnst & Kring, 1997; McGlashan & Fenton, 1992):

- Poorer premorbid functioning
- Lower educational level
- Signs of brain dysfunction or structural abnormalities, including reduced blood flow and metabolism in certain areas of the brain, enlarged ventricles
- Poorer performance on neuropsychological tests
- More gradual onset, few if any remissions during the early years of the disorder
- Progressive decline in functioning that leads to enduring disability

Positive symptoms tend to occur during acute episodes and then disappear. Even when the individual is free of the more dramatic positive features of the disorder, such as hallucinations and delusions, she or he may continue to be impaired by the persistence of the more enduring negative characteristics of blunted emotions and poverty of speech. Positive symptoms, such as thought disorder and delusions, may also persist into the residual phase in some cases, making it difficult for the person to adjust to the demands of community living (Harrow et al., 1995). Thought disorder and delusional activity may persist even when antipsychotic medication is continued.

Type I–Type II Schizophrenia

An intriguing possibility is that positive and negative symptom patterns represent different subtypes of schizophrenia: Type I and Type II, respectively (Crow, 1980a, 1980b, 1980c). Type I schizophrenia is characterized by positive symptoms (for example, hallucinations, delusions, and looseness of associations), abrupt onset, retained intellectual ability, and a more favorable response to antipsychotic medication. This type of schizophrenia may involve an underlying disturbance in the supply or regulation of dopamine in the brain, since antipsychotic drugs that regulate dopamine function generally have a favorable impact on positive symptoms. Type II schizophrenia corresponds to a pattern consisting of negative symptoms (flattened or blunted affect, social withdrawal, poverty of speech), greater chronicity and intellectual impairment, and poorer response to antipsychotic drugs. This pattern suggests a different developmental process than Type I schizophrenia, perhaps one that involves structural damage or atrophy in the brain.

The Type I–Type II distinction remains controversial, as evidence does not clearly support the existence of two distinct behavior patterns in schizophrenia. Some investigators (e.g., Kay, 1990; Mortimer et al., 1990) find that only a minority of people with schizophrenia can be classified as exhibiting either predominantly positive or negative symptoms. Positive and negative symptoms may not define distinct subtypes of schizophrenia but rather separate dimensions that can coexist in the same individual.

Perhaps, as recent research suggests, a three-dimensional model is most appropriate for grouping schizophrenic symptoms (Andreasen et al., 1995; Arndt et al., 1995). One dimension, a *psychotic dimension,* consists of delusional thinking and hallucinations. A *negative dimension* comprises negative symptoms such as flat affect and poverty of speech and thought. The third dimension, labeled a *disorganized dimension,* includes inappropriate affect and thought disorder (disordered thought and speech). Although schizophrenic symptoms seem to cluster into these three dimensions, there is considerable overlap among the dimensions. Thus, it does not appear these dimensions represent distinct subtypes of schizophrenia. Still, it remains an open question whether or not different underlying neurobiological processes give rise to these different constellations of symptoms.

THEORETICAL PERSPECTIVES

The understanding of schizophrenia has been approached from the major theoretical perspectives. The causes of schizophrenia remain unknown but are generally believed to involve the interaction of biological, psychological, social, and environmental influences.

Psychodynamic Perspectives

According to the psychodynamic perspective, schizophrenia represents the overwhelming of the ego by primitive sexual or aggressive impulses from the id. These impulses threaten the ego and give rise to intense intrapsychic conflict. Under such threat, the person regresses to an early period in the oral stage, referred to as *primary narcissism.* In this period, the infant has not yet learned that the world and itself are two distinct entities. ("Secondary" narcissism describes self-involvement at a later age, such as during adolescence.) Be-

cause the ego mediates the relationship between the self and the outer world, this breakdown in ego functioning accounts for the detachment from reality that is typical of schizophrenia. Input from the id causes fantasies to become mistaken for reality, giving rise to hallucinations and delusions. Primitive impulses may also carry more weight than social norms and be expressed in bizarre, socially inappropriate behavior.

Freud's followers, such as Erik Erikson and Harry Stack Sullivan, placed more emphasis on interpersonal than intrapsychic factors. Sullivan (1962), for example, who devoted much of his life's work to schizophrenia, emphasized the importance of impaired mother-child relationships, arguing they can set the stage for gradual withdrawal from other people. In early childhood, anxious and hostile interactions between the child and parent lead the child to take refuge in a private fantasy world. A vicious cycle ensues: The more the child withdraws, the less opportunity there is to develop a sense of trust in others and the social skills necessary to establish intimacy. Then the weak bonds between the child and others prompt social anxiety and further withdrawal. This cycle continues until young adulthood. Then, faced with an increasing set of demands at school or work and in intimate relationships, the person becomes

Withdrawing into oneself? Henry Stack Sullivan and some other psychodynamic theorists see people with schizophrenia as withdrawing into private fantasy worlds, largely because of severely disturbed relationships with their mothers.

overwhelmed with anxiety and withdraws completely into a world of fantasy.

Critics of Freud's views point out that schizophrenic behavior and infantile behavior are not much alike, so that schizophrenia cannot be explained by regression. Critics of Freud and modern psychodynamic theorists note that psychodynamic explanations are *post hoc,* or retrospective. Early child-adult relationships are recalled from the vantage point of adulthood rather than observed longitudinally. Psychoanalysts have not been able to demonstrate that certain early childhood experiences or family patterns predict schizophrenia.

Learning Perspectives

Although learning theory may not account for schizophrenia, the principles of conditioning and observational learning may play a role in the development of some forms of schizophrenic behavior. From this perspective, people may learn to "emit" schizophrenic behaviors when they are more likely than normal behavior to be reinforced, as suggested by Ullmann and Krasner (1975).

Ullmann and Krasner focused on the reinforcement value of social stimulation. Children who later develop schizophrenia may grow up in nonreinforcing environments because of disturbed family patterns or other environmental influences. Thus, they never learn to respond appropriately to social stimuli. Instead, as Sullivan too had argued, they attend increasingly to private or idiosyncratic stimuli. Other people perceive them as strange, and they suffer social rejection. In a vicious cycle, rejection spurs feelings of alienation; alienation, in turn, engenders more bizarre behavior. Patterns of bizarre behavior may be maintained by the unintentional reinforcement they receive from some people in the form of attention and expressions of sympathy.

Support for this view is found in operant conditioning studies in which bizarre behavior is shaped by reinforcement. Experiments involving people with schizophrenia show, for example, that reinforcement affects the frequency of bizarre versus normal verbalizations and that hospital patients can be shaped into performing odd behaviors. In a classic case example, Haughton and Ayllon (1965) conditioned a 54-year-old woman with chronic schizophrenia to cling to a broom. A staff member gave her the broom to hold and, when she did, another staff member gave her a cigarette. This pattern was repeated several times. Soon the woman could not be parted from the broom. But the fact that reinforcement can influence people to engage in peculiar behavior does not demonstrate that the bizarre behaviors characterizing schizophrenia can be accounted for by learning.

TRUTH *or* FICTION REVISITED

12.6 *True.* A 54-year-old woman hospitalized with schizophrenia was in fact conditioned to cling to a broom by being given cigarettes as reinforcers. The issue is the extent to which principles of learning can account for the bizarre behavior patterns shown by people with schizophrenia.

There are other shortcomings to these behavioral explanations. For example, many of us grow up in harsh or punishing circumstances, but do not retreat into private worlds of fantasy or display bizarre behavior. Many people with schizophrenia also grow up in homes that are supportive and socially reinforcing. Moreover, schizophrenic behaviors fall into patterns that are unlikely to occur by chance and then be reinforced to the point they become learned habits.

Social-Cognitive Perspectives Social-cognitive theorists suggest that modeling of schizophrenic behavior can occur within the mental hospital. In that setting, patients may begin to model themselves after their fellow patients who act strangely. Hospital staff may inadvertently reinforce schizophrenic behavior by paying more attention to those patients who exhibit more bizarre behavior. This understanding is consistent with the observation that schoolchildren who disrupt the class garner more attention from their teachers than well-behaved children do.

Perhaps some forms of schizophrenic behavior can be explained by the principles of modeling and reinforcement. However, many people come to display schizophrenic behavior patterns without prior exposure to other people with schizophrenia. In fact, the onset of schizophrenic behavior patterns is more likely to lead to hospitalization than to result from hospitalization.

Biological Perspectives

Though we still have much to learn about the biological underpinnings of schizophrenia, we've come to see that biology plays a determining role.

Genetic Factors Evidence that schizophrenia is strongly influenced by genetic factors is compelling (Cannon et al., 1998; Gottesman, 1991, 1993; Kendler & Diehl, 1993; Kendler et al., 1997). Schizophrenia, like many other disorders, tends to run in families (Erlenmeyer-Kimling, et al., 1997). Cross-cultural evidence from studies in such countries as Sweden, Iceland, and Ireland as well as in the United States shows an increased risk of schizophrenia in people who have biological relatives with the disorder (Kendler et al., 1993c; Erlenmeyer-Kimling et al., 1997). Overall, people who have biological relatives with schizophrenia have about a tenfold greater risk of developing schizophrenia than do members of the general population (APA, 1994; Kendler & Diehl, 1993).

Further supporting a genetic linkage, evidence shows the closer the genetic relationship between people diagnosed with schizophrenia and their family members, the greater the likelihood (or concordance rate) of schizophrenia in their relatives. Figure 12.1 shows the pooled results of European studies on family incidence of schizophrenia conducted from 1920 to 1987.

Yet more support for a genetic contribution to schizophrenia is found in twin studies, which show concordance rates for the disorder among identical or monozygotic (MZ)

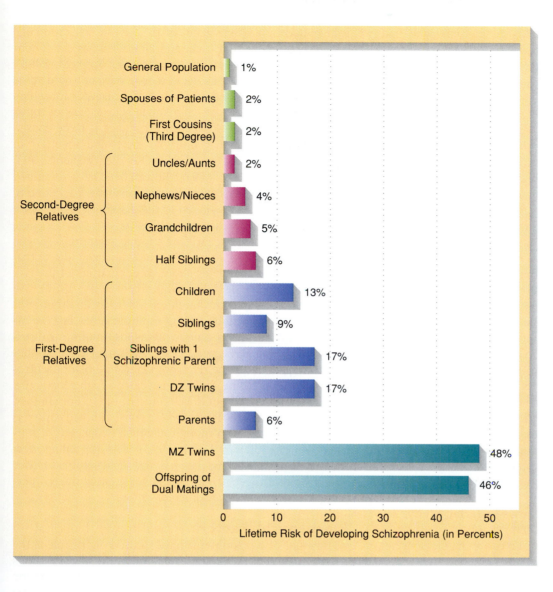

FIGURE 12.1 *The familial risk of schizophrenia.*
Generally speaking, the more closely one is related to people who have developed schizophrenia, the greater the risk of developing schizophrenia oneself. Monozygotic (MZ) twins, whose genetic heritages overlap fully, are much more likely than dizygotic (DZ) twins, whose genes overlap by 50%, to be concordant for schizophrenia.

Source: Adapted from Gottesman et al. (1987).

twins of about 48% on the average, which is more than twice the rate found among fraternal or dizygotic (DZ) twins (about 17%) (Gottesman, 1991; Plomin, Owen, & McGuffin, 1994). A twins study in Norway found an even greater spread: 48% concordance in MZ twins versus 3.6% in DZ twins (Onstad, Skre, Torgensen, & Kringlen, 1991).

Although the results of twin studies are strongly suggestive of a genetic component in the risk of schizophrenia, the fact that MZ twins share 100% genetic similarity but are discordant for schizophrenia in about half of the cases shows that schizophrenia is determined, at least in part, by other-than-genetic factors.

Although familial association (tendencies for twins and other family members to share the same or similar disorders) is consistent with a genetic explanation, it does not prove the disorders in question are genetically transmitted. Families share common environments, not just common genes. We should also note another possible *environmental* factor in common between MZ twins. MZ twins may be subject prenatally to a greater risk of shared viral illnesses than DZ twins because most MZ twins, unlike DZ twins, share

fetal blood circulation in the early stages of pregnancy and thus may be more likely to share infections (J. O. Davis & Phelps, 1995; Davis, Phelps, & Bracha, 1995). However, no one has thus far identified any prenatal viral agent linked to the later development of schizophrenia.

Because of the limitations of family and twin studies, researchers have turned to adoption studies. By examining adopted children who are reared apart from their biological parents, investigators can better sort out genetic from environmental influences. Adoption studies provide the strongest evidence for a genetic contribution to schizophrenia (Gottesman, McGuffin, & Farmer, 1987). In an early study, Heston (1966) located 47 children of mothers who had schizophrenia (so-called *high-risk*, or HR children) who were adopted or sent to live with relatives soon after birth. The lifetime risk for schizophrenia among these adoptees was 16.6%, as compared to 0% among a group of 50 reference cases of adoptees who were also reared by foster mothers but whose biological mothers did not have schizophrenia.

In a Danish study, United States and Danish researchers examined official registers and found 39 HR adoptees who had been reared apart from biological mothers who had schizophrenia (D. Rosenthal et al., 1968, 1975). Three of the 39 HR adoptees (8%) were diagnosed with schizophrenia, as compared to 0% of a reference group of 47 adoptees whose biological parents had no psychiatric history. In addition, the HR adoptees had a higher incidence of schizophrenia-spectrum disorders.

Other investigators have approached the question of heredity in schizophrenia from the opposite direction. United States researcher Seymour Kety and Danish colleagues (Kety, Rosenthal, Wender, Schulsinger, & Jacobsen, 1975; Kety et al., 1978) used official records to find 33 index cases of children in Copenhagen, Denmark, who had been adopted early in life and were later diagnosed with schizophrenia. They compared the rates of diagnosed schizophrenia in the biological and adoptive relatives of the index cases with those of the relatives of a matched reference group that consisted of adoptees with no psychiatric history. The results strongly supported the genetic explanation. The incidence of diagnosed schizophrenia was greater among the biological relatives of the adoptees who had schizophrenia than among the biological relatives of the control adoptees. Adoptive relatives of both the index cases and control cases showed similar, *low* rates of schizophrenia. Similar results were found in later research that extended the scope of the investigation to the rest of Denmark (Kety et al., 1994). It thus appears that family linkages in schizophrenia follow shared genes, not shared environments, as does thought disorder associated with schizophrenia (Moldin, 1994; Kinney et al., 1997).

Still another approach, the **cross-fostering study,** has yielded additional evidence of genetic factors in schizophrenia. In this approach, investigators compare the incidence of schizophrenia among children whose biological parents either had or didn't have schizophrenia and who were reared by adoptive parents who either had or didn't have schizophrenia. Another Danish study by Wender and his colleagues (Wender, Rosenthal, Kety, Schulsinger, & Welner, 1974) found the incidence of schizophrenia related to the presence of schizophrenia in the children's biological parents but not in their adoptive parents. High-risk children (children whose biological parents had schizophrenia) were almost twice as likely to develop schizophrenia as those of nonschizophrenic biological parents, regardless of whether or not they were reared by a parent with schizophrenia. It is also notable that adoptees whose biological parents did not suffer from schizophrenia were placed at no greater risk of developing schizophrenia by being reared by an adoptive parent with schizophrenia than by a nonschizophrenic parent. In sum, a genetic relationship with a person with schizophrenia seems to be the most prominent risk factor for developing the disorder.

Models of Genetic Transmission The mode of genetic transmission in schizophrenia remains unknown (Carey & DiLalla, 1994). We know that some disorders, such as Huntington's disease and muscular dystrophy, are transmitted by a single gene. In the case of schizophrenia, however, evidence from twin and family studies is not consistent with a single-gene model (Kendler & Diehl, 1993). Another reason the single-gene theory may not hold up is that we have yet to find any behavioral disorder for which conclusive evidence exists of a single-gene means of transmission (Kendler, 1994). Instead, evidence is more consistent with the view that multiple genes are involved in determining risk for schizophrenia (Kendler & Diehl, 1993; Moldin & Gottesman, 1997). Researchers have identified several chromosomes, especially chromosomes 22, 6, and 8, that may contain genes linked to the disorder (Talan, 1995; DeAngelis, 1997; Kendler et al., 1996c).

In sum, the evidence to date strongly supports a genetic component in schizophrenia. Recent estimates indicate that genetic factors account for about three quarters of the risk of developing the disorder (Gottesman et al., 1987). We don't yet understand the mode of inheritance, although it appears that interactions among multiple genes may be involved in establishing a genetic predisposition for the disorder (Buchsbaum & Hazlett, 1998; Hallmayer et al., 1992). However, genetics alone does not determine risk of schizophrenia. For one thing, people may carry a high genetic risk of schizophrenia and not develop the disorder. For another, the rate of concordance among MZ twins, as noted earlier, is well below 100%, even though identical twins carry identical genes (Kendler & Diehl, 1993). The prevailing view today, which we discuss later, is the *diathesis-stress model*, which holds that schizophrenia involves a complex interplay of genetic and environmental factors.

Biochemical Factors Contemporary biological investigations of schizophrenia have focused on the role of the neurotransmitter dopamine. The **dopamine theory** posits that schizophrenia involves an overreactivity of dopamine receptors in the brain—the receptor sites on postsynaptic neurons into which molecules of dopamine lock (Haber & Fudge, 1997).

People with schizophrenia do not appear to produce more dopamine than other people. Instead, they appear to *utilize* more of it. But why? Research suggests that people with schizophrenia may have a greater-than-normal number of dopamine receptors in their brains or have receptors that are overly sensitive to dopamine (K. L. Davis et al., 1991; Gur & Pearlson, 1993).

The major source of evidence for the dopamine model is found in the effects of antipsychotic drugs called major tranquilizers or **neuroleptics.** The most widely used neuroleptics belong to a class of drugs called **phenothiazines,** which includes such drugs as Thorazine, Mellaril, and Prolixin. Neuroleptic drugs block dopamine receptors, thereby reducing the level of dopamine activity (Kane, 1996). As a consequence, neuroleptics inhibit excessive transmission of neural impulses that may give rise to schizophrenic behavior. Researchers suspect that a particular type of dopamine receptor, the D2 receptor, is involved because most neuroleptics act principally on this receptor ("Schizophrenia

Update—Part I," 1995). However, the issue is clouded because some newer antipsychotic drugs, such as clozapine, have little effect on D2 receptors but have a stronger effect on another type of dopamine receptor called the D4 receptor.

Another source of evidence supporting the role of dopamine in schizophrenia is based on the actions of amphetamines, a class of stimulant drugs. These drugs increase the concentration of dopamine in the synaptic cleft by blocking its reuptake by presynaptic neurons. When given in large doses to normal people, these drugs can lead to abnormal behavior states that mimic paranoid schizophrenia.

Overall, evidence points to irregularities in schizophrenia patients in the neural pathways in the brain that utilize dopamine (Meador-Woodruff et al., 1997). The specific nature of this abnormality remains unclear. We can't yet say whether the abnormality involves overreactivity of particular dopamine pathways or more complex interactions among dopamine systems. One possibility is that overreactivity of dopamine receptors may be involved in producing more flagrant behavior patterns (positive symptoms) but not the negative symptoms or deficits associated with schizophrenia. Decreased, rather than increased, dopamine reactivity may be connected with some of the negative symptoms of schizophrenia (Bodkin et al., 1996; Earnst & Kring, 1997; Okubo et al., 1997). We should also note that other neurotransmitters, such as norepinephrine, serotonin, and GABA, also appear to be involved in schizophrenia (Busatto et al., 1997; Kapur & Remington, 1996; "Schizophrenia Update—Part I," 1995).

Viral Infections   Could schizophrenia be caused by a slow-acting virus that attacks the developing brain of a fetus or newborn child? Prenatal rubella (German measles), a viral infection, is a cause of later mental retardation. Could another virus give rise to schizophrenia?

Viral infections are more prevalent in the winter months. The viral theory could account for findings of an excess number of people with schizophrenia being born in the winter (Pallast et al., 1994). However, we have yet to find an identified viral agent we can link to schizophrenia. Thus, we must consider the viral theory of schizophrenia to be intriguing but inconclusive. Even if a viral basis for schizophrenia were discovered, it would probably account for but a small fraction of cases (Meltzer, 1987).

Brain Abnormalities   If schizophrenia is a brain disease, as it is widely believed to be, what is the nature of the disease process? Researchers are using modern brain-imaging techniques, including PET scans, EEGs, CT scans, and MRIs, to probe the inner workings of the brains of people with schizophrenia to find out. Evidence from these studies shows various abnormalities in the brains of people with schizophrenia (Bertolino et al., 1996; Gur et al., 1998; Ismail et al., 1998; Lim et al., 1998; Marsh et al., 1997; Rajkowska, Selemon, & Goldman-Rakic, 1998; Zipursky et al., 1998).

The most prominent findings involve enlargements of brain ventricles (the hollow spaces in the brain) (Dwork, 1997; Lauriello et al., 1997; Nopoulos, Flaum, & Andreasen, 1997). Ventricular enlargement is a sign of structural deterioration of brain tissue (cell loss). It is found in about 3 of 4 schizophrenia patients (Coursey, Alford, & Safarjan, 1997). Still, not all people with schizophrenia show evidence of enlarged ventricles or other signs of structural damage to brain tissue. This leads researchers to suspect that there may be several forms of schizophrenia that have different causal processes. One form may involve a degenerative loss of brain tissue (Knoll et al., 1998).

Researchers suspect that structural damage to the brains of schizophrenia patients may occur long before the initial onset of the disorder, most probably prenatally or very early in life (Akbarian et al., 1996; Gur et al., 1998). One theory points to prenatal complications occurring during the period of 13 to 15 weeks of fetal development when certain brain structures are forming (Davis & Bracha, 1996). Early-occurring brain damage, together with a genetic vulnerability, may predispose some individuals to schizophrenia. The source of brain damage remains an open question. Among the suspected causes are viral infections, birth complications such as anoxia (oxygen deprivation), brain traumas suffered early in life or during prenatal development, environmental influences in childhood, or genetic defects leading to abnormal brain development.

Another line of research points to possible neurotransmitter disturbances. By tracking blood flow in the brain and using brain imaging techniques, such as the PET scan, EEG, and MRI, researchers find consistent evidence of reduced brain activity in the frontal lobes, specifically in an area called the *prefrontal cortex* (Andreasen et al., 1997; Goldman-Rakic & Selemon, 1997). The prefrontal cortex, the part of the frontal lobes in the cerebral cortex lying in front of the motor cortex, is involved in performing various cognitive and emotional functions, the kinds of functions often impaired in people with schizophrenia. Among other functions, the prefrontal cortex serves as a kind of mental clipboard for holding information needed to guide organized behavior (Casanova, 1997). Imbalances in neurotransmitters in these neural pathways may be involved in explaining disturbed brain circuitry (Goldman-Rakic & Selemon, 1997). Abnormalities in the complex circuitry of the frontal lobes may explain why people with schizophrenia have difficulty organizing their thoughts and behavior and performing higher level cognitive tasks, such as formulating concepts, prioritizing information, and formulating goals and plans (Andreasen et al., 1994; Glantz & Lewis, 1997). The prefrontal cortex is also involved in regulating attention, so findings of reduced activity coincide with neuropsychological evidence of deficits in attention among people with schizophrenia. These are intriguing findings that may provide clues as to the biological bases of schizophrenia. (See Figures 12.2, 12.3, and 12.4.)

Other evidence points to defects in brain circuitry involving brain regions lying below the cortex, especially the **hippocampus** and **amygdala**, two structures in the **limbic**

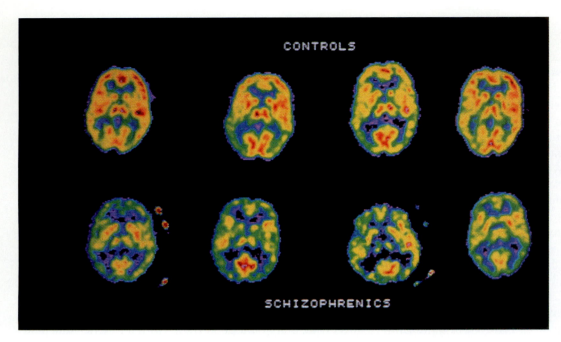

CONTROLS

SCHIZOPHRENICS

FIGURE 12.2 *PET scans of people with schizophrenia versus normals.*
Positron emission tomography (PET scan) evidence of the metabolic processes of the brain show relatively less metabolic activity (indicated by less yellow and red) in the frontal lobes of the brains of people with schizophrenia. PET scans of the brains of four normal people are shown in the top row, and PET scans of the brains of four people with schizophrenia are shown below.

system (Bogerts, 1997; Coursey, Alford, & Safarjan, 1997; Haber & Fudge, 1997). The limbic system plays key roles in regulating emotions and higher mental functions, including memory. These structures send projections to the prefrontal cortex, which interprets information received from lower brain centers (DeAngelis, 1997). Imbalances in neurotransmitter function may also be involved in disrupting these brain processes.

TYING IT TOGETHER: THE DIATHESIS-STRESS MODEL

In 1962, psychologist Paul Meehl proposed an integrative model that led to the development of the diathesis-stress model. Meehl suggested that certain people possess a genetic predisposition to schizophrenia that is expressed

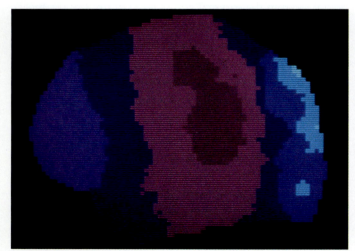
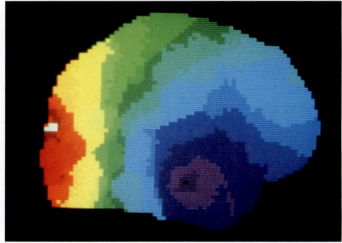

FIGURE 12.3 *CET maps of the brains of a person with schizophrenia as compared to normal individuals.*
In computer electroencephalographic topography (CET), a computer generates a map of the electrical activity of the brain from input from electrodes placed at multiple sites on the scalp. The regions of the brain are color coded so that areas of relatively greater activity are indicated by warm colors (yellows and oranges) and areas of relative inactivity are indicated by cool colors (blues and purples). Here we see evidence of lower levels of alpha-wave activity in the occipital lobe of the brain of a person with schizophrenia (left) as compared to a composite of 16 normal subjects (right). Alpha waves usually occur during times of relaxation or rest.

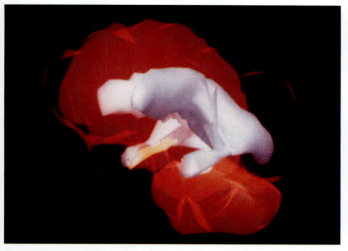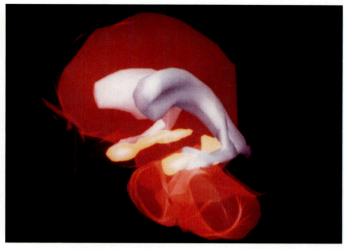

FIGURE 12.4 *Structural changes in the brain of a person with schizophrenia (left) as compared with that of a normal subject.*
The magnetic resonance imaging (MRI) of the brain of a person with schizophrenia (left) shows a relatively shrunken hippocampus (yellow) and relatively enlarged, fluid-filled ventricles (gray) when compared to the structures of the normal subject (right). The MRI was conducted by schizophrenia researcher Nancy C. Andreasen.

Source: Gershon, E. S., & Rieder, R. O. (1992). Major disorders of mind and brain. *Scientific American, 267*(No. 3), p. 128.

behaviorally only if they are reared in stressful environments (Meehl, 1962, 1972).

More recently, Zubin and Spring (1977) formulated the diathesis-stress model, which views schizophrenia in terms of the interaction of a *diathesis,* in the form of a genetic predisposition to develop the disorder, with a level of environmental *stress* that exceeds the individual's stress threshold or coping resources. Environmental stressors may include family conflict, child abuse (Read, 1997), emotional deprivation, loss of supportive figures, or environmental insults such as early brain trauma. On the other hand, if environmental stress remains below the person's stress threshold, schizophrenia may never develop in persons at genetic risk (see Figure 12.5).

But what is the biological basis for the diathesis? Despite the widely held belief that schizophrenia is a brain disease (Buchanan & Carpenter, 1997), researchers are still asking

the question, "Where is the pathology?" (J. R. Stevens, 1997). No one has yet been able to find any specific brain abnormality present in all individuals who receive a schizophrenia diagnosis (Stevens, 1997; Powchik et al., 1998).

Perhaps it shouldn't surprise us that a "one-size fits all" model doesn't apply. Schizophrenia is a complex disorder characterized by different subtypes and symptom complexes. There may be different causal processes in the brain explaining different forms of schizophrenia or even different *schizophrenias* (Braff & Swedlow, 1997; Buchanan & Carpenter, 1997; Knoll et al., 1998).

We noted two possible causal processes, one involving structural damage to brain tissue, the other involving disturbed neurotransmitter functioning that disrupts complex brain circuits involved in thought, perception, emotions, and attention. The welter of confusing thoughts and perceptions, social withdrawal, and bizarre behavior that characterize

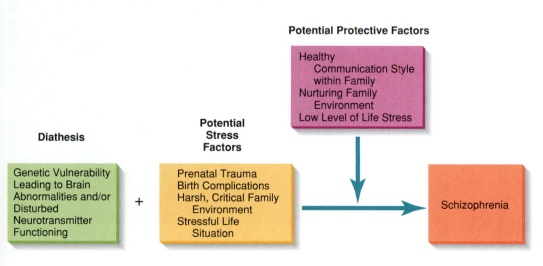

FIGURE 12.5 *Diathesis-stress model of schizophrenia.*

schizophrenia may be the result of disturbed neurotransmitter functioning in brain circuits involving the prefrontal cortex and its connections to lower brain regions (Andreasen et al., 1997; Goldman-Rakic & Selemon, 1997; Weinberger, 1997). These neural networks are involved in processing information efficiently and turning it into meaningful thoughts and behavior. A defect in this circuitry may be involved in explaining the more flagrant, positive features of schizophrenia such as hallucinations, delusions, and thought disorder.

Another potential causal process involves structural damage to the brain, as evidenced by the presence of enlarged ventricles. Ventricular enlargement may play a greater role in explaining negative symptomatology and chronic cognitive impairment than the more flagrant features of the disorder (Earnst & Kring, 1997; Gur et al., 1994).

Research Evidence Supporting the Diathesis-Stress Model

There are several lines of evidence supporting the diathesis-stress model. One line of support is the fact that schizophrenia tends to develop in late adolescence or early adulthood, around the time that young people typically face the increased stress associated with developmental challenges relating to establishing independence and finding a role in life. Other evidence shows that psychosocial stress, such as carping criticisms from family members, worsens symptoms in people with schizophrenia, increasing risks of relapse (S. King & Dixon, 1996). However, the question of whether stress directly triggers the initial onset of schizophrenia in genetically vulnerable individuals still remains open to debate (E. F. Walker & Diforio, 1997).

Other sources of stress that may contribute to the development of schizophrenia in genetically vulnerable individuals involve sociocultural factors associated with poverty, such as overcrowding, poor diet and sanitation, impoverished housing, and inadequate health care (Kety, 1980). Supportive evidence for a link between social class and schizophrenia comes from a classic study by Hollingshead and Redlich (1958) in New Haven, Connecticut. They found that the rate of schizophrenia was twice as high among the lowest socioeconomic class than among the second lowest. More recent evidence from the ECA (Keith, Regier, & Rae, 1991) and NCS (Kendler et al., 1996b) studies showed a higher prevalence of schizophrenia and schizophrenia-type disorders among lower income people. In the ECA study, schizophrenia was five times more prevalent at the lowest rung of the socioeconomic ladder than it was at the highest (Keith, Regier, & Rae, 1991). Schizophrenia and schizophreniform disorder are also more common among the unemployed, a group usually at the lowest rungs of the socioeconomic ladder (Kendler et al., 1996b).

Whereas low socioeconomic status may be a contributor or antecedent to schizophrenia, an alternative possibility is that it represents a *consequence* of the disorder. People with schizophrenia may drift downward in social status because they lack the social skills and cognitive abilities to function at higher levels. Disproportionate numbers of individuals with schizophrenia may thus wind up in an impoverished status.

Evidence for the hypothesis that people who suffer from schizophrenia drift downward in socieconomic status is mixed. Some evidence is supportive (R. J. Turner & Wagonfield, 1967); other evidence is not (Dunham, 1965; Hollingshead & Redlich, 1958). Perhaps both views are partly correct. Although many people with schizophrenia drift downward occupationally in comparison to the occupations held by their fathers, many are also reared in families from the lower socioeconomic classes. The stresses of poverty may thus play a role in the development of schizophrenia. Family sources of stress may also play a role in the development of schizophrenia, as we will see in our discussion of family theories.

Perhaps the strongest support for the diathesis-stress model comes from longitudinal studies of HR children who are at increased genetic risk of developing the disorder by virtue of having one or more parents with schizophrenia. **Longitudinal studies** of HR children (offspring of parents with schizophrenia) support the central tenet of the diathesis-stress model that heredity interacts with environmental influences in determining vulnerability to schizophrenia. Longitudinal studies track individuals over extended periods of time. Ideally they begin before the emergence of the disorder or behavior pattern in question and follow its course. In this way, investigators may identify early characteristics that predict the later development of a particular disorder, such as schizophrenia. These studies require a commitment of many years and substantial cost. Because

Protective factors in high-risk children. A supportive and nurturing environment may reduce the likelihood of developing schizophrenia among high-risk children.

schizophrenia occurs only in 1% to 2% of the general population, researchers have focused on HR children because they are more likely to develop the disorder. Children who have one parent with schizophrenia have about a 10% to 25% chance of developing schizophrenia, and those with two parents have about a 45% risk (Erlenmeyer-Kimling et al., 1997; Gottesman, 1991; "Schizophrenia Update—Part I," 1995).

TRUTH *or* FICTION REVISITED

12.7 *False.* Children of parents who both have schizophrenia have slightly less than a 50% chance (45%) of developing the disorder themselves.

Finnish researchers followed 112 HR children ("index cases") who were adopted at birth (Tienari et al., 1987, 1990). These index cases were compared with a reference group of 135 cases—matched adopted children of nonschizophrenic biological parents. The evidence to date shows a much higher rate of schizophrenia in the index cases than among the control cases, 5% versus 1%, respectively (Tienari, 1991, 1992). There was also a greater prevalence of other psychotic disorders in the index cases (4%) than among the controls (0%).

Consistent with the diathesis-stress model, environmental factors appear to have played a role in the Finnish study. All of the index cases who developed schizophrenia or other psychotic disorders were reared by disturbed adoptive families (Tienari et al., 1987, 1990). Moreover, index children reared by disturbed adoptive families were more likely to have developed other serious psychological problems, such as borderline personality, than those reared by more functional families. Some of the disturbed families were rigid and tended to cope with family conflict by denying it. Others were chaotic; they showed low levels of trust and high levels of anxiety. The evidence from the Finnish study indicates that a combination of genetic factors and a disruptive family environment increases the risk of schizophrenia and other psychotic disorders. A serious drawback to the Finnish study, however, is that it is retrospective, not prospective. The disturbed family relationships could thus represent the reaction of the families to the emergence of behavioral problems in their troubled offspring rather than a contributing factor in its own right (Kendler & Diehl, 1993).

Researchers have also compared HR children and other children to search for factors, or markers, that may predispose HR children to schizophrenia (e.g., Szymanski et al., 1991). If we understand these early indicators, we may be able to understand the processes that lead to schizophrenia. We may also be able to identify children at greatest risk and devise intervention programs that may possibly prevent the development of schizophrenia.

The best known longitudinal study of HR children was undertaken by Sarnoff Mednick and his colleagues in Denmark (Mednick & Schulsinger, 1965). In 1962, the Mednick group identified 207 HR children (children whose mothers had schizophrenia) and 104 reference subjects who were matched for factors such as gender, social class, age, and education but whose mothers did not have schizophrenia (Mednick, Parnas, & Schulsinger, 1987). The children from both groups ranged in age from 10 to 20 years, with a mean of 15 years. None showed signs of disturbance when first interviewed.

Five years later, at an average age of 20, the children were reexamined. By then 20 of the HR children were found to have demonstrated abnormal behavior, although not necessarily a schizophrenic episode (Mednick & Schulsinger, 1968). The children who showed abnormal behavior, referred to as the HR "sick" group, were then compared with a matched group of 20 HR children from the original sample who remained well functioning (an HR "well" group) and a matched group of 20 low-risk (LR) subjects. It turned out that the mothers of the HR "well" offspring had experienced easier pregnancies and deliveries than those of the HR "sick" group or the LR group. Seventy percent of the mothers of the HR "sick" children had serious complications during pregnancy or delivery. Perhaps, consistent with the diathesis-stress model, complications during pregnancy or childbirth or shortly after birth cause brain damage (a stress factor) that in combination with a genetic vulnerability leads to severe mental disorders in later life (Berquier & Ashton, 1991). A more recent study in Finland provided a supportive link in showing an association between fetal and postnatal abnormalities and the development of schizophrenia in adulthood (P. B. Jones et al., 1998). The low rate of complications during pregnancy and birth in the HR "well" group in the Danish study suggests that normal pregnancies and births may actually help protect HR children from developing abnormal behavior patterns (Mednick et al., 1987).

Evaluation of these same HR subjects in the late 1980s, when they averaged 42 years of age and had passed through the period of greatest risk for development of schizophrenia, showed a significantly higher percentage of schizophrenia in the HR group than the LR comparison group, 16% versus 2%, respectively (Parnas et al., 1993). Additionally, the HR group had a significantly greater frequency of schizophrenic-spectrum disorders, such as schizotypal and paranoid personality disorders. In total, 43% of the children whose mothers had schizophrenia were diagnosed with a schizophrenia-spectrum disorder at some point in their lifetimes. These results, like those of the Finnish study, show a strong familial association for schizophrenia between mothers and their children. An Israeli study paralleled the Danish and Finnish studies in finding a significantly greater risk of schizophrenia in a sample of HR children (8% with diagnosed schizophrenia) as compared to LR controls (0%) by the age of 30 (Ingraham et al., 1995).

Protective and Vulnerability Factors in HR Children

Evidence from longitudinal studies of HR children indicates that environmental factors, including the quality of parenting and possible prenatal or perinatal complications, interact with genetic factors in the causal pathway that leads to schizophrenia. Certain environmental factors, such as good parenting, may actually have a protective role in preventing the development of the disorder in people at increased genetic risk.

The HR children who developed schizophrenia in the Mednick study had poorer relationships with their parents than HR children who eventually became schizotypal or showed no pattern of abnormal behavior (Mednick et al., 1987). Other HR studies show similar patterns. A study at Emory University, for instance, indicates that poor rearing by parents with schizophrenia may be associated with early developmental problems in HR children (Goodman, 1987).

Investigators are also looking for early indicators of schizophrenia in HR children. In one U.S. study, researchers found striking evidence of deficiencies in attention and social competence in HR children (Weintraub, 1987). The classmates of HR children tended to see them as being different and described them as withdrawn, abrasive, and socially inept. Other researchers found evidence of greater than expected frequencies of problems in social, intellectual, and emotional development in HR children through the age of 5 (Goodman, 1987; Sameroff, Seifer, Zax, & Barocas, 1987). It is too early to tell whether the early developmental problems identified by these researchers in HR children predict the development of schizophrenia. Recently re-ported evidence from the Israeli HR study shows that poor attentional skills in the preteen to early teenage years predicted which high-risk children would go on to develop a schizophrenic-spectrum disorder in early adulthood (A. F. Mirsky, Ingraham, & Kugelmass, 1995; Mirsky et al., 1995).

Although the reasons are unclear, some HR children are apparently invulnerable to developing schizophrenia, even when they are reared in stressful environments (Weintraub, 1987). Perhaps invulnerable children have some yet unidentified physiological factor that protects them from developing schizophrenia (Marcus et al., 1987). Perhaps environmental factors such as availability of a supportive family environment protect them.

There is some evidence that healthful styles of parental communication, including parental ability to express positive feelings, contributes to the school adjustment of HR children (Wynne, Cole, & Perkins, 1987). The Emory University study found that the most socially competent HR children had the most positive child rearing environments—even within poor single-parent families. These environments often included a secondary caregiver who helped meet their needs, such as a boyfriend of the mother or a relative (Goodman, 1987).

Although these longitudinal studies have not yet run their course, a number of factors have emerged that may place HR children at greater or lesser risk for developing schizophrenia (see Table 12.2). A limitation of studying HR

TABLE 12.2

Possible Risk Factors Associated with Vulnerability to Schizophrenia in the Biological Children of People with Schizophrenia ("HR" children)

High-Risk (Vulnerability) Factors	Low-Risk (Protective) Factors
Maternal anxiety during pregnancy[a]	Lesser severity of maternal illness[b]
Psychotic status of mother in the period of 6 months to 2 years following the birth[a]	Older age of mothers[b]
Severity of maternal mental illness[c]	Higher education and IQ of mother[b]
Negative attitudes of mother toward pregnancy[a]	Prior work experience of mother[b]
Low social class[c]	Presence of secondary caregiver (e.g., spouse, boyfriend, or other relative)[b]
Family conflict, marital discord, and lack of parenting skills[d]	Mother's healthy communication with the child, father's expression of positive emotions in a free play situation, and balance between child-initiated and parent-initiated activities in free play situation[e]
Chronic mental illness in the mentally disturbed parent[e]	
Deviant (confused) communication style and expression of hostile feelings toward the child[e]	Absence of severe environmental trauma in the form of pregnancy and birth complications[f]
Poor attentional skills in the preteen to early teenage years[f]	Supportive and nurturing rearing environment[g]
Complications during pregnancy and delivery[g]	

[a]Swedish high-risk study (McNeil & Kaiij, 1978).
[b]Emory University Project on Children of Disturbed Parents (Goodman, 1987).
[c]Rochester Longitudinal Study (Sameroff et al., 1987).
[d]Stony-Brook High-Risk Project (Weintraub, 1987).
[e]University of Rochester Child and Family Study (Wynne et al., 1987).
[f]Israeli high-risk study (Mirsky, Ingraham, & Kugelmass, 1995; Mirsky et al., 1995).
[g]Danish high-risk study (Mednick et al., 1987).

children as a model of the development of schizophrenia is that it is not clear whether the "markers" that seem to increase vulnerability among children whose parents had schizophrenia will generalize to the majority of people with schizophrenia whose parents did not have the disorder (Goldstein, 1987a).

Family Theories

Disturbed family relationships have long been regarded as playing a role in the development and course of schizophrenia (Miklowitz, 1994).

The Schizophrenogenic Mother   Early family theories of schizophrenia focused on the role of a "pathogenic" family member, such as the **schizophrenogenic mother** (Fromm-Reichmann, 1948, 1950). In what some feminists view as historic psychiatric sexism, the schizophrenogenic mother was described as cold, aloof, overprotective, and domineering. She was characterized as stripping her children of self-esteem, stifling their independence, and forcing them into dependency on her. Children reared by such mothers were believed to be at special risk for developing schizophrenia if their fathers were passive and failed to counteract the pathogenic influences of the mother. Despite extensive research, however, mothers of people who develop schizophrenia do not fit the stereotypical picture of the schizophrenogenic mother (Hirsch & Leff, 1975).

The Double-Bind Hypothesis   In the 1950s, family theorists began to focus on the role of disturbed communications in the family. One of the more prominent theories, put forth by Bateson, Jackson, Haley, and Weakland (1956), was that **double-bind communications** contributed to the development of schizophrenia. A double-bind communication transmits two mutually incompatible messages. In a double-bind communication with a child, a mother might freeze up when the child approaches her and then scold the child for keeping a distance. Whatever the child does, she or he is wrong. With repeated exposure to such double binds, the child's thinking may become disorganized and chaotic. The double-binding mother prevents discussion of her inconsistencies because she cannot admit to herself that she is unable to tolerate closeness. Note this vignette:

> *A young man who had fairly well recovered from an acute schizophrenic episode was visited in the hospital by his mother. He was glad to see her and impulsively put his arm around her shoulders whereupon she stiffened. He withdrew his arm and she asked, "Don't you love me anymore?" He then blushed and she said, "Dear, you must not be so easily embarrassed and afraid of your feelings." The patient was able to stay with her only a few minutes more and following her departure he assaulted an aide.*
>
> BATESON ET AL., 1956, P. 251

Perhaps double-bind communications serve as a source of family stress that increases the risk of schizophrenia in genetically vulnerable individuals. In more recent years, investigators have broadened the investigation of family factors in schizophrenia by viewing the family in terms of a system of relationships among the members, rather than singling out mother-child or father-child interactions. Research has begun to identify stressful factors in the family that may interact with a genetic vulnerability in leading to the development of schizophrenia. Two principal sources of family stress that have been studied are patterns of deviant communications and negative emotional expression in the family.

Communication Deviance   Communication deviance describes a pattern characterized by unclear, vague, disruptive, or fragmented parental communication and by parental inability to focus in on what the child is saying (Miklowitz, 1994). Parents who are high in communication deviance tend to attack their children personally rather than offer constructive criticism and may subject them to double-bind communications. They also tend to interrupt the child with intrusive, negative comments. They are prone to telling the child what she or he "really" thinks rather than allowing the child to formulate her or his own thoughts and feelings. Parents of people with schizophrenia show higher levels of communication deviance than parents of people without schizophrenia (Miklowitz, 1994; Miklowitz et al., 1991). Communication deviance may be one of the stress-related factors that increases the risk of development of schizophrenia in vulnerable individuals (M. J. Goldstein, 1987). Then too, the causal pathway may work in the opposite direction. Perhaps communication deviance is a parental reaction to the behavior of disturbed children. Parents may learn to use odd language as a way of coping with children who continually interrupt and confront them (Miklowitz et al., 1991). Or perhaps parents and children share genetic traits that become expressed as disturbed communications and increased vulnerability toward schizophrenia, without there being a causal link between the two.

Expressed Emotion   Another measure of disturbed family communications is called expressed emotion (EE). EE involves the tendency of family members to be hostile, critical, and unsupportive of their schizophrenic family members. People with schizophrenia whose families are high in EE tend to show poorer adjustment and have higher rates of relapse following release from the hospital (Butzlaff & Hooley, 1998; King & Dixon, 1995). Expressed emotion in relatives is also associated with a greater risk of relapse from major depression and alcoholism (Fichter et al., 1997; Hinrichsen & Pollak, 1997; Hooley & Licht, 1997).

TRUTH *or* FICTION REVISITED

12.8 *True.*   Schizophrenia patients in families characterized by hostile, critical, and unsupportive family members are at greater risk of relapse than those from more supportive families.

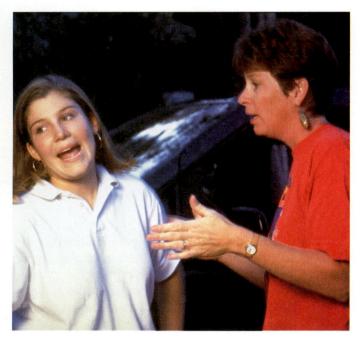

Expressed emotion and schizophrenia. Expressed emotion is a family stress factor that can increase the risk of relapse in people with schizophrenia and other disorders.

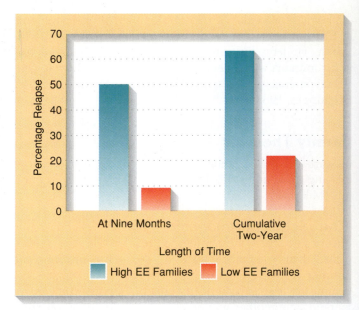

FIGURE 12.6 *Relapse rates of people with schizophrenia in high and low EE families.*
People with schizophrenia whose families are high in expressed emotion (EE) are at greater risk of relapse than those whose families are low in EE. Whereas low-EE families may help protect the family member with schizophrenia from environmental stressors, high-EE families may impose additional stress.

Source: Adapted from Leff & Vaughn (1981).

Low EE families may actually serve to protect, or buffer, the individual with schizophrenia from the adverse impact of outside stressors and help prevent recurrent episodes (Strachan, 1986) (see Figure 12.6). Yet family interactions are a two-way street. Family members and patients influence each other and are influenced in turn. Disruptive behaviors by the schizophrenic family member frustrate other members of the family, prompting them to respond in a less supportive and more critical and hostile way. This in turn can exacerbate the schizophrenic individual's disruptive behavior (Bellack & Mueser, 1993; Rosenfarb et al., 1995).

Families of people with schizophrenia tend to have little if any preparation or training for coping with the stressful demands of caring for them (Winefield & Harvey, 1994). Rather than focusing so much on the negative influence of high EE family members, we should learn to understand better the negative day-to-day interactions between people with schizophrenia and their family members that lead to high levels of expressed emotion. Recent evidence shows that families can be helped to reduce the level of expressed emotion (Penn & Mueser, 1996).

Research on expressed emotion and family stress factors helps focus attention on the need for family intervention programs (reviewed later in this chapter) that help prepare families for the burdens of caregiving and assist them in learning more adaptive ways of relating to one another. This, in turn, may reduce the stress imposed on the family member with schizophrenia and improve family harmony.

Family Factors in Schizophrenia: Causes or Sources of Stress There is no evidence to support the belief that family factors, such as negative family interac-

tions, can lead to schizophrenia in children who do not have a genetic vulnerability. What then is the role of family factors in schizophrenia? Within the diathesis-stress model, disturbed patterns of emotional interaction and communication in the family represent a source of potential stress that may increase the risks of developing schizophrenia among people with a genetic predisposition for the disorder. Perhaps these increased risks could be minimized or eliminated if families are taught to handle stress and to be less critical and more supportive of the members of their families with schizophrenia. Counseling programs that help family members of people with chronic schizophrenia learn to express their feelings without attacking or criticizing the person with schizophrenia may prevent family conflicts that damage the person's adjustment (Spiegel & Wissler, 1986). The family member with schizophrenia may also benefit from efforts to reduce the level of contact with relatives who fail to respond to family interventions.

TREATMENT

There is no cure for schizophrenia. Treatment of the disorder is often multifaceted, incorporating pharmacological, psychological, and rehabilitative approaches. Most people treated for schizophrenia in organized mental-health settings receive some form of antipsychotic medication, which is intended to control the more flagrant behavior patterns, such as hallucinations and delusions, and decrease the risk of recurrent episodes.

Cultural Differences in Expressed Emotion

Relationships between expressed emotion and rates of recurrence of schizophrenia have been drawn largely from research with non-Hispanic White samples in England and the United States (Karno et al., 1987). Because family patterns are often influenced by cultural factors, researchers have begun to explore whether the EE construct has value in predicting recurrence of schizophrenia in other cultures. Some cross-cultural support for the prognostic value of the construct comes from a study of low-income, relatively unacculturated Mexican American family members of people with schizophrenia (Karno et al., 1987). Paralleling findings with the non-Hispanic White British and American families, high levels of EE (that is, critical, hostile, and emotionally overinvolved attitudes and behaviors) among key family members in the Mexican American sample were associated with an increased risk of relapse among people with schizophrenia who lived with their families after hospitalization. Evidence from samples of both Mexican American families and Anglo-American families with high levels of expressed emotion show them to be more likely than low EE families to view the psychotic behavior of a schizophrenic family to lie within the person's control (Weisman et al., 1993, 1998). The anger and criticism of high EE family members may stem from the perception that patients can and should exert greater control over their aberrant behavior.

We also have evidence for cultural variations in expressed emotion. Much lower prevalences of high EE behaviors, as compared with the (non-Hispanic) White British and American families, were found among a sample of Mexican American families and other families from northern India who had family members with schizophrenia (Wig et al., 1987). The (non-Hispanic) White families thus tended to be more openly critical of the members of their families who had schizophrenia than were family members from these other cultural backgrounds. The specific components of EE may also vary across cultures (Martins, de Lemos, & Bebbington, 1992).

Other researchers find that the extended family structure often found in traditional cultures may offer an emotional and financial buffer against the hardships imposed by the behavioral excesses and deficiencies of people with schizophrenia. In Western cultures, these burdens are more likely to be borne by the nuclear family (Lefley, 1990). Such differences remind us of the need to take cultural factors into account when examining relationships between family factors and schizophrenia.

The construct of expressed emotion may also have prognostic significance in predicting the course of other disorders. In a recent study in Egypt, depressed patients who experienced relapses reported higher levels of expressed emotion within their families than did nonrelapsers (Okasha et al., 1994).

Biological Approaches

The advent in the 1950s of antipsychotic drugs—also referred to as major tranquilizers or *neuroleptics*—revolutionized the treatment of schizophrenia and provided the impetus for large-scale releases of mental patients to the community (deinstitutionalization). Antipsychotic medication has helped control the more flagrant behavior patterns of schizophrenia and reduced the need for long-term hospitalization when taken on a maintenance basis (Kane, 1996; Sheitman et al., 1998). Yet for many chronic schizophrenia patients today, entering a hospital is like going through a revolving door. That is, they are repeatedly admitted and discharged within a relatively brief time frame. Many are simply discharged to the streets once they are stabilized on medication and receive little if any follow-up care, which often leads to a pattern of chronic homelessness punctuated by brief stays in the hospital. Only a small proportion of people with schizophrenia who are discharged from long-term care facilities are successfully reintegrated into the community (Bellack & Mueser, 1990).

Commonly used antipsychotic drugs include the phenothiazines *chlorpromazine* (Thorazine), *thioridazine* (Mellaril), *trifluoperazine* (Stelazine), and *fluphenazine* (Prolixin), and *haloperidol* (Haldol), which is a chemically distinct from the phenothiazines but produces similar effects.

Though we can't say with certainty how these drugs work, it appears that they derive their therapeutic effect from blocking dopamine receptors in the brain. This reduces dopamine activity, which seems to quell the more flagrant signs of schizophrenia, such as hallucinations and delusions. The effectiveness of antipsychotic drugs has been repeatedly demonstrated in double-blind, placebo-controlled studies. Yet a substantial minority of people with schizophrenia receive little benefit from traditional neuroleptics, and no clear-cut factors determine who will best respond (Kane & Marder, 1993).

One of the major drawbacks of traditional neuroleptics is that they work better on positive symptoms, such as hallucinations and delusions, than on the more enduring negative symptoms, such as apathy, withdrawal, and poverty of speech. A newer type of antipsychotic drug, clozapine (trade name Clozaril), appears to help alleviate negative as well as positive symptoms of schizophrenia (Sheitman et al., 1998). Clozapine is also more effective in patients who have failed to respond to the more traditional antipsychotics (Rosenheck et al., 1997; Young et al., 1998).

The major risk of long-term treatment with neuroleptic drugs (possibly excluding clozapine) is a potentially disabling side effect called **tardive dyskinesia** (TD). TD is an involuntary movement disorder that can affect any body part (Hansen, Casey, & Hoffman, 1997). It is irreversible in many cases, even when the neuroleptic medication is withdrawn. It occurs most often in patients who are treated with neuroleptics for 6 months or longer and can take different forms, the most common of which is frequent eye blinking. Common signs of TD include involuntary chewing and eye movements, lip smacking and puckering, facial grimacing, and involuntary movements of the limbs and trunk. In some cases, the movement disorder is so severe that patients have difficulties breathing, talking, or eating. Overall, about 1 in 4 people receiving long-term treatment with neuroleptics eventually develop TD (Jeste & Caligiuri, 1993). TD is more common among older people and among women (Hansen, Casey, & Hoffman, 1997). Unfortunately, we lack a safe and effective treatment for TD (M. F. Egan, Apud, & Wyatt, 1997; Sheitman et al., 1998). Although TD tends to gradually improve or stabilize over a period of years, many people with TD remain persistently and severely disabled.

The risk of these potentially disabling side effects requires physicians to weigh the risks and benefits of long-term treatment with these drugs carefully. Investigators have altered drug regimens in the attempt to reduce the risk of TD, such as by stopping medication in stable outpatients and starting it again when early symptoms reappear. However, intermittent medication schedules are associated with a twofold increase in the risk of relapse and have not been shown to lower the risk of TD (Kane, 1996).

A new generation of drugs, called atypical antipsychotic drugs (clozapine, risperidone, and olanzapine), has been introduced that offer the promise of controlling schizophrenic symptoms with fewer neurological side effects than conventional antipsychotics (Luchins et al., 1998; Marzuk & Barchas, 1997; Sheitman et al., 1998; Tollefson et al., 1997; Tran et al., 1997; Zimbroff et al., 1997). They also appear to be more effective in treating negative symptoms of schizophrenia than conventional antipsychotics. One of these atypical antipsychotics, *clozapine*, is the only known drug that carries a minimal risk of TD (Conley & Buchanan, 1997; Kane, 1996). However, other side effects limit its use, especially the risk of agranulocytosis, a potentially lethal disorder in which the body produces inadequate supplies of white blood cells. The disorder affects 1% to 2% of patients who use the drug (Kane & Marder, 1993). There are also promising findings that olanzapine may reduce the risk of TD relative to conventional antipsychotics (Tollefson et al., 1997), but more research is needed to reach a more definitive conclusion about the level of risk associated with either olanzapine or risperidone (Egan, Apud, & Wyatt, 1997).

Antipsychotic drugs help control the more flagrant or bizarre features of schizophrenia but are not a cure. People with chronic schizophrenia typically receive maintenance doses of antipsychotic drugs once their flagrant symptoms abate. Continued medication reduces the rate of relapse (P. L. Gilbert et al., 1995; Schooler et al., 1997) but is no panacea. Many patients, perhaps 15% to 20% per year, will relapse even if they are maintained on continued medication (Kane, 1996). Yet estimates are that 75% of patients with schizophrenia who have been in remission for a year or more will relapse within 12 to 18 months if their medication is withdrawn (Kane, 1996). Still, not all people with schizophrenia require antipsychotic medication to maintain themselves in the community. Unfortunately, no one can yet predict which patients can manage effectively without continued medication.

TRUTH *or* **FICTION** REVISITED

12.9 *False.* Antipsychotic drugs help control the symptoms of schizophrenia but cannot cure the disorder.

Medication alone is insufficient to meet the multifaceted needs of people with schizophrenia. Drug therapy needs to be supplemented with psychoeducational programs to help patients develop better social skills and adjust to demands of community living. A wide array of treatment components are needed within a comprehensive model of care, including such elements as antipsychotic medication, medical care, family therapy, social skills training, crisis intervention, rehabilitation services, and housing and other social services (Marder et al., 1996; Penn & Mueser, 1996). Programs also need to ensure a continuity of care between the hospital and the community.

Sociocultural Factors in Treatment Ethnic or racial differences may come into play in determining medication dosages for effective treatment of schizophrenia and sensitivity to side effects. Asians, for example, tend to require smaller doses of neuroleptics than Caucasians to achieve an optimal response. Asians also tend to experience more side effects from the same dosage.

Ethnicity may also play a role in the family's involvement in the treatment process. Researchers report that in a study of 26 Asian Americans and 26 non-Hispanic White Americans with schizophrenia, family members of the Asian American patients were more frequently involved in the treatment program (K. Lin et al., 1991). For example, the Asian American patients were more likely to be accompanied to their medication evaluation sessions by family members. The authors believe the greater family involvement among Asian Americans represents the relatively stronger sense of family responsibility in Asian cultures. Non-Hispanic White

Americans are more likely to emphasize individualism and self-responsibility. Maintaining connections between the person with schizophrenia and the family and larger community is part of the cultural tradition in many Asian cultures, as well as in other parts of the world, such as in Africa. The seriously mentally ill of China, for instance, retain strong supportive links to their families and workplaces, which helps increase their chances of being reintegrated into community life (Liberman, 1994). In traditional healing centers for the treatment of schizophrenia in Africa, the strong support that patients receive from the family and community members, together with a community-centered lifestyle, are identified as important elements of successful care (Peltzer & Machleidt, 1992).

There is clear value in working with the family in treating schizophrenia in Asian Americans as in other groups. Researchers find that failure to include the family often compromises the value of therapy for Asian Americans and causes many of them to drop out of therapy prematurely (T. Y. Lin et al., 1978). Researchers in a hospital in Great Britain reported that living with family members was among the factors that might explain the lower relapse and rehospitalization rates found among Asian people with schizophrenia as compared to White or Afro-Caribbean people (Birchwood et al., 1992). Family interactions are not necessarily harmonious or conducive of better outcomes, however, as research on expressed emotion makes clear. Neglect or rejection of the person with schizophrenia within the family may play an important role in premature treatment termination and poorer outcomes.

Psychoanalytic Approaches

Freud did not believe traditional psychoanalysis was well suited to the treatment of schizophrenia. The withdrawal into a fantasy world that typifies schizophrenia prevents the individual with schizophrenia from forming a meaningful relationship with the psychoanalyst. The techniques of classical psychoanalysis, Freud wrote, must "be replaced by others; and we do not know yet whether we shall succeed in finding a substitute" (cited in Arieti, 1974, p. 532).

Other psychoanalysts such as Harry Stack Sullivan and Frieda Fromm-Reichmann adapted psychoanalytic techniques specifically for the treatment of schizophrenia. However, research has failed to demonstrate the effectiveness of psychoanalytic or psychodynamic therapy for schizophrenia. In light of negative findings, some critics have argued that further research on the use of psychodynamic therapies for treating schizophrenia is not warranted (e.g., Klerman, 1984). However, promising results are reported for a form of individual therapy called *personal therapy* that is grounded in the diathesis-stress model. Personal therapy helps patients cope more effectively with stress and helps them build social skills, such as learning how to deal with criticism from others. Among patients living with their families, personal therapy was shown to reduce relapse rates and improve social functioning (Hogarty et al., 1997).

Learning-Based Approaches

Although few behavior therapists believe faulty learning causes schizophrenia, learning-based interventions have been shown to be effective in modifying schizophrenic behavior and assisting people with the disorder in developing more adaptive behaviors that can help them adjust more effectively to living in the community. Therapy methods include the following techniques: (1) selective reinforcement of behavior (such as providing staff attention for appropriate behavior and extinguishing bizarre verbalizations through withdrawal of staff attention); (2) the token economy, in which individuals are rewarded for appropriate behavior with tokens, such as plastic chips, that can be exchanged for tangible reinforcers such as desirable goods or privileges; and (3) social skills training, in which clients are taught conversation skills and other appropriate social behaviors through coaching, modeling, behavior rehearsal, and feedback.

Social-Learning Programs Promising results have emerged from studies applying intensive learning-based approaches in hospital settings. A classic study by Paul and Lentz (1977) showed that a psychosocial treatment program improved adaptive behavior in the hospital, decreased need for medication, and lengthened community tenure following release in relation to a traditional, custodial-type treatment condition and a *milieu* approach that emphasized patient participation in decision making (see Figure 12.7). The psychosocial program was based on a token-economy system in which patients could earn tokens for engaging in adaptive behaviors, such as attending meetings, maintaining proper grooming, and using appropriate verbal communications. Tokens could be exchanged later for rewards such as food, privacy time, passes, and other privileges. Signs were posted that listed the numbers of tokens available for performing specific behaviors and the numbers of tokens needed to earn particular rewards.

Overall, token economies have proven to be more effective than intensive milieu treatment and traditional custodial treatment in improving social functioning and reducing psychotic behavior (Glynn & Mueser, 1992; Mueser & Liberman, 1995). However, the many prerequisites may limit the applicability of this approach. Such programs require strong administrative support, skilled treatment leaders, extensive staff training, and continuous quality control (Glynn & Mueser, 1986).

Recently, investigators have reported promising results in using cognitive-behavioral approaches in reducing or even eliminating hallucinations or delusions in patients with schizophrenia (S. Bouchard et al., 1996). More research is needed to demonstrate the clinical utility of using CBT to treat psychotic symptoms in general clinical practice.

Social Skills Training Social skills training (SST) involves programs that help individuals acquire a range of social and vocational skills. People with schizophrenia are often deficient in basic social skills involving assertiveness, interviewing skills, and general conversational skills—skills

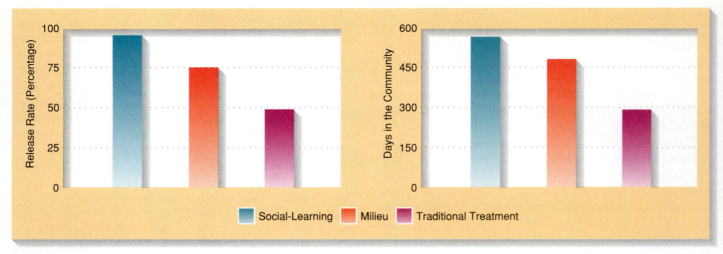

FIGURE 12.7 *Some measures of outcome from the Paul and Lentz study.*
This figure shows the release rates and community tenure (days in the community) of people with schizophrenia in the three conditions studied by Paul and Lentz: (1) social-learning-based treatment, (2) milieu
treatment, and (3) traditional hospital treatment. Nearly all of the subjects in the social-learning program
(97.5%) were able to be discharged and to remain in the community for a minimum of 90 days, as compared
to 71% of the milieu-therapy participants and 45% of the control (standard treatment) participants. Subjects
in the social-learning program also remained in the community longer than subjects who received the other
conditions.

Source: Glynn & Mueser (1986).

that may be needed to adjust successfully to community living. Controlled studies have shown that SST can improve a
wide range of social skills, increase social adjustment, reduce psychiatric symptoms, and improve community functioning in persons with schizophrenia (Hunter, Bedell, &
Corrigan, 1997; Marder et al., 1996; Penn, 1998; Smith,
Bellack, & Liberman, 1996). Social skills training has also
been shown to reduce relapse rates during the first year following treatment (Bellack & Mueser, 1993). Yet it remains
to be seen whether social skills training can produce a substantial payoff in helping patients adapt to community living
(Dilk & Bond, 1996; Penn, 1998; Penn & Mueser, 1996).

Although different approaches to skills training have
been developed, the basic model uses role-playing exercises
within a group format. Participants practice skills such as
starting or maintaining conversations with new acquaintances and receive feedback and reinforcement from the
therapist and other group members. The first step might
be a dry run in which the participant role-plays the targeted
behavior, such as asking strangers for bus directions. The
therapist and other group members then praise the effort
and provide constructive feedback. Role playing is aug-
mented by techniques such as modeling (observation of the
therapist or other group members enacting the desired behavior), direct instruction (specific directions for enacting
the desired behavior), shaping (reinforcement for successive
approximations to the target behavior), and coaching (therapist use of verbal or nonverbal prompts to elicit a particular
desired behavior in the role play). Participants are given
homework assignments to practice the behaviors in the settings in which they live, such as on the hospital ward or in

the community. The aim is to enhance generalization or
transfer of training to other settings. Training sessions may
also be run in stores, restaurants, schools, and other *in vivo*
settings.

Similar skills training techniques have been used to
help people with schizophrenia develop better work skills.
Your first author was involved in a study in a sheltered
workshop setting which showed that people with chronic
schizophrenia achieved significant increases in their work
productivity following participation in a work skills training
program containing the following elements: direct instruction in specific job tasks, step-by-step modeling of task
performance, and rehearsal of tasks with corrective and positive feedback from the trainer and co-workers (Sauter &
Nevid, 1991).

Psychosocial Rehabilitation

People with schizophrenia typically have difficulties functioning in social and occupational roles. These problems limit
their ability to adjust to community life even in the absence
of overt psychotic behavior. Many older long-hospitalized
individuals who have been resettled in the community are
particularly ill-prepared to handle the tasks of daily living,
such as cooking, shopping, or traveling around town. Many
younger individuals with schizophrenia have markedly deficient social skills, even though they have spent only short
periods of time in mental hospitals (W. A. Anthony & Liberman, 1986).

A number of self-help clubs (commonly called clubhouses) and more structured psychosocial rehabilitation

centers have sprung up to help people with schizophrenia find a place in society. Many centers were launched by non-professionals or by people with schizophrenia themselves, largely because mental-health agencies often failed to provide comparable services (Anthony & Liberman, 1986). The clubhouse movement began in 1948 with the founding of Fountain House by a group of formerly hospitalized people with schizophrenia (Foderaro, 1994). There are now more than 200 clubhouses modeled after Fountain House across the country, and some 50 more in other countries including Sweden, Japan, and Australia. Although no one actually lives in the clubhouse, it serves as a kind of self-contained community that provides members with social support and help in finding educational opportunities and paid employment. Multiservice rehabilitation centers typically offer housing as well as job and educational opportunities. These centers often make use of skills training approaches to help clients learn how to handle money, resolve disputes with family members, develop friendships, take buses, cook their own meals, shop, and so on.

The rehabilitation model teaches that people with emotional or physical disabilities can achieve their potentials if they are given the support and structure they need and if the expectations and demands placed on them are consistent with their capabilities. Both the client and the family should be helped to adjust their expectations to attainable levels (Anthony & Liberman, 1986).

Family Intervention Programs

Family conflicts and negative family interactions can heap stress on family members with schizophrenia, increasing the risk of recurrent episodes (Marsh & Johnson, 1997). Researchers and clinicians have worked with families of people with schizophrenia to help them cope with the burdens of care and assist them in developing more cooperative, less confrontative ways of interrelating. The specific components involved in family interventions vary among programs, but they tend to share certain common features, such as a focus on the practical aspects of everyday living, educating family members about schizophrenia, teaching them how to relate in a less hostile way to family members with schizophrenia, improving communication in the family, and fostering effective problem-solving and coping skills for handling family problems and disputes.

Structured family-intervention programs can reduce rates of relapse among people with schizophrenia (Baucom et al., 1998; Marsh & Johnson, 1997; Penn & Mueser, 1996). However, the benefits appear to be modest, and questions remain about whether recurrences are prevented or merely delayed. We should also note that not all people with schizophrenia live with their families. Perhaps similar psychoeducational programs can be applied to nonfamily environments in which people with schizophrenia live, such as foster-care homes or board-and-care homes (Strachan, 1986).

In sum, no single treatment approach meets all the needs of people with schizophrenia. The conceptualization of schizophrenia as a lifelong disability underscores the need for long-term treatment interventions involving antipsychotic medication, family interventions, psychological interventions, vocational training, and social system support such as provision of decent housing. These interventions should be coordinated and integrated within a comprehensive model of treatment to be most effective in helping the individual achieve maximal social adjustment (Coursey, Alford, & Safarjan, 1997; Liberman, Kopelowicz, & Young, 1994). Treatment services are also more likely to improve client functioning in certain areas, such as improving work or independent living, when they are specifically targeted toward those areas (Brekke et al., 1997). This model may consist of drug therapy, hospitalization as needed, hospital-based social-learning programs, family intervention programs, skills training programs, social self-help clubs, and rehabilitation programs.

DELUSIONAL DISORDER

Many of us, perhaps even most of us, feel suspicious of other people's motives at times. We may feel others have it in for us or believe others are talking about us behind our backs. For most of us, however, paranoid thinking does not take the form of outright delusions. The diagnosis of **delusional disorder** applies to people who hold persistent, clearly delusional beliefs, often involving paranoid themes. Delusional disorder is an uncommon but not rare disorder that is believed to affect about 3 people in 1,000 (APA, 1994).

In delusional disorders, the delusional beliefs concern events that may possibly occur, such as the infidelity of a spouse, persecution by others, or attracting the love of a famous person. The apparent plausibility of these beliefs may lead others to take them seriously and check them out before concluding they are unfounded. Apart from the delusion, the individual's behavior does not show evidence of obviously bizarre or odd behavior, as we see in the following case:

Mr. Polsen, a married 42-year-old postal worker, was brought to the hospital by his wife because he had been insisting that there was a contract out on his life. Mr. Polsen told the doctors that the problem had started some four months ago when he was accused by his supervisor of tampering with a package, an offense that could have cost him his job. When he was exonerated at a formal hearing, his supervisor was "furious" and felt publicly humiliated, according to Mr. Polsen. Shortly afterwards, Mr. Polsen reported, his co-workers began avoiding him, turning away from him when he walked by, as if they didn't want to see him. He then began to think that they were talking about him behind his back, although he could never clearly make out what they were saying. He gradually became convinced that his co-workers were avoiding him because his boss had put a contract on his life. Things remained about the same for two months, when Mr. Polsen began to notice several

The Love Delusion

Erotomania, or the love delusion, is a delusional disorder in which the individual believes he or she is loved by someone else, usually someone famous or of high social status. In reality, the individual may have only a passing or nonexistent relationship with the alleged lover (R. L. Goldstein, 1986). Although the love delusion was once thought to be predominantly a female disorder, recent reports suggest it may not be a rarity among men. It has been suggested, for example, that John Hinckley, Jr., who attempted to assassinate then-president Ronald Reagan reportedly to impress actress Jodie Foster, could be considered as having erotomania (A. Stone, 1984). Although women with erotomania may have a potential for violence when their attentions are rebuffed, men with this condition appear more likely to threaten or commit acts of violence in the pursuit of the objects of their unrequited desires (Goldstein, 1986). Antipsychotic medications may reduce the intensity of the delusion but do not appear to eliminate the delusion (Segal, 1989). Nor is there evidence that psychotherapy helps people with erotomania. The prognosis is thus bleak, and people with erotomania may harass their love objects for many years. Mental health professionals also need to be aware of the potential for violence in the management of people who possess these delusions of love (Goldstein, 1986; Segal, 1989).

TRUTH _or_ FICTION REVISITED

12.10 _True._ Some people do suffer from the delusion that they are loved by a famous person. They are said to have a delusional disorder, erotomanic type.

The following cases provide some examples of the love delusion:

> _Mr. A., a 35-year-old man, was described as a "love-struck" suitor of a daughter of a former President of the United States. He was arrested for repeatedly harrassing the woman in an attempt to win her love, although they were actually perfect strangers. Refusing to adhere to the judge's warnings to stop pestering the woman, he placed numerous phone calls to her from prison and was later transferred to a psychiatric facility, still declaring they were very much in love._
>
> _Mr. B. was arrested for breaching a court order to stop pestering a famous pop singer. A 44-year-old farmer, Mr. B. had followed his love interest across the country, constantly bombarding her with romantic overtures. He was committed to a psychiatric hospital, but maintained the belief that she'd always wait for him._
>
> _Then there was Mr. C., a 32-year-old businessman, who believed a well-known woman lawyer had fallen in love with him following a casual meeting. He constantly called and sent flowers and letters, declaring his love. While she repeatedly rejected his advances and eventually filed criminal charges for harrassment, he felt that she was only testing his love by placing obstacles in his path. He abandoned_

> _large white cars cruising up and down the street where he lived. This frightened him and he became convinced there were hit men in these cars. He then refused to leave his home without an escort and would run home in panic when he saw one of these cars approaching. Other than the reports of his belief that his life was in danger, his thinking and behavior appeared entirely normal on interview. He denied experiencing hallucinations and showed no other signs of psychotic behavior, except for the queer beliefs about his life being in danger. The diagnosis of Delusional Disorder, Persecutory type seemed the most appropriate, since there was no_
>
> _evidence that a contract had been taken on his life (hence, a persecutory delusion) and there was an absence of other clear signs of psychosis that might support a diagnosis of a schizophrenic disorder._
>
> ADAPTED FROM SPITZER ET AL., 1994, PP. 177–179

Mr. Polsen's delusional belief that "hit teams" were pursuing him was treated with antipsychotic medication in the hospital setting and faded in about 3 weeks. His belief that he had been the subject of an attempted "hit" stuck in his mind, however. A month following admission, he stated, "I guess my boss has called off the contract. He couldn't get away with it now without publicity" (Spitzer et al., 1994, p. 179).

Is one of these people in love with you? People with *erotomania*—that is, the love delusion—may believe that they are loved by a celebrity or "star" (such as singer Mariah Carey, left, or actor Leonardo DiCaprio, right) or someone of high social status, even though they have never met.

> *his wife and business and his functioning declined.*
> *When the woman continued to reject him, he began*
> *sending her threatening letters and was committed*
> *to a psychiatric facility.*
>
> ADAPTED FROM GOLDSTEIN, 1986, P. 802

Although delusions frequently occur in schizophrenia, delusional disorders are believed to be distinct from schizophrenia. Persons with delusional disorders do not exhibit the confused or jumbled thinking characteristic of schizophrenia. Hallucinations, when they occur, are not as prominent. Delusions in schizophrenia are embedded within a larger array of disturbed thoughts, perceptions, and behavior. In delusional disorders, the delusion itself may be the only clear sign of abnormality. Also, the paranoid content in paranoid schizophrenia is generally less coherent and more bizarre than that of delusional disorders. Whereas people who have schizophrenia may believe their minds are controlled by "psychics" or other external forces, paranoid thinking in delusional disorders often seems plau-

sible. Unlike people with schizophrenia, persons with delusional disorders are generally able to function effectively in their work, although their interpersonal relationships may suffer because of their delusional concerns. Such people appear quite normal when their delusions are not being discussed.

Delusional disorders should also be distinguished from another disorder in which paranoid thinking is present—paranoid personality disorder. People with paranoid personality disorders may hold exaggerated or unwarranted suspicions of others but not the outright delusions that are found among people with delusional disorders or paranoid schizophrenia. A person with paranoid personality disorder may believe he was passed over for a promotion because

TABLE 12.3

Types of Delusional Disorders

Type	Description
Erotomanic type	Delusional beliefs that someone else, usually someone of higher social status, such as movie star or political figure, is in love with you.
Grandiose Type	Inflated beliefs about your worth, importance, power, knowledge, or identity, or beliefs that you hold a special relationship to a deity or a famous person. Cult leaders who believe they have special mystical powers of enlightenment may have delusional disorders of this type.
Jealous Type	Delusions of jealousy in which the person may become convinced, without due cause, that his or her lover is unfaithful. The delusional person may misinterpret certain clues as signs of unfaithfulness, such as spots on the bedsheets.
Persecutory Type	The most common type of delusional disorder, persecutory delusions involve themes of being conspired against, followed, cheated, spied upon, poisoned or drugged, or otherwise maligned or mistreated. Persons with such delusions may repeatedly institute court actions, or even commit acts of violence, against those who they perceive are responsible for their mistreatment.
Somatic Type	Delusions involving physical defects, disease, or disorder. Persons with these delusions may believe that foul odors are emanating from their bodies, or that internal parasites are eating away at them, or that certain parts of their body are unusually disfigured or ugly, or not functioning properly despite evidence to the contrary.
Mixed Type	Delusions typify more than one of the other types; no single theme predominates.

Source: Adapted from *DSM-IV* (APA, 1994).

his boss had it in for him, but he would not maintain the unfounded belief his boss had put a contract on his life.

Various kinds of delusional disorders are described in Table 12.3. Delusional disorders are relatively uncommon. Once a delusion is established, it may persevere, although the individual's concern about it may wax and wane over the years. In other cases, the delusion may disappear entirely for periods of time and then recur. Sometimes the disorder disappears permanently.

SUMMARY

History of the Concept of Schizophrenia

Emil Kraepelin was the first to describe the syndrome we identify as schizophrenia. He labeled the disorder *dementia praecox* and believed it was a disease that develops early in life and follows a progressively deteriorating course. Eugen Bleuler renamed the disorder *schizophrenia* and believed its course is more variable. He also distinguished between primary symptoms (the four As) and secondary symptoms. Kurt Schneider distinguished between first-rank symptoms that define the disorder and second-rank symptoms that occur in schizophrenia and other disorders.

Prevalence of Schizophrenia

Schizophrenia is believed to affect about 1% of the population.

Phases of Schizophrenia

Schizophrenia usually develops in late adolescence or early adulthood. Its onset may be abrupt or gradual. The period of deterioration preceding the onset of acute symptoms is called the prodromal phase. An acute episode involves the emergence of clear psychotic features. The residual phase is characterized by a level of functioning that was typical of the prodromal phase.

Schizophrenia-Spectrum Disorders

Schizophrenia-spectrum disorders refer to schizophrenic-type disorders that range in severity from milder personality disorders, such as schizotypal and schizoid types, to schizophrenia itself and schizoaffective disorder.

Features of Schizophrenia

Among the more prominent features of schizophrenia are disorders in the content of thought (delusions) and form of thought (thought disorder), as well as the presence of perceptual distortions (hallucinations) and emotional disturbances (flattened or inappropriate affect). There are also dysfunctions in the brain processes that regulate attention to the external world.

Types of Schizophrenia

The disorganized type describes a type of schizophrenia associated with grossly disorganized behavior and thought processes. The catatonic type describes a type of the disorder associated with grossly impaired motor behaviors, such as maintenance of fixed postures and muteness for long periods of time. The paranoid type involves the presence of paranoid delusions or frequent auditory hallucinations. The undifferentiated type is a catchall category, which applies to cases involving schizophrenic episodes that don't clearly fit the other types. The residual type applies to individuals with schizophrenia who do not have prominent psychotic behaviors at the time of evaluation.

Dimensions of Schizophrenia

Researchers have identified various dimensions of schizophrenia, including the process-reactive dimension, a dimension characterized by positive versus negative symptomatology, and Type I versus Type II schizophrenia.

Theoretical Perspectives

In the traditional psychodynamic model, schizophrenia represents a regression to a psychological state corresponding to early infancy in which the proddings of the id produce bizarre, socially deviant behavior and give rise to hallucinations and delusions. Learning theorists propose that some form of schizophrenic behavior may result from lack of social reinforcement, which leads to gradual detachment from the social environment and increased attention to an inner world of fantasy. Modeling and selective reinforcement of bizarre behavior may explain some schizophrenic behaviors in the hospital setting.

Research has demonstrated strong linkages between biological factors and schizophrenia. Evidence for genetic factors comes from studies of family patterns of schizophrenia, twin studies, and adoption studies. The mode of genetic transmission remains unknown. Environmental factors also play a role in schizophrenia, and many researchers have adopted the diathesis-stress model to account for the interaction between a genetic predisposition (diathesis) and stress arising from environmental factors.

Most researchers believe the neurotransmitter dopamine plays a role in schizophrenia, especially in the more flagrant features of the disorder. Viral factors may also be involved, but definite proof of viral involvement is lacking. Evidence of brain dysfunctions and structural damage in schizophrenia is accumulating, but researchers are uncertain about causal pathways. Family factors such as communication deviance and expressed emotion may act as sources of stress that increase the risk of development or recurrence of schizophrenia among people with a genetic predisposition.

Treatment

Treatment of schizophrenia tends to be multifaceted, incorporating pharmacological and psychosocial approaches. Antipsychotic medication is not a cure but tends to stem the more flagrant aspects of the disorder and to reduce the need for hospitalization and the risk of recurrent episodes.

Psychoanalytic approaches have not been shown to be effective in treating schizophrenia. Learning-based approaches, such as token-economy systems and social skills training, have achieved some success in increasing adaptive behavior among people with schizophrenia. Psychosocial-rehabilitation approaches help people with schizophrenia adapt more successfully to occupational and social roles in the community. Family-intervention programs help families cope with the burdens of care, communicate more clearly, and learn more helpful ways of relating to the patient.

Delusional Disorder

People with delusional disorder hold delusional beliefs that are apparently plausible and less bizarre than schizophrenic delusions. The delusion itself is often the only clear sign of abnormality, whereas schizophrenic delusions are embedded within a more general pattern of disturbed thoughts, perceptions, and behaviors.

REVIEW QUESTIONS

1. What is schizophrenia? How is it diagnosed? How have conceptualizations of schizophrenia changed over the years? How is schizophrenia distinguished from other disorders within the schizophrenic spectrum?

2. What are the features associated with the different phases of schizophrenia?

3. What disturbances in attention, perception, emotions, thought processes, self-identity, and behavior are associated with schizophrenia?

4. What are the ways in which theorists have distinguished between types and dimensions of schizophrenia?

5. What have we learned about the biological bases of schizophrenia? What don't we know?

6. How does the diathesis-stress model account for the development of schizophrenia? What evidence exists to support the model?

7. What treatment approaches, including biological and psychosocial interventions, are used in treating schizophrenia? What benefits do they have? What risks are associated with conventional forms of drug therapy?

8. What are the features associated with the subtypes of delusional disorder? How is delusional disorder distinguished from schizophrenia?

© Rufino Tamayo
Dos Caras

13

Abnormal Behavior in Childhood and Adolescence

TRUTH or FICTION?

13.1 Many behavior patterns deemed normal for children would be considered abnormal among adults.

13.2 Maternal smoking during pregnancy may put children at increased risk of attention-deficit hyperactivity disorder (ADHD).

13.3 Some people can recall verbatim every story they read in a newspaper.

13.4 Children who are hyperactive are often given depressants to help calm them down.

13.5 Some children refuse to go to school because they believe that terrible things may happen to their parents while they are away.

13.6 Major depression rarely occurs before adulthood.

13.7 Therapists have used Puerto Rican folktales to help Puerto Rican children adjust to the demands of living in mainstream U.S. society.

13.8 Problems of persistent bedwetting in childhood generally persist into adolescence.

When you have completed your study of Chapter 13, you should be able to:

1. Discuss ways of determining what is normal and abnormal in childhood and adolescence.

2. Discuss risk factors for psychological disorders in childhood and adolescence.

3. Discuss features, theoretical perspectives, and treatments of autism.

4. Discuss features and causes of mental retardation and methods of intervention.

5. Discuss the savant syndrome.

6. Discuss types, features, theoretical perspectives, and remediation of learning disorders.

7. Describe types of communication disorders.

8. Discuss types, features, theoretical perspectives, and treatments of attention-deficit and disruptive behavior disorders.

9. Discuss features and treatment of anxiety disorders and depression in childhood and adolescence.

10. Discuss the problem of adolescent suicide.

11. Discuss theoretical perspectives on enuresis and encopresis and ways of treating them.

*I*nsanity is hereditary.
You can get it from your children.

SAM LEVENSON

At the age of 5½, your second author's daughter Jordan would do the following in the course of a day:

- Repeat verbatim several scenes from the Mel Brooks films *Spaceballs* and *Young Frankenstein*
- Change her clothing five or six times
- Drink orange juice from a baby bottle
- Play "Heart and Soul" on the piano a dozen times
- Punch her 7-year-old sister and her father
- Awaken several times during the night screaming
- Curse like a marine (or like a Mel Brooks film character)
- Curl up on a couch and play with her toes
- Demand that one of her parents help wipe her after she made "poo"
- Lisp
- Attain (prekindergarten) achievement test scores in the 99th percentile

After the monster goes wild, Igor, Dr. Frankenstein's assistant in *Young Frankenstein,* confesses to the good doctor that he had found the brain of "Abby Someone" for the experiment in rejuvenation. "Abby who?" asks Dr. Frankenstein. "Abby Normal," admits Igor.

Many times Jordan's parents asked themselves whether her behavior was normal or, well, "abby-normal." To determine what is normal and abnormal among children and adolescents, not only do we consider the criteria outlined in Chapter 1, but we also weigh what is to be expected given the child's age, gender, family and cultural background, and the sundry developmental transformations that are taking place. Many problems are first identified when the child enters school. They may have existed earlier but been tolerated, or unrecognized as problematic, in the home. Sometimes the stress of starting school contributes to their onset.

NORMAL AND ABNORMAL IN CHILDHOOD AND ADOLESCENCE

There are diverse criteria for defining abnormal behavior in children, just as there are in adults. Some children and adolescents exhibit bizarre behavior patterns. Others engage in self-defeating behavior, such as refusing to eat or going on a binge and then making themselves vomit. Others display deficiencies in intellectual growth, as in **mental retardation.** Some act in ways that are socially inappropriate, as in conduct disorders. Other disorders, such as those that involve anxiety and depression, are mainly characterized by distress in the child. Keep in mind, however, that what is socially acceptable at one age, such as intense fear of strangers at about 9 months, may be socially unacceptable at more advanced ages. Many behavior patterns that would be considered abnormal among adults—such as intense fear of strangers and lack of bladder control—are perfectly normal for children at certain ages.

Problems in childhood and adolescence often have a special poignancy. Many of them occur at ages when children have little capacity to cope. Many of them prevent children from fulfilling their developmental potentials.

Psychotherapy with children has been approached from various perspectives and differs in important respects from therapy with adults. Children may not have the verbal skills to express their feelings through speech or the ability to sit in a chair through a therapy session. Therapy methods must be tailored to the level of the child's cognitive, physical, social, and emotional development. For example, psychodynamic therapists have developed techniques of **play therapy** in which children enact family conflicts symbolically through their play activities, such as by playacting with dolls or puppets. Or they might be given drawing materials and asked to draw pictures, in the belief that their drawings will reflect their underlying feelings.

Just how common are mental health problems among America's children and adolescents? Although we lack a nationwide sample, a large random sample of 1,710 high school students in nine schools in Oregon showed a high rate of psychological disorders. One in 3 students showed evidence of having a diagnosable psychological disorder at some point in their lives; 10% had a current disorder (Lewinsohn et al., 1993). Depressive disorders and anxiety disorders topped the list of diagnosable disorders.

Despite the prevalence of psychological disorders among the young, fewer than 1 in 5 children in the United States who have psychological problems that warrant treatment actually receive any type of mental health treatment (Kendall, 1994). Children who have *internalized* problems, such as anxiety and depression, are at higher risk of going untreated than are children with *externalized* problems (problems involving acting out or aggressive behavior) that tend to be disruptive or annoying to others.

Psychological problems among children and adolescents in the United States appear to be on the rise. Research was conducted comparing parent and teacher ratings of child problems such as withdrawal, physical complaints, anxiety/depression, social problems, delinquent behavior, and attention problems, among other behavioral problems. The results showed increased problems across the board in the period from 1976 to 1989, among boys and girls, Black children and White children, younger and older children, and children from higher and lower socioeconomic levels (Achenbach & Howell, 1993). Among the largest changes were increased apathy or lack of motivation, greater dislike of school and feelings of unhappiness or sadness, and reduced amount of time spent with friends (Goleman, 1993d). Although the research study was not designed to address the underlying reasons for the rise in reported child problems, speculation centers on changing social conditions, such as the rise in single-parent families leading to reductions in the amount of time that parents spend with their children, as well as less parental monitoring and greater levels of violence in the streets (Goleman, 1993d).

RISK FACTORS FOR DISORDERS IN CHILDHOOD AND ADOLESCENCE

The problems encountered in childhood and adolescence are varied, yet a number of risk factors apply to many if not most of them. One primary risk factor is gender. Boys are at greater risk for developing childhood problems ranging from autism to hyperactivity to elimination disorders. Problems of anxiety and depression also affect boys more often than girls, by a ratio of about 3 to 1 (Achenbach, 1982). In adolescence, however, anxiety and mood disorders become more common among girls and remain so throughout adulthood. The eating disorders of anorexia and bulimia, which usually begin in adolescence, predominantly affect girls. Here we examine other risk factors for developmental disorders.

Biological Risk Factors

Prenatal factors, birth complications, premature birth, and low birth weight all heighten the risk of maladaptive behavior in childhood (Lewis, Dlugokinski, Caputo, & Griffin, 1988). Although serious illnesses may increase the risk of behavioral and emotional problems, run-of-the-mill bacterial and viral infections apparently do not increase the risk of these problems. Genetic factors appear to play a role in many behavioral problems of children and adolescents, including hyperactivity and attentional disorders, learning disorders, autism, antisocial and oppositional behavior, anxiety disorders, and eating disorders (e.g., Comings, 1997; Zahn-Waxler et al., 1996).

Psychosocial Risk Factors

Stress apparently heightens the risk of psychological and behavioral as well as physical problems among children. In one study of children aged 6 to 9, undesirable life events and daily hassles predicted maladaptive behavior (Wertlieb, Weigel, & Feldsten, 1987). Family conflicts and instabilities appear to contribute to anxieties, depression, and conduct disorders in children and to eating disorders in adolescents. Inconsistent or harsh parenting practices are often associated with externalizing problems, such as conduct disorder, and internalizing problems, such as depression.

Researchers find evidence of a chain of events linking stressful life events experienced by the parents to depressed mood in adolescent children (Ge et al., 1994). Parental stress may lead parents to become depressed, which may lead them to be less tolerant of their children and more reliant on harsh or inconsistent parenting behaviors, which in

Multicultural Influences on Judgments of Children's Behavior as Normal or Abnormal

Cultural beliefs help determine whether people view behavior as normal or abnormal. People who base judgments of normality only on standards derived from their own cultures risk being ethnocentric when they view the behavior of people in other cultures as abnormal (Kennedy, Scheirer, & Rogers, 1984). The problem is of special concern regarding child psychopathology. Because children rarely label their own behavior as abnormal, definitions of normality depend largely on how a child's behavior is filtered through the lenses by which parents in a particular culture view that behavior (M. C. Lambert et al., 1992; Weisz et al., 1988). Cultures may vary with respect to the types of behaviors they classify as unacceptable or abnormal as well the threshold for labeling child behaviors as deviant or socially unacceptable. Researchers find that parents in different cultures do judge the unusualness of behavior from different perspectives (Lambert et al., 1992).

For example, researchers posed the question, "When a child has psychological problems, what determines whether adults will consider the problem serious or whether they will seek professional help?" (Weisz et al., 1988, p. 601). To explore this question, researchers presented vignettes to Thai and American parents, teachers, and clinical psychologists. The vignettes depicted two children, one with problems characterized by "overcontrol" (for example, shyness and fears) and one with problems characterized by undercontrol (for example, disobedience and fighting). The Thai parents rated *both* sets of problems as less serious (see Figure 13.1) and worrisome than American parents and as more likely to improve without treatment as time

passed. Such an interpretation is embedded within traditional Thai-Buddhist beliefs and values. Thai-Buddhist values tolerate broad variations in children's behavior. They assume that change is inevitable and children's behavior will eventually change for the better. Differences between cultural groups were greater for parents and teachers than for psychologists, which suggests that professional training in a common scientific tradition might offset cultural differences.

How serious is this problem? Thai parents might judge the behavior shown by these children to be less serious than American parents would. Thai-Buddhist values tolerate broad variations in children's behavior and assume that it will change for the better.

turn may raise the risk that their children may become depressed. Yet the relationship between the child and parent is a two-way street: Parents influence and are influenced by their children's behavior. In a recent study, interactions between mothers and young children (2.5 to 6.5 years of age) were observed (Dumas, Serketich, & LaFreniere, 1995). Mothers of anxious children attempted to control their children's behavior by being coercive and nonresponsive. The children attempted to control their mothers' behaviors by becoming resistant and coercive. The relationship itself could be characterized as coercive, not just the behavior of the child or parent individually.

Cognitive factors such as expectancies are also intertwined with maladaptive behavior patterns in childhood. For example, when presented with social opportunities, such as happening upon another child who has a ball, outgoing, popular children are likely to report thinking something like, "I was thinking that he/she would be nice and let me play." Socially withdrawn children are more likely to have expectancies such as "I was afraid that she/he didn't want me to play" (Stefanek, Ollendik, Baldock, Francis, & Yaeger, 1987). Aggressive children also report self-defeating expectancies, particularly the assumption that others intend them ill. Children's expectancies, like those of adults, influence their

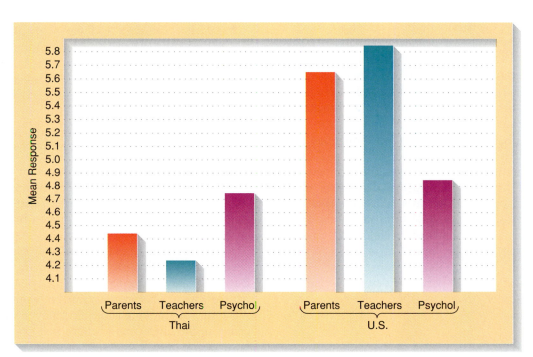

FIGURE 13.1 *Ratings by Thai and U.S. parents of the seriousness of children's behavioral problems.* Researchers presented vignettes of children with problems characterized by overcontrol (for example, shyness and fears) and undercontrol (for example, disobedience and fighting) to Thai and American parents. The Thai parents rated both sets of problems as less serious and worrisome than American parents, and as more likely to improve without treatment. The Thai parents apparently assume that people change and that their children's behavior will eventually change for the better.

Source: Weisz et al. (1988).

actions and can become self-fulfilling prophecies—for better or worse.

Rejection by peers and parents appears to place children at increased risk. A 40-year longitudinal study of 253 males first contacted between the ages of 5 and 9 found that social rejection placed them at significant risk in later life for premature death, conviction for felonies, and various disorders, including alcoholism (McCord, 1983). Cause and effect are somewhat clouded, however. Although social rejection is painful for most children (and adults), children sometimes display maladaptive behaviors that prompt rejection and portend later difficulties.

Children who suffer parental abuse or severe neglect are at greater risk in adolescence of lowered intelligence and depression and suicide, among other problems (discussed in Chapter 15). They are also more likely than other children to be arrested for a crime as adolescents ("Study finds severe effects from childhood abuse," 1991) and as adults (Widom, 1989a). Abuse can also disturb patterns of attachment and exploratory behavior (Dodge, Pettit, & Bates, 1994). Abused children are less apt than nonabused peers to venture out to explore their surroundings.

Various biological and psychosocial factors thus appear to place children and adolescents at risk for maladaptive behavior patterns. Now let us consider some of these problems, beginning with **pervasive developmental disorders.**

PERVASIVE DEVELOPMENTAL DISORDERS

Pervasive developmental disorders involve markedly impaired behavior or functioning in multiple areas of development. These disorders generally become evident in the first few years of life and are often associated with mental retardation (APA, 1994). They were generally classified as forms of *psychoses* in early editions of the DSM. They were thought to reflect childhood forms of adult psychoses such as schizophrenia because they share features such as social and emotional impairment, oddities of communication, and stereotyped motor behaviors. Research has shown that they are distinct from schizophrenia and other psychoses, however. Only very rarely in these children is there evidence of the prominent hallucinations or delusions that would justify a diagnosis of schizophrenia. Pervasive developmental disorders are now classified separately from psychotic disorders. The label of schizophrenia with childhood onset is reserved for the relatively rare instances in which schizophrenia develops in childhood (L. K. Jacobsen, et al. 1997). There are several variations of pervasive developmental disorders; autistic disorder, or autism, is the major type.

Autism

Peter nursed eagerly, sat and walked at the expected ages. Yet some of his behavior made us vaguely uneasy. He never put anything in his mouth. Not his fingers nor his toys—nothing. . . .

More troubling was the fact that Peter didn't look at us, or smile, and wouldn't play the games that seemed as much a part of babyhood as diapers. He rarely laughed, and when he did, it was at things that didn't seem funny to us. He didn't cuddle, but sat upright in my lap, even when I rocked him. But children differ and we were content to let Peter be himself. We thought it hilarious when my brother, visiting us when Peter was 8 months old, observed that "That kid has no social instincts, whatsoever." Although Peter was a first child, he was not isolated. I frequently put him in his playpen in front of the house, where the schoolchildren stopped to play with him as they passed. He ignored them, too.

It was Kitty, a personality kid, born two years later, whose responsiveness emphasized the degree of Peter's difference. When I went into her room for the late feeding, her little head bobbed up and she greeted me with a smile that reached from her head to her toes. And the realization of that difference chilled me more than the wintry bedroom.

Peter's babbling had not turned into speech by the time he was 3. His play was solitary and repetitive. He

tore paper into long thin strips, bushel baskets of it every day. He spun the lids from my canning jars and became upset if we tried to divert him. Only rarely could I catch his eye, and then saw his focus change from me to the reflection in my glasses. . . .

[Peter's] adventures into our suburban neighborhood had been unhappy. He had disregarded the universal rule that sand is to be kept in sandboxes, and the children themselves had punished him. He walked around a sad and solitary figure, always carrying a toy airplane, a toy he never played with. At that time, I had not heard the word that was to dominate our lives, to hover over every conversation, to sit through every meal beside us. That word was autism.

ADAPTED FROM EBERHARDY, 1967

Autism, or *autistic disorder,* is one of the severest disorders of childhood. It is a chronic, lifelong condition. Children with autism, such as Peter, seem utterly alone in the world, despite parental efforts to bridge the gulf that divides them.

Autism derives from the Greek *autos,* meaning "self." The term *autism* was first used in 1906 by the Swiss psychiatrist Eugen Bleuler to refer to a peculiar style of thinking among people with schizophrenia. (Autism is one of Bleuler's "four As.") Autistic thinking is the tendency to view oneself as the center of the universe, to believe that external events somehow refer to oneself. In 1943, another psychiatrist, Leo Kanner, applied the diagnosis "early infantile autism" to a group of disturbed children who seemed unable to relate to others, as if they lived in their own private world. Unlike children suffering from mental retardation, the children with autism seemed to shut out any input from the outside world, creating a kind of "autistic aloneness" (Kanner, 1943).

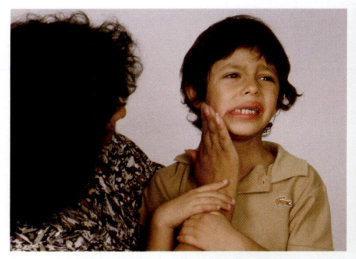

Autism. Autism, one of the most severe childhood disorders, is characterized by pervasive deficits in the ability to relate to and communicate with others, and by a restricted range of activities and interests. Children with autistic disorder lack the ability to relate to others and seem to live in their own private worlds.

Autism is a rare disorder. A large community-based study in the state of Utah showed a prevalence of autism in only 4 persons among 10,000 people, a prevalence rate of 0.04% (Ritvo et al., 1989). The Utah researchers found that rates of autism did not vary with race, religion, or parent's occupation or educational level.

Autism typically becomes evident in toddlers between 18 and 30 months of age, mostly among boys (Rapin, 1997). Autism seems always to have been with Peter. In the case of Eric, however, the disorder apparently developed between the ages of 12 and 24 months:

"People used to say to me they hoped they [would have] a baby just like mine," Sarah said of Eric, 3 years old at the time. As an infant, Eric smiled endearingly, laughed, and hugged. He uttered a dozen words by his first birthday. By 16 months he had memorized the alphabet and could read some signs. "People were very impressed," Sarah said.

Gradually, things changed, but it took months for Sarah to realize that Eric had a problem. At the age of 2, other members of Eric's play group bubbled with conversation. Eric had abandoned words completely. Instead, Eric combined letters and numbers in idiosyncratic ways, such as "B–T–2–4–6–Z–3."

Eric grew increasingly withdrawn. His diet was essentially self-limited to peanut butter and jelly sandwiches. He spent hour after hour arranging letters and

numbers on a magnetic board. But the "symptom" that distressed Sarah most was impossible to measure: when she gazed into Eric's eyes, she no longer saw a "sparkle."

ADAPTED FROM D. MARTIN, 1989

Children with autism are often described by their parents as having been "good babies" early in infancy. This generally means they were not demanding. As they develop, however, they begin to reject physical affection, such as cuddling, hugging, and kissing (Schopler & Mesibov, 1984). Their speech development begins to fall behind the norm. Although Eric did quite well through his first 16 months, there are often signs of social detachment beginning as early as the first year of life, such as failure to look at other people's faces (Osterling & Dawson, 1994). The clinical features of the disorder appear prior to 3 years of age (APA, 1994). Autism is four to five times more common among males than females (APA, 1994).

Features of Autism   Perhaps the most poignant feature of autism is the child's utter aloneness (see Table 13.1). Other features include language and communication problems and ritualistic or stereotyped behavior. Mutism may occur or, if some language skills are present, they may be characterized by peculiar usage, as in echolalia (parroting back what the child has heard in a high-pitched monotone); pronoun reversals (using "you" or "he" instead of "I"); use of words that have meaning only to those who have intimate

---

TABLE 13.1

Diagnostic Features of Autistic Disorder

A. Diagnosis requires a combination of features from the following groups. Not all of the features from each group need be present for a diagnosis to be made.

(1) Impaired social interactions	1. Impairment in the nonverbal behaviors such as facial expressiveness, posture, gestures, and eye contact that normally regulate social interaction
	2. Does not develop age-appropriate peer relationships
	3. Failure to express pleasure in the happiness of other people
	4. Does not show social or emotional reciprocity (give and take)
(2) Impaired communication	1. Delay in development of spoken language (nor is there an effort to compensate for this lack through gestures)
	2. When speech development is adequate, there is nevertheless lack of ability to initiate or sustain conversation
	3. Shows abnormalities in form or content of speech (e.g., stereotyped or repetitive speech, as in echolalia; idiosyncratic use of words; speaking about the self in the second or third person—using "you" or "he" to mean "I")
	4. Does not show spontaneous social or imaginative (make-believe) play
(3) Restricted, repetitive, and stereotyped behavior patterns	1. Shows restricted range of interests
	2. Insists on routines (e.g., always uses same route to go from one place to another)
	3. Shows stereotyped movements (e.g., hand flicking, head banging, rocking, spinning)
	4. Shows preoccupation with parts of objects (e.g., repetitive spinning of wheels of toy car) or unusual attachments to objects (e.g., carrying a piece of string)

B. Onset occurs prior to the age of 3 through display of abnormal functioning in at least one of the following: social behavior, communication, or imaginative play.

Source: Adapted from the *DSM-IV* (APA, 1994).

knowledge of the child; and tendencies to raise the voice at the end of sentences, as if asking a question. Nonverbal communication may also be impaired or absent. For example, children with autistic disorder may not engage in eye contact or display facial expressions. Although they may be unresponsive to others, researchers find they are capable of displaying strong emotions, especially strong negative emotions such as anger, sadness, and fear (Capps et al., 1993; Kasari et al., 1993).

A primary feature of autism is repeated purposeless stereotyped movements interminably—twirling, flapping the hands, or rocking back and forth with the arms around the knees. Some children with autism mutilate themselves, even as they cry out in pain. They may bang their heads, slap their faces, bite their hands and shoulders, or pull out their hair. They may also throw sudden tantrums or panics. Another feature of autism is aversion to environmental changes—a feature termed "preservation of sameness." When familiar objects are moved even slightly from their usual places, children with autism may throw tantrums or cry continually until their placement is restored. Like Eric, children with autistic disorder may insist on eating the same food every day.

Children with autism are bound by ritual. The teacher of a 5-year-old girl with autistic disorder learned to greet her every morning by saying, "Good morning, Lily, I am very, very glad to see you" (S. Diamond, Baldwin, & Diamond, 1963). Although Lily would not respond to the greeting, she would shriek if the teacher omitted even one of the *verys*.

Children who develop autism appear to have failed to develop a differentiated self-concept (Ferrari & Matthews, 1983). Nearly all normal 2-year-olds recognize their reflections in a mirror, but about 30% of 3- to 12-year-old children with autism fail to recognize themselves (Spiker & Ricks, 1984). Despite their unusual behavior, children with autism are often quite attractive and often have an "intelligent look" about them. However, as measured by scores on standardized tests, their intellectual development tends to lag below the norm. Three of four people with autism show evidence of mental retardation (Rapin, 1997). The Utah study revealed that 60% of children with autism scored below 70 on standardized IQ tests (Ritvo et al., 1989). Perhaps 5% to 30% of children with autistic disorder score in the average range on intelligence tests (Yirmiya & Sigman, 1991). Even those who function at an average level of intelligence show deficits in activities requiring the ability to symbolize, such as recognizing emotions, engaging in symbolic play, and conceptual problem solving. They also display difficulty in attending to tasks that involve interacting with other people. The relationship between autism and intelligence is clouded, however, by difficulties in administering standardized IQ tests to these children. Testing requires cooperation, a skill that is dramatically lacking in children with autism. At best, we can only estimate their intellectual ability.

Theoretical Perspectives The causes of autism remain unknown. Early views of autism focused on patholog-ical family relationships. Kanner and his colleagues (e.g., Kanner & Eisenberg, 1955) suggested that children with autism were reared by cold, detached parents who were dubbed "emotional refrigerators." Psychoanalyst Bruno Bettelheim (1967) also focused on the family by suggesting that extreme self-absorption is the child's defense against parental rejection. The parents rear the child in an emotionally and socially desolate atmosphere in which the child's efforts to develop language and social skills wither. The child surrenders efforts to develop mastery over the external world and withdraws into a world of fantasy. The pathological insistence on preservation of sameness represents the child's rigid, defensive efforts to impose order and predictability.

Research, however, has not supported the assumption—so devastating to many parents—that they are in fact frosty and remote (W. Hoffmann & Prior, 1982). Of course there is truth to the notion that children with autism and their parents do not relate to one another very well, but causal connections are clouded. Rather than rejecting their children and thus fostering autism, parents may grow somewhat aloof because their efforts to relate to their children repeatedly meet with failure. Aloofness then becomes a result of autism, not a cause.

Psychologist O. Ivar Lovaas and his colleagues (Lovaas, Koegel, & Schreibman, 1979) offer a cognitive-learning perspective on autism. They suggest that children with autism have perceptual deficits that limit them to processing only one stimulus at a time. As a result, they are slow to learn by means of classical conditioning (association of stimuli). From the learning-theory perspective, children become attached to their primary caregivers because they are associated with primary reinforcers such as food and hugging. Children with autism, however, attend either to the food or the cuddling and do not connect it with the parent.

Cognitive theorists have focused on the kinds of cognitive deficits shown by children with autism and the possible relationships among them. Rutter (1983), for example, suggests that cognitive and language deficits are primary and give rise to social problems. Children with autism appear to have difficulty integrating information from various senses. At times they seem hypersensitive to stimulation. At other times they are so insensitive that an observer might wonder whether or not they are deaf. Perceptual-cognitive deficits seem to diminish their capacity to make use of information—to comprehend and apply social rules.

But what is the basis of these perceptual and cognitive deficits? The sundry impairments associated with autism, including mental retardation, language deficits, bizarre motor behavior, even seizures, suggest an underlying neurological basis involving some form of brain damage (McBride, Anderson, & Shapiro, 1996; Zilbovicius et al., 1992). MRI scans do show structural differences in the brains of boys and men with autistic disorder, including enlarged ventricles indicative of a loss of brain cells (Haznedar et al., 1997; Piven et al., 1995, 1997). Yet researchers have yet to pinpoint any causal process in the brain that could account for autism (H. J. Garber & Ritvo, 1992; Rapin, 1997; Zilbovicius et al.,

1992, 1995). Perhaps autism stems from multiple causes involving more than one type of brain abnormality (Ritvo & Ritvo, 1992).

Researchers also suspect that genetics plays a significant role in autism (Rapin, 1997). Rates of concordance for autistic disorder are about 60% for identical (MZ) twins versus about 10% for fraternal (DZ) twins, which suggests a strong genetic component in the development of the disorder (Plomin, Owen, & McGuffin, 1994). Researchers also suspect that multiple genes are involved and interact with other factors, possibly environmental or biological, in giving rise to autism (McBride, Anderson, & Shapiro, 1996; Hallmayer et al., 1996). Still, the causes of autism remain a mystery.

Treatment   Psychodynamically oriented treatments for autism have included psychotherapy, play therapy, and placement of children in residential facilities largely governed by Bruno Bettelheim's ideas. The residences aim to provide children with the warmth presumed to be lacking in the home. Unconditional support is intended to help the children form secure attachments to other people who then become introjected as positive self-images (Sanders, 1974). Children are also given the chance to influence their environments. Their demands are met so long as they are not self-injurious. Evidence from controlled studies supporting the effectiveness of these approaches remains lacking, however.

Although most behaviorists do not contend that autism is caused by faulty learning, they suggest that principles of learning may be helpful in treating autistic behavior. Operant conditioning methods (that is, systematic use of rewards and punishments) have been used to increase the child's ability to attend to others and to play with other children and to stop self-mutilative behavior. Techniques such as extinction (withholding reinforcement following a response) are sometimes effective for such behaviors as head-banging, but a great many unreinforced trials (trials that are ignored), even a thousand or more, may be required to eliminate the response. The problem seems to be that many repetitive behavior patterns—for example, rocking and self-injurious behaviors—are maintained by internal reinforcements such as increased stimulation. Therefore, withdrawal of social reinforcers may have little if any effect.

Use of aversive stimulation such as spanking and, in extreme cases, electric shock, is more effective than extinction. Brief bursts of mild but painful electrical stimulation can eliminate self-mutilation within a minute of application (Lovaas, 1977). Using electric shock with children raises moral, ethical, and legal concerns, of course. Lovaas has countered that failure to eliminate self-injurious behavior places the child at greater risk of physical harm and denies children the opportunity to participate in other kinds of therapy. The use of aversive stimulation should be combined with positive reinforcement for acceptable alternative behaviors.

Because children who suffer from autism show behavioral deficits, a central focus of behavior modification is the development of new behavior. New behaviors are maintained by reinforcements, so it is important to teach these children, who often respond to people as they would to a piece of furniture, to accept people as reinforcers. People can be established as reinforcers by pairing praise with primary reinforcers such as food. Then social reinforcement (praise) and primary reinforcers (food) can be used to shape and model toileting behaviors, speech, and social play. The involvement of families and residential treatment personnel in these behavioral programs prompts the maintenance and generalization of behavioral changes (S. R. Anderson et al., 1986; Romanczyk, 1986).

Although there is no cure for autism, some structured treatment programs have yielded promising results. The most effective treatment programs focus on behavioral, educational, and communication deficits and are highly intensive and structured, offering a great deal of individual instruction (Rapin, 1997). In a classic study conducted by O. Ivar Lovaas (1987) at UCLA, children suffering from autism received more than 40 hours of one-to-one behavior modification each week for at least 2 years. Significant intellectual and educational gains were reported for 9 of the 19 children (47%) in the program. The children who improved achieved normal IQ scores and were able to succeed in the first grade. Only 2% of a control group that did not receive the intensive treatment achieved similar gains. Treatment gains were well maintained at the time of a follow-up when the children were 11 years old (McEachin, Smith, & Lovaas, 1993).

Another leading program, housed at the University of North Carolina, involves a collaborative effort between the university and the state government. This comprehensive program incorporates home teaching, individualized instruction in specialized public school classes, parental training and counseling, and job training and placement. Fewer than 10% of participating children needed to be institutionalized, as compared to 39% to 74% of children with autism overall (Sleek, 1994). Although these results are promising, longer term follow-ups remain to be reported.

Biological approaches have had some limited impact in the treatment of autism. This may be changing. One line of research has shown that drugs that enhance serotonin activity, such as SSRIs, can reduce repetitive thoughts and behavior and aggression and lead to some improvement in social relatedness and language use in adults with autism (Longhurst, Potenza, & McDougle, 1997; McDougle et al., 1996). The effects of these drugs on children with autism remain to be seen. Other research has focused on drugs normally used to treat schizophrenia, such as Haldol, which blocks dopamine activity. Several controlled studies show Haldol to be helpful in many cases in reducing social withdrawal and repetitive motor behavior (such as rocking behavior), aggression, hyperactivity and self-injurious behavior (McBride, Anderson, & Shapiro, 1996). We have not seen drugs lead to consistent improvement in the cognitive and language development in children with autism.

The Long-Term View   Autistic traits generally continue into adulthood to one degree or another. Yet some

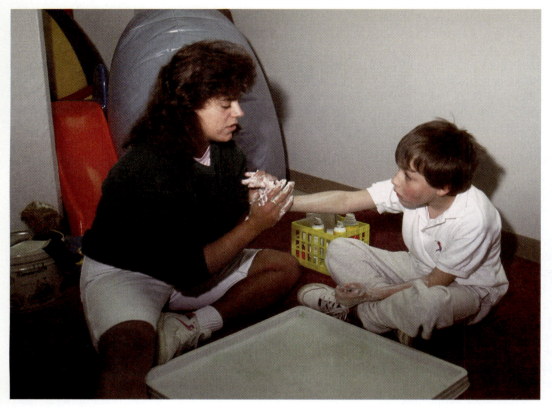

Establishing contact. One of the principal therapeutic tasks in working with children with autism is the establishment of interpersonal contact. Psychodynamic therapists emphasize the importance of continual support to help the child form secure attachments. Behavior therapists use reinforcers to increase adaptive social behaviors, such as paying attention to the therapist and playing with other children. Behavior therapists may also use punishments to suppress self-mutilative behavior.

autistic children do go on to achieve college degrees and function independently (Rapin, 1997). Others need continuing treatment throughout their lives, even institutionalized care. Even the highest functioning adults with the disorder manifest deficient social and communication skills and a highly limited range of interests and activities (APA, 1994).

MENTAL RETARDATION

Mental retardation involves a broad delay in the development of cognitive and social functioning. The course of development of children with mental retardation is variable. Many improve over time, especially if they receive support, guidance, and enriched educational opportunities. Children with mental retardation who are reared in impoverished environments may fail to improve or may deteriorate further in relation to other children.

Mental retardation is generally assessed by a combination of formal intelligence tests and observation of adaptive functioning. The *DSM-IV* uses three criteria in diagnosing mental retardation: (1) an IQ score of approximately 70 or below on a test such as the Wechsler Intelligence Scale for Children (WISC) or the Stanford-Binet, (2) evidence of impaired functioning in adaptive behavior, and (3) onset of the disorder before age 18. People whose behavior is impaired fail to meet the standards of behavior that are expected of someone of the same age within a given cultural setting. They do not develop comparable social and communication skills or become adequately independent and self-sufficient. For infants, task-related judgments of subaverage intellec-

tual functioning may be used in place of IQ scores because tests of infant intelligence either do not yield reliable IQ scores, or IQ scores at all.

The *DSM-IV* classifies mental retardation according to level of severity, as shown in Table 13.2. Most children with mental retardation (about 85%) fall into the mildly retarded range. These children are generally capable of meeting basic academic demands such as learning to read simple passages. As adults they are generally capable of independent functioning, although they may require some guidance and support. Table 13.3 provides a description of the deficits and abilities associated with various degrees of mental retardation.

Not all systems of classification of mental retardation are based on level of severity. The American Association of Mental Retardation (AAMR), an organization composed of leading professionals in the field, classifies mental retardation according to the intensity of support needed by the individual in various areas of functioning (AAMR, 1992). Some individuals need only intermittent support that varies in intensity from time to time on an *as needed basis;* others require more constant or pervasive support requiring extensive commitment of staff and resources. This system of classification attempts to match the level of support needed to the individual's ability to function in work, school, and home environments.

Causes of Retardation

In many cases, mental retardation can be traced to biological causes, including chromosomal and genetic disorders, infectious diseases, and brain damage. However, more than half

TABLE 13.2

Levels of Mental Retardation

Degree of Severity	Approximate IQ Range	Percentage of People with Mental Retardation Within the Range
Mild Mental Retardation	50–70	Approximately 85%
Moderate Mental Retardation	35–49	10
Severe Mental Retardation	20–34	3–4
Profound Mental Retardation	Below 20	1–2

Source: Adapted from the *DSM-IV* (APA, 1994).

of the cases of mental retardation remain unexplained, with most of these cases falling in the mild range of severity (Flint et al., 1995). These unexplained cases may involve cultural or familial causes, such as being raised in an impoverished home environment. Or perhaps they involve an interaction of environmental and genetic factors, the nature of which remains poorly understood (Thaper et al., 1994).

Down Syndrome and Other Chromosomal Abnormalities The most common chromosomal abnormality linked to mental retardation is **Down syndrome**

(formerly called Down's syndrome), which is characterized by an extra or third chromosome on the 21st pair of chromosomes, resulting in 47 chromosomes rather than the normal complement of 46. Down syndrome occurs in about 1 in 800 births. It usually occurs when the 21st pair of chromosomes in either the egg or the sperm fails to divide normally, resulting in an extra chromosome. Chromosomal abnormalities become more likely as parents age (Hamamy et al., 1990), so expectant couples in their thirties or older often undergo prenatal genetic tests to detect Down syndrome and other genetic abnormalities. Down syndrome

TABLE 13.3

Levels of Retardation, Typical Ranges of IQ Scores, and Types of Adaptive Behaviors Shown

Approximate IQ Score Range	Preschool Ages 0–5 Maturation and Development	School Age 6–21 Training and Education	Adult 21 and Over Social and Vocational Adequacy
Mild 50–70	Often not noticed as retarded by casual observer, but is slower to walk, feed self, and talk than most children.	Can acquire practical skills and useful reading and arithmetic to a 3rd to 6th grade level with special education. Can be guided toward social conformity.	Can usually achieve social and vocational skills adequate to self-maintenance; may need occasional guidance and support when under unusual social or economic stress.
Moderate 35–49	Noticeable delays in motor development, especially in speech; responds to training in various self-help activities.	Can learn simple communication, elementary health and safety habits, and simple manual skills; does not progress in functional reading or arithmetic.	Can perform simple tasks under sheltered conditions; participates in simple recreation; travels alone in familiar places; usually incapable of self-maintenance.
Severe 20–34	Marked delay in motor development; little or no communication skill; may respond to training in elementary self-help—e.g., self-feeding.	Usually walks, barring specific disability; has some understanding of speech and some response; can profit from systematic habit training.	Can conform to daily routines and repetitive activities; needs continuing direction and supervision in protective environment.
Profound Below 20	Gross retardation; minimal capacity for functioning in sensorimotor areas; needs nursing care.	Obvious delays in all areas of development; shows basic emotional responses; may respond to skillful training in use of legs, hands, and jaws; needs close supervision.	May walk, may need nursing care, may have primitive speech; will usually benefit from regular physical activity; incapable of self-maintenance.

Source: Rathus, S. A. (1996). *Psychology,* (6th ed.). Fort Worth: Harcourt Brace, p. 353.

can be traced to a defect in the mother's chromosomes in about 95% of cases, with the remainder attributable to defects in the father's sperm.

People with Down syndrome are recognizable by certain physical features, such as a round face; broad, flat nose; and small, downward-sloping folds of skin at the inside corners of the eyes that gives the impression of slanted eyes. Children with Down syndrome are also characterized by a protruding tongue; small, squarish hands and short fingers; a curved fifth finger; and disproportionately small arms and legs in relation to their bodies. Nearly all of these children have mental retardation and many suffer from physical problems, such as malformations of the heart and respiratory difficulties. Sadly, most die by middle age. In their later years, they tend to suffer memory losses and experience childish emotions that represent a form of senility.

Children with Down syndrome suffer various deficits in learning and development. They tend to be uncoordinated and to lack proper muscle tone, which makes it difficult for them to carry out physical tasks and engage in play activities like other children. Down syndrome children suffer memory deficits, especially for information presented verbally, which makes it difficult for them to learn in school. They also have difficulty following instructions from teachers and expressing their thoughts or needs clearly in speech. Despite their disabilities, most can learn to read, write, and perform simple arithmetic, if they receive appropriate schooling and the right encouragement.

Although less common than Down syndrome, chromosomal abnormalities on the sex chromosome may also result in mental retardation, such as in Klinefelter's syndrome and Turner's syndrome. Klinefelter's syndrome, which only occurs among males, is characterized by the presence of an extra X sex chromosome, resulting in an XXY sex chromosomal pattern rather than the XY pattern that men normally have. Estimates of the prevalence of Klinefelter's syndrome range from 1 in 500 to 1 in 1,000 male births (Brody, 1993c). Men with this XXY pattern fail to develop appropriate secondary sex characteristics, resulting in small, underdeveloped testes, low sperm production, enlarged breasts, poor muscular development, and infertility. Mild retardation or learning disabilities frequently occur among these men. Men with Klinefelter's syndrome often don't discover they have the condition until they undergo tests for infertility.

Found only among females is Turner's syndrome, which is characterized by the presence of a single X sex chromosome instead of the normal two. Although such girls develop normal external genitals, their ovaries remain poorly developed, producing reduced amounts of estrogen. As women, they tend to be shorter than average and infertile. They also tend to show evidence of mild retardation, especially in skills relating to math and science.

Fragile X Syndrome and Other Genetic Abnormalities

Fragile X syndrome is the most common type of inherited mental retardation. It is the second most common form of retardation overall, after Down syndrome (Angier, 1991a; "Blood test can detect retardation," 1993; Plomin, Owen, & McGuffin, 1994). The disorder is believed to be caused by a mutated gene on the X sex chromosome (Hagerman, 1996). The defective gene is located in an area of the chromosome that appears fragile, hence the name *fragile X syndrome*. Fragile X syndrome causes mental retardation in every 1,000 to 1,500 males and (generally less severe) mental handicaps in every 2,000 to 2,500 females (Angier, 1991a; Rousseau et al., 1991). The effects of fragile X syndrome range from mild learning disabilities to retardation so profound that those affected can hardly speak or function.

Females normally have two X sex chromosomes, whereas males have only one. For females, having two X sex chromosomes seems to provide some protection against the disorder if the defective gene turns up on one of the two chromosomes (Angier, 1991a). This may explain why the disorder usually has more profound effects on males than on females. Yet the mutation does not always manifest itself. Many males and females carry the fragile X mutation but show no clinical evidence of it. Yet they can pass along the syndrome to their offspring.

A genetic test can detect the presence of the mutation by direct DNA analysis (Rousseau et al., 1991) and may be of help to prospective parents in genetic counseling. Prenatal testing of the fetus is also possible (G. R. Sutherland et al., 1991). Although there is no treatment for fragile X syndrome, identifying the defective gene is the first step toward understanding how the protein produced by the gene functions to produce the disability, which may lead to the development of treatments for the disorder (Angier, 1991a).

Phenylketonuria (PKU) is a genetic disorder that occurs in 1 in 10,000 births (Plomin, Owen, & McGuffin,

Learning to function. Although persons with Down syndrome suffer from deficits in learning and development, most can learn to function productively with encouragement and training.

1994). It is caused by a recessive gene that prevents the child from metabolizing the amino acid *phenylalanine,* which is found in many foods. Consequently, phenylalanine and its derivative, phenylpyruvic acid, accumulate in the body, causing damage to the central nervous system that results in mental retardation and emotional disturbance. The presence of PKU can be detected among newborns by analyzing blood or urine samples. Although there is no cure for PKU, children with the disorder may suffer less damage or develop normally if they are placed on a diet low in phenylalanine soon after birth (Brody, 1990). Such children receive protein supplements that compensate for their nutritional loss.

Tay-Sachs disease is also caused by recessive genes. A fatal degenerative disease of the central nervous system, it mostly afflicts Jews of Eastern European ancestry. About 1 in 25 American Jews is a carrier of the recessive gene responsible for the disorder. The chance that both members of a Jewish couple carry the gene is thus about 1 in 625. Children who are afflicted by Tay-Sachs suffer gradual loss of muscle control, deafness and blindness, retardation and paralysis, and eventually die before the age of 5.

Today, various prenatal tests exist that can detect the presence of genetic disorders. In *amniocentesis,* which is usually conducted about 14 to 15 weeks following conception, a sample of amniotic fluid is drawn with a syringe from the amniotic sac that contains the fetus. Cells from the fetus can then be separated from the fluid, allowed to grow in a culture, and examined for the presence of biochemical and chromosomal abnormalities, including Down syndrome. Blood tests are used to detect carriers of Tay-Sachs disease and other disorders.

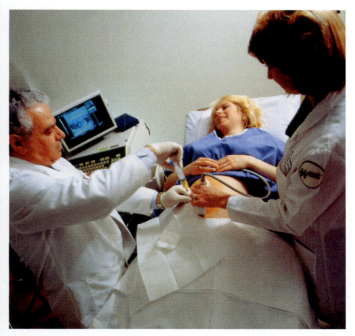

Amniocentesis. In amniocentesis, a physician extracts a sample of amniotic fluid to test for biochemical and chromosomal abnormalities. Here the physician uses ultrasound to determine the location of the fetus to help prevent accidental injury to it while placing the syringe in the mother's abdomen.

In the future, it may be possible to control the effects of defective genes during prenatal development. Today, however, expectant couples who are informed that their unborn children are genetically defective grapple with the often agonizing decision about whether or not to have an abortion. The question of abortion in such cases raises painful moral and personal dilemmas, not only for the affected families but for society at large.

Prenatal Factors   Some cases of mental retardation are caused by maternal infections or substance abuse during pregnancy. Rubella (German measles) in the mother, for example, can be passed along to the unborn child, causing brain damage that results in retardation and possibly playing a role in autism. Although the mother may experience mild symptoms or none at all, the effects on the fetus can be tragic. Other maternal diseases that may cause retardation in the child include syphilis, **cytomegalovirus,** and genital herpes.

Widespread programs that immunize women against rubella before pregnancy and tests for syphillis during pregnancy have reduced the risk of transmission of these infections to children. Most children who contract genital herpes from their mothers do so during delivery by coming into contact with the herpes simplex virus that causes the disease in the birth canal. Caesarean sections (C-sections) reduce the risk of the baby's coming into contact with the virus during outbreaks.

Drugs that the mother ingests during pregnancy may pass through the placenta to the child. Some can cause severe birth deformities and mental retardation. Children whose mothers drink alcohol during pregnancy are often born with fetal alcohol syndrome (described in Chapter 9), which is characterized by mental retardation and various physical abnormalities, such as a flattened nose, widely separated eyes, reduced head size, and lower than average height and weight. FAS is among the most prominent causes of mental retardation. Maternal smoking during pregnancy has also been linked to the development of attention deficit hyperactivity disorder in children (Milberger et al., 1996).

TRUTH or FICTION REVISITED

13.2 *True.*   Maternal smoking during pregnancy is associated with an increased risk of ADHD in children.

Birth complications, such as oxygen deprivation or head injuries, place children at increased risk for neurological disorders, including mental retardation. Prematurity also places children at risk of retardation and other developmental problems. Brain infections, such as encephalitis and meningitis, or traumas during infancy and early childhood can cause mental retardation and other health problems. Children who ingest toxins, such as paint chips containing lead, may also suffer brain damage that produces mental retardation.

Cultural-Familial Causes   Most cases of mental retardation fall in the mild range of severity. In most of these cases, there is no apparent biological cause or distinguishing physical feature that sets these children apart from other children. Psychosocial factors such as an impoverished home or social environment that is intellectually unstimulating, or parental neglect or abuse, may play a causal or contributing role in the development of mental retardation in such children. Supporting a family linkage is evidence from a study in Atlanta in which mothers who failed to finish high school were four times more likely than better educated mothers to have children with mild retardation (Drews et al., 1995).

In these cases, retardation is considered to be **cultural-familial.** Children in impoverished families may lack toys, books, or opportunities to interact with adults in intellectually stimulating ways. Consequently, they may fail to develop appropriate language skills or they become unmotivated to learn the skills that are valued in contemporary society. Economic burdens, such as the need to hold multiple jobs, may prevent their parents from spending time reading to them, talking to them at length, and exposing them to creative play or trips to museums and parks. They may spend most of their days glued to the TV set. The parents, most of whom were also reared in poverty, may lack the reading or communication skills to help shape the development of these skills in their children. A vicious cycle of poverty and impoverished intellectual development may be repeated from generation to generation.

Children with this form of retardation may respond dramatically when provided with enriched learning experiences, especially at the earlier ages. Social programs such as Head Start have helped children at risk of cultural-familial retardation to function within the normal range of ability (e.g., Barnett & Escobar, 1990).

Intervention   The services that children with mental retardation require to meet the developmental challenges they face depend in part on the level of severity and type of retardation (Dykens & Hodapp, 1997; Snell, 1997). With appropriate training, children with mild retardation may approach a sixth-grade level of competence. They can acquire vocational skills that allow them to support themselves at a basic level through meaningful work. Many such children can be mainstreamed in regular classes. At the other extreme, children with more severe or profound mental retardation may need institutional care or placement in a residential care facility in the community, such as a group home. Placement in an institution is often based on the need to control destructive or aggressive behavior, not because of severity of the individual's intellectual impairment. Consider the case of a child with moderate retardation:

The mother pleaded with the emergency room physician to admit her 15-year-old son, claiming that she couldn't take it anymore. Her son, a Down syndrome patient with an IQ of 45, had alternated since the age of 8 between living in institutions and at home. Each visiting

day he pleaded with his mother to take him home, and after about a year at each placement, she would bring him home but find herself unable to control his behavior. During temper tantrums, he would break dishes and destroy furniture and had recently become physically assaultive toward his mother, hitting her on the arm and shoulder during a recent scuffle when she attempted to stop him from repeatedly banging a broom on the floor.

ADAPTED FROM SPITZER ET AL., 1989, PP. 338–340

In 1975, Congress passed the Education for All Handicapped Children Act, Public Law 94-142, which required public schools to provide children with handicapping conditions free public education appropriate to their needs. PL 94-142 was an impetus for a massive increase in special education programs for children with mental retardation and other handicapping conditions such as physical disability. To ensure the appropriateness of the educational experience, school officials must adapt the educational program to the needs of the individual child. This often involves a multidisciplinary approach, in which professionals from different disciplines evaluate the child and recommend services and training experiences that are suited to the child's special needs. Some communities, however, have been slow to conform with the law because Congress has not appropriated the funds needed to ensure compliance. Local governments may be unwilling to raise taxes to pay for special education services.

Controversy remains concerning whether children with mental retardation should be mainstreamed in regular classes or placed in special education classes. Although some children with mild retardation may achieve better when they are mainstreamed, others may not do so well in regular classes. They may find them to be overwhelming and withdraw from their schoolmates. There has also been a trend toward deinstitutionalization of people with more severe mental retardation, a policy shift motivated in large part by public outrage over the appalling conditions that existed in many institutions serving this population. The Developmentally Disabled Assistance and Bill of Rights Act, which Congress passed in 1975, provided that persons with mental retardation have the right to receive appropriate treatment in the least restrictive treatment setting. Nationwide, the population of institutions for people with mental retardation shrunk by nearly two thirds from the 1970s to the 1990s.

People with mental retardation who are capable of functioning in the community have the right to receive less restrictive care than is provided in large institutions. Many are capable of living outside the institution and have been placed in supervised group homes. Residents typically share household responsibilities and are encouraged to participate in meaningful daily activities, such as training programs or sheltered workshops. Others live with their families and attend structured day programs. Adults with mild retardation often work in outside jobs and live in their own apartments

Imparting Skills. In 1975, Congress enacted legislation that requires public schools to provide children with disabilities with educational programs that meet their individual needs.

or share apartments with other persons with mild retardation. Although the large-scale dumping of mental patients in the community from psychiatric institutions resulted in massive social problems and swelled the ranks of America's homeless population (see Chapter 3), deinstitutionalization of people with mental retardation has largely been a success story that has been achieved with rare dignity (Winerip, 1991).

Children and adults with mental retardation may need psychological counseling to help them adjust to life in the community. Many have difficulty making friends and may become socially isolated. Problems with self-esteem are also common, especially because people who have mental retardation are often demeaned and ridiculed. Supportive counseling may be supplemented with behavioral techniques that help them acquire skills in areas such as hygiene, work, and social relationships.

Behavioral approaches can be used to teach basic hygienic behaviors such as toothbrushing, self-dressing, and hair-combing. In the example of toothbrushing, the therapist might first define the component parts of the targeted behavior (for example, picking up the toothbrush, wetting the toothbrush, taking the cap off the tube, putting the paste on the brush, etc.) (Kissel, Whitman, & Reid, 1983). The therapist might then shape the desired behavior by using such techniques as *verbal instruction* (for example, "Jim, pick up the toothbrush"); *physical guidance* (physically guiding the client's hand in performing the desired response); and *reward* (use of positive verbal reinforcement) for successful completion of the desired response ("That's really good, Jim"). Such behavioral techniques have been shown to be effective in teaching a simple but remunerative vocational

skill (that is, stamping return addresses on envelopes) to a group of adult women with such severe mental retardation that they were essentially nonverbal (Schepis, Reid, & Fitzgerald, 1987). These techniques may also help people with severe mental retardation develop adaptive capacities that can enable them to perform more productive roles.

Other behavioral treatment techniques include social skills training, which focuses on increasing the individual's ability to relate effectively to others, and anger management training to help individuals develop more effective ways of handling conflicts without aggressive acting out (W. Huang & Cuvo, 1997; C. M. Nezu & Nezu, 1994; Rose, 1996). Punishment, which typically involve the use of *time-out* procedures (the temporary removal from reinforcing environments) or *aversives* (e.g., mildly painful stimuli, such as brief electric shocks), are used to control aggressive or destructive behavior in some settings, especially on inpatient units. The use of aversives is controversial and the subject of an ongoing debate within the field, as it is in the field of autism (Spreat & Behar, 1994). Social skills training may also be used to increase conversational skills and job interviewing skills.

Children with mental retardation stand perhaps a three to four times greater chance of developing other psychological disorders, such as attention-deficit-hyperactivity disorder (ADHD), depression, or anxiety disorders (Borthwick-Duffy, 1994). As many as 3 of 4 boys with fragile X syndrome, for example, develop ADHD (Matson & Sevin, 1994). Mental health professionals have been slow to recognize the prevalence of mental health problems among people with mental retardation, perhaps because of a long-held conceptual distinction between emotional impairment on the one hand and intellectual deficits on the other (Ollendick &

A CLOSER LOOK

Savant Syndrome

Got a minute? Try the following:

1. Without referring to a calendar, calculate the day of the week that March 15, 2079, will fall on.

2. List the prime numbers between 1 and 1 billion. (Hint: the list starts 1, 2, 3, 5, 7, 11, 13, 17 . . .)

3. Repeat verbatim the newspaper stories you read over coffee this morning.

4. Sing accurately every note played by the first violin in Beethoven's Ninth Symphony.

These tasks are impossible for all but a very few. Ironically, people who are most likely to be able to accomplish these feats suffer from autism, mental retardation, or both. Such a person is commonly called an *idiot savant.* The term savant is derived from the French *savoir,* meaning "to know." The label *savant syndrome* is preferable to the pejorative term *idiot savant,* in referring to someone with severe mental deficiencies who possesses some remarkable mental abilities. The prevalence of the savant syndrome among people with mental retardation is estimated at about .06%, or about 1 case in 2,000 (A. L. Hill, 1977). Prevalence rates are reported to be higher among autistic populations. Most people with savant syndrome, like most people with autism, are male (Treffert, 1988). Among a sample of 5,400 people with autism, 531 cases (9.8%) were reported by parents to have the savant syndrome (Rimland, 1978). Because they want to think of their children as special, however, parents might overreport the incidence of the savant syndrome.

Several hundred people with the savant syndrome have been described in this century. They are reported to have shown remarkable but circumscribed mental skills, such as calendar calculating, rare musical talent, even accomplished poetry (Dowker, Hermelin, & Pring, 1996)—all of which stand in contrast to their limited general intellectual abilities. People with the savant syndrome also have outstanding memories. Just as we learn about health by studying illness, we may be able to learn more about normal mechanisms of memory by studying people in whom memory stands apart from other aspects of mental functioning (e.g., S. J. Kelly, Macaruso, & Sokol, 1997).

The savant syndrome phenomenon occurs more frequently in males by a ratio of about 6 to 1. The spe-

cial skills of people with the savant syndrome tend to appear out of the blue and may disappear as suddenly. Some people with the syndrome engage in lightning calculations. A 19th-century enslaved person in Virginia, Thomas Fuller, "was able to calculate the number of seconds in 70 years, 17 days, and 12 hours in a minute and one half, taking into account the 17 leap years that would have occurred in the period" (S. C. Smith, 1983). There are also cases of persons with the syndrome who were also blind but could play back any musical piece, no matter how complex, or repeat long passages of foreign languages without losing a syllable. Some people with the syndrome make exact estimates of elapsed time. One could reportedly repeat verbatim the contents of a newspaper he had just heard; another could repeat backward what he had just read (Tradgold, 1914, cited in Treffert, 1988).

TRUTH *or* **FICTION** REVISITED

13.3 *True.* Ability to recall news stories verbatim is found in some individuals with the savant syndrome.

Various theories have been presented to explain the savant syndrome (Treffert, 1988). Some believe that children with the savant syndrome have unusually well-developed memories, which allow them to record and scan vast amounts of information. It has been suggested that people with the savant syndrome may inherit two sets of hereditary factors, one for retardation and the other for special abilities. Perhaps it is coincidental that their special abilities and their mental handicaps were inherited in common. Other theorists suggest that the left and right hemispheres of their cerebral cortexes are organized in an unusual way. This latter belief is supported by research suggesting that the special abilities they possess often involve skills associated with right hemisphere functioning. Still other theorists suggest they learn special skills to compensate for their lack of more general skills, perhaps as a means of coping with their environment, or perhaps as a means of earning social reinforcements. Perhaps their skills in concrete functions, such as calculation, compensate for their lack of abstract thinking ability. Linguists such as Noam Chomsky theorize that people are neurologically "prewired" to grasp the deep structure that underlies all human languages. Perhaps, as the neurologist Oliver

CHAPTER 13

Savant syndrome. Dustin Hoffman (left) won the Oscar for best actor for his portrayal in the film *Rainman* of a man with autism who showed a remarkable capacity for numerical calculation. Tom Cruise (right) played his brother. Hoffman was able to capture the sense of emotional detachment and isolation of his character.

Sacks speculates, the brain circuits of some people with the savant syndrome are wired with a "deep arithmetic"—an innate structure for perceiving mathematical relationships that is analogous to the prewiring that allows people to perceive and produce language. Another speculation attributes the savant syndrome to prolonged periods of sensory deprivation. A barren social environment could have prompted concentration on "trivial" pursuits—for example, memorizing obscure facts or learning calendar calculating. Among people with the savant syndrome who are blind or deaf, sensory deprivation takes on a literal meaning. Among people with autism, attending to minute details may derive from their inability to focus on stimuli beyond an extremely narrow range. Yet many individuals with the savant syndrome do not have sensory disabilities and were not socially deprived; they were reared in stimulus-rich environments.

Recent research has pointed to possible gender-linked left hemisphere damage occurring prenatally or congenitally. Compensatory right hemisphere development might then take place, establishing specialized brain circuitry that processes concrete and narrowly defined kinds of information (Treffert, 1988). An environment that reinforces savant abilities and provides opportunities for practice and concentration would give further impetus to the development of these unusual abilities. Still the savant syndrome remains a mystery.

Ollendick, 1982; A. M. Nezu, 1994). Many professionals even assumed (wrongly) that people with mental retardation were worry free and somehow immune from psychological problems (Nezu, 1994). Given these commonly held beliefs, it is perhaps not surprising that many of the psychological problems of people with mental retardation have gone unrecognized and untreated (Reiss & Valenti-Hein, 1994).

LEARNING DISORDERS

Nelson Rockefeller served as governor of New York State and as vice president of the United States. He was brilliant and well educated. However, despite the best of tutors, he always had trouble reading. Rockefeller suffered from **dyslexia,** which derives from the Greek roots *dys-,* meaning "bad," and *lexikon,* meaning "of words." Dyslexia is the most common type of **learning disorder** (also called a *learning disability*) (Shaywitz, 1998). It accounts for perhaps 80% of cases of learning disability. Mental retardation involves a general delay in intellectual development. People with learning disorders, by contrast, may be generally intelligent, even gifted, but show inadequate development in reading, math, or writing skills that impairs school performance or daily activities.

About 5% of children in U.S. public schools are identified as having a learning disorder (APA, 1994). Learning disorders tend to run a chronic course. The more severe the problem is in childhood, the more likely it is to affect adult development (Spreen, 1988). Children with learning disorders tend to perform poorly in school. They are often viewed as failures by their teachers and their families. It is not surprising that most of them develop low expectations and problems in self-esteem by the age of 9. Moreover, their academic and personal problems tend to worsen as time passes (Wenar, 1983).

Authorities do not all agree on the definition of learning disorders. One approach considers children to have a learning disorder if they perform at two grade levels or more below their age levels or grade levels (Morris, 1988). However, children advance more rapidly at younger ages, so a second grader performing at a kindergarten level is relatively more deficient than an eighth grader performing at a sixth grade level. A specific cutoff point, such as the 2-year discrepancy, seems arbitrary. A second approach considers children to have a learning disorder when they underperform on standardized tests of specific academic skills in relation to what children of comparable intelligence achieve. The intelligence-achievement gap is the criterion suggested in the DSM. Recent evidence, however, challenges the validity of the achievement-IQ discrepancy for defining learning disability (Fletcher et al., 1994; Stanovich & Siegel, 1994).

Some authorities limit the diagnosis of learning disorder to children who are "at least average" in intelligence, so as to more clearly distinguish learning disorders from mental retardation. However, there is no universally accepted standard for determining what is meant by "at least average" (Morris, 1988). Sometimes an IQ score of 90 is used as the lower boundary of average intelligence. In other cases, IQ scores as low as 70 are considered low average as opposed to mentally retarded. Some authorities believe that even children whose IQ scores fall within the retarded range may be considered to have a learning disorder if their achievement on tests of academic skills does not keep pace with that of children of comparable potential.

An act of Congress, the Congressional Education for All Handicapped Children Act of 1975, drew a distinction among learning disorders and learning problems that stem from causes such as mental retardation; emotional disorders; perceptual or motor handicaps; and cultural, economic, or environmental disadvantage. The exclusion of learning problems that might be attributable to such environmental causes as cultural or economic disadvantage from the purview of learning disorders has drawn fire on political and scientific grounds. It has been argued, for example, that attributing the disproportionately high incidence of academic failures among poor children to impoverished environments, as opposed to potentially treatable learning disorders, is tantamount to expecting them to fail (Morris, 1988). The underlying message to the child—and the child's school system—seems to be: Why bother to make special efforts to help them succeed in school? Refusal to accept failure from poor children, on the other hand, might encourage them—and their teachers—to do everything they can to remediate specific deficits in learning.

Types of Learning Disorders

There are several types of learning disorders, including *mathematics disorder, disorder of written expression,* and *reading disorder.*

Mathematics Disorder   Children with deficiencies in arithmetic skills are said to have *mathematics disorder.* They may have problems understanding basic mathematical terms or operations, such as addition or subtraction; decoding mathematical symbols (+, = etc.); or learning multiplication tables. The problem may become apparent as early as the first grade (age 6) but is not generally recognized until about the third grade (age 8).

Disorder of Written Expression   *Disorder of written expression* is the problem of children with grossly deficient writing skills. The impairment may be characterized by errors in spelling, grammar, or punctuation, or by difficulty in composing sentences and paragraphs. Severe writing difficulties generally become apparent by age 7 (second grade), although milder cases may not be recognized until the age of 10 (fifth grade) or later.

Reading Disorder   Reading disorder—*dyslexia*—characterizes children who have poorly developed skills in recognizing words and comprehending written text. Dyslexia is believed to affect 4% to 5% of the U.S. population—about 12 million people (Blakeslee, 1991). Children with dyslexia may read laboriously and distort, omit, or substitute words when reading aloud. They may have trouble decoding letters. They may perceive letters upside down (*w* for *m*) or in reversed images (*b* for *d*). Dyslexia is usually apparent by the age of 7, coinciding with the second grade, although it is sometimes recognized in 6-year-olds. Though it was earlier believed that the problem affected mostly boys, more recent studies find similar rates between boys and girls (Shaywitz, 1998). Among children with reading disorder, boys are more likely than girls to exhibit disruptive behavior as an accompanying feature of the disability and so are more likely to be referred for evaluation. More careful diagnostic surveys find more similar rates of the disorder in boys and girls (APA, 1994). Children and adolescents with dyslexia tend to be more prone to depression, to have lower self-worth and feelings of competence in their academic work, and to have signs of attention-deficit hyperactivity disorder than do their peers (Boetsch, Green, & Pennington, 1996).

Theoretical Perspectives

Hypotheses of the origins of learning disorders tend to focus on cognitive-perceptual problems and possible underlying neurological factors. Many children with learning disorders have problems with visual or auditory perception. They may lack the capacity to copy words or to discriminate geometric shapes. Other children have short attention spans or show hyperactivity, which may also be suggestive of an underlying brain abnormality.

Much of the research on learning disorders has focused on dyslexia. Though no one can say with certainty what causes dyslexia, evidence is mounting that points to one or more abnormalities in the brain. One line of research has identified defective brain circuitry involved in reading (Shaywitz et al., 1998). This abnormality makes it difficult to break down written words into their component sounds

Dyslexia. Children with dyslexia have difficulty decoding words. Note the reversal of the letters *w* and *l* in the word *owl* in this picture of a girl with dyslexia completing a writing exercise.

(Shaywitz, 1998). Another line of research implicates brain abnormalities involving the senses of vision, hearing, and touch (Blakeslee, 1991). There is evidence of impaired visual processing in people with dyslexia that would be consistent with a defect in a major visual relay station in the brain involved in sequencing the flow of visual information from the retina to the visual cortex of the brain (Livingstone et al., 1991). Inspection of the autopsied brains of people who had dyslexia showed this relay station was smaller and less well organized than that in other people. As a result, the brains of people with dyslexia may not be able to decipher a rapid succession of visual stimuli, such as those involved in decoding letters and words. Words may thus become blurry, fuse together, or seem to jump off the page—problems reported by people with dyslexia (Blakeslee, 1991). Dysfunctions in other sensory pathways involving the sense of hearing and even the sense of touch may also be involved in learning disorders.

Recent research suggests that some forms of dyslexia may be traceable to an abnormality in the brain circuits responsible for processing rapidly flowing auditory information (Blakeslee, 1994b). This flaw in brain circuitry may make it difficult to understand rapidly occurring speech sounds, such as the sounds corresponding to the letters "b" and "p" in syllables like "ba" and "pa." Problems discerning the differences between many basic speech sounds can make it difficult for people with dyslexia to learn to speak correctly and later, perhaps, to learn to read. They continue to have problems distinguishing in rapid speech between words like "boy" and "toy" or "pet" and "bet." If defects in brain circuitry responsible for the relaying and processing of sensory data are involved in learning disorders, as the evidence now suggests, this may lead the way to the development of specialized treatment programs to help children adjust to their sensory capabilities.

Genetic factors appear to be involved in brain abnormalities associated with dyslexia (Shaywitz, 1998; Wingert & Kantrowitz, 1997). People whose parents have dyslexia are at greater risk themselves (see Figure 13.2) (Vogler, De-Fries, & Dekker, 1985). Moreover, higher rates of concordance (agreement) for dyslexia are found between identical (MZ) than fraternal (DZ) twins, 70% vs. 40%, respectively (Plomin, Owen, & McGuffin, 1994). Suspicion has focused on the role that particular genes may play in causing subtle defects in brain circuitry involved in reading.

Researchers suspect that one of the genes responsible for the disorder may be located on a region of a chromosome that contains the genes that control the development of the immune system (Blakeslee, 1994c; "U.K. researchers say dyslexia is hereditary," 1998). This may explain the unusually high incidence of autoimmune diseases, such as rheumatoid arthritis, ulcerative colitis, and asthma, in people with dyslexia. Autoimmune diseases involve a breakdown in the body's regulation of the immune system. We also find a higher than average frequency of reading problems in students with immune disorders (Tonnessen et al., 1994). Because not all people with dyslexia have an increased risk of

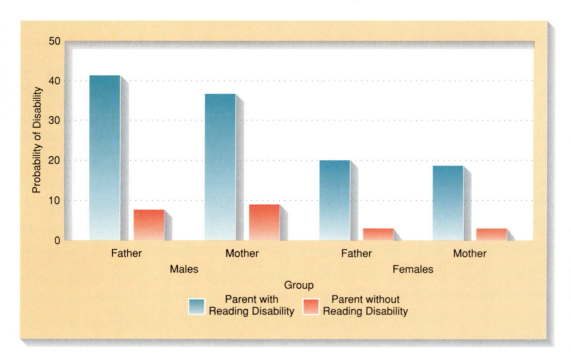

FIGURE 13.2 *Familial risk of developmental reading disorder (Dyslexia).* Boys are at greater risk than girls of developing dyslexia, and children of both genders whose parents with dyslexia are at relatively greater risk. Although these data are consistent with a genetic explanation of the etiology of dyslexia, it is also possible that parents with dyslexia do not provide their children with the types of stimulation such as books and reading bedtime stories that foster reading skills.

Source: Adapted from Vogler et al. (1985).

immune disorders, the genetic linkage may apply only to a particular subtype of dyslexia. Other genes may be involved in other forms of the disorder.

Intervention

Interventions for learning disorders have generally been approached from the following perspectives (Lyon & Moats, 1988):

1. *The psychoeducational model.* Psychoeducational approaches emphasize children's strengths and preferences, rather than attempt to correct assumed underlying deficiencies. For example, a child who retains auditory information better than visual information might be taught verbally, for example using tape recordings, rather than by using written materials.

2. *The behavioral model.* The behavioral model assumes that academic learning is built on a hierarchy of basic skills, or "enabling behaviors." In order to read effectively, one must first learn to recognize letters, then attach sounds to letters, then combine letters and sounds into words, and so on. The child's learning competencies are assessed to determine where deficiencies lie in the hierarchy of skills. An individualized program of instruction and reinforcement helps the child acquire the skills to perform academic tasks.

3. *The medical model.* This model assumes that learning disorders are symptoms of biologically based deficiencies in cognitive processing. Proponents suggest that remediation should be directed at the underlying pathology rather than the learning disability. If the child has a visual defect that makes it difficult to follow a line of text, treatment should aim to remediate the visual deficit, perhaps through visual-tracking exercises. Improvement in reading ability would be expected to follow.

4. *The neuropsychological model.* This approach borrows from the psychoeducational and medical models. It assumes that learning disorders reflect underlying biologically based deficits in processing information (medical model). It also assumes that remediation should be academic in focus (psychoeducational). Subject matter should be adapted to bypass inefficient brain regions and appeal to more efficient or intact neural systems.

5. *The linguistic model.* The linguistic approach focuses on children's basic language deficiencies, such as failing to recognize how sounds and words are strung together to create meaning, which can give rise to problems in reading, spelling, and finding the words to express themselves. Adherents to this model teach language skills sequentially, helping the student grasp the structure and use of words (Shaywitz, 1998; R. K. Wagner & Torgesen, 1987).

6. *The cognitive model.* This model focuses on how children organize their thoughts when they learn academic material. Within this perspective, children are helped to learn by (1) recognizing the nature of the learning task, (2) applying effective problem-solving strategies to complete tasks, and (3) monitoring the success of their strategies. Children with arithmetic problems might be guided to break down a math problem into its component tasks, think through the steps necessary to complete each task, and evaluate their performance at each step to judge how to proceed. Children are shown a systematic approach to problem solving that can be applied to diverse academic tasks.

Evaluation The medical model is currently limited by lack of evidence that underlying deficiencies are correctable or that such improvements foster academic skills (Hinshaw, 1992; Lyon & Moats, 1988). There is also a lack of evidence for the psychoeducational approach (S. Brady, 1986; Lyon &

Moats, 1988). Although the neuropsychological approach has not yet been fully tested, interventions focused on changing the child's learning strategies in order to circumvent apparent underlying neuropsychological deficits have thus far failed to demonstrate significant gains in children with severe forms of learning disability (Hinshaw, 1992). The interventions showing the most promising results to date are those that provide direct instruction in the academic skills in which the child is deficient, such as oral and written language skills (Hinshaw, 1992). The behavioral model has also shown some promising results toward improving performance of children who are deficient in reading and arithmetic skills (Koorland, 1986). Whether the gains from behavioral training generalize to classroom performance beyond the training setting remains to be seen. The linguistic approach has received some support, but not enough to advocate widespread use in treating children with reading and spelling deficiencies (Lyon & Moats, 1988). The cognitive model, too, has received some support, but many children with learning disorders have not developed enough basic knowledge in their problem areas to use it to think through problems (Lyon & Moats, 1988).

Many children who have learning disorders are placed in special education programs or classes. Yet programs for learning-disabled children vary widely in quality, and we still lack firm evidence demonstrating their long-term effectiveness (Hinshaw, 1992; Wingert & Kantrowitz, 1997).

COMMUNICATION DISORDERS

Communication disorders involve difficulties in understanding or using language. The category of communication disorders includes *expressive language disorder, mixed receptive/expressive language disorder, phonological disorder,* and *stuttering.* Each of these disorders interferes with academic or occupational functioning or ability to communicate socially. Table 13.4 contains a listing of the *DSM-IV* classification of learning disorders and communication disorders.

Expressive language disorder involves impairment in the use of spoken language, such as slow vocabulary development, errors in tense, difficulties recalling words, and problems producing sentences of appropriate length and complexity for the individual's age. Affected children may also have a phonological (articulation) disorder, compounding their speech problems.

Mixed receptive/expressive language disorder refers to children who have difficulties both understanding and producing speech. There may be difficulty understanding words or sentences. In some cases, children have difficulty understanding certain word types (such as words expressing differences in quantity—*large, big,* or *huge*), spatial terms (such as *near* or *far*), or sentence types (such as sentences that begin with the word *unlike*). Other cases are marked by difficulties understanding simple words or sentences.

Phonological disorder involves difficulties in articulating the sounds of speech in the absence of defects in the oral speech mechanism or neurological impairment. Children with the disorder may omit, substitute, or mispronounce certain sounds—especially *ch, f, l, r, sh* and *th* sounds, which are usually articulated properly by the early school years. It may sound as if they are uttering "baby talk." In more severe cases, there are problems articulating sounds usually mastered during the preschool years: *b, m, t, d, n,* and *h.* Speech therapy is often helpful, and milder cases often resolve themselves by the age of 8.

Stuttering involves disturbances in the ability to speak fluently with appropriate timing of speech sounds. The lack of normal fluency must be inappropriate for the person's age in order to justify the diagnosis. Stuttering usually begins between 2 and 7 years of age and affects about 1 child in 100 before puberty (APA, 1994). The disorder is characterized by one or more of the following characteristics: (1) repetitions of sounds and syllables; (2) prolongations of certain sounds; (3) interjections of inappropriate sounds; (4) broken words, such as pauses occurring within a spoken word; (5) blocking of speech; (6) circumlocutions (substitutions of alternative words to avoid problematic words); (7) displaying an excess of physical tension when emitting words; and (8) repetitions of monosyllabic whole words (for example, "I-I-I-I am glad to meet you.") (APA, 1994). Stuttering occurs predominantly among males by a ratio of about 3 to 1. Stuttering remits in upward of 80% of children, typically before age 16. As many as 60% of cases show remission without any treatment. Stuttering is believed to involve an

TABLE 13.4

DSM-IV Classification of Learning Disorders and Communication Disorders

Learning Disorders	Reading Disorder
	Mathematics Disorder
	Disorder of Written Expression
Communication Disorders	Expressive Language Disorder
	Mixed Receptive/Expressive Language Disorder
	Phonological Disorder
	Stuttering

Source: Adapted from the *DSM-IV* (APA, 1994).

interaction of genetic and environmental factors (Felsenfeld, 1996; Yairi, Ambrose; & Cox, 1996). Underlying social anxiety or social phobias maybe involved in some cases, at least among adults with stuttering problems (De-Carle & Pato, 1996; Schneier, Wexler, & Liebowitz, 1997; M. B. Stein, Baird, & Walker, 1996).

ATTENTION-DEFICIT AND DISRUPTIVE BEHAVIOR DISORDERS

The category of *attention-deficit and disruptive behavior disorders* refers to a diverse range of problem behaviors, including *attention-deficit/hyperactivity disorder* (ADHD), *conduct disorder* (CD), and *oppositional defiant disorder* (ODD). These disorders are socially disruptive and usually more upsetting to other people than to the children who receive these diagnoses. Although there are differences among these disorders, the rate of comorbidity (co-occurrence) among these disorders is very high (Jensen, Martin, & Cantwell, 1997).

Attention-Deficit/Hyperactivity Disorder

Many parents believe their children are not attentive toward them—that they run around on whim and do things in their own way. Some inattention, especially in early childhood, is normal enough. In **attention-deficit/hyperactivity disorder** (ADHD), however, children display impulsivity, inattention, and **hyperactivity** that are considered inappropriate to their developmental levels.

ADHD is divided into three subtypes: a predominantly inattentive type, a predominantly hyperactive or impulsive type, or a combination type characterized by high levels of both inattention and hyperactivity-impulsivity (APA, 1994). The disorder is usually first diagnosed during elementary school, when problems with attention or hyperactivity-impulsivity make it difficult for the child to adjust to school. Although signs of hyperactivity are often observed earlier, many overactive toddlers do not go on to develop ADHD.

ADHD is far from rare. An estimated 2 million American children have ADHD, making it the nation's leading childhood psychiatric disorder (Hancock, 1996). The disorder is believed to affect 3% to 6% of schoolage children (elementary through high school) (Goldman et al., 1998; J. C. Hill & Schoener, 1996). Boys are 3 to 9 times more likely than girls to be identified as having ADHD (Angier, 1991b). Although inattention appears to be the basic problem, there are associated problems such as inability to sit still for more than a few moments, bullying, temper tantrums, stubbornness, and failure to respond to punishment (see Table 13.5).

Activity and restlessness impair the ability of children with ADHD to function in school. They seem incapable of sitting still. They fidget and squirm in their seats, butt into other children's games, have outbursts of temper, and may engage in dangerous behavior, such as running into the street without looking. All in all, they can drive parents and teachers to despair.

Where does "normal" age-appropriate overactivity end and hyperactivity begin? Assessment of the degree of hyperactive behavior is crucial because many normal children are called "hyper" from time to time. Some critics of the ADHD

TABLE 13.5

Diagnostic Features of Attention-Deficit-Hyperactivity Disorder (ADHD)

Kind of Problem	Specific Behavior Pattern
Lack of attention	Fails to attend to details or makes careless errors in schoolwork, etc. Has difficulty sustaining attention in schoolwork or play Doesn't appear to pay attention to what is being said Fails to follow through on instructions or to finish work Has trouble organizing work and other activities Avoids work or activities that require sustained attention Loses work tools (e.g., pencils, books, assignments, toys) Becomes readily distracted Forgetful in daily activities
Hyperactivity	Fidgets with hands or feet or squirms in his or her seat Leaves seat in situations such as the classroom in which remaining seated is required Is constantly running around or climbing on things Has difficulty playing quietly
Impulsivity	Frequently "calls out" in class Fails to wait his/her turn in line, games, etc.

In order to receive a diagnosis of ADHD, the disorder must begin by the age of 7; must have significantly impaired academic, social, or occupational functioning; and must be characterized by a designated number of clinical features shown in this table occurring over a 6-month period in at least two settings such as at school, at home, or at work.

Source: Adapted from the *DSM-IV* (APA, 1994).

diagnosis argue that it merely labels children who are difficult to control as mentally disordered or sick. Most children, especially boys, are highly active during the early school years. Proponents of the diagnosis counter that there is a difference in quality between normal overactivity and ADHD. Normally overactive children are usually goal directed and can exert voluntary control over their own behavior. But children with ADHD appear hyperactive without reason and do not seem to be able to conform their own behavior to the demands of teachers and parents. Put it another way: Most children can sit still and concentrate for a while when they want to do so; children who are hyperactive seemingly cannot.

Children with ADHD tend to do more poorly in school than their peers. They may fail to follow or remember instructions or complete assignments. They are more likely to have learning disabilities, to repeat grades, and to be placed in special education classes (Faraone et al., 1993). They also stand a greater risk than their peers of having mood disorders, anxiety disorders, and problems getting along with family members (Biederman et al., 1996). Although they tend to be of average or above average intelligence, they often underachieve in school. They are frequently disruptive in the classroom and tend to get into fights (especially the boys). Not surprisingly, they tend to be unpopular with their classmates. Though ADHD symptoms tend to decline with age, the disorder often persists into adolescence and adulthood (Downey et al., 1997; Goldman et al., 1998; J. C. Hill & Schoener, 1997; Roy-Byrne et al., 1997). Children with ADHD are more likely than their peers to go on to become delinquents, be suspended from school, and to require continued interventions during adolescence (N. M. Lambert, Hartsough, Sassone, & Sandoval, 1987) (see Figure 13.3).

Continued problems with maintaining attention or feelings of restlessness in adulthood may make it difficult to work at a desk job or participate in sedentary activities. An estimated 0.8% (8 in 1,000) of 20-year-olds and 0.05% (5 in 10,000) 40-year-olds are believed to have ADHD (Hill & Schoener, 1996). Still, many adults who were diagnosed with ADHD in childhood show no evidence of impaired social, academic, or occupational functioning.

Theoretical Perspectives Although the causes of ADHD are not known, both environmental and biological influences are believed involved (Arnold, O'Leary, & Edward, 1997; L. J. Seidman et al., 1997). Skills in handling children's misbehavior, marital conflict, parental stress, and father involvement are examples of environmental factors that may play a part in the development of ADHD.

Neuropsychological testing, EEG studies, and MRI studies point to possible subtle brain abnormalities in some children and adolescents with ADHD (Castellanos et al., 1996; Chabot & Serfontein, 1996; Seidman et al., 1997). EEG tests point to possible abnormalities in areas of the brain involved in regulating processes of attention, arousal, and communication between the left and right hemispheres (Chabot & Serfontein, 1996).

Increasing evidence points to a significant genetic component in ADHD (F. Levy et al., 1997). Relatives of both boys and girls with attention-deficit disorder also have an increased prevalence of the disorder themselves, which is suggestive of a familial mode of transmission, possibly genetic in origin (LaHoste et al., 1996). Stronger evidence comes from findings of higher concordance rates for ADHD among monozygotic (MZ) twins than DZ (dizygotic) twins, supporting a genetic linkage (Sherman et al., 1997). Mothers of children with ADHD often had difficult pregnancies,

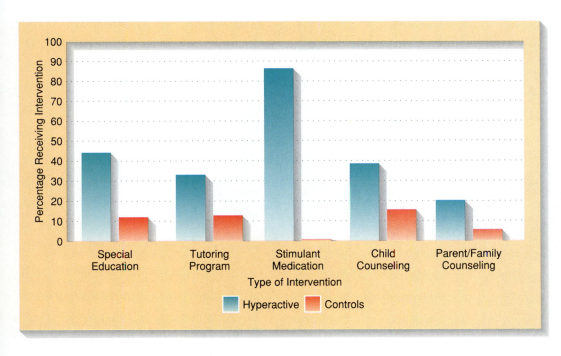

FIGURE 13.3 *Interventions received by adolescents who were earlier diagnosed as hyperactive.* Adolescents who were diagnosed as hyperactive during childhood were more likely than other adolescents to receive the kinds of interventions shown in this figure.

Source: Adapted from Lambert et al. (1987).

which is suggestive of prenatal influences. Children who have ADHD are also more likely than other children to have mothers who abused alcohol or other drugs, or smoked during pregnancy, which may have resulted in developmental defects. As infants, children with ADHD were more prone to neurological disorders, such as encephalitis and seizures.

One widely held hypothesis is that the brains of children with ADHD may be less mature than those of unaffected children, which may make children with ADHD less capable of restraining impulsive behavior. Brain scans using MRI do show evidence of developmental abnormalities in the brains of many boys with ADHD (Castellanos et al., 1994). The hypothesis gains further support from the observed gender ratio of affected children because the nervous systems of boys mature more slowly than those of girls. We shall also see that the effects of stimulants on children with ADHD also offer some support to the hypothesis of organic causes. Still, despite evidence suggestive of biological factors, we lack a definitive biological explanation of ADHD.

Is sugar to blame for hyperactivity? Many parents and teachers are quick to blame sugar intake. They assume that sugar heightens children's activity levels because it provides a quick source of energy. Evidence shows that ingestion of sugar in children does increase blood levels of the hormone epinephrine, which stimulates the sympathetic nervous system and can lead to such symptoms as shakiness and sweating (T. W. Jones et al., 1995). Yet evidence from controlled studies fails to show that sugar intake has any general effects on disruptive behavior or academic performance in children, even in children with hyperactivity (Kolata, 1994a; Wolraich et al., 1994; "Study disputes link of sugar to hyperactivity," 1995). It remains possible that sugar may affect some overly sensitive children (Wolraich et al., 1994). If sugar or artificial sweeteners do have any behavioral effects on behavior at all, they are at best subtle (Kolata, 1994a). Still, the clear relationships of sugar to tooth decay, poor nutrition, and obesity argue against excessive consumption (Milich, Wolraich, & Lindgren, 1986).

Treatment   It appears paradoxical that the drugs used to help ADHD children calm down and attend better in school, which include Ritalin (methylphenidate) and Cylert (pemoline), belong to a class of stimulants. Although the use of stimulant medication is not without its critics, it is clear that these drugs can help many children with ADHD calm down and concentrate better on tasks and schoolwork, perhaps for the first times in their lives (Goldman et al., 1998; Greenhill, 1998; T. Spencer et al., 1996). These drugs not only improve attention in ADHD children, but also reduce impulsivity; overactivity; and disruptive, annoying, or aggressive behavior (Hinshaw, 1991, 1992; Klorman et al., 1994; Gillberg et al., 1997). Stimulant medication appears to be safe and effective when carefully monitored and successful in helping about 3 of 4 children with ADHD ("Attention Deficit Disorder—Part II," 1995; Hinshaw, 1991, 1992; Wolraich et al., 1990; Spencer et al., 1996). Improvements are noted at home as well as in school. The normal (voluntary) high activity levels shown in physical education classes and on weekends are not disrupted, however.

TRUTH *or* FICTION REVISITED

13.4 *False.* Children with ADHD are often given stimulant drugs such as Ritalin, not depressants. These stimulants have a paradoxical effect of calming them down and increasing their attention spans.

We do not know what accounts for the seemingly paradoxical effects of stimulants in calming children with ADHD,

Attention-deficit/hyperactivity disorder (ADHD). ADHD is more common in boys than girls and is characterized by attentional difficulties, restlessness, impulsivity, excessive motor behavior (continuous running around or climbing), and temper tantrums.

although it is suspected that these drugs work by altering levels of neurotransmitters in the brain or the sensitivity of receptors in the brain to these chemicals ("Attention Deficit Disorder—Part II," 1995). Though the precise mechanisms are not well understood, we've learned that these drugs heighten dopamine activity in the frontal lobes of the brain, the area that regulates attention and control of impulsive behavior (Hancock, 1996). Thus, the drugs may help children focus their attention and avoid acting-out impulsively (B. J. Casey et al., 1997).

Use of stimulants has achieved such widespread use that by 1995, 1 million children in the United States were taking Ritalin, more than twice as many as in 1990 (Hancock, 1996; Kolata, 1996).

Although stimulant medication can help reduce restlessness and increase attention, it is hardly a panacea. There remains no solid evidence showing that stimulant medication improves academic performance or leads to better outcomes in adulthood ("Attention Deficit Disorder—Part II," 1995; Rutter, 1997). Relapses often occur soon after the child stops taking the medication (Greenhill, 1998). As in the case of Eddie, the range of effectiveness is limited:

Nine-year-old Eddie is a problem in class. His teacher complains that he is so restless and fidgety that the rest of the class cannot concentrate on their work. He hardly ever sits still. He is in constant motion, roaming the classroom, talking to other children while they are working. He has been suspended repeatedly for outrageous behavior, most recently swinging from a fluorescent light fixture and unable to get himself down. His mother reports that Eddie has been a problem since he was a toddler. By the age of 3 he had become unbearably restless and demanding. He has never needed much sleep and always awakened before anyone else in the family, making his way downstairs and wrecking things in the living room and kitchen. Once, at the age of 4, he unlocked the front door and wandered into traffic, but was rescued by a passer by.

Psychological testing shows Eddie to be average in academic ability, but to have a "virtually nonexistent" attention span. He shows no interest in television or in games or toys that require some concentration. He is unpopular with peers and prefers to ride his bike alone or to play with his dog. He has become disobedient at home and at school and has stolen small amounts of money from his parents and classmates.

Eddie has been treated with methylphenidate (Ritalin), but it was discontinued because it had no effect on his disobedience and stealing. However, it did seem to reduce his restlessness and increase his attention span at school.

ADAPTED FROM SPITZER ET AL., 1989, PP. 315–317

Then there is the question of side effects. Although short-term side effects (e.g., loss of appetite or insomnia)

usually subside within a few weeks of treatment or may be eliminated by lowering the dose, concerns have been raised about whether stimulants might retard a child's growth. Although these drugs do slow the child's growth for a few years, researchers find no evidence that they alter eventual height (Gittelman-Klein & Mannuzza, 1990). It appears that the rate of growth in children who were treated with stimulants rebounds during adolescence ("Attention Deficit Disorder— Part II," 1995).

With so many children on Ritalin and similar drugs, critics claim that we are too ready to seek a "quick fix" for problem behavior in children rather than examine other factors contributing to the child's problem, such as problems in the family. As one pediatrician put it, "It takes time for parents and teachers to sit down and talk to kids. . . It takes less time to get a child a pill" (Hancock, 1996, p. 52). Whatever the benefits of stimulant medication, medication alone typically fails to bring the social and academic behavior of children with ADHD into a normal range (Hinshaw, 1992). Drugs cannot teach new skills. So attention has focused on whether a combination of stimulant medication and behavioral or cognitive-behavioral techniques can produce greater benefits than either approach alone. Cognitive-behavioral treatment of ADHD combines behavior modification, typically based on the use of reinforcement (for example, a teacher praising the child with ADHD for sitting quietly) and cognitive modification (for example, training the child to silently talk him or herself through the steps involved in solving academic problems). Thus far the evidence is suggestive but not conclusive in favor of the combination approach (Greenhill, 1998; Hinshaw, Klein, & Abikoff, 1998).

Conduct Disorder

Although they both involve disruptive behavior, **conduct disorder** differs in important ways from ADHD. Whereas children with ADHD seem literally incapable of controlling their behavior, children with conduct disorders purposefully engage in patterns of antisocial behavior that violate social norms and the rights of others (Hinshaw, 1987). Whereas children with ADHD throw temper tantrums, children diagnosed as conduct disordered are intentionally aggressive and cruel. Like antisocial adults, many conduct-disordered children are callous and apparently do not experience guilt or remorse for their misdeeds. They may steal or destroy property. In adolescence they may commit rape, armed robbery, even homicide. They may cheat in school— when they bother to attend—and lie to cover their tracks. They frequently engage in substance abuse and sexual activity.

Conduct disorders are much more common among boys than girls, especially the childhood-onset type in which characteristic features of the disorder appear before age 10 (APA, 1994). Conduct disorder typically takes a somewhat different form in boys than girls. In boys, conduct disorder is more likely to be manifested by stealing, fighting, vandalism, or disciplinary problems at school, whereas in girls it is more likely to involve lying, truancy, running away, substance use, and prostitution (APA, 1994).

Children with conduct disorders frequently have academic problems, such as poor reading, math, and expressive language skills, but their disorders do not prevent them from paying attention in class. Although there are differences between ADHD and conduct disorder, some children with conduct disorder also display a pattern of short attention span and hyperactivity that may justify a double diagnosis.

Conduct disorder is typically a chronic or persistent disorder (Lahey et al., 1995). Longitudinal studies show that elementary school children with conduct disorders are more likely than other children to engage in delinquent acts as early adolescents (Spivack, Marcus, & Swift, 1986; Tremblay et al., 1992). Antisocial behavior in the form of delinquent acts (stealing, truancy, vandalism, fighting or threatening others, and so on) during early adolescence (ages 14 to 15) has also been found to predict alcohol and substance abuse in late adolescence, especially among boys (M. H. Boyle et al., 1992). Another form of conduct disorder may involve a cluster of personality traits that have different origins than antisocial behavior (Wooton et al., 1997). These personality traits include callousness (uncaring, mean, cruel) and an unemotional way of relating to others.

Oppositional Defiant Disorder

Debate continues among professionals over the issue of whether conduct disorder (CD) and **oppositional defiant disorder** (ODD) are separate disorders or variations of a common disruptive behavior disorder (Rey, 1993). Or perhaps ODD is a precursor or milder form of conduct disorder (Abikoff & Klein, 1992; Biederman et al., 1996). At present, the two disorders are conceptualized as related but separate disorders, with ODD related more closely to nondelinquent (oppositional) conduct disturbance and conduct disorder involving delinquent behavior in the form of truancy, stealing, lying, and aggressivity (Rey, 1993). Yet oppositional defiant disorder, which typically develops earlier than CD, may lead to the development of a conduct disorder (Loeber, Lahey, & Thomas, 1991).

Children with ODD tend to be negativistic and defiant of authority, which is exhibited by their tendency to argue with parents and teachers and refuse to follow requests or directives from adults. They may deliberately annoy other people, become easily angered or lose their temper, become touchy or easily annoyed, blame others for their mistakes or misbehavior, feel resentful toward others, or act in spiteful or vindictive ways toward others (Angold & Costello, 1996; APA, 1994). The disorder typically begins before age 8 and develops gradually over a period of months or years. It typically starts in the home environment but may extend to other settings, such as school.

ODD is one of the most common diagnoses among children (Doll, 1996). Studies show that among children diagnosed with a psychological disorder, about 1 in 3 are judged to meet criteria for ODD (Rey, 1993). A recent view of epidemiological studies estimated the prevalence of ODD among children in the general community at about 6% (Rey, 1993). ODD is more common overall among boys than girls. However, this overall effect masks a gender shift over age. Among children 12 years of age or younger, ODD appears to be more than twice as common among boys. Yet among adolescents, a higher prevalence is reported in girls (Rey, 1993). By contrast, most studies find conduct disorder to be more common in boys than girls across all age groups.

Theoretical Perspectives   The causal factors in ODD remain obscure, with some theorists pointing to oppositionality as an expression of a type of child temperament described as the "difficult-child" type (Rey, 1993). Others believe that unresolved parent-child conflicts or overly strict parental control may lie at the root of the disorder. Psychodynamic theorists look at ODD as a sign of fixation at the anal stage of psychosexual development expressed in the form of rebelliousness against parental wishes (J. Egan, 1991). Learning theorists view child oppositional behaviors arising from parental use of inappropriate reinforcement strategies. In this view, parents may inappropriately reinforce oppositional behavior by "giving in" to the child's demands whenever the child refuses to comply with the parent's wishes, which can become a pattern.

Family factors are also implicated in the development of conduct disorder. Some forms of conduct disorder appear to be linked to ineffective parenting styles, such as failure to

Oppositional defiant disorder (ODD).   ODD is characterized by negativistic and oppositional behavior in response to directives from parents, teachers, or other authority figures. Children with ODD may act spitefully or vindictively towards others, but don't typically show the cruelty, aggressivity and delinquent behavior associated with conduct disorder. Yet questions remain about whether the two disorders are truly distinct or are variations of a common underlying disorder involving disruptive behavior patterns.

provide positive reinforcement for appropriate behavior and use of harsh and inconsistent discipline for misbehavior. Families of children with CD tend to be characterized by negative, coercive interactions (Dadds et al., 1992). Children with CD are often very demanding and noncompliant in relating to their parents and other family members. Family members often reciprocate by using negative behaviors, such as threatening or yelling at the child or using physical means of coercion. Parental aggression against children with conduct behavior problems is common, including pushing, grabbing, slapping, spanking, hitting, or kicking (Jourile et al., 1997). Parents of children with ODD and severe CD display high rates of antisocial personality disorder and substance abuse (Frick et al., 1992). It's not too much of a stretch to speculate that parental modeling of antisocial behaviors can lead to antisocial conduct in their children.

Conduct disorders often occur in a context of parental distress, such as marital conflict. Another factor is maternal depression. Depressed mothers tend to perceive their children as more disruptive than others view them. They also tend to display poor parenting behaviors—such as vague and interrupted commands—that may foster disruptive behavior in their children (Forehand et al., 1988). Mothers of children with conduct disorders are also more likely than other mothers to be inconsistent in their use of discipline and less able to supervise their children's behavior (Frick et al., 1992). Maternal smoking during pregnancy has also been linked to a greater likelihood of conduct disorder in sons (Wakschlag et al., 1997). Perhaps maternal smoking affects the developing fetus in ways that lead to conduct problems, or perhaps there are other characteristics of mothers who smoke, such as ineffective parenting skills, that set the stage for childhood behavior problems.

Some investigations focus on the ways in which children with disruptive behavior disorders process information. For example, children who are overly aggressive in their behavior tend to be biased in their processing of social information: They may assume that others intend them ill when they do not (Lochman, 1992). They usually blame others for the scrapes they get into. They believe that they are misperceived and treated unfairly. They may believe that aggression will yield positive outcomes (Dodge et al., 1997). They are also less able than their peers to generate alternative (nonviolent) responses to social provocations (Lochman & Dodge, 1994).

Genetic factors may interact with family or other environmental factors in the development of conduct disorder in children and antisocial behavior in adolescence (T. G. O'Connor et al., 1998; Slutske et al., 1997, 1998). Genetic factors may also be involved in the development of oppositional defiant disorder.

Treatment The treatment of conduct disorders remains a challenge. Though there is no established pharmacological treatment approach, a recent study indicates that Ritalin may be effective in reducing antisocial behavior in CD children and adolescents (R. G. Klein et al., 1997). Psychotherapy has not generally been shown to help disruptive children change their behavior. Placing children with conduct disorders in programs or treatment settings with explicit rules and clear rewards for obeying them may offer greater promise (e.g., Henggeler et al., 1986). Such programs usually rely on operant conditioning procedures that involve systematic use of rewards and punishments.

Many children with conduct disorders, especially boys, display aggressive behavior and have problems controlling their anger. Many can benefit from programs designed to help them learn anger-coping skills that they can use to handle conflict situations without resorting to violent behavior. Cognitive-behavioral therapy has been used to teach boys who engage in antisocial and aggressive behavior to reconceptualize social provocations as problems to be solved rather than as challenges to their manhood that must be answered with violence. They have been trained to use calming self-talk to inhibit impulsive behavior and control anger when they experience social taunts or provocations and to generate and try out nonviolent solutions to social conflicts (Kazdin, Siegel, & Bass, 1992; Lochman & Lenhart, 1993). Other programs present child models on videotape demonstrating skills of anger control. The results of these programs appear promising (Kazdin & Weisz, 1998; Webster-Stratton & Hammond, 1997). Sometimes the disruptive child's parents are brought into the treatment process (Kazdin et al., 1992).

Henggeler and his colleagues (e.g., Henggeler et al., 1997) have developed a "family-ecological" approach based on Urie Bronfenbrenner's (1979) ecological theory. Like Bronfenbrenner, Henggeler sees children as embedded within various social systems—family, school, criminal justice, community, and so on. He focuses on how juvenile offenders affect and are affected by the systems with which they interact. The techniques themselves are not unique. Rather, the family-ecological approach tries to change children's relationships with multiple systems to end disruptive interactions. This multiple systems or *multisystemic therapy* (MST) approach has shown promising results in the treatment of juvenile offenders in terms of reducing the frequency of subsequent arrests in comparison with youths who received typical youth services from a county youth services department (Henggeler, Melton, & Smith, 1992; Henggeler et al., 1997; Kazdin, 1998; Kazdin & Weisz, 1998).

The following example illustrates the involvement of the parents in the behavioral treatment of a case of oppositional defiant disorder:

Billy was a 7-year-old second grader referred by his parents. The family was relocated frequently because the father was in the navy. Billy usually behaved when his father was taking care of him, but he was noncompliant with his mother and yelled at her when she gave him instructions. His mother was incurring great stress in the effort to control Billy, especially when her husband was at sea.

Billy had become a problem at home and in school during the first grade. He ignored and violated rules in both settings. Billy failed to carry out his chores and frequently yelled at and hit his younger brother. When he acted up, his parents would restrict him to his room or the yard, take away privileges and toys, and spank him. But all of these measures were used inconsistently. He also played on the railroad tracks near his home and twice the police had brought him home after he had thrown rocks at cars.

A home observation showed that Billy's mother often gave him inappropriate commands. She interacted with him as little as possible and showed no verbal praise, physical closeness, smiles, or positive facial expressions or gestures. She paid attention to him only when he misbehaved. When Billy was noncompliant, she would yell back at him and then try to catch him to force him to comply. Billy would then laugh and run from her.

Billy's parents were informed that the child's behavior was a product of inappropriate cueing techniques (poor directions), a lack of reinforcement for appropriate behavior, and lack of consistent sanctions for misbehavior. They were taught the appropriate use of reinforcement, punishment, and **time out.** *The parents then charted Billy's problem behaviors to gain a clearer idea of what triggered and maintained them. They were shown how to reinforce acceptable behavior and use time out as a contingent punishment for misbehavior. Billy's mother was also taught relaxation training to help desensitize her to Billy's disruptions. Biofeedback was used to enhance the relaxation response.*

During a 15-day baseline period, Billy behaved in a noncompliant manner about four times per day. When treatment was begun, Billy showed an immediate drop to about one instance of noncompliance every two days. Follow-up data showed that instances of noncompliance were maintained at a bearable level of about one per day. Fewer behavioral problems in school were also reported, even though they had not been addressed directly.

ADAPTED FROM S. J. KAPLAN, 1986, PP. 227–230

ANXIETY IN CHILDHOOD AND ADOLESCENCE

Anxieties and fears are a normal feature of childhood, just as they are a normal feature of adult life. Children face many fears and anxieties that are deemed normal because they are commonplace and seem to reflect natural cognitive-developmental processes. For example, during the second half of the first year, it is normal for children to develop separation anxiety from caregivers and fear of strangers. Other common childhood anxieties concern supernatural and imaginary creatures, being left alone or in the dark, attack by animals, noise, pain, and injury. Certain fears tend to decline during the first 6 years, such as fears of noises, strange people and objects, and pain. Other fears tend to increase, such as fears of animals, of the dark, of social ridicule, and of true sources of danger. These trends are quite normal. Many adolescents also feel anxious from time to time. Many anxiety problems in adolescence quickly resolve on their own without formal treatment (D. B. Clark et al., 1994).

Anxiety is considered abnormal, however, when it is excessive and interferes with normal academic or social functioning or becomes troubling or persistent. Children, like adults, may suffer from various anxiety disorders, including phobias and generalized anxiety disorder (GAD). Children may also show the more general pattern of avoidance of social interactions that characterizes *avoidant personality disorder. Separation anxiety disorder,* however, is a diagnostic category that applies only to children and adolescents.

Generalized anxiety disorder and phobic disorders are common among adolescents, but panic disorder and obsessive-compulsive disorder are not (Clark et al., 1994). Anxiety disorders often co-occur (one may have social phobia and a specific phobia, for example) or occur together with other disorders, especially depression (D. A. Cole, Truglio, & Peeke, 1997; D. A. Cole et al., 1998). Estimates indicate that more than a third of adolescents with anxiety disorders also have a depressive disorder (Clark et al., 1994). Anxiety disorders in adolescence appear more common in girls than boys (Lewinsohn et al., 1998). Anxiety disorders in childhood or adolescence may set the stage for anxiety disorders in adulthood (Pollack et al., 1996). Many adults with anxiety disorders suffered from separation anxiety or GAD as children (Kendall, 1994).

Children who are socially avoidant or have social phobias typically have normal needs for affection and acceptance, and they develop warm relationships with family members. Their avoidance of people outside the family interferes with their development of peer relationships, however. They tend to be shy and withdrawn. They usually avoid playgrounds and other children in the neighborhood. Their distress at being around other children at school can also impede their academic progress. Such problems tend to develop after normal fear of strangers fades, at age $2\frac{1}{2}$ or later. Problems with anxiety may be complicated by depression and isolation because anxious children typically fail to establish social relationships outside the immediate family. In some cases, children avoid other children because of lack of experience in relating to them, although they can relate relatively well to adults.

Children with GAD are generally apprehensive and fretful. Although specific and social phobias may also be found in these children, their worries are not limited to one or two specific objects or events. Their fears extend to future events, such as visits to the doctor and tests, and to past events, such as whether or not they said the right thing to a peer or responded to a test item correctly. They are also greatly concerned about their competence in social relationships, school, and sports. Children with GAD often report anxiety-

Social avoidance. Socially avoidant children tend to be excessively shy and withdrawn and have difficulty interacting with other children.

related physical symptoms such as headaches and stomachaches. Here we focus on an anxiety disorder that is unique to children and adolescents: separation anxiety disorder.

Separation Anxiety Disorder

It is normal for children to show anxiety when they are separated from their caregivers (Ainsworth & Bowlby, 1991). Mary Ainsworth (1989), who has chronicled the development of attachment behaviors, notes that separation anxiety is a normal feature of the child-caregiver relationship and begins during the first year. The sense of security normally provided by bonds of attachment apparently encourages children to explore their environments and become progressively independent of their caregivers (Bowlby, 1988).

Separation anxiety disorder is diagnosed when separation anxiety is persistent and excessive or inappropriate for the child's developmental level. That is, 3-year-olds ought to be able to attend preschool without nausea and vomiting brought on by anxiety, and 6-year-olds ought to be able to attend first grade without persistent dread that they or their parents will come to harm. Children with this disorder tend to cling to their parents and follow them around the house. They may voice concerns about death and dying and insist that someone stay with them while they are falling asleep. Other features of the disorder include nightmares, stomachaches, nausea and vomiting when separation is anticipated (as on school days), pleading with parents not to leave, or throwing tantrums when parents are about to depart. They may refuse to attend school for fear that something will happen to their parents while they are away. The disorder affects about 4% of children and young adolescents and occurs more frequently, according to community-based studies, among females (APA, 1994). The disorder may persist into adulthood, leading to an exaggerated concern about the well-being of one's children and spouse and difficulty tolerating any separation from them.

TRUTH *or* FICTION REVISITED

13.5 *True.* Some children with separation anxiety disorder do refuse to go to school because they believe that terrible things may happen to their parents while they are away.

In previous years, separation anxiety disorder was usually referred to as *school phobia*. Separation anxiety disorder may occur at preschool ages, however. Today, most cases in which younger children refuse to attend school are viewed as stemming from separation anxiety. In adolescence, however, refusal to attend school is also frequently connected with academic and social concerns, in which cases the label of separation anxiety disorder would not apply.

The development of separation anxiety disorder frequently follows a stressful life event, such as illness, the death of a relative or pet, or a change of schools or homes. Alison's problems followed the death of her grandmother:

Alison's grandmother died when Alison was 7 years old. Her parents decided to permit her request to view her grandmother in the open coffin. Alison took a tentative glance from her father's arms across the room, then

Separation anxiety. In separation anxiety disorder, a child shows persistent anxiety when separated from her or his parents that is inconsistent with her or his developmental level. Such children tend to cling to their parents and resist even brief separations.

asked to be taken out of the room. Her 5-year-old sister took a leisurely close-up look, with no apparent distress.

Alison had been concerned about death for two or three years by this time, but her grandmother's passing brought on a new flurry of questions: "Will I die?," "Does everybody die?," and so on. Her parents tried to reassure her by saying, "Grandma was very, very old, and she also had a heart condition. You are very young and in perfect health. You have many, many years before you have to start thinking about death."

Alison also could not be alone in any room in her house. She pulled one of her parents or her sister along with her everywhere she went. She also reported nightmares about her grandmother and, within a couple of days, insisted on sleeping in the same room with her parents. Fortunately, Alison's fears did not extend to school. Her teacher reported that Alison spent some time talking about her grandmother, but her academic performance was apparently unimpaired.

Alison's parents decided to allow Alison time to "get over" the loss. Alison gradually talked less and less about death, and by the time 3 months had passed, she was able to go into any room in her house by herself. She wanted to continue to sleep in her parents' bedroom, however. So her parents "made a deal" with her. They would put off the return to her own bedroom until the school year had ended (a month away), if Alison

would agree to return to her own bed at that time. As a further incentive, a parent would remain with her until she fell asleep for the first month. Alison overcame the anxiety problem in this fashion with no additional delays.

THE AUTHORS' FILES

Theoretical understandings of excessive anxiety in children to some degree parallel explanations of anxiety disorders in adults. Psychoanalytic theorists argue that childhood anxieties and fears, like their adult counterparts, symbolize unconscious conflicts. Cognitive theorists focus on the role of cognitive biases underlying anxiety reactions. In support of the cognitive model, investigators find that highly anxious children show cognitive biases in processing information, such as interpreting ambiguous situations as threatening, expecting negative outcomes, thinking poorly of themselves and of their ability to cope, and engaging in negative self-talk (Daleiden & Vasey, 1997; Prins & Hanewald, 1997; Treadwell & Kendall, 1996). Expecting the worst, combined with low self-confidence, encourages avoidance of feared activities—with friends, in school, and elsewhere. Negative expectations may also heighten feelings of anxiety to the point where they impede performance. Learning theorists suggest that the occurrence of generalized anxiety may touch on broad themes, such as fears of rejection or failure, that carry across situations. Perhaps underlying fears of rejection or self-perceptions of inadequacy generalize to most areas of social interaction and achievement.

Whatever the causes, overanxious children may profit from the anxiety-control techniques we discussed in Chapter 5, such as gradual exposure to phobic stimuli and relaxation training. Cognitive techniques such as replacing anxious self-talk with coping self-talk may also be helpful (Kendall, 1994). Cognitive-behavioral approaches appear to be effective in treating various childhood anxiety disorders (Kazdin & Weisz, 1998; Kendall et al., 1997; Knox, Albano, & Barlow, 1996).

DEPRESSION IN CHILDHOOD AND ADOLESCENCE

The stereotype is that childhood is the happiest time of life. Most children enjoy protection from their parents and are unencumbered by adult responsibilities. From the perspective of aging adults, their bodies seem made of rubber and free of aches. They have apparently boundless energy.

Despite the stereotype, depression is common among children and adolescents. Estimates indicate that perhaps 8% to 9% of children in the 10- to 13-year age range experience major depression during any given 1-year period (Goleman, 1994a). Although rare, major depression has even been found among preschoolers. Although there is no discernible gender difference in the risk of depression in childhood, a prominent gender difference appears after the age of 15, with adolescent girls becoming about twice as likely to become depressed as adolescent boys (Hankin et al., 1998; Lewinsohn, Roder, & Seeley, 1994; Nolen-Hoeksema & Girgus, 1994).

The basic features of depression in children and adolescents are similar to those in adults (Kovacs, 1996). Depressed children and adolescents typically show a greater sense of hopelessness, display more cognitive errors and negative attributions (e.g., blaming themselves for negative events), and have lower perceived competence or self-efficacy and lower self-esteem than do their nondepressed peers (Lewinsohn et al., 1994; Tems et al., 1993). They often report feelings of sadness, crying, and apathy as well as insomnia, fatigue, and poor appetite. They may refuse to attend school, express fears of their parents' dying, and cling to their parents or retreat to their rooms. They may have suicidal thoughts or attempt suicide.

The average length of a major depressive episode in childhood or adolescence is about 11 months, but an individual episode may last for as long as 18 months in some cases (Goleman, 1994a). Moderate levels of depression, however, may persist for years, severely impacting school performance and social functioning (Nolen-Hoeksema & Girgus, 1994). Childhood depression is often a harbinger of future depressive episodes. About 3 of 4 children who become depressed from age 8 to 13 have a recurrence later in life (Goleman, 1994a).

Children who experience depression may also lack skills in various domains, including performance in school, acceptance by peers, and athletic performance (Seroczynski, Cole, & Maxwell, 1997). They may find it hard to concentrate in school and may suffer from impaired memory, making it difficult for them to keep their grades up (Goleman, 1994a). They often keep their feelings to themselves, which may prevent their parents from recognizing the problem and seeking help for them. Negative feelings may also be expressed in the form of anger, sullenness, or impatience, leading to conflicts with parents that in turn can accentuate and prolong the depression in the child.

Childhood depression rarely occurs by itself (Hammen & Compas, 1994). Depressed children typically experience other psychological disorders, especially anxiety disorders and conduct or oppositional defiant disorders (Angold & Costello, 1993; Hammen & Compas, 1994). Eating disorders are also common among female adolescents who become depressed (Rohde, Lewinsohn, & Seeley, 1991). Overall, childhood depression increases the chances of the child having another psychological disorder by at least 20-fold (Angold & Costello, 1993).

The depressed child or adolescent may also fail to label what they are feeling as depression. They may not report feelings of sadness even though they appear tearful and sad (Goleman, 1994a). Part of the problem is cognitive-developmental. Children are not usually capable of recognizing internal feeling states until about the age of 7. The capacity for **concrete operations** by about that age apparently contributes to the development of self-perception of internal feeling states (Glasberg & Aboud, 1982). But children may not be able to identify negative feeling states like depression in themselves until adolescence (R. W. Larson, Raffaelli, Richards, Ham, & Jewell, 1990). Even adolescents may not recognize what they are experiencing as depression.

Depression in childhood may be "masked" by behaviors that do not appear directly related to depression. Conduct disorders, academic problems, physical complaints, and even hyperactivity may stem, now and then, from unrecognized depression. Among adolescents, aggressive and sexual *acting out* may also be signs of underlying depression (G. A. Carlson, 1980).

Correlates and Treatment of Depression in Childhood and Adolescence

Some of the correlates of childhood depression are situational. Exposure to stressful life events, such as parental conflict or unemployment, places children, especially younger children, at increased risk for depression (Nolen-Hoeksema, Girgus, & Seligman, 1992). Depression and suicidal behavior in childhood are frequently related to family problems and conflicts. Stressful life events and a lack of social support from friends and family also figure in the profile of adolescents who become depressed (Lewinsohn et al.,

Is this child too young to be depressed? Although we tend to think of childhood as the happiest and most carefree time of life, depression is actually quite common among children and adolescents. Depressed children may report feelings of sadness and lack of interest in previously enjoyable activities. Many, however, do not report or are not aware of feelings of depression, even though they may look depressed to observers. Depression may also be masked by other problems, such as conduct or school-related problems, physical complaints, and overactivity.

1994). Depression in adolescents may be triggered by such stressful life events as conflicts with parents and dissatisfaction with school grades. Interestingly, the relationship between loss of a parent in childhood and later depression during childhood or adolescence is not a consistent finding; some studies show a connection, whereas others do not (Lewinsohn et al., 1994).

As children mature and their cognitive abilities increase, however, cognitive factors, such as attributional styles, appear to play a relatively stronger role in the development of depression. Older children (sixth and seventh graders) who adopt a more helpless or pessimistic explanatory style (attributing negative events to internal, stable, and global causes and positive events to external, unstable, and specific causes) are more likely than children with an optimistic explanatory style to report features of depression (Nolen-Hoeksema et al., 1992). Researchers also find that adolescents who are depressed tend to hold more dysfunctional attitudes and to adopt a more helpless explanatory style than do their peers (Lewinsohn et al., 1994). Like their adult counterparts, children and adolescents with depression tend to adopt a cognitive style that is characterized by negative attitudes toward themselves and the future (J. Garber, Weiss, & Shanley, 1993). All in all, the distorted cognitions of depressed children include the following:

1. Expecting the worst (pessimism)
2. Catastrophizing the consequences of negative events
3. Assuming personal responsibility for negative outcomes, even when it is unwarranted
4. Selectively attending to the negative aspects of events

Although there are links between cognitive factors and depression, it remains to be determined whether children become depressed because they think depressing thoughts, whether depression causes changes in cognitive style, or whether depression and cognitive styles interact in more complex ways. Genetic factors appear to play a role in explaining depressive symptoms, at least among adolescents (O'Connor et al., 1998). The role of genetics in childhood depression requires further study, however (Kovacs et al., 1997).

Self-perceptions of incompetence have been linked to low self-esteem, helplessness, and depression in children and adolescents (e.g., Nolen-Hoeksema et al., 1992). Self-perception of incompetence is not always a cognitive distortion, of course. Children who are perceived by peers as having multiple incompetencies—difficulties performing in academic, social, and athletic domains, for example—are at greater risk of developing depression than children who are perceived by their peers as having fewer incompetencies (D. A. Cole, 1991). Depressed children may be less likely to receive social reinforcements from their peers because of failure to perform as well as others in the classroom or at play. For some children as for some adults, treatment of depression may involve fostering social and other skills.

Adolescent girls may face a greater risk of depression because they tend to face more social challenges than boys during adolescence—challenges such as pressures to narrow their interests and pursue feminine-typed activities (Nolen-Hoeksema & Girgus, 1994). It may be that girls who adopt a more passive, ruminative style of coping as children may be at greatest risk of becoming depressed when they face socially restrictive attitudes that devalue their accomplishments and abilities in relation to those of boys, when they face restrictions placed on social roles and activities deemed appropriate for their gender, and when they encounter sexual pressures or abuse.

Accumulating evidence supports the effectiveness of cognitive-behavioral therapy (CBT) in treating depression in childhood and adolescence (Brent et al., 1997; Kaslow & Thompson, 1998; Reinecke, Ryan, & DuBois, 1998). Though individual approaches vary, CBT usually involves a coping-skills model in which children or adolescents receive social skills training (e.g., learning how to start a conversation or make friends) to increase the likelihood of obtaining social reinforcement (Kazdin & Weisz, 1998). CBT typically also includes training in problem-solving skills and ways of increasing the frequency of rewarding activities and of countering depressive styles of thinking. In addition, family therapy may be useful in helping families resolve their conflicts and reorganize their relationships in ways that members can become more supportive of each other.

The earlier generation of antidepressants failed to show superior results to placebos in treating childhood or adolescent depression (R. L. Fisher & Fisher, 1996; Pellegrino, 1996; Rutter, 1997; Sommers-Flanagan & Sommers-Flanagan, 1996). We cannot assume that drugs that may be effective in adults will work as well, or be as safe, when used in children (Bitiello & Jensen, 1997). However, the drug Prozac, one of the new generation of SSRI antidepressants, has been shown to produce better results than a placebo control in relieving severe and persistent depression in children and adolescents (Emslie et al., 1997). Still, the complete elimination of depressive symptoms was rare.

Psychoanalysis, cognitive-behavioral therapy, play therapy, drug therapy, family therapy—these are a sample of the kinds of therapies commonly used to help children in the United States cope with adjustment problems and patterns of abnormal behavior. Yet research suggests that culturally sensitive therapies, ones specifically tailored to the cultural backgrounds and needs of children from diverse cultural groups, are also of value.

Costantino and his colleagues (1986), for example, adapted traditional Puerto Rican folktales, or *cuentos,* as modeling examples in treating Puerto Rican children with behavior problems. The *cuentos* featured child protagonists who served as models for adaptive behavior. The stories were read aloud by the therapists and the children's mothers, and were followed by group discussion of the behavior and feelings of the main character and the moral of the story. The final element in such sessions was role playing, in

Cognitive Disorders and Disorders Related to Aging

14.1 A man with a brain tumor patted the heads of fire hydrants and parking meters in the belief that they were children.

14.2 The most often identified cause of delirium is ingestion of toxic mushrooms.

14.3 After a motorcycle accident, a medical student failed to recognize the woman he had married a few weeks earlier.

14.4 Dementia is a normal part of the aging process.

14.5 People who occasionally become forgetful in middle age are probably suffering from the early stages of Alzheimer's disease.

14.6 A common pain reliever found in most people's medicine cabinets has been found to reduce the risk of Alzheimer's disease when taken regularly.

14.7 A famous folksinger and songwriter was misdiagnosed with alcoholism and spent several years in mental hospitals until the correct diagnosis was made.

14.8 A railroad worker in the 19th century suffered an accident in which a metal rod went clear through his brain, but he was able to get up, dust himself off, and speak to his coworkers.

14.9 A form of dementia is linked to a sexually transmitted disease.

When you have completed your study of Chapter 14, you should be able to:

1. Describe the basic features of cognitive disorders, how they are classified and problems in diagnosing them.

2. Discuss features and causes of delirium and amnestic disorders.

3. Discuss the basic features of dementia and the relationship between dementia and normal aging.

4. Discuss problems of anxiety, sleep, and depression among older people, including relationships between memory problems and depression.

5. Discuss Alzheimer's disease with respect to its incidence, features, progression, biological bases, and treatment.

6. Discuss vascular dementia and dementia due to Pick's disease, Parkinson's disease, Huntington's disease, HIV disease, and Creutzfeldt-Jakob disease.

7. Discuss psychological problems resulting from head trauma, brain tumors, nutritional disorders, endocrine disorders, and brain infections.

In *The Man Who Mistook His Wife for a Hat*, neurologist Oliver Sacks (1985a) tells of Dr. P., a distinguished musician and teacher who had lost the ability to recognize objects visually. For example, Dr. P. failed to recognize the faces of his students at the music school. When a student spoke, however, Dr. P. immediately recognized his or her voice. Not only did the professor fail to discriminate faces visually, but sometimes he perceived faces where none existed. He patted the heads of fire hydrants and parking meters, which he took to be children. He warmly addressed the rounded knobs on furniture. These peculiarities were generally dismissed as jokes and laughed off by Dr. P. and his colleagues. After all, Dr. P. was well known for his oddball humor and jests. But Dr. P.'s music remained as accomplished as ever, his general health seemed fine, and so these misperceptions seemed little to be concerned about.

TRUTH ⬤or FICTION REVISITED

14.1 *True.* A man with a brain tumor patted the heads of fire hydrants and parking meters in the belief that they were children. The tumor caused dysfunction in the parts of his brain that processed visual information.

Not until 3 years later did Dr. P. seek a neurological evaluation. His ophthalmologist had found that although Dr. P.'s eyes were healthy, he had problems interpreting visual stimulation. So he made the referral to Dr. Sacks, a neurologist. When Sacks engaged Dr. P. in conversation, Dr. P.'s eyes fixated oddly on miscellaneous features of Dr. Sack's face—his nose, then his right ear, then his chin, sensing parts of his face but apparently not connecting them in a meaningful pattern. When Dr. P. sought to put on his shoe after a physical examination, he confused his foot with the shoe. When preparing to leave, Dr. P. looked around for his hat, and then . . .

> [Dr. P.] reached out his hand, and took hold of his wife's head, tried to lift it off, to put it on. He had apparently mistaken his wife for a hat! His wife looked as if she was used to such things.
>
> SACKS, 1985A, P. 10

Dr. P.'s peculiar behavior may seem amusing to some, but his loss of visual perception was tragic. Although Dr. P. could identify abstract forms and shapes—a cube, for example—he no longer recognized the faces of his family, or his own. Some features of particular faces would strike a chord of recognition. For example, he could recognize a picture of Einstein from the distinctive hair and mustache, and a picture of his own brother from the square jaw and big teeth. But he was responding to isolated features, not grasping the facial patterns as wholes.

Sacks recounts a final test:

> It was still a cold day, in early spring, and I had thrown my coat and gloves on the sofa.
> "What is this?" I asked, holding up a glove.
> "May I examine it?" he asked, and, taking it from me, he proceeded to examine it as he had examined the geometrical shapes.
> "A continuous surface," he announced at last, "infolded on itself. It appears to have"—he hesitated—"five outpouchings, if this is the word."
> "Yes," I said cautiously. "You have given me a description. Now tell me what it is."
> "A container of some sort?"

"Yes," I said, "and what would it contain?"

"It would contain its contents!" said Dr. P., with a laugh. "There are many possibilities. It could be a change-purse, for example, for coins of five sizes. It could . . ."

I interrupted the blarney flow. "Does it not look familiar? Do you think it might contain, might fit, a part of your body?"

No light of recognition dawned on his face.

No child would have the power to see and speak of "a continuous surface . . . infolded on itself," but any child, any infant, would immediately know a glove as a glove, see it as familiar, as going with a hand. Dr. P. didn't. He saw nothing as familiar. Visually, he was lost in a world of lifeless abstractions.

SACKS, 1985A, P. 13.

Later, we might add, Dr. P. accidentally put the glove on his hand, exclaiming, "My God, it's a glove!" (Sacks, 1985a, p. 13). His brain immediately seized the pattern of **tactile** information, although his visual brain centers were powerless to provide a confirmatory interpretation. Dr. P., that is, showed lack of visual knowledge—a symptom referred to as visual **agnosia**, derived from Greek roots meaning "without knowledge." Still, Dr. P.'s musical abilities and verbal skills remained intact. He was able to function, to dress himself, take a shower, and eat his meals by singing various songs to himself—for example, eating songs and dressing songs—that helped him coordinate his actions. However, if his dressing song was interrupted while he was dressing himself, he would lose his train of thought and be unable to recognize not only the clothes his wife had laid out but also his own body. When the music stopped, so did his ability to make sense of the world. Sacks later learned that Dr. P. had a

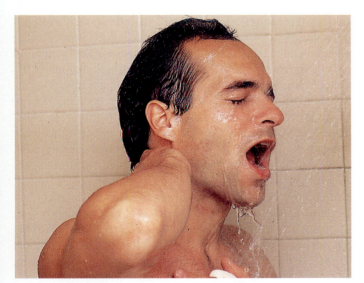

Does his singing help him coordinate his actions? In a celebrated case study, Dr. Oliver Sacks discussed the case of "Dr. P.," who was discovered to be suffering from a brain tumor that impaired his ability to interpret visual cues. Yet he could continue to eat meals and wash and dress himself so long as he could sing to himself.

massive tumor in the area of the brain that processes visual information. Dr. P. was apparently unaware of his deficits, having filled his visually empty world with music in order to function and imbue his life with meaning and purpose.

Dr. P.'s case is unusual in the peculiarity of his symptoms, but it illustrates the universal dependence of psychological functioning on an intact brain. The case also shows how some people adjust—sometimes so gradually that the changes are all but imperceptible—to developing physical or organic problems. Dr. P.'s visual problems might have been relatively more debilitating in a person who was less talented or who had less social support to draw on. In this chapter, we focus on various psychological problems, especially cognitive disorders, that arise from injuries or diseases that affect the brain.

COGNITIVE DISORDERS

Cognitive disorders involve disturbances in thinking or memory that represent a marked change from the individual's prior level of functioning (APA, 1994). Cognitive disorders are not psychologically based; they are caused by physical or medical conditions or drug use or withdrawal that affect the functioning of the brain. In some cases the specific cause of the cognitive disorder can be identified; in others, it cannot be pinpointed. Although these disorders are biologically based, we can see in the case of Dr. P. that psychological and environmental factors play key roles in determining the impact and range of disabling symptoms as well as the individual's ability to cope with deterioration of cognitive and physical abilities.

Our ability to perform cognitive functions—to think, reason, and store and recall information—is dependent on the functioning of the brain. Cognitive disorders arise when the brain is either damaged or impaired in its ability to function due to injury, illness, exposure to toxins, or use or abuse of psychoactive drugs. When brain damage results from an injury or stroke, deterioration in intellectual, social, and occupational functioning can be rapid and severe. In the case of a progressive form of deterioration, such as **Alzheimer's disease,** the decline is more gradual but leads eventually to a state of virtual helplessness. People who suffer from cognitive disorders may become completely dependent on others to meet basic needs in feeding, toileting, and grooming. In other cases, although some assistance in meeting the demands of daily living may be required, people are able to function at a level that permits them to live semi-independently.

There are three major types of cognitive disorders: delirium, amnestic disorders, and dementia (see Table 14.1).

Diagnostic Problems

The diagnosis of cognitive disorders can be a difficult task. Brain damage may result in a variety of symptoms, depending on such factors as the location and extent of the damage, the person's coping ability, and, as in the case of Dr. P., the availability of social support. Damage to a given area of the brain may not produce the same symptoms in different people because of minor structural or functional differences, because of subtle differences in the site of the damage, or because of psychological factors—such as histories of learning—that interact with organic factors. Moreover, organic factors sometimes cause abnormal behavior patterns such as depression, disorientation, and suspiciousness. These patterns resemble those occurring in other mental disorders, such as depressive disorders and schizophrenia.

Neurological examinations and neuropsychological testing are used to detect brain damage. Imaging techniques such as CT and PET scans probe for organic defects that are not revealed by neurological examination. CT scans generally help clinicians identify structural defects such as tumors, whereas PET scans provide insight into apparently structurally intact regions that are made dysfunctional by strokes or other causes. Many organic conditions are treatable or reversible, particularly when they are diagnosed early. A timely and thorough physical evaluation can thus spell the difference between recovery and impairment—in some cases, between life and death. The detection of underlying physical pathology, such as a brain tumor, also leads to very different approaches to treatment than is the case for other psychological disorders. For example, cognitive disorders caused by brain tumors may be successfully treated with surgery, not by psychotherapy. However, psychotherapy and rehabilitation counseling play important roles in a comprehensive treatment approach that aims at helping people with physically based cognitive impairment cope more effectively and function more independently.

The extent and location of brain damage largely determine the range and severity of impairment. By and large, the more widespread the damage, the greater and more exten-

sive the impairment in functioning. The location of the damage is also critical because many brain structures or regions perform specialized functions. Damage to the temporal lobe, for example, is associated with defects in memory and attention, whereas damage to the occipital lobe may result in visual-spatial deficits, such as Dr. P.'s loss of ability to recognize familiar faces.

Delirium

Delirium derives from the Latin roots *de-*, meaning "from," and *lira,* meaning "line" or "furrow." It means straying from the line, or the norm, in perception, cognition, and behavior. Delirium involves a state of extreme mental confusion in which people have difficulty concentrating and speaking clearly and coherently (see Table 14.2). People suffering from delirium may find it difficult to tune out irrelevant stimuli or shift their attention to new tasks. They may speak excitedly, but their speech carries little if any meaning. Disorientation as to time (not knowing the current date, day of the week, or time) and place (not knowing where you are) is common. Disorientation to person (the identities of oneself and others) is not. People in a state of delirium may experience terrifying hallucinations, especially visual hallucinations. Disturbances in perceptions often occur, such as misinterpretations of sensory stimuli (for example, confusing an alarm clock for a fire bell), or illusions (for instance, feeling as if the bed has an electrical charge passing through it). There can be a dramatic slowing down of movement into a state resembling catatonia. There may be rapid fluctuations between restlessness and stupor. Restlessness is characterized by insomnia; agitated, aimless movements; even bolting out of bed or striking out at nonexistent objects. This may alternate with periods in which victims have to struggle to stay awake.

Delirium can result from a variety of medical conditions including head trauma; metabolic disorders, such as hypoglycemia (low blood sugar); fluid or electrolyte imbalances; seizure disorders (epilepsy); deficiencies of the B vitamin thiamine; brain lesions; and various diseases that affect the functioning of the central nervous system, including Parkinson's disease, Alzheimer's disease, viral encephalitis (a type of brain infection), liver disease, and kidney disease (APA, 1994). Delirium may also occur due to exposure to toxic substances (such as eating certain poisonous mushrooms), as a side effect of using certain medications, or during states of drug or alcohol intoxication. Delirium may also result from abrupt cessation of use of psychoactive substances, especially alcohol, usually after periods of chronic, heavy use. People with chronic alcoholism who abruptly stop drinking may experience a form of delirium called **delirium tremens** or DTs. Although there are many known causes of delirium, in many cases the specific cause cannot be identified.

Whatever the cause, delirium involves a generalized disturbance of the brain's metabolic processes and imbalances in the levels of neurotransmitters. As a result, the ability to process information is impaired and confusion reigns.

TABLE 14.2
Features of Delirium

	Level of Severity		
	Mild	**Moderate**	**Severe**
Emotion	Apprehension	Fear	Panic
Cognition and perception	Confusion, racing thoughts	Disorientation, delusions	Meaningless mumbling, vivid hallucinations
Behavior	Tremors	Muscle spasms	Seizures
Autonomic activity	Abnormally fast heartbeat (tachycardia)	Perspiration	Fever

Source: Adapted from Freemon, 1981, p. 82.

The abilities to think and speak clearly, to interpret sensory stimuli accurately, and to attend to the environment decline. Delirium may occur abruptly, as in cases resulting from seizures or head injuries, or gradually over hours or days, as in cases involving infections, fever, or metabolic disorders. During the course of delirium, the person's mental state will often fluctuate between periods of clarity ("lucid intervals"), which are most common in the morning, and periods of confusion and disorientation. Delirium is generally worse in the dark and following sleepless nights.

Unlike dementia, in which there is a steady deterioration of mental ability, states of delirium often clear up spontaneously when the underlying organic or drug-related cause is resolved. The course of delirium is relatively brief, usually lasting about a week but rarely longer than a month. However, if the underlying cause persists or leads to further deterioration, delirium may progress to coma or death.

The DTs

Withdrawal from psychoactive drugs, especially alcohol, is recognized as the most commonly occurring cause of delirium (Freemon, 1981).

TRUTH *or* FICTION REVISITED

14.2 *False.* Though ingestion of certain types of poisonous mushrooms may result in delirium, the most frequently identified cause of delirium is abrupt withdrawal from alcohol or other drugs.

The diagnosis of *alcohol withdrawal delirium* describes a condition that has historically been called **delirium tremens,** or the DTs. The DTs usually occur following abrupt withdrawal from alcohol after years of heavy drinking. Tremors become evident within the first hours of withdrawal. Convulsive seizures may occur after 24 hours, then subside, and the person may appear normal for the next day or two (Freemon, 1981). Then an acute period of delirium begins in which the patient may be terrorized by wild and frightening hallucinations, like "bugs crawling down walls"

or on the skin. The DTs can last for a week or more and are best treated in a hospital setting, where the patient can be carefully monitored and the symptoms treated with mild tranquilizers and environmental support. The following case illustrates the cognitive disturbance associated with the DTs:

A divorced carpenter, 43 years of age, is brought to a hospital emergency department by his sister. She reports that he has at least a 5-year history of consuming large amounts of alcohol (a fifth of cheap wine) on a daily basis. He has had many blackouts from drinking, and he has lost several jobs due to drinking. He ran out of money three days earlier, at which time he stopped drinking abruptly, and he has been begging for money to buy his meals. On examination, he seems keyed up, talking almost non-stop in an unfocused and rambling manner. He appears confused and believes that the doctor is his brother, calling him by his brother's name. There is evidence of a hand tremor, and he picks at "bugs" that he believes he sees on the hospital bedsheets. He is disoriented as to place and time; he apparently thinks that he is in a parking lot of a supermarket rather than a hospital. He is apprehensive and fears that an impending holocaust is about to end the world. He has difficulty concentrating. His perceptions apparently drift into hallucinations of fiery car crashes that seem to be prompted by sounds of hospital carts crashing against each other in the hallways.

ADAPTED FROM SPITZER ET AL., 1994, PP. 263–264

Amnestic Disorders

Amnestic disorders (commonly called amnesias) are characterized by a dramatic decline in memory functioning that is not connected with states of delirium or dementia. Amnesia involves an inability to learn new information (deficits in short-term memory) or to recall previously accessible information or past events from one's life (deficits in long-term memory). Problems with short-term memory may be revealed by an inability to remember the names of, or to recognize, people whom the person met 5 or 10 minutes earlier. Immediate memory, as measured by ability to repeat back a series of numbers, seems to be unimpaired in states of amnesia. The number series is unlikely to be recalled later, however, no matter how often it is rehearsed.

Unlike the memory disorders of dissociative amnesia and dissociative fugue discussed in Chapter 6, amnestic disorder results from a physical cause. Amnestic disorders frequently follow a traumatic event, such as a blow to the head, an electric shock, or an operation. A head injury may prevent people from remembering events that occurred shortly before the accident. The victim of an automobile accident or a football player who is knocked unconscious may be unable to remember events that occurred within several minutes of the injury. The automobile accident victim may not remember anything that transpired after getting into the car. The football player who is rendered amnestic from a blow to the head during the game may not remember anything after leaving the locker room. In some cases memories for the remote past are retained but recent memories are lost. People with amnesia may be more likely to remember events from their childhood than last evening's dinner, for example. Consider the following case:

> A medical student was rushed to the hospital after he was thrown from a motorcycle. His parents were with him in his hospital room when he awakened. As his parents were explaining what had happened to him, the door suddenly flew open and his flustered wife, whom he had married a few weeks earlier, rushed into the room, leaped onto his bed, and began to caress him and expressed her great relief that he was not seriously injured. After several minutes of expressing her love and reassurance, his wife departed and the flustered student looked at his mother and asked: "Who is she?"
>
> ADAPTED FROM FREEMON, 1981, P. 96

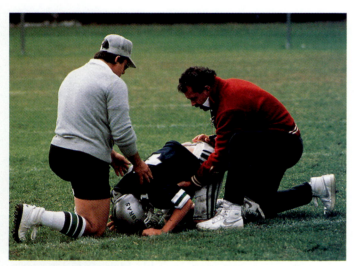

Amnestic disorder. An amnestic disorder syndrome can follow a traumatic injury such as a blow to the head. This football player may not be able to recall the events that happened just prior to his being tackled, nor the collision itself.

The medical student's long-term memory loss not only included memories dating to the accident but also further back to the time before he was married or had met his wife. Like most victims of posttraumatic amnesia, the medical student recovered his memory fully.

TRUTH *or* FICTION REVISITED

14.3 *True.* After a motorcycle accident, a medical student failed to recognize the woman he had married a few weeks earlier.

People with an amnestic disorder may experience disorientation, more commonly involving disorientation as to place (not knowing where one is at the time) and time (not knowing the day, month, and year) than disorientation as to self (not knowing one's own name). They may also lack insight into their memory loss and attempt to deny or mask their memory deficits even when evidence to the contrary is presented to them (APA, 1994). They may also attempt to fill the gaps in their memories with imaginary events. Or they may admit they have a memory problem but appear apathetic about it, showing a kind of emotional blandness.

Although people with amnestic disorder may suffer profound memory losses, their general intelligence tends to remain within a normal range. Memory loss in pure amnesia may thus be distinguished from that occurring in progressive dementias such as Alzheimer's disease, in which memory and intellectual functioning both deteriorate. Early detection and diagnosis of the causes of memory problems are vital to many sufferers, because 20% to 30% of them are correctable (D. Cohen, 1986).

Other causes of amnesia include brain surgery, sudden loss of oxygen to the brain (**hypoxia**); infection; **infarction** (blockage) of the blood vessels supplying the brain, and chronic, heavy use of certain psychoactive substances, most commonly alcohol.

Alcohol-Induced Persisting Amnestic Disorder (Korsakoff's Syndrome)

A common cause of amnestic disorder is thiamine deficiency linked to chronic abuse of alcohol. Alcohol abusers tend to take poor care of their nutritional needs and may not follow a diet rich enough in vitamin B_1, or thiamine. Thiamine deficiencies may produce an irreversible form of memory loss called **alcohol-induced persisting amnestic disorder,** which is more commonly known as **Korsakoff's syndrome.** The word *persisting* is used because the memory deficits persist long after the time the individual was drinking or underwent withdrawal (APA, 1994). Korsakoff's syndrome is not limited to people with chronic alcoholism, however. It has been reported in other groups who experience thiamine deficiencies during times of deprivation, such as among prisoners of war.

Korsakoff's syndrome produces substantial losses in short- and long-term memories and an inability to form new memories. These memory deficits are believed to result from the loss of brain tissue due to bleeding. Despite their memory losses, patients with Korsakoff's syndrome may retain their general level of intelligence. They are often described as being superficially friendly but lacking in insight, unable to discriminate between actual events and wild stories they invent to fill the gaps in their memories. They sometimes become grossly disoriented and confused and require custodial care.

Korsakoff's syndrome often follows an acute attack of **Wernicke's disease,** another brain disorder caused by thiamine deficiency. Wernicke's disease is characterized by confusion and disorientation, difficulty maintaining balance while walking (**ataxia**), and paralysis of the muscles that control eye movements. These symptoms may pass, but the person is often left with Korsakoff's syndrome and enduring memory impairment. If, however, Wernicke's disease is treated promptly with major doses of vitamin B_1, Korsakoff's syndrome may not develop. Once Korsakoff's syndrome has set in, it is usually permanent, although slight improvement is possible with treatment.

Dementia

Dementia involves a profound deterioration in mental functioning characterized by gross memory impairment and by one or more of the cognitive deficits listed in Table 14.3 (APA, 1994). Like other forms of cognitive disorder, dementia is acquired at some point during life, which means the person was not born with cognitive impairment. The impairment is of sufficient magnitude to impair social or occupational functioning.

There are more than 70 known causes of dementia including brain diseases, such as Alzheimer's disease and Pick's disease, and infections or disorders that affect the functioning of the brain, such as meningitis, HIV disease, and encephalitis. In some cases the dementia can be halted or reversed, especially when it is caused by certain types of tumors and treatable infections or when it results from depression or substance abuse. Most dementias are progressive and irreversible, however, such as dementia due to the Alzheimer's disease (G. W. Small et al., 1997).

Dementia most often affects people in later life. Some decline in cognitive functioning occurs normally with aging. Dementia, however, is not a product of normal aging but a sign of underlying pathology or disease process in the brain. Screening and testing on neurological and neuropsychological tests can help distinguish dementias from normal aging processes. Generally speaking, the decline in intellectual functioning in dementia is more rapid and severe.

Most dementias occur in people over the age of 80 (Skoog et al., 1993). Dementias that begin after age 65 are called late-onset or **senile dementias.** Those that begin at 65 or earlier are termed early-onset or **presenile dementias.** Dementia of the Alzheimer's type is the most common form

TABLE 14.3

Cognitive Deficits in Dementia

Cognitive Deficit	Definition	Description
Aphasia	Impaired ability to comprehend and/or produce speech.	There are several types of aphasia. In sensory or receptive aphasia, people have difficulty understanding written or spoken language but retain the ability to express themselves through speech. In motor aphasia, the ability to express thoughts through speech is impaired, but the person can understand spoken language. A person with a motor aphasia may not be able to summon up the names of familiar objects or may scramble the normal order of words.
Apraxia	Impaired ability to perform purposeful movements despite an absence of any defect in motor functioning.	There may be an inability to tie a shoelace or button a shirt, although the person can describe how these activities should be performed and despite the fact that there is nothing wrong with the person's arm or hand. The person may have difficulty pantomiming the use of an object (e.g. combing one's hair).
Agnosia	Inability to recognize objects despite an intact sensory system.	Agnosias may be limited to specific sensory channels. A person with a visual agnosia may not be able to identify a fork when shown a picture of the object, although he or she has an intact visual system and may be able to identify the object if allowed to touch it and manipulate it by hand. Auditory agnosia is marked by impairment in the ability to recognize sounds; in tactile agnosia, people are unable to identify objects (such as coins or keys) by holding them or touching them.
Disturbance in Executive Functioning	Deficits in planning, organizing, or sequencing activities or in engaging in abstract thinking.	An office manager who formerly handled budgets and scheduling loses the ability to manage the flow of work in the office or adapt to new demands. An English teacher loses the ability to extract meaning from a poem or story.

Source: Adapted from *DSM-IV* (APA, 1994).

Dementia. Dementia involves a deterioration of mental abilities such as memory, reasoning, language, thinking, and skills involved in carrying through a series of purposeful movements. Here we see how the staff at a nursing home use a chalkboard to help orient a man suffering from dementia.

of dementia, accounting for more than half of cases overall (Loebel, Dager, & Kitchell, 1993). Vascular dementia, the second most common form of dementia, most often affects people in later life but at somewhat earlier ages than dementia due to Alzheimer's disease.

Estimates indicate that 20% or more of the population over the age of 85 suffer from dementias, especially dementia due to Alzheimer's disease and vascular dementia (APA, 1994). A recent study in Sweden found an even higher prevalence of dementia (30%) among a sample of 85-year-old White women (Skoog et al., 1993). As we see next, dementia is not the only psychological problem associated with aging.

PSYCHOLOGICAL DISORDERS RELATED TO AGING

How old would you be if you didn't know how old you was?

SATCHEL PAIGE

Old age isn't so bad when you consider the alternative.

MAURICE CHEVALIER

Many physical changes occur with aging. Changes in calcium metabolism cause the bones to grow brittle and heighten the risk of breaks from falls. The skin grows less elastic, creating wrinkles and folds. The senses become less keen, so older people see and hear less acutely. Older people need more time (called *reaction time*) to respond to stimuli, whether they are driving or taking intelligence tests. For example, older drivers require more time to react to traffic signals and other cars. The immune system functions less effectively with increasing age, so people become more vulnerable to illness as they age. Cognitive changes occur as well.

Cognitive Changes in Later Life

Most of us experience mild declines in memory by about the age of 50. We also tend to experience minor deterioration of visual-spatial skills by age 60 and some slight decrements in language skills and abstract thinking ability by about age 70 (NIH, 1987). Reductions in brain levels of dopamine that naturally occur as we age may play a role in the decline in cognitive functioning (Volkow et al., 1998). However, despite earlier beliefs that people naturally grow senile as they age, the processes of normal aging involve modest declines in intellectual abilities. The significant, marked declines in intellectual functioning that characterize dementia are not a normal function of the aging process but rather a sign of a degenerative brain disorder.

TRUTH *or* **FICTION** REVISITED

14.4 *False.* Dementia is not a normal part of the aging process. It is a sign of a degenerative brain disease.

People in later life tend to experience some drop-off in general cognitive ability as measured by tests of intelligence, or IQ tests. The decline is sharpest on timed items, such as the performance scales of the Wechsler Adult Intelligence Scale. Although a decline in cognitive ability (reading comprehension, spatial ability as in map reading, or basic mathematical reasoning) in later life is common, it is not universal. Studies show that 20% to 30% of people in their eighties perform about as well on intelligence tests as those in their thirties and forties (Goleman, 1994d). Some abilities, such as vocabulary or accumulated knowledge, hold up rather well in later life; so-called *fluid memory,* the ability to

What changes take place as we age? How do they affect our moods? Although some declines in cognitive and physical functioning are connected with aging, older adults who remain active and engage in rewarding activities can be highly satisfied with their lives.

form new memories or recall from memory events that were recently experienced, is more likely to decline, beginning by about age 60.

We understand little about the causes of these declines in cognitive functioning. Loss of motivation and of sensory acuity play a part. B. F. Skinner (1983) contended that much of the decline reflects an "aging environment," not an aging person. That is, much of the behavior of older people goes unreinforced, especially after retirement. Some cognitive changes may reflect psychological problems, such as depression, rather than the physical aspects of aging. If the underlying problem is treated, cognitive performance may well improve. Depression often goes unrecognized among older people, however. Moreover, older people with mental health problems are much more likely to seek help from their medical doctors than from a community mental health center or clinic (M. A. Phillips & Murrell, 1994).

Anxiety Disorders and Aging

Like other psychological problems, anxiety disorders can affect people at any stage of life. However, evidence based on a compilation of studies conducted from 1970 through the early 1990s showed that anxiety disorders were generally less prevalent among older than younger adults (Flint,

1994). The most frequently occurring anxiety disorders in older adults are generalized anxiety disorder (GAD) and phobic disorders. Panic disorder is rare. Most cases of agoraphobia affecting older adults tend to be of recent origin and may involve the loss of social support systems due to the death of a spouse or close friends. Then again, some older individuals who are frail may have realistic fears of falling on the street and may be misdiagnosed as agoraphobic if they refuse to leave the house alone. Generalized anxiety may arise from the perception that one lacks control over one's life, which may arise in later life as the person contends with infirmity, loss of friends and loved ones, and lessened economic opportunities. Use of mild tranquilizers to quell feelings of anxiety are common among older adults. Generalized anxiety and phobias among older people often occur comorbidly (concurrently) with depression. In some cases, anxiety arises secondarily from depression and may be relieved when the underlying mood disorder is successfully treated. Cognitive-behavior therapy, supportive therapy, and use of antianxiety drugs can be helpful in treating generalized anxiety disorder in older adults (L. S. Schneider, 1996; Stanley, Beck, & Glassco, 1996).

Depression and Aging

Depression to varying degrees is commonplace, even epidemic, among people in later life—the most common emotional problem they face (Unützer et al., 1997). In some cases depression in the elderly is a continuation of a lifelong pattern of recurrent depression, while in other cases it first arises in later life. The National Institute on Aging estimates that at least 15% of people over the age of 65 suffer from some degree of depression that impairs the quality of their lives, though not necessarily at a level of severity that would meet criteria for a major depressive disorder. Still, estimates are that 3% of Americans in the 65+ age group suffer from a diagnosable major depressive disorder (Brody, 1994b). Rates of depression are even higher among residents of nursing homes. Suicide is also most frequent among older people. Depression in later life is also associated with a faster rate of physical decline and a higher mortality rate (Brenda et al., 1998; Zubenko et al., 1997). Depression may be linked to a higher mortality rate because of coexisting medical conditions or perhaps because of a lack of compliance with taking necessary medications.

Older people of color have many of the same concerns as other older adults, such as reduced opportunities for social participation and loneliness, but they are also likely to have encountered social stresses such as discrimination and poverty, and, among immigrant groups, acculturative stress and English language deficiency. A history of discrimination and prejudice may make it difficult for people of color to trust therapists who are not of their own racial or ethnic group (A. O. Freed, 1992). The importance of acculturative stress was underscored in a recent study of older Mexican American adults that showed those who were minimally acculturated to U.S. society to have greater rates of depression than either highly acculturated or bicultural individuals (Zamanian et al., 1992).

Depressive disorders occur commonly in people suffering from various brain disorders, several of which, such as Alzheimer's disease and stroke, disproportionately affect older people (Teri, 1992). Researchers estimate that depressive disorders occur in as many as half of stroke victims and about a third to a half of people affected by Alzheimer's disease or Parkinson's disease (e.g., Devanand et al., 1997; Mega et al., 1996; Migliorelli et al., 1995). In the case of Parkinson's disease, depression may be not only a reaction to coping with the disease; it may also result from neurobiological changes in the brain that are caused by the disease (Rao, DiClemente, & Ponton, 1992).

Depression in older adults presents with similar features as depression at younger ages, with the exception of a greater prevalence of delusions in older patients (Kovacs, 1996a). Factors associated with the risk of depression in later life include lower income level, impairment in daily functioning, poor health, living alone, and lack of social support (Alexopoulos et al., 1996a; Lebowitz et al., 1997; Zeiss et al. 1996). Genetic factors appear to play a moderate role in depression among older adults, but environmental factors appear even stronger (McGue & Christensen, 1997).

The availability of social support appears to buffer the effects of stress, bereavement, and illness, thereby reducing the risk of depression. Social support is especially important to older people who are challenged because of physical disability (LaGory & Fitzpatrick, 1992). However, coping with living with a depressed spouse can take its toll, leading to an increased risk of depression in the spouse (Tower & Kasl, 1996).

On the other hand, participation in volunteer organizations and religious institutions is associated with a lower risk of depression among older people (Palinkas, Wingard, & Barrett-Connor, 1990). These forms of social participation may provide not only a sense of meaning and purpose but also a needed social outlet.

Consider an interesting gender difference related to social support. Researchers report that older men in their sample were more likely to experience depression following the loss of a close family member (other than their spouses) than were older women (Siegel & Kuykendall, 1990). Older men who were widowed and who did not belong to a church or synagogue, and who consequently had less available social supports, were most at risk of depression. The researchers suspect that widowers have more limited social support networks than widows and are less likely to have confidants outside marriage who might provide support. This belief is supported by other findings that friends are the most frequent source of support for older women, regardless of their marital status (Palinkas et al., 1990). For older men, however, spouses represent the most frequent sources of support.

Older people may be especially vulnerable to depression because of the stress of coping with life changes associated with the so-called golden years—retirement; physical

Depression and aging. Depression is the most common psychological problem faced by older adults. Rates of suicide are also highest among people in later life. What are some of the factors that might account for the high rates of depression and suicide in older people?

illness or incapacitation; placement in a residential facility or nursing home; the deaths of a spouse, siblings, lifetime friends, and acquaintances; or the need to care for a spouse whose condition is declining. Retirement, whether voluntary or forced, may sap the sense of meaningfulness in life and lead to a loss of role identity. Deaths of relatives and friends not only induce grief but remind older people of their own advanced age as well as reducing the availability of social support. Older adults may feel incapable of forming new friendships or finding new goals in life.

Evidence suggests that the chronic strain of coping with a family member with dementia can lead to depression in the caregiver, even in the absence of any prior vulnerability to depression. Nearly half of Alzheimer's caregivers become depressed (McNaughton et al., 1995; G. W. Small et al., 1997).

Despite the prevalence of depression in older people, physicians often fail to recognize it or to treat it appropriately (Koenig et al., 1997; Lyness et al., 1997). In one study of more than 500 elderly people in Ontario who committed suicide, nearly 9 of 10 were found to have gone untreated (Duckworth & McBride 1996). Health care providers may be less likely to recognize depression among older people than in middle-aged or young people because they tend to focus more on the older patient's physical complaints or because depression in older people is often masked by physical complaints and sleeping problems.

Memory Functioning and Depression Most older people with memory deficits do not suffer from Alzheimer's disease. They are more likely to have memory losses due to depression or other factors such as chronic alcohol use or the effects of small strokes (Bäckman & Forsell, 1994; Kolata, 1994b). Many older depressed adults who have associated memory deficits are misdiagnosed as having Alzheimer's disease (Kaszniak & Scogin, 1995). Unlike irreversible dementias such as those resulting from Alzheimer's disease, memory loss and cognitive impairment that can accompany depression in older adults often lifts when the underlying depression is resolved. However, when depression occurs among patients already afflicted with dementia, as in Alzheimer's disease, a rapid and dramatic worsening of cognitive functioning may occur.

Depression and memory loss in older people may also accompany bereavement. Such problems may be resolved as grief resolves and survivors learn to cope on their own, however:

> *Mrs. A. was a 71-year-old retired schoolteacher. Her husband died after a 3-year bout with intestinal cancer. Although his death was expected and prepared for, she was nevertheless overcome by emotion. She had been a highly functioning, scholarly woman who read widely, yet Mrs. A. was suddenly unable to think clearly. She noticed her striking forgetfulness. So did her children, who had come to support her during the period of mourning. Mrs. A. had difficulty recalling where she had placed things. Now and then she forgot the day of the week and the date. She felt incapable of shopping for groceries because it was too arduous to make change. Although she would make lists as a way of reminding herself of her chores, she would misplace the lists and forget about them. She could not concentrate to read or watch television. If she did watch for a while, she did not remember what she had seen. She recurrently called her children by the wrong name, and was particularly prone to calling her son by her deceased husband's name. As the weeks elapsed, however, the forgetfulness, disorientation, and diminished capacity for concentration gradually dissipated. After about half a year, Mrs. A returned to her normal level of intellectual functioning and has continued to function adequately.*
>
> ADAPTED FROM SALZMAN AND GUTFREUND, 1986, P. 258

Some depressed older people complain of memory problems even though their memory functioning is average or above average (J. M. Williams, Little, Scates, & Blockman, 1987). Perceptions of memory impairment among some depressed older people may be a kind of cognitive distortion, one that is characteristic of the tendency of depressed people in general to devalue their abilities.

Treating Depression in Older People Evidence indicates that treatments for depression that are effective for younger people, such as antidepressant medication, cognitive behavior therapy, and interpersonal psychotherapy, as well as ECT, are also effective in treating geriatric depression (D. A. Casey & Davis, 1996; Dew et al., 1997; Flint & Rifat,

1998; Zeiss & Breckenridge, 1997). In fact, older adults benefit as much, though perhaps more slowly, from pharmacological and psychological interventions as mid-life or younger adults (Reynolds et al., 1996). This finding should help put to rest the belief that psychotherapy is not appropriate for older people. We lack evidence, however, showing whether any particular form of psychotherapy is clearly superior in treating depression in older people.

Although antidepressant medication can help relieve depression in older people, several factors may complicate the use of drugs with older adults, such as poor adherence to medication due to a greater sensitivity to side effects and coexisting medical diseases that may interfere with proper dosing (Depression Guideline Panel, 1993b). Psychological treatment can avoid these potential pitfalls. In one example of a psychological approach, Zeiss and Lewinsohn (1986) developed a cognitive-behavioral treatment model tailored to the life problems of people as they age. Therapists helped depressed older people cope more effectively with life changes, such as the loss of loved ones or physical illness. Therapists also helped older people challenge self-defeating attitudes, such as the belief that they are too old to change or to learn new behaviors.

In another example, Teri (1992) describes a behavioral treatment of depression for patients with dementia that she developed at the University of Washington. Her approach assumes that depressive behaviors are maintained through reinforcement contingencies, and, consequently, she seeks to alter the patterns of reinforcement available to older people. For example, Teri helps clients identify activities they can still enjoy and encourages them to increase their rate of participation in these activities. She also helps clients create conditions under which they can retain as much independence as possible and in which their remaining cognitive and functional abilities are maximized. Drug therapy may be considered when behavior therapy fails.

Another clinical trial compared two other forms of group therapy for depression among people in later life, social problem-solving therapy (PST) and reminiscence therapy (RT) (Arean et al., 1993). PST trains participants in the core skills of problem solving: identifying problems, generating alternative solutions, selecting the optimal solution, implementing the solution, and evaluating the outcome. RT is based on a life review approach. Participants are encouraged to examine their lives and to accept their shortcomings as well as their successes, to resolve past conflicts, and to focus on goals that will enhance the meaning of their lives in the future. Both psychological treatments produced significant reductions in depressive features as compared to a control condition, with PST producing significantly greater reductions than RT. These findings indicate that group therapies, particularly PST, appear to be effective treatment approaches for depression in later life.

Sleep Problems and Aging

Sleep problems, especially insomnia and sleep apnea, are common among older people. Insomnia in late adulthood is actually more prevalent than depression (K. Morgan, 1996). People are more likely to experience sleep problems as they age, which may to a certain extent reflect age-related changes in sleep physiology. However, sleep problems may be a feature of other disorders, such as depression, dementia, and anxiety disorders (Monane, 1993). Psychosocial factors, such as loneliness and the related difficulty of sleeping alone after loss of a spouse, may also be involved. Dysfunctional cognitions, such as excessive concerns about the negative consequences of losing sleep and perceptions of hopelessness and helplessness about controlling sleep, may play a role in perpetuating insomnia in older people (Morin et al., 1993a).

Pharmacological approaches to treating insomnia are often used, but problems relating to long-term use of tranquilizing medication, such as the development of dependence and withdrawal symptoms, caution against long-term use. Researchers find older people with persistent insomnia to be more accepting of behavioral approaches, similar to those described in Chapter 10, than pharmacological approaches (Morin et al., 1992). Evidence shows that behavior therapy is effective in treating insomnia in later life and that older adults are as capable of benefiting from the treatment as younger adults (Morin et al., 1993b; Murtagh & Greenwood, 1995).

A study of sleep apnea (temporary cessation of breathing during sleep) in a geriatric population showed that between 25% and 42% of the people studied had five or more apneas per hour of sleep (Ancoli-Israel et al., 1991). Apnea may involve more than a sleep problem; it is also linked to an increased risk of dementia and of heart attacks and strokes (Ancoli-Israel et al., 1991; Strollo & Rogers, 1996).

Dementia of the Alzheimer's Type

Alzheimer's disease (AD) is a degenerative brain disease that leads to a progressive and irreversible dementia, characterized by loss of memory and the ability to reason. It accounts for more than half of the cases of dementia in the general population (see Figure 14.1) (Selkoe, 1992; Tune, 1998). Alzheimer's disease is estimated to shorten the life span by an average of 8 years and causes an estimated 17,000 deaths annually in the United States, 98% of which involve people age 65 or older (National Center for Health Statistics, 1996a).

Although AD is strongly connected with aging, it is a disease and not a consequence of normal aging of the brain. Alzheimer's afflicts more than 4 million Americans, about 1 in 10 Americans over the age of 65 and almost half of those over the age of 85 (S. S. Hall, 1998; Ricks, 1997). Women are at higher risk of developing the disease than are men (Gao et al., 1998). With an aging population and wider use of life-prolonging medical advances, AD is expected to become an even larger problem, striking an estimated 14 million Americans by the year 2050 (National Broadcasting Service, 1997; Cable News Network, 1997b). The economic costs of AD are estimated at more than $100 billion a year in the United States (Kolata, 1995b). Notable individuals who

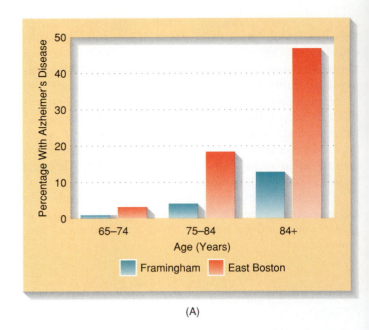

(A)

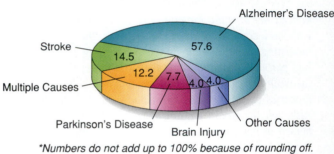

(B)

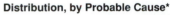

Some Treatable Causes of Dementia

Medications	Certain Tumors or Infections of the Brain
Emotional Depression	Blood Clots Pressing on the Brain
Vitamin B_{12} Deficiency	Metabolic Imbalances (Including Thyroid,
Chronic Alcoholism	Kidney or Liver Disorders)

(C)

FIGURE 14.1 *Prevalence of Alzheimer's disease among older population of two communities in Massachusetts and distribution of probable causes of dementia.*
Studies of East Boston and Framingham in Massachusetts show that the prevalence of Alzheimer's disease increases with age among older people. The figures reported for Framingham are lower than those reported in East Boston, most probably because the Framingham study employed narrower criteria in diagnosing the disease. Note in Part B that Alzheimer's disease is considered the probable cause in most cases of dementia (57.6%).

have suffered from the disease include the artists Willem de Kooning and Norman Rockwell, the actress Rita Hayworth, the boxer Sugar Ray Robinson, and former president Ronald Reagan (R. Cooke, 1994).

The dementia associated with AD involves a progressive deterioration of mental abilities involving memory, language, and problem-solving ability. Isolated memory losses are not indicative of AD (e.g., forgetting where one put one's glasses) and may occur normally as part of the aging process. However, suspicion of AD is raised when cognitive impairment is more severe and pervasive, affecting the individual's ability to meet the ordinary responsibilities of daily work and social roles. Over the course of the illness, people with AD may get lost in parking lots or in stores, or even in their own homes (Kolata, 1994b). The wife of an AD patient describes how AD has affected her husband: "With no cure, Alzheimer's robs the person of who he is. It is painful to see Richard walk around the car several times because he can't find the door" (Morrow, 1998a, p. D4). Agitation, wandering behavior, and aggressive behavior become common as the disease progresses (Aarsland, et al., 1996; Devanand et al., 1997). People with AD may become confused or delusional in their thinking and sense their mental ability is slipping away but not understand why it is happening. Bewilderment and fear may lead to paranoid delusions or beliefs that their loved ones have betrayed them, robbed them, or don't care about them ("Update on Alzheimer's Disease, Part I," 1995). They may forget the names of their loved ones or fail to recognize them. They may even forget their own names. A listing of the features of Alzheimer's disease is presented in Table 14.4.

Psychotic features such as delusions and/or hallucinations were found in about 1 in 3 people with AD in one study (Jeste et al., 1992). The appearance of psychotic symptoms appears to be connected with greater cognitive impairment and more rapid deterioration. People with Alzheimer's disease are frequently depressed or suicidal, but their doctors may overlook the danger signs or disregard them (Teri & Wagner, 1992).

Alzheimer's disease was first described in 1907 by the German physician Alois Alzheimer (1864–1915). During an autopsy of a 56-year-old woman who had suffered from severe dementia, he found two brain abnormalities that are now regarded as signs of the disease: plaques (portions of degenerative brain tissue) and neurofibrillary tangles (twisted bundles of nerve cells) (see Figure 14.2). The darkly shaded areas in the photo to the right in Figure 14.2 show the diminished brain activity associated with Alzheimer's disease.

Diagnosis   There is no clear-cut diagnostic test for AD. The diagnosis of AD is generally based on a process of exclusion and given only when other possible causes of dementia are eliminated. Other medical and psychological conditions may mimic AD, such as severe depression resulting in memory loss and impaired cognitive functioning. Consequently, misdiagnoses may occur, especially in the early stages of the disease. A confirmatory diagnosis of AD can be made only upon inspection of brain tissue by biopsy or autopsy (Davies, 1988). However, biopsy is rarely

TABLE 14.4

Features of Alzheimer's Disease

1. *Forgetfulness:* Memory loss is the cardinal symptom of Alzheimer's disease. While some level of forgetfulness is normally associated with aging, the severe memory losses that occur in Alzheimer's disease are not part of a normal aging process. In early stages, the person may lose the ability to remember relatively trivial material, such as forgetting names, dates, or places. They may also be able to recall events from their childhood or remote past better than they remember more recent events, giving an impression that their memory is intact. As the disease progresses, they begin to forget more meaningful events, like being unable to remember the last time they ate.

2. *Agitation and Aggression:* The person with Alzheimer's disease may engage in pacing or fidgeting behavior, or hostile displays of aggressive behavior including yelling, throwing, or hitting. Even people who had never before engaged in hostile or aggressive behaviors may become unable to control themselves.

3. *Depression:* Depression is common among people with Alzheimer's disease, and often involves impaired concentration, sleep disturbances, and suicidal feelings. Whether the depression is due to the brain damage associated with the disease itself, or represents a reaction to the recognition of loss of mental ability, or some combination of these factors, remains unclear.

4. *Incontinence:* The person may experience a loss of urinary or bowel control, generally occurring in the later stages of the illness.

5. *Suspicion, Paranoia, and Psychotic Behavior:* The ability to discern reality may become impaired. Individuals may come to believe that someone is attempting to harm them or is stealing their possessions, or that their spouses are unfaithful to them. Delusions may develop in which individuals may believe that their spouses are actually other people. Auditory or visual hallucinations may occur.

6. *Wandering:* A dangerous and difficult management problem, the person may wander off due to restlessness or pacing and be unable to find the way back.

7. *Language Difficulties:* Aphasia (difficulties finding words or forming grammatical sentences) and difficulties comprehending written or spoken language are frequent features of Alzheimer's disease. Individuals may be able to read, but not understand what they have read. In later stages, the individual's speech may be limited to uttering repetitive sounds.

8. *Apraxia:* Apraxia, or the inability to carry through purposeful movements, may develop. Individuals may have difficulty using utensils, dressing themselves, or writing. Apraxias usually develop after memory and language dysfunctions have become significant.

9. *Sleep difficulties:* Restlessness at night and problems falling sleep or maintaining sleep are quite common.

Source: Adapted from Jarvik & Trader, 1988; Used with permission from Rathus, 1996.

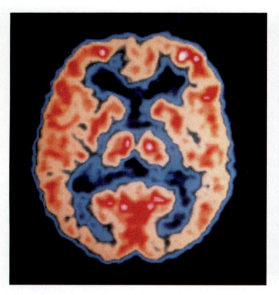
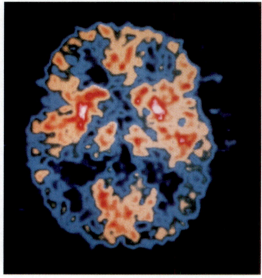

FIGURE 14.2 *PET scans of brains from a healthy aged adult (left) and a patient with Alzheimer's disease (right).* The darkly shaded areas in the photo to the right suggest how the neurological changes associated with Alzheimer's disease (as marked by the excess of dark shading) impair brain activity.

Source: Robert P. Friedland, Case Western Reserve University, courtesy of Clinical Neuroimaging, © 1988 by John Wiley and Sons, Inc.

performed because of the risk of hemorrhaging or infection, and autopsy, of course, occurs too late to help the patient.

Scientists have been searching for years for a diagnostic test for AD. Recent efforts have focused on identifying markers of AD. Specialists at Harvard University, for example, have developed a test that measures levels of a protein in the brain associated with AD (Morrow, 1998a). Such techniques are promising but require further study.

Features of Alzheimer's Disease   The dementia associated with AD progresses steadily and becomes well advanced after about 3 years (Cooke, 1994). Earlier age of onset of AD appears to be associated with poorer cognitive functioning, even when the duration of the illness is taken into account. AD that strikes people earlier in life may involve a more severe form of the disease.

The early stages of the disease are marked by limited memory problems and subtle personality changes (see Table 14.5). People may at first have trouble managing their finances; remembering recent events or basic information such as telephone numbers, area codes, zip codes, and the names of their grandchildren; and performing numerical computations (Reisberg et al., 1986). A business manager who once handled millions of dollars may become unable to add two numbers (Davies, 1988). There may be subtle personality changes, such as signs of withdrawal in people who had been outgoing or irritability in people who had been gentle. In these early stages, people with AD generally appear neat and well groomed and are generally cooperative and socially appropriate.

As AD progresses to a level of moderate severity, assistance may be required in managing everyday tasks. People

Some notable individuals with Alzheimer's disease.   Alzheimer's disease (AD) has struck a number of notable people, including the artist Norman Rockwell (left), the actress Rita Hayworth (middle), and former President Ronald Reagan (right), here shown with his wife Nancy at his first public appearance after being diagnosed with AD.

TABLE 14.5

The Global Deterioration Scale (GDS) for Assessment of Alzheimer's Disease

GDS Stage	Clinical Phase	Clinical Characteristics	Diagnosis
1 = No cognitive decline	Normal	No subjective complaints of memory deficit. No memory deficit evident on clinical interview.	Normal
2 = Very mild cognitive decline	Forgetfulness	Subjective complaints of memory deficits. No objective deficits in employment or social situations. Appropriate concern with respect to symptomatology.	Normal aged
3 = Mild cognitive decline	Early confusional	Earliest clear-cut deficits. Decreased performance in demanding employment and social settings. Objective evidence of memory deficit obtained only with an intensive interview. Mild to moderate anxiety accompanies symptoms.	Compatible with incipient Alzheimer's disease
4 = Moderate cognitive decline	Late confusional	Clear-cut deficit on careful clinical interview. Inability to perform complex tasks. Denial is dominant defense mechanism. Flattening of affect and withdrawal from challenging situations occur.	Mild Alzheimer's disease
5 = Moderately severe cognitive decline	Early dementia	Patients can no longer survive without some assistance. Patients are unable during interview to recall a major relevant aspect of their current lives. Persons at this stage retain knowledge of many major facts regarding themselves and others. They invariably know their own names and generally know their spouses and children's names. They require no assistance with using the toilet and eating, but may have some difficulty choosing the proper clothing to wear.	Moderate Alzheimer's disease
6 = Severe cognitive decline	Middle dementia	May occasionally forget the name of the spouse upon whom they are entirely dependent for survival. Will be largely unaware of all recent events and experiences in their lives. Will require some assistance with activities of daily living. Personality and emotional changes occur.	Moderately severe Alzheimer's disease
7 = Very severe cognitive decline	Late dementia	All verbal abilities are lost. Frequently there is no speech at all—only grunting. Incontinent of urine; requires assistance toileting and feeding. Loses basic psychomotor skills (for example, ability to walk).	Severe Alzheimer's disease

Source: Reprinted with permission from Reisberg et al., 1982. Copyright © 1982 by American Psychiatric Association.

with AD in the moderately severe range may be unable to select clothes for the season or the occasion. They may be unable to recall their addresses or names of family members. When they drive, they begin making mistakes, such as failing to stop at stop signs or accelerating when they should be braking.

Some people with AD are not aware of their deficits. Others deny them. At first they may attribute their problems to other causes, such as stress or fatigue. Denial may protect people with AD in the early or mild stages of the disease from recognition that their intellectual abilities are in decline (Reisberg et al., 1986). Denial is suspected when there is a clear discrepancy between the realities of their condition and their reported perceptions of their condition. On the other hand, the recognition that one's mental abilities are slipping away may lead to depression.

Cognitive impairment becomes more severe as the disease progresses. At the moderately severe level, people encounter difficulties in various aspects of personal functioning, such as toileting and bathing themselves (Reisberg et al., 1986). There are large gaps in their memories for recent events. They may not be able to recall their complete addresses but may remember parts of them. Or they may forget the name of the president but be able to recall his last name if given the first name. They may fail to recognize familiar people or forget their names. They often make mistakes in recognizing themselves in mirrors (Mendez et al., 1992). Memory for remote events is also affected. People with advanced AD may be unable to recall the names of their schools, parents, or birthplaces. They may no longer be able to speak in full sentences. Verbal responses may be limited to a few words.

Movement and coordination functions deteriorate. People with AD at the moderately severe level may begin walking in shorter, slower steps. They may no longer be able to sign their names, even when assisted by others. They may have difficulty handling a knife and fork. Agitation becomes a prominent feature at this stage, and victims may act out in response to the threat of having to contend with an environment that no longer seems controllable. They may pace or fidget or display aggressive behavior such as yelling, throwing, or hitting. Patients may wander off because of restlessness and be unable to find their way back.

People with advanced AD may start talking to themselves or experience visual hallucinations or paranoid delusions. They may believe someone is attempting to harm them or is stealing their possessions, or that their spouses are unfaithful to them. They may believe their spouses are actually other people.

At the most severe stage, cognitive functions decline to the point where people become essentially helpless. They become incontinent, are unable to communicate, walk, or even sit up, and require assistance in toileting and feeding. They may be entirely mute and inattentive to the environment. In the end state, seizures, coma, and death result.

Several of the principal features of Alzheimer's disease, including disorientation, memory loss, and behavior problems, are illustrated by the following case:

A 65-year-old draftsman began to have problems remembering important details at work; at home he began to have difficulty keeping his financial records up-to-date and remembering to pay bills on time. His intellectual abilities progressively declined, forcing him eventually to retire from his job. Behavioral problems began to appear at home, as he grew increasingly stubborn and even verbally and physically abusive toward others when he felt thwarted.

On neurological examination, he displayed disorientation as to place and time, believing that the consultation room was his place of employment and that the year was "1960 or something," when it was actually 1982. He had difficulty with even simple memory tests, failing to remember any of six objects shown to him ten minutes earlier, not recalling the names of his parents or siblings, or the name of the president of the United States. His speech was vague and filled with meaningless phrases. He couldn't perform simple arithmetical computations, but he could interpret proverbs correctly.

Shortly following the neurological consultation, the man was placed in a hospital since his family was no longer able to control his increasingly disruptive behavior. In the hospital, his mental abilities continued to decline, while his aggressive behavior was largely controlled by major tranquilizers (antipsychotic drugs). He was diagnosed as suffering from a primary degenerative

dementia of the Alzheimer type. He died at age 74, some 8 years following the onset of his symptoms.

ADAPTED FROM SPITZER ET AL., 1989, PP. 131–132

The Global Deterioration Scale, or GDS (Reisberg, Ferris, DeLeon, & Crook, 1982), shows the magnitude or "stage" of cognitive decline associated with normal aging and with various degrees of severity of Alzheimer's disease (see Table 14.5). Keep in mind, however, that forgetfulness among the aged may fall within the spectrum of normal aging. It is not necessarily an early sign of Alzheimer's disease. A study of 40 people who averaged 69 years of age and complained of forgetfulness (GDS Stage 2) were found $3\frac{1}{2}$ years later to be alive and functioning well in the community (Reisberg et al., 1986). Only 5% of them showed notable cognitive deterioration during the $3\frac{1}{2}$ years. People in later life (and some of us not quite that advanced in years) complain of not remembering names as well as they used to, or of forgetting names that were once well known to them. Although mild forgetfulness may concern people, it need not impair their social or occupational functioning (Reisberg et al., 1986).

TRUTH *or* FICTION REVISITED

14.5 *False.* Occasional memory loss or forgetfulness in middle life may be a normal consequence of the aging process and is not a sign of the early stages of Alzheimer's disease.

Impact on the Family: A Funeral That Never Ends Alzheimer's disease touches on people's deepest fears, namely fears of losing control of one's mind, one's thoughts, one's actions, one's environment. Families who helplessly watch their loved ones slowly deteriorate have been described as attending a "funeral that never ends" (M. K. Aronson, 1988). Living with a person with advanced AD may seem like living with a stranger, so profound are the changes in the person's personality and behavior.

At least 2 of 3 persons with AD and related disorders live at home (Gurland & Cross, 1986). Eventually, they come to require round-the-clock attention from family members, placing incredible strains on the members of the family who shoulder the burden of care. Spouses usually provide the bulk of care, often with the assistance of their children, principally their daughters or daughters-in-law (Aronson, 1988). The children, usually middle-aged, are caught (some describe it as being "sandwiched") between the demands of caring for a parent with dementia and tending to their own children, marriages, and careers. The stress caused by the symptoms of advanced AD, such as wandering away, aggressiveness, destructiveness, incontinence, screaming, and remaining awake at night all contribute to the level of stress imposed on caregivers (Gurland & Cross, 1986).

Families who can no longer shoulder the burden of care may seek to place the person with AD in a nursing home or

Alzheimer's disease. Alzheimer's disease can devastate patients' families. Spouses usually provide the bulk of daily care. This man has been caring for his wife for several years, and he believes that his hugs and kisses sometimes prompt his wife to murmur his name.

long-term care facility. A recent study showed that as many as two thirds of family caregivers who keep relatives with dementia at home with them decide to institutionalize them within a period of 18 months, generally because they can no longer cope with the burdens of caregiving (A. C. Cohen et al., 1993). Problems of aggressive behavior and incontinence were among the factors that distinguished people with dementia who eventually became institutionalized from those who remained with their families.

Generally speaking, it is the ability of the family to support the AD patient financially and emotionally, and not the degree of dementia or impairment of functioning, that determines whether or not afflicted people become institutionalized (Aronson, 1988). About 60% of nursing home residents suffer from dementias of one type or another (Davies, 1988). Because Medicare, the system of health care for older Americans, does not cover long-term custodial care in nursing homes for people with dementia, families must either foot the bill themselves or seek subsidized care (Medicaid) for indigent patients.

Self-help groups have been established to provide families whose loved ones have AD with emotional support and opportunities to share information about the disease. More than 1,000 support groups—composed of individuals who are living through or have lived through caring for family members with AD—have been started by the Alzheimer's Disease and Related Disorders Association (ADRDA) (J. Marks, 1988).

Theoretical Perspectives We don't know either what causes AD or how to either prevent it or cure it. AD may involve multiple causes, so we may need to look for different causal pathways. We do know that plaques, the steel-wool-like clumps that form in the brains of people with Alzheimer's disease, are composed of a material called *beta amyloid,* which consists of fibrous protein fragments. For some unknown reason, possibly involving a genetic mutation, these fragments break off from a larger protein during metabolism and cluster together in strings that attract remnants of other nerve cells, forming plaques. The formation of these plaques may be responsible for destroying adjacent brain tissue, leading to the death of brain cells across a large area of the brain, which in turn leads to the memory loss, confusion, and other symptoms of the disease (Angier, 1990a).

Recent discoveries have begun to shed some light on the puzzle of AD. Scientists in 1997 reported finding a protein that exists in high concentrations in the brains of AD patients that seems to work with beta amyloid to kill brain cells (Yan et al., 1997). Another group reported finding yet another type of plaque in the brains of AD patients that was made from a different material than beta amyloid (Trojanowski et al., 1997). As these pieces of the puzzle begin to fit together, scientists are hopeful of finding a target that might lead to an effective treatment.

Genetic factors appear to play a large role in AD. Consistent with a genetic contribution, higher concordance rates were found among monozygotic (MZ) twin pairs (78%) than among dizygotic twin pairs (39%) (Bergem et al., 1997). Late-onset AD has been linked to a gene involved in production of a protein called *apolipoprotein E* (APOe), which transports cholesterol through the bloodstream ("The race for Alzheimer's treatments," 1997). This protein appears to be involved in the formation of the plaques and neurofibrillary tangles associated with Alzheimer's disease (M. F. Weiner, 1996). However, this particular gene may account for only a small percentage of Alzheimer's cases (National Institute on Aging, 1997). In 1998 another gene involved in APOe production was linked to AD (Bullido et al., 1998). Still other genes may be involved in different forms of the disease, including defects in genes involved in cell metabolism, the process of converting food into energy, and in production of beta amyloid (L. M. Fisher, 1997; Pericak-Vance et al., 1997; Rogaeva et al., 1998).

Researchers believe genetic factors may be even stronger in early-onset (prior to age 70) than late-onset AD (Li et al., 1995). In 1995, scientists reported that a rare but severe form of Alzheimer's disease that can afflict young people, even people in their thirties, is linked to a mutation on another single gene (Sherrington et al., 1995). Whether the actions of this gene can teach us something about the more common form of the disease that primarily affects older adults remains an open question.

Other biochemical research focuses on the possible role of neurotransmitter imbalances in the brain, especially imbalances of the neurotransmitter acetylcholine (ACh). People with AD have reduced levels of ACh in their brains,

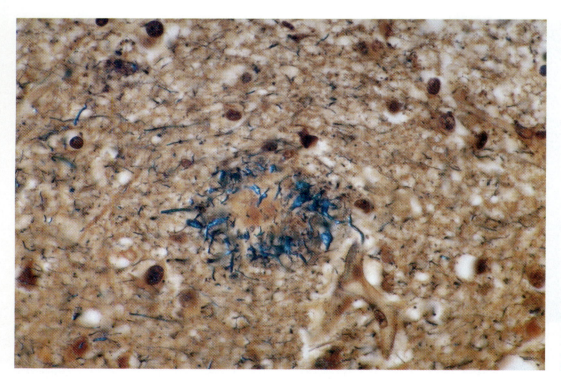

Plaques linked to Alzheimer's disease. In Alzheimer's disease, nerve tissue in the brain degenerates, forming steel wool-like clumps or plaques composed of beta-amyloid protein fragments.

which may be due to the death of brain cells in an area of the brain, the nucleus basalis of Meynert, that manufactures ACh .

Treatment Drug therapies have focused on raising the levels of ACh in the brain. One such drug is *tacrine* (trade name Cognex), which inhibits the breakdown of ACh by decreasing the action of an enzyme that metabolizes or breaks down ACh. Tacrine is no panacea. It produces modest benefits at best in improving memory and language functioning and is associated with side effects such as headaches, nausea, vomiting, diarrhea, rash, and elevated enzyme levels that could lead to liver damage (Tune, 1998). The drug may be most useful in treating patients in the mild to moderate range of severity of AD . Another recently approved drug, *donepezil,* also increases acetylcholine but has fewer side effects than tacrine. Yet its effects on boosting mental functioning are also modest at best ("FDA Approves Second Drug for Alzheimer's," 1996; "The race for Alzheimer's treatments," 1997). All in all, presently available drugs to combat AD, and those in the pipeline, may slow the progression of the disease but are far from a cure (Weingartner et al., 1996).

Though we still lack an effective and safe treatment for AD, evidence shows that high doses of vitamin E may help slow the progression of the disease (Sano et al., 1997). A natural herbal extract, *ginkgo biloba,* has also slowed deterioration in AD patients and even led to some modest improvements in some (Le Bars et al., 1997). These substances, vitamin E and *ginkgo* extract, may help protect brain cells in AD patients. Other promising results come from the use of estrogen replacement therapy with older women with AD,

which appears to help older women retain more memory functioning (Cable News Network, 1996). Whether these findings will translate into clinical benefits in treating AD patients remains to be seen (Jarman, 1998).

People who are suspected of having AD should be evaluated quickly because other conditions that produce AD-like symptoms, such as stroke or depression, may be treatable or reversible. Early diagnosis allows those afflicted and their families to set aside money and make other plans to ensure adequate continuing care. The use of memory aids, such as color-coding food or personal belongings, may help people with AD cope with declining cognitive ability. Use of written notes may help AD patients partially compensate for memory deficits and better organize their behavior. Tranquilizing medication may be used to help control the emotional agitation and inappropriate behavior that accompanies severe dementias. Antidepressant medication and psychological treatment in the form of behavior therapy may help reduce depression that accompanies AD (Taragano et al., 1997; Teri et al., 1997). Cognitive functioning may also improve as the depression responds to treatment. Caretakers often need assistance from trained counselors to help them deal more effectively with the behavioral problems associated with AD, such as agitation and physical or verbal aggression.

On the prevention front, researchers report that people who regularly take the commonly used pain reliever ibuprofen, a type of anti-inflammatory drug (brand names *Advil, Nuprin,* or *Motrin*), are much less likely than others to develop AD (Hager & Peyser, 1997). We can't say for sure why ibuprofen may reduce the risk of AD, but perhaps it curbs the brain inflammation associated with the disease (Weiner,

Examining Your Attitudes Toward Aging

What are your assumptions about late adulthood? Do you see older people as basically different from the young in their behavior patterns and their outlooks, or just as a few years more mature?

T F 1. By age 60 most couples have lost their capacity for satisfying sexual relations.

T F 2. Older people cannot wait to retire.

T F 3. With advancing age people become more externally oriented, less concerned with the self.

T F 4. As individuals age, they become less able to adapt satisfactorily to a changing environment.

T F 5. General satisfaction with life tends to decrease as people become older.

T F 6. As people age they tend to become more homogeneous—that is, all old people tend to be alike in many ways.

T F 7. For the older person, having a stable intimate relationship is no longer highly important.

T F 8. The aged are susceptible to a wider variety of psychological disorders than young and middle-aged adults.

To evaluate the accuracy of your attitudes toward aging, mark each of the following items true (T) or false (F). Then turn to the answer key at the end of the chapter.

T F 9. Most older people are depressed much of the time.

T F 10. Church attendance increases with age.

T F 11. The occupational performance of the older worker is typically less effective than that of the younger adult.

T F 12. Most older people are just not able to learn new skills.

T F 13. When forced to make a decision, older people are more cautious and take fewer risks than younger persons.

T F 14. Compared to younger persons, older people tend to think more about the past than the present or the future.

T F 15. Most people in later life are unable to live independently and reside in nursing home–like institutions.

Source: Rathus, S. A. & Nevid, J. S. (1995). *Adjustment and Growth: The Challenges of Life.* (6th ed.). Fort Worth, TX: Harcourt Brace College Publishers, p.440. Reprinted with permission.

1996). Anti-inflammatory drugs such as ibuprofen carry a risk of serious side effects when taken over the long term, so experts do not recommend using them to prevent Alzheimer's. Researchers hope that other anti-inflammatory drugs can be developed that won't have dangerous side effects ("Can ordinary pain relievers prevent Alzheimer's," 1997).

TRUTH or FICTION REVISITED

14.6 *True.* Recent evidence links regular use of the pain reliever ibuprofen to reduced risk of AD. However, physicians caution against routine use of the drug for this purpose because of the risks of side effects.

Vascular Dementia

The brain, like other living tissues, depends on the bloodstream to supply it with oxygen and glucose and to carry away its metabolic wastes. A stroke (also called a *cerebrovascular accident* or CVA) occurs when part of the brain becomes damaged because of a disruption in its blood supply, usually as the result of a blood clot that becomes lodged in an artery that services the brain and obstructs circulation. The areas of the brain that are affected may be damaged or destroyed, leaving the victim with disabilities in motor, speech, and cognitive functions. Death may also occur. Vascular dementia (formerly called *multi-infarct dementia*) is a form of dementia that results from repeated strokes. (An infarct refers to the death of tissue caused by insufficient blood supply.) Vascular dementia accounts for about 20% of cases of dementia ("Update on Alzheimer's Disease," Part I, 1995) and appears to be more common in men than women (APA, 1994). Like dementia of the Alzheimer's type, it is most prevalent among people in later life, especially after age 75. Unlike AD, heredity does not appear to play a major role in vascular dementia (Bergem et al., 1997).

Strokes and Vascular Dementia There are three major types of stroke. In a *cerebral thrombosis,* a blood clot forms in an artery that provides blood to the brain, which blocks circulation to brain tissue. In a *cerebral embolism,* circulation is blocked by a blood clot or another substance, such as an air bubble or fatty globule, that travels from elsewhere in the body and becomes lodged in an artery that services the brain. *Atherosclerosis* (the buildup of fatty deposits along the interior walls of blood vessels) narrows arteries, making it more likely that blood clots will form and block the supply of blood to the brain, which increases the likelihood of these types of stroke.

The most severe type of stroke is a *cerebral hemorrhage*, which is caused by a blood vessel rupturing in the brain. Blood from the ruptured vessel leaks into sensitive brain tissue, damaging or destroying it. A weakness in the vessel wall that permits it to rupture may be a congenital defect or the result of hypertension, which may gradually weaken the walls of blood vessels. Sometimes the cause remains unknown. The effects of a cerebral hemorrhage depend on the size of the ruptured vessel and the area of the brain affected. Victims typically experience a sudden loss of consciousness and lapse into a coma, which may be accompanied by convulsions.

The effects of a stroke depend on the extent of the brain damage and can be severe—fatal, in fact, especially a cerebral hemorrhage. Some trivial ("silent") strokes do not affect key brain regions and produce only minor effects. Most stroke victims need to adjust to some degree of permanent impairment, however. Survivors may experience paralysis or loss of sensation on one side of the body, loss of speech (aphasia), and impaired memory. Some cannot walk on their own. Many victims find it difficult to adjust to their loss of functioning. As a consequence, they may have unstable moods that fluctuate between depression and rage.

Single strokes may produce gross impairments in specific functions, such as aphasia, but single strokes do not typically cause the more generalized cognitive declines that characterize dementia. Vascular dementia generally results from multiple strokes that occur at different times and that have cumulative effects on a wide range of mental abilities.

Features of Vascular Dementia   The symptoms of vascular dementia are similar to those of dementia of the Alzheimer's type, including impaired memory and language ability, agitation and emotional instability, and loss of ability to care for one's own basic needs. However, AD is characterized by an insidious onset and a gradual decline of mental functioning, while vascular dementia typically occurs abruptly and follows a stepwise course of deterioration involving a pattern of rapid declines in cognitive functioning that are believed to reflect the effects of additional strokes (Brinkman, Largen, Cushman, Braun, & Block, 1986). Certain cognitive functions in people with vascular dementia may remain relatively intact in the early course of the disorder, leading to a pattern of patchy deterioration in which islands of mental competence remain while other abilities suffer gross impairment, depending on the particular areas of the brain that have been damaged by multiple strokes.

DEMENTIAS AND OTHER PSYCHOLOGICAL PROBLEMS DUE TO GENERAL MEDICAL CONDITIONS

We have examined relationships between aging and psychological disorders such as dementia and depression. Next we consider a number of physical disorders which affect psychological functioning in various ways.

Dementia Due to Pick's Disease

Pick's disease causes a progressive dementia that is symptomatically similar to AD. Symptoms include memory loss and social inappropriateness, such as a loss of modesty or the display of flagrant sexual behavior. Diagnosis is confirmed only upon autopsy by the *absence* of the neurofibrillary tangles and plaques that are found in AD and by the presence of other abnormal structures—Pick's bodies—in nerve cells. Pick's disease is believed to account for perhaps 5% of dementias. Unlike AD, it begins most often between the ages of 50 and 60 (APA, 1994), and the risk declines with advancing age after 70 (Heston & Mastry, 1982). Men are more likely than women to suffer from Pick's disease.

Pick's disease appears to run in families, and a genetic component is suspected in its etiology (Heston, White, & Mastry, 1987). It has been estimated that members of the immediate family of victims of Pick's disease have an overall risk of 17% of contracting the disease by age 75 (Heston et al., 1987).

Dementia Due to Parkinson's Disease

Dementia occurs in approximately 20% to 60% of people with **Parkinson's disease** (APA, 1994), a slowly progressing neurological disorder that was first identified by the physician James Parkinson in 1817. Parkinson treated several patients who suffered from a degenerative process that was characterized by shaking or tremors, rigidity, disturbances in posture (leaning forward), and lack of control over body movements. Parkinson's disease afflicts between 400,000 and 1 million people in the United States (Cowley, 1992; "Update on Alzheimer's Disease, Part I," 1995), including former heavyweight champion Muhammad Ali. It affects men and women about equally and most often strikes between the ages of 50 and 69 (Knight, Godfrey, & Shelton, 1988).

People with Parkinson's disease may be able to exercise control over their shaking or tremors, but only briefly. Some cannot walk at all. Others walk laboriously, in a crouch. Some execute voluntary body movements with difficulty, have poor control over fine motor movements, such as finger control, and have sluggish reflexes. They may look expressionless, as if they are wearing masks, a symptom that apparently reflects the degeneration of brain tissue that controls facial muscles. It is particularly difficult for patients to engage in sequences of complex movements, such as those required to sign their names. People with Parkinson's disease may be unable to coordinate two movements at the same time, as seen in this description of a Parkinson's patient who had difficulty walking and reaching for his wallet at the same time:

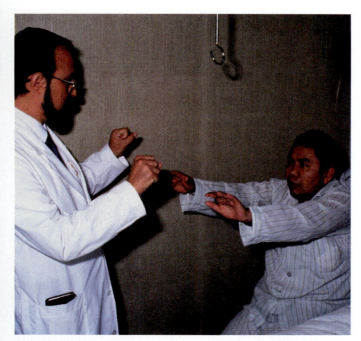

Parkinson's disease. Parkinson's disease is characterized by tremors, rigidity, disturbances in posture, and lack of control over body movements. There is also evidence of cognitive and perceptual impairment, especially during the later stages of the disease. Here a physician examines a Parkinson's patient for signs of motor impairment.

A 58-year-old man was walking across the hotel lobby in order to pay his bill. He reached into his inside jacket pocket for his wallet. He stopped walking instantly as he did so and stood immobile in the lobby in front of strangers. He became aware of his suspended locomotion and resumed his stroll to the cashier; however, his hand remained rooted in his inside pocket, as though he were carrying a weapon he might display once he arrived at the cashier.

ADAPTED FROM KNIGHT ET AL., 1988

Parkinson's disease involves the destruction of brain cells in an area of the brain stem called the *substantia nigra* ("black substance"), which is involved in controlling body movements. In some cases, the damage or destruction appears to be drug induced (Widner et al., 1992), resulting from side effects of major tranquilizers such as Thorazine or Stelazine. Other suspected causes include viral infections that affect the brain, exposure to environmental toxins, and arteriosclerosis (Knight et al., 1988). In most cases, however, the cause is unknown.

Despite the severity of motor disability, cognitive functions seem to remain intact during the early stages of the disease. Dementia is more common in the later stages of the disease or among those with more severe forms of the disease (APA, 1994). The form of dementia associated with Parkinson's disease typically involves a slowing down of thinking processes, impaired ability to think abstractly or plan or organize a series of actions, and difficulty retrieving memories. Overall, the cognitive impairments associated with Parkinson's disease tend to be more subtle than those associated with Alzheimer's disease (Knight et al., 1988). People with Parkinson's disease often become socially withdrawn and are at greater-than-average risk for depression (Cummings, 1992). Depression may be due to difficulty in coping with the disease or to the biochemical changes that are part and parcel of the disease (S. M. Rao, Huber, & Bornstein, 1992).

The cells in the substantia nigra that are destroyed in Parkinson's disease are involved in the manufacture and storage of the neurotransmitter dopamine (C. R. Freed et al., 1992). Why these cells die remains a mystery, but some forms of the disease are believed to be inherited (Leary, 1996a). In 1998, researchers reported finding a mutation of a particular gene that causes a rare condition similar to Parkinson's disease (Kitada et al., 1998). Other genetic defects may be involved in Parkinson's itself.

Environmental influences such as infections or exposure to toxic chemicals may also be involved. Whatever the underlying cause, the symptoms of the disease—the uncontrollable tremors, shaking, rigid muscles, and difficulty moving—are tied to deficiencies in the amount of dopamine in the brain. The drug L-dopa increases the levels of dopamine in the brain and had brought hope to Parkinson's patients when it was first used in treating the disease in the 1970s. L-Dopa is converted in the brain into dopamine.

L-Dopa helps control the symptoms of the disease and slows its progression, but it does not cure it. About 80% of people with Parkinson's disease show significant improvement in their tremors and motor symptoms following treatment with L-dopa. After a few years, however, L-dopa begins to lose its effectiveness and the disease continues to progress. The drug is often rendered useless within 10 years of treatment (Cowley, 1992). Use of another drug, deprenyl, may allow a delay in taking L-dopa for a period of nearly 9 months (The Parkinson Study Group, 1993). The longer that treatment with L-dopa can be delayed, experts say, the better for the patient (Talan, 1993b). Several other drugs are in the experimental stage, offering hope for further advances in treatment.

Research raises hopes that significant progress in combating the disease may be in the offing. Two research groups independently reported finding a brain chemical that protects and stimulates the nerve cells that die or are disabled in Parkinson's disease (Hefti et al., 1991; Hyman et al., 1991). Whether or not these findings lead to a means of protecting these nerve cells from damage or rejuvenating disabled cells remains to be determined.

Another promising treatment approach involves delivering deep brain stimulation by means of electrodes that are surgically implanted in the brain and connected through an opening behind the ear to a battery-driven generator controlled by a hand-held device (Talan, 1995). Deep brain stimulation has helped quiet tremors in some Parkinson's patients but is considered experimental at this time.

Other research groups (e.g., Freed et al., 1992; Spencer et al., 1992; Widner et al., 1992) have transplanted dopamine-producing neurons from the brains of aborted fetuses into the brains of people with Parkinson's disease. The hope is that fetal cells will take root in the recipient's brain and produce dopamine, replenishing the loss of this vital brain chemical in Parkinson sufferers (Cowley, 1992). Many of the people receiving the brain tissue implants gained more control over motor and speech functions and showed less need of L-dopa. However, they were not restored to normal (Cowley, 1992). Fetal tissue is used because it is more plastic than tissue from deceased children or adults (that is, more adaptable to surviving and functioning in the host brain), and it is also less likely to stimulate an immune response in the host and thus be rejected (Garry et al., 1992).

Many questions are raised by this treatment approach, however. Some are moral and ethical. A debate is underway, for example, about whether it is proper to use tissues from electively aborted fetuses in research or treatment (Garry et al., 1992; Kassirer & Angell, 1992). Some people worry that successful therapy of this sort could lead to the purposeful conception and abortion of fetuses for medical purposes. Other questions about this approach reflect the early stage of the research (Fahn, 1992). For example: Exactly how much fetal tissue is effective? How long do benefits last? Will the brain of the host regulate dopamine secretion by transplanted cells? Will this treatment reverse Parkinson's disease or merely delay its progress?

Dementia Due to Huntington's Disease

Huntington's disease, also known as Huntington's chorea, was first recognized by the neurologist George Huntington in 1872. Huntington's disease involves a progressive deterioration of the basal ganglia, especially of the *caudate nucleus* and the *putamen,* which primarily affects neurons that produce ACh and **GABA.**

Symptoms of the disease may appear in childhood but usually begin in the prime of adulthood, between the ages of 30 and 50. The most prominent physical symptoms of the disease are involuntary, jerky movements of the face (grimaces), neck, limbs, and trunk—in contrast to the poverty of movement that typifies Parkinson's disease. These twitches are termed *choreiform,* which derives from the Greek *choreia,* meaning "dance." Unstable moods, alternating with states of apathy, anxiety, and depression, are common in the early stages of the disease. As the disease progresses, paranoia may develop and people may become suicidally depressed. Difficulties retrieving memories in the early course of the disease may develop into dementia as the disease progresses. Eventually, there is loss of control of bodily functions, leading to death, which generally occurs within 15 years after the onset.

Huntington's disease afflicts 30,000 Americans; 150,000 others are at risk of developing the disease (Angier, 1993b). Men and women are equally likely to develop the

disease (APA, 1994). One of the victims of the disease was the folksinger Woody Guthrie, who gave us the beloved song, "This Land Is Your Land," among many others. He died of Huntington's disease in 1967, after 22 years of battling the malady. Because of the odd, jerky movements associated with the disease, Guthrie, like many other Huntington's victims, was misdiagnosed as suffering from alcoholism. He spent several years in a number of mental hospitals before the correct diagnosis was made.

TRUTH *or* **FICTION** **REVISITED**

14.7 *True.* The folksinger and songwriter was Woody Guthrie, whose Huntington's disease went misdiagnosed for years.

Huntington's disease is caused by a single defective gene on chromosome 4 (Tamminga, 1997). The gene is apparently connected with *mitochondria,* which are factors in cells that manufacture energy and fuel basic life processes. In addition to producing cognitive and motor impairments, problems in energy metabolism cause people with Huntington's disease to lose weight rapidly (A. Young, 1992). As a by-product of energy metabolism gone awry, lactic acid builds up and kills cells in the brain. Researchers are therefore investigating the potential benefits of drugs and vitamins that lower levels of lactic acid (Young, 1992).

Huntington's disease is transmitted genetically from either parent to children of either gender. People who have a parent with Huntington's disease stand a 50% chance of inheriting the gene. People who inherit the gene eventually contract the disease.

Woody Guthrie. The folksinger Woody Guthrie died from Huntington's disease in 1967, after 22 years of battling the disease.

Until recently, children of Huntington's disease victims had to wait until the symptoms developed—usually in midlife—to learn whether they had inherited the disease. A genetic test has been developed that can detect carriers of the defective gene, those who will eventually develop the disease should they live long enough. Eventually, perhaps, genetic engineering may provide a means of modifying the defective gene or its effects. Researchers are also closely scrutinizing the effects of transplants of fetal brain tissue into the brains of people with Parkinson's disease because variations of this procedure might have benefits for people with Huntington's disease (Fahn, 1992). Because researchers have not yet developed ways to cure or control Huntington's disease, some potential carriers, such as folksinger Arlo Gurthie, whose father was Woody Guthrie, prefer not knowing whether they have inherited the gene. Meanwhile, research continues. One promising development in experimental work with monkeys involves the use of brain implants that release a substance that protects the kind of brain cells killed off by Huntington's disease ("Tests Suggest Possible Protection from Huntington's Symptoms," 1997). We don't yet know whether the use of such implants could be used to treat the disease in humans.

Dementia Due to HIV Disease

Human immunodeficiency virus (HIV), the virus that causes AIDS, can invade the central nervous system , causing a cognitive disorder—dementia due to HIV disease. The most typical signs of dementia due to HIV disease are forgetfulness and impaired concentration and problem-solving ability (APA, 1994). Common behavioral features of the dementia are apathy and social withdrawal. As AIDS progresses, the dementia grows more severe, taking the form of delusions, disorientation, further impairments in memory and thinking processes, and perhaps even delirium. In its later stages, the dementia may resemble the profound deficiencies found among people with advanced Alzheimer's disease.

Dementia is rare in persons with HIV who have not yet developed full-blown AIDS. Yet as many as 1 in 4 people with AIDS develop some form of cognitive impairment that may progress to dementia (CMHS, 1994). Signs of mental intellectual impairment short of full-blown dementia may also occur earlier than the onset of AIDS (Baldeweg et al., 1997). People with HIV who show early signs of intellectual impairment appear to be at greater risk of early death from AIDS ("Cognitive Impairment Linked To Early Death In HIV-Infected Patients," 1996; Wilkie et al., 1998).

Dementia Due to Creutzfeldt-Jakob Disease

Creutzfeldt-Jakob disease is a fatal illness affecting the central nervous system. The cause is a *slow virus*, a virus that produces an infection that develops slowly in the body. Dementia is a common feature of the disease. The disease typically affects people in the 40- to 60 year-old age range, although it may develop in adults at any age (APA, 1994). There are no treatments for the disease, and death usually results within months of onset of symptoms. In about 5% to 15% of cases there is evidence of familial transmission, which suggests that a genetic component may be involved in determining susceptibility to the disease. Several dozen people in Great Britain are believed to have died from a variation of Creutzfeldt-Jakob disease spread by eating meat infected with "mad cow disease" (bovine spongiform encephalopathy) ("Clues found in brain-killing process," 1998).

Dementia Due to Head Trauma

Head trauma can injure the brain. Such injury is caused by jarring, banging, or cutting brain tissue, usually because of accident or assault. There are several types of brain traumas, including concussions, contusions, and lacerations. Progressive dementia due to head trauma is more likely to result from multiple head traumas (as in the case of boxers who receive multiple blows to the head during their careers) than to a single blow or head trauma (APA, 1994). Yet even a single head trauma can have psychological effects, and, if severe enough, can lead to physical disability or death. Specific changes in personality following traumatic injury to the brain vary with the site and extent of the injury, among other factors (Prigatano, 1992). Damage to the frontal lobe, for example, is associated with a range of emotional changes involving alterations of mood and personality (Stuss, Gow, & Hetherington, 1992).

Concussion   One type of brain trauma is the **concussion**—epidemic among football players and boxers—which involves the momentary loss of consciousness resulting from a violent blow to, or jarring of, the head. In a concussion, the brain is shaken against the skull in a manner similar to Jell-O moving about in a bowl (Thigpen, 1994). The loss of consciousness may last from a second or two to a few minutes. The person may experience lingering symptoms such as dizziness, headaches, memory deficits, anxiety, depression, and difficulties concentrating for a few days or weeks following the incident, but recovery is usually complete. Thus, football players and prize-fighters can often recover completely from being knocked out, without lingering cognitive effects. However, in some severe cases chronic memory or attentional problems may result (Blakeslee, 1995a). Repeated concussions may also lead to permanent neurological damage.

Severe concussions may produce delirium and agitation, and sufferers may have amnesia for the events directly preceding the injury. In some cases in which the concussion was sustained as the result of an extremely frightening incident, the person may go on to develop a posttraumatic stress disorder (PTSD) characterized by recurrent, intrusive images of the traumatic event (Blakeslee, 1995a).

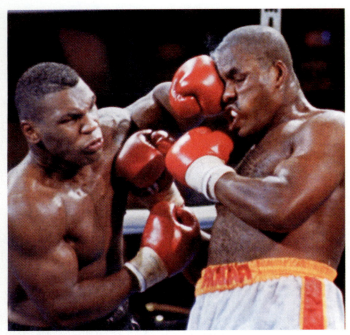

Heading toward a concussion? Concussions are epidemic among boxers and some other athletes, such as football players. Concussions involve transient loss of consciousness from a blow to the head. Severe cases can produce delirium and agitation.

TRUTH *or* **FICTION** REVISITED

14.8 *True.* The 19th century railroad worker who had a metal rod go clear through his brain and lived to tell about it was Phineas Gage. Though the wound healed, the injury affected his personality, so much so that others who knew him said that "Gage is no longer Gage."

Contusion A more serious type of brain trauma, a **contusion,** is produced by jarring the brain so hard that the soft brain tissue is pounded against the hard bone of the skull and bruised. A coma typically results and may last for hours or days. Hemorrhaging may require surgery to repair the damage or stop the bleeding. Upon awakening, victims may have problems with cognitive functions and speech, but functioning is usually regained in about a week. Repeated concussions and contusions, however, such as those incurred by professional boxers, can cause lasting brain damage and give rise to dementia and emotional instability. Boxers who suffer from this condition, called the "punch-drunk syndrome" or *traumatic encephalopathy* (*encephalopathy* derives from Greek roots meaning "something wrong in the head"), experience cognitive and physical symptoms such as slurring of speech, shaky or unsteady gait, emotional problems, memory deficits, dizziness, and tremors.

Laceration The most serious type of brain trauma, a **laceration,** is an injury caused by a foreign object that pierces the skull and damages brain tissue. The extent of the damage is related to the location and extent of the injury. Although a severe laceration can cause immediate death, survivors often suffer permanent brain damage that results in major mental and physical impairments. Sometimes, however, the victim "luckily" experiences only minor damage or no permanent effects. In the classic case of Phineas Gage, the effects were more subtle:

Brain Tumors Benign and malignant (cancerous) brain tumors can cause serious cognitive disorders in addition to the threats they pose to our physical health (see Figure 14.3). The skull prevents the brain from expanding, so even a benign tumor can press against and damage the surrounding tissue. Malignant brain tumors can be primary (that is, originate in the brain), or secondary (spread, or *metastasize* to the brain from other cancerous sites in the body). In either case, they are made up of cells that proliferate rapidly and destroy adjacent healthy cells.

The symptoms produced by a brain tumor depend on the tumor's size and location. Memory problems sometimes represent the first signs of a tumor. Recurrent headaches are another sign. Because such early signs also occur in many other disorders, the possibility of a brain tumor is often overlooked. As the tumor grows, symptoms worsen, giving rise to persistent, severe headaches; seizures; disorientation; memory impairment; vomiting; changes in vision; motor impairment; and, in some cases, dementia. The personality may also be affected. Depression, flat or blunted affect, and confusion are some of the personality changes observed in people with brain tumors. Some people with brain tumors become slovenly in their dress or careless in their work. Some tumors are operable and can be removed by surgery, so early detection and treatment are critical. Inoperable malignancies sometimes respond to radiation.

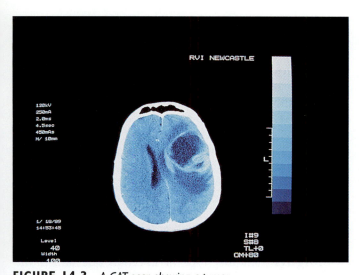

FIGURE 14.3 *A CAT scan showing a tumor.*
This CAT scan of a 67-year-old man shows a tumor on the left side of the brain (the right side of the photograph). The tumor is the dark, roughly circular region.

Nutritional Deficiencies

Nutritional imbalances or deficiencies may also affect cognitive functioning. People with chronic alcoholism, as noted in the section on amnestic disorders, may neglect their diets and develop such disorders as *alcohol-induced persisting amnestic disorder* (more widely known as *Korsakoff's syndrome*) as a result.

A deficiency of niacin, a B vitamin, causes **pellagra,** which derives its name from the Latin *pellis,* meaning "skin," and the Greek *agra,* meaning "seizure." Pellagra gives rise to physical symptoms, such as diarrhea and skin eruptions (hence the name), and to psychological symptoms, such as anxiety, depression, loss of memory for recent events, and problems in concentration. If left untreated, hallucinations and delirium may result, and eventually death. Because of greater attention to diet and an improved standard of living, pellagra is now uncommon in the United States. It is more common in developing countries where diets are nutritionally unbalanced and consist mainly of cornmeal. Except in the most advanced cases, treatment with a diet rich in niacin and other key vitamins is an effective treatment.

Beriberi (a reduplication of the Sinhalese word meaning "weakness") is another disease caused by thiamine deficiency. It is associated with chronic alcoholism and in other cases of people whose diets are lacking in thiamine, and sometimes occurs together with pellagra. Beriberi is characterized by neurological disorders that produce difficulties in memory and concentration, irritability, fatigue and lethargy, lack of appetite, insomnia, irritability, and loss of appetite.

Endocrine Disorders

Because hormones are released directly into the bloodstream and travel throughout the body, including the brain, overactivity or underactivity of endocrine glands can affect psychological as well as physical functions.

The thyroid gland secretes **thyroxin,** which is involved in the regulation of the metabolic rate. Hyperthyroidism (also called *Grave's disease*) is caused by oversecretion of thyroxin, which accelerates the metabolism and produces weight loss, "bug eyes," and psychological effects such as excitability, insomnia, anxiety, restlessness, even transient delusions or hallucinations. Former president George Bush and first lady Barbara Bush were treated for Grave's disease.

Hypothyroidism, which results from abnormally low levels of thyroxin, may cause **cretinism** in childhood, a condition characterized by stunted growth and mental retardation. In adulthood, hypothyroidism, also called *myxedema,* slows the metabolism and is associated with physical changes, such as dry skin and weight gain, and psychological changes, such as sluggishness and fatigue, difficulties in concentration and memory, depression, and dementia in some cases. The widespread use of iodized salt, which prevents thyroid deficiencies, has greatly reduced the occurrence of hypothyroidism in the United States.

The adrenal glands, which are located above the kidneys, consist of an outer layer, or cortex, and an internal core, or medulla. The adrenal cortex secretes steroids, which enhance resistance to stress and regulate metabolism of carbohydrates. Underactivity of the adrenal cortex may result in **Addison's disease** (after the English physician, Thomas Addison), which is characterized by weight loss, low blood pressure, fatigue, irritability, lack of motivation, social withdrawal, and depression. President John Kennedy suffered from Addison's disease. Cortical overactivity, or **Cushing's syndrome** (after the American physician, Harvey Cushing), is a relatively rare disease generally affecting young women. Cushing's syndrome is characterized by physical symptoms,

Grave's disease. Former President George Bush and First Lady Barbara Bush both suffered from Grave's disease, which is caused by oversecretion of thyroxin.

John Kennedy. Another former President, John Fitzgerald Kennedy, suffered from Addison's disease, which results from a deficiency in the secretion of cortical steroids by the adrenal cortex.

such as weight gain, fatigue, and muscle weakness, and psychological features, such as negative mood states that may fluctuate between depression and anxiety.

Infections of the Brain

Infections of the brain may damage or destroy neural tissue and have profound mental and physical effects. We consider three major types of brain infection—encephalitis, meningitis, and neurosyphilis.

Encephalitis **Encephalitis** is derived from Greek roots meaning "inflammation" (*-itis*) in "the head" (*kephale*). An inflammation of the brain may be caused by various types of infection or by other conditions, such as lead poisoning. Most brain infections involve viruses that may be carried by mosquitoes, ticks, and other insects. Inanimate objects that penetrate the brain, such as shrapnel or bullets, cause structural damage, may carry infectious organisms, and also leave openings that allow other infectious organisms to enter. In other cases, infections from other parts of the body spread to the brain.

An epidemic of encephalitis, suspected of being caused by an influenza virus carried by mosquitoes, spread throughout Europe and the United States around the time of World War I. It was called "sleeping sickness" because it induced

prolonged periods of lethargy and sleepiness, which were followed by periods of irritability and excitability. Epidemics of encephalitis are practically unknown today in developed nations, but outbreaks of encephalitis—along with infestations of insects—continue to plague developing nations.

Delirium can occur during the acute phase of encephalitis, and convulsions and coma occur in some cases. Changes in personality also occur, especially in young children, and survivors may be left with psychological symptoms such as irritability, restlessness, depression, and dementia. There is usually an apparently complete physical recovery, but some effects may linger: tremors, paralysis in the arms or legs, speech and hearing problems, and, in the case of afflicted infants, mental retardation.

Meningitis Another type of infection that afflicts the central nervous system, **meningitis**, involves acute inflammation of the membranes, or meninges (from the Greek *meningos,* meaning "membrane"), that cover the spinal cord and brain. Various microbes, such as viruses, bacteria, and protozoa, may cause meningitis. The most common cause is the meningococcus (from the Greek *kokkos,* meaning "kernel" or "berry") bacterium, which is also responsible for most epidemics. If treated early with antibiotics, this form of meningitis can generally be cured. If left untreated, however, it may lead to coma and death. Victims typically experience a high fever, convulsions, severe headache, muscle stiffness and pain, vomiting, drowsiness, impaired concentration, irritability, and memory impairment. When contracted in infancy, meningitis, like encephalitis, may cause mental retardation because of its effects on developing brain tissue.

Neurosyphilis **General paresis** (from the Greek *parienai,* meaning "to relax") is a form of dementia—or "relaxation" of the brain in its most negative connotation—that results from neurosyphilis, a form of syphilis in which the disease organism directly attacks the brain and central nervous system. General paresis is of historical significance to abnormal psychology. The 19th century discovery of the connection between this form of dementia and a concrete physical illness, syphilis, strengthened the medical model and held out the promise that organic causes would eventually be found for other abnormal behavior patterns.

Syphilis is a sexually transmitted disease caused by the bacterium *Treponema pallidum.* Syphilis is almost always transmitted through genital, oral-genital, or anal contact with an infected person, but it may also be transmitted from mother to fetus through the placenta. If left untreated, syphilis undergoes several stages of development, beginning with the appearance of a painless chancre (a round hard sore with raised edges) at the site of the infection about 2 to 4 weeks following contact. Although the chancre disappears spontaneously within a few weeks, the infection continues to fester. During the secondary stage, beginning a few weeks to a few months later, a skin rash appears, which consists of reddish raised bumps. This rash also eventually disappears, and the infection enters a latency stage, which may last from 1 to 40 years, in which the infection appears dormant. The bacteria are multiplying and invading sites throughout the body, however. They sometimes destroy nerve cells in the spinal cord that control motor responses. Sometimes they attack brain tissue. In the late stage of the infection, the damage caused by the bacteria produces a wide range of symptoms, including—when the brain is attacked directly—a form of dementia called general paresis.

General paresis is associated with physical symptoms such as tremors, slurred speech, impaired motor coordination, and, eventually, paralysis—all of which are suggestive of *relaxed* control over the body. Psychological signs include shifts in mood states, blunted emotional responsiveness, and irritability; delusions; changes in personal habits, such as suspension of personal grooming and hygiene; and progressive intellectual deterioration, including impairments of memory, judgment, and comprehension. Some people with general paresis grow euphoric and entertain delusions of grandiosity. Others become lethargic and depressed. Eventually, people with general paresis lapse into a state of apathy and confusion, characterized by the inability to care for themselves or to speak intelligibly. Death eventually ensues, either because of renewed infection or because of the damage caused by the existing infection.

TRUTH *or* FICTION REVISITED

14.9 *True.* The dementia called general paresis results from a form of syphilis called neurosyphilis.

Late-stage syphilis once accounted for 10% to 30% of admissions to psychiatric hospitals. However, advances in detection and the development of antibiotics that cure the infection has sharply reduced the incidences of late-stage syphilis and the development of general paresis. The effectiveness of treatment depends on when antibiotics are introduced and the extent of central nervous system damage. In cases where extensive tissue damage has been done, antibiotics can stem the infection and prevent further damage, thereby producing some improvement in intellectual performance. They cannot restore people to their original levels of functioning, however.

SUMMARY

Cognitive Disorders

Cognitive disorders involving disturbances of thinking or memory that represent a marked decline in functioning are caused by physical or medical conditions or drug use or withdrawal that affect the functioning of the brain.

Delirium is a state of mental confusion characterized by symptoms such as impaired attention, disorientation, disorganized thinking and rambling speech, reduced level of consciousness, and perceptual disturbances. Delirium is most commonly caused by alcohol withdrawal, as in the form of delirium tremens (DTs).

Amnestic disorders involve deficits in short-term or long-term memory. The most common cause of amnestic syndrome is alcohol amnestic disorder, or Korsakoff's syndrome, which involves a thiamine deficiency typically associated with patterns of chronic alcohol abuse.

Dementia involves cognitive deterioration or impairment, as evidenced by memory deficits, impaired judgment, personality changes, and disorders of higher cognitive functions such as problem-solving ability and abstract thinking. Dementia is not a normal consequence of aging but a sign of a degenerative brain disorder. There are various causes of dementias, including Alzheimer's disease and Pick's disease.

Psychological Disorders Related to Aging

Generalized anxiety disorder and phobic disorders are the most commonly occurring anxiety disorders among older people. Depression is common among people in later life and may be associated with memory deficits that can lift as the depression clears, which is not the case in the more progressive dementias, such as those caused by Alzheimer's disease. Certain sleep disorders, such as insomnia and sleep apnea, are also common among older people.

Dementia of the Alzheimer's type and vascular dementia primarily affect people in later life. Alzheimer's disease (AD) involves a progressive deterioration in cognitive and personality functioning and self-care skills. There is no cure or effective treatment for AD. Research into its causes has focused on genetic factors and imbalances in neurotransmitters, especially acetylcholine. Vascular dementia results from multiple strokes (blood clots that block the supply of blood to parts of the brain, damaging or destroying brain tissue).

Dementias and Other Psychological Problems Due to General Medical Conditions

Various other medical conditions can lead to dementias, including Pick's disease, Parkinson's disease, Huntington's disease, HIV disease, and Creutzfeldt-Jakob disease; head trauma; and brain tumor. Still other medical conditions, such as cerebral hemorrhage, nutritional disorders, endocrine disorders, and infections of the brain and spinal cord, have psychological effects.

Pick's disease is denoted by the presence of Pick's bodies in the nerve cells and the absence of the neurofibrillary tangles and plaques found in AD. Parkinson's disease is characterized by involuntary shaking or tremors, motor disabilities, and possible cognitive impairment. Parkinson's disease involves destruction of brain tissue in the substantia nigra area of the brain, which is involved in controlling body movements. The disease involves reductions in the level of dopamine in the brain.

Huntington's disease is a genetically transmitted disease that involves progressive deterioration in the basal ganglia, which primarily affects neurons that produce ACh and GABA. The symptoms usually first appear between the ages of 30 and 50 and involve involuntary, jerky movements of the face (grimaces), neck, limbs, and trunk, or so-called choreiform movements, which are accompanied by dementia. The disease is progressive and death usually occurs within 15 years.

Human immunodeficiency virus (HIV) can attack the central nervous system, causing a progressive decline in mental and motor functioning. Creutzfeldt-Jacob disease is caused by a slow-acting virus.

Head traumas may injure the brain by jarring, banging, or cutting brain tissue. Dementia is more likely to occur from multiple head traumas than a single incident. Delirium, agitation, and amnesia may result from severe concussions. Contusions can lead to coma, cognitive impairment, and emotional problems. Lacerations can be lethal or lead to permanent major cognitive impairment.

Brain tumors, whether benign or malignant, can cause psychological difficulties such as memory impairment, changes in personality, disorientation, and dementia.

Pellagra, a nutritional disorder caused by deficiencies of niacin, can lead to psychological problems such as anxiety, depression, loss of memory for recent events, problems in concentration, and hallucinations and delirium. Beriberi is caused by thiamine deficiency and often produces impairment in memory and concentration, lethargy, lack of appetite, and irritability. Hyperthyroidism can lead to psychological effects such as excitability, insomnia, anxiety, and restlessness. In childhood, hypothyroidism can result in cretinism, which is characterized by stunted growth and mental retardation. In adulthood, hypothyroidism slows the metabolism and is associated with psychological changes such as sluggishness and fatigue, difficulties in concentration and memory, depression, and possibly dementia. Underactivity of the adrenal cortex may cause Addison's disease, which is associated with weight loss, low blood pressure, fatigue, irritability, lack of motivation, social withdrawal, and depression. Overactivity of the adrenal cortex can produce Cushing's syndrome, which is characterized by various physical and emotional problems.

Encephalitis, an inflammation of the brain, is often associated with states of delirium, and convulsions or coma during acute stages. Meningitis is an infection of the central nervous system that involves an acute inflammation of the membranes that cover the spinal cord and brain. Both encephalitis and meningitis can lead to mental retardation if contracted during infancy. Neurosyphilis is a sexually transmitted disease in which the brain is attacked by the bacterium that causes syphilis, which can result in a state of dementia called general paresis.

Scoring Key for Attitudes Toward Aging Scale

1. False. Most healthy couples continue to engage in satisfying sexual activities into their seventies and eighties.
2. False. This is too general a statement. Those who find their work satisfying are less desirous of retiring.
3. False. In late adulthood, we tend to become more concerned with internal matters—our physical functioning and our emotions.
4. False. Adaptability remains reasonably stable throughout adulthood.
5. False. Age itself is not linked to noticeable declines in life satisfaction. Of course, we may respond negatively to disease and losses, such as the death of a spouse.
6. False. Although we can predict some general trends for older adults we can also do so for younger adults. Older adults, like their younger counterparts, are heterogeneous in personality and behavior patterns.
7. False. Older adults with stable intimate relationships are more satisfied.
8. False. We are susceptible to a wide variety of psychological disorders at all ages.
9. False. Only a minority are depressed.
10. False. Actually, church attendance declines, but not verbally expressed religious beliefs.
11. False. Although reaction time may increase and general learning ability may undergo a slight decline, older adults usually have little or no difficulty at familiar work tasks. In most jobs, experience and motivation are more important than age.
12. False. Learning may just take a bit longer.
13. False.
14. Older adults do not direct a higher proportion of thoughts toward the past than do younger people. Regardless of our age, we may spend more time daydreaming at any age if we have more time on our hands.
15. Fewer than 10% of older adults require some form of institutional care.

1. What are cognitive disorders? How are they classified? What problems arise in diagnosing them?

2. What are the features and causes of delirium, amnestic disorders, Korsakoff's syndrome, and dementia?

3. What is Alzheimer's disease? What have we learned about the biological underpinnings of the disease? What don't we know? What treatment approaches are used to help Alzheimer's sufferers?

4. What other forms of dementia are discussed in the chapter? What are their features and causes?

5. What is Parkinson's disease? What causes it? How is it treated? What new lines of research are discussed in the chapter that may lead to more effective treatments? What are some of the ethical issues involved in these lines of research?

6. What is Huntington's disease? What causes it? What promising lines of research are cited in the text that may lead to possible treatments for the disease?

7. What are the psychological features associated with head trauma, nutritional disorders, endocrine disorders, and brain infections?

© **Andy Warhol**
Guns, 1982

CHAPTER  15

Violence and Abuse

TRUTH or FICTION?

15.1 We are more likely to be hurt or killed by strangers than by people we know.

15.2 Despite all the talk about crime, the United States has a relatively low homicide rate among young men compared to other industrialized countries.

15.3 A male teen in the United States stands a greater chance of dying from a gunshot wound than from all natural causes of death combined.

15.4 Though alcohol use is linked to aggression, it is rarely involved in homicides.

15.5 Women who remain with men who abuse them suffer from a form of masochism.

15.6 The most common form of child maltreatment is physical abuse.

15.7 Women are more likely to be raped by men they know than by strangers.

15.8 Child molesters typically use physical force to compel children into performing sexual acts.

15.9 In some cases, sexual relations between clients and therapists are therapeutically justified.

1. Discuss the conditions under which violent behavior may be classified as either normal or abnormal.

2. Discuss relationships between violent behavior and psychological disorders.

3. Discuss biological, social-cognitive, cognitive, and sociocultural perspectives on aggression and relationships among anger, frustration, and aggression.

4. Discuss the problem of spousal abuse, with attention to prevalence, patterns of abuse, sociocultural factors, and psychological characteristics of abusers.

5. Discuss the problem of child maltreatment with respect to the types of maltreatment, risk factors involved, causes, effects on children, and treatment and prevention efforts.

6. Discuss the types of rape, incidence of rape, effects on survivors, theoretical perspectives on the causes of rape, and treatment approaches directed toward rape survivors and rapists.

7. Describe the prevalence and patterns of child sexual abuse, the characteristics of abusers, effects on survivors, and efforts directed toward treatment and prevention.

8. Discuss the types, prevalence, and effects of sexual harassment.

There was a time not so long ago when people would leave their doors unlocked, walk through city parks long into the night, and open their front doors to strangers without hesitation. Today, the fear of crime, especially the fear of violent crime, has come to govern our behavior increasingly. We live behind triple-locked doors, equip our homes and cars with the most sophisticated security systems, and travel in groups when venturing out at night in unfamiliar places. Some of us rarely if ever go out at night, even in our own neighborhoods. The wail of car alarms on city streets is a constant although annoying reminder of how the fear of crime affects our everyday life.

We are a nation obsessed with crime. Video crews travel alongside police cruisers to bring television viewers into the netherworld of criminal activity. Police dramas sandwich murders, rapes, and other violent crimes between commercial breaks. Movies featuring organized crime or violent rampages by alienated youth fill the theaters.

We are much more likely to be hurt or killed by people we know than by strangers. A recent study of emergency room patients treated for violence-related injuries showed that nearly half had been injured by people they knew, often someone they knew intimately—a current or former spouse, boyfriend or girlfriend ("Study finds half of victims know attackers," 1997).

TRUTH *or* FICTION REVISITED

15.1 *False.* We are much more likely to be hurt or killed by someone we know than by a stranger.

By international standards, the United States stands out as a violent culture. Homicide is the second leading cause of death, after accidents, among young people in the 15 to 24 age range (Lore & Schultz, 1993). It is the leading cause of death among Black males in this age group (Coontz & Franklin, 1997). The murder rate in the United States is nearly 10 times what it is in Japan; the robbery rate is nearly 150 times greater! (Kristof, 1995). The homicide rate in the United States among young men is especially high (see Figure 15.1), exceeding by a wide margin the homicide rates of 21 other developed nations (Fingerhut & Kleinman, 1990).

TRUTH *or* FICTION REVISITED

15.2 *False.* The United States leads the industrialized world in the homicide rate among young men.

Although other factors are clearly involved in the high rate of homicides in the United States, a contributing factor is easy access to firearms. About 3 of 4 homicides of young people result from the use of firearms, as compared to fewer than 1 in 4 in other developed nations (Kristof, 1995; "Cracking Down on Teen-Age Homicide," 1996). A 1997 national survey showed that 1 in 5 teenagers in the United States carries a weapon ("One in Five Teen-agers is Armed, a Survey Finds," 1998). The percentage of homicides involving the use of firearms has been rising steadily, up to 72% in 1994 ("Homicide Trends Show Record Rate of Firearm-Related Deaths," 1996). More male teens in the United States die from firearms than from all natural causes combined (M. L. Rosenberg, 1993). It is too easy for many young people in the United States to acquire guns, and an alarming number of them carry them (O'Donnell & Clifford, 1995). In Japan, which virtually prohibits private ownership of handguns and exacts stiff penalties for carrying a loaded pistol, only 38 murders by firearms were recorded in 1994, as compared to more than 16,000 in the United States in 1993, the latest year for which statistics were available (Kristof, 1995). Or put

International Homicide Rates

Austria
Japan
West Germany
Denmark
Portugal
England/Wales
Poland
Ireland
Greece
France
Switzerland
Netherlands
Belgium
Sweden
Australia
Canada
Finland
Norway
Israel
New Zealand
Scotland
United States

Number per 100,000
0   5   10   15   20   25

FIGURE 15.1 *Homicide rates: U.S. versus other developed countries.* The homicide rate among young men in the U.S. far exceeds the rates in other developed countries. The easy availability of firearms is clearly a contributing factor to the high rate of homicides in the U.S.

another way, the number of homicides *on any given day* in the United States in which guns are involved exceed the number in Japan for a whole year! Although the homicide rate in the United States remains high, there is good news. The murder rate overall, and homicides of young persons involving the use of firearms, began dropping in the early 1990s (Butterfield, 1996; Fingerhut, Ingram, & Feldman, 1998). Moreover, violent crime overall declined steadily during the early to mid-1990s, the longest period of decline in 25 years (Butterfield, 1997a, 1997c). By 1996, the rate of violent crime had fallen to the lowest level since the federal government started tracking it in 1973 (Butterfield, 1997a).

TRUTH or FICTION REVISITED

15.3 *True.* A male teenager is more likely to die from a gunshot wound than from all natural causes combined.

In this chapter we focus on violent and abusive behavior. We will see that violence and abuse take many forms, from outright physical aggression to sexual harassment. We will also see that the search for the origins of violent and abusive behavior is best approached from a multifactorial model that takes into account sociocultural, psychological, and biological factors.

VIOLENCE AND ABNORMAL BEHAVIOR

In Chapter 1 we introduced you to the idea that abnormal behavior can be defined in a number of ways, including unusualness, social deviance or unacceptability, faulty perceptions or interpretations of reality, severe personal distress, maladaptiveness, and dangerousness. Given these definitions, is violent behavior abnormal?

The answer largely depends on the context in which the behavior occurs. The behavior of a professional football player or hockey player may indeed be violent, but it is not what we would usually consider to be abnormal, except perhaps if it exceeds the boundaries of what would be considered sporting. (In hockey, it may be difficult to know where to draw the line.) Prize-fighters earn their livings in a sport that is by its nature violent. Even though the physical pounding a prize-fighter endures in the ring may lead to the development of physical and psychological disorders (see discussion of punch-drunk syndrome in Chapter 14), prize-fighting is not classified as abnormal behavior.

Warfare or combat is also inherently violent and certainly dangerous to self and others. Yet we don't typically consider the violent behavior of soldiers who fight wars or the general officers who direct them as abnormal. Perhaps we might consider the behavior of the nations themselves that wage war or their leaders as abnormal. But those who risk their lives and commit violent acts against soldiers of other nations are generally seen as loyal or patriotic, perhaps even heroic, not abnormal.

Where, then, do we draw the line between violent behavior that is deemed normal and that deemed abnormal?

America the violent. The homicide rate in the U.S. is 10 times what it is in Japan. Young men in the U.S. are more likely to die as the result of homicide than young men in any of the other developed nations listed in Figure 15.1. These empty shoes of young gunshot victims are a poignant reminder of the many needless deaths caused by homicides.

We adopt the following standard. We consider violent behavior to be abnormal if it (1) occurs outside a socially sanctioned context, and (2) is either self-defeating or dangerous (harmful to oneself or others). The football player who slams an opponent into the ground is rewarded with a multimillion dollar contract; the one who slams his wife against the wall commits a violent act that is abnormal as well as criminal. The spouse abuser's behavior is clearly dangerous (harmful to others and perhaps to self), socially unacceptable, and also maladaptive or self-defeating, because it can lead to arrest, marital dissolution, and retaliation, as well as failing to resolve the underlying conflict. It may also be associated with severe personal distress.

Violence and Psychological Disorders

A common perception exists that people with psychological disorders are especially prone to violence. Some people with psychological disorders do commit violent acts, just as assuredly as do some people without diagnosable psychological disorders. The great majority of people with psychological disorders, however, are nonviolent (Lamberg, 1998). Substance or alcohol abuse and a history of criminal behavior are much more strongly tied to violent crimes than mental disorders (Bonta, Law, & Hanson, 1998; Lamberg, 1998).

On the other hand, evidence points to an increased risk of violence associated with some mental disorders, such as schizophrenia, especially during times of active hallucinations and delusions (Hodgkins et al., 1996, 1998; Link & Stueve, 1998; Monahan, 1992). Most of the violent acts committed by former patients occur within their networks of families and friends (Link & Stueve, 1998; Steadman et al., 1998). Factors such as substance abuse and poor adherence to medication in people with severe mental disorders (schizophrenia or bipolar disorder) are also linked to a higher risk of violent behavior (e.g., Eronen et al., 1996; Modestin, Berger, & Ammann, 1996; Steadman et al., 1998; Swartz et al, 1998; Tiihonen et al., 1997).

As many as 1 in 2 people with schizophrenia have either an alcohol or illicit drug dependence disorder (Miller & Brown, 1997; "Substance abuse and schizophrenia," 1997; Ziedonis & Trudeau, 1997). People with these dual diagnoses are labeled *MICAs* (*mentally ill chemical abusers*). They sometimes engage in violent behavior when they stop taking their psychiatric medication and return to using alcohol or drugs. Alcohol and other drugs may contribute to violence by impairing behavioral controls over impulses. We should also note that violent behavior is sometimes a feature of antisocial personality disorder (see Chapter 8) and conduct disorder in children and adolescents (see Chapter 13). All told, however, only a small proportion of aggressive or violent behavior on our streets and in our homes can be attributed to diagnosable psychological disorders. We need to consider other explanations derived from biological, social-cognitive, and sociocultural perspectives to provide a fuller accounting of violent and abusive behavior.

PERSPECTIVES ON AGGRESSION

Are human beings basically aggressive by nature? Or is aggression learned behavior? There is no shortage of opinions among observers of the human condition as to the origins of

Youth and gun violence. At Columbine High School in Colorado in April 1999, two students killed 12 fellow students and a teacher in a violent rampage before turning their guns on themselves.

human aggression. We have yet to come to any generally accepted theory of violence and aggression. Here, let us consider how several of the major theoretical perspectives have approached the problem. We also offer our own speculations on what these perspectives may teach us about our capacity to aggress and do violence against others.

Biological Perspectives

The animal world is not a peaceable kingdom. Animals in their natural habitat face a constant struggle to survive as either prey or predator. The classic biological view of aggression holds that it is an inborn pattern of behavior, or **instinct.** According to this view, predators are naturally aggressive because aggression serves a survival function. A predator is more likely to survive and be around long enough to pass along its genetic inheritance to its offspring if it "instinctively" attacks its prey. Within species, aggression usually occurs among males and typically involves a way of establishing dominance or access to mates. The more aggressive males may thus have greater access to the most fertile females and be more likely to pass along their genetic inheritance to future generations, presumably including the genes controlling aggressive behavior, than would their more placid brethren.

To what extent might human aggression be instinctual? Might there be a biological basis to human aggression? And if so, what are the neurobiological mechanisms that underlie it?

An early proponent of the belief that human aggression is a product of instinct was Sigmund Freud. As he looked upon the destruction and devastation that human beings had wrought in the Great War (what World War I was called at the time), Freud came to believe there must be an underlying instinct that accounts for human aggression, which he dubbed the "death instinct." The "death instinct" was basically self-destructive in its aim, having as its ultimate purpose the return to the tension-free state that preceded birth. The death instinct can give rise to self-destructive behaviors, including suicide. Sometimes it is turned against others in the form of outward aggression, violence, and warfare. In Freud's view, instinctual impulses such as aggression and sex strive for expression and must be released in some form. The ego is responsible for finding socially appropriate outlets for channeling these impulses. Thus, aggressive impulses may be "vented" by participating in rough-and-tumble sports such as football or hockey or by seeking to "trounce" your opponent in tennis or bridge. They may also be expressed vicariously, such as by watching a violent movie or sporting event. The venting of aggressive impulses, which is termed **catharsis,** is believed to act as something of a safety valve, an acceptable way of "letting off steam." Outward aggression arises when the ego is unable to contain these destructive impulses, which can occur if the ego is weak or overtaxed.

Sociobiological Views **Sociobiology** is the doctrine that holds that behavioral traits, not just physical traits such as hair color or height, can be transmitted genetically. Sociobiologists believe that behavioral traits that increased the chances our earliest ancestors would survive and be able to reproduce may have been passed along genetically from generation to generation, perhaps all the way down the genetic highway to us, even though these traits may no longer be adaptive in modern civilization. The period of time since the dawning of modern civilization is but a brief moment in our history as a species, a mere blink of the eye. Sociobiologists believe that aggressiveness may be one such trait that had survival value to our earliest ancestors, who eked out a bare-bones existence by hunting and killing other animals and collecting edible roots and shrubs.

The sociobiologists would not be surprised by the popularity of simulated violence among young people, especially young boys, in the form of violent video games. In *Mortal Kombat,* one of the most popular video games, the loser is decapitated. The sociobiologists may well see the attraction to violence in media and in video games as a by-product of our aggressive inheritance. Consistent with the evolutionary perspective, ample evidence exists showing boys and men to be more aggressive than girls or women (Knight, Fabes, & Higgins, 1996).

Instinct theories of aggression and sociobiological viewpoints remain controversial. For one thing, critics contend that culture and learning play more important roles in human behavior, not heredity. They point to differences in aggression existing cross-culturally and among individuals in a given culture as evidence that aggressive behavior in humans is not instinctive or controlled by our genes. Some individuals as well as some cultures are warlike and aggressive, whereas others are essentially nonviolent and peaceful. Although diversity in human aggression argues against its instinctive basis, more contemporary evolutionary models argue for an interactionist approach, which posits that biological factors interact with social and environmental factors in creating conditions that lead to aggressive behavior (Buss & Shackelford, 1997). Evidence is accumulating that points to biology playing an important role in the complex interplay of factors underlying aggressive behavior.

Neurobiological Bases of Aggression Investigations of brain mechanisms in aggression have focused attention on the role of the hypothalamus. If we electrically stimulate certain parts of the hypothalamus of other animals such as rats and monkeys, we can elicit attack behavior or other stereotypical violent responses. This leads us to believe that the hypothalamus may act as a control center in regulating aggressive behavior, at least in other animals. However, the human brain is much more complex than that of other species, and our behavior depends more on learning than on neural reflexes. Whatever brain mechanisms may be involved in regulating aggression in humans may be subject to the overriding influences of culture and learning.

Contemporary neurobiological research on aggression has focused largely on the role of neurotransmitters, especially serotonin (see nearby "A Closer Look" feature), and on the male sex hormone testosterone (e.g., Virkkunen & Linnoila, 1993; Virkkunen et al., 1994). Testosterone is implicated in aggression in part because men tend to be more aggressive than women. Although testosterone is produced in both men and women, the levels in men are much higher. Researchers find that teenage boys with higher levels of testosterone are more likely to respond aggressively to

provocations than their peers (Olweus, 1987). Other researchers report that violent criminals have unusually high levels of testosterone (e.g., Virkkunen & Linnoila, 1993). Higher testosterone levels are also found among female prisoners who are higher in aggressive dominance (Dabbs & Hargrove, 1997).

Researchers also find cross-cultural evidence supporting a link between testosterone and aggressive behavior in adult men. A study of bushmen from the !Kung San tribe of Namibia, Africa, showed that men with higher levels of testosterone were more violent than those with lower levels (Christiansen & Winkler, 1992). Because these studies are correlational in nature, we cannot conclude that testosterone plays a causal role in aggression. Yet it gives us reason to believe that high levels of testosterone may be a link in a chain that leads to aggressive behavior. The picture is clouded, however, by other evidence, admittedly preliminary in nature, that links lowered levels of testosterone to aggressive behavior in men ("Testosterone wimping out?," 1995). Although more research is needed on the links between testosterone and aggression in men, it is possible that either excesses or deficits of the hormone may be involved in mediating aggressive behavior in men.

More evidence of biological factors in human aggression comes from genetic studies of criminality and violent behavior (DiLalla & Gottesman, 1991). Are propensities toward violent behavior inherited? Evidence from both twin studies and adoptee studies points to a genetic contribution to criminality (DiLalla & Gottesman, 1991). However, not all criminals are violent; some commit property offenses. The heritability of violent criminality per se is less clear and remains to be more fully explored in future research.

An instinct to aggress? A male stickleback fish will "instinctively" attack other male sticklebacks that intrude upon its territory, or even a cardboard cut-out made to resemble a male stickleback. Some theorists believe that aggression in humans is also a product of instinct. Yet the diversity in human aggression that exists both within and across cultures argues strongly against its instinctive basis.

Serotonin and Aggression: Does It Put the Brakes on Violent Impulses?

The neurotransmitter serotonin has been implicated in a number of psychological disorders, including depression (see Chapter 7), obsessive-compulsive disorder (see Chapter 5), and bulimia (see Chapter 10). Imbalances of serotonin are even believed to account for migraine headaches (see Chapter 4). Now researchers are investigating links between serotonin and aggressive behavior.

Serotonin acts as an inhibitory neurotransmitter in some parts of the brain, especially the *limbic system,* a part of the brain involved in regulating primitive drives such as hunger, thirst, and aggression. The limbic system also plays key roles in learning, memory, and the regulation of emotions. Researchers suspect that serotonin helps put the brakes on primitive behaviors, including acts of impulsive aggression (Cowley & Underwood, 1998). In one study, men who had committed crimes involving acts of impulsive violence were found to have abnormally low levels of serotonin in their brains, whereas men who had committed violent criminal acts involving premeditation and planning had normal levels of serotonin (Toufexis, 1993). Serotonin activity has also been implicated in aggressive behavior in young boys (Pine et al., 1997). Dysfunctions in serotonin activity may also have implications for explaining the impulsive, aggressive behavior observed in people with certain personality disorders, such as borderline personality disorder (Siever & Trestman, 1993).

In animal research, investigators find that if you destroy certain parts of the brain involved in serotonin production, the level of aggressive behavior increases (Siever & Trestman, 1993). This can be observed in greater mouse-killing behavior in rats. Other research shows that more dominant male monkeys have higher levels of serotonin than lower-ranking males. A leading investigator, John Mann of Columbia University, calls serotonin a "behavioral seat belt" because of its role as a restraining mechanism on impulsive behavior, including sexual and aggressive impulses (Coccaro et al., 1998; Cowley & Underwood, 1998). Yet other researchers are taking more of a "wait and see" attitude. They believe it is premature to make any definitive statements about the role of serotonin in human aggression (M. E. Berman, Tracy, & Coccaro, 1997).

If serotonin deficiencies play a role in aggressive behavior, it stands to reason that SSRI-type antidepressants, which increase serotonin, may help curb aggressive outbursts. Though work in this area is only beginning, a recent study found that Prozac, a type of SSRI, reduced certain forms of aggression in personality disorder patients who had histories of impulsive violence but not major depression or bipolar disorder (Coccaro & Kavoussi, 1997). Though much of the research attention has been focused on serotonin, other neurotransmitters may also be involved in controlling aggressive behavior.

Social-Cognitive Perspectives

Social-cognitive theorists such as Albert Bandura (1973, 1986) propose that aggression is learned behavior acquired by the same principles of learning that explain the acquisition of other behaviors. The roles of modeling and reinforcement are highlighted in the learning of aggressive behavior. Children may learn to imitate violent behavior they observe at home, in the schoolyard, or on television or in other media. If they are then reinforced for acting aggressively, such as by getting their way with their peers or earning peer approval or respect, their tendency to aggress may become stronger over time. A child's exposure to aggressive models may begin in the home in the form of witnessing spousal violence or suffering violence firsthand in the form of physical abuse or punishment meted out by parents. One lesson the child may draw from such experiences is that violence in the context of interpersonal relationships is an acceptable way of getting others to do what you want them to do, or of punishing them when they fail to comply with your requests. Children may also be exposed to peers who model aggressive behavior in the schoolyard or playground and to fictional characters in action movies whose aggressive behavior is rewarded, even glamorized.

Psychologist David Lykken (1993) points to a lack of proper socialization as a root cause of violence in our society. He argues that the inability or unwillingness of parents, especially single parents, to socialize their children—to teach them right from wrong—leads children to become overly aggressive.

Social-cognitive theorists also incorporate roles for expectancies and competencies in explaining aggressive behavior. People who expect that aggressive behavior will produce positive outcomes are more likely to act in kind. People who

The Effects of Media Violence

Much of human learning occurs by observation. Television is also one of our major sources of informal observational learning. According to psychologist Leonard Eron (1993), the child who watches 2 to 4 hours of television a day will have seen 8,000 murders and another 100,000 acts of violence by the time she or he has finished elementary school. But does media violence cause real violence? If there are causal connections between media violence and real violence, what can parents and educators do to prevent the fictional from spilling over into the real world?

Classic experiments have shown that children tend to imitate the aggressive behavior they see on television, whether the models are cartoons or real people (e.g., Bandura, Ross, & Ross, 1963) (see Figure 15.2). In study after study, children and adults who view violence in the media later show higher levels of aggressive behavior than people who are not exposed to media violence (DeAngelis, 1993; Liebert, Sprafkin, & Davidson, 1989). Aggressive video games apparently have similar effects. In one study, 5- to 7-year-olds played one of two video games (Schutte, Malouff, Post-Gordon, & Rodasts, 1988)—one (*Karateka*) in which villains were destroyed by being hit or kicked; the other (*Jungle Hunt*) in which the character swung nonviolently from vine to vine to cross a jungle. Afterward the children were observed in a playroom. Those who had played *Karateka*—both boys and girls—were significantly more likely to hit their playmates and an inflated doll. Based on accumulated research, psychologists have come to believe that media violence does contribute directly to aggression [Huesmann, 1993; National Institute of Mental Health (NIMH), 1982].

Effects of Media Violence

Social scientists believe that media violence contributes to aggressive behavior in several ways. For one thing, media violence models aggressive "skills." Acquisition of these skills, in turn, may enhance children's aggressive competencies. They also learn the lesson that violence pays off when they see a television hero earn respect and approval for vanquishing an opponent by acting aggressively. For another thing, aggressive behavior that might otherwise be inhibited by fear of punishment may be *disinhibited* by exposure to media violence. In other words, people may be more likely to express aggressive impulses that would otherwise have been controlled when they are exposed to media characters who act violently, especially when the characters are similar to the observers and are depicted as "getting away" with aggres-

sive behavior or are even rewarded for it. Media violence and aggressive video games also increase viewers' levels of arousal. People are more likely to engage in aggressive behavior under high levels of arousal. Media violence also has cognitive effects that may result in violent behavior, such as priming or arousing aggressive thoughts and memories in viewers (Berkowitz, 1988) and providing viewers with aggressive scripts—that is, ideas on how to behave in situations that seem to parallel those they have observed (Huesmann & Miller, 1994). Lastly, we become used to, or habituated to, many stimuli that impinge on us repeatedly. Repeated exposure to TV violence may lead to an habituation, a kind of "numbing," of our emotional response to real violence (Huesmann, 1993). Children's TV remains steeped in violence, with a recent study finding that 58% of children's shows contained violent content (Seppa, 1997). If children who are routinely exposed to violence in the media come to perceive violence as the norm, they may become more accepting of violence as a means of resolving conflicts and may place less value on constraining aggressive urges (Eron, 1993; Huesmann, 1993).

The Selection Factor

Although media violence encourages aggression in viewers, it has its greatest impact on children who are already considered the most aggressive by their teachers (Josephson, 1987). There also seems to be a circular relationship between viewing media violence and aggressive behavior (DeAngelis, 1993). Yes, TV violence

What's Johnny learning? Research evidence supports the view that exposure to violent media contributes to aggressive behavior in children. What mechanisms may account for these effects?

FIGURE 15.2 *A classic experiment in the imitation of aggressive models.*
Research by Albert Bandura and his colleagues has shown that children frequently imitate the aggressive behavior that they observe. In the top row, an adult model strikes a clown doll. The lower rows show a boy and a girl imitating the aggressive behavior.

contributes to aggressive behavior, but aggressive children are also more likely to tune in and stay tuned to it. Media violence also interacts with other contributors to violence. For example, parental rejection and use of physical punishment further increase the likelihood of aggression in children. Harsh home life may further confirm the TV viewer's vision of the world as a violent place and further encourage reliance on television for companionship.

What to Do
The question repeatedly arises as to whether media violence should be curtailed in an effort to stem community violence. The controversy pits two widely held social values against one another: freedom of expression and need of society to curtail violent behavior of its members.

What, then, should be done? First of all, the threat should be placed in context. Media violence may be a contributor to aggressive behavior but does not automatically trigger it. Many other factors, including the quality of the home environment, are involved. The de-

velopment of warm loving attachments to others can buffer the effects of exposure to violent media. Second, Huesmann and his colleagues (Huesmann, Eron, Klein, Brice, & Fischer, 1983) have shown that we as parents and educators can do many things to mitigate the impact of media violence. For example, children who watch violent shows are rated by peers as being significantly less aggressive when they are informed of the following:

1. The violent behavior they observe in the media does not represent the behavior of most people.

2. The apparently aggressive behaviors they watch are not real. They reflect camera tricks, special effects, and stunts.

3. Most people resolve conflicts by nonviolent means.

Cognitive factors also come into play. If children are taught that violence is not an appropriate way of handling interpersonal conflicts, they may be deterred from acting aggressively in such situations. Moreover, parents and educators can help children acquire more

(box continues on following page)

The Effects of Media Violence

adaptive, nonviolent ways of solving interpersonal problems. Finally, efforts are underway at the legislative level to provide parents with a device that will allow them to block transmission of violent programming on television. The so-called V-chip is embedded in the television receiver and receives a signal from broadcasters that particular programs carry violent material. Parents can then program their TV sets to block transmission of violent programs. Critics of the V-chip argue that it represents a form of censorship. Proponents counter that it merely provides parents with the ability to exercise choice concerning the type of programming they want in their homes. What do you think?

Source: Adapted from Rathus, 1996. Used with permission.

lack competencies for solving interpersonal problems without resorting to aggression may be more likely to act aggressively in conflict situations.

Social-cognitive theorists argue against the catharsis view of aggression. The expression of aggression, even in controlled situations such as a sporting event, may not reduce the potential for aggression but actually increase it by providing additional opportunities for reinforcement.

Violence may also beget violence from one generation to another. Many people who engage in abusive or violent behavior were themselves abused as children. Physically abused children often begin to show violent behavior early in childhood (D. L. Davis & Boster, 1992). Neglected children may be at even greater risk of becoming violent later in life (Widom, 1989a, 1989b). However, the pathway between child abuse (which includes physical abuse, neglect, and maltreatment) and later violent or abusive behavior is neither direct nor certain. Most studies show that the majority of abused children do not become delinquents or violent offenders (Widom, 1989a, 1989b). Child abuse may lead to other outcomes, such as withdrawal or self-destructive behavior, rather than outward aggression. We need to expand our knowledge of how other factors, such as exposure to violence in media, interact with child abuse to increase the potential for later violent behavior.

The intergenerational transmission of violent behavior may involve a modeling effect. If children are abused, or if they observe one parent battering the other, they may learn that violent behavior is an acceptable means of dealing with interpersonal conflicts. Children who are exposed to violence in the home or were abused themselves may fail to establish secure, loving attachments with their parents and a sense of empathy and respect for the feelings of others, which may set the stage for wanton acts of violent cruelty toward others. It is also conceivable that there is a genetic component underlying the intergenerational transmission of violent behavior (DiLalla & Gottesman, 1991).

Childhood exposure to crime and violence is widespread, especially among urban youth. A recent study of urban high school students showed that 93% reported having witnessed a violent act and 44% had been victimized themselves (Berman et al., 1997). Not surprisingly, young people exposed to violence, or who have been victims themselves, are at greater risk of mental health problems, including PTSD, depression, anxiety, as well as trouble with teachers, than are their nonvictimized peers (Boney-McCoy & Finkelhor, 1996; Freeman, Shaffer, & Smith, 1996).

Posttraumatic stress disorder (PTSD) in these young people may include difficulties concentrating due to intrusive memories of the experience, anxious reactions, and disruptions of sleeping and eating patterns (Osofsky, 1995). In the urban high school sample, about 1 in 3 (34.5%) of the students who were exposed to violence developed diagnosable PTSD. Children exposed to violence may also become withdrawn or depressed and fail to thrive. All told, estimates indicate that more than one third of young people in the United States in the 10- to 16-year age range, more than 6 million youngsters, have been victims of violence.

Cognitive Perspectives

Cognitive psychologists focus on the ways in which people interpret confrontative or conflict situations (Berkowitz, 1994). When people see other people's motives as hostile, they are more likely to act aggressively than when they form a more benign interpretation of the other's behavior. Evidence shows that young people who have problems with aggression tend to distort other people's motives. They tend to assume other people intend them harm when they do not (Crick & Dodge, 1994). In a similar way, men who commit date rape may misread the woman's expressed wishes, believing that the woman is merely playing "hard to get" when she resists his sexual overtures. Cognitive theorists also recognize that people are more likely to act aggressively when they magnify the importance of a perceived insult (e.g., Lochman & Dodge, 1994).

Sociocultural Perspectives

From the sociocultural perspective, violent behavior is rooted in underlying social causes, many of which go hand in hand, such as poverty, lack of opportunity, family breakdown, and exposure to deviant role models. Social stressors such as prolonged unemployment also play a role. Data drawn from the Epidemiologic Catchment Area (ECA) study showed that people who were nonviolent and employed when first interviewed but were later laid off were nearly six times more likely to engage in violent behavior than others who remained employed (Catalano et al., 1993). In countries such as Japan, which are characterized by social cohesiveness, strong family ties, and a relatively balanced distribution of wealth, violent crime is but a small fraction of what it is in the more fragmented United States society (Kristof, 1995). Children in the United States who grow up in economically disadvantaged, inner-city neighborhoods show higher levels of aggression than do less disadvantaged children (Guerra et al., 1995). In helping to explain the poverty-aggression connection, let us note that poorer children are generally exposed to greater levels of life stress, including stress associated with exposure to neighborhood violence. They also tend to be more accepting of aggressive behavior (Guerra et al., 1995). Children who are exposed to more life stress and those who adopt more accepting beliefs concerning aggression tend to behave more aggressively than do other children.

Another factor linking poverty and violent behavior is the gang subculture. In America's poorer neighborhoods, a subculture of violence has sprung up, organized around deviant peer groups, or gangs, in which protecting "turf" and proving one's manhood by taking up the gun or the knife has become the social norm. To young people who feel alienated from society and who hold little or no hope for their future, the sense of belongingness and acceptance that comes from joining a gang can be a tempting lure that may be difficult to resist, especially for those youngsters from disintegrated or disrupted families who are unable to provide them with support and moral guidance.

Sociocultural theorists also examine the role of violence as a social influence tactic. Violence, or the threat of violence, may be viewed as a form of coercion used to get people to comply with one's wishes, whether it involves strong-arm tactics of organized crime "enforcers" or abusive spouses who demand that their partners accede to their demands.

Sociocultural perspectives on violence also consider how cultural values and methods of child rearing have a way of breeding violence. In other cultures, such as in Thailand and Jamaica, aggression in children is actively discouraged and politeness and deference is fostered (Tharp, 1991). By contrast, our culture socializes children to be competitive and independent. Cultural differences may explain findings that children in Thailand and Jamaica are more likely than U.S. children to be "overcontrolled" and to complain of sleeping problems, fears, and physical problems, whereas children in the U.S. are more likely to be "undercontrolled" and perceived by others as argumentative, disobedient, and belligerent (Tharp, 1991).

Homicide Rates and Ethnicity   Homicide rates in the United States vary across racial/ethnic groups. Although African Americans constitute about 13% of the population,

Sociocultural roots of violence. According to the sociocultural perspective, violent behavior is rooted in social ills, such as poverty, family breakdown, and social decay that gives rise to deviant subcultures, such as gangs.

about 50% of the murder victims in the United States are African American (U.S. Department of Justice, 1994). Homicides committed by or against young African Americans are especially high [Centers for Disease Control (CDC), 1991]. The chances of African American men in the 15 to 34 age range becoming victims of homicide are about nine times greater than the chances of non-Hispanic White American men in the same age range. The rate of homicides committed by young men is more than seven times greater among African Americans (85.6 per 100,000) than non-Hispanic White Americans (11.2 per 100,000). The odds of becoming a victim of homicide are almost as great among young Hispanic American men as young African American men (Tardiff et al., 1994). In the great majority of homicides in the United States, the victim and the perpetrator were of the same race and knew each other. Blacks tend to kill Blacks; Whites tend to kill Whites.

In explaining ethnic differences in homicide rates, we need to consider underlying social causes. One factor is poverty. Homicide rates are higher among lower income groups, and African Americans and Hispanic Americans as a group are disproportionately represented among the more economically disadvantaged segments of our society. A second factor is the proliferation of firearms, especially in poorer, predominantly minority communities. A study of all homicides committed in New York City in the early 1990s found that young Black, Hispanic American, and Asian males were more likely to be killed by firearms than were Whites. Another factor is illicit drug use, which is often linked to street crime, especially in poorer communities.

Alcohol and Aggression

Alcohol use is implicated in nearly 40% of violent crimes, including about 50% of homicides, at least 25% of serious assaults, and more than 25% of rapes (Collins & Messerschmidt, 1993; S. E. Martin, 1992). The U.S. Justice Department estimates that more than 1 of 3 adult offenders had been drinking just preceding the commission of their crimes (CNN On-line, 1998a).

TRUTH *or* FICTION REVISITED

15.4 *False.* Alcohol use is implicated in about 50% of homicides and plays a role in many cases of other violent crimes.

A cross-cultural study of violent crime data from 11 countries in different parts of the world showed that in nearly 2 of 3 violent crimes overall, the perpetrator had been drinking at the time the crime was committed (Murdoch, Pihl, & Ross, 1990). The risks of homicide, suicide, and violent death are greater among alcohol and illicit drug uses than nonusers (Rivara et al., 1997). Even people living with alcohol or drug users who don't drink or use drugs themselves are at greater risk of being killed than are people living in drug-free households (Wren, 1997a).

Alcohol and aggression. Alcohol use figures prominently in many forms of aggressive behavior, from barroom brawls to violent crimes.

Although these linkages between alcohol and aggressive behavior are correlational, a growing body of experimental findings points to alcohol playing a causal role in both verbal and physical aggression (Giancola & Zeichner, 1997; Ito, Miller, & Pollock, 1996; Pihl & Peterson, 1993). Several factors may be involved in explaining alcohol's effects. For one thing, alcohol may have certain cognitive effects, such as reducing the ability to weigh the consequences of one's behavior, which may lead in some circumstances to acts of impulsive violence that have unfortunate consequences. Alcohol use may also lead to a loosening of the inhibitions or restraints (a process called *disinhibition*) that normally curtail impulsive behavior, including acts of impulsive violence. Alcohol also has a relaxing effect and may make the person less sensitive to anxiety-arousing cues relating to potential punishment that might ordinarily serve to inhibit aggressive behavior. Perhaps, too, people may act aggressively when drinking because of their expectations about the effects of alcohol, rather than because of its biochemical properties per se. Alcohol and other drugs may also make it more difficult for people to perceive the motives of others accurately (R. N. Parker, 1993), leading them to perceive a malevolent intent in other's behavior that can trigger a violent response.

Not everyone who drinks becomes aggressive, however (Lau, Pihl, & Peterson, 1995). Relationships between violent behavior and alcohol or other drug use are complex and may be moderated by a number of factors, including the dosage level and the user's biological sensitivity to the drug's effects, the user's relationship to the victim, the setting of the encounter, as well as other situational, individual, and sociocultural factors (Chermack & Giancola, 1997; S. E. Martin, 1992). For example, some people become more violent when they drink than do others, and violent behavior tends to occur more often when people drink in some situations, such as sporting events, than in others. Differences in the levels or actions of the neurotransmitter serotonin may also be involved. Researchers have linked tendencies to become violent under the influence of alcohol to low levels of serotonin in the brain, which suggests a deficiency of serotonin may lower the threshold for violent behavior following alcohol use (Virkkunen & Linnoila, 1993). All in all, it appears that the interplay of alcohol and violent behavior involves complex relationships between the chemical effects of alcohol on the brain and environmental cues, which under certain circumstances may lead to violent behavior.

Emotional Factors in Violent Behavior

Emotional factors, especially frustration and anger, often figure prominently in aggressive behavior. Frustration is the emotional state associated with the thwarting or blocking of one's attempt to achieve a goal. According to the classic *frustration-aggression* hypothesis, frustration always produces aggression, and aggression is always a consequence of frustration. Consider the following example. Let's say you attend a movie but are unable to enjoy it because someone sitting in front of you is constantly talking and says you should be the one to move if it bothers you so much. You may feel frustrated because your goal of enjoying the movie is thwarted, but will you attack the person you hold responsible? Perhaps, but perhaps not. We've come to recognize that although frustration often plays a role in aggression, it may lead to responses other than aggression. In the preceding example, you might leave the theater or complain to the manager rather than instigating a fight. Moreover, aggression often has causes other than frustration. For example, aggression may involve a response to a direct provocation or it may involve other motives, such as retaliation for perceived wrongdoing. Aggression in response to frustration is more likely when it induces anger and when the person blames the other person for being responsible for the situation.

Anger is often a catalyst or instigator of violent or aggressive behavior. A husband strikes his wife in a "fit of anger" when he feels frustrated that dinner is not waiting for him when he returns from work. The child abuser lashes out in anger when the child fails to comply quickly enough to his or her demands. In the schoolyard, a slight provocation is blown out of proportion, eliciting an angry response that quickly escalates into a physical confrontation.

Problems with controlling anger figure prominently in personality disorders, especially borderline and antisocial personality disorders. People with borderline personality disorder often show a lack of control over their anger, having frequent temper outbursts or displays of impulsive, aggressive behavior directed at themselves or others. People with antisocial personalities may channel feelings of resentment and anger against family or society in general into violent or aggressive behavior. But anger management is a problem not only for people with personality disorders. In Chapter 4, we noted how problems related to anger and hostility are implicated as risk factors in cardiovascular disorders. We saw in Chapter 13 how children and adolescents with conduct disorders often have problems controlling their anger and need to learn anger coping skills, such as calming self-talk, to handle conflict situations without resorting to violent behavior. Cognitive-behavior therapists have made important inroads in helping people with anger-management problems, as we discuss further in the nearby "A Closer Look" section.

 TYING IT TOGETHER

Human aggression is a complex behavior that cannot be explained by any single cause. Although some aggressive displays in other animals may be a product of "instinct," instinct theories fail to account for the variation in aggressive behavior in humans. A terrorist bombing, a mugging on a street corner, organized warfare, and a husband slamming his wife against the wall are all considered forms of aggression, but the motives that underlie them reflect different political, social, and psychological factors.

Although we cannot reduce human aggression to the level of instinct, increasing evidence points to roles for biological factors in human aggression. Biology may have more to teach us about the more impulsive forms of violent behavior, such as explosive acts of rage, than the more calculated forms of violence, such as reprisals for perceived wrongdoing or premeditated, violent crimes. Biological factors may also play a more direct role in lowering the threshold for violence in people who use alcohol or other drugs.

We also need to consider roles for culture and learning. Violent behavior is practically unknown in some cultures but all too common in others, including, unfortunately, our own. Children are exposed to cultural attitudes that legitimize certain forms of violence. Young boys learn from peer influences and from television and movie role models that conflicts are settled with fists or weapons rather than words. Cognitive factors such as ways of interpreting provocations, expectations that violence will lead to positive outcomes, and tendencies to practice angering self-statements in conflict situations help account for individual differences in aggressive behavior.

Consider one possible causal pathway involving multiple factors leading to impulsive violence. Young people who are exposed to aggressive role models in the home and the community may learn that violent behavior is an acceptable way to respond to conflict, perhaps even the expected way. They may lack resources for handling stress or channeling anger in more constructive ways. We can further speculate that a biological predisposition for impulsive, violent behavior, perhaps mediated by a serotonin imbalance, may further increase the potential for violence in people exposed to these learning experiences. Alcohol use may also enter the mix of factors that raises the potential for violence, perhaps even to a greater extent in people with these biological vulnerabilities.

(continued on page 530)

Anger Management

Cognitive-behavioral therapists assist people with anger control problems by helping them identify and correct anger-inducing thoughts they experience in situations in which they are provoked by others. Clients are taught to scrutinize the fleeting thoughts they have in confrontative situations and to recognize the cognitive distortions underlying these thoughts, such as tendencies to personalize a stranger's rudeness as a personal affront and demanding that others live up to their expectations.

Psychologist Ray Novaco (1974, 1977) developed a treatment program for anger control based on *stress inoculation therapy*, a type of cognitive-behavioral treatment that helps people manage anticipated stressors by developing new coping skills, such as self-relaxation, and by countering disruptive thoughts that occur in confrontative situations (e.g., "Who does he think he is? I'll show him!") with more adaptive self-statements (e.g., "Relax, don't get steamed up. The guy's just a jerk."). Like a vaccine that inoculates you against a virus by exposing you to an inert variant of the microbe, stress inoculation therapy exposes participants to a managed "dose" of the stressor by having them imagine themselves keeping their "cool" in confrontative situations by practicing coping responses and adaptive self-statements. Other cognitive-behavioral approaches, such as problem-solving therapy, are also used to help people with anger-management problems generate alternative, nonviolent solutions to conflict situations. A key facet in these treatment programs is helping people rethink provocations as problems to be solved rather than as threats demanding an aggressive response.

Anger-management training programs have been used with a number of different groups, including adults with anger control problems and violent youth. Treatment programs for violent youth often require a broader, multifaceted approach that involves cognitive, behavioral, and emotional components (Davis & Boster, 1992; Deffenbacher et al., 1996). The cognitive component helps participants rethink minor provocations so they don't flare out of control and to use calming self-talk in angering situations. The behavioral component may include training in relaxation skills, to help participants calm themselves down in angering situations, and in social problem-solving skills, which helps them develop alternative ways of coping with confrontative situations. The emotional component may involve the opportunity to receive emotional support within the context of supportive group therapy sessions.

Coping with Frustrating or Confrontative Situations
What we tell ourselves about the motives that underlie other people's behavior can increase our arousal and prompt an aggressive response. Let us suggest a few coping responses that may help you tone down your response to frustrating or confrontative situations:

1. *Attend to your internal states of arousal.* When you feel yourself getting "hot under the collar," tell yourself, "Stop and think." Take stock of any angering thoughts you may have.

2. *Pause for a moment to consider the evidence.* Are you taking the situation too personally? Are you overreacting to it? Are you jumping to conclusions about the other person's motives? Are there other ways of viewing the person's behavior, other than as a personal affront?

3. *Practice adaptive self-statements,* such as "I can deal with this. Easy does it."

4. *Practice a competing response to anger, such as calming mental imagery, or meditative or self-relaxation exercises.* Or disrupt an anger response by taking a walk around the block, watching TV, or reading. Or, to

Anger and aggression. Anger is often an instigator of aggressive behavior. What techniques do cognitive-behavioral therapists use to help people control anger and manage frustrating or confrontative situations without resorting to violence?

paraphrase Mark Twain, count to 10 when you're feeling angry. If that doesn't work, count to 100. The time-honored technique of counting to 10 interrupts the tendency to respond impulsively to provocations. It gives you extra time to collect your thoughts and, even more importantly, to diffuse any self-angering thoughts with some rational counters: "Hey, calm down. This is not worth getting bent out of shape. Stay cool."

5. *Counter anger with empathy.* Rather than saying, "What a despicable person he is to act that way," think, "Maybe he's having a rough day," or, "She's just jealous of me and is acting out like a child." Or, "He must be a very unhappy person to act that way." Or, "She may have reasons—or thinks she has reasons—for acting this way. Anyway, that's her problem, not mine. Don't take it so personally. Better to focus on solving this problem rather than getting steamed."

6. *Think through alternative, nonviolent solutions to the problem or situation and formulate a plan of action.*

7. *Give yourself a mental pat on the back for coping assertively, not aggressively, in the situation.*

Table 15.1 offers examples of angering self-statements and rational alternatives for some common confrontative situations:

TABLE 15.1

Anger Management: Substituting Rational Responses for Angering Self-Statements

Situation	Angering Self-Statement	Rational Alternative
A provocateur says, "So what are you going to do about it?"	"That jerk. Who does he think he is? I'll teach him a lesson he won't forget!"	"He must really have a problem if he acts this way. But that's his problem. I don't have to act at his level."
You get caught in a monster traffic jam.	"Why does this always happen to me? I can't stand this."	"This may be inconvenient, but it's not the end of the world. Don't blow it out of proportion. Everyone gets caught in traffic every now and then. Just relax and listen to some music."
You're waiting behind someone in the checkout line at the supermarket who has to cash a check. It seems like it's taking hours.	"He (she) has some nerve holding up the line. It's so unfair for someone to make other people wait. I'd like to tell him off!"	"It will only take a few minutes. People have a right to cash their checks in the market. Just relax and read a magazine off the rack while you wait."
You're cruising looking for a parking spot when suddenly another car cuts you off and seizes a vacant parking space.	"No one should be allowed to treat me like this. I'd like to punch him out."	"Don't expect other people to always be considerate of your interests. Stop personalizing things."
		"Relax, there's no sense going to war over this."
Your spouse or partner comes home several hours later than expected, without calling ahead.	"It's so unfair. I can't let him (her) treat me like this."	"Make it fair. Explain how you feel without putting him (her) down."
You're watching a movie at the theater and someone sitting next to you is talking throughout the picture.	"Don't they have any regard for other people's rights? I'm so angry with these people I can tear their heads off."	"Even if they're inconsiderate it doesn't mean I have to get angry about it or ruin my enjoyment of the movie. If they don't quiet down when I ask them, I'll just change my seat or call the manager."
A person insults you or treats you disrespectfully.	"I just can't walk away from this like nothing happened."	"Of course you can. When did anger ever settle anything? There are better ways of handling this than getting steamed."

What can be done to prevent violence? One illustrative example comes from the state of Washington, where school children are exposed to nonaggressive ways of handling problem situations. The curriculum focuses on the following skills:

1. *Empathy training,* which helps children identify their own feelings and become more aware of other children's feelings;

2. *Anger management training,* in which children are taught coping skills to control anger;

3. *Impulse control training,* in which students learn problem-solving skills to handle problem situations.

The program has had some success in reducing physically aggressive behavior and foster mor appropriate social behavior. What can each of us do in our own lives to counter violence?

SPOUSE ABUSE

Although the O.J. Simpson case may have brought the problem of domestic violence into the public eye, battering or spouse abuse is a national crisis. Surveys show that each year in the United States, at least 2 million women are severely beaten by their male partners (Koss et al., 1994) and about 1 of 8 husbands engages in at least one act of spousal violence (Holtzworth-Munroe, 1995). Nearly 2,000 women die as the result of these beatings. About 1 in 8 women report being subjected to acts of physical

Spouse abuse. About one in four couples in the U.S. report incidences of domestic violence. Though both spouses may abuse each other, women suffer a much greater incidence of severe abuse at the hands of their partners and resulting physical injuries.

aggression by their partners during the preceding year (K. D. O'Leary, 1995).

Women stand a greater chance of being attacked, raped, injured, or killed by their current or former male partners than by other types of assailants (Koss et al., 1994). Yet it may surprise you to learn that evidence from community samples in the United States and other countries such as New Zealand show that women are as likely as men are, if not more likely, to commit acts of violence against their partner (Magdol et al., 1997; Margolin & Burman, 1993). In about half of the couples in which partner abuse occurs, both partners engage in acts of physical abuse against one another. However, the sheer frequency of battering does not take into account differences in the severity of the abuse. Women are much more likely than men to suffer severe abuse and to sustain physical injuries, including severe injuries such as broken bones and damage to internal organs (Margolin & Burman, 1993; O'Leary, 1995). For this reason, our focus is on the male batterer.

Different motivations may be involved in accounting for partner violence in men and women. One hypothesis gaining interest is that men tend to attack while women tend to react. That is, male violence toward women may stem from factors that threaten their traditional position of dominance in relationships, such as unemployment and drug abuse. Violence perpetrated by women may arise from the stress of coping with an abusive partner (Magdol et al., 1997).

Although spouse abuse cuts across all strata of our society, it is more commonly reported among people of lower socioeconomic levels. This may reflect a greater level of stress experienced by people who are struggling financially. It may also reflect a reporting bias, a tendency for upper income groups to use personal physicians who may be less inclined to report incidents of domestic violence than health care providers in public facilities who tend to serve less affluent groups (Margolin & Burman, 1993). Some evidence suggests that income disparity between husband and wife, with the wife earning more than the husband, contributes to wife abuse, not poverty per se (McCloskey, 1996).

Ethnic or racial group differences appear unrelated to the risk of spouse abuse when we take into account socioeconomic level and other sociodemographic factors (Margolin & Burman, 1993). The lack of opportunity and alienation from the larger society experienced by many economically disadvantaged people, including many ethnic minority group members, increases the potential for mental health problems and violence and abuse within domestic relationships (Nelson et al., 1992).

Psychological Characteristics of Male Batterers

Although there is no one psychological profile of male batterers, they tend to show higher levels of hostility, impulsivity, verbal aggression, early problem behavior, and antisocial and borderline personality traits than nonbatterers (Aldarondo, 1996; Else et al., 1993; Magdol et al., 1998). Male batterers also tend to externalize or minimize blame for their actions and feel inadequate or dissatisfied with themselves (Flournoy & Wilson, 1991). Other characteristics associated with increased risk of battering include youthful age, lower income and occupational and educational status, high levels of stress, problem behaviors during adolescence, lack of assertive self-expression, exposure to parental violence in childhood, being the victim of physical abuse by one's mother during teenage years, and alcohol use, especially heavy use (Feldman, 1997; Magdol et al., 1998; Van-Der Pahlen et al., 1997).

Patterns of Abuse

Battering typically occurs within a larger pattern of abuse. Male batterers are more likely than nonbatterers to physically abuse their children, to sexually aggress against their spouses, and to have witnessed family violence during childhood (Hotaling & Sugarman, 1986). Acts of physical abuse by male partners are not usually isolated incidents but typically occur as a recurrent pattern in the relationship (Straus, 1990). Battering often starts before marriage vows are taken, and although it may involve milder forms of aggression at first, such as pushing and grabbing, it may escalate if nothing is done to stop it (Holtzworth-Monroe, 1995).

Relationship factors, especially marital conflict, also play a role in initiating and maintaining spousal abuse (Aldarondo, 1996). Moreover, as compared to nonviolent couples, physically aggressive couples show poorer problem-solving skills (Anglin & Holtzworth-Munroe, 1997). They also focus less of their efforts on solving their problems while showing more negative interactions in which angry responses from one spouse beget angry responses from the other (Margolin & Burman, 1993).

Spousal violence often follows an event that serves as a trigger for the abuser to lose control (G. Ryan, 1993). The triggering event may involve criticism or rejection from the spouse or incidents that lead the man to feel trapped, insecure, or threatened (Bitler, Linnoila, & George, 1994). The use of alcohol or other drugs further raises the risk that such events will lead to a battering episode. A recent analysis of some 62 episodes of domestic violence showed that about 90% of the assailants reported using alcohol or other drugs on the day of the assault (Brookoff et al., 1997).

Male batterers often have low self-esteem and a sense of personal inadequacy (Murphy, Meyer, & O'Leary, 1994). They may become excessively dependent on their wives for emotional support and feel threatened if they perceive their partners becoming more independent or developing separate interests from their own. Spousal violence may represent an inappropriate way of responding to this emotional threat. Abusers also tend to have poor problem-solving skills in handling conflict situations with their spouses (Else et al., 1993), which may explain (although not condone) why they turn to the use of physical force when a triggering event occurs.

Sociocultural Viewpoints

Writing from a sociocultural perspective, feminist theorists consider domestic violence to be a product of the differential power relationships that exist between men and women in our society. Men are socialized into dominant roles in which they expect women to be subordinate to their wishes (Koss et al., 1994). Cross-cultural evidence shows that the husband's need for control is an underlying contributor to wife abuse (M. I. Wilson & Daly, 1996). Men also learn that aggressive displays of masculine power are socially sanctioned and are even glorified in some settings, such as on the athletic field. These role expectations, together with a willingness to accept interpersonal violence as an appropriate means of resolving differences, create a context for spousal abuse in situations in which the man's sense of control is threatened when he perceives his partner as failing to meet his needs or respect his wishes. Men who batter may also have less power in their relationships and may attempt to make up for their lack of power by using physical force.

Feminist theorists further point out that domestic violence exists because our society condones it (Gardiner, 1992). The man who beats his wife may be taken aside and "talked to" by a police officer, rather than arrested on the spot. Even if he is arrested and convicted, his punishment is likely to be less severe (sometimes just a "slap on the wrist") than if he had assaulted a stranger.

Effects of Spouse Abuse

In addition to the risk of physical injury, domestic violence can lead to posttraumatic stress disorder (PTSD) and other psychological effects, especially depression and low self-esteem (Cascardi et al., 1995; O'Leary, 1995; C. G. Watson et al., 1997). Rates of PTSD in battered women have ranged from 60% (Astin et al., 1995) in one study to 78% in another (Watson et al., 1997). These rates were about three times higher than among comparison groups of non-battered women. Typically, the more severe the abuse, the greater the level of psychological distress. Battering may also be a contributing factor to alcohol or substance use disorders. Domestic violence may also lead the abused woman to flee the abusive situation, which in the absence of other resources may lead to homelessness (Toro et al., 1995). For the male abuser, battering may lead to a severing of family ties that may also ultimately lead to homelessness.

Exposure to domestic violence also takes an emotional toll on the children. More than 3 million children in the United States witness violence between their parents each year (DeAngelis, 1995b). In a recent study of 62 incidents of domestic violence in Memphis, Tennessee, children witnessed 85% of the assaults (Brookoff et al., 1997). Witnessing interparental violence has direct negative effects on the child's emotional health and behavior, leading in many cases to depression and behavior problems (DeAngelis, 1995a). Even nonphysical forms of parental aggression, such as insults, threats, or kicking furniture, are associated with more behavioral and emotional problems in children (Jouriles et al., 1996). Parental modeling of spouse abuse may also set the stage for perpetuating an intergenerational pattern of spousal abuse from generation to generation. Clearly, it sets a poor example by modeling the use of violence as an acceptable means of resolving interpersonal conflicts. Many abusers, as well as many battered spouses, also have histories of being emotionally or physically abused during childhood. Moreover, spouse abuse often occurs in a context in which children are physically abused by the offender as well (McCloskey, 1996). The greater the frequency of spousal violence, the more likely that children too will suffer physical abuse at the hands of the violent father or mother (S. M. Ross, 1996).

Why Don't Battered Women Just Leave?

About half of the abused women who seek professional assistance return to their abusive husbands or partners (Strube, 1988). Why do women remain in abusive relationships or take back abusive partners after a separation? Are they driven by unconscious, masochistic needs to punish themselves?

Professionals who work with abused women argue that women in abusive relationships are better understood as trauma survivors than as masochists (Strube, 1988). Battered women have much in common with other trauma survivors, such as former political hostages and victims of kidnapping. Leonore Walker (1979) coined the term *battered woman syndrome* to describe the traumatizing effects of battering, which include feelings of helplessness and impaired coping ability, that can make it difficult for the battered woman to leave the abuser and establish a new life on her own. Compounding their problems, many battered wives lack the economic means to establish an independent household of their own for themselves and their children. Consequently, many fear becoming destitute if they leave the batterer.

Spousal violence may exact a greater emotional toll than other forms of trauma because the agent of abuse is someone whom the woman trusted and loved and with whom she may need to continue a relationship, especially if children are involved. Betrayal of trust may intensify the woman's emotional reactions and further impair her ability to cope.

A review of the literature on the effects of spousal violence identifies several psychological factors that may affect the battered woman's ability to cope effectively (Follingstad, Neckerman, & Vormbrock, 1988):

1. *Shattering the myth of personal invulnerability.* Most people maintain an illusion that they are somehow immune to the traumas or tragic events that befall others, such as violent crime, crippling traffic accidents, or fatal cancers (Janoff-Bulman & Frieze, 1983). This illusion, which helps maintain a sense of personal security, may be shattered in women exposed to spousal abuse, leaving them feeling vulnerable. If a woman is brutalized by the man in whom she had placed her trust, she may come to think that other bad things will also befall her. The shield of invulnerability cracks. Her sense of safety and security in her own home that most of us take for granted may be destroyed.

2. *Reduced problem-solving ability.* Trauma may hamper the woman's ability to weigh alternative solutions to her problems. Survivors may become so preoccupied with the immediate problem of preventing recurrent beatings that they cannot focus on ways of making the larger life changes that will extricate them and their children from the marriages. Women may even come to believe that they cannot take control of events and that submission is the only realistic way of preventing further abuse (B. Cooper, 1976). Some abused woman women sink to a state of despair in which they essentially "give up" trying and decide to return to the abuser rather than seek alternatives (K. D. Newman, 1993).

3. *Stress-related reactions.* Battered women may experience a form of posttraumatic stress disorder that can further impair their coping ability. Like soldiers who have had traumatic combat experiences, battered women may reexperience beatings in the form of nightmares, flashbacks, and

What about the children? Children too are affected by spousal abuse. Children exposed to interparental abuse may become depressed or develop behavioral problems. Childhood exposure may also set the stage for the perpetuation of spousal abuse from one generation to another. Many children are also beaten by the abusers.

intrusive images of abuse. They may become numbed to their environment, have sleep disturbances, feel anxious in the presence of cues or reminders of beatings, and avoid situations or stimuli connected with beatings. Anxiety and feelings of dread may lead the battered woman to withdraw from the outside world and cut off support from other people. Feelings of pessimism, anger, guilt, and depression are also common, along with suicidal thoughts and attempts. Problems with alcohol or drug abuse may also develop, further impairing the woman's ability to function effectively.

4. *Thought conversion.* Hostages and kidnap victims who are held for a lengthy period of time sometimes experience a conversion in attitudes and come to regard their captors with positive or sympathetic feelings, at the same time developing negative feelings toward potential rescuers. In a similar way, battered women who are subjected to chronic abuse may come to view their tormenters in more sympathetic terms.

5. *Finding meaning in the abuse.* According to existential psychiatrist Viktor Frankl (1963), people have a basic psychological need to find meaning in their experiences, even in brutal abuse. Some battered women may try to find meaning in the abuse, or even justify it, by using rationalization. Rationalizations (e.g., "He didn't really mean it . . . it was really the alcohol . . . it was really my fault.") as well as the use of denial (e.g., "It wasn't really that bad.") tend to perpetuate abusive relationships.

6. *Learned helplessness.* Domestic violence can lead to feelings of helplessness, which can sap the woman's motivation to seek to overcome the trauma and make it less likely she will seek help to extricate herself from the abusive relationship (L. E. Walker, 1979; K. Wilson et al., 1992). Helplessness may develop as the abused woman finds that her repeated attempts to make changes in the relationship fail or when her requests for external help are met with frustrating "run-arounds" or lack of concern from criminal justice or mental-health personnel. She may come to believe that nothing she can do will prevent the battering or extricate herself from the situation.

7. *Difficulties handling troubling emotions.* Battered women may have difficulty handling their anger toward the abuser, perhaps because they have learned, from his example, that anger is a dangerous or uncontrollable emotion (Carmen, Riecker, & Mills, 1984). Unexpressed anger may become redirected inward in the form of self-blame and self-loathing, which, in turn, can lead to feelings of resignation and depression and to self-destructive behaviors ranging from substance abuse to suicide attempts. Depression may further hamper the woman's ability to change her life.

We also need to take into account the cultural expectations placed on women. Women in many cultures are expected to adhere to a self-sacrificial ideal that a woman's role is to sacrifice her needs for the sake of her children and family. If she is abused, she may see her role as "suffering in silence" lest her response to the situation threaten family stability. Yet she may face a conflict between two conflicting moral values: (1) that "good women provide a strong family base for their children," and (2) that "people should not harm those they love" (Pilowsky, 1993). The turning point to taking effective action may come when she asserts as a stronger moral imperative the belief that self-respect and self-care are the moral rights of every woman.

In sum, battered women are trauma survivors, not masochists. Labeling them as masochists has the unfortunate effect of blaming the victim for the abuse. When we see battered women as survivors, rather than as masochists, we supplant blaming them with an effort to understand the psychological factors that may lead them to feel trapped in their relationships. Such understanding may facilitate the development of programs to help abused women make hard decisions and counteract tendencies toward rationalization, self-hatred, and denial. Viewing the woman who suffers abuse as a survivor also shifts blame away from her and onto the batterer, where it belongs.

TRUTH *or* FICTION REVISITED

15.5 *False.* Battered women are trauma survivors, not masochists. Labeling them as masochists has the unfortunate effect of blaming the victim for the abuse.

Treatment of Batterers and Abused Spouses

Before treatment can begin, the battering must stop. Only then can any therapeutic attempt at healing or reconciliation begin. Couples therapy or family therapy may be useful in treating couples and families with a history of domestic violence (Kirschner & Kirschner, 1992; K. D. O'Leary, 1995). In some cases, each spouse receives individual therapy along with marital or couples therapy. The therapist may help the couple understand rage as an expression of a sense of inner powerlessness and assist them to understand each other's emotional pain better and learn more productive ways of handling anger and resolving conflicts without resorting to violence (Mones & Panitz, 1994). In some cases the relationship cannot be saved, and the couple may need help in coping with the consequences of divorce.

Group therapy for male batterers may also be used to provide a place where batterers can feel secure enough to express their inner feelings and where they will be confronted by other group members if they avoid taking responsibility for their abusive behavior. Support groups for battered women are also available in many communities and are often led by women who were formerly abused themselves (O'Leary, 1995). In addition to providing mutual support, these groups help battered women recognize the cycle of violence, develop escape strategies, weigh alternatives to marriage, enhance self-esteem, and decrease self-blame.

Abusers may be mandated by the courts to receive treatment as an alternative to incarceration. Unfortunately, evidence casts doubt on whether court-mandated treatment reduces future acts of spouse abuse as compared to the deterrent effects of traditional criminal justice penalties (Rosenfeld, 1992). Another problem is that many abusers simply stop attending therapy, despite a court order requiring their attendance.

CHILD ABUSE

More than 3 million cases of alleged child maltreatment are reported annually in the United States (Daro & Wiese, 1995). Among these, more than a million cases are substantiated by child protective agencies, representing 16 of every 1,000 U.S. children. More than 1,000 children in the United States die each year as the result of abuse or neglect. As horrific as these numbers are, they greatly understate the problem, as most incidents of child maltreatment are never publicly identified. The great majority of deaths involve children under the age of 5; nearly half involve children under 1 year of age. However, older children are more likely to suffer physical abuse than newborns to 2-year-olds (Cappelleri, Eckenrode, & Powers, 1993). Boys and girls are about equally likely to suffer physical abuse. A 1998 national survey of high school boys in the United States found 1 in 8 reporting they had been either physically or sexually abused (Lewin, 1998). Physical abuse was far more common than sexual abuse.

Child abuse is also a major problem in Canada and other countries. A random sample of households in Ontario, Canada, showed that 31% of the adult men and 21% of the adult women reported a history of physical abuse in childhood (MacMillan et al., 1997).

Although the mother is identified as the abuser in about 60% of cases of physical abuse (DeAngelis, 1995b), it should be recognized that mothers assume a disproportionate share of child-care responsibilities and constitute the great majority of single-parent heads of households. Like other forms of violence and abuse, child abuse cuts across ethnic, racial, and national boundaries. Although reliable statistics in other countries are often hard to come by, a survey in the African nation of Nigeria revealed a large percentage of children and adolescents reported having seen an abused or neglected child and believed that child abuse and neglect were widespread in their country (Ebigbo, 1993). Sad to say, child abuse may well be universal, although prevalences may vary from country to country.

What Is Child Abuse?

Child abuse includes several types of physical, sexual, and emotional maltreatment or neglect of children. Although definitions of the specific types of abuse vary, a useful set of definitions was developed by the New York State Federation on Child Abuse and Neglect (New York City Board of Education, 1984) (see Table 15.2). Despite these definitions, it can be difficult to determine where to draw the line between "acceptable" spanking or hitting and child abuse. Neglect is the most common form of child maltreatment, representing nearly half (49%) of substantiated cases according to a recent report (Daro & Wiese, 1995). Physical abuse accounts for 21% of cases, sexual abuse for 11%, emotional maltreatment for 3%, and other forms for 16% (see Figure 15.3).

TRUTH *or* **FICTION** **REVISITED**

15.6 *False.* The most common form of child maltreatment is neglect.

Mandatory reporting laws in all 50 states require mental-health professionals, including psychologists, social workers,

Child abuse. There are more than one million substantiated cases of child abuse reported in the U.S. each year. More than 1,000 U.S. children die each year as the result of abuse or neglect at the hands of their parents or caretakers. Here we see a memorial organized by community residents in New York City after the death of a 6-year-old victim of child abuse.

TABLE 15.2

Types of Child Abuse

Type of Abuse	Definition
Physical Abuse	Nonaccidental physical injury of a child caused by a parent or caretaker. The injuries may range from superficial bruises to broken bones, burns, and serious internal injuries and may result in death in some cases.
Physical Neglect	Failing to provide children with, or withholding from them, adequate food, shelter, clothing, hygiene, medical care, or supervision needed to promote their growth and development.
Sexual Abuse	The sexual exploitation of children involving acts ranging from nontouching offenses, such as exhibitionism, to genital fondling, sexual intercourse, or involving them in the production of pornography.
Emotional Maltreatment	The use of constant harsh criticism of the child involving the use of verbally abusive language, or emotional neglect, which is characterized by the withholding of physical and emotional contact needed to promote normal emotional development and in some extreme cases, physical development.

Source: Adapted from Alpert & Green, 1992, pp. 228–229.

and marriage and family counselors, to notify child protective officials if they come to know of child abuse or have reasonable suspicions that abuse is occurring (Ebert, 1992). Despite mandatory reporting laws, a great many cases of child abuse go unreported.

Factors in Child Abuse

A number of parental factors are associated with an increased risk of child abuse, including stress, witnessing family violence in one's family of origin, being abused during one's own childhood, failure to develop an appropriate attachment to one's children, poor anger-management skills, alcohol or substance abuse, holding rigid rules concerning child rearing, and acceptance of violence as a means of re-

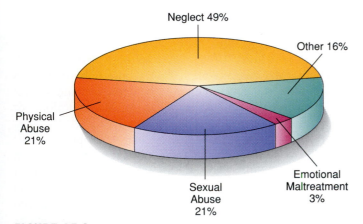

FIGURE 15.3 *Cases of child maltreatment by type.*
This figure shows the breakdown of substantiated cases of child maltreatment reported by child protective agencies in 36 states in the U.S. for 1993 and 1994. Child neglect was the most frequent type of child maltreatment, followed by physical abuse.

Source: National Committee to Prevent Child Abuse (NCPCA); Daro & Wiese (1995).

solving conflicts and controlling children's behavior (Belsky, 1993; Pogge, 1992). Moreover, teenage parents, undereducated parents, single parents, and parents from lower income levels are more likely than other parents to physically abuse their children (Christmas, Wodarski, & Smokowski, 1996; DeAngelis, 1995b).

Many people who abuse or neglect children suffer from mental disorders, including alcohol-related disorders, mood disorders, and anxiety disorder (Egami et al., 1996). Parental stress is a major risk factor in its own right and may underlie other risk factors such as poverty and single parenthood (Pogge, 1992). Sources of stress include unemployment or job-related problems, medical problems, financial pressures, marital conflict, and living in an unstable and unsafe environment. Not surprisingly, incidents of child abuse tend to increase during times of rising unemployment. There appears to be no discernible difference in the risk of child abuse across ethnic groups or even socioeconomic levels when one takes into account the level of life stressors to which parents are subjected (Pogge, 1992).

Child abuse does not arise out of vacuum but may be seen as progressing through a series of increasingly coercive behaviors on the part of the abusive parent (D. A. Wolfe, 1987). Cognitive factors, such as blaming the child for the abuse (e.g., "If he didn't want to get hit, he should not have left his clothes lying around"), serve to justify the abuse and may contribute to the progression to more abusive behaviors. Abusive parents tend to see their children's misbehavior as intentional, even when it is not. They also rely more heavily on physical punishment and less on reasoning as a means of controlling their children than do nonabusive parents (Belsky, 1993). They often lack appropriate parenting and problem-solving skills for dealing with child behavior problems and have a low tolerance for demands made by children (Milner, 1993; Pogge, 1992). Yet, it does not appear that parents who physically abuse their children are more likely than nonabusers to have diagnosable psychological disorders (Pogge, 1992). Nor do they have any clearly identifiable psychological traits that set them apart.

The stress of adapting to changing family structures is another recognized risk factor in child maltreatment (Pogge, 1992). A great many families in our society have disintegrated or are in the process of coming apart at the seams. Stressors such as economic hardship and drug and alcohol abuse often figure prominently in family disruption. For some parents, the stressful demands of adjusting to these changes can lead to feelings of powerlessness and lower self-esteem, which in turn can lead to child neglect or to irrational, impulsive acts of physical abuse of children.

Modeling of excessive use of physical punishment by parents may help explain the intergenerational transmission of child abuse. When children observe their own parents using physical violence when they are stressed or angry, they may come to view violence as an acceptable coping response for handling noncompliant children.

Child Maltreatment: An Integrative Approach

Psychologist Jay Belsky (1993) applies an integrative model toward understanding the origins of child abuse. He speaks of various "contexts of maltreatment" that need to be considered in reaching a broader understanding of the factors contributing to child maltreatment. The *developmental context* takes into account the intergenerational transmission of abuse. The *immediate interactional context* takes into account the deficits in parenting skills and problematic parent-child interactions that are associated with abusive behavior. Then there is the broader context of *community, cultural,* and perhaps even *evolutionary* factors. Community factors linked to abuse include social isolation and limited social ties. Cultural factors include the acceptability of corporal punishment as an appropriate means of disciplining children. In the cultural context in which some forms of hitting are deemed acceptable, child maltreatment becomes abnormal only to the extent that its severity deviates from the social norm. The willingness of society to tolerate violence, even to glorify it in movies and certain sporting events, may set the stage for bringing violence into the home in the form of child abuse, spousal abuse, or both.

Although on a personal level we may abhor violence against children, Belsky suggests there may be a broader evolutionary context that underlies abuse and neglect. Under conditions in which there is not enough food or other needed resources to go around to ensure survival of all, parents may neglect the needs of their children or select among them whom to provide for. This point is certainly controversial and rests on a tenuous assumption that behavioral proceses leading to child abuse or neglect are somehow imprinted in our genes and represent a genetic lineage from our ancient human ancestors whose survival may have depended on it. Belsky's larger point is that child abuse and neglect are multiply determined by a number of factors that operate in different contexts or at different levels of analysis. No one factor is invariably associated with abuse or neglect—not inadequate parenting skills nor a childhood history of abuse. Although abusers are more likely than nonabusers to have been abused in childhood, most abused children do not abuse their own children as adults (Kaufman & Zigler, 1989). We need to develop a better understanding of how various factors combine and interact with each other to increase the risk of abuse and neglect in a given family. We also need to discriminate between physical abuse and neglect because these forms of maltreatment don't always occur together and may reflect a different constellation of factors.

Effects of Child Abuse

The physical injuries suffered by physically abused children are disturbing and often tragic, ranging from welts and bruises to broken bones and massive internal injuries, which sometimes result in death. The emotional wounds of abuse and neglect may run even deeper and be longer lasting. Abused or neglected children often have difficulties forming healthy attachments to others. They may lack the capacity for empathy or fail to develop a sense of conscience or concern about the welfare of others. They may act out in ways that mirror the cruelty they've experienced in their lives, such as by torturing or killing animals, setting fires, or aggressing against smaller, more vulnerable children.

Other common psychological effects of neglect and abuse are lowered self-esteem, depression, suicidal thinking, and failure to venture beyond the home in order to explore the outside world (N. M. Stone, 1993). In one study, about 1 in 4 abused children made suicidal attempts or threats (Stone, 1993). Abused children often show immature behaviors such as bed-wetting or thumb-sucking (Conger, 1992). Child abuse is also associated with an increased risk in later life of bulimia (Rorty, Yager, & Rossotto, 1994), dissociative identity disorder (multiple personality) (Coons, 1994), anxiety disorders (M. B. Stein et al., 1996), PTSD, depression and substance abuse (Duncan et al., 1996; J. McCauley et al., 1997), borderline personality disorder (Weaver & Clum, 1995), and various physical health problems (McCauley et al., 1997). Abused children, even preschoolers, are also more apt to be depressed and aggressive than nonabused children (Kazdin, Moser, Kolbus, & Bell, 1985).

Physical abuse disrupts the normal development of attachment between the child and adult caregivers, which can make it more difficult for children to develop healthy peer relationships (K. A. Dodge et al., 1994). Researchers find that children who were physically abused in early childhood (before age 5) were perceived in their early school years by their peers, teachers, and mothers as less popular, more disliked, and more withdrawn than nonabused children (Dodge et al., 1994). Failure to develop positive peer relationships can lead to emotional problems and conduct disturbances in adolescence and adulthood.

Physical abuse can lead to neuropsychological deficits that impair verbal, perceptual, and motor skills; diminish performance on intelligence tests; and interfere with academic achievement (Ammerman et al., 1986; Tarter, Hegedus, Winsten, & Alterman, 1984). Physical abuse is also associated with poor self-perceptions and depression in school-age children. Abused children often assume that they must have done something terribly wrong to have prompted their parents to punish them so severely. Self-blaming attributions can lead to diminished self-esteem and depression. Yet some maltreated children are apparently resilient in the face of abuse and are able to function well socially and academically (Kaufman et al., 1994). We don't understand the mechanisms that underlie resilience to abuse. Nor do we know if resilient children are apt to develop problems in their interpersonal relationships later in life.

For a period of 20 years, Widom (1991) has been tracking the development of 908 people who were abused or neglected during childhood and comparing them to a group of nonabused controls. After accounting for differences relating to social class and race, the abused or neglected group were

- more likely to have been arrested during adolescence and adulthood,
- more likely to engage in criminal violence or to become repeat offenders,
- less likely to be employed and held lower paying jobs, completed fewer years of education, scored lower on tests of intelligence, and had higher suicide rates.

Child Abuse Treatment

Given the scope of the problem, child maltreatment clearly represents a national emergency. Government efforts at the federal and state levels to deal with the problem have thus far been largely unsuccessful, despite the expenditures of billions of dollars annually (Alpert & Green, 1992). Nonetheless, some progress has been made in treating physically abusive parents and their children, with most gains reported in the use of behavioral and cognitive-behavioral programs that focus on training the parents in various skills relating to stress management, anger control, and parenting techniques (D. A. Wolfe & Wekerle, 1993). Parent training programs aim at helping the abusive parents learn to cope better with stress and improve their interactions with their children (DeAngelis, 1995b). Yet we still lack long-term follow-ups to determine whether such programs have lasting benefits in preventing recurrent episodes of child abuse.

Although therapists who work with abusive families recognize the importance of ethnic and cultural issues in planning treatment programs, research exploring the development of culturally sensitive treatment interventions remains lacking. We also know little about the effects of child abuse treatment programs that target the children themselves, in part because virtually all programs are geared toward treating the abusive parents (DeAngelis, 1995a). Also

lacking are studies specifically targeting child neglect as distinguished from physical or emotional abuse, despite evidence that neglect can have even more damaging consequences than physical abuse (DeAngelis, 1995b). In fact, nearly half of the child fatalities due to maltreatment are the result of neglect, not physical abuse (Daro & Wiese, 1995).

Preventing Child Abuse

Much of the focus in preventing child abuse has centered on training new and expectant parents, and especially teen parents, in parenting skills. Although skills-training approaches have been shown to increase parenting knowledge and to enhance child-rearing skills, we still await evidence from large well-controlled studies that such programs succeed in reducing the rates of child abuse in at-risk families (Wekerle & Wolfe, 1993). A major limitation in the research to date is that virtually all participants in these parenting programs are women; the needs of men who are potentially at risk of becoming abusive parents have yet to be addressed on any widespread basis.

Because the stresses associated with poverty are a major contributing factor to child maltreatment, significant progress in the battle against child abuse and neglect may come only when we are able to deter young women from having children, especially multiple children, if they lack the social and financial resources to support them (Belsky, 1993; Christmas et al., 1996). Yet child abuse is not limited to young parents or the poor. Finding solutions to the problems of child abuse will necessarily involve comprehensive efforts that address the multifaceted needs of at-risk families and families in crisis from across the socioeconomic spectrum.

RAPE

We now turn to consider the problem of sexual aggression. We use the term *sexual aggression* broadly to include both acts of outright sexual violence, such as rape or sexual assault, as well as sexual harassment, in which one person aggresses against another sexually by subjecting the other person to unwanted sexual overtures, demands, or lewd comments. Sexual molestation of children is also by definition a form of sexual aggression, even if no direct force is used to obtain sexual favors, because children by virtue of their developmental level are deemed incapable of providing informed consent.

The person who commits rape, like those who commit other forms of violent behavior, does not necessarily have a diagnosable mental disorder within the DSM system. Yet, like other forms of violence discussed in this chapter, rape can be considered abnormal in that it is socially unacceptable, violates social norms, and is grievously harmful to its victims. Rape may also be associated with some clinical syndromes, especially some forms of sexual sadism.

Forcible rape refers to the use of force, violence, or threats of violence to coerce someone into sexual intercourse. **Statutory rape** is defined as sexual intercourse with a person who is unable to give consent, either because of being under the age of consent or because of mental disability, even though the person may cooperate with the rapist.

Incidence of Rape

More than 500,000 women are believed to be sexually assaulted each year in the United States. (U.S. Bureau of Justice Statistics, 1995). Of these, 170,000 involve completed rapes and 140,000 involve attempted rapes. Most rapes go unreported to police. Yet the prevalence of rapes reported to authorities in the United States is 20 times greater than the rate in Japan and 13 times greater than the rate in Great Britain ("Women under assault," 1990). There is some good news to report, however. The numbers of reported rapes began declining during the mid-1990s. Unreported rapes also appear to be on the decline (Butterfield, 1997b). Whether this decline represents an ebbing of sexual crimes against women remains to be seen.

Victimization Surveys

Victimization surveys provide information about unreported as well as reported rapes (Harney & Muehlenhard, 1991). They involve random samples of individuals who are asked to give information regarding any experiences they've had in which they were sexually coerced or assaulted. A large-scale survey of 3,187 women and 2,972 men attending 32 colleges across the nation revealed a disturbingly high percentage of the women reporting they had experienced rape

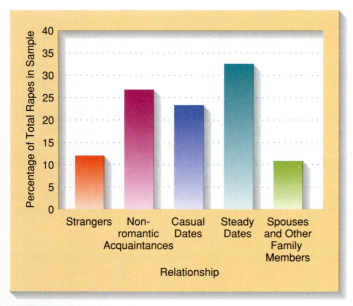

FIGURE 15.4 *Relative percentages of stranger rapes and acquaintance rapes.*
According to a large-scale survey of more than 3,000 college women at 32 colleges, the great majority of rapes of college women were committed by men whom the women were acquainted with, including dates, nonromantic acquaintances, and family members.

Source: Adapted from Koss (1988).

(15.4%) or attempted rape (12.1%) (Koss, Gidycz, & Wisniewski, 1987). In nearly 90% of the rapes, the woman was acquainted with the assaulter (Koss, 1988; see Figure 15.4). Acquaintance rapes are especially likely to be underreported to police because the victims may not perceive them as crimes. About 1 in 13 men surveyed (7.7%) admitted to committing or attempting rape (Koss et al., 1987).

Based on a compilation of official records and victimization surveys, researchers estimate that between 14% and 25% of U.S. women have been raped or will be raped at some point during their lifetimes (Calhoun & Atkeson, 1991; Koss, 1993; Polaschek, Ward, & Hudson, 1997). In about four of five cases of rapes overall (and nearly 9 of 10 in the college survey), the woman was acquainted with the assailant (Gibbs, 1991; "Unsettling Report on an Epidemic of Rape," 1992), though typically they were not usually intimate acquaintances or lovers (Koss, 1988).

TRUTH *or* **FICTION** **REVISITED**

15.7 True. In about four of five cases of rape, the assailant was someone the woman knew.

Who Is at Risk?

Any woman is at risk, including women and girls of all ages, races, and socioeconomic levels.[1] However, younger women are most at risk, especially adolescent girls. More than half of the reported rapes in the United States are committed against girls under the age of 18; about one in six rapes are committed against girls under the age of 12 ("U.S. finds heavy toll of rapes on young," 1994). The younger the woman, the more likely she is to be acquainted with the assailant.

Date rape is a kind of acquaintance rape. Men who commit date rape may assume that the woman's willingness to accompany him home, or even acceptance of a date, signifies assent to sexual activity, or that women are somehow obligated to reciprocate with sex if their dates take them to dinner and treat them to a good time. Other date rapists presume that women who go to singles bars and similar places are in effect expressing tacit agreement to sexual activity ("looking for it") with any men who show interest in them. Date rapists may also assume that women who resist their advances are merely trying to avoid looking "easy." Unlike stranger rape, in which wholesale force or threats are used from the beginning, date rape usually follows a chain of steps from gentle urging to more intense advances to outright physical coercion (Gibbs, 1991). Many women who experience nonconsensual intercourse in a dating situation do not consider it to be rape. They may attribute the act to a serious communication problem or to another type of crime or do not perceive themselves as having been victimized, even when the act clearly meets the legal definition of rape (Layman, Gidycz, & Lynn, 1996).

---

[1]Although male rapes do occur, the great majority of cases involve women who are raped.

Date rape. Many rape awareness workshops, like the one depicted here, have been held on college campuses in order to combat the problem of date rape on campus.

Date rape is not the only form of dating violence. Dating violence involving use of physical force, such as hitting, is common; in one study conducted at the University of Maine, 1 in 5 students had experienced some form of dating violence in a recent dating relationship (C. L. Stacy et al., 1994).

Theoretical Perspectives

There is no single kind of rape or rapist (Siegel, 1992). Rapists are no more likely than other offenders to have the kinds of psychological disorders coded on Axis I of the *DSM-IV* (Polaschek et al., 1997). Some rapists who have feelings of shyness and inadequacy report that they cannot find willing partners. They lack social skills for interacting with the opposite gender (Overholser & Beck, 1986). Others are basically antisocial and tend to act out on their impulses regardless of the cost to the victim. Many antisocial rapists have long records as violent offenders (Siegel, 1992). Many were sexually abused themselves as children (Dhawan & Marshall, 1996). For still other rapists, violent cues appear to enhance sexual arousal, so they are motivated to combine sex with aggression (Barbaree & Marshall, 1991). College men who report having used force or threat of force to gain sexual favors showed greater penile arousal in a laboratory study in response to depictions of rape scenes than did noncoercive men (Lohr, Adams, & Davis, 1997). Cues such as the woman in the rape depiction showing pain or fear, or the man acting forcibly, dampened sexual arousal in noncoercive men but not in the coercive men. In other words, when noncoercive men are physiologically aroused they are put off by cues of nonconsent or use

of force. But coercive men are not. Other rapists, who were abused as children, may humiliate women as a way of expressing anger and power over women and of taking revenge.

Psychological Factors Groth and Hobson (1983) argue that the seeking of sexual gratification has little to do with rape. On the basis of clinical experience with more than 1,000 rapists, Groth and Hobson hypothesize the existence of three basic kinds of rape: anger rape, power rape, and sadistic rape. The anger rape is a savage, unpremeditated attack triggered by feelings of hatred and resentment. Anger rapists often use more force than necessary to gain compliance to take revenge for humiliations they have suffered—or believe they have suffered—at the hands of women. The power rapist is basically motivated by the desire to control another person. Groth and Hobson suggest that power rapists use rape to try "to resolve disturbing doubts about [their] masculine identity and worth, [or] to combat deep-seated feelings of insecurity and vulnerability" (p. 165). Sadistic rapes frequently employ torture and **bondage**, merging sex and aggression. Sadistic rapists are most likely to mutilate their victims.

Sociocultural Factors Rape is a form of social deviance, not a symptom of a diagnosable psychological disorder. Though some rapists show evidence of psychopathology, especially psychopathic traits, on psychological tests (S. L. Brown & Forth, 1997; Herkov et al., 1996), many do not. The "normality" of many rapists suggests that socialization factors play an important role.

Some sociocultural theorists argue that our culture actually breeds rapists by socializing men into sexually dominant and aggressive roles associated with stereotypical concepts of masculinity (e.g., G. C. Hall & Barongan, 1997; Lisak, 1991). Sexually coercive college men tend to have a hypermasculine personality orientation, adhere more strictly to traditional gender roles, view women as adversaries in the "mating game," and hold more accepting attitudes toward the use of violence against women than noncoercive men (e.g., O'Donohue, McKay, & Schewe, 1996; Polaschek et al., 1997). They are also more prone to blame rape victims than rapists and more sexually aroused by portrayals of rape than are men who hold less rigid stereotypes. Sociocultural influences also reinforce themes that may underlie rape, such as the cultural belief that a masculine man is expected to be sexually assertive and overcome a woman's resistance until she "melts" in his arms (Stock, 1991).

College men on dates frequently perceive their dates' protests as part of an adversarial sex game. One male undergraduate said, "Hell, no" when asked whether a date had consented to sex. He added, ". . . but she didn't say no, so she must have wanted it, too . . . It's the way it works" (Celis, 1991). Consider the comments of Jim, a man who raped a woman he had just met at a party (Trenton State College, 1991):

She looked really hot, wearing a sexy dress that showed off her great body. We started talking right away. I knew that she liked me by the way she kept smiling and touching my arm while she was speaking. She seemed pretty relaxed so I asked her back to my place for a drink . . . When she said yes, I knew that I was going to be lucky!

When we got to my place, we sat on the bed kissing. At first, everything was great. Then, when I started to lay her down on the bed, she started twisting and saying she didn't want to. Most women don't like to appear too easy, so I knew that she was just going through the motions. When she stopped struggling, I knew that she would have to throw in some tears before we did it.

She was still very upset afterwards, and I just don't understand it! If she didn't want to have sex, why did she come back to the room with me? You could tell by the way she dressed and acted that she was no virgin, so why she had to put up such a big struggle I don't know.

Accepting a date is not the equivalent of consenting to intercourse. Accompanying a man to his room or apartment is not the equivalent of consenting to intercourse. Kissing and petting are not the equivalent of consenting to intercourse. When a women fails to consent or says no, the man must take no for an answer.

Effects of Rape

Women who are raped suffer more than the rape itself. Many survivors are distraught in the weeks following the attack. They cry often and suffer insomnia. They report loss of appetite, headaches, irritability, anxiety and depression, and menstrual irregularity. Some become sullen, withdrawn, and mistrustful. Some women show an unrealistic composure, which often gives way to venting of feelings later on. Because of society's tendency to blame the victim for the assault, some survivors also have misplaced feelings of guilt, shame, and self-blame. Some women also fear notifying their husbands and boyfriends about the assault, for fear they will be blamed or considered unfaithful. Survivors often develop sexual dysfunctions such as lack of sexual desire and difficulty becoming sexually aroused (Letourneau et al., 1996). Of a sample of 222 rape survivors, nearly 90% reported a lack of sexual desire and some fear of sex (Becker, Skinner, & Abel, 1983). At the very least, many women do not reap the level of sexual enjoyment they had experienced before the assault (Calhoun & Atkeson, 1991). Many rape survivors also express fears of contracting AIDS from the assault. Many show signs of posttraumatic stress disorder (PTSD), including intrusive memories of the rape, nightmares, emotional numbing, and heightened autonomic arousal (Foa, Riggs, & Gershuny, 1995; M. A. Jenkins et al., 1998; Valentiner et al., 1996). Women with a history of sexual assault are also more likely than nonassaulted women to report physical health problems and poor general health overall (Golding, 1994).

Psychological problems experienced by rape survivors often continue through at least the first year following the sexual assault (Kimerling & Calhoun, 1994). About 1 in 4 rape survivors continue to encounter psychological problems such as depression and anxiety for a number of years after the attack (Calhoun & Atkeson, 1991; Koss et al., 1994).

Treatment of Rape Survivors

Treatment of rape survivors is often a two-phase process that first assists women in coping with the immediate aftermath of rape and then helps them with their long-term adjustment. Crisis intervention provides women with emotional support and information to help them see to their immediate needs, as well as helping them develop strategies for coping with the trauma (Resick & Schnicke, 1990). Longer-term treatment may be designed to help rape survivors cope with undeserved feelings of guilt and shame, lingering feelings of anxiety and depression, and the interpersonal and sexual problems they may develop with the men in their lives. Unfortunately, most rape survivors do not seek help from mental health professionals, rape crisis centers, or rape survivor assistance programs (Kimerling & Calhoun, 1994). The cultural stigma associated with seeking help for mental health problems may discourage a fuller utilization of psychological services.

CHILD SEXUAL ABUSE

Few crimes are as heinous as sexual abuse of children. The emotional consequences of sexual abuse can be severe and

Rape crisis counseling. Rape-crisis centers help rape survivors cope with the trauma of rape. They provide them with emotional support and help them obtain medical, psychological, and legal services.

Rape Prevention

Given the incidence of rape, it is useful to be aware of strategies that may prevent it. By listing strategies for rape prevention, we do not mean to imply that rape survivors are somehow responsible for falling prey to an attack. The responsibility for any act of sexual violence lies with the perpetrator, not with the person who is assaulted, and perhaps with society for fostering attitudes that underlie sexual violence. On a societal level, we need to do a better job of socializing young men to acquire prosocial and respectful attitudes toward women. Exposure to feminist, egalitarian, and multicultural education may help promote more respectful attitudes in young men (Hall & Barongan, 1997; Kershner, 1996).

Preventing Stranger Rape

- Establish signals and plans with other women in the building or neighborhood.
- List first initials only in the phone directory and on the mailbox.
- Use dead-bolt locks.
- Lock windows and install iron grids on first-floor windows.
- Keep doorways and entries well lit.
- Have keys handy for the car or the front door.
- Do not walk by yourself after dark.
- Avoid deserted areas.
- Do not allow strange men into the apartment or the house without checking their credentials.
- Keep the car door locked and the windows up.
- Check out the backseat of the car before getting in.
- Don't live in a risky building.
- Don't give rides to hitchhikers (that includes women hitchhikers).
- Don't converse with strange men on the street.
- Shout "Fire!" not "Rape!" People flock to fires but circumvent scenes of violence.

Preventing Date Rape

- Avoid getting into secluded situations until you know your date very well. Some men interpret a date's willingness to accompany them to their room as an agreement to engage in sexual activity.
- Be wary when a date attempts to control you in any way, such as frightening you by driving rapidly or taking you some place you would rather not go.
- Stay sober. We often do things we would not otherwise do—including sexual activity with people we might otherwise reject—when we have had too many drinks. Be aware of your limits.
- Be very assertive and clear concerning your sexual intentions. Some rapists, particularly date rapists, tend to misinterpret women's wishes. If their dates begin to implore them to stop during kissing or petting, they construe pleading as "female game-playing." So if kissing or petting is leading where you don't want it to go, speak up.
- When dating a person for the first time, try to date in a group.
- Encourage your college or university to offer educational programs about date rape. The University of Washington, for example, offers students lectures and seminars on date rape and provides women with escorts to get home. Many universities require all incoming students to attend orientation sessions on rape prevention.
- Talk to your date about his attitudes toward women. If you get the feeling that he believes that men are in a war with women, or that women try to "play games" with men, you may be better off dating someone else.

Sources: Boston Women's Health Book Collective, 1984; Rathus & Fichner-Rathus, 1994.

long lasting, leading to emotional problems and difficulties developing intimate relationships that last long into the future. The number of reported cases of child sexual abuse jumped threefold during the 1980s and early to mid-1990s, to about 150,000 incidents annually according to recent estimates (DeAngelis, 1995b). Yet the reported cases are, like reported rape statistics, only the tip of the iceberg. Perhaps only a third or a quarter of actual cases are reported to authorities (Alter-Reid, Gibbs, Lachenmeyer, Sigal, & Mossoth, 1986). A national telephone victimization survey of more than 2,600 U.S. adults revealed that nearly 27% of the women and 16% of the men reported having been sexually abused as children (Finkelhor et al., 1990). An Ontario, Canada, study of a random sample of households found 13% of the women and 4% of the men reporting a history of sexual abuse in childhood (MacMillan et al., 1997). As shocking as these figures may be, surveys may undershoot the mark, as people may not be willing to report abuse. Although girls are more likely than boys to be sexually abused, estimates are that boys constitute perhaps one fifth to one third of sexually abused children (DeAngelis, 1995b; Finkelhor, 1990).

Sexual abuse, like other forms of violence and abuse, cuts across all socioeconomic and family background characteristics (Finkelhor, 1993). Neither social class nor ethnicity appears to be associated with relative risk. However, children from less cohesive or disintegrating families appear more likely to be victimized than children from intact families (Finkelhor, 1984). The average age at which children are first sexually abused ranges between 7 and 10 for boys and 6 and 12 for girls (Knudsen, 1991).

Patterns of Child Sexual Abuse

Sexual abuse of children includes a range of sexual acts such as fondling, kissing, exhibitionism, touching of genitals, oral sex, anal intercourse, and, among girls, vaginal intercourse (Knudsen, 1991). Because children are not deemed capable of giving voluntary consent, any sexual act between an adult and a child is considered a form of sexual abuse, even if there is no force or physical threat used or the child gives consent.

Sexual abuse of boys or girls is more likely to be committed by family members than by strangers, but girls are more likely than boys to be abused by a family member or acquaintance (Faller, 1989). Boys are more often threatened or suffer physical injuries during a sexual assault than is the case with girls (Knudsen, 1991). A recent study at the University of New Mexico found that while the frequency of childhood sexual abuse (about 30% overall) was similar between Hispanic and non-Hispanic White college women, Hispanic women reported that perpetrators were more likely to be extended family members and less likely to be members of the immediate family or non-family members than did non-Hispanic White women (Arroyo, Simpson, & Aragon, 1997).

It may surprise you to learn that physical force is seldom used by the abuser. Most of the time the abuser is able to use manipulation, deception, or threat of force to obtain the child's compliance rather than direct force. Children are not worldly wise and are typically submissive to adult authority. They may be easily misled or manipulated by an unscrupulous adult, especially when the abuser is someone with whom the child has had a trusting relationship. Threat of force may be used if guile and deception fail to achieve compliance. Although most abused children suffer one incident of abuse, in some cases a pattern of abuse occurs that continues for a period of months or even years. Children who are abused by family members are most likely to suffer repeated incidents of abuse.

TRUTH or FICTION REVISITED

15.8 False. In most cases, the abuser is able to use manipulation, deception, or threat of force to obtain the child's compliance rather than direct force.

The most common type of abuse of girls or boys involves genital fondling (Knudsen, 1991). In one female sample, intercourse occurred in only 4% of cases, as compared to genital fondling, which occurred in 38%, and exhibitionism, which occurred in 20% (Knudsen, 1991). However, in cases in which girls are abused by a family member, a common pattern involves a gradual progression of abuse beginning with affectional fondling during the preschool years, progressing to oral sex or mutual masturbation during middle childhood, and then vaginal or anal intercourse beginning in preadolescence or adolescence (Waterman & Lusk, 1986).

Characteristics of Abusers

The great majority of abusers of both boys and girls are men (Thomlison et al., 1991). Authorities in the field estimate that perhaps 95% of cases of abuse involving young girls, and perhaps 80% involving young boys, are perpetrated by men (Finkelhor & Russell, 1984). Although most abusers are adult males, some are adolescent males, many of whom were abused themselves as young boys and may be imitating their own victimization (Muster, 1992). Gay males and lesbians account for only a small percentage of abusers of either boys or girls.

Despite the popular stereotype, most abusers do not fit the profile of the proverbial stranger hanging around the schoolyard. Most cases of child sexual abuse, perhaps as many as 75% to 80%, involve assailants who have some kind of relationship with the child or the child's family, typically a relative or step-relative, a family friend, or a neighbor (Waterman & Lusk, 1986). In many cases (estimates range from 10% to 50% of cases), the molester is a family member, typically a father, uncle, or stepfather.

Family members who discover that a child has been abused are less likely to report the abuse to authorities when the offender is a family member, perhaps because to do so might shame the family and out of concern that they might be held accountable for failing to protect the child. In a Boston study, none of the parents whose children were abused by family members notified the authorities, as compared to about 1 in 4 parents whose children were abused by acquaintances and about 3 of 4 whose children were abused by strangers (Finkelhor, 1984).

In an early study, Gebhard and his colleagues (1965) found that many fathers who had sexually abused their daughters were religiously devout, fundamentalistic, and moralistic. Such men, when sexually frustrated, may be less likely to find extramarital and extrafamilial sexual outlets. In many cases, the father is under stress but does not find adequate emotional and sexual support from his wife (Gagnon, 1977). He may turn to a daughter as a wife surrogate. The girl is often mature enough to have assumed household chores and may become, in her father's eyes, the "woman of the house." The wife may be surprised by revelations of incest, despite obvious clues and even the daughter's repeated complaints. Sometimes the wife seems involved in a tacit conspiracy to allow the abuse to continue to preserve the family or because of fear of the abuser.

Banning (1989) offers a sociocultural explanation of why a disproportionate number of molesters are men. Banning argues that men are socialized in our culture to seek younger and weaker partners they can more easily dominate. In the extreme, this pattern can lead to sexual interest in young girls, who because of their age can be more easily dominated than adult women. Yet child molestation may also be motivated by pedophilia, an unusual pattern of sexual arousal characterized by a sexual interest in children, sometimes to the exclusion of more appropriate (adult) stimuli (see Chapter 11).

A cycle of sexual abuse and other forms of sexual violence is a common finding, with children who suffer sexual abuse becoming sexual offenders themselves as adults (Dhawan & Marshall, 1996; Romano & De-Luca, 1996).

Effects of Child Sexual Abuse

Children who suffer sexual abuse seldom report it to others, sometimes because of fear of retaliation from the abuser and sometimes because they fear being blamed for it. Often the symptoms of abuse are "masked" and become expressed as school problems, fears, or eating or sleeping problems. These changes can have many causes, so more direct evidence is needed to confirm abuse. No single behavioral pattern is reliably associated with child sexual abuse (Miller-Perrin & Wurtele, 1988). Sometimes a pediatrician discovers physical evidence of sexual abuse.

Child survivors of sexual abuse are more likely than others to develop psychological problems, including anxiety, depression, anger and aggressive behavior, poor self-esteem, eating disorders, premature sexual behavior or promiscuity, drug abuse, self-destructive behavior including suicide attempts, lack of trust, low self-esteem, social withdrawal, psychosomatic problems such as stomachaches and headaches, PTSD symptoms, and sexual dysfunctions in adulthood (Boney-McCoy & Finkelhor, 1996; Sarwer & Durlak, 1996; Swanston et al., 1997; Toth & Cicchetti, 1996). Regressive behavior, in the form of thumbsucking, or recurrences of childhood fears, such as fear of the dark or of strangers, are not uncommon. Late adolescence and early adulthood is a particularly difficult time for survivors of child sexual abuse, as unresolved feelings of anger and guilt and a deep sense of mistrust can prevent the expected development of intimate relationships (Jackson et al., 1990). Women who suffered sexual abuse as children are also more likely than other women to suffer sexual and physical abuse as adults (Messman & Long, 1996). Though much of the research on effects of childhood sexual abuse has focused on female survivors, a significant proportion of male survivors also suffer adverse psychological effects into adulthood (Dhaliwal et al., 1996). It is a myth to believe that sexual abuse has little effect on boys (G. R. Holmes, Offen, & Waller, 1997).

Effects are not limited to psychological hardships; sexually abused girls may also suffer hormonal and possible

So there really was a monster in her bedroom.

For many kids, there's a real reason to be afraid of the dark.

Last year in Indiana, there were 6,912 substantiated cases of sexual abuse. The trauma can be devastating for the child and for the family. So listen closely to the children around you.

If you hear something you don't want to believe, perhaps you should. For helpful information on child abuse prevention, contact the LaPorte County Child Abuse Prevention Council, 7451 Johnson Road, Michigan City, IN 46360. (219) 874-0007

LaPorte County Child Abuse Prevention Council

So there really was a monster in her bedroom. Not all monsters are imagined. Some, like incest perpetrators, are family members.

immunological problems (DeAngelis, 1995a). In one recent study, sexually abused girls produced excess levels of stress hormones (epinephrine and norepinephrine) and the neurotransmitter dopamine, which can be taken as a sign that the body is overstressed or hyperaroused (De Bellis et al., 1994).

Adolescents who were sexually abused during childhood are more likely than their nonabused peers to become delinquent, suicidal, and sexually active (DeAngelis, 1995b). Psychological distress can be enduring, lasting well into middle or even late adulthood (McCauley et al., 1997). However, a recent meta-analysis based on college students who reported child sexual abuse found that the effects were typically neither pervasive nor intense (Rind, Tromovitch, & Bauserman, 1998).

Some child survivors retreat into a personal fantasy world or refuse to leave the house. We noted in Chapter 6 how many cases of dissociative identity disorder (multiple personality) have been linked to a history in childhood of retreating into fantasy to cope with sexual abuse. Childhood sexual abuse is also linked to the later development of borderline personality disorder (J. B. Murray, 1993b; Weaver & Clum, 1995). Many survivors of childhood sexual abuse— like many rape survivors—develop posttraumatic stress disorder or related symptoms during childhood or in later life, or show such signs of the disorder as flashbacks, nightmares, emotional numbing, and feelings of detachment from others (Boney-McCoy & Finkelhor, 1996).

Although the effects of child sexual abuse are more similar than not between boys and girls (e.g., both genders tend to experience fears and sleep disturbances), there are some important differences. The clearest gender difference is that boys tend to develop "externalized" behavior problems such as excessive aggressive behavior, whereas girls tend to experience "internalized" problems, such as depression (Finkelhor, 1990; Gomez-Schwartz, Horowitz, & Cardarelli, 1990).

Although long-term effects of child sexual abuse are common, they appear to be greater among survivors who were abused by their fathers or stepfathers, who were abused at an earlier age, who were subjected to penetration, who suffered more prolonged and severe abuse, or who were forced to submit or threatened with physical force (Beitchman et al., 1992; DeAngelis, 1995b). Adult survivors of childhood sexual abuse who blame themselves for the abuse tend to have more psychological problems than those who blame the perpetrator (Feinauer & Stuart, 1996). The use of cognitive coping skills in adulthood, such as disclosing and discussing the abuse but not dwelling on it, appears to differentiate well-adjusted and poorly adjusted college women who suffered sexual abuse as children (Himelein & McElrath, 1996).

When the offender is a father or other family member, the effects of abuse are amplified by the deep feeling of the betrayal of trust by the offender as well as by their mothers or other family members whom they perceive as having failed to protect them. They may have felt powerless to control their bodies or their lives and may find it difficult ever to develop a trusting relationship in adulthood.

Treating Survivors of Child Sexual Abuse

Because most cases of child sexual abuse go unreported, survivors of abuse may not receive psychotherapy for overcoming trauma-related feelings of anger and (misplaced)

Survivors of child sexual abuse. Most cases of child sexual abuse go unreported. This means that survivors of abuse may not receive any psychological counseling to help them deal with their traumatic experiences until adulthood, if then.

guilt until adulthood. Sex therapy may help adult survivors overcome sexual dysfunctions and fears (Douglas, Matson, & Hunter, 1989). Group therapy may help them face their feelings in a supportive setting with people who have undergone similar trauma (P. C. Alexander et al., 1989).

When sexual abuse is uncovered in childhood, a multicomponent treatment approach may be recommended, including individual therapy for the child survivor, joint therapy with the child and nonoffending parent, and family therapy (Celano et al., 1996; J. A. Cohen & Mannarino, 1997). Therapy with the child survivor typically focuses on providing support, addressing issues of betrayal and powerlessness, and helping the child see that he or she is not to blame.

Preventing Child Sexual Abuse

Sexual abuse prevention includes community efforts, such as enactment and enforcement of laws requiring teachers and helping professionals to report cases of suspected child sexual or physical abuse to child protective services. Many states have enacted laws that require convicted sex offenders to register with the local police. These laws, called "Megan's laws," after a 7-year-old New Jersey girl who was killed by a neighbor with a history of sexual assault, are intended to let

Ethnic Group Differences in the Effects of Sexual Abuse

Little is known about differences among ethnic groups in the effects of child sexual abuse. In one of the few studies reported to date, researchers at a child sex abuse clinic compared samples of Asian American, African American, Hispanic American, and non-Hispanic White American child survivors (Rao et al., 1992). The results showed that Asian American children were more likely to develop suicidal thoughts and less likely to display anger overtly or engage in sexual acting out than were children from the other groups.

Gail Wyatt (1990) investigated childhood sexual abuse in a sample of 126 African American women and 122 non-Hispanic White women in Los Angeles County. The subjects were matched on such variables as marital status, number of children, and education.

The operational definition of childhood sexual abuse was broad, including acts such as exhibitionism, fondling, oral sex, and sexual intercourse. The prevalence of abuse was similar in both groups. Nearly 1 woman in 2 had suffered at least one incident of abuse, and nearly 40% of these incidences had gone unreported to authorities. The African American women were somewhat less likely to report abuse to their immediate family members or to the police. However, they were nearly twice as likely to have informed extended family members as were the White women, a finding that underscores the importance of the extended family among African Americans. African American women were more likely than White women (35% versus 22%) to avoid reporting abuse for fear of repercussions. The African American women may have felt more vulnerable to the financial adversity that their families would have had to endure if the abuser—often their mothers' boyfriends or their stepfathers on whom the family was financially dependent—had been forced to leave the home. White women more often expressed fear of being blamed for the abuse as a reason for nonreporting (36%) than did African American women (23%).

The psychological impact of abuse was similar for both groups. Women from both groups were likely to have felt violated and to harbor feelings of fear, disgust, and anger. Sexual problems in adulthood were also common in both groups. However, the African American women were more prone to report that the abusive experiences from childhood came to affect their general attitudes toward men and led them to avoid men who in some ways reminded them of their abusers. Yet broadly speaking, the similarities in the responses of the two groups of women eclipsed the differences.

---

members of the community know of the presence of sex offenders (Weber, 1996).

At the individual level, school-based sexual abuse prevention programs have been established that now reach about 2 of 3 children in the United States (Goleman, 1993c). Although these programs vary in their content, most teach children to avoid contact with strangers and to distinguish between acceptable touching (a member of their family embracing them affectionately or patting them on the head) and "bad" or unacceptable touching. Trainers need to pitch their presentation to the child's developmental level and be aware that some children may need extra instruction to distinguish the forms of touching that should be avoided. Generally speaking, most children, even grammar-school aged children, can learn the basic concepts of sexual abuse prevention (Tutty, 1992).

Evidence attesting to the efficacy of child sexual abuse prevention programs remains limited. However, the results from a national study were encouraging, as researchers found that the better school-based prevention programs were helpful in preparing children to handle a potential encounter with a molester (Goleman, 1993c). Children who participated in training were more likely than comparison children to use such strategies as yelling or running away, or saying no if they were threatened by an abuser. They were also more likely to report incidents to adults. Still, the researchers noted there is considerable room for improvement in many programs.

Children also need to be taught that in some cases they may be unable to say "no" when confronted with a threatening adult, even if they would like to say "no" and know it would be the "right thing" to do (Waterman et al., 1986). Most prevention programs teach children that it is not their fault if they are unable to fend off a molester, but encourage them to "never keep a bad or scary secret" and "always tell your parents" if they are molested or threatened, especially if the molester tells them not to say anything.

Children are more likely to report incidents of sexual abuse if they are reassured that they will be believed and not be blamed, that their parents will continue to love them, and if they are made to feel secure that they and their families will be protected from the abuser. Assuring the credibility of children's reports of sexual abuse remains a thorny issue, however, as children are easily suggestible and can be led to believe that abuse occurred even when it did not, especially if investigators direct the inquiry in ways that plant ideas in the children's minds. Recall too (see Chapter 6) the controversy that has swirled around the issue of recovered memories of childhood sexual or physical abuse that the individual only becomes aware of at some point in adulthood, often during therapy or hypnosis. The judicial system is faced with the daunting challenge of distinguishing between true and faulty memories, especially when there is an absence of independent verification of abuse.

Another important element in the prevention of sexual violence, including rape and child sexual abuse, is the development of effective treatment programs for offenders. Sooner or later, virtually all sex offenders are released from prison. Yet do prison-based programs help reduce the potential for future abuse?

Treatment of Sex Offenders

Convicted rapists and child molesters are criminals and typically sentenced to prison as a form of punishment, not treatment. They may receive psychological treatment during their incarceration in the hope it will help prepare them for their eventual release and deter them from committing future offenses when they do reenter society. Treatment programs are more likely to be successful when they address the long-term adjustment of the sex offender and do not expect a permanent "cure" to result from a single round of prison-based treatment sessions (Hanson, Steffy, & Gauthier, 1993). The most widely used form of treatment for incarcerated sex offenders is group therapy, predicated on the belief that although sex offenders may trick counselors, they cannot so readily fool each another (D. Kaplan, 1993).

Group therapy may be supplemented by cognitive-behavior therapy techniques such as covert sensitization, which we discussed in Chapter 11. Also coming into greater use is *empathy training,* which attempts to increase the offender's sensitivity toward his victim by having him write about his crime from what he imagines would be the victim's perspective. The fact remains, however, that the great majority of incarcerated sex offenders receive little or nothing in the way of psychological treatment in prison (Goleman, 1992a).

A biologically based treatment involves the use of antiandrogen (testosterone-reducing) drugs such as Depo-Provera. These drugs lower the sex drive, which it is hoped will help offenders control their urges to offend, at least so long as they continue using the drug (Ingersoll & Patton, 1991). Unlike castration, the effects of antiandrogens are reversible when the drugs are discontinued. However, problems with compliance with taking the drugs consistently presents a major obstacle to their widespread use. Moreover,

Sex offenders. The great majority of incarcerated sex offenders receive little if any psychological treatment in prison. Here, teenage sex offenders in a state school participate in a group therapy session.

taking antiandrogens does not help rapists resolve the psychological factors underlying their sexual attacks, particularly resentment and anger toward women and needs for dominance and power. Nor does it assist men with pedophilia to learn to respond to more adaptive erotic cues, rather than images of children. Nor do drugs provide offenders with opportunities to develop social skills they need to develop consensual sexual relationships. Despite these drawbacks, the use of antiandrogens appears to be about equal in effectiveness to cognitive-behavioral treatments in curbing recidivism of sex offenders, with both treatment approaches producing medium-sized treatment effects in reducing recidivism in relation to an absence of treatment (G. C. Hall, 1995). Antiandrogens may also be helpful when they are used in conjunction with psychological counseling (Leary, 1998; Marshall et al., 1991)

Overall, efficacy studies of treatment of sex offenders show a modest benefit in reducing recidivism rates associated with comprehensive cognitive-behavioral treatment, or psychological treatment combined with antiandrogen therapy (Hall, 1995; Polaschek et al., 1997). Generally speaking, better outcomes are achieved with child molesters and exhibitionists than with rapists. Not surprisingly, recidivism rates are higher among sex offenders who fail to complete treatment and who show deviant sexual interest, such as penile arousal to child pornography (Hanson & Bussiére, 1998). More extreme measures, such as surgical castration (removal of the testes) have been used in some European countries but not as yet in the United States. The effects of surgical castration on recidivism are not clear.

One treatment alternative that remains largely unexplored is targeting men who are sexually attracted to children or have a predisposition to rape *before* they commit abusive acts. Perhaps early intervention can prevent sexual violence from occurring. Unfortunately, most men who would likely be good candidates for early intervention do not come forward for treatment until they are convicted of a sexual crime.

SEXUAL HARASSMENT

Sexual coercion is not limited to rape or outright sexual assault. **Sexual harassment** is a form of sexual coercion in which one person subjects another to unwanted sexual comments, overtures, gestures, physical contact, or direct demands for sexual favors as a condition of employment, retention, or advancement (see Table 15.3). Sexual harassment can occur in many settings, including the workplace, school, or therapist's consulting room. The great majority of cases of sexual harassment involve men harassing women. Sexual harassment in the workplace is considered a form of sex discrimination, and employers can be held accountable if sexual harassment creates a hostile or abusive work environment or interferes with an employee's work performance. A 1998 decision by the U.S. Supreme Court held that persons can bring a sexual harassment action even if they did not suffer any career setback, such as a dismissal or loss of a promotion, as the result of the harassment (Greenhouse, 1998). Employers can be accountable if they either *knew* that harassment was occurring or *should have known* and failed to correct the situation promptly (McKinney & Maroules, 1991).

Although sexual harassment may involve many motives, it typically has more to do with the abuse of power than with sexual motivation (Goleman, 1991). Harassers usually hold a dominant position in relation to the person who is harassed and abuse their authority by taking advantage of the other person's vulnerability. Resentment and hos-

TABLE 15.3
Examples of Sexual Harassment
Verbal harassment or abuse
Subtle pressure for sexual activity
Remarks about a person's clothing, body, or sexual activities
Leering or ogling at a person's body
Unwelcome touching, patting, or pinching
Brushing against a person's body
Demands for sexual favors accompanied by implied or overt threats concerning one's job or student status
Physical assault

Source: Adapted from Powell, 1991.

tility directed at women who venture beyond the traditional gender boundaries and enter traditional male occupations may be expressed in the form of sexual taunts and overtures by men as a way of "keeping women in their place" (Fitzgerald, 1993a).

Although sexual harassment is prohibited by law, and people subjected to harassment can sue to have the harassment stopped or can obtain monetary awards for emotional damages they suffer, relatively few formal complaints are filed. Fewer than 5% of women experiencing sexual harassment file a formal complaint (Goleman, 1991). Why? For one thing, harassment may be difficult to prove because it usually occurs without corroborating witnesses or evidence. Like survivors of rape, people who are harassed may fear

Sexual harassment? Sexual harassment is behavior of a sexual nature that is unwelcome by the recipient. Sexual harassment on the job creates a work environment that is hostile or abusive to the person on the receiving end. It may also interfere with the person's ability to perform his or her job. Would you say that the man's behavior here could be interpreted as harassment? What would you do if you were sexually harassed?

How to Resist Sexual Harassment

What would you do if you were sexually harassed by an employer or a professor? How would you handle it? Would you try to ignore it and hope it would stop? What actions might you take? We offer some suggestions, adapted from Powell (1991), that may be helpful. Recognize, however, that responsibility for sexual harassment always lies with the perpetrator and the organization that permits sexual harassment to take place, not with the person subjected to the harassment.

1. *Convey a professional attitude.* Harassment may be stopped cold by responding to the harasser with a businesslike, professional attitude. If a harassing professor suggests that you come back after school to review your term paper so the two of you will be undisturbed, set limits assertively. Tell the professor that you'd feel more comfortable discussing the paper during regular office hours. The harasser should quickly get the message that you wish to maintain a strictly professional relationship. If the harasser persists, do not blame yourself. You are responsible only for your own actions. When the harasser persists, a more direct response may be appropriate: "Professor Jones, I'd like to keep our relationship on a purely professional basis, okay?"

2. *Avoid being alone with the harasser.* If you are being harassed by your professor but need some advice about preparing your term paper, approach him or her after

class when other students are milling about, not privately during office hours. Or bring a friend to wait outside the office while you consult the professor.

3. *Maintain a record.* Keep a record of all incidents of harassment as documentation in the event you decide to lodge an official complaint. The record should include the following: (1) where the incident took place; (2) the date and time; (3) what happened, including the exact words that were used, if you can recall them; (4) how you felt; and (5) the names of any witnesses. Some people who have been subjected to sexual harassment have carried a hidden tape recorder during contacts with the harasser. Such recordings may not be admissible in a court of law, but they are persuasive in organizational grievance procedures. A hidden tape recorder may be illegal in your state, however. It is thus advisable to check the law.

4. *Talk with the harasser.* It may be uncomfortable to address the issue directly with a harasser, but doing so puts the offender on notice that you are aware of the harassment and want it to stop. It may be helpful to frame your approach in terms of a description of the specific offending actions (e.g., "When we were alone in the office, you repeatedly attempted to touch me or brush up against me"); your feelings about the offending behavior ("It made me feel like my

---

that they will not be believed or will suffer retaliation by the harasser, lose their jobs, or have their reputations soured in the industries in which they work.

What should you do if you are sexually harassed? The nearby "A Closer Look" section discusses some options for you to consider.

Prevalence of Sexual Harassment

Sexual harassment is the most frequently occurring form of sexual victimization in the United States (Fitzgerald, 1993a). Some 42% of women and 14% of men who responded to a survey of federal employees by the U.S. Merit System Protection Board reported they had been subjected to sexual harassment in the workplace (DeWitt, 1991); 38% of women responding to a 1991 national poll reported experiencing harassment in the form of unwanted sexual advances or comments from supervisors or other men in positions of authority (Kolbert, 1991). Overall, estimates indicate that

about 1 woman in 2 is likely to encounter some form of sexual harassment in her academic or work environment at some point in her life (Fitzgerald & Shullman, 1993). Sexual harassment even extends downward to teenage workers. A recent survey of 16- and 17-year-old girls with jobs found that nearly half (49%) said they had been victims of sexual harassment (Goodstein & Connelly, 1998).

Sexual harassment directed at women is especially common in worksites that are traditional male preserves, such as the construction site, the shipyard, and the firehouse (Fitzgerald, 1993a). Cross-cultural research shows high frequencies of sexual harassment in other developed countries that have been studied; in Japan, about 70% of women report incidents of harassment; in Europe, about 50% (Castro, 1992).

Sexual harassment on college campuses is also common. A survey of 2,000 college women showed that about half had been subjected to sexual harassment from professors, most commonly in the form of crude or degrading remarks

privacy was being violated. I'm very upset about this and haven't been sleeping well"); and what you would like the offender to do ("So I'd like you to agree never to attempt to touch me again, okay?"). Having a talk with the harasser may stop the harassment. If the harasser denies the accusations, it may be necessary to take further action.

5. *Write a letter to the harasser.* Set down on paper a record of the offending behavior, and put the harasser on notice that the harassment must stop. Your letter might (1) *describe what happened* ("Several times you have made sexist comments about my body"); (2) *describe how you feel* ("It made me feel like a sexual object when you talked to me that way"); and (3) *describe what you would like the harasser to do* ("I want you to stop making sexist comments to me").

6. *Seek support.* Support from people you trust can help you through the often trying process of resisting sexual harassment. Talking with others allows you to express your feelings and receive emotional support, encouragement, and advice. In addition, it may strengthen your case if you have the opportunity to identify and talk with other people who have been harassed by the offender.

7. *Consider filing a complaint.* Companies and organizations, such as universities and colleges, are required by law to respond reasonably to complaints of sexual harassment. In large organizations, a designated official (sometimes an ombudsman, affirmative action officer, or sexual harassment adviser) is usually charged to handle such complaints. Set up an appointment with this official to discuss your experiences. Ask about the grievance procedures in the organization and your right to confidentiality. Have available a record of the dates of the incidents, what happened, how you felt about it, and so on.

The two major government agencies that handle charges of sexual harassment are the Equal Employment Opportunity Commission (look under the government section of your phone book for the telephone number of the nearest office) and your state Human Rights Commission (listed in your phone book under state or municipal government). These agencies may offer advice on how you can protect your legal rights and proceed with a formal complaint.

8. *Consider legal remedies.* Sexual harassment is illegal and actionable. If you are considering legal action, consult an attorney familiar with this area of law. You may be entitled to back pay (if you were fired for reasons arising from the sexual harassment), job reinstatement, and punitive damages.

Source: Adapted from Nevid et al., 1995. Reprinted with permission.

(Fitzgerald et al., 1988). Nearly 1 in 3 reported unwanted sexual attention, and 1 in 10 reported unwanted sexual contact, including fondling and outright sexual assaults. A compilation of results from various studies showed that 7% to 27% of men also reported some exposure to sexual harassment on campus (McKinney & Maroules, 1991).

Sexual harassment may also occur between doctor and patient, or between therapist and client. Professionals may use their power and influence to pressure patients or clients into having sexual relations. In some cases, harassment is disguised by unscrupulous therapists who make it seem that sexual contact would be therapeutically beneficial. Clients tend to perceive therapists as experts whose suggestions carry great authority. Thus, they may be vulnerable to exploitation by therapists who abuse the trust that clients place in their hands. Let's be absolutely clear here: There is no therapeutic justification for a therapist having sex with a client. The ethical codes of psychologists and other mental-health professionals specifically prohibit any kind of sexual contact between therapists and clients. There is no therapeutic justification for sexual relations between client and therapist. Any therapist who makes a sexual overture toward a client, or tries to persuade a client to have sexual relations, is acting unethically. Professionals too may be sexually harassed. Survey show that more than one third of female doctors (Frank, Brogan, & Schiffman, 1998) and more than one half of female psychologists (deMayo, 1997) report they have been sexually harassed by patients.

TRUTH *or* **FICTION** **REVISITED**
15.9 *False.* There is no therapeutic justification for sexual relations between a client and therapist. It is unethical conduct on the part of the therapist.

Effects of Sexual Harassment

Sexual harassment, like other forms of sexual abuse, can have damaging psychological effects (Koss et al., 1994).

Studies show that 75% of people who were subjected to sexual harassment experienced some psychological effects, such as anxiety, lowered self-esteem, and increased irritability and anger (Gruber & Bjorn, 1986; Loy & Stewart, 1984). Women subjected to sexual taunts or outright demands for sexual favors in the workplace may feel forced to resign. Women attending college who are unable to stop sexual harassment by professors may drop courses, switch majors, or even transfer to other schools, often at great personal sacrifice (Fitzgerald, 1993a, 1993b). Forms of sexual harassment such as verbal taunts, sexual teasing, and staring may even have effects similar to those of sexual abuse, leading to disturbances in body image and eating behavior (Weiner & Thompson, 1997).

The effects of sexual harassment are compounded by the attitude held by many in our society that people who complain of harassment or rape are somehow to blame for their difficulties (Powell, 1991). People who bring harassment complaints may be perceived as exaggerating the incident or taking things too seriously. Women, especially, are subjected to stereotypical expectations that they are to be nice and demure—to be passive and never to "make a scene." A woman who seeks to protect her rights by filing a complaint may be labeled as a "troublemaker." "Women are damned if they assert themselves and victimized if they don't" (Powell, 1991, p. 114).

* * * * * *

We focused in this chapter on various forms of interpersonal aggression, of one person acting violently toward another. Yet, throughout history, human aggression in the form of organized conflict and warfare has claimed far more lives than individual aggression and has left widespread devastation in its wake. As we look toward the new millennium, we might wonder whether psychologists and other social scientists might help usher in a new age of peace. Might psychologists be able to use their skills in conflict resolution to mediate conflicts that give rise to war? Can psychologists succeed where leaders of government, kings and queens, and philosophers and great historic figures have failed? Certainly the causes of organized warfare are complex, which belies any attempt at finding a simple solution. Yet, perhaps psychologists can use their unique perspectives to help "give peace a chance." For example, the cognitive perspective might give us insights into ways in which leaders of nations interpret situations that might set the stage for a warlike response to international conflicts. Perhaps we can address tendencies for leaders to believe that aggression is both a necessary and justified reaction when one's "national honor" is challenged. The efforts toward the development of a "peace psychology" are only beginning (see Feshbach, 1994). We cannot say whether the effort will succeed, but we can say it would be a far greater shame not to try.

SUMMARY

Violent or aggressive behavior is generally considered abnormal when it is not socially sanctioned and results in harm to self or others.

Violence and Abnormal Behavior

Although most people with psychological disorders are nonviolent, an increased potential for violent behavior is associated with some abnormal behavior patterns, such as schizophrenia or bipolar disorder compounded by alcohol or substance abuse.

Perspectives on Aggression

Beliefs in the instinctual basis of human aggression fail to account for the diversity in aggressive behavior we see among humans. A model of multiple causation takes into account the contributions and interactions of biological, psychological, and sociocultural factors.

Spouse Abuse

Spousal battering typically occurs within a larger pattern of abuse that may also involve child abuse and sexual aggression against the spouse. Relationship problems, alcohol use, and feelings of inadequacy and low self-esteem on the part of the batterer often figure prominently in battering relationships. Battering incidents often follow a triggering event that leads the abuser to lose control. Sociocultural theorists view spousal abuse as arising from the differential power relationships between men and women in our society. Women in abusive relationships are survivors of trauma, not masochists.

Child Abuse

There are several different forms of child abuse or maltreatment, including neglect, physical abuse, sexual abuse, and emotional maltreatment. Neglect is the most frequently occurring form of abuse. Stress, poor parenting and anger-management skills, and a history of being physically abused during childhood or witnessing family violence are implicated among various risk factors for predicting which parents are at increased risk of abusing their children. Effects of child abuse range from physical injuries, even death, to emotional consequences, such as difficulties forming healthy attachments, low self-esteem, suicidal thinking, depression, and failure to explore the outside world, among other problems. The emotional and behavioral consequences of child abuse and neglect often extend into adulthood.

Rape

Rape is a violent crime, not a sexual disorder. The desires to dominate women or express hatred toward them may be more prominent motives for rape than sexual desire. A sociocultural perspective suggests that cultural attitudes, such as stereotypes of male aggressiveness and social dominance, underlie propensities to rape. Rape survivors often suffer a range of immediate and long-term effects.

Child Sexual Abuse

Any sexual act involving children is a form of sexual abuse, even if no direct force or threat of force is used, or the child consents. The great majority of assailants had some prior relationship with the child or child's family. Effects of child sexual abuse include a range of emotional and behavioral problems. Survivors may have difficulty forming intimate attachments in adulthood. Child sex abuse prevention programs focus on helping children handle potential encounters with molesters and report instances of abuse should they occur.

Sexual Harassment

Sexual harassment involves unwelcome sexual comments, overtures, gestures, physical contact, or direct demands for sexual favors as a condition of employment, retention, or advancement. Sexual harassment may occur in many places, including the workplace, school, or doctor's or therapist's office. Sexual harassment typically has more to do with the abuse of power than sexual motivation. It is often used by men as a tactic to "keep women in their place," especially in situations that have been traditional male preserves. Like other forms of abuse, sexual harassment can have damaging psychological consequences.

REVIEW QUESTIONS

1. What criteria are used to classify violent behavior as abnormal?

2. How are psychological disorders implicated in violent behavior?

3. How are the roots of violent behavior conceptualized within biological, social-cognitive, cognitive, and sociocultural perspectives? Why is there a need for multiple models or perspectives?

4. How is violent behavior related to anger and frustration? How do psychologists help people with anger management problems?

5. What have we learned about patterns of spousal abuse, child maltreatment, rape, and child sexual abuse; the risk factors involved; and the characteristics of abusers? What can be done about preventing these forms of violence and abuse? What efforts are made to treat sex offenders? How successful are these treatment programs?

6. What is sexual harassment? How common is it? What effects does it have? What can a person do to resist it?

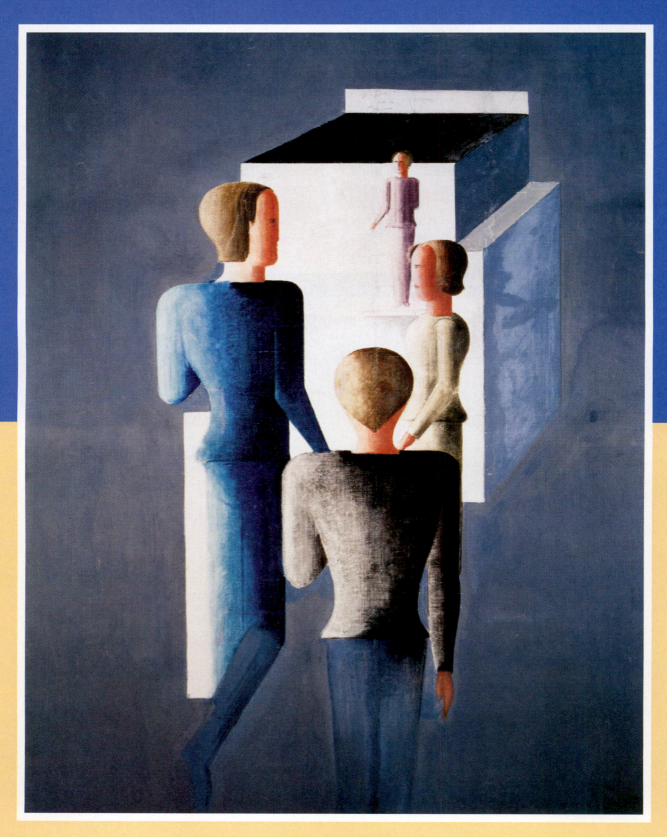

© Oskar Schlemmer
Quatre figures et cube, 1928

CHAPTER

Abnormal Psychology and Society

1. Describe the legal procedures for psychiatric commitment and the safeguards established to prevent abuses.

2. Discuss the controversy concerning psychiatric commitment.

3. Discuss the problem faced by psychologists and other professionals who are given the task of attempting to predict dangerousness.

4. Discuss the legal bases of the right to treatment and right to refuse treatment.

5. Discuss the landmark cases that established the legal precedents for the insanity plea.

6. Distinguish between the "not-guilty-by-reason-of-insanity" verdict and the "guilty-but-mentally-ill verdict."

7. Distinguish between the insanity plea and the principle of competency to stand trial.

8. Discuss the "duty to warn" obligation for therapists and describe the landmark case on which it is based.

Larry Hogue—the "wild man" of West 96th Street. Hogue, a homeless veteran of the Vietnam War who dwells in the alleyways and doorways of Manhattan's Upper West Side. Hogue, a middle-aged man who goes barefoot in winter, eats from garbage cans, and mutters to himself (Dugger, 1992). Hogue, who reportedly stalked a teacher and threatened to cook and eat her fawn-colored Akita. Hogue, who reportedly becomes violent when he smokes crack and was once arrested for pushing a schoolgirl in front of a school bus (E. Shapiro, 1992). (Miraculously, she escaped injury.) Hogue, who had been shuttled in and out of state psychiatric hospitals and prisons more than 40 times (Wickenhaver, 1992). Hogue, for whom the criminal justice systems and mental health systems are nothing but revolving doors. Hogue, whom many regard as the living embodiment of the cracks in our mental health, criminal justice, and social services systems.

Typically, Hogue would improve during a brief hospital stay and be released, only to return to using crack instead of his psychiatric medication. His behavior would then deteriorate (Dugger, 1994).

What does society do about Larry Hogue? What does society do about Joyce Brown?

Joyce Brown? Joyce Brown was a middle-aged woman who also lived on the streets of New York. At one time she slept above a hot air vent on the sidewalk on the Upper East Side of Manhattan, in the midst of some of the most expensive real estate in the world. Sometimes she was observed defecating in her clothes or on the sidewalk. She hurled insults at strangers and refused to go to a shelter, preferring to live in the streets, despite the obvious dangers of potential attack and the risks of exposure to the elements.

In New York, a program had begun to provide outreach services to homeless people in need of psychological treatment. Teams of specialists, each consisting of a nurse, a social worker, and a psychiatrist, were charged with the task of identifying and monitoring behaviorally disordered homeless people, helping them obtain services, bringing them soup and sandwiches, and taking them to the hospital if they were deemed to represent an immediate threat to themselves or others under the authority provided by state laws governing psychiatric commitment, even if it was against the individual's will.

Brown had been picked up and brought against her will to a city hospital for evaluation, where she was diagnosed with paranoid schizophrenia and judged to be in need of treatment. She resisted treatment and claimed that she had a right to live her life as she saw fit, even if it offended other people. As long as she committed no crime, what right did society have to deprive her of her liberty? Yes, she admitted, she had defecated in the streets. But there were no public rest rooms available, and establishments such as restaurants had refused her access.

The mayor at the time, Ed Koch, argued that the city had held her against her will, not because she offended passersby, but because it was compassionate to help those who cannot fend for themselves. Joyce Brown sued for release, and while her case meandered through the courts, she remained in the hospital, although her doctors were prevented from medicating her against her will. Because she refused medication, the doctors released her, claiming there was little they could do for her. Though we've lost track of Joyce Brown, Larry Hogue turned up again in 1998 in his old haunts on the Upper West Side of Manhattan, where he was seen panhandling. Local residents expressed fears that he would return to terrorizing them (Holloway, 1998).

The cases of Larry Hogue and Joyce Brown touch on the more general issue of how to balance the rights of the individual with the rights of

"The Wild Man of West 96th Street." Larry Hogue, the so-called Wild Man of West 96th St. in New York City, has become a symbol of the cracks in the mental health, criminal justice, and social services systems.

society. Do people, for example, have the right to live on the streets under unsanitary conditions? There are those who argue that a just and humane society has the right and responsibility to care for people who are perceived incapable of protecting their own best interests, even if "care" means involuntarily committing them to a psychiatric institution. Do people who are obviously mentally disturbed have the right to refuse treatment? Do psychiatric institutions have the right to inject them with antipsychotic and other drugs against their will? Should mental patients with a history of disruptive or violent behavior be hospitalized indefinitely or permitted to live in supervised residences in the community once their conditions are stabilized? When severely disturbed people break the law, should society respond to them with the criminal justice system or with the mental-health system?

In this chapter we consider psychiatric commitment and other issues that arise from society's response to abnormal behavior, such as the rights of patients in institutions, the use of the **insanity defense** in criminal cases, and the responsibility of professionals to warn individuals who may be placed at risk by the dangerous behavior of their clients. We conclude by considering a major challenge facing society today: What can we as a society do to prevent psychological disorders from arising or lessening their impact if they do arise?

PSYCHIATRIC COMMITMENT

Legal placement of people in psychiatric institutions against their will is called **civil,** or psychiatric, **commitment.** Through civil commitment, individuals who are deemed to be mentally disordered and to be a threat to themselves or others may be involuntarily confined to psychiatric institutions to provide them with treatment and help ensure their own safety and that of others. Civil commitment should be distinguished from legal or criminal commitment, in which an individual who has been acquitted of a crime by reason of insanity is placed in a psychiatric institution for treatment. In **legal commitment**, a criminal's unlawful act is judged by a court of law to be the result of a mental disorder or defect that should be dealt with by having the individual committed to a psychiatric hospital where treatment can be provided, rather than having the individual incarcerated in a prison.

Civil commitment should also be distinguished from voluntary hospitalization, in which an individual voluntarily seeks treatment in a psychiatric institution and can, with adequate notice, leave the institution when she or he so desires. Even in such cases, however, when hospital staff perceive that a voluntary patient who is requesting discharge presents a threat to her or his own welfare or to others, the staff may petition the court to change the patient's legal status from voluntary to involuntary.

Involuntary placement of an individual in a psychiatric hospital usually requires that a petition be filed by a relative or a professional. Psychiatric examiners may be empowered by the court to evaluate the person in a timely fashion, after which a judge hears psychiatric testimony and decides whether or not to commit the individual. In the event of commitment, the law usually requires periodic legal review and recertification of the patient's involuntary status. The legal process is intended to ensure that people are not "warehoused" indefinitely in psychiatric hospitals. Hospital staff must demonstrate the need for continued inpatient treatment.

Legal safeguards are usually in place to protect people's civil rights in commitment proceedings. Defendants have the right to due process and to be assisted by an attorney, for example. On the other hand, when individuals are deemed to present a clear and imminent threat to themselves or others, the court may order immediate hospitalization until a more formal commitment hearing can be held. Such emergency powers are usually limited to a specific period, such as 72 hours. During this time a formal commitment petition must be filed with the court, or the individual has a right to be discharged.

Standards for psychiatric commitment have been tightened over the past generation, and the rights of individuals who are subject to commitment proceedings more strictly protected. In the past, psychiatric abuses were more commonplace. People were often committed without clear evidence that they posed a threat. Not until 1979, in fact, did the U.S. Supreme Court rule, in *Addington v. Texas,* that in order for individuals to be hospitalized involuntarily, they must be judged to be both "mentally ill" and to present a clear and present danger to themselves or others. Thus, people cannot be committed because of their eccentricity. People must be judged mentally ill and to present a clear and present danger to themselves or others in order for them to be psychiatrically committed.

16.1 *False.* People cannot be committed because they are eccentric. The U.S. Supreme Court has determined that people must be judged mentally ill and present a clear and present danger to themselves or others to be psychiatrically committed.

Few would argue that contemporary tightening of civil commitment laws provides greater protection of the rights of the individual. Even so, some critics of the psychiatric system have called for the complete abolition of psychiatric commitment on the grounds that commitment deprives the individual of liberty in the name of therapy, and that such a loss of liberty cannot be justified in a free society. Perhaps the most vocal and persistent critic of the civil commitment statutes is psychiatrist Thomas Szasz (Szasz, 1970). Szasz argued that the label of *mental illness* is a societal invention that transforms social deviance into medical illness. In Szasz's view, people should not be deprived of their liberty because their behavior is perceived to be socially deviant or disruptive. According to Szasz, people who violate the law should be prosecuted for criminal behavior, not confined to a psychiatric hospital. Although psychiatric commitment may prevent some people from acting violently, it *does* violence to many more by depriving them of liberty:

> The mental patient, we say, *may be* dangerous: he may harm himself or someone else. But we, society, *are* dangerous: we rob him of his good name and of his liberty, and subject him to tortures called "treatments." (Szasz, 1970, p. 279)

Szasz's strident opposition to institutional psychiatry and his condemnation of psychiatric commitment have focused attention on abuses in the mental-health system. Szasz has also convinced many professionals to question the legal, ethical, and moral bases of coercive psychiatric treatment in the forms of involuntary hospitalization and forced medication. Many caring and concerned professionals draw the line at abolishing psychiatric commitment, however. They argue that people may not be acting in their considered best interests when they threaten suicide or harm to others, or when their behavior becomes so disorganized that they cannot meet their basic needs.

PREDICTING DANGEROUSNESS

In order to be psychiatrically committed, people must be judged to be dangerous to themselves or others. Professionals are thus responsible for making accurate predictions of dangerousness to determine whether people should be involuntarily hospitalized or maintained involuntarily in the hospital. But how accurate are professionals in predicting dangerousness? Do professionals have special skills or clinical wisdom that renders their predictions accurate, or are their predictions no more accurate than those of laypeople?

Unfortunately, the accuracy of mental health professionals in making predictions of dangerousness leaves much to be desired. Mental health professionals tend to *overpredict* dangerousness—that is, to label many individuals as dangerous when they are not (Monahan, 1981). Clinicians tend to err on the side of caution in overpredicting the potential for dangerous behavior, perhaps because they believe that failure to predict violence may have more serious consequences than overprediction. On the other hand, overprediction of dangerousness deprives many people of liberty on the basis of fears that turn out to be groundless. According to Szasz and other critics of the practice of psychiatric commitment, the commitment of the many to prevent the violence of the few is a form of preventive detention that violates the basic principles on which the United States was founded.

16.2 *False.* Psychologists and other mental health professionals who rely on their clinical judgments are not very accurate when it comes to predicting dangerousness of the people they treat. The best predictor of future violence is a history of past violence.

The leading professional organizations, the American Psychological Association (1978) and the American Psychiatric Association (1974), have both gone on record as stating that neither psychologists nor psychiatrists, respectively, can reliably predict violence among the people they treat. As a leading authority in the field, John Monahan of the University of Virginia, put the issue, "When it comes to predicting violence, our crystal balls are terribly cloudy" (E. Rosenthal, 1993, p. A1).

Predictions of dangerousness based on the clinical judgments of psychologists and psychiatrists may be somewhat more accurate than predictions based on chance alone (Lidz, Mulvey, & Gardner, 1993). However, they are generally less accurate than predictions based on evidence of past violent behavior (Mossman, 1994; Gardner et al., 1996). Basically clinicians do not possess any special knowledge or ability for predicting violence beyond that of the average person. In fact, a layperson supplied with information concerning an individual's past violent behavior may be more accurate in predicting the individual's potential for future violence than the clinician who bases a prediction solely on information obtained from a clinical interview (Mossman, 1994). Unfortunately, although past violent behavior may be the best predictor of future violence, hospital staff may not be permitted access to criminal records or may lack the time or resources to track down these records (Rosenthal, 1993). The prediction problem has been cited by some as grounds for the abandonment of dangerousness as a criterion for civil commitment.

Although their crystal balls may be cloudy, mental-health professionals who work in institutional settings continue to be called on to make these predictions—deciding who to commit and who to discharge based largely on how they appraise the potential for violence. Clinicians may be more successful in predicting violence by basing predictions on a composite of factors, including evidence of past violent behavior, than on any single factor (C. E. Shaffer, Waters, & Adams, 1994). One study in Louisiana reported a 75% accuracy rate in classifying inmates as dangerous or nondangerous in a sample consisting of psychiatric inpatients and prison inmates based on a cluster of variables including age, race, vocational history, juvenile arrest record, marital status, and previous psychiatric hospitalization (Shaffer et al., 1994). Another variable that may increase predictability is substance abuse. The potential for violence is heightened in people with serious psychiatric disorders when they drink or use crack or other drugs (Rosenthal, 1993; Tardiff et al., 1997).

Problems in Predicting Dangerousness

Various factors may lead to inaccurate predictions of dangerousness, including the following.

The Post Hoc Problem Recognizing violent tendencies after a violent incident occurs (post hoc) is easier than predicting it (ad hoc). It is often said that hindsight is 20/20. Like Monday morning quarterbacking, it is easier to piece together fragments of people's prior behaviors as evidence of their violent tendencies *after* they have committed acts of violence. Predicting a violent act before the fact is a more difficult task, however.

The Problem in Leaping from the General to the Specific Generalized perceptions of violent tendencies may not predict specific acts of violence. Most people who have "general tendencies" toward violence may never act out on them. Nor is classification within a diagnostic category that is associated with aggressive or dangerous behavior, such as antisocial personality disorder, a sufficient basis for predicting specific violent acts in individuals (J. D. Bloom & Rogers, 1987).

Problems in Defining Dangerousness One difficulty in assessing the predictability of dangerousness is the lack of agreement in defining the criteria for labeling behavior as violent or dangerous. There is no universal agreement on the definition of violence or dangerousness. Most people would agree that crimes such as murder, rape, and assault are acts of violence. There is less agreement, even among authorities, for labeling other acts—for example, driving recklessly, harshly criticizing one's spouse or children, destroying property, selling drugs, shoving into people at a tavern, or stealing cars—as violent or dangerous.

Szasz argues that decisions on which dangerous acts are considered grounds for commitment are value judgments:

> Drunken drivers are dangerous both to themselves and to others. They injure and kill many more people than, for example, persons with paranoid delusions of persecution. Yet, people labeled "paranoid" are readily committable, while drunken drivers are not.
>
> Some types of dangerous behavior are even rewarded. Race-car drivers, trapeze artists, and astronauts receive admiration and applause. . . . Thus, it is not dangerousness in general that is at issue, but rather the manner in which one is dangerous. (Szasz, 1963, p. 46)

Should she be committed to a psychiatric institution? People must be judged as dangerous in order to be psychiatrically hospitalized against their wills. This photograph of emergency workers pulling a woman away from a ledge after she threatened to jump leaves little doubt about the dangerousness of her behavior. But professionals have not demonstrated that they can reliably predict future dangerousness.

Professional boxers, football players, and hockey players reap huge financial rewards and public acclaim for engaging in violent and dangerous behaviors that are *socially acceptable*. Some suggest that corporate executives who expose consumers or employees to risks to their health or personal safety are guilty of commiting corporate violence (or *suite* crime as opposed to *street* crime), which accounts for more deaths and injuries than all other types of crimes (Monahan, Novaco, & Geis, 1979). Consider, for example, the dangerousness of business owners and corporate executives who produce and market cigarettes despite widespread knowledge of the death and disease caused by these substances. Clearly, the determination of which behaviors are regarded as dangerous involves moral and political judgments within a given social context (Monahan, 1981).

Base-Rate Problems The prediction of dangerousness is complicated by the fact that violent acts such as murder, assault, or suicide are infrequent or rare events at the individual level within the general population, even if newspaper headlines sensationalize them regularly. Other rare events—such as earthquakes—are also difficult to predict with any degree of certainty concerning when or where they will strike.

The relative difficulty of making predictions of infrequent or rare events is known as the *base-rate problem*. Consider as an example the problem of suicide prediction. If the suicide rate in a given year has a low base rate of about 1% of a clinical population, the likelihood of accurately predicting that any given person in this population will commit

suicide is not very favorable. You would be correct 99% of the time if you predicted that any given individual in this population would *not* commit suicide in a given year. But to predict the nonoccurrence of suicide in every case would mean you would fail to predict the relatively few cases in which suicide does occur, even though virtually all of your predictions would likely be correct. Yet predicting the one likely case of suicide among each 100 people in the population is likely to be tricky. You are likely to be wrong more often than not if you made predictions of suicide in a given year in only 3 cases out of 100 (even if 1 of the 3 did commit suicide).

When clinicians make predictions, they weigh the relative risks of incorrectly failing to predict the occurrence of a behavior (a *false negative*) against the consequences of incorrectly predicting it (a *false positive*). Clinicians often err on the side of caution by overpredicting dangerousness. Say that a person makes a veiled threat to harm herself or himself ("I don't know how I can go on. I often feel that I'd like to take all the pills at once and end it all."). The clinician might decide the person is a serious suicide risk and needs to be hospitalized, voluntarily or involuntarily. If the person is hospitalized and suicide does not occur, the clinician is in a position to claim that the hospitalization may have prevented suicide. On the other hand, had the clinician not sought commitment and had the person committed suicide, the clinician could be accused of exercising poor professional judgment. From the clinician's perspective, erring on the side of caution might seem like a no-lose situation. Yet many people who are committed to an institution under

(A)

(B)

(C)

Who is the most dangerous? Is it the apparently drunk driver (a)? Is it the institutionalized psychiatric patient (b)? Or is it the scheming corporate executives (c)? Critics of the mental health system, such as psychiatrist Thomas Szasz, point out that drunk drivers account for more injuries and deaths than do people with paranoid schizophrenia, although the latter are more likely to be committed. Others have suggested that those corporate executives who knowingly make decisions that jeopardize the health of employees and consumers to maximize profits are guilty of corporate violence that accounts for more deaths and injuries than other types of crime.

such circumstances are denied their liberty when they would not actually have taken their lives.

The Unlikelihood of Disclosure of Direct Threats of Violence How likely is it that truly dangerous people will disclose their intentions to a health professional who is evaluating them or to their own therapist? The client in therapy is not likely to inform a therapist of a clear threat such as "I'm going to kill _____ next Wednesday morning." Threats are more likely to be vague and nonspecific, as in "I'm so sick of _____; I could kill her," or "I swear he's driving me to murder." In such cases, therapists must infer dangerousness from hostile gestures and veiled threats. Vague, indirect threats of violence are less reliable indicators of dangerousness than specific, direct threats.

The Difficulty of Predicting Behavior in the Community from Behavior in the Hospital Much of the research on the accuracy of clinical predictions of dangerousness is based on the predictions of the long-term dangerousness of hospitalized patients when they are discharged. Clinicians base such predictions largely on patients' behavior in the hospital. Violent or dangerous behavior may be situation specific, however. A model patient who is able to adapt to a structured environment like that of a psychiatric hospital may be unable to cope with pressures of independent communal life. Accuracy is improved when predictions of potential violence are based on the person's past community behavior, such as a history of violent incidents, rather than on the person's behavior in the hospital setting (Klassen & O'Connor, 1988).

PATIENTS' RIGHTS

We have considered society's right to hospitalize involuntarily people who are judged to be mentally ill and to pose a threat to themselves or others. What happens following commitment, however? Do involuntarily committed patients have the right to receive or demand treatment? Or can society just warehouse them in psychiatric facilities indefinitely without treating them? Consider the opposite side of the coin as well: May people who are involuntarily committed refuse treatment? Such issues—which have been brought into public light by landmark court cases—fall under the umbrella of *patients' rights.* Generally speaking, the history of abuses in the mental-health system, as highlighted in such popular books and movies as *One Flew Over the Cuckoo's Nest,* have led to a tightening of standards of care and adoption of legal guarantees to protect patients' rights. The legal status of some issues, such as the right to treatment, remains unsettled, however.

Right to Treatment

One might assume that mental-health institutions which accept people for treatment will provide them with treatment.

What are the rights of mental patients?   Popular books and films such as *One Flew Over the Cuckoo's Nest* starring Jack Nicholson have highlighted many of the abuses of mental hospitals. In recent years, a tightening of standards of care and the adoption of legal safeguards have led to better protection of the rights of patients in mental hospitals.

Not until the 1972 landmark federal court case of *Wyatt v. Stickney,* however, did a federal court establish a minimum standard of care to be provided by hospitals. The case was a class action suit against Stickney, the commissioner of mental health for the State of Alabama, brought on behalf of Ricky Wyatt, a mentally retarded young man, and other patients at a state hospital and school in Tuscaloosa.

The federal district court in Alabama held both that the hospital had failed to provide treatment to Wyatt and others and that living conditions at the hospital were inadequate and dehumanizing. The court described the hospital dormitories as "barnlike structures" that afforded no privacy to the residents. The bathrooms had no partitions between stalls, the patients were outfitted with shoddy clothes, the wards were filthy and crowded, the kitchens were unsanitary, and the food was substandard. In addition, the staff was inadequate in numbers and poorly trained. The court held that mental hospitals must, at a minimum, provide the following:

1. A humane psychological and physical environment,
2. Qualified staff in numbers sufficient to administer adequate treatment, and
3. Individualized treatment plans (*Wyatt v. Stickney,* 334 Supp., p. 1343, 1972).

The court established that the state was obliged to provide adequate treatment for people who were involuntarily confined to psychiatric hospitals. The court further ruled that to commit people to hospitals for treatment involuntarily, and then not to provide treatment, violated their rights to due process under the law.

A listing of some of the rights granted institutionalized patients under the court's ruling is shown in Table 16.1. Although the ruling of the court was limited to Alabama, many other states have followed suit and revised their mental hospital standards to ensure that involuntarily committed patients are not denied basic rights.

TRUTH **or** FICTION REVISITED

16.3 *False.* The Alabama case of *Wyatt v. Stickney* established certain patient rights, including the right not to be required to perform work that is performed for the sake of maintaining the facility.

Other court cases have further clarified patients' rights.

O'Connor v. Donaldson   The 1975 case of Kenneth Donaldson is another landmark in patients' rights. Donaldson, a former patient at a state hospital in Florida, sued two hospital doctors on the grounds that he had been involuntarily confined without receiving treatment for 14 years, despite the fact that he posed no serious threat to himself or others. Donaldson had been originally committed on the basis of a petition filed by his father who had perceived him as delusional. Despite the facts that Donaldson received no treatment during his confinement and was denied grounds privileges and occupational training, his repeated requests

Kenneth Donaldson.   Donaldson points to the U.S. Supreme Court decision that ruled that people who are considered mentally ill but not dangerous cannot be confined against their will if they can be maintained safely in the community.

for discharge were denied by the hospital staff. He was finally released when he threatened to sue the hospital. Once discharged, Donaldson did sue his doctors and was awarded damages of $38,500 from O'Connor, the superintendent of the hospital. The case was eventually argued before the U.S. Supreme Court.

TABLE 16.1

Partial Listing of the Patient's Bill of Rights Under *Wyatt v. Stickney*

1. Patients have rights to privacy and to be treated with dignity.

2. Patients shall be treated under the least restrictive conditions that can be provided to meet the purposes that commitment was intended to serve.

3. Patients shall have rights to visitation and telephone privileges unless special restrictions apply.

4. Patients have the right to refuse excessive or unnecessary medication. In addition, medication may not be used as a form of punishment.

5. Patients shall not be kept in restraints or isolation except in emergency conditions in which their behavior is likely to pose a threat to themselves or others and less restrictive restraints are not feasible.

6. Patients shall not be subject to experimental research unless their rights to informed consent are protected.

7. Patients have the right to refuse potentially hazardous or unusual treatments, such as lobotomy, electroconvulsive shock, or aversive behavioral treatments.

8. Unless it is dangerous or inappropriate to the treatment program, patients shall have the right to wear their own clothing and keep possessions.

9. Patients have rights to regular exercise and to opportunities to spend time outdoors.

10. Patients have rights to suitable opportunities to interact with the opposite gender.

11. Patients have rights to humane and decent living conditions.

12. No more than six patients shall be housed in a room and screen or curtains must be provided to afford a sense of privacy.

13. No more than eight patients shall share one toilet facility, with separate stalls provided for privacy.

14. Patients have a right to nutritionally balanced diets.

15. Patients shall not be required to perform work that is performed for the sake of maintenance of the facility.

Court testimony established that although the hospital staff had not perceived Donaldson to be dangerous during his hospitalization, they had refused to release him. The hospital doctors argued that continued hospitalization had been necessary because they had believed that Donaldson was unlikely to adapt successfully to community living. The doctors had prescribed antipsychotic medications as a course of treatment, but Donaldson had refused to take them because of his Christian Science beliefs. As a result, he received only custodial care.

The U.S. Supreme Court held that "mental illness [alone] cannot justify a State's locking a person up against his will and keeping him indefinitely in simple custodial confinement . . . There is still no constitutional basis for confining such persons involuntarily if they are dangerous to no one and can live safely in freedom" (p. 2493). The ruling addressed patients who are not considered dangerous. It is not yet clear whether the same constitutional rights would be applied to committed patients who are judged to be dangerous.

In its ruling on *O'Connor v. Donaldson*, the Supreme Court did not deal with the larger issue of the rights of patients to receive treatment. The ruling does not directly obligate state institutions to treat involuntarily committed, nondangerous people because the institutions may elect to release them instead.

The Supreme Court did touch on the larger issue of society's rights to protect itself from individuals who are perceived as offensive. In delivering the opinion of the court, Justice Potter Stewart wrote,

> May the State fence in the harmless mentally ill solely to save its citizens from exposure to those whose ways are different? One might as well ask if the State, to avoid public uneasiness, could incarcerate all who are physically unattractive or socially eccentric. Mere public intolerance or animosity cannot constitutionally justify the deprivation of a person's physical liberty (*O'Connor v. Donaldson*, 95 S. Ct. 2486, 1975).

Youngberg v. Romeo In a 1982 case, *Youngberg v. Romeo*, the U.S. Supreme Court more directly addressed the issue of the patient's right to treatment. Even so, it seemed to retreat somewhat from the patients' rights standards established in *Wyatt v. Stickney*. Nicholas Romeo, a 33-year-old profoundly retarded man who was unable to talk or care for himself, had been institutionalized in a state hospital and school in Pennsylvania. While in the state facility he had a history of injuring himself through his violent behavior and was often kept in restraints. The case was brought by the patient's mother who alleged that the hospital was negligent in not preventing his injuries and for routinely using physical restraints for prolonged periods while not providing adequate treatment.

The Supreme Court ruled that involuntarily committed patients, such as Nicholas, have a right to be confined in less restrictive conditions, such as being freed from physical restraints whenever it is reasonable to do so. The Supreme

Court ruling also included a limited recognition of the committed patient's right to treatment. The Court held that institutionalized patients have a right to minimally adequate training to help them function free of physical restraints, but only to the extent that such training can be provided in *reasonable* safety. The determination of reasonableness, the Court held, should be made on the basis of the judgment of the qualified professionals in the facility. The federal courts should not interfere with the internal operations of the facility, the Court held, because "there's no reason to think judges or juries are better qualified than appropriate professionals in making such decisions" (p. 2462). The courts should only second-guess the judgments of qualified professionals, the Supreme Court held, when such judgments are determined to depart from professional standards of practice. But the Supreme Court did not address the broader issues of the rights of committed patients to receive training that might eventually enable them to function independently outside the hospital.

The related issue of whether people with severe psychological disorders who reside in the community have a constitutional right to receive mental-health services (and whether states are obliged to provide these services) continues to be argued in the courts at both the state and federal levels (Perlin, 1994).

Right to Refuse Treatment

Consider the following scenario. A person, John Citizen, is involuntarily committed to a mental hospital for treatment. The hospital staff determines that John suffers from a psychotic disorder, paranoid schizophrenia, and should be treated with antipsychotic medication. John, however, decides not to comply with treatment. He claims that the hospital has no right to treat him against his will. The hospital staff seeks a court order to mandate treatment, arguing it makes little sense to commit people involuntarily unless the hospital is empowered to treat them as the staff deems fit.

Does an involuntary patient, such as John, have the right to refuse treatment? If so, does this right conflict with states' rights to commit people to mental institutions to receive treatment for their disorders? One might also wonder whether people who are judged in need of involuntary hospitalization are competent enough to make decisions about which treatments are in their best interests.

The rights of committed patients to refuse psychotropic medications was tested in the 1979 case of *Rogers v. Okin*, in which a Massachusetts federal district court imposed an injunction on a Boston state hospital that prohibited the forced medication of patients except in emergency situations. The court ruled that committed patients could not be forcibly medicated, except in the case of emergency—for example, when patients' behaviors pose a significant threat to themselves or others. The court recognized that a patient may be unwise to refuse medication, but that a patient with or without a mental disorder has the right to exercise bad judgment so long as the effects of the "error" do not impose "a danger of physical harm to himself, fellow patients, or hospital staff."

Many professionals were outraged by this court ruling. As one psychiatrist put it, patients who refused medications would literally find themselves "rotting with their rights on" (Gutheil, 1980). Others, however, viewed the court decision in more favorable terms, seeing it as a means of ensuring that hospitalized patients would be treated with greater dignity and would be more likely to receive proper treatment (R. Cole, 1982). Despite dire predictions to the contrary, legal protections ensuring patients' rights to refuse psychiatric treatments do not appear to have had seriously damaging or disruptive effects on mental-health services or on the people receiving these services (Kapp, 1994).

Although statutes and regulations vary from state to state, cases in which hospitalized patients refuse medications are often first brought before an independent review panel. If the panel rules against the patient, the case may then be brought before a judge, who makes the final decision about whether or not the patient is to be forcibly medicated. In actual practice, the number of refusals of medication is generally low, about 10% overall (Appelbaum & Hoges, 1986). Furthermore, between 70% and 90% of refusals that reach the review process are eventually overridden. Hospitalized patients in a recent study who refused medication tended to be more assaultive, were more likely to require seclusion and restraint, and had longer hospitalizations than compliant patients (J. A. Kasper et al., 1997). However, refusal episodes tended to be brief, about 3 days on average, and all initial refusers were eventually treated.

Let us note that voluntarily admitted patients have always had the right to refuse treatment. They may also sign themselves out of the hospital, even if their doctors believe that they should remain. But there's a catch: Hospitals may petition the court to change patients' commitment status from voluntary to involuntary if the staff believes that patients are dangerous and in need of treatment. The judge must concur, however, for the change to carried out.

Our discussion of legal issues and abnormal behavior now turns to the controversy concerning the **insanity defense.**

THE INSANITY DEFENSE

As President Ronald Reagan stepped out of the Washington Hilton on March 31, 1981, gunshots rang out. Secret Service agents formed a human shield around the president as another agent shoved him into a waiting limousine, which then sped away to a hospital. At first, the president did not know he had been wounded. He said later that it sounded like firecrackers. Agents seized the gunman, John Hinckley, a 25-year-old drifter. Not only had the president been wounded. James Brady, his press secretary, was hit by a stray bullet that shattered his spine, leaving him partially paralyzed. A Secret Service agent was also shot.

Hinckley had left a letter in his hotel room revealing his hope that his assassination of the president would impress a young actress, Jodie Foster. Hinckley had never met Foster but had a crush on her.

There was never any question at the trial that Hinckley had fired the wounding bullets, but the prosecutor was burdened to demonstrate beyond a reasonable doubt that Hinckley had had the capacity, at the time of the assassination attempt, to control his behavior and appreciate its wrongfulness. The defense presented testimony that portrayed Hinckley as an incompetent schizophrenic who suffered under the delusion that he would achieve a "magic union" with Foster as a result of killing the president. The prosecutor portrayed Hinckley as making a conscious and willful choice to kill the president. The prosecution further argued that whatever mental disorder Hinckley might have had did not prevent him from controlling his behavior.

The jury sided with the defense, finding Hinckley not guilty by reason of insanity. The verdict led to a public outcry across the country, with many calling for the abolition of the insanity defense. Public opinion polls taken several days after the Hinckley verdict was returned showed the public had little confidence in the psychiatric testimony that had been offered at the trial (Slater & Hans, 1984). One objection focused on the fact that once the defense presented evidence to support a plea of insanity, the federal prosecutor had the responsibility of proving *beyond a reasonable doubt* that the defendant was sane. It can be difficult enough to demonstrate that someone is sane or insane in the present, so imagine the problems that attend proving someone *was* sane at the time a criminal act was committed.

Was he insane when he committed his crime? John W. Hinckley, Jr. attempted to assassinate President Ronald Reagan in 1981 but was found not guilty by reason of insanity. The public outrage over the Hinckley verdict led to a reexamination of the insanity plea in many states.

Jodie Foster. John Hinckley reportedly attempted to assassinate President Reagan in order to impress Ms. Foster, whom he had seen in the film *Taxi Driver* but never met. In the film, Robert DeNiro, who portrayed a person with paranoid schizophrenia, rescued Foster's character from a life of prostitution. Hinckley's attorneys claimed that their client experienced similar rescue fantasies. Foster is seen here in the film *The Silence of the Lambs.*

TRUTH *or* FICTION REVISITED

16.4 ***True.*** A man who was seen by millions of TV viewers attempting to assassinate President Reagan was found "not guilty by reason of insanity" by a court of law.

In the aftermath of the Hinckley verdict, the federal government and a number of states have changed their statutes to shift the burden of proof to the defense to prove *insanity*. Presently, 38 states impose on the defendant the burden of proving insanity (Ogloff, Roberts, & Roesch, 1993). Even the American Psychiatric Association went on record as stating that psychiatric expert witnesses should not be called on to render opinions about whether defendants can control their behavior. In the opinion of the psychiatric association, these are not medical judgments that psychiatrists are trained to provide.

Perceptions of the use of the insanity defense tend to stray far from the facts. The general public grossly overestimates the number of cases in which the insanity defense is used and how often it succeeds. While a recent survey showed the public estimates that the insanity defense is used in about 1 in 3 felony cases, in actuality it occurs in fewer than 1% of cases (Silver, Cirincione, & Steadman, 1994; Steadman et al., 1993). A study in Baltimore showed that the insanity defense plea was used there in a minuscule 1/100th of 1% of indictments brought to trial (Janofsky et al., 1996). Whereas the public believes that 44% of defendants who

claim insanity are acquitted, the actual figure (based on a review of records in eight states) was 26% (Silver et al., 1994; Steadman et al., 1993). In actual practice, out of 1,000 felony cases, there are fewer than 10 in which the insanity defense is used, and only about 2 or 3 in which it is used successfully. Thus, despite public perceptions to the contrary, the use of the insanity defense is actually rather rare, and the rate of acquittals is rarer still ("Insanity: A defense of last resort," 1992).

TRUTH *or* FICTION REVISITED

16.5 ***False.*** The insanity defense is rarely used in felony cases, and the rate of acquittals based on the defense is even rarer.

Nor do psychiatric experts offer conflicting testimony to the degree that the public generally believes. In a study in Alaska, psychiatrists who were called as expert witnesses agreed with each other's testimony 79% of the time (M. R. Phillips, Wolf, & Coons, 1988). Conflicting psychiatric testimony was presented in only 1.5% of all criminal cases in the Alaskan study in which psychiatric testimony was presented, and in 7 of 10 of these cases the defendant was found guilty. However uncommon, when battles between opposing witnesses did occur, the result was unlikely to lead to acquittal.

The public also overestimates the proportion of defendants acquitted on the basis of insanity who are set free rather than confined to mental health institutions and underestimates the length of hospitalization of those who are confined (Silver et al., 1994). The net result of these findings is that although changes in the insanity defense, or its abolition, may prevent some few flagrant cases of abuse, they are not likely to afford the public much broader protection.

Although the public outrage over the Hinckley and other celebrated insanity verdicts has led to a reexamination of the insanity defense (see feature "The GMBI Verdict"), society has long held to the doctrine of free will as a basis for determining responsibility for wrongdoing. The doctrine of free will, as applied to criminal responsibility, requires that people can be held guilty of a crime only if they are judged to have been in control of their actions at the time of commission of the crime. Not only must it be determined by a court of law that a defendant had committed a crime beyond a reasonable doubt, but the issue of the individual's state of mind must be considered as well in determining guilt. The court must thus rule not only on whether a crime was committed, but on whether or not an individual is held *morally* responsible and *deserving* of punishment. The insanity defense is based on the belief that when a criminal act derives from a distorted state of mind, and not from the exercise of free will, the individual should not be punished but rather treated for the underlying mental disorder. The insanity defense has a long legal history.

Legal Bases of the Insanity Defense

We can find in modern law three major court rulings that bear on the insanity defense. The first involved a case in

The GBMI Verdict—Guilty But Mentally Ill

In 1975, well before the Hinckley verdict, Michigan became the first state to adopt a new legal standard—the GBMI, or "guilty-but-mentally-ill," verdict. The GBMI verdict offers juries the option of finding a defendant both guilty and mentally ill, if they determine the defendant is mentally ill but the mental illness did not cause the defendant to commit the crime. The GBMI verdict provides that people so convicted may be imprisoned but also receive treatment while in prison. Their mental condition may also be taken into account in future parole hearings (Maeder, 1985). In the wake of the Hinckley acquittal, six additional states adopted the GBMI verdict, with four of these states adopting the verdict in the very month following the Hinckley verdict (Maeder, 1985). The GBMI verdict has now been adopted in 13 states as a supplement to, not a replacement for, the insanity defense (Ogloff et al., 1993).

The GBMI verdict is something of an in-between determination, in that the defendant is neither acquitted nor found guilty in the traditional sense of the term (Ogloff et al., 1993). The verdict has sparked a great deal of controversy. Although GBMI was intended to reduce the number of NGRI (not guilty by reason of insanity) verdicts, this outcome has apparently not occurred. In Michigan, for example, approximately the same number of insanity acquittals were returned in the years directly preceding and following the adoption of the GBMI alternative, approximately 50 to 60 per year (G. A. Smith & Hall, 1982). About 34 defendants per year, on the average, received the GBMI verdict in Michigan in the years following its passage, and these defendants would probably have been found guilty anyway had the GBMI verdict not been available (Smith & Hall, 1982).

In a celebrated case, John E. du Pont, an heir to the du Pont family fortune, was found guilty but mentally ill following trial for the 1996 murder of Olympic gold medalist, wrestler David Schultz ("Du Pont heir found guilty of murder but mentally ill," 1997). Du Pont was subsequently remanded to a state psychiatric hospital for treatment, rather than prison. At trial, it was reported that du Pont exhibited bizarre behavior, and suffered from delusions of being spied upon by Nazis and of having his body inhabited by bugs.

It is also clear that the availability of mental-health treatment in prison settings, and the consideration of mental-health criteria in parole hearings, is not limited to GBMI defendants. All in all, the GBMI verdict appears to be a social experiment that has not yet proved its usefulness and is seen by some as merely a means of stigmatizing defendants who are found guilty as also being mentally ill (Maeder, 1985).

Ohio in 1834 in which it was ruled that people cannot be held responsible if they are compelled to commit criminal actions because of impulses they are unable to resist.

The second major legal test of the insanity defense is referred to as the M'Naghten rule, based on a case in England in 1843 of a Scotsman, Daniel M'Naghten, who had intended to assassinate the prime minister of England, Sir Robert Peel. Instead, he killed Peel's secretary whom he had mistaken for the prime minister. M'Naghten claimed that the voice of God had commanded him to kill Sir Robert. The English court acquitted M'Naghten on the basis of insanity, finding that the defendant had been " . . . labouring under such a defect of reason, from disease of the mind, as not to know the nature and quality of the act he was doing; or, if he did know it, that he did not know he was doing what was wrong." The M'Naghten rule, as it has come to be called, holds that people do not bear criminal responsibility if, by reason of a mental disease or defect, they either have no knowledge of their actions or are unable to tell right from wrong.

To find the third major case that helped lay the foundation for the modern insanity defense we must jump more than 100 years to 1954 and the case of *Durham v. United States*. In this case, the presiding judge, David Bazelon, held that the "accused [person] is not criminally responsible if his unlawful act was the product of mental disease or mental defect" (pp. 874–875). Under the Durham rule, juries were expected to decide not only whether the accused suffered from a mental disease or defect but also whether this mental condition was causally connected to the criminal act. The court recognized that criminal intent is a precondition of criminal responsibility:

> The legal and moral traditions of the western world require that those who, of their own free will and with evil intent . . . commit acts which violate the law, shall be criminally responsible for those acts. Our traditions also require that where such acts stem from and are the product of a mental disease or defect . . . moral blame shall not attach, and hence there will not be criminal responsibility. (*Durham v. United States*, 214 F2d 862, D.C. circ. 1954)

Daniel M'Naghten. The murder trial of Daniel M'Naghten, held in the Old Bailey, London, in 1843.

The intent of the Durham rule was to reject as outmoded the two earlier standards of legal insanity, the irresistible impulse rule and the "right-wrong" principle under the M'Naghten rule. Judge Bazelon argued that the "right-wrong test" was outmoded because the concept of "mental disease" is broader than the ability to recognize right from wrong. The legal basis of insanity should thus not be judged on but one feature of a mental disorder, such as deficient reasoning ability. The irresistible impulse test was denied because the court recognized that in certain cases, criminal acts arising from "mental disease or defect" may occur in a cool and calculating manner rather than in the manner of a sudden, irresistible impulse.

The Durham rule, however, has proved to be unworkable for several reasons, such as a lack of precise definitions of such terms as *mental disease* or *mental defect* (Maeder, 1985). Courts were confused, for example, about issues such as whether a personality disorder, like antisocial personality disorder, constituted a "disease." It also proved difficult for juries to draw conclusions about whether an individual's "mental disease" was causally connected to the criminal act. Without clear or precise definitions of terms, juries came to rely increasingly on expert psychiatric testimony, often serving as little more than rubber stamps as their verdicts endorsed the testimony of expert witnesses (Maeder, 1985).

By 1972, the Durham rule had failed and was replaced in many jurisdictions by a set of legal guidelines formulated by the American Law Institute (ALI) to define the legal basis of insanity (Maeder, 1985). Currently, 22 states have adopted the ALI guidelines, or some variation of these standards (Ogloff et al., 1993). These guidelines, which essentially combine the M'Naghten principle with the irresistible impulse principle, include the following provisions:

1. A person is not responsible for criminal conduct if at the time of such conduct as a result of mental disease or defect he lacks substantial capacity either to appreciate the criminality (wrongfulness) of his conduct or to conform his conduct to the requirements of law.

2. . . . the terms "mental disease or defect" do not include an abnormality manifested only by repeated criminal or otherwise antisocial conduct. (American Law Institute, 1962, p. 66)

The first guideline incorporates aspects of the M'Naghten test (being unable to appreciate right from wrong) and the irresistible impulse test (being unable to conform one's behavior to the requirements of law) of insanity. The second guideline asserts that repeated criminal behavior (like a pattern of drug dealing) is not sufficient in itself to establish a mental disease or defect that might relieve the individual of criminal responsibility. Although many legal authorities believe that the ALI guidelines are an improvement over earlier tests, questions remain as to whether a jury composed of ordinary citizens can be expected to make complex judgments about the defendant's state of mind, even on the basis of expert testimony. Under the ALI guidelines, juries must determine whether defendants lack substantial capacity to be aware of, or capable of, conforming their behavior to the law. By adding the term *substantial capacity* to the legal test, the ALI guidelines may also broaden the legal basis of the insanity defense because this may imply that defendants need not be completely incapable of controlling their criminal actions in order to meet the legal test of not guilty by reason of insanity.

Under our system of justice, juries must struggle with the complex question of determining criminal responsibility, not merely criminal actions. But what of those individuals who successfully plead not guilty by reason of insanity? Should they be committed to a mental institution for a fixed sentence, as they might have been had they been incarcerated in a penal institution? Or should their commitments be of an indeterminate term and their release depend on their mental status? The legal basis for answering such questions was decided in the following case of a man, Michael Jones, whose acquittal by reason of insanity resulted in involuntary commitment to a mental hospital for a period that turned out to be seven times longer than the maximum prison sentence for the crime.

Determining the Term of Criminal Commitment The issue of determinate versus indeterminate commitment was addressed in the case of Michael Jones (*Jones v. United States*), who was arrested in 1975 and charged with petty larceny for attempting to steal a jacket from a Washington, D.C., department store. Jones was first committed to a public mental hospital, St. Elizabeth's Hospital (which, incidentally, is the hospital where John Hinckley remains committed as of this writing). Jones was diagnosed by a hospital psychologist as suffering from paranoid schizophrenia and was kept hospitalized until he was judged competent to stand trial, about 6 months later. Jones offered a plea of not guilty by reason of insanity, which the court accepted without challenge, remanding him to St. Elizabeth's. Despite the fact that Jones's crime carried a maximum sentence of 1 year in prison, Jones's repeated attempts to obtain release were denied in subsequent court hearings.

His appeal was eventually heard by the U.S. Supreme Court *7 years* after he was hospitalized. The Supreme Court reached its decision in 1983. It ruled against Jones's appeal and affirmed the decision of the lower courts that he was to remain in the hospital. The Supreme Court thereby established a principle that individuals who are acquitted by reason of insanity "constitute a special class that should be treated differently" than civilly committed individuals. They may be committed for an indefinite period to a mental institution under criteria that require a less stringent level of proof of dangerousness than would ordinarily be applied in cases of civil commitment. Thus, people found not guilty by reason of insanity may remain confined to a mental hospital for many years longer than they would have been sentenced to prison had they been found guilty.

TRUTH *or* FICTION REVISITED

16.6 *True.* People who are found not guilty of a crime by reason of insanity may remain confined in a mental hospital indefinitely—for many years longer than they would have been sentenced to prison, if they had been found guilty.

Among other things, the Supreme Court ruling in *Jones v. the United States* provides that the usual and customary sentences that the law provides for particular crimes have no bearing on criminal commitment. In the words of the Court,

different considerations underlie commitment of an insanity acquittee. As he was not convicted, he may not be punished. His confinement rests on his continuing illness and dangerousness. . . . There simply is no necessary correlation between severity of the offense and length of time necessary for recovery (*Jones v. United States*, 103 S.Ct. 3043, 1983).

The ruling held that a person who is criminally committed may be confined "to a mental institution until such time as he has regained his sanity or is no longer a danger to society" (p. 3053). As in the case of Michael Jones, insanity acquittees may remain confined in a mental institution for longer than they would have been sentenced to prison. It is also possible, however, that such persons could be released earlier than they might have been released from prison, if their "mental condition" is found to have improved. A person acquitted of a serious crime by virtue of the insanity defense may even be released within a few weeks or months, although, practically speaking, it is doubtful that improve-

ment would be established so quickly. Public outrage over a speedy release, especially for a major crime, might also prevent rapid release.

The indeterminateness of legal or criminal commitment raises various questions. Is it reasonable to deny people like Michael Jones their liberty for an indefinite and possibly lifelong term for a relatively minor crime, such as petty larceny? On the other hand, is justice served by acquitting perpetrators of heinous crimes by reason of insanity and then allowing them the opportunity for an early release if they are deemed by professionals to be able to rejoin society?

The Supreme Court's ruling in *Jones v. United States* seems to imply that we must separate the notion of legal sentencing from that of legal or criminal commitment. The former, in which sentences are scaled according to the seriousness of the crime, rests on the principle that the punishment should fit the crime. In legal or criminal commitment, however, persons acquitted of their crimes by reason of insanity are guiltless in the eyes of the law. They must be treated, not punished, until such time that their mental status has improved to the point that permits them to reenter society safely.

Perspectives on the Insanity Defense

The insanity defense places special burdens on juries. In assessing criminal responsibility, the jury is expected to determine not only that a crime was committed by the accused, but also the defendant's state of mind at the time of commission of the crime. In rejecting the Durham decision, courts have relieved psychiatrists and other expert witnesses from bearing the burden of responsibility for determining whether or not the defendant's behavior is a product of a "mental disease or defect." But is it reasonable to assume that juries of people from all walks of life are better able to assess defendants' states of mind than mental health professionals? In particular, how can a jury evaluate the testimony of expert conflicting witnesses? The task imposed on the jury is made even more difficult by the mandate to decide whether or not the defendant was mentally incapacitated *at the time* of the crime. The defendant's courtroom behavior may bear little resemblance to his or her behavior during the crime.

Another challenge to the insanity defense has been raised by Thomas Szasz and others who deny the existence of mental illness itself. If mental illness does not exist, then the insanity defense becomes groundless. Szasz argues that the insanity defense is ultimately degrading because it strips people of personal responsibility for their behavior. People who break laws are criminals, Szasz argues, and should be prosecuted and sentenced accordingly. Acquittal of defendants by reason of insanity treats them as nonpersons, as unfortunates who are not deemed to possess the basic human qualities of free choice, self-determination, and personal responsibility. We are each responsible for our behavior, Szasz contends, and we should each be held accountable for our misdeeds.

Szasz argues that the insanity defense has historically been invoked in crimes which were particularly heinous or perpetrated against persons of high social rank. When persons of low social rank commit crimes against persons of higher status, Szasz argues, the effect of the insanity defense is to direct attention away from the social ills that may have motivated the crime. Despite Szasz's contention, however, the insanity defense is invoked in many cases of less shocking crimes or in cases involving persons from similar social classes.

How, then, are we to evaluate the insanity defense? To abolish the insanity defense in all forms would be to reverse hundreds of years of a legal tradition that has recognized that people are not to be held responsible for their criminal behavior when their ability to control themselves is impaired by a mental disorder or defect.

Consider a hypothetical example. John Citizen commits a crime, say a heinous crime like murder, while acting on a delusional belief that the victim was intent on assassinating him. The accused claims that voices from his TV set informed him of the identity of the assailant and commanded him to kill the assailant to save himself and other potential victims. Cases like this are thankfully rare. Few mentally disturbed persons, even few people with psychotic features, commit violent crimes, and even fewer commit murder.

In reaching a judgment on the insanity plea, we need to consider whether we believe that the law should allow special standards to apply in cases such as our hypothetical case, or whether one standard of criminal responsibility should apply to all. If we assert the legitimacy of the insanity defense in some cases, we still need a standard of insanity that can be interpreted and applied by juries of ordinary citizens. The furor over the Hinckley verdict suggests that issues concerning the insanity plea remain unsettled.

COMPETENCY TO STAND TRIAL

There is a basic rule of law that those who stand accused of crimes must be able to understand the charges and proceedings brought against them and be able to participate in their own defense. The concept of competency to stand trial should not be confused with the legal defense of insanity. A defendant can be held competent to stand trial but judged not guilty by reason of insanity. A clearly delusional person, for example, may understand the court proceedings and be able to confer with defense counsel, but still be acquitted by reason of insanity. On the other hand, a person may be incapable of standing trial at a particular time, but be tried and acquitted or convicted at a later time when competency is restored.

TRUTH *or* FICTION REVISITED

16.7 *True*. A defendant can be held competent to stand trial but still be judged not guilty of a crime by reason of insanity.

Far more people are confined to mental institutions on the basis of a determination that they lack competency to stand trial than on the basis of an insanity verdict. There may be 45 people committed under the competency-to-stand-trial criteria for every one committed following a verdict of not guilty by reason of insanity (Steadman, 1979).

People who are declared incompetent to stand trial are generally confined to a mental institution until they are deemed competent or a determination is made that they are unlikely ever to regain competency. Abuses may occur, however, if the accused are kept incarcerated for indefinite periods awaiting trial. In earlier years, it was not uncommon for people who were declared incompetent to have their trials delayed for months or years until they were judged ready to stand trial, if indeed they were ever judged to be competent. In 1972, however, the U.S. Supreme Court ruled in the case of *Jackson v. Indiana* that a person could not be kept in a mental hospital awaiting trial longer than it would take to determine whether treatment was likely to restore competency. If it did not seem the person would ever become competent, even with treatment, the individual would have to be either released or committed under the procedures for civil commitment.

A 1992 ruling by the U.S. Supreme Court, in the case of *Medina v. California*, held that the burden of proof for determining incompetence to stand trial lies with the defendant, not the state (Greenhouse, 1992). This decision may speed the trials of many people who commit crimes and whose competency is in question.

THE DUTY TO WARN

One of the most difficult dilemmas a therapist may face is whether or not to disclose confidential information that may protect third parties from harm. Part of the difficulty lies in determining whether or not the client has made a bona fide threat against another person. The other part of the dilemma is that information a client discloses in psychotherapy is generally protected as privileged communication, which carries a right to confidentiality. But this right is not absolute. Courts have determined that a therapist is obliged to breach confidentiality under certain conditions, such as when there is clear and compelling evidence that an individual poses a serious threat to others.

In 1976, a California case, *Tarasoff v. the Regents of the University of California,* established the legal basis for the therapist's **duty to warn.**

The Tarasoff Case

In 1969, a graduate student at the University of California at Berkeley, Prosenja Poddar, a native of India, became depressed when his romantic overtures toward a young woman, Tatiana Tarasoff, were rebuffed. Poddar entered psychotherapy with a psychologist at a student health facility, during the course of which he informed the psychologist that he intended to kill Tatiana when she returned from her summer vacation. The psychologist, concerned about Poddar's potential for violence, first consulted with his colleagues

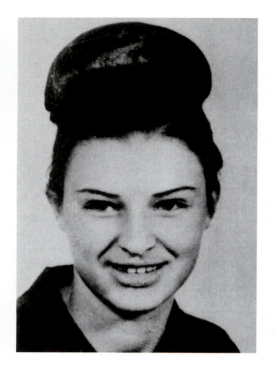 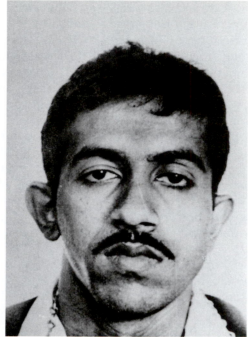

Tatiana Tarasoff (left) *and Prosenjit Poddar* (right). Poddar, Tatiana's killer, was a rejected suitor who had made threats against her to his therapist at a university health center. Poddar was subsequently convicted of voluntary manslaughter in her death. A suit brought by Tatiana's parents against the university led to a landmark court ruling that established an obligation of therapists to warn third parties of threats made against them by their clients.

and then notified the campus police. He informed them that Poddar was dangerous and recommended he be taken to a facility for psychiatric treatment.

Poddar was subsequently interviewed by the campus police. They believed that he was rational and released him after he promised to keep his distance from Tatiana. Poddar then terminated treatment with the psychologist, and shortly afterward killed Tatiana. He shot her with a pellet gun when she refused to allow him entry to her home and then repeatedly stabbed her as she fled into the street. Poddar was found guilty of the lesser sentence of voluntary manslaughter, rather than murder, based on testimony of three psychiatrists that Poddar suffered from diminished mental capacity and paranoid schizophrenia. Under California law, his diminished capacity prevented the finding of malice that was necessary for conviction on a charge of first- or second-degree murder. Following a prison term, Poddar returned to India, where he reportedly made a new life for himself (Schwitzgebel & Schwitzgebel, 1980).

Tatiana's parents, however, sued the university. They claimed that the university health center had failed in its responsibility to warn Tatiana of the threat made against her by Poddar. The Supreme Court of the State of California agreed with the parents. They ruled that a therapist who has reason to believe that a client poses a serious threat to another person is obligated to warn the potential victim. This obligation is not met by notifying police. This ruling imposed on therapists a duty-to-warn obligation when their clients show the potential for violence by making threats against others.

The ruling recognized that the rights of the intended victim outweigh the rights of confidentiality. Under *Tarasoff,*

the therapist does not merely have a *right* to breach confidentiality and warn potential victims of danger, but is *obligated* by law to divulge such confidences to the victim.

TRUTH *or* FICTION REVISITED

16.8 False. Therapists are required in many states to reveal confidential information to third parties who have been threatened by their clients.

The duty-to-warn provision poses ethical and practical dilemmas for psychologists and other psychotherapists. Psychotherapists, in states that apply the *Tarasoff* obligation, have a duty to assess the potential violence of their clients, *even though professionals are not generally able to predict dangerousness with a high degree of accuracy.* Under *Tarasoff,* then, therapists may actually feel obliged to protect their personal interests and those of others by breaching confidentiality on the mere suspicion that their clients harbor violent intentions toward third parties. Because there are very few cases in which clients' threats are carried out, the *Tarasoff* ruling may serve to deny many clients their rights to confidentiality in order to prevent such rare instances. Although some clinicians may "overreact" to *Tarasoff* and breach confidentiality without sufficient cause, it can be argued that the interests of the few potential victims outweigh the interests of the many who may suffer a loss of confidentiality.

Although therapists apparently possess no special ability to predict dangerousness, the *Tarasoff* ruling obliges them to judge whether or not their clients' disclosures indicate a clear intent to harm others. In the *Tarasoff* case, the threat was obvious enough to prompt the therapist to breach confidentiality by requesting the help of campus police. In most cases, however, threats are not so clear cut. There remains a lack of clear criteria for determining whether or not a therapist "should have known" that a client was dangerous before a violent act occurs (Fulero, 1988). In the absence of guidelines that specify the criteria therapists should use to fulfill their duty to warn, they must rely on their best subjective judgments.

Although the intent of the *Tarasoff* decision was to protect potential victims, it may inadvertently increase the risks of violence when applied to clinical practice (A. Stone, 1976). For example,

1. *Clients may be less willing to confide in their therapists.* Under the obligations imposed on therapists by *Tarasoff*, clients may be less willing to confide violent urges to their therapists, making it more difficult for therapists to help them diffuse these feelings before they are acted upon.

2. *Potentially violent people may be less likely to enter therapy.* People with violent tendencies may be less willing to enter therapy for fear that disclosures made to a therapist may be revealed.

3. *Therapists may be less likely to probe violent tendencies for fear of legal complications.* To protect themselves and their careers, therapists may avoid asking clients questions concerning potential violence in the belief that they are legally protected if they remain ignorant of them (T. P. Wise, 1978). Therapists might also avoid accepting patients for treatment who are believed to have violent tendencies.

It is unclear whether *Tarasoff* has protected lives or endangered lives. It is clear, however, that *Tarasoff* has raised concerns for clinicians who are trying to meet their legal responsibilities under *Tarasoff* and their clinical responsibilities to their clients.

A recent survey of psychiatric residents in San Francisco showed that nearly half had issued Tarasoff-type warnings (R. L. Binder & McNiel, 1996). In most cases, the intended victim had already been aware of the threat. Most of the patients were told by their therapists that warnings had been issued. Though issuing a warning produced no clear effects on the therapeutic relationship in most cases, negative effects were reported in some cases.

In the wake of the *Tarasoff* decision, we might also ask, "How far might the duty to warn be extended?" Might a therapist be responsible for protecting society at large when more generalized threats are made that do not identify a specific victim? To date, the *Tarasoff* ruling has not been extended to cases in which generalized threats are made (Knapp & VanderCreek, 1982). In Vermont, however, the *Tarasoff* decision has been extended to include a duty to warn in situations when threats against property are made (*Peck v. Counseling Service of Addison County*, 1985).

The *Tarasoff* decision carries the force of law only in California (DeBell & Jones, 1997b). Other states vary in terms of their statutes that apply in duty-to-warn cases. Therapists must be aware of the statutes and legal precedents that exist in the particular states in which they practice. Therapists must also not lose sight of the primary therapeutic responsibility to their clients when legal issues arise. They must balance the obligation to meet their responsibilities under duty-to-warn provisions with the need to help their clients resolve the feelings of rage and anger that give rise to violent threats.

* * * * * * * *

We opened this book by noting that despite the public impression that abnormal behavior affects only the few, it actually affects nearly every one of us in one way or another. Let us close by suggesting that if we all work together to foster research into the causes, treatment, and prevention of abnormal behavior, perhaps we can meet the multifaceted challenges that abnormal behavior poses to so many of us and to our society at large.

SUMMARY

Psychiatric Commitment

The legal process by which people are placed in psychiatric institutions against their will is called psychiatric or civil commitment. Psychiatric commitment is intended to provide treatment to people who are deemed to suffer from mental disorders and to pose a threat to themselves or others. Legal or criminal commitment, by comparison, involves the placement of a person in a psychiatric institution for treatment who has been acquitted of a crime by reason of insanity. In voluntary hospitalization, people voluntarily seek treatment in a psychiatric facility and can leave of their own accord, unless a court rules otherwise.

Predicting Dangerousness

Although people must be judged dangerous to be placed involuntarily in a psychiatric facility, mental-health professionals have not demonstrated any special ability to predict dangerousness. Factors that may account for the failure to predict dangerousness include (1) recognizing violent tendencies post hoc is easier than predicting it, (2) generalized perceptions of violent tendencies may not predict specific acts of violence, (3) lack of agreement in defining violence or dangerousness, (4) base-rate problems, (5) unlikelihood of direct threats of violence, and (6) predictions based on hospital behavior may not generalize to community settings.

Patients' Rights

Landmark court cases have clarified patients' rights in psychiatric facilities. In *Wyatt v. Stickney,* a court in Alabama imposed a minimum standard of care. In *O'Connor v. Donaldson,* the U.S. Supreme Court ruled that nondangerous mentally ill people could not be held in psychiatric facilities against their will if such people could be maintained safely in the community. In *Youngberg v. Romeo,* the U.S. Supreme Court ruled that involuntarily confined patients have a right to less restrictive types of treatment and to receive training to help them function. Court rulings, such as that of *Rogers v. Okin* in Massachusetts, have established that patients have a right to refuse medication, except in case of emergency.

The Insanity Defense

Three court cases established legal precedents for the insanity defense. In 1834, a court in Ohio applied a principle of irresistible impulse as the basis of an insanity defense. The M'Naghten rule, based on a case in England in 1843, treated the failure to appreciate the wrongfulness of one's action as the basis of legal insanity. The *Durham* rule was based on a case in the United States in 1954 in which it was held that persons did not bear criminal responsibility if their criminal behavior was the product of "mental disease or mental defect." Another set of standards developed by the American Law Institute that combines the M'Naghten and irresistible impulse principles has been adopted in some form in 22 states. People who are criminally committed may be hospitalized for an indefinite period of time, with their eventual release dependent on a determination of their mental status.

Competency to Stand Trial

People who are accused of crimes but are incapable of understanding the charges against them or assisting in their own defense can be found incompetent to stand trial and remanded to a psychiatric facility. In the case of *Jackson v. Indiana,* the U.S. Supreme Court placed restrictions on the length of time a person judged incompetent to stand trial could be held in a psychiatric facility.

The Duty to Warn

Although information disclosed by a client to a therapist generally carries a right to confidentiality, the California *Tarasoff* ruling held that therapists have a duty or obligation to warn third parties of threats made against them by their clients.

1. Under what conditions can a person be involuntarily hospitalized? What rights does a person have who has been committed?

2. How successful are professionals in predicting dangerousness? What factors limit their ability to predict dangerous behavior?

3. What are the legal rights of individuals regarding the right to treatment and the right to refuse treatment? What landmark cases were involved in establishing these rights?

4. What are the legal precedents for the insanity plea? How common are insanity pleas? How successful are they?

5. What happens to a defendant who is found not guilty by reason of insanity?

6. What is the difference between the NGRI and GBMI verdicts?

7. What is the difference between competency to stand trial and the plea of not guilty by reason of insanity?

8. What is the "duty to warn"? What landmark case established the duty? What concerns have therapists raised about the duty to warn?

GLOSSARY

A

Abnormal psychology. The branch of psychology that deals with the description, causes, and treatment of abnormal behavior patterns.

Abstinence violation effect. The tendency in people trying to maintain abstinence from a substance, such as alcohol or cigarettes, to overreact to a lapse with feelings of guilt and a sense of resignation that may then trigger a full-blown relapse.

Acculturation. The process of adapting to a new or different culture.

Acetylcholine. A type of neurotransmitter that is involved in the control of muscle contractions. Abbreviated *ACh*.

Acrophobia. Excessive, irrational fear of heights.

Acute stress disorder. A traumatic stress reaction occurring in the days and weeks following exposure to a traumatic event.

Addiction. Impaired control over the use of a chemical substance accompanied by physiological dependence on the substance.

Addison's disease. A disease caused by underactivity of the adrenal cortex.

Adjustment disorder. A maladaptive reaction to an identified stressor or stressors that occurs shortly following exposure to the stressor(s) and results in impaired functioning or signs of emotional distress that exceed what would normally be expected in the situation. The reaction may be resolved if the stressor is removed or the individual learns to adapt to it successfully.

Affect. (AF-fect). Emotion or feeling state that is attached to objects, ideas, or life experiences.

Agnosia. A disturbance of sensory perception.

Agonist. A compound that activates the same receptors as another drug or naturally produced substance.

Agoraphobia. Excessive, irrational fear of open places.

AIDS dementia complex. A form of dementia that is believed to result from an infection of the brain caused by the AIDS virus.

Al-Anon. An organization sponsoring support groups for family members of people with alcoholism.

Alarm reaction. The first stage of the general adaptation syndrome following response to a stressor, it is characterized by heightened sympathetic activity.

Alcohol persisting amnestic disorder. See *Korsakoff's syndrome*.

Alcoholism. Physiological dependence on alcohol that results in impaired personal, social, or physical functioning.

Alzheimer's disease. A progressive brain disease characterized by gradual loss of memory and intellectual functioning, personality changes, and eventual loss of ability to care for oneself.

Ambivalent. Holding conflicting feelings toward another person or goal, such as both loving and hating the same person.

Ambulatory. Able to walk about on one's own.

Amenorrhea. Absence of menstruation—a symptom of anorexia nervosa.

Amnestic disorders. Disturbances of memory associated with inability to learn new material and recall past events.

Amphetamine psychosis. A psychotic state induced by ingestion of amphetamines.

Amphetamines. Types of stimulants, such as Dexedrine and Benzedrine. Abuse can trigger an amphetamine psychosis that mimics acute episodes of schizophrenia.

Amygdala. One of a pair of almond-shaped structures in the limbic system that are involved in emotion and memory.

Anal-expulsive. In psychodynamic theory, a personality type characterized by excessive self-expression, such as extreme sloppiness or messiness.

Anal fixation. In psychodynamic theory, attachment to objects and behaviors that characterized the anal stage.

Analgesia. A state of relief from pain without loss of consciousness.

Analogue. Something that resembles something else in many respects.

Analogue study. A method of research that involves the simulation of naturally occurring conditions in a controlled setting.

Anal-retentive. In psychodynamic theory, a personality type characterized by excessive needs for self-control, such as extreme neatness and punctuality.

Anal stage. The second stage of psychosexual development in Freud's theory, in which gratification is achieved through anal activities, such as by the elimination of bodily wastes.

Analytical psychology. Jung's psychodynamic theory, which emphasizes such concepts as the collective unconscious, the existence of archetypes, and the notion of the self as a unifying force of personality.

Anhedonia. A state characterized by inability to experience pleasure.

Anorexia nervosa. An eating disorder, primarily affecting young women, which is characterized by maintenance of an abnormally low body weight, distortions of body image, intense fears of gaining weight, and, in females, amenorrhea.

Antagonist drugs. Drugs that block the actions of other drugs.

Antecedents. Factors of events that precede other events. Antecedents may or may not be causally connected to the events that follow.

Antibodies. Substances produced by white blood cells that identify and target antigens for destruction.

Antidepressants. Types of drugs that act to relieve depression. Tricyclics, MAO-inhibitors, and serotonin re-uptake inhibitors are the major classes of antidepressants.

Antigens. A substance that triggers an immune-system reponse to it. (The contraction for *anti*body *gen*erator.)

Antisocial personality disorder. A type of personality disorder that is characterized by a chronic pattern of antisocial and irresponsible behavior and lack of remorse. Also referred to as *psychopathy* and *sociopathy*.

Anxiety. An emotional state characterized by physiological arousal, unpleasant feelings of tension, and a sense of apprehension, foreboding, and dread about the future.

Anxiety disorder. A type of mental disorder in which anxiety is the prominent feature. Formerly labeled *neurosis*.

Aphasia. Impaired ability to understand or express oneself through speech.

Apnea. Temporary cessation of breathing.

Archetypes. Jung's concept of primitive images or concepts that reside in the collective unconscious.

Arteriosclerosis. A disease involving thickening and hardening of the arteries.

Assertiveness training. A set of techniques in behavior therapy, generally consisting of modeling, feedback, and behavior rehearsal, that is intended to train clients to become more self-expressive and capable of standing up for their rights.

Asylum. Historic: an institution that cared for the mentally ill. Also, a safe place or refuge.

Ataxia. Loss of muscle coordination.

Atherosclerosis. A disease process consisting of arteriosclerosis with the deposition of fatty substances along the walls of the arteries.

Attention-deficit/hyperactivity disorder. A behavior disorder of childhood that is characterized by excessive motor activity and inability to focus one's attention.

Attributional style. A personal style for explaining cause-and-effect relationships between events.

Aura. A warning sign or cluster of symptoms preceding the occurrence of a migraine headache or epileptic seizure.

Authentic. In the humanistic-existential model, a term that describes choices and actions that reflect upon our true feelings and needs.

Autism. (1) The absorption in daydreaming and fantasy. (2) A disorder in childhood characterized by failure to relate to others, lack of speech, disturbed motor behaviors, intellectual impairment, and demands for sameness in the environment. Also one of Bleuler's "Four As," describing one of the primary symptoms of schizophrenia.

Automatic thoughts. Thoughts that seem to pop into one's mind. In Aaron Beck's theory, automatic thoughts that reflect cognitive distortions induce negative feelings such as anxiety or depression.

Autonomic nervous system. The division of the peripheral nervous system that regulates the activities of glands and involuntary functions, such as respiration, heartbeat, and digestion. Abbreviated *ANS*. Also see *sympathetic* and *parasympathetic* branches of the ANS.

Aversive conditioning. A behavior therapy technique in which a maladaptive response is paired with exposure to an aversive stimulus, such as electric shock or nausea, so that a conditioned aversion develops toward the stimuli associated with the mal-

adaptive response. Also termed *aversion therapy*.

Avoidant disorder of childhood or adolescence. A childhood behavior disorder characterized by excessive fear and avoidance of strangers.

Avoidant personality disorder. A type of personality disorder characterized by avoidance of social relationships due to fears of rejection.

Axon. The long, thin part of the neuron along which nervous impulses travel.

B

Barbiturates. Types of depressants that are sometimes used to relieve anxiety or induce sleep, but which are highly addictive.

Basal ganglia. Ganglia located between the thalamus and the cerebrum in the brain that are involved in the coordination of motor activity.

Baseline. A period of time preceding the implementation of a treatment. Used to gather data regarding the rate of occurrence of the target behavior before treatment is introduced.

Behavioral assessment. The approach to clinical assessment that focuses on the objective recording or description of the problem behavior, rather than inferences about personality traits.

Behavioral interview. An approach to clinical interviewing that focuses on relating the problem behavior to antecedent stimuli and reinforcement consequences.

Behavioral rating scale. A method of behavioral assessment that involves the use of a scale to record the frequency of occurrence of target behaviors.

Behavior genetics. The field of study that addresses the role of genetics in the explanation of behavior.

Behaviorism. The school of psychology that defines psychology as the study of observable or overt behavior and focuses on investigating the relationships between stimuli and responses.

Behaviorist. One who adheres to the school of behaviorism.

Behavior modification. The application of principles of learning to the bringing about of desired behavioral changes.

Behavior therapy. See *behavior modification*.

Benzodiazepines. The class of minor tranquilizers that includes Valium and Librium.

Bereavement. The normal experience of suffering following the loss of a loved one.

Beriberi. A nutritional disorder caused by thiamine deficiency.

Biofeedback training. A method of feeding back to the individual information about bodily functions so that the person is able

to gain better control over these functions. Abbreviated *BFT*.

Biological markers. Biological characteristics that identify people with greater vulnerability to particular disorders.

Biological psychiatry. The movement within modern psychiatry that focuses on biological explanations and treatments of mental disorders.

Bipolar. Characterized by opposites, as in *bipolar disorder*.

Bipolar disorder. A disorder characterized by mood swings between states of extreme elation and severe depression. Formerly called *manic-depression*.

Bisexuals. People who are attracted to and interested in forming romantic relationships with members of both genders.

Blind. In the context of research design, a state of being unaware of whether or not one has received a treatment.

Blocking. (1) A disruption of self-expression of threatening or emotionally laden material. (2) In people with schizophrenia, a condition of suddenly becoming silent with loss of memory for what they had just discussed.

Body mass index. A person's weight, adjusted for height, calculated by dividing one's weight (in kilograms) by the square of one's height (in meters). Abbreviated *BMI*.

Bondage. A form of sadomasochism involving the binding of the arms or legs of oneself or one's partner during sexual activity.

Borderline personality disorder. A type of personality disorder that is characterized by abrupt shifts in mood, lack of a coherent sense of self, and unpredictable, impulsive behavior.

Bottoming out. A state of despair characterized by financial ruin, suicide attempts, and shattered family relationships that is experienced by many pathological gamblers.

Brain electrical activity mapping. A method of brain imaging that involves the computer analysis of data from multiple electrodes that are placed on the scalp in order to reveal areas of the brain with relatively higher or lower levels of electrical activity. Abbreviated *BEAM*.

Breathing-Related Sleep Disorder. A sleep disorder in which sleeping is repeatedly disrupted due to difficulties breathing normally.

Brief psychotic disorder. A psychotic disorder lasting from a day to a month that often follows exposure to a major stressor.

Bulimia nervosa. An eating disorder characterized by a recurrent pattern of binge eating followed by self-induced purging and accompanied by persistent overconcern with body weight and shape.

C

Cardiovascular disease. A disease or disorder of the cardiovascular system, such as coronary heart disease and hypertension.

Case. In the context of abnormal psychology, an individual who is identified as having a particular disorder or as receiving a treatment.

Case study. A carefully drawn biography that is typically constructed on the basis of clinical interviews, observations, psychological tests, and, in some cases, historical records.

Castration anxiety. In psychodynamic theory, the boy's unconscious fear that he will be castrated as a form of punishment for having incestuous wishes for his mother.

Cataplexy. The brief, sudden loss of muscular control, typically lasting from a few seconds to as long as two minutes.

Catastrophize. To exaggerate or magnify the negative consequences of events; to "blow things out of proportion."

Catatonic type. The subtype of schizophrenia characterized by gross disturbances in motor activity, such as catatonic stupor.

Catecholamine hypothesis. The belief that decreased availability of norepinephrine produces depression, while increased levels produce mania.

Catecholamines. A group of chemically related substances that function as neurotransmitters in the brain (dopamine and norepinephrine) and as hormones (epinephrine and norepinephrine).

Catharsis. (1) The discharge of states of tension associated with repression of threatening impulses or material. (2) The free expression or purging of feelings. Also called *abreaction*.

Causal relationship. A relationship between two factors or events in which one is necessary and sufficient to bring about the other. Also called a *cause-and-effect relationship*.

Central nervous system. The brain and spinal cord.

Cerebellum. A part of the hindbrain involved in coordination and balance.

Cerebral cortex. The wrinkled surface area of the cerebrum, often referred to as gray matter because of the appearance produced by the high density of cell bodies. Associative thinking is generally assumed to occur in the cerebral cortex.

Cerebrum. The large mass of the forebrain, consisting of two hemispheres.

Childhood schizophrenia. The development of a schizophrenic disorder in childhood; considered a relatively rare occurrence.

Choleric. Having or showing bad temper.

Chromosomes. The structures found in the nuclei of cells that carry the units of heredity, or *genes*.

Circadian rhythm sleep disorder. A sleep disorder characterized by disruption of sleep due to a mismatch in sleep schedules between the body's internal sleep-wake cycle and the demands of the environment. Formerly called *sleep-wake schedule disorder*.

Cirrhosis of the liver. A disease of the liver caused by chronic protein deficiency, often associated with prolonged alcohol abuse, because people who abuse alcohol may not follow a proper diet.

Civil commitment. The legal process involved in placing an individual in a mental institution, even against his or her will. Also called *psychiatric commitment*.

Clanging. In people with schizophrenia, the tendency to string words together because they rhyme or sound alike.

Classical conditioning. A simple form of learning in which a previously neutral stimulus (the conditioned stimulus) comes to elicit the response (the conditioned response) that is usually elicited by a second stimulus as a result of being paired repeatedly with the second stimulus. Also called *Pavlovian conditioning*.

Claustrophobia. Excessive, irrational fear of tight, small places.

Client-centered therapy. Another name for Carl Rogers' *person-centered therapy*.

Closed-ended questions. Questionnaire or test items that have a limited range of response options.

Cocaine. A stimulant derived from coca leaves.

Coefficient alpha. A measure of internal consistency or reliability: the average inter-correlation among the items composing a particular scale or test.

Cognition. Mental processes such as sensation and perception, memory, intelligence, language, thought, and problem solving.

Cognitive disorders. A category of mental disorders characterized by impaired cognitive abilities and daily functioning in which biological causation is either known or presumed.

Cognitive restructuring. A cognitive therapy method that involves replacing irrational or self-defeating thoughts and attitudes with rational alternatives.

Cognitive-specificity hypothesis. In Aaron Beck's theory, the belief that links different feeling states such as depression and anxiety to particular kinds of automatic thoughts.

Cognitive therapy. (1) The name of Aaron Beck's kind of psychotherapy, which challenges the distorted thought patterns that give rise to or exacerbate clients' problems. (2) More generally, a form of psychotherapy that addresses clients' cognitive processes, usually their self-defeating attitudes.

Cognitive triad of depression. In Aaron Beck's theory, the view that depression derives from the adoption of negative views of oneself, the environment, and the future.

Collective unconscious. In Carl Jung's theory, the hypothesized storehouse of archetypes and racial memories.

Comatose. In a coma, a state of deep prolonged unconsciousness.

Community psychology. The branch of psychology that focuses on changing social systems in the community in the interest of preventing and remedying maladaptive behavior.

Competencies. In social-learning theory, a type of person variable characterized by knowledge and skills.

Compulsion. A repetitive or ritualistic behavior that the person feels compelled to perform, such as compulsive hand-washing.

Compulsion to utter. In psychodynamic theory, the urge to verbally express repressed material.

Computed tomography. The generation of a computer-enhanced image of the internal structures of the brain by means of passing a narrow X-ray beam through the head at different angles. Abbreviated *CT scan*.

Concordance. Agreement.

Concrete operations. The stage of cognitive development in Jean Piaget's theory that corresponds to the development of logical thought processes involving the relationships among objects with respect to such properties as conservation and reversibility.

Concurrent validity. A type of test validity that is determined on the basis of the statistical relationship or correlation between the test and a criterion measure taken at the same point in time.

Concussion. A blow to, or jarring of, the head that results in momentary loss of consciousness or disruption of brain functioning.

Conditional positive regard. In Carl Rogers's theory, valuing other people on the basis of whether their behavior meets with one's approval.

Conditioned response. (1) In classical conditioning, a learned or acquired response to a previously neutral stimulus. (2) A response to a conditioned stimulus. Abbreviated *CR*.

Conditioned stimulus. A previously neutral stimulus that comes to evoke a conditioned response following repeated pairings with a stimulus (unconditioned stimulus) that had already evoked that response. Abbreviated *CS*.

Conditions of worth. Standards by which one judges the worth or value of oneself or others.

Conduct disorder. A pattern of abnormal behavior in childhood characterized by disruptive, antisocial behavior.

Congruence. In Carl Rogers's theory, the fit between one's self-concept and one's thoughts, behaviors, and feelings. One of the principal characteristics of effective person-centered therapists.

Conscious. Aware.

Construct. (CON-struct). A hypothetical concept such as *id* or *hunger* that is proposed to exist within people and help explain behavior.

Construct validity. (1) The degree to which a test or instrument measures the hypothetical construct that it purports to measures. (2) In experiments, the degree to which treatment effects can be accounted for by the theoretical mechanisms or constructs that are represented by the independent variables.

Content validity. (1) The degree to which the content of a test or measure represents the content domain of the construct it purports to measure. (2) The degree to which the content of a test or measure covers a representative sample of the behaviors associated with the construct dimension or trait in question.

Continuous amnesia. A form of dissociative amnesia in which the person loses the memory of all events occurring since the problem began.

Contrasted groups approach. A method of concurrent validity in which group membership is used as the criterion by which the validity of a test is measured. The ability of the test to differentiate between two or more comparison groups (for example, people with schizophrenia vs. normals) is taken as evidence of concurrent validity.

Controlled social drinking. A controversial approach to treating problem drinkers in which the goal of treatment is the maintenance of controlled social drinking in moderate amounts, rather than total abstinence.

Control subjects. Subjects who do not receive the experimental treatment or manipulation but for whom all other conditions are held constant.

Contusion. Brain trauma caused by jarring the brain with sufficient force that the brain is shifted and pressed against the skull, causing structural damage to the soft brain tissue.

Conversion disorder. A type of somatoform disorder characterized by loss or impairment of physical function in the absence of any organic causes that might account for the changes. Formerly called *hysteria* or *hysterical neurosis*.

Corpus callosum. A thick bundle of fibers that connects the two hemispheres of the brain.

Correlation. A relationship or association between two or more variables. A correlation between variables may suggest, but does not prove, that a causal relationship exists between the them.

Correlation coefficient. A statistic that expresses the strength and direction (positive or negative) of the relationship between two variables.

Corticosteroids. Steroids manufactured by the adrenal cortex that are involved in regulating the metabolism of carbohydrates and which increase resistance to stress by stemming inflammation and allergic reactions. Also called *cortical steroids*.

Countertransference. In psychoanalysis, the transfer of feelings that the analyst holds towards other persons in her or his life onto the client.

Covert sensitization. A technique of aversive conditioning that aims to help a client discontinue undesired behavior by associating the behavior with imagined aversive stimuli.

Crack. The hardened, smokable form of cocaine.

Creative self. In Alfred Adler's theory, the self-aware part of the personality that strives to achieve its potential.

Cretinism. A disorder caused by thyroid deficiency in childhood that is characterized by stunted growth and mental retardation.

Criterion validity. The degree to which a test or instrument correlates with an independent, external criterion (standard) representing the construct or trait that the test or instrument is intended to measure. There are two general types of criterion validity: concurrent validity and predictive validity.

Cross-fostering study. A method of determining heritability of a trait or disorder by examining differences in prevalence among adoptees reared by either adoptive parents or biological parents who possessed the trait or disorder in question. Evidence that the disorder followed biological rather than adoptive parentage favors the heritability of the trait or disorder.

Cultural-familial retardation. A milder form of mental retardation that is believed to result, or at least be influenced by, impoverishment in the child's home environment.

Culture-bound. Referring to patterns of behavior that are found within only one or a few cultural contexts.

Cushing's syndrome. A relatively rare disease that is caused by overactivity of the adrenal cortex and involves both physical and psychological changes.

Cyclothymic disorder. A mood disorder characterized by a chronic pattern of mild mood swings between depression and mania that are not of sufficient severity to be classified as bipolar disorder.

Cytomegalovirus. A source of infection that, in pregnant women, carries a risk of mental retardation to the unborn child.

D

Defense mechanisms. In psychodynamic theory, the reality-distorting strategies used by the ego to shield itself from conscious awareness of anxiety-evoking or troubling material.

Deinstitionalization. The practice of discharging large numbers of hospitalized mental patients to the community and of reducing the need for new admissions through the development of alternative treatment approaches such as halfway houses and crisis intervention services.

Delirium. A state of mental confusion, disorientation, and extreme difficulties focusing attention.

Delirium tremens. A withdrawal syndrome that often occurs following a sudden decrease or cessation of drinking in chronic alcoholics; it is characterized by extreme restlessness, sweating, disorientation, and hallucinations. Abbreviated *DTs*.

Delta-9–tetrahydrocannabinol. The major active ingredient in marijuana. Abbreviated *THC*.

Delusion. A firmly held but inaccurate belief that persists despite evidence that it has no basis in reality.

Delusional disorder. A type of psychosis characterized by the presence of persistent delusions, often of a paranoid nature, that do not have the bizarre quality of the type often found in paranoid schizophrenia. Other than the delusion itself, the person's behavior may appear entirely normal.

Dementia. A state of deterioration of mental functioning, involving impairment of memory, thinking, judgment, use of language, and ability to carry through purposeful movements, and eventually resulting in personality changes.

Dementia praecox. The term given by Kraepelin to the disorder we now call schizophrenia.

Demonological model. The model that explains abnormal behavior in terms of supernatural forces, such as possession by or a pact with the devil.

Dendrites. The rootlike structures at the end of the neuron that receive nerve impulses from other neurons.

Dependent personality disorder. A type of personality disorder characterized by difficulties making independent decisions and overly dependent behaviors.

Dependent variable. A measure of outcome in a scientific study that is assumed to be dependent on the effects of the independent variable.

Depersonalization. Feelings of unreality or detachment from one's self or one's body, as if one were a robot or functioning on automatic pilot, or observing oneself from outside.

Depersonalization disorder. A disorder characterized by persistent or recurrent episodes of depersonalization.

Depressant. A drug that lowers the level of activity of the central nervous system.

Derealization. Loss of the sense of reality of one's surroundings, experienced in terms of strange changes in one's environment (for example, people or objects changing size or shape), or in the sense of the passage of time.

Description. In science, the representation of observations without interpretation or inferences as to their nature or meaning. Description can be contrasted with inference, which is the process of drawing conclusions based on observations.

Desperation phase. The latter stage of pathological gambling in which the gambler hits *rock bottom*.

Determinant. (1) A factor that establishes (gives rise to) and sets limits, as on behavior. (2) A factor that is believed to govern responses to the Rorschach inkblot test—properties such as form, shading, texture, or color, and sense of movement implied by the features of the blot or the percept that the respondent imposes on the blot.

Detoxification. The process of ridding the system of alcohol or drugs under supervised conditions in which withdrawal symptoms can be monitored and controlled.

Deviation IQ. An intelligence quotient that is derived by determining the deviation between the individual's score and the norm (mean).

Dialogue. In Gestalt therapy, a technique in which one enacts a confrontation between two opposing parts of one's personality, such as between one's top dog and underdog.

Diathesis-stress. A model of abnormal behavior that posits that abnormal behavior patterns, such as schizophrenia, involve the interaction of genetic and environmental influences. In this model, a genetic predisposition, or diathesis, increases the individual's vulnerability to develop the disorder in response to stressful life circumstances. If, however, the level of stress is kept under the person's particular threshold, the disorder may never develop, even among people with the genetic predisposition.

Disorganized type. The subtype of schizophrenia that is characterized by disorganized behavior, bizarre delusions, and vivid hallucinations. Formerly *hebephrenic schizophrenia*.

Disorientation. A state of mental confusion or lack of awareness with respect to time, place, or the identity of oneself or others.

Displacement. In psychodynamic theory, a type of defense mechanism that involves the transferring of impulses toward threatening or unacceptable objects onto more acceptable or safer objects.

Disruptive behavior disorders. A category of behavior disorders in childhood involving socially disruptive behavior patterns, including attention-deficit hyperactivity disorder, conduct disorder, and oppositional defiant disorder.

Dissociative amnesia. A type of dissociative disorder in which a person experiences memory losses in the absence of any identifiable organic cause. But general knowledge and skills are usually retained.

Dissociative disorder. A category of disorders involving sudden changes in consciousness or self-identity, including dissociative amnesia, dissociative fugue, and dissociative identity disorder, and depersonalization disorder.

Dissociative fugue. A type of dissociative disorder in which one suddenly flies from one's life situation, travels to a new location, assumes a new identity, and has amnesia for past personal material. The person usually retains skills and other abilities and may appear to others in the new environment to be leading a normal life.

Dissociative identity disorder. A dissociative disorder in which a person has two or more distinct, or alter, personalities.

Distress. A state of physical or emotional pain or suffering.

Dizygotic twins. Twins who develop from separate fertilized eggs. Also called fraternal twins. Abbreviated *DZ twins*. Often contrasted with *monozygotic (MZ) twins* in studies of heritability of particular traits or disorders.

Dopamine. A neurotransmitter of the catecholamine class that is involved in Parkinson's disease and is believed to play a role in schizophrenia (see *Dopamine theory*).

Dopamine theory. The biochemical theory of schizophrenia that proposes that schizophrenia involves the action of dopamine.

Double-bind communications. A pattern of communication involving the transmission of contradictory or mixed messages without acknowledgment of the inherent conflict; posited by some theorists to play a role in the development of schizophrenia.

Double depression. Persons diagnosed with both *major depressive disorder* and *dysthymic disorder*.

Down syndrome. A condition caused by a chromosomal abnormality involving an extra chromosome on the 21st pair ("trisomy 21"), it is characterized by mental retardation and various physical abnormalities. Formerly called *mongolism* and *Down's syndrome*.

Drive for superiority. In Adler's theory, a term describing the desire to compensate for feelings of inferiority.

Duty to warn. An obligation imposed on therapists to warn third parties of threats made against them by the therapists' clients. The *Tarasoff* case established the legal basis for duty-to-warn provisions.

Dyslexia. A type of learning disorder characterized by impaired reading ability.

Dyspareunia. Persistent or recurrent pain experienced during or following sexual intercourse.

Dyssomnias. A category of sleep disorders involving disturbances in the amount, quality, or timing of sleep.

Dysthymic disorder. A mild but chronic type of depressive disorder.

E

Eclectic. The adoption of principles or techniques from various systems or theories.

Ego. In psychodynamic theory, the psychic structure corresponding to the concept of the self. The ego is governed by the reality principle and is responsible for finding socially acceptable outlets for the urgings of the id. The ego is characterized by the capacity to tolerate frustration and delay gratification.

Ego analyst. Psychodynamically oriented therapists who are influenced by ego psychology.

Ego dystonic. Behavior or feelings that are perceived to be foreign or alien to one's self-identity.

Ego-dystonic homosexuality. A term used in the DSM to refer to a sense of discomfort with their sexual orientation that may be experienced by gay males or lesbians who would prefer to have a heterosexual orientation.

Ego ideal. In Freud's view, the configuration of higher social values and moral ideals embodied in the superego.

Ego identity. In Erik Erikson's view, the sense of personal identity: the achievement of a firm sense of who one is and what one stands for.

Ego psychology. The approach of modern psychodynamic theorists that posits that the ego has energy and strivings of its own apart from the id. Ego psychologists focus more on the conscious strivings of the ego than on the hypothesized unconscious functioning of the id.

Ego syntonic. Behavior or feelings that are perceived as natural or compatible parts of the self.

Electra complex. In psychodynamic theory, the term used to describe the conflict in the young girl during the phallic stage of development involving her longing for her father and her resentment of her mother.

Electroconvulsive therapy. The induction of a convulsive seizure by means of passing an electric current through the head; used primarily in the treatment of severe depression. Abbreviated *ECT*.

Electrodermal response. Changes in the electrical conductivity of the skin following exposure to a stimulus.

Electroencephalograph. An instrument for measuring the electrical activity of the brain (brain waves). Abbreviated *EEG*.

Electrolytes. Nonmetallic substances that serve as electrical conductors. In the body, electrolytes, such as dissolved salt, play vital roles in cell functioning, such as the maintenance of appropriate fluid balance in cells.

Electromyograph. An instrument for measuring muscle tension which is often used in biofeedback training. Abbreviated *EMG*.

Emotion-focused coping. A style of coping with stress that attempts to minimize emotional responsiveness rather than deal with the source of stress directly (for example, the use of denial to avoid thinking about the stress, or the use of tranquilizers to quell feelings of anxiety).

Empathetic understanding. In Carl Rogers's theory, the ability to understand a client's experiences and feelings from the client's frame of reference. It is considered one of the principal characteristics of effective person-centered therapists.

Encephalitis. An inflammation of the brain.

Encoding. The stage of information processing that involves the modification of information for placement in memory.

Encopresis. Loss or lack of bowel control beyond the age of expected control that cannot be accounted for by physical causes.

Encounter group. A specialized form of group therapy or group process that focuses on increased self-awareness in a setting that encourages open expression of feelings.

Endocrine system. The system of ductless glands in the body that directly secrete hormones into the bloodstream.

Endogenous. Referring to abnormal behavior patterns that appear to arise from one's nature (genetic factors) rather than one's nurture (environmental influences).

Endorphins. Natural substances that function as neurotransmitters in the brain and are similar in their effects to morphine.

Enuresis. Loss or lack of bladder control beyond the age of expected control that cannot be accounted for by physical causes.

Epidemiological method. A method of research involved in tracking the rates of occurrence of particular disorders among different groups.

Epinephrine. A hormone produced by the adrenal medulla that is involved in stimulating the sympathetic division of the autonomic nervous system. Also called *adrenaline*.

Erogenous zone. A part of the body that is sensitive to sexual stimulation.

Eros. Freud's concept of the basic life instinct, which seeks to preserve and perpetuate life.

Erotomania. A form of delusional disorder characterized by delusional beliefs that one is loved by someone of high social status, even though one may have only a passing or even a non-existent relationship with the alleged lover. Also called the *love delusion*.

Estrogen. A female sex hormone involved in promoting growth of female sexual characteristics and regulating the menstrual cycle.

Etiology. Cause or origin; the study of causality. Plural, *etiologies*.

Exhaustion stage. The third stage of the general adaptation syndrome (GAS), which is characterized by a lowering of resistance, increased parasympathetic activity, and possible physical deterioration.

Exhibitionism. A type of paraphilia almost exclusively occurring in males, in which the man experiences persistent and recurrent sexual urges and sexually arousing fantasies involving the exposure of his genitals to a stranger and either has acted upon these urges or feels strongly distressed by them.

Exorcism. A ritual intended to expel demons or evil spirits from a person believed to be possessed.

Expectancies. In social-learning theory, a person variable describing people's predictions. Expectancies may refer to signs that suggest the occurrence of other events and to the outcomes of particular behaviors, as in "if-then" statements.

Experimental method. A scientific method that aims to discover cause-and-effect relationships by means of manipulating the independent variable(s) and observing their effects on the dependent variable(s).

Experimental subject. (1) In an experiment, a subject receiving a treatment or intervention, in contrast to a *control subject*. (2) More generally, one who participates in an experiment.

External attribution. In the reformulated helplessness theory, a type of attribution involving the belief that the cause of an event involves factors outside the self. Contrast with *internal attribution*.

External validity. A type of experimental validity involving the degree to which the experimental results can be generalized to other settings and populations.

Extinguish. In classical conditioning, to weaken a conditioned response by presenting the conditioned stimulus in the absence of the unconditioned stimulus. In operant conditioning, to weaken a previously reinforced response by withholding or withdrawing reinforcement.

Extraversion. A personality trait describing someone whose interests and attention are directed to people and things outside the self. Extraverted people tend to be sociable, outgoing, and self-expressive. Opposite of *introversion*.

F

Face validity. An aspect of content validity: the degree to which the content of a test or measure bears an apparent or obvious relationship to the constructs or traits it is purported to measure.

Factitious disorder. A type of mental disorder characterized by the intentional fabrication of psychological or physical symptoms for no apparent gain.

Factor analysis. A statistical technique for determining relationships that exist among items, such as items on psychological tests or personality scales.

False negative. An incorrect appraisal that people are free of a particular disorder when in fact they are not.

Family therapy. A form of therapy in which the family unit is treated as the client.

Fat cells. Cells that store fat. Also called *adipose tissue*.

Fear. An unpleasant, negative emotion characterized by the perception of a specific threat, sympathetic nervous system activity, and tendencies to avoid the feared object.

Fear-stimulus hierarchy. An ordered series of increasingly more fearful stimuli. Used in the behavioral techniques of *systematic desensitization* and *gradual exposure*.

577

Feedback. Information about one's behavior.

Female sexual arousal disorder. A type of sexual dysfunction in women, involving difficulties becoming sexually aroused, as defined by a lack of vaginal lubrication or failure to maintain sufficient lubrication to complete the sexual act, or lack of sexual excitement or pleasure during sexual activity.

Fetal alcohol syndrome. A cluster of symptoms appearing in children whose mothers drank alcohol during certain stages of pregnancy, characterized by distinct facial features and developmental delays. Abbreviated *FAS*.

Fetishism. A type of paraphilia in which a person uses an inanimate object or a body part (*partialism*) as a focus of sexual interest and as a source of arousal.

Fight-or-flight reaction. The hypothesized inborn tendency to respond to a threat by means of fighting the threat or fleeing.

First-rank symptoms. In Kurt Schneider's view, the primary features of schizophrenia, such as hallucinations and delusions, which distinctly characterize the disorder.

Fixation. In psychodynamic theory, arrested development in the form of attachment to objects of an earlier stage that occurs as the result of excessive or inadequate gratification at that stage.

Flashback. (1) The vivid re-experiencing of a past event, which may be difficult to distinguish from current reality. (2) The experience of sensory distortions or hallucinations occurring days or weeks after usage of LSD or other hallucinogenic drugs that mimics the drug's effects.

Forced-choice format. A method of structuring test questions that requires respondents to select among a set number of possible answers.

Forcible rape. The legal term for rape or forced sexual intercourse with a nonconsenting person.

Form level. The appropriateness of fit between a person's response to a Rorschach ink blot and the features of the blot itself.

Four As. In Bleuler's view, the primary characteristics of schizophrenia: (*loose*) *associations*, (*blunted or inappropriate*) *affect*, *ambivalence*, and *autism*.

Frame of reference. In Carl Rogers's view, the person's unique patterning of attitudes, perceptions, and beliefs about the world, according to which the person evaluates events.

Free association. In psychoanalysis, the method of verbalizing thoughts as they occur without any conscious attempt to edit or censure them.

Freebasing. A method of ingesting cocaine by means of heating the drug with ether to separate its most potent component (its "free base") and then smoking the extract.

Frotteurism. A type of paraphilia, characterized by recurrent sexual urges or sexually arousing fantasies involving bumping and rubbing against nonconsenting persons for sexual gratification and the person had either acted upon these urges or is strongly distressed by them.

Frustration. (1) The thwarting of a motive or pursuit of a goal. (2) The emotion produced by the thwarting of a motive or pursuit of a goal.

Functional analysis. Analysis of behavior in terms of antecedent stimuli and and consequent stimuli (potential reinforcers).

G

GABA. Gamma-aminobutyric acid (GABA), an inhibitory neurotransmitter, believed to play a role in anxiety.

Galvanic skin response. A measure of the change in electrical activity of the skin caused by increased activity of the sweat glands that accompanies states of sympathetic nervous system arousal, such as when the person is anxious. Abbreviated *GSR*.

Gamma-aminobutyric acid (GABA). See *GABA*.

Gastrointestinal disorders. Disorders of the stomach and intestines, such as ulcers or colitis.

Gender identity. One's psychological sense of being female or being male.

Gender-identity disorder. A disorder in which the individual believes that her or his anatomic gender is inconsistent with her or his psychological sense of being female or male.

Gender roles. The characteristic ways in which males and females are expected to behave within a given culture.

General adaptation syndrome. In Selye's view, the body's three-stage response to states of prolonged or intense stress. Abbreviated *GAS*.

Generalized amnesia. A form of dissociative amnesia in which people lose memories of their entire lives, although they retain their basic habits, tastes, and skills.

Generalized anxiety disorder. A type of anxiety disorder characterized by general feelings of dread and foreboding and heightened states of sympathetic arousal. Formerly referred to as *free-floating anxiety*.

General paresis. A degenerative brain disorder that occurs during the final stage of syphillis.

Genes. The units found on chromosomes that carry heredity.

Genetic predisposition. A tendency to develop a behavior pattern that is determined by one's heredity.

Genetics. The science of heredity.

Genital stage. In psychodynamic theory, the fifth stage of psychosexual development that corresponds to mature sexuality and is characterized by the expression of libido through sexual intercourse with an adult member of the opposite gender.

Genotype. (1) The genetic constitution of an individual or a group. (2) The sum total of traits that one inherits from one's parents.

Genuineness. In Carl Rogers's view, the ability to recognize and express one's true feelings. Genuineness is considered to be a characteristic of the effective person-centered therapist.

Gestalt therapy. The approach to psychotherapy originated by Fritz Perls that seeks to help people integrate the conflicting parts of their personalities through directive exercises designed to help people perceive their whole selves.

Global attribution. In the reformulated helplessness theory, a type of attribution involving the belief that the cause of an event involved generalized, rather than specific factors. Contrast with *specific attribution*.

Gonads. The sex glands of an organism that have reproductive functions; the testes in men, the ovaries in women.

Gradual exposure. In behavior therapy, a method of overcoming fears through a stepwise process of direct exposure to increasingly fearful stimuli.

Group therapy. A form of psychotherapy in which several individuals receive treatment at the same time in a group format.

H

Halfway house. A protected or supervised environment in the community, which provides a bridge or compromise between living in the psychiatric hospital and independent community living.

Hallucination. A perception that occurs in the absence of an external stimulus that is confused with reality.

Hallucinogenic. A substance that gives rise to hallucinations.

Hashish. A drug derived from the resin of the marijuana plant—*Cannabis sativa*. Often called *hash*.

Health psychology. The branch of psychology involved in the study of the relationships between psychological factors (e.g., coping styles, belief patterns, overt behaviors) and physical illness. Health psychology seeks to apply knowledge of these relationships to help people lower their risk of developing disease or improving their ability to cope with disease through making adaptive behavioral and cognitive changes.

Hemoglobin. The red compound found in red blood cells that carries oxygen from the lungs to the tissues and carries away carbon dioxide from the tissues to the lungs.

Heroin. A type of opiate or narcotic drug derived from morphine that has strong addictive properties.

Heterosexism. The culturally based belief system that holds that only reproductive sexuality is psychologically healthy and morally correct.

Heterozygote. A plant or animal that is a hybrid, inheriting genes for two unlike characteristics.

Hierarchy of needs. In Abraham Maslow's theory, the ordered series of needs that motivate behavior.

High strain. Referring to jobs that impose great stress on workers.

Hippocampus. One of a pair of structures in the limbic system that are involved in processes of memory.

Histrionic personality disorder. A type of personality disorder characterized by excessive need to be the center of attention and to receive reassurance, praise, and approval from others. Such persons often appear overly dramatic and emotional in their behavior.

Homophobia. Hatred and fear of lesbians and gay males.

Homosexuality. The sexual orientation characterized by erotic interest in, and development of romantic relationships with, members of one's own gender.

Homozygotes. A plant or organism having genes with like characteristics.

Hormones. Substances secreted by endocrine glands that regulate bodily functions and promote the development or growth of body structures.

Humors. Historic: the vital bodily fluids considered responsible for one's disposition and health, as in Hippocrates's belief that the health of the body and mind depended on the balance of four humors in the body: phlegm, black bile, blood, and yellow bile.

Huntington's disease. A degenerative disease that is transmitted genetically and is characterized by jerking and twisting movements, psychotic behavior, and mental deterioration.

Hydrocarbons. Chemical compounds consisting of hydrogen and carbon that are a constituent of cigarette smoke.

Hyperactivity. An abnormal behavior pattern found most often in young boys that is characterized by difficulties maintaining attention and extreme restlessness.

Hypersomnia. A condition relating to a pattern of excessive sleepiness during the day.

Hypertension. High blood pressure.

Hyperthyroidism. A physical condition caused by excesses of the hormone thyroxin, it is characterized by excitability, insomnia, and weight loss. Also called *Graves' disease.*

Hyperventilation. A pattern of overly rapid breathing associated with anxiety in which one breathes off too much carbon dioxide, leading to feelings of light-headedness and further distress.

Hypnosis. A trance-like state induced by suggestion in which one is generally passive and responsive to the commands of the hypnotist.

Hypnotics. Drugs, such as sedatives and anesthetics, that induce partial or complete unconsciousness and that are commonly used in the treatment of sleep disorders.

Hypoactive sexual desire disorder. Persistent or recurrent lack of sexual interest or sexual fantasies.

Hypochondriasis. A somatoform disorder that is characterized by persistent beliefs that one has a serious medical condition despite the lack of medical evidence to support such beliefs.

Hypoglycemia. A metabolic disorder involving low levels of blood sugar that is characterized by lack of energy, dizziness, and shakiness.

Hypomanic episodes. Mild manic episodes.

Hypothalamus. A structure in the lower middle part of the brain that is involved in regulating body temperature, emotion, and motivation.

Hypothesis. An assumption that is tested through experimentation.

Hypothyroidism. A physical condition caused by deficiencies of the hormone thyroxin that is characterized by sluggishness and lowered metabolism.

Hypoxia. Deficiencies in the supply of oxygen to the brain or other organs.

Hypoxyphilia. A paraphilia in which a person seeks sexual gratification by being deprived of oxygen by means of using a noose, plastic bag, chemical, or pressure on the chest.

Hysteria. Former term for *conversion disorder.*

I

Id. In psychodynamic theory, the unconscious psychic structure that is present at birth. The id contains instinctive drives and is governed by the pleasure principle.

Ideas of persecution. A form of delusional thinking characterized by false beliefs that one is being persecuted or victimized by others.

Ideas of reference. A form of delusional thinking in which a person reads personal meaning into the behavior of others or external events that are completely independent of the person.

Identification. (1) In psychodynamic theory, the process of incorporating the personality or behavior of others. (2) In social-learning theory, a process of imitation by which children acquire behaviors similar to those of role models.

Identity diffusion. See *role diffusion.*

Immune surveillance theory. The belief that cancer results from a breakdown in the body's immune system in which the immune system fails to mark and destroy mutant cells, allowing them to spread.

Immune system. The body's system for recognizing and destroying antigens (foreign bodies) that invade the body, mutated cells, and worn-out cells.

Impotence. See *male erectile disorder.*

Impulse control disorders. Disorders involving the failure to control impulses that result in harm to oneself or others, such as pathological gambling or kleptomania.

Incidence. The number of new cases of a disorder occurring within a specific period of time.

Independent variable. A factor in an experiment that is manipulated so that its effects can be measured or observed.

Individual psychology. The psychodynamic theory developed by Alfred Adler.

Individual response specificity. The belief that people respond to the same stressor in idiosyncratic ways.

Infarction. The development of an infarct, or area of dead or dying tissue, resulting from the blocking or obstruction of blood vessels normally serving that tissue.

Inference. A conclusion that is drawn from data.

Inferiority complex. In Adler's view, the feelings of inferiority that are believed to be a central source of motivation.

Inflammation. The response to an injured part in which increased blood flow brings an increased number of white blood cells and results in reddening, warming, and swelling of the area.

Inhibited orgasm. Persistent or recurrent delay in achieving orgasm following an adequate period of sexually stimulating activity.

Inquiry. In Rorschach terminology, the phase of the testing process in which the examiner poses probing questions to uncover the factors that determined the subject's responses.

Insanity defense. A form of legal defense in which a defendant in a criminal case pleads innocence on the basis of insanity.

Insight. In psychotherapy, the attainment of awareness and understanding of one's true motives and feelings.

Insomnia. A term applying to difficulties falling asleep, remaining asleep, or achieving restorative sleep.

Institutionalization syndrome. A behavioral pattern characteristic of patients in institutional settings that is marked by dependency, obedience to authority, and passivity.

Intake interview. The process of gathering information from new clients through the use of a structured series of questions.

Intelligence. (1) The global capacity to understand the world and cope with its challenges. (2) The trait or traits associated with successful performance on intelligence tests.

Intelligence quotient. A measure of intelligence derived on the basis of scores on an intelligence test. It is called a quotient because it was originally derived by dividing a respondent's *mental age* by her or his actual age. Abbreviated *IQ*.

Internal attribution. In the reformulated helplessness theory, a type of attribution involving the belief that the cause of an event involved factors within oneself. Contrasted with *external attribution*.

Internal consistency. Reliability as measured by the cohesiveness or interrelationships of the items on a test or scale.

Internal validity. A type of experimental validity involving the degree to which manipulation of the independent variable(s) can be causally related to changes in the dependent variable(s).

Interpretation. In psychoanalysis, an explanation of a client's behavior or verbalizations offered by the analyst.

Interrater reliability. A measure of reliability of a test based on the agreement between raters.

Intoxication. A state of drunkenness.

Introjection. In psychodynamic theory, the process of unconsciously incorporating features of the personality of another person within one's own ego structure.

In vivo. In real life.

Involuntary. Automatic or without conscious direction, as in the cases of bodily processes such as heartbeat and respiration.

K

Kleptomania. An impulse control disorder characterized by compulsive stealing.

Knob. The swollen ending of an axon terminal.

Koro syndrome. A culture-related somatoform disorder, found primarily in China, in which people fear that their genitals are shrinking and retracting into the body.

Korsakoff's syndrome. A form of brain damage that is associated with chronic thiamine deficiency. The syndrome is associated with chronic alcoholism and is characterized by memory loss, disorientation, and the tendency to invent memories to replace lost memories (confabulation). Also called *alcohol persisting amnestic disorder*.

L

La belle indifférence. A French term describing the lack of concern over one's symptoms displayed by some people with conversion disorder.

Laceration. The most serious type of brain trauma, this involves an injury to the brain that is caused by a foreign object that pierces the skull, such as a bullet or a piece of shrapnel.

Latency stage. According to psychoanalytic theory, the fourth stage of psychosexual development, which is characterized by repression of sexual impulses.

Latent content. In psychodynamic theory, the underlying or symbolic content of dreams.

Learned helplessness. In Seligman's model, a behavior pattern characterized by passivity and perceptions of lack of control that develops because of a history of failure to be able to exercise control over one's environment.

Learning disorder. Noted deficiency in a specific learning ability, which is remarkable because of the individual's general intelligence and exposure to learning opportunities.

Legal commitment. The legal process involved in confining a person found "not guilty by reason of insanity" in a mental institution; also called *criminal commitment*.

Leukocytes. White blood cells. Leukocytes comprise part of the body's immune system.

Libido. In psychodynamic theory, the energy of Eros, the life instinct. Generally, sexual drive or energy.

Limbic system. A group of forebrain structures, consisting of the amygdala, hippocampus, thalamus, and hypothalamus that are involved in processes of learning and memory and basic drives involving hunger, thirst, sex, and aggression.

Lipoprotein. A cluster of fat and protein that serves as a vehicle for transporting fats through the blood system.

Localized amnesia. A form of dissociative amnesia in which memory is lost for all events occurring during a particular period of time.

Locus of control. One's perception of the site (internal or external) of the capacity to generate reinforcement. People who believe that they have the capacity to generate or attain reinforcements are said to have an internal locus of control. People who rely on others or luck for reinforcement are said to have an external locus of control.

Longitudinal studies. Research studies in which subjects are followed over time. Longitudinal studies have helped researchers identify factors in early life that may predict the later development of disorders such as schizophrenia.

Losing phase. A middle phase of a "gambling career" in which losses begin to mount and gambling may increase in the attempt to break even.

LSD. See *lysergic acid diethylamide*.

Lysergic acid diethylamide. A type of hallucinogenic drug.

M

Magnetic resonance imaging. Formation of a computer-generated image of the anatomical details of the brain by measuring the signals that these structures emit when the head is placed in a strong magnetic field. Abbreviated *MRI*.

Major depressive disorder. A severe mood disorder characterized by the occurrence of major depressive episodes in the absence of a history of manic episodes. Major depressive disorder is characterized by a range of features such as depressed mood, lack of interest or pleasure in usual activities, lack of energy or motivation, and changes in appetite or sleep patterns.

Major tranquilizer. A type of tranquilizer used primarily in the treatment of psychotic behavior, such as Thorazine. Also called an *antipsychotic* drug.

Male erectile disorder. A sexual dysfunction in males, characterized by difficulty in achieving or maintaining erection during sexual activity.

Malingering. Faking illness so as to avoid or escape work or other duties, or to obtain benefits.

Manic. Relating to mania, as in the manic phase of a bipolar disorder.

Manic episode. A period of unrealistically heightened euphoria, extreme restlessness, and excessive activity characterized by disorganized behavior and impaired judgment. Alternates with major depressive episodes in bipolar disorder.

Manifest content. In psychodynamic theory, the reported content or apparent meaning of dreams.

Mantra. In meditation, a resonant sounding word or sound that is repeated to induce a state of relaxation and a narrowing of consciousness.

Marijuana. An hallucinogenic-type drug derived from the *Cannabis sativa* plant.

Markers. (1) Characteristics that identify individuals who are most vulnerable to a particular disorder or who are already afflicted with the disorder. Studies of HR (high-risk) children aim to identify potential markers for schizophrenia. The DST (dexamethasone suppression test) may represent a possible biological marker for depression.

Medical model. A biological perspective in which abnormal behavior is viewed as symptomatic of underlying illness.

Medulla. An area of the hindbrain involved in the regulation of heartbeat and respiration.

Melancholia. A state of severe depression.

Meningitis. An inflammation of the meninges, or membranes covering the brain and spinal cord, often caused by a bacterial infection.

Menopause. The cessation of menstruation.

Mental age. The age equivalent that corresponds to the person's level of intelligence, as measured by performance on the Stanford Binet Intelligence Scale.

Mental retardation. (1) A generalized delay or impairment in the development of intellectual and adaptive abilities. (2) Substantially lower intellectual functioning, as determined by an IQ of 70 or below.

Mental status examination. A structured clinical evaluation to determine various aspects of the client's mental functioning.

Meta-analysis. A statistical technique for combining the results of different studies into an overall average. In psychotherapy research, meta-analysis is used to compute the average benefit or size of effect associated with psychotherapy overall, or with different forms of therapy, in relation to control groups.

Metabolic rate. The rate at which energy is consumed in the body.

Methadone. An artificial narcotic that lacks the rush associated with heroin, which is used to help people addicted to heroin abstain from it without incurring an abstinence syndrome.

Model. In social-learning theory, a person whose behavior patterns are imitated by others.

Modeling. In behavior therapy, a technique for helping a client acquire new behavior by means of having the therapist or members of a therapy group demonstrate a target behavior that is then imitated by a client.

Monoamine oxidase (MAO) inhibitors. Antidepressants that act to increase the availability of neurotransmitters in the brain by inhibiting the actions of an enzyme, monoamine oxidase, that normally breaks down, or degrades, neurotransmitters (norepinephrine and serotonin) in the synaptic cleft.

Monogenic model. A single-gene model of genetic transmission in schizophrenia.

Monozygotic twins. Twins who develop from the same fertilized egg and therefore share identical genes. Also called identical twins. Abbreviated *MZ twins*. Contrast with fraternal, or *dizygotic (DZ) twins*.

Mood. The pervasive quality of an individual's emotional experience, as in depressed mood, anxious mood, or elated mood.

Mood disorder. A type of disorder characterized by disturbances of mood, as in depressive disorders (*major depressive disorder* or *dysthymic disorder*) or bipolar disorders (bipolar disorder and *cyclothymic disorder*).

Moral principle. In psychodynamic theory, the principle that governs the superego to set moral standards and enforce adherence to them.

Moral therapy. A 19th century treatment philosophy that emphasized that hospitalized mental patients should be treated with care and understanding in a pleasant environment, not shackled in chains.

Morphine. A strongly addicting, narcotic drug derived from the opium poppy that relieves pain and induces feelings of well-being.

Motor cortex. The part of the cerebral cortex, located in the frontal lobe, that is involved in controlling muscular responses.

Mourning. Normal feelings or expressions of grief following a loss. See *bereavement*.

Movement. In Rorschach terminology, responses to the Rorschach test that involve perceptions of the figures as animated (for example, running, dancing, or flying), which may be suggestive of intelligence and creativity on the part of the respondent.

Multifactorial-polygenic model. A model of genetic transmission of schizophrenia that maintains that schizophrenia is caused by the interactive or combined effects of multiple genes and environmental influences.

Multi-infarct dementia. A form of mental deterioration that is caused by multiple strokes or other forms of brain damage.

Multiphasic. Referring to several aspects of the personality, as in the Minnesota Multiphasic Personality Inventory.

Münchausen syndrome. A type of factitious disorder characterized by the feigning of medical symptoms for no apparent purpose other than getting admitted or remaining in hospitals.

Musterbation. Albert Ellis's term for a type of rigid thought pattern characterized by the tendency to impose absolutist expectations on oneself: One thinks that one "must" achieve a certain goal, as in "I *must* get an A in this course or else!"

Myocardial infarction. A breakdown of the tissue of the heart due to an obstruction of the blood vessels that supply blood to the affected area—a heart attack.

Myocarditis. An inflammation of the muscle tissue of the heart (myocardium).

N

Naloxone. A drug that prevents users from becoming high if they subsequently take heroin. Some people are placed on naloxone after being withdrawn from heroin to prevent return to heroin.

Naltrexone. A chemical cousin of naloxone that blocks the high from alcohol as well as opiates and is now approved for use in treating alcoholism.

Narcissistic personality disorder. A type of personality disorder characterized by the adoption of an inflated self-image and demands for constant attention and admiration, among other features.

Narcolepsy. A sleep disorder characterized by sudden, irresistible episodes of sleep ("sleep attacks").

Narcotics. Drugs, such as opiates, that are used for pain relief and treatment of insomnia, but which have strong addictive potential.

Naturalistic-observation method. A method of scientific research in which the behavior of subjects is carefully and unobtrusively observed and measured in their natural environments.

Negative correlation. A statistical relationship between two variables such that increases in one variable are associated with decreases in the other.

Negative reinforcer. A reinforcer whose removal increases the frequency of an operant behavior. Anxiety, pain, and social disapproval often function as negative reinforcers; that their removal tends to increase the rate of the immediately preceding behavior. Contrast with *positive reinforcer*.

Negative symptoms. The deficits or behavioral deficiencies associated with schizophrenia, such as social skills deficits, social withdrawal, flattened affect, poverty of speech and thought, psychomotor retardation, failure to experience pleasure in pleasant activities.

Neo-Freudians. A term used to describe the "second generation" of theorists who followed in the Freudian tradition. On the whole, neo-Freudians (such as Jung, Adler, Horney, Sullivan) placed greater emphasis on the importance of cultural and social influences on behavior and lesser importance on sexual impulses and the functioning of the id.

Neologisms. A type of disturbed thinking associated with schizophrenia involving the coining of new words.

Neuroleptics. A group of antipsychotic drugs used in the treatment of schizophrenia, such as the phenothiazines (Thorazine, Mellaril, etc.).

Neurons. Nerve cells.

Neuropsychology. The field of psychology that focuses on the study of relationships between the brain and behavior.

Neurosis. The type or types, respectively, of nonpsychotic behavioral disturbances characterized chiefly by the use of defensive behaviors to control anxiety, in which the person is generally able to function but is impaired in some aspect(s) of functioning. Plural: *neuroses.*

Neurotic anxiety. In psychodynamic theory, the feelings of anxiety that stem from the unconscious perception of threat that unacceptable impulses may rise to the level of consciousness or become expressed in overt behavior.

Neuroticism. A trait describing a general neurotic quality involving such characteristics as anxious, worrisome behavior, apprehension about the future, and avoidance behavior.

Neurotransmitter. A chemical substance that serves as a type of messenger by transmitting neural impulses from one neuron to another.

Nicotine. A stimulant found in tobacco.

Nightmare disorder. A sleep disorder characterized by recurrent awakenings from sleep due to the occurrence of frightening nightmares. Formerly called *dream anxiety disorder.*

Nonspecific treatment factors. The characteristics that are not specific to any one form of psychotherapy, but tend to be shared by psychotherapies, such as the attention a client receives from a therapist and the therapist's encouragement of the client's sense of hope and positive expectancies.

Norepinephrine. A type of neurotransmitter of the catecholamine class.

Nuclear magnetic resonance. See *magnetic resonance imaging.*

O

Obesity. Excessive body weight or plumpness, often defined as weighing at least 20% above one's ideal body weight.

Objective tests. Tests that allow a limited, specified range of response options or answers so that they can be scored objectively.

Object-relations. The person's relationships to the internalized representations or "objects" of other's personalities that have been introjected within the person's ego structure. See *object-relations theory.*

Object-relations theory. In psychodynamic theory, the viewpoint that focuses on the influences of the internalized representations (called "objects") within the person's ego structure of the personalities of parents and other figures of strong attachment.

Obsession. A recurring or nagging thought or image that seems beyond the individual's ability to control.

Obsessive-compulsive personality disorder. A type of personality disorder characterized by rigid ways of relating to others, perfectionistic tendencies, lack of spontaneity, and excessive attention to details.

Oedipus complex. In psychodynamic theory, the conflict that occurs during the phallic stage of development in which the boy incestuously desires his mother and perceives his father as a rival for his mother's love and attention. The counterpart in girls involves incestuous desires to possess the father, combined with jealous rivalry with the mother for father's love and resentment of the mother, whom she blames for lacking a penis.

Open-ended questions. A type of question that provides an unlimited range of response options.

Operant conditioning. A form of learning in which the organism acquires new behaviors on the basis of reinforcement.

Opiate. A type of depressant drug with strong addictive properties that is derived from the opium poppy and provides relief from pain and feelings of euphoria.

Opioid. A natural or synthetic (artificial) drug with opiate-like properties and effects.

Oppositional defiant disorder. A disorder in childhood or adolescence characterized by excessive oppositionality or tendencies to refuse requests from parents and others.

Optimum level of arousal. The level of arousal associated with peak performance and maximum feelings of well-being.

Oral stage. In psychodynamic theory, the first of Freud's stages of psychosexual development, during which pleasure is primarily sought through such oral activities as sucking and biting.

Orienting response. An unlearned pattern of responses to an incoming stimulus, including pupil dilation, particular brain wave patterns associated with states of attention, and changes in the electrical conductivity of the skin (GSR).

Osteoporosis. A physical disorder caused by calcium deficiency that is characterized

by extreme brittleness of the bones. (From the Greek *osteon,* meaning "bone," and the Latin *porus,* meaning "pore.")

Overanxious disorder. A disorder in childhood or adolescence characterized by excessive anxiety or worrisome behavior.

P

Panic disorder. A type of anxiety disorder characterized by the repeated occurrence of episodes of intense anxiety or panic.

Paranoid. Referring to irrational suspicions.

Paranoid personality disorder. A type of personality disorder characterized by persistent suspiciousness of the motives of others, but not to the point of holding clear-cut delusions.

Paranoid type. A subtype of schizophrenia characterized by hallucinations and systematized delusions, commonly involving themes of persecution.

Paraphilias. Sexual deviations or types of sexual disorders in which the person experiences recurrent sexual urges and sexually arousing fantasies involving nonhuman objects (such as articles of clothing), inappropriate or nonconsenting partners (for example, children), or situations producing humiliation or pain to oneself or one's partner. The person has either acted upon such urges or is strongly distressed by them.

Parasomnias. A category of sleep disorders involving the occurrence of abnormal behaviors or physiological events occurring during sleep or at the transition between wakefulness and sleep.

Parasympathetic. Relating to the activity of the parasympathetic branch of the autonomic nervous system. See *sympathetic division.*

Parkinson's disease. A progressive disease of the basal ganglia, it is characterized by muscle tremor and shakiness, rigidity, difficulty walking, poor control over fine body movements, lack of facial muscle tonus, and cognitive impairment in some cases, especially in later stages of the disorder.

Pathogen. An organism such as a bacterium or virus that can cause disease.

Pathological gambler. A person who gambles habitually despite consistent losses. A compulsive gambler.

Peak experience. In humanistic theory, a brief moment of rapture that stems from the realization that one is on the path toward self-actualization.

Pellagra. A disease caused by deficiency of niacin characterized by skin eruptions and various behavioral features.

Penile strain gauge. A device for measuring the size of penile erection.

Performance anxiety. Fear relating to the threat of failing to perform adequately.

Peripheral nervous system. The part of the nervous system that consists of the somatic nervous system and the autonomic nervous system.

Perseveration. The persistent repetition of the same thought or response.

Personality disorders. Types of abnormal behavior patterns involving excessively rigid patterns of behaviors, or ways of relating to others, that ultimately become self-defeating because their rigidity prevents adjustment to external demands.

Person-centered therapy. Carl Rogers's method of psychotherapy, emphasizing the establishment of a warm, accepting therapeutic relationship that frees clients to engage in the process of self-exploration and self-acceptance.

Person variables. In social-learning theory, the influences on behavior of characteristics relating to the person, including encoding strategies, competencies, expectancies, subjective values, and self-regulatory systems and plans.

Pervasive developmental disorder. A disorder characterized by gross impairment in the development of a broad array of skills relating to social, cognitive, and language functioning.

Phallic stage. In psychodynamic theory, Freud's third stage of psychosexual development, characterized by sexual interest focused on the phallic region and the development of incestuous desires for the parent of the opposite gender and rivalry with the parent of the same gender (the Oedipus complex).

Phenothiazines. A group of antipsychotic drugs or "major tranquilizers" used in the treatment of schizophrenia.

Phenotype. The representation of the total array of traits of an organism, as influenced by the interaction of nature (genetic factors) and nurture (environmental factors).

Phenylketonuria. A genetic disorder that prevents the metabolization of phenylpyruvic acid, leading to mental retardation. Abbreviated *PKU*.

Phlegmatic. Slow and stolid.

Phobia. An excessive, irrational fear that is out of proportion to the degree of danger in a stimulus or a situation.

Phrenologist. Practitioner of the study of bumps on a person's head as indications of the individual's underlying traits or characteristics.

Physiological dependence A state of physical dependence on a drug in which the user's body comes to depend upon a steady supply of the drug.

Pick's disease. An form of dementia, similar in its features to Alzheimer's disease, but characterized by the presence of specific abnormalities (Pick's bodies) in nerve cells and the absence of the neurofibrillary tangles and plaques found in Alzheimer's disease.

Placebo. (pluh-SEE-bo). An inert medication or form of bogus treatment that is intended to control for the effects of expectancies. Sometimes referred to as a "sugar pill."

Play therapy. A form of psychodynamic therapy with children in which play activities and objects are used as a means of helping children symbolically enact family conflicts or express underlying feelings or personal problems.

Pleasure principle. In psychodynamic theory, the governing principle of the id, involving the demands for immediate gratification of instinctive needs.

Polygenic. Traits or characteristics that are determined by more than one gene.

Polymorphously perverse. In psychodynamic theory, the belief that humans are born with the capacity of achieving sexual gratification through various ways, such as heterosexual, homosexual, and autoerotic (pleasure from one's body organs) activities.

Polysomnographic. Relating to the simultaneous measurement of multiple physiological responses during sleep or attempted sleep.

Pons. A brain structure, located in the hindbrain, which is involved in respiration.

Population. A total group of people, other organisms, or events.

Pornography. Portrayals of explicit sexual activity that are intended to sexually arouse the observer.

Positive correlation. A statistical relationship between two variables such that increases in one variable are associated with increases in the other.

Positive reinforcers. Types of reinforcers that increase the frequency of behavior when they are presented. Food and social approval are generally, but not always, positive reinforcers. Contrast with *negative reinforcer*.

Positive symptoms. The more flagrant features of schizophrenia associated with behavioral excesses, such as hallucinations, delusions, bizarre behavior, and thought disorder.

Positron-emission tomography. A brain imaging technique in which a computer-generated image of the neural activity of regions of the brain is formed by tracing the amounts of glucose used in the various regions. Abbreviated *PET scan*.

Possession. In demonology, a type of superstitious belief in which abnormal behavior is taken as a sign that the individual has become possessed by demons or the Devil, usually as a form of retribution or the result of making a pact with the Devil.

Postpartum depression. Persistent and severe mood changes that occur following childbirth.

Posttraumatic stress disorder. A type of disorder involving impaired functioning following exposure to a traumatic experience, such as combat, physical assault or rape, natural or technological disasters, etc., in which the person experiences such problems as reliving or reexperiencing the trauma, intense fear, avoidance of event-related stimuli, generalized "numbing" of emotional responsiveness, and heightened autonomic arousal.

Preconscious. In psychodynamic theory, descriptive of material that lies outside of present awareness but which can be brought into awareness by focusing attention. See also *unconscious*.

Predictive validity. The degree to which a test response or score is predictive of some criterion behavior (such as school performance) in the future.

Prefrontal cortex. The area of the frontal lobes lying in front of the motor cortex, it is involved in higher mental processes involving thinking, planning, attention, memory, speech, and language.

Prefrontal lobotomy. A form of psychosurgery in which certain neural pathways in the brain are severed in the attempt to control disturbed behavior.

Pregenital. In psychodynamic theory, referring to characteristics that are typical of stages of psychosexual development that precede the genital stage.

Premature ejaculation. A type of sexual dysfunction involving a persistent or recurrent pattern of ejaculation occurring during sexual activity at a point before the man desires it.

Prepared conditioning. The belief that people are genetically prepared to acquire fear responses to certain classes of stimuli, such as fears of large animals, snakes, heights, or even strangers. Although the development of such phobias may have had survival value to our prehistoric ancestors, such behavior patterns may be less functional today.

Presenile dementias. Dementias that begin at age 65 or earlier.

Presenting problem. The complaint that prompts initial contact with a helping professional.

Pressured speech. An outpouring of speech in which words seem to surge urgently for expression, as in a manic state.

Prevalence. The overall number of cases of a disorder existing in the population during a given period of time.

Primary gains. In psychodynamic theory, the relief from anxiety obtained through the development of a neurotic symptom.

Primary process thinking. In psychodynamic theory, the mental process in infancy by which the id seeks gratification of primitive impulses by means of imagining that it possesses what it desires. Thinking which is illogical, magical, and fails to discriminate between reality and fantasy.

Primary reinforcers. Natural reinforcers or stimuli that have reinforcement value without learning. Water, food, warmth, and relief from pain are examples of primary reinforcers. Contrast with *secondary reinforcer*.

Primary sex characteristics. The characteristics that distinguish the genders and are directly involved in reproduction, such as the sex organs.

Proband. The initial diagnosed case of a given disorder.

Problem-focused coping. A form of coping with stress characterized by directly confronting the source of the stress.

Problem-solving therapy. A form of therapy that focuses on helping people develop more effective problem-solving skills.

Process schizophrenia. A type of schizophrenia characterized by gradual onset, poor premorbid functioning, and poor outcomes. Contrast with *reactive schizophrenia*.

Prodromal phase. (1) A stage in which the early features or signs of a disorder become apparent. (2) In schizophrenia, the period of decline in functioning that precedes the development of the first acute psychotic episode.

Progesterone. A female sex hormone involved in promoting the growth and development of the sex organs and helping to maintain pregnancy.

Prognosis. A prediction of the probable course or outcome of a disorder.

Projection. In psychodynamic theory, a defense mechanism in which one's own impulses are attributed to another person.

Projective test. A psychological test that presents ambiguous or vague stimuli onto which the examinee is believed to project on her own personality and unconscious motives in making a response. The Rorschach and thematic apperception test (TAT) are examples of projective tests.

Prophylactic. Relating to a device, drug, or remedy designed to preserve health or prevent disease.

Psychiatric commitment. See *civil commitment*.

Psychiatrist. A physician who specializes in the diagnosis and treatment of emotional disorders.

Psychic. (1) Relating to mental phenomena. (2) A person who claims to be sensitive to supernatural forces.

Psychic determinism. The belief that emotions and behavior are caused by the interplay of internal mental processes.

Psychoactive. Describing chemical substances or drugs that have psychological effects.

Psychoanalysis. (1) The theoretical model of personality developed by Sigmund Freud. (2) The method of psychotherapy developed by Sigmund Freud.

Psychoanalytic theory. The theoretical model of personality developed by Freud. Also called *psychoanalysis*.

Psychodrama. The method of group therapy developed by Moreno in which people express emotional responses and enact conflicts with significant others in their lives through dramatized role-enactments.

Psychodynamic model. The theoretical model of Freud and his followers in which behavior is viewed as the product of clashing forces within the personality.

Psychological dependence. Reliance, as on a substance, although one may not be physiologically dependent on the substance.

Psychological hardiness. A cluster of stress-buffering traits characterized by commitment, challenge, and control.

Psychological resilience. The capacity to recover mentally and emotionally from, or to make adaptive adjustments to, adversity.

Psychologist. A person with advanced graduate training in psychology. A clinical psychologist is a type of psychologist who specializes in abnormal behavior.

Psychometric approach. A method of psychological assessment that seeks to use psychological tests to identify and measure the reasonably stable traits in an individual's personality, which are believed to largely determine the person's behavior.

Psychomotor retardation. A general slowing down of motor behavior and psychological functioning.

Psychoneuroimmunology. The field of scientific investigation that studies relationships between psychological factors, such as coping styles, attitudes, and behavior patterns, and immunological functioning.

Psychopharmacology. The field of study that examines the effects of drugs on behavior and psychological functioning and that explores the use of psychoactive drugs in the treatment of emotional disorders.

Psychophysiological. Referring to physiological correlates or underpinnings of psychological events.

Psychosexual. Descriptive of the stages of human development in Freud's theory in which sexual energy (libido) becomes expressed through different erogenous zones of the body during different developmental stages.

Psychosis. A type of major psychological disorder in which people show impaired ability to interpret reality and difficulties in meeting the demands of daily life. Schizophrenia is a prominent example of a psychotic disorder. Plural: *psychoses*.

Psychosocial. Relating to interpersonal relationships and social interactions that influence behavior and development.

Psychosocial development. Erikson's theory of personality development that extends through multiple stages of development from infancy through old age.

Psychotherapy. A method of helping involving a systematic interaction between a therapist and a client that brings psychological principles to bear on influencing the client's thoughts, feelings, or behaviors in order to help that client overcome abnormal behavior or adjust to problems in living.

Psychotropic drugs. Drugs that are used in the treatment of emotional disorders whose main effects are psychological or behavioral.

Punishments. Unpleasant stimuli that suppress the frequency of the behaviors they follow.

R

Random sample. A sample that is drawn in such a way that every member of a population has an equal probability of being selected.

Rape trauma syndrome. A cluster of symptoms that victims often experience in the aftermath of rape.

Rapid flight of ideas. A characteristic of manic behavior involving rapid speech and changes of topics.

Rapid smoking. A method of aversive conditioning in which cigarettes are inhaled more rapidly than usual, making smoking an aversive experience.

Rapport. In psychotherapy, the interpersonal relationship between a therapist and a client that is characterized by harmony, trust, and cooperation.

Rational-emotive behavior therapy. Albert Ellis's method of cognitive therapy, which focuses on helping clients challenge and correct irrational beliefs that produce emotional and behavioral difficulties.

Rationalization. In psychodynamic theory, a type of defense mechanism involving a process of self-deception in the form of finding justifications for unacceptable impulses, ideas, or behavior.

Reactive schizophrenia. A type of schizophrenia characterized by a relatively abrupt onset that is believed to be precipitated by stressful or traumatic events. Contrast with *process schizophrenia*.

Reality anxiety. The concept in psychodynamic theory relating to reality-based fear.

Reality principle. In psychodynamic theory, the governing principle of the ego that involves consideration of what is socially acceptable and practical in gratifying needs.

Reality testing. The ability to perceive the world accurately and to distinguish reality from fantasy.

Rebound anxiety. The occurrence of strong anxiety following withdrawal from a tranquilizer.

Receptor site. A part of a dendrite on the receiving neuron that is structured to receive a neurotransmitter.

Rehearsal. In behavior therapy, a practice opportunity in which a person enacts a desired response and receives feedback from others.

Reinforcement. A stimulus that increases the frequency of the response that it follows. See *positive* and *negative*, and *primary* and *secondary* reinforcers.

Relapse. A recurrence of a problem behavior or disorder.

Relapse-prevention training. A cognitive-behavioral technique that is used in the treatment of addictive behaviors that involves the use of behavioral and cognitive strategies to resist temptations and prevent lapses from becoming relapses.

Relaxation training. A technique for acquiring skills of self-relaxation, such as progressive muscle relaxation.

Reliability. In psychological assessment, the consistency of a measuring instrument, such as a psychological test or rating scale. There are various ways of measuring reliability, such as test-retest reliability, internal consistency, and inter-rater reliability. Also see *validity*.

REM sleep. REM (rapid eye-movement) sleep is the stage of sleep associated with dreaming that is characterized by the appearance of rapid eye movements under the closed eyelids.

Repressed memories. Recollections of events, typically from childhood, that were forgotten or repressed until they surfaced into awareness at a later time, usually during adulthood.

Repression. In psychodynamic theory, a type of defense mechanism involving the ejection from awareness of anxiety-provoking ideas, images, or impulses, without the conscious awareness that one has done so.

Residual phase. In schizophrenia, the phase of the disorder that follows an acute

phase, characterized by a return to a level of functioning that was typical of the prodromal phase.

Resistance. During psychoanalysis, the blocking of thoughts or feelings that would evoke anxiety if they were consciously experienced. Resistance may also take the form of missed sessions by the client or the client's verbal confrontation with the analyst as threatening material is about to be uncovered.

Resistance stage. In Selye's view, the second stage of the general adaptation syndrome, involving the attempt to withstand prolonged stress and preserve bodily resources. Also called the *adaptation stage*.

Response. A reaction to a stimulus.

Reticular activating system. A part of the brain involved in processes of attention, sleep, and arousal. Abbreviated *RAS*.

Reverse tolerance. The acquisition of decreased tolerance for a psychoactive drug such that lesser amounts of the substance become capable, over time, of producing the same effects as greater amounts.

Reward. A pleasant stimulus or event that increases the frequency of the behavior it follows.

Role diffusion. In Erikson's theory, a state of confusion, aimlessness, insecurity, and heightened susceptibility to the suggestions of others that is associated with the failure to acquire a firm sense of ego identity during adolescence.

S

Sadomasochism. Sexual activities between partners involving the attainment of gratification by means of inflicting and receiving pain and humiliation.

Sample. Part of a population.

Sanguine. A cheerful disposition.

Sanism. The negative stereotyping of people who are identified as mentally ill.

Schizoaffective disorder. A type of psychotic disorder in which individuals experience both severe mood disturbance and features associated with schizophrenia.

Schizoid personality disorder. A type of personality disorder characterized by a persistent lack of interest in social relationships, flattened affect, and social withdrawal.

Schizophrenia. An enduring psychosis that involves failure to maintain integrated personality functioning, impaired reality testing, and disturbances in thinking. Common features of schizophrenia include delusions, hallucinations, flattened or inappropriate affect, and bizarre behavior. Also see *schizophreniform disorder, schizotypal personality disorder,* and *brief reactive psychosis*.

Schizophreniform disorder. A psychotic disorder lasting less than 6 months in duration with features that resemble schizophrenia.

Schizophrenogenic mother. The type of mother, described as cold but also overprotective, that was believed to be capable of causing schizophrenia in her children. Research has failed to support the validity of this concept.

Schizotypal personality disorder. A type of personality disorder characterized by eccentricities or oddities of thought and behavior but without clearly psychotic features.

Secondary gains. Side-benefits associated with neuroses or other disorders, such as expressions of sympathy and increased attention from others, and release from ordinary responsibilities.

Secondary process thinking. In psychodynamic theory, the reality-based thinking processes and problem-solving activities of the ego.

Secondary reinforcers. Stimuli that gain reinforcement value through their association with established reinforcers. Money and social approval are typically secondary reinforcers. Contrast with *primary reinforcer*.

Secondary sex characteristics. The physical traits that differentiate men from women but which are not directly involved in reproduction, such as the depth of the voice and the distribution of bodily hair.

Second-rank symptoms. In Goldstein's view, symptoms associated with schizophrenia that also occur in other mental disorders.

Sedatives. Types of depressant drugs that reduce states of tension and restlessness and induce sleep.

Selection factor. A kind of confound or bias in experimental studies in which differences between experimental and control groups are due to differences in the types of subjects comprising the groups, rather than to the independent variable. It is called a selection factor because it involves a bias in the process by which subjects were selected for the treatment and control groups.

Selective abstraction. In Beck's theory, a type of cognitive distortion involving the tendency to selectively focus only on the parts of one's experiences that reflect upon one's flaws and to ignore those aspects that reveal one's strengths or competencies.

Selective amnesia. A type of dissociative amnesia involving the loss of memory for disturbing events that occurred during a certain time period.

Self. The center of one's consciousness that organizes one's sensory impressions and governs one's perceptions of the world. The sum total of one's thoughts, sensory impressions, and feelings.

Self-actualization. In humanistic psychology, the tendency to strive to become all that one is capable of being. The motive that drives one to reach one's full potential and express one's unique capabilities.

Self-efficacy expectations. Our beliefs that we can accomplish certain tasks or bring about desired results through our own efforts.

Self-esteem. One's sense of worth or value as a human being.

Self-ideals. The mental image or representation of what we expect ourselves to be.

Self-insight. Awareness of the relationships between one's behavior and one's motivations, needs, and wants.

Self-monitoring. In behavioral assessment, the process of recording or observing one's own behavior, thoughts, or emotions.

Self-psychology. Hans Kohut's theory, which describes processes that normally lead to the achievement of a cohesive sense of self or, in narcissistic personality disorder, to a grandiose but fragile sense of self.

Self-spectatoring. The tendency to observe one's behavior as if one were a spectator of oneself. People with sexual dysfunctions often become self-spectators in the sense of focusing their attention during sexual activity on the response of their sex organs rather than on their partners or the sexual stimulation itself.

Senile dementias. Forms of dementia that begin following the age of 65.

Sensate focus exercises. In sex therapy, the mutual pleasuring activities between the partners that is focused on the partners taking turns giving and receiving physical pleasure.

Sensitivity. The ability of a test or diagnostic instrument to identify people as having a given characteristic or disorder who truly have the characteristic or disorder.

Sensorium. The person's entire sensory apparatus. The term is used by clinicians to refer to the client's focusing of attention, capacity for concentration, and level of awareness of the world.

Sensory cortex. The part of the cerebral cortex, located in the parietal lobe, that receives sensory stimulation.

Separation anxiety disorder. A childhood disorder characterized by extreme fears of separation from parents or others upon whom the child is dependent.

Separation-individuation. In Margaret Mahler's theory, the process by which young children come to separate psychologically from their mothers and come to perceive themselves as separate and distinct persons.

Serotonin. A type of neurotransmitter, imbalances of which have been linked to mood disorders and anxiety.

Serotonin-reuptake inhibitor. A type of antidepressant medication that prevents serotonin from being taken back up by the transmitting neuron, thus increasing its action.

Serum cholesterol. A fatty substance (cholesterol) in the blood serum that has been implicated in cardiovascular disease.

Set point. A value that regulatory mechanisms in the body attempt to maintain. For example, these regulatory mechanisms may try to maintain a certain body weight by adjusting the rate of metabolism.

Sexual aversion disorder. A type of sexual dysfunction characterized by aversion to, and avoidance of, genital sexual contact.

Sexual masochism. A type of paraphilia characterized by sexual urges and sexually arousing fantasies involving receiving humiliation or pain in which the person has either acted upon these urges or is strongly distressed by them.

Sexual sadism. A type of paraphilia or sexual deviation characterized by recurrent sexual urges and sexually arousing fantasies involving inflicting humiliation or physical pain on sex partners in which the person has either acted upon these urges or is strongly distressed by them.

Significant. In statistics, a magnitude of difference that is taken as indicating meaningful differences between groups because of the low probability that it occurred by chance.

Simple schizophrenia. See *schizotypal personality disorder*.

Single-case experimental designs. A type of case study in which the subject (case) is used as his or her own control by varying the conditions to which the subject is exposed (by use of a *reversal* phase) or by means of a *multiple-baseline* design.

Situation variables. In social-learning theory, the external influences on behavior, such as rewards and punishments.

Sleep disorders. A diagnostic category representing persistent or recurrent sleep-related problems that cause significant personal distress or impaired functioning.

Sleep terror disorder. A sleep disorder characterized by repeated episodes of sleep terror resulting in abrupt awakenings.

Sleepwalking disorder. A type of sleep disorder involving repeated episodes of sleepwalking.

Social-learning theory. A learning-based theory that emphasizes observational learning and incorporates roles for both situation and person variables in determining behavior.

Social phobia. An excessive fear of engaging in behaviors that involve public scrutiny.

Social-skills training. In behavior therapy, a technique for helping people acquire or improve their social skills. Assertiveness training can be considered a form of social-skills training.

Sociocultural perspective. A model of abnormal behavior that places emphasis on the social and cultural influences that lead to deviant behavior, rather than on pathological influences within the person. More broadly, the model that interprets behavior within a larger social and cultural context.

Sodium lactate. A chemical substance that has been found to induce panic in some people, especially among panic-prone people.

Soma. A cell body.

Somatic nervous system. The division of the peripheral nervous system that relays information from the sense organs to the brain and transmits messages from the brain to the skeletal muscles, resulting in body movements.

Somatization disorder. A type of somatoform disorder involving recurrent multiple complaints which cannot be explained by any clear physical causes. Also called *Briquet's syndrome*.

Somatoform disorders. Disorders in which people complain of physical (somatic) problems, although no physical abnormality can be found. See *conversion disorder, hypochondriasis,* and *somatization disorder*.

Somatosensory cortex. That part of the cerebral cortex that is involved in the perception of tactile stimulation and in the regulation of voluntary motor activity.

Specific attribution. In the reformulated helplessness theory, a type of attribution involving the belief that the cause of an event involved specific, rather than generalized, factors. Contrasted with *global attribution*.

Specificity. The ability of a test or diagnostic instrument to avoid classifying people as having a characteristic or disorder who truly do not have the characteristic or disorder.

Specific phobia. A persistent but excessive fear of a specific object or situation, such as a fear of heights or of small animals.

Splitting. A term describing the inability of some persons (especially people with borderline personalities) to reconcile the positive and negative aspects of themselves and others into a cohesive integration, resulting in sudden and radical shifts between strongly positive and strongly negative feelings.

Spontaneous recovery. The recurrence of an extinguished response as a function of the passage of time.

Spontaneous remission. The sudden resolution of a psychological or physical problem or disorder. Resolution of such a problem without treatment.

Stable attribution. In the reformulated helplessness theory, a type of attribution involving the belief that the cause of an event involved stable, rather than changeable, factors. Contrast with *unstable attribution.*

Standardized interview. A highly structured form of clinical interviewing that makes use of a series of specific questions to help the clinician reach a diagnosis.

Standard scores. Scores that indicate the relative standing of raw scores in relation to the distribution of normative scores. For example, raw scores on the MMPI scales are converted into standard scores that indicate the degree to which each of the individual raw scores deviates from the mean.

Statutory rape. A legal term referring to sexual intercourse with a minor, even with the minor's consent.

Steroids. A group of hormones including testosterone, estrogen, progesterone, and corticosteroids.

Stimulus. (1) An aspect of the environment that produces a change in an organism's behavior (a response). (2) A form of physical energy, such as sound or light, that impinges on the senses.

Stratified random sample. A random sample that was drawn in such a way that certain identified subgroups within the population were represented in the sample in relation to their numbers in the population.

Stress. The demand made on an organism to adapt or adjust.

Stressor. A source of stress.

Structural family therapy. A form of family therapy that analyzes the structure of the family unit in terms of the role relationships and communications that exist within the family.

Structural hypothesis. In Freud's theory, the belief that the clashing forces within the personality could be divided into three psychic structures: the id, the ego, and the superego.

Structured interview. A means by which an interviewer obtains clinical information from a client by asking a fairly standard series of questions concerning such issues as the client's presenting complaints or problems, mental state, life circumstances, and psychosocial or developmental history.

Stupor. A state of relative or complete unconsciousness in which the person is not generally aware of, or responsive to, the environment, as in a *catatonic stupor.*

Subjective values. The values that individuals place on objects or events.

Substance abuse. The continued use of a psychoactive drug despite the knowledge that it is causing or contributing to a persistent or recurrent social, occupational, psychological, or physical problem.

Substance dependence. Impaired control over the use of a psychoactive drug and continued or even increased use despite awareness that the substance is disrupting one's life. Substance dependence is often characterized by physiological dependence.

Superego. In psychodynamic theory, the psychic structure that represents the incorporation of the moral values of the parents and important others and that floods the ego with guilt and shame when it falls short of meeting those standards. The superego is governed by the moral principle and consists of two parts, the conscience and the ego-ideal.

Supermales. Males who possess the XYY chromosomal structure, which has been associated with exaggerated male characteristics such as heavier beards, and which was linked in some earlier research to violent tendencies in some cases.

Survey method. A method of scientific research in which large samples of people are questioned by use of a survey instrument.

Survivor guilt. The feelings of guilt often experienced by survivors of calamities.

Symbiotic. (1) In biology, the living together of two different but interdependent organisms. (2) In Mahler's object-relations theory, the term used to describe the state of oneness that normally exists between mother and infant in which the infant's identity is fused with the mother's.

Sympathetic. Pertaining to the division of the autonomic nervous system that becomes active to meet the demands of stress, as in adjusting to cold temperatures, or in expending bodily reserves of energy through physical exertion or through emotional reactions, such as anxiety or fear. See *parasympathetic.*

Symptom substitution. The appearance of a new symptom as a substitute for one which has been removed or suppressed. In psychodynamic terms, a symptom, such as phobia, represents an indirect expression of an unconscious conflict. In this view, the removal of a symptom without the resolution of the underlying conflict would be expected to lead to the emergence of another symptom that would represent the continuing conflict.

Synapse. A junction between the terminal knob of one neuron and the dendrite or soma of another through which the nerve impulses pass.

Syndrome. A cluster of symptoms that is characteristic of a particular disorder.

Syphilis. A type of sexually transmitted disease, implicated in its final stages of causing a mental disorder called *general paresis.*

Systematic desensitization. A behavior therapy technique for overcoming phobias by means of exposure (in imagination or by means of slides) to progressively more fearful stimuli while one remains deeply relaxed.

Systems perspective. The view that problems reflect the systems (family, social, school, ecological, etc.) in which they are embedded.

T

Tachycardia. Abnormally rapid heart beat.

Tactile. Pertaining to the sense of touch.

Taijin-kyofu-sho. A psychiatric syndrome found in Japan that involves excessive fear of offending or causing embarrassment to others. Abbreviated *TKS.*

Tardive dyskinesia. A movement disorder characterized by involuntary movements of the face, mouth, neck, trunk, or extremities that is caused by long-term use of antipsychotic medications.

Tay-Sachs disease. A disease of lipid metabolism that is genetically transmitted and generally results in death in early childhood.

Temporal stability. The consistency of test responses across time, as measured by test-retest reliability.

Terminals. In neuropsychology, the small branching structures found at the tips of axons.

Testosterone. A male sex hormone (steroid), produced by the testes, that is involved with promoting growth of male sexual characteristics and sperm.

Test-retest reliability. A method for measuring the reliability of a test by means of comparing (correlating) the scores of the same test subjects on separate occasions.

Thalamus. A structure in the brain that is involved in relaying sensory information to the cortex and in processes relating to sleep and attention.

Theory. (1) A plausible or scientifically defensible explanation of events. (2) A formulation of the relationships underlying observed events. Theories are helpful to scientists because they provide a means of organizing observations and lead to predictions about future events.

Therapeutic community. A treatment setting, such as in a special ward in a hospital or in a community residence, in which the interactions among the residents and staff are structured to serve a therapeutic purpose.

Thermistor. A small device that is strapped to the skin for registering body temperature, as used in biofeedback training.

Thought disorder. Disturbances in thinking characterized by various features, especially the breakdown in logical associations between thoughts.

Thought insertion. A type of delusion in which people believe that their thoughts have been planted in their minds from external sources.

Thyroxin. A hormone produced by the thyroid gland that increases the metabolic rate.

Time out. A behavioral technique in which an individual who emits an undesired behavior is removed from an environment in which reinforcers are available and placed in an unreinforcing environment for a period of time as a form of punishment. Time out is frequently used in behavioral programs for modifying behavior problems in children, in combination with positive reinforcement for desirable behavior.

Token economies. Behavioral treatment programs in institutional settings in which a controlled environment is constructed such that people are reinforced for desired behaviors by receiving tokens (such as poker chips) that may be exchanged for desired rewards or privileges.

Tolerance. Physical habituation to a drug so that with frequent usage, higher doses are needed to attain similar effects.

Transcendental meditation. A popular form of meditation introduced to the United States by the Maharishi Mahesh Yogi that focuses on the repeating of a mantra to induce a meditative state. Abbreviated *TM*.

Transference relationship. In psychoanalysis, the client's transfer or generalization to the analyst of feelings and attitudes the client holds toward important figures in his or her life.

Transvestic fetishism. A type of paraphilia in heterosexual males characterized by recurrent sexual urges and sexually arousing fantasies involving dressing in female clothing in which the person has either acted upon these urges or is strongly distressed by them. Also termed *transvestism*.

Trephining. A harsh, prehistoric practice of cutting a hole in a person's skull, possibly as an ancient form of surgery for brain trauma, or possibly as a means of releasing the demons that prehistoric people may have believed caused abnormal behavior in the afflicted persons.

Trichotillomania.. A type of impulse control disorder involving persistent failure to resist urges to pull one's own hair out, producing noticeable hair loss.

Tricyclics. A group of antidepressant drugs that increase the activity of norepinephrine and serotonin in the brain by interfering with the reuptake of these neurotransmitters by transmitting neurons. Also called *TCAs* (tricyclic anti-depressants).

Tumescence. A swelling or a swollen part, as in penile tumescence (erection).

Two-factor model. O. Hobart Mowrer's belief that both operant and classical conditioning are involved in the acquisition of phobic responses. Basically, the fear component of phobia is acquired by means of classical conditioning (pairing of a previously neutral stimulus with an aversive stimulus), while the avoidance component is acquired by means of operant conditioning (relief from anxiety negatively reinforces avoidance behavior).

Type A behavior pattern. A pattern of behavior characterized by a sense of time urgency, competitiveness, and hostility. Abbreviated *TABP*.

U

Ulcers. Open sores, as in the stomach lining.

Unconditional positive regard. In Carl Rogers's view, the expression of unconditional acceptance of another person's basic worth as a person, regardless of whether one approves of all of the behavior of the other person. The ability to express unconditional positive regard is considered a quality of an effective person-centered therapist.

Unconditioned response. An unlearned response or a response to an unconditioned stimulus. Abbreviated *UR* or *UCR*.

Unconditioned stimulus. A stimulus that elicits an instinctive or unlearned response from an organism. Abbreviated *US* or *UCS*.

Unconscious. (1) In psychodynamic theory, pertaining to impulses or ideas that are not readily available to awareness, in many instances because they are kept from awareness by means of *repression*. (2) Also in psychodynamic theory, the part of the mind that contains repressed material and primitive urges of the id. (3) More gener-

ally, a state of unawareness or loss of consciousness.

Unipolar. Pertaining to a single pole or direction, as in unipolar (depressive) disorders. Contrast with *bipolar disorder*.

Unobtrusive. Not interfering.

Unstable attribution. In the reformulated helplessness theory, a type of attribution involving the belief that the cause of an event involved changeable, rather than stable, factors. Contrasted with *stable attribution*.

V

Vacillate. To move back and forth.

Vaginal plethysmograph. A device for measuring sexual arousal in females as a function of the amount of blood congestion in the vaginal cavity.

Vaginismus. A type of sexual dysfunction characterized by the recurrent or persistent contraction of the muscles surrounding the vaginal entrance, making penile entry while attempting intercourse difficult or impossible.

Validity. (1) With respect to tests, the degree to which a test measures the traits or constructs that it purports to measure. (2) With respect to experiments, the degree to which an experiment yields scientifically accurate and defensible results.

Validity scales. Groups of test items that serve to detect whether the results of a particular test are valid or whether a person responded in a random manner or in a way that was intended to create a favorable or unfavorable impression.

Variables. Conditions that are measured (dependent variables) or manipulated (independent variables) in scientific studies.

Voyeurism. A type of paraphilia characterized by recurrent sexual urges and sexually arousing fantasies involving the act of watching unsuspecting others who are naked, in the act of undressing, or engaging in sexual activity, in which the person has either acted upon these urges or is strongly distressed by them.

W

Waxy flexibility. A feature of catatonic schizophrenia in which a person's limbs are moved into a certain posture or position, which the person then rigidly maintains for a lengthy period of time.

Weaning. The process of accustoming a child to eat solid food, rather than seek nourishment through breast feeding or sucking a baby bottle.

Wernicke's disease. A brain disorder associated with chronic alcoholism that is characterized by confusion, disorientation, and difficulties maintaining balance while walking (ataxia). If left untreated, it may lead to *Korsakoff's syndrome*.

Winning phase. The first stage in a "gambling career," marked by perceptions of gambling as a pleasant pastime, in which early winnings boost self-esteem. But pathological gamblers eventually progress to stages of *losing* and *desperation*.

Withdrawal syndrome. The characteristic cluster of withdrawal symptoms following the sudden reduction or abrupt cessation of use of a psychoactive substance after physiological dependence has developed.

World view. The prevailing view of the times. (English translation of the German *Weltanschauung*.)

REFERENCES

A

Aarsland, D., et al. (1996). Relationship of aggressive behavior to other neuropsychiatric symptoms in patients with Alzheimer's disease. *American Journal of Psychiatry, 153,* 243–247.

Abenhaim, L., et al. (1996). Appetite-suppressant drugs and the risk of primary pulmonary hypertension. *The New England Journal of Medicine, 335,* 609–616.

Aber, J. L., & Allen, J. P. (1987). Effects of maltreatment of young children on young children's socioemotional development: An attachment theory perspective. *Developmental Psychology, 23,* 406–414.

Abikoff, H., & Klein, R. G. (1992). Attention-deficit hyperactivity and conduct disorder: Comorbidity and implications for treatment. *Journal of Consulting and Clinical Psychology, 60,* 881–892.

Abraham, K. (1948). The first pregenital stage of the libido (1916). In D. Bryan & A. Strachey (Eds.), *Selected papers of Karl Abraham, M. D.* London: The Hogarth Press.

Abrahamson, D. J., Barlow, D. H., Beck, J. G., Sackheim, D. K., & Kelly, J. D. (1985). The effects of attentional focus and partner responsiveness on sexual responding: Replication and extension. *Archives of Sexual Behavior, 14,* 361–371.

Abramowitz, J. (1996). Variants of exposure and response prevention in the treatment of obsessive-compulsive disorder: A meta-analysis. *Behavior Therapy, 27,* 583–600.

Abrams, D. B., et al. (1987). Psychosocial stress and coping in smokers who relapse or quit. *Health Psychology, 6,* 289–303.

Abrams, K. K., Allen, L., & Gray, J. J. (1993). Disordered eating attitudes and behaviors, psychological adjustment and ethnic identity: A comparison of Black and White female college students. *International Journal of Eating Disorders, 14,* 49–57.

Abramson, L. T., Seligman, M. E. P., & Teasdale, J. D. (1978). Learned helplessness in humans: Critique and reformulation. *Journal of Abnormal Psychology, 87,* 49–74.

Achenbach, T. M. (1978). The Child Behavior Profile: I. Boys aged 6 through 11. *Journal of Consulting and Clinical Psychology, 46,* 478–488.

Achenbach, T. M. (1982). *Developmental psychopathology* (2nd ed.). New York: Wiley.

Achenbach, T. M., & Edelbrock, C. S. (1979). The child behavior profile: I. Boys aged 12–16 and girls aged 6–11 and 12–16. *Journal of Consulting and Clinical Psychology, 47,* 223–233.

Achenbach, T. M., & Howell, C. T. (1993). Are American children's problems getting worse? A 13–year comparison. *Journal of American Academy of Child and Adolescent Psychiatry, 32,* 1145–1154.

Acierno, R. E., Hersen, M., & Van Hasselt, V. B. (1993). Interventions for panic disorder: A critical review of the literature. *Clinical Psychology Review, 13,* 393–408.

Ackerman, M. D., & Carey, M. P. (1995). Psychology's role in the assessment of erectile dysfunction: Historical precedents, current knowledge, and methods. *Journal of Consulting and Clinical Psychology, 63,* 862–876.

Ackerman, S. H., Manaker, S., & Cohen, M. I. (1981). Recent separation and the onset of peptic ulcer disease in older children and adolescents. *Psychosomatic Medicine, 43,* 305–310.

Ackourey, K. (1991). Insuring Americans with disabilities: How far can Congress go to protect traditional practices? *Emory Law Journal, 40,* 1183–1225.

Adams, K. M. (1984). Luria left in the lurch: Unfulfilled promises are not valid tests. *Journal of Clinical Neuropsychology, 6,* 455–458.

Adler, J. (1994, December 19). The endless binge. *Newsweek,* pp. 72–73.

Adler, N. E., et al. (1994). Socioeconomic status and health. The challenge of the gradient. *American Psychologist, 49,* 15–24.

Affleck, G., Tennen, H., Croog, S., & Levine, S. (1987). Causal attribution, perceived benefits, and morbidity after a heart attack: An 8–year study. *Journal of Consulting and Clinical Psychology, 55,* 29–35.

Agras, W. S. (1993). "Pharmacologic and cognitive-behavioral treatment for bulimia nervosa": Reply. *American Journal of Psychiatry, 150,* 1570.

Agras, W. S., et al. (1996). Maintenance following a very-low-calorie diet. *Journal of Consulting and Clinical Psychology, 64,* 610–613.

Agras, W. S., et al. (1997). One-year follow-up of cognitive-behavioral therapy for obese individuals with binge eating disorder. *Journal of Consulting and Clinical Psychology, 65,* 343–347.

AIDS policy: Confidentiality and disclosure. (1988). Official Actions. *American Journal of Psychiatry, 145,* 541.

Ainsworth, M. D. S. (1989). Attachments beyond infancy. *American Psychologist, 44,* 709–716.

Ainsworth, M. D. S., & Bowlby, J. (1991). An ethological approach to personality development. *American Psychologist, 46,* 333–341.

Ainsworth, M. D., et al. (1978). *Patterns of attachment: A psychological study of the Strange situation.* Hillsdale, NJ: Erlbaum.

Akbarian, S., et al. (1996). Maldistribution of interstitial neurons in prefrontal white matter of the brains of schizophrenic patients. *Archives of General Psychiatry, 53,* 425–436.

Akhtar, A. (1987). Schizoid personality disorder: A synthesis of developmental, dynamic, and descriptive features. *American Journal of Psychotherapy, 41,* 499–517.

Akhtar, N., & Bradley, E. J. (1991). Social information processing deficits of aggressive children: Present findings and implications for social skills training. *Clinical Psychology Review, 11,* 621–644.

Akhtar, S. (1988). Four culture-bound psychiatric syndromes in India. *The International Journal of Social Psychiatry, 34,* 70–74.

Akiskal, H. S. (1983). Dysthymic disorder: Psychopathology of proposed chronic depressive subtypes. *American Journal of Psychiatry, 140,* 11–20.

Alaia, S. L. (1992). Life effects of narcolepsy: Measures of negative impact, social support, and psychological well-being. *Loss, Grief and Care, 5,* 1–22.

Albert, M. S., Naeser, M. A., Duffy, F. H., & McAnulty, G. (1986). CT and EEG validators for Alzheimer's disease. In L. W. Poon (Ed.), *Handbook for clinical memory assessment of older adults* (pp. 383–392). Washington, DC: American Psychological Association.

Alcohol and Health. (1987). Rockville, MD: National Institute of Alcohol Abuse and Alcoholism.

Alcohol and the Heart: Consensus Emerges (1996, January). *Harvard Heart Letter, 6* (5).

Aldarondo, E. (1996). Risk marker analysis of the cessation and persistence of wife assault. *Journal of Consulting and Clinical Psychology, 64,* 1010–1019.

Aldrich, M. S. (1992). Narcolepsy. *Neurology, 42,* (7, Suppl 6) 34–43.

Alexander, A. B. (1981). Asthma. In S. N. Haynes & L. Gannon (Eds.), *Psychosomatic disorders: A psychophysiological approach to etiology and treatment.* New York: Praeger Books.

Alexander, F. (1939). Emotional factors in essential hypertension. *Psychosomatic Medicine, 1,* 153–216.

Alexander, F. (1950). *Psychosomatic medicine.* New York: Norton.

Alexander, P. C., et al. (1989). A comparison of group treatments of women sexually abused as children. *Journal of Consulting and Clinical Psychology, 57,* 479–483.

Alexopoulos, G. S., et al. (1996a). Disability in geriatric depression. *American Journal of Psychiatry, 153,* 877–885.

Alexopoulos, G. S., et al. (1996b). Recovery in geriatric depression. *Archives of General Psychiatry, 153,* 305–312.

Allderidge, P. (1979). Hospitals, madhouses and asylums: Cycles in the care of the insane. *British Journal of Psychiatry, 134,* 1476–1478.

Allen, J. R., & Setlow, V. P. (1991). Heterosexual transmission of HIV: A view of the future. *Journal of the American Medical Association, 266,* 1695–1696.

Allen, L. S., & Gorski, R. A. (1992). Sexual orientation and the size of the anterior commissure in the human brain. *Proceedings of the National Academy of Sciences USA, 89,* 7199–7202.

Allison, D. B., et al. (1994). A genetic analysis of relative weight among 4,020 twin pairs, with an emphasis on sex effects. *Health Psychology, 13,* 362–365.

Alloy, L. B., & Abramson, L. Y. (1988). Depressive realism: Four theoretical perspectives. In L. B. Alloy (Ed.), *Cognitive processes in depression* (pp. 223–265). New York: Guilford Press.

Alloy, L. B., & Clements, C. M. (1992). Illusion of control: Invulnerability to negative affect and depressive symptoms after laboratory and natural stressors. *Journal of Abnormal Psychology, 101,* 2234–2245.

Alpert, J. L., & Green, D. (1992). Child abuse and neglect: Perspectives on a national emergency. *Journal of Social Distress and the Homeless, 1,* 223–236.

Alter-Reid, K., Gibbs, M.S., Lachenmeyer, J. R., Sigal, J., & Mossoth, N. A. (1986). Sexual abuse of children: A review of the empirical findings. *Clinical Psychology Review, 6,* 249–266.

Altman, L. K. (1990a, April 18). Scientists see a link between alcoholism and a specific gene. *The New York Times,* pp. A1, A18.

Altman, L. K. (1990b, May 29). The evidence mounts on passive smoking. *The New York Times*, pp. C1, C8.

Altman, L. K. (1991, June 18). W.H.O. says 40 million will be infected with AIDS virus by 2000. *The New York Times*, p. C3.

Altman, L. K. (1993a, June 15). Conference ends with little hope for AIDS cure. *The New York Times*, pp. C1, C3.

Altman, L. K. (1993b, December 22). Study suggests high rate of impotence. *The New York Times*, p. C13.

Altman, L. K. (1994a, February 22). Stomach microbe offers clues to cancer as well as ulcers. *The New York Times*, p. C3.

Altman, L. K. (1994b, November 1). AIDS drugs fail to curb dementia and nerve damage. *The New York Times*, p. C3.

Altman, L. K. (1995, January 31). AIDS is now the leading killer of Americans from 25 to 44. *The New York Times*, p. C7.

Alzheimer's terrible toll. (1995, October 2). *Newsweek*, p. 36.

Amador, X. F., et al. (1998). Suicidal behavior in schizophrenia and its relationship to awareness of illness. *American Journal of Psychiatry, 153*, 1185–1188.

American Association of Mental Retardation (AAMR) (1992). *Mental retardation: Definition, classification, and systems of supports* (9th ed.). Washington, DC: Author.

American Heart Association (1990) *Heart and stroke facts*. Publication No. 55–00376. New York: Author.

American Law Institute. (1962). *Model penal code: Proposed official draft*. Philadelphia: Author.

American Medical Association. (1997, October 22/29). Suicides can still be prevented: People who talk about it do do it. *Science News Updates* [On-line].

American Psychiatric Association. (1974). *Clinical aspects of the violent individual*. Washington, DC: Author.

American Psychiatric Association (1987a). Diagnostic and statistical manual of mental disorders (3rd ed., rev.). Washington, DC: Author.

American Psychiatric Association. (1987b). Dexamethasone suppression test: An overview of its current status in psychiatry. Washington, DC: Author.

American Psychiatric Association. (1988). AIDS policy: Confidentiality and disclosure. *American Journal of Psychiatry, 145*, 541.

American Psychiatric Association. (1990). *The practice of electroconvulsive therapy*. Washington, DC: American Psychiatric Press.

American Psychiatric Association. (1991). Editorial. The APA task force report on benzodiazepine dependence, toxicity, and abuse. (Editorial), *American Journal of Psychiatry, 148*, 151–152.

American Psychiatric Association. (1993a). *DSM-IV Draft Criteria (3/1/93)*. Task Force on DSM-IV. Washington, DC: American Psychiatric Press.

American Psychiatric Association. (1993b). Practice guidelines for eating disorders. *American Journal of Psychiatry, 150*, 207–228.

American Psychiatric Association. (1994). *DSM-IV: Diagnostic and statistical manual of mental disorders* (4th ed.). Washington, DC: Author.

American Psychological Association. (1978). Report of the Task Force on the Role of Psychology in the Criminal Justice System. *American Psychologist, 33*, 1099–1113.

American Psychological Association, Committee on Lesbian and Gay Concerns. (1991). Avoiding heterosexual bias in language. *American Psychologist, 46*, 973–974.

American Psychological Association. (1992). *Big world, small screen: The role of television in American society*. Washington, DC: Author.

America's New Profile. (1994, November 28). *Business Week*, p. 32.

Amering, M., & Katschnig, H. (1990). Panic attacks and panic disorder in cross-cultural perspective. *Psychiatric Annals, 20*, 511–516.

Amering, M., et al. (1997). Embarrassment about the first panic attack predicts agoraphobia in panic disorder patients. *Behaviour Research and Therapy, 35*, 517–521.

Ames, M. A., & Houston, D. A. (1990). Legal, social, and biological definitions of pedophilia. *Archives of Sexual Behavior, 19*, 333–342.

Ammerman, R. T., Cassissi, J. E., Herson, M., et al. (1986). Consequences of physical abuse and neglect in children. *Clinical Psychology Review, 6*, 291–310.

Ancoli-Israel, S., et al., (1991). Dementia in institutionalized elderly: Relation to sleep apnea. *Journal of the American Geriatrics Society, 39*, 258–263.

Andersen, B. L. (1992). Psychological interventions for cancer patients to enhance the quality of life. *Journal of Consulting and Clinical Psychology, 60*, 552–568.

Andersen, B. L. (1997, July). Psychological interventions for individuals with cancer. *Clinician's Research Digest, Supplemental Bulletin 16*, 1–2.

Anderson, E. M., & Lambert, M. J. (1995). Short-term dynamically oriented psychotherapy: A review and meta-analysis. *Clinical Psychology Review, 15*, 503–514.

Anderson, L. P. (1991). Acculturative stress: A theory of relevance to black Americans. *Clinical Psychology Review, 11*, 685–702.

Anderson, S. R., et al. (1986). Transitional residential programming for autistic individuals. *Behavior Therapist, 9*, 205–211.

Andreasen, N. C. (1986). Scale for the assessment of thought, language, and communication (TLC). *Schizophrenia Bulletin, 12*, 473–482.

Andreasen, N. C. (1987a). The diagnosis of schizophrenia. *Schizophrenia Bulletin, 13*, 1–8.

Andreasen, N. C. (1987b). Creativity and mental illness: Prevalence rates in writers and their first-degree relatives. *American Journal of Psychiatry, 144*, 1288–1292.

Andreasen, N. C. & Flaum, M. (1991). Schizophrenia: The characteristic symptoms. *Schizophrenia Bulletin, 17*, 27–49.

Andreasen, N. C., & Grove, W. M. (1986). Thought, language, and communication in schizophrenia: Diagnosis and prognosis. *Schizophrenia Bulletin, 12*, 348–359.

Andreasen N. C., et al. (1994). Regional brain abnormalities in schizophrenia measured with magnetic resonance imaging. *Journal of the American Medical Association, 272*, 1763–1769.

Andreasen, N. C., et al. (1995). Symptoms of schizophrenia: Methods, meanings, and mechanisms. *Archives of General Psychiatry, 52*, 341–351.

Andreasen, N. C., et al. (1997). Hypofrontality in schizophrenia: Distributed dysfunctional circuits in neuroleptic-naive patients. *The Lancet, 349*, 1730–1734.

Andrews, E. L. (1997, September 9). In Germany, humble herb is a rival to Prozac. *The New York Times*, pp. C1, C7.

Andrews, G., & Harvey, R. (1981). Does psychotherapy benefit neurotic patients? *Archives of General Psychiatry, 38*, 1203–1208.

Anger doubles risk of attack for heart disease patients. (1994, March 19). *The New York Times*, p. A8.

Angier, N. (1990a, May 29). Scientists link protein fragments to Alzheimer's. *The New York Times*, p. C3.

Angier, N. (1990b, December 13). If anger ruins your day, it can shrink your life. *The New York Times*, p. B23.

Angier, N. (1991a, May 30). Gene causing common type of retardation is discovered. *The New York Times*, pp. A1, B11.

Angier, N. (1991b, August 4). Kids who can't sit still. *The New York Times*, Section 4A, pp. 30–33.

Angier, N. (1991c, August 30). Zone of brain linked to men's sexual orientation. *The New York Times*, pp. A1, D18.

Angier, N. (1993a, July 1). Report suggests homosexuality is linked to genes. *The New York Times*, pp. A12, D21.

Angier, N. (1993b, November 11). Action of gene in Huntington's disease is proving a tough puzzle. *The New York Times*, p. C3.

Angier, N. (1994, December 1). Researchers link obesity in humans to flaw in a gene. *The New York Times*, p. A1.

Angier, N. (1995, November 2). Study links brain to transsexuality. *The New York Times*, p. B15.

Angier, N. (1996, November 29). People haunted by anxiety appear to be short on a gene. *The New York Times*, pp. A1, B17.

Anglin, K., & Holtzworth-Munroe, A. (1997). Comparing the responses of maritally violent and nonviolent spouses to problematic marital and nonmarital situations: Are the skills deficits of physically aggressive husbands and wives global? *Journal of Family Psychology, 11*, 301–313.

Angold, A., & Costello, E. J. (1993). Depressive comorbidity in children and adolescents: Empirical, theoretical, and methodological issues. *American Journal of Psychiatry, 150*, 1779–1791.

Angold, A., & Costello, J. (1996). Toward establishing an empirical basis for the diagnosis of oppositional defiant disorder. *Journal of the American Academy of Child and Adolescent Psychiatry, 35*, 1205–1212.

Anonymous. (1985, June 13). Schizophrenia—A mother's agony over her son's pain. *Chicago Tribune*, Section 5:1–3.

Anthenelli, R. M., et al. (1994). A comparative study of criteria for subgrouping alcoholics: The primary/secondary diagnostic scheme versus variations of the Type 1/Type 2 criteria. *American Journal of Psychiatry, 151*, 1468–1474.

Anthony, J.C., & Helzer, J. E. (1991). Syndromes of drug abuse and dependence. In L. N. Robins & D. A. Regier (Eds.), *Psychiatric disorders in America: The Epidemiologic Catchment Area Study* (pp. 116–154). New York: The Free Press.

Anthony, J. C., Warner, L. A., & Kessler, R. C. (1994). Comparative epidemiology of dependence on tobacco, alcohol, controlled substances, and inhalants: Basic findings from the National Comorbidity Survey. *Experimental and Clinical Psychopharmacology, 2*, 244–268.

Anthony, W. A., Cohen, M., & Kennard, W. (1990). Understanding the current facts and principles of mental health systems planning. *American Psychologist, 45*, 1249–1256.

Anthony, W. A., & Liberman, R. P. (1986). The practice of psychiatric rehabilitation: Historical, conceptual, and research base. *Schizophrenia Bulletin, 12*, 542–559.

Anthony, W. Z. (1978). Brief intervention in a case of childhood trichotillomania by self-monitoring. *Journal of Behavior Therapy and Experimental Psychiatry, 9*, 173–175.

Anton, R. F. (1994). Medications for treating alcoholism. *Alcohol Health and Research World, 18*, 265– 271.

Antoni, M. H., Levine, J., Tischer, P., Green, C., & Millon, T. (1986). Refining personality assessments by combining MCMI high-point profiles and MMPI codes: IV. MMPI 89/98. *Journal of Personality Assessment, 50*, 65–72.

Antoni, M. H., Tischer, P., Levine, J., Green, C., & Millon, T. (1985). Refining personality assessments by combining MCMI high-point profiles and MMPI codes, Part I: MMPI code 28/82. *Journal of Personality Assessment, 49*, 392–398.

Antonuccio, D. O., Thomas, M., & Danton, W. G. (1997). A cost-effectiveness analysis of cognitive behavior therapy and fluoxetine (Prozac) in the treatment of depression. *Behavior Therapy, 28*, 187–210.

Antony, M. M., Brown, T. A., & Barlow, D. H. (1997). Response to hyperventilation and CO_2 inhalation of subjects with types of specific phobia, panic disorder, or no mental disorder. *American Journal of Psychiatry, 154*, 1089–1095.

APA Task Force on Laboratory Tests in Psychiatry. (1987). *American Journal of Psychiatry, 144*, 1253–1262.

Appelbaum, P. S., & Hoges, K. (1986). The right to refuse treatment: What the research reveals. *Behavioral Sciences and the Law, 4,* 279–292.

Arana, G. W., Baldessarini, R. J., Ornstein, M. (1985). The dexamethasone suppression test for diagnosis and prognosis in psychiatry: Commentary and review. *Archives of General Psychiatry, 42,* 1193–1204.

Arana, J. D. (1990). Characteristics of homeless mentally ill inpatients. *Hospital and Community Psychiatry, 41,* 674–676.

Arean, P. A., et al. (1993). Comparative effectiveness of social problem-solving therapy and reminiscence therapy as treatments for depression in older adults. *Journal of Consulting and Clinical Psychology, 61,* 1003–1010.

Arenson, K. W. (1997, December 15). Fraternity leaders appear to be the first in line for alcohol. *The New York Times,* p. A20.

Arieti, S. (1974). *Interpretation of schizophrenia* (2nd ed.). New York: Basic Books.

Arkin, R. M., Detchon, C. S., & Maruyama, G. M. (1982). Roles of attribution, affect, and cognitive interference in test anxiety. *Journal of Personality and Social Psychology, 43,* 1111–1124.

Arkowitz, H. (1995). Common factors or processes of change in psychotherapy? *Clinical Psychology: Science and Practice, 2,* 94–100.

Arndt, J., & Greenberg, J. (1996). Fantastic accounts can take many forms: False memory construction? Yes. Escape from self? We don't think so. *Psychological Inquiry, 7,* 127–132.

Arndt, S., et al. (1995). A longitudinal study of symptom dimensions in schizophrenia: Prediction and patterns of change. *Archives of General Psychiatry, 52,* 352–360.

Arnett, P. A. (1997). Autonomic responsivity in psychopaths: A critical review and theoretical proposal. *Clinical Psychology Review, 17,* 903–936.

Arnett, P. A., Smith, S. S., & Newman, J. P. (1997). Approach and avoidance motivation in psychopathic criminal offenders during passive avoidance. *Journal of Personality and Social Psychology, 72,* 1413–1428.

Arnold, E. H., O'Leary, S. G., & Edward, G. H. (1997). Father involvement and self-reported parenting of children with attention deficit-hyperactivity disorder. *Journal of Consulting and Clinical Psychology, 65,* 337–342.

Arnow, B, Kenardy, J., & Agras, W. S. (1992). Binge eating among the obese: A descriptive study. *Journal of Behavioral Medicine, 15,* 155–170.

Arntz, A. (1994) Treatment of borderline personality disorder: A challenge for cognitive-behavioral therapy. *Behaviour Research and Therapy, 32,* 419–430.

Arntz, A., & van den Hout, M. (1996). Psychological treatments of panic disorder without agoraphobia: Cognitive therapy versus applied relaxation. *Behaviour Research and Therapy, 34,* 113–121.

Aronson, M. K. (1988). Patients and families: Impact and long-term-management implications. In M. K. Aronson, (Ed.), *Understanding Alzheimer's disease.* (pp. 74–78). New York: Charles Scribners & Sons.

Aronson, T. A. (1989). A critical review of psychotherapeutic treatments of the borderline personality: Historical trends and future directions. *Journal of Nervous and Mental Disease, 177,* 511–528.

Arroyo, J. A., Simpson, T. L., & Aragon, A. S. (1997). Childhood sexual abuse among Hispanic and non-Hispanic White college women. *Hispanic Journal of Behavioral Sciences, 19,* 57–68.

Asaad, G., & Shapiro, B. (1986). Hallucinations: Theoretical and clinical overview. *American Journal of Psychiatry, 143,* 1088–1097.

Asarnow, J. R., Carlson, G. A., & Guthrie, D. (1987). Coping strategies, self-perceptions, hopelessness, and perceived family environments in depressed and suicidal children. *Journal of Consulting and Clinical Psychology, 55,* 361–366.

Asarnow, R. F., et al. (1991). Span of apprehension in schizophrenia. In J. Zubin, S. Steinhauer, & J. Gruzelier (Eds)., *Handbook of schizophrenia: Vol. 5. Neuropsychology, psychophysiology, and information-processing* (pp. 353–370). Amsterdam: Elsevier Science.

Astley, S. J., et. al. (1992). Analysis of facial shape in children gestationally exposed to marijuana, alcohol, and/or cocaine. *Pediatrics, 89,* 67–77.

Atkinson, R. L. (1997). Use of drugs in the treatment of obesity. *Annual Revue of Nutrition, 17,* 383–403.

Attention Deficit Disorder—Part II. (1995, May). *The Harvard Mental Health Letter, 11* (11), 1–3.

Augusto, A., et al. (1996). Post-natal depression in an urban area of Portugal: Comparison of childbearing women and matched controls. *Psychological Medicine, 26,* 135–141.

Avins, A. L., & Browner, W. S. (1998). Improving the prediction of coronary heart disease to aid in the management of high cholesterol levels: What a difference a decade makes. *Journal of the American Medical Association, 279,* 445–449.

Ax, R. K., Forbes, M. R., & Thompson, D. D. (1997). Prescription privileges for psychologists: A survey of predoctoral interns and directors of training. *Professional Psychology: Research and Practice, 28,* 509–514.

Ayllon, T., & Haughton, E. (1962). Control of the behavior of schizophrenic patients by food. *Journal of the Experimental Analysis of Behavior, 5,* 343–352.

Azar, B. (1994, May). New mania treatment is major breakthrough. *APA Monitor,* p. 28.

Azar, B. (1997, May). Nature, nurture: Not mutually exclusive. *APA Monitor, 28* (5), pp. 1, 28.

Azar, B. (1995, September). The bond between mother and child. *APA Monitor, 26* (9), p. 28.

Azrin, N. H., & Peterson, A. L. (1989). Reduction of an eye tick by controlled blinking. *Behavior Therapy, 20,* 467–473.

B

Babcock, J. C., et al. (1993). Power and violence: The relation between communication patterns, power discrepancies, and domestic violence. *Journal of Consulting and Clinical Psychology, 61,* 40–50.

Bäckman, L., & Forsell, Y. (1994). Episodic memory functioning in a community-based sample of old adults with major depression: Utilization of cognitive support. *Journal of Abnormal Psychology, 103,* 361–370.

Baddeley, A. D. (1992). Working memory. *Science, 225,* 556–559.

Baer, J. S., et al. (1992). An experimental test of three methods of alcohol risk reduction with young adults. *Journal of Consulting and Clinical Psychology, 60,* 974–979.

Bailey, J. M., & Pillard, R. C. (1991). A genetic study of male sexual orientation. *Archives of General Psychiatry, 48,* 1089–1096.

Bailey, J. M., et al. (1994). Heritable factors influence sexual orientation in women. *Archives of General Psychiatry, 50,* 217–223.

Baird, T. D., & August, G. J. (1985). Familial heterogeneity in infantile autism. *Journal of Autism and Developmental Disorders, 15,* 315–321.

Baker, R.C., & Kirschenbaum, D. S. (1993). Self-monitoring may be necessary for successful weight control. *Behavior Therapy, 24,* 377–394.

Bakish, D., et al. (1996). A double-blind placebo-controlled trial comparing fluvoxamine and imipramine in the treatment of panic disorder with or without agoraphobia. *Psychopharmacology Bulletin, 32,* 135–141.

Baldeweg, T., et al. (1997). Neurophysiological changes associated with psychiatric symptoms in HIV-infected individuals without AIDS. *Biological Psychiatry, 41,* 474–487.

Baldwin, A. R., Oei, T. P., & Young, R. (1994). To drink or not to drink: The differential role of alcohol expectancies and drinking refusal self-efficacy in quantity and frequency of alcohol consumpton. *Cognitive Therapy & Research, 17,* 511–530.

Ball, J. C., & Ross, A. (1991). *The effectiveness of methadone maintenance treatment.* New York: Springer-Verlag.

Ball, S. A., et al. (1995). Subtypes of cocaine abusers: Support for a Type A-Type B distinction. *Journal of Consulting and Clinical Psychology, 63,* 115–124.

Ball, S. A., et al. (1997). Personality, temperament and character dimensions and the DSM-IV personality disorders in substance abusers. *Journal of Abnormal Psychology, 106,* 545–553.

Balleza, M. (1992, October 9). A new mental disorder appears in abuse cases. *The New York Times,* p. D16.

Balter, M. (1997). AIDS research: New hope in HIV disease. *Science, 275.*

Banaji, M. R., & Kihlstrom, J. F. (1996). The ordinary nature of alien abduction memories. *Psychological Inquiry, 7,* 132–135.

Bancroft, J. (1990). Commentary: Biological contributions to sexual orientation. In D. P. McWhirter, S. A. Sanders, & J. M. Reinisch (Eds.), *Homosexuality/heterosexuality: Concepts of sexual orientation* (pp. 101–111). New York: Oxford University Press.

Bandura, A. (1973). *Aggression: A social learning analysis.* Englewood Cliffs, NJ: Prentice-Hall.

Bandura, A. (1982). Self-efficacy mechanism in human agency. *American Psychologist, 37,* 122–147.

Bandura, A. (1986). *Social foundations of thought and action: A social-cognitive theory.* Englewood Cliffs, NJ: Prentice-Hall.

Bandura, A., Barr-Taylor, C., Williams, S. L., Mefford, I. N., Barchas, J. D. (1985). Catecholamine secretion as a function of perceived coping self-efficacy. *Journal of Consulting and Clinical Psychology, 53,* 406–414.

Bandura, A., Blanchard, E. B., & Ritter, B. (1969). The relative efficacy of desensitization and modeling approaches for inducing behavioral, affective, and cognitive changes. *Journal of Personality and Social Psychology, 13,* 173–199.

Bandura, A., Jeffery, R. W., & Wright, C. L. (1974). Efficacy of participant modeling as a function of response induction aids. *Journal of Abnormal Psychology, 83,* 56–64.

Bandura, A., Ross, S. A., & Ross, D. (1963). Imitation of film-mediated aggressive models. *Journal of Abnormal and Social Psychology, 66,* 3–11.

Banning, A. (1989). Mother-son incest: Confronting a prejudice. *Child Abuse and Neglect, 13,* 563–570.

Barbaree, H. E., & Marshall, W. L. (1991). The role of male sexual arousal in rape: Six models. *Journal of Consulting and Clinical Psychology, 59,* 621–631.

Barber, M. E. et al. (1998). Aborted suicide attempts: A new classification of suicidal behavior. *American Journal of Psychiatry, 155,* 385–389.

Barber, T. X. (1970). *LSD, marihuana, yoga, and hypnosis.* Chicago: Aldine.

Barkham, M., et al. (1996). Dose-effect relations in time-limited psychotherapy for depression. *Journal of Consulting and Clinical Psychology, 64,* 927–935.

Barkin, R., Braun, B. G., & Kluft, R. P. (1986). The dilemma of drug therapy for multiple personality disorder. In B. G. Braun (Ed.), *Treatment of multiple personality disorder.* Washington, DC: American Psychiatric Press.

Barkley, R. A., et al. (1976). Evaluation of a token system for juvenile delinquents in a residential setting. *Journal of Behavior Therapy and Experimental Psychiatry, 7,* 227–230.

Barkley, R. A. (1981). *Hyperactive children: A handbook for diagnosis and treatment.* New York: Guilford Press.

Barkley, R. A., DuPaul, G. J., & McMurray, M. B. (1990). Comprehensive evaluation of attention deficit disorder with and without hyperactivity as defined by research criteria. *Journal of Consulting and Clinical Psychology, 58,* 775–789.

Barlow, D. H. (1988). *Anxiety and its disorders: The nature and treatment of anxiety and panic.* New York: Guilford Press.

Barlow, D. H. (1994). Psychological interventions in the era of managed competition. *Clinical Psychology: Science and Practice, 1,* 109–122.

Barlow, D. H., Brown, T. A., & Craske, M. G. (1994). Definitions of panic attacks and panic disorder in DSM-IV: Implications for research. *Journal of Abnormal Psychology, 103,* 553–554.

Barlow, D. H., Craske, M. G., Cerny, J. A., & Klosko, J. S. (1989). Behavioral treatment of panic disorder. *Behavior Therapy, 20,* 261–282.

Barlow, D. H., Esler, J. L., & Vitali, A. E. (1998). Psychosocial treatments for panic disorders, phobias, and generalized anxiety disorder. In P. E. Nathan & J. M. Gorman (Eds.), *A guide to treatments that work* (pp. 288–318). New York: Oxford University Press.

Barlow, D. H., & Lehman, C. L. (1996). Advances in the psychosocial treatment of anxiety disorders: Implications for national health care. *Archives of General Psychiatry, 53,* 727–735.

Barlow, D. H., Sackheim, D. K., & Beck, J. G. (1983). Anxiety increases sexual arousal. *Journal of Abnormal Psychology, 92,* 49–54.

Barnett, P. A., & Gotlib, I. (1988). Psychosocial functioning and depression: Distinguishing among antecedents, concomitants, and consequences. *Psychological Bulletin, 104,* 97–126.

Barnett, W. S., & Escobar, C. M. (1990). Economic costs and benefits of early intervention. In S. J. Meisels & J. P. Shonkoff (Eds.), *Handbook of early childhood intervention.* New York: Cambridge University Press.

Baron, M., Gruen, R., Asnis, L., & Lord, S. (1985). Familial transmission of schizotypal and borderline personality disorder. *Journal of Clinical Psychology, 142,* 927–934.

Barrow, S. M., et al. (1989). *Effectiveness of programs for the mentally ill homeless.* New York: New York State Psychiatric Institute.

Barsky, A. J., Wyshak, G., & Klerman, G. L. (1992). Psychiatric comorbidity in DSM–III–R hypochondriasis. *Archives of General Psychiatry, 49,* 101–108.

Barsky, A. J. et al. (1994). Histories of childhood trauma in adult hypochondriacal patients. *American Journal of Psychiatry, 151,* 397–401.

Barsky, A. J., et al. (1998). A prospective 4- to 5-year study of DSM-III-R hypochondriasis. *Archives of General Psychiatry, 55,* 737–744.

Bartecchi, C. E., MacKenzie, T. D., & Schrier, R. W. (1994). The human costs of tobacco use (First of two parts). *New England Journal of Medicine, 330,* 907–912.

Bartlett, J. G. (1993). Zidovudine now or later? *The New England Journal of Medicine, 329,* 351–352. (Editorial)

Basch, M. F. (1980). *Doing psychotherapy.* New York: Basic Books.

Baskin, D. (1984). Cross-cultural conceptions of mental illness. *Psychiatric Quarterly, 56,* 45–53.

Baskin, D., Bluestone, H., & Nelson, M. (1981). Ethnicity and psychiatric diagnosis. *Journal of Clinical Psychology, 37,* 529–537.

Basoglu, M., et al. (1997). Double-blindness procedures, rater blindness, and ratings of outcome. *Archives of General Psychiatry, 54,* 744–748.

Basow, S. (1992). *Gender: Stereotypes and roles* (3rd ed.). Pacific Grove, CA: Brooks/Cole.

Bateson, G. D., Jackson, D., Haley, J., & Weakland, J. (1956). Toward a theory of schizophrenia. *Behavioral Science, 1,* 251–264.

Battaglia, M., et al. (1995). A family study of schizotypal disorder. *Schizophrenia Bulletin, 21,* 33–45.

Baucom, D. H., et al. (1998). Empirically supported couple and family interventions for marital distress

and adult mental health problems. *Journal of Consulting and Clinical Psychology, 66,* 53–88.

Beardslee, W. R., Bemporad, J., Keller, M. B., & Klerman, G. L. (1983). Children of parents with major affective disorder: A review. *American Journal of Psychiatry, 140,* 825–832.

Beautrais, A. L., et al. (1996). Prevalence and comorbidity of mental disorders in persons making serious suicide attempts: A case-control study. *American Journal of Psychiatry, 153,* 1009–1014.

Beauvais, F., & LaBoueff, S. (1985). Drug and alcohol abuse intervention in American Indian communities. Special Issue: Intervening with special populations. *International Journal of the Addictions, 20,* 139–171.

Bebbington, P. (1993). Transcultural aspects of affective disorders. *International Review of Psychiatry, 5,* 145–156.

Beck, A. T. (1976). *Cognitive therapy and the emotional disorders.* New York: International Universities Press.

Beck, A. T. (1985). Theoretical perspectives on clinical anxiety. In A. H. Tuma, & J. D. Maser (Eds.), *Anxiety and the anxiety disorders.* Hillsdale, NJ: Erlbaum.

Beck, A. T. (1991). Cognitive therapy: A 30-year retrospective. *American Psychologist, 46,* 368–375.

Beck, A. T. (1993). Cognitive therapy: Past, present, and future. *Journal of Consulting and Clinical Psychology, 61,* 194–198.

Beck, A. T., Brown, G., Steer, R. A., Eidelson, J. I., & Riskind, J. H. (1987). Differentiating anxiety and depression: A test of the cognitive content-specificity hypothesis. *Journal of Abnormal Psychology, 96,* 179–183.

Beck, A. T., & Clark, D. A. (1997). An information processing model of anxiety: Automatic and strategic processes. *Behaviour Research and Therapy, 35,* 49–58.

Beck, A. T., Emery, G., & Greenberg, R. L. (1985). *Anxiety disorders and phobias: A cognitive perspective.* New York: Basic Books.

Beck, A. T., Freeman, A., & Associates. (1990). *Cognitive therapy of personality disorders.* New York: Guilford Press.

Beck, A. T., Rush, A. J., Shaw, B. F., & Emery, G. (1979). *Cognitive therapy of depression.* New York: Guilford Press.

Beck, A. T., Ward, C. H., Mendelson, M., Mock, J., & Erbaugh, J. (1961). An inventory for measuring depression. *Archives of General Psychiatry, 4,* 561–571.

Beck, A. T., & Young, J. E. (1985). Depression. In D. H. Barlow (Ed.), *Clinical handbook of psychological disorders* (pp. 206–244). New York: Guilford Press.

Beck, A. T., et al. (1990). Relationship between hopelessness and ultimate suicide: A replication with psychiatric outpatients. *American Journal of Psychiatry, 147,* 190–195.

Beck, A. T., et al. (1991). Factor analysis of the Dysfunctional Attitude Scale in a clinical population. *Psychological Assessment, 3,* 478–483.

Beck, A. T. et al. (1992). A crossover study of focused cognitive therapy for panic disorder. *American Journal of Psychiatry, 149,* 778–783.

Beck, D., Casper, R., & Andersen, A. (1996). Truly late onset of eating disorders: A study of 11 cases averaging 60 years of age at presentation. *International Journal of Eating Disorders, 20,* 389–395.

Beck, J. G. (1984). The effect of performance demand and attentional focus on sexual responding in functional and dysfunctional men. Unpublished doctoral dissertation, State University of New York at Albany.

Beck, J. G. (1993). Vaginismus. In W. O'Donohue & J. H. Geer (Eds.), *Handbook of sexual dysfunctions: Assessment and treatment.* (pp. 381–397). Boston: Allyn & Bacon.

Beck, J. G., & Barlow, D. H. (1986). The effects of anxiety and attentional focus on sexual responding: II.

Cognitive and affective patterns in erectile dysfunction. *Behaviour Research and Therapy, 24,* 19–26.

Beck, J. G. (1995). Hypoactive sexual desire disorder: An overview. *Journal of Consulting and Clinical Psychology, 63,* 919–927.

Beck, M. (1994, August 1). An epidemic of obesity. *Newsweek,* pp. 62–63.

Becker, D., & Lamb, S. (1994). Sex bias in the diagnosis of borderline personality disorder and posttraumatic stress disorder. *Professional Psychology: Research and Practice, 25,* 55–61.

Becker, J. A. V., Skinner, L. J., & Abel, G. G. (1983). Sequelae of sexual assault: The survivor's perspective. In J. G. Greer & I. R. Stuart (Eds.), *The sexual aggressor* (pp. 240–266). New York: Van Nostrand Reinhold.

Begleiter, H., Parjesz, B., Bihari, B., & Kissin, B. (1984). Event-related brain potentials in boys at risk for alcoholism. *Science, 225,* 1493–1496.

Begley, S. (1993, July 26). Does DNA make some men gay? *Newsweek,* p. 59.

Begley, S. (1993, December 6). When DNA isn't destiny. *Newsweek,* pp. 53–55.

Begley, S. (1995, November 20). Lights of madness. *Newsweek,* pp. 76–77.

Begley, S. (1998, January 26). Is everybody crazy? *Newsweek,* pp. 48–56.

Beidel, D. C., & Turner, S. M. (1986). A critique of the theoretical bases of cognitive-behavioral theories and therapy. *Clinical Psychology Review, 6,* 177–199.

Beitchman, J. H., et al. (1992). A review of the long-term effects of child sexual abuse. *Child Abuse and Neglect, 16,* 101–118.

Beitman, B. D., Goldfried, M. R., & Norcross, J. C. (1989). The movement toward integrating the psychotherapies: An overview. *American Journal of Psychiatry, 146,* 138–147.

Bekker, M. H. J. (1996). Agoraphobia and gender: A review. *Clinical Psychology Review, 16,* 129–146.

Bell, A. P., & Weinberg, M. S. (1978). *Homosexualities: A study of diversity among men and women.* New York: Simon and Schuster.

Bell, A. P., Weinberg, M. S., & Hammersmith, S. K. (1981). *Sexual preference: Its development in men and women.* Bloomington, IN: University of Indiana Press.

Bellack, A. S. (1992). Cognitive rehabilitation for schizophrenia: Is it possible? Is it necessary? *Schizophrenia Bulletin, 18,* 43–50.

Bellack, A. S., & Mueser, K. T. (1990). Schizophrenia. In A. S. Bellack, M. Hersen, & A. E. Kazdin (Eds.), *International handbook of behavior modification and therapy.* (2nd ed.) (pp. 353–370). New York: Plenum Press.

Bellack, A. S., & Mueser, K. T. (1993). Psychosocial treatment for schizophrenia. *Schizophrenia Bulletin, 19,* 317–336.

Bellack, A. S., Turner, S. M., Hersen, M., & Luber, R. F. (1984). An examination of social skills training for chronic schizophrenic patients. *Hospital and Community Psychiatry, 35,* 1023–1028.

Bellivier, F., et al. (1998). Association between the tryptophan hydroxylase gene and manic-depressive illness. *Archives of General Psychiatry, 55,* 33–37.

Belsky, J. (1993). Etiology of child maltreatment: A developmental-ecological analysis. *Psychological Bulletin, 114,* 413–434.

Bemporad, J. R. (1996). Self-starvation through the ages: Reflections on the pre-history of anorexia nervosa. *International Journal of Eating Disorders, 19,* 217–237.

Bender, L. (1938). A visual motor gestalt test and its clinical use. *Research Monograph of the American Orthopsychiatric Association, 3,* XI, 176.

Benet, S. (1974). *Abkhasians: The long living people of the Caucasus.* New York: Holt, Rinehart & Winston.

Benjamin, L., & Wonderlich, S. A. (1994). Social perceptions and borderline personality disorder: The relation to mood disorders. *Journal of Abnormal Psychology, 103,* 610–624.

Bennett, D. (1985). Rogers: More intuition in therapy. *APA Monitor, 16,* 3.

Ben-Porath, Y. S., Butcher, J. N., & Graham, J. R. (1991). Contribution of the MMPI-2 content scales to the differential diagnosis of schizophrenia and major depression. *Psychological Assessment, 3,* 634–640.

Ben-Porath, Y., McCully, E., & Almagor, M. (1993). Incremental validity of the MMPI-2 Content Scales in the assessment of personality and psychopathology by self-report. *Journal of Personality Assessment, 63,* 557–575.

Benson, H. (1975). *The relaxation response.* New York: Morrow.

Benson, H., Manzetta, B. R., & Rosner, B. (1973). Decreased systolic blood pressure in hypertensive subjects who practiced meditation. *Journal of Clinical Investigation, 52,* 8.

Bentall, R. P. (1990). The illusion of reality: A review and integration of psychological research on hallucinations. *Psychological Bulletin, 107,* 82–95.

Bentall, R. P., Haddock, G., & Slade, P. (1994). Cognitive behavior therapy for persistent auditory hallucinations: From theory to therapy. *Behavior Therapy, 25,* 51–66.

Bentler, P. M. (1976). A typology of transsexualism: Gender identity theory and data. *Archives of Sexual Behavior, 5,* 567–584.

Beratis, S., Gabriel, J., & Hoidas, S. (1994). Age at onset in subtypes of schizophrenic disorders. *Schizophrenia Bulletin, 20,* 287–296.

Berenbaum, H., & Fujita, F. (1994). Schizophrenia and personality: Exploring the boundaries and connections between vulnerability and outcome. *Journal of Abnormal Psychology, 103,* 148–158.

Berenbaum, H., & Oltmanns, T. F. (1990). Emotional experience and expression in schizophrenia and depression. *Journal of Abnormal Psychology, 101,* 37–44.

Bergem, A. L. M., et al. (1997). Heredity in late-onset Alzheimer's disease and vascular dementia. *Archives of General Psychiatry, 54,* 264–270.

Berger, P. A. (1978). Medical treatment of mental illness. *Science, 200,* 974–981.

Bergler, E. (1957). *Homosexuality: Disease or way of life.* New York: Hill & Wang.

Bergner, R. M. (1997). What is psychopathology? And so what? *Clinical Psychology: Science and Practice, 4,* 235–248.

Berkman, L. F., & Breslow, L. (1983). *Health and ways of living: The Alameda County Study.* New York: Oxford University Press.

Berkman, L. F., & Syme, S. L. (1979). Social networks, host resistance, and mortality: A nine-year follow-up study of Alameda County residents. *American Journal of Epidemiology, 109,* 186–204.

Berkowitz, L. (1988). Frustrations, appraisals, and aversively stimulated aggression. *Aggressive Behavior, 14,* 3–11.

Berkowitz, L. (1994). Is something missing? Some observations prompted by the cognitive-neoassociationist view of anger and emotional aggression. In L. R. Huesmann (Ed.), *Aggressive behavior: Current perspectives.* New York: Plenum Press.

Berlin, I. N. (1987). Effects of changing Native American cultures on child development. *Journal of Community Psychology, 15,* 299–306.

Berman, M. E., Fallon, A. E., & Cocarro, E. F. (1998). The relationship between personality psychopathology and aggressive behavior in research volunteers. *Journal of Abnormal Psychology, 107,* 651–658.

Berman, M. E., Tracy, J. I., & Coccaro, E. F. (1997). The serotonin hypothesis of aggression revisited. *Clinical Psychology Review, 17,* 651–665.

Berman, S. L., et al. (1997). The impact of exposure to crime and violence on urban youth. *American Journal of Orthopsychiatry, 66,* 329–336.

Bernstein, A. S. (1987). Orienting response research in schizophrenia: Where we have come and where we might go. *Schizophrenia Bulletin, 13,* 623–641.

Bernstein, D. P., et al. (1996). Childhood antecedents of adolescent personality disorders. *American Journal of Psychiatry, 153,* 907–913.

Bernstein, E. M., & Putnam, F. W. (1986). Development, reliability, and validity of a dissociation scale. *The Journal of Nervous and Mental Disease, 174,* 727–735.

Bernstein, I. L. (1985). Learned food aversions in the progression of cancer and its treatment. In N. S. Braverman & P. Bernstein (Eds.), *Experimental assessments and clinical application of conditioned food aversions. Annals of the New York Academy of Sciences, 443.*

Bernstein, R. L., & Gaw, A. C. (1990). Koro: Proposed classification for DSM–IV. *American Journal of Psychiatry, 147,* 1670–1674.

Berquier, A., & Ashton, R. (1991). A selective review of possible neurological etiologies of schizophrenia. *Clinical Psychology Review, 11,* 645–661.

Berrettini, W. H., et al. (1997). A linkage study of bipolar illness. *Archives of General Psychiatry, 54,* 27–35.

Bertolino, A., et al. (1996). Regionally specific pattern of neurochemical pathology in schizophrenia as assessed by multislice proton magnetic resonance spectroscopic imaging. *American Journal of Psychiatry, 153,* 1554–1563.

Bettelheim, B. (1967). *The empty fortress.* New York: Free Press.

Beutler, L. E. (1995). Common factors and specific effects. *Clinical Psychology: Science and Practice, 2,* 79–82.

Beutler, L. E., et al. (1985). Comparative follow-up evaluations: Patients with inflatable and noninflatable penile protheses. Manuscript submitted for publication.

Beutler, L. E., et al. (1987). Group cognitive therapy and alprazolam in the treatment of depression in older adults. *Journal of Consulting and Clinical Psychology, 55,* 550–556.

Bhurgra, D., & De Silva, P. (1993). Sexual dysfunction across cultures. *International Review of Psychiatry, 5,* 243–252.

Bianchi, S. M., & Spain, D. (1997). *Women, work and family in America.* Population Reference Bureau.

Bick, P. A., & Kinsbourne, M. (1987). Auditory hallucinations and subvocal speech in schizophrenic patients. *American Journal of Psychiatry, 144,* 222–225.

Bickel, W. K., et al. (1997). Effects of adding behavioral treatment to opioid detoxification with buprenorphine. *Journal of Consulting and Clinical Psychology, 65,* 803–810.

Bieber, I. (1976). A discussion of "Homosexuality: The ethical challenge." *Journal of Consulting and Clinical Psychology, 44,* 163–166.

Biederman, J., et al. (1996). Is childhood oppositional defiant disorder a precursor to adolescent conduct disorder? Findings from a four-year follow-up study of children with ADHD. *Journal of the American Academy of Child and Adolescent Psychiatry, 35,* 1193–1204.

Biederman, J. S., et al. (1996). A prospective 4–year follow-up study of attention-deficit hyperactivity and related disorders. *Archives of General Psychiatry, 53,* 437–446.

Bierut, L. J., et al. (1998). Familial transmission of substance dependence: Alcohol, marijuana, cocaine, and habitual smoking. *Archives of General Psychiatry, 55,* 982–988.

Bigler, E. D., & Ehrenfurth, J. W. (1981). The continued inappropriate singular use of the Bender Visual Motor Gestalt Test. *Professional Psychology, 12,* 562–569.

Binder, J. L., & Strupp, H. H. (1997). Negative process: A recurrently discovered and underestimated facet of therapeutic process and outcome in the individual psychotherapy of adults. *Clinical Psychology: Science and Practice, 4,* 121–139.

Binder, R. L., & McNiel, D. E. (1996). Application of the Tarasoff ruling and its effect on the victim and the therapeutic relationship. *Psychiatric Services, 47,* 1212–1215.

Biofeedback applications as central or adjunctive treatment. (1997, April). *Clinician's Research Digest, 15* (4), 5.

Biran, M. (1988). Cognitive and exposure treatment for agoraphobia: Re-examination of the outcome research. *Journal of Cognitive Psychotherapy: An International Quarterly, 2,* 165–178.

Birchwood, M., et al. (1992). The influence of ethnicity and family structure on relapse in first-episode schizophrenia: A comparison of Asian, Afro-Caribbean, and White patients. *British Journal of Psychiatry, 161,* 783–790.

Birnbaum, M. H., Martin., H., & Thomann. K. (1996). Visual function in multiple personality disorder. *Journal of the American Optometric Association, 67,* 327–334.

Bitiello, B., & Jensen, P. S. (1997). Medication development, testing in children and adolescents. *Archives of General Psychiatry, 54,* 871–876.

Bitler, D. A., Linnoila, M., & George, D. T. (1994). Psychosocial and diagnostic characterisics of individual intitiating domestic violence. *Journal of Nervous and Mental Disease, 182,* 583–585.

Blackman, S. J. (1996). Has drug culture become an inevitable part of youth culture? A critical assessment of drug education. *Educational Review, 48,* 131–142.

Blackwood, H. R., et al. (1996). A locus for bipolar affective disorder on chromosome 4p. *Nature Genetics, 12,* 427–430.

Blair, C. D., & Lanyon, R. I. (1981). Exhibitionism: A critical review of the etiology and treatment. *Psychological Bulletin, 89,* 439–463.

Blakeley, M. K. (1985). Is one woman's sexuality another woman's pornography? The question behind a major legal battle. *Ms.,* pp. 37–47, 120–123.

Blakeslee, S. (1988, September 8). New groups aim to help parents face grief when a newborn dies. *The New York Times,* p. B13.

Blakeslee, S. (1990, September 20). Study links emotions to second heart attacks. *The New York Times,* p. B8.

Blakeslee, S. (1991, September 15). Study ties dyslexia to brain flaw affecting vision and other senses. *The New York Times,* pp. A1, A30.

Blakeslee, S. (1994a, January 19). Geologists seek clues to fault that caused quake. *The New York Times,* p. A. 18.

Blakeslee, S. (1994b, August 16). New clue to cause of dyslexia seen in mishearing of fast sounds. *The New York Times,* pp. C1, C10.

Blakeslee, S. (1994c, October 18). Researchers find gene that may link dyslexia with immune disorders. *The New York Times,* p. C3.

Blakeslee, S. (1995a, August 2). Rethinking the handling of mild concussions. *The New York Times,* p. C9.

Blakeslee, S. (1995b, August 9). Two new treatments for erectile ills. *The New York Times,* p. C8.

Blakeslee, S. (1997a, June 27). Brain studies tie marijuana to other drugs. *The New York Times,* p. A16.

Blakeslee, S. (1997b, December 16). Suicide rate higher in 3 gambling cities, study says. *The New York Times,* p. A16.

Blakeslee, S. (1998, May 14). Two studies shed new light on cocaine's effect on brain. *The New York Times,* p. A20.

Blanchard, E. B. (1992). Psychological treatment of benign headache disorders. *Journal of Consulting and Clinical Psychology, 60,* 537–551.

Blanchard, E. B., Andrasik, F., Guarnieri, P., Neff, D. F., & Rodichok, L. D. (1987). Two-, three-, and four-year follow-up on the self-regulatory treatment of chronic headache. *Journal of Consulting and Clinical Psychology, 55,* 257–259.

Blanchard, E. B., & Diamond, S. (1996). Psychological treatment of benign headache disorders. *Professional Psychology, 27,* 541–547.

Blanchard, E. B., Kalb, L. C., Pallmeyer, T. P., & Gerardi, R. (1982). The development of a psychophysiological assessment procedure for posttraumatic stress disorder in Vietnam veterans. *Psychiatric Quarterly, 4,* 220–229.

Blanchard, E. B., et al. (1985). Behavioral treatment of 250 chronic headache patients: A clinical replication series. *Behavior Therapy, 16,* 308–327.

Blanchard, E. B., et al. (1990). A controlled evaluation of thermal biofeedback and thermal feedback combined with cognitive therapy in the treatment of vascular headache. *Journal of Consulting and Clinical Psychology, 58,* 216–224.

Blanchard, J. J., Kring, A. M., & Neale, J. M. (1994). Flat affect in schizophrenia: A test of neuropsychological models. *Schizophrenia Bulletin, 20,* 311–325.

Blanchard, R., & Hucker, S. J. (1991). Age, transvestism, bondage, and concurrent paraphilic activities in 117 fatal cases of autoerotic asphyxia. *British Journal of Psychiatry, 159,* 371–377.

Blanchard, R., Steiner, B. W., & Clemmensen, L. H. (1985). Gender dysphoria, gender reorientation, and the clinical management of transsexualism. *Journal of Consulting and Clinical Psychology, 53,* 295–304.

Blashfield, R. K., & Draguns, J. G. (1976). Evaluative criteria for psychiatric classification. *Journal of Abnormal Psychology, 85,* 140–150.

Blatt, S. (1986). Where have we been and where are we going? *Journal of Personality Assessment, 50,* 343–346.

Blatt, S. J., et al. (1995). Impact of perfectionism and need for approval on the brief treatment of depression: The National Institute of Mental Health Treatment of Depression Collaborative Research Program revisited. *Journal of Consulting and Clinical Psychology, 63,* 125–132.

Blatt, S. J., et al. (1996). Interpersonal factors in brief treatment of depression: Further analyses of the National Institute of Mental Health Treatment of Depression Collaborative Research Program. *Journal of Consulting and Clinical Psychology, 64,* 162–171.

Blatt, S. J., et al. (1998). When and how perfectionism impedes the brief treatment of depression: Further analyses of the National Institute of Mental Health Treatment of Depression Collaborative Research Program. *Journal of Consulting and Clinical Psychology, 66,* 423–428.

Blazer, D., et al. (1991). The association of age and depression among the elderly: An epidemiologic exploration. *Journal of Gerontology, 46,* 210–215.

Blazer, D. G., et al. (1994). The prevalence and distribution of major depression in a National Comorbidity Survey. *American Journal of Psychiatry, 151,* 979–986.

Blehar, M. C., Weissman, M. M., Gershon, E. S., & Hirschfeld, R. M. A. (1988). Family and genetic studies of affective disorders. *Archives of General Psychiatry, 45,* 289–292.

Bliss, E. L. (1984). A symptom profile of patients with multiple personalities, including MMPI results. *The Journal of Nervous and Mental Disease, 172,* 197–202.

Bliss, E. L., & Jeppsen, E. A. (1985). Prevalence of multiple personality among inpatients and outpatients. *American Journal of Psychiatry, 142,* 250–251.

Blood test can detect retardation. (1993, October 6). *New York Daily News,* p. 10.

Bloom, B. L. (1992). Computer assisted psychological intervention: A review and commentary. *Clinical Psychology Review, 12,* 169–197.

Bloom, J. D., & Rogers, J. L. (1987). The legal basis of forensic psychiatry: Statutorily mandated psychiatric diagnosis. *American Journal of Psychiatry, 144,* 847–853.

Blumenthal, D. (1988, October 9). Dieting reassessed. *The New York Times Magazine, Part 2: The Good Health Magazine,* pp. 24–25, 53–54.

Blumenthal, R., & Endicott, J. (1997). Barriers to seeking treatment for major depression. *Depression and Anxiety, 4,* 273–278.

Blumenthal, S. J. (1985). Suicide and suicide prevention. (Comm. Pub. No. 98-497). Washington, DC: U. S. Government Printing Office.

Bodkin, J., et al. (1996). Treatment of negative symptoms in schizophrenia and schizoaffective disorder by selegiline augmentation of antipsychotic medication. *Journal of Nervous & Mental Disease, 184,* 295–301.

Boetsch, E. A., Green, P. A., & Pennington, B. F. (1996). Psychosocial correlates of dyslexia across the life span. *Development and Psychopathology, 8,* 539–562.

Bogerts, B. (1993). Recent advances in the neuropathology of schizophrenia. *Schizophrenia Bulletin, 19,* 431–445.

Bogerts, B. (1997). The temporolimbic system theory of positive schizophrenic symptoms. *Schizophrenia Bulletin, 23,* 423–435.

Bond, A. J. (1996). Understanding drug treatment in mental health care. New York: Wiley.

Boney-McCoy, S., & Finkelhor, D. (1996). Is youth victimization related to trauma symptoms and depression after controlling for prior symptoms and family relationships? A longitudinal, prospective study. *Journal of Consulting and Clinical Psychology, 64,* 1406–1416.

Bonta, J., Law, M., & Hanson, K. (1998). The prediction of criminal and violent recidivism among mentally disordered offenders: A meta-analysis. *Psychological Bulletin, 123,* 123–142.

Boor, M. (1982). The multiple personality epidemic. *Journal of Nervous and Mental Disease, 170,* 302–304.

Booth-Kewley, S., & Friedman, H. S. (1987). Psychological predictors of heart disease: A quantitative review. *Psychological Bulletin, 101,* 343–362.

Boren, T., Faulk, P., Roth, K. A., Larson, G., & Normark, S. (1993). Attachment of *Helicobacter pylori* to human gastric epithelium mediated by blood group antigens. *Science, 262,* 1892–1895.

Borkovec, T. D., & Costello, E. (1993). Efficacy of applied relaxation and cognitive-behavioral therapy in the treatment of generalized anxiety disorder. *Journal of Consulting and Clinical Psychology, 61,* 611–619.

Borkovec, T. D., Mathews, A. M., Chambers, A., Ebrahimi, S., Lytle, R., & Nelson, R. (1987). The effects of relaxation training with cognitive therapy or nondirective therapy and the role of relaxation-induced anxiety in the treatment of generalized anxiety. *Journal of Consulting and Clinical Psychology, 55,* 883–888.

Bornstein, M. R., Bellack, A. S., & Hersen, M. (1977). Social-skills training for unassertive children: A multiple-baseline analysis. *Journal of Applied Behavior Analysis, 10,* 183–195.

Bornstein, R. F. (1992). The dependent personality: Developmental, social, and clinical perspectives. *Psychological Bulletin, 112,* 3–23.

Bornstein, R. F. (1996a). Construct validity of the Rorschach Oral Dependency Scale: 1967–1995. *Psychological Assessment, 8,* 200–205.

Bornstein, R. F. (1996b). Sex differences in dependent personality disorder prevalence rates. *Clinical Psychology Science and Practice, 3,* 1–12.

Bornstein, R. F. (1997). Dependent personality disorder in the DSM-IV and beyond. *Clinical Psychology: Science and Practice, 4,* 175–187.

Borthwick-Duffy, S. A. (1994). Epidemiology and prevalence of psychopathology in individuals with dual diagnoses. *Journal of Consulting and Clinical Psychology, 62,* 17–27.

Boskind-White, M., & White, W. C. (1983). *Bulimarexia: The binge-purge cycle.* New York: W. W. Norton.

Boskind-White, M., & White, W. C., Jr. (1986). Bulimarexia: A historical-sociocultural perspective. In K. D. Brownell & J. P. Foreyt, (Eds.), *Handbook of eating disorders: Physiology, psychology, and treatment of obesity, anorexia, and bulimia* (pp. 353–378). New York: Basic Books.

Boston Women's Health Book Collective. (1984). *The new our bodies, ourselves.* New York: Simon & Schuster.

Botelho, R. J., & Richmond, R. (1996). Secondary prevention of excessive alcohol use: Assessing the prospects of implementation. *Family Practice, 13,* 182–193.

Bouchard, C. (1997). Obesity in adulthood—the importance of childhood and parental obesity. *The New England Journal of Medicine, 337,* 926–927.

Bouchard, C., Shephard, R. J., & Stephens, T. (Eds.). (1993). *Physical activity, fitness, and health: Consensus statement,* p. 61. Proceedings of the Second International Consensus Symposium on Physical Activity, Fitness, and Health, Toronto, Ontario, Canada, May 1992. Champaign, IL: Human Kinetics.

Bouchard, S., et al. (1996). Cognitive restructuring in the treatment of psychotic symptoms in schizophrenia: A critical analysis. *Behavior Therapy, 27,* 257–277.

Bouchard, T. J., Jr. (1994). Genes, environment, and personality. *Science, 264,* 1700–1701.

Bouwer, C., & Stein, D. J. (1997). Association of panic disorder with a history of traumatic suffocation. *American Journal of Psychiatry, 154,* 1566–1570.

Bowden, C. L., et al. (1994). Efficacy of divalproex vs. lithium and placebo in the treatment of mania. *Journal of the American Medical Association, 271,* 918–924.

Bowden, C. L., et al. (1996). Relation of serum valproate concentration to response in mania. *American Journal of Psychiatry, 153,* 765–770.

Bowers, T. G., & Clum, G. A. (1988). Relative contribution of specific and nonspecific treatment effects: Meta-analysis of placebo-controlled behavior therapy research. *Psychological Bulletin, 103,* 315–323.

Bowlby, J. (1988). *A secure base.* New York: Basic Books.

Boyd, J. H., & Weissman, M. M. (1981). Epidemiology of affective disorders: A reexamination and future directions. *Archives of General Psychiatry, 38,* 1039–1046.

Boyd-Franklin, N. (1989). *Black families in therapy: A multisystems approach.* New York: Guilford Press.

Boyle, M. H., et al. (1992). Predicting substance use in late adolescence: Results from the Ontario Child Health Study Follow-up. *American Journal of Psychiatry, 149,* 761–767.

Boyle, P. (1993). The hazards of passive—and active—smoking. *New England Journal of Medicine, 328,* 1708–1709.

Braddock, D. (1992). Community mental health and mental retardation services in the United States: A comparative study of resource allocation. *American Journal of Psychiatry, 149,* 175–183.

Braddock, L. (1986). The dexamethasone suppression test: Fact and artifact. *British Journal of Psychiatry, 148,* 363–374.

Brady, E. U., & Kendall, P. C. (1992). Comorbidity of anxiety and depression in children and adolescents. *Psychological Bulletin, 111,* 244–255.

Brady, S. (1986). Short-term memory, phonological processing, and reading ability. *Annals of Dyslexia, 36,* 138–153.

Braff, D. L. (1993). Information processing and attention dysfunction in schizophrenia. *Schizophrenia Bulletin, 19,* 233–259.

Braff, D. L., & Saccuzzo, D. P. (1985). The time course of information-processing deficits in schizophrenia. *American Journal of Psychiatry, 142,* 170–174.

Braff, D. L., & Swerdlow, N. R. (1997). Neuroanatomy of schizophrenia. *Schizophrenia Bulletin, 23,* 509–512.

Braun, B. G. (Ed.), (1986). *Treatment of multiple personality disorder.* Washington, DC: American Psychiatric Press.

Braun, B. G. (1990). Multiple personality disorder: An overview. *American Journal of Occupational Therapy, 44,* 971–976.

Brawman-Mintzer, O., et al. (1993). Psychiatric comorbidity in patients with generalized anxiety disorder. *American Journal of Psychiatry, 150,* 1216–1218.

Bray, J. H., & Jouriles, E. N. (1995). Treatment of marital conflict and prevention of divorce. *Journal of Marital and Family Therapy, 21,* 461–473.

Breaux, C., Matsuoka, J. K., & Ryujin, D. H. (1995, August). National utilization of mental health services by Asian/Pacific Islanders. Paper presented at the meeting of the American Psychological Association, New York, NY.

Breggin, P. R. (1992, September 18). U.S. hasn't given up linking genes to crime. *The New York Times,* p. A34.

Breiter, H. C., et al. (1996). Functional magnetic resonance imaging of symptom provocation in obsessive-compulsive disorder. *Archives of General Psychiatry, 53,* 595–606.

Brekke, J. S., et al. (1997). The impact of service characteristics on functional outcomes from community support programs for persons with schizophrenia: A growth curve analysis. *Journal of Consulting and Clinical Psychology, 65,* 464–475.

Bremmer, J. D., et al. (1996). Chronic PTSD in Vietnam combat veterans: Course of illness and substance abuse. *American Journal of Psychiatry, 153,* 369–375.

Brems, C., & Johnson, M. E. (1997). Clinical implications of the co-occurrence of substance use and other psychiatric disorders. *Professional Psychology: Research and Practice, 28,* 437–447.

Brenda, W. J. H., et al. (1998). Depressive symptoms and physical decline in community-dwelling older persons. *Journal of the American Medical Association, 279,* 1720–1726.

Brent, D. A., et al. (1997). A clinical psychotherapy trial for adolescent depression comparing cognitive, family, and supportive therapy. *Archives of General Psychiatry, 54,* 877–885.

Breslau, N., et al. (1996). Sleep disturbance and psychiatric disorders: A longitudinal epidemiological study of young adults. *Biological Psychiatry, 39,* 411–418.

Breslau, N., et al. (1997a). Sex differences in posttraumatic stress disorder. *Archives of General Psychiatry, 54,* 1044–1048.

Breslau, N., et al. (1997b). Psychiatric sequelae of posttraumatic stress disorder in women. *Archives of General Psychiatry, 54,* 81–87.

Breslau, N., et al. (1998). Major depression and stages of smoking: A longitudinal investigation. *Archives of General Psychiatry, 55,* 161–166.

Breslow, N. (1989). Sources of confusion in the study and treatment of sadomasochism. *Journal of Social Behavior and Personality, 4,* 263–274.

Brill, A. A. (1938). Introduction. In A. A. Brill (Ed.). *The basic writings of Sigmund Freud* (pp. 3–34). New York: Random House.

Brinkman, S. D., Largen, J. W., Jr., Cushman, L., Braun, P. R., & Block, R. (1986). Clinical validators: Alzheimer's disease and multi-infarct dementia. In L. W. Poon (Ed.), *Handbook for clinical memory assessment of older adults.* (pp. 307–313). Washington, DC: American Psychological Association.

Brodsky, B. S., et al. (1997). Characteristics of borderline personality disorder associated with suicidal behavior. *American Journal of Psychiatry, 154,* 1715–1719.

Brody, J. E. (1988a, May 5). Sifting fact from myth in the face of asthma's growing threat to American children. *The New York Times,* p. B19.

Brody, J. E. (1988b, October 11). Studies unmask origins of brutal migraines. *The New York Times,* pp. C1, C10.

Brody, J. E. (1990, June 7). A search to bar retardation in a new generation. *The New York Times,* B9.

Brody, J. E. (1992a, May 15). Study finds liquid diet works (but not for the 50% who quit). *The New York Times,* p. B7.

Brody, J. E. (1992b, June 16). Suicide myths cloud efforts to save children. *The New York Times,* pp. C1, C3.

Brody, J. E. (1992c, September 30). Myriad masks hide an epidemic of depression. *The New York Times,* p. C12.

Brody, J. E. (1993a, November 10). The leading killer of women: Heart disease. *The New York Times,* p. C17.

Brody, J. E. (1993b, December 8). Deciding how, or whether, to treat menopause. *The New York Times,* p. C16.

Brody, J. E. (1993c, December 15). Living with a common genetic abnormality. *The New York Times,* p. C17.

Brody, J. E. (1994a, January 5). Heart diseases are persisting in study's second generation. *The New York Times,* p. C12.

Brody, J. E. (1994b, February 9). Depression in the elderly: Old notions hinder help. *The New York Times,* p. C13.

Brody, J. E. (1994c, December 6). Rise in obesity in U.S. is explored by experts. *The New York Times,* p. C11.

Brody, J. E. (1994d, December 28). Wine for the heart: Over all, risks may outweigh benefits. *The New York Times,* p. C10.

Brody, J. E. (1995a, January 18). Dysthymia: Help for chronic sadness. *The New York Times,* p. C8.

Brody, J. E., (1995b, August 2). With more help available for impotence, few men seek it. *The New York Times,* p. C9.

Brody, J. E. (1996a, August 7). Relaxation method may aid health. *The New York Times,* p. C10.

Brody, J. E. (1996b, November 14). Decline seen in death rates from cancer as a whole. *The New York Times,* p. A21.

Brody, J. E. (1996c, November 20). Controlling anger is good medicine for the heart. *The New York Times,* p. C15.

Brody, J. E. (1997a, March 26). Race and weight. *The New York Times,* p. C8.

Brody, J. E. (1997b, December 30). Despite the despair of depression, few men seek treatment. *The New York Times,* p. F7.

Brody, J. E. (1997c, September 10). For some with mild depression, an herb may be a gentle remedy. *The New York Times,* p. C10.

Brody, J. E. (1998, June 16). Gaining weight on sugar-free, fat-free diets. *The New York Times,* p. F7.

Brody, N. (1990). Behavior therapy versus placebo: Comment on Bowers and Clum's meta-analysis. *Psychological Bulletin, 107,* 106–109.

Broman, C. L. (1996). Coping with personal problems. In H. W. Neighbors & J. S. Jackson (Eds.), *Mental health in black America* (pp. 117–129). Thousand Oaks, CA: Sage Publications.

Bronfrenbrenner, U. (1979). *The ecology of human development: Experiments by nature and design.* Cambridge, MA: Harvard University Press.

Broocks, A., et al. (1998). Comparison of aerobic exercise, clomipramine, and placebo in the treatment of panic disorder. *American Journal of Psychiatry, 155,* 603–609.

Brookoff, D., et al. (1997). Characteristics of participants in domestic violence: Assessment at the scene of domestic assault. *Journal of the American Medical Association, 277,* 1369–1373.

Broussard, B. A., et. al. (1991). Prevalence of obesity in American Indians and Alaska Natives. *American Journal of Clinical Nutrition, 53* (6 Suppl), 1535S–1542S.

Brown, D. R. (1996). Marital status and mental health. In H. W. Neighbors & J. S. Jackson (Eds.), *Mental health in black America* (pp. 77–94). Thousand Oaks, CA: Sage Publications.

Brown, D. R., Ahmed, F., Gary, L.E., & Milburn, N. G. (1995). Major depression in a community sample of African Americans. *American Journal of Psychiatry,* 373–378.

Brown, G. W., et al. (1994). Life events and endogenous depression: A puzzle reexamined. *Archives of General Psychiatry, 51,* 525–534.

Brown, J. (1987). A review of meta-analyses conducted on psychotherapy outcome research. *Clinical Psychology Review, 7,* 1–24.

Brown, L. S. (1992). A feminist critique of the personality disorders. In L. Brown & M. Balou (Eds.), *Personality and psychopathology: Feminist reappraisals.* (pp. 206–228). New York: Guilford Press.

Brown, L S. (1997, November). Recovered memories of abuse: Research and clinical update. *Clinician's Research Digest, Supplemental Bulletin, 17,* 1–2.

Brown, L., & Root, M. P. P. (Eds.). (1990). *Diversity and complexity in feminist therapy.* New York: Haworth.

Brown, R. A., et al. (1997). Cognitive-behavioral treatment for depression in alcoholism. *Journal of Consulting and Clinical Psychology, 65,* 715–726.

Brown, R. T., Wynne, M. E., & Medenis, R. (1985). Methylphenidate and cognitive therapy: A comparison of treatment approaches with hyperactive boys. *Journal of Abnormal Child Psychology, 13,* 69–87.

Brown, S. A. (1985a). Expectancies versus background in the prediction of college drinking patterns. *Journal of Consulting and Clinical Psychology, 53,* 123–130.

Brown, S. A. (1985b). Reinforcement expectancies and alcohol treatment outcome after one year. *Journal of Studies on Alcohol, 46,* 304–308.

Brown, S. A., Creamer, V. A., & Stetson, B. A. (1987). Adolescent alcohol expectancies in relation to personal and parental drinking patterns. *Journal of Abnormal Psychology, 96,* 117–121.

Brown, S. L., & Forth, A. E. (1997). Psychopathy and sexual assault: Static risk factors, emotional precursors, and rapist subtypes. *Journal of Consulting and Clinical Psychology, 65,* 848–857.

Brown, T. A., Chorpita, B. F., & Barlow, D. H. (1998). Structural relationships among dimensions of the DSM-IV anxiety and mood disorders and dimensions of negative affect, positive affect, and autonomic arousal. *Journal of Abnormal Psychology, 107,* 179–192.

Brownell, K. D. (1991). Dieting and the search for the perfect body: Where physiology and culture collide. *Behavior Therapy, 22,* 1–12.

Brownell, K. D. (1994, December 15). Get slim with higher taxes. *The New York Times,* p. A29.

Brownell, K. D., & Rodin, J. (1994). The dieting maelstrom: Is it possible and advisable to lose weight? *American Psychologist, 49,* 781–791.

Brownell, K. D., & Wadden, T. A. (1992). Etiology and treatment of obesity: Understanding a serious, prevalent, and refractory disorder. *Journal of Consulting and Clinical Psychology, 60,* 505–517.

Bruce, T. J. (1996). Predictors of alprazolam discontinuation with and without cognitive behavior therapy for panic disorder: A reply. *American Journal of Psychiatry, 153,* 1109–1110.

Bruch, H. (1973). *Eating disorders: Obesity, anorexia and the person within.* New York: Basic Books.

Bruch, M. A. (1997). Positive thoughts or cognitive balance as a moderator of the negative life events–dysphoria relationship: A reexamination. *Cognitive Therapy and Research, 21,* 25–38.

Bryant, R. A., & Harvey, A. G. (1997). Acute stress disorder: A critical review of diagnostic issues. *Clinical Psychology Review, 17,* 757–773.

Bryant, R. A., & Harvey, A. G. (1998). Relationship between acute stress disorder and posttraumatic stress disorder following mild traumatic brain injury. *American Journal of Psychiatry, 155,* 625–629.

Buchanan, R. W., & Carpenter, W. T., Jr. (1997). The neuroanatomies of schizophrenia. *Schizophrenia Bulletin, 23,* 367–372.

Buchsbaum, M. S., & Hazlett, E. A. (1998). Positron emission tomography studies of abnormal glucose metabolism in schizophrenia. *Schizophrenia Bulletin, 24,* 343–364.

Buchsbaum, M. S., et al. (1984). The Genain quadruplets: Electrophysiological, positron emission and x-ray tomographic studies. *Psychiatry Research, 13,* 95–108.

Buchsbaum, M. S., et al. (1996). PET and MRI of the thalamus in never-medicated patients with schizophrenia. *American Journal of Psychiatry, 153,* 191–199.

Bullido, M. J., et al. (1998). A polymorphism in the regulatory region of APOE associated with risk for Alzheimer's dementia. *Nature Genetics, 18,* 69–71.

Bullman, T. A., & Kang, H. K. (1994). Posttraumatic stress disorder and the risk of traumatic deaths among Vietnam veterans. *Journal of Nervous and Mental Disease, 182,* 604–610.

Bulluck, P. (1998, March 20). Black youths' rate of suicide rising sharply, studies find. *The New York Times,* pp. A1, A16.

Burgess, A. W., & Hartman, C. R. (1986). *Sexual exploitation of patients by health professionals.* New York: Praeger.

Buriel, R., Calzada, S., & Vazquez, R. (1982). The relationship of traditional Mexican American culture to adjustment and delinquency among three generations of Mexican American male adolescents. *Hispanic Journal of Behavioral Sciences, 4,* 41–55.

Burish, T. G., Snyder, S. L., & Jenkins, R. A. (1991). Preparing patients for cancer chemotherapy: Effect of coping preparation and relaxation interventions. *Journal of Consulting and Clinical Psychology, 59,* 518–525.

Burke, K. C., et al. (1990). Age at onset of selected mental disorders in five community populations. *Archives of General Psychiatry, 47,* 511–518.

Burnam, M. A., Hough, R. L., Karno, M., Escobar, J. I., & Telles, C. A. (1987). Acculturation and lifetime prevalence of psychiatric disorders among Mexican Americans in Los Angeles. *Journal of Health and Social Behavior, 28,* 89–102.

Burnam, M. A., et al. (1988). Sexual assault and mental disorders in a community population. *Journal of Consulting and Clinical Psychology, 56,* 843–850.

Burns, D. D. (1980). *Feeling good: The new mood therapy.* New York: Morris.

Burns, D. D., & Beck, A. T. (1978). Modification of mood disorders. In J. P. Foreyt and D. P. Rathjen (Eds.), *Cognitive behavior therapy: Research and application* (pp. 109–134). New York: Plenum Press.

Burns, D. D., & Nolen-Hoeksema, S. (1992). Therapeutic empathy and recovery from depression in cognitive-behavioral therapy: A structural equation model. *Journal of Consulting and Clinical Psychology, 60,* 441–449.

Burros, M. (1994, July 17). Despite awareness of risks, more in U.S. are getting fat. *The New York Times,* pp. A1, A8.

Busatto, G. F., et al. (1997). Correlation between reduced in vivo benzodiazepine receptor binding and severity of psychotic symptoms in schizophrenia. *American Journal of Psychiatry, 154,* 56–63.

Buss, D. M., & Shackelford, T. K. (1997). Human aggression in evolutionary psychological perspective. *Clinical Psychology Review, 17,* 605–619.

Butler, A. C., & Beck, A. T. (1995, Summer). Cognitive therapy for depression. *The Clinical Psychologist, 48,* 3–5.

Butler, A. C., & Beck, A. T. (1996, Summer). Cognitive therapy for depression. *The Clinical Psychologist, 49,* 6–7.

Butler, G. (1989). Issues in the application of cognitive and behavioral strategies to the treatment of social phobia. *Clinical Psychology Review, 9,* 91–106.

Butler, L. D., et al. (1996). Hypnotizability and traumatic experience: A diathesis-stress model of dissociative symptomatology. *American Journal of Psychiatry, 153*(Suppl), 42–63.

Butler, M. (1985). Guidelines for feminist therapy. In L. Rosewater & L. Walker (Eds.), *Handbook of feminist therapy: Women's issues in psychotherapy* (pp. 32–38). New York: Springer.

Butler, R. N., & Lewis, M. I. (1982). *Aging and Mental Health* (3rd ed.). St. Louis: C. V. Mosby.

Butterfield, F. (1996, May 6). Major crimes fell in '95, early data by F.B.I. indicate. *The New York Times,* pp. A1, B8.

Butterfield, F. (1997a, January 5). Serious crime decreased for fifth year in a row. *The New York Times,* p. A10.

Butterfield, F. (1997b, February 3). '95 Data show sharp drop in reported rapes. *The New York Times,* pp. A1, A14.

Butterfield, F. (1997c, June 2). Homicides plunge 11 percent in U.S., F.B.I. report says. *The New York Times,* pp. A1, B10.

Butterfield, F. (1997d, November 16). Number of victims of crime fell again in '96, study says. *The New York Times,* p. A18.

Butzlaff, R. L., & Hooley, J. M. (1998). Expressed emotion and psychiatric relapse. *Archives of General Psychiatry, 55,* 547–552.

Byrne, D. (1977). The imagery of sex. In Money, J., & Musaph, H. (Eds.), *Handbook of sexology* (pp. 327–350). New York: Elsevier/North Holland.

C

Cable News Network. (1996, November 29). *Estrogen may help Alzheimer's sufferers keep their memory.* Author.

Cable News Network. (1997a, February 4). *Miscarriage feeds major depression.* Author.

Cable News Network. (1997b, February 5). *Big jump in Alzheimer's cases forecast.* Author.

Cable News Network. (1997c, February 6). *Researchers find promising therapy for Parkinson's.* Author.

Cable News Network. (1997d, March 23). *Program helps mentally ill avoid homelessness.* Author.

Cable News Network. (1997e, April 16). *As smoking goes passé in U.S., Third World lights up.* Author.

Cable News Network. (1997f, May 15). *FDA approves antidepressant to stop smoking.* Author.

Cable News Network. (1998a, April 6). Alcohol remains large factor in violent crime. *CNN Interactive,* [On-line].

Cable News Network. (1998b, May 20). New studies show a genetic link to the complex disease of alcoholism *Cable News Network Web Posting.* [On-line].

Cacioppo, J. T., von Hippel, W., & Ernst, J. M. (1997). Mapping cognitive structures and processes through verbal content: The thought-listing technique. *Journal of Consulting and Clinical Psychology, 65,* 928–940.

Caetano, R. (1987). Acculturation and drinking patterns among U.S. Hispanics. *British Journal of Addiction, 82,* 789–799.

Caine, E. D., Ebert, M. H., & Weingartner, H. (1977). An outline for the analysis of dementia: The memory disorder of Huntington's disease. *Neurology, 27,* 1087–1092.

Caldwell, C. H. (1996). Predisposing, enabling, and need factors related to patterns of help-seeking among African American women. In H. W. Neighbors & J.S. Jackson (Eds.), *Mental health in black America.* (pp. 146–160). Thousand Oaks, CA: Sage Publications.

Calhoon, S. K. (1996). Confirmatory factor analysis of the Dysfunctional Attitude Scale in a student sample. *Cognitive Therapy and Research, 20,* 81–91.

Calhoun, K. S., & Atkeson, B. M. (1991). *Treatment of rape victims: Facilitating social adjustment.* New York: Pergamon Press.

Califia, P. (1997). *Sex changes: The politics of transgenderism.* San Francisco: Cleis.

Calne, D. B. (1977). Developments in the pharmacology and therapeutics of Parkinsonism. *Annals of Neurology, 1,* 111–119.

Cameron, L. D., & Nicholls, G. (1998). Expression of stressful experiences through writing: Effects of a self-regulation manipulation for pessimists and optimists. *Health Psychology, 17,* 84–92.

Cameron, N. (1963). *Personality development and psychopathology: A dynamic approach.* Boston: Houghton Mifflin.

Campbell, D. T., & Stanley, J. C. (1963). Experimental and quasi-experimental designs for research on teaching. In N. L. Gage (Ed.), *Handbook of research on teaching.* Chicago: Rand McNally.

Campbell, S. B., & Cohn, J. F. (1991). Prevalence and corrrelates of postpartum depression in first-time mothers. *Journal of Abnormal Psychology, 100,* 594–599.

Can ordinary pain relievers prevent Alzheimer's. (1997, June). *UC Berkeley Wellness Letter, 13* (9), pp. 1–2.

Can stress make you sick? (1998). *Harvard Health Letter, 23* (6), pp. 1–3.

Cannon, T. D., & Marco, E. (1994). Structural brain abnormalities as indicators of vulnerability to schizophrenia. *Schizophrenia Bulletin, 20,* 89–102.

Cannon, T. D., et al. (1998). The genetic epidemiology of schizophrenia in a Finnish twin cohort: A population-based modeling study. *Archives of General Psychiatry, 55,* 67–74.

Capps, L. et al. (1993). Parental perception of emotional expressiveness in children with autism. *Journal of Consulting and Clinical Psychology, 61,* 475–484.

Carani, C., et al. (1990). Effects of androgen treatment in impotent men with normal and low levels of free testosterone. *Archives of Sexual Behavior, 19,* 223–234.

Card, J. J. (1987). Epidemiology of posttraumatic stress disorder in a national cohort of Vietnam veterans. *Journal of Clinical Psychology, 43,* 6–17.

Cardin, V. A., McGill, C. W., & Falloon, I. R. H. (1986). An economic analysis: Costs, benefits, and effectiveness. In I. R. H. Falloon (Ed.), *Family management of schizophrenia.* (pp. 115–123). Baltimore: Johns Hopkins University Press.

Carey, B. (1998, January /February). The sunshine supplement. *Health,* pp. 52–55.

Carey, G. (1992). Twin imitation for antisocial behavior: Implications for genetic and family environment research. *Journal of Abnormal Psychology, 101,* 18–25.

Carey, G., & DiLalla, D. L. (1994). Personality and psychopathology: Genetic perspectives. *Journal of Abnormal Psychology, 103,* 32–43.

Carey, M. P., & Burish, T. G. (1987). Providing relaxation training to cancer chemotherapy patients: A comparison of three delivery techniques. *Journal of Consulting and Clinical Psychology, 55,* 732–737.

Carey, M. P., & Burish, T. G. (1988). Etiology and treatment of the psychological side effects associated with cancer chemotherapy: A critical review and discussion. *Psychological Bulletin, 104,* 307–325.

Carey, M. P., Faulstich, M. E., Gresham, F. M., Ruggiero, L., & Enyart, P. (1987). Children's Depression Inventory: Construct and discriminant validity across clinical and nonreferred (control) populations. *Journal of Consulting and Clinical Psychology, 55,* 755–761.

Carey, M. P., Wincze, J. P., & Meisler, A. W. (1998). Sexual dysfunction: Male erectile disorder. In D. H. Barlow, *Clinical handbook for psychological disorders* (pp. 442–480). New York: Guilford Publication.

Carini, M. A., & Nevid, J. S. (1992). Social appropriateness and impaired perspective in schizophrenia. *Journal of Clinical Psychology, 48,* 170–177.

Carlat, D. J., & Camargo, C. A. (1991). Review of bulimia nervosa in males. *American Journal of Psychiatry, 148,* 831–843.

Carlat, D. J., Camargo, C. A., & Herzog, D. B. (1997). Eating disorders in males: A report on 135 patients. *American Journal of Psychiatry, 154,* 1127–1132.

Carlin, A. S., Hoffman, H. G., & Weghorst, S. (1997). Virtual reality and tactile augmentation in the treatment of spider phobia. *Behaviour Research and Therapy, 35,* 1153–1158.

Carlson, E. B., & Rosser-Hogan, R. (1994). Cross-cultural response to trauma: A study of traumatic experiences and posttraumatic symptoms in Cambodian refugees. *Journal of Traumatic Stress, 7,* 43–58.

Carlson, G. A. (1980). Unmasking masked depression in children and adolescents. *American Journal of Psychiatry, 137,* 445–449.

Carlson, G. A., & Garber, J. (1986). Developmental issues in the classification of depression in children. In M. Rutter, C. Izard, & P. Read (Eds.), *Depression in young people: Developmental and clinical perspectives* (pp. 399–434). New York: Guilford Press.

Carlson, G. A., & Miller, D. C. (1981). Suicide affective disorder and women physicians. *American Journal of Psychiatry, 138,* 1330–1335.

Carmelli, D., Swan, G. E., Robinette, D., & Fabstiz, R. (1992). Genetic influences on smoking—a study of male twins. *The New England Journal of Medicine, 327,* 829–833.

Carmen, E. H., Rieker, P. P., & Mills, T. (1984). Victims of violence and psychiatric illness. *American Journal of Psychiatry, 141,* 378–383.

Carroll, K. M., & Rounsaville, B. J. (1992). Contrast of treatment-seeking and untreated cocaine abusers. *Archives of General Psychiatry, 49,* 464–471.

Carter, C. S., et al. (1997). Anterior cingulate gyrus dysfunction and selective attention deficits in schizophrenia: H2O PET study during single-trial Stroop task performance. *American Journal of Psychiatry, 154,* 1670–1675.

Carter, J. C., & Fairburn, C. G. (1998). Cognitive-behavioral self-help for binge eating disorder: A controlled effectiveness study. *Journal of Consulting and Clinical Psychology, 66,* 616–623.

Carter, M. M., et al. (1995). Effects of a safe person on induced distress following a biological challenge in panic disorder with agoraphobia. *Journal of Abnormal Psychology, 104,* 156–163.

Carver, C. S., & Gaines, J. G. (1987). Optimism, pessimism, and postpartum depression. *Cognitive Therapy & Research, 11,* 449–462.

Casanova, M. R. (1997). Functional and anatomical aspects of prefrontal pathology in schizophrenia. *Schizophrenia Bulletin, 23,* 517–519.

Cascardi, M., et al. (1995). Characteristics of women physically abused by their spouses and who seek treatment regarding marital conflict. *Journal of Consulting and Clinical Psychology, 63,* 616–623.

Casey, B. J., et al. (1997). Implication of right frontostriatal circuitry in response inhibition and attention-deficit hyperactivity disorder. *Journal of the American Academy of Child and Adolescent Psychiatry, 36,* 374–383.

Casey, D. A., & Davis, M. H. (1996). Electroconvulsive therapy in the very old. *General Hospital Psychiatry, 18,* 436–439.

Castellanos, F., et al. (1994). Quantitative morphology of the caudate nucleus in attention deficit hyperactivity disorder. *American Journal of Psychiatry, 151,* 1791–1796.

Castellanos, F. X., et al. (1996). Quantitative brain magnetic resonance imaging in attention-deficit hyperactivity disorder. *Archives of General Psychiatry, 53,* 607–616.

Castle, D. J., et al. (1995). Gender differences in schizophrenia: Hormonal effect or subtypes? *Schizophrenia Bulletin, 21,* 1–12.

Castonguay, L. G., et al. (1996). Predicting the effect of cognitive therapy for depression: A study of unique and common factors. *Journal of Consulting and Clinical Psychology, 64,* 497–504.

Castro, J. (1992, January 20). Sexual harassment: A guide. *Time Magazine,* p. 37.

Catalano, R., et al. (1993). Using ECA survey data to examine the effect of job layoffs on violent behavior. *Hospital and Community Psychiatry, 44,* 874–879.

Caton, C. L. M., et al. (1990). An evaluation of a mental health program for homeless men. *American Journal of Psychiatry, 147,* 286–289.

Caudill, B. D., & Marlatt, G. A. (1975). Modeling influences in social drinking: An experimental analogue. *Journal of Consulting and Clinical Psychology, 43,* 405–415.

Celano, M., et al. (1996). Treatment of traumagenic beliefs among sexually abused girls and their mothers: An evaluation study. *Journal of Abnormal Child Psychology, 24,* 1–17.

Celis, W. (1991, January 2). Students trying to draw line between sex and an assault. *The New York Times,* pp. 1, B8.

Centers for Disease Control. (1991). Homicide among young black males—United States, 1978–1987. *Journal of the American Medical Association, 265,* 183–184.

Centers for Disease Control. (1993). Update: Acquired immunodeficiency syndrome—United States, 1992. *Morbidity and Mortality Weekly Report, 42* (No. 28), pp. 547–557.

Center for Mental Health Services (CMHS) (1994). Mental health statistics. Office of Consumer, Family and Public Information, Center for Mental Health Services, U.S. Department of Health and Human Services. Rockville, MD: Author.

Chabot, R. J., & Serfontein, G. (1996). Quantitative electroencephalographic profiles of children with attention deficit disorder. *Biological Psychiatry, 40,* 951–963.

Chadda, R. K., & Ahuja, N. (1990). Dhat syndrome: A sex neurosis of the Indian subcontinent. *British Journal of Psychiatry, 156,* 577–579.

Chakos, M. H., et al. (1996). Incidence and correlates of tardive dyskinesia in first episode of schizophrenia. *Archives of General Psychiatry, 53,* 313–319.

Chambless, D. L. (1996, June). Identification of empirically supported psychological interventions. *Clinician's Research Digest, Supplemental Bulletin 14.*

Chambless, D. L., & Gillis, M. M. (1993). Cognitive therapy of anxiety disorders. *Journal of Consulting and Clinical Psychology, 61,* 248–260.

Chambless, D. L., & Hollon, S. D. (1998). Defining empirically supported therapies. *Journal of Consulting and Clinical Psychology, 66,* 7–18.

Chambless, D. L., et al. (1998, Winter). Update on empirically validated therapies, II. *The Clinical Psychologist, 51,* 3–16.

Chan, D. W. (1991). The Beck Depression Inventory: What difference does the Chinese version make? *Psychological Assessment, 3,* 616–622.

Chang, E. C. (1997). Irrational beliefs and negative life stress: Testing a diathesis-stress model of depressive symptoms. *Personality and Individual Differences, 22,* 115–117.

Chang, S. C. (1984). Review of I. Yamashita "Taijin-kyofu." *Transcultural Psychiatric Research Review, 21,* 283–288.

Chaplin, T. C., Rice, M. E., & Harris, G. T. (1995). Salient victim suffering and the sexual responses of child molesters. *Journal of Consulting and Clinical Psychology, 63,* 249–255.

Chartrand, S. (1996, August 12). Mixers for 'cocktails' used to delay AIDS. *The New York Times,* p. D2.

Chase, M. (1998, March 2). A new diet drug hits the marketplace, with potential risks. *The Wall Street Journal,* p. B1.

Chemtob, C. M., et al. (1997). Cognitive-behavioral treatment for severe anger in posttraumatic stress disorder. *Journal of Consulting and Clinical Psychology, 65,* 184–189.

Chen, M. S. (1991, February). Lay-led smoking cessation approach for Southeast Asian men. Paper presented at the program on "Smoking Cessation Strategies for Minorities." National Heart, Lung & Blood Institute, National Institutes of Health, Bethseda, MD.

Chermack, S. T., & Giancola, P. R. (1997). The relation between alcohol and aggression: An integrated biopsychosocial conceptualization. *Clinical Psychology Review, 17,* 621–649.

Chesno, F. A., & Kilmann, P. R. (1975). Effects of stimulation intensity on sociopathic avoidance learning. *Journal of Abnormal Psychology, 84,* 144–151.

Chess, S., Korn, S. J., & Fernandez, P. B. (1971). *Psychiatric disorders of children with congenital rubella.* New York: Brunner/Mazel.

Cheung, F. (1991). The use of mental health services by ethnic minorities. In H. F. Myers et al. (Eds.), *Ethnic minority perspectives on clinical training and services in psychology* (pp. 23–31). Washington, DC: American Psychological Association.

Cheung, F. M., & Ho, R. M. (1997). Standardization of the Chinese MMPI-A in Hong Kong: A preliminary study. *Psychological Assessment, 9,* 499–502.

Cheung, F., Song, W., & Butcher, J. N. (1991). An infrequency scale for the Chinese MMPI. *Psychological Assessment, 3,* 648–653.

Chick, D., et al. (1993). The relationship between MMPI personality scales and clinician-generated DSM-III-R personality disorder diagnoses. *Journal of Personality Assessment, 6,* 264–276.

Childhood sexual abuse and bulimic behavior in a nationally representative sample. (July 1996). *American Journal of Public Health* [News release].

Childs, E. K. (1990). Therapy, feminist ethics, and the community of color with particular emphasis on the treatment of Black women. In H. Lerman & N. Porter (Eds.), *Feminist ethics in psychotherapy* (pp. 195–203). New York: Springer.

Ching, J. W. J., et al. (1995). Perceptions of family values and roles among Japanese Americans: Clinical considerations. *American Journal of Orthopsychiatry, 65,* 216–224.

Chipperfield, B., & Vogel-Sprott, M. (1988). Family history of problem drinking among young male social drinkers: Modeling effects on alcohol consumption. *Journal of Abnormal Psychology, 97,* 423–428.

Chowdhury, A. N. (1996). The definition and classification of Koro. *Culture, Medicine and Psychiatry, 20,* 41–65.

Christensen, A., et al. (1983). Parental characteristics and interactional dysfunction in families with child behavioral problems: A preliminary investigation. *Journal of Abnormal Child Psychology, 11,* 153–166.

Christiansen, B. A., & Goldman, M. S. (1983). Alcohol related expectancies versus demographic/background variables in the prediction of adolescent drinking. *Journal of Consulting and Clinical Psychology, 52,* 249–257.

Christiansen, K., & Winkler, E. M. (1992). Hormonal, anthropometrical, and behavioral correlates of physical aggression in Kung San men of Namibia. *Aggressive Behavior, 18,* 271–280.

Christiansen, P. E., et al. (1996). Paroxetine and amitriptyline in the treatment of depression in general practice. *Acta Psychiatr Scand, 93,* 158–163.

Christmas, A. L., Wodarski, J. S., & Smokowski, P. R. (1996). Risk factors for physical child abuse: A practice theoretical paradigm. *Family Therapy, 23,* 233–248.

Ciarrocchi, J. W., Kirschner, N. M., & Fallik, F. (1991). Personality dimensions of male pathological gamblers, alcoholics, and dually addicted gamblers. *Journal of Gambling Studies, 7,* 133–141.

Cinciripini, P. M., et al. (1996). Behavior therapy, and the transdermal nicotine patch: Effects on cessation outcome, affect, and coping. *Journal of Consulting and Clinical Psychology, 64,* 314–323.

Clark, D. A. (1997). Twenty years of cognitive assessment: Current status and future directions. *Journal of Consulting and Clinical Psychology, 65,* 996–1000.

Clark, D. A., Beck, A. T., & Beck, J. S. (1994). Symptom differences in major depression, dysthymia, panic disorder, and generalized anxiety disorder. *American Journal of Psychiatry, 151,* 205–209.

Clark, D. A., Cook, A., & Snow, D. (1998). Depressive symptom differences in hospitalized, medically ill, depressed psychiatric inpatients and nonmedical controls. *Journal of Abnormal Psychology, 107,* 38–48.

Clark, D. A., et al. (1996). Is the relationship between anxious and depressive cogntions and symptoms linear or curvilinear? *Cognitive Therapy & Research, 20,* 135–154.

Clark, D. B., et al. (1994). Anxiety disorders in adolescence: Characteristics, prevalence, and comorbidities. *Clinical Psychology Review, 14,* 113–137.

Clark, D. M. (1986). A cognitive approach to panic. *Behaviour Research and Therapy, 24,* 461–470.

Clark, D. M., et al. (1997). Misinterpretation of body sensations in panic disorder. *Journal of Consulting and Clinical Psychology, 65,* 203–213.

Clark, L. A., & Watson, D. (1991). Tripartite model of anxiety and depression: Psychometric evidence and taxonomic implications. *Journal of Abnormal Psychology, 100,* 316–336.

Clark, L. A., Watson, D., & Mineka, S. (1994). Temperament, personality, and the mood and anxiety disorders. *Journal of Abnormal Psychology, 103,* 103–116.

Clark, S. E., & Loftus, E. F. (1996). The construction of space alien abduction memories. *Psychological Inquiry, 7,* 140–143.

Clarkin, J. F., Pildonis, P. A., & Magruder, K. M. (1996). Psychotherapy of depression implications for reform of the health care system. *Archives of General Psychiatry, 53,* 717–723.

Cleckley, H. (1976). *The mask of sanity* (5th ed.). St. Louis: Mosby.

Cleghorn, J. M., et al. (1992). Toward a brain map of auditory hallucinations. *American Journal of Psychiatry, 149,* 1062–1069.

Cloninger, C. R. (1987). Neurogenetic adaptive mechanisms in alcoholism. *Science, 236,* 410–416.

Cloninger, C. R., Sigvardsson, S., & Bohman, M. (1996). Type I and type II alcoholism: An update. *Alcohol Health and Research World, 20,* 18–23.

Clues found in brain-killing process. (1998, February 10). *The New York Times,* p. F7.

Clum, G. A., Clum, G. A., & Surls, R. (1993). A meta-analysis of treatments for panic disorder. *Journal of Consulting and Clinical Psychology, 61,* 317–326.

Coccaro, E. F., & Kavoussi, R. J. (1997). Fluoxetine and impulsive aggressive behavior in personality-disordered subjects. *Archives of General Psychiatry, 54,* 1081–1088.

Coccaro, E. F. et al. (1998). Correlates with aggression and serotonin function in personality-disordered subjects: Cerebrospinal fluid vasopressin levels. *Archives of General Psychiatry, 55,* 708–714.

Cockerham, W. C., Kunz, G., & Lueschen, G. (1989). Alcohol use and psychological distress: A comparison of Americans and West Germans. *The International Journal of the Addictions, 24,* 951–961.

Coffey, C. E., & Weiner, R. D. (1990). Electroconvulsive therapy: An update. *Hospital and Community Psychiatry, 41,* 515–521.

Cognitive impairment linked to early death in HIV-infected patients. (1996, March 29). *Reuters News Service.*

Cohen, A. C., et al. (1993). Factors determining the decision to institutionalize dementing individuals: A prospective study. *The Gerontologist, 22,* 714–720.

Cohen, D. (1986). Psychopathological perspectives: Differential diagnosis of Alzheimer's disease and related disorders. In L. W. Poon (Ed.), *Handbook for clinical memory assessment of older adults.* (pp. 81–88). Washington, DC: American Psychological Association.

Cohen, F. L., Ferrans, C. E., & Eshler, B. (1992). Reported accidents in narcolepsy. *Loss, Grief and Care, 5,* 71–80.

Cohen, J. A., & Mannarino, A. P. (1997). A treatment study for sexually abused preschool children: Outcome during a one-year follow-up. *Journal of the American Academy of Child and Adolescent Psychiatry, 36,* 1228–1235.

Cohen, L. A. (1987, November). Diet and cancer. *Scientific American,* 42–48, 533–534.

Cohen, O. J., & Fauci, A. S. (1998). Transmission of multidrug-resistant human immunodeficiency virus: The wake up call. *New England Journal of Medicine, 339,* 341–343.

Cohen, S., Evans, G. W., Stokols, D., & Krantz, D. S. (1986). *Behavior, health, and environmental stress.* New York: Plenum Publishing.

Cohen, S., Tyrrell, D. A. J., & Smith, A. P. (1991). Psychological stress and susceptibility to the common cold. *The New England Journal of Medicine, 325,* 606–612.

Cohen, S., Tyrrell, D. A. J., & Smith, A. P. (1993). Negative life events, perceived stress, negative affect, and susceptibility to the common cold. *Journal of Personality and Social Psychology, 64,* 131–140.

Cohen, S., et al. (1997). Social ties and susceptibility to the common cold. *Journal of the American Medical Association, 277,* 1940–1944.

Cohen-Kettenis, P. T., & van Goozen, S. H. M. (1997). Sex reassignment of adolescent transsexuals: A follow-up study. *Journal of the American Academy of Child and Adolescent Psychiatry, 36,* 263–271.

Cohn, C. K. (1997). Genetic risk factors for bipolar disorder. *American Journal of Psychiatry, 154,* 1484.

Cohn, L. D., et al. (1987). Body-figure preferences in male and female adolescents. *Journal of Abnormal Psychology, 96,* 276–279.

Colditz, G. A. (1992). Economic costs of obesity. *American Journal of Clinical Nutrition, 55,* 503S–507S.

Cole, D. A. (1991). Preliminary support for a competency-based model of depression in children. *Journal of Abnormal Psychology, 100,* 181–190.

Cole, D. A., Truglio, R., & Peeke, L. (1997). Relation between symptoms of anxiety and depression in children: A multitrait-multimethod-multigroup assessment. *Journal of Consulting and Clinical Psychology, 65,* 110–119.

Cole, D. A., et al. (1998). A longitudinal look at the relation between depression and anxiety in children and adolescents. *Journal of Consulting and Clinical Psychology, 66,* 451–460.

Cole, R. (1982). Patient's rights vs. doctor's rights: Which should take precedence? In A. E. Doudera & J. P. Swazy (Eds.), *Refusing treatments in mental health institutions: Values and conflict.* Ann Arbor, MI: AUPHA Press.

Cole, S. W., Kemeny, M. E., & Taylor, S.E. (1997). Social identity and physical health: Accelerated HIV progression in rejection-sensitive gay men. *Journal of Personality and Social Psychology, 72,* 320–335.

Coleman, D., & Baker, F. M. (1994). Misdiagnosis of schizophrenia in older, Black veterans. *Journal of Nervous and Mental Disease, 182,* 527–528.

Coleman, E. (1987). Bisexuality: Challenging our understanding of sexual orientation. *Sexuality and Medicine, 1,* 225–242.

Coleman, H. L. K., Wampold, B. E., & Casali, S. L. (1995). Ethnic minorities' ratings of ethnically similar and European-American counselors: A meta-analysis. *Journal of Counseling Psychology, 42,* 55–64.

Collins, J. J., & Messerschmidt, P. M. (1993). Epidemiology of alcohol-related violence. *Alcohol Health and Research World, 17,* 93–100.

Collins, P. H. (1990). *Black feminist thought: Knowledge, consciousness, and the politics of empowerment.* Boston: Unwin Hyman.

Colvin, C. R., & Block, J. (1994). Do positive illusions foster mental health? An examination of the Taylor and Brown formulation. *Psychological Bulletin, 16,* 3–20.

Comas-Diaz, L., & Griffith, E. (1988). Introduction: On culture and psychotherapeutic care. In L. Comas-Diaz & E. Griffith (Eds.), *Clinical guidelines in cross-cultural mental health.* New York: Wiley.

Combs, B. J., Hales, D. R., & Williams, B. K. (1980). *An invitation to health.* Menlo Park, CA: Benjamin/Cummings.

Comings, D. E. (1997). Genetic aspects of childhood behavioral disorders. *Child Psychiatry and Human Development, 27,* 139–150.

Commission on the Review of the National Policy toward Gambling, (1978). *Gambling in America: The final report.* Washington, DC: U.S. Government Printing Office.

Compas, B. E., et al. (1998). Sampling of empirically supported psychological treatments from health psychology: Smoking, chronic pain, cancer, and bulimia nervosa. *Journal of Consulting and Clinical Psychology, 66,* 89–112.

Conduct Problems Prevention Research Group (1992). A developmental and clinical model for the prevention of conduct disorders: The FAST Track Program. *Development and Psychopathology, 4,* 509–527.

Conger, R. E., (1992). Child abuse and self-esteem in latency-aged children. *American Journal of Forensic Psychology, 10,* 41–45.

Conley, R. R., & Buchanan, R. W. (1997). Evaluation of treatment-resistant schizophrenia. *Schizophrenia Bulletin, 23,* 663–674.

Connors, G. J., et al. (1997). The therapeutic alliance and its relationship to alcoholism treatment participation and outcome. *Journal of Consulting and Clinical Psychology, 65,* 588–598.

Considine, R. V., et al. (1996). Serum immunoreactive-leptin concentration in normal weight and obese humans. *The New England Journal of Medicine, 334,* 292–295.

Consumer Reports. (1995, November). Mental health: Does therapy help? pp. 734–739.

Consumers Union (1995, January). Secondhand smoke: Is it a hazard? *Consumer Reports,* pp. 27–33.

Conte, H. R. (1986). Multivariate assessment of sexual dysfunction. *Journal of Consulting and Clinical Psychology, 54,* 149–157.

Conte, H. R., Plutchik, R., Wild, K., & Karasu, T. B. (1986). Combined psychotherapy and pharmacotherapy for depression: A systematic analysis of the evidence. *Archives of General Psychiatry, 43,* 471–479.

Cook, T. D., & Campbell, D. T. (1979). *Quasi-experimentation: Design and analysis issues for field settings.* Chicago: Rand McNally.

Cooke, D. J., & Michie, C. (1997). An item response theory analysis of the Hare Psychopathy Checklist—Revised. *Psychological Assessment, 9,* 3–14.

Cooke, R. (1994, November 8). Memory's foe: Progress seen in battle vs. brain killer. *New York Newsday,* p. A16.

Cooke, R. (1995, February 14). Development with mice may aid Alzheimer's study. *New York Newsday,* pp. 27, 29.

Cookson, W. O. C. M., & Moffatt, M. R. (1997). Asthma—An epidemic in the absence of infection? *Science 275,* 41–42.

Coolidge, F. L., & Segal, D. L. (1998). Evolution of personality disorder diagnosis in the *Diagnostic and Statistical Manual of Mental Disorders. Clinical Psychology Review, 18,* 585–599.

Cooney, N. L., et al. (1997). Alcohol cue reactivity, negative-mood reactivity, and relapse in treated alcoholic men. *Journal of Abnormal Psychology, 106,* 243–250.

Coons, P. M. (1986). Treatment progress in 20 patients with multiple personality disorder. *Journal of Nervous and Mental Disease, 174,* 715–721.

Coons, P. M. (1994). Confirmation of childhood abuse in child and adolescent cases of multiple personality disorder and dissociative disorder not otherwise specified. *Journal of Nervous and Mental Disease, 182,* 461–464.

Coons, P. M., Bowman, E. S., & Pellow, T. A. (1989). Post-traumatic aspects of the treatment of victims of sexual abuse and incest. *Psychiatric Clinics of North America, 12,* 325–327.

Coontz, S., & Franklin, D. (1997, October 28). When the marriage penalty is marriage. *The New York Times,* p. A23.

Cooper, A. J., et al. (1990). A female sex offender with multiple paraphilias: A psychologic, physiologic (laboratory sexual arousal) and endocrine case study. *Canadian Journal of Psychiatry, 35,* 334–337.

Cooper, B. (1976). *Counselor training manual No. 2—Crisis intervention.* Ann Arbor, MI: NOW Domestic Violence and Spouse Assault Fund.

Cooper, M. L., et al. (1992). Stress and alcohol use: Moderating effects of gender, coping, and alcohol expectancies. *Journal of Abnormal Psychology, 101,* 139–152.

Cooper, P. J., & Steere, J. (1995). A comparison of two psychological treatments for bulimia nervosa: Implications for models of maintenance. *Behaviour Research and Therapy, 33,* 875–885.

Corbitt, E. M., & Widiger, T. A. (1995). Sex differences among the personality disorders: An exploration of the data. *Clinical Psychology: Science and Practice, 2,* 225–238.

Cordes, C. (1985). Common threads found in suicide. *APA Monitor, 16*(10), 11.

Cordova, M. J., et al. (1995). Frequency and correlates of posttraumatic-stress-disorder-like symptoms after treatment for breast cancer. *Journal of Consulting and Clinical Psychology, 63,* 981–986.

Cormier, W. H., & Cormier, L. S. (1985). *Interviewing strategies for helpers.* Monterey, CA: Brooks/Cole.

Cornblatt, B. A., & Kilep, J. G. (1994). Impaired attention, genetics, and the pathophysiology of schizophrenia. *Schizophrenia Bulletin, 20,* 31–46.

Cornelius, J. R., et al. (1997). Fluoxetine in depressed alcoholics: A double-blind, placebo-controlled trial. *Archives of General Psychiatry, 54,* 700–705.

Cornes, C. L., & Frank, E. (1994). Interpersonal psychotherapy for depression. *The Clinical Psychologist, 47*(3), 9–10.

Coronado, S. F., & Peake, T. H. (1992). Culturally sensitive therapy: Sensitive principles. *Journal of College Student Psychotherapy, 7,* 63–72.

Coronary disease: Taking emotions to heart. (1996, October). *Harvard Health Letter, 21* (11), pp. 1–3.

Coryell, W. (1996). Psychotic depression. *Journal of Clinical Psychiatry, 57*(3, Suppl), 27–31.

Coryell, W., Endicott, J., & Keller, M. (1992a). Major depression in a nonclinical sample: Demographic and clinical risk factors for first onset. *Archives of General Psychiatry, 49,* 117–125.

Coryell, W., Endicott, J., & Keller, M. (1992b). Rapidly cycling affective disorder: Demographics, diagnosis, family history, and course. *Archives of General Psychiatry, 49,* 126–131.

Coryell, W., Endicott, J., Maser, J. D., Keller, M., et al. (1995). Long-term stability of polarity distinctions in the affective disorders. *American Journal of Psychiatry, 152,* 385–390.

Coryell, W., & Winokur, G. (1992). Course and outcome. In E. S. Paykel (Ed.), *Handbook of affective disorders* (2nd ed.), (pp. 89–110). New York Guilford Press.

Coryell, W., et al. (1996). Importance of psychotic features to long-term course in major depressive disorder. *American Journal of Psychiatry, 153,* 483–489.

Cosgray, R. E., et al. (1991). Death from auto-erotic asphyxiation in a long-term psychiatric setting. *Perspectives in Psychiatric Care, 27,* 21–24.

Costa, P. T., Jr., & McCrae, R. R. (1985). Hypochondriasis, neuroticism, and aging: When are somatic

complaints unfounded? *American Psychologist, 40,* 19–28.

Costantino, G., et al. (1986). Cuento therapy: A culturally sensitive modality for Puerto Rican children. *Journal of Consulting and Clinical Psychology, 54,* 639–645.

Côté, G., et al. (1994). Reduced therapist contact in the cognitive behavioral treatment of panic disorder. *Behavior Therapy, 25,* 123–145.

Coursey, R. D., Alford, J., & Safarjan, B. (1997). Significant advances in understanding and treating serious mental illness. *Professional Psychology: Research and Practice, 28,* 205–216.

Cowen, E. L. (1985). Person-centered approaches to primary prevention in mental health: Situation-focused and competence-enhancement. *American Journal of Community Psychology, 13,* 31–48.

Cowley, G. (1992, December 7). Progress on Parkinson's: Tissue from aborted fetuses can bring relief. *Newsweek,* p. 68.

Cowley, G. (1994, November 14). What's high cholesterol? *Newsweek,* p. 53.

Cowley, G. (1995a, January 30). A new assault on addiction. *Newsweek,* p. 51.

Cowley, G., & Underwood, A. (1998, January 5). A little help from serotonin. *Newsweek,* pp. 78–81.

Cox, B. J., et al. (1992). Situations and specific coping strategies associated with clinical and nonclinical panic attacks. *Behavior Research & Therapy, 30,* 67–69.

Cox, W. M., & Klinger, E. (1988). A motivational model of alcohol use. *Journal of Abnormal Psychology, 97,* 168–180.

Coyne, J. C. (1976). Toward an interactional description of depression. *Psychiatry, 39,* 14–27.

Coyne, J. C., Kessler, R. C., Tal, M., Turnbull, J., Wortman, C. B., Greden, J. F. (1987). Living with a depressed person. *Journal of Consulting and Clinical Psychology, 55,* 347–352.

Cracking down on teen-age homicide. (1996, July 13). *The New York Times,* p. A18.

Craighead, L. (1984). Sequencing of behavior therapy and pharmacotherapy for obesity. *Journal of Consulting and Clinical Psychology, 52,* 190–199.

Craighead, L. W., Agras, W. S. (1991). Mechanisms of action in cognitive-behavioral and pharmacological interventions for obesity and bulimia nervosa. *Journal of Consulting and Clinical Psychology, 59,* 115–125.

Craighead, W. E., Craighead, L. W., & Ilardi, S. S. (1995). Behavior therapies in historical perspective. In B. Bongar & L. E. Beutler (Eds.), *Comprehensive textbook of psychotherapy: Theory and practice.* (pp. 64–83). New York: Oxford University Press.

Craske, M. G. (1991). Phobic fear and panic attacks: The same emotional states triggered by different cues? *Clinical Psychology Review, 11,* 599–620.

Craske, M. G., Brown, T. A., & Barlow, D. H. (1991). Behavioral treatment of panic disorder: A two-year follow-up. *Behavior Therapy, 22,* 289–304.

Creamer, M., Burgess, P., & Pattison, P. (1992). Reaction to trauma: A cognitive processing model. *Journal of Abnormal Psychology, 101,* 452–459.

Crews, D., & Moore, M. C. (1986). Evolution of mechanisms controlling mating behavior. *Science, 231,* 121–125.

Crick, N. R., & Dodge, K. A. (1994). A review and reformulation of social information-processing mechanisms in children's social adjustment. *Psychological Bulletin, 115,* 74–101.

Crits-Christoph, P. (1992). The efficacy of brief dynamic psychotherapy: A meta-analysis. *American Journal of Psychiatry, 149,* 151–158.

Crits-Christoph, P., & Siqueland, L. (1996). Psychosocial treatment for drug abuse: Selected review and recommendations for national health care. *Archives of General Psychiatry, 53,* 749–756.

Cronin, A. (1993, June 27). Two viewfinders, two views of Gay America. *The New York Times,* Section 4, p. 10.

Croop, R. S., Faulkner, E. B., & Labriola, D. F. (1997). The safety profile of naltrexone in the treatment of alcoholism: Results from a multicenter usage study. *Archives of General Psychiatry, 54,* 1130–1135.

Cross-National Collaborative Group (1992). The changing rate of major depression: Cross-national comparisons. *Journal of the American Medical Association, 268,* 3098–3105.

Crow, T. J. (1980a). Molecular pathology of schizophrenia: More than one disease process? *British Medical Journal, 280,* 66–68.

Crow, T. J. (1980b). Positive and negative schizophrenic symptoms and the role of dopamine. *British Journal of Psychiatry, 137,* 383–386.

Crow, T. J. (1980c). Positive and negative schizophrenic symptoms and the role of dopamine: A debate. *British Journal of Psychiatry, 137,* 379–383.

Cuéllar, I., & Roberts, R. E. (1997). Relations of depression, acculturation, and socioeconomic status in a Latino sample. *Hispanic Journal of Behavioral Sciences, 19,* 230–238.

Cui, X-J, & Vaillant, G. E. (1997). Does depression generate negative life events? *Journal of Nervous and Mental Disease, 185,* 145–150.

Cullen, E. A., & Newman, R. (1997). In pursuit of prescription privileges. *Professional Psychology: Research and Practice, 28,* 197–200.

Cummings, J. L. (1992). Depression and Parkinson's disease: A review. *American Journal of Psychiatry, 149,* 443–454.

Cunningham, F. G., & Gilstrap, L. C. (1991). Maternal serum alpha-fetoprotein screening. *The New England Journal of Medicine, 325,* 55–57.

Curb, J. D., & Marcus, E. B. (1991). Body fat and obesity in Japanese-Americans. *American Journal of Clinical Nutrition, 53,* 1552S–1555S.

Curran, P. J., Stice, E., & Chassin, L. (1997). The relation between adolescent alcohol use and peer alcohol use: A longitudinal random coefficients model. *Journal of Consulting and Clinical Psychology, 65,* 130–140.

Curry, S., Marlatt, G. A., Gordon, J. R. (1987). Abstinence violation effect: Validation of an attributional construct with smoking cessation. *Journal of Consulting and Clinical Psychology, 55,* 145–149.

D

Dabbs, J. M., & Hargrove, M. F. (1997). Age, testosterone, and behavior among female prison inmates. *Psychosomatic Medicine, 59,* 477–480.

Dadds, M. R., Heard, P. M., & Rapee, R. M. (1992). The role of family intervention in the treatment of child anxiety disorders: Some preliminary findings. *Behavior Change, 9,* 171–177.

Dadds, M., R., et al. (1992). Childhood depression and conduct disorder: II. An analysis of family interaction patterns in the home. *Journal of Abnormal Psychology, 101,* 505–513.

Dahl, R. E. (1992). The pharmacologic treatment of sleep disorders. *Psychiatric Clinics of North America, 15,* 161–178.

Daleiden, E. L., & Vasey, M. W. (1997). An information-processing perspective on childhood anxiety. *Clinical Psychology Review, 17,* 407–429.

Daley, S. E., et al. (1997). Predictors of the generation of episodic stress: A longitudinal study of late adolescent women. *Journal of Abnormal Psychology, 106,* 251–259.

Damasio, A. R. (1997). Towards a neuropathology of emotion and mood. *Nature, 386,* 769–770.

Darnton, J. (1994, September 21). Report says smoking causes a global epidemic of death. *The New York Times,* p. B8.

Daro, D., & Wiese, D. (1995). Current trends in child abuse reporting and fatalities: NCPCA's 1994 annual fifty state survey. Chicago, IL: National Committee to Prevent Child Abuse.

Darrow, S. L., et al. (1992). Sociodemographic correlates of alcohol consumption among African-American and White women. *Women and Health, 18,* 35–51.

Davies, P. (1988). Alzheimer's disease and related disorders: An overview. In M. K. Aronson (Ed.), *Understanding Alzheimer's disease* (pp. 3–14). New York: Scribner's.

Davis, J. O., & Bracha, H. S. (1996). Prenatal growth markers in schizophrenia: A monozygotic co-twin control study. *American Journal of Psychiatry, 153,* 1166–1172.

Davis, J. O., & Phelps. J. A. (1995). Twins with schizophrenia: Genes or germs? *Schizophrenia Bulletin, 21,* 13–18.

Davis, J. O., Phelps, J. A., & Bracha, H. S. (1995). Prenatal development of monozygotic twins and concordance for schizophrenia. *Schizophrenia Bulletin, 21,* 357–366.

Davis, K. L., et al. (1991). Dopamine in schizophrenia: A review and reconceptualization. *American Journal of Psychiatry, 148,* 1474–1486.

Davis, K. L., et al. (1992). A double-blind, placebo-controlled multicenter study of tacrine for Alzheimer's disease. *The New England Journal of Medicine, 327,* 1253–1259.

Davison, G. C., Vogel, R. S., & Coffman, S. G. (1997). Think-aloud approaches to cognitive assessment and the articulated thoughts in simulated situations paradigm. *Journal of Consulting and Clinical Psychology, 65,* 950–958.

Dean, A., Kolody, B., Wood, P., & Matt, G. E. (1992). The influence of living alone on depression in elderly persons. *Journal of Aging and Health, 4,* 3–18.

DeAngelis, T. (1993a). It's back: TV violence, concern for kid viewers. APA Monitor, 24(8), p. 16.

DeAngelis, T. (1994a, May). Vets, minorities, single moms make up homeless population. *APA Monitor,* p. 39.

DeAngelis, T. (1994b, November). Ethnic-minority issues recognized in DSM-IV. *APA Monitor,* p. 36.

DeAngelis, T. (1995a, April). New threat associated with child abuse. *APA Monitor, 26(4),* pp. 1, 38.

DeAngelis, T. (1995b). Research documents trauma of abuse. *APA Monitor, 26(4),* p. 34.

DeAngelis, T. (1997, January). Chromosomes contain clues on schizophrenia. *APA Monitor, 28 (1),* p. 26.

DeBell, C., & Jones, R. D. (1997a). As good as it seems? A review of EMDR experimental research. *Professional Psychology: Research and Practice, 28,* 153–163.

DeBell, C., & Jones, R. D. (1997b). Privileged communication at last? An overview of *Jaffee v. Redmond. Professional Psychology: Research and Practice, 28,* 559–566.

De Bellis, M. D., et al. (1994). Urinary catecholamine excretion in sexually abused girls. *Journal of the American Academy of Child and Adolescent Psychiatry, 33,* 320–327.

De-Carle, A. J., & Pato, M. T. (1996). Social phobia and stuttering. *American Journal of Psychiatry, 153,* 1367–1368.

Deckel, A. W., Hesselbrock, V., & Bauer, L. (1996). Antisocial personality disorder, childhood delinquency, and frontal brain functioning: EEG and neuropsychological findings. *Journal of Clinical Psychology, 52,* 639–650.

Decker, T .W., Cline-Elsen, J., & Gallagher, M. (1992). Relaxation therapy as an adjunct in radiation oncology. *Journal of Clinical Psychology, 48,* 388–393

Deffenbacher, J. L., & Suinn, R. M. (1988). Systematic desensitization and the reduction of anxiety. *The Counseling Psychologist, 16,* 9–30.

Deffenbacher, J. L., et al. (1996). Anger reduction in early adolescents. *Journal of Counseling Psychology, 43,* 149–157.

Dekker, J. (1993). Inhibited male orgasm. In W. O'Donohue & J. H. Geer (Eds.), *Handbook of sexual dysfunctions: Assessment and treatment* (pp. 279–301). Boston: Allyn & Bacon.

De La Cancela, V., & Guzman, L. P. (1991). Latino mental health service needs: Implications for training psychologists. In H. F. Myers et al. (Eds.), *Ethnic minority perspectives on clinical training and services in psychology* (pp. 59–64). Washington, DC: American Psychological Association.

De Leon, M. J., et al. (1983). Computed tomography and positron emission transaxial tomography evaluations of normal aging and Alzheimer's disease. *Journal of Cerebral Blood Flow and Metabolism, 3,* 391–394.

DeLeon, P. H., et al. (1997). Ethics and public policy formulation: A case example related to prescription privileges. *Professional Psychology: Research and Practice, 28,* 518–525.

Delprato, D. J., & Midgley, B. D. (1992). Some fundamentals of B. F. Skinner's behaviorism. *American Psychologist, 47,* 1507–1520.

De Mayo et al., as cited in Fried, L. P. (1998). Risk factors for 5-year mortality in older adults: The cardiovascular health study *Journal of the American Medical Association, 279,* 585–592.

deMayo, R. A. (1997). Patient sexual behavior and sexual harassment: A national survey of female psychologists. *Professional Psychology: Research and Practice, 28,* 58–62.

Dement, W. C. (1992). The proper use of sleeping pills in the primary care setting. *Journal of Clinical Psychiatry, 53,* (12, Suppl) 50–56.

DeMyer, M. K., Hingenten, J. N., & Jackson, R. K. (1981). Infantile autism reviewed: A decade of research. *Schizophrenia Bulletin, 7,* 338–451.

Denicoff, K. D., et al. (1997). Valproate prophylaxis in a prospective clinical trial of refractory bipolar disorder. *American Journal of Psychiatry, 154,* 1456–1458.

Denneby, J. A., et al. (1996). Case-control study of suicide by discharged psychiatry patients. *British Medical Journal, 312,* 1580.

Dennis, D. L., et al. (1991). A decade of research and services for homeless mentally ill persons. *American Psychologist, 46,* 1129–1138.

Denollet, J., et al. (1996). Personality as independent predictor of long-term mortality in patients with coronary heart disease. *Lancet, 347,* 417–421.

Depression Guideline Panel (1993a). *Depression in primary care: Vol. 1. Detection and diagnosis.* Clinical Practice Guideline No. 5. Rockville, MD: U.S. Department of Health and Human Services, Public Health Service, Agency for Health Care Policy and Research (AHCPR Pub. No. 93–0550).

Depression Guideline Panel (1993b). *Depression in primary care: Vol. 2. Treatment of major depression.* Clinical Practice Guideline No. 5. Rockville, MD: U.S. Department of Health and Human Services, Public Health Service, Agency for Health Care Policy and Research (AHCPR Pub. No. 93–0551).

DeRubeis, R. J., & Crits-Christoph, P. (1998). Empirically supported individual and group psychological treatments for adult mental disorders. *Journal of Consulting and Clinical Psychology, 66,* 37–52.

DeRubeis, R. J., et al. (1990). How does cognitive therapy work? Cognitive change and symptom change in cognitive therapy and pharmacotherapy for depression. *Journal of Consulting and Clinical Psychology, 58,* 862–869.

De Silva, P. (1993). Post-traumatic stress disorder: Cross-cultural aspects. *International Review of Psychiatry, 5,* 217–229.

Desmond, E. W. (1987, November). Out in the open: Changing attitudes and new research give fresh hope to alcoholics. *Time Magazine,* pp. 80–90.

Devan, G. S. (1987). Koro and schizophrenia in Singapore. *British Journal of Psychiatry, 150,* 106–107.

Devanand, D. P., et al. (1994). Does ECT alter brain structure? *American Journal of Psychiatry, 151,* 957–970.

Devanand, D. P., et al. (1997). Psychopathologic features in mild to moderate Alzheimer's Disease. *Archives of General Psychiatry, 54,* 257–263.

DeVeaugh-Geiss J. (1994). Pharmacologic therapy of obsessive compulsive disorder. *Advances in Pharmacology, 30,* 35–52.

Devins, G. M., Binik, Y. M., Hollomby, D. J., Barre, P. E., & Guttmann, R. D. (1981). Helplessness and depression in end-stage renal disease. *Journal of Abnormal Psychology, 90,* 531–545.

Devor, E. J. (1993). Why there is no gene for alcoholism. *Behavior Genetics, 23,* 145–151.

Devor, E. J. (1994). A developmental-genetic model of alcoholism: Implications for genetic research. *Journal of Consulting and Clinical Psychology, 62,* 1108–1115.

Dew, M. A., et al. (1997). Temporal profiles of the course of depression during treatment: Predictors of pathways toward recovery in the elderly. *Archives of General Psychiatry, 54,* 1016–1024.

DeWitt, K. (1991, October 31). The evolving concept of sexual harassment. *The New York Times,* Sec. 1, p. 28.

De Young, M. (1982). *The sexual victimization of children.* Jefferson, NC: McFarland & Company.

Dhaliwal, G. K., et al. (1996). Adult male survivors of childhood sexual abuse: Prevalence, sexual abuse characteristics, and long-term effects. *Clinical Psychology Review, 16,* 619–639.

Dhawan, S., & Marshall, W. L. (1996). Sexual abuse histories of sexual offenders. *Sexual Abuse Journal of Research and Treatment, 8,* 7–15.

Diamond, E. L. (1982). The role of anger and hostility in essential hypertension and coronary heart disease. *Psychological Bulletin, 92,* 410–433.

Diamond, S., Baldwin, R., & Diamond, R. (1963). *Inhibition and choice.* New York: Harper & Row.

DiLalla, D. L., Carey, G., Gottesman, I. I., & Bouchard, T. J., Jr. (1996). Heritability of MMPI personality indicators of psychopathology in twins reared apart. *Journal of Abnormal Psychology, 105,* 491–499.

DiLalla, L. F., & Gottesman, I. I. (1991). Biological and genetic contributors to violence: Widom's untold tale. *Psychological Bulletin, 109,* 125–129.

Dilk, M., N., & Bond, G. R. (1996). Meta-analytic evaluation of skills training research for individuals with severe mental illness. *Journal of Consulting and Clinical Psychology, 64,* 1337–1346.

Dilsaver, S. C., et al. (1996). Treatment of bipolar depression with carbamazepine: Results of an open study. *Biological Psychiatry, 40,* 935–937.

Dinh, K. T., et al. (1995). Children's perceptions of smokers and nonsmokers: A longitudinal study. *Health Psychology, 14,* 32–40.

Dixon, L., et al. (1997). Assertive community treatment and medication compliance in the homeless mentally ill. *American Journal of Psychiatry, 154,* 1302–1304.

Do you have a cancer gene? (1990, May 13). *U.S. News & World Report,* pp. 67–77.

Doane, J. A., Faloon, I. R H., Goldstein, M. J., & Mintz, J. (1985). Parental affective style and the treatment of schizophrenia. *Archives of General Psychiatry, 42,* 34–42.

Dobson, K. S., & Shaw, B. F. (1995). Cognitive therapies in practice. In B. Bongar & L. E. Beutler (Eds.), *Comprehensive textbook of psychotherapy: Theory and practice.* (pp. 159–172). New York: Oxford University Press.

Dodge, K. A. (1985). Attributional bias in aggressive children. *Advances in Cognitive Behavioral Research and Therapy, 4,* 73–110.

Dodge, K. A., Pettit, G. S., & Bates, J. E. (1994). Effects of physical maltreatment on the development of peer relations. *Development and Psychopathology, 6,* 43–55.

Dodge, K. A., et al. (1997). Reactive and proactive aggression in school children and psychiatrically impaired chronically assaultive youth. *Journal of Abnormal Psychology, 106,* 37–51.

Dodge, L. J. T., Glasgow, R. E., & O'Neill, H. K. (1982). Bibliotherapy in the treatment of female orgasmic dysfunction. *Journal of Consulting and Clinical Psychology, 50,* 442–443.

Doering, S., et al. (1998). Predictors of relapse and rehospitalzation in schizophrenia and schizoaffective disorder. *Schizophrenia Bulletin, 24,* 87–98.

Doleys, D. M. (1977). Behavioral treatments for nocturnal enuresis in children: A review of the literature. *Psychological Bulletin, 8,* 30–54.

Doll, B. (1996). Prevalence of psychiatric disorders in children and youth: An agenda for advocacy by school psychology. *School Psychology Quarterly, 11,* 20–46.

Donnerstein, E. I. (1980). Aggressive erotica and violence against women. *Journal of Personality and Social Psychology, 39,* 269–277.

Donnerstein, E. I., & Linz, D. G. (1984). Sexual violence in the media: A warning. *Psychology Today, 18*(1), 14–15.

Donnerstein, E. I., & Linz, D. G. (1987). *The question of pornography.* New York: The Free Press.

Douglas, A. R., Matson, I. C., & Hunter, S. (1989). Sex therapy for women incestuously abused as children. *Sexual and Marital Therapy, 4,* 143–159.

Douglas, V. I., Parry, P., Marton, P., Garson, C. (1976). Assessment of a cognitive training program for hyperactive children. *Journal of Abnormal Child Psychology, 4,* 389–410.

Dow, S. (1981). Retarded ejaculation. *Journal of Sex and Marital Therapy, 7,* 49–53.

Dowker, A., Hermelin, B., & Pring, L. (1996). A savant poet. *Psychological Medicine, 26,* 913–924.

Downey, K. K., et al. (1997). Adult attention deficit hyperactivity disorder: Psychological test profiles in a clinical population. *Journal of Nervous & Mental Disease, 185,* 32–38.

Doyne, E. J., et al. (1987). Running versus weight lifting in the treatment of depression. *Journal of Consulting and Clinical Psychology, 55,* 748–754.

Drake, R. E., & Vaillant, G. E. (1985). A validity study of axis II of DSM III. *American Journal of Psychiatry, 142,* 553–558.

Drake, R. E., et al. (1991). Housing instability and homelessness among rural schizophrenic patients. *American Journal of Psychiatry, 148,* 211–215.

Drevets, W. C., et al. (1997) Subgenual prefrontal cortex abnormalities in mood disorders. *Nature, 386,* 824–827.

Drewnowski, A. (1997). Taste preferences and food intake. *Annual Review of Nutrition, 17,* 237–253.

Drewnowski, A., et al. (1994). Eating pathology and DSM-III-R bulimia nervosa: A continuum of behavior. *American Journal of Psychiatry, 151,* 1217–1219.

Drews, C. D., et al. (1995). Variation in the influence of selected sociodemographic risk factors for mental retardation. *American Journal of Public Health, 85,* 329–334.

Drummond, D. C., & Glautier, S. (1994). A controlled trial of cue exposure treatment in alcohol dependence. *Journal of Consulting and Clinical Psychology, 62,* 809–817.

Dryden, W. (1984). *Rational-emotive therapy: Fundamentals and innovations.* London: Croom Helm.

Dubbert, P. M. (1992). Exercise in behavioral medicine. *Journal of Consulting and Clinical Psychology, 60,* 613–618.

Dubovsky, S. (1998, April). Are community rates of psychiatric disorders accurate? *Journal Watch for Psychiatry, 4,* p. 36.

Duckworth, G., & McBride, H. (1996). Suicide in old age: A tragedy of neglect. *Canadian Journal of Psychiatry, 41,* 217–222.

Duffy, A., et al. (1998). Psychiatric symptoms and syndromes among adolescent children of parents with lithium-responsive or lithium-nonresponsive bipolar disorder. *American Journal of Psychiatry, 155,* 431–433.

Duffy, F. H. (1994). The role of quantified electroencephalography in psychological research. In G. Dawson & K. W. Fischer (Eds.), *Human behavior and the developing brain.* (pp. 93–132). New York: Guilford Press.

Dugger, C. W. (1992, September 3). Threat only when on crack, homeless man foils system. *The New York Times,* pp. A1, B4.

Dugger, C. W. (1994, July 15). Larry Hogue is arrested in Westchester. *The New York Times,* pp. B1, B2.

Dugger, C. W. (1995, January 23). Slipping through cracks and out the door. *The New York Times,* pp. B1, B2.

Dulit, R. A., et al. (1994). Clinical correlates of self-mutilation in borderline personality disorder. *American Journal of Psychiatry, 151,* 1305–1311.

Duman, R. S., Heninger, G. R., & Nestler, E. J. (1997). A molecular and cellular theory of depression. *Archives of General Psychiatry, 54,* 597–606.

Dumas, J. E., Serketich, W. J., & LaFreniere, P. J. (1995). "Balance of power": A transactional analysis of control in mother-child dyads involving socially competent, aggressive, and anxious children. *Journal of Abnormal Psychology, 104,* 104–113.

Duncan, R. D., et al. (1996). Childhood physical assault as a risk factor for PTSD, depression, and substance abuse: Findings from a national survey. *American Journal of Orthopsychiatry, 66,* 437–447.

Dunham, H. W. (1965). *Community and schizophrenia: An epidemiological analysis.* Detroit: Wayne State University Press.

Du Pont heir found guilty of murder but mentally ill. (1997, February 26). *The New York Times,* p. A10.

Durham v. United States, 214 F. 2d 862 (DC Circ 1954).

Durkheim, E. (1958). *Suicide.* (J. A. Spaulding & G. Simpson, Trans.). New York: Free Press. (Original work published 1897).

Dutton-Douglas, M. A., & Walker, L. E. A. (1988). Introduction to feminist therapies. In M. A. Dutton-Douglas & L. Walker (Eds.), *Feminist psychotherapies: Integration of therapeutic and feminist systems* (pp. 3–11). Norwood, NJ: Ablex.

Duvoisin, R. C. (1996). Recent advances in the genetics of Parkinson's disease. *Advances in Neurology, 69,* 33–40.

Dwork, A. J. (1997). Postmortem studies of the hippocampal formation in schizophrenia. *Schizophrenia Bulletin, 23,* 385–402.

Dwyer, M. (1988). Exhibitionism/voyeurism. *Journal of Social Work and Human Sexuality, 7,* 101–112.

Dykens, E. M., & Hodapp, R. M. (1997). Treatment issues in genetic mental retardation syndromes. *Professional Psychology: Research and Practice, 28,* 263–270.

E

Earnst, K .S., & Kring, A. M. (1997). Construct validity of negative symptoms: An empirical and conceptual review. *Clinical Psychology Review, 17,* 167–189.

Eaton, W. W., Dryman, A., & Weissman, M. M. (1991). Panic and phobia. In L. N. Robins & D. A. Regier (Eds.), *Psychiatric disorders in America: The Epidemiologic Catchment Area Study* (pp. 155–179). New York: The Free Press.

Eaton, W. W., et al. (1994). Panic and panic disorder in the United States. *American Journal of Psychiatry, 151,* 413–420.

Eaton, W. W., et al. (1997). Natural history of diagnostic interview schedule/DSM-IV major depression: The Baltimore Epidemiologic Catchment Area follow-up. *Archives of General Psychiatry, 54,* 993–999.

Eberhardy, F. (1967). The view from "the couch." *Journal of Child Psychological Psychiatry, 8,* 257–263.

Ebert, B. W. (1992). Mandatory child abuse reporting in California. Special section: American academy of forensic psychology. *Forensic Reports, 5,* 335–350.

Ebigbo, P. O. (1993). Situation analysis of child abuse and neglect in Nigeria. *Journal of Psychology in Africa, 1,* 159–178.

Eckert, E. D., Bouchard, T. J., Bohlen, J., & Heston, L .L. (1986). Homosexuality in monozygotic twins reared apart. *British Journal of Psychiatry, 148,* 421–425.

Eckhardt, C. I., Barbour, K. A., & Stuart, G. L. (1997). Anger and hostility in maritally violent men: Conceptual distinctions, measurement issues, and literature review. *Clinical Psychology Review, 17,* 333–358.

Eckhardt, C. I., & Deffenbacher, J. L. (1995). Diagnosis of anger disorders. In H. Kassinove (Ed.), *Anger disorders: Definition, diagnosis, and treatment* (pp. 27–47). Washington, DC: Taylor & Francis.

Eckhardt, M. J., et al. (1981). Health hazards associated with alcohol consumption. *Journal of the American Medical Association, 246,* 648–666.

Edelson, E. (1998, March 9). Migraines come into focus. *Newsday,* p. C7.

Edwards, E. D., & Egbert-Edwards, M. (1990). American Indian adolescents: Combating problems of substance use and abuse through a community model. In A. R. Stiffman & L. E. Davis (Eds.), *Ethnic issues in adolescent mental health* (pp. 285–302). Newbury Park, CA: Sage Publications.

Egami, Y., et al. (1996). Psychiatric profile and sociodemographic characteristics of adults who report physically abusing or neglecting children. *American Journal of Psychiatry, 153,* 921–928.

Egan, J. (1991). Oppositional defiant disorder. In J. M. Wiener (Ed.). *Textbook of child and adolescent psychiatry.* Washington, DC: American Psychiatric Press.

Egan, M. F., Apud, J., & Wyatt, R. J. (1997). Treatment of tardive dyskinesia. *Schizophrenia Bulletin, 23,* 583–609.

Egeland, J. A., et al. (1983). Amish study, II: The impact of cultural factors on diagnosis of bipolar illness. *American Journal of Psychiatry, 140,* 67–71.

Ehlers, A. (1995). A 1-year prospective study of panic attacks: Clinical course and factors associated with maintenance. *Journal of Abnormal Psychology, 104,* 164–172.

Ehlers, A., & Breuer, P. (1992). Increased cardiac awareness in panic disorder. *Journal of Abnormal Psychology, 101,* 371–382.

Ehlers, A., Margraf, J., Roth, W. T., Barr-Taylor, C., & Birbaumer, N. (1988). Anxiety induced by false heart rate feedback in patients with panic disorder. *Behaviour Research and Therapy, 26,* 1–11.

Ehlers, A., Mayou, R. A., & Bryant, B. (1998). Psychological predictors of chronic posttraumatic stress disorder after motor vehicle accidents. *Journal of Abnormal Psychology, 107,* 508–519.

Ehlich, P. J., et al. (1997). PTSD after a peacekeeping mission. *American Journal of Psychiatry, 154,* 1319–1320.

Ehrhardt, A. A. (1992). Trends in sexual behavior and the HIV pandemic [Editorial]. *American Journal of Public Health, 82,* 1459–1461.

Eiberg, H., Berendt, I., & Mohr, J. (1995). Assignment of dominant inherited nocturnal euresis (ENUR1) to chromosome 13q. *Nature Genetics, 10,* 354–356.

Eisdorder, C., & Cohen, D. (1980). Diagnostic criteria for primary neuronal degeneration of the Alzheimer type. *Journal of Family Practice, 11,* 553–557.

Eisenbruch, M. (1992). Toward a culturally sensitive DSM: Cultural bereavement in Cambodian refugees and the traditional healer as taxonomist. *Journal of Nervous and Mental Disease, 180,* 8–10.

Eisler, I., et al. (1997). Family and individual therapy in anorexia nervosa: A 5-year follow-up. *Archives of General Psychiatry, 54,* 1025–1030.

Eisler, R. M., Blanchard, E. B., Fitts, H., & Williams, J. G. (1978). Social skill training with & without modeling for schizophrenic & non-psychotic hospitalized psychiatric patients. *Behavioral Modification, 2,* 147–172.

Elderly's suicide rate is up 9% over 12 years. (1996, January 12). *The New York Times,* p. A14.

Elkin, I., et al. (1989). National Institute of Mental Health treatment of depression collaborative research program: General effectiveness of treatments. *Archives of General Psychiatry, 46,* 971–982.

Elkin, I., et al. (1995). Initial severity and differential treatment outcome in the National Institute of Mental Health Treatment of Depression Collaborative Research Program. *Journal of Consulting and Clinical Psychology, 63,* 841–847.

Elkins, I. J., et al. (1992). Span of apprehension in schizophrenic patients as a function of distractor masking and laterality. *Journal of Abnormal Psychology, 101,* 53–60.

Ellason, J. W., & Ross, C. A. (1997). Two-year follow-up of inpatients with dissociative identity disorder. *American Journal of Psychiatry, 154,* 832–839.

Ellickson, P. L., Hays, R. D., & Bell, R. M. (1992). Stepping through the drug use sequence: Longitudinal scalogram analysis of initiation and regular use. *Journal of Abnormal Psychology, 101,* 441–451.

Elliott, A. J., et al. (1998). Randomized, placebo-controlled trial of paroxetine versus imipramine in depressed HIV-positive outpatients. *American Journal of Psychiatry, 155,* 367–372.

Elliott, D. M. (1997). Traumatic events: Prevalence and delayed recall in the general population. *Journal of Consulting and Clinical Psychology,* 811–820.

Ellis, A. (1985). Cognition and affect in emotional disturbance. *American Psychologist, 40,* 471–472.

Ellis, A. (1987). The impossibility of achieving consistently good mental health. *American Psychologist, 42,* 364–375.

Ellis, A. (1993). Reflections on rational-emotive therapy. *Journal of Consulting and Clinical Psychology, 61,* 199–201.

Ellis, A. (1996). *Better, deeper, and more enduring brief therapy: The rational emotive behavior therapy approach.* New York: Brunner/Mazel.

Ellis, A. (1977a). Anger: How to live with and without it. Secaucus, NJ: Citadel Press.

Ellis, A. (1977b). The basic clinical theory of rational-emotive therapy. In A. Ellis & R. Grieger (Eds.), *Handbook of rational-emotive therapy.* New York: Springer.

Ellis, A., & Dryden, W. (1987). *The practice of rational emotional therapy.* New York: Springer.

Ellis, A., Young, J., & Lockwood, G. (1989). Cognitive therapy and rational-emotive therapy: A dialogue. *Journal of Cognitive Psychotherapy, 1,* 205–256.

Ellis, L. (1990). Prenatal stress may effect sex-typical behaviors of a child. *Brown University Child Behavior and Development Letter, 6*(1), pp. 1–3.

Ellis, L., & Ames, M. A. (1987). Neurohormonal functioning and sexual orientation: A theory of homosexuality-heterosexuality. *Psychological Bulletin, 101,* 233–258.

Else, L., et al. (1993). Personality characteristics of men who physically abuse women. *Hospital and Community Psychiatry, 44,* 54–58.

Emmanuel, N. P., Lydiard, R. B., & Ballenger, J. C. (1992). Fluoxeine treatment of voyeurism. *American Journal of Psychiatry, 148,* 471–472.

Emslie, G. J., et al. (1997). A double-blind, randomized, placebo-controlled trial of fluoxetine in children and adolescents with depression. *Archives of General Psychiatry, 54,* 1031–1037.

Engdahl, B., et al. (1997). Posttraumatic stress disorder in a community group of former prisoners of war: A normative response to severe trauma. *American Journal of Psychiatry, 154,* 1576–1581.

Engels, G. I., Garnefski, N., & Diekstra, R. F. W. (1993). Efficacy of rational-emotive therapy: A quantitative analysis. *Journal of Consulting and Clinical Psychology, 61,* 1083–1090.

Epping-Jordan, J. E., Compas, B. E., & Howell, D. C. (1994). Predictors of cancer progression in young adult men and women: Avoidance, intrusive thoughts, and psychological symptoms. *Health Psychology, 13,* 539–547.

Epstein, L. H., & Perkin, K. A. (1988). Smoking, stress, and coronary heart disease. *Journal of Consulting and Clinical Psychology, 56,* 342–349.

Epstein, S. (1994). Trait theory as personality theory: Can a part be as great as the whole? *Psychological Inquiry, 5,* 120–122.

Erdman, H. P., et al. (1987). A comparison of the Diagnostic Interview Schedule and clinical diagnosis. *American Journal of Psychiatry, 144,* 1477–1480.

Erikson, E. H. (1963). *Childhood and society.* New York: W. W. Norton.

Erikson, E. H. (1975). *Life history and the historical moment.* New York: W. W. Norton.

Erlenmeyer-Kimling, L., & Cornblatt, B. (1987). The New York High-Risk Project: A follow-up report. *Schizophrenia Bulletin, 13,* 451–461.

Erlenmeyer-Kimling, L., et al. (1997). The New York high-risk project: Prevalence and comorbidity of Axis I disorders in offspring of schizophrenic parents at 25-year follow-up. *Archives of General Psychiatry, 54,* 1096–1102.

Ernsberger, P. (1987). Complications of the surgical treatment of obesity. *American Journal of Psychiatry, 144,* 833–834.

Ernst, N. D., & Harlan, W. R. (1991). Obesity and cardiovascular disease in minority populations: Executive summary. *American Journal of Clinical Nutrition, 53,* 1507S–1511S.

Eron, L. D. (1993). Cited in DeAngelis, T. (1993b). It's back: TV violence, concern for kid viewers. *APA Monitor, 24*(8), p. 16.

Eronen, M., et al. (1996). Schizophrenia and homicidal behavior. *Schizophrenia Bulletin, 22,* 83–89.

Escobar, J. I. (1998). Immigration and mental health: Why are immigrants better off? *Archives of General Psychiatry, 55,* 781–782.

Esterling, B. A., et al. (1994a). Chronic stress, social support, and persistent alterations in the natural killer cell response to cytokines in older adults. *Health Psychology, 13,* 291–298.

Esterling, B. A., et al. (1994b). Emotional disclosure through writing or speaking modulates latent Epstein-Barr virus antibody titers. *Journal of Consulting and Clinical Psychology, 62,* 130–140.

Evans, D. A., et al. (1989). Prevalence of Alzheimer's disease in a community population of older persons. *Journal of the American Medical Association, 262,* 2551–2556.

Evans, G. D., & Murphy, M. J. (1997). The practicality of predoctoral prescription training for psychologists: A survey of directors of clinical training. *Professional Psychology: Research and Practice, 28,* 113–117.

Evans, R. B. (1969). Childhood parental relationships of homosexual men. *Journal of Consulting and Clinical Psychology, 33,* 129–135.

Exner, J. E. (1991). *The Rorschach: A comprehensive system: Vol. 2. Interpretation.* New York: Wiley.

Exner, J. E. (1993). *The Rorschach: A comprehensive system: Vol. 1. Basic foundations* (3rd ed.). New York: Wiley.

Extinguishing Alzheimer's. (1998, June 23). *The New York Times,* p. F7.

F

Fabian, J. L. (1991). "Koro: Proposed classification for DSM-IV": Comment. *American Journal of Psychiatry, 148,* 1766.

Fabian, W. D., Jr., & Fishkin, S. M. (1981). A replicated study of self-reported changes in psychological ab-

sorption with marijuana intoxication. *Journal of Abnormal Psychology, 90,* 546–553.

Fabrega, H., Jr. (1992). Diagnosis interminable: Toward a culturally sensitive DSM-IV. *Journal of Nervous and Mental Disease, 180,* 5–7.

Fabrega, H., Jr., Mezzich, J., & Ulrich, R. F. (1988). Black-white differences in psychopathology in an urban psychiatric population. *Comprehensive Psychiatry, 29,* 285–297.

Fahn, S. (1992). Fetal-tissue transplants in Parkinson's disease. *The New England Journal of Medicine, 327,* 1589–1590.

Fairburn, C. G. (1997). Eating disorders. In D. M. Clark and C. G. Fairburn (Eds.), *Science and practice of cognitive behaviour therapy* (pp. 209–241). New York: Oxford University Press.

Fairburn, C. G., Cooper, Z., & Cooper, P. J. (1986). The clinical features and maintenance of bulimia nervosa. In K. D. Brownell & J. P. Foreyt (Eds.), *Handbook of eating disorders* (pp. 389–404). New York: Basic Books.

Fairburn, C. G., Kirk, J., O'Connor, M., & Cooper, P. J. (1986). A comparison of two psychological treatments for bulimia nervosa. *Behaviour Research and Therapy, 24*(6), 629–643.

Fairburn, C. G., & Wilson, G. T. (Eds.). (1993). *Binge eating: Nature, assessment, and treatment.* New York: Guilford Press.

Fairburn, C. G., et al. (1991). Three psychological treatments for bulimia nervosa: A comparative trial. *Archives of General Psychiatry, 48,* 463–469.

Fairburn, C. G., et al. (1997). Risk factors for bulimia nervosa: A community-based case-control study. *Archives of General Psychiatry, 54,* 509–517.

Fairweather, G. W., Sanders, D. H., Maynard, H., Cressler, D. L., & Bleck, D. S. (1969). *Community life for the mentally ill: An alternative to institutional care.* Chicago: Aldine.

Falk, B., Hersen, M., & Van Hasselt, V. B. (1994). Assessment of post-traumatic stress disorder in older adults: A critical review. *Clinical Psychology Review, 14,* 383–415.

Faller, K. C. (1989). Characteristics of a clinical sample of sexually abused children: How boy and girl victims differ. *Child Abuse and Neglect, 13,* 281–291.

Fallon, A. E., & Rozin, P. (1985). Sex differences in perceptions of desirable body shape. *Journal of Abnormal Psychology, 94,* 102–105.

Fallon, B. A., et al. (1993). Fluoxetine for hypochondriacal patients without major depression. *Journal of Clinical Psychopharmacology, 13,* 438–441.

Falloon, I. R. H., et al. (1982). Family management in the prevention of exacerbations of schizophrenia. *New England Journal of Medicine, 306,* 1437–1440.

Falloon, I. R. H., et al. (1985). Family management in the prevention of morbidity of schizophrenia: Clinical outcome of a two-year longitudinal study. *Archives of General Psychiatry, 42,* 887–896.

Fals-Stewart, W., Marks, A. P., & Schafer, J. (1993). A comparison of behavioral group therapy and individual behavior therapy in treating obsessive-compulsive disorder. *Journal of Nervous and Mental Disease, 181,* 189–193.

Falste, R. (1988, October 9). The myth about teenagers. *The New York Times Magazine (The Good Health Report Magazine).* pp. 19, 76.

Fann, W. E., Karacan, I., Pokerny, A. D., & Williams, R. L. (1982). *Phenomenology and the treatment of psychophysiological disorders.* New York: Spectrum Publications.

Faraone, S. V., Kremen, W. S., & Tsuang, M. T. (1990). Genetic transmission of major affective disorders: Quantitative models and linkage analyses. *Psychological Bulletin, 108,* 109–127.

Faraone, S. V., & Tsuang, M. T. (1985). Quantitative models of the genetic transmission of schizophrenia. *Psychological Bulletin, 98,* 41–66.

Faraone, S. V., et al. (1993). Intellectual performance and school failure in children with attention deficit hyperactivity disorders and their siblings. *Journal of Abnormal Psychology, 102,* 616–623.

Farber, B. A., Brink, D. C., & Raskin, P. M. (1996). *The psychotherapy of Carl Rogers: Cases and commentary* (pp. 74–75). New York: The Guilford Press.

Farberman, R. K. (1997). Public attitudes about psychologists and mental health care: Research to guide the American Psychological Association Public Education Campaign. *Professional Psychology: Research and Practice, 28,* 128–136.

Farr, C. B. (1994). Benjamin Rush and American psychiatry. *American Journal of Psychiatry, 151 (Suppl.),* 65–73.

Farrell, A. D., Camplair, P. S., & McCullough, L. (1987). Identification of target complaints by computer interview: Evaluation of the Computerized Assessment System for Psychotherapy Evaluation and Research. *Journal of Consulting and Clinical Psychology, 55,* 691–700.

Farrell, A. D., & White, K. S. (1998). Peer influences and drug use among urban adolescents: Family structure and parent/adolescent relationship as protective factors. *Journal of Consulting and Clinical Psychology, 66,* 248–258.

Fava, M. (1991). Does fluoxetine increase the risk of suicide? *The Harvard Mental Health Letter, 7(7),* 8.

Fava, M., et al. (1994). Dyfsunctional attitudes in major depression: Changes with pharmacotherapy. *Journal of Nervous and Mental Disease, 182,* 45–49.

Fawcett, J., et al. (1990). Time-related predictors of suicide in major affective disorder. *American Journal of Psychiatry, 147,* 1189–1194.

Fawzy, F. I., & Fawzy, N. W. (1994). A structured psychoeducational intervention for cancer patients. *General Hospital Psychiatry, 16,* 149–192.

Fawzy, F. I., et al. (1990). A structured psychiatric intervention for cancer patients. *Archives of General Psychiatry, 47,* 729–735.

Fay, R. E., et al. (1989). Prevalence and patterns of same-gender sexual contact among men. *Science, 243,* 338–348.

FDA approves Paxil for treating additional mental disorders. (1996, July). *APA Monitor, 27* (7), p. 4.

FDA approves second drug for Alzheimer's, (1996, November 27). *The New York Times,* p. C8.

Feder, B. J. Increase in teen-age smoking sharpest among black males. (1996, May 24). *The New York Times,* p. A20.

Feder, H. H. (1984). Hormones and sexual behavior. *Annual Review of Psychology, 35,* 165–200.

Feighner, J. P. (1982). Benzodiazepines as antidepressants. *Modern Problems in Pharmopsychiatry, 18,* 197–213.

Feinauer, L. L., Stuart, D. A. (1996). Blame and resilience in women sexually abused as children. *American Journal of Family Therapy, 24,* 31–40.

Feldman, C. M. (1997). Childhood precursors of adult interpartner violence. *Clinical Psychology: Science and Practice, 4,* 307–333.

Felsenfeld, S. (1996). Progress and needs in the genetics of stuttering. *Journal of Fluency Disorders, 21,* 77–103.

Fenichel, O. (1945). *The psychoanalytic theory of neurosis.* New York: W. W. Norton.

Fenton, W. S., et al. (1997). Symptoms, subtype, and suicidality in patients with schizophrenia spectrum disorders. *American Journal of Psychiatry, 154,* 199–204.

Ferguson-Peters, M. (1985). Racial socialization of young Black children. In H. & J. L. McAdoo (Eds.), *Black children* (pp. 159–173). Beverly Hills, CA: Sage Publications.

Ferrando, S. J., et al. (1997). Selective serotonin reuptake inhibitor treatment of depression in symptomatic HIV infection and AIDS: Improvement in affective and somatic symptoms. *General Hospital Psychiatry, 19,* 89–97.

Ferrans, C. E., Cohen, F. L., & Smith, K. M. (1992). The quality of life of persons with narcolepsy. *Loss, Grief and Care, 5,* 23–32.

Ferrari, M., & Matthews, W. S. (1983). Self-recognition deficits in autism: Syndrome-specific or general developmental delay? *Journal of Autism and Developmental Disorders, 13,* 317–325.

Feshbach, S. (1994). Nationalism, patriotism, and aggression: A clarification of functional differences. In L. R. Huesmann (Ed.), *Aggressive behavior: Current perspectives.* (pp. 275–291) New York: Plenum Press.

Feske, U. (1998). Eye movement desensitization and reprocessing treatment for posttraumatic stress disorder. *Clinical Psychology: Science and Practice, 5,* 171–81.

Feske, U., & Chambless, D. L. (1996). Cognitive behavioral versus exposure only treatment for social phobia: A meta-analysis. *Behavior Therapy, 26,* 695–720.

Feske, U., & Goldstein, A. J. (1997). Eye movement desensitization and reprocessing treatment for panic disorder: A controlled outcome and partial dismantling study. *Journal of Consulting and Clinical Psychology, 65,* 1026–1035.

A few brisk walks a month are linked to living longer. (1998, February 11). *The New York Times,* p. A14.

Fibel, B., & Hale, W. D. (1978). The generalized expectancy for success scale: A new measure. *Journal of Consulting and Clinical Psychology, 46,* 924–931.

Fichter, M. M., et al. (1997). Family climate and expressed emotion in the course of alcoholism. *Family Process, 36,* 202–221.

Fieve, R. R. (1975). *Moodswings: The third revolution in psychiatry.* New York: Morrow.

Fingerhut, L. A., Ingram, D. D., & Feldman, J. J. (1998). Homicide rates among U.S. teenagers and young adults: Differences by mechanism, level of urbanization, race, and sex, 1987 through 1995. *Journal of the American Medical Association, 280,* 423–427.

Fingerhut, L. A., & Kleinman, J. C. (1990). International and interstate comparisons of homicide among young males. *Journal of the American Medical Association, 263,* 3292–3295.

Finkelhor, D. (1980). Sex among siblings: A survey on prevalence, variety, and effects. *Archives of Sexual Behavior, 9,* 171–194.

Finkelhor, D. (1984). *Child sexual abuse: Theory and research.* New York: Free Press.

Finkelhor, D. (1990). Early and long-term effects of child sexual abuse: An update. *Professional Psychology: Research and Practice, 21,* 325–330.

Finkelhor, D. (1993). Epidemiological factors in the identification of child abuse. Special issue: Clinical recognition of sexually abused children. *Child Abuse and Neglect, 17,* 67–70.

Finkelhor, D., & Hotaling, G. T. (1984). Sexual abuse in the National Incidence Study of Child Abuse and Neglect: An appraisal. *Child Abuse and Neglect, 8,* 22–33.

Finkelhor, D., & Russell, D. (1984). Women as perpetrators: Review of the evidence. In D. Finkelhor (Ed.), *Child sexual abuse: Theory and research.* New York: The Free Press

Finkelhor, D., et al. (1990). Sexual abuse in a national survey of adult men and women: Prevalence, characteristics, and risk factors. *Child Abuse and Neglect, 14,* 19–28.

Finkelstein, J. R. J., et al. (1997). Attentional dysfunctions in neuroleptic-naive and neuroleptic-withdrawn schizophrenic patients and their siblings. *Journal of Abnormal Psychology, 106,* 203–212.

Finn, S. (1996). *Using the MMPI-2 as therapeutic assessment.* Minneapolis, MN: University of Minnesota Press.

Finney, J. W., & Monahan, S. C. (1996). The cost-effectiveness of treatment for alcoholism: A second approximation. *Journal of Studies on Alcohol, 57,* 229–243.

Fishbain, D. A. (1991). "Koro: Proposed classification for DSM-IV": Comment. *American Journal of Psychiatry, 148,* 1765–1766.

Fishbain, D. A., & Goldberg, M. (1991). The misdiagnosis of conversion disorder in a psychiatric emergency service. *General Hospital Psychiatry, 13,* 177–181.

Fisher, J. D., & Fisher, W. A. (1992). Changing AIDS-risk behavior. *Psychological Bulletin, 111,* 455–474.

Fisher, J. D., et al. (1994). Empirical tests of an information-motivation-behavioral skills model of AIDS-preventive behavior with gay men and heterosexual university students. *Health Psychology, 13,* 238–250.

Fisher, L. M. (1997, April 30). Alzheimer's team finds a new genetic link. *The New York Times,* p. A16.

Fisher, M., et al. (1995). Eating disorders in adolescents: A background paper. *Journal of Adolescent Health, 16,* 420–437.

Fisher, R. L., & Fisher, S. (1996). Antidepressants for children: Is scientific support necessary? *Journal of Nervous & Mental Disease, 184,* 99–102.

Fisher, S., & Greenberg, R. (1978). (Eds.). *The scientific evaluation of Freud's theories and therapy: A book of readings.* New York: Basic Books.

Fisman, S., & Takhar, J. (1996). "Fear of alien abduction": Reply. *Journal of the American Academy of Child and Adolescent Psychiatry, 35,* 556–557.

Fitzgerald, L. F. (1993a). Sexual harassment: Violence against women in the workplace. *American Psychologist, 48,* 1070–1076.

Fitzgerald, L. F. (1993b). *Sexual harassment in higher education: Concepts and issues.* Washington, DC: National Education Association.

Fitzgerald, L. F., & Shullman, S. L. (1993). Sexual harassment: A research analysis and agenda for the 1990's. *Journal of Vocational Behavior, 42,* 5–27.

Fitzgerald, L. F., et al. (1988). The incidence and demensions of sexual harassment in academia and the workplace. *Journal of Vocational Behavior, 32,* 152–175.

Fizzle anger. (1996, February). *Prevention,* p. 24.

Fleming, M. Z., Cohen, D., Salt, P., Jones, D., & Jenkins, S. (1981). A study of pre- and postsurgical transsexuals: MMPI characteristics. *Archives of Sexual Behavior, 10,* 161–170.

Fleming, M. Z., MacGowan, B. R., Robinson, L., Spitz, J., & Salt, P. (1982). The body image of the postoperative female-to-male transsexual. *Journal of Consulting and Clinical Psychology, 50,* 461–462.

Fletcher, J. M., et al. (1994). Cognitive profiles of reading disability: Comparisons of discrepancy and low achievement definitions. *Journal of Educational Psychology, 86,* 6–23.

Flint, A. J. (1994). Epidemiology and comorbidity of anxiety disorders in the elderly. *American Journal of Psychiatry, 151,* 640–649.

Flint, A. J., & Rifat, S. L. (1998). Two-year outcome of psychotic depression in late life. *American Journal of Psychiatry, 155,* 178–183.

Flint, J., et al. (1995). The detection of subtelomeric chromosomal rearrangements in idiopathic mental retardation. *Nature Genetics, 9,* 132–140.

Flournoy, P. S., & Wilson, G. L. (1991). Assessment of MMPI profiles of male batterers. *Violence and Victims, 6,* 309–320.

Fluoxetine Bulimia Nervosa Collaborative Study Group. (1992). Fluoxetine in the treatment of bulimia nervosa: A multicenter, placebo-controlled, double-blind trial. *Archives of General Psychiatry, 49,* 139–147.

Foa, E. B. (1990, August/September). Obsessive-compulsive disorder. In American Psychiatric Association, *DSM-IV Update.* Washington, DC: American Psychiatric Association.

Foa, E. B. (1996). The efficacy of behavioral therapy with obsessive-compulsives. *The Clinical Psychologist, 49,* 19–21.

Foa, E.B., & Kozak, M. J. (1995). *DSM-IV* field trial: Obsessive-compulsive disorder. *American Journal of Psychiatry, 152,* 90–96.

Foa, E. B., & Meadows, E. A. (1997). Psychosocial treatments for posttraumatic stress disorder: A critical review. *Annual Review of Psychology, 48,* 449–480.

Foa, E. B., Riggs, D. S., & Gershuny, B. S. (1995). Arousal, numbing, and intrusion: Symptom structure of PTSD following assault. *American Journal of Psychiatry, 152,* 115–120.

Foderaro, L. W. (1994, November 8). "Clubhouse" helps mentally ill find the way back. *The New York Times,* p. B1.

Fokias, D., & Tyler, P. (1995). Social support and agoraphobia: A review. *Clinical Psychology Review, 15,* 347–366.

Folkman, S., & Lazarus, R. S. (1986). Stress processes and depressive symptomatology. *Journal of Abnormal Psychology, 95,* 107–113.

Follette, W. C., & Houts, A. C. (1996). Models of scientific progress and the role of theory and taxonomy development: A case study of the DSM. *Journal of Consulting and Clinical Psychology, 64,* 1120–1132.

Follingstad, D. R., Neckerman, A. P., & Vormbrock, J. (1988). Reactions to victimization and coping strategies of battered women: The ties that bind. *Clinical Psychology Review, 8,* 373–390.

Folstein, S., & Rutter, M. (1978). A twin study of individuals with infantile autism. In M. Rutter & E. Schopler (Eds.), *Autism: A reappraisal of concepts and treatment.* New York: Plenum Press.

Fonagy, P., et al. (1995). Attachment, the reflective self, and borderline states: The predictive specificity of the Adult Attachment Interview and pathological emotional development. In S. Goldberg & R. Muir (Eds.), *Attachment theory: Social, developmental, and clinical perspectives* (pp. 233–278). Hillsdale, NJ: Analytic Press.

Fontana, A., & Rosenheck, R. (1994). Posttraumatic stress disorder among Vietnam theater veterans: A causal model of etiology in a community sample. *Journal of Nervous and Mental Disease, 182,* 677–684.

Fontham, E. T. H., et al. (1994). Environmental tobacco smoke and lung cancer in nonsmoking women: A multicenter study. *Journal of the American Medical Association, 271,* 1752–1759.

Forehand, R., Brody, G., Slotkin, J., Fauber, R., McCombs, A., & Long, N. (1988). Young adolescent and maternal depression: Assessment, interrelations, and family predictors. *Journal of Consulting and Clinical Psychology, 56,* 422–426.

Forehand, R., Brody, G., & Smith, K. (1986). Contributions of child behavior and marital dissatisfaction to maternal perceptions of child maladjustment. *Behaviour Research & Therapy, 24,* 43–48.

Forehand, R., Lautenschlager, G. J., Faust, J., & Graziano, W. G. (1986). Parent perceptions and parent-child interactions in clinic-referred children: A preliminary investigation of the effect of maternal depressive moods. *Behaviour Research and Therapy, 24,* 73–75.

Foster, G. D., & Kendall, P. C. (1994). The realistic treatment of obesity: Changing the scales of success. *Clinical Psychology Review, 14,* 701–736.

Foster, G. D., et al. (1997). What is a reasonable weight loss? Patients' expectations and evaluations of obesity treatment outcomes. *Journal of Consulting and Clinical Psychology, 65,* 79–85.

Foster, S. L., & Cone, J. D. (1986). Design and use of direct observation procedures. In A. R. Ciminiero, K. S. Calhoun, & H. E. Adams (Eds.), *Handbook of behavioral assessment* (2nd ed.) (pp. 253–324). New York: John Wiley & Sons.

Fowles, D. C. (1993). Electrodermal activity and antisocial behavior: Empirical findings and theoretical issues. In J. C. Roy et al. (Eds.), *Psychological theories of drinking and alcoholism* (pp. 181–226). New York: Guilford Press.

Foy, D. W., Resnick, H. S., Sipprele, R. C., & Carroll, E. M. (1987). Premilitary, military, and postmilitary factors in the development of combat-related posttraumatic stress disorder. *The Behavior Therapist, 10,* 3–9.

Frank, E. (1991). Interpersonal psychotherapy as a maintenance treatment for patients with recurrent depression. *Psychotherapy, 28,* 259–266.

Frank, E., Brogan, D., & Schiffman, M. (1998). Harassment among US women physicians. *Archives of Internal Medicine, 158,* 352–358.

Franklin, M. E., & Foa, E. B. (1998). Cognitive-behavioral treatments for obsessive compulsive disorder. In P. E. Nathan & J. M. Gorman (Eds.), *A guide to treatments that work* (pp. 339–357). New York: Oxford University Press.

Fraser, J. S. (1996). All that glitters is not always gold: Medical offset effects and managed behavioral health care. *Professional Psychology: Research & Practice, 27,* 335–344.

Frauenglass, S., et al. (1997). Family support decreases influence of deviant peers on Hispanic adolescent's substance use. *Journal of Clinical Child Psychology, 26,* 15–23.

Fredrikson, M., Annas, P., & Wik, G.(1997). Parental history, aversive exposure and the development of snake and spider phobia in women. *Behaviour Research and Therapy, 35,* 23–28.

Freed, A. O. (1992). Discussion: Minority elderly. *Journal of Geriatric Psychiatry; 25,* 105–111.

Freed, C. R., et al. (1992). Survival of implanted fetal dopamine cells and neurologic improvement 12 to 46 months after transplantation for Parkinson's disease. *The New England Journal of Medicine, 327,* 1549–1555.

Freeman, L. N., Shaffer, D,. & Smith, H. (1996). The neglected victims of homicide: The needs of young siblings of murder victims. *American Journal of Orthopsychiatry, 66,* 337–345.

Freedman, D. K. (1994). [Review of *Comprehensive handbook of psychotherapy integration.*] *Journal of Psychotherapy Integration, 4,* 89–91.

Freedman, R., et al. (1987). Neurobiological studies of sensory gating in schizophrenia. *Schizophrenia Bulletin, 13,* 669–678.

Freemon, F. R. (1981). *Organic mental disease.* Jamaica, NY: Spectrum.

Freeston, M. H., et al. (1997). Cognitive-behavioral treatment of obsessive thoughts: A controlled study. *Journal of Consulting and Clinical Psychology, 65,* 405–413.

Freiberg, P., (1995). Psychologists examine attacks on homosexuals. *APA Monitor, 26 (6),* 30–31.

Freimer, N. B., et al. (1996). Genetic mapping using haplotype, association and linkage methods suggests a locus for severe bipolar disorder (BPI) at 18q22-q23. *Nature Genetics, 12,* 436–441.

French, S. A., & Jeffery, R. W. (1994). Consequences of dieting to lose weight: Effects on physical and mental health. *Health Psychology, 13,* 195–212.

French, S. A., et al. (1995). Frequent dieting among adolescents: Psychosocial and health behavior correlates. *American Journal of Public Health, 85,* 695–710.

Freud, S. (1957). Mourning and melancholia (1917). In J. Rickman (Ed.), *A general selection from the works of Sigmund Freud.* Garden City, NY: Doubleday.

Freud, S. (1959a). *Analysis of a phobia in a 5–year–old boy.* In A. & J. Strachey (Ed. & Trans.), *Collected papers.* Vol. 3, New York: Basic Books. (Original work published 1909).

Freud, S. (1959b). *Group psychology and the analysis of the ego.* (James Strachey, ed. and trans.). London: Hogarth Press. (Original work published 1922).

Freud, S. (1964). New introductory lectures. In *Standard edition of the complete psychological works of Sigmund Freud* (Vol. 22). London: Hogarth (Original work published in 1933).

Freund, K., & Blanchard, R. (1986). The concept of courtship disorder. *Journal of Sex and Marital Therapy, 12,* 79–92.

Frick, P. J., et al. (1992). Familial risk factors to oppositional defiant disorder and conduct disorder: Parental psychopathology and maternal parenting. *Journal of Consulting and Clinical Psychology, 60,* 49–55.

Friedman, D., & Squires-Wheeler, E. (1994). Event-related potentials (ERPs) as indicators of risk for schizophrenia. *Schizophrenia Bulletin, 20,* 63–74.

Fried, P. A., Watkinson, B., & Siegel, L. S. (1997). Reading and language in 9- to 12-year olds prenatally exposed to cigarettes and marijuana. *Neurotoxicology and Teratology, 19,* 171–183.

Friedman, M. A., & Brownell, K. D. (1995). Psychological correlates of obesity: Moving to the next research generation. *Psychological Bulletin, 117,* 3–20.

Friedman, M., & Rosenman, R. H. (1974). *Type A behavior and your heart.* New York: Harper & Row.

Friedman, M., & Ulmer, D. (1984). *Treating Type A behavior and your heart.* New York: Fawcett Crest.

Friedman, M., et al. (1986). Alteration of type A behavior and its effect on cardiac recurrences in postmyocardial infarction patients: Summary results of the recurrent coronary prevention project. *American Heart Journal, 112,* 653–665.

Friedman, S. S. (1996). Girls in the 90's. Eating disorders: *The Journal of Treatment and Prevention, 4,* 238–244.

Fromm-Reichmann, F. (1948). Notes on the development of treatment of schizophrenics by psychoanalytic psychotherapy. *Psychiatry, 11,* 263–273.

Fromm-Reichmann, F. (1950). *Principles of intensive psychotherapy.* Chicago: University of Chicago Press.

Frueh, B. C., et al. (1996). Trauma management therapy: A preliminary evaluation of a multicomponent behavioral treatment for chronic combat-related PTSD. *Behaviour Research and Therapy, 34,* 533–543.

Fuchs, C. S., et al. (1995). Alcohol consumption and mortality among women. *The New England Journal of Medicine, 332,* 1245–1250.

Fulero, S.M. (1988). *Tarasoff:* 10 years later. *Professional Psychology: Research and Practice, 19,* 184–190.

Fullerton, D. I., Cayner, J. J., & McLaughlin-Reidel, T. (1978). Results of a token economy. *Archives of General Psychiatry, 35,* 1451–1453.

Funder, D. C. (1994). Explaining traits. *Psychological Inquiry, 5,* 125–126.

Fyer, M. R., et al. (1993). A direct interview family study of social phobias. *Archives of General Psychiatry, 50,* 286–293.

G

Gabbard, G. O., et al. (1997). The economic impact of psychotherapy: A review. *American Journal of Psychiatry, 154,* 147–155.

Gadow, K. D. (1985). Relative efficacy of pharmacological, behavioral, and combination treatment for enhancing academic performance. *Clinical Psychology Review, 5,* 513–533.

Gagnon, J. H. (1977). *Human Sexualities.* Glenview, IL: Scott Foresman.

G.A.I.N.S. Project. (1990). American Indian Health Care Association. 2345 E. Sixth Street, St. Paul, Minnesota.

Galassi, J. P. (1988). Four cognitive-behavioral approaches: Additional considerations. *The Counseling Psychologist, 16*(1), 102–105.

Gall, R., Isaac, L., & Kryger, M. (1993). Quality of life in mild obstructive sleep apnea. *Sleep, 16,* (Suppl), S59–S61.

Games, D., et al. (1995). Alzheimer-type neuropathology in transgenic mice overexpressing V717F β-amyloid precursor protein. *Nature, 373,* 523–527.

Garber, H. J., & Ritvo, E. R. (1992). Magnetic resonance imaging of the posterior fossa in autistic adults. *American Journal of Psychiatry, 149,* 245–247.

605

Gao, S., et al. (1998). The relationships between age, sex, and the incidence of dementia and Alzheimer's disease: A meta-analysis. *Archives of General Psychiatry, 55,* 809–815.

Garb, H. N. (1997). Race bias, social class bias, and gender bias in clinical judgment. *Clinical Psychology: Science and Practice, 4,* 99–120.

Garber, H. R., et al. (1989). A magnetic resonance imaging study of autism: Normal fourth ventricle size and absence of pathology. *American Journal of Psychiatry, 146,* 532–534.

Garber, J., Weiss, B., & Shanley, N. (1993). Cognitions, depressive symptoms, and development in adolescents. *Journal of Abnormal Psychology, 102,* 47–57.

Garcia, M., & Marks, G. (1989). Depressive symptomatology among Mexican-American adults: An examination with the CES-D scale. *Psychiatry Research, 27,* 137–148.

Gard, M. C. E., & Freeman, C. P. (1996). The dismantling of a myth: A review of eating disorders and socio-economic status. *International Journal of Eating Disorders, 20,* 1–12.

Gardiner, S. (1992). Out of harm's way: Intervention with children in shelters. Special Issue: Feminist perspectives in child and youth care practices. *Journal of Child and Youth Care, 7,* 41–48.

Gardner, W., et al. (1996). Clinical versus actuarial predictions of violence in patients with mental illnesses. *Journal of Consulting and Clinical Psychology, 64,* 602–609.

Garfield, S. L. (1982). Eclecticism and integration in psychotherapy. *Behavior Therapy, 13,* 610–623.

Garfield, S. L. (1994) Eclecticism and integration in psychotherapy : Developments and issues. *Clinical Psychology: Science and Practice, 1,* 123–137.

Garner, D. M. (1993). Binge eating in anorexia nervosa. In C. G. Fairburn, & G. T. Wilson (Eds.), *Binge eating: Nature, assessment, and treatment* (pp. 50–76). New York: Guilford.

Garner, D. M., & Wooley, S. C. (1991). Confronting the failure of behavioral and dietary treatments for obesity. *Clinical Psychology Review, 11,* 729–780.

Garner, D. M., Garfinkel, P. E., Schwartz, D. M., & Thompson, M. G. (1980). Cultural expectations of thinness in women. *Psychological Reports, 47,* 483–491.

Garry, D. J., et al. (1992). Are there really alternatives to the use of fetal tissue from elective abortions in transplantation research? *The New England Journal of Medicine, 327,* 1592–1595.

Garssen, B., de Ruiter, C., & Van Dyck, R. (1992). Breathing retraining: A rational placebo? *Clinical Psychology Review, 12,* 141–153.

Garssen, B., et al. (1996). Hyperventilation and panic attack. *American Journal of Psychiatry, 153,* 513–518.

Gater, R., et al. (1998). Sex differences in the prevalence and detection of depressive and anxiety disorders in general health care settings: Report from the World Health Organization collaborative study on psychological problems in general health care. *Archives of General Psychiatry, 55,* 405–413.

Gatz, M. (Ed.). (1995). *Emerging issues in mental health and aging.* Washington, DC: American Psychological Association.

Gatz, M., et al. (1992). Importance of shared genes and shared environments for symptoms of depression in older adults. *Journal of Consulting and Clinical Psychology, 60,* 701–708.

Gauthier, J., Coté, G., & French, D. (1994). The role of home practice in the thermal biofeedback treatment of migraine headache. *Journal of Consulting and Clinical Psychology, 62,* 180–184.

Gauthier, J. G., Ivers, H., & Carrier, S. (1996). Non-pharmacological approaches in the management of recurrent headache disorders and their comparison and combination with pharmacotherapy. *Clinical Psychology Review, 16,* 543–571.

Gawin, F. H. (1991). Cocaine addiction: Psychology and neurophysiology. *Science, 251,* 1581.

Gawin, F. H., & Ellinwood, E. H. (1988). Cocaine and other stimulants: Actions, abuse, and treatment. *New England Journal of Medicine, 318,* 1173–1182.

Gawin, F. H., et al. (1989). Desipramine facilitation of initial cocaine abstinence. *Archives of General Psychiatry, 46,* 117–121.

Gaziano, J. M. (1993). Moderate alcohol intake, increased levels of high-density lipoprotein and its subfractions, and decreased risk of myocardial infarction. *New England Journal of Medicine, 329,* 1829–1834.

Ge, X., et al. (1994). Parents' stressful life events and adolescent depressed mood. *Journal of Health and Social Behavior, 35,* 28–44.

Ge, X., et al. (1996). Parenting behaviors and the occurrence and co-occurrence of adolescent depressive symptoms and conduct problems. *Developmental Psychology, 32,* 717–731.

Gebhard, P. H., Gagnon, J. H., Pomeroy, W. B., & Christenson, C. V. (1965). *Sex offenders: An analysis of types.* New York: Harper & Row.

Geer, J., Heiman, J., & Leitenberg, H. (1984). *Human sexuality.* Englewood Cliffs, NJ: Prentice-Hall.

Gelfin, Y., Gorfine, M., & Lerer, B. (1998). Effect of clinical doses of fluoxetine on psychological variables in healthy volunteers *American Journal of Psychiatry, 155,* 290–292.

Gelman, D. (1988, August 29). Treating war's psychic wounds: Stress disorder among Vietnam vets may be rising. *Newsweek,* pp. 62–64.

Gelman, D. (1994, April 18). The mystery of suicide. *Newsweek,* pp. 44–49.

Georgotas, A., & McCue, R. E. (1986). Benefits and limitations of major pharmacological treatment for depression. *American Journal of Psychotherapy, 40,* 370–376.

Geringer, W. M., et al. (1993). Knowledge, attitudes, and behavior related to condom use and STDs in a high risk population. *Journal of Sex Research, 30,* 75–83.

Gershon, E. S., & Rieder, R. O. (1992). Major disorders of mind and brain. *Scientific American, 267*(3), 126–133.

Gfroerer, J. C., Greenblatt, J. C., & Wright, D. A. (1997). Substance use in the US college-age population: Differences according to educational status and living arrangement. *American Journal of Public Health, 87,* 62–65.

Ghanshyam, N., et al. (1995). Platelet serotonin-2A receptors: A potential biological marker for suicidal behavior. *American Journal of Psychiatry, 152,* 850–855.

Giancola, P. R., & Zeichner, A. (1997). The biphasic effects of alcohol on human physical aggression. *Journal of Abnormal Psychology, 106,* 598–607.

Gibbs, N. (1991, June 3). When is it rape? *Time Magazine,* pp. 48–54.

Gibson, B., Sanbonmatsu, D. M., & Posavac, S. S. (1997). The effects of selective hypothesis testing on gambling. *Journal of Experimental Psychology: Applied, 3,* 126–142.

Gidron, Y., & Davidson, K. (1996). Development and preliminary testing of a brief intervention for modifying CHD-predictive hostility components. *Journal of Behavioral Medicine, 19,* 203–220.

Gil, K. M., et al. (1990). The relationship of negative thoughts to pain and psychological distress. *Behavior Therapy, 21,* 349–362 .

Gilbert, P. L., et al. (1995). Neuroleptic withdrawal in schizophrenic patients: A review of the literature. *Archives of General Psychiatry, 52,* 173–188.

Gilbert, S. (1997a, January 22). Lag seen in aid for depression. *The New York Times,* p. C9.

Gilbert, S. (1997b, June 25). Social ties reduce risk of a cold. *The New York Times,* p. C11.

Gillberg, C., et al. (1997). Long-term stimulant treatment of children with attention-deficit hyperactivity disorder symptoms: A randomized, double-blind, placebo-controlled trial. *Archives of General Psychiatry, 54,* 857–864.

Gillin, J. C. (1991). The long and the short of sleeping pills. *The New England Journal of Medicine, 324,* 1735–1736.

Gillum, R. R. (1996). The epidemiology of cardiovascular disease in Black Americans. [Editorial]. *The New England Journal of Medicine, 335,* 1597–1599.

Ginns, E I., et al. (1996). A genome-wide search for chromosomal loci linked to bipolar affective disorder in the Old Order Amish. *Nature Genetics, 12,* 431–435.

Gitlin, M. J., & Pasnau, R. O. (1989). Psychiatric syndromes linked to reproductive function in women: A review of current knowledge. *American Journal of Psychiatry, 146,* 1413–1422.

Gittelman-Klein, R., & Mannuzza, S. (1990). Hyperactive boys almost grown up. *Archives of General Psychiatry, 45,* 1131–1134.

Gladue, B. A., & Bailey, J. M. (1995). Aggressiveness, competitiveness, and human sexual orientation. *Psychoneuroendocrinology, 20,* 475–485.

Glantz, K., et al. (1996). Virtual reality (VR) for psychotherapy: From the physical to the social environment. *Psychotherapy, 33,* 464–473.

Glantz, L. A., & Lewis, D A. (1997). Reduction of synaptophysin immunoreactivity in the prefrontal cortex of subjects with schizophrenia: Regional and diagnostic specificity. *Archives of General Psychiatry, 54,* 943–952.

Glara, M. A., et al. (1993). Perceptions of self and other in major depression. *Journal of Abnormal Psychology, 102,* 93–100.

Glasberg, R., & Aboud, F. (1982). Keeping one's distance from sadness: Children's self-reports of emotional experience. *Developmental Psychology, 18,* 287–293.

Glaser, R., Kiecolt-Glaser, J. K., Speicher, C. E., & Holliday, J. E. (1985). Stress, loneliness, and changes in herpes virus latency. *Journal of Behavioral Medicine, 8,* 249–260.

Glaser, R., Rice, J., Speicher, C. E., Stout, J. C., & Kiecolt-Glaser, J. K. (1986). Stress depresses interferon production by leukocytes concomitant with a decrease in natural killer cell activity. *Behavioral Neuroscience, 100,* 675–678.

Glaser, R., et al. (1987). Stress-related immune suppression: Health implications. *Brain, Behavior, and Immunity, 1,* 7–20.

Glaser, R., et al. (1991). Stress-related activation of Epstein-Barr virus. *Brain, Behavior, and Immunity, 5,* 219–232.

Glaser, R., et al. (1993). Stress and the memory T-cell response to the Epstein-Barr virus in healthy medical students. *Health Psychology, 12,* 435–442.

Glaser, R., Peral, D. K., Kiecolt-Glaser, J. K., & Malarkey, W. B. (1994). Plasma cortisol levels and reactivation of laten Epstein-Barr virus in response to examination stress. *Psychoneuroendocrinology, 19,* 765–772.

Glass, C. R., & Arnkoff, D. B. (1997). Questionnaire methods of cognitive self-statement assessment. *Journal of Consulting and Clinical Psychology, 65,* 911–927.

Gleaves, D. H. (1996). The sociocognitive model of dissociative identity disorder: A reexamination of the evidence. *Psychological Bulletin, 120,* 42–59.

Glenn, S. S., Ellis, J., & Greenspoon, J. (1992). On the revolutionary nature of the operant as a unit of behavioral selection. *American Psychologist, 47,* 1329–1326.

Glenn, S. W., & Nixon, S. J. (1991). Applications of Cloninger's subtypes in a female alcoholic sample. *Alcoholism: Clinical and Experimental Research, 15,* 851–857.

Gleser, G., Green, B., & Winget, C. (1981). *Prolonged psychosocial effects of disaster: A study of Buffalo Creek.* New York: Academic Press.

Glynn, S., & Mueser, K. T. (1986). Social learning for chronic mental inpatients. *Schizophrenia Bulletin, 12,* 648–668.

Glynn, S., & Mueser, K. T. (1992). Social learning. In R. P. Liberman (Ed.), *Handbook of psychiatric rehabilitation* (pp. 127–152). New York: Macmillan.

Goeders, N. E., & Smith, J. E. (1983). Cortical dopaminergic involvement in cocaine reinforcement. *Science, 221,* 773–775.

Goenjian, A. K., et al. (1996). Basal cortisol, dexamethasone suppression of cortisol, and MHPG in adolescents after the 1988 earthquake in Armenia. *American Journal of Psychiatry, 153,* 929–934.

Goetz, K. L., & Price, T. R. P. (1994). The case of koro: Treatment response and implications for diagnostic classification. *Journal of Nervous and Mental Disease, 182,* 590–591.

Goff, D. C. (1993). "Is anything consistent over time?": Reply. *Journal of Nervous and Mental Disease, 181,* 605.

Goff, D, C., & Summs, C. A. (1993). Has multiple personality disorder remained consistent over time? A comparison of past and recent cases. *Journal of Nervous and Mental Disease, 181,* 595–600.

Goisman, R. M., et al. (1994). Panic, agoraphobia, and panic disorder with agoraphobia: Data from a multicenter anxiety disorders study. *Journal of Nervous and Mental Disease, 182,* 72–79.

Gold, S. R., & Gold, R. G. (1993). Sexual aversions: A hidden disorder. In W. O'Donohue & J. H. Geer (Eds.), *Handbook of sexual dysfuntions: Assessment and treatment* (pp. 83–102). Boston: Allyn & Bacon.

Goldberg, C. (1998, September 11). Little drop in college binge drinking. *The New York Times,* p. A14.

Goldbloom, D. S., et al. (1997). A randomized controlled trial of fluoxetine and cognitive behavioral therapy for bulimia nervosa: Short-term outcome. *Behavior Research and Therapy, 35,* 803–811.

Golden, C. J., Hammeke, T. A., & Purisch, A. D. (1980). *The Luria-Nebraska Neuropsychological Battery: Manual.* Los Angeles: Western Psychological Services.

Golden, T. (1990a, March 12). Was illness at bridges in the minds of workers. *The New York Times,* pp. B1, B4.

Golden, T. (1990b, April 2). Ill, possibly violent, and no place to go. *The New York Times,* pp. A1, B4.

Goldfarb, L. A., Dynens, E. M., & Gerrard, M. (1985). The Goldfarb fear of fat scale. *Journal of Personality Assessment, 49,* 329–332.

Goldfried, M. R., & Norcross, J. C. (1995). Integrative and eclectic therapies in historical perspective. In B. Bongar & L E. Beutler (Eds.), *Comprehensive textbook of psychotherapy: Theory and practice* (pp. 254–273). New York: Oxford University Press.

Golding, J. M. (1994). Sexual assault history and physical health in randomly selected Los Angeles women. *Health Psychology, 13,* 130–138.

Goldman, D., & Bergen, A. (1998). General and specific inheritance of substance abuse and alcoholism. *Archives of General Psychiatry, 55,* 964–965.

Goldman, L. S. , et al. (1998). Attention-deficit/hyperactivity disorder in children and adolescents. *Journal of the American Medical Association, 279,* 1100–1107.

Goldman-Rakic, P. S., & Selemon, L. D. (1997). Functional and anatomical aspects of prefrontal pathology in schizophrenia. *Schizophrenia Bulletin, 23,* 437–458.

Goldstein, A. (1976). Opioid peptides (endorphins) in pituitary and brain. *Science, 193,* 1081–1086.

Goldstein, I., et al. (1998). Oral sildenafil in the treatment of erectile dysfunction. *The New England Journal of Medicine, 338,* 1397–1404.

Goldstein, M. J. (1987). The UCLA high-risk project. *Schizophrenia Bulletin, 13,* 505–514.

Goldstein, M. J., Rodnick, E. H., Evans, J. R., May, P. R. A., & Steinberg, M. R. (1978). Drug and family therapy in the aftercare of acute schizophrenics. *Archives of General Psychiatry, 35,* 1169–1177.

Goldstein, M. J., & Tsuang, M. T. (1990). Gender and schizophrenia: An introduction and synthesis of findings. *Schizophrenia Bulletin, 16,* 179–183.

Goldstein, R. B., et al. (1991). The prediction of suicide: Sensitivity, specificity, and predictive value of a multivariate model applied to suicide among 1906 patients with affective disorders. *Archives of General Psychiatry, 48,* 418–422.

Goldstein, R. B., et al. (1994). Psychiatric disorders in relatives of probands with panic disorder and/or major depression. *Archives of General Psychiatry, 51,* 383–394.

Goldstein, R. L. (1986). Erotomania. *American Journal of Psychiatry, 143,* 802.

Goleman, D. (1988a, October 18). Chemistry of sexual desire yields its elusive secrets. *The New York Times,* pp. C1, C 15.

Goleman, D. (1988b, November 1). Narcissism looming larger as root of personality woes. *The New York Times,* pp. C1, C16.

Goleman, D. (1988c, December 13). Obsessive disorder: Secret toll is found. *The New York Times,* pp. C1, C11.

Goleman, D. (1990a, June 26). Scientists pinpoint brain irregularities in drug addicts. *The New York Times,* pp. C1, C7.

Goleman, D. (1990b, December 6). Women's depression is higher. *The New York Times.*

Goleman, D. (1991, October 22). Sexual harassment: It's about power, not lust. *The New York Times,* pp. C1, C12.

Goleman, D. (1992a, April 14). Therapies offer hope for sex offenders. *The New York Times,* pp. C1, C11.

Goleman, D. (1992b, October 14). Study ties genes to drinking in women as much as in men. *The New York Times,* p. C14.

Goleman, D. (1992c, December 8). A rising cost of modernity: Depression. *The New York Times,* pp. C1, C13.

Goleman, D. (1993a, September 1). New addiction approach get results. *The New York Times,* p. C10.

Goleman, D. (1993b, September 22). Scientist trace "voices" in schizophrenia. *The New York Times,* p. C12.

Goleman, D. (1993c, October 6). Abuse-prevention efforts aid children. *The New York Times,* p. C13.

Goleman, D. (1993d, December 7). New study portrays the young as more and more troubled. *The New York Times,* p. C16.

Goleman, D. (1993e, December 7). Stress and isolation tied to a reduced life span. *The New York Times,* p. C5.

Goleman, D. (1994a, January 11). Childhood depression may herald adult ills. *The New York Times,* pp. C1, C10.

Goleman, D. (1994b, February 13). 2 drugs get a new use: Soothing mania. *The New York Times,* p. C 12.

Goleman, D. (1994c, April 19). Revamping psychiatrists' bible. *The New York Times,* p. C1, C11.

Goleman, D. (1994d, April 26). Mental decline in aging need not be inevitable. *The New York Times,* p. C1, C10.

Goleman, D. (1995a, January 4). At last, a psychiatric manual on children too little to talk. *The New York Times,* p. C8.

Goleman, D. (1995b, May 2). Biologists find site of working memory. *The New York Times,* pp. C 1, C9.

Goleman, D. (1995c, June 13). Provoking a patient's worst fears to determine the brain's role. *The New York Times,* pp. C1, C10.

Goleman, D. (1995d, June 21). "Virtual reality" conquers fear of heights. *The New York Times,* p. C11.

Goleman, D. (1995e, July 1). A genetic clue to bedwetting is located. *The New York Times,* p. A8.

Goleman, D. (1995f, November 9). Hallucinating patients give doctors a clue. *The New York Times,* p. B11.

Goleman, D. (1995g, October 4). Eating disorder rates surprise experts. *The New York Times,* p. C11.

Goleman, D. (1996a, February 15). Psychotherapy found to produce changes in brain function similar to drugs. *The New York Times,* p. B12.

Goleman, D. (1996b, August 13). Brain images of addiction in action show its neural basis. *The New York Times,* pp. C1, C3.

Gomez-Schwartz, B., Horowitz, J., & Cardarelli, A. (1990). *Child sexual abuse: The initial effects.* Newbury Park, CA: Sage Publications.

Gonzalez, D. (1992, November 15). What's the problem with "Hispanic"? Just ask a "Latino." *The New York Times,* Section 4, p. 6.

Goodman, S. H. (1987). Emory University project on children of disturbed parents. *Schizophrenia Bulletin, 13,* 411–423.

Goodstein, L., & Connelly, M. (1998, April 30). Teenage poll finds a turn to the traditional. *The New York Times,* p. A20.

Gordis, E. (1995). The National Institute on Alcohol Abuse and Alcoholism. *Alcohol Health & Research World, 19,* 5–11.

Gordon, C. M., & Carey, M. P. (1996). Alcohol's effects on requisites for sexual risk reduction in men: An initial experimental investigation. *Health Psychology, 15,* 56–60.

Gordon, T., & Doyle, J. T. (1987). Drinking and mortality: The Albany Study. *American Journal of Epidemiology, 125,* 263–270.

Gordon, S., & Snyder, C. W. (1989). *Personal issues in human sexuality: A guidebook for better sexual health* (2nd ed.). Boston: Allyn & Bacon.

Gormally, J., Sipps, G., Raphael, R., Edwin, D., & Varvil-Weld, D. (1981). The relationship between maladaptive cognitions and social anxiety. *Journal of Consulting and Clinical Psychology, 49,* 300–301.

Gortner, E. T., et al. (1998). Cognitive-behavioral treatment for depression: Relapse prevention. *Journal of Consulting and Clinical Psychology, 66,* 377–384.

Gorwood, P., et al. (1995). Gender and age at onset in schizophrenia: Impact of family history. *American Journal of Psychiatry, 152,* 208–212.

Gosselin, C., & Wilson, G. (1980). *Sexual variations.* New York: Simon & Schuster.

Gotlib, I. H. (1984). Depression and general psychopathology in university students. *Journal of Abnormal Psychology, 93,* 19–30.

Gotlib, I. H., et al. (1991). Prospective investigation of postpartum depression: Factors involved in onset and recovery. *Journal of Abnormal Psychology, 100,* 122–132.

Gotlib, I. H., et al. (1993). Negative cognitions and attributional style in depressed adolescents: An examination of stability and specificity. *Journal of Abnormal Psychology, 102,* 607–615.

Gottesman, I. I. (1991). *Schizophrenia genetics: The origins of madness.* New York: Freeman.

Gottesman, I. I. (1993). Origins of schizophrenia: Past as prologue. In R. Plomin and G. E. McClearn (Eds.), *Nature, nurture & psychology* (pp. 213–216). Washington, DC: American Psychological Association.

Gottesman, I. I. (1997). Twins: En route to QTLs for cognition. *Science, 276,* 1522–1523.

Gottesman, I. I., McGuffin, P., & Farmer, A. E. (1987). Clinical genetics as clues to the "real" genetics of schizophrenia. *Schizophrenia Bulletin, 13,* 23–47.

Gould, M. S., et al. (1996). Psychosocial risk factors of child and adolescent completed suicide. *Archives of General Psychiatry, 53,* 1155–1162.

Gould, R., Miller, B. L., Goldberg, M. A., & Benson, D. F. (1986). The validity of hysterical signs and symptoms. *The Journal of Nervous and Mental Disease, 174,* 593–597.

Gould, R. A., Otto, M. W., & Pollack, M. H. (1995). A meta-analysis of treatment outcome for panic disorder. *Clinical Psychology Review, 15,* 819–844.

Gould, R. A., et al. (1997). Cognitive-behavioral and pharmacological treatment for social phobia: A meta-analysis. *Clinical Psychology: Science and Practice, 4,* 291–306.

Graber, B. (1993). Medical aspects of sexual arousal disorders. In W. O'Donohue & J. H. Geer (Eds.), *Handbook of sexual dysfunctions: Assessment and treatment* (pp. 103–156). Boston: Allyn & Bacon.

Graber, B., et al. (1994). Prediction of eating problems: An 8-year study of adolescent girls. *Developmental Psychology, 30,* 823–834.

Grachev, I. D., et al., (1998). Structural abnormalities of frontal neocortex in obsessive-compulsive disorder. *Archives of General Psychiatry, 55,* 181–182.

Grady, D. (1997, October 23). Antidepressant is found to help smokers quit. *The New York Times,* p. A17.

Grady, D. (1997a, January 21). Brain-tied gene defect may explain why schizophrenics hear voices. *The New York Times,* pp. C1, C3.

Grady, D. (1997b, March 21). Study plays down the importance of a sleep disorder. *The New York Times,* p. A26.

Grady, D. (1997c, December 11). Drink a day can lower death rate by 20 percent. *The New York Times,* p. A22.

Graham, J. R. (1993). *MMPI-2: Assessing personality and psychopathology.* (2nd ed.). New York: Oxford University Press.

Graham, J. R., & Strenger, V. E. (1988). MMPI characteristics of alcoholics: A review. *Journal of Consulting and Clinical Psychology, 56,* 197–205.

Grange, D., Telch, C. F., & Tibbs, J. (1998). Eating attitudes and behaviors in 1,435 South African caucasian and non-caucasian college students. *American Journal of Psychiatry, 155,* 250–254.

Grant, B. F. (1997). Prevalence and correlates of alcohol use and DSM-IV alcohol dependence in the United States: Results of the National Longitudinal Alcohol Epidemiologic Survey. *Journal of Studies on Alcohol, 58,* 464–473.

Grant, B. F., et al. (1994). Prevalence of DSM-IV Alcohol Abuse and Dependence: United States, 1992. *Alcohol Health & Research World, 18,* 243–248.

Grant, I., & Heaton, R. K. (1990). Human immunodeficiency virus-type 1 (HIV-1) and the brain. *Journal of Consulting and Clinical Psychology, 58,* 22–30.

Grassi, B., et al. (1997). Efficacy of paroxetine for the treatment of depression in the context of HIV infection. *Pharmacopsychiatry, 30,* 70–71.

Green, A. H. (1978). Self-destructive behavior in battered children. *American Journal of Psychiatry, 135,* 579–582.

Green, A. I., & Salzman, C. (1990). Clozapine: Benefits and risks. *Hospital and Community Psychiatry, 41,* 379–380.

Green, R., Mandel, J., Hotvedt, M., Gray, J., & Smith, L. (1986). Lesbian mothers and their children: A comparison with solo parent heterosexual mothers and their children. *Archives of Sexual Behvaior, 15,* 167–184.

Greenberg, R. P., & Bornstein, R. F. (1988a). The dependent personality: I. Risk for physical disorders. *Journal of Personality Disorders, 2,* 126–135.

Greenberg, R. P., & Bornstein, R. F. (1988b). The dependent personality: II. Risk for psychological disorders. *Journal of Personality Disorders, 2,* 136–143.

Greenberg, R. P., Bornstein, R. F., Greenberg, M. D., & Fisher, S. (1992). A meta-analysis of antidepressant outcome under "blinder" conditions. *Journal of Consulting and Clinical Psychology, 60,* 664–669.

Greenberg, R. P., et al. (1994). A meta-analysis of fluoxetine outcome in the treatment of depression. *Journal of Nervous and Mental Disease, 182,* 547–551.

Greene, B. A. (1985). Considerations in the treatment of Black patients by white therapists. *Psychotherapy, 22,* 389–393.

Greene, B. A. (1986). When the therapist is white and the patient is Black: Considerations for psychotherapy in the feminist heterosexual and lesbian communities. *Women & Therapy, 5,* 41–65.

Greene, B. A. (1990). Sturdy bridges: The role of African American mothers in the socialization of African American children. *Women & Therapy, 10,* 205–225.

Greene, B. A. (1992a). Racial socialization: A tool in psychotherapy with African American children. In L. Vargas & J. Koss, (Eds.), *Working with culture: Psychotherapeutic interventions with ethnic minority children and adolescents* (pp. 63–81). San Francisco: Jossey Bass.

Greene, B. A. (1992b). Black feminist psychotherapy. In E. Wright (Ed.), *Psychoanalysis and feminism: A critical dictionary* (pp. 34–35). Oxford, U.K.: Basil Blackwell.

Greene, B. A. (1992c). Still here: A perspective on psychotherapy with African American women. In J. Chrisler & D. Howard (Eds.), *New directions in feminist psychology.* New York: Springer.

Greene, B. A. (1993a, Spring). Psychotherapy with African American women: The integration of feminist and psychodynamic approaches. *Journal of Training and Practice in Professional Psychology, 7,* 49–66.

Greene, B. A. (1993b). African American women. In L. Comas-Diaz & B. Greene (Eds.), *Women of color and mental health.* New York: Guilford Press.

Greene, B. (1997a, June). Psychotherapy with African American women: Integrating feminist and psychodynamic models. *Journal of Smith College Studies in Social Work Special Issue: Theoretical, Policy, Research and Clinical Perspectives for Social Work Practice with African Americans, 67,* 299–322.

Greene, B., & Sanchez, J. (1997b). Diversity: Advancing an inclusive feminist psychology. In J. Worell & N. Johnson (Eds.), *New directions in education and training for feminist psychology practice* (pp.173–202). Washington, DC: American Psychological Association.

Greene, B. (In press). Gender, sex and culture: Gender and culture. In A. Kazdin (Ed.), *Encyclopedia of Psychology.* Washington, DC: American Psychological Association Press and Oxford University Press.

Greenhill, L. L. (1998). Childhood attention deficit hyperactivity disorder: Pharmacological treatments. In P. E. Nathan, & J. M. Gorman (Eds.), *A guide to treatments that work* (pp. 42–64). New York: Oxford University Press.

Greenhouse, C. J. (1998). Tuning to a key of gladness. *Law and Society Review, 32,* 5–21.

Greenhouse, L. (1992, June 23). Defendants must prove incompetency. *The New York Times,* p. A17.

Greenwald, A. G. (1975). Consequences of prejudice against the null hypothesis. *Psychological Bulletin, 82,* 1–20.

Greenwald, R. (1996). The information gap in the EMDR controversy. *Professional Psychology: Research & Practice, 27,* 67–72.

Greist, J., et al. (1995). Double-blind parallel comparison of three dosages of sertraline and placebo in outpatients with obsessive-compulsive disorder. *Archives of General Psychiatry, 52,* 289–295.

Grier, W., & Cobbs, P. (1968). *Black rage.* New York: Basic Books.

Griffith, J. (1983). Relationship between acculturation and psychological impairment in adult Mexican-Americans. *Hispanic Journal of Behavioral Sciences, 5,* 431–459.

Griffith, J. (1985). A community survey of psychological impairment among Anglo- and Mexican Americans and its relationship to service utilization. *Community Mental Health Journal, 21,* 28–41.

Grissett, N. I., & Norvell, N. K. (1992). Perceived social support, social skills and quality of relationships in bulimic women. *Journal of Consulting and Clinical Psychology, 60,* 293–299.

Grisso, T., & Appelbaum, P. S. (1992). Is it unethical to offer predictions of future violence? *Law and Human Behavior, 16,* 621–633.

Grissom, R. J. (1996). The magical number .7 +- .2: Meta-meta-analysis of the probability of superior outcome in comparisons involving therapy, placebo, and control. *Journal of Consulting and Clinical Psychology, 64,* 973–982.

Grob, G. N. (1983). *Mental illness and American society, 1875–1940.* Princeton, NJ: Princeton University Press.

Gross, J. (1994a, January 19). Aftershocks in paradise: Hearts are trembling too. *The New York Times,* p. A17.

Gross, J. (1994b). Asperger syndrome: A label worth having? *Educational Psychology in Practice, 10,* 104–110.

Grossman, D. C., et al. (1997). Effectiveness of a violence prevention curriculum among children in elementary school: A randomized controlled trial. *Journal of the American Medical Association, 277,* 1605–1611.

Groth, A., & Hobson, W. (1983). The dynamics of sexual assault. In L. Schlesinger & E. Revitch (Eds.), *Sexual dynamics of antisocial behavior.* Springfield, IL: Thomas.

Grover, S. A., Coupal, L., & Hu, X. P. (1995). Identifying adults at increased risk of coronary disease. How well do the current cholesterol guidelines work? *Journal of the American Medical Association, 274,* 801–806.

Gruber, J. E., & Bjorn, L. (1986). Women's responses to sexual harassment: An analysis of sociocultural, organizational, and personal resource models. *Social Science Quarterly, 67,* 814–826.

Grünbaum, A. (1985). Cited in Goleman, D. J. (1985, January 15). Pressure mounts for analyst to prove theory is scientific. *The New York Times,* pp. C1, C9.

Grunberg, N. E. (1991). Smoking cessation and weight gain. *The New England Journal of Medicine, 324,* 768–769.

Guarnaccia, P. J. (1993). *Ataques de nervois* in Puerto Rico: Culture-bound syndrome or popular illness? *Medical Anthropology, 15,* 157–170.

Guarnaccia, P. J., Angel, R., & Worobey, J. L. (1991). The impact of marital status and employment status on depressive affect for Hispanic Americans. *Journal of Community Psychology, 19,* 136–149.

Guarnaccia, P. J., & Rodriguez, O. (1996). Concepts of culture and their role in the development of culturally competent mental health services. *Hispanic Journal of Behavioral Sciences, 18,* 419–443.

Guarnaccia, P. J., Rubio-Stipec, M., & Canino, G. (1989). *Ataques de nervios* in the Puerto Rican diagnostic interview schedule: The impact of cultural categories on psychiatric epidemiology. *Culture, Medicine and Psychaitrty, 13,* 275–295.

Guerra, N. G., et al. (1995). Stressful events and individual beliefs as correlates of economic disadvantage and aggression among urban children. *Journal of Consulting and Clinical Psychology, 63,* 518–528.

Gullette, E. C. D., et al. (1997). Effects of mental stress on myocardial ischemia during daily life. *Journal of the American Medical Association, 277,* 1521–1526.

Gunderson, J. G. (1996). The borderline patient's intolerance of aloneness: Insecure attachments and therapist availability. *American Journal of Psychiatry, 153,* 752–758.

Gunderson, J. G., & Phillips, K. A. (1991). A current view of the interface between borderline personality disorder and depression. *American Journal of Psychiatry, 148,* 967–975.

Gunderson, J. G., & Singer, M. T. (1986). Defining borderline patients: An overview. In M. H. Stone (Ed.), *Essential papers on borderline disorders* (pp. 453–474). New York: New York University Press.

Gur, R. E., & Pearlson, G. D. (1993). Neuroimaging in schizophrenia research. *Schizophrenia Bulletin, 19,* 337–353.

Gur, R. E., et al. (1994). Clinical subtypes of schizophrenia: Differences in brain and CSF volume. *American Journal of Psychiatry, 151,* 343–350.

Gur, R. E., et al., (1998). A follow-up magnetic resonance imaging study of schizophrenia: Relationship of neuroanatomical changes to clinical and neurobehavioral measures. *Archives of General Psychiatry, 55,* 145–152.

Gurin, G. (1996). Forward. In H. W. Neighbors & J. S. Jackson (Eds.), *Mental health in black America* (pp. vii–x). Thousand Oaks, CA: Sage Publications.

Gurland, B. J., & Cross, P. S. (1986). Public health perspectives on clinical memory testing of Alzheimer's disease and related disorders. In L. W. Poon (Ed.), *Handbook for clinical memory assessment of older adults* (pp. 11–20). Washington, DC: American Psychological Association.

Gutheil, T. G. (1980). In search of true freedom: Drug refusal, involuntary medication, and "rotting with your rights on." *American Journal of Psychiatry, 137,* 327–328.

Guthrie, P. C., & Mobley, B. D. (1994). A comparison of the differential diagnostic efficiency of three personality disorder inventories. *Journal of Clinical Psychology, 50,* 656–665.

Gutierrez, P. M., & Silk, K. R. (1998). Prescription privileges for psychologists: A review of the psychological literature. *Professional Psychology: Research and Practice, 29,* 213–222.

Guydish, J., et al. (1998). Drug abuse day treatment: A randomized clinical trial comparing day and residential treatment programs. *Journal of Consulting and Clinical Psychology, 66,* 280–289.

Guze, S. B. (1993). Genetics of Briquet's syndrome and somatization disorder: A review of family, adoption, and twin studies. *Annals of Clinical Psychiatry, 5,* 225–230.

H

Haaga, D. A. F. (1995). Metatraits and cognitive assessment: Application to attributional style and depressive symptoms. *Cognitive Therapy and Research, 19,* 121–142.

Haaga, D., & Davidson, G. C. (1993). An appraisal of rational-emotive therapy. *Journal of Consulting and Clinical Psychology, 61,* 215–220.

Haaga, D. A. F., Dyck, M. J., & Ernst, D. (1991). Empirical status of cognitive theory of depression. *Psychological Bulletin, 110,* 215–236.

Haapasalo, J., & Tremblay, R. E. (1994). Physically aggressive boys from ages 6 to 12: Family background, parenting behavior, and prediction of delinquency. *Journal of Consulting and Clinical Psychology, 62,* 1044–1052.

Haber, S. N., & Fudge, J. L. (1997). The interface between dopamine neurons and the amygdala: Implications for schizophrenia. *Schizophrenia Bulletin, 23,* 471–482.

Häfner, H., et al. (1998). Causes and consequences of the gender difference in age at onset of schizophrenia. *Schizophrenia Bulletin, 24,* 99–113.

Hager, M., & Peyser, M. (1997, March 24). Battling Alzheimer's. *Newsweek,* p. 66.

Hagerman, R. J. (1996). Fragile X syndrome. *Child and Adolescent Psychiatric Clinics of North America, 5,* 895–911.

Hall, G. C. (1995). Sexual offender recidivism revisited: A meta-analysis of recent treatment studies. *Journal of Consulting and Clinical Psychology, 63,* 802–809.

Hall, G. C., & Barongan, C. (1997). Prevention of sexual aggression: Sociocultural risk and protective factors. *American Psychologist, 52,* 5–14.

Hall, R. L. (1996). Escaping the self or escaping the anomaly? *Psychological Inquiry, 7,* 143–148.

Hall, R. L., & Greene, B. (1996). The sins of omission and commission: Women, psychotherapy and the psychological literature. *Women & Therapy, 18,* 1, 5–31.

Hall, S. M., et. al. (1994). Continuity of care and desipramine in primary cocaine abusers. *Journal of Nervous and Mental Disease, 182,* 570–575.

Hall, S. S. (1998, February 15). Our memories, our selves. *The New York Times Magazine,* pp. 26–33, 49, 56–57.

Hallmayer, J., et al. (1992). Exclusion of linkage between the serotonin₂ receptor and schizophrenia in a large Swedish kindred. *Archives of General Psychiatry, 49,* 216–219.

Hallmayer, J., et al. (1996). Autism and the X chromosome: Multipoint sib-pair analysis. *Archives of General Psychiatry, 53,* 985–989.

Hamamy, H., et al. (1990). Consanguinity and the genetic control of Down syndrome. *Clinical Genetics, 37,* 24–29.

Hamburger, S. D., et al. (1997). Childhood-onset schizophrenia: Biological markers in relation to clinical characteristics. *American Journal of Psychiatry, 154,* 64–68.

Hamer, D. H., Hu, S., Magnuson, V. L., Hu, N., & Pattatucci, A. M. L. (1993, July 16). A linkage between DNA markers on the X chromosome and male sexual orientation. *Science, 261,* 321–327.

Hammen, C., & Compas, B. E. (1994). Unmasking unmasked depression in children and adolescents: The problem of comorbidity. *Clinical Psychology Review, 14,* 585–603.

Hammen, C., & de Mayo, R. (1982). Cognitive correlates of teacher stress and depressive symptoms: Implications for attributional models of depression. *Journal of Abnormal Psychology, 91,* 96–101.

Hammen, C., & Gitlin, M. (1997). Stress reactivity in bipolar patients and its relation to prior history of disorder. *American Journal of Psychiatry, 154,* 856–857.

Hammen, C., et al.(1992). Psychiatric history and stress: Predictors of severity of unipolar depression. *Journal of Abnormal Psychology, 101,* 45–52.

Hammond, O. (1988). Needs assessment and policy development: Native Hawaiians as Native Americans. *American Psychologist, 43,* 383–387.

Hancock, L. (1996, March 18). Mother's little helper. *Newsweek,* pp. 51–56.

Hankin, B. L., et al. (1998). Development of depression from preadolescence to young adulthood: Emerging gender differences in a 10–year longitudinal study. *Journal of Abnormal Psychology, 107,* 128–140.

Hansen, T. E., Casey, D. E., & Hoffman, W. F. (1997). Neuroleptic intolerance. *Schizophrenia Bulletin, 23,* 567–582.

Hanson, R. K., & Bussiere, M. T. (1998). Predicting relapse: A meta-analysis of sexual offender recidivism studies. *Journal of Consulting and Clinical Psychology, 66,* 348–362.

Hanson, R. K., Steffy, R. A., & Gauthier, R. (1993). Long-term recidivism of child molesters. *Journal of Consulting and Clinical Psychology, 61,* 646–652.

Harding, J. J. (1989). Postpartum psychiatric disorders: A review. *Comprehensive Psychiatry, 30,* 109–112.

Hare, R. D. (1965). Temporal gradient of fear arousal in psychopaths. *Journal of Abnormal Psychology, 70,* 442–445.

Hare, R. D. (1986). Criminal psychopaths. In J. C. Yuille (Ed.), *Police selection and training: The role of psychology* (pp. 187–206). Dordrecht, Netherlands: Martinos Nijhoff.

Hare, R. D. (1993). *Without conscience: The disturbing world of the psychopaths among us.* New York: Pocket Books.

Hare, R. D., Frazelle, J., & Cox, D. N. (1978). Psychopathy and physiological responses to threat of an aversive stimulus. *Psychophysiology, 15,* 165–172.

Hare, R. D., Hart, S. D., & Harpur, T. J. (1991). Psychopathy and the DSM-IV criteria for antisocial personality disorder. *Journal of Abnormal Psychology, 100,* 391–398.

Harney, P. A., & Muehlenhard, C. L. (1991). Rape. In E. Grauerholz & M. A. Koralewski (Eds.), *Sexual coercion: A sourcebook on its nature, causes, and prevention* (pp. 3–16). Lexington, MA: Lexington Books.

Harpur, T. J., & Hare, R. D. (1994). Assessment of psychopathy as a function of age. *Journal of Abnormal Psychology, 103,* 604–609.

Harrell, T. H., & Ryon, N. B. (1983). Cognitive-behavioral assessment of depression: Clinical validation of the Automatic Thoughts Questionnaire. *Journal of Consulting and Clinical Psychology, 51,* 721–725.

Harris, L. (1988). *Inside America.* New York: Vintage.

Harrow, M., & Marengo, J. T. (1986). Schizophrenic thought disorder at followup: Its persistence and prognostic significance. *Schizophrenia Bulletin, 12,* 373–393.

Harrow, M., & Quinlan, D. M. (1985). *Disordered thinking and schizophrenic psychopathology.* New York: Gardner Press.

Harrow, M., et al. (1995). Vulnerability to delusions over time in schizophrenia and affective disorders. *Schizophrenia Bulletin, 21,* 95–109.

Hart, B. M., Reynolds, N. J., Baer, D. M., Brawley, E. R., & Harris, F. R. (1968). Effects of contingent and non-contingent social reinforcement on the cooperative play of a pre-school child. *Journal of Applied Behavior Analysis, 1,* 73–76.

Hartung, C. M., & Widiger, T. A. (1998). Gender differences in the diagnosis of mental disorders: Conclusions and controversies of the DSM-IV. *Psychological Bulletin, 123,* 260–278.

Harvey, P. D., et al. (1997). Age-related differences in formal thought disorder in chronically hospitalized schizophrenic patients: A cross-sectional study. *American Journal of Psychiatry, 154,* 205–210.

Hatfield, E., Sprecher, S., & Traupman, J. (1978). Men's and women's reactions to sexually explicit films: A serendipitous finding. *Archives of Sexual Behavior, 6,* 583–592.

Haughton, E., & Ayllon, T. (1965). Production and elimination of symptomatic behavior. In L. P. Ullmann & L. Krasner (Eds.), *Case studies in behavior modification.* New York: Holt, Rinehart and Winston.

Hauser, W. A., & Hesdorffer, D. C. (1990). *Epilepsy: Frequency, causes and consequences.* New York: Demos.

Havassy, B. E., Hall, S. M., & Wasserman, D. A. (1991). Social support and relapse: Commonalities among alcoholics, opiate users, and cigarette smokers. *Addictive Behaviors, 16,* 235–246.

Hawkrigg, J. J. (1975). Agoraphobia. *Nursing Times, 71,* 1280–1282.

Hawton, K. (1991). Sex therapy. Special Issue: The changing face in behavioral psychotherapy. *Behavioral Psychotherapy, 19,* 131–136.

Hawton, K., & Catalan, J. (1990). Sex therapy for vaginismus: Characteristics of couples and treatment outcomes. *Sexual and Marital Therapy, 5,* 39–48.

Hawton, K., Catalan, J., & Fagg, J. (1992). Sex therapy for erectile dysfunction: Characteristics of couples, treatment outcome, and prognostic factors. *Archives of Sexual Behavior, 21,* 161–175.

Haznedar, M. M., et al. (1997). Anterior cingulate gyrus volume and glucose metabolism in autistic disorder. *American Journal of Psychiatry, 154,* 1047–1050.

Hazuda, H. P., et al. (1991). Obesity in Mexican American subgroups: Findings from the San Antonio heart study. *American Journal of Clinical Nutrition, 53,* 1529S–1534S.

Heart disease higher in Mexican-Americans. (1997, March 18). *Newsday,* p. A17.

Heart disease: Still the leading cause of death in the U.S. (1996, April 8). *Reuters News Service.*

Heatherton, T. F., et al. (1997). A 10-year longitudinal study of body weight, dieting, and eating disorder symptoms. *Journal of Abnormal Psychology, 106,* 117–125.

Heckers, S. (1997). Neuropathology of schizophrenia: Cortex, thalamus, basal ganglia, and neurotransmitter-specific projection systems. *Schizophrenia Bulletin, 23,* 403–421.

Hefti, F., et al. (1991). Promotion of neuronal survival in vitro by thermal proteins and poly(dicarboxylic)amino acids. *Brain Research, 15,* 273–283.

Hegel, M. T., Ravaris, C. L., & Ahles, T. A. (1994). Combined cognitive-behavioral and time-limited alprazolam treatment of panic disorder. *Behavior Therapy, 25,* 183–195.

Heiby, E., & Becker, J. D. (1980). Effect of filmed modeling on the self-reported frequency of masturbation. *Archives of Sexual Behavior, 9,* 115–122.

Heiby, E. M., Campos, P. E., Remick, R. A., & Keller, F. D. (1987). Dexamethasone suppression and self-reinforcement correlates of clinical depression. *Journal of Abnormal Psychology. 96,* 70–72.

Heidrich, S. M., Forsthoff, C. A., & Ward, S. E. (1994). Psychological adjustment in adults with cancer: The self as mediator. *Health Psychology, 13,* 346–353.

Heikkinen, M. E., et al. (1997). Psychosocial factors and completed suicide in personality disorders. *Acta Psychiatrica Scandinavica, 95,* 49–57.

Heim, N. (1981). Sexual behavior of castrated sex offenders. *Archives of Sexual Behavior, 10,* 11–20.

Heiman, J. R., & LoPiccolo, J. (1987). *Becoming orgasmic* (2nd ed.). Englewood Cliffs, NJ: Prentice-Hall Books.

Heiman, J. R., & Rowland, D. L. (1983). Affective and physiological sexual patterns: The effects of instructions on sexually functional and dysfunctional men. *Journal of Psychosomatic Research, 27,* 105–116.

Heimberg, R. G. (1989). Cognitive and behavioral treatments for social phobia: A critical analysis. *Clinical Psychology Review, 9,* 107–128.

Heimberg, R. G., et al. (1987). Attributional style, depression, and anxiety: An evaluation of the specificity of depressive attributions. *Cognitive Therapy & Research, 11,* 537–550.

Hellerstein, D., Frosch, W., & Koenigsberg, H. W. (1987). The clinical significance of command hallucinations. *American Journal of Psychiatry, 144,* 219–221.

Hellerstein, D. J., et al. (1993). A randomized double-blind study of fluoxetine versus placebo in the treatment of dysthymia. *American Journal of Psychiatry, 150,*1169–1175.

Helweg-Larsen, M. , & Collins, B. E. (1994). The UCLA Multidimensional Condom Attitudes Scale: Documenting the complex determinants of condom use in college students. *Health Psychology, 13,* 224–237.

Helzer, J. E., Burnam, A., & McEvoy, L. T. (1991). Alcohol abuse and dependence. In L. N. Robins & D. A. Regier (Eds.), *Psychiatric disorders in America: The Epidemiologic Catchment Area Study* (pp. 81–115). New York: The Free Press.

Helzer, J. E., & Schuckit, M. A. (1990, August/September). Substance use disorders. In American Psychiatric Association, *DSM-IV Update.* Washington, DC: American Psychiatric Association.

Helzer, J. E., et al. (1985). A comparison of clinical and diagnostic interview schedule diagnoses. *Archives of General Psychiatry, 42,* 657–666.

Hendin, H., & Haas, A. P. (1991). Suicide and guilt as manifestation of PTSD in Vietnam combat veterans. *American Journal of Psychiatry, 148,* 586–591.

Henggeler, S. W., et al. (1986). Multisystemic treatment of juvenile offenders: Effects on adolescent behavior and family interaction. *Developmental Psychology, 22,* 132–141.

Henggeler, S. W., Melton, G. B., & Smith, L. A. (1992). Family preservation using multisystemic therapy: An effective alternative to incarcerating serious juve-

nile offenders. *Journal of Consulting and Clinical Psychology, 60,* 953–961.

Henggeler, S. W., et al. (1997). Multisystemic therapy with violent and chronic juvenile offenders and their families: The role of treatment fidelity in successful dissemination. *Journal of Consulting and Clinical Psychology, 65,* 821–833.

Henker, B., & Whalen, C. K. (1980). The changing faces of hyperactivity: Retrospect and prospect. In C. K. Whalen and B. Henker (Eds.), *Hyperactive children* (pp. 321–363). New York: Academic Press.

Henkin, W. A. (1985). Toward counseling the Japanese in America: A cross-cultural primer. *Journal of Counseling and Development, 63,* 500–503.

Herbert, J. D., Hope, D. A., & Bellack, A. S. (1992). Validity of the distinction between generalized social phobia and avoidant personality disorder. *Journal of Abnormal Psychology, 101,* 332–339.

Herek, G.M. (1996). Heterosexism and homophobia. In R.P. Cabaj & T. S. Stein (Eds.), *Textbook of homosexuality and mental health* (pp. 101–113). Washington, DC: American Psychiatric Association Press.

Herkov, M. J., et al. (1996). MMPI differences among adolescent inpatients, rapists, sodomists, and sexual abusers. *Journal of Personality Assessment, 66,* 81–90.

Herman, C. P., & Polivy, J. (1980). Restrained eating. In A. J. Stunkard (Ed.), *Obesity* (pp. 208–225). Philadelphia: Saunders.

Herman, C. P., Polivy, J., Lank, C. N., & Heatherton, T. F. (1987). Anxiety, hunger, and eating behavior. *Journal of Abnormal Psychology, 96,* 264–269.

Hermann, B., & Whitman, S. (1992). Psychopathology in epilepsy: The role of psychology in altering paradigms of research, treatment, and prevention. *American Psychologist, 47,* 1134–1138.

Hermann, C., Blanchard, E. B., & Flor, H. (1997). Biofeedback treatment for pediatric migraine: Prediction of treatment outcome. *Journal of Consulting and Clinical Psychology, 65,* 611–616.

Herrell, J. M. (1975). Sex differences in emotional response to "erotic literature". *Journal of Consulting and Clinical Psychology, 43,* 921.

Herron, W. G. (1987). Evaluating the process-reactive dimension. *Schizophrenia Bulletin, 13,* 357–359.

Hertz, M .R. (1986). Rorschach bound: A 50–year memoir. *Journal of Personality Assessment, 50,* 396–416.

Herzog, D. B., Keller, M. B., & Lavori, P. W. (1988). Outcome in anorexia and bulimia nervosa: A review of the literature. *The Journal of Nervous and Mental Disease, 176,* 131–143.

Herzog, W., Schellberg, D., & Deter, H. C. (1997). First recovery in anorexia nervosa patients in the long-term course: A discrete-time survival analysis. *Journal of Consulting and Clinical Psychology, 65,* 169–177.

Heston, L. L. (1966). Psychiatric disorders in foster home reared children of schizophrenic mothers. *British Journal of Psychiatry, 112,* 819–825.

Heston, L. L., & Mastry, A. R. (1982). Age at onset of Pick's and Alzheimer's dementia: Implications for diagnosis and research. *Journal of Gerontology, 37,* 422–424.

Heston, L. L., White, J. A., & Mastri, A. R. (1987). Pick's disease: Clinical genetics and natural history. *Archives of General Psychiatry, 44,* 409–411.

Heuch, I., et al. (1983). Use of alcohol, tobacco and coffee, and risk of pancreatic cancer. *British Journal of Cancer, 48,* 637–643.

Hewitt, P. L., Flett, G. L., & Ediger, E. (1996). Perfectionism and depression: Longitudinal assessment of a specific vulnerability hypothesis. *Journal of Abnormal Psychology, 105,* 276–280.

Hilchey, T. (1994, November 11). High anxiety raises risk of heart failure in men, study finds. *The New York Times,* p. A17.

Hilchey, T. (1995, May 14). Sleep disorder may affect many truck drivers, researchers say. *The New York Times,* p. A28.

Hill, A. L. (1987). Idiot savants: The rate of incidence. *Perceptual and Motor Skills, 44,* 161–162.

Hill, J. C., & Schoener, E. P. (1996). Age-dependent decline of attention deficit hyperactivity disorder. *American Journal of Psychiatry, 153,* 1143–1146.

Hill, J. C. & Schoener, E. P. (1997). Advancing age, declining ADHD: Reply. *American Journal of Psychiatry, 154,* 1324–1325.

Hill, M. A. (1992). Light, circadian rhythms, and mood disorders: A review. *Annuals of Clinical Psychiatry, 4,* 131–146.

Hill, S. Y. (1980). Introduction: The biological consequences. In *Alcoholism and alcohol abuse among women: Research issues.* Rockville, MD: National Institute on Alcohol Abuse and Alcoholism.

Hill, J. O., & Peters, J. C. (1998). Environmental contributions to the obesity epidemic. *Science, 280,* 1371–1374.

Hilts, P. J. (1991, October 9). Report is critical of mental clinics. *The New York Times,* p. L25.

Hilts, P. J. (1995a, April 19). Black teen-agers are turning away from smoking, but Whites puff on. *The New York Times.*

Hilts, P. J. (1995b, July 20). Survey finds surge in smoking by young. *The New York times,* p. B9

Himelein, M. J., & McElrath, J. V. (1996). Resilient child sexual abuse survivors: cognitive coping and illusion. *Child Abuse and Neglect, 20,* 747–758.

Hinden, B. R., et al. (1997). Covariation of the anxious-depressed syndrome during adolescence: Separating fact from artifact. *Journal of Consulting and Clinical Psychology, 65,* 6–14.

Hinrichsen, G. A., & Pollak, S. (1997). Expressed emotion and the course of late-life depression. *Journal of Abnormal Psychology, 106,* 336–340.

Hinshaw, S. P. (1987). On the distinction between attentional deficits/hyperactivity and conduct problems/aggression in child psychopathology. *Psychological Bulletin, 101,* 443–463.

Hinshaw, S. P. (1991). Stimulant medication and the treatment of aggression in children with attentional deficits. *Journal of Clinical Child Psychology, 20,* 301–312.

Hinshaw, S. P. (1992). Academic underachievement, attention deficits, and aggression: Comorbidity and implications for intervention. *Journal of Consulting and Clinical Psychology, 60,* 893–903.

Hinshaw, S. P., Lahey, B. B., & Hart, E. L. (1993). Issues of taxonomy and comorbidity in the development of conduct disorder. *Development and Psychopathology, 5,* 31–49.

Hinshaw, S. P., Klein, R. G., & Abikoff, H. (1998). Childhood attention deficit hyperactive disorder: Nonpharmacological and combination treatments. In P. E. Nathan & J. M. Gorman (Eds.), *A guide to treatments that work* (pp. 26–41). New York: Oxford University Press.

Hirayama, T. (1989). Association between alcohol consumption and cancer of the sigmoid colon: Observations from a Japanese cohort study. *Lancet,* pp. 725–727.

Hirsch, S. R., & Leff, J. P. (1975). *Abnormalities in parents of schizophrenics.* Oxford, U.K.: Oxford University Press.

Hirschfeld, R. M. A., & Cross, C. (1982). Epidemiology of affective disorders. *Archives of General Psychiatry, 39,* 35–46.

Hirschfeld, R. M. A., et al. (1997). The National Depressive and Manic-Depressive Association consensus statement on the undertreatment of depression. *Journal of the American Medical Association, 277,* 333–340.

Hobbins, J. C. (1991). Diagnosis and management of neural-tube defects today. *The New England Journal of Medicine, 324,* 690–691.

Hodgins, D. C., el-Guebaly, N., & Armstrong, S. (1995). Prospective and retrospective reports of mood states before relapse to substance use. *Journal of Consulting and Clinical Psychology, 63,* 400–407.

Hodgins, S., et al. (1996). Mental disorder and crime evidence from a Danish birth cohort. *Archives of General Psychiatry, 53,* 489–496.

Hodgins, S., et al. (1998). In reply. *Archives of General Psychiatry, 55,* 87–88.

Hoelscher, T. J., Lichstein, K. L., Fischer, S., & Hegarty, T. B. (1987). Relaxation treatment of hypertension: Do home relaxation tapes enhance treatment outcome? *Behavior Therapy, 18,* 33–37.

Hoffman, A. (1971). LSD discoverer disputes "chance" factor in finding. *Psychiatric News, 6,* 23–26.

Hoffman, S. G., et al. (1995). Psychophysiological differences between subgroups of social phobia. *Journal of Abnormal Psychology, 104,* 224–231.

Hoffman, W., & Prior, M. (1982). Neuropsychological dimensions of autism in children: A test of the hemispheric dysfunction hypothesis. *Journal of Clinical Neuropsychology, 4,* 27–42.

Hogarty, G. E., Schroeder, N. R., Ulrich, R., Mussare, N., Peregino, F., & Herron, E. (1979b). Fluphenazine and social therapy in the aftercare of schizophrenic patients. *Archives of General Psychiatry, 36,* 1283–1294.

Hogarty, G. E., et al. (1986). Family psychoeducation, social skills training, and maintenance chemotherapy in the aftercare of schizophrenia. *Archives of General Psychiatry, 43,* 633–642.

Hogarty, G. E., et al. (1997). Three-year trials of personal therapy among schizophrenic patients living with or independent of family, II: Effects on adjustment of patients. *American Journal of Psychiatry, 154,* 1514–1524.

Hogg, R. S., et al. (1998). Improved survival among HIV-infected individuals following initiation of antiretroviral therapy. *Journal of the American Medical Association, 279,* 450–454.

Holahan, C. J., et al. (1995). Social support, coping, and depressive symptoms in a late-middle-aged sample of patients reporting cardiac illness. *Health Psychology, 14,* 152–163.

Holland, A. J., Sicotte, N., & Treasure, J. (1988). Anorexia nervosa: Evidence of a genetic basis. *Journal of Psychosomatic Research, 32,* 561–571.

Hollander, E., et al. (1992). Serotonergic function in obsessive-compulsive disorder: Behavioral and neuroendocrine responses to oral m-chlorophenylpiperazine and fenfluramine in patients and health volunteers. *Archives of General Psychiatry, 49,* 21–28.

Hollestedt, C., et al. (1983). Outcome of pregnancy in women treated at an alcohol clinic. *Acta Psychiatrica Scandanavia, 67,* 236–248.

Hollingshead, A. B., & Redlich, F. C. (1958). *Social class and mental illness: A community study.* New York: Wiley.

Hollon, S. D., & Beck, A. T. (1979). Cognitive therapy for depression. In P. C. Kendall and S. D. Hollon (Eds.), *Cognitive-behavioral interventions: Theory, research and procedures* (pp. 153–196). Orlando, FL: Academic Press.

Hollon, S. D., Evans, M. D., & DeRubeis, R. J. (1990). Cognitive mediation of relapse prevention following treatment for depression: Implications of differential risk. In R. E. Ingram (Ed.), *Contemporary psychological approaches to depression: Theory, research, and treatment* (pp. 117–136). New York: Plenum Press.

Hollon, S. D., & Kendall, P. C. (1980). Cognitive self-statements in depression: Development of an automatic thoughts questionnaire. *Cognitive Therapy and Research, 4,* 383–395.

Hollon, S. D., Shelton, R. C., & Davis, D. D. (1993). Cognitive therapy for depression: Conceptual issues and clinical efficacy. *Journal of Consulting and Clinical Psychology, 61,* 270–275.

Hollon, S. D., Shelton, R. C., & Loosen, P. T. (1991). Cognitive therapy and pharmacotherapy for depression. *Journal of Consulting and Clinical Psychology, 59,* 88–99.

Holloway, L. (1998, February 12). A mental patient skips care and West Siders worry again. *The New York Times,* p. B5.

Holmes, D. S., Solomon, S., Cappo, B. M., & Greenberg, J. L. (1983). Effects of transcendental meditation versus resting on physiological and subjective arousal. *Journal of Personality and Social Psychology, 44,* 1244–1252.

Holmes, G. R., Offen, L., & Waller, G. (1997). See no evil, hear no evil, speak no evil: Why do relatively few male victims of childhood sexual abuse receive help for abuse-related issues in adulthood? *Clinical Psychology Review, 17,* 69–88.

Holmes, T. H., & Rahe, R. H. (1967). The social readjustment rating scale. *Journal of Psychosomatic Research, 11,* 213–218.

Holmes, W. C., et al. (1997). Human immunodeficiency virus (HIV) infection and quaity of life: The potential impact of axis I psychiatric disorders in a sample of 95 seropositive men. *Psychosomatic Medicine, 59,* 187–192.

Holroyd, K. A., et al. (1991). A comparison of pharmacological (amitryptyline HCl) and nonpharmacological (cognitive-behavioral) therapies for chronic tension headaches. *Journal of Consulting and Clinical Psychology, 59,* 387–393.

Holt, C. S., Heimberg, R. G., & Hope, D. A. (1992). Avoidant personality disorder and the generalized subtype of social phobia. *Journal of Abnormal Psychology, 101,* 318–325.

Holtzworth-Munroe, A. (1995). Marital violence. *The Harvard Mental Health Letter, 12,* pp. 4–6.

Holzman, P. S. (1987). Recent studies of psychophysiology in schizophrenia. *Schizophrenia Bulletin, 13,* 49–75.

Holzman, P. S., Shenton, M. E., & Solovay, M. R. (1986). Quality of thought disorder in differential diagnosis. *Schizophrenia Bulletin, 12,* 360–372.

Holzman, P. S., et al. (1997). Smooth pursuit eye tracking in twins: A critical commentary. *Archives of General Psychiatry, 54,* 429–431.

Homer, C. J. (1997). Asthma disease management. *The New England Journal of Medicine, 337,* 1461–1463.

Homicide trends show record rate of firearm-related deaths. (1996, June 7). *Reuters News Service.*

Hooley, J. M., & Licht, D. M. (1997). Expressed emotion and causal attributions in the spouses of depressed patients. *Journal of Abnormal Psychology, 106,* 298–306.

Hopkins, J., Campbell, S. B., & Marcus, M. (1987). Role of infant-related stressors in postpartum depression. *Journal of Abnormal Psychology, 96,* 237–241.

Horne, L. R., Van Vactor, J. C., & Emerson, S. (1991). Disturbed body image in patients with eating disorders. *American Journal of Psychiatry, 148,* 211–215.

Hotaling, G. T., & Sugarman, D. B. (1986). An analysis of risk markers in husband to wife violence: The current state of knowledge. *Violence and Victims, 1,* 101–124.

Hough, R. L., et al. (1987). Utilization of health and mental services by Los Angeles Mexican Americans and non-Hispanic whites. *Archives of General Psychiatry, 44,* 702–709.

House, J. S., Robbins, C., & Metzner, H. L. (1982). The association of social relationships and activities with mortality: Prospective evidence from the Tecumseh Community Health Study. *American Journal of Epidemiology, 116,* 123–140.

Houts, A. C. (1996, Winter). Behavioral treatment of enuresis. *The Clinical Psychologist, 49,* 5–6.

Houts, A. C., Berman, J. S., & Abramson, H. (1994). Effectiveness of psychological and pharmacological treatments for nocturnal enuresis. *Journal of Consulting and Clinical Psychology, 62,* 373–745.

How hard do you really need to exercise? (1995, July). *Tufts University Diet & Nutrition Letter, 13,* pp. 4–6.

Howard, K. I., Kopta, S. M., Krause, M. S., & Orlinksy, D. E. (1986). The dose-effect relationship in psychotherapy. *American Psychologist, 41,* 159–164.

Howard, K. I., et al. (1996). Patterns of mental health service utilization. *Archives of General Psychiatry, 53,* 696–703.

Howard-Pitney, B., et al. (1992). Psychological and social indicators of suicide ideation and suicide attempts in Zuni adolescents. *Journal of Consulting and Clinical Psychology, 60,* 473–476.

Howland, R. H., & Thase, M. E. (1993). A comprehensive review of cyclothymic disorder. *Journal of Nervous and Mental Disease, 18,* 485–493.

Hsu, K. G. (1989). The gender gap in eating disorders: Why are the eating disorders more common among women? *Clinical Psychology Review, 9,* 393–407.

Hsu, L. K. G. (1990). *Eating disorders.* New York: Guilford Press.

Huang, L. H. (1994). An integrative approach to clinical assessment and intervention with Asian-American adolescents. *Journal of Clinical Child Psychology, 23,* 21–31.

Huang, W., & Cuvo, A. J. (1997). Social skills training for adults with mental retardation in job-related settings. *Behavior Modification, 21,* 3–44.

Huang, Z., et al. (1997). Dual effects of weight and weight gain on breast cancer risk. *Journal of the American Medical Association, 278,* 1407–1411.

Hublin, C., et al. (1997). Prevalence and genetics of sleepwalking: A population-based twin study. *Neurology, 48,* 177–181.

Hudson, J. I., Pope, H. G., & Jonas, J. M. (1984). Treatment of bulimia with antidepressants: Theoretical considerations and clinical findings. In A. J. Stunkard & E. Stellar (Eds.), *Eating and its disorders* (pp. 259–273). New York: Raven Press.

Hudson, J. I., Pope, H. G., Jr., Jonas, J. M., & Yurgelun-Todd, D. (1983). Family history study of anorexia nervosa and bulimia. *British Journal of Psychiatry, 142,* 133–138, 428–429.

Hudziak, J. J., et al. (1996). Clinical study of the relation of borderline personality disorder to Briquet's syndrome (hysteria), somatization disorder, antisocial personality disorder, and substance abuse disorders. *American Journal of Psychiatry, 153,* 1598–1606.

Huesmann, L. R., Eron, L. D., Klein, R., Brice, P., & Fischer, P. (1983). Mitigating the imitation of aggressive behaviors by changing children's attitudes about media violence. *Journal of Personality and Social Psychology, 44,* 899–910.

Huesmann, L. R., & Miller, L. S. (1994). Long-term effects of repeated exposure to media violence in childhood. In L. R. Huesmann (Ed.), *Aggressive behavior: Current perspectives.* New York: Plenum Press.

Huesmann, R. (1993). Cited in DeAngelis, T. (1993). It's back: TV violence, concern for kid viewers. *APA Monitor, 24*(8), 16.

Hugdahl, K., & Ohman, A. (1977). Effects of instruction on acquisition and extinction of electrodermal response to fear-relevant stimuli. *Journal of Experimental Psychology: Human Learning and Memory, 3,* 608–618.

Hughes, J. R., Gust, S. W., & Pechacek, T. F. (1987). Prevalence of tobacco dependence and withdrawal. *American Journal of Psychiatry, 144,* 205–208.

Hughes, P. L., Wells, L. A., Cunningham, C. J., & Ilstrup, D. M. (1986). Treating bulimia with desipramine. *Archives of General Psychiatry, 43,* 182–186.

Hull, J. G., & Young, R. D. (1983). Self-consciousness, self-esteem, and success-failure as determinants of alcohol consumption in male social drinkers. *Journal of Personality and Social Psychology, 44,* 1097–1109.

Humphrey, L. L. (1986a). Family dynamics in bulimia. In S. C. Feinstein et al. (Eds.), *Adolescent psychiatry.* Chicago: University of Chicago Press.

611

Humphrey, L. L. (1988). Family wide distress in bulimia. In D. Cannon & T. Baker (Eds.), *Addictive disorders: Psychological assessment and treatment*. New York: Praeger.

Hunt, T., & Weber, J. (Producers). (1989). *NOVA: Confronting the Killer Gene* [Telecast]. Boston: WGBH Educational Foundation.

Hunter, R. H., Bedell, J. R., & Corrigan, P. W. (1997). Current approaches to assessment and treatment of persons with serious mental illness. *Professional Psychology: Research & Practice, 28*, 217–228.

The Huntington's Disease Collaborative Research Group. (1993). A novel gene containing a trinucleotide repeat that is expanded and unstable on Huntington's disease chromosomes. *Cell 72*, 971–983.

Hurlburt, G., & Gade, E. (1984). Personality differences between Native American and Caucasian women alcoholics: Implications for alcoholism counseling. *White Cloud Journal, 3*, 35–39.

Hurlburt, R. T. (1997). Randomly sampling thinking in the natural environment. *Journal of Consulting and Clinical Psychology, 65*, 941–949.

Hurt, R. D., et al. (1997). A comparison of sustained-release bupropion and placebo for smoking cessation. *The New England Journal of Medicine, 337*, 1195–1202.

Hurt, R. D., et al. (1998). Nicotine nasal spray for smoking cessation. *Mayo Clinic Proceedings, 73*, 118–125.

Hyman, C., et al. (1991). BDNF is a neurotrophic factor for dopaminergic neurons of the substantia nigra. *Nature, 21*, 230–232.

I

Ilardi, S. S., & Craighead, W. E. (1994). The role of nonspecific factors in cognitive-behavior therapy for depression. *Clinical Psychology: Science and Practice, 1*, 138–156.

Imber, S. D., et al. (1990). Mode-specific effects among three treatments for depression. *Journal of Consulting and Clinical Psychology, 58*, 352–359.

Impotence drug is easier to use. (1997, May). *Harvard Health Letter, 22* (7), p. 8.

Ingersoll, S. L, & Patton, S. O. (1991). *Treating perpetrators of sexual abuse*. Lexington, MA: Lexington Books.

Ingraham, L. J., et al. (1995). Twenty-five year followup of the Israeli High-Risk Study: Current and lifetime psychopathology. *Schizophrenia Bulletin, 21*, 183–192.

Ingram, R. E. (1990). Self-focused attention in clinical disorders: Review and a conceptual model. *Psychological Bulletin, 107*, 156–176.

Ingram, R. E. (1991). Tilting at windmills: A response to Pyszczynski, Greenberg, Hamilton, and Nix. *Psychological Bulletin, 110*, 544–550.

Insanity: A defense of last resort. (1992, February 3). *Newsweek*, p. 49

Institute of Medicine. (1990). *Broadening the base of treatment for alcohol problems*. Washington, DC: National Academy Press.

Irle, E., et al. (1998). Obsessive-compulsive disorder and ventromedial frontal lesions: Clinical and neuropsychological Findings. *American Journal of Psychiatry, 155*, 255–263.

Ironson, G. et al. (1997). Posttraumatic stress symptoms, intrusive thoughts, loss, and immune function after hurricane Andrew. *Psychosomatic Medicine, 59*, 128–141.

Isay, R. A. (1990). Psychoanalytic theory and the therapy of gay men. In D. P. McWhirter, S. A. Sanders, & J. M. Reinisch (Eds.), *Homosexuality/heterosexuality: Concepts of sexual orientation* (pp. 283–303). New York: Oxford University Press.

Isay, R. A. (1993, April 23). Sex survey may say most about society's attitudes to gays. *The New York Times*, Section 4, p. 16. (Letter)

Ismail, B. T., et al. (1998). Neurological abnormalities in schizophrenia: Clinical, etiological and demographic correlates. *Schizophrenia Research, 30*, 229–238.

Isometsä, E. T., et al. (1996). Suicide among subjects with personality disorders. *American Journal of Psychiatry, 153*, 667–673.

Israel, G. E., & Tarver II, D. E. (1997). *Transgender care: Recommended guidelines, practical information, and personal accounts*. Philadelphia: Temple University Press.

Ito, T. A., Miller, N., & Pollock, V. E. (1996). Alcohol and aggression: A meta-analysis on the moderating effects of inhibitory cues, triggering events, and self-focused attention. *Psychological Bulletin, 120*, 60–82.

J

Jablensky, A., et al. (1992). Schizophrenia: Manifestations, incidence and course in different cultures: A World Health Organization ten-country study. *Psychological Medicine, 20*, (Monograph Suppl.), 1–97.

Jackson, J. S., & Neighbors, H. W. (1996). Changes in African American resources and mental health: 1979 to 1992. In H. W. Neighbors & J.S. Jackson (Eds.), *Mental health in black America* (pp. 189–212). Thousand Oaks, CA: Sage Publications.

Jackson, J., et al. (1990). Young adult women who report childhood intrafamilial sexual abuse: Subsequent adjustment. *Archives of Sexual Behavior, 19*, 211–221.

Jacobsen, F. M., Wehr, T. A., Skewer, R. A., Sack, D. A., & Rosenthal, N. E. (1987). Morning versus midday phototherapy of seasonal affective disorder. *American Journal of Psychiatry, 144*, 1301–1305.

Jacobsen, L. K., et al. (1997). Cerebrospinal fluid monoamine metabolites in childhood-onset schizophrenia. *American Journal of Psychiatry, 154*, 69–74.

Jacobson, N. S., & Hollon, S. D. (1996a). Cognitive-behavior therapy versus pharmacotherapy: Now that the jury's returned its verdict, it's time to present the rest of the evidence. *Journal of Consulting and Clinical Psychology, 64*, 74–80.

Jacobson, N. S., & Hollon, S. D. (1996b). Prospects for future comparisons between drugs and psychotherapy: Lessons from the CBT-versus-pharmacotherapy. *Journal of Consulting and Clinical Psychology, 64*, 104–108.

Jacobson, N. S., Wilson, L., & Tupper, C. (1988). The clinical significance of treatment gains resulting from exposure-based interventions for agoraphobia: A reanalysis of outcome data. *Behavior Therapy, 19*, 539–554.

Jacobson, N. S., et al. (1996). A component analysis of cognitive-behavioral treatment for depression. *Journal of Consulting and Clinical Psychology, 64*, 295–304.

Jaffe, A. J., et al. (1996). Naltrexone, relapse prevention, and supportive therapy with alcoholics: An analysis of patient treatment matching. *Journal of Consulting and Clinical Psychology, 64*, 1044–1053.

Jamison, K. K., & Akiskal, H. S. (1983). Medication compliance in patients with bipolar disorder. *Psychiatric Clinics of North America, 6*, 175–192.

Janerich, D. T., et al. (1990). Lung cancer and exposure to tobacco smoke in the household. *The New England Journal of Medicine, 323*, 632–636.

Janet, P. (1889). *L'automatisme psychologique*. Paris: Alcan.

Janoff-Bulman, R., & Frieze, I. (1983). A theoretical perspective for understanding reactions to victimization. *Journal of Social Issues, 39*, 1–17.

Janofsky, J. S., et al. (1996). Insanity defense pleas in Baltimore City: An analysis of outcome. *American Journal of Psychiatry, 153*, 1464–1468.

Janssen, H. J. E. M., et al. (1997). A prospective study of risk factors predicting grief intensity following pregnancy loss. *Archives of General Psychiatry, 54*, 56–61.

Jarman, B. (1998, February). Advances in understanding and treating Alzheimer's disease. *Journal Watch for Psychiatry, 4* (2), 18.

Javier, R. A. (1993). Cited in Rathus, S. A. (1993). *Psychology*, 5th ed. Fort Worth, TX: Harcourt Brace Jovanovich.

Javier, R. A., & Nevid, J. (1993, July). *El uso de "cuento" como estrategia de intervencion en un programa de cesacion de fumar para los hispano-parlantes*. Paper presented at the XXIV Interamerican Congress of Psychology, Santiago, Chile.

Jeffery, R. W. (1991). Population perspectives on the prevention and treatment of obesity in minority populations. *American Journal of Clinical Nutrition, 53* (6 Suppl), 1621A–1624S.

Jeffery, R. W. (1988). Dietary risk factors and their modification in cardiovascular disease. *Journal of Consulting and Clinical Psychology, 56*, 350–357.

Jellinek, E. M. (1960). *The disease concept of alcoholism*. New Haven, CT: College and University Press.

Jemmott, J. B., et al. (1983, June 25). Academic stress, power motivation, and decrease in secretion rate of salivary secretory immunoglobin A. *Lancet*, 1400–1402.

Jenike, M. A., et al. (1996). Cerebral structural abnormalities in obsessive-compulsive disorder: A quantitative morphometric magnetic resonance imaging study. *Archives of General Psychiatry, 53*, 625–632.

Jenike, M. A., et al. (1997). Placebo-controlled trial of fluoxetine and phenelzine for obsessive-compulsive disorder. *American Journal of Psychiatry, 154*, 1261–1264.

Jenkins, C. D. (1988). Epidemiology of cardiovascular diseases. *Journal of Consulting and Clinical Psychology, 56*, 324–332.

Jenkins, C. D., et al. (1994). Quantifying and predicting recovery after heart surgery. *Psychosomatic Medicine, 56*, 203–212.

Jenkins, J. H. (1988). Ethnopsychiatric interpretations of schizophrenic illness: The problem of *nervios* within Mexican-American families. *Culture, Medicine, and Psychiatry, 12*, 301–329.

Jenkins, J. H., & Karno, M. (1992). The meaning of expressed emotion: Theoretical issues raised by cross-cultural research. *American Journal of Psychiatry, 149*, 9–21.

Jenkins, M. A. et al. (1998). Learning and memory in rape victims with posttraumatic stress disorder. *American Journal of Psychiatry, 155*, 278–279.

Jenny, C., Roesler, T.A., & Poyer, K.L. (1994). Are children at risk for sexual abuse by homosexuals? *Pediatrics, 94*, 41–44.

Jensen, P. S., Martin, D., & Cantwell, D. P. (1997). Comorbidity in ADHD: Implications for research practice, and DSM-V. *Journal of the American Academy of Child and Adolescent Psychiatry, 36*, 1065–1079.

Jeste, D. V., & Caligiui, M. P. (1993). Tardive dyskinesia. *Schizophrenia Bulletin, 19*, 303–315.

Jeste, D. V., et al. (1992). Cognitive deficits of patients with Alzheimer's disease with and without delusions. *American Journal of Psychiatry, 149*, 184–188.

Jian, W., et al. (1996). Mental stress–induced myocardial ischemia and cardiac events. *Journal of the American Medical Association, 275*, 1651–1656.

Jimerson, D. C,. et al. (1997). Decreased serotonin function in bulimia nervosa. *Archives of General Psychiatry, 54*, 529–534.

Johnson, C., & Flach, A. (1985). Family characteristics of 105 patients with bulimia. *American Journal of Psychiatry, 142*, 1321–1324.

Johnson, F. N. (Ed.). (1975). *Lithium research and therapy*. New York: Academic Press.

Johnson, J. D. (1985). A mechanism to inhibit input activation and its dysfunction in schizophrenia. *British Journal of Psychiatry, 146*, 429–435.

Johnson, K. M., & Lando, H. (1991, February). Smoking cessation strategies for minorities. Paper presented at the program on "Smoking Cessation Strategies for Minorities." National Heart, Lung & Blood Institute, National Institutes of Health, Bethesda, MD.

Johnson, K. W., et al. (1995). Panel II: Macrosocial and environmental influences on minority health. *Health Psychology, 14*, 601–612.

Johnson, R. E., & Crowley, J. E. (1996). An analysis of stress denial. In H. W. Neighbors & J.S. Jackson (Eds.), *Mental health in black America* (pp. 62–76). Thousand Oaks, CA: Sage Publications.

Johnson, R. J., & McFarland, B. H. (1996). Lithium use and discontinuation in a health maintenance organization. *American Journal of Psychiatry, 153,* 993–1000.

Johnson, S. L., & Miller, I. (1997). Negative life events and time to recovery from episodes of bipolar disorder. *Journal of Abnormal Psychology, 106,* 449–457.

Johnson, S. L., & Roberts, J. E. (1995). Life events and bipolar disorder: Implications from biological theories. *Psychological Bulletin, 117,* 434–449.

Johnson, W. G., Tsoh, J. Y., & Varnado, P. J. (1996). Eating disorders: Efficacy of pharmacological and psychological interventions. *Clinical Psychology Review, 16,* 457–478.

Johnston, L. D., Bachman, J. G., & O'Malley, P. M. (1992, January 25). *Monitoring the future: A continuing study of the lifestyles and values of youth.* The University of Michigan News and Information Services: Ann Arbor, MI.

Johnston, L. D., O'Malley, P. M., & Bachman, J. G. (1991). *Drug use among American high school seniors, college students and young adults.* DHHS Publication No. (ADM) 91-1835. Rockville, MD: National Institute on Drug Abuse.

Johnston, L. D., O'Malley, P. M., and Bachman, J. G. (1996). *National Survey Results on Drug Use from The Monitoring the Future Study, 1975–1995. Volume I. Secondary School Students.* U.S. Department of Health and Human Services, Public Health Service, National Institutes of Health: National Institute on Drug Abuse.

Joiner, T. E., Alfano, M. S., & Metalsky, G. I. (1992). When depression breeds contempt: Reassurance seeking, self-esteem, and rejection of depressed college students by their roommates. *Journal of Abnormal Psychology, 101,* 165–173.

Joiner, T. E., Jr., Catanzaro, S. J., & Laurent, J. (1996). Tripartite structure of positive and negative affect, depression, and anxiety in child and adolescent psychiatric inpatients. *Journal of Abnormal Psychology, 105,* 401–409.

Joiner, T. E., et al. (1997). The modified scale for suicidal ideation: Factors of suicidality and their relation to clinical and diagnostic variables. *Journal of Abnormal Psychology, 106,* 260–265.

Joint Commission on Mental Illness and Health. (1961). *Action for mental health: Final report of the Joint Commission on Mental Illness and Health.* New York: Basic Books.

Jones, E. (1953). *The life and work of Sigmund Freud.* New York: Basic Books.

Jones v. United States, 103 S. Ct. 3043 (1983).

Jones, F. (1997, March). Eloquent Anonymity. [Review of the book *Lush Life: A Biography of Billy Strayhorn*]. *Readings: A Journal of Reviews and Commentary in Mental Health, 12,* (1), 10–14.

Jones, M. C. (1924). A laboratory study of fear: The case of Peter. *Pedogogical Seminary, 31,* 308–315.

Jones, M. C. (1974). Albert, Peter, and John B. Watson. *American Psychologist, 29,* 581–583.

Jones, P. B., et al. (1998). Schizophrenia as a long-term outcome of pregnancy, delivery, and perinatal complications: A 28-year follow-up of the 1966 North Finland general population birth cohort. *American Journal of Psychiatry, 155,* 355–364.

Jones, T. W., et al. (1995). Enhanced adrenomedullary response and increased susceptibility to neuroglycopenia. *Journal of Pediatrics, 126,* 171–177.

Joseph, A. M., et al. (1996). The safety of transdermal nicotine as an aid to smoking cessation in patients with cardiac diseases. *The New England Journal of Medicine, 335,* 1792–1798.

Josephson, W. D. (1987). Television violence and children's aggression: Testing the priming, social script,

and disinhibition prediction. *Journal of Personality and Social Psychology, 53,* 882–890.

Jouriles, E. N., et al. (1996). Physical violence and other forms of marital aggression: Links with children's behavior problems. *Journal of Family Psychology, 10,* 223–234.

Jouriles, E. N., et al. (1997). Psychometric properties of family members' reports of parental physical aggression toward clinic-referred children. *Journal of Consulting and Clinical Psychology, 65,* 309–318.

Judd, L. J. (1997). The clinical course of unipolar major depressive disorders. *Archives of General Psychiatry, 54,* 989–991.

Junginger, J., Barker, S., & Coe, D. (1992). Mood theme and bizzareness of delusions in schizophrenia and mood psychosis. *Journal of Abnormal Psychology, 101,* 287–292.

Jurkovic, G. J. (1980). The juvenile delinquent as a moral philosopher: A structural-developmental perspective. *Psychological Bulletin, 88,* 709–727.

Just, M. A., & Carpenter, P.A. (1992). A capacity theory of comprehension: Individual difference in working memory. *Psychological Review, 99,* 122–149.

Just, N., & Alloy, L. B. (1997). The response styles theory of depression: Tests and an extension of the theory. *Journal of Abnormal Psychology, 106,* 221–229.

K

Kadden, R. M. (1994). Cognitive-behavioral approaches to alcoholism treatment. *Alcohol Health & Research World, 18,* 279–286.

Kahn, M. W. (1982). Cultural clash and psychopathology in three aboriginal cultures. *Academic Psychology Bulletin, 4,* 553–561.

Kahn, M. W., Hannah, M., Hinkin, C., Montgomery, C., Pitz, D. (1987). Psychopathology on the streets: Psychological assessment of the homeless. *Professional Psychology: Research & Practice, 18,* 580–586.

Kahn, M. W., Henry, J., & Lejero, L. (1981). Indigenous mental health paraprofessionals on an Indian reservation. In M. O. Wagonfeld & S. S. Rakin (Eds.), *Paraprofessionals in human services.* New York: Human Sciences Press.

Kalichman, S. C., & Sikkema, K. J. (1994). Psychological sequelae of HIV infection and AIDS: Review of empirical findings. *Clinical Psychology Review, 14,* 611–632.

Kammeyer, K. C. W. (1990). *Marriage and family: A foundation for personal decisions.* (2nd ed.). Boston: Allyn & Bacon.

Kammeyer, K. C. W., Ritzer, G., & Yetman, N. R. (1990). *Sociology: Experiencing changing societies.* Boston: Allyn & Bacon.

Kane, J. M. (1996). Drug therapy: Schizophrenia. *The New England Journal of Medicine, 334,* 34–41.

Kane, J. M., & Marder, S. R., (1993). Psychopharmacologic treatment of schizophrenia. *Schizophrenia Bulletin, 19,* 287–302.

Kane, J. M., & Marder, S. R. (1994). Response to Fuchs. *Schizophrenia Bulletin, 20,* 23–24.

Kane, J. M., Rifkin, A., Woerner, M., & Sarantakos, S. (1986a). Dose response relationships in maintenance drug treatment for schizophrenia. *Psychopharmacology Bulletin, 22,* 205–235.

Kane, J. M., Woerner, M., S., Borenstein, M., Wegner, J., & Lieberman, J. (1986b). Integrating incidence and prevalence of tardive dyskinesia. *Psychopharmacology Bulletin, 22,* 254–258.

Kane, J. M., et al. (1985). High-dose versus low-dose strategies in the treatment of schizophrenia. *Psychopharmacology Bulletin, 21,* 533–537.

Kannel, W. B., McGee, D. L., & Castelli, W. P. (1984). Latest perspectives on cigarette smoking and cardiovascular disease: The Framingham Study. *Journal of Cardiac Rehabilitation, 4,* 267–277.

Kanner, A. D., Coyne, J. C., Schaefer, C., & Lazarus, R. S. (1981). Comparison of two modes of stress

measurement: Daily hassles and uplifts versus major life events. *Journal of Behavioral Medicine, 4,* 1–39.

Kanner, L., (1943). Autistic disturbances of affective content. *Nervous Child, 2,* 217–240.

Kanner, L., & Eisenberg, L. (1955). Notes on the follow-up studies of autistic children. In P. Hoch & J. Zubin (Eds), *Psychopathology of childhood.* New York: Grune & Stratton.

Kantor, M. (1998). *Homophobia: Description, development and dynamics of gay bashing.* Westport, CT: Praeger.

Kaplan, A. S., & Woodside, D. B. (1987). Biological aspects of anorexia nervosa and bulimia nervosa. *Journal of Consulting and Clinical Psychology, 55,* 645–653.

Kaplan, D. (1993, January 18). The incorrigibles. *Newsweek,* pp. 48–50.

Kaplan, H. S. (1974). *The new sex therapy: Active treatment of sexual dysfunctions.* New York: Brunner/Mazel.

Kaplan, H. S. (1987). *Sexual aversion, sexual phobias, and panic disorder.* New York: Brunner/Mazel.

Kaplan, H. S. (1995). *The sexual desire disorders: Dysfunctional regulation of sexual motivation.* New York: Brunner/Mazel.

Kaplan, M. (1996). *Clinical practice with caregivers of dementia patients.* Washington, DC: Taylor & Francis.

Kaplan, S. J. (1986). *The private practice of behavior therapy: A guide for behavioral practitioners.* New York: Plenum Press.

Kapp, M. B. (1994). Treatment and refusal rights in mental health: Therapeutic justice and clinical accommodation. *American Journal of Orthopsychiatry, 64,* 223–234.

Kapur, S., & Remington, G. (1996). Serotonin-dopamine interaction and its relevance to schizophrenia. *American Journal of Psychiatry, 153,* 466–476.

Karasek, R. A., Baker, D., Marxer, F., Ahlbom, A., & Theorell, T. (1981). Job decision latitude, job demands, and cardiovascular disease: A prospective study of Swedish men. *American Journal of Public Health, 71,* 694–705.

Karel, M. J. (1997). Aging and depression: Vulnerability and stress across adulthood. *Clinical Psychology Review, 17,* 847–879.

Karlen, N. (1995, May 29). Greetings from Minnesober. *The New York Times Magazine,* pp. 32–35.

Karno, M., et al. (1987). Expressed emotions and schizophrenic outcome among Mexican-American Families. *Journal of Nervous and Mental Disease, 175,* 143–151.

Karno, M., et al. (1988). The epidemiology of obsessive-compulsive disorder in five US communities. *Archives of General Psychiatry, 45,* 1094–1099.

Kasari, D., et al. (1993). Affective development and communication in children with autism. In A. P. Kaiser & D. B. Gray (Eds.), *Enhancing children's communication: Research foundation for intervention* (pp. 201–222). New York: Brookes.

Kaslow, N.J., & Thompson, M. P. (1998). Applying the criteria for empirically supported treatments to studies of psychosocial interventions for child and adolescent depression. *Journal of Consulting and Clinical Psychology, 27,* 146–155.

Kasper, J. A., et al. (1997). Prospective study of patients' refusal of antipsychotic medication under a physician discretion review procedure. *American Journal of Psychiatry, 154,* 483–489.

Kasper, M. E., Rogers, R., & Adams, P. A. (1996). Dangerousness and command hallucinations: An investigation of psychotic inpatients. *Bulletin of the American Academy of Psychiatry and the Law, 24,* 219–224.

Kassett, J. A., et al. (1989). Psychiatric disorders in the first-degree relatives of probands with bulimia nervosa. *American Journal of Psychiatry, 146,* 1468–1471.

Kassirer, J. P., & Angell, M. (1992). The use of fetal tissue in research on Parkinson's disease. *The New England Journal of Medicine, 327,* 1591–1592.

Kassirer, J. P., & Angell, M. (1998). Losing weight — An ill-fated new year's resolution. *The New England Journal of Medicine, 338,* 52–54.

Kaszniak, A. W., & Scogin F. R. (1995). Assessment of dementia and depression in older adults. *The Clinical Psychologist, 48,* 17–24.

Katz, J. N. (1995). The invention of heterosexuality. New York: Dutton.

Katz, R., & McGuffin, P. (1993) . The genetics of affective disorders. In L. J. Chapman, J. P. Chapman, & D. Fowles (Eds.), *Progress in experimental personality and psychopathology research.* New York: Springer.

Kaufman, J., & Zigler, E. (1989). The intergenerational transmission of child abuse. In D. Cicchetti & V. Carlson (Eds.), *Child maltreatment: Theory and research on the causes and consequences of child abuse and neglect* (pp. 129–150). Cambridge: Cambridge University Press.

Kaufman, J., et al. (1994). The use of multiple informants to assess children's maltreatment experience. *Journal of Family Violence, 9,* 227–248.

Kaul, T.J., & Bednar, R.L. (1986). Experiential group research: Results, questions, and suggestions. In S.L. Garfield & A.E. Bergin (Eds.), *Handbook of psychotherapy and behavior change: An evaluative analysis* (3rd ed.). New York: Wiley.

Kawachi, I., et al. (1994). Prospective study of phobic anxiety and risk of coronary heart disease in men. *Circulation, 89,* 1992–1997.

Kay, S. R. (1990). Significance of the positive-negative distinction in schizophrenia. *Schizophrenia Bulletin, 16,* 635–652.

Kazdin, A. E. (1984). *Behavior modification in applied settings.* Homewood, NJ: Dorsey Press.

Kazdin, A. E. (1992). *Research design in clinical psychology* (2nd ed.). Boston: Allyn & Bacon.

Kazdin, A. E. (1998). Psychosocial treatments for conduct disorder in children. In P. E. Nathan, & J. M. Gorman (Eds.), *A guide to treatments that work* (pp. 65–89). New York: Oxford University Press.

Kazdin, A. E., Esveldt-Dawson, K., French, N. H., & Unis, A. S. (1987). Problem-solving skills training and relationship therapy in the treatment of antisocial child behavior. *Journal of Consulting and Clinical Psychology, 55,* 76–85.

Kazdin, A. E., Moser, J., Colbus, D., & Bell, R. (1985). Depressive symptoms among physically abused and psychiatrically disturbed children. *Journal of Abnormal Psychology, 94,* 298–307.

Kazdin, A. E., Siegel, T. D., & Bass, D. (1992). Cognitive problem-solving skills training and parent management training in the treatment of antisocial behavior in children. *Journal of Consulting and Clinical Psychology,* 733–747.

Kazdin, A. E., & Weisz, J. R. (1998). Identifying and developing empirically supported child and adolescent treatments. *Journal of Consulting and Clinical Psychology, 66,* 19–36.

Keane, T. M. (1998). Psychological and behavioral treatments for post-traumatic stress disorder. In P. E. Nathan & J. M. Gorman (Eds.), *A guide to treatments that work* (pp. 398–407). New York: Oxford University Press.

Keane, T. M., & Kaloupek, D. G. (1996, Winter). Cognitive behavior therapy in the treatment of posttraumatic stress disorder. *The Clinical Psychologist, 49,* 7–8.

Kearins, J. M. (1981). Visual spatial memory in Australian aboriginal children in desert regions. *Cognitive Psychology, 13,* 434–460.

Keck, P. E., Jr., & McElroy, S. L. (1998). Pharmacological treatment of bipolar disorders. In P. E. Nathan & J. M. Gorman (Eds.), *A guide to treatments that work* (pp. 249–269). New York: Oxford University Press.

Keefe, R. S. E., et al. (1997). Eye tracking, attention, and schizotypal symptoms in nonpsychotic relatives of patients with schizophrenia. *Archives of General Psychiatry, 54,* 169–176.

Keel, P. K., et al. (1999). Long-term outcome of bulimia nervosa. *Archives of General Psychiatry, 56,* 63–69.

Keesey, R. E. (1980). A set-point analysis of the regulation of body weight. In A. J. Stunkard (Ed.), *Obesity.* Philadelphia: Saunders.

Keesey, R. E. (1986). A set-point theory of obesity. In K. D. Brownell & J. P. Foreyt (Eds.), *Handbook of eating disorders: Physiology, psychology, and treatment of obesity, anorexia, and bulimia.* New York: Basic Books.

Keiller, S. W., & Graham, J. R. (1993). The meaning of low scores on MMP-2 Clinical Scales of normal subjects. *Journal of Personality Assessment, 62,* 211–223.

Keith, S. J., Regier, D. A., & Rae, D. S. (1991). Schizophrenic disorders. In L. N. Robins & D. A. Regier (Eds.), *Psychiatric disorders in America: The Epidemiologic Catchment Area Study* (pp. 33–52). New York: The Free Press.

Keller, M. B. (1990). Diagnostic and course of illness variables pertinent to refractory depression. In A. Tasman, et al. (Eds.), *Review of psychiatry,* Vol. 9. Washington, DC: American Psychiatric Press.

Keller, M. B., First, M., & Koscis, J. H. (1990, August/September). Major depression and dysthymia. In American Psychiatric Association, *DSM-IV Update.* Washington, DC: American Psychiatric Association.

Keller, M. B., et al. (1993). Bipolar I: A five-year prospective follow-up. *Journal of Nervous and Mental Disease, 181,* 238–245.

Keller, M.B, Hirschfeld, R.M.A., & Hanks, D.L. (1997). Double depression: A distinctive subtype of unipolar depression. *Journal of Affective Disorders, 45,* 65–73.

Kellner, R. (1990). Somatization: Theories and research. *Journal of Nervous & Mental Disease, 178,* 150–160.

Kellner, R. (1992). Diagnosis and treatment of hypochondriacal syndromes. *Psychosomatics, 33,* 278–289.

Kelly, J. A., Brasfield, T. L., & St. Lawrence, J. S. (1991). Predictors of vulnerability to AIDS risk behavior relapse. *Journal of Consulting and Clinical Psychology, 59,* 163–166.

Kelly, J. A., & Kalichman, S. C. (1995). Increased attention in human sexuality can improve HIV-AIDS prevention efforts: Key research issues and directions. *Journal of Consulting and Clinical Psychology, 63,* 907–918.

Kelly, J. A., Wildman, B. G., & Berler, E. S. (1980). Small group behavioral training to improve the job interview skills repertoire of mildly retarded adolescents. *Journal of Applied Behavior Analysis, 13,* 461–471.

Kelly, J. A., et al. (1989). Behavioral intervention to reduce AIDS risk activities. *Journal of Consulting and Clinical Psychology, 57,* 60–67.

Kelly, J. A. et al. (1992). AIDS/HIV risk behavior among the chronic mentally ill. *American Journal of Psychiatry, 149,* 886–889.

Kelly, J. A., et al. (1995). Factors predicting continued high-risk behavior among gay men in small cities: Psychological, behavioral, and demographic characteristics related to unsafe sex. *Journal of Consulting and Clinical Psychology, 63,* 101–107.

Kelly, J. A., et al. (1998). Implications of HIV treatment advances for behavioral research on AIDS: Protease inhibitors and new challenges in HIV secondary prevention. *Health Psychology, 17,* 310–319.

Kelly, S. J., Macaruso, P., & Sokol, S. M. (1997). Mental calculation in an autistic savant: A case study. *Journal of Clinical and Experimental Neuropsychology, 19,* 172–184.

Kendall, P. C. (1994). Treating anxiety disorders in children: Results of a randomized clinical trial. *Journal of Consulting and Clinical Psychology, 62,* 100–110.

Kendall, P. C., & Braswell, L. (1985). *Cognitive-behavioral therapy for impulsive children.* New York: The Guilford Press.

Kendall, P. C., & Southam-Gerow, M. A. (1996). Long-term follow-up of a cognitive-behavioral therapy for anxiety-disordered youth. *Journal of Consulting and Clinical Psychology, 64,* 724–730.

Kendall, P. C., & Williams, C. L. (1981). Behavioral and cognitive-behavioral approaches to outpatient treatment with children. In W. E. Craighead, A. E. Kazdin, & M. J. Mahoney (Eds.), *Behavior modification: Principles, issues, and applications* (2nd ed.), Boston: Houghton Mifflin.

Kendall, P. C., et al. (1992). Comorbidity of anxiety and depression in youth: Treatment implications. *Journal of Consulting and Clinical Psychology, 60,* 869–880.

Kendall, P. C., et al. (1997). Therapy for youths with anxiety disorders: A second randomized clinical trial. *Journal of Consulting and Clinical Psychology, 65,* 366–380.

Kendell, R. E. (1983). Hysteria. In G. F. M. Russell & L. A. Hersov (Eds.), *Handbook of psychiatry (Vol. 4). The neuroses and personality disorders* (pp. 232–246). Cambridge: Cambridge University Press.

Kendler, K. (1992). Cited in Goleman, D. (1992, October 14). Study ties genes to drinking in women as much as in men. *The New York Times,* p. C14.

Kendler, K. S. (1994). Twin studies of psychiatric illness: Current status and future directions. *Archives of General Psychiatry, 50,* 905–918.

Kendler, K. S. (1997). The diagnostic validity of melancholic major depression in a population-based sample of female twins. *Archives of General Psychiatry, 54,* 299–304.

Kendler, K. S., & Diehl, S. R. (1993). The genetics of schizophrenia: A current, genetic-epidemiologic perspective. *Schizophrenia Bulletin, 19,* 261–295.

Kendler, K. S., & Gardner, C. O. (1998). Boundaries of major depression: An evaluation of DSM-IV criteria. *American Journal of Psychiatry, 155,* 172–177.

Kendler, K. S., Gruenberg, A. M., & Kinney, D. K. (1994). Independent diagnoses of adoptees and relatives as defined by DSM-III in the Provincial and National Samples of the Danish Adoption Study of schizophrenia. *Archives of General Psychiatry, 51,* 456–468.

Kendler, K. S., Gruenberg, A. M., Tsuang, M.T. (1985). Psychiatric illness in first-degree relatives of schizophrenic and surgical control patients, a family study using DSM-III criteria. *Archives of General Psychiatry, 42,* 770–779.

Kendler, K. S., Neale, M. C., Kessler, R. C., et al. (1993f). A longitudinal study of 1-year prevalence of major depression in women. *Archives of General Psychiatry, 50,* 843–852.

Kendler, K. S., & Prescott, C. A. (1999). A population-based twin study of lifetime major depression in men and women. *Archives of General Psychiatry, 56,* 39–44.

Kendler, K. S., & Walsh, D. (1995). Schizotypal personality disorder in parents and the risk for schizophrenia in siblings. *Schizophrenia Bulletin, 21,* 47–52.

Kendler, K. S., et al. (1991). The genetic epidemiology of bulimia nervosa. *American Journal of Psychiatry, 148,* 1627–1637.

Kendler, K. S. et al. (1992a). A population-based twin study of major depression in women: The impact of varying definitions of illness. *Archives of General Psychiatry, 49,* 257–266.

Kendler, K. S., et al. (1992b). Generalized anxiety disorder in women. *Archives of General Psychiatry, 49,* 267–272.

Kendler, K. S., et al. (1992c). The genetic epidemiology of phobias in women: The interrelationship of agoraphobia, social phobia, situational phobia, and simple phobia. *Archives of General Psychiatry, 49,* 273–281.

Kendler, K. S., et al. (1992d). A population-based twin study of alcoholism in women. *Journal of the American Medical Association, 268,* 1877–1882.

Kendler, K. S., et al. (1993a). A pilot Swedish twin study of affective illness, including hospital- and population-ascertained subsamples. *Archives of General Psychiatry, 50,* 699–706.

Kendler, K. S., et al. (1993b). The lifetime history of major depression in women: Reliability of diagnosis and heritability. *Archives of General Psychiatry, 50,* 863–870.

Kendler, K. S., et al. (1993c). The Roscommon Family Study. I. Methods, diagnosis of probands, and risk of schizophrenia in relatives. *Archives of General Psychiatry, 50,* 527–540.

Kendler, K. S., et al. (1993d). The Roscommon Family Study. III. Schizophrenia-related personality disorders in relatives. *Archives of General Psychiatry, 50,* 781–788.

Kendler, D. S., et al. (1993e). The prediction of major depression in women: Toward an integrated etiologic model. *American Journal of Psychiatry, 150,* 1139–1148.

Kendler, K. S., et al. (1994). A twin-family study of alcoholism in women. *American Journal of Psychiatry, 151,* 707–715.

Kendler, K. S., et al. (1996a). The identification and validation of distinct depressive syndromes in a population-based sample of female twins. *Archives of General Psychiatry, 53,* 391–399.

Kendler, K. S., et al. (1996b). Lifetime prevalence, demographic risk factors, and diagnostic validity of nonaffective psychosis as assessed in a US community sample: The National Comorbidity Survey. *Archives of General Psychiatry, 53,* 1022–1031.

Kendler, K. S., et al. (1996c). Evidence for a schizophrenia vulnerability locus on chromosome 8p in the Irish study of high-density schizophrenia families. *American Journal of Psychiatry, 153,* 1534–1540.

Kendler, K .S., et al. (1997). Resemblance of psychotic symptoms and syndromes in affected sibling pairs from the Irish study of high-density schizophrenia families: Evidence for possible etiologic heterogeneity. *American Journal of Psychiatry, 154,* 191–198.

Kennedy, S., Scheirer, J., & Rogers, A. (1984). The price of success: Our monocultural science. *American Psychologist, 390,* 966–967.

Kernberg, O. F. (1975). *Borderline conditions and pathological narcissism.* New York: Jason Aronson.

Kershner, R. (1996). Adolescent attitudes about rape. *Adolescence, 31,* 29–33.

Kessler, D. A., et al. (1997). The legal and scientific basis for FDA's assertion of jurisdiction over cigarettes and smokeless tobacco. *Journal of the American Medical Association, 277,* 405–409.

Kessler, R. C. (1994). The National Comorbidity Survey: Preliminary results and future directions. *International Journal of Methods in Psychiatric Research, 4,* 114.1–114.13.

Kessler, R. C., et al. (1990). Clustering of teenage suicides after television news stories about suicides: A reconsideration. *American Journal of Psychiatry, 145,* 1379–1383.

Kessler, R. C., et al. (1991). Stressful life events and symptom onset in HIV infection. *American Journal of Psychiatry, 148,* 733–738.

Kessler, R. C. et al. (1993). Sex and depression in the National Comorbidity Survey I: Lifetime prevalence, chronicity and recurrence. *Journal of Affective Disorders, 29,* 85–96.

Kessler, R. C., et al. (1994). Lifetime and 12-month prevalence of DSM-III-R psychiatric disorders in the United States: Results from the National Comorbidity Survey. *Archives of General Psychiatry, 51,* 8–19.

Kessler, R. C. et al. (1995). Posttraumatic stress disorder in the National Comorbidity Survey. *Archives of General Psychiatry, 52,* 1048–1060.

Kessler, R. C., et al. (1997a). Differences in the use of psychiatric outpatient services between the United States and Ontario. *The New England Journal of Medicine, 336,* 551–557.

Kessler, R. C., et al. (1997b). Lifetime co-occurrence of DSM-III-R alcohol abuse and dependence with other psychiatric disorders in the National Comorbidity Survey. *Archives of General Psychiatry, 54,* 313–321.

Kessler, R. C., et al. (in press). Comorbidity of DSM-III-R major depressive disorder in the general population : Results from the U.S. National Comorbidity Survey.

Kety, S. S. (1980). The syndrome of schizophrenia: Unresolved questions and opportunities for research. *British Journal of Psychiatry, 136,* 421–436.

Kety, S. S., Rosenthal, D., Wender, P. H., Schulsinger, F., & Jacobsen, B. (1975). Mental illness in the biological and adoptive families of adoptive individuals who have become schizophrenic: A preliminary report based on psychiatric interviews. In R. R. Fieve, D. Rosenthal, & H. Brill (Eds.), *Genetic research in psychiatry.* Baltimore: The Johns Hopkins University Press.

Kety, S. S., Rosenthal, D., Wender, P. H., Schulsinger, F., & Jacobsen, B. (1978). The biological and adoptive families of adopted individuals who become schizophrenic. In C. Wynne, R. L. Cromwell, & S. Mathysse (Eds.), *The nature of schizophrenia* (pp. 25–37). New York: John Wiley & Sons.

Kety, S., et al. (1994). Mental illness in the biological and adoptive relatives of schizophrenic adoptees: Replication of the Copenhagen study in the rest of Denmark. *Archives of General Psychiatry, 51,* 442–455.

Keyes, D. (1982). *The minds of Billy Milligan.* New York: Bantam Books.

Kiecolt-Glaser, J. K., & Glaser, R. (1992). Psychoneuroimmunology: Can psychological interventions modulate immunity? *Journal of Consulting and Clinical Psychology, 60,* 569–575.

Kiecolt-Glaser, J. K., Speicher, C. E., Holliday, J. E., & Glaser, R. (1984). Stress and the transformation of lymphocytes in Epstein-Barr virus. *Journal of Behavioral Medicine, 7,* 1–12.

Kiecolt-Glaser, J. K., et al. (1985). Psychosocial enhancement of immunocompetence in a geriatric population. *Health Psychology, 4,* 25–41.

Kiecolt-Glaser, J. K., et al. (1987a). Chronic stress and immunity in family caregivers of Alzheimer's disease victims. *Psychosomatic Medicine, 49,* 523–535.

Kiecolt-Glaser, J. K., et al. (1987b). Marital quality, marital disruption, and immune function. *Psychosomatic Medicine, 49,* 13–34.

Kiecolt-Glaser, J. K., et al. (1988). Marital discord and immunity in males. *Psychosomatic Medicine, 50,* 213–229.

Kiecolt-Glaser, J., et al. (1995). Slowing of wound healing by psychological stress. *Lancet, 346,* 1194–1196.

Kiesler, C. A. (1982). Mental hospitalization and alternative care. *American Psychologist, 37,* 349–360.

Kiesler, C. A., & Sibulkin, A. E. (1987). *Mental hospitalization: Myths and facts about a national crisis.* Newbury Park, CA: Sage.

Killen, J. D., Fortmann, S. P., Newman, B., & Varady, A. (1990). Evaluation of a treatment approach combining nicotine gum with self-guided behavioral treatments for smoking relapse prevention. *Journal of Consulting and Clinical Psychology, 58,* 85–92.

Killen, J. D., et al. (1986). Self-induced vomiting and laxative and diuretic use among teenagers. *Journal of the American Medical Association, 225,* 1417–1449.

Killen, J. D., et al. (1996). Weight concerns influence the development of eating disorders: A 4-year prospective study. *Journal of Consulting and Clinical Psychology, 64,* 936–940.

Kim, S. C., & Seo, K. K., (1998). Efficacy and safety of fluoxetine, sertraline, and clomipramine in patients with prompter ejaculation: A double-blind, placebo controlled study. *Journal of Urology, 159,* 425–427.

Kimball, D. P. (1988). *Biological psychology.* New York: Holt, Rinehart, & Winston.

Kimerling, R., & Calhoun, K. S. (1994). Somatic symptoms, social support, and treatment seeking among sexual assault victims. *Journal of Consulting and Clinical Psychology, 62,* 333–340.

King, C., III., et al. (1998). Adolescent exposure to cigarette advertising in magazines: An evaluation of brand-specific advertising in relation to youth readership. *Journal of the American Medical Association, 279,* 516–520.

King, D. W., et al. (1995). Alternative representations of war zone stressors: Relationship to posttraumatic stress disorder in male and female Vietnam veterans. *Journal of Abnormal Psychology, 104,* 184–196.

King, D. W., et al. (1996). Prewar factors in combat-related posttraumatic stress disorder: Structural equation modeling with a national sample of female and male Vietnam veterans. *Journal of Consulting and Clinical Psychology, 64,* 520–531.

King, L. A., et al. (1998). Resilience–recovery factors in post–traumatic stress disorder among female and male Vietnam veterans: Hardiness, postwar social support, and additional stressful life events. *Journal of Personality and Social Psychology, 74,* 420–434.

King, S., & Dixon, M. J. (1995). Expressed emotion, family dynamics, and symptom severity in a predictive model of social adjustment for schizophrenic young adults. *Schizophrenia Research, 14,* 121–132.

Kinney, D. K., et al. (1997). Thought disorder in schizophrenic and control adoptees and their relatives. *Archives of General Psychiatry, 54,* 475–479.

Kinsey, A. C., Pomeroy, W. B., & Martin, C. E. (1948). *Sexual behavior in the human male.* Philadelphia: Saunders.

Kinsey, A. C., Pomeroy, W. B., Martin, C. E., & Gebhard, P. H. (1953). *Sexual behavior in the human female.* Philadelphia: Saunders.

Kirmayer, L. J., Robbins, J. M., & Paris, J. (1994). Somatoform disorders: Personality and the social matrix of somatic distress. *Journal of Abnormal Psychology, 103,* 125–136.

Kirschner, D. A., & Kirschner, S. (1992). Comprehensive family therapy in the treatment of spouse abuse. *Psychotherapy in Private Practice, 10,* 67–76.

Kissel, R. C., Whitman, T. L., & Reid, D. H. (1983). An institutional staff training and self-management program for developing multiple self-care skills in severely-profoundly retarded individuals. *Journal of Applied Behavior Analysis, 16,* 395–415.

Kitada, T., et al. (1998). Mutations in the parkin gene cause autosomal recessive juvenile parkinsonism. *Nature, 392,* 605–608.

Kitayama, S., et al. (1997). Individual and collective processes in the construction of the self: Self-enhancement in the United States and self-criticism in Japan. *Journal of Personality and Social Psychology, 72,* 1245–1267.

Kivlahan, D. R., Marlatt, G. A., Fromme, K., Coppel, D. B., & Williams, E. (1990). Secondary prevention with college drinkers: Evaluation of an alcohol skills training program. *Journal of Consulting and Clinical Psychology, 58,* 805–810.

Klag, M. J. (1991). Cited in Leary, W. E. (1991, February 6). Social links are seen in black stress. *The New York Times,* p. A16.

Klassen, D., O'Connor, W. A. (1988). Predicting violence in schizophrenic and non-schizophrenic patients: A prospective study. *Journal of Community Psychology, 16,* 217–227.

Klatsky, A. L., Freidman, G. D., & Siegelaub, A. B. (1981). Alcohol and mortality: A ten-year Kaiser-Permanente experience. *Annals of Internal Medicine, 95,* 139–145.

Kleiman, D. (1988, November 7) A day in a mental hospital, a dream of life outside. *The New York Times,* pp. B1, B2.

Klein, D. F. (1993). False suffocation alarms, spontaneous panics, and related conditions: An integrative hypothesis. *Archives of General Psychiatry, 50,* 306–317.

Klein, D. F. (1994). "Klein's suffocation theory of panic": Reply. *Archives of General Psychiatry, 51,* 506.

Klein, D. N., Taylor, E. B., Dickstein, S., & Harding, K. (1988). Primary early-onset dysthymia: Comparison with primary nonbipolar nonchronic major depression on demographic, clinical, familial, personality, and socioenvironmental characteristics and short-term outcome. *Journal of Abnormal Psychology, 97,* 387–398.

Klein, D. N., et al. (1998). Thirty-month naturalistic follow-up study of early-onset dysthymic disorder: Course, diagnostic stability, and prediction of outcome. *Journal of Abnormal Psychology, 107,* 338–348.

Klein, M. (1981). On Mahler's autistic and symbiotic phases: An exposition and evaluation. *Psychoanalysis and Contemporary Thought, 4,* 69–105.

Klein, M., et al. (1952). *Developments in psychoanalysis.* London: Hogarth Press.

Klein, R. G., et al. (1997). Clinical efficacy of methylphenidate in conduct disorder with and without attention deficit hyperactivity disorder. *Archives of General Psychiatry, 4,* 1073–1080.

Kleiner, L., & Marshall, W. L. (1985). Relationship difficulties and agoraphobia. *Clinical Psychology Review, 5,* 581–595.

Kleinfield, N. R. (1993, August 29). Legal gambling faces higher odds. *The New York Times,* Section IV, p. 3.

Kleinman, A. (1987). Anthropology and psychiatry: The role of culture in cross-cultural research on illness. *British Journal of Psychiatry, 151,* 447–454.

Klem, M. L., et al. (1997). A descriptive study of individuals successful at long-term maintenance of substantial weight loss. *American Journal of Clinical Nutrition, 11,* 98–106.

Klepinger, D. H., et al. (1993). Perceptions of AIDS risk and severity and their association with risk-related behavior among U.S. men. *Family Planning Perspectives, 25,* 74–82.

Klerman, G. L. (1984). Ideology & science in the individual psychotherapy of schizophrenia. *Schizophrenia Bulletin, 10,* 608–612.

Klerman, G. L., & Weissman, M. M. (1989). Increasing rates of depression. *Journal of the American Medical Association, 261,* 2229–2235.

Klerman, G. L., Weissman, M. M., Rounsaville, B. J., & Chevron, E. S. (1984). *Interpersonal psychotherapy of depression.* New York, NY: Basic Books.

Klerman, G. L., et al. (1991). Panic attacks in the community: Social morbidity and health care utilization. *Journal of the American Medical Association, 265,* 742–746.

Klesges, R. C., Ward, K. D., & DeBon, M. (1996). Smoking cessation: A succcessful behavioral/pharmacological interface. *Clinical Psychology Review, 16,* 479–496.

Klesges, R. C., et al. (1997). How much weight gain occurs following smoking cessation? A comparison of weight gain using both continuous and point prevalence abstinence. *Journal of Consulting and Clinical Psychology, 65,* 286–291.

Klorman, R., et al. (1988). Effects of methylphenidate on attention-deficit hyperactivity disorder with and without aggressive/noncompliant features. *Journal of Abnormal Psychology, 97,* 413–422.

Klorman, R., et al. (1994). Clinical and cognitive effects of methylphenidate on children with attention deficit disorder as a function of aggression/oppositionality and age. *Journal of Abnormal Psychology, 103,* 206–221.

Klosko, J. S., et al. (1990). A comparison of alprazolam and behavior therapy in treatment of panic disorder. *Journal of Consulting and Clinical Psychology, 58,* 77–84.

Kluft, R. P. (1984a). An introduction to multiple personality disorder. *Psychiatric Annals, 14,* 19–24.

Kluft, R. P. (1984b). Multiple personality in childhood. *Psychiatric Clinics of North America, 7,* 121–135.

Kluft, R. P. (1986). Three high functioning multiples. *Journal of Nervous and Mental Disease, 174,* 722–726.

Kluft, R. P. (1987). First-rank symptoms as a diagnostic clue to multiple personality disorder. *American Journal of Psychiatry, 144,* 293–298.

Kluft, R. P. (1988). The dissociative disorders. In J. Talbott, R. Hales, & S. Yudofsky (Eds.), *Textbook of psychiatry,* Washington, DC: American Psychiatric Press.

Knapp, S., & Vandercreek, L. (1982). *Tarasoff:* Five years later. *Professional Psychology, 13,* 511–516.

Knight, G. P., Fabes, R. A., & Higgins, D A. (1996). Concerns about drawing causal inferences from meta-analyses: An example in the study of gender differences in aggression. *Psychological Bulletin, 119,* 410–421.

Knight, R. G., Godfrey, H. P. D., & Shelton, E. J. (1988). The psychological deficits associated with Parkinson's disease. *Clinical Psychology Review, 8,* 391–410.

Knoll, J. L., IV, et al. (1998). Heterogeneity of the psychoses: Is there a neurodegenerative psychosis? *Schizophrenia Bulletin, 24,* 365–379.

Knox, L S., Albano, A. M., & Barlow. D. H. (1996). Parental involvement in the treatment of childhood obsessive compulsive disorder: A multiple-baseline examination incorporating parents. *Behavior Therapy, 27,* 93–114.

Knudsen, D. D. (1991). Child sexual coercion. In E. Grauerholz & M. A. Koralewski (Eds.), *Sexual coercion: A sourcebook on its nature, causes, and prevention* (pp. 17–28). Lexington, MA: Lexington Books.

Kobak, K. A., et al. (1996). Computer-administered clinical rating scales: A review. *Psychopharmacology, 127,* 291–301.

Kobak, K. A., et al. (1997). A computer-administered telephone interview to identify mental disorders. *Journal of the American Medical Association, 278,* 905–910.

Kobasa, S. C. (1979). Stressful life events, personality, and health: An inquiry into hardiness. *Journal of Personality and Social Psychology, 37,* 1–11.

Kobasa, S. C., Maddi, S. R., & Kahn, S. (1982). Hardiness and health: A prospective study. *Journal of Personality and Social Psychology, 42,* 168–177.

Kobasa, S. C., Maddi, S. R., & Zola, M. A. (1983). Type A and hardiness. *Journal of Behavioral Medicine, 6,* 41–51.

Kockott, G., & Fahrner, E. (1988). Male-to-female and female-to-male transsexuals: A comparison. *Archives of Sexual Behavior, 17,* 539–545.

Kocsis, J. H., et al. (1996). Maintenance therapy for chronic depression: A controlled clinical trial of desipramine. *Archives of General Psychiatry, 53,* 769–774.

Kocsis, J. H., et al. (1997). Double-blind comparison of sertraline, imipramine, and placebo in the treatment of dysthymia: Psychosocial outcomes. *American Journal of Psychiatry, 154,* 390–395.

Koenig, H. G., et al. (1997). Use of antidepressants by nonpsychiatrists in the treatment of medically ill hospitalized depressed elderly patients. *American Journal of Psychiatry, 154,* 1369–1375.

Kogan, A. O., & Guilford, P. M. (1998). Side effects of short-term 10,000-lux light therapy. *American Journal of Psychiatry, 155,* 293–294.

Kogon, M. M., et al. (1997). Effects of medical and psychotherapeutic treatment on the survival of women with metastatic breast carcinoma. *Cancer, 80,* 225–230.

Kohlenberg, R. J. (1973). Behaviorist approach to multiple personality: A case study. *Behavior Therapy, 4,* 137–140.

Kohut, H. (1966). Forms and transformations of narcissism. *Journal of the American Psychoanalytic Association, 14,* 243–272.

Kolata, G. (1990, May 24). Where fat is problem, heredity is the answer, studies find. *The New York Times,* p. B9.

Kolata, G. (1991a, November 9). For heterosexuals, diagnosis of AIDS is often unmercifully late. *The New York Times,* p. 32.

Kolata, G. (1991b, March 21). Chemical is found to shield cells in Parkinson's disease. *The New York Times,* p. B10.

Kolata, G. (1992, July 5). Appetite suppressants aid obese. *The New York Times,* p. B1.

Kolata, G. (1994a, February 3). Sweeteners-hyperactivity link is discounted. *The New York Times,* p. A19.

Kolata, G. (1994b, November 11). A simpler test for Alzheimer's is reported. *The New York Times,* p. A20.

Kolata, G. (1995a, January 19). Identifying asthma risk in children. *The New York Times,* p. A21.

Kolata, G. (1995b, February 9). Landmark in Alzheimer research: Breeding mice with the disease. *The New York Times,* p. A20.

Kolata, G. (1995c, March 9). Metabolism found to adjust for a body's natural weight. *The New York Times,* pp. A1, A22.

Kolata, G. (1996, December 17). Ritalin use is lower than thought. *The New York Times,* p. C3

Kolata, G. (1998, March 28). U.S. approves sale of impotence pill; huge market seen. *The New York Times,* pp. A1, A8.

Kolbert, E. (1991, October 11). Sexual harassment at work is pervasive, survey suggests. *The New York Times,* pp. A1, A17.

Kolbert, E. (1994, January 21). Demons replace dolls and bicycles in world of children of the quake. *The New York Times,* p. A19.

Kolko, D. J. (1988). Educational programs to promote awareness and prevention of child sexual victimization: A review and methodological critique. *Clinical Psychology Review, 8,* 195–209.

Kolko, D. J., & Rickard-Figueroa, J. L. (1985). Effects of video games on the adverse corollaries of chemotherapy in pediatric oncology patients: A single-case analysis. *Journal of Consulting and Clinical Psychology, 53,* 223–228.

Koorland, M. A. (1986). Applied behavior analysis and the correction of learning disabilities. In J. K. Torgesen & B. Y. L. Wong (Eds.), *Psychological and educational perspectives on learning disabilities* (pp. 297–328). Orlando, FL: Academic Press.

Kopta, S. M., et al. (1994). Patterns of symptomatic recovery in psychotherapy. *Journal of Consulting and Clinical Psychology, 62,* 1009–1016.

Koran, L. M., Thienemann, M. L., & Davenport, R. (1996) Quality of life for patients with obsessive-compulsive disorder. *American Journal of Psychiatry, 153,* 783–788.

Koran, L., et al. (1996). Fluvoxamine versus clomipramine for obsessive-compulsive disorder: A double-blind comparison. *Journal of Clinical Psychopharmacology, 16,* 121–129.

Koran, L., et al. (1997). Rapid benefit of intravenous pulse loading of clomipramine in obsessive-compulsive disorder. *American Journal of Psychiatry, 154,* 396–401.

Koss, M. P. (1988). Stranger and acquaintance rape: Are there differences in the victim's experience? *Psychology of Women Quarterly, 12,* 1–24.

Koss, M. P. (1993). Rape: Scope, impact, interventions, and public policy responses. *American Psychologist, 48,* 1062–1069.

Koss, M. P., Gidycz, C. A., & Wisniewski, N. (1987). The scope of rape: Incidence and prevalence of sexual aggression and victimization in a national sample of higher education students. *Journal of Consulting and Clinical Psychology, 55,* 162–170.

Koss, M. P., et al. (1994). *No safe haven: male violence against women at home, at work, and in the community.* Washington, D C American Psychological Association.

Kosson, D. S. (1996). Psychopathy and dual-task performance under focusing conditions. *Journal of Abnormal Psychology, 105*, 391–400.

Kosson, D. S., Smith, S. S., & Newman, J. P. (1990). Evaluating the construct validity of psychopathy in black and white male inmates: Three preliminary studies. *Journal of Abnormal Psychology, 99*, 250–259.

Kotler, M. (1997). Excess dopamine D4 receptor (D4DR) exon III seven repeat allele in opioid-dependent subjects. *Molecular Psychiatry, 2*, 251–254.

Kotses, H., et al. (1991). Long-term effects of biofeedback-induced facial relaxation on measures of asthma severity in children. *Biofeedback and Self Regulation, 16*, 1–21.

Kovacs, M. (1996). Presentation and course of major depressive disorder during childhood and later years of the life span. *Journal of the American Academy of Children and Adolescent Psychiatry, 35*, 705–715.

Kovacs, M., & Beck, A. T. (1978). Maladaptive cognitive structure in depression. *American Journal of Psychiatry, 135*, 525–533.

Kovacs, M., et al., (1997). A controlled family history study of childhood-onset depressive disorder. *Archives of General Psychiatry, 54*, 613–623.

Kozol, N. J., Crider, R. A., Brodsky, M. D., & Adams, E. H. (1985). *Epidemiology of heroin: 1964–1984.* Rockville, MD: National Institute on Drug Abuse.

Kraepelin, E. (1909–1913). *Psychiatrie* (8th ed.). Leipzig: J. A. Barth.

Kramer, M. S. et al. (1998, September 11). Distinct mechanism for antidepressant activity by blockade of central substance P receptors. *Science,* pp. 1640–1645.

Kramer, P. (1993). *Listening to Prozac.* New York: Penguin Books.

Krantz, D. S., Contrada, R. J., Hills, D. R., & Friedler, E. (1988). Environmental stress and biobehavioral antecedents of coronary heart disease. *Journal of Consulting and Clinical Psychology, 56*, 333–341.

Krantz, S. E., & Moos, R. H. (1988). Risk factors at intake predict nonremission among depressed patients. *Journal of Consulting and Clinical Psychology, 56*, 863–869.

Kranzler, H. R., et al. (1996). Comorbid psychiatric diagnosis predicts three year outcomes in alcoholics: A posttreatment natural history study. *Journal of Studies in Alcohol, 57*, 619–626.

Kraus, R. F., & Buffler, P. A. (1979) Sociocultural stress and the American native in Alaska: An analysis of changing patterns of psychiatric illness and alcohol abuse among Alaska natives. *Culture, Medicine, and Psychiatry, 11*–15.

Kresin, D. (1993) Medical aspects of inhibited sexual desire disorder. In W. O'Donohue & J. H. Geer (Eds.), *Handbook of sexual dysfunctions: Assessment and treatment* (pp. 15–52). Boston: Allyn & Bacon.

Krieger, N., & Sidney, S. (1996). Racial discrimination and blood pressure: The CARDIA study of young black and white adults. *American Journal of Public Health, 86*, 1370–1378.

Kring, A. M., & Neale, J. M. (1996). Do schizophrenic patients show a disjunctive relationship among expressive, experiential, and psychophysiological components of emotion? *Journal of Abnormal Psychology, 105*, 249–257.

Kring A. M. et al. (1993). Flat affect in schizophrenia does not reflect diminished subjective experience of emotion. *Journal of Abnormal Psychology, 102*, 507–517.

Kristof, N. D. (1995, May 14). Japanese say no to crime: Tough methods, at a price. *The New York Times,* pp. A1, A8.

Kruesi, M. J. P., et al. (1987). Effects of sugar and aspartame on aggression and activity in children. *American Journal of Psychiatry, 144*, 1487–1490.

Kruesi, M. J., et al. (1992). Paraphilias: A double-blind cross-over comparison of clomipramine versus desipramine. *Archives of Sexual Behavior, 21*, 587–593.

Krug, E., et al. (1998). Suicide after natural disasters. *The New England Journal of Medicine, 338*, 373–378.

Kruger, T. E., & Jerrells, T. R. (1992). Potential role of alcohol in human immunodeficiency virus infection. *Alcohol Health & Research World, 16*, 57–63.

Krupnick, J. L., et al. (1996). The role of therapeutic alliance in psychotherapy and pharmacotherapy outcome: Findings in the National Institute of Mental Health Treatment of Depression Collaborative Research Program. *Journal of Consulting and Clinical Psychology, 64*, 532–539.

Kuczmarski, R. J. (1992). Prevalence of overweight and weight gain in the United States. *American Journal of Clinical Nutrition, 55* (Suppl.), 495S–502S.

Kuczmarksi, R. J., et al. (1994). Increasing prevalence of overweight among U.S. adults. *Journal of the American Medical Association, 272*, 205–211.

Kuiper, N. A., & Martin, R. A. (1993). Humor and self-concept. *Humor International Journal of Humor Research, 6*, 251–270.

Kupfer, D. J, & Reynolds, C. F. (1997). Current concepts: Management of insomnia. *The New England Journal of Medicine, 336*, 341–346.

Kupfersmid, J. (1995). Does the Oedipus complex exist? *Psychotherapy, 32*, 535–547.

Kurdek, L. A., & Schmitt. J. P. (1986). Relationship quality of partners in heterosexual married, heterosexual cohabiting, gay, and lesbian relationships. *Journal of Personality and Social Psychology, 51*, 711–720.

Kutchins, H., & Kirk, S. A. (1995, May). DSM-IV: Does bigger and newer mean better? *The Harvard Mental Health Letter, 11* (11), 4–6.

Kwon, S., & Oei, T. P. S. (1994). The roles of two levels of cognitions in the development, maintenance, and treatment of depression. *Clinical Psychology Review, 14*, 331–358.

L

Lacks, P. E., Bertelson, A. D., Ganz, L., & Kunkel, J. (1983). The effectiveness of three behavioral treatments for different degrees of sleep-onset insomnia. *Behavior Therapy, 14*, 593–605.

Lacks, P., & Morin, C. M. (1992). Recent advances in the assessment and treatment of insomnia. Special Issue: Behavioral medicine: An update for the 1990s. *Journal of Consulting and Clinical Psychology, 60*, 586–594.

LaCroix, A. Z., & Haynes, S. G. (1987). Gender differences in the stressfulness of workplace roles: A focus on work and health. In R. Barnett, G. Baruch, & L. Biener (Eds.), *Gender and stress.* (pp. 96–121). New York: The Free Press.

Ladouceur, R., & Walker, M. (1996). A cognitive perspective on gambling. In P. M. Salkovskis (Ed.), *Trends in cognitive and behavioural therapies* (pp. 89–120). New York: Wiley.

Lager, B., et al. (1994). Phototherapy for seasonal affective disorder: A blind comparison of three different schedules. *American Journal of Psychiatry, 151*, 1081–1083.

LaGory, M., & Fitzpatrick, K. (1992). The effects of environmental context on elderly depression. *Journal of Aging and Health, 4*, 459–479.

LaGreca, A. M., et al. (1996). Symptoms of posttraumatic stress in children after hurricane Andrew: A prospective study. *Journal of Consulting and Clinical Psychology, 64*, 712–723.

Lahey, B. B., et al. (1994). DSM-IV field trials for oppositional defiant disorder and conduct disorder in children and adolescents. *American Journal of Psychiatry, 151*, 1163–1171.

Lahey, B. B., et al. (1995). Four-year longitudinal study of conduct disorder in boys: Patterns and predictors of persistence. *Journal of Abnormal Psychology, 104*, 83–93.

LaHoste, G. J., et al. (1996). Dopamine D4 receptor gene polymorphism is associated with attention deficit hyperactivity disorder. *Molecular Psychiatry, 1*, 121–124.

Laing, R. D. (1964). Is schizophrenia a disease? *International Journal of Social Psychiatry, 10*, 184–193.

Laing, R. D. (1976, July 20). Round the bend. *New Statesman.*

Lamb, D. H. et al. (1994). Sexual and business relationship between therapists and former clients. *Psychotherapy, 31*, 270–278.

Lamb, H. R., & Lamb, D. M. (1990). Factors contributing to homelessness among the chronically and severely mentally ill. *Hospital and Community Psychiatry, 41*, 301–305.

Lamberg, L. (1998). Mental illness and violent acts: Protecting the patient and the public. *Journal of the American Medical Association, 280*, 407–408.

Lambert, M. C., et al. (1992). Jamaican and American adult perspectives on child psychopathology: Further exploration of the threshold model. *Journal of Consulting and Clinical Psychology, 60*, 146–149.

Lambert, M. J., & Bergin, A. E. (1994). The effectiveness of psychotherapy. In A. E. Bergin & S.L. Garfield (Eds.), *Handbook of psychotherapy and behavior change* (4th ed., pp. 72–113). New York: Wiley.

Lambert, M. J., & Okiishi, J. C. (1997). The effects of the individual psychotherapist and implications for future research. *Clinical Psychology: Science and Practice, 4*, 66–75.

Lambert, N. M., Hartsough, C. S., Sassone, D., & Sandoval, J. (1987). Persistence of hyperactivity symptoms from childhoood to adolescence and associated outcomes. *American Journal of Orthopsychiatry, 57*, 22–32.

Landerman, L. R., et al. (1994). The relationship between insurance coverage and psychiatric disorder in predicting use of mental health services. *American Journal of Psychiatry, 151*, 1785–1790.

Landolt, H. P., et al. (1996). Late-afternoon ethanol intake affects nocturnal sleep and the sleep EEG in middle-aged men. *Journal of Clinical Psychopharmacology , 16*, 428–436.

Lane, E. (1994, December 6). Losing weight isn't enough. *New York Newsday,* p. A6.

Lang, J. G., Munoz, R. F, Bernal, G., & Sorenson, J. L. (1982). Quality of life and psychological well-being in a bicultural Latino community. *Hispanic Journal of Behavioral Sciences, 4*, 433–450.

Lang, P. J. (1968). Fear reduction and fear behavior: Problems in treating a construct. In J. M. Schlein (Ed.), *Research in psychotherapy, Vol. III* (pp. 90–102). Washington, D C: American Psychological Association.

Langenbucher, J. W., & Chung, T. (1995). Onset and staging of DSM-IV alcohol dependence using mean age and survival-hazard methods. *Journal of Abnormal Psychology, 104*, 346–354.

Langford, H. G., et al. (1985). Dietary therapy slows the return of hypertension after stopping prolonged medication. *Journal of the American Medical Association, 253*, 657–664.

Laporte, L., & Guttman, H. (1996). Traumatic childhood experiences as risk factors for borderline and other personality disorders. *Journal of Personality Disorders, 10*, 247–259.

Lara, M. E., Leader, J., & Klein, D. N. (1997). The association between social support and course of depression: Is it confounded with personality? *Journal of Abnormal Psychology, 106*, 478–482.

Larisch, R., et al. (1997). In vivo evidence for the involvement of dopamine D2 receptors in striatum and anterior cingulate gyrus in major depression. *Neuroimage, 5*, 251–260.

Larson, E. W., et al. (1992). Disulfiram treatment of patients with both alcohol dependence and other psychiatric disorders: A review. *Alcoholism: Clinical and Experimental Research, 16,* 125–130.

Larson, R. W., Raffaelli, M., Richards, M. H., Ham, M., & Jewell, L. (1990). Ecology of depression in late childhood and early adolescence: A profile of daily states and activities. *Journal of Abnormal Psychology, 99,* 92–102.

Last draw for smokers. (1996, October). *UC Berkeley Wellness Letter, 13,* 2–3.

Lau, M. A., Pihl, R. O., & Peterson, J. B. (1995). Provocation, acute alcohol intoxication, cognitive performance, and aggression. *Journal of Abnormal Psychology, 104,* 150–155.

Laumann, E. O., Gagnon, J. H., Michael, R. T., & Michaels, S. (1994). *The social organization of sexuality: Sexual practices in the United States.* Chicago: University of Chicago Press.

Lauriello, J., et al. (1997). Similar extent of brain dysmorphology in severely ill women and men with schizophrenia. *American Journal of Psychiatry, 154,* 819–825.

Lawson, D. M. (1983). Alcoholism. In M. Hersen (Ed.), *Outpatient behavior therapy: A clinical guide* (pp. 143–172). New York: Grune & Stratton.

Lawson, W. B. (1986) Racial and ethnic factors in psychiatric research. *Hospital and Community Psychiatry, 37,* 50–54.

Layman, M. J. Gidycz, C. A., & Lynn, S. J. (1996). Unacknowledged versus acknowledged rape victims: Situational factors and posttraumatic stress. *Journal of Abnormal Psychology, 105,* 124–131.

Lazarus, R. S., DeLongis, A., Folkman, S., & Gruen, R. (1985). Stress and adaptational outcomes: The problem of confounded measures. *American Psychologist, 40,* 770–779.

Lazarus, R. S., & Folkman, S. (1984). *Stress, appraisal, and coping.* New York: Springer.

Lear, M. W. (1988, July 3). Mad malady. *New York Times Magazine,* pp. 21–22.

Leary, W. E. (1998, Feburary 12). New therapy offers promise in treatment of pedophiles. *The New York Times,* p. A11.

Leary, W. E. (1995a, January 18). Heroin medication approved as treatment for alcoholism. *The New York Times,* p. A18.

Leary, W. E. (1995b, February 22). A hospital sees gain for blacks on cancer. *The New York Times,* p. C10.

Leary, W. E. (1996a, November 15). Scientists identify site of gene tied to some cases of Parkinson's. *The New York Times,* p. A19.

Leary, W. E. (1996b, December 18). Responses of alcoholics to therapies seem similar. *The New York Times,* p. A17.

Leary, W. E. (1997, January 14). Researchers investigate (horrors!) nicotine's potential benefits. *The New York Times,* p. C3.

Leathers, S. J., Kelley, M.A., & Richman, J. A. (1997). Postpartum depressive symptomatology in new mothers and fathers: Parenting, work, and support. *Journal of Nervous and Mental Disease, 185,* 129–139.

Leavitt, F., & Labott, S. M. (1997). Criterion-related validity of Rorschach analogues of dissociation. *Psychological Assessment, 9,* 244–249.

Le Bars, P. L., et al. (1997). A placebo-controlled, double-blind, randomized trial of an extract of ginkgo biloba for dementia. *Journal of the American Medical Association, 278,* 1327–1332.

Lebowitz, B. D., et al. (1997). Diagnosis and treatment of depression in late life: Consensus statement update. *Journal of the American Medical Association, 278,* 1186–1190.

Lechtenberg, R. (1984). *Epilepsy and the family.* Cambridge, MA: Harvard University Press.

Ledray, L. E. (1990). Counseling rape victims: The nursing challenge. *Perspectives in Psychiatric Care, 26,* 21–27.

Lee, C. C., & Richardson, B. L. (1991). *Multicultural issues in counseling: New approaches to diversity.* Alexandria, VA: AACD.

Lee, T. H. (1996, May). Marijuana's cognitive effects persist. *Journal Watch for Psychiatry, 2* (5), 41.

Lee, T. M. C., et al. (1998). Seasonal affective disorder. *Clinical Psychology: Science and Practice, 5,* 275–290.

Leedham, B., et al. (1995). Positive expectations predict health after heart transplantation. *Health Psychology, 14,* 74–79.

Lefcourt, H. M., & Martin, R. A. (1986). *Humor and life stress: Antidote to adversity.* New York: Springer-Verlag.

Leff, J. (1977). International variations in the diagnosis of schizophrenia. *British Journal of Psychiatry, 131,* 329–338.

Leff, J., & Vaughn, C. (1981). The role of maintenance therapy and relatives' expressed emotion in relapse of schizophrenia: A two-year follow-up. *British Journal of Psychiatry, 139,* 102–104.

Lefley, H. P. (1990). Culture and chronic mental illness. *Hospital and Community Psychiatry, 41,* 277–286.

Lehman, A. F., et al. (1997). A randomized trial of assertive community treatment for homeless persons with severe mental illness. *Archives of General Psychiatry, 54,* 1038–1043.

Lehrer, M., et al. (1994). Relaxation and music therapies for asthma among patients prestabilized on asthma medication. *Journal of Behavioral Medicine, 17,* 1–24.

Lehrer, P. M., Sargunaraj, D., & Hochron, S. (1992). Psychological approaches to the treatment of asthma. *Journal of Consulting and Clinical Psychology, 60,* 639–643.

Leibel, R. L., Rosenbaum, M., & Hirsch, J. (1995). Changes in energy expenditure resulting from altered body weight. *New England Journal of Medicine, 332,* 621–628.

Leibenluft, E. (1996). Women with bipolar illness: Clinical and research issues. *American Journal of Psychiatry, 153,* 163–173.

Leibowitz, S. F. (1986). Brain monoamines and peptides: Role in the control of eating behavior. *Federation Proceedings, 45,* 1396–1403.

Leishman, K. (1987, February). Heterosexuals and AIDS. *The Atlantic Monthly,* 39–58.

Leitenberg, H., Rosen, J. C., Gross, J., Nudelman, S., & Vara, L. S. (1988). Exposure plus response-prevention treatment of bulimia nervosa. *Journal of Consulting and Clinical Psychology, 56,* 535–541.

Leitenberg, H., Yost, L. W., & Carroll-Wilson, M. (1986). Negative cognitive errors in children: Questionnaire development, normative data, and comparisons between children with and without self-reported symptoms of depression, low self-esteem, and evaluation anxiety. *Journal of Consulting and Clinical Psychology, 54,* 528–536.

Lejoyeux, M., et al. (1996). Phenomenology and psychopathology of uncontrolled buying. *American Journal of Psychiatry, 153,* 1524–1529.

Lemanske, R. F., Jr, & Busse, W. W. (1997). Asthma. *Journal of the American Medical Association, 278,* 1855–1873.

Leon, G. R., et al. (1995). Prospective analysis of personality and behavioral vulnerabilities and gender influences in the later development of disordered eating. *Journal of Abnormal Psychology, 104,* 140–149.

LePera, P. (1990). ACS runs Uptown out of town. *Cancer News, 44* (2), 20.

Lerman, C., et al. (1999). Evidence suggesting the role of specific genetic factors in cigarette smoking. *Health Psychology, 18,* 14–20.

Lesch, K. P., et al. (1996). Association of anxiety-related traits with a polymorphism in the serotonin transporter gene regulatory region. *Science, 274,* 1527–1531.

Le Shan, L. (1966). An emotional life-history pattern associated with neoplastic disease. *Annals of New York Academy of Sciences, 125,* 780–792.

Leshner, A. I. (1996). Understanding drug addiction: Implications for treatment. *Hospital Practice, 37,* 47–54, 57–59.

Leshner, A. I. (1997). Drug abuse and addiction treatment research. *Archives of General Psychiatry, 54,* 691–694.

Lesieur, H. R., & Blume, S. B. (1991). Evaluation of patients treated for pathological gambling in a combined alcohol, substance abuse and pathological gambling treatment unit. *British Journal of Addiction, 86,* 1017–1028.

Lesieur, H. R., Blume, S. B., & Zoppa, R. M. (1986). Alcoholism, drug abuse, and gambling. *Alcoholism: Clinical and Experimental Research, 10,* 33–38.

Lesser, I. (1992, December). Ethnic differences in response to psychotropic drugs. Paper presented at a symposium, *Anxiety Disorders in African Americans,* presented by the State University of New York Health Science Center at Brooklyn, Brooklyn, NY.

Letourneau, E., & O'Donohue, W. (1993). Sexual desire disorders. In W. O'Donohue & J. H. Geer (Eds.), *Handbook of sexual dysfunctions: Assessment and treatment.* (pp. 53–81). Boston: Allyn & Bacon.

Letourneau, E. J., et al. (1996). Comorbidity of sexual problems and posttraumatic stress disorder in female crime victims. *Behavior Therapy, 27,* 321–336.

LeVay, S. (1991). A difference in hypothalamic structure between heterosexual and homosexual men. *Science, 253,* 1034–1037.

Levenson, J. L., & Bemis, C (1991). The role of psychological factors in cancer onset and progression. *Psychosomatics, 32,* 124–132.

Levine, D., et al. (1991, February). Church-based smoking cessation strategies in urban blacks. Paper presented at the program on "Smoking Cessation Strategies for Minorities." National Heart, Lung & Blood Institute, National Institutes of Health, Bethesda, MD.

Levine, J., Warrenburg, S., Kerns, R., Schwartz, G., Delaney, R., Fontana, A., Gradman, A., Smith, S., Scott, A., & Cascione, R. (1987). The role of denial in recovery from coronary heart disease. *Psychosomatic Medicine, 49,* 109–117.

Levitan, R. D., Rector, N. A., & Bagby, R. M. (1998). Negative attributional style in seasonal and nonseasonal depression. *American Journal of Psychiatry, 155,* 428–430.

Levitan, R. D., et al. (1997). Hormonal and subjective responses to intravenous metachlorophenylpiperazine in bulimia nervosa. *Archives of General Psychiatry, 54,* 521–527.

Levy, D. L. (1994). Eye tracking and schizophrenia: A selective review. *Schizophrenia Bulletin, 20,* 47–62.

Levy, F., et al. (1997). Attention-deficit hyperactivity disorder: A category or a continuum? Genetic analysis of a large-scale twin study. *Journal of the American Academy of Child and Adolescent Psychiatry, 36,* 741–744.

Levy, S. R., Jurkovic, G. L., & Spirito, A. (1995). A multisystems analysis of adolescent suicide attempters. *Journal of Abnormal Child Psychology, 23,* 221–234.

Lewandowski, L. M., et al. (1997). Meta-analysis of cognitive-behavioral treatment studies for bulimia. *Clinical Psychology Review, 17,* 703–718.

Lewin, T. (1998, June 26). One in eight boys of high-school age has been abused, survey shows. *The New York Times,* p. 11

Lewinsohn, P. M. (1974). A behavioral approach to depression. In R. J. Friedman & M. M. Katz (Eds.), *The psychology of depression: Contemporary theory and research.* Washington, DC: Winston-Wiley.

Lewinsohn, P. M, Antonuccio, D., Steinmetz, J., & Terry, L, (1984). *The coping with depression course: A psychoeducational intervention for unipolar depression.* Eugene, OR: Castalia.

Lewinsohn, P. M., Duncan, E. M., Stanton, A. K., & Hautzinger, M. (1986). Age at first onset for nonpolar depression. *Journal of Abnormal Psychology, 95,* 378–383.

Lewinsohn, P. M. , Gotlib, I. H., & Seeley, J. R. (1997). Depression-related psychosocial variables: Are they specific to depression in adolescents? *Journal of Abnormal Psychology, 106*, 365–375.

Lewinsohn, P. M., & Libet, J. M. (1972). Pleasant events, activity schedules and depression. *Journal of Abnormal Psychology, 79*, 291–295.

Lewinsohn, P. M., Rohde, P., & Seeley, J. R. (1994). Psychosocial risk factors for future adolescent suicide attempts. *Journal of Consulting and Clinical Psychology, 62*, 297–305.

Lewinsohn, P. M., Rohde, P., & Seeley, J. R. (1996). Adolescent suicidal ideation and attempts: Prevalence, risk factors, and clinical implications. *Clinical Psychology: Science and Practice, 3*, 25–46.

Lewinsohn, P., Steinmetz, J., Larson, D., & Franklin, J. (1981). Depression-related cognitions: Antecedent or consequence? *Journal of Abnormal Psychology, 90*. 213–219.

Lewinsohn, P. M., Teri., L, & Wasserman, D. (1983). Depression. In M. Hersen (Ed.), *Outpatient behavior therapy: A practical guide* (pp. 81–108). New York: Grune & Stratton.

Lewinsohn, P. M. , et al. (1990). Cognitive-behavioral treatment for depressed adolescents. *Behavior Therapy, 21*, 385–401.

Lewinsohn, P. M., et al. (1991). Cognitive-behavioral treatment for depressed adolescents. *Behavior Therapy, 21*, 385-401.

Lewinsohn, P. M., et al. (1993). Adolescent psychopathology: I. Prevalence and incidence of depression and other DSM-III-R disorders in high school students. *Journal of Abnormal Psychology, 102*, 133–144.

Lewinsohn, P. M. et al. (1994). Adolescent psychopathology: II. Psychosocial risk factors for depression. *Journal of Abnormal Psychology, 103*, 302–315.

Lewinsohn, P. M., et al. (1998). Gender differences in anxiety disorders and anxiety symptoms in adolescents. *American Journal of Psychiatry, 107*, 109–117.

Lewis, D. O. (1993). From abuse to violence: Psychophysiological consequences of maltreatment. *Annual Progress in Child Psychiatry and Child Development*, 507–527.

Lewis, D. O., et al. (1997). Objective documentation of child abuse and dissociation in 12 murderers with dissociative identity disorder. *American Journal of Psychiatry, 154*, 1703–1710.

Lewis, J. M. (1998). For better or worse: Interpersonal relationships and individual outcome. *American Journal of Psychiatry, 155*, 582–589.

Lewis, R. J., Dlugokinski, E. L., Caputo, L. M., & Griffin, R. B. (1988). Children at risk for emotional disorders: Risk and resource dimensions. *Clinical Psychology Review, 8*, 417–440.

Lewis-Hall, F. (1992, December). *"Overview of DSM-III-R: Focus on panic disorder and obsessive-compulsive disorder."* Paper presented at a symposium, *Anxiety Disorders in African Americans*, presented by the State University of New York Health Science Center at Brooklyn, Brooklyn, NY.

Lex, B. W. (1987). Review of alcohol problems in ethnic minority groups. *Journal of Consulting and Clinical Psychology, 55*, 293–300.

Ley, R. (1985). Blood, breath, and fears: A hyperventilation theory of panic attacks and agoraphobia. *Clinical Psychology Review, 5*, 271–285.

Ley, R. (1991). The efficacy of breathing retraining and the centrality of hyperventilation in panic disorder: A reinterpretation of experimental findings. *Behaviour Research and Therapy, 29*, 301–304.

Ley, R. (1996). Panic attacks: Klein's false suffocation alarm, Taylor and Rachman's data, and Ley's dyspneic-fear theory. *Archives of General Psychiatry, 53*, 83.

Ley, R. (1997). The Ondine curse, false suffocation alarms, trait-state suffocation fear, and dyspnea-

suffocation fear in panic attacks. *Archives of General Psychiatry, 54*, 677.

Li, G., et al. (1995). Age at onset and familial risk in Alzheimer's disease. *American Journal of Psychiatry, 152*, 424-430.

Liberman, R. P. (1994). Treatment and rehabilitation of the seriously mentally ill in China: Impressions of a society in transition. *American Journal of Orthopsychiatry, 64*, 68–77.

Liberman, R. P., Kopelowicz, A., & Young, A. S. (1994). Biobehavioral treatment and rehabilitation of schizophrenia. *Behavior Therapy, 25*, 89–107.

Lichtenstein, E., & Glasgow, R. E. (1992). Smoking cessation: What have we learned over the past decade? *Journal of Consulting and Clinical Psychology, 60*, 518–527.

Lichtenstein, E., Glasgow, R. E., & Abrams, D. B. (1986). Social support in smoking cessation: In search of effective interventions. *Behavior Therapy, 17*, 607–619.

Lichtenstein, E., Harris, D., Birchler, G., Wahl, J., & Schmahl, D. (1973). Comparison of rapid smoking, warm, smoky air, and attention placebo in the modification of smoking behavior. *Journal of Consulting and Clinical Psychology, 40*, 92–98.

Lichstein, K. L., & Riedel, B.W. (1995). Behavioral assessment and treatment of insomnia: A review with an emphasis on clinical application. *Behavior Therapy, 25*, 659–688.

Lidz, C. W., Mulvey, E. P., & Gardner, W. (1993) The accuracy of predictions of violence to others. *Journal of the American Medical Association, 269*, 1007–1011.

Lieber, C. S. (1990, January 14). Cited in "Barroom biology: How alcohol goes to a woman's head." *The New York Times*, p. E24.

Liebert, R. M., Sprafkin, J. N., & Davidson, E. S. (1989). *The early window: Effects of television on children and youth* (3rd. ed.). New York: Pergamon Press.

Liebowitz, M. R., Gorman, J. M., Fyer, A. J., & Klein, D. F. (1985b). Social phobia: Review of a neglected anxiety disorder. *Archives of General Psychiatry, 42*, 729–736.

Liebowitz, M. R., et al. (1985a). Specificity of lactate infusions in social phobia vesus panic disorders. *American Journal of Psychiatry, 142*, 947–949.

Liebowitz, M. R., et al. (1994). Atacqaue de nervios and panic disorder. *American Journal of Psychiatry, 151*, 871–875.

Lied, E. R., & Marlatt, G. A. (1979). Modeling as a determinant of alcohol consumption: Effect of subject sex and prior drinking history. *Addictive Behaviors, 4*, 47–54.

Lief, H.I., & Hubschman, L. (1993). Orgasm in the postoperative transsexual. *Archives of Sexual Behavior, 22*, 145–155.

Lightsey, O. W., Jr. (1994a). Positive automatic cognitions as moderators of the negative life event–dysphoria relationship. *Cognitive Therapy and Research, 18*, 353–365.

Lightsey, O. W., Jr. (1994b). "Thinking positive" as a stress buffer: The role of positive automatic cognitions in depression and happiness. *Journal of Counseling Psychology, 41*, 325–334.

Lilienfeld, S. O. (1994). Conceptual problems in the assessment of psychopathy. *Clinical Psychology Review, 14*, 17–38.

Lilienfeld, S. O. (1997). The relation of anxiety sensitivity to higher and lower order personality dimensions: Implications for the etiology of panic attacks. *Journal of Abnormal Psychology, 106*, 539–544.

Lilienfeld, S. O., & Andrews, B. P. (1996). Identifying noncriminal psychopaths. *Journal of Personality Assessment, 66*, 488–524.

Lilienfeld, S. O., & Marino, L. (1995). Mental disorder as a Roschian concept: A critique of Wakefield's "harmful dysfunction" analysis. *Journal of Abnormal Psychology, 104*, 411–420.

Lillie-Blanton, M., Anthony, J. C., & Schuster, C. R. (1993). Probing the meaning of racial/ethnic group comparsions in crack cocaine smoking. *Journal of the American Medical Association, 269*, 993–997.

Lim, K. O., et al. (1996). Cortical gray matter volume deficit in patients with first-episode schizophrenia. *American Journal of Psychiatry, 153*, 1548–1553.

Lim, K. O., et al. (1998). Proton magnetic resonance spectroscopic imaging of cortical gray and white matter in schizophrenia. *Archives of General Psychiatry, 55*, 346–352.

Lin, K., et al. (1991). Ethnicity and family involvement in the treatment of schizophrenic patients. *Journal of Nervous & Mental Disease, 179*, 631–633.

Lin, T. Y., et al. (1978). Ethnicity and patterns of help-seeking. *Culture, Medicine, and Psychiatry, 2*, 3–14.

Lindsey, K. P., & Paul, G. L. (1989). Involuntary commitments to public mental institutions: Issues involving the overrepresentation of blacks and assessment of relevant functioning. *Psychological Bulletin, 106*, 171–183.

Linehan, M. M. (1993). *Cognitive-behavioral treatment of borderline personality disorder*. New York: Guilford Press.

Linehan, M. M., Camper, P., Chiles, J. A., Strosahl, K., & Shearin, E. (1987). Interpersonal problem solving and parasuicide. *Cognitive Therapy and Research, 11*, 1–12.

Linehan, M., et al. (1991). Cognitive-behavioral treatment of chronically parasuicidal borderline patients. *Archives of General Psychiatry, 48*, 1060–1064.

Linehan, M. M., et al. (1994). Interpersonal outcome of cognitive behavioral treatment for chronically suicidal borderline patients. *American Journal of Psychiatry, 151*, 1771–1776.

Ling, G. S. F., et al. (1984). Separation of morphine analgesia from physical dependence. *Science, 226*, 462–464.

Link, B. G., & Stueve, A. (1998). New evidence on the violence risk posed by people with mental illness. *Archives of General Psychiatry, 55*, 403–404.

Linnoila, V. M., & Virkkunen M. (1992). Aggression, suicidality, and serotonin. *Journal of Clinical Psychiatry, 53*, (10, Suppl) 46–51.

Linton, T. E., & Juul, K. D. (1980). Mainstreaming: Time for reassessment. *Educational Leadership, 37*, 433–437.

Linz, D. (1985). *Sexual violence in the media: Effects on male viewers and implications for society*. Unpublished doctoral dissertation, University of Wisconsin-Madison.

Linz, D. (1989). Exposure to sexually explicit materials and attitudes toward rape: A comparison of study results. *Journal of Sex Research, 26*, 50–84.

Linz, D., Donnerstein, E., & Penrod, S. (1988). The effects of long-term exposure to violent and sexually degrading depictions of women. *Journal of Personality and Social Psychology, 55*, 758–767.

Lipsey, M. W., & Wilson, D. B. (1993). The efficacy of psychology, educational, and behavioral treatment: Confirmation from meta-analysis. *American Psychologist, 48*, 1181–1209.

Lipsey, M. W., & Wilson, D. B. (1995). Reply to comments on Lispey and Wilson (1993). *American Psychologist, 50*, 113–115.

Lipton, R. B., et al. (1998). Efficacy and safety of acetaminophen, aspirin, and caffeine in alleviating migraine headache pain. *Archives of Neurology, 55*, 210–217.

Lisak, D. (1991). Sexual aggression, masculinity, and fathers. *Signs, 16*, 238–262.

Litman, G., & Topman, A. (1983). Outcome studies on techniques in alcoholism treatment. In M. Galanter (Ed.), *Recent developments in alcoholism* (Vol. 1). New York: Plenum Press.

Litman R,.E., et al. (1997). A quantitative analysis of smooth pursuit eye tracking in monozygotic twins

619

discordant for schizophrenia. *Archives of General Psychiatry, 54,* 417–428.

Litz, B. T. (1992). Emotional numbing in combat-related post-traumatic stress disorder: A critical review and reformulation. *Clinical Psychology Review, 12,* 417–432.

Litz, B.T., Orsillo, S. M., & Friedman, M. (1997). Post-traumatic stress disorder associated with peacekeeping duty in Somalia for US military personnel: Reply. *American Journal of Psychiatry, 154,* 1483.

Litz, B. T., et al. (1997a). Warriors as peacekeepers: Features of the Somalia experience and PTSD. *Journal of Consulting and Clinical Psychology, 65,* 1001–1010.

Litz, B.T., et al. (1997b). Posttraumatic stress disorder associated with peacekeeping duty in Somalia for U.S. military personnel. *American Journal of Psychiatry, 154,* 178–184.

Liu, W., et al. (1990). The mental health of Asian American teenagers: A research challenge. In A. Stiffman & L. Davis (Eds.), *Ethnic issues in adolescent mental health* (pp. 92–112). Newbury Park. CA: Sage Publications.

Livesley, W. J. (1985). The classification of personality disorder, II: The problem of criteria. *Canadian Journal of Psychiatry, 30,* 359–362.

Livesley, W. J., West, M., Tanney, A. (1985). Historical comment on DSM-III schizoid and avoidant personality disorders. *American Journal of Psychiatry, 142,* 1344–1347.

Livesley, W. J., West, M., & Tanney, A. (1986). Doctor Livesley and associates reply. *American Journal of Psychiatry, 143,* 1062–1063.

Livesley, W. J., et al. (1993). Genetic and environmental contributions to dimensions of personality disorder. *American Journal of Psychiatry, 150,* 1826–1831.

Livesley, W. J., et al. (1994). Categorical distinctions in the study of personality disorder: Implications for classification. *Journal of Abnormal Psychology, 103,* 6–17.

Livingston, I. L. (1993). Stress, hypertension, and young Black Americans: The importance of counseling. *Journal of Multicultural Counseling and Development, 21,* 132–142.

Livingstone, M., et al. (1991). Physiological and anatomical evidence for a magnocellular defect in developmental dyslexia. *Proceedings of the National Academy of Sciences, 88,* 7943–7947.

Lobo, B. L., & Greene, W. L. (1997). Insomnia. *The New England Journal of Medicine, 336,* 1919.

Lochman, J. E. (1992). Cognitive-behavioral intervention with agressive boys: Three-year follow-up and preventive effects. *Journal of Consulting and Clinical Psychology, 60,* 426–432

Lochman, J. E., & Dodge, K. A. (1994). Social-cognitive processes of severely violent, moderately aggressive, and nonaggressive boys. *Journal of Consulting and Clinical Psychology, 62,* 366–374.

Lochman, J. E., & Lenhart, L. (1993). Anger coping intervention for aggressive children: Conceptual models and outcome effects. *Clinical Psychology Review, 13,* 785–805.

Loebel, J. P., Dager, S. R., & Kitchcell, M. A. (1993). Alzheimer's disease. In D. L. Dunner (Ed.), *Current psychiatric therapy* (pp. 59–65). Philadelphia: Saunders.

Loeber, R., & Farrington, D. P. (1994). Problems and solutions in longitudinal and experimental studies of child psychopathology and delinquency. *Journal of Consulting and Clinical Psychology, 62,* 887–900.

Loeber, R., Lahey, B. B., & Thomas, C. (1991). Diagnostic conundrum of oppositional defiant disorder and its comorbid conditions: Effects of age and gender. *Journal of Consulting and Clinical Psychology, 59,* 379–390.

Loewenstein, R. J. (1991). Psychogenic amnesia and psychogenic fugue: A comprehensive review. *Annual Review of Psychiatry, 10,* 223–247.

Loftus, E. F. (1993). The reality of repressed memories. *American Psychologist, 48,* 518–537.

Loftus, E. F. (1996). The myth of repressed memory and the realities of science. *Clinical Psychology: Science and Practice, 3,* 356–365.

Loftus, E., & Ketcham, K. (1994). *The myth of repressed memory: False memories and allegations of sexual abuse.* New York: St. Martin's Press.

Lohr, B. A., Adams, H. E., & Davis, J. M. (1997). Sexual arousal to erotic and aggressive stimuli in sexually coercive and noncoercive men. *Journal of Consulting and Clinical Psychology, 106,* 230–242.

Longhurst, J. G., Potenza, M. N., & McDougle, C. J. (1997). Autism. *The New England Journal of Medicine, 337,* 1555–1557.

Lonigan, C. J., Carey, M. P., & Finch, A. J., Jr. (1994). Anxiety and depression in children and adolescents: Negative affectivity and the utility of self-reports. *Journal of Consulting and Clinical Psychology, 62,* 1000–1008.

López, S. R., & Hernandez, P. (1986). How culture is considered in evaluations of psychopathology. *The Journal of Nervous and Mental Diseases, 176,* 598–606.

López, S. R., & Núñez, J. A. (1987) Cultural factors considered in selected diagnostic criteria and interview schedules. *Journal of Abnormal Psychology, 96,* 270–272.

López Viets, V. C., & Miller, W. R. (1997). Treatment approaches for pathological gamblers. *Clinical Psychology Review, 17,* 689–702.

LoPiccolo, J. (1985, September 19–22). *Advances in diagnosis and treatment of sexual dysfunction.* Paper presented at the 28th annual meeting of the Society for the Scientific Study of Sex, San Diego.

LoPiccolo, J. (1990). Sexual dysfunction. In A. S. Bellack, M. Hersen, & A. E. Kazdin (Eds.).*International handbook of behavior modification therapy* (2nd ed) (pp. 557–564). New York: Plenum Press.

LoPiccolo, J. (1992). Post-modern sex therapy for erectile failure. In R. C. Rosen & S. R. Leiblum (Eds.), *Erectile disorders: Assessment and treatment* (pp. 171–197). New York: Guilford Press.

LoPiccolo, J., & Friedman, J. (1988). Broad-spectrum treatment of low sexual desire: Integration of cognitive, behavioral, and systemic therapy. In S. Leiblum & R. Rosen (Eds.), *Sexual desire disorders.* New York: Guilford Press.

LoPiccolo, J., & Stock, W. E. (1986). Treatment of sexual dysfunction. *Journal of Consulting and Clinical Psychology, 54,* 158–167.

Loranger, A. W., et al. (1994). The international personality disorder examination: The World Health Organization/Alcohol, Drug, Abuse and Mental Health Administration International Pilot Study of Personality Disorders. *Archives of General Psychiatry, 51,* 215–224.

Loranger, A. W. (1996). Dependant personality disorder: Age, sex, and Axis I comorbidity. *Journal of Nervous and Mental Disease, 184,* 17–21.

Lore, R. K., & Schultz, L. A. (1993). Control of human aggression: A comparative perspective. *American Psychologist, 48,* 16–25.

Lorefice, L. S. (1991). Fluoxetine treatment of a fetish. *Journal of Clinical Psychiatry, 52,* 41.

Loring, M., & Powell, B. (1988). Gender, race, and DSM III: A study of objectivity of psychiatric diagnostic behavior. *Journal of Health & Social Behavior, 29,* 1–22.

Lovaas, O. I. (1977). *The autistic child: Language development through behavior modification.* New York: Halstead Press.

Lovaas, O. I. (1987). Behavioral treatment and normal educational and intellectual functioning in young autistic children. *Journal of Consulting and Clinical Psychology, 55,* 3–9.

Lovaas, O. I., Freitag, G., Kinder, M. I., Rubenstein, B. D., Schaeffer, B., & Simmons, J. Q. (1966). Establishment of social reinforcers in two schizophrenic children on the basis of food. *Journal of Experimental Child Psychology, 4,* 109–125.

Lovaas, O. I., Koegel, R. L., & Schreibman, L. (1979). Stimulus overselectivity in autism: A review of the research. *Psychological Bulletin, 86,* 1236–1254.

Lowe, M. R., Gleaves, D. H., Murphy-Eberenz, K. P. (1998). On the relation of dieting and bingeing in bulimia nervosa. *Journal of Abnormal Psychology, 107,* 263–271.

Loy, P. H., & Stewart, L. P. (1984). The extent and effects of the sexual harassment of working women. *Sociological Focus, 17,* 31–43.

Lubin, B., Larsen, R. M., & Matarazzo, J. D. (1984). Patterns of psychological test usage in the United States: 1935–1982. *American Psychologist, 39,* 451–454.

Lubin, B., Larsen, R. M., Matarazzo, J. D., & Seever, M. (1985). Psychological test usage patterns in five professional settings. *American Psychologist, 40,* 857–861.

Luborsky, I., et al. (1996). Factors in outcomes of short-term dynamic psychotherapy for chronic vs. nonchronic major depression. *Journal of Psychotherapy: Practice and Research, 5,* 152–159.

Luborsky, L., Barber, J. P., & Beutler, L. (1993). Introduction to special section: A briefing on curative factors in dynamic psychotherapy. *Journal of Consulting and Clinical Psychology, 61,* 539–541.

Luborsky, L., et al. (1988). *Who will benefit from psychotherapy? Predicting therapeutic outcomes.* New York: Basic Books.

Luchins, D. J., et al. (1998). Alteration in the recommended dosing schedule for risperidone. *American Journal of Psychiatry, 155,* 365–366.

Ludolph, P. S. (1985). How prevalent is multiple personality? *American Journal of Psychiatry, 142,* 1526–1527.

Luntz, B., K., & Widom, C. S. (1994). Antisocial personality disorder in abused and neglected children grown up. *American Journal of Psychiatry, 151,* 670–674.

Lurigio, A. J., & Lewis, D. A. (1989). Worlds that fail: A longitudinal study of urban mental patients. *Journal of Social Issues, 45,* 79–90.

Lutgendorf, S. K., et al. (1997). Cognitive-behavioral stress management decreases dysphoric mood and herpes simplex virus-type 2 antibody titer in symptomatic HIV-seropositive gay men. *Journal of Consulting and Clinical Psychology, 65,* 31–43.

Lydiard, R. B., Brawman-Mintzer, O., & Ballenger, J. C. (1996). Recent developments in the psychopharmacology of anxiety disorders. *Journal of Consulting and Clinical Psychology, 64,* 660–668.

Lyketsos, C. G. et al. (1993). Depressive symptoms as predictors of medical outcomes in HIV infection. *Journal of the American Medical Association, 270,* 2563–2567.

Lyketsos, C. G., et al. (1996). Changes in depressive symptoms as AIDS develops. *American Journal of Psychiatry, 153,* 1430–1437.

Lykken, D. T. (1957). A study of anxiety in the sociopathic personality. *Journal of Abnormal and Social Psychology, 55,* 6–10.

Lykken, D. T. (1993). Predicting violence in the violent society. *Applied and Preventive Psychology, 2,* 13–20.

Lykken, D. T. (1994). On the causes of crime and violence: A reply to Aber and Rappaport. *Applied and Preventive Psychology, 3,* 55–58.

Lykken, D. T. Cited in Goleman, D. A set point for happiness. *The New York Times,* July 21, 1996, p. E2.

Lynch, J. W., Kaplan, G. A., & Shema, S. J. (1997). Cumulative impact of sustained economic hardship on physical, cognitive, psychological, and social functioning. *The New England Journal of Medicine, 337,* 1889–1895.

Lyness, J. M., et al. (1997). Screening for depression in elderly primary care patients. *Archives of Internal Medicine, 157,* 449–454.

Lyon, F. R., & Moats, L. C. (1988). Critical issues in the instruction of the learning disabled. *Journal of Consulting and Clinical Psychology, 56,* 830–835.

Lyons, J. S., Rosen, A. J., & Dysken, M. W. (1985). Behavioral effects of tricyclic drugs in depressed patients. *Journal of Consulting and Clinical Psychology, 53*, 17–24.

M

Macklin, M. L., et al. (1998). Lower precombat intelligence is a risk factor for posttraumatic stress disorder. *Journal of Consulting and Clinical Psychology, 66*, 323–326.

MacLean, W. E., et al. (1992). Psychological adjustment of children with asthma: Effects of illness severity and recent stressful life events. *Journal of Pediatric Psychology, 17*, 159–171.

MacMillan, H. L., et al. (1997). Prevalence of child physical and sexual abuse in the community: Results from the Ontario health supplement. *Journal of the American Medical Association, 278*, 131–135.

MacPhillamy, D. J., & Lewinsohn, P. M. (1974). Depression as a function of levels of desired and obtained pleasure. *Journal of Abnormal Psychology, 83*, 651–657.

Maddi, S. R., & Kobasa, S. C. (1984). *The hardy executive: Health under stress.* Homewood, IL: Dow Jones–Irwin.

Maddi, S. R., & Khoshaba, D. M. (1994). Hardiness and mental health. *Journal of Personality Assessment, 63*, 265–274.

Maeder, T. (1985). *Crime and madness: The origins and evolution of the insanity defense.* New York: Harper & Row.

Magdol, L., et al. (1997). Gender differences in partner violence in a birth cohort of 21-year olds: Bridging the gap between clinical and epidemiological approaches. *Journal of Consulting and Clinical Psychology, 65*, 68–78.

Magdol, L,. et al. (1998). Developmental antecedents of partner abuse: A prospective longitudinal study. *Journal of Abnormal Psychology, 107*, 375–389.

Magee, W. J., et al. (1996). Agoraphobia, simple phobia, and social phobia in the National Comorbidity Survey. *Archives of General Psychiatry, 53*, 159–168.

Maher, W. B., & Maher, B. A. (1985). Psychopathology: I. From ancient times to the eighteenth century. In G. A. Kimble & K. Schlesinger (Eds.), *Topics in the history of psychology* (Vol. 2). Hillsdale, NJ: Erlbaum.

Mahler, M., & Kaplan, L. (1977). Developmental aspects in the assessment of narcissistic and so-called borderline personalities. In P. Hartocollis (Ed.), *Borderline personality disorders: The concept, the syndrome, the patient* (pp. 71–85). New York: International Universities Press.

Mahler, M. S., Pine, F., & Bergman, A. (1975). The borderline syndrome: The role of the mother in the genesis and psychic structure of the borderline personality. *International Journal of Psychoanalysis, 56*, 163–177.

Maier, S. F., & Seligman, M. E. P. (1976). Learned helplessness: Theory and evidence. *Journal of Experimental Psychology (General), 105*, 3–46.

Maier, S. F., Watkins, L. R., & Fleshner, M. (1994). Psychoneuroimmunology; The interface between behavior, brain, and immunity. *American Psychologist, 49*, 1004–1017.

Maier, T. (1995, February 21). Drug hailed as a "magic bullet" has skeptics. *Newsday*, p. B23.

Maier, W., et al. (1994). Personality disorders among the relatives of schizophrenia patients. *Schizophrenia Bulletin, 20*, 481–493.

Mail, P., & McDonald, D. (1980). *Tulapai to Tokay.* New Haven: HRAF Press.

Maj, M. (1991) A family study of DSM–III–R schizoaffective disorder, depressive type, compared with schizophrenia and psychotic and nonpsychotic major depression. *American Journal of Psychiatry, 148*, 612–616.

Maj, M., et al. (1994a). Validity of rapid cycling as a course specifier for bipolar disorder. *American Journal of Psychiatry, 151*, 1015–1019.

Maj, M., et al. (1994b). WHO Neuropsychiatric AIDS Study, Cross-sectional phase I: Study design and psychiatric findings. *Archives of General Psychiatry, 51*, 39–49.

Malamuth, N. M. (1984). Aggression against women: Cultural and individual causes. In N. M. Malamuth & E. Donnerstein (Eds.), *Pornography and sexual aggression* (pp. 19–52). Orlando, FL: Academic Press.

Malamuth, N. M., & Check, J. V. P. (1981). The effects of mass media exposure on acceptance of violence against women: A field experiment. *Journal of Research in Personality, 15*, 436–446.

Maldonado, R., et al. (1997). Absence of opiate rewarding effects in mice lacking dopamine D2 receptors. *Nature, 388*, 586–589.

Maldonado, J. R., Butler, L. D., & Spiegel, D. (1998). Treatments for dissociative disorders. In P. E. Nathan & J. M. Gorman (Eds.), *A guide to treatments that work* (pp. 423–446). New York: Oxford University Press.

Maletsky, B. M. (1980). Self-referred vs. court-referred sexually deviant patients: Success with assisted covert sensitization. *Behavior Therapy, 11*, 306–314.

Maletzky, B. M. (1991). *Treating the sexual offender.* Newbury Park, CA: Sage Publications

Maletzky, B. M. (1998). The paraphilias: Research and treatment. In P. E. Nathan, & J. M. Gorman (Eds.), *A guide to treatments that work* (pp. 472–500). New York: Oxford University Press.

Malgady, R. G., Rogler, L. H., & Costantino, G. (1990). Culturally sensitive psychotherapy for Puerto Rican children and adolescents: A program of treatment outcome research. *Journal of Consulting and Clinical Psychology, 58*, 704–712.

Malloy, P. F., Fairbank, J. A., & Keane, T. M. (1983). Validation of a multimethod assessment of posttraumatic stress disorder in Vietnam veterans. *Journal of Consulting and Clinical Psychology, 51*, 488–494.

Malmo, R. B., & Shagass, C. (1949). Physiological study of symptom mechanism in psychiatric patients under stress. *Psychosomatic Medicine, 11*, 25–29.

Maloney, M. P., & Ward, M. P. (1976). *Psychological assessment: A conceptual approach.* New York: Oxford University Press.

Mandal, M. K., Pandey, R., & Prasad, A. B. (1998). Facial expression of emotions and schizophrenia: A review. *Schizophrenia Bulletin, 24*, 399–412.

Mann, J., Tarantola, D., & Netter, T.W. (1992). *AIDS in the world 1992.* Cambridge, MA: Harvard University Press.

Mann, J. J., (1996). Demonstration in vivo of reduced serotonin responsivity in the brain of untreated depressed patients. *American Journal of Psychiatry, 153*, 174–182.

Mann, J. J., et al. (1996). Postmortem studies of suicide victims. In S. J. Watson (Ed.), *Biology of schizophrenia and affective disease* (pp. 179–221). Washington, DC: American Psychiatric Press.

Mann, J. J., & Malone, K. M. (1997). Cerebrospinal fluid amines and higher-lethality suicide attempts in depressed inpatients. *Biological Psychiatry, 41*, 162–171.

Mannuzza, S., Gittelman-Klein, R., Bonagura, N., Horowitz-Konig, P. H., & Shenker, R. (1988). Hyperactive boys almost grown up: II. Status of subjects without a mental disorder. *Archives of General Psychiatry, 45*, 13–18.

Mannuzza, S., et al. (1991). Hyperactive boys almost grown up: V. Replication of psychiatric status. *Archives of General Psychiatry, 48*, 77–83.

Mapou, R. L., & Law, W. A. (1994). Neurobehavioral aspects of HIV disease and AIDS: An update. *Professional Psychology: Research and Practice, 25*, 132–140.

Marangell, L. B., et al. (1997). Inverse relationship of peripheral thyrotropin-stimulating hormone levels to brain activity in mood disorders. *American Journal of Psychiatry, 154*, 224–230.

Marcus, D. K., & Nardone, M. E. (1992). Depression and interpersonal rejection. *Clinical Psychology Review, 12*, 433–449.

Marcus, J., et al. (1987). Review of the NIMH Israeli Kibbutz-City study and the Jerusalem infant development study. *Schizophrenia Bulletin, 13*, 425–438.

Marder, S. R., et al. (1996). Two-year outcome of social skills training and group psychotherapy for outpatients with schizophrenia. *American Journal of Psychiatry, 153*, 1585–1592.

Marengo, J., & Harrow, M. (1987). Schizophrenic thought disorder at follow-up: A persistent or episodic course? *Archives of General Psychiatry, 44*, 651–659.

Margolin, G., & Burman, B. (1993). Wife abuse versus marital violence: Different terminologies, explanations, and solutions. *Clinical Psychology Review, 13*, 59–73.

Margraf, J., Ehlers, A., Roth, W. T. (1986). Biological models of panic disorder and agoraphobia: A review. *Behaviour Research and Therapy, 24*, 553–567.

Mark, D. H. (1998). Editor's Note. *Journal of the American Medical Association, 279*, 151.

Marklund, M., et al. (1998). The effect of a mandibular advancement device on apneas and sleep in patients with obstructive sleep apnea. *Chest, 113*, 707–713.

Markman, H. J., Floyd, F. J., Stanley, S. M., & Staraasli, R. D. (1988). Prevention of marital distress: A longitudinal investigation. *Journal of Consulting and Clinical Psychology, 56*, 210–217.

Markovitz, J. H., et al. (1993). Psychological predictors of hypertension in the Framingham Study: Is there tension in hypertension? *Journal of the American Medical Association, 270*, 2439–2443.

Markowitz, J. C., et al. (1998). Treatment of depressive symptoms in human immunodeficiency virus–positive patients. *Archives of General Psychiatry, 55*, 452–457.

Marks, I., et al. (1998a). Computer-aided treatments of mental health problems. *Clinical Psychology: Science and Practice, 5*, 151–170.

Marks, I., et al. (1998b). Treatment of posttraumatic stress disorder by exposure and/or cognitive restructuring: A controlled study. *Archives of General Psychiatry, 55*, 317–325.

Marks, I. M. (1982). Toward an empirical clinical science: Behavioral psychotherapy in the 1980's. *Behavior Therapy, 13*, 63–81.

Marks, I. M., et al. (1989). The "efficacy" of alprazolam in panic disorder and agoraphobia: A critique of recent reports. *Archives of General Psychiatry, 46*, 668–670.

Marks, J. (1978). *The benzodiazepines: Use, overuse, misuse, abuse.* Baltimore: University Park Press.

Marks, J. (1988). Alzheimer support groups: A framework for survival. In M. K. Aronson (Ed.), *Understanding Alzheimer's disease* (pp. 188–197). New York: Scribner's.

Marks, M., & De Silva, P. (1994). The "match/mismatch" mode of fear: Empirical status and clinical implications. *Behaviour Research and Therapy, 32*, 759–770.

Marks, M. P., et al. (1992). Are anxiety symptoms and catastrophic cognitions directly related? *Journal of Anxiety Disorders, 5*, 247–254.

Marlatt, G. A. (1978). Craving for alcohol, loss of control, and relapse: A cognitive-behavioral analysis. In P. E. Nathan, G. A. Marlatt, & T. Loberg (Eds.), *Alcoholism: New directions in behavioral research and treatment* (pp. 271–314). New York: Plenum Press.

Marlatt, G. A., Demming, B., & Reid, J. B. (1973). Loss of control drinking in alcoholics: An experimental analogue. *Journal of Abnormal Psychology, 81*, 233–241.

Marlatt, G. A., & Gordon, J. R. (1980). Determinants of relapse: Implications for the maintenance of behavior change. In P. O. Davidson & S. M. Davidson (Eds.), *Behavioral medicine: Changing health lifestyles.* New York: Brunner/Mazel.

Marlatt, G. A., & Gordon, J. R. (1985). *Relapse prevention: Maintenance strategies in the treatment of addictive behaviors.* New York: The Guilford Press.

Marlatt, G. A., & Rohsenow, D. J. (1981). The think-drink effect. *Psychology Today, 15* (12), 60–69.

Marlatt, G. A. (1993). Harm reduction for alcohol problems: Moving beyond the controlled drinking controversy. *Behavior Therapy, 24,* 461–504.

Marlatt, G. A., et al. (1998). Screening and brief intervention for high-risk college student drinkers: Results from a 2-year follow-up assessment. *Journal of Consulting and Clinical Psychology, 66,* 604–615.

Marriott, M. (1992, November 21). Fervid debate on gambling: Disease or moral weakness? *The New York Times,* pp. A1, A22.

Marsh, D. T., & Johnson, D. L. (1997). The family experience of mental illness: Implications for intervention. *Professional Psychology: Research & Practice, 28,* 229–237.

Marsh, L., et al. (1997). Structural magnetic resonance imaging abnormalities in men with severe chronic schizophrenia and an early age at clinical onset. *Archives of General Psychiatry, 54,* 1104–1112.

Marshall, D. (1971). Sexual behavior on Mangaia. In D. Marshall & R. Suggs (Eds.), *Human sexual behavior: Variations in the ethnographic spectrum.* Englewood Cliffs, NJ: Prentice-Hall.

Marshall, W. L. (1989). Pornography and sex offenders. In D. Zillmann & J. Bryant (Eds.), *Pornography: Research advances and policy considerations* (pp. 185–214). Hillsdale, NJ: Erlbaum.

Marshall, W. L., Eccles, A., & Barbaree, H. E. (1991). The treatment of exhibitionists: A focus on sexual deviance versus cognitive and relationship features. *Behaviour Research and Therapy, 29,* 129–135.

Marshall, W. L., et al. (1991). Treatment outcome with sex offenders. *Clinical Psychology Review, 11,* 465–485.

Martelli, M. F., Auerbach, S. M., Alexander, J., & Mercuri, L. G. (1987). Stress management in the health care setting: Matching interventions with patient coping styles. *Journal of Consulting and Clinical Psychology, 55,* 201–207.

Martin, D. (1989, January 25). Autism: Illness that can steal a child's sparkle. *The New York Times,* p. B1.

Martin, P. R., & Seneviratne, H. M. (1997). Effects of food deprivation and a stressor on head pain. *Health Psychology, 16,* 310–318.

Martin, R. A., & Lefcourt, H. M. (1983). Sense of humor as a moderator of the relation between stressors and moods. *Journal of Personality and Social Psychology, 45,* 1313–1324.

Martin, R. A., et al. (1993). Humor, coping with stress, self-concept, and psychological well-being. *Humor International Journal of Humor Research, 6,* 89–104.

Martin, R. L., et al. (1985). Mortality in a follow-up of 500 psychiatric outpatients: I. Total mortality. *Archives of General Psychiatry, 42,* 47–54.

Martin, S. E. (1992). The epidemiology of alcohol-related interpersonal violence. *Alcohol Health and Research World, 16,* 230–237.

Martinez, F. D., Cline, M., & Burrows, B. (1992). Increased incidence of asthma in children of smoking mothers. *Pediatrics, 89,* 21–26.

Martins, C., de Lemos, A. I., & Bebbington, P. E. (1992). A Portuguese/Brazilian study of expressed emotion. *Social Psychiatry and Psychiatric Epidemiology, 27,* 22–27.

Marton, K. I. (1997). Sleep apnea: Are its consequences exaggerated? *Journal Watch for Psychiatry, 3,* 51.

Marx, E. M., Williams, J. M. G., & Claridge, G. C. (1992). Depression and social problem solving. *Journal of Abnormal Psychology, 101,* 78–86.

Marzuk, P. M., & Barchas, J. D. (1997) Psychiatry. *Journal of the American Medical Association, 277,* 1892–1894.

Maslow, A. H. (1963). The need to know and the fear of knowing. *Journal of General Psychology, 68,* 111–124.

Mason, M. (1994, September). Why ulcers run in families. *Health,* pp. 44, 48.

Masters, W. H., & Johnson, V. E. (1966). *Human sexual response.* Boston: Little, Brown.

Masters, W. H., & Johnson, V. E. (1970). *Human sexual inadequacy.* Boston: Little, Brown.

Masters, W. H., & Johnson, V. E. (1979). *Homosexuality in perspective.* Boston: Little, Brown.

Matefy, R. (1980). Role-playing theory of psychedelic flashbacks. *Journal of Consulting and Clinical Psychology, 48,* 551–553.

Mathews, A. M. (1990). Why worry? The cognitive function of anxiety. *Behaviour Research & Therapy, 28,* 455–468.

Matochik, J. A., et al. (1994). Cerebral glucose metabolism in adults with attention deficit hyperactivity disorder after chronic stimulant treatment. *American Journal of Psychiatry, 151,* 658–664.

Matson, J. L., & Sevin, J. A. (1994). Theories of dual diagnosis in mental retardation. *Journal of Consulting and Clinical Psychology, 62,* 6–16.

Matt, G., E., & Navarro, A. M. (1997). What meta-analyses have and have not taught us about psychotherapy effects: A review and future directions. *Clinical Psychology Review, 17,* 1–32.

Matthews, K. A., et al. (1990). Influences of natural menopause on psychological characteristics and symptoms of middle-aged healthy women. *Journal of Consulting and Clinical Psychology, 58,* 345–351.

Mattick, R. P., & Peteres, L. (1988). Treatment of severe social phobia: Effects of guided exposure with and without cognitive restructuring. *Journal of Consulting and Clinical Psychology, 56,* 251–260.

Mavissakalian, M. (1987). Initial depression and response to imipramine in agoraphobia. *Journal of Nervous & Mental Disease, 175,* 358–361.

Mavissakalian, M., Michelson, L., Greenwald, D., Kornblith, S., & Greenwald, M. (1983). Cognitive-behavioral treatment of agoraphobia: paradoxical intention vs. self-statement training. *Behaviour Research and Therapy, 21,* 75–86.

Mavissakalian, M. R., & Perel, J. M. (1989). Imipramine dose-response relationship in panic disorder with agoraphobia. *Archives of General Psychiatry, 46,* 127–131.

Mayo-Smith, M. F. (1997). Pharmacological management of alcohol withdrawal. A meta-analysis and evidence-based practice guideline. American Society of Addiction Medicine Working Group on Pharmacological Management of Alcohol Withdrawal. *Journal of the American Medical Association, 278,* 144–151.

Maypole, D. E., & Anderson, R. B. (1987). Culture-specific substance abuse prevention for Blacks. *Community Mental Health Journal, 23* (2), 135–139.

Mays, V. M. (1985). The Black American and psychotherapy: The dilemma. *Psychotherapy, 22,* 379–388.

Mays, V. M., Caldwell, C. H., & Jackson, J. S. (1996). Mental health symptoms and service utilization patterns of help-seeking among African American women. In H. W. Neighbors & J.S. Jackson (Eds.), *Mental health in black America* (pp. 161–176). Thousand Oaks, CA: Sage Publications.

Mazure, C. M. (1998). Life stressors as risk factors in depression. *Clinical Psychology: Science and Practice, 5,* 291–313.

Mazziotta, J. C. (1996). Mapping mental illness: A new era. *Archives of General Psychiatry, 53,* 574–576.

McBride, P. A., Anderson, G. M., & Shapiro, T. (1996). Autism research: Bringing together approaches to pull apart the disorder. *Archives of General Psychiatry, 53,* 980–983.

McCabe, S. B., & Gotlib, I H. (1995). Selective attention and clinical depression: Performance on a deployment-of-attention task. *Journal of Abnormal Psychology, 104,* 241–245.

McCarty, D. et al. (1991). Alcoholism, drug abuse, and the homeless. *American Psychologist, 46,* 1139–1148.

McCaul, M. E, & Furst, J. (1994). Alcoholism treatment in the United States. *Alcohol Health & Research World, 18,* 253–260.

McCauley, E., Mitchell, J. R., Burke, P., & Moss, S. (1988). Cognitive attributes of depression in children and adolescents. *Journal of Consulting and Clinical Psychology, 56,* 903–908.

McCauley, J., et al. (1997). Clinical characteristics of women with a history of childhood abuse: Unhealed wounds. *Journal of the American Medical Association, 277,* 1362–1368.

McClelland, D. C., Alexander, C., & Marks, E. (1982). The need for power, stress, immune functions, and illness among male prisoners. *Journal of Abnormal Psychology, 91,* 61–70.

McCloskey, L. A. (1996). Socioeconomic and coercive power within the family. *Gender and Society, 10,* 449–463.

McConaghy, N. (1990). Sexual deviation. In A. S. Bellack, M. Hersen, & A.E. Kazdin (Eds.), *International handbook of behavior modification and therapy* (2nd ed.) (pp. 565–580). New York: Plenum Press.

McCord, J. (1983). A 40-year perspective on effects of child abuse and neglect. *Child Abuse and Neglect, 7,* 265–270.

McCord, W., & McCord, J. (1964). *The psychopath: An essay on the criminal mind.* New York: D. Van Nostrand.

McCormick, J.K, & Kalb, C. (1998, June 15). Dying for a drink. *Newsweek,* pp. 30–34.

McCormick, R. A., Taber, J., Kruedelbach, N., Russo, A. (1987). Personality profiles of hospitalized pathological gamblers: The California Personality Inventory. *Journal of Clinical Psychology, 43,* 521–527.

McCrady, B. S. (1993). Alcoholism. In D. H. Barlow (Ed.), *Clinical handbook of psychological disorders* (2nd ed.), (pp. 362–393). New York: Guilford Press.

McCrady, B. S. (1994). Alcoholics Anonymous and behavior therapy: Can habits be treated as diseases? Can diseases be treated as habits? *Journal of Consulting and Clinical Psychology, 62,* 1159–1166.

McCrady, B. S., & Langenbucher, J. W. (1996). Alcohol treatment and health care system reform. *Archives of General Psychiatry, 53,* 737–746.

McCranie, E. W., & Bass, J. D. (1984). Childhood family antecedents of dependency and self-criticism: Implications for depression. *Journal of Abnormal Psychology, 93,* 3–8.

McCreadie, R. G., Main, C. J., & Dunlap, R. A. (1978). Token economy, pimozide and chronic schizophrenia. *British Journal of Psychiatry, 133,* 179–181.

McCullough, J. P., et al. (1996). Differential diagnosis of chronic depressive disorders. *Psychiatric Clinics of North America, 19,*.55–71.

McCutchan, J. A. (1990). Virology, immunology, and clinical course of HIV infection. *Journal of Consulting and Clinical Psychology, 58,* 5–12.

McDermut, J. F., Haaga, D. A. F., & Bilek, L. A. (1997). Cognitive bias and irrational beliefs in major depression and dysphoria. *Cognitive Therapy and Research, 21,* 459–476.

McDougle, C. J., et al. (1996). A double-blind, placebo-controlled study of fluvoxamine in adults with autistic disorder. *Archives of General Psychiatry, 53,* 1001–1008.

McEachin, J. J., Smith, T., & Lovaas, O. I. (1993). Long-term outcome for children with autism who received early intensive behavioral treatment. *American Journal on Mental Retardation, 97,* 359–372.

McElroy, S. L., et al. (1992). The DSM-III-R impulse control disorders not elsewhere classified; Clinical characteristics and relationship to other psychiatric disorders. *American Journal of Psychiatry, 149,* 318–325.

622 REFERENCES

McElroy, S. L., et al. (1996). A randomized comparison of divalproex oral loading versus haloperidol in the initial treatment of acute psychotic mania. *Journal of Clinical Psychiatry, 57,* 142–146.

McGee, R., & Feehan, M. (1991). Are girls with problems of attention underrecognized? *Journal of Psychopathology and Behavioral Assessment, 13,* 187–198.

McGinnis, J. M., & Foege, W. H. (1993). Actual causes of death in the United States. *Journal of the American Medical Association, 270,* 2207–2212.

McGlashan, T. H., & Fenton, W. S. (1992). The positive-negative distinction in schizophrenia: Review of natural history validators. *Archives of General Psychiatry, 49,* 63–72.

McGonagle, K. A., et al. (in press). DSM-III-R dysthymia in the community: Results from the National Comorbidity Survey.

McGue, M. (1993). From proteins to cognitions: The behavioral genetics of alcoholism. In R. Plomin & G. E. McClearn (Eds.), *Nature, nurture & psychology* (pp. 245–268). Washington, D C: American Psychological Association.

McGovern, F. J., & Nevid, J. S. (1986). Evaluation apprehension on psychological inventions in a prison-based setting. *Journal of Consulting and Clinical Psychology, 54,* 576–578.

McGovern, P.G., et al. (1996). Recent trends in acute coronary heart disease. *The New England Journal of Medicine, 334,* 884–890.

McGrath, E., Keita, G. P., Strickland, B. R., & Russo, N. F. (1990). *Women and depression: Risk factors and treatment issues.* Washington DC: American Psychological Association.

McGue, M., & Christensen, K. (1997). Genetic and environmental contributions to depression symptomatology: Evidence from Danish twins 75 years of age and older. *Journal of Abnormal Psychology, 106,* 439–448.

McGue, M., & Gottesman, I. I. (1989). A single dominant gene still cannot account for the transmission of schizophrenia. *Archives of General Psychiatry, 46,* 478–479.

McGue, M., & Pickens, R. W., Sivkis, D. S. (1992). Sex and age effects on the inheritance of alcohol problems: A twin study. *Journal of Abnormal Psychology, 101,* 3–17

McGuffin, P., & Katz, R. (1986). Nature, nurture and affective disorder. In J. W. W. Deakin (Ed.), *The biology of depression. Proceedings of a meeting of the Biological Group of the Royal College of Psychiatrists held at Manchester University, 1985.* (pp. 26–52). Washington, DC: American Psychiatric Press.

McGuffin, P., et al. (1996). Hospital-based twin register of the heritability of DSM-IV unipolar depression. *Archives of General Psychiatry, 53,* 129–136.

McGuire, P. K., Shah, G. M. S., & Murray, R. M. (1993). Increased blood flow in Broca's area during auditory hallucinations in schizophrenia. *The Lancet, 342,* 703–706.

McKay, J. R., et al. (1995). Effect of random versus nonrandom assignment in a comparison of inpatient and day hospital rehabilitation for male alcoholics. *Journal of Consulting and Clinical Psychology, 63,* 70–78.

McKinney, K., & Maroules, N. (1991). Sexual harassment. In E. Grauerholz & M. A. Koralewski (Eds.), *Sexual coercion: A sourcebook on its nature, causes, and prevention* (pp. 29–44). Lexington, MA: Lexington Books.

McKusick, L., et al. (1987, June). Prevention of HIV infection among gay and bisexual men: Two longitudinal studies. Paper presented to the Third International Conference on AIDS, Washington, DC.

McLeer, S. V. (1994). Psychiatric disorders in sexually abused children. *Journal of the American Academy of Child and Adolescent Psychiatry, 33,* 313–319.

McLellan, A. T., et al. (1993). The effects of psychosocial services in substance abuse treatment. *Journal of the American Medical Association, 269,* 1953–1959.

McLellan, A. T., et al. (1994). Similarity of outcome predictors across opiate, cocaine, and alcohol treatments: Role of treatment services. *Journal of Consulting and Clinical Psychology, 62,* 1141–1158.

McLin, W. M. (1992). Introduction to issues in psychology and epilepsy. *American Psychologist, 47,* 1124–1125.

McMahon, R. J. (1994). Diagnosis, assessment, and treatment of externalizing problems in children: The role of longitudinal data. *Journal of Consulting and Clinical Psychology, 62,* 901–917.

McMillen, J. C., Smith, E . M., & Fisher, R. H. (1997). Perceived benefit and mental health after three types of disaster. *Journal of Consulting and Clinical Psychology, 65,* 733–739.

McMillen, J. C., Zuravin, S., & Rideout, G. B. (1995). Perceived benefit from child sexual abuse. *Journal of Consulting and Clinical Psychology, 63,* 1037–1043.

McMurtrie, B. (1994, July 19). Overweight fatten ranks. *New York Newsday,* p. A26.

McNally, R. (1987). Preparedness and phobias: A review. *Psychological Bulletin, 101,* 283–303.

McNally, R. J. (1990). Psychological approaches to panic disorder: A review. *Psychological Bulletin, 108,* 403–419.

McNally, R. J., Cassiday, K. L., & Calamari, J. E. (1990). Taijin-kyofu-sho in a Black American woman: Behavioral treatment of a "culture-bound" anxiety disorder. *Journal of Anxiety Disorders, 4,* 83–87.

McNally, R. J., & Eke, M. (1996). Anxiety sensitivity, suffocation fear, and breath-holding duration as predictors of response to carbon dioxide challenge. *Journal of Abnormal Psychology, 105,* 146–149.

McNally, R. J., Riemann, B., C., & Kim, E. (1990). Selective processing of threat cues in panic disorder. *Behaviour Research & Therapy, 28,* 407–412.

McNally, R. J., et al. (1995). Clinical versus nonclinical panic: A test of suffocation false alarm theory. *Behaviour Research & Therapy, 33,* 127–131.

McNaughton, 10 Cl & F, 200, 8 Eng. Rep. 718 (H & L) 1843.

McNaughton, M. E., et al. (1995). The relationship among stress, depression, locus of control, irrational beliefs, social support, and health in Alzheimer's disease caregivers. *Journal of Nervous and Mental Disease, 183,* 78–85.

McNeil, T. F., & Kaiij,L. (1978). Obstetrical factos in the development of schizophrenia: Complications in the births of preschizophrenics and in reproduction by schizophrenic patients. In L. C. Wynne, R. L. Cromwell, & S. Matthysse (Eds.), *The nature of schizophrenia: New approaches to research and treatment.* New York: Wiley

McNulty, J. L., et al. (1997). Comparative validity of MMPI-2 scores of African American and Caucasian mental health center clients. *Psychological Assessment, 9,* 464–470.

McQuiston, J. T. (1997, February 5). New mother on Long Island suffering from depression is found, apparently a suicide. *The New York Times,* p. B5.

Mead, M. (1935). *Sex and temperament in three primitive societies.* New York: Morrow.

Meador-Woodruff, J. H., et al. (1997). Dopamine receptor transcript expression in striatum and prefrontal and occipital cortex: Focal abnormalities in orbitofrontal cortex in schizophrenia . *Archives of General Psychiatry, 54,* 1089–1095.

Medalia, A., et al. (1998). Effectiveness of attention training in schizophrenia. *Schizophrenia Bulletin, 24,* 147–152.

Mednick, S. A. (1970). Breakdown in individuals at high risk for schizophrenia: Possible predispositional perinatal factors. *Mental Hygiene, 54,* 50–63.

Mednick, S. A., Moffitt, T. E., & Stack, S. (1987). *The causes of crime: New biological approaches.* New York: Cambridge University Press.

Mednick, S. A., Parnas, J., & Schulsinger, F. (1987). The Copenhagen High-Risk project, 1962–86. *Schizophrenia Bulletin, 13,* 485–495.

Mednick, S. A., & Schulsinger, F. (1965). A longitudinal study of children with a high risk for schizophrenia: A preliminary report. In S. Vandenberg (Ed.), *Methods and goals in human behavior genetics.* (pp. 255–296). New York: Academic Press.

Mednick, S. A., & Schulsinger, F. (1968). Some premorbid characteristics related to breakdown in children with schizophrenic mothers. In D. Rosenthal & S. S. Kety (Eds.), *The transmission of schizophrenia* (pp. 267–291). New York: Pergamon Press.

Meehan, P. J., et al. (1991). Attempted suicide among young adults: Progress toward a meaningful estimate of prevalence. *American Journal of Psychiatry, 149,* 41–44.

Meehl, P. E. (1962). Schizotaxia, schizotypy, schizophrenia. *American Psychologist, 17,* 827–838.

Meehl, P. E. (1972). A critical afterword. In I. I. Gottesman & J. Shields (Eds.), *Schizophrenia and genetics: A twin study vantage point* (pp. 367–415). New York: Academic Press.

Mega, M. S., et al. (1996). The spectrum of behavioral changes in Alzheimer's disease. *Neurology, 46,* 130–135.

Mehrabian, A., & Weinstein, L. (1985). Temperament characteristics of suicide attempters. *Journal of Consulting and Clinical Psychology, 53,* 544–546.

Meichenbaum, D. (1993). Changing conceptions of cognitive behavior modification: Retrospect and prospect. *Journal of Consulting and Clinical Psychology, 61,* 202–204.

Meichenbaum, D., & Deffenbacher, J. L. (1988). Stress inoculation training. *The Counseling Psychologist, 16* (1), 69–90.

Meichenbaum, D., & Turk, D. (1976). The cognitive-behavioral management of anxiety, anger, and pain. In P. O. Davidson (Ed.), *The behavioral management of anxiety, depression, and pain.* New York: Brunner/Mazel.

Meier, B. (1997, December 10). Among girls, blacks smoke much less. *The New York Times,* p. A22.

Meisler, A. W., & Carey, M. P. (1990). A critical reevaluation of nocturnal penile tumescence monitoring in the diagnosis of erectile dysfunction. *Journal of Nervous and Mental Disease, 178,* 78–89.

Meissner, W. W. (1980). Psychoanalysis and sexual disorders. In B. J. Wolman & J. Money (Eds.), *Handbook of human sexuality.* Englewood Cliffs, NJ: Prentice-Hall.

Melchert, T. P. (1996). Childhood memory and a history of different forms of abuse. *Professional Psychology: Research and Practice, 27,* 438–446.

Mellor, C. S. (1970). First rank symptoms of schizophrenia. *British Journal of Psychiatry, 177,* 15–23.

Meltzer, H. Y. (1987). Biological studies in scizophrenia. *Schizophrenia Bulletin, 13,* 77–111.

Mendelson, J. H., Miller, K. D., Mello, N. K., Pratt, H., & Schmitz, R. (1982). Hospital treatment of alcoholism: A profile of middle income Americans. *Alcoholism: Clinical and Experimental Research, 6,* 377–383.

Mendez, M. et al. (1992). Disturbances of person identification in Alzheimer's disease: A retrospective study. *Journal of Nervous & Mental Disease, 180,* 94–96.

Mendlewicz, J., & Rainer, J. D. (1977). Adoption study supporting genetic transmission in manic depressive illness. *Nature, 268,* 326–329.

Merckelbach, H., Arntz, A., & de Jong, P. (1991). Conditioning experiences in spider phobics. *Behaviour Research and Therapy, 29,* 301–304.

Merckelbach, H., et al. (1996). The etiology of specific phobias: A review. *Clinical Psychology Review, 16,* 337–361.

Merikangas, K. R., et al. (1998). Familial transmission of substance use disorders. *Archives of General Psychiatry, 55,* 973–979.

623

Messenger, J. (1971). Sex and repression in an Irish folk community. In D. Marshall & R. Suggs (Eds.), *Human sexual behavior: Variations in the ethnographic spectrum*. Englewood Cliffs, NJ: Prentice-Hall.

Messman, T. L., & Long, P. J. (1996). Child sexual abuse and its relationship to revictimization in adult women: *Clinical Psychology Review, 16,* 397–420.

Meyer, G. J. (1997). Assessing reliability: Critical corrections for a critical examination of the Rorschach comprehensive system. *Psychological Assessment, 9,* 480–489.

Meyer, G. J., & Handler, L. (1997). The ability of the Rorschach to predict subsequent outcome: A meta-analysis of the Rorschach Prognostic Rating Scale. *Journal of Personality Assessment, 69,* 1–38.

Meyer, J. K., & Reter, D. J. (1979). Sex reassignment: Follow-up. *Archives of General Psychiatry, 36,* 1010–1015.

Meyer. T. (1997, March 6). *Associated Press Report.*

Meyer, T. J., & Mark, M. M. (1995). Effects of psychosocial interventions with adult cancer patients: A meta-analysis of randomized experiments. *Health Psychology, 14,* 101–108.

Michels, R., & Marzuk, P. M. (1993). Progress in psychiatry.[Second of two parts]. *New England Journal of Medicine, 329,* 628–638.

Michelson, L. K., & Marchione, K. (1991). Behavioral, cognitive, and pharmacological treatments of panic disorder with agoraphobia: Critique and synthesis. *Journal of Consulting and Clinical Psychology, 59,* 100–114.

Michelson, L., et al. (1990). Panic disorder: Cognitive-behavioral treatment. *Behaviour Research & Therapy, 28,* 141–151.

Michelson, L. K. et al. (1996). A comparative outcome and follow-up investigation of panic disorder with agoraphobia: The relative and combined efficacy of cognitive therapy, relaxation training, and therapist-assisted exposure. *Journal of Anxiety Disorders, 10,* 297–330.

Migliorelli, R., et al. (1995). Prevalence and correlates of dysthymia and major depression among patients with Alzheimer's disease. *American Journal of Psychiatry, 152,* 37–44.

Miklowitz, D. J. (1994). Family risk indicators in schizophrenia. *Schizophrenia Bulletin, 20,* 137–149.

Miklowitz, D. J., et al. (1991). Communication deviance in families of schizophrenic and manic patients. *Journal of Abnormal Psychology, 100,* 163–173.

Milberger, S. , et al. (1996). Is maternal smoking during pregnancy a risk factor for attention deficit hyperactivity disorder in children? *American Journal of Psychiatry, 153,* 1138–1142.

Milich, R., Wolraich, M., & Lindgren, S. (1986). Sugar and hyperactivity: A critical review of empirical findings. *Clinical Psychology Review, 6,* 493–513.

Miller, B. J. (1978). *The complete medical guide.*(4th ed.). New York: Simon and Schuster.

Miller, E. (1987). Hysteria: Its nature and explanation. *British Journal of Clinical Psychology, 26,* 163–173.

Miller, I. W., & Norman, W. H. (1986). Persistence of depressive cognitions within a sub-group of depressed patients. *Cognitive Therapy and Research, 10,* 211–224.

Miller, N. S., Gold, M. S., & Mahler, J. C. (1991). Violent behaviors associated with cocaine use: Possible pharmacological mechanisms. *International Journal of the Addictions, 26,* 1077–1088.

Miller, S. D., et al. (1991). Optical differences in multiple personality disorder: A second look. *Journal of Nervous & Mental Disease, 179,* 132–135.

Miller, T. Q., et al. (1991). Reasons for the trend toward null findings in research on Type A behavior. *Psychological Bulletin, 110,* 469–485.

Miller, T. Q, et al. (1996). Meta-analytic review of research on hostility and physical health. *Psychological Bulletin, 119,* 322–348.

Miller, W.R., & Brown, S. A., (1997). Why psychologists should treat alcohol and drug problems. *American Psychologist, 52,* 1269–1279.

Miller, W. R., & Hester, R. K. (1986). Inpatient alcoholism treatment: Who benefits? *American Psychologist, 41,* 794–805.

Miller, W. R., Leckman, A. L., Delaney, H. D., & Tinkcom, M. (1992). Long-term follow-up of behavioral self-control training. *Journal of Studies on Alcohol, 53,* 249–261.

Miller, W. R., & Muñoz, R. F. (1983). *How to control your drinking,* (2nd ed.). Albuquerque, NM: University of New Mexico Press.

Miller-Perrin, C. L., & Wurtele, S. K. (1988). The child sexual abuse prevention movement: A critical analysis of primary and secondary approaches. *Clinical Psychology Review, 8,* 313–329.

Millon, T. (1981). *Disorders of personality DSM-III: Axis II.* New York: Wiley.

Millon, T. (1982). *Millon Clinical Multiaxial Inventory manual* (3rd ed.). Minneapolis: National Computer Systems.

Milner, J. S. (1993). Social information processing and physical child abuse. *Clinical Psychology Review, 13,* 275–294.

Minarik, M. L., & Ahrens, A. H. (1996). Relations of eating and symptoms of depression and anxiety to the dimensions of perfectionism among undergraduate women. *Cognitive Research & Therapy, 20,* 155–169.

Mineka, S. (1991, August). Paper presented to the annual meeting of the American Psychological Association, San Francisco. (Cited in Turkington, C. [1991]). Evolutionary memories may have phobia role. *APA Monitor, 22* (11), 14.

Minuchin, S. (1974). *Families and family therapy.* Cambridge, MA: Harvard University Press.

Minuchin, S., Rosman, B. L., & Baker, L. (1978). *Psychosomatic Families: Anorexia nervosa in context.* Cambridge, MA: Harvard University Press.

Miranda, J., Persons, J. B., & Nix-Byers, C. (1990). Endorsement of dysfunctional beliefs depends on current mood state. *Journal of Abnormal Psychology, 99,* 237–241.

Mirsky, A. F., Ingraham, L. J., & Kugelmass, S. (1995). Neuropsychological assessment of attention and its pathology in the Israeli cohort. *Schizophrenia Bulletin, 21,* 193–204.

Mirsky, A. F., et al., (1995). Overview and summary: Twenty-five-year followup of high-risk children. *Schizophrenia Bulletin, 21,* 227–239.

Mirsky, I. A. (1958). Physiologic, psychologic and social determinants in the etiology of duodenal ulcer. *American Journal of Digestive Diseases, 3,* 285–315.

Mischel, W. (1979). On the interface of cognition and personality: Beyond the person-situation debate. *American Psychologist, 34,* 740–754.

Mitchell, J. E., & Eckert, E. D. (1987). Scope and significance of eating disorders. *Journal of Consulting and Clinical Psychology, 55,* 628–634.

Mitler, M. M. (1993). Daytime sleepiness and cognitive functioning in sleep apnea. *Sleep, 16,* S68–S70.

Mittelmark, M. B., et al. (1986). Community-wide prevention of cardiovascular disease: Education strategies of the Minnesota Heart Health Program. *Preventive Medicine, 15,* 1–17.

Mittelmark, M. B., et al. (1987). Predicting experimentation with cigarettes: The Childhood Antecedents of Smoking Study. *American Journal of Public Health, 77,* 206–208.

Mizes, J. S., Landolf-Fritsche, B., & Grossman-McKee, D. (1987). Patterns of distorted cognitions in phobic disorders: An investigation of clinically severe simple phobics, social phobics, and agoraphobics. *Cognitive Therapy & Research, 11,* 583–592.

Modell, J. G., et al. (1997). Comparative sexual side effects of bupropion, fluoxetine, paroxetine, and sertraline. *Clinical Pharmacology and Therapeutics, 61,* 476–487.

Modestin, J. (1992). Multiple personality disorder in Switzerland. *American Journal of Psychiatry, 149,* 88–92.

Modestin, J., Berger, A., & Ammann, R. (1996). Mental disorder and criminality: Male alcoholism. *Journal of Nervous & Mental Disease, 184,* 393–402.

Mohr, D. C. (1995). Negative outcome in psycotherapy: A critical review. *Clinical Psychology: Science and Practice, 2,* 1–27.

Mohr, D. C., & Beutler, L. E. (1990). Erectile dysfunction: A review of diagnostic and treatment procedures. *Clinical Psychology Review, 10,* 123–150.

Mokuau, N. (1990). The impoverishment of native Hawaiians and the social work challenge. *Health and Social Work, 15,* 235–242.

Moldin, S. O. (1994). Indicators of liability to schizophrenia: Perspectives from genetic epidemiology. *Schizophrenia Bulletin, 20,* 169–184.

Moldin, S. O., & Gottesman, I I. (1997). At issue: Genes, experience, and change in schizophrenia–positioning in the 21st century. *Schizophrenia Bulletin, 23,* 547–561.

Moldin, S. O. Reich, T., & Rice, J. P. (1991). Current perspective on the genetics of unipolar depression. *Behavior Genetics, 21,* 211–242.

Monahan, J. (1981). *A clinical prediction of violent behavior: DHHS Publication, Adm. 81-921.* Rockville, MD: National Institutes of Mental Health.

Monahan, J. (1992). Mental disorder and violent behavior: Perceptions and evidence. *American Psychologist, 47,* 511–521.

Monahan, J., Novaco, R., & Geis, G. (1979). Corporate violence: Research strategies for community psychology. In T. Sarbin (Ed.), *Challenges to the criminal justice system.* New York: Human Sciences.

Monahan, J., & Steadman, H. J. (1983). Crime and mental disorder: An epidemiological approach. In A. Morris & M. Tomroy (Eds.), *Crime and justice: An annual review of research* (Vol. 4, pp. 145–189). Chicago: University of Chicago Press.

Monane, M. (1992). Insomnia in the elderly. Roundtable Conference: Low-dose benzodiazepine therapy in the treatment of insomnia. *Journal of Clinical Psychiatry, 53,* (6, Suppl), 23–28.

Moncher, M. S., Holden, G. W., & Trimble, J. E. (1990). Substance abuse among Native-American youth. *Journal of Consulting and Clinical Psychology, 58,* 408–415.

Mones, A. G., & Panitz, P. E. (1994). Marital violence: An integrated systems approach. *Journal of Social Distress and the Homeless, 3,* 39–51.

Money, J. (1987). Sin, sickness, or status? Homosexual gender identity and psychoneuroendocrinology. *American Psychologist, 42,* 384–399.

Money, J. (1994). The concept of gender identity disorder in childhood and adolescence after 39 years. *Journal of Sex and Marital Therapy, 20,* 163–177.

Money, J., & Lamacz, M. (1990). *Vandalized lovemaps.* Buffalo, NY: Prometheus Books.

Montague, C. T., et al. (1997). Congenital leptin deficiency is associated with severe early-onset obesity in humans. *Nature, 387,* 903–908.

Monti, P. M., et al. (1987). Reactivity of alcoholics and nonalcoholics to drinking cues. *Journal of Abnormal Psychology, 96,* 122–126.

Monti, P. M., et al. (1994). Cue exposure with coping skills treatment for male alcoholics: A preliminary investigation. *Journal of Consulting and Clinical Psychology, 61,* 1011–1019.

Moon, J. R., & Eisler, R. M. (1983). Anger control: An experimental comparison of three behavioral treatments. *Behavior Therapy, 14,* 493–505.

Moos, R. H., Cronkite, R. C., & Moos, B. S. (1998). Family and extrafamily resources and the 10-year course of treated depression. *Journal of Abnormal Psychology, 107,* 450–460.

Moran, M. G. (1991). Psychological factors affecting pulmonary and rheumatologic diseases: A review. *Psychosomatics, 32,* 14–23.

Morgan, C. A., et al. (1997). Startle reflex abnormalities in women with sexual assault-related PTSD. *American Journal of Psychiatry, 154,* 1076–1080.

Morgan, K. (1996). Mental health factors in late-life insomnia. *Reviews in Clinical Gerontology, 6,* 75–83.

Morgenstern, J., et al. (1997). The comorbidity of alcoholism and personality disorders in a clinical population: Prevalence rates and relation to alcohol typology variables. *Journal of Abnormal Psychology, 106,* 74–84.

Morihisa, J. M., Duffy, F. H., & Wyatt, R. J. (1983). Brain electrical activity mapping (BEAM) in schizophrenic patients. *Archives of General Psychiatry, 40,* 719–728.

Morin, C. M, & Azrin, N. H. (1988). Behavioral and cognitive treatments of geriatric insomnia. *Journal of Consulting and Clinical Psychology, 56,* 748–753.

Morin, C. M., & Ware, J. C. (1996). Sleep and psychopathology. *Applied and Preventive Psychology, 5,* 211–224.

Morin, C. M., & Wooten, V. (1996). Psychological and pharmacological approaches to treating insomnia: Critical issues in assessing their separate and combined effects. *Clinical Psychology Review, 16,* 521–542.

Morin, C. M., et al. (1992). Patients' acceptance of psychological and pharmacological therapies for insomnia. *Sleep, 15,* 302–305.

Morin, C. M., et al. (1993a). Dysfunctional beliefs and attitudes about sleep among older adults with and without insomnia complaints. *Psychology and Aging, 8,* 463–467.

Morin, C. M. et al. (1993b). Cognitive-behavior therapy for late-life insomnia. *Journal of Consulting and Clinical Psychology, 61,* 137–146.

Morokoff, P. J. (1993). Female sexual arousal disorder. In W. Donohue and J. H. Greer (Eds.), *Handbook of sexual dysfunctions: Assessment and treatment* (pp. 157–199). Boston: Allyn & Bacon.

Morris, R. D. (1988). Classification of learning disabilities: Old problems and new approaches. *Journal of Consulting and Clinical Psychology, 56,* 789–794.

Morrison, J. (1989). Childhood sexual histories of women with somatization disorder. *American Journal of Psychiatry, 146,* 239–241.

Morrison, R. L., & Bellack, A. S. (1984). Social skills training. In A. S. Bellack (Ed.), *Schizophrenia: Treatment, management and rehabilitation.* (pp. 247–279). Orlando, FL: Grune & Stratton.

Morrison, R. L., & Bellack, A. S. (1987). Social functioning of schizophrenic patients: Clinical and research issues. *Schizophrenia Bulletin, 13,* 715–725.

Morrow, D. J. (1998a, March 5). Stumble on the road to market. *The New York Times,* p. D1.

Morrow, D. J. (1998b, April 21). Pfizer drug for impotence leads market. *The New York Times,* pp. D1, D4.

Mortimer, A. M., et al. (1990). The positive-negative dichotomy in schizophrenia. *British Journal of Psychiatry, 157,* 41–49.

Moss, M., Frank, E., & Anderson, B. (1990). The effects of marital status and partner support on rape trauma. *American Journal of Orthopsychiatry, 60,* 379–391.

Moss, F., et al. (1985). Sobriety and American Indian problem drinkers. *Alcoholism Treatment Quarterly, 2,* 81–96.

Mossman, D. (1994). Assessing predictions of violence: Being accurate about accuracy. *Journal of Consulting and Clinical Psychology, 62,* 783–792.

Mossman, D., & Perlin, M. L. (1992). Psychiatry and the homeless mentally ill: A reply to Dr. Lamb. *American Journal of Psychiatry, 149,* 951–957.

Mowrer, O. H. (1948). Learning theory and the neurotic paradox. *American Journal of Orthopsychiatry, 18,* 571–610.

Mrazek, P. J., & Haggerty, R. J. (Eds.) (1994). *Reducing risks of mental disorders: Frontiers for preventive intervention research.* Washington, DC: National Academy Press.

Mueser, K. T., Bellack, A. S., & Blanchard, J. J. (1992). Comorbidity of schizophrenia and substance abuse: Implications for treatment. *Journal of Consulting and Clinical Psychology, 60,* 845–856.

Mueser, K. T., & Liberman, R. P. (1995). Behavior therapy in practice. In B. Bongar & L. E. Beutler (Eds.), *Comprehensive textbook of psychotherapy: Theory and practice* (pp. 84–110). New York: Oxford.

Muir, G., Lonsway, K. A., & Payne, D. L. (1996). Rape myth acceptance among Scottish and American students. *Journal of Social Psychology, 136,* 261–262.

Mumford, D. B. (1993). Eating disorders in different cultures. *International Review of Psychiatry, 5,* 109–113.

Mundo, E., et al. (1997). Long-term pharmacotherapy of obsessive-compulsive disorder: A double-blind controlled study. *Journal of Clinical Psychopharmacology, 17,* 4–10.

Muñoz, R. F., Mrazek, P. J., & Haggerty, R. J. (1996). Institute of Medicine Report on Prevention of Mental Disorders: Summary and commentary. *American Psychologist, 51,* 1116–1121.

Murdoch, D., Pihl, R. O., & Ross, D. (1990). Alcohol and crimes of violence: Present issues. *International Journal of the Addictions, 25,* 1065–1081.

Murphy, C. M., Meyer, S. L., & O'Leary, K. D. (1994). Dependency characteristics of partner assaultive men. *Journal of Abnormal Psychology, 103,* 729–735.

Murray, C. B., & Peacock, M. J. (1996). A model-free approach to the study of subjective well-being. In H. W. Neighbors & J.S. Jackson (Eds.), *Mental health in black America.* (pp. 14–26). Thousand Oaks, CA: Sage Publications.

Murray, H. A. (1943). *Thematic Apperception Test: Pictures and manual.* Cambridge, MA: Harvard University Press.

Murray, J. B. (1989a). Alcoholism: Etiologies proposed and therapeutic approaches tried. *Genetic, Social, and General Psychology Monographs, 115,* 81–121.

Murray, J. B. (1989b). Geophysical variables and behavior: VLII. Seasonal affective disorder and phototherapy. *Psychological Reports, 64,* 787–801.

Murray, J. B. (1993a). Review of research on pathological gambling. *Psychological Reports, 72,* 791–810.

Murray, J. B. (1993b). Relationship of childhood sexual abuse to borderline personality disorder, posttraumatic stress disorder, and multiple personality disorder. *Journal of Psychology, 127,* 657–676.

Murray, J. B. (1994a). Dimensions of multiple personality disorder. *The Journal of Genetic Psychology, 155,* 233–246.

Murray, J. B. (1997). Munchausen syndrome/Munchausen syndrome by proxy. *Journal of Psychology, 131,* 343–352.

Murray, R. M., & Reveley, A. M. (1986). Genetic aspects of schizophrenia: Overview. In A. Kerr and P. Snaith (Eds.), *Contemporary issues in schizophrenia* (pp. 261–267). Avon, UK: The Bath Press.

Murray, R. M., et al. (1983). Current genetic and biological approaches to alcoholism. *Psychiatric Developments, 2,* 179–192.

Murstein, B. I., & Mathes, S. (1996). Projection on projective techniques & pathology: The problem that is not being addressed. *Journal of Personality Assessment, 66,* 337–349.

Murtagh, D. R. R., & Greenwood, K. M. (1995). Identifying effective psychological treatments for insomnia: A meta-analysis. *Journal of Consulting and Clinical Psychology, 63,* 79–89.

Muster, N. J., (1992). Treating the adolescent victim-turned-offender. *Adolescence, 27,* 441–450.

Myers, H. F., et al. (1995). Behavioral risk factors related to chronic diseases in ethnic minorities. *Health Psychology, 14,* 622–631.

N

Naber, D., & Hippius, H. (1990). The European experience with the use of clozapine. *Hospital and Community Psychiatry, 41,* 886–890.

Nadler, L. B. (1985). The epidemiology of pathological gambling: Critique of existing research and alternative strategies. *Journal of Gambling Behavior, 1,* 35–50.

Nakawatase, T. V., Yamamoto, J., & Saaso, T. (1993, July/August). Association between fast-flushing response and alcohol use among Japanese Americans. *Prevention Pipeline,* p. 72 (Abstract).

Nathan, P. E. (1988). The addictive personality is the behavior of the addict. *Journal of Consulting and Clinical Psychology, 56,* 183–188.

Nathan, P. E. (1994). DSM-IV: Empirical, accessible, not yet ideal. *Journal of Clinical Psychology, 50,* 103–110.

Nathan, P. E., & Skinstad, A. H. (1987). Outcomes of treatment for alcohol problems: Current methods, problems, and results. *Journal of Consulting and Clinical Psychology, 55,* 332–340.

National Academy of Sciences, National Research Council (1989). *Diet and health: Implications for reducing chronic disease risk.* Washington, DC: National Academy Press.

National Broadcasting Service. (1997, October 20). *Indepth: The tragedy of Alzheimer's disease.* National Broadcasting Service.

National Cancer Institute (1991, August 22). Cited in *The New York Times,* Lung cancer is said to overtake heart trouble as smokers' peril. P. B10.

National Cancer Institute (NCI) (1994). *Cancer facts, sites and types: Racial differences in breast cancer survival.* Author.

National Center for Health Statistics (1967): *Suicide in the United States, 1950–1964.* Washington, DC: US Department of Health, Education, and Welfare.

National Center for Health Statistics (NCHS). (1996a). Mortality trends for Alzheimer's disease. *Vital and Health Statistics,* Series 20, No. 28.

National Center for Health Statistics. (1996b). News releases and fact sheets. *Highlights of a new report from the National Center for Health Statistics (NCHS), Monitoring health care in America: Quarterly fact sheet.* Washington, DC: US Department of Health, Education, and Welfare.

National Center for Infant Clinical Programs. *Diagnostic classfication of mental health and developmental disorders of infancy and early childhood.* Arlington, VA: Author.

National Highway Traffic Safety Administration (1988). *Fatal accident reporting system: 1987.* Washington, DC: US Department of Transportation.

National Institute on Aging (1997). *New findings on Alzheimer's disease offer clues on causes, diagnosis, and treatments.* Bethesda, MD: Author.

National Institute on Alcohol Abuse and Alcoholism. (1990). *7th Special Report to Congress on Alcohol and Health.* Rockville, MD: Author.

National Institutes of Health. (1987). *Differential diagnosis of dementing diseases.* NIH Consensus Development Conference Statement, Vol 6, No. 11. Bethesda, MD: Author.

National Institutes of Health (1991, Sept. 15–27). *Treatment of panic disorder.* Consensus Development Conference Consensus Statement. Bethesda, MD: Author.

National Institute of Mental Health. (NIMH) (1982). *Television and behavior: Ten years of scientific progress and implications for the eighties.* Washington, DC: Author.

National Task Force on the Prevention and Treatment of Obesity (1993). Very low-calorie diets. *Journal of the American Medical Association, 270,* 967–974.

National Task Force on the Prevention and Treatment of Obesity (1994). Weight cycling. *Journal of the American Medical Association, 272,* 1196–1202.

National Task Force on the Prevention and Treatment of Obesity (1996). Long-term pharmacotherapy in the management of obesity. *Journal of the American Medical Association, 276,* 1907–1915.

NBC Nightly News. (1996, November 11). National Broadcasting Company.

Ndetei, D. M., & Singh, A. (1983). Hallucinations in Kenyan schizophrenic patients. *Acta Psychiatrica Scandinavica, 67,* 144–147.

Ndetei, D. M., & Vadher, A. (1984). A comparative cross-cultural study of the frequencies of hallucination in schizophrenia. *Acta Psychiatrica Scandinavica, 70,* 545–549.

Neal, A. M., & Turner, S. M. (1991). Anxiety disorders research with African Americans: Current status. *Psychological Bulletin, 109,* 400–410.

Needles, D. J., & Abramson, L. Y. (1990). Positive life events, attributional style, and hopelessness: Testing a model of recovery from depression. *Journal of Abnormal Psychology, 99,* 156–165.

Neff, J. A., & Hoppe, S. K. (1993). Race/ethnicity, acculturation, and psychological distress: Fatalism and religiosity as cultural resources. *Journal of Community Psychology, 21,* 3–20.

Negy, C., & Snyder, D. K. (1997). Ethnicity and acculturation: Assessing Mexican American couples' relationships using the marital satisfaction inventory—revised. *Psychological Assessment, 9,* 414–421.

Neiger, B. L. (1988). Adolescent suicide: Character traits of high-risk teenagers. *Adolescence, 23,* 469–475.

Neighbors, H. (1992, December). *The help seeking behavior of black Americans: A summary of the National Survey of Black Americans.* Paper presented at a symposium, Anxiety Disorders in African Americans, presented by the State University of New York Health Science Center at Brooklyn, Brooklyn, NY.

Neighbors, H. W., & Jackson, J. S. (1996). *Mental health in black America: Psychosocial problems and help-seeking behavior.* In H. W. Neighbors & J.S. Jackson (Eds.), Mental health in black America (pp. 1–13). Thousand Oaks, CA: Sage Publications.

Nelson, C. B., Heath, A. C., Kessler, R. C. (1998). Temporal progression of alcohol dependence symptoms in the U. S. household population: Results from the National Comorbidity Survey, *Journal of Consulting and Clinical Psychology, 66,* 474–483.

Nelson, J. C., & Davis, J. M. (1997). DST studies in psychotic depression: A meta-analysis. *American Journal of Psychiatry, 154,* 1497–1503.

Nelson, J. C., Mazure, C. M., & Jatlow, P. I. (1990). Value of the DST for predicting response of patients with major depression to hospitalization and desipramine. *American Journal of Psychiatry, 147,* 1488–1492.

Nelson, S. H., et. al. (1992). An overview of mental health services for American Indians and Alaska natives in the 1990s. *Hospital and Community Psychiatry, 43,* 257–261.

Nemiah, J. C. (1978). Psychoneurotic disorders. In A. M. Nicholi (Ed.), *Harvard guide to modern psychiatry.* Cambridge, MA: Harvard University Press.

Neugebauer, R. (1979). Medieval and early modern theories of mental illness. *Archives of General Psychiatry, 36,* 477–484.

Neugebauer, R., et al. (1997). Major depressive disorder in the 6 months after miscarriage. *Journal of the American Medical Association, 277,* 383–388.

Nevid, J. S. (1996). Smoking cessation with ethnic minorities: Themes and approaches. *Journal of Social Distress and the Homeless, 5,* 1–16.

Nevid, J. S., Capurso, R., & Morrison, J. K. (1980). Patient's adjustment to family-care as related to their perceptions of real-ideal differences in treatment environments. *American Journal of Community Psychology, 8,* 117–120.

Nevid, J. S., Fichner-Rathus, L., & Rathus, S. A. (1995). *Human sexuality in a world of diversity* (2nd ed.). Boston: Allyn & Bacon.

Nevid, J.S., & Javier, R.A. (1992, June). *"SI, PUEDO" smoking cessation program for Hispanic Smokers.* Poster presentation at the Fourth National Forum on Cardiovascular Health, Pulmonary Disorders, and Blood Resources, Minority Health Issues for an Emerging Majority, National Heart, Lung, and Blood Institute, National Institutes of Health, Washington, DC.

Nevid, J. S., & Javier, R. A. (1997). Preliminary investigation of a culturally-specific smoking cessation intervention for Hispanic smokers. *American Journal of Health Promotion, 11,* 198–207.

Nevid, J. S., Javier, R. A., & Moulton, J. (1996). Factors predicting participant attrition in a community-based culturally-specific smoking cessation program for Hispanic smokers. *Health Psychology, 15,* 226–229.

Nevid, J. S., Lavi, B., & Primavera, L. H. (1986). Cluster analysis of training orientations in clinical psychology. *Professional Psychology: Research and Practice, 17,* 367–370.

Nevid, J. S., Lavi, B., & Primavera, L. H. (1987). Principal components analysis of therapeutic orientations of doctoral programs in clinical psychology. *Journal of Clinical Psychology, 43,* 723–729.

Nevid, J. S., Rathus, S. A., & Rubenstein, H. R. (1998). *Health in the new millennium* (pp. 143–165). New York: Worth.

Neville, H. A., et al. (1996). The impact of multicultural training on white racial identity attitudes and therapy competencies. *Professional Psychology: Research & Practice, 27,* 83–89.

A new drug for schizophrenia wins approval from the FDA. (1996, October 2). *The New York Times,* p. A21.

New York City Board of Education (1984). *Child abuse and neglect prevention training manual: Working together to make a difference.* New York: Office of the Chief Executive for Instruction, Office of Student Progress, and Guidance Services Unit.

Newlin, D. B. (1989). The skin-flushing response: Autonomic, self-report, and conditioned response to repeated administrations of alcohol in Asian men. *Journal of Abnormal Psychology, 98,* 421–425.

Newman, D. L., et al. (1996). Psychiatric disorder in a birth cohort of young adults: Prevalence, comorbidity, clinical significance, and new case incidence from ages 11 to 21. *Journal of Consulting and Clinical Psychology, 64,* 552–562.

Newman, J. P., Patterson, C. M., & Kosson, D. S. (1987). Response preservation in psychopaths. *Journal of Abnormal Psychology, 96,* 145–148.

Newman, J. P., & Wallace, J. F. (1993). Psychopathy and cognition. In K. S. Dobson & P. C. Kendall (Eds.), *Psychopathology and cognition.* (pp. 293–349). New York: Academic Press.

Newman, K. D. (1993). Giving up: Shelter experiences of battered women. *Public Health Nursing, 10,* 108–113.

Newman, L. S., & Baumeister, R. F. (1996). Toward an explanation of the UFO abduction phenomenon: Hypnotic elaboration, extraterrestrial sadomasochism, and spurious memories. *Psychological Inquiry, 7,* 99–126.

Newman, M. G., & Borkovec, T. D. (1995). Cognitive-behavioral treatment of generalized anxiety disorder. *The Clinical Psychologist, 48,* 5–7.

Newman, M .G., et al. (1997). Comparison of palmtop-computer-assisted brief cognitive-behavioral treatment to cognitive-behavioral treatment for panic disorder. *Journal of Consulting and Clinical Psychology, 65,* 178–183.

Newmark, C. S., Frerking, R. A., Cook, L., & Newmark, L. (1973). Endorsement of Ellis's irrational beliefs as a function of psychopathology. *Journal of Clinical Psychology, 29,* 300–302.

Newsweek (1992, February 3). Insanity: A defense of last resort. *Newsweek,* p. 49.

Nezu, A. M., (1994). Introduction to special section: Mental retardation and mental illness. *Journal of Consulting and Clinical Psychology, 62,* 4–5.

Nezu, A. M., & Ronan, G. F. (1985). Life stress, current problems, problem solving, and depressive symptoms: An integrative model. *Journal of Consulting and Clinical Psychology, 53,* 693–697.

Nezu, C. M., & Nezu, A. M. (1994). Outpatient psychotherapy for adults with mental retardation and concomitant psychopathology: Research and clinical imperatives. *Journal of Consulting and Clinical Psychology, 62,* 34–42.

NIAAA report links drinking and early death. (1990, October). *The Addiction Letter, 6* p. 5.

Niccols, G. A. (1994). Fetal alcohol syndrome: Implications for psychologists. *Clinical Psychology Review, 14,* 91–111.

Nicholson, R. A., & Berman, J. S. (1983). Is follow-up necessary in evaluating psychotherapy? *Psychological Bulletin, 93,* 261–278.

Nicholson, R. A., et al. (1997). Utility of MMPI-2 indicators of response distortion: Receiver operating characteristic analysis. *Psychological Assessment, 9,* 471–479.

Nickerson, K. J., Helms, J. E., & Terrell, F. (1994). Cultural mistrust, opinions about mental illness, and Black students' attitudes toward seeking psychological help from White counselors. *Journal of Counseling Psychology, 41,* 378–385.

Niederehe, G. (1986). Depression and memory impairment in the aged. In L. W. Poon (Ed.), *Handbook for clinical memory assessment of older adults* (pp. 226–237). Washington, D C : American Psychological Association.

Nigg, J. T., & Goldsmith, H.H. (1994). Genetics of personality disorders: Perspectives from personality and psychopathology research. *Psychological Bulletin, 115,* 346–380.

Nigg, J. T., et al. (1992). Malevolent object representations in borderline personality disorder and major depression. *Journal of Abnormal Psychology, 101,* 61–67.

Niles, M. A., et al. (1995). Predictors of initial smoking cessation and relapse through the first 2 years of the Lung Health Study. *Journal of Consulting and Clinical Psychology, 63,* 60–69.

Nishizawa, S., et al. (1997). Differences between males and females in rates of serotonin synthesis in human brain. *Proceedings of the National Academy of Science, 94,* 5308–5313.

Nolen-Hoeksema, S. (1991). Responses to depression and their effects on the duration of depressive episodes. *Journal of Abnormal Psychology, 100,* 569–582.

Nolen-Hoeksema, S., & Girgus, J. S. (1994). The emergence of gender differences in depression during adolescence. *Psychological Bulletin, 115,* 424–443.

Nolen-Hoeksema, S., Girgus, J. S., & Seligman, M. E. P. (1992). Predictors and consequences of childhood depressive symptoms: A 5-year longitudinal study. *Journal of Abnormal Psychology, 101,* 405–422.

Nolen-Hoeksema, S., McBride, A., & Larson, J. (1997). Rumination and psychological distress among bereaved partners. *Journal of Personality and Social Psychology, 72,* 855–862.

Nolen-Hoeksema, S., Morrow, J., & Fredrickson, B. L. (1993). Response styles and the duration of episodes of depressed mood. *Journal of Abnormal Psychology, 102,* 20–28.

Nopoulos, P., Flaum, M., & Andreasen, N. C. (1997). Sex differences in brain morphology in schizophrenia. *American Journal of Psychiatry, 154,* 1648–1654.

Norris, F. H. (1992). Epidemiology of trauma: Frequency and impact of different potentially traumatic events on different demographic groups. *Journal of Consulting and Clinical Psychology, 60,* 409–418.

North, C. S., Smith, E. M., & Spitznagel, E. L. (1994). Posttraumatic stress disorder in survivors of a mass shooting. *American Journal of Psychiatry, 151,* 82–88.

Norton, G. R., Harrison, B., Hauch, J., & Rhodes, L. (1985). Characteristics of people with infrequent panic attacks. *Journal of Abnormal Psychology, 94,* 216–221.

Norton, G. R., & Rhodes, L. (1983). Characteristics of people with infrequent panic attacks: A preliminary analysis. Unpublished manuscript: University of Winnipeg.

NOVA. (1989, March 28). Confronting the killer gene. Boston: WGBH Educational Foundation.

Novaco, R. W. (1974). A treatment program for the management of anger through cognitive and relaxation control. Doctoral Dissertation, Indiana University.

Novaco, R. W. (1977). A stress inoculation approach to anger management in the training of law enforcement officers. American Journal of Community Psychology, 5, 327–346.

Nowell, P. D., et al. (1997). Benzodiazepines and zolpidem for chronic insomnia: A meta-analysis of treatment efficacy. Journal of the American Medical Association, 278, 2170–2177.

Nowell, P. D., et al. (1998). Effective treatments for selected sleep disorders. In P. E. Nathan, & J. M. Gorman (Eds.), A guide to treatments that work (pp. 531-543). New York:Oxford University Press.

Noyes, R. (1994). Psychiatric comorbidity among patients with hypochondriasis. General Hospital Psychiatry, 16, 78–87.

Noyes, R., et al. (1993). The validity of DSM-III-R hypochondriasis. Archives of General Psychiatry, 50, 961–970.

Nussbaum, M., et al. (1985). Follow-up investigation of patients with anorexia nervosa. The Journal of Pediatrics, 106, 835–840.

O

Obot, I. S. (1996). Problem drinking, chronic disease, and recent life events. In H. W. Neighbors & J.S. Jackson (Eds.), Mental health in black America. (pp. 45–61). Thousand Oaks, CA: Sage Publications.

O'Brien, C. P. (1996). Recent developments in the pharmacotherapy of substance abuse. Journal of Consulting and Clinical Psychology, 64, 677–686.

O'Brien, C. P., & McKay, J. (1998). Psychopharmacological treatments of substance use disorders. In P. E. Nathan & J. M. Gorman (Eds.), A guide to treatments that work (pp. 127–155). New York: Oxford University Press.

O'Brien, C. P., & McLellan, A. T. (1997). Addiction medicine. Journal of the American Medical Association, 277, 1840–1841.

Ochs, R. (1998, March 9). Alcohol: Sorting the contradictions. New York Newsday.

O'Connor, R. D. (1969). Modification of social withdrawal through symbolic modeling. Journal of Applied Behavior Analysis, 2, 15–22.

O'Connor v. Donaldson, 95 S. Ct. 2486 (1975).

O'Connor, T. G., et al. (1998). Co-occurrence of depressive symptoms and antisocial behavior in adolescence: A common genetic liability. Journal of Abnormal Psychology, 107, 27–37.

O'Donnell, Clifford R. (1995). Firearm deaths among children and youth. American Psychologist, 50, 771–776.

O'Donohue, W., Dopke, C. A., & Swingen, D. N. (1997). Psychotherapy for female sexual dysfunction: A review. Clinical Psychology Review, 17, 537–566.

O'Donohue, W., Letourneau, E., & Geer, J. H. (1993). Premature ejaculation. In W. O'Donohue & J. H. Geer (Eds.), Handbook of sexual dysfunctions: Assessment and treatment (pp. 303–333). Boston: Allyn & Bacon.

O'Donohue, W., McKay, J. S., & Schewe, P. A. (1996). Rape: The roles of outcome expectancies and hypermasculinity. Sexual Abuse Journal of Research and Treatment, 8, 133–141.

Oei, T. P. S., & Shuttlewood, G. J. (1996). Specified and nonspecific factors in psychotherapy: A case of cognitive therapy for depression. Clinical Psychology Review, 16, 83–103.

Oetting, E. R., & Beauvais, F. (1990). Adolescent drug use: Findings of national and local surveys. Journal of Consulting and Clinical Psychology, 58, 385–394.

Oetting, E. R., Beauvais, F., & Edwards, R. (1988). Alcohol and Indian youth: Social and psychological correlates and prevention. Journal of Drug Issues, 18, 87–102.

O'Farrell, T. J., et al. (1996). Cost-benefit and cost-effectiveness analyses of behavioral marital therapy as an addition to outpatient alcoholism treatment. Journal of Substance Abuse, 8, 145–166.

Office of Technology Assessment, U.S. Congress (1987, April). Losing a million minds: Confronting the tragedy of Alzheimer's disease (OTA-BA-323). Washington, DC : U.S. Government Printing Office.

Ogles, B. M., Lambert, M. J., & Sawyer, J. D. (1995). Clinical significance of the National Institute of Mental Health Treatment of Depression Collaborative Research program data. Journal of Consulting and Clinical Psychology, 63, 321–326.

Ogloff, J. R. P., Roberts, C. F., & Roesch, R. (1993). The insanity defense: Legal standards and clinical assessment. Applied & Preventive Psychology, 2, 163–178.

O'Hara, M. W., Zekoski, E. M., Philipps, L. H., & Wright, E. J. (1990). Journal of Abnormal Psychology, 99, 3–15.

O'Hara, M. W., et al. (1991). Prospective study of postpartum blues: Biological and psychosocial factors. Archives of General Psychiatry, 48, 801–806.

Ohman, A., Fredrikson, M., Hugdahl, K., & Rimmo, P. (1976). The premise of equipotentiality in human classical conditioning: Conditioned electrodermal responses to potentially phobic stimuli. Journal of Experimental Psychology: General, 105, 313–337.

Okasha, A. et al. (1994). Expressed emotion, perceived criticism and relapse in depression: A replication in an Egyptian community. American Journal of Psychiatry, 151, 1001–1005.

Okazaki, S. (1997). Sources of ethnic differences between Asian American and White American college students on measures of depression and social anxiety. Journal of Abnormal Psychology, 106, 52–60.

Okubo, Y., et al. (1997). Decreased prefrontal dopamine D1 receptors in schizophrenia revealed by PET. Nature, 385, 634–636.

Oldham, J. M. (1994). Personality disorders: Current perspectives. Journal of the American Medical Association, 272, 213–220.

O'Leary, A. (1990). Stress, emotion, and human immune functions. Psychological Bulletin, 108, 382–383.

O'Leary, D. S., et al. (1996). Auditory attentional deficits in patients with schizophrenia: A positron emission tomography study. Archives of General Psychiatry, 53, 633–641.

O'Leary, K. D. (1995, July). Assessment and treatment of partner abuse. Clinician's Research Digest, Supplemental Bulletin 12, pp. 1–2.

O'Leary, K. D., Malone, J., & Tyree, A. (1994). Physical aggression in early marriage: Prerelationship and relationship effects. Journal of Consulting and Clinical Psychology, 62, 594–602.

O'Leary, K. D., Pelham, W. E., Rosenbaum, A., & Price, G. H. (1976). Behavioral treatment of hyperkinetic children: An experimental evolution of its usefulness. Clinical Pediatrics, 15, 510–515.

Olesen, J. (1994). Understanding the biologic basis of migraine. New England Journal of Medicine, 331, 1713–1714.

Olfson, M., et al. (1998) Use of ECT for the inpatient treatment of recurrent major depression. American Journal of Psychiatry, 155, 22–29.

Olinger, J. L., Kuiper, N. A., & Shaw, B. F. (1987). Dysfunctional attitudes and stressful life events: An interactive model of depression. Cognitive Therapy & Research, 11, 25–40.

Ollendick, T. H., & Ollendick, D. G. (1982). Anixety disorders. In J. L. Matson & R. P. Barrett (Eds.),

Psychopathology in the mentally retarded (pp. 77–119). Orlando, FL: Grune and Stratton.

Ollendick, T. H. et al., (1992). Journal of Consulting and Clinical Psychology, 60, 80–87.

Olmsted, M. P., & Garner, D. M. (1986). The significance of self-induced vomiting as a weight-control method among non-clinical samples. International Journal of Eating Disorders, 5, 683–700.

Olweus, D. (1987). Testosterone and adrenaline. In S. K. Mednick et al. (Eds.), The causes of crime: New biological approaches (pp. 263–282). Cambridge, UK: Cambridge University Press.

O'Malley, S. S., et al. (1996a). Experience of a slip among alcoholics treated with naltrexone or placebo. American Journal of Psychiatry, 153, 281–283.

O'Malley, S. S., et al. (1996b). Six-month follow-up of naltrexone and psychotherapy for alcohol dependence. Archives of General Psychiatry, 53, 217–224.

One in five teen-agers is armed, a survey finds. The New York Times, p. A19.

Onstad, S., Skre, I., Torgensen, S., & Kringlen, E. (1991). Twin concordance for DSM-III-R schizophrenia. Acta Psychiatrica Scandinavica, 83, 395–401.

Ordman, A. M., & Kirschenbaum, D. S. (1986). Bulimia: Assessment of eating, psychological adjustment, and familial characteristics. International Journal of Eating Disorders, 5, 865–876.

Organista, K. C., Munoz, R. F., & Gonzalez, G. (1994). Cognitive-behavioral therapy for depression in low-income and minority medical outpatients: Description of a program and exploratory analyses. Cognitive Therapy and Research, 18, 241–259.

Orgata, S. N., et al. (1990). Childhood sexual and physical abuse in adult patients with borderline personality disorders. American Journal of Psychiatry, 147, 1008–1013.

Ormel, J. et al. (1994). Common mental disorders and disability across cultures. Journal of the American Medical Association, 272, 1741–1748.

Ornberg, B., & Zalewski, C. (1994). Assessment of adolescents with the Rorschach: A critical review. Assessment, 1, 209–217.

Orne, M. T., et al. (1996). "Memories" of anomalous and traumatic autobiographical experiences: Validation and consolidation of fantasy through hypnosis. Psychological Inquiry, 7, 168–172.

Orr, S. P., et al. (1995). Physiologic responses to loud tones in Vietnam veterans with posttraumatic stress disorder. Journal of Abnormal Psychology, 104, 75–82.

Orsillo, S. M., et al. (1996). Current and lifetime psychiatric disorders among veterans with war zone-related posttraumatic stress disorder. Journal of Nervous & Mental Disease, 184, 307–313.

Osofsky, J. D. (1995). The effects of exposure to violence on young children. American Psychologist, 50, 782–788.

Öst, L. (1987). Age of onset in different phobias. Journal of Abnormal Psychology, 96, 223–229.

Öst, L. (1992). Blood and injection phobia: Background and cognitive, physiological, and behavioral variables. Journal of Abnormal Psychology, 101, 68–74.

Osterling, J., & Dawson, G. (1994). Early recognition of children with autism: A study of first birthday home videotapes. Journal of Autism and Developmental Disorder, 24, 247–257.

O'Sullivan, M., J., & Lasso, B. (1992). Community mental health services for Hispanics: A test of the culture compatibility hypothesis. Hispanic Journal of Behavioral Sciences, 14, 455–468.

Ouimette, P. C., Finney, J. W., & Moos, R. H. (1997). Twelve-step and cognitive-behavioral treatment for substance abuse: A comparison of treatment effectiveness. Journal of Consulting and Clinical Psychology, 65, 230–240.

Overholser, J. C., & Beck, S. (1986). Multimethod assessment of rapists, child molesters, and three control groups on behavioral and psychological measures. *Journal of Consulting and Clinical Psychology, 54,* 682–687.

Overmier, J. B. L., & Seligman, M. E. P. (1967). Effect of inescapable shock upon subsequent escape and avoidance learning. *Journal of Comparative and Physiological Psychology, 63,* 28–33.

P

Padgett, V. R., Brislin-Slütz, J. A., & Neal, J. A. (1989). Pornography, erotica, and attitudes toward women: The effects of repeated exposure. *Journal of Sex Research, 26,* 479–491.

Palinkas, L. A., Wingard, D. L., & Barrett-Connor, E. (1990). The biocultural context of social networks and depression among the elderly. *Social Science and Medicine, 4,* 441–447.

Pallast, E. G. M., et al. (1994). Excess seasonality of births among patients with schizophrenia and seasonal ovopathy. *Schizophrenia Bulletin, 20,* 269–276.

Panic attacks and panic disorder—Part I. (1996, April). *The Harvard Mental Health Letter, 12* (10), 1–3.

Pansarasa, C., & Nevid, J. S. (1995, August). *Division of labor and marital satisfaction: Roles of moderating variables.* Poster session presented at the meeting of the American Psychological Association, New York, NY.

Papolos, D. F., Yu, Y. M., Rosenbaum, E., & Lachman, H. M. (1996). Modulation of learned helplessness by 5-hydroxtryptamine2A receptor antisense oligodeoxynucleotides. *Psychiatry Research, 63,* 197–203.

Papp, L. A., et al. (1997). Respiratory psychophysiology of panic disorder: Three respiratory challenges in 98 subjects. *American Journal of Psychiatry,154,* 557–1565.

Park, J. Y., et al. (1984). The flushing response to alcohol use among Koreans and Taiwanese. *Journal of Studies on Alcohol, 45,* 481–485.

Parker, K. C. H., Hanson, R. K., & Hinsley, J. (1988). MMPI, Rorschach, and WAIS: A meta-analytic comparison of reliability, stability, and validity. *Psychological Bulletin, 103,* 367–373.

Parker, R. N. (1993). The effects of context on alcohol and violence. Special Issue: Alcohol, aggression, and injury. *Alcohol: Health and Research World, 17,* 117–122.

The Parkinson Study Group (1993). Effects of tocopherol and deprenyl on the progression of disability in early Parkinson's disease. *New England Journal of Medicine, 328,* 176–182.

Parnas, J., et al. (1993). Lifetime DSM-III-R diagnostic outcomes in the offspring of schizophrenic mothers: Results from the Copenhagen High-Risk Study. *Archives of General Psychiatry, 50,* 707–714.

Partinen, M., & Telakivi, T. (1992). Epidemiology of obstructive sleep apnea syndrome. *Sleep, 15* (6, Suppl), S1–S4.

Pasewark, R. A., & Pantle, M. L. (1979). Insanity plea: Legislators' view. *American Journal of Psychiatry, 136,* 222–223.

Pate, R. R., et al. (1995). Physical activity and public health: A recommendation from the Centers for Disease Control and Prevention and the American College of Sports Medicine. *Journal of the American Medical Association, 273,* 402–407.

Patrick, C. J., Cuthbert, B. N., & Lang, P. J. (1994). Emotion in the criminal psychopath: Fear image processing. *Journal of Abnormal Psychology, 103,* 523–534.

Patterson, G. R. (1993). Orderly change in a stable world: The antisocial trait as a chimera. *Journal of Consulting and Clinical Psychology, 61,* 911–919.

Patterson, G. R., Reid, J. B., & Dishion, T. J. (1992). *Antisocial boys.* Eugene, OR: Castalia.

Paul, G. (1967). Strategy of outcome research in psychotherapy. *Journal of Consulting and Clinical Psychology, 31,* 109–118.

Paul, G. L. (1969). Outcome of systematic desensitization II: Controlled investigations of individual treat-

ment, technique variations, and current status. In C. M. Franks (Ed.), *Behavior therapy: Appraisal and status.* New York: McGraw-Hill.

Paul, G. L., & Lentz, R. J. (1977). *Psychosocial treatment of chronic mental patients: Milieu versus social-learning programs.* Cambridge, MA: Harvard University Press.

Paulesu, E., Frith, C. D., & Frackowisk, R. S. J. (1993). The neural correlates of the verbal component of working memory. *Nature, 362,*342–344.

Pauli, P., et al. (1991). Anxiety induced by cardiac perceptions in patients with panic attacks: A field study. *Behaviour Research & Therapy, 29,* 137–145.

Pauli, P., et al. (1997). Behavioral and neurophysiological evidence for altered processing of anxiety-related words in panic disorder. *Journal of Abnormal Psychology, 106,* 213–220.

Pauly, I. B. (1981). Outcome of sex reassignment surgery for transsexuals. *Australian & New Zealand Journal of Psychiatry, 15,* 45–51.

Pavlov, I. (1927). *Conditioned reflexes.* London: Oxford University Press.

Paykel, E. S. (1979). Predictors of treatment response. In E. S. Paykel & A. Coppen (Eds.), *Psychopharmacology of affective disorders.* Oxford, UK: Oxford University Press.

Paykel, E. S. (1982). Life events and early environments. In E. S. Paykel (Ed.), *Handbook of affective disorders.* New York: Guilford Press.

Paykel, E. S., & Hale, A. S. (1986). Recent advances in the treatment of depression. In J. W. Deakin (Ed.), *The biology of depression*(pp. 153–173). Proceedings of a meeting of the Biological Group of the Royal College of Psychiatrists held at Manchester University, 1985. Washington, D C: American Psychiatric Press.

Peck v. Counseling Service of Addison County, 499 A.2d 422, Vermont Supreme Court Docket 83–062 (June 14, 1985).

Pelham, W. E., Jr., & Murphy, H. A. (1986). Attention deficit and conduct disorders. In M. Hersen (Ed.), *Pharmacological and behavioral treatment: An integrative approach.* New York: Wiley.

Pelham, W. E., et al.(1985). Behavioral and stimulant treatment of hyperactive children: A therapy study with methylphenidate probes in a within-subjects design. *Journal of Applied Behavior Analysis, 13,* 221–236.

Pellegrino, D. D. (1996). Clinical judgment, scientific data, and ethics: Antidepressant therapy in adolescents and children. *Journal of Nervous & Mental Disease, 184,* 106–108.

Peltzer, K., & Machleidt, W. (1992). A traditional (African) approach towards the therapy of schizophrenia and its comparison with western models. *Therapeutic Communities International Journal for Therapeutic and Supportive Organizations, 13,* 229–242.

Pendery, M. L., Maltzman, I. M., & West, L. J. (1982). Controlled drinking by alcoholics? New findings and a re-evaluation of a major affirmative study. *Science, 217,* 169–174.

Penn, D. L. (1998, June). Assessment and treatment of social dysfunction in schizophrenia. *Clinician's Research Digest,* Supplemental Bulletin 18.

Penn, D. L., & Mueser, K. T. (1996). Research update on the psychosocial treatment of schizophrenia. *American Journal of Psychiatry, 153,* 607–617.

Pennebaker, J. W., Kiecolt-Glaser, J. K., & Glaser, R. (1988). Disclosure of traumas and immune function: Health implications for psychotherapy. *Journal of Consulting and Clinical Psychology, 56,* 239–245.

Penner, L. A., Thompson, J. K., & Coovert, D. L. (1991). Size overestimation among anorexics: Much ado about very little? *Journal of Abnormal Psychology, 100,* 90–93.

Perez, F. I., Stump, D. A., Gay, J. R. A., & Hart, V. R. (1976). Intellectual performance in multi-infarct dementia and Alzheimer's disease: A replication study. *Canadian Journal of Neurological Sciences, 3,* 181–187.

Perez, F. I., et al. (1975). Analysis of intellectual and cognitive performance in patients with multi-infarct dementia, vertebrobasilar insuffiency with dementia, and Alzheimer's disease. *Journal of Neurology, Neurosurgery, and Psychiatry, 38,* 533–540.

Perez-Stable, E. (1991, May). *Health promotion among Latinos: What are the priorities?* Chancellor's Distinguished Lecture, University of California, Irvine.

Pericak-Vance, M. A., et al. (1997). Complete genomic screen in late-onset familial Alzheimer's disease: Evidence for a new focus on chromosome 12. *Journal of the American Medical Association, 278,* 1237–1241.

Perilstein, R. D., Lipper, S., & Friedman, L. J. (1991). Three cases of paraphilias responsive to fluoxetine treatment. *Journal of Clinical Psychiatry, 52,* 169–170.

Perlin, M. L. (1994). Law and the delivery of mental health services in the community. *American Journal of Orthopsychiatry, 64,* 194–208.

Perlman, J. D., & Abramson, P. R. (1982). Sexual satisfaction among married & cohabitating individuals. *Journal of Consulting and Clinical Psychology, 50,* 458–460.

Perna, G., et al. (1996). Family history of panic disorder and hypersensitivity to CO_2 in patients with panic disorder. *American Journal of Psychiatry, 153,* 1060–1064.

Perri, M. G., et al. (1997). Effects of group-versus home-based exercise in the treatment of obesity. *Journal of Consulting and Clinical Psychology, 65,* 278–285.

Perry, C. L., Klepp, K., & Shultz, J. M. (1988). Primary prevention of cardiovascular disease: Community-wide strategies for youth. *Journal of Consulting and Clinical Psychology, 56,* 358–364.

Perry, C. L., et al. (1987). Promoting healthy eating and physical activity patterns among adolescents: Slice of life. *Health Education Research: Theory and Practice, 2,* 93–104.

Perry, P. J., et al. (1991). Clozapine and norclozapine plasma concentrations and clinical response of treatment-refractory schizophrenic patients. *American Journal of Psychiatry, 148,* 231–235.

Persons, J. B., Thase, M. E., & Crits-Christoph, P. (1996). The role of psychotherapy in the treatment of depression: Review of two practice guidelines. *Archives of General Psychiatry, 53,* 283–290.

Peterson, C., Villanova, P., & Raps, C S. (1985). Depression and attributions: Factors responsible for inconsistent results in the published literature. *Journal of Abnormal Psychology, 94,* 165–168.

Peterson, E. D., et al. (1997). Racial variation in the use of coronary-revascularization procedures — Are the differences real? Do they matter? *The New England Journal of Medicine, 336 ,* 480–486.

Pettingale, K. W. (1985). Towards a psychobiological model of cancer: Biological considerations. Special issue: Cancer and the mind. *Social Science and Medicine, 20,*779-787.

Pfohl, B. (1991). Histrionic personality disorder: A review of available data and recommendations for DSM-IV. *Journal of Personality Disorders, 5,* 150–166.

Philipps, L. H., & O'Hara, M. W. (1991). Prospective study of postpartum depression: $4^1/_2$-year follow-up of women and children. *Journal of Abnormal Psychology, 100,* 151–155.

Phillips, E. L., Phillips, E. A., Fixsen, D. L., & Wolf, M. M. (1971). Achievement place: Modifications of the behaviors of pre-delinquent boys within a token economy. *Journal of Applied Behavior Analysis, 4,* 45–59.

Phillips, M. A., & Murrell, S. A. (1994). Impact of psychological and physical health, stressful events, and social support on subsequent mental health help seeking among older adults. *Journal of Consulting and Clinical Psychology, 62,* 275.

Phillips, M. R., Wolf, S., & Coons, D. J. (1988). Psychiatry and the criminal justice system: Testing the myths. *American Journal of Psychiatry, 145,* 605–610.

Phinney, J. (1989). Stages of ethnic identity in minority group adolescents. *Journal of Early Adolescence, 9,* 34–49.

Phinney, J., & Alipuria, L. (1990). Ethnic identity in older adolescents from four ethnic groups. *Journal of Adolescence, 13,* 171–183.

Phinney, J., Lochner, B. & Murphy, R. (1990). Ethnic identity development and psychological adjustment in adolescence. In A. Stiffman & L. Davis (Eds.), *Ethnic issues in adolescent mental health.* Newbury Park. CA: Sage Publications.

Pickar, D., et al. (1992). Clinical and biological response to clozapine in patients with schizophrenia: Cross-over comparison with fluphenazine. *Archives of General Psychiatry, 49,* 345–353.

Pihl, R. O., & Peterson, J. B. (1993). Alcohol, drug use and aggressive behavior. In S. Hodgins (Ed.), *Mental disorder and crime* (pp. 263–283). Newbury Park, CA: Sage Publications.

Pihl, R. O., Peterson, J., & Finn, P. (1990). Inherited predispostion to alcoholism: Characteristics of sons of male alcoholics.*Journal of Abnormal Psychology, 99,* 291–301.

Pike, K. M. (1998). Long-term course of anorexia nervosa: Response, relapse, remission., and recovery. *Clinical Psychology Review, 18,* 447–475.

Pike, K. M., & Rodin, J. (1991). Mothers, daughters, and disordered eating. *Journal of Abnormal Psychology, 101,* 198–204.

Pillard, R. C. (1990). The Kinsey Scale: Is it familial? In D. P. McWhirter, S. A. Sanders, & J. M. Reinisch (Eds.), *Homosexuality/heterosexuality: Concepts of sexual orientation* (pp. 88–100). New York: Oxford University Press.

Pillard, R. C., & Weinrich, J. D. (1986). Evidence of familial nature of male homosexuality. *Archives of Sexual Behavior, 43,* 808–812.

Pilowsky, J. E. (1993). The courage to leave: An exploration of Spanish-speaking women victims of spousal abuse. *Canadian Journal of Community Mental Health, 12,* 15–29.

Pimental, P. A., et al. (1997). Changing psychologists' opinions about prescriptive authority: A little information goes a long way. *Professional Psychology: Research and Practice, 28,* 123–127.

Pinderhughes, E. (1989). *Understanding race, ethnicity and power: Keys to efficacy in clinical practice.* New York: Free Press.

Pine, D.S, et al. (1997). Neuroendocrine response to fenfluramine challenge in boys: Associations with aggressive behavior and adverse rearing. *Archives of General Psychiatry, 54,* 839–846.

Piven, J., et al. (1995). An MRI study of brain size in autism. *American Journal of Psychiatry, 152,* 1145–1149.

Piven, J., et al. (1997). An MRI study of the corpus callosum in autism. *American Journal of Psychiatry, 154,* 1051–1056.

Pliszka, S. R. (1991). Antidepressants in the treatment of child and adolescent psychopathology. *Journal of Clinical Child Psychology, 3,* 313–320.

Plomin, R., DeFries, J., McClearn, G. E., & Rutter, M. (1997). *Behavioral genetics* (3rd ed.). New York: Freeman.

Plomin, R., Owen, M. J., & McGuffin, P. (1994). The genetic basis of complex human behaviors. *Science, 264,* 1733–1739.

Pogge, D. L. (1992). Risk factors in child abuse and neglect. *Journal of Social Distress and the Homeless, 1,* 237–248.

Polaschek, D. L. L., Ward, T., & Hudon, S. M. (1997). Rape and rapists: Theory and treatment. *Clinical Psychology Review, 17,* 117–144.

Polcin, D. L. (1992). Issues in the treatment of dual diagnosis clients who have chronic mental illness. *Professional Psychology: Research and Practice, 23,* 30–37.

Polivy, J., & Herman, C. P. (1987). Diagnosis and treatment of normal eating. *Journal of Consulting and Clinical Psychology, 55,* 635–644.

Pollack, M. H., et al. (1996). Relationship of childhood anxiety to adult panic disorder: Correlates and influence on course. *American Journal of Psychiatry, 153,* 376–381.

Pollack, M. H., et al. (1998). Sertaline in the treatment of panic disorder. *Archives of General Psychiatry, 55,* 1010-1016.

Polledri, P. (1996). Munchausen syndrome by proxy and perversion of the maternal instinct. *Journal of Forensic Psychiatry, 7,* 551–562.

Pollock, V. E. (1992). Meta-analysis of subjective sensitivity to alcohol in sons of alcoholics. *American Journal of Psychiatry, 149,* 1534–1538.

Polymeropoulos, M. H., et al. (1996). Mapping of a gene for Parkinson's disease to chromosome 4q21–q23. *Science, 274,* 1197–1199.

Pope, H. G., Hudson, J. L., Yurgelun-Todd, D., & Hudson, M. S., (1984). Prevalence of anorexia nervosa and bulimia in three student populations. *International Journal of Eating Disorders, 3,* 45–51

Pope, H. G., Jr., Jones, J. M., Hudson, J., Cohen, B. M., & Gunderson, J. G. (1983). The validity of DSM-III borderline personality disorder. *Archives of General Psychiatry, 40,* 23–30.

Pope, H. G., Jr., & Yurgelun-Todd, D. (1996). The residual cognitive effects of heavy marijuana use in college students. *Journal of the American Medical Association, 275,* 521–527.

Pope, K.S. (1994, August). Sexual involvement between therapists and patients. *The Harvard Mental Health Letter, 11* (2), 5–6.

Popham, R. E., Schmidt, W., & Israelstam, S. (1984). Heavy alcohol consumption and physical health problems: A review of the epidemiologic evidence. In R. G. Smart et al. (Eds.), *Research advances in alcohol and drug problems,* (Vol. 8.). New York: Plenum Press.

Popper, K. (1985). Cited in Goleman (1985).

Posner, M. I. (1997). Introduction: Neuroimaging of cognitive processes. *Cognitive Psychology, 33,* 2–4.

Potter, J. D. (1997). Hazards and benefits of alcohol. *The New England Journal of Medicine, 337,* 1763–1764.

Potter, W. Z., & Rudorfer, M. V. (1993). Electroconvulsive therapy—a modern medical procedure. *New England Journal of Medicine, 328,* 882–883.

Poulakis, Z., & Wertheim, E. H. (1993). Relationships among dysfunctional congitions, depressive symptoms, and bulimic tendencies. *Cognitive Therapy and Research, 17,* 549–559.

Powchik, P. et al. (1998). Postmortem studies in schizophrenia. *Schizophrenia Bulletin, 24,* 325–341.

Powell, E. (1991). *Talking back to sexual pressure.* Minneapolis: CompCare Publishers.

Prescott, C. A., et al. (1994). Genetic and environmental influences on lifetime alcohol-related problems in a volunteer sample of older twins. *Journal of Studies on Alcohol, 55,* 184–202.

Press, A., et al. (1985, March 18). The war against pornography. *Newsweek,* pp. 58–66.

Pressman, M. R. (1986). Sleep and sleep disorders: An introduction. *Clinical Psychology Review, 6,* 1–9.

Price, L. H., & Heninger, G. R. (1994). Lithium in the treatment of mood disorders. *New England Journal of Medicine, 331,* 591–598.

Prichard, J. C. (1835). *Treatise on insanity.* London: Gilbert & Piper.

Prigatano, G. P. (1992). Personality disturbances associated with traumatic brain injury. *Journal of Consulting and Clinical Psychology, 60,* 360–368.

Prince, M. (1906). *The dissociation of a personality: A biographical study in abnormal psychology.* New York: Longmans, Green.

Prince, R., & Tcheng-Laroche, F. (1987). Culture-bound syndromes and international disease classification. *Culture, Medicine, and Psychiatry, 11,* 3–19.

Prins, P. J. M., & Hanewald, G. J. F. P. (1997). Self-statements of test-anxious children: Thought-listing and questionnaire approaches. *Journal of Consulting and Clinical Psychology, 65,* 440–447.

Prochaska, J. O., et al. (1994). Stages of change and decisional balance for 12 problem behaviors. *Health Psychology, 13,* 39–46.

Project MATCH Research Group. (1997). Matching alcoholism treatments to client heterogeneity: Project MATCH posttreatment drinking outcomes. *Journal of Studies on Alcohol, 58,* 7–29.

Prudic, J., et al. (1996). Resistance to antidepressant medications and short-term clinical response to ETC. *American Journal of Psychiatry, 153,* 985–992.

Public Broadcasting Service (1997, December 23). *Easy money: Frontline.* Author.

Pulley, B. (1997, December 7). Study finds legality spreads the compulsion to gamble. *The New York Times,* p. A17.

Pumariega, A. J. (1986). Acculturation and eating attitudes in adolescent girls: A comparitive correlational study. *Journal of the American Academy of Child Psychiatry, 25,* 276–279.

Putnam, F. W., & Carlson, E. B. (1994). "Screening for mulitple personality disorder with the Dissociative Experiences Scale": A reply. *American Journal of Psychiatry, 151,* 1249–1250.

Putnam, F. W., Guroff, J. J., Silberman, E. K., Barban, L., & Post, R. M. (1986). The clinical phenomenology of multiple personality disorder: Review of 100 recent cases. *Journal of Clinical Psychiatry, 47,* 285–293.

Pyeritz, R. E. (1997). Family history and genetic risk factors. *Journal of the American Medical Association, 278,* 1284–1285.

Pyle, R. L., Halvorson, P. A., & Goff, G. M. (1986). The increasing prevalence of bulimia in freshman college students. *International Journal of Eating Disorders, 5,* 631–647.

Pyszczynski, T., & Greenberg, G. (1985). Depression and preference for self-focusing stimuli after success and failure. *Journal of Personality and Social Psychology, 49,* 1066–1075.

Pyszczynski, T., & Greenberg, G. (1986). Evidence for a depressive self-focusing style. *Journal of Research in Personality, 20,* 95–106.

Pyszczynski, T., & Greenberg, J. (1987). Self-regulatory perseveration and the depressive self-focusing style: A self-awareness theory of reactive depression. *Psychological Bulletin, 102,* 122–138.

Q

Quay, H. C. (1965). Psychopathic personality as pathological stimulation seeking. *American Journal of Psychiatry, 122,* 180–183.

Quitkin, F. M., et al. (1996). Chronological milestones to guide drug change. When should clinicians switch antidepressants? *Archives of General Psychiatry, 53,* 785–792.

R

Rabkin, J. G., et al. (1991). Depression, distress, lymphocyte subsets, and human immunodeficiency virus symptoms on two occasions in HIV-positive homosexual men. *Archives of General Psychiatry, 48,* 111–119.

Rabkin, J. G., et al. (1997). Stability of mood despite HIV illness progression in a group of homosexual men. *American Journal of Psychiatry, 154,* 231–238.

The race for Alzheimer's treatments. (1997, May). *Harvard Health Letter, 22,*1–3.

Rachman, S. J. (1994). Overprediction of fear: A review. *Behaviour Research and Therapy, 32,* 683–690.

Rachman, S., & Bichard, S. (1988). The overprediction of fear. *Clinical Psychology Review, 8,* 303–312.

Rachman, S., & Levitt, K. (1985). Panics and their consequences. *Behaviour Research and Therapy, 23,* 600.

Rachman, S., Levitt, K., & Lopatka, C. (1988). Experimental analyses of panic: III. Claustrophobic subjects. *Behaviour Research and Therapy, 26,* 41–52.

Rajfer, J., et al. (1992). Nitric oxide as a mediator of relaxation of the corpus cavernosum in response to nonadrenergic, noncholinergic neurotransmission. *The New England Journal of Medicine, 326,* 90–94.

Rajkowska, G., Selemon, L. D., & Goldman-Rakic, P. S. (1998). Neuronal and glial somal size in the prefrontal cortex. *Archives of General Psychiatry, 55,* 215–224.

Rakel, R. E. (1993). Insomnia: Concerns of the family physician. *Journal of Family Practice, 36,* 551–558.

Rao, K., DiClemente, R. J., & Ponton, L. E. (1992). Child sexual abuse of Asians compared with other populations. *Journal of the American Academy of Child and Adolescent Psychiatry, 31,* 880–886.

Rao, S. M., Huber, S. J., & Bornstein, R. A. (1992). Emotional changes with multiple sclerosis and Parkinson's disease. *Journal of Consulting and Clinical Psychology, 60,* 369-378.

Rapee, R. (1985). Distinction between panic disorder and generalized anxiety disorder: Clinical presentation. *Australian and New Zealand Journal of Psychiatry, 19,* 227–232.

Rapee, R. M. (1987). The psychological treatment of panic attacks: Theoretical conceptualization and review of evidence. *Clinical Psychology Review, 7,* 427–438.

Rapee, R. M. (1991). Generalized anxiety disorder: A review of clinical features and theoretical concepts. *Clinical Psychology Review, 11,* 419–440.

Rapee, R. M. (1994). Detection of somatic sensations in panic disorder. *Behaviour Research and Therapy, 32,* 825–831.

Rapee, R. M., Litwin, E. M., & Barlow, D. H. (1990). Impact of life events on subjects with panic disorder and on comparison subjects. *American Journal of Psychiatry, 147,* 640–644.

Rapin, I. (1997). Autism. *The New England Journal of Medicine, 337,* 97–104.

Rasmussen, T., & Milner, B. (1975). Clinical and surgical studies of the cerebral speech areas in man. In K. J. Zulch, O. Creutzfeldt, & G. C. Galbraith (Eds.), *Cerebral localization.* Berlin: Springer-Verlag.

Rathus, S. A. (1978). Treatment of recalcitrant ejaculatory incompetence. *Behavior Therapy, 9,* 962.

Rathus, S. A. (1993). *Psychology* (5th ed.). Fort Worth: Harcourt Brace Jovanovich.

Rathus, S. A., & Fichner-Rathus, L. (1994). *Making the most of college* (2nd ed.). Englewood Cliffs, NJ: Prentice Hall.

Rathus, S. A., & Nevid, J. S. (1977). *Behavior therapy.* Garden City, NY: Doubleday.

Rathus, S. A., Nevid, J. S., & Fichner-Rathus, L. (1993) *Human sexuality in a world of diversity.* Boston: Allyn & Bacon.

Rathus, S. A., Senna, J., & Siegel, L. (1974). Delinquent behavior and academic investment among suburban youth. *Adolescence, 9,* 481–494.

Ratti, L. A., Humphrey, L. L., & Lyons, J. S. (1996). Structural analysis of families with a polydrug-dependent, bulimic, or normal adolescent daughter. *Journal of Consulting & Clinical Psychology, 64,* 1255–1262.

Rauch, S. L. (1996). A symptom provocation study of posttraumatic stress disorder using positron emission tomography and script-driven imagery. *Archives of General Psychiatry, 53,* 380–387.

Rauch, S. L., & Jenike, M. A. (1998). Pharmacological treatment of obsessive compulsive disorder. In P. E. Nathan & J. M. Gorman (Eds.), *A guide to treatments that work* (pp. 358–376). New York: Oxford University Press.

Rauschenberger, S. L., & Lynn, S. J. (1995). Fantasy proneness, DSM-III-R Axis I psychopathology, and dissociation. *Journal of Abnormal Psychology, 104,* 373–380.

Ravussin, E., et al. (1988). Reduced rate of energy expenditure as a risk factor for body-weight gain. *The New England Journal of Medicine, 318,* 467–472.

Rax, S. (1993). Structural cerebral pathology in schizophrenia: Regional or diffuse? *Journal of Abnormal Psychology, 102,* 445–452.

Razin, A. M., Swencionis, C., & Zohman, L. R. (1986). Reduction of physiological, behavioral, and self-report responses in Type A behavior: A preliminary report. *International Journal of Psychiatry in Medicine, 16,* 31–47.

Read, J. (1997). Child abuse and psychosis: A literature review and implications for professional practice. *Professional Psychology: Research and Practice, 28,* 448–456.

Redd, W. H. (1995). Behavioral research in cancer as a model for health psychology. *Health Psychology, 14,* 99–100.

Reed, G.M., et al. (In press). Negative HIV-specific expectancies and AIDS-related bereavement as predictors of symptom onset in asymptomatic HIV seropositive gay men. *Health Psychology.*

Regier, D. A., et al. (1998). Limitations of diagnostic criteria and assessment instruments for mental disorders: Implications for research and policy. *Archives of General Psychiatry, 55,* 109–115.

Reich, J. (1987). Prevalence of DSM-III-R self-defeating (masochistic) personality disorder in normal and outpatient populations. *Journal of Nervous and Mental Diseases, 175,* 52–54.

Reich, J. (1996). The morbidity of DSM-III-R dependent personality disorder. *Journal of Nervous & Mental Disease, 184,* 22–26.

Reich, J., & Noyes, R. (1986). Letters to the Editor: Differentiating schizoid and avoidant personality disorders. *American Journal of Psychiatry, 143,* 1061–1063.

Reichman, M. E. (1994). Alcohol and breast cancer. *Alcohol Health and Research World, 18,* 182–183.

Reid, B. V., & Whitehead, T. L. (1992). Introduction. In T. L. Whitehead & B. V. Reid (Eds.), *Gender constructs and social issues* (pp. 1–9). Chicago: University of Illinois.

Reid, J. B. (1993). Prevention of conduct disorder before and after school entry: Relating interventions to developmental findings. *Development and Psychopathology, 5,* 243–262.

Reid, W. H., & Balis, G. U. (1987). Evaluation of the violent patient. In R. E. Hales and A. J. Frances (Eds.), *American Psychiatric Association Annual Review* (Vol. 6). Washington, D C: American Psychiatric Press.

Reid, W. J. (1986). Antisocial personality. In R. Michels and J. O. Cavenar, Jr. (Eds.), *Psychiatry* (Vol. 1). New York: Basic Books.

Renfrey, G. S. (1992). Cognitive-behavior therapy and the Native American client. *Behavior Therapy, 23,* 321–340.

Reinisch, J. M. (1990). *The Kinsey Institute new report on sex: What you must know to be sexually literate.* New York: St. Martin's Press.

Reisberg, B., Ferris, S. H., DeLeon, M. J., & Crook, T. (1982). The Global Deterioration Scale for Assessment of Primary Degenerative Dementia. *American Journal of Psychiatry, 139,* 1136–1139.

Reisberg, B., et al. (1986). Assessment of presenting symptoms. In L. W. Poon (Ed.), *Handbook for clinical memory assessment of older adults.* (pp. 108–128). Washington, D C: American Psychological Association.

Reisner, A. D. (1994). Multiple personality disorder diagnosis: A house of cards? *American Journal of Psychiatry, 151,* 629.

Reisner, A. D. (1996). Repressed memories: True and false. *Psychological Record, 46,* 563–579.

Reiss, B. F. (1980). Psychological tests in homosexuality. In J. Marmor (Ed.), *Homosexual behavior* (pp. 296–311). New York: Basic Books.

Reiss, S. (1987). Theoretical perspectives on the fear of anxiety. *Clinical Psychology Review, 7,* 585–596.

Reiss, S., Peterson, R. A., Gursky, D. M., & McNally, R. J. (1986). Anxiety sensitivity, anxiety frequency and the predictions of fearfulness. *Behaviour Research and Therapy, 24,* 1–8.

Reiss, S., & Valenti-Hein, D. (1994). Development of a psychopathology rating scale for children with mental retardation. *Journal of Consulting and Clinical Psychology, 62,* 28–33.

Reinecke, M. A., Ryan, N. E., & DuBois, D. L. (1998). Cognitive-behavioral therapy of depression and depressive symptoms during adolescence: A review and meta-analysis. *Journal of the American Academy of Child and Adolescent Psychiatry, 37,* 26–34.

Renneberg, B., et al. (1990). Intensive behavioral group treatment of avoidant personality disorder. *Behavior Therapy, 21,* 363–377.

Report: Adolescent suicide rates rise. (1995, April 21). *New York Newsday,* p. A54.

Researchers identify cognitive process that contributes to gambling behavior. (1997, May). *APA News Release.*

Resick, P. A., & Schnicke, M. K. (1990). Treating symptoms in adult victims of sexual assault. *Journal of Interpersonal Violence, 5,* 488–506.

Resnick, M., et al. (1992, March 24). *Journal of the American Medical Association.* Cited in Young Indians prone to suicide, study finds. *The New York Times,* March 25, 1992, p. D24.

Review Panel. (1981). Coronary-prone behavior and coronary heart disease: A critical review. *Circulation, 63,* 1199–1215.

Rexrode, K. M., et al. (1997). A prospective study of body mass index, weight change, and risk of stroke in women. *Journal of the American Medical Association, 277,* 1539–1545.

Rey, J. M. (1993). Oppositional defiant disorder. *American Journal of Psychiatry, 150,* 1769–1778.

Rey, J. M. (1994). Comorbidity between disruptive disorders and depression in referred adolescents. *New Zealand Journal of Psychiatry, 28,* 106–113.

Rey, J. M., Stuart, G. W., Platt, J. M., Bashir, M. R., & Richards, I. M. (1988). DSM-III Axis IV revisited. *American Journal of Psychiatry, 145,* 286–292.

Reynolds, C. F., III, et al. (1996). Treatment outcome in recurrent major depression: A post hoc comparison of elderly ("Young Old") and midlife patients. *American Journal of Psychiatry, 153,* 1288–1292.

Ribeiro, S. C. M., et al. (1993). The DST as a predictor of outcome in depression: A meta-analysis. *American Journal of Psychiatry, 150,* 1618–1629.

Rich, C. L., Fowler, R. C., Fogarty, L. A., & Young, D. (1988). San Diego Suicide Study: III. Relationships between diagnoses and stressors. *Archives of General Psychiatry, 45,* 589–592.

Rich, C. L., Ricketts, J. E., Thaler, R. C., & Young, D. (1988). Some differences between men and women who commit suicide. *American Journal of Psychiatry, 145,* 718–722.

Richards, J. C., Edgar, L. V., & Gibbon, P. (1996). Cardiac acuity in panic disorder. *Cognitive Therapy and Research, 20,* 361–376.

Ridley, C. R. (1984). Clinical treatment of the nondisclosing Black client: A therapeutic paradox. *American Psychologist, 39,* 1234–1244.

Riese, W. (1954). Auto-observation of aphasia: Reported by an eminent 19th century medical scientist. *Bulletin of the History of Medicine, 28,* 237–242.

Riether, A. M., & Stoudemire, A. (1988). Psychogenic fugue states: A review. *Southern Medical Journal, 81,* 568–571.

Riley, V. (1981). Psychoneuroendocrine influences on immunocompetence and neoplasia. *Science, 212,* 1100–1109.

Rimer, S. (1993, December 13). With millions taking Prozac, a legal drug culture arises. *The New York Times,* p. A1, B8.

Rimland, B. (1977). Comparative effects of treatment on child's behavior (drugs, therapies, schooling and several non-treatment events.). *Institute for Child Behaviour Research,* Publication 34.

Rimland, B. (1978). The savant capabilities of autistic children and their cognitive implications. In G. Serban (Ed.), *Cognitive defects in the development of mental illness.* New York: Brunner-Mazel.

Rind, B., Tromovitch, P., & Bauserman, R. (1998). Meta-analytic examination of assumed properties of child sexual abuse using college samples. *Psychological Bulletin, 124,* 22–53.

Ritvo, E. R., & Ritvo, R. (1992). "The UCLA-University of Utah Epidemiologic Survey of Autism: The etiologic role of rare diseases": Reply. *American Journal of Psychiatry, 149,* 146–147.

Ritvo, E. R. et al. (1989). The UCLA-University of Utah Epidemiologic Survey of autism: Prevalence. *American Journal of Psychiatry, 146,* 194–199.

Rivara, F. P., et al. (1997). Alcohol and illicit drug abuse and the risk of violent death in the home. *Journal of the American Medical Association, 278,* 569–575.

Rivas-Vazquez, R. A., & Blais, M. A. (1997). Selective serotonin reuptake inhibitors and atypical antidepressants: A review and update for psychologists. *Professional Psychology: Research and Practice, 28,* 526–536.

Robin, R. W., et al. (1997). Prevalence and characteristics of trauma and posttraumatic stress disorder in a southwestern American Indian community. *American Journal of Psychiatry, 154,* 1582–1588.

Robins, C. J., & Hayes, A. M. (1993). An appraisal of cognitive therapy. *Journal of Consulting and Clinical Psychology, 61,* 205–214.

Robins, L. N., Helzer, J. E., Croughan, J., & Ratcliff, K. S. (1981). National Institute of Mental Health: Diagnostic Interview Schedule. *Archives of General Psychiatry, 41,* 949–958.

Robins, L. N., Locke, B. Z., & Reiger, D. A. (1991). An overview of psychiatric disorders in America. In L. N. Robins & D. A. Regier (Eds.), *Psychiatric disorders in America: The Epidemiologic Catchment Area Study* (pp. 328–366). New York: The Free Press.

Robins, L. N., & Regier, D. A. (Eds.)(1991). *Psychiatric disorders in America: The Epidemiologic Catchment Area Study.* New York: The Free Press.

Robins, L. N., Tipp, J., & Przybeck, T. (1991). Antisocial personality. In L. N. Robins & D. A. Regier (Eds.), *Psychiatric disorders in America: The Epidemiologic Catchment Area Study* (pp. 258–290). New York: The Free Press.

Robins, L. N., et al. (1984). Lifetime prevalence of specific psychiatric disorders in three sites. *Archives of General Psychiatry, 41,* 949–958.

Robinson, D., et al. (1995). Reduced caudate nucleus volume in obsessive-compulsive disorder. *Archives of General Psychiatry, 52,* 393–398.

Robinson, T., et al. (1996). Ethnicity and body dissatisfaction: Are Hispanic and Asian girls at increased risk of eating disorders. *Journal of Adolescent Health, 19,* 384–393.

Rocha, B. A., et al. (1998). Increased vulnerability to cocaine in mice lacking the serotonin-1 B receptor. [Letter]. *Nature, 393,* 175.

Rock, C. L., & Curran-Celentano. J. (1996). Nutritional management of eating disorders. *The Psychiatric Clinics of North America, 19,* 701–713.

Rodin, J., Bartoshuk, L., Peterson, C., & Schank, D. (1990). Bulimia and taste: Possible interactions. *Journal of Abnormal Psychology, 99,* 32–39.

Rodin, J., & Slochower, J. (1976). Externality in the nonobese: The effects of environmental responsiveness on weight. *Journal of Personality and Social Psychology, 33,* 338–344.

Rodriguez, N., et al. (1997). Posttraumatic stress disorder in adult female survivors of childhood sexual abuse: A comparison study. *Journal of Consulting and Clinical Psychology, 65,* 53–59.

Rodríguez de Fonseca, F., et al. (1997). Activation of corticotropin-releasing factor in the limbic system during cannabinoid withdrawal. *Science, 276,* 2050–2054.

Roehrs, T. A., et al. (1992). Rebound insomnia in normals and patients with insomnia after abrupt and tapered discontinuation. *Psychopharmacology, 108,* 67–71.

Rogaeva, E., et al. (1998). Evidence for an Alzheimer disease susceptibility locus on chromosome 12 and for further locus heterogeneity. *Journal of the American Medical Association, 280,* 619–622.

Rogan, A. (1986, Fall). Recovery from alcoholism: Issues for black and Native American alcoholics. *Alcohol Health and Research World, 10,* 42–44.

Rogers, C. R. (1951). *Client-centered therapy.* Boston: Houghton Mifflin.

Rogers, R., et al. (1990). The clinical presentation of command hallucinations in a forensic population. *American Journal of Psychiatry, 147,* 1304–1307.

Rogler, L. H., Cortes, D. E., & Malgady, R. G. (1991). Acculturation and mental health status among Hispanics: Convergence and new directions for research. *American Psychologist, 46,* 584–597.

Rogosch, F. A., & Cicchetti, D. (1994). Illustrating the interface of family and peer relations through the study of child maltreatment. Special Issue: From family to peer group: Relations between relationships systems. *Social Development, 3,* 291–308.

Rohan, W. P. (1982). The concept of alcoholism: Assumptions and issues. In E. M. Pattison & E. Kaufman (Eds.), *Encyclopedic handbook of alcoholism* (pp. 31–39). New York: Gardner Press.

Rohde, P., Lewinsohn, P. M., & Seeley, J. R. (1991). Comorbidity of unipolar depression: II. Comorbidity with other mental disorders in adolescents and adults. *Journal of Abnormal Psychology, 101,* 214–222.

Romanczyk, R. G. (1986). Some thoughts on future trends in the education of individuals with autism. *The Behavior Therapist, 8,* 162–164.

Romano, E., & De-Luca, R. V. (1996). Characteristics of perpetrators with histories of sexual abuse. *International Journal of Offender Therapy and Comparative Criminology, 40,* 147–156.

Room, R. (1984). Alcohol and ethnography: A case of problem deflation? *Current Anthropology, 25* (2), 169–191.

Rorty, M., Yager, J., & Rossotto, E. (1994). Childhood sexual, physical and psychological abuse in bulimia nervosa. *American Journal of Psychiatry, 151,* 1122–1126.

Rose, J. (1996). Anger management: A group treatment program for people with mental retardation. *Journal of Developmental and Physical Disabilities, 8,* 133–149.

Rosen, L. A., et al. (1988). Effects of sugar (sucrose) on children's behavior. *Journal of Consulting and Clinical Psychology, 56,* 583–589.

Rosen, R. C., (1996). Erectile dysfunction: The medicalization of male sexuality. *Clinical Psychology Review, 16,* 497–519.

Rosen, R. C., & Leiblum, S. R. (1995). Treatment of sexual disorders in the 1990s: An integrated approach. *Journal of Consulting and Clinical Psychology, 63,* 877–890.

Rosenbaum, M., & Patterson, K. M. (1995). Group psychotherapy in historical perspective. In B. Bongar & L. E. Beutler (Eds.), *Comprehensive textbook of psychotherapy: Theory and practice* (pp. 173–188). New York: Oxford University Press.

Rosenberg D. R., et al. (1997a). Frontostriatal measurement in treatment-naive children with obsessive-compulsive disorder. *Archives of General Psychiatry, 54,* 824–830.

Rosenberg, D. R., et al. (1997b). Oculomotor response inhibition abnormalities in pediatric obsessive-compulsive disorder. *Archives of General Psychiatry, 54,* 831–838.

Rosenberg, H. (1993). Prediction of controlled drinking by alcoholics and problem drinkers. *Psychological Bulletin, 113,* 129–130.

Rosenberg, J. L., et al. (1997). Applying science to violence prevention. *Journal of the American Medical Association, 277,* 1641–1642.

Rosenberg, M. L. (1993). Promoting safety and nonviolent conflict resolution in adolescence. In S. G. Millstein, A. C. Petersen, & E. O. Nightingale (Eds.), *Promoting adolescent health: Third symposium on research opportunities in adolescence.* New York: Carnegie Council on Adolescent Development.

Rosencheck, R., Fontana, A. & Cottrol, C. (1995). Effects of clinician-veteran racial pairing in the treatment of posttraumatic stress disorder. *American Journal of Psychiatry, 152,* 555–563.

Rosenfarb, I. S., et al. (1995). Expressed emotion and subclinical psychopathology observable within the transactions between schizophrenic patients and their family members. *Journal of Abnormal Psychology, 104,* 259–267.

Rosenfeld, B. D. (1992). Court-ordered treatment of spouse abuse. *Clinical Psychology Review, 12,* 205–226.

Rosenheck, R., & Fontana, A. (1994). A model of homelessness among male veterans of the Vietnam War generation. *American Journal of Psychiatry, 151,* 421–427.

Rosenheck, R., et al. (1997). A comparison of clozapine and haloperidol in hospitalized patients with refractory schizophrenia. *The New England Journal of Medicine, 337,* 809–815.

Rosenman, R. H., Brand, R. J., Jenkins, D. D., Friedman, M., Straus, R., & Wurm, M. (1975). Coronary heart disease in the Western Collaborative Group Study: Final follow-up experience of $8\frac{1}{2}$ years. *Journal of the American Medical Association, 233,* 872–877.

Rosenthal, D., et al. (1968). Schizophrenics' offspring reared in adoptive homes. In D. Rosenthal & S. S. Kety (Eds.), *The transmission of schizophrenia.* Oxford: Pergamon Press.

Rosenthal, D., et al. (1975). Parent-child relationships and psychopathological disorder in the child. *Archives of General Psychiatry, 32,* 466–476.

Rosenthal, E. (1990, August 28). The spread of AIDS: A mystery unravels. *The New York Times,* pp. C1, C2.

Rosenthal, E. (1993, April 9). Who will turn violent? Hospitals have to guess. *The New York Times,* pp. A1, C12.

Rosenthal, R. J. (1992). Pathological gambling. *Psychiatric Annals, 22,* 72–78.

Roskies, E., et al. (1986). The Montreal Type A intervention project: Major findings. *Health Psychology, 5,* 45–69.

Rosman, B. L., Minuchin, S., & Liebman, R. (1976). Input and outcome of family therapy of anorexia nervosa. In J. L. Claghorn (Ed.), *Successful psychotherapy.* New York: Brunner/Mazel.

Ross, A. D. (1981). *Psychological disorders of childhood: A behavioral approach to theory, research & practice* (2d. ed.). New York: McGraw Hill.

Ross, C. A. (1989). *Multiple personality disorder: Diagnosis, clinical features and treatment.* New York: Wiley.

Ross, C. A., Joshi, S., & Currie, R. (1990). Dissociative experiences in the general population. *American Journal of Psychiatry, 147,* 1547–1552.

Ross, C. A., Norton, G. R., & Wozney, K. (1989). Multiple personality disorder: An analysis of 236 cases. *Canadian Journal of Psychiatry, 34,* 413–418.

Ross, C. A., et al. (1990). Structured interview data on 102 cases of multiple personality disorder from four centers. *American Journal of Psychiatry, 147,* 596–601.

Ross, C. A., et al. (1991). The frequency of multiple personality disorder among psychiatric inpatients. *American Journal of Psychiatry, 148,* 1717–1720.

Ross, M., & Need, J. (1989). Effects of adequacy of gender reassignment surgery on psychological adjustment: A follow-up of fourteen male-to-female patients. *Archives of Sexual Behavior, 18,* 145–153.

Ross, S. M. (1996). Risk of physical abuse to children of spouse-abusing parents. *Child Abuse and Neglect, 20,* 589–598.

Rost, K. M., Akins, R. N., Brown, F. W., & Smith, G. R. (1992). The comorbidity of DSM-III-R personality disorders in somatization disorder. *General Hospital Psychiatry, 14,* 322–326.

Rothbaum, B. O. (1996). Virtual reality exposure therapy in the treatment of fear of flying: A case report. *Behaviour Research and Therapy, 34,* 477–481.

Rothbaum, B. O., et al. (1995). Effectiveness of computer-generated (virtual reality) graded exposure in the treatment of acrophobia. *American Journal of Psychiatry, 152,* 626–628.

Rothblum, E. (1983). Sex role stereotypes and depression in women. In V. Franks & E. Rothblum (Eds.), *The stereotyping of women: Its effects on mental health* (pp. 83–111). New York: Springer.

Rotheram-Borus, M. J., Trautman, P. D., Dopkins, S. C., & Shrout, P. E. (1990). Cognitive style and pleasant activities among female adolescent suicide attempters. *Journal of Consulting and Clinical Psychology, 58,* 554–561.

Rotter, J. B. (1966). Generalized expectancies for internal vs external control of reinforcement. *Psychological Monographs, 1,* 210–609.

Rotter, J. B. (1972). Beliefs, social attitudes, and behavior: A social learning analysis. In J. B. Rotter, J. E. Chance, & E. J. Phares (Eds.), *Applications of a social learning theory of personality.* New York: Holt, Rinehart and Winston.

Rousseau, F., et al., (1991). Direct diagnosis by DNA analysis of the fragile X syndrome of mental retardation. *New England Journal of Medicine, 325,* 1673–1681.

Rowland, D. L., Cooper, S. E., & Slob, A. K. (1996). Genital and psychoaffective response to erotic stimulation in sexually functional and dysfunctional men. *Journal of Abnormal Psychology, 105,* 194–203.

Roy, A., et al. (1991). Suicide in twins. *Archives of General Psychiatry, 48,* 29–32.

Roy-Byrne, P., et al. (1997). Adult attention-deficit hyperactivity disorder: Assessment guidelines based on clinical presentation to a specialty clinic. *Comprehensive Psychiatry, 38,* 133–140.

Roy-Byrne, P. P., & Cowley, D. S. (1998). Pharacological treatment of panic, generalized anxiety, and phobic disorders. In P.E. Nathan & J. M. Gorman (Eds.), *A guide to treatments that work* (pp. 319-338). New York: Oxford University Press.

Rozin, P., & Fallon, A. (1988). Body image, attitudes to weight, and misperceptions of figure preferences of the opposite sex: A comparison of men and women in two generations. *Journal of Abnormal Psychology, 97,* 342–345.

Rubin, L. J. (1996). Childhood sexual abuse: False accusations of "false memory"? *Professional Psychology: Research and Practice, 27,* 447–451.

Ruderman, A. J., & Besbeas, M. (1992). Psychological characteristics of dieters and bulimics. *Journal of Abnormal Psychology, 101,* 383–390.

Ruiz, R. A. (1981). Cultural and historical perspectives in counseling Hispanics. In D. W. Sue (Ed.), *Counseling the culturally different: Theory and practice* (pp. 186–215). New York: Wiley.

Rush, A. J., & Weissenburger, J. E. (1994). Do thinking patterns predict depressive symptoms? *Cognitive Therapy and Research, 10,* 225–236.

Russo, N. F. (1990). Overview: Forging research priorities for women's mental health. *American Psychologist, 45,* 368–373.

Rutter, M. (1983). Cognitive deficits in the pathogenesis of autism. *Journal of Child Psychology & Psychiatry, 24,* 513–531.

Rutter, M., & Garmezy, N. (1983). Developmental psychopathology. In P. H. Mussen (Ed.), *Handbook of child psychology: Vol. 4, socialization, personality, and social development* (pp. 776–911). New York: Wiley.

Ryan, G. (1993). Working with perpetrators of sexual abuse and domestic violence. *Pastoral Psychology, 41,* 303–319.

Ryan, N. D., et al. (1987). The clinical picture of major depression in children and adolescents. *Archives of General Psychiatry, 44,* 854–861.

S

Sabol, S. Z., et al. (1999). A genetic association for cigarette smoking behavior. *Health Psychology, 18,* 7–13.

Sachdev, P., & Hay, P. (1996). Site and size of lesion and psychosurgical outcome in obsessive-compulsive disorder: A magnetic resonance imaging study. *Biological Psychiatry, 39,* 739–742.

Sack, K. (1995, March 21). Pataki, in switch, seeks cuts in programs for mentally ill. *The New York Times,* pp. A1, B6.

Sack, W. H., Clarke, G.N., & Seeley, J. (1996). Multiple forms of stress in Cambodian adolescent refugees. *Child Development, 67,* 107–116.

Sack, W. H., et al. (1994). The Khmer Adolescent Project: I. Epidemiological findings in two generations of Cambodian refugees. *Journal of Nervous and Mental Disease, 182,* 387–395.

Sackheim, H. A., Prudic, J., & Devanand, D. P. (1990). Treatment of medication-resistant depression with electroconvulsive therapy. In A. Tasman, et al., (Eds.), *Review of psychiatry,* Vol. 9. Washington, DC: American Psychiatric Press.

Sackheim, H. A., et al. (1994). Effects of stimulus intensity and electrode placement on the efficacy and cognitive effects of electroconvulsive therapy. *New England Journal of Medicine, 328,* 839–846.

Sackeim, H.A., et al. (1996). The effects of electroconvulsive therapy on quantitative electroencephalograms: Relationship to clinical outcome. *Archives of General Psychiatry, 53,* 814–824.

Sacks, O. (1985a). *The man who mistook his wife for a hat and other clinical tales.* New York: Summit.

Sacks, O. (1985b, February 20). The twins. *New York Review of Books.* pp. 16–20.

Sadker, M., & Sadker, D. (1985). Sexism in the schoolroom of the 1980s. *Psychology Today, 19,* 54–57.

Safran, J. D., & Messer, S. B. (1997). Psychotherapy integration: A postmodern critique. *Clinical Psychology: Science and Practice, 4,* 140–152.

St. Lawrence, J. S., et al. (1995a). Comparison of education versus behavioral skills training interventions in lowering sexual HIV-risk behavior of substance-dependent adolescents. *Journal of Consulting and Clinical Psychology, 63,* 154–157.

St. Lawrence, J. S., et al. (1995b). Cognitive-behavioral intervention to reduce African American adolescents' risk for HIV infection. *Journal of Consulting and Clinical Psychology, 63,* 221–237.

Sajjad, S. H. A. (1991). Classification of koro. *American Journal of Psychiatry, 148,* 1279.

Sakheim, D. K. (1984). *Waking assessment of erectile potential: The validation of a laboratory procedure to aid in the differential diagnosis of psychogenic and organic impotence.* Unpublished doctoral dissertation, State University of New York at Albany.

Salgado de Snyder, V. N. (1987). Factors associated with acculturative stress and depressive symptomatology among married Mexican immigrant women. *Psychology of Women Quarterly, 11,* 475–488.

Salgado de Snyder, V. N., Cervantes, R. C., & Padilla, A. M. (1990). Gender and ethnic differences in psychosocial stress and generalized distress among Hispanics. *Sex Roles, 22,* 441–453.

Salisbury, D. F., et al. (1998). First-episode schizophrenic psychosis differs from first-episode affective psychosis and controls in P300 amplitude over left temporal lobe. *Archives of General Psychiatry, 55,* 173–180.

Salkovskis, P. M., & Clark, D. M. (1993). Panic disorder and hypochondriasis. Special Issue: Panic, cognitions and sensations. *Advances in Behaviour Research and Therapy, 15,* 23–48.

Salkovskis, P. M., Clark, D. M., & Hackmann, A. (1991). Treatment of panic attacks using cognitive therapy without exposure or breathing retraining. *Behaviour Research & Therapy, 29,* 161–166.

Salkovskis, P. M., & Warwick, H. M. (1986). Morbid preoccupations, health anxiety. and reassurance: A cognitive-behavioral approach to hypochondriasis. *Behaviour Research and Therapy, 24,* 597–602.

Salokangas, R. K. R., & Saarinen, S. (1998). Deinstitutionalization and schizophrenia in Finland: I. Discharged patients and their care. *Schizophrenia Bulletin, 24,* 457–467.

Saltz, E., et al. (1994). Attacking the personal fable: Role-play and its effect on teen attitudes toward sexual abstinence. *Youth and Society, 26,* 223–242.

Salzman, C., & Gutfreund, M. J. (1986). Clinical techniques and research strategies for studying depression and memory. In L. W. Poon (Ed.), *Handbook for clinical memory assessment of older adults* (pp. 257–267). Washington, DC: American Psychological Association.

Samara, F. E., et al. (1997). Effect of valproate on the pharmacokinetics and pharmacodynamics of lorazepam. *Journal of Clinical Pharamacology, 37,* 422–450.

Sameroff, A., Seifer, R., Zax, M., & Barocas, R. (1987). Early indicators of developmental risk: Rochester Longitudinal Study. *Schizophrenia Bulletin, 13,* 383–394.

Sammons, M. T., & Brown, A. B. (1997). The Department of Defense psychopharmacology demonstration project: An evolving program for postdoctoral education in psychology. *Professional Psychology: Research and Practice, 28,* 107–112.

Sanchez, E. G., & Mohl, P. C. (1992). Psychotherapy with Mexican-American patients. *American Journal of Psychiatry, 149,* 626–630.

Sanchez-Craig, M., Annis, H. M., Bornet, A. R., & MacDonald, K. R. (1984). Random assignment to abstinence or controlled drinking: Evaluation of a cognitive-behavioral program for problem drinkers. *Journal of Consulting and Clinical Psychology, 52,* 390–403.

Sanchez-Craig, M., & Wilkinson, D.A. (1986/1987). Treating problem drinkers who are not severely dependent on alcohol. *Drugs and Society, 1,* 39–67.

Sanders, B., & Green, J. A. (1995). The factor structure of the Dissociative Experiences Scale in college students. *Dissociation Progress in the Dissociative Disorders, 7,* 23–27.

Sanders, J. (1974, September). *An autistic child in residential treatment.* Paper presented at American Psychological Association meeting, New Orleans.

Sanders, S. A., Reinisch, J. M., & McWhirter, D. P. (1990). Homosexuality/heterosexuality: An overview. In D. P. McWhirter, S. A. Sanders, & J. M. Reinisch (Eds.) *Homosexuality/Heterosexuality: Concepts of sexual orientation* (pp. xix–xxvii). New York: Oxford University Press.

Sanderson, W. C., & Barlow, D. H. (1990). A description of patients diagnosed with DSM-III-R generalized anxiety disorder. *Journal of Nervous & Mental Disease, 178,* 588–591.

Sano, M., et al. (1997). A controlled trial of selegiline, alpha-tocopherol, or both as treatment for Alzheimer's disease. *New England Journal of Medicine, 336,* 1216–1222.

Santiago, J. M., McCall-Perez, F., Gorcery, M., & Beigel, A. (1985). Long-term psychological effects of rape in 35 rape victims. *American Journal of Psychiatry, 142,* 1338–1340.

Sar, V., et al. (1996). Structured interview data on 35 cases of dissociative identity disorder in Turkey. *American Journal of Psychiatry, 153,* 1329–1333.

Sarbin, T. R. (1994). Dissociation: State, trait or skill? *Contemporary Hypnosis, 11,* 47–54.

Sarwer, D. B., & Durlak, J. A. (1996). Childhood sexual abuse as a predictor of adult female sexual dysfunction: A study of couples seeking sex therapy. *Child Abuse and Neglect, 20,* 963–972.

Sass, L. (1982, August 22). The borderline personality. *The New York Times Magazine,* pp. 12–15, 66–67.

Sateia, M. J. (1987). Behavioral modification in the treatment of smoking. *Psychiatric Medicine, 5,* 375–387.

Satel, S. L., Soutwick, S., M., & Gawin, F. H. (1991). Clinical features of cocaine-induced paranoia. *American Journal of Psychiatry, 148,* 495–498.

Satir, V. (1967). *Conjoint family therapy.* (rev. ed.). Palo Alto, CA: Science and Behavior Books.

Sato, T. (1997). Seasonal affective disorder and phototherapy: A critical review. *Professional Psychology: Research and Practice, 28,* 164–169.

Sauter, A. W., & Nevid, J. S. (1991). Work skills training with chronic schizophrenic sheltered workers. *Rehabilitation Psychology, 36,* 255–264.

Saypol, D. C., Peterson, G. A., Howards, S. S., & Yanzel, J. J. (1983). Impotence: Are the newer diagnostic methods a necessity? *Journal of Urology, 130,* 260–262.

Scarr, S., et al. (1981). Personality resemblance among adolescents and their parents in biologically related and adoptive families. *Journal of Personality and Social Psychology, 40,* 885–898.

Schachter, S., & Latané, B. (1964). Crime, cognition, and the autonomic nervous system. In D. Levine (Ed.), *Nebraska symposium on motivation* (Vol. 12, pp. 221–273). Lincoln, NE: University of Nebraska Press.

Schafer, D. W. (1986). Recognizing multiple personality patients. *American Journal of Psychotherapy, 40,* 500–510.

Schafer, J. & Brown, S. (1991). Marijuana and cocaine effect expectancies and drug use patterns. *Journal of Consulting and Clinical Psychology, 59,* 558–565.

Scheff, T. J. (1966). *Being mentally ill: A sociological theory.* Chicago: Aldine.

Scheflin, A. W., & Brown, D. (1996). Repressed memory or dissociative amnesia: What the science says. *Journal of Psychiatry and Law, 24,* 143–188.

Scheier, L., M., Botvin, G. J., & Baker, E. (1997). Risk and protective factors as predictors of adolescent alcohol involvement and transitions in alcohol use: A prospective analysis. *Journal of Studies on Alcohol, 58,* 652–7667.

Scheier, M. F., & Carver, C. S. (1985). Optimism, coping, and health: Assessment and implications of generalized outcome expectancies. *Health Psychology, 4,* 219–247.

Scheier, M. F., & Carver, C. S. (1992). Effects of optimisim on psychological and physical well-being: Theoretical overview and empirical update. Special issue: Cognitive perspectives in health psychology. *Cognitive Therapy and Research, 16,* 201–228.

Scheier, M. F., et al. (1989). Dispositional optimism and recovery from coronary artery bypass surgery: The beneficial effects on physical and psychological well-being. *Journal of Personality and Social Psychology, 57,* 1024–1040.

Schepis, M. R., Reid, D. H., & Fitzgerald, J. R. (1987). Group instruction with profoundly retarded persons: Acquisition, generalization, and maintenance of a remunerative work skill. *Journal of Applied Behavior Analysis, 20,* 97–105.

Schiavi, R. C. (1990). Chronic alcoholism and male sexual dysfunction. *Journal of Sex and Marital Therapy, 16,* 23–33.

Schizophrenia Update—Part I (1995, June). *The Harvard Mental Health Letter, 11,* 1–4.

Schmahl, D. P., Lichtenstein, E., & Harris, D. E. (1972). Successful treatment of habitual smokers with warm, smoky air and rapid smoking. *Journal of Consulting and Clinical Psychology, 38,* 105–111.

Schmauk, F. J. (1970). Punishment, arousal, and avoidance learning in sociopaths. *Journal of Abnormal Psychology, 76,* 325–335.

Schmidt, N. B., Lerew, D. R., & Jackson, R. J. (1997). The role of anxiety sensitivity in the pathogenesis of panic: Prospective evaluation of spontaneous panic attacks during acute stress. *Journal of Abnormal Psychology, 106,* 355–364.

Schmidt, N. B., Telch, M. J., & Jaimez, T. L. (1996). Biological challenge manipulation of PCO_2 levels: A test of Klein's (1993) suffocation alarm theory of panic. *Journal of Abnormal Psychology, 105,* 446–454.

Schmidt, N. B., Trakowski, J. H., & Staab, J. P. (1997). Extinction of panicogenic effects of a 35% CO_2 challenge in patients with panic disorder. *Journal of Abnormal Psychology, 106,* 630–638.

Schmitt, E. (1995, May 29). Victorious in war, not yet at peace. *The New York Times,* Section 4, pp. 1, 4.

Schneider, K. (1957). Primäre und sekundäre Symptome bei der Schizophrenia. *Fortschritte der Neurologie Psychiatrie, 25,* 487–490.

Schneider, L. S. (1996). Overview of generalized anxiety disorder in the elderly. *Journal of Clinical Psychiatry, 57* (Suppl 7), 34–45.

Schneier, F. R., Wexler, K. B., & Liebowitz, M. R. (1997). Social phobia and stuttering. *American Journal of Psychiatry, 154,* 131.

Schoenfeld, H., Margolin, J., & Baum, S. (1987). Münchausen syndrome as a suicide equivalent: Abolition of syndrome by psychotherapy. *American Journal of Psychotherapy, 41,* 604–612.

Schoenman, T. J. (1984). The mentally ill witch in text books of abnormal psychology: Current status and implications of a fallacy. *Professional Psychiatry, 15,* 299–314.

Scholing, A., & Emmelkamp, P. M. G. (1996). Treatment of generalized social phobia: Results at long-term follow-up. *Behaviour Research and Therapy, 34,* 447–452.

Schooler, N. R., et al. (1997). Relapse and rehospitalization during maintenance treatment of schizophrenia. *Archives of General Psychiatry, 54,* 453–463.

Schopler, E., & Mesibov, G. B. (Eds.) (1984). *The effects of autism on the family.* New York: Plenum Press.

Schork, K. (1990, August 19). The despair of Pakistan's women: Not even Benazir Bhutto could stop the repression. *Washington Post.*

Schott, E. D. E., & Stunkard, A. J. (1987). Bulimia vs. bulimic behaviors on a college campus. *Journal of American Medical Association, 258,* 1213–1215.

Schotte, D. E., & Clum, G. A. (1982). Suicide ideation in a college population: A test of a model. *Journal of Consulting and Clinical Psychology, 50,* 690–696.

Schotte, D. E., & Clum, G. A. (1987). Problem-solving skills in suicidal psychiatric patients. *Journal of Consulting and Clinical Psychology, 55,* 49–54.

Schotte, D. E., Cools, J., & Payvar, S. (1990). Problem-solving deficits in suicidal patients: Trait vulnerability or state phenomenom? *Journal of Consulting and Clinical Psychology, 58,* 562–564.

Schou, M. (1997). Forty years of lithium treatment. *Archives of General Psychiatry, 54,* 9–13.

Schreiner-Engel, P., et al. (1989). Low sexual desire in women: The role of reproductive hormones. *Hormones and Behavior, 23,* 221–234.

Schretlen, D. J. (1988). The use of psychological tests to identify malingered symptoms of mental disorder. *Clinical Psychology Review, 8,* 451–476.

Schteingart, J. S., et al. (1995). Homeless and child functioning in the context of risk and protective factors moderating child outcomes. *Journal of Clinical Child Psychology, 24,* 320–331.

Schuckit, M. A. (1983). Subjective responses to alcohol in sons of alcoholics and control. *Archives of General Psychiatry, 41,* 879–884.

Schuckit, M. A. (1987). Biological vulnerability to alcoholism. *Journal of Consulting and Clinical Psychology, 55,* 301–309.

Schuckit, M. A. (1996). Recent developments in the pharmacotherapy of alcohol dependence. *Journal of Consulting and Clinical Psychology, 64,* 669–676.

Schuckit, M. A., & Rayes, U. (1979). Ethanol ingestion: Differences in blood acetaldehyde concentrations in relatives of alcoholics. *Science, 203,* 54–55.

Schuckit, M. A., & Smith, T. L. (1996). An 8-year follow-up of 450 sons of alcoholic and control subjects. *Archives of General Psychiatry, 53,* 202–210.

Schulsinger, F. (1972). Psychopathy: Heredity and environment. *International Journal of Mental Health, 1,* 190–206.

Schulsinger, H. (1976). A ten year follow-up of children of schizophrenic mothers: A clinical assessment. *Acta Psychiatrica Scandinavica, 53,* 371–386.

Schutte, N. S., Malouff, J. M., Post-Gorden, J. C., & Rodasts, A. L. (1988). Effect of playing videogames on children's aggressive and other behavior. *Journal of Applied Social Psychology, 18,* 454–460.

Schwartz, B. S., et al. (1998). Epidemiology of tension-type headache. *Journal of the American Medical Association, 279,* 381–383.

Schwartz, J. M., et al. (1996). Systematic changes in cerebral glucose metabolic rate after successful behavior modification treatment of obsessive-compulsive disorder. *Archives of General Psychiatry, 53,* 109–113.

Schwartz, M. F., & Masters, W. H. (1984). The Masters and Johnson treatment program for dissatisfied homosexual men. *American Journal of Psychiatry, 141,* 173–181.

Schwartz, P. J. (1997). Effects of meta-chlorophenylpiperazine infusions in patients with seasonal affective disorder and healthy control subjects. *Archives of General Psychiatry, 54,* 375–385.

Schwartz, P. J., et al. (1996). Winter seasonal affective disorder: A follow-up study of the first 59 patients of the National Institute of Mental Health seasonal studies program. *American Journal of Psychiatry, 153,* 1028–1036.

Schwartz, R. M. (1986). The internal dialogue: On the asymmetry between positive and negative thoughts. *Cognitive Therapy & Research, 10,* 591–605.

Schwartz, R. M., & Michelson, L. (1987). States-of-mind model: Cognitive balance in the treatment of agoraphobia. *Journal of Consulting and Clinical Psychology, 55,* 557–565.

Schwenk, T. L. (1998, February). A turbulent year for diet pills. *Journal Watch for Psychiatry, 4* (2), p. 16.

Schwitzgebel, R. L., & Schwitzgebel, R. K. (1980). *Law and psychological practice.* New York: Wiley & Sons.

Scientists say gene is linked to asthma. (1994, June 7). *The New York Times,* p. C14.

Scogin, F., et al. (1996). Negative outcomes: What is the evidence on self-administered treatments? *Journal of Consulting and Clinical Psychology, 64,* 1086–1089.

Scott, J. E., & Schwalm, L. A. (1988). Rape rates and the circulation rates of adult magazines. *Journal of Sex Research, 24,* 241–250.

Scroppo, J. C., Drob, S. L., Weinberger, J. L., & Eagle, P. (1998). Identifying dissociative identity disorder: A self-report and projective study. *Journal of Abnormal Psychology, 107,* 272–284.

Sears, R. R., Maccoby, E. E., & Levin, H. (1957). *Patterns of child rearing.* New York: Harper & Row.

The Sedentary Society. (1996, August). *Harvard Heart Letter, 6,* 3–4.

Seeman, M. V. (1997). Psychopathology in women and men: Focus on female hormones. *American Journal of Psychiatry, 154,* 1641–1647.

Segal, J. H. (1989). Erotomania revisited: From Kraepelin to DSM-III-R. *American Journal of Psychiatry, 146,* 1261–1266.

633

Segal, Z. V., et al. (1992). Cognitive and life stress predictors of relapse in remitted unipolar depressed patients: Test of the congruency hypothesis. *Journal of Abnormal Psychology, 101*, 26–36.

Segerstrom, S. C., et al. (1998). Optimism is associated with mood, coping, and immune change in response to stress. *Journal of Personality and Social Psychology, 74*, 1646–1655.

Segraves, R. (1988). Drugs and desire. In S. Leiblum & R. Rosen (Eds.), *Sexual desire disorders*. New York: Guilford Press.

Segraves, R. T., & Althof, S. (1998). Psychotherapy and pharmacotherapy of sexual dysfunctions. In P. E. Nathan, & J. M. Gorman (Eds.), *A guide to treatments that work* (pp. 447-471). New York: Oxford University Press.

Segrin, C., & Abramson, L. Y. (1994). Negative reactions to depressive behaviors: A communication theories analysis. *Journal of Abnormal Psychology, 103*, 655–668.

Segrin, C., & Dillard, J. P. (1992). The international theory of depression: a meta-analysis of the research literature. *Journal of Social and Clinical Psychology, 11*, 43-70.

Seidenberg, M., & Berent, S. (1992). Childhood epilepsy and the role of psychology. *American Psychologist, 47*, 1130–1133.

Seidman, L. J., et al. (1997). Toward defining a neuropsychology of attention deficit-hyperactivity disorder: Performance of children and adolescents from a large clinically referred sample. *Journal of Consulting and Clinical Psychology, 65*, 150–160.

Seidman, S. N., & Rieder, R. O. (1994). A review of sexual behavior in the United States. *American Journal of Psychiatry, 151*, 330–341.

Seligman, M. E. P. (1973). Fall into helplessness. *Psychology Today, 7*, 43–48.

Seligman, M. E. P. (1975). *Helplessness: On depression, development, and death*. San Francisco: Freeman.

Seligman, M. E. P. (1991). *Learned optimism*. New York: Knopf.

Seligman, M. E. P. (1995). The effectiveness of psychotherapy: The *Consumer Reports* Survey. *American Psychologist, 50*, 965–974.

Seligman, M. E. P. (1998, August). *Prevention of depression and positive psychology*. Paper presented at the meeting of the American Psychological Association, San Francisco.

Seligman, M. E. P., & Maier, S. F. (1967). Failure to escape traumatic shock. *Journal of Experimental Psychology, 74*, 1–9.

Seligman, M. E. P., & Rosenhan, D. L. (1984). *Abnormal psychology*. New York: W. W. Norton.

Seligman, M. E. P., et al. (1988). Explanatory style change during cognitive therapy for unipolar depression. *Journal of Abnormal Psychology, 97*, 13–18.

Seligmann, J. (1994, December 12). A gene that says, "No more." *Newsweek*, p. 86.

Selkoe, D. J. (1992). Aging brain, aging mind. *Scientific American, 267*(3), 134–142.

Selvin, B. W. (1993, June 1). Transsexuals are coming to terms with themselves and society. *New York Newsday*, pp. 55, 58, 59.

Selye, H. (1976). *The stress of life*. (Rev. ed.) New York: McGraw-Hill.

Semans, J. (1956). Premature ejaculation: A new approach. *Southern Medical Journal, 49*, 353–358.

Seppa, N. (1997, June). Children's TV remains steeped in violence. *APA Monitor, 28* (6), p. 36.

Seroczynski, A. D., Cole, D. A., & Maxwell, S. E. (1997). Cumulative and compensatory effects of competence and incompetence on depressive symptoms in children. *Journal of Abnormal Psychology, 106*, 586–597.

Seto, M. C., & Barbaree, H. E. (1995). The role of alcohol in sexual aggression. *Clinical Psychology Review, 15*, 545–566.

Shader, R., & Greenblatt, D. J. (1993). Use of benzodiazepines in anxiety disorders. *New England Journal of Medicine, 328*, 1398–1405.

Shadish, W. R., Jr., Lurigio, A. J., & Lewis, D. A. (1989). After deinstitutionalization: The present and future of mental health long-term care policy. *Journal of Social Issues, 45*, 1–15.

Shadish, W. R., & Ragsdale, K. (1996). Random versus nonrandom assignment in controlled experiments: Do you get the same answer? *Journal of Consulting and Clinical Psychology, 64*, 1290–1305.

Shadish, W. et al. (1993). Effects of family and marital psychotherapies: A meta-analysis. *Journal of Consulting and Clinical Psychology, 61*, 992–1002.

Shadish, W. R., et al. (1997). Evidence that therapy works in clinically representative conditions. *Journal of Consulting and Clinical Psychology, 65*, 355–365.

Shaffer, C. E., Jr., Waters, W. F., & Adams, S. G., Jr. (1994). Dangerousness: Assessing the risk of violent behavior. *Journal of Consulting and Clinical Psychology, 62*, 1064–1068.

Shaffer, D. (1994). Attention deficit hyperactivity disorder in adults. *American Journal of Psychiatry, 151*, 633–638.

Shaffer, D., Gould, M., & Hicks, R. C. (1994). Worsening suicide rate in black teenagers. *American Journal of Psychiatry, 151*, 1810–1812.

Shaffer, D., et al. (1996). Psychiatric diagnosis in child and adolescent suicide. *Archives of General Psychiatry, 53*, 339–348.

Shagass, C., Straumanis, J. J., Roemer, R. A., & Amadeo, M. (1979). Temporal variability of somatosensory, visual, and auditory evoked potentials in schizophrenia. *Archives of General Psychiatry, 36*, 1341–1351.

Shalev, A. Y., et al. (1996). Predictors of PTSD in injured trauma survivors: A prospective study. *American Journal of Psychiatry, 153*, 219–225.

Shapiro, C. M., et al. (1993). Alleviating sleep-related discontinuance symptoms associated with benzodiazepine withdrawal: A new approach. *Journal of Psychosomatic Research, 37* (Suppl 1), 55–57.

Shapiro, D. A., et al. (1994). Effects of treatment duration and severity of depression on the effectiveness of cognitive-behavioral and psychodynamic-interpersonal psychotherapy. *Journal of Consulting and Clinical Psychology, 62*, 522–534.

Shapiro, D. A., et al. (1995). Effects of treatment duration and severity of depression on the maintenance of gains after cognitive-behavioral and psychodynamic interpersonal psychotherapy. *Journal of Consulting and Clinical Psychology, 63*, 378–387.

Shapiro, E. (1992, August 22). Fear returns to sidewalks of West 96th Street. *The New York Times*, pp. B3–B4.

Shapiro, F. (1989). Eye movement desensitization: A new treatment for post-traumatic stress disorder. *Journal of Behavior Therapy and Experimental Psychiatry, 20*, 211–217.

Shapiro, F. (1995). *Eye movement desensitization and reprocessing: Basic principles, protocols, and procedures*. New York: Guilford Press.

Shapiro, L. 1998, (June 15). Fat, fatter: But who's counting? *Newsweek*, p. 55.

Sharan, P., et al. (1996). Preliminary report of psychiatric disorders in survivors of a severe earthquake. *American Journal of Psychiatry, 153*, 556–558.

Sharp, D. M., et al. (1996). Fluvoxamine, placebo, and cognitive behavior therapy used alone and in combination in the treatment of panic disorder and agrophobia. *Journal of Anxiety Disorders, 10*, 219–242.

Shaw, J. (1989). The unnecessary penile implant. *Archives of Sexual Behavior, 18*, 455–460.

Shaw, R., Cohen, F., Doyle, B, & Palesky, J. (1985). The impact of denial and repressive style on information gain and rehabilitation outcomes in myocardial infarction patients. *Psychosomatic Medicine, 47*, 262–273.

Shaywitz, S. E. (1998). Dyslexia. *The New England Journal of Medicine, 338*, 307–312.

Shaywitz, S., Cohen, D., & Shaywitz, B. (1980). Behavior and learning difficulties in children of normal intelligence born to alcoholic mothers. *The Journal of Pediatrics, 96*, 978–982.

Shaywitz, S. E., et al. (1998). Functional disruption in the organization of the brain for reading in dyslexia. *Proceedings of the National Academy of Sciences of the United States of America, 95*, 2636–2641.

Shea, M. T., Widiger, T. A., & Klein, M. H. (1992). Comorbidity of personality disorders and depression: Implications for treatment. *Journal of Consulting and Clinical Psychology, 60*, 857–868.

Shea, M. T., et al. (1992). Course of depressive symptoms over follow-up: Findings from the National Institue of Mental Health Treamtent of Depression Collaborative Research Program. *Archives of General Psychiatry, 49*, 782–787.

Shea, S., et al. (1992). Predisposing factors for severe, uncontrolled hypertension in an inner-city minority population. *The New England Journal of Medicine, 327*, 776–781.

Sheitman, B. B., et al. (1998). Pharmacological treatments of schizophrenia. In P. E. Nathan, & J. M. Gorman (Eds.), *A guide to treatments that work* (pp. 167-189). New York: Oxford University Press.

Shekelle, R. B., Gale, M., & Norusis, M. (1985). Type A score (Jenkins Activity Survey) and risk of recurrent coronary heart disease in the Aspirin Myocardial Infarction Study. *American Journal of Cardiology, 56*, 221–225.

Sher, K. J., & Trull, T. J. (1994). Personality and disinhibitory psychopathology: Alcoholism and antisocial personality disorder. *Journal of Abnormal Psychology, 103*, 92–102.

Sherbourne, C. D., Hays, R. D., & Wells, K. B. (1995). Personal and psychosocial risk factors for physical and mental health outcomes and course of depression among depressed patients. *Journal of Consulting and Clinical Psychology, 63*, 345–355.

Sheridan, C. L., & Radmacher, S. A. (1992). *Health psychology: Challenging the biomedical model*. New York: Wiley.

Sherman, D. K., et al. (1997). Twin concordance for attention deficit hyperactivity disorder: A comparison of teachers' and mothers' reports. *American Journal of Psychiatry, 154*, 532–535.

Shern, D. L., et al. (1997). Housing outcomes for homeless adults with mental illness: Results from the second round McKinney program. *Psychiatric Services, 48*, 239–241.

Sherrington, R., et al. (1995). Cloning of a gene bearing missense mutations in early-onset familial Alzheimer's disease. *Nature, 375*, 754–760.

Sherwin, B., Gelfand, M., & Brender, W. (1985). Androgen enhances sexual motivation in females: A prospective crossover study of sex steroid administration in the surgical menopause. *Psychosomatic Medicine, 47*, 339–351.

Sheung-Tak,C. (1996). A critical review of Chinese koro. *Culture, Medicine and Psychiatry, 20*, 67–82.

Shiffman, S., et al. (1996). Progression from a smoking lapse to relapse: Prediction from abstinence violation effects, nicotine dependence, and lapse characteristics. *Journal of Consulting and Clinical Psychology, 64*, 993–1002.

Shneidman, E. S. (1985). *Definition of suicide*. New York: Wiley.

Shontz, F. C., & Green, P. (1992). Trends in research on the Rorschach: Review and recommendations. *Applied and Preventive Psychology, 1*, 149–156.

Shopper, M. (1996). Fear of alien abduction. *Journal of the American Academy of Child and Adolescent Psychiatry, 35*, 555–556.

Short, K. H., & Johnston, C. (1997). Stress, maternal distress, and children's adjustment following immigration: The buffering role of social support. *Journal of Consulting and Clinical Psychology, 65,* 494–503.

Shumaker, S. A., & Hill, D. R. (1991). Gender differences in social support and physical health. *Health Psychology, 10,* 102–11.

Shweder, R. (1985). Cross-cultural study of emotions. In A. Kleinman & B. Good (Eds.), *Culture and depression.* Berkeley: University of California Press.

Siegel, J. M., & Kuykendall, D. H. (1990). Loss, widowhood, and psychological distress among the elderly. *Journal of Consulting and Clinical Psychology, 58,* 519–524.

Siegel, L. J. (1992). *Criminology,* 4th ed. St. Paul, MN: West Publishing Co.

Siever, L., & Trestman, R. L. (1993). The serotonin system and aggressive personality disorder. *International Clinical Psychopharmacology, 8* (Suppl. 2), 33–39.

Siever, L. J., et al. (1990). Increased morbid risk for schizophrenia-related disorders in relatives of schizotypal personality disordered patients. *Archives of General Psychiatry, 47,* 634–640.

Sigvardsson, S., Bohman, M.B., & Cloninger, C. (1996). Replication of the Stockholm adoption study of alcoholism: Confirmatory cross-fostering analysis. *Archives of General Psychiatry, 53,* 681–687.

Silbersweig, D. A., et al. (1995). A functional neuroanatomy of hallucinations in schizophrenia. *Nature, 378,* 176–179.

Silver, E., Cirincione, C., & Steadman, H. J. (1994). Demythologizing inaccurate perceptions of the insanity defense. *Law and Human Behavior, 18,* 63–70.

Silverman, K., Evans, S. M., Strain, E. C., & Griffiths, R. R. (1992). Withdrawal syndrome after the double- blind cessation of coffee consumption. *The New England Journal of Medicine, 327,* 1109–1114.

Silverton, L., Finell, K. M., Mednick, S. A., & Schulsinger, F. (1985). Low birth weight and ventricular enlargement in a high-risk sample. *Journal of Abnormal Psychology, 94,* 405–409.

Simeon, D., et al. (1997). Feeling unreal: 30 Cases of DSM-III-R depersonalization disorder. *American Journal of Psychiatry, 154,* 1107–1113.

Simon, G. E. (1998). Management of somatoform and factitious disorders. In P. E. Nathan & J. M. Gorman(Eds.), *A guide to treatments that work* (pp. 408-422). New York: Oxford University Press.

Simpson, H. B., Nee, J. C., & Endicott, J. (1997). First-episode major depression: Few sex differences in course. *Archives of General Psychiatry, 54,* 633–639.

Singh, G. (1985). Dhat syndrome revisisted. *Indian Journal of Psychiatry, 27,* 119–122.

Sintchak, J., & Geer, J. (1975). A vaginal plethysmograph system. *Psychophysiology, 12,* 113–115.

Sitharthan, T., et al. (1997). Cue exposure in moderation drinking: A comparison with cognitive-behavior therapy. *Journal of Consulting and Clinical Psychology, 65,* 878–882.

Skaar, K. L., et al. (1997). Smoking cessation 1: An overview of research. *Behavioral Medicine, 23,* 5–13.

Skinner, B. F. (1938). *The behavior of organisms: An experimental analysis.* New York: Appleton.

Skinner, B. F. (1983). Intellectual self-management in old age. *American Psychologist, 38,* 239–244.

Skodol, A. E., Gallaher, P. E., & Oldham, J. M. (1996). Excessive dependency and depression: Is the relationship specific? *Journal of Nervous & Mental Disease, 184,* 165–171.

Skoog, I., et al. (1993). A population-based study of dementia in 85–year-olds. *New England Journal of Medicine, 328,* 153-158.

Slater, D., & Hans, V. P. (1984) Public opinion of forensic psychiatry following the Hinckley verdict. *American Journal of Psychiatry, 141,* 675–679.

Sleek, S. (1994, January). Many methods employed to breach autism's walls. *APA Monitor,* pp. 30–31.

Sleeping pills for chronic insomnia: A meta-analysis. (1998, February). *Journal Watch for Psychiatry, 4* (2), 11.

Slutske, W. S., et al. (1997). Modeling genetic and environmental influences in the etiology of conduct disorder: A study of 2,682 adult twin pairs. *Journal of Abnormal Psychology, 106,* 266–279.

Slutske, W. S., et al. (1998). Common genetic risk factors for conduct disorder and alcohol dependence. *Journal of Abnormal Psychology, 107,* 363–374.

Small, G. W., et al. (1997). Diagnosis and treatment of Alzheimer's disease and related disorders: Consensus Statement of the American Association for Geriatric Psychiatry, the Alzheimer's Association, and the American Geriatrics Society. *Journal of the American Medical Association, 278,* 1363–1371.

Small, J. G., et al. (1997). Quetiapine in patients with schizophrenia: A high- and low-dose double-blind comparison with placebo. *Archives of General Psychiatry, 54,* 549–557.

Smelson, R. A., & Lindeken, S. (1996) Screening for pathological gambling among substance misusers. *British Journal of Psychiatry, 169,* 523.

Smith, D. (1982). Trends in counseling and psychotherapy. *American Psycologist, 37,* 802–809.

Smith, E. E., & Jonides, J. (1997). Working memory: A view from neuroimaging. *Cognitive Psychology, 33,* 5–42.

Smith, G. A., & Hall, J. A. (1982). Evaluating Michigan's Guilty but Mentally Ill verdict: An empirical study. *University of Michigan Journal of Law Reform, 16,* 77.

Smith, G. R. (1994). The course of somatization and its effects on utilization of health care resources. *Psychosomatics, 35,* 263–267.

Smith, G. R., et al. (1991). Antisocial personality disorder in primary care patients with somatization disorder. *Comprehensive Psychiatry, 32,* 367–372.

Smith, G. T., et al. (1995). Expectancy for social faciliation from drinking: The divergent paths of high-expectancy and low-expectatncy adolescents. *Journal of Abnormal Psychology, 104,* 32–40.

Smith, J. E., & Krejci, J. (1991). Minorities join the majority: Eating disturbances among Hispanic and Native American youth. *International Journal of Eating Disorders, 10,* 179–186.

Smith, J. N., & Baldessarini, R. J. (1980). Changes in prevalence, severity, and recovery in tardive dyskinesia with age. *Archives of General Psychiatry, 37,* 1368–1373.

Smith, M. E., & Fremouw, W. J. (1987). A realistic approach to treating obesity. *Clinical Psychology Review, 7,* 449–465.

Smith, M. L., & Glass, G. V. (1977). Meta-analysis of psychotherapy otucome studies. *American Psychologist, 32,* 752–760.

Smith, M. L., Glass, G. V., & Miller, T. I. (1980). *The benefits of psychotherapy.* Baltimore, MD: Johns Hopkins University Press.

Smith, R. E., Smoll, F. L., & Ptacek, J. T. (1990). Conjunctive moderator variables in vulnerability and reliency research: Life stress, social support, and coping skills, and adolescent sport injuries. *Journal of Personality and Social Psychology, 58,* 360–370.

Smith, R. J. (1978). *The great mental calculators.* New York: Columbia University Press.

Smith, S. C. (1983). *The great mental calculators.* New York: Columbia University Press.

Smith, S. S., & Newman, J. P. (1990). Alcohol and drug abuse-dependence disorders in psychopathic and nonpsychopathic criminal offenders. *Journal of Abnormal Psychology, 99,* 430–439.

Smith, T. E., Bellack, A. S., Liberman, R. P. (1996). Social skills training for schizophrenia: Review and future directions. *Clinical Psychology Review, 16,* 599–617.

Smith, T. W., Snyder, C. R., & Perkins, S. C. (1983). The self-serving function of hypochondriacal complaints: Physical symptoms as self-handicapping strategies. *Journal of Personality and Social Psychology, 44,* 787–797.

Smith-Warner, S. A. et al. (1998). Alcohol and breast cancer in women: A pooled analysis of cohort studies. *Journal of the American Medical Association, 279,* 535–540.

Smoking will be world's biggest killer. (1996, September 17). *Newsday,* p. A21.

Smyth, J. M. (1998). Written emotional expression: Effect sizes, outcome types, and moderating variables. *Journal of Consulting and Clinical Psychology, 66,* 174–184.

Snell, M. E. (1997). Teaching children and young adults with mental retardation in school programs: Current research. *Behaviour Change, 14,* 73–105.

Snyder, S. H. (1980). *Biological aspects of mental disorder.* New York: Oxford University Press.

Sobell, M. B., & Sobell, L. C. (1973). Alcoholics treated by individualized behavior therapy: One year treatment outcome. *Behaviour Research & Therapy, 11,* 599–618.

Sobell, M. B., & Sobell, L. C. (1976). Second year treatment outcome of alcoholics treated by individualized behavior therapy: Results. *Behaviour Research and Therapy, 14,* 195–215.

Sobell, M. B., & Sobell, L. C. (1984). The aftermath of heresy: A response to Pendery et al.'s critique of "Individualized behavior therapy for alcoholics." *Behaviour Research and Therapy, 22,* 413–440.

Sobin, C., & Sackeim, H. A. (1997). Psychomotor symptoms of depression. *American Journal of Psychiatry, 154,* 4–17.

Solano, L., et al. (1993). Psychosocial factors and clinical evolution in HIV-1 infection: A longitudinal study. *Journal of Psychosomatic Research, 37,* 39–51.

Solomon, D. A., et al. (1997). Recovery from major depression: A 10-year prospective follow-up across multiple episodes. *Archives of General Psychiatry, 54,* 1001–1006.

Solomon, G F., et al. (1997, March/April). Shaking up immunity: Psychological and immunologic changes after a natural disaster. *Psychosomatic Medicine, 59,* 114–127.

Somervell, P. D., et al. (1989) The prevalence of major depression in black and white adults in five United States communities. *American Journal of Epidemiology, 130,* 725–735.

Sommers-Flanagan, J., & Sommers-Flanagan, R. (1996). Efficacy of antidepressant medication with depressed youth: What psychologists should know. *Professional Psychology: Research & Practice, 27,* 145–153.

Sorenson, S. B., & Golding, J. M. (1988). Suicide ideation and attempts in Hispanics and non-Hispanic Whites: Demographic and psychiatric disorder issues. *Suicide and Life-Threatening Behavior, 18,* 205–218.

Sorenson, S. B., & Rutter, C. M. (1991). Transgenerational patterns of suicide attempt. *Journal of Consulting and Clinical Psychology, 59,* 861–866.

Sorenson, S. B., Rutter, C. M., & Aneshensel, C. S. (1991). Depression in the community: An investigation into age of onset. *Journal of Consulting and Clinical Psychology, 59,* 541–546.

Southwick, S. M., Morgan, C. A. III, Darnell, A., Bremner, D., Nicolaou, A. L., Nagy, L. M., Charney, D. S. (1995). Trauma-related symptoms in veterans of Operation Desert Storm: A 2-year follow-up. *American Journal of Psychiatry, 152,* 1150–1155.

Southwick, S., & Yehuda, R. (1993). The interaction between pharmacotherapy and psychotherapy in the treatment of posttraumatic stress disorder. *American Journal of Psychiatry, 150,* 404–410.

Southwick, S. M., et al. (1993). Trauma-related symptoms in veterans of Operation Desert Storm: A preliminary report. *American Journal of Psychiatry, 150,* 1524–1528.

Southwick, S. M., et al .(1997). Noradrenergic and sero-tonergic function in posttraumatic stress disorder. *Archives of General Psychiatry, 54,* 749–758.

Spangler, D. L., et al. (1997). Comparison of cognitive models of depression: Relationships between cognitive constructs and cognitive diathesis-stress match. *Journal of Abnormal Psychology, 106,* 395–403.

Spanos, N. P. (1978). Witchcraft in histories of psychiatry: A critical analysis and an alternative conceptualization. *Psychological Bulletin, 85,* 417–439.

Spanos, N. P. (1994). Multiple identity enactments and multiple personality disorder: A sociocognitive perspective. *Psychological Bulletin, 116,* 143–165.

Spanos, N. P., Weekes, J. R., & Bertrand, L. D. (1985). Multiple personality: A social psychological perspective. *Journal of Abnormal Psychology, 94,* 362–376.

Spark, R. F. (1991). *Male sexual health: A couple's guide.* Mount Vernon, NY: Consumer Reports Books.

Spector, I. P., & Carey, M. P. (1990). Incidence and prevalence of the sexual dysfunctions: A critical review of the empirical literature. *Archives of Sexual Behavior, 19,* 389–408.

Speigel, D., & Cardena, E. (1991). Disintegrated experience: The dissociative disorders revisited. *Journal of Abnormal Psychology, 100,* 366–378.

Spencer, D. D., et al. (1992). Unilateral transplantation of human fetal mesencephalic tissue into the caudate nucleus of patients with Parkinson's disease. *The New England Journal of Medicine, 327,* 1541–1548.

Spencer, D. J. (1983). Psychiatric dilemmas in Australian aborigines. *International Journal of Social Psychiatry, 29* (3), 208–214.

Spencer, T., et al. (1996). Pharmacotherapy of attention-deficit hyperactivity disorder across the life cycle. *Journal of the American Academy of Child and Adolescent Psychiatry, 35,* 409–432.

Spiegel, D. A., & Bruce, T. J. (1997). Benzodiazepines and exposure-based cognitive behavior therapies for panic disorder: Conclusions from combined treatment trials. *American Journal of Psychiatry, 154,* 773–781.

Spiegel, D. S., & Wissler, T. (1986). Family environment as a predictor of psychiatric rehospitalization. *American Journal of Psychiatry, 143,* 56–60.

Spiegel, D., et al. (1989, October 14). Effect of psychosocial treatment on survival of patients with metastatic breast cancer. *Lancet,* pp. 888–891.

Spiker, D., & Ricks, M. (1984). Visual self-recognition in autistic children: Developmental relationships. *Child Development, 55,* 214–225.

Spitzer, R. L. (1991). An outsider-insider's views about revising the DSMs. *Journal of Abnormal Psychology, 100,* 294–296.

Spitzer, R. L. (1998). Diagnosis and need for treatment are not the same. *Archives of General Psychiatry, 55,* 120.

Spitzer, R. L., & Forman, J. B. (1979). DSM-III field trials: II. Initial experience with the multiaxial system. *American Journal of Psychiatry, 136,* 818–820.

Spitzer, R. L., Gibbon, M., Skodol, A. E., Williams, J. B. W., & First, M. B. (1989). *DSM-III-R casebook.* Washington, DC: American Psychiatric Press.

Spitzer R. L., et al. (1991). Results of a survey of forensic psychiatrists. *American Journal of Psychiatry, 148,* 875–879.

Spitzer, R. L., et al. (1992). Binge eating disorder: A multisite field trial of the diagnostic criteria. *International Journal of Eating Disorders, 11,* 191–203.

Spitzer, R. L., et al. (1994). *DSM-IV case book* (4th ed.). Washington, D C: American Psychiatric Press.

Spivack, G., Marcus, J., & Swift, M. (1986). Early classroom behaviors and later misconduct. *Developmental Psychology, 22,* 124–131.

Spohr, H. L., Willms, J., & Steinhausen, H. C. (1993). Prenatal alcohol exposure and long-term developmental consequences. *Lancet, 341,* 907–910.

Spreat, S., & Behar, D. (1994). Trends in the residential (inpatient) treatment of individuals with a dual diagnosis. *Journal of Consulting and Clinical Psychology, 62,* 43–48.

Spreen, O. (1988). Prognosis of learning disability. *Journal of Consulting and Clinical Psychology, 56,* 836–842.

Stacy, A. W., Newcomb, M. D., & Bentler, P. M. (1991). Cognitive motivation and drug use: A 9-year longitudinal study. *Journal of Abnormal Psychology, 100,* 502–515.

Stacy, C. L., et al. (1994). It's not all moonlight and roses: Dating violence at the University of Maine, 1982–1992. *College Student Journal, 28,* 2–9.

Stader, S. R., & Hokanson, J. E. (1998). Psychosocial antecedents of depressive symptoms: An evaluation using daily experiences methodology. *Journal of Abnormal Psychology, 107,* 17–26.

Stamler, J. (1985). The marked decline in coronary heart disease mortality rates in the United States, 1968–1981: Summary of findings and possible explanations. *Cardiology, 72,* 11–12.

Stamler, J., et al. (1986). Is the relationship between serum cholesterol and risk of premature death from coronary heart disease continuous and graded? Findings in 356,222 primary screenees of the Multiple Risk Factor Intervention Trial (MRFIT). *Journal of the American Medical Association, 256,* 2823–2828.

Stanley, M. A., Beck, J. G., & Glassco, J. D. (1996). Treatment of generalized anxiety in older adults: A preliminary comparison of cognitive-behavioral and supportive approaches. *Behavior Therapy, 27,* 565–581.

Stanley, M. A., & Turner, S. M. (1995). Current status of pharmacological and behavioral treatment of obsessive-compulsive disorder. *Behavior Therapy, 26,* 163–186.

Stanovich, K. E., & Siegel, L. S. (1994). Phenotypic performance profile of children with reading disabilities: A regression-based test of the phonological-core variable-difference model. *Journal of Educational Psychology, 86,* 24–53.

Stanton, M. D., & Shadish, W. R. (1997). Outcome, attrition, and family/couples treatment for drug abuse: A meta-analysis and review of the controlled, comparative studies. *Psychological Bulletin, 122,* 170–191.

Steadman, H. J. (1979). *Beating a rap: Defendants found incompetent to stand trial.* Chicago: University of Chicago Press.

Steadman, H. J., et al. (1993). *Before and after Hinckley: Evaluating insanity defense reform.* New York: Guilford Press.

Steadman, H. J., et al. (1998).Violence by people discharged from acute psychiatric inpatient facilities and by others in the same neighborhoods. *Archives of General Psychiatry, 55,* 393–401.

Steele, C. M., & Southwick, L. (1985). Alcohol and social behavior I: The psychology of drunken excess. *Journal of Personality and Social Psychology, 48,* 18–34.

Steer, R. A., et al. (1994). Psychometric properties of the Cognition Checklist with psychiatric outpatients and university students. *Psychological Assessment, 6,* 67–70.

Steer, R. A., et al. (1995). Common and specific dimensions of self-reported anxiety and depression: A replication. *Journal of Abnormal Psychology, 104,* 542–545.

Stefanek, M. E., Ollendick, T. H., Baldock, W. P., Francis, G., & Yaeger, N. J. (1987). Self-statements in aggressive, withdrawn, and popular children. *Cognitive Therapy and Research, 11,* 229–239.

Stein, D., et al. (1998). The association between attitudes toward suicide and suicidal ideation in adolescents. *Acta Psychiatrica Scandinavia, 97,* 195–201.

Stein, D. M., & Lambert, M. J. (1995). Graduate training in psychotherapy: Are therapy outcomes enhanced? *Journal of Consulting and Clinical Psychology, 63,* 182–196.

Stein, M. B., Baird, A., & Walker, J. R. (1996). Social phobia in adults with stuttering. *American Journal of Psychiatry, 153,* 278–280.

Stein, M. B., Walker, J. R., & Forde, D. R. (1996). Public-speaking fears in a community sample: Prevalence, impact on functioning, and diagnostic classification. *Archives of General Psychiatry, 53,* 169–174.

Stein, M. B., et al. (1996). Childhood physical and sexual abuse in patients with anxiety disorders and in a community sample. *American Journal of Psychiatry, 153,* 275–277.

Stein, M. B., et al. (1998). Paroxetine treatment of generalized social phobia (social anxiety disorder). *Journal of the American Medical Association, 280,* 708–713.

Steinberg, L., Dornbusch, S. M., & Brown, B. B. (1992). Ethnic differences in adolescent achievement: An ecological perspective. *American Psychologist, 47,* 723–729.

Steinberg, M. (1991) The spectrum of depersonalization: Assessment and treatment. *Annual Review of Psychiatry, 10,* 223–247.

Steinhausen, H. C., et al. (1993). Long-term psychopathological and cognitive outcome of children with fetal alcohol syndrome. *Journal of the American Academy of Child and Adolescent Psychiatry, 32,* 990–994.

Steketee, G., & Foa, E. B. (1985). Obsessive-compulsive disorder. In D. H. Barlow (Ed.), *Clinical handbook of psychological disorders* (pp. 69–144). New York: Guilford Press.

Stemberger, R. R., et al. (1995). Social phobia: An analysis of possible developmental factors. *Journal of Abnormal Psychology, 194,* 526–531.

Sterngold, J. (1995, October 22). Imagine the Internet as electronic casino. *The New York Times,* Sect. E, p. 3.

Steven, J. E. (1995, January 30). Virtual therapy. *The Boston Globe,* pp. 25, 29.

Stevens, J. R. (1997). Anatomy of schizophrenia revisited. *Schizophrenia Bulletin, 23,* 373–383.

Stevens, J. et al. (1998). The effect of age on the association between body-mass index and mortality. *The New England Journal of Medicine, 338,* 1–7.

Stewart, M. W., et al. (1994). Differential relationships between stress and disease activity for immunologically distinct subgroups of people with rheumatoid arthritis. *Journal of Abnormal Psychology, 1103,* 251–258.

Stice, E. (1994). Review of the evidence for a sociocultural model of bulimia nervosa and an exploration of the mechanisms of action. *Clinical Psychology Review, 14,* 633–661.

Stice, E., et al. (1994). Relation of media exposure to eating disorder symptomatology: An examination of mediating mechanisms. *Journal of Abnormal Psychology, 103,* 836–840.

Stock, W. E. (1991). Feminist explanations: Male power, hostility, and sexual coercion. In E. Grauerholz & M. A. Koralewski (Eds.), *Sexual coercion: A sourcebook on its nature, causes, and prevention* (pp. 61–73). Lexington, MA: Lexington Books.

Stokols, D. (1992). Establishing and maintaining healthy environments: Toward a social ecology of health promotion. *American Psychologist, 47,* 6–22.

Stolberg, S. G. (1998a, March 13). New cancer cases decreasing in U.S. as deaths do, too. *The New York Times,* p. A1, A14.

Stolberg, S. G. (1998b). Rise in smoking by young blacks erodes a success story. *The New York Times,* p. A24.

Stoller, R. J. (1969). Parental influences in male transexualism. In R. Green & J. Money (Eds.), *Transexualism and sex reassignment.* Baltimore: Johns Hopkins University Press.

Stone, A. (1976). The *Tarasoff* decisions: Suing psychotherapists to safeguard society. *Harvard Law Review, 90,* 358–378.

Stone, A. (1984). *Law, psychiatry and morality.* Washington, DC: American Psychiatric Press.

Stone, A.A., et al. (1994). Daily events are associated with a secretory immune response to an oral antigen in men. *Health Psychology, 13,* 440–446.

Stone, M. H. (1980). *The borderline syndromes: Constitution, personality, and adaptation.* New York: McGraw-Hill.

Stone, N. M. (1993). Parental abuse as a precursor to childhood onset depression and suicidality. *Child Psychiatry and Human Development, 24,* 13–24.

Stover, E. S., et al. (1996). Perspectives from the National Institute of Mental Health: Preventing or living with AIDS. *Annals of Behavioral Medicine, 18,* 58–60.

Strachan, A. M. (1986). Family intervention for the rehabilitation of schizophrenia: Toward protection and coping. *Schizophrenia Bulletin, 12,* 678–698.

Strakowski, S. M. (1994). Diagnostic validity of schizophreniform disorder. *American Journal of Psychiatry, 15,* 815–824.

Strakowski, S. M., et al. (1996). Suicidality among patients with mixed and manic bipolar disorder. *American Journal of Psychiatry, 153,* 674–676.

Straube, E. (1979). On the meaning of electrodermal nonresponding in schizophrenia. *Journal of Nervous and Mental Disease, 167,* 601–611.

Straus, M. A. (1990). The national family violence surveys. In M. A. Straus & R. J. Gelles (Eds.), *Physical violence in American families: Risk factors and adaptation to violence in 8,145 families* (pp. 3–16). New Brunswick, NJ: Transaction.

Streissguth, A. P. (1994). A long-term perspective of FAS. *Alcohol Health and Research World, 18,* 74–81.

Streissguth, A. P., Barr, H. M., Sampson, P. D., Darby, B. L., & Martin, D. C. (1989). IQ at age 4 in relation to maternal alcohol use and smoking during pregnancy. *Developmental Psychology, 25,* 3–11.

Streissguth, A. P., et al. (1984). Interuterine alcohol and nicotine exposure: Attention and reaction time in 4–year-old children. *Developmental Psychology, 20,* 533–541.

Stretch, R. H. (1987). Posttraumatic stress disorder among U.S. Army reservists: Reply to Nezu & Carnevale. *Journal of Consulting and Clinical Psychology, 55,* 272–273.

Strober, M. (1986). Psychopathology of adolesence revisited. *Clinical Psychology Review, 6,* 199–209.

Strober, M., & Humphrey, L. L. (1987). Familial contributions to the etiology and course of anorexia nervosa and bulimia. *Journal of Consulting and Clinical Psychology, 55,* 654–659.

Strollo, P. J., & Rogers, R. M. (1996). Obstructive sleep apnea. *The New England Journal of Medicine, 334,* 99–104.

Strube, M. J. (1988). The decision to leave an abusive relationship: Empirical evidence and theoretical issues. *Psychological Bulletin, 104,* 236–250.

Strunk, R. C., Mrazek, D. A., Fuhrman, A. S. W., & LaBrecque, J. F. (1985). Physiologic and psychological characteristics associated with deaths due to asthma in childhood: A case-controlled study. *Journal of the American Medical Association, 254,* 1193–1198.

Strupp, H. H. (1992). The future of psychodynamic psychotherapy. *Psychotherapy, 29,* 21–27.

Stuart, F., Hammond, C., & Pett, M. (1987). Inhibited sexual desire in women. *Archives of Sexual Behavior, 16,* 91–106.

Stubbs, E. G., Ritvo, E. R., & Mason-Brothers, A. (1985). Autism and shared parental HLA antigens. *Journal of Child Psychiatry, 24,* 182–185.

Study disputes link of sugar to hyperactivity. (1995, November 22). *The New York Times,* p. C7.

Study finds few sufferers die of asthma. (1994, December 8). *The New York Times,* p. A27.

Study finds half of victims know attackers. (1997, August 25). *The New York Times,* p. A. 16.

Study finds pattern in college binge drinking. (1995, April 6). *The New York Times,* p. A21.

Stunkard, A. J., & Sørensen, T. I. A. (1993). Obesity and socioeconomic status—a complex relation. *New England Journal of Medicine, 329,* 1036–1037.

Stunkard, A. J., & Wadden, T. A. (1992). Psychological aspects of severe obesity. *American Journal of Clinical Nutrition, 55* (Suppl.), 524S–432S.

Stunkard, A. J., et al. (1986). An adoption study of human obesity. *New England Journal of Medicine, 314,* 193, 198.

Stunkard, A. J., et al. (1990). A separated twin study of the body mass index. *The New England Journal of Medicine, 322,* 1483–1487.

Sturm, R., & Wells, K. B (1995). How can care for depression become more cost-effective? *Journal of the American Medical Association, 273,* 51–58.

Stuss, D. T., Gow, C. A., & Hetherington, C. R. (1992). "No longer Gage." Frontal lobe dysfunction and emotional changes. *Journal of Consulting and Clinical Psychology, 60,* 349–359.

Substance abuse and schizophrenia. (1997, November). *Clinician's Research Digest,* p. 5.

Sue, S. (1988). Psychotherapeutic services for ethnic minorities: Two decades of research findings. *American Psychologist,43,*301–308.

Sue, S., et al. (1976). Conceptions of mental illness among Asian and Caucasian American students. *Psychological Reports, 38,* 703–708.

Sue, S., et al. (1991). Community mental health services for ethnic minority groups: A test of the cultural responsiveness hypothesis. *Journal of Consulting and Clinical Psychology, 59,* 533–540.

Sue, S., et al. (1995). Psychopathology among Asian Americans: A model minority? *Cultural Diversity and Mental Health, 1,* 39–51.

Sullivan, H. S. (1962). *Schizophrenia as a human process.* New York: Norton.

Suls, J., Wan, C. K., & Blanchard, E. B. (1994). A multilevel data-analytic approach for evaluation of relationships between daily life stressors and symptomatology: Patients with irritable bowel syndrome. *Health Psychology, 13,* 103–113.

Surgeon General's Report. (1989). *Reducing the health consequences of smoking: 25 years of progress.* Atlanta: Centers for Disease Control.

Surveys find few adults exercise enough. (1996, August 10). *The New York Times,* p. A12.

Sutherland, A J., & Rodin, G. M. (1990). Factitious disorders in a general hospital setting: Clinical features and a review of the literature. *Psychosomatics, 31,* 392–399.

Sutherland, G. R., et al., (1991). Prenatal diagnosis of fragile X syndrome by direct detection of the unstable DNA sequence. *The New England Journal of Medicine, 325,* 1720–1722.

Sutker, P. B., Uddo-Crane, M., & Allain, A. N., Jr. (1991). Clinical and research assessment of posttraumatic stress disorder: A conceptual overview. *Psychological Assessment, 3,* 520–530.

Sutker, P. B., et al. (1995). War zone stress, personal resources, and PTSD in Persian Gulf War returnees. *Journal of Abnormal Psychology, 104,* 444–452.

Suzdak, P. D., Glowa, J. R., Crawley, J. N., & Schwartz, R. D. (1986). A selective imidazobenzodiazepine antagonist of ethanol in the rat. *Science, 225,* 1243–1247.

Svikis, D. S., Velez, M. L., & Pickens, R. W. (1994). Genetic aspects of alcohol use and alcoholism in women. *Alcohol Health & Research World, 18,* 192–196.

Swaim, R. C., Oetting E. R., Edwards, R. W., & Beauvais, F. (1989). Links from emotional distress to adolescent drug use: A path model. *Journal of Consulting and Clinical Psychology, 57,* 227–231.

Swanston, H. Y., et al. (1997). Sexually abused children 5 years after presentation: A case-control study. *Pediatrics, 100,* 600–608.

Swartz, M., et al. (1991). Somatization disorder. In L. N. Robins & D. A. Regier (Eds.), *Psychiatric disorders in America: The Epidemiologic Catchment Area Study* (pp. 220–257). New York: The Free Press.

Swartz, M. S., et al. (1998). Violence and severe mental illness: The effects of substance abuse and nonadherence to medication. *American Journal of Psychiatry,155,* 226–231.

Swayze, V. W., et al. (1990). Structural brain abnormalities in bipolar affective disorder; Ventricular enlargement and focal signal hyperintensities. *American Journal of Psychiatry, 47,* 1054–1059.

Sweeney, J. A., et al. (1994). Eye tracking dysfunction in schizophrenia: Characterization of component eye movement abnormalities, diagnostic specificity, and the role of attention. *Journal of Abnormal Psychology, 103,* 222–230.

Sweeney, P. D., Anderson, K., Bailey, S. (1986). Attributional style in depression: A meta-analytic review. *Journal of Personality and Social Psychology, 50,* 974–991.

Sylvain, C., Ladouceur, R., & Boisvert, J.-M. (1997). Cognitive and behavioral treatment of pathological gambling: A controlled study. *Journal of Consulting and Clinical Psychology, 65,* 727–732.

Szanto, K., et al. (1996). Suicide in elderly depressed patients. Is active vs. passive suicidal ideation a clinically valid distinction? *American Journal of Geriatric Psychiatry, 4,* 197–207.

Szasz, G., et al. (1987). Induction of penile erection by intracavernosal injection: A double-blind comparison of phenoxybenzamine versus papaverine-phentolamine versus saline. *Archives of Sexual Behavior, 16,* 371–378.

Szasz, T. S. (1961). *The myth of mental illness.* New York: Harper & Row.

Szasz, T. S. (1963). *Law, liberty and psychiatry.* New York: MacMillan.

Szasz, T. S. (1970). *Ideology and insanity: Essays on the psychiatric dehumanization of man.* New York: Doubleday Anchor.

Szasz, T. S. (1984). *The therapeutic state: Psychiatry in the mirror of current events.* Buffalo: Prometheus.

Szymanski, S., Kane, J. M., & Lieberman, J. A. (1991). A selective review of biological markers in schizophrenia. *Schizophrenia Bulletin, 17,* 99–111.

T

Tafoya, T.N. (1996). Native two-spirit people. In R.P. Cabaj & T. S. Stein (Eds.), *Textbook of homosexuality and mental health* (pp.603–617). Washington, DC: American Psychiatric Press.

Tafti, M., et al. (1992). Sleep in human narcolepsy revisited with special reference to prior wakefulness duration. *Sleep, 15,* 344–351.

Takeuchi, D. T., Mokuau, N., & Chun, C. (1992). Mental health services for Asian Americans and Pacific Islanders. Special Issue: Multicultural mental health and substance abuse services. *Journal of Mental Health Administration, 19,* 237–245.

Takriti, A. (1987). Male sexual dysfunction in Jordan. Unpublished paper. (Cited in Bhurgra & De Silva, 1993).

Talan, J. (1993a, October 12). Prozac: A face-lift for the mind? *New York Newsday,* pp. 61, 64.

Talan, J. (1993b, January 26). Drug for Parkinson's puts off use of stronger medication, report says. *New York Newsday,* p. 59.

Talan, J. (1994, May 24). Is panic attack a false alarm? *Newsday,* pp. B27, B33.

Talan, J. (1995, October 31). Path to treatment? *Newsday,* pp. A 4, 49.

637

Talan, J. (1996a, June 5). Study: Mental stress tied to heart attacks. *Newsday*, p. A35.

Talan, J. (1996b, November 19). New suicide findings. *Newsday*, p. B26.

Talbott, E., et al. (1985). Occupational noise exposure, noise-induced hearing loss, and the epidemiology of high blood pressure. *American Journal of Epidemiology, 121,* 501–514.

Tamminga, C. A. (1997). Clinical genetics, II. *American Journal of Psychiatry, 154,* p. 1046.

Tanda, G., Pontien, & Chiara (1997). Cannabinoid and heroin activation of mesolimbic dopamine transmission by a common opioid receptor mechanism. *Science, 276,* 2048–2050.

Tannahill, R. (1980). *Sex in history.* New York: Stein and Day.

Taragano, F. E., et al. (1997). A double-blind, randomized, fixed-dose trial of fluoxetine vs. amitriptyline in the treatment of major depression complicating Alzheimer's disease. *Psychosomatics, 38,* 246–252.

Tarasoff v. Regents of the University of California, 131 Cal Rptr. 14, 551 P. 2d 344 (1976).

Tardiff, K., et al. (1994). Homocide in New York City: Cocaine use and firearms. *Journal of the American Medical Association, 272,* 43–46.

Tardiff, K., et al. (1997). Violence by patients admitted to a private psychiatric hospital. *American Journal of Psychiatry, 154,* 88–93.

Tarter, R., Hegedus, A. M., Winsten, N. E., & Alterman, A. I. (1984). Neuropsychological, personality, and family characteristics of physically abused delinquents. *Journal of the American Academy of Child Psychiatry, 23,* 668–674.

Task Force on Promotion and Dissemination of Psychological Procedures. (1995). Training in and dissemination of empirically validated psychological treatments: Report and recommendations. *The Clinical Psychologist, 48*(1), 3–24.

Task Force Report, American Psychiatric Association. (1980). Effects of antipsychotic drugs: Tardive dyskinesia. *American Journal of Psychiatry, 37,* 1163–1171.

Taylor, C. B., Killen, J. D., and the Editors of Consumer Reports Books (1991). *The facts about smoking.* Yonkers, NY: Consumer Reports Books.

Taylor, R. J., Hardison, C. B., & Chatters, L. M. (1996). Kin and nonkin as sources of informal assistance. In H. W. Neighbors & J.S. Jackson (Eds.), *Mental health in black America* (pp. 130–145). Thousand Oaks, CA: Sage Publications.

Taylor, S. (1995). Assessment of obsessions and compulsions: Reliability, validity, and sensitivity to treatment effects. *Clinical Psychology Review, 15,* 261–296.

Taylor, S. E., & Brown, J. D. (1994). Positive illusions and well-being revisited: Separating fact from fiction. *Psychological Bulletin, 116,* 21–27.

Taylor, S., & Rachman, S. J. (1994). Klein's suffocation theory of panic. *Archives of General Psychiatry, 51,* 505–506.

Taylor, S., et al. (1996). Suffocation false alarms and efficacy of cognitive behavioral therapy for panic disorder. *Behavior Therapy, 27,* 115–126.

Teicher, M. H., et al. (1997). Circadian rest-activity disturbances in seasonal affective disorder. *Archives of General Psychiatry, 54,* 124–130.

Telch, C. F., & Telch, M. J. (1986). Group coping skills instruction and supportive group therapy for cancer patients: A comparison of strategies. *Journal of Consulting and Clinical Psychology, 54,* 802–808.

Tems, C. L., et al. (1993). Cognitive distortions in depressed children and adolescents: Are they state dependent or traitlike? *Journal of Clinical Child Psychology, 22,* 316–326.

Teri, L. (1992, November). Clinical problems in older adults. *Clinician's Research Digest* (Supplemental Bulletin #9).

Teri. L. & Wagner, A. (1992). Alzheimer's disease and depression. *Journal of Consulting and Clinical Psychology, 60,* 379–391.

Teri, L., et al. (1997). Behavioral treatment of depression in dementia patients: A controlled clinical trial. *Journal of Gerontology: Psychological Sciences, 52B,* 159–166.

Terman, M., et al. (1996). Predictors of response and nonresponse to light treatment for winter depression. *American Journal of Psychiatry, 153,*1423–1429.

Terry, D. J., Mayocchi, L., & Hynes, G. J. (1996). Depressive symptomatology in new mothers: A stress and coping perspective. *Journal of Abnormal Psychology, 105,* 220–231.

Testosterone wimping out? (1995, July). *Newsweek,* p. 61.

Tests suggest possible protection from Huntington's symptoms. (1997, March 27). *The New York Times,* p. A 20.

Teunisse, R. J., et al. (1996). Visual hallucinations in psychologically normal people: Charles Bonnnet's syndrome. *Lancet, 347,* 794–797.

Thakker, J., & Ward, T. (1998). Culture and classification: The cross-cultural application of the DSM-IV. *Clinical Psychology Review, 18,* 501–529.

Thaper, A., et al. (1994). The genetics of mental retardation. *British Journal of Psychiatry, 164,* 747–758.

Tharp, R. G. (1991). Cultural diversity and treatment of children. *Journal of Consulting and Clinical Psychology, 59,* 799–812.

Thase, M.E. (1997a). In reply. *Archives of General Psychiatry, 54,* 1973.

Thase, M. E. (1997b). Sertraline and imipramine for the treatment of dysthymia: Reply. *Archives of General Psychiatry, 54,* 973.

Thase, M. E., & Kupfer, D. J. (1996). Recent developments in the pharmacotherapy of mood disorders. *Journal of Consulting and Clinical Psychology, 64,* 646–659.

Thase, M. E., et al (1991). Cognitive behavior therapy of endogenous depression: I. An outpatient clinical replication series. *Behavior Therapy, 22,* 457–467.

Thase, M. E., et al. (1996). A placebo-controlled, randomized clinical trial comparing sertraline and imipramine for the treatment of dysthymia. *Archives of General Psychiatry, 53,* 777–784.

Thase, M. E., et al. (1997). Treatment of major depression with psychotherapy or psychotherapy-pharmacotherapy combinations. *Archives of General Psychiatry, 54,* 1009–1015.

Theorell, T. (1992). Critical life changes: A review of research. *Psychotherapy and Psychosomatics, 57,* 108–117.

Thigpen, D. E. (1994, December 12). Chin music. *Time,* pp. 71–72.

Thoits, P. A. (1983). Dimensions of life events as influences upon the genesis of psychological distress and associated conditions: An evaluation and synthesis of the literature. In H. B. Kaplan (Ed.), *Psychosocial stress: Trends in theory and research.* New York: Academic Press.

Thomas, A. M., & LoPiccolo, J. (1994). Sexual functioning in persons with diabetics: Issues in research, treatment, and education.*Clinical Psychology Review, 14,*61–86.

Thomlison, B., et al. (1991). Characteristics of Canadian male and female child sexual abuse victims. Special Issue: Child sexual abuse. *Journal of Child and Youth Care, Fall,* 65–76.

Thompson, C. E., Worthington, R., & Atkinson, D. R. (1994). Counselor content orienation, counselor race, and Black women's cultural mistrust and self-disclosures. *Journal of Counseling Psychology, 41,* 155–161.

Thompson, L. (1991, January, 15). Health status of Hispanics: Nation's fastest-growing minority lacks access to medical care. *Washington Post.*

Thoreson, C. E., & Mahoney, M. J. (1974). *Behavioral self-control.* New York: Holt, Rinehart, & Winston.

Thun, M. J., et al. (1997). Alcohol consumption and mortality among middle-aged and elderly U.S. adults. *The New England Journal of Medicine, 337,* 1705–1714.

Tienari, P. (1991). Interaction between genetic vulnerability and family environment: The Finnish adoptive family study of schizophrenia. *Acta Psychiatrica Scandinavica, 84,* 460–465.

Tienari, P. (1992). Implications of adoption studies on schizophrenia. *British Journal of Psychiatry, 161,* (18, Suppl) 52–58.

Tienari, P., et al. (1987). Genetic and psychosocial factors in schizophrenia: The Finnish Adoptive Family Study. *Schizophrenia Bulletin,13,* 477–484.

Tienari, P., et al. (1990). Adopted-away offspring of schizophrenics and controls: The Finnish adoptive family study of schizophrenia. In L. Robins & M. Rutter (Eds.), *Straight and devious pathways from childhood to adulthood.* New York: Cambridge University Press.

Tiihonen, J., et al. (1992). Modified activity of the human auditory cortex during auditory hallucinations. *American Journal of Psychiatry, 149,* 255–257.

Tiihonen, J., et al. (1997). Specific major mental disorders and criminality: A 26-year prospective study of the 1996 Northern Finland Birth Cohort.*American Journal of Psychiatry, 154,* 840–845.

Timbrook, R. E., & Graham, J. R. (1994). Ethnic differences on the MMPI-2? *Psychological Assessment, 6,* 212–217.

Timpson, J., et al. (1988). Depression in a Native Canadian in Northwestern Ontario: Sadness, grief or spiritual illness? *Canada's Mental Health, 36* (2–3), 5–8.

Tinker, J. E., & Tucker, J. A. (1997). Motivations for weight loss and behavior change strategies associated with natural recovery for obesity. *Psychology of Addictive Behaviors, 11,* 98–106.

Tobin, D. L. Johnson, C. L., & Dennis, A. B. (1992). Divergent forms of purging behavior in bulimia nervosa patients. *International Journal of Eating Disorders, 11,* 17–24.

Tobin, J. (1996). A case of Koro in a 20-year-old Irish male. *Irish Journal of Psychological Medicine, 13,* 72–73.

Tolchin, M. (1989, July 19). When long life is too much: Suicide rises among elderly. *The New York Times,* pp. A1, A15.

Tollefson, G. D., et al. (1997a). Olanzapine versus haloperidol in the treatment of schizophrenia and schizoaffective and schzophreniform disorders: Results of an international collaborative trial. *American Journal of Psychiatry, 154,* 448– 456.

Tollefson, G. D., et al. (1997b). Blind, controlled, long-term study of the comparative incidence of treatment-emergent tardive dyskinesia with olanzapine or halperidol. *American Journal of Psychiatry, 154,* 1248–1254.

Tomes, H. (1993). It's in the nation's interest to break abuse cycle. *APA Monitor, 24* (3), 28.

Tondo, L., et al. (1998). Lithium maintenance treatment of depression and mania in Bipolar I and Bipolar II disorders. *American Journal of Psychiatry, 155,* 638–645.

Tonnesen, P., Norregaard, J., Simonsen, K., & Sawe, U. (1991). A double-blind trial of a 16-hour transdermal nicotine patch in smoking cessation. *The New England Journal of Medicine, 325,* 311–315.

Tonnessen, F. E., et al. (1994). Immune disorders and dyslexia: A study of asthmatic children. *Reading & Writing, 6,* 151–160.

Torgersen, S. (1983). Genetic factors in anxiety disorders. *Archives of General Psychiatry, 40,* 1085–1089.

Torgersen, S. (1986). Genetic factors in moderately severe and mild affective disorder. *Archives of General Psychiatry, 43,* 222–226.

Torgersen, S., et al. (1993). "True" schizotypal personality disorder: A study of co-twins and relatives of schizophrenic probands. *American Journal of Psychiatry, 150,* 1661–1667.

Toro, P. A., et al. (1995). Distinguishing homelessness from poverty: A comparative study. *Journal of Consulting and Clinical Psychology, 63,* 280–289.

Toro, P. A., et al. (1997). Evaluating an intervention for homeless persons: Results of a field experiment. *Journal of Consulting and Clinical Psychology, 65,* 476–484.

Toth, S. L., & Cicchetti, D. (1996). Patterns of relatedness, depressive symptomatology, and perceived competence in maltreated children. *Journal of Consulting and Clinical Psychology, 64,* 32–41.

Toubiana, Y. H., Milgram, N. A., Strich, Y., & Edelstein, A. (1988). Crisis intervention in a school-community disaster: Principles and practice. *Journal of Community Psychology, 16,* 228–240.

Touchette, N. (1991). Bad rap for Prozac? *The Journal of NIH Research, 3,* 42–47.

Toufexis, A. (1993, April 19). Seeking the roots of violence. *Time Magazine* pp. 52–53.

Tough new warning on diet is issued by Cancer Society. (1996, September 17). *The New York Times,* p. A16.

Tower, R. B., & Kasl, S. V. (1996). Depressive symptoms across older spouses: Longitudinal influences. *Psychology and Aging, 11,* 683–697.

Tracy, J. I, Josiassen, R. C., & Bellack, A. S. (1995). Neuropsychology of dual diagnosis: Understanding the combined effects of schizophrenia and substance use disorders. *Clinical Psychology Review, 15,* 67–98.

Tradgold, A. F. (1914). *Mental deficiency.* New York: Wainwood.

Tran, P. V., et al. (1997). Double-blind comparison of alanzepine versus risperidone in the treatment of schizophrenia and other psychotic disorders. *Journal of Clinical Psychopharmacology, 17,* 407–418.

Transdermal Nictotine Study Group. (1991). Transdermal nicotine for smoking cessation: Six-month results from two multicenter, controlled clinical trials. *Journal of the American Medical Association, 266,* 3133–3138.

Trappler, B., & Friedman, S. (1996). Posttraumatic stress disorder in survivors of the Brooklyn Bridge shooting. *American Journal of Psychiatry, 153,* 705–707.

Trask, P. C., & Sigmon, S. T. (1997). Munchausen syndrome: A review and new conceptualization. *Clinical Psychology: Science and Practice, 4,* 346–358.

Traven, N. D., et al. (1995). Coronary heart disease mortality and sudden death: Trends and patterns in 35- to 44-year-old white males, 1970-1990. *American Journal of Epidemiology, 142,* 45–52.

Treadwell, K. R. H., & Kendall, P. C. (1996). Self-talk in youth with anxiety disorders: States of mind, content specificity, and treatment outcome. *Journal of Consulting and Clinical Psychology, 64,* 941–950.

Treaster, J. B. (1991a, January 25). Drop in youth's cocaine use may reflect social shift.*The New York Times* p.A18.

Treaster, J. B. (1991b, October 29). Costly and scarce, marijuana is a high more are rejecting. *The New York Times,* p. A1.

Treatment of Drug Abuse and Addiction—Part I. (1995, August). *The Harvard Mental Health Letter, 12,* pp. 1–4.

Treatment of alcoholism—Part II. (1996, September) *The Harvard Mental Health Letter, 13,* 1–5.

Treffert, D. A. (1988). The idiot savant: A review of the syndrome. *American Journal of Psychiatry, 145,* 563–572.

Tremblay, R. E., et al. (1992). Early disruptive behavior, poor school achievement, delinquent behavior, and delinquent personality: Longitudinal analyses. *Journal of Consulting and Clinical Psychology, 60,* 64–72.

Trenton State College. (1991, Spring). *Sexual Assault Victim Education and Support Unit (SAVES-U) Newsletter.*

Treves, T. A. (1991). Epidemiology of Alzheimer's disease. *Psychiatric Clinics of North America, 14,* 251–265.

Trichopoulos, D., Li, F. P., & Hunter, D. J. (1996). What causes cancer? *Scientific American, 275,* pp. 80–87.

Trimble, J. E. (1991). The mental health service and training needs of American Indians. In H. F. Myers et al. (Eds.), *Ethnic minority perspectives on clinical training and services in psychology* (pp. 43–48). Washington, D C: American Psychological Association.

Trojanowski, J. Q., et al. (1997). Strategies for improving the postmortem neuropathological diagnosis of Alzheimer's disease. *Neurobiology of Aging, 18,*(4S), S75-S79.

Truman, D. M., Tokar, D. M., & Fischer, A. R. (1996). Dimensions of masculinity: Relations to date rape supportive attitudes and sexual aggression in dating situations. *Journal of Counseling and Development, 74,* 555–562.

Tseng, W. et al. (1992). Koro epidemics in Guangdong, China: A questionnaire survey. *Journal of Nervous & Mental Disease, 180,* 117–123.

Tsoh, J. Y., et al. (1997). Smoking cessation 2: Components of effective intervention. *Behavioral Medicine, 23,* 15–27.

Tsuang, D., & Coryell, W. (1993). An 8-year follow-up of patients with DSM-III-R psychotic depression, schizoaffective disorder, and schizophrenia. *American Journal of Psychiatry, 150,* 1182–1188.

Tsuang, M. T., Simpson, J.C., & Fleming, J. A. (1992). Epidemiology of suicide. *International Review of Psychiatry, 4,* 117–129.

Tsuang, M. T., et al. (1998). Co-occurence of abuse of different drugs in men: The role of drug-specific and shared vulnerabilities. *Archives of General Psychiatry, 55,* 967–972.

Tune, L. (1998). Treatments for dementia. In P. E. Nathan, & J. M. Gorman (Eds.), *A guide to treatments that work* (pp. 90–126). New York: Oxford Press.

Turner, R. J., & Wagonfield, M. O. (1967). Occupational mobility and schizophrenia. *American Sociological Review, 32,* 104–113.

Turner, S. M. (1992, December). Behavioral treatment of anxiety disorders in African-Americans. Paper presented at a symposium, *Anxiety Disorders in African Americans,* presented by the State University of New York Health Science Center at Brooklyn, Brooklyn, NY.

Turner, S. M. (1996 November). Nature and treatment of social phobia. *Clinician's Research Digest,* Supplemental Bulletin 15.

Turner, S. M., & Beidel, D. C. (1989). Social phobia: Clinical syndrome, diagnosis, and comorbidity. *Clinical Psychology Review, 9,* 3–18.

Turner, S. M., Beidel, D. C., & Costello, A. (1987). Psychopathology in the offspring of anxiety disorder patients. *Journal of Consulting and Clinical Psychology, 55,* 229–235.

Turner, S. M., Beidel, D. C., Dancu, C. V., & Keys, D. J. (1986a). Psychopathology of social phobia and comparison to avoidant personality disorder. *Journal of Abnormal Psychology, 95,* 389–394.

Turner, S. M., Beidel, D. C., & Jacob, R. G. (1994). Social phobia: A comparison of behavior therapy and atenolol. *Journal of Consulting and Clinical Psychology, 62,* 350–358.

Turner, S. M., Beidel, D. C., & Townsley, R. M. (1990). Social phobia; Relationship to shyness. *Behaviour Research & Therapy, 28,* 497–505.

Turner, S. M., Beidel, D. C., & Townsley, R. M. (1992). Social phobia: A comparison of specific and generalized subtypes and avoidant personality disorder. *Journal of Abnormal Psychology, 101,* 326–331.

Turner, S. M., & Luber, R. F. (1980). The token economy in day hospital settings: Contingency management or information feedback. *Journal of Behavior Therapy and Experimental Psychiatry, 11,* 89–94.

Turner, S. M., McCann, B. S., Beidel, D. C., & Mezzich, J. E. (1986b). DSM-III classification of the anxiety disorders: A psychometric study. *Journal of Abnormal Psychology, 95,* 168–172.

Turovksy, J., & Barlow, D. H. (1995, Summer). Albany Panic Control Treatment (PCT) for panic disorder and agoraphobia. *The Clinical Psychologist, 48* (3), pp. 5–6.

Tutty, L. M. (1992). The ability of elementary school children to learn child sexual abuse prevention concepts. *Child Abuse and Neglect, 16,* 369–384.

U

Uchino, B. N., Cacioppo, J. T., & Keicolt-Glaser, J. K. (1996). The relationship between social support and physiological processes: A review with emphasis on underlying mechanisms and implications for health. *Psychological Bulletin, 119,* 488–531.

U.K. researchers say dyslexia is hereditary. (1998, February 22). *Reuters News Service.*

Ullmann, L. P., & Krasner, L. (1975). *A psychological approach to abnormal behavior* (2nd ed.). Englewood Cliffs, NJ: Prentice-Hall.

Unlocking the secrets of serotonin. (1996, August). *University of Texas Lifetime Health Letter, 8,* pp. 1, 6.

Unsettling report on an epidemic of rape. (1992 May 4) *Time Magazine,* p. 15.

Unützer, J., et al. (1997). Depressive symptoms and the cost of health services in HMO patients aged 65 years and older: A 4-year prospective study *Journal of the American Medical Association, 277,* 1618–1623.

Update on Alzheimer's Disease. Part I. (1995, February). *Harvard Mental Health Letter, 11* (6), 1–5.

U. S. Bureau of the Census. (1989). *Statistical Abstract of the United States: 1989.* (109th ed.). Washington, DC: U. S. Government Printing Office.

U. S. Bureau of the Census. (1994). *Statistical Abstract of the United States: 1994.* (114th ed.). Washington, DC: U. S. Government Printing Office.

U. S. Bureau of Justice Statistics. (1995). *National Crime Victimization Survey.* Washington, DC: Author.

U.S. Department of Health and Human Services (USDHHS). (1982). *The health consequences of smoking: Cardiovascular disease.* (DHHS Publication No. PHS 84–50204). Rockville, MD: Author.

U.S. Department of Health and Human Services (USDHHS). (1986a). *NIDA capsules: Designer drugs.* No. 10. U.S. Department of Health and Human Services (USDHSS)., Public Health Service, Alcohol, Drug Abuse, and Mental Health Administration, National Institute on Drug Abuse. Rockville, MD: National Institute on Drug Abuse.

U.S. Department of Health and Human Services (USDHHS). (1986b). *NIDA capsules: Heroin.* No. 11. U.S. Department of Health and Human Services (USDHSS), Public Health Service, Alcohol, Drug Abuse, and Mental Health Administration, National Institute on Drug Abuse. Rockville, MD: National Institute on Drug Abuse.

U.S. Department of Health and Human Services (USDHHS). (1986c). *NIDA capsules: PCP (phencyclidine).* No. 134 U.S. Department of Health and Human Services (USDHSS). Public Health Service, Alcohol, Drug Abuse, and Mental Health Administration, National Institute on Drug Abuse. Rockville, MD: National Institute on Drug Abuse.

U.S. Department of Health and Human Services (USDHHS). (1991a). *Healthy people 2000: National health promotion and disease prevention objectives.* Washington, DC: U.S. Government Printing Office.

U.S. Department of Health and Human Services (USDHHS). (1991b). *Vital statistics of the United States 1988.* (Vol. 2. Part A. Mortality.) Washington, DC: U.S. Government Printing Office. (DHHS Pub. No. PHS 91–1101).

U.S. Department of Health and Human Services (USDHHS). (1991c). *Alcohol research: Promise for the* decade. (USDHHS, Public Health Service, Alcohol, Drug Abuse, and Mental Health Administration, National Institute on Alcohol Abuse and Alcoholism, Pub. No. ADM-92-1990). Washington, DC: Author.

U.S. Department of Health and Human Services (USDHHS). (1992). *NIDA capsules: LSD (lysergic acid diethylamide)* No. 39. U.S. Department of Health and Human Services, Public Health Service, Alcohol, Drug Abuse, and Mental Health Administration, National Institute on Drug Abuse. Rockville, MD: National Institute on Drug Abuse.

U.S. Department of Health and Human Services (USDHHS). (1993). *National household survey on drug abuse: Highlights 1991.* (DHHS Publication No. (SMA) 93-1979). Washington, DC: U.S. Government Printing Office.

USDHHS. (1994, December 23). *Cigarette Smoking Among Adults - U.S., 1993. Morbidity and Mortality Weekly Report, 43,* Washington, DC: U.S. Government Printing Office.

U.S. Department of Health and Human Services. (1996). Health, United States 1995. *HHS issues annual report, with special profile of women's health.* Rockville, MD: Author.

U.S. Department of Justice. (1986). *Attorney general's commission on pornography: Final report.* Washington, DC: U.S. Government Printing Office.

U.S. Department of Justice (1994). *Crime in the United States: 1993.* Uniform crime reports. Washington, DC: Author.

U.S. Department of Justice, Federal Bureau of Investigation. (1990). *Uniform crime reports. (1990). Rape statistics.* Washington, DC: U. S. Government Printing Office.

U.S. finds heavy toll of rapes on young. (1994, June 23). *The New York Times,* p. A12.

U.S. Senate Committee on the Judiciary. (1991). Violence against women: The increase of rape in America 1990. *Response to the Victimization of Women and Children, 14,* 20–23.

V

Vaillant, G. E. (1996). A long-term follow-up of male alcohol abuse. *Archives of General Psychiatry, 53,* 243–249.

Valdivieso, S., et al. (1996). Growth hormone response to clonidine and the cortisol response to dexamethasone in depressive patients. *Psychiatry Research, 60,* 23–32.

Valentiner, D. P., et al. (1996). Coping strategies and posttraumatic stress disorder in female victims of sexual and nonsexual assault. *Journal of Abnormal Psychology, 105,* 455–458.

Van Balkom, A. J. L. M., et al. (1997). A meta-analysis of the treatment of panic disorder with or without agoraphobia : A comparison of psychopharmacological, cognitive-behavioral, and combination treatments. *Journal of Nervous & Mental Disease, 185,* 510–516.

Van Den Hout, M., Arntz, A., & Hoekstra, R. (1994). Exposure reduced agoraphobia but not panic, and cognitive therapy reduced panic but not agoraphobia. *Behaviour Research and Therapy, 32,* 447–451.

Van Den Hout, M.A., Van Der Molen, M., Griez, E., Lousberg, H., & Nansen, A. (1987). Reduction of CO_2-induced anxiety in panic attacks after repeated CO_2 exposure. *American Journal of Psychiatry, 144,* 788–791.

Van Der Molen, G. M., Van Den Hout, M. A., Vroemen, J., Loustberg, H. et al. (1986). Cognitive determinants of lactate-induced anxiety. *Behaviour Research and Therapy, 24,* 677–680.

Van Der Pahlen, B., et al. (1997). Early antecedents of spouse abuse. *Aggressive Behavior, 23,* 239–243.

Van Dyke, C., & Byck, R. (1982). Cocaine. *Scientific American, 44* (3), 128–141.

Van Italie, T. B. (1985). Health implications of overweight and obesity in the United States. *Annals of Internal Medicine, 103,* 938–988.

Van Kammen, D, P. (1977). γ-Aminobutyric acid (GABA) and the dopamine hypothesis of schizophrenia. *American Journal of Psychiatry, 134,* 138–143.

Van Praag, H.M. (1988). Editorial: Biological psychiatry. *Journal of Nervous and Mental Disease, 176,* 195–199.

Van Son, M. J. M., Mulder, G., & Londen, A. V. (1990). The effectiveness of dry bed training for nocturnal enuresis in adults. *Behaviour Research and Therapy, 28,* 347–349.

Van Wyk, P. H., & Geist, C. S. (1984). Psychosocial development of heterosexual, bisexual, and homosexual behavior. *Archives of Sexual Behavior, 13,* 505–544.

Vega, W. A., et al. (1998). Lifetime prevalence of DSM-III-R psychiatric disorders among urban and rural Mexican Americans in California. *Archives of General Psychiatry, 55,* 771–778.

Venables, P. H. (1996). Schizotypy and maternal exposure to influenza and to cold temperature: The Mautitius study. *Journal of Abnormal Psychology, 105,* 53–60.

Vernberg, J. M., & Vogel, J. M. (1993). Interventions with children after disasters. *Journal of Clinical Child Psychology, 22,* 485–498.

Virkkunen, M. (1990). Biochemical findings in habitual violence and impulsivity: A review. *Psychiatria Fennica, 21,* 119–132.

Virkkunen, M., & Linnoila, M. (1993). Brain serotonin, Type II alcoholism and impulsive violence. *Journal of Studies on Alcohol,* (Suppl. 11), 163–169.

Virkkunen, M., et al. (1994). CSF biochemistries, glucose metabolism, and diurnal activity rhythms in alcoholic, violent offenders, fire setters, and healthy volunteers. *Archives of General Psychiatry, 51,* 20–27.

Vitaro, F., Arseneault, L., & Tremblay, R. E. (1997). Dispositional predictors of problem gambling in male adolescents. *American Journal of Psychiatry, 154,* 1769–1770.

Vitousek, K., Watson, S., & Wilson, G. T. (1998). Enhancing motivation for change in treatment-resistant eating disorders. *Clinical Psychology Review, 18,* 391–420.

Vogler, G. P., DeFries, J. C., & Decker, S. N. (1985). Family history as an indicator of risk for reading disability. *Journal of Learning Disabilities, 18,* 419–421.

Volavka., J., et al. (1996). The electroencephalogram after alcohol administration in high-risk men and the development of alcohol use disorders 10 years later: Preliminary findings. *Archives of General Psychiatry, 53,* 258–263.

Volberding, P. A., et al. (1990). Zidovudine in asymptomatic human immunodeficiency virus infection. *New England Journal of Medicine, 322,* 941–949.

Volberg, R. A., & Steadman, R. A. (1992). Accurately depicting pathological gamblers: Policy and treatment implications. *Journal of Gambling Studies, 8,* 401–412.

Volkow, N. D., et al. (1997). Relationship between subjective effects of cocaine and dopamine transporter occupancy. *Nature, 386,* 827–830.

Volkow, N. D., et al. (1998). Association between decline in brain dopamine activity with age and cognitive and motor impairment in healthy individuals. *American Journal of Psychiatry, 155,* 344–349.

Volpicelli, J. R., et al. (1992). Naltrexone in the treatment of alcohol dependence. *Archives of General Psychiatry, 49,* 876–880.

Volpicelli, J. R., et al. (1994). Naltrexone and the treatment of alcohol dependence. *Alcohol Health & Research World, 18,* 272–278.

Volpicelli, J. R., et al. (1997). Naltrexone and alcohol dependence: Role of subject compliance. *Archives of General Psychiatry, 54,* 737–742.

W

Wachtel, P. L. (1991). Toward a more seamless psychotherapeutic integration. *Journal of Psychotherapy Integration, 1,* 43–54.

Wadden, T. A., Foster, G. D., & Letizia, K. A. (1994). One-year behavioral treatment of obesity: Comparison of moderate and severe caloric restriction and the effects of weight maintenance therapy. *Journal of Consulting and Clinical Psychology, 62,* 165–171.

Wadden, T. A., et al. (1997). Exercise in the treatment of obesity: Effects of four interventions on body composition, resting energy expenditure, appetite, and mood. *Journal of Consulting and Clinical Psychology, 65,* 269–277.

Wadden, T. A., et al. (1998). Exercise and the maintenance of weight loss: 1-year follow-up of a controlled clinical trial. *Journal of Consulting and Clinical Psychology, 66,* 429–433.

Wade, C. & Tavris, C. (1994). The longest war: Gender and culture. In W.J. Lonner & R.S. Malpass (Eds.), *Psychology and culture* (pp. 121–126). Boston: Allyn & Bacon.

Wade, W. A., Treat, T. A., & Stuart, G. L. (1998). Transporting an empirically supported treatment for panic disorder to a service clinic setting: A benchmarking strategy. *Journal of Consulting and Clinical Psychology, 66,* 231–239.

Wagner, B. M. (1997). Family risk factors for child and adolescent suicidal behavior. *Psychological Bulletin, 121,* 246–298.

Wagner, R. K., & Torgesen, J. K. (1987). The nature of phonological processing and its causal role in the acquisition of reading skills. *Psychological Bulletin, 101,* 192–212.

Wakefield, H., & Underwager, R. (1996). Commentary on Kenneth Pope's review. *Clinical Psychology: Science and Practice, 3,* 366–371.

Wakefield, J. C. (1992a). The concept of mental disorder: On the boundary between biological facts and social values. *American Psychologist, 47,* 373–388.

Wakefield, J. C. (1992b). Disorder as harmful dysfunction: A conceptual critique of DSM-III-R's definition of mental disorder. *Psychological Review, 99,* 232–247.

Wakefield, J. C. (1997). Normal inability versus pathological disability: Why Ossorio's definition of mental disorder is not sufficient. *Clinical Psychology: Science and Practice, 4,* 249–258.

Wakeling, A. (1996). Epidemology of anorexia nervosa. *Psychiatry Research, 62,* 3–9.

Wakschlag, L. S., et al. (1997). Maternal smoking during pregnancy and the risk of conduct disorder in boys. *Archives of General Psychiatry, 54,* 670–676.

Waldinger, M. D., Hengeveld, M. W., & Zwinderman, A. H. (1994). Paroxetine treatment of premature ejaculation: A double-blind, randomized, placebo-controlled study. *American Journal of Psychiatry, 151,* 1377–1379.

Walker, C. E., Hedberg, A., Clement, P. W., & Wright, L. (1981). *Clinical procedures for behavior therapy.* Englewood Cliffs, NJ: Prentice-Hall.

Walker, E. F., & Diforio, D. (1997). Schizophrenia: A neural diathesis-stress model. *Psychological Review, 104,* 667–685.

Walker, L. E. (1979). *The battered woman.* New York: Harper & Row.

Walker, L.E. (1988). The battered woman syndrome. In G. T. Hotaling, D. Finkelhor, J. T. Kirkpatrick, and M. A. Straus (Eds.), *Family abuse and its consequences: New directions in research* (pp. 139–148). Newbury Park, CA: Sage Publications.

Wallace, C. J., & Liberman, R. P. (1985). Social skills training for patients with schizophrenia: A controlled clinical trial. *Psychiatry Research, 15,* 239–247.

Wallace, J. (1985). The alcoholism controversy. *American Psychologist, 40,* 372–373.

Wallen, J. (1992). Providing culturally appropriate mental health services for minorities. Special Issue: Multicultural mental health and substance abuse services. *Journal of Mental Health Administration, 19,* 288–295.

Waller, N. G., & Ross, C. A. (1997). The prevalence of biometric structure of pathological dissociation in the general population: Taxometric and behavior genetic findings. *Journal of Abnormal Psychology, 106,* 499–510.

Walsh, B. T., et al. (1997). Medication and psychotherapy in the treatment of bulimia nervosa. *American Journal of Psychiatry, 154,* 523–531.

Wampold, B .E., et al. (1997a). A meta-analysis of outcome studies comparing bona fide psychotherapies: Empirically, "All must have prizes." *Psychological Bulletin, 122,* 203–215.

Wampold, B. E., et al. (1997b). The flat earth as a metaphor for the evidence for uniform efficacy of bona fide psychotherapies: Reply to Crits-Christoph (1997) and Howard et al. (1997). *Psychological Bulletin, 122,* 226–230.

Warheit, G. J., Vega, W. A., Auth, J., & Meinhardt, K. (1985). Psychiatric symptoms and dysfunctions among Anglos and Mexican Americans: An epidemiological study. In J. R. Greenley (Ed.), *Research in community and mental health* (pp. 3–32). London: JAI Press.

Warner, L. A., et al. (1995). Prevalence and correlates of drug use and dependence in the United States. *Archives of General Psychiatry, 52,* 219–229.

Waterman, J., & Lusk, R. (1986). Scope of the problem. In K. MacFarlane et al. (Eds.), *Sexual abuse of young children: Evaluation and treatment* (pp. 315–332). New York: Guilford Press.

Waterman, J. (1986). Overview of treatment issues. In K. MacFarlane et al. (Eds.), *Sexual abuse of young children: Evaluation and treatment* (pp. 197–203). New York: Guilford Press.

Waterman, J., et al. (1986). Challenges for the future. In K. MacFarlane, et al. (Eds.), *Sexual abuse of young children: Evaluation and treatment* (pp. 315–332). New York: Guilford Press.

Waterman, J. (1986). Overview of treatment issues. In K. MacFarlane et al. (Eds.), *Sexual abuse of young children: Evaluation and treatment* (pp. 197–203). New York: Guilford.

Watson, C. G., et al. (1997). Lifetime prevalences of nine common psychiatric/personality disorders in female domestic abuse survivors. *Journal of Nervous & Mental Disease, 185,* 645–647.

Watson, D., et al., (1995a). Testing a tripartite model: I. Evaluating the convergent and discriminant validity of anxiety and depression symptom scales. *Journal of Abnormal Psychology, 104,* 3–14.

Watson, D., et al. (1995b). Testing a tripartite model: II. Exploring the symptom structure of anxiety and depression in student, adult, and patient samples. *Journal of Abnormal Psychology, 104,* 15–25.

Watson, J. D., & Crick, F. H. C. (1953). Molecular structure of nucleic acids: A structure for deoxyribose nucleic acid. *Nature, 171,* 737–738.

Watters, W. W. (1986). Supra-biological factors in the assessment of males seeking penile prostheses. *Canadian Journal of Psychiatry, 31,* 25–31.

Weaver, T. L., & Clum, G. A. (1995). Psychological distress associated with interpersonal violence: A meta-analysis. *Clinical Psychology Review, 15,* 115–140.

Webber P., Fox, P., & Burnette, D. (1994). Living alone with Alzheimer's disease: Effects on health and social service utilization patterns. *Gerontologist, 34,* 8–14.

Weber, B. (1996, July 6). First arrests in New York under sex-offender law. *The New York Times,* p. B24.

Webster-Stratton, C., & Hammond, M. (1997). Treating children with early-onset conduct problems: A comparison of child and parent training interventions. *Journal of Consulting and Clinical Psychology, 65,* 93–109.

Wechsler, D. (1945). A standardized memory scale for clinical use. *Journal of Psychology, 19,* 87–95.

Wechsler, D. (1975). Intelligence defined and undefined: A relativistic appraisal. *American Psychologist, 30,* 135–139.

Wechsler, H., et al. (1994). Health and behavioral consequences of binge drinking in college: A national survey of students at 140 campuses. *Journal of the American Medical Association, 272,* 1672–1677.

As weight goes up so does breast cancer risk. (1996, July). *Tufts University Diet & Nutrition Letter, 14,* 1–2.

Weinberg, G. (1972). *Society and the healthy homosexual.* New York: St. Martin's Press.

Weinberger, D. R., et al. (1986). Physiological dysfunction of dorsolateral prefrontal cortex in schizophrenia: I. Regional cerebral blood flow (rCBF) evidence. *Archives of General Psychiatry, 43,* 935– 939.

Weinberger, D. R. (1997). On localizing schizophrenic neuropathology. *Schizophrenia Bulletin, 23,* 537–540.

Weinberger, J. (1995). Common factors aren't so common: The common factors dilemma. *Clinical Psychology: Science and Practice, 2,* 45–69.

Weiner, I. B. (1994). The Rorschach inkblot method (RIM) is not a test: Implications for theory and practice. *Journal of Personality Assessment, 62,* 498–504.

Weiner, I. B. (1996). Some observations on the validity of the Rorschach inkblot method. *Psychological Assessment, 8,* 206–213.

Weiner, K. E., & Thompson, J. K (1997). Overt and covert sexual abuse: Relationship to body image and eating disturbance. *International Journal of Eating Disorders, 22,* 273–284.

Weiner, M. (1988). A crisis as a challenge. In M. K. Aronson (Ed.), *Understanding Alzheimer's Disease.* New York: Charles Scribner's & Sons.

Weiner, M. (1989, November 26). Evidence points to aluminum's link with Alzheimer's disease. *The New York Times,* p. E12.

Weiner, M. F. (1996, July). What new treatments for Alzheimer's disease are being explored? *The Harvard Mental Health Letter, 13* (1), p. 8.

Weiner, M. F. (1997). Current status of the Rorschach inkblot method. *Journal of Personality Assessment, 68,* 5–19.

Weingartner, H. J., et al. (1996). Conceptual and practical issues in the development and assessment of drugs that would enhance cognition. In D. Herrmann, C. McEvoy, C. Hertzog, P. Hertel, & M. K. Johnson (Eds.), *Basic and applied memory research: Practical applications, Vol. 2* (pp. 439–454) Mahwah, NJ: Erlbaum.

Weinraub, B. (1994, January 19). Movie and museum worlds are suffering with the rest. *The New York Times,* p. A17.

Weintraub, S. (1987). Risk factors in schizophrenia: The Stony Brook High-Risk Project. *Schizophrenia Bulletin, 13,* 439–450.

Weisman, A., et al. (1993). An attributional analysis of expressed emotion in Mexcian-American families with schizophrenia. *Journal of Abnormal Psychology, 102,* 601–606.

Weisman, A. G., et al. (1998). Expressed emotion, attributions, and schizophrenia symptom dimensions. *Journal of Abnormal Psychology, 107,* 355–359.

Weiss, B., Dodge, K. A., Bates, J. E., & Pettit, G. S. (1992). Some consequences of early harsh discipline: Child aggression and a maladaptive social information processing style. *Child Development, 63,* 1321–1335.

Weiss, G. (1985). Follow-up studies on outcome of hyperactive children. *Psychopharmacology Bulletin, 21,* 169–177.

Weiss, R. (1992). Update on nicotine patches: With help, they help some. *The New York Times,* p. C15.

Weiss, R. D, & Mirin, S. M. (1987). *Cocaine.* Washington, DC: American Psychiatric Press Inc.

Weissman, A. N., & Beck, A. T. (1978, November). *Development and validation of the Dysfunctional Attitudes Scale: A preliminary investigation.* Paper presented at the meeting of the American Educational Research Association, Toronto, Canada.

Weissman, M. (1986). The relationship between panic disorder and agoraphobia: An epidemiologic perspective. *Psychopharmacology Bulletin, 22,* 787–791.

Weissman, M., et al. (1981). Depressed outpatients. Results one year after treatment with drugs and/or interpersonal psychotherapy. *Archives of General Psychology, 18,* 51–55.

Weissman, M. M., & Markowtiz, J. C. (1994). Interpersonal psychotherapy: Current status. *Archives of General Psychiatry, 51,* 599–606.

Weissman, M. M. et al. (1989). Suicidal ideation and suicide attempts in panic disorder and attacks. *The New England Journal of Medicine, 321,* 1209–1214.

Weissman, M. M., et al. (1991). Affective disorders. In L. N. Robins & D. A. Regier (Eds.), *Psychiatric disorders in America: The Epidemiologic Catchment Area Study* (pp. 53–80). New York: The Free Press.

Weissman, M. M., et al. (1994). The cross-national epidemiology of obsessive compulsive disorder. *Journal of Clinical Psychiatry, 55* (Suppl. 3), 5–10.

Weissman, M. M., et al. (1997). The cross-national epidemiology of panic disorder. *Archives of General Psychiatry, 54,* 305–309.

Weissman, M. W., et al. (1996). Cross-national epidemiology of major depression and bipolar disorder. *Journal of the American Medical Association, 276,* 293–299.

Weisz, J. R., et al. (1987). Epidemiology of behavioral and emotional problems among Thai and American children: Parent reports for ages 6 to 11. *Journal of the American Academy of Child and Adolescent Psychiatry, 26,* 890–897.

Weisz, J. R., et al. (1988). Thai and American perspectives on over- and undercontrolled child behavior problems: Exploring the threshold model among parents, teachers, and psychologists. *Journal of Consulting and Clinical Psychology, 56,* 601–609.

Weisz, J. R., et al. (1995). Effects of psychotherapy with children and adolescents revisited: A meta-analysis of treatment outcome studies. *Psychological Bulletin, 117,* 450–468.

Wekerle, C., & Wolfe, D. A. (1993). Prevention and child physical abuse and neglect: Promising new directions. *Clinical Psychology Review, 13,* 501–540.

Welch, M. R., & Kartub, P. (1978). Socio-cultural correlates of incidence of impotence: A cross-cultural study. *Journal of Sex Research, 14,* 218–230.

Welch, S.L., & Fairburn, C.G. (1996). Childhood sexual and physical abuse as risk factors for the development of bulimia nervosa. *Child Abuse and Neglect, 20,* 633–642.

Weller, E. (1997, July). Long-term impact of exposure to suicide. *Journal Watch for Psychiatry, 2* (7), 55.

Weltzin, T. E., et al. (1994). Prediction of reproductive status in women with bulimia nervosa by past high weight. *American Journal of Psychiatry, 151,* 136–138.

Wenar, C. (1983). *Psychopathology from infancy through adolescence: A developmental approach.* New York: Random House.

Wender, P. H., Rosenthal, D., Kety, S. S., Schulsinger, F., & Welner, J. (1974). Cross-fostering: A research strategy for clarifying the role of genetic and experiential factors in the etiology of schizophrenia. *Archives of General Psychiatry, 30,* 121–128.

Wenzlaff, R. M., & Grozier, S. A. (1988). Depression and the magnification of failure. *Journal of Abnormal Psychology, 97,* 90–93.

Wertlieb, D., Weigel, C., & Feldstein, M. (1987). Stress, social support, and behavior symptoms in middle childhood. *Journal of Clinical Child Psychology, 16,* 204–211.

West, C., et al. (1995, August). Black/white differences in coping with the aftermath of Hurricane Andrew.

641

Paper presented at the meeting of the American Psychological Association, New York, NY.

West, M. A. (1985). Meditation and somatic arousal reduction. *American Psychologist, 40,* 717–719.

Westermeyer, J. (1984). The role of ethnicity in substance abuse. In B. Stimmel (Ed.), *Cultural and sociologial aspects of alcoholism and substance abuse* (pp. 9–18). New York: Haworth Press.

Wetzler, S. (1990). The Millon Clinical Multiaxial Inventory (MCMI): A review. *Journal of Personality Assessement, 55,* 445–464.

Whalen, C. K., et al. (1987). Natural social behaviors in hyperactive children: Dose effects of methylphenidate. *Journal of Consulting and Clinical Psychology, 55,* 187–193.

What is catatonia? (1995, February). *Harvard Mental Health Letter, 11* (8), p. 8.

What is PTSD? *American Journal of Psychiatry,* [Editorial]*154,* 143–145.

Whiffen, V. E. (1988). Vulnerability to postpartum depression: A prospective multivariate study. *Journal of Abnormal Psychology, 97,* 467–474.

Whiffen, V. E. (1992). Is postpartum depression a distinct diagnosis? *Clinical Psychology Review, 12,* 485–508.

Whiffen, V. E., & Gotlib, I. H. (1993). Comparison of postpartum and nonpostpartum depression: Clinical presentation, psychiatric history, and psychosocial functioning. *Journal of Consulting and Clinical Psychology, 61,* 485–493.

Whitam, F. L., Diamond, M., & Martin, J. (1993). Homosexual orientation in twins: A report on 61 pairs and three triplet sets. *Archives of Sexual Behavior, 22,* 187–206.

Whitehead, W. E., & Bosmajian, L. S. (1982). Behavioral medicine approaches to gastrointestinal disorders. *Journal of Consulting and Clinical Psychology, 50,* 972–983.

Wickelgren, I. (1997, June 27). Marijuana: Harder than thought? *Science, 276,* 1967.

Wickenhaver, J. (1992, September 8). After the "Wild Man": Can an insane system be cured? *Manhattan Spirit,* pp. 13, 28.

Wickizer, T. M., Lessler, D., & Travis, K .M. (1996). Controlling inpatient psychiatric utilization through managed care. *American Journal of Psychiatry, 153,* 339–345.

Widiger, T. A. (1991). DSM-IV reviews of the personality disorders: Introduction to special series. *Journal of Personality Disorder, 5,* 122–134.

Widiger, T. A. (1992). Generalized social phobia versus avoidant personality disorder: A commentary on three studies. *Journal of Abnormal Psychology, 101,* 340–343.

Widiger, T. A. (1994, November). DSM-IV: Rationale and highlights. *Clinician's Research Digest,* (Supplemental Bulletin 11), pp. 1–2.

Widiger, T. A., & Costa, P. T., Jr. (1994). Personality and personality disorders. *Journal of Abnormal Psychology, 103,* 78–91.

Widiger, T. A., & Weissman, M. M. (1991). Epidemiology of borderline personality disorder. *Hospital and Community Psychiatry, 10,* 1015–1021.

Widiger, T. A., et al. (1991). Toward an empirical classification for the *DSM-IV. Journal of Abnormal Psychology, 100,* 280–288.

Widner, H., et al. (1992). Bilateral fetal mesencephalic grafting in two patients with Parkinsonism induced by 1-methyl-4-phenyl-1,2,3,6-tetrahydropyridine (MPTP). *The New England Journal of Medicine, 327,* 1556–1563.

Widom, C.S. (1989a). Child abuse, neglect, and adult behavior: Research design and findings on criminality, violence, and child abuse. *American Journal of Orthopsychiatry, 59,* 355–367.

Widom, C. S. (1989b). Does violence beget violence? A critical examination of the literature. *Psychological Bulletin, 106,* 3–28.

Widom, C. S. (1991). Childhood victimization: Risk factor for delinquency. In M. E. Colten & S. Gore (Eds.), *Adolescent stress: Causes and consequences* (pp. 201–221). New York: DeGruyter.

Wiersma, D., et al. (1998). Natural course of schizophrenic disorders: A 15-year follow-up of a Dutch incidence cohort. *Schizophrenia Bulletin, 24,* 75–85.

Wig, N. N., et al. (1987). Distribution of expressed emotion components among relatives of schizophrenic patients in Aarhus and Chandigarh. *British Journal of Psychiatry, 151,* 160–165.

Wilbur, C. B. (1986). Psychoanalysis and multiple personality disorder. In B. G. Braun (Ed.), *Treatment of multiple personality disorder.* Washington, DC: American Psychiatric Press.

Wilkie, F. L., et al. (1998). Mild cognitive impairment and risk of mortality in HIV-1 infection. *Journal of Neuropsychiatry and Clinical Neuroscience, 10,* 125–132.

Wilkinson, D. J. C., et al. (1998). Sympathetic activity in patients with panic disorder at rest, under laboratory mental stress, and during panic attacks. *Archives of General Psychiatry, 55,* 511–520.

William, W. (1994). The society of Alcoholics Anonymous: 105th annual meeting of the American Psychiatric Association (1949, Montreal, Canada). *American Journal of Psychiatry, 151* (6, Suppl.), 259–262.

Williams, B. F., et al. (1994). Fetal alcohol syndrome: Developmental characteristics and directions for further research. *Education and Treatment of Children, 17,* 86–97.

Williams, D. H. (1986). The epidemiology of mental illness in Afro-Americans. *Hospital and Community Psychiatry, 37,* 42–49.

Williams, E. E., & Ellison, F. (1996). Culturally informed social work practice with American Indian clients: Guidelines for non-Indian social workers. *Social Work, 41,* 147–151.

Williams, J. B., et al. (1992). The Structured Clinical Interview for DSM-III— (SCID). II: Multisite test-retest reliability. *Archives of General Psychiatry, 49,* 630–636.

Williams, J. B. W. (1985). The multiaxial system of DSM III: Where did it come from and where should it go? It's origins and critics. *Archives of General Psychiatry, 42,* 175–180.

Williams, J. M. (1984). *The psychological treatment of depression: A guide to the theory and practice of cognitive-behavior therapy.* New York: The Free Press.

Williams, J. M., Little, M. M., Scates, S., & Blockman, N. (1987). Memory complaints and abilities among depressed older adults. *Journal of Consulting and Clinical Psychology, 55,* 595–598.

Williams, K., E., Chambless, D. L., & Ahrens, A. (1997). Are emotions frightening? An extension of the fear of fear construct. *Behaviour Research and Therapy, 35,* 239–248.

Williams, L. (1989, November 22). Psychotherapy gaining favor among blacks. *The New York Times,* pp. A1, C7.

Williams, M. (1985). Alcohol and ethnic minorities: Black Americans—an update. *Alcohol Health and Research World, 9,* 52–54.

Williams, P. G., Wiebe, D. J., & Smith, T. W. (1992). Coping processes as mediators of the relationship between hardiness and health. *Journal of Behavioral Medicine, 15,* 237–255.

Williams, R. B., et al. (1997). Psychosocial correlates of job strain in a sample of working women. *Archives of General Psychiatry, 54,* 543–548.

Williams, S. L., & Falbo, J. (1996). Cognitive and performance-based treatments for panic attacks in people with varying degrees of agoraphobic disability. *Behaviour Research and Therapy, 34,* 253–264.

Williamson, G. M., & Schulz, R. (1992). Physical illness and symptoms of depression among elderly outpatients. *Psychology and Aging, 7,* 343–351.

Wilson, C. C. (1987). Physiological responses of college students to a pet. *Journal of Nervous and Mental Disease, 175,* 606–612.

Wilson, G. T. (1987). Chemical aversion conditioning treatment for alcoholism: A re-analysis. *Behaviour Research and Therapy, 25,* 503–516.

Wilson, G. T. (1991). Chemical aversion conditioning in the treatment of alcoholism: Further comments: *Behaviour Research & Therapy, 29,* 415–419.

Wilson, G. T. (1994). Behavioral treatment of childhood obesity: Theoretical and practical implications. *Health Psychology, 13,* 371–372.

Wilson, G. T. (1996). Treatment of bulimia nervosa: When CBT fails. *Behaviour Research and Therapy, 34,* 197–212.

Wilson, G. T. (1997). Behavior therapy at century close. *Behavior Therapy, 28,* 449–457.

Wilson, G. T., & Fairburn, C. G. (1998). Treatment for eating disorders. In P. E. Nathan, & J. M. Gorman (Eds.), *A guide to treatments that work* (pp. 501–530). New York: Oxford University Press.

Wilson, G. T., & Walsh, T. (1991). Eating disorders in the *DSM-IV. Journal of Abnormal Psychology, 100,* 362–365.

Wilson, K., et al. (1992). Levels of learned helplessness in abused women. *Women and Therapy, 13,* 53–67.

Wilson, K. G., et al. (1992). Panic attacks in the nonclinical population: An empirical approach to case identification. *Journal of Abnormal Psychology, 101,* 460–468.

Wilson, K. K. (1997). *The disparate classification of gender and sexual orientation in American psychiatry.* [Online]. Available: http://www.priory.com/psych/disparat.htm

Wilson, M. I., & Daly, M. (1996). Male sexual proprietariness and violence against wives. *Current Directions in Psychological Science, 5,* 2–7.

Wilson, S. A., Becker, L. A., & Tinker, R. H. (1995). Eye movement desensitization and reprocessing (EMDR) treatment for psychologically traumatized individuals. *Journal of Consulting and Clinical Psychology, 63,* 928–937.

Wilson, S. A., Becker, L. A., & Tinker, R. H. (1997). Fifteen-month follow-up of eye movement desensitization and reprocessing (EMDR) treatment for posttraumatic stress disorder and psychological trauma. *Journal of Consulting and Clinical Psychology, 65,* 1047-1056.

Wilson, W. H. (1996). Time required for initial improvement during clozapine treatment of refractory schizophrenia. *American Journal of Psychiatry, 153,* 951–952.

Winefield, H. R., & Harvey, E. J. (1994). Needs of family caregivers in chronic schizophrenia. *Schizophrenia Bulletin, 20,* 557–566.

Winerip, M. (1991, December 18). Soldier in battle for the retarded. *The New York Times,* pp. B1, B6.

Wingert, P., & Kantrowitz, B. (1997, October 27). Why Andy couldn't read. *Newsweek,* pp. 54–64.

Winokur, G., et al. (1993). A prospective follow-up of patients with bipolar and primary unipolar affective disorders. *Archives of General Psychiatry, 50,* 457–465.

Winston, A., et al. (1991). Brief psychotherapy of personality disorders. *Journal of Nervous & Mental Disease, 179,* 188–193.

Winston, A., et al. (1994). Short-term psychotherapy of personality disorders. *American Journal of Psychiatry, 51,* 190–194.

Wirz-Justice, A., et al. (1993). Light therapy in seasonal affective disorder is independent of time of day or circadian phase. *Archives of General Psychiatry, 50,* 929–937.

Wise, E. H., & Barnes, D. R. (1986). The relationship among life events, dysfunctional attitudes, and depression. *Cognitive Therapy and Research, 10,* 257–266.

Wise, R. A. (1988). The neurobiology of craving. *Journal of Abnormal Psychology, 97,* 118–132.

Wise, T. P. (1978). Where the public peril begins: A survey of psychotherapists to determine the effects of *Tarasoff*. *Stanford Law Review, 135*, 165–190.

Wittchen, H., et al. (1994). DSM-III-R generalized anxiety disorder in the National Comorbidity Survey. *Archives of General Psychiatry, 51*, 355–363.

Wlazlo, Z., et al. (1990). Exposure in vivo vs. social skills training for social phobia: Long-term outcome and differential effects. *Behaviour Research & Therapy, 28*, 181–193.

Wolchick, S. A., et al. (1980). The effects of emotional arousal on subsequent sexual arousal in men. *Journal of Abnormal Psychology, 89*, 595–598.

Wolfe, B. E., & Goldfried, M. R. (1988). Research on psychotherapy integration: Recommendations and conclusions from an NIMH workshop. *Journal of Consulting and Clinical Psychology, 56*, 448–451.

Wolfe, D. A. (1987). *Child abuse: Implications for child development and psychopathology*. Newbury Park, CA: Sage Publications.

Wolfe, D. A., & Wekerle, C. (1993). Treatment strategies for child physical abuse and neglect: A critical progress report. *Clinical Psychology Review, 13*, 475–500.

Wolfe, J. et al. (1994). Posttraumatic stress disorder and war-zone exposure as correlates of perceived health in female Vietnam War veterans. *Journal of Consulting and Clinical Psychology, 62*, 1235–1240.

Wolpe, J. (1958). *Psychotherapy by reciprocal inhibition*. Stanford, CA: Stanford University Press.

Wolpe, J., & Lazarus, A. A. (1966). *Behavior therapy techniques*. New York: Pergamon Press.

Wolpe, J., & Rachman, S. (1960). Psychoanalytic "evidence": A critique based on Freud's case of Little Hans. *Journal of Nervous and Mental Disease, 131*, 135–147.

Wolraich, M. L., et al. (1990). Stimulant medication use by primary care physicians in the treatment of attention-deficit hyperactivity disorder. *Pediatrics, 86*, 95–101.

Wolraich, M. L., et al. (1994). Effects of diets high in sucrose or aspartame on the behavior and cognitive performance of children. *New England Journal of Medicine, 330*, 301–307.

Women under assault. (1990, July 16). *Newsweek*, p. 23.

Wonderlich, S. A., et al. (1997). Relationship of childhood sexual abuse and eating disorders. *Journal of the American Academy of Child and Adolescent Psychiatry, 36*, 1107–1115.

Wong, J. L., & Whitaker, D. J. (1993). Depressive mood states and their cognitive and personality correlates in college students: They improve over time. *Journal of Clinical Psychology, 49*, 615–621.

Wong, S. E., Massel, H. K., Mosk, M. D., & Liberman, R. P. (1986). Behavioral approaches to the treatment of schizophrenia. In G. D. Burrows, T. R. Norman, & G. Rubenstein (Eds.), *Handbook of studies on schizophrenia* (pp. 79–100). New York: Elsevier.

Wood, J. M., Nezworski, M. T., & Stejskal, W. J. (1996). The comprehensive system for the Rorschach: A critical examination. *Psychological Science, 7*, 3–10.

Wood, J. M., Nezworski, M. T., & Stejskal, W. J. (1997). The reliability of the comprehensive system for the Rorschach: A comment on Meyer. *Psychological Assessment, 9*, 490–494.

Wood, J. M., et al. (1992). Effects of 1989 San Francisco earthquake on frequency and content of nightmares. *Journal of Abnormal Psychology, 101*, 219–234.

Woodward, A. M., Dwinell, A. D., & Arons, B. S. (1992). Barriers to mental health care for Hispanic Americans: A literature review and discussion. *Journal of Mental Health Administration, 19*, 224–236.

Woody, S., & Rachman, S. (1994). Generalized anxiety disorder (GAD) as an unsuccessful search for safety. *Clinical Psychology Review, 14*, 743–753.

Woody, S. R. (1996). Effects of focus of attention on anxiety levels and social performance of individuals with social phobia. *Journal of Abnormal Psychology, 105*, 61–69.

Wootton, J. M., et al. (1997). Ineffective parenting and childhood conduct problems: The moderating role of callous-unemotional traits. *Journal of Consulting and Clinical Psychology, 65*, 301–308.

Wren, C. S. (1997a, August 20). Saying "no" to drugs but dying in violence. *The New York Times*, p. A16.

Wren, C. S. (1997b, December 21). Survey suggests leveling off in use of drugs by students. *The New York Times*, p. A24.

Wright, J., et al. (1997). Health effects of obstructive sleep apnea and the effectiveness of continuous positive airway pressure: A systematic review of the research evidence. *British Medical Journal, 314*, 851–860.

Wulfert, E., Greenway, D. E., & Dougher, M. J. (1996). A logical functional analysis of reinforcement-based disorders: Alcoholism and pedophilia. *Journal of Consulting and Clinical Psychology, 64*, 1140–1151.

Wyatt v. Stickney, 334 F. Supp. 1341 (1972).

Wyatt, G. E. (1990). The aftermath of child sexual abuse of African American and White American women: The victim's experience. *Journal of Family Violence, 5*, 61–81.

Wyer, R. S., Jr., Bodenhausen, G. V., & Gorman, T. F. (1985). Cognitive mediators of reactions to rape. *Journal of Personality and Social Psychology, 48*, 324–338.

Wynne, L. C., Cole, R. E., & Perkins, P. (1987). University of Rochester Child and Family Study: Risk research in progress. *Schizophrenia Bulletin, 13*, 463-476.

X

Xing-jia Cui, X.J., & Vaillant, G. E. (1996). Antecedents and consequences of negative life events in adulthood: A longitudinal study. *American Journal of Psychiatry, 152*, 21–26.

Y

Yairi,. E., Ambrose, N., & Cox, N. (1996). Genetics of stuttering: A critical review. *Journal of Speech and Hearing Research, 39*, 771–784.

Yan, S. D., et al. (1997). An intracellular protein that binds amyloid-B peptide and mediates neurotoxicity in Alzheimer's disease. *Nature, 389*, 689–695.

Yeh, M., Takeuchi, D. T., & Sue, S. (1994). Asian-American children treated in the mental health system: A comparison of parallel and mainstream outpatient service centers. *Journal of Clinical Child Psychology, 23*, 5–12.

Yehuda, R., et al. (1996). Dissociation in aging holocaust survivors. *American Journal of Psychiatry, 153*, 935–940.

Yehuda, R., Marshall, R., & Giller, E. L., Jr. (1998). Psychopharmacological treatment of post-traumatic stress disorder. In P.E. Nathan & J. M. Gorman (Eds.), *A guide to treatments that work* (pp. 377-397). New York: Oxford University Press.

Yeung, P. P., & Greenwald, S. (1992). Jewish Americans and mental health: Results of the NIMH Epidemiologic Catchment Area Study. *Social Psychiatry and Psychiatric Epidemiology, 27*, 292–297.

Yirmiya, N., & Sigman, M. (1991). High functioning individuals with autism: Diagnosis, empirical findings, and theoretical issues. *Clinical Psychology Review, 11*, 669–683.

Yong, L.C., et al. (1996). Prospective study of relative weight and risk of breast cancer: The breast cancer detection demonstration project follow-up study, 1979 to 1987–1989. *American Journal of Epidemiology, 143*, 985–995.

Yonkers, K. A., et al. (1998). Is the course of panic disorder the same in women and men? *American Journal of Psychiatry, 155*, 596–602.

You needn't starve to keep off lost pounds (1990, February). *Tufts University Diet & Nutrition Letter, 12* (7), p. 7.

Young, A. (1992). Cited in Blakeslee, S. (1992, October 27). Unusual clues help in long fight to solve Huntington's disease. *The New York Times*, p. C3.

Young, M. A., et al. (1994). Interactions of risk factors in predicting suicide. *American Journal of Psychiatry, 51*, 434–435.

Young, M. A., et al. (1996). Stable trait components of hopelessness: Baseline and sensitivity to depression. *Journal of Abnormal Psychology, 105*, 155–165.

Young, T., et al. (1993). The occurrence of sleep-disordered breathing among middle-aged adults. *New England Journal of Medicine, 328*, 1230–1235.

Young, T., et al. (1996). The gender bias in sleep apnea diagnosis. *Archives of Internal Medicine, 156*, 2445–2451.

Young, T. J., & French, L. A. (1996). Suicide and homicide rates among U.S. Indian health service areas: The income inequality hypothesis. *Social Behavior and Personality, 24*, 365–366.

Young, T. K., & Sevenhuyser, G. (1989). Obesity in northern Canadian Indians: patterns, determinants, and consequences. *American Journal of Clinical Nutrition, 49*, 786–793.

Youngberg v. Romeo, 102 S. Ct. 2452, 2463 (1982).

Yuen, N., et al. (1996). The rate and characteristics of suicide attempters in the native Hawaiian adolescent population. *Suicide and Life Threatening Behavior, 26*, 27–36.

Yung, P. M. B., & Keltner, A. A. (1996). A controlled comparison on the effect of muscle and cognitive relaxation procedures on blood pressure: Implications for the behavioural treatment of borderline hypertensives. *Behaviour Research and Therapy, 34*, 821–826.

Yurgelun-Todd, D. A., et al. (1996). Functional magnetic resonance imaging of schizophrenic patients and comparison subjects during word production. *American Journal of Psychiatry, 153*, 200–205.

Z

Zahn-Waxler, C., et al. (1996). Behavior problems in 5-year-old monozygotic and dizygotic twins: Genetic and environmental influences, patterns of regulation, and internalization of control. *Development and Psychopathology, 8*, 103–122.

Zalewski, C., & Archer, R. P. (1991). Assessment of borderline personality disorder: A review of MMPI and Rorschach findings. *Journal of Nervous & Mental Disease, 179*, 338–345.

Zalewski, C. E., & Gottesman, I. I. (1991). (Hu)Man versus mean revisited: MMPI group data and psychiatric diagnosis. *Journal of Abnormal Psychology, 100*, 562–568.

Zamanian, K., et al. (1992). Acculturation and depression in Mexican-American elderly. *Gerontologist, 11*, 109–121.

Zanardi, R., et al. (1996). Double-blind controlled trial of sertraline versus paroxetine in the treatment of delusional depression. *American Journal of Psychiatry, 153*, 1631–1633.

Zanarini, M. C., et al. (1997). Reported pathological childhood experiences associated with the development of borderline personality disorder. *American Journal of Psychiatry, 154*, 1101–1106.

Zane, N., & Sue, S. (1991). Culturally responsive mental health services for Asian Americans: Treatment and training issues. In H. F. Myers et al. (Eds.), *Ethnic minority perspectives on clinical training and services in psychology* (pp. 49–58). Washington, DC: American Psychological Association.

Zatzick, D. F., et al. (1997). Posttraumatic stress disorder and functioning and quality of life outcomes in a nationally representative sample of male Vietnam veterans. *American Journal of Psychiatry, 154*, 1690–1695.

Zeiss, A. M., & Breckenridge, J. S. (1997). Treatment of late life depression: A response to the NIH Consensus Conference. *Behavior Therapy, 28*, 3–21.

Zeiss, A. M. & Lewinsohn, P. M. (1986). Adapting behavioral treatment for depression to meet the needs of the elderly. *The Clinical Psychologist, 98–100.*

Zeiss, A. M., et al. (1996). Relationship of physical disease and functional impairment to depression in older people. *Psychology and Aging, 11,* 572–581.

Zhou, J-N., et al. (1995). A sex difference in the human brain and its relation to transsexuality. *Nature, 378,* 68–70.

Ziedonis, D. M., & Trudeau, K. (1997). Motivation to quit using substances among individuals with schizophrenia: Implications for a motivation-based treatment model. *Schizophrenia Bulletin, 23,* 229–238.

Zilbergeld, B., & Evans, M. (1980). The inadequacy of Masters & Johnson. *Psychology Today, 14,* 29–34, 47–53.

Zilbovicius, M. et al. (1992). Regional cerebral blood flow in childhood autism: A SPECT study. *American Journal of Psychiatry, 149,* 924–930.

Zilbovicius, M., et al. (1995). Delayed maturation of the frontal cortex in childhood autism. *American Journal of Psychiatry, 152,* 248–252.

Zillmann, D. (1989). Effects of prolonged consumption of pornography. In D. Zillmann & J. Bryant (Eds.), *Pornography: Research advances and policy considerations* (pp. 127–157). Hillsdale, NJ: Erlbaum.

Zillmann, D., & Weaver, J. B. (1989). Pornography and men's sexual callousness toward women. In D. Zillmann & J. Bryant (Eds.), *Pornography: Research advances and policy considerations* (pp. 95–125). Hillsdale, NJ: Erlbaum.

Zima, B. T., et al. (1996). Mental health problems among homeless mothers: Relationship to service use and child mental health problems. *Archives of General Psychiatry, 53,* 332–338.

Zimbroff, D. L., et al. (1997). Controlled, dose-response study of sertindole and haloperidol in the treatment of schizophrenia. *American Journal of Psychiatry, 154,* 782–791.

Zipursky, R. B., et al. (1998). Cerebral gray matter volume deficits in first episode psychosis. *Archives of General Psychiatry. 55,* 540–546.

Zlotnick, C., Elkin, I., & Shea, M. T. (1998). Does the gender of a patient or the gender of a therapist affect the treatment of patients with major depression? *Journal of Consulting and Clinical Psychology, 66,* 655–659.

Zoellner, L. A., Craske, M., G., & Rapee, R. M. (1996). Stability of catastrophic cognitions in panic disorder. *Behaviour Research and Therapy, 34,* 399–402.

Zorumski, C. F., & Isenberg, K. E. (1991). Insights into the structure and function of GABA-benzodiazepine receptors: Ion channels and psychiatry. *American Journal of Psychiatry, 148,* 162–172.

Zotter, D. L, & Crowther, J. H. (1991). The role of cognitions in bulimia nervosa. *Cognitive Therapy & Research, 15,* 413–426.

Zubenko, G. S., et al. (1997). Mortality of elderly patients with psychiatric disorders. *American Journal of Psychiatry, 154,* 1360–1368.

Zubin, J., & Spring, B. (1977). Vulnerability—New view of schizophrenia. *Journal of Abnormal Psychology, 86,* 103–126.

Zucker, K. J., & Green, R. (1992). Psychosexual disorders in children and adolescents. *Journal of Child Psychology and Psychiatry, 33,* 107–151.

Zuckerman, M. (1980). Sensation seeking. In H. London & J. Exner (Eds.), *Dimensions of personality.* New York: Wiley.

Zuger, A. (1998, February). Uneven progress in AIDS treatment. *Journal Watch for Psychiatry, 4* (2), 18.

Zweig-Frank, H., & Paris, J. (1991). Parents' emotional neglect and overprotection according to the recollections of patients with borderline personality disorder. *American Journal of Psychiatry, 148,* 648–651.

PHOTO CREDITS

Chapter 9 Page 304 Christopher Richard Wynne Nevinson, *A Bursting Shell,* 1915, London, Tate Gallery, Art Resource; p. 308 (left) Walter Bibikow/The Image Bank; (right) Lawrence Migdale/Tony Stone Images; p. 309 MGM-Pathe/Kobal Collection; p. 313 Robert Harbison; p. 316 Collins/Monkmeyer Press; p. 319 (top left) D. Wells/The Image Works; (top right) Dean Conger/Corbis; (bottom) Paul Chesley/Tony Stone Images; p. 322 Don Farrall/PhotoDisc, Inc.; p. 324 Joel Gordon Photography; p. 326 (left) Bureau of Alcohol, Tobacco, and Firearms; (right) Nick Koudis/reprinted with the permisssion of the American Cancer Society; p. 329 Rousseau/The Image Works; p. 332 Robert Essel/The Stock Market; p. 334 (left) Richard Hutchings/PhotoEdit; (right) Jeff Greenberg/Omni-Photo Communications, Inc.; p. 338 Joel Gordon Photography; p. 339 H. Kanus/Photo Researchers, Inc.; p. 341 Trinity Press International.

Chapter 10 Page 348 Scala/Art Resource, N.Y.; p. 351 Kelley Chin/AP/Wide World Photos; p. 352 Tony Freeman/PhotoEdit; p. 354 Jill Greenberg © 1998, The Walt Disney Co. Reprinted with permission of Discover Magazine; p. 356 Esbin/Anderson/Omni-Photo Communications, Inc.; p. 360 Tony Freeman/PhotoEdit; p. 362 Joel Gordon Photography; p. 370 Uniphoto Picture Agency; p. 371 PhotoDisc, Inc.; p. 373 Ogust/The Image Works.

Chapter 11 Page 378 SuperStock, Inc.; 381 (left) George Holton/Photo Researchers, Inc.; (right) Lee Snyder/Photo Researchers, Inc.; p. 383 (left) *San Francisco Examiner;* (right) Bob McLeod/*San Francisco Examiner;* p. 386 Roy Morsch/The Stock Market; p. 388 Randy Matusow/Monkmeyer Press; p. 391 Douglas Mason/Woodfin Camp & Associates; p. 392 Fredrik D. Bodin; p. 395 Roy Morsch/The Stock Market; p. 402 Ira Wyman/Sygma; p. 405 AP/Wide World Photos.

Chapter 12 Page 408 Paul Klee, *Love Song During the New Moon,* Bern, Kunstmuseum, Switzerland/Giraudon/Art Resource, NY; p. 411 (top) Corbis; (bottom) The Granger Collection; p. 412 R. Flynt/The Image Works; p. 414 Dion Ogust/The Image Works; p. 417 Peter Ginter/The Image Bank; p. 419 VSA Very Special Arts Gallery; p. 422 Benyas-Kaufman Photographers, Inc.; p. 423 (left) Grunnitis/Monkmeyer Press; (right) Mitchell Funk/The Image Bank; p. 425 Corbis; p. 430 (top) M. Buchsbaum/Mt.Sinai Hospital/Medical Arts Studio; (bottom) Nancy C. Andreasen, M.D./University of Iowa Hospitals & Clinics; p. 431 Nancy C. Andreasen, M.D./University of Iowa Hospitals & Clinics/Gershon, E.S., & Rieder, R.O. (1992) Major disorders of mind and brain, *Scientific American,* 267, p. 128; p. 432 Amy Etra/PhotoEdit; p. 436 Cindy Charles/Liaison Agency, Inc.; p. 443 (left) Villard-Niviere/SIPA Press; (right) Kalpesh Lathigra/FSP/Liaison Agency, Inc.

Chapter 13 Page 446 Rufino Tamayo (1899-1991), *Dos Caras,* Schalkwijk/Art Resource; p. 450 Tony Freeman/PhotoEdit; p. 452

Erika Stone; p. 456 Goodwin/Monkmeyer Press; p. 458 Greenlar/The Image Works; p. 459 Yoav Levy/Phototake NYC; p. 461 Paul Conklin/PhotoEdit; p. 463 Stephen Vaughn/Globe Photos, Inc.; p. 465 Will & Deni McIntyre/Photo Researchers, Inc.; p. 470 Michael Weisbrot and Family; p. 472 Jack Star/PhotoDisc, Inc.; p. 475 Jeff Greenberg/PhotoEdit; p. 476 David Young-Wolff/PhotoEdit; p. 477 Jean Claude LeJeune/Stock Boston; p. 479 Lawrence Migdale/Photo Researchers, Inc.

Chapter 14 Page 484 Bellows, George (1882–1925), *Portrait of Mr. and Mrs. Philip Wase,* National Museum of American Art, Smithsonian Institution, Washington, DC; p. 487 Frank Siteman/Stock Boston; p. 490 Jeff Persons/Stock Boston; p. 492 Ira Wyman/Sygma; p. 493 Steve Weber/Tony Stone Images; p. 494 Mel Curtis/PhotoDisc, Inc.; p. 498 (top) Robert P. Friedland, M.D., Case Western Reserve University; (bottom left) John Bryson/Sygma; (bottom center) Studio X/Liaison Agency, Inc.; (bottom right) Mark J. Terrill/AP/Wide World Photos; p. 501 AP/Wide World Photos; p. 502 Cecil Fox/Science Source/Photo Researchers, Inc.; p. 505 David Leah/Science Photo Library/Photo Researchers, Inc.; p. 506 Robin Carson, photographer. Used by permission of Woody Guthrie Publications, Inc.; p. 508 AP/Wide World Photos; p. 509 (top) Simon Fraser/Science Photo Library/Photo Researchers, Inc.; (bottom) The White House Photo Office; p. 510 Ted Streshinsky/Corbis.

Chapter 15 Page 514 Warhol, Andy, *Guns,* The Andy Warhol Foundation for the Visual Arts/ARS/Art Resource, NY; p. 518 Wally McNamee/Sygma; p. 519 Ed Andrieski/AP/Wide World Photos; p. 520 David Thompson/Oxford Scientific Films, Ltd.; p. 522 Byron/Monkmeyer Press; p. 523 Albert Bandura; p. 525 Harvey Finkle/Impact Visuals Photo & Graphics, Inc.; p. 526 J.P. Laffont/Sygma; p. 528 Ted Spiegel/Corbis; p. 530 Esbin Anderson/The Image Works; p. 532 Les Stone/Sygma; p. 534 Stephen Ferry/Liaison Agency, Inc.; p. 539 Steve McCurry/Magnum Photos, Inc.; p. 540 R.Sidney/The ImageWorks; p. 543 LaPorte County Child Abuse Prevention Council; p. 544 Doug Plummer; p. 546 Bob Daemmrich/Stock Boston; p. 547 John Coletti/Index Stock Imagery, Inc.

Chapter 16 Page 552 Oskar Schlemmer (1888–1943), *Quatre figures et cube,* 1928, Stuttgart, Staatsgalerie, Germany; p. 555 Ed Bailey/AP/Wide World Photos; p. 557 AP/Wide World Photos; p. 558 (A) Stacy Pick/Stock Boston; (B) Peter Southwick/Stock Boston; (C) Tom McCarthy/Index Stock Imagery, Inc.; p. 559 Kobal Collection; p. 560 AP/Wide World Photos; p. 562 AP/Wide World Photos; p. 563 Orion Pictures Corporation (Courtesy Kobal); p. 565 The Granger Collection; p. 568 AP/Wide World Photos.

UBJECT INDEX

Ego psychology, 25
Ego syntonic, 276
Elavil (amitriptyline), 114, 116, 256, 261
Electra complex, 23
Electroconvulsive therapy (ECT), 115, 117
  for mood disorders/depression, 266
Electrodermal response, 83
Electroencephalograph (EEG), 83
Electromyograph (EMG), 83, 151
Elimination disorders, 480–482
Ellis, Albert, 33–34, 98, 187, 195, 252
Emotion-focused coping, 140
Emotions
  coronary heart disease and, 158–159
  personality disorders and lack of, 298–299
  schizophrenia and disturbances of, 421
  violent behavior and, 527
Empathy, 96
Encephalitis, 510
Encopresis, 482
Endocrine disorders, aging and, 509–510
Endocrine system, 131–133
Endogenous depression, reactive versus, 238–239
Endorphins, 322
Enuresis, 480–482
Environmental factors, health and illness and, 145, 148
Epidemiological method, 43–44
Epidemiologic Catchment Area (ECA) study, 39
  aggression and, 525
  antisocial personality disorders and, 280
  anxiety disorders and, 175, 191
  major depressive disorder and, 238
  manic episode and, 246
  somatization disorder and, 224
Epinephrine, 132–133, 142
Epstein-Barr virus, 134–135
Erikson, Erik, 25, 425
Erogenous zones, 22
Eros, 22
Erotomania, 442–443
Estrogen, 133
Ethics, research, 40
Ethnic differences
  abnormal behavior and, 5, 6–8
  alcoholism and, 318–320
  anxiety disorders and, 191
  bulimia nervosa and, 353
  cancer and, 159–160
  child sexual abuse and, 545
  coronary heart disease (CHD) and, 156–157
  depression and, 7–8, 238
  eating disorders and, 353, 354
  expressed emotion and, 437
  gender identity disorder and, 384–385
  health and illness and, 143–145
  homicide rates and, 525–526

major depressive disorder and, 238
mental health and, 38–39
psychological resilience and, 150–151
responses to psychotropic medications and, 117–118
schizophrenia and, 413, 414, 438–439
smoking and, 326, 327
suicide and, 267
use of mental health services and, 118–119
Ethnic issues
  assessment of abnormal behavior and, 63–64
  DSM and, 59
  matching clients with therapists, 109
  in psychotherapy, 108–112
Ethyl alcohol (ethanol), 314
Etiological assumption, 171
Event-related potentials, (ERPs), 418
Exhaustion stage, 138
Exhibitionism, 387–388
Existential therapies, 97
Exorcism, 11
Expectancies, 31
Expectancy effects, 91
Experimental method, 41–43
Experimental subjects, 41–42
Exposure, gradual, 194
Expressed emotion (EE), 435–436, 437
External attribution, 255
External validity, 43
Extinction, 185
Eye movement desensitization and reprocessing (EDR), 199
Eye movement dysfunction, 418

Face validity, 62
Factitious disorder, 221
  Münchausen syndrome, 228–229
Falling out, 61
False negatives, 77
Family and marital therapy, 104
Family history/factors
  See also Genetic differences
  coronary heart disease and, 154
  eating disorders and, 357–358
  gender identity disorder and, 384
  personality disorders and, 296–297
  schizophrenia and, 435–436
Fat cells, 363
Fear
  anxiety disorders and overprediction of, 186
  phobic disorders and, 175
Fear reduction, methods of, 99–100
Feedback, 47
Female orgasmic disorder, 396–397
Female sexual arousal disorder, 396
Feminist therapy, 112–113
Fenfluramine, 365–366
Fetal alcohol syndrome (FAS), 318, 320–321, 459

Fetishism, 388–389
  transvestic, 389
Fight-or-flight reaction, 137
First-rank symptoms, 412
Fixation, 23
Flashbacks, 329
Flooding, 198
Fluid memory, 492–493
Fluoxetine (Prozac), 115, 116, 193, 227, 230, 256, 261–262, 265
Fluphenazine (Prolixin), 114, 116, 437
Flurazepam (Dalmane), 114, 116
Forced-choice formats, 72
Forcible rape, 537
Foster, Jodie, 442, 562
Four As of schizophrenia, 411–412
Fragil X syndrome, 458
Frankl, Victor, 97
Free association, 93–94
Freebasing, 323–324
Free-stimulus hierarchy, 194
Freud, Sigmund, 15, 16, 171, 226, 293, 323, 439
  depression and, 248
  displacement and, 184
  evaluation of, 26–27
  instinct and, 519
  normality versus abnormality and, 25–26
  psychoanalysis, 22, 92–96, 227
  stages of psychosexual development, 22–24
  structural hypothesis, 21
  structure of the mind, 20–21
Frotteurism, 390
Fugue, dissociative, 212–213
Functional analysis, 78, 101

GABA, 317, 506
Galen, 11
Galvanic skin response (GSR), 83, 298–299, 418
Gambling, pathological, 312–313
Gamma aminobutyric acid (GABA), 189–190
Garland, Judy, 321
GBMI (guilty-but-mentally-ill) verdict, 564
Gender bias, 241
Gender differences
  alcoholism and, 315–316
  anorexia nervosa and, 351–352
  bipolar disorder and, 244
  child sexual abuse and, 542
  coping styles and, 240
  coronary heart disease and, 154
  depression and, 237–238, 240–241, 476–477
  fragil X syndrome and, 458
  Klinefelter's syndrome and, 458
  schizophrenia and, 415
  sleep terror disorder and, 372
  smoking and, 326

Waxy flexibility, 422
Weaning, 23
Weschler, David, 68–69, 70
Wechsler scales, 69, 70, 456
Wellbutrin (buproprion), 261
Wells, H. G., 323
Wernicke's disease, 491
Weyer, Johann, 13
White Americans, non-Hispanic
   antisocial personality disorders and,
      280
   anxiety disorders and, 191
   bulimia nervosa in, 353
   cancer and, 144, 159–160
   coronary heart disease and, 156–157
   expressed emotion and, 437
   homicide rates for, 526

major depressive disorder and, 238
mental health of, 39
schizophrenia and, 424, 438–439
smoking and, 326, 327
substance dependence and, 310
suicide and, 267
use of mental health services and, 118
Witchcraft, 11–13
Withdrawal syndromes, 308, 309, 314,
   322
World Health Organization (WHO), 7,
   52, 299, 325, 412
Worldview, 8
Writing, therapeutic benefits of, 136
Written expression disorder, 464
Wyatt v. Stickney, 559, 560

Xanax (alprazolam), 114, 116, 193
X-Files, 220

Youngberg v. Romeo, 561
Yo-yo dieting, 367

Zar, 61
Zoloft (sertraline), 115, 116, 193, 261
Zolpidem (Ambien), 372
Zoophilia, 392
Zyban (bupropion), 338